MAPPING THE LAW

Essays in Memory of Peter Birks

Peter Brian Herrenden Birks
(1941–2004)

Mapping the Law

Essays in Memory of Peter Birks

Edited by
ANDREW BURROWS
and
LORD RODGER OF EARLSFERRY

OXFORD
UNIVERSITY PRESS

*This book has been printed digitally and produced in a standard specification
in order to ensure its continuing availability*

OXFORD
UNIVERSITY PRESS

Great Clarendon Street, Oxford OX2 6DP

Oxford University Press is a department of the University of Oxford.
It furthers the University's objective of excellence in research, scholarship,
and education by publishing worldwide in

Oxford New York

Auckland Cape Town Dar es Salaam Hong Kong Karachi
Kuala Lumpur Madrid Melbourne Mexico City Nairobi
New Delhi Shanghai Taipei Toronto
With offices in
Argentina Austria Brazil Chile Czech Republic France Greece
Guatemala Hungary Italy Japan South Korea Poland Portugal
Singapore Switzerland Thailand Turkey Ukraine Vietnam

Oxford is a registered trade mark of Oxford University Press
in the UK and in certain other countries

Published in the United States
by Oxford University Press Inc., New York

ISBN 978-0-19-920655-1

Printed and bound by CPI Antony Rowe, Eastbourne

Biographical Outline of Peter Birks 1941–2004

Educated at Trinity College, Oxford, and University College, London

Degrees and Honours

MA (Oxon), LLM (Lond), DCL (Oxon), LLD (Edinburgh)
Fellow of the British Academy, 1989
Fellow of the Royal Society for the Encouragement of Arts, Manufactures
    and Commerce, 1992
Fellow of University College London, 1993
Elected to Membership of Accademia dei Giusprivatisti Europei
    (Academy of European Private Lawyers), 1994
Honorary Fellow, Trinity College, Oxford, 1994
Queen's Counsel (honoris causa) 1995
Doctor of Law (honoris causa) Regensburg, 1996
Doctor of Law (honoris causa) De Montfort, 1999
Foreign Member, Royal Netherlands Academy, 2001
President of the Society of Legal Scholars, 2002–3
Doctor of Law (honoris causa) Nijmegen, 2003

Chronological Outline of Academic Career

Teaching Associate, Northwestern University Law School, 1964–5
Lecturer, University College London, 1967–71
Law Fellow, Brasenose College, Oxford and, concurrently, CUF Lecturer
    (Law), University of Oxford, 1971–81
Professor of Civil Law, University of Edinburgh, 1981–8
Professor of Law, University of Southampton, 1988–9
Regius Professor of Civil Law, University of Oxford, and Professorial
    Fellow of All Souls College, Oxford, 1989–2004

Visiting Posts

Mallesons Stephen Jacques Visiting Professor, Australian National University, 1989
Visiting Scholar, Albert Ludwigs University, Freiburg-im-Breisgau, 1992
Wisselleerstoelhouder, Catholic University of Nijmegen, 1994–96
Visiting Scholar, University of Western Australia, 1993, 1995
Distinguished Visitor, University of Hong Kong, 1991, 1995
Distinguished Visitor Academy of Law, Singapore, 1995
University of Auckland Research Foundation Scholar, 1997
Miegunyah Distinguished Visitor, University of Melbourne, 1998
Centennial Visiting Fellow, Victoria University, Wellington, 1999
Visiting Professor University of Texas at Austin, 2000
Professor of Anglo-American Law, University of Leiden, 2001–2004

Addresses given at the Memorial Service for Peter Birks on 20 November 2004 in the University Church of St Mary the Virgin, Oxford

First Address (given by Andrew Burrows)

As I was taught by Peter Birks and taught with him, I have been asked to say some words about Peter as a teacher and as a colleague here in the Oxford Law Faculty.

I first met Peter thirty years ago when I came to Brasenose for my Oxford entrance interview. He was interviewing with the senior law tutor at BNC, John Davies, who, in customary fashion, began the interview by trying to relax me with some general questions. Peter said nothing during those first ten minutes but I was very conscious of him sitting restlessly on the settee. Then suddenly, pushing his hand back through the mop of hair that he then had, he said this, 'I am a Roman barber. I have set up stall in an open square. As I am shaving the beard of a customer, my hand is knocked by a ball kicked by boys playing nearby and I slash the face of my customer. Should I, the barber, have to pay compensation to the injured customer?' I cannot recall what answer I gave but I vividly remember the feeling of nervous excitement as whatever I said and whichever way I turned Peter was there firing another variation at me as we explored aspects of negligence and causation and volenti.

Tutorials in Brasenose with Peter engendered similar feelings of excitement tinged with fright. Peter was so passionate about the subjects he was teaching and so anxious for his students to share in the enterprise of constructing clear and elegant pictures of the law. But it could be nerve-racking because he would sometimes ask fiendishly difficult questions and expect us to come up with acceptable answers. Many people here may remember the grandfather clock that he had in his room. It had a very loud tick and Peter would ask these questions and we would sit in silence sometimes for several minutes with just the clock ticking away while Peter waited for us to come up with some sort of answer that he could use to guide us further towards the truth. He was also a meticulous marker of essays. Earlier this week I found one of my tutorial essays entitled 'The Relationship between the Doctrine of Consideration and the Doctrine of

Promissory Estoppel'. In typical Peter style there is half a page of tightly written comments at the end, which begin, 'Very Good but Fundamentally Flawed'.

When I returned to Oxford as a Tutorial Fellow it was a particularly great privilege to teach with Peter on the Restitution postgraduate BCL seminars (which I had attended as a student a decade earlier when being run by Peter and Jack Beatson). By now Peter had become the Regius Professor of Civil Law and, following on from the great pioneering work of Robert Goff and Gareth Jones, he had published his seminal book *An Introduction to the Law of Restitution*. Lord Rodger will be saying more about Peter's scholarship but it is noteworthy here that, for Peter, research and teaching complemented each other so that it was natural for him to continue to use the Restitution seminars to develop his published views. Those seminars constituted the most rewarding experience as a teacher that I have ever had. And it was all down to Peter. He assumed that the students had carefully read the cases on the reading list and knew what the judges had said; and Peter would take it on from there, provoking and challenging them with his latest interpretations and forever being able to cut through the detail with a masterly, decisive, crisp explanation. At times the depth of Peter's knowledge was simply breathtaking. He could move seamlessly from the latest case through English Legal History to Roman law to German law. In Peter's legal world there was no place for misleading labels and fictions and so it was that, in those seminars, we first heard the new precise language that so permeated Peter's work: unjust factors, subtractive enrichment, stultification, disimpoverishment, and so on. What was being discussed was at the cutting edge of the law and many of Peter's views as to what the law was, or what it ought to be—which was just about the only distinction that he did not draw sharply—have subsequently become law. Of course, Peter was never afraid to change his mind in the search for an ever more precise and stylish picture of the law so that as one came to the seminar one could never be sure what he was going to say. Indeed it was possible for what was indisputably correct one year to be indisputably incorrect the next—and vice versa. That all added to the fun. It was a two-hour seminar. We never had a break and we always ran out of time. Peter adored it and the students adored him. It is no surprise that many came to Oxford primarily to attend his seminars and that many went into academia, or out into practice, preaching the Birksian message of the importance of clear classification and of transparent rationality in the law.

Peter was not only a gifted teacher. He was an inspirational and dedicated doctoral supervisor, as several here today will testify. He regarded a DPhil as a joint project in which there was as much for him to learn as for the supervisee. It is a humbling experience to see in his rooms at All Souls a shelf laden with the bound theses of his many doctoral students.

Peter was a warm and entertaining companion but I am not sure he ever really switched off from thinking about law or legal matters. When they were under nines, his son Theodore and my oldest son played in the same football team. I was once acting as linesman in a match but that didn't stop Peter expecting me to explain, as I was trying to concentrate on the offsides, when, if ever, you could refuse restitution because of a change of position that was not a disenrichment. I also remember going round to Peter's house in Boar's Hill one Sunday lunchtime to drop off a book. Peter was there under the trees in the garden working away with a rake and looking very relaxed. As he saw me he came over and said, 'I've had a really good hour's gardening. I've sorted out *Boulter v Barclays Bank*. The Court of Appeal has definitely got the burden of proof point wrong.'

Never attracted by practice, Peter regarded working in a university law school as a privilege in enabling one to search for the truth unhindered by the demands of clients or the fear of falling out with an employer. In the Oxford Law Faculty, as well as being our intellectual leader, he worked tirelessly and selflessly for the faculty's well-being. He would respond with an unconditional yes to any request to take on extra teaching or an administrative task or supervision. In addition to serving on many other committees, he was twice Director of Graduate Studies (Research), three times Chairman of FHS or BCL examiners, Chairman of the Management Committee at the Centre for Socio-Legal Studies, the person behind the Clarendon Law Lecture Series now in its tenth year, and, taking huge amounts of his time and energy over several years, he was the driving force behind the creation in 1994 of the Oxford Institute of Legal Practice and was still Chair of its Board of Studies until a few weeks before he died. And it is not as if he did these jobs in a token way. On the contrary, he threw himself into them and often spearheaded important and lasting reforms.

There have been many great figures in the long and distinguished history of the Oxford Law Faculty. But surely no one has combined the roles of teacher, supervisor, administrator, and scholar with such brilliance and such passionate commitment as Peter Birks.

There are many here today who became academic lawyers because of Peter and many others whom he helped in some way through his work. We are so grateful to him for being our mentor, our generous friend, and our inspirational colleague.

I want to conclude by reading a small extract from the cover of his *Introduction to the Law of Restitution*. Over the years, I have read this extract to students both here and abroad and although Peter would not express it in quite the same way today—in particular, he would be referring to the law of unjust enrichment rather than the law of restitution—this passage will for me be a poignant reminder forever of Peter's passion and enthusiasm for the subject and indeed for the study of law generally.

Restitution is an area of the law no smaller and no less important than, say, Contract, Tort, or Trusts. A series of intellectual and historical accidents has, however, scattered its raw material to the fringes of other subjects. Homes have been found for it under dishonest or opaque labels: quasi-contract . . . constructive trust, money had and received, and so on. Dispersed in this way, Restitution has escaped the revolution in legal learning which has happened over the past century. It has been the age of the textbook. Successive editions have settled the case-law of other subjects into well-tried and now familiar patterns. The case-law of Restitution remains disorganized: its textbooks have only just begun to be written . . . It is the last major area to be mapped and in some sense the most exciting subject in the modern canon. There is everything to play for.

Second Address (given by Alan Rodger)

We are here to give thanks for the life of Peter Birks. In the short time available it would be impossible to outline his career, far less all his achievements. But it is scarcely necessary to do so, since most of the story is well known to this congregation, if only from the two excellent obituaries which appeared shortly after Peter's death in July. In any event, we have come here from far and wide because Peter was one of the best loved, as well as one of the most distinguished, scholars in the history of the Oxford Law Faculty. What we are trying to capture today are some of those qualities that made him so.

Inevitably, on a University and College occasion such as this, the focus is on *iura virumque*, laws and the man. The double aspect is not inappropriate since the qualities that shaped the private man were essentially those that made the academic lawyer. First and foremost, Peter was a man of passions. For that reason, his public career could never have been one of smooth progress against the background of a serene and ordered private life. Rather—as Peter would readily acknowledge—until his late thirties, his relationships often seemed to bring more misery than happiness both to himself and, unfortunately, to those around him. Inevitably, that misery took its toll. But, in 1979, just when he was at his lowest ebb, he met Jackie; and, at a stroke, his life changed. Or, as he put it more passionately, in the words from *Fidelio* that he used in dedicating his Restitution book to her: 'Your faithfulness has saved my life'. Peter believed that, quite literally. His life began anew; Peter and Jackie married on 29 October 1984—significantly enough, the notional date that he gave to the preface to *Restitution*. In due course, Theodore was born. No doubt, Peter's family still had to make sacrifices, but, for the rest of his days, his home life was supremely happy and secure. With this dramatic change, his academic life too could flourish as never before. Even Jackie might admit that the statistics go far towards proving the point: in the 11 years from 1969 to 1980, Peter published 13 items; in the following 11 years, from 1981 to 1992, he published 52. Doubtless, the advent of computers also had something to do with the upsurge. The early printers, spewing forth lengths of faintly printed text, gave terrifyingly concrete form to Peter's enthusiasms. Six feet on the intricacies of Roman procedure could be daunting, to say the least.

From the outset, Peter had no doubt about his vocation as an academic lawyer. Not for him the temptations of practice: though he was delighted to be made an honorary QC in 1995, he had never qualified as a solicitor or barrister and it did not cross his mind that he might be better as a practitioner or sitting as a judge. He had no desire to concoct arguments that might serve the needs of the hour or of some particular client. This did not mean that he underestimated the role of litigation or of the courts. On the contrary, he always insisted that 'the law was an intellectual and academic discipline which derived its autonomy, its difficulty and its satisfactions from its focus on litigation and, ultimately, adjudication'. But he wanted to take part in that difficult intellectual and academic discipline, rather than in the underlying litigations or adjudications. With this unclouded perception of his role, Peter did not suffer from the kind of inferiority complex that, at one time, crippled academic lawyers in this country. Let practitioners practise and judges judge; academics had their own job to do. And for Peter that job was, ultimately, more important than the others.

Not only more important, but more enjoyable too. Peter simply loved what he did. If he could never really see the point of taking holidays and was bad at the so-called work–life balance, this was because he was far too busy enjoying himself, in the congenial surroundings of Brasenose or All Souls, working with friends who happened also to be his colleagues and pupils. His ability to transmit this enjoyment to others was central to his success. He made any project seem not only worthwhile but enormous fun. Why did even hung-over young men and women prise themselves from their beds to attend the restitution classes which he loved to schedule, quite deliberately, for the early morning? Surely, because, under his leadership, the classes were both the most rigorous, and the most enjoyable, show in town. There were jokes galore but, above all, a feeling that the participants were lucky to be spending a couple of hours engaged together on an unendingly fascinating exercise. Similarly, more often than not, letters or, latterly, emails on a matter of business would contain a devastating aside on some absurdity or pomposity that had caught his eye. If you found yourself sitting near Peter at dinner, you knew that an entertaining evening was in prospect.

There was more to it than that, however. Like Justinian—not a comparison he would have permitted—Peter believed that there is a *cupida legum iuventus*, that there are young people eager to learn the law. Teaching, whether in Oxford or elsewhere, was therefore not a chore, but an opportunity to engage with them. He regretted not having been able himself to study full-time for a higher degree. In compensation, he was a devoted supervisor of his DPhil students, tirelessly questioning and probing but, above all, encouraging. His reward was a succession of fine theses which turned into important books. To his intense pride, his pupils went on to distinguished careers in practice and in universities throughout the Commonwealth and beyond. For instance, in Germany you constantly come across successful young lawyers who delight in recalling his restitution classes. It is no accident, either, that Peter received honorary degrees, for example, from Nijmegen and Regensburg. By his teaching, as well as his writing, Peter maintained and spread the influence of Oxford. And if in his approach one could sometimes detect imperial echoes, Peter was, after all, a son of the Raj. Indeed, while, to his regret, the sun might be setting on the Privy Council in Downing Street, Peter was a kind of one-man Privy Council, welcoming the contributions of scholars and courts everywhere, but aiming to bring order and reason to the common law throughout the world. Outbursts of legal nationalism, whether in Scotland or in the far Antipodes, he treated with particular contempt, precisely because he saw them as introducing essentially irrational considerations into an area where they had no valid role to play.

Although Peter is best known for his work on unjust enrichment, his first love was Roman Law, which he learned in lively discussions with his tutor at Trinity, the charismatic John Kelly. At University College London the ebullient Tony Thomas encouraged his interest in the subject, and most of his early published work was on Roman Law. His Roman Law articles have many of the hallmarks that distinguish his work on English Law: a refined sensitivity to language and a concern with the precise wording of the pleadings, with what the parties would have said in court and, more generally, with the procedures that they used. Most importantly, perhaps, when the judges came to decide the cases, where did they find the law in the days before it was written down? In all this, the influence of English legal historians, especially Toby Milsom and Sir John Baker, is unmistakable and it gave Peter's work on Roman Law its distinctive character.

For Peter, at least, there was nothing strange in applying insights from English legal history to Roman Law. For instance, his fascination with fictions in both systems meant that, when, in 1983, he was shown the text of the recently discovered *Tabula Contrebiensis* from first century BC Spain, he immediately spotted—what other scholars had missed—that the second of the two formulae contained a remarkable and sophisticated fiction. Peter's insight proved to be the key to unravelling the inscription. And perhaps the key to unravelling Peter's career and his understanding of the role of the Regius Professor of Civil Law lies in his belief—which had also been the belief of Rudolf Jhering—that, fundamentally, Roman and English lawyers were doing the same kind of work—work, besides, which only trained lawyers could do. So, as Peter liked to remark—if not rebuked by the Lord Chief Justice for using Latin—Ulpian could sit in the appellate committee of the House of Lords on Monday morning, whereas, not being a lawyer, even so omniscient a Roman historian as Sir Ronald Syme could not. The study of Roman Law was therefore an essentially legal pursuit not remote from, but complementary to, the study of modern law, and vice versa. Peter's work on Roman Law flowed into his work on English Law.

Contrary to what is sometimes suggested, Peter's concentration on modern law in his more recent publications did not mean that his enthusiasm for, or commitment to, the study of Roman Law had diminished. A moment's conversation with him would have exploded that myth. Moreover, his unfulfilled ambition was to write a history of the Roman law of delict, for which he had prepared the way in a series of penetrating articles on the Lex Aquilia. But, although Peter loved the countless intellectual puzzles to be found on every page of the Digest, he was not seduced by them. He, at least, never doubted that the importance of Roman Law for university education today lies in the Institutes of Gaius and Justinian, which offer a unique overview of the grammar of a legal system—the distinctions between property and obligations, between ownership and possession, etc. In Peter's judgment, only Barry Nicholas's *Introduction to Roman Law* could provide some of the same necessary insights. But the Institutes were the genuine article and so, along with Grant McLeod, Peter produced a marvellously readable translation of Justinian's version.

Peter loved the (true) story of the Scottish advocate who said to the judge in an insolvency case, 'Speaking personally, I have never seen much difference between rights *in rem* and rights *in personam*'. The story appealed to him because it demonstrated so clearly the pitfalls which lie in wait for lawyers, even intelligent lawyers, who have never had an opportunity to absorb the basic concepts. Hence Peter's very real concern about the proliferation of conversion courses, which profess to turn botanists into lawyers in the space of a year. Of course, when friends screwed up their courage to confess to him that their son or daughter had actually embarked on one of these courses, Peter tended to say, 'Oh, well, Sophie's different: I'm sure it will be all right in *her* case'. But he felt real anger—bitterness would not be too strong a word—at what he saw as the unthinking way in which, with the connivance of the profession, English law faculties had abandoned the study of Roman Law and so had deprived their students of the insights which that study offered. Even his beloved Oxford had taken a step in the same direction while he was on sabbatical leave in Freiburg. In Oxford Peter could, and did, fight relentlessly, and successfully, to maintain the position of Roman Law. He did so, not out of any selfish motive, but because he believed, with every fibre of his being, that today's students, just as much as their sixth-century counterparts, deserve the best possible start to their legal lives.

As early as 1971 Peter devoted a paper to the group of quasi-delicts in Roman Law. This is surely one of the dreariest topics known to man and one which not even Peter could really cheer up. In his view, however, it was a current legal problem deserving our attention, because it related to the manner in which a great legal system classified obligations. Years later, Peter felt unable to acquit his hero, Gaius, of responsibility for introducing the vocabulary of quasi-contracts and quasi-delicts, but he added, in mitigation, that Gaius probably did not expect 'them to do two thousand years of taxonomic service'. In the 1971 article we find a throwaway line that quasi-contractual obligation 'should be based on the redress of unjust enrichment'. In those few words one can already detect the beginnings of his thinking on restitution or, as he later came to see the subject, unjust enrichment.

At the very core of his revolutionary work on this subject lay questions of classification or taxonomy. Jackie introduced him to some undergraduate texts on taxonomy in the natural sciences and reminded him of Darwin. Soon his articles and books began to be peopled, so to speak, with aquatic and herbivorous animals, as well as wolves, dingos, labradors, and six other breeds of dog. Those of us who had tended to skip over such abstract issues soon found ourselves confronted with grids, boxes, and maps, which were subtly revised as publication followed publication. Where was it all going?

The answer was that it was eventually going to end in a fundamental reassessment of Peter's own work on the English law of restitution. Nothing could better illustrate the importance which he attached to these issues of classification. For him the classes which he so painstakingly identified were not mere inventions which one could apply or not apply to the law, at will. Rather, for Peter, when Gaius set out the classifications, he was in effect giving the results of a discovery which he had made about the nature of legal systems. That discovery had indeed been imperfect, especially so far as unjust enrichment was concerned. Peter's aim, therefore, was to go further. Eventually, he reached a point where he had to change the entire focus of his work from the response of restitution to the event of unjust enrichment. That done, he set out to show how the obligation to reverse an unjust enrichment operated in English law. At first, he thought that English law worked differently but, under the pressure of the arguments of one of his restitution pupils, Dr Sonja Meier, a German lawyer, he came to believe that this could not be so and that the 'no basis' approach had to be followed in English law too. Moreover, he thought that, coincidentally, the courts had in effect reached the same position in the swaps cases. Hence, in what was to be the last year of his life, there came forth his book on Unjust Enrichment—the New Testament, as one of his colleagues has called it. The thesis has met with resistance, as he knew that it would, but Peter's view was that, ultimately, there was no answer to the criticisms of the old approach and so there could be no going back. Even his critics pay generous tribute to the sheer power and intellectual honesty of his argument. Whatever the personal cost, Peter felt compelled to make the argument and then, when he knew that he was fatally ill, to revise it.

Time and the courts will tell whether the new approach prevails and, if so, in what form. It is not only sad, but a great misfortune for the law, that Peter is not here to take his part in the arguments as they develop. That is no mere conventional compliment to an academic lawyer, such as judges frequently pay in after-dinner speeches or on occasions like this. Although, in a rather unattractive conceit, judges sometimes like to portray themselves as brutish day labourers who look to academic lawyers for a deeper understanding of the law, the truth is that only comparatively rarely do academics actually produce those novel fundamental insights. But one who did, to an exceptional extent, was Peter. To accord him his own highest accolade, Peter was 'the real thing'. Quite simply, everyone recognizes that he knew far more about unjust enrichment and its impact on other fields of private law than anyone else in the world. Judges do not scatter references to his writings through their opinions in order to give a spurious impression of intellectual depth. They refer to Peter because they find in his work insights into the law which they could never hope to achieve for themselves. In most areas of unjust enrichment, it is Peter who has guided the courts. In Scotland, for example, two short articles which he wrote during his time as a professor at Edinburgh were sufficient to reinvigorate a previously moribund area of the law.

Sometimes critics in any given system might feel that he had rationalized some of the cases in a manner that would have surprised the authors of the judgments. But, in a very real sense, that was to miss the point: in his view, Peter was fitting the cases into the true structure of the law which he had worked out or—as I think he would have put it—which he had uncovered. In that respect, his writings more closely resemble the jurisprudence of German or French professors. It is therefore no coincidence that he was the first British academic lawyer to be honoured with an obituary in the *Juristen Zeitung*. In this kind of scholarly work, the opinions of the judges are just as likely to be criticized as those of other academic writers. The fact that, thanks to Peter, among others, the courts now welcome constructive writing of this kind means that the standing of British academic lawyers is higher today than at any time in the past.

Perhaps of all things, his role in that development would have pleased Peter, the immediate Past President of the Society of Legal Scholars. It has rightly been said that the Society owes a greater debt to him than to anyone in living memory. During his time as Secretary of the Society of Public Teachers of Law between 1989 and 1996, he not only embarked on a root-and-branch reform of its structures but somehow found time to organize a remarkable series of Saturday seminars in All Souls which attracted senior judges, practitioners, and academics from around the world. The whole point of these occasions was that everyone took part on an equal footing and that they all learned from one another. That was Peter's vision of how our understanding of the law would grow.

Unavoidably, my time has run out before the tale of Peter's life and works is even half told. That is, perhaps, as it should be, since it is all too clear that Peter's life too came to a close when there were still many things which he wished to say and do. In fact, however, he achieved an extraordinary amount and his influence was felt all over the legal world. Above all, Peter laid the intellectual foundations of a whole area of the law. That is given to very few.

With Peter's death, the legal world has lost one of its most inspiring figures; his University and colleges one of their most faithful servants; his family and friends a warm-hearted, generous, entertaining, and loyal companion. In our sadness we all have much, very much, for which to be grateful.

Foreword

This collection of essays has been written by his colleagues, friends and former pupils in honour of Peter Birks. Peter's interest in law was all-embracing—there was no part of the legal map he would have regarded as *terra incognita*—but these essays deal with the sections of that map which were closest to his heart. They constitute a remarkable testimony to his influence; there could be no better memorial to his work. It is particularly welcome that the editors have included the moving addresses they gave at Peter's Memorial Service, which captured so much of his personality and achievements, both the intellectual eminence of the scholar and the warmth and kindness of the man. It is good to have these addresses in permanent form.

There is little that I can, or would wish to, add. I came to know Peter during the ten years he spent as an Official Fellow of Brasenose College. Peter was the best of colleagues, not just for the other law tutors (Peter and I were subsequently joined by Hugh Collins), but for the Fellowship as a whole. He was as generous with his friendship as he was with his energy and enthusiasm. He was a brilliantly successful college tutor, demanding and inspiring, taking infinite pains with his pupils. All Brasenose lawyers of that decade will recognize Andrew Burrows's account (in his memorial address) of a Birks tutorial.

One of Peter's most admirable qualities was his strong sense of loyalty, as a virtue to be practised lifelong not only to his friends but also, just as strongly, to his institutions. He became very attached to Brasenose, and remained in close touch long after his departure. In that sense, it can be said that he never did depart. At one period, he even came from Edinburgh to Oxford on a fortnightly basis to teach Roman Law to Brasenose first year students. That was an heroic undertaking, travelling by the Edinburgh—London coach throughout Friday night (having taken two sleeping tablets, of a brand now withdrawn due to its alarming side-effects), and arriving by the London—Oxford coach on Saturday morning in time to give a full set of tutorials.

Peter's other great personal quality was his generosity; that generous spirit which led him to give so much time and thought to helping or supporting the work of others, whether they were pupils, research students, or colleagues. My own debt to him is immeasurable. Advice, comments, suggestions, vigorous discussion were always available and were always warmly encouraging. Peter was a great morale booster: after two hours in his company all things seemed possible.

The contributors to this distinguished collection of essays would no doubt have hoped to produce a book to mark his retirement. We can imagine the pleasure with which he would have received it. Since, however, the book has to serve as a memorial, we must be grateful to them that they have produced a worthy one.

John Davies

Acknowledgements

We are grateful to Eric Descheemaeker, who was one of Peter's doctoral students at the time of his death, for compiling the list of Peter's publications. We are also grateful to Tony Weir, Fellow of Trinity College, Cambridge, for his translation from German into English of Essay 23. Oxford University Press has done an excellent job turning the essays into the fitting memorial intended and we would particularly like to thank Darcy Ahl, Gwen Booth, John Louth, and Virginia Williams. Thanks are also due to Alan Rodger's judicial assistant, Charles Banner, and Andrew Burrows's secretary, Lyn Hambridge.

Contents

I THE ENGLISH LAW OF UNJUST ENRICHMENT AND RESTITUTION

IV LEGAL HISTORY

Table of Cases

GERMAN CASES (IN CHRONOLOGICAL ORDER)

Table of Legislation

Roman Law

JUSTINIANIC LEGAL SOURCES

List of Contributors

Sir John Baker is Downing Professor of the Laws of England in the University of Cambridge; Fellow of St Catharine's College, Cambridge.

Sir Jack Beatson is one of Her Majesty's judges; formerly Rouse Ball Professor of English Law, University of Cambridge.

Andrew Burrows is Norton Rose Professor of Commercial Law in the University of Oxford; Fellow of St Hugh's College, Oxford.

John W Cairns is Professor of Legal History, University of Edinburgh.

Robert Chambers is Professor of Law, King's College London.

Mindy Chen-Wishart is Fellow and Tutor in Law, Merton College, Oxford.

Gerhard Dannemann is Professor of British Legal, Economic, and Social Structures, Humboldt University, Berlin.

Eric Descheemaeker is Fellow and Tutor in Law, St Catherine's College, Oxford.

James Edelman is Fellow and Tutor in Law, Keble College, Oxford; Adjunct Professor, University of Western Australia.

Joshua Getzler is Fellow and Tutor in Law, St Hugh's College, Oxford.

Sir Roy Goode is Emeritus Professor of Law in the University of Oxford; Emeritus Fellow of St John's College, Oxford.

Jeffrey Hackney is Fellow and Tutor in Law, Wadham College, Oxford.

Tony Honoré is Emeritus Fellow of All Souls College, Oxford; formerly Regius Professor of Civil Law, University of Oxford.

David Ibbetson is Regius Professor of Civil Law in the University of Cambridge; Fellow of Corpus Christi College, Cambridge.

David Johnston is a Queen's Counsel; formerly Regius Professor of Civil Law, University of Cambridge.

Gareth Jones is Downing Professor Emeritus of the Laws of England in the University of Cambridge; Fellow of Trinity College, Cambridge.

Thomas Krebs is Fellow and Tutor in Law, Brasenose College, Oxford.

Ewan McKendrick is Professor of English Private Law in the University of Oxford; Fellow of Lady Margaret Hall, Oxford.

Gerard McMeel is Professor of Law, University of Bristol.

Hector MacQueen is Professor of Private Law, University of Edinburgh.

Sonja Meier is at the Max Planck Institute for Comparative and International Private Law, Hamburg.

Ernest Metzger is Douglas Professor of Civil Law, University of Glasgow.

Lord Millett is a former Lord of Appeal in Ordinary.

Charles Mitchell is Professor of Law, King's College, London.

Arianna Pretto-Sakmann is Associate-in-Law, Columbia Law School, New York; formerly Fellow and Tutor in Law, Brasenose College, Oxford.

Lord Rodger of Earlsferry is a Lord of Appeal in Ordinary.

Francis Rose is Professor of Commercial Law, University of Bristol.

Eltjo Schrage is Professor of Law, University of Amsterdam.

Lionel Smith is James McGill Professor of Law, Faculty of Law, McGill University.

Robert Stevens is Fellow and Tutor in Law, Lady Margaret Hall, Oxford.

William Swadling is Fellow and Tutor in Law, Brasenose College, Oxford.

Graham Virgo is Reader in English Law in the University of Cambridge; Fellow of Downing College, Cambridge.

Joseph Georg Wolf is Emeritus Professor of Roman Law, Albert Ludwigs University, Freiburg-im-Breisgau.

Reinhard Zimmermann is the Director of the Max Planck Institute of Comparative and International Private Law, Hamburg.

Introduction

Andrew Burrows and Alan Rodger

Peter Birks, the Regius Professor of Civil Law at Oxford, who died on 6 July 2004, was the most influential English academic lawyer of his generation. He was a passionate believer in the rationality of law, in correct classification of the elements of the law, and in showing how they related to one another—hence the mapping analogy in the title of this collection. Peter inspired generations of students and fellow academics with his writing, teaching, and charismatic personality. The essays in this volume, written in his honour by his colleagues and friends (many of them former students), reflect his principal academic interests in the English, and comparative, law of unjust enrichment and restitution, in Roman law, and in legal history. For Peter these were not disparate areas, unconnected with one another. On the contrary, he carried over the ideas which he developed in the area of Roman law or English legal history or in examining modern German law into his work on contemporary English law and, in particular, into his work on unjust enrichment. This is perhaps most obviously shown by the use which he made of the Roman scheme of classification, to be found in his beloved Gaius, in analysing the structure of English private law. Given his catholic interests, we hesitate to say that Peter would have singled out the English law of unjust enrichment and restitution as his favourite subject, but it is certainly the one for which he is best known throughout the English-speaking legal world. It is therefore appropriate to begin the book with the essays on that topic.

1. The English Law of Unjust Enrichment and Restitution

This first part contains fifteen essays on aspects of the substantive law of unjust enrichment and restitution. But the first essay, by Francis Rose, sets the scene by offering a personal perspective on the development of the English law of restitution, both through the courts and especially through the work of academics. Some of this story, including features of Peter's role, has not previously been told. The essay leaves us with the 'cliff-hanging' question, which only time will resolve, of whether Peter's last book *Unjust Enrichment*[1] has correctly predicted the new

---

[1] (2nd edn, 2005).

world: if not, in Rose's poignant words, 'we shall never know whether theory might have been turned into practice by the force of Birks's intellect and personality'.

For convenience, the fifteen essays on the substantive English law of unjust enrichment and restitution are divided into three sections: general concepts; some particular unjust factors; and property, insolvency, and restitution.

1.1. General Concepts

Essay 2, by Andrew Burrows, analyses the new scheme in *Unjust Enrichment*[2] for answering the question whether an enrichment is *unjust*. It is argued that 'absence of basis' should not replace the traditional common law 'unjust factors' but should instead be used as a valuable cross-check in difficult or novel cases. There was therefore no need for Peter to say that 'Almost everything of mine now needs calling back for burning'.[3]

Robert Stevens then explores three controversial issues on *enrichment*. How is enrichment by services to be quantified? How is an enrichment established where it comprises an incomplete contractual performance? Can enrichment be established where title to the asset transferred does not pass? His answer to the last of these is particularly important in its firm rejection of the view, also explored in Lionel Smith's essay (see below), that unjust enrichment has no role to play where the claimant retains title to the asset in question.

In the fourth essay, Gareth Jones offers his thoughts on *change of position*, which is the most important defence, both theoretically and practically, to a claim for unjust enrichment. He principally examines the under-explored question of the impact of public policy on change of position. But his essay also looks at the following: the role of change of position in claims for rescission; whether change of position is a defence to 'claims based on the claimant's title'; and whether it is useful (he argues not) to confine one's articulated reasoning to it being 'equitable' or 'inequitable' on the facts to uphold the defence.

Graham Virgo's influential multi-causal view of restitution as being under-pinned by three principles (the reversal of unjust enrichment, the giving up of wrongful profits, and the vindication of property) is well-known. In his contribution to this volume he explores the role of *fault* across that wide area. He concludes that it plays a different role in different parts of the law of resti-tution and that a proper analysis is being hampered by the lack of clarity in the terminology used to describe the various types of fault.

There then follow three essays by former doctoral students of Peter Birks, who (in addition to their other writings) have made major contributions to our understanding of the law by the publication of books based on their DPhil theses.[4] In this volume they have retuned to the subject-matter of their theses.

---

[2] ibid, chs 5 and 6.   [3] ibid, p xii.
[4] See C Mitchell, *The Law of Subrogation* (1994); L Smith, *The Law of Tracing* (1997); J Edelman, *Gain-Based Damages* (2002). Essay 13 is by a fourth doctoral student of Peter Birks's,

Charles Mitchell's essay on *subrogation* (Essay 6) shows how cases on 'reviving subrogation' over the last decade, most importantly *Banque Financière de la Cité SA v Parc (Battersea) Ltd*,[5] constitute a major judicial advance in explaining and clarifying the law of subrogation. But as the essay goes on to point out, some old habits die hard and some difficult questions still remain (such as the precise impact of reviving subrogation on third parties).

Lionel Smith, giving hope to us all, claims in Essay 7 that, thirteen years on, he is still not sure he understands *tracing* very well. He then proceeds to show how some of the new and controversial arguments made by Peter in *Unjust Enrichment* were, to a greater or lesser degree, influenced by his understanding of the nature of claims to traceable proceeds. Particularly significant is the concluding observation that Smith's worries about lack of fit between unjust enrichment and claims to traceable proceeds are reduced if one adopts Peter's final vision for the law of unjust enrichment.

The first section is concluded by James Edelman's essay on *gain-based damages for wrongs* and their relation to compensation. He argues that 'damages' simply means a money award for a wrong; that recent cases have continued to recognize the distinction he drew in his book on the subject[6] between restitutionary damages and disgorgement damages; but that a 'rights-based' measure of compensatory damages, which, he argues, has been applied in many non-commercial wrongs cases, will normally render restitutionary damages superfluous.

1.2. Some Particular Unjust Factors

The second group of essays focuses on what, applying the traditional common law 'unjust factors' approach to unjust enrichment, would be regarded as principal unjust factors: namely, mistake and the *Woolwich* principle,[7] duress, undue influence, and failure of consideration. The last three of these essays will also be of direct interest to contract lawyers.

In Essay 9, Jack Beatson looks at the relationship between the *Woolwich* principle and other common law grounds for restitution, in particular mistake of law. He argues (writing before an appeal to the House of Lords) that the Court of Appeal's reasoning in *Deutsche Morgan Grenfell Group plc v IRC*,[8] denying restitution of 'overpaid' tax, cannot be supported. He points out, however, that the decision might be 'saved' if one applied Peter's radical thesis that absence of basis, and not mistake of law, triggered the restitutionary claim so that the extended limitation period for mistaken payments would be inapplicable.

Robert Chambers, whose book, based on his DPhil thesis, *Resulting Trusts* (1997), has again had a major impact on our understanding of the subject.

[5] [1999] 1 AC 221. [6] See n 4 above.

[7] It was laid down by the House of Lords in *Woolwich Building Society v Inland Revenue Commissioners* [1993] 1 AC 70 that a payment demanded of a citizen ultra vires by a public authority is recoverable as of right. [8] [2005] EWCA Civ 78, [2005] STC 329.

In the tenth essay Ewan McKendrick examines three aspects of duress: the setting aside of a contract for duress, the recovery of a non-contractual benefit because of duress, and the award of compensatory damages for duress. Particularly significant are his acceptance of the view that a threatened breach of contract is always illegitimate pressure for the purposes of economic duress, and his rejection of any difference in the causation test to be applied as between duress of the person and economic duress.

Mindy Chen-Wishart's essay on undue influence (Essay 11) rejects the claimant-sided consent-based view of the doctrine favoured by Peter. On the other hand, like Peter, she rejects a defendant-sided 'wrongful act' explanation. This leads her to suggest that the best explanation lies in a 'relational theory of undue influence'. This goes beyond a 'single factor' explanation but in essence views the doctrine as requiring the defendant to protect the claimant or to ensure that the claimant can protect herself.

In Essay 12 Gerard McMeel looks at the relationship between contract and claims for unjust enrichment (principally for failure of consideration) and argues that, on its true construction, a contract can rule out or limit a restitutionary claim for unjust enrichment even when the contract has been discharged and even where there is no direct contractual link between the claimant and defendant. Focusing on three different contexts (where there is a subsisting contract, where there is a discharged contract, and where there is a mere 'contractual setting' between the claimant and defendant) he sees the central question about the relationship between contract and unjust enrichment as being whether a contract, as a matter of construction, ousts an otherwise arguable restitutionary claim. He labels this a 'construction' approach, although one might equally perhaps call it a 'contracting-out of restitution' approach.

1.3. Property, Insolvency, and Restitution

In this final section on restitution in English law, some perplexingly difficult questions on property, insolvency, and restitution are explored. It begins with Essay 13 by Robert Chambers, another of Peter's star doctoral students, whose book on *Resulting Trusts*[9] (based on his doctoral thesis) has greatly enhanced our understanding of a complex topic. Here Chambers returns to that area and argues that seeing resulting trusts as effecting restitution of unjust enrichment can provide the paradigm for understanding all property rights to restitution of unjust enrichment.

Peter Millett does not agree with the Chambers/Birks approach to the relationship between unjust enrichment and property law. In his contribution (Essay 14) he reproduces some correspondence between himself and Peter as to the correct analysis of *FC Jones v Jones*.[10] Given Peter's death, Lord Millett regrets

---

[9] (1997).   [10] [1997] Ch 159.

that he had the last word on this. But the second edition of *Unjust Enrichment* shows that Peter remained committed to his 'unjust enrichment' analysis of *Jones v Jones*. In his words, 'The only satisfactory explanation is that [Mrs Jones] was unjustly enriched at [the trustee in bankruptcy's] expense to the extent of the whole sum'.[11]

William Swadling's essay (Essay 15) focuses on when, if ever, a mistake in relation to a delivery of goods prevents title in the goods passing to the deliveree. When, in other words, is the delivery unjust? This question is of importance to unjust enrichment lawyers (in recognizing that there may be more than one way of framing a claim) even if one does not agree with Swadling that the existence of a claim in tort for unjust delivery precludes a claim for unjust enrichment.[12] He concludes that it is not clear that mistake should ever prevent title from passing and that three leading cases laying down the contrary are flawed.

In the final essay, Roy Goode examines the extent to which it is helpful to analyse the statutory provisions on the avoidance of transactions in insolvency proceedings as reversing an unjust enrichment. In the light of the policy of the relevant sections, he concludes that the common law rules of unjust enrichment (eg defences such as change of position) have no role to play except as regards, what he terms, 'transaction-related cross-claims' by the defendant.

2. The Comparative Law of Unjust Enrichment and Restitution

As we have already noted, Peter was receptive to ideas in other modern legal systems. More particularly, he openly acknowledged the significance of German law and juristic writings in bringing about the shift in thinking which gave rise to *Unjust Enrichment*. It seems fitting therefore to begin with four essays which deal with aspects of German law on this topic.

Reinhard Zimmermann was a close friend for many years and Peter was quick to recognize the significance of his *Law of Obligations: Roman Foundations of the Civilian Tradition*[13] which provided the first substantial and readable text from which students could trace the development of legal doctrines from Ancient Rome to the present day. In Essay 17, wearing his comparative law hat, Zimmermann explains how the German law relating to restitution after termination for breach of contract has been changed by the provisions which were inserted into the BGB (Bürgerliches Gesetzbuch: the German Civil Code) with effect from 1 January 2002. He concludes by setting those reforms in their wider European context.

In the preface to *Unjust Enrichment* Peter acknowledged the particular part which the comparative work of Sonja Meier had played in his fundamental

---

[11] *Unjust Enrichment* (2nd edn, 2005) 82.
[12] This issue (whether retention of title preludes unjust enrichment) is examined in the essays of Robert Stevens and Lionel Smith. [13] (1990).

change to an absence of basis approach. Like everyone else, she regrets that his early death meant that she was not able to explore his new approach with Peter, but in Essay 18 she sets out her views. She welcomes the new approach to transfer, while exploring some of the difficulties which may lie ahead in adopting that approach in other areas of the law. Finally, on the basis of the experience in German law, she counsels against any tendency to over-generalize the lack of basis approach and suggests that it is preferable to concentrate on the justification for granting restitution in particular situations.

When he worked in Oxford, Gerhard Dannemann was part of the team which conducted the famous restitution seminars for the BCL. His particular role was to draw illustrations and arguments from a comparison between English and German law. In his essay (19) he too examines the new approach adopted by Peter in *Unjust Enrichment* and, in the light of the experience of German law, he suggests ways in which three particular areas of English law may have to be developed and analysed more deeply if the new approach is to work coherently.

Thomas Krebs is another former doctoral pupil of Peter's. His thesis[14] dealt with comparative aspects of German and English law at the very time when Peter's views were shifting. Here, in Essay 20, Krebs concentrates on the so-called *Eingriffskondiktion* and begins by sketching the way that German scholars and courts developed various theories to identify cases in which restitution should and should not be granted, with the attribution theory eventually becoming predominant. He goes on to suggest that, if English law moves in the direction advocated by Peter, then some version of the attribution doctrine may prove helpful in developing a theoretical basis for identifying those infringements of a party's rights for which restitution may be an appropriate response. The lessons of German law further lead him to suggest that the idea that restitution is triggered by a wrong may be flawed.

In Essay 21, Hector MacQueen takes us north of the border where Peter spent some years as Professor of Civil Law at Edinburgh University. Although he had never had occasion previously to look into the Scots law of unjust enrichment, Peter soon produced two remarkable papers which were to shake this area of Scots law to its core. The author traces the various ways in which Peter's influence was brought to bear not only on academics and law reformers but on the Scottish courts, culminating in decisions which sought to set the law off on a new and more coherent path.

3. Roman Law

This section opens with an essay (22) by Alan Rodger on the interpretation of the term *damnum iniuria*, the harm to property for which the Lex Aquilia

---

[14] On which he based his book, *Restitution at the Crossroads: A Comparative Study* (2001).

supplied a remedy. In particular, he suggests that the expression is an asyndeton in which *iniuria* refers to unlawful harm. While the suggestion runs counter to the interpretation which Peter adopted in one of his essays, the theme may be appropriate since exploration of *iniuria* in its various manifestations was one of Peter's abiding interests.

The next essay (23), by Georg Wolf, is inspired by the Lex Irnitana, a copy of the Flavian municipal law which was discovered in the south of Spain in 1981. It offered many new insights into the working of the Roman legal system and, more particularly, into the procedures of the Roman courts. From the first moment when he heard about the new discovery, after dinner in John Richardson's home in St Andrews, Peter became passionately interested in the new text. The essay highlights the importance of law in spreading that essentially urban Roman culture which has helped to shape Western civilization.

Ernie Metzger wrote a doctoral thesis, largely devoted to the Lex Irnitana, under Peter's supervision.[15] In Essay 24 he uses the provisions of chapter 84 of the statute and other texts to argue that what may at first sight appear simply to be requirements that the judge should adjourn proceedings in particular circumstances are better seen as a mechanism for ensuring that the parties' right to a fair trial is observed.

Arianna Pretto-Sakmann also wrote a doctoral thesis under Peter's supervision, on personal property.[16] She opens her essay (25) with an entertaining sketch of the way that Peter used animals, in particular the classification of animals, to illustrate his legal arguments. Then she goes on to look in detail at some aspects of the Roman law relating to bees, including the Aquilian liability of a defendant who burned bees—a topic which Peter liked to ponder in discussion with students and colleagues.

The influence of Roman law in the development of modern legal systems was only possible because of the work of the group of lawyers in sixth-century Constantinople who compiled the Digest. For almost four decades Tony Honoré, Peter's predecessor as Regius Professor of Civil Law, has been shedding light on the way that Justinian's compilers went about their mammoth task of reading and editing. In Essay 26 he returns to the vexed topic of the group of works known as the Appendix. With a wealth of detailed argument, he supports the thesis that the Appendix comprises works which were not available to the compilers until the process of reading was already under way. The compilers first shared these new works out among the existing groups but then changed their minds and allotted them to a separate ad hoc committee.

In Essay 27 David Johnston takes us backwards and forwards between classical Roman Law and the later developments which helped to shape thinking in modern law. He reminds us that, like history books, law books tend to be written

---

[15] Published as *A New Outline of the Roman Civil Trial* (1997).
[16] Published as *Boundaries of Personal Property: Shares and Sub-Shares* (2005).

by the victors with the result that doctrines which ultimately failed to prosper are rather overlooked. Drawing attention to two ultimately unsuccessful doctrines in contract and delict, he ponders why they failed in practice, even though, at first sight, they might seem to have been attractive, at least from the standpoint of legal theory.

Eltjo Schrage begins his essay (28) in the tenements of ancient Rome but then shows how medieval and later lawyers tackled the problem of the enrichment of a landlord which was liable to happen if, on the termination of the lease, a tenant was not allowed to remove the improvements which he had made to the landlord's property. He eventually brings the story right up to the present day with an examination of recent changes in practice and in the Dutch Civil Code, which have sought to meet the legitimate claims of tenants without forcing landlords to pay for improvements which they do not want.

4. Legal History

Peter's thinking about the way that Roman law developed was heavily influenced by the thinking of his colleagues on the development of actions in English law. In his essay (29) John Baker recalls how Peter would go off to hear Professor Milsom at the London School of Economics and would return to University College London 'freighted with new ideas' which he could apply to Roman law. Developing one of the major themes which attracted Peter, Baker discusses how the action on the case for deceit developed at a time when lawyers operated in a world where the categories of contract and tort were as yet unknown. In particular, under reference to the proceedings in *Lopus v Chandeler*, he shows how at the beginning of the seventeenth century, relying on earlier views, some of the judges were prepared to contemplate the possibility of giving a remedy for false misrepresentation, in the absence of a firm warranty—a step which was not actually taken until 1789.

With his colleague, Jeffrey Hackney, in Essay 30 we are back in the law of leases and on that boundary between obligations and property which so interested Peter. Starting from the modern law on a tenant's denial of his landlord's title, he uncovers two distinct strands in the medieval law which are often confused and then shows how a supposed analogy with denial of rent was used to help rationalize the law of conversion in *Isaack v Clark*.[17]

In Essay 31 Joshua Getzler, a colleague of Peter's who shared his passion for Roman law and legal history, takes us to another of the frontiers in the law which Peter liked to patrol, the division between law and equity. The duties of fiduciaries were a constantly recurring theme in his work and in this essay Getzler examines *Keech v Sandford*,[18] which is usually regarded as the starting-point of

---

[17] (1615) 2 Bulstr 306.   [18] (1726) Cas T King 61.

the doctrine that a fiduciary cannot profit from his office. He explores both the reason why an apparently rather obscure decision was to come to have such great influence and the material in earlier cases which helped shape Lord Chancellor King's thinking.

In his essay (32) John Cairns takes an institution, slavery, which was a recognized part of Roman society and discusses the problems which it caused in the very different social conditions of eighteenth-century Scotland. The pursuer in a divorce action wished to call a slave from the Caribbean to give evidence of his wife's adultery. Cairns analyses the ensuing legal debate about the competence of a slave to give evidence and shows how the very fact that Scots law did not recognize or regulate slavery led to uncertainty and potential confusion.

In a world where lawyers are obsessed with the latest cases, Peter was always concerned to draw attention to the sophistication of lawyers of earlier generations. So, for instance, he would come back time and again to Lord Mansfield's judgment in *Moses v Macferlan*.[19] And he greatly admired Sir William Jones's *Essay on the Law of Bailments*.[20] Against the background of Jones's life and career, in the concluding essay in the volume David Ibbetson shows how, even though he went on to devote a great deal of attention to classification in the natural world, unlike Peter, Jones did not apply the same approach to the analysis of the law.

To some the collection may seem to lack a coherent theme. But to Peter, and to anyone who knew Peter, that is not so: they all deal with topics which would have been of immediate interest to him. In that very real sense they are a tribute to him. While the rest of us would struggle to understand, far less to assess, all the essays, it is an inspiring, if somewhat daunting, thought that Peter would have had an easy familiarity with, and clear views on, every chapter. Acutely aware of his high standards, the authors have tried to produce essays which would, at least, have stimulated him—whether into acceptance or into determined rejection. While we mourn the fact that we will never actually know Peter's views on the essays, still more do we mourn our inability to relive the intellectual excitement of debating the issues with him. But our sadness at that loss is tempered by the knowledge that, as the pages of this book make clear, Peter's influence is undimmed.

---

[19] (1760) 2 Burr 1005.   [20] (1781).

PART I

THE ENGLISH LAW OF
UNJUST ENRICHMENT
AND RESTITUTION

1

The Evolution of the Species

Francis Rose [*]

In our last conversation, Peter Birks and I were discussing the development of the law of Restitution, in particular its teaching, and the fact that there were parts of its history which should be recorded before they are forgotten. Within current constraints, this chapter cannot be other than a preliminary, incomplete, and therefore unbalanced and distorted, sketch. Some important events and players are not mentioned. No doubt there are errors. On this occasion, errors and omissions must be accepted. But two things can be done. One is to offer a personal perspective on a story that, not inappropriately for the honorand, touches on elements of legal history, restitution, legal education, and personal anecdotes which are not universally known. The other is to make a start on a picture constructed from elements which do not easily fit together and which needs continuing work in order to be better understood. Rather like the recent history of the law of Restitution.

Holmes[1] has famously observed that 'The life of the law has not been logic; it has been experience'.[2] Those who are content with merely identifying rules of law may be satisfied with the knowledge that legal rules in part emerge from factual circumstances, adversarial arguments, ignorance, and control by precedent. But, in absolute terms, Holmes's dichotomy is defeatist and wrong. By its nature, law needs to be just and consistent, as well as flexible. Practice and theory need to be reconciled. And principles and rules must be adaptable to new challenges.

The need for this in the previously underdeveloped area of Restitution has simply reflected a general problem which has become increasingly noticeable over the past four decades. There have been great societal, political, economic, and technological changes. The volume and variety of law and its recorded forms have proliferated enormously, with massive and complicated new legislation, both primary and secondary, domestic and international; more, and more specialist, law reports, law journals, and books; and many more specialist legal

---

[*] Professor of Commercial Law, University of Bristol.

[1] For convenience, and with no disrespect, individuals in this essay are generally referred to by surname only. [2] OW Holmes, *The Common Law* (1881), 1.

subjects studied within a grossly inflated educational system. The necessity for
well-informed and skilled guidance through the ever more complicated maze has
been steadily gathering strength since the 1960s, the decade in which Peter Birks
embarked upon the law.[3]

It was an opportune moment for one whose career was dedicated to mapping
the law, both as an explorer of new territory and as one who learned his car-
tographical proficiency in the more familiar world, employing his skills in
attempting both to plan routes into the unknown and to correct and update past
trails, so as to produce an harmonious whole.

Typically of students like himself, Birks became a member of an inn of court.[3a]
As his reputation in the new world of Restitution grew, he was frequently called
upon to advise and to speak to practitioners and judges. And in 1995 he was
appointed a Queen's Counsel *ad honorem*.[4] But he never completed his journey to
qualification as a barrister and resisted invitations to more formal links with
practice, fiercely determined to maintain the appearance and reality of independence and impartiality in his quest for the correct exposition of the law. For him
the best way to this was the route which professed academic freedom.

The adjective 'academic' is not infrequently used in a perjorative sense, to
signify unpractical or trivial; but it more correctly signifies belonging to a
learned, scholarly, society. In this sense, it is well exemplified by 'classical'
Roman law scholarship. In Birks's words, 'Under the influence of modern
contract writing, or pop music, law students tend now to use "classical" to mean
"old fashioned" or "out of date"; but it means, in this context, law that is
ordered, detailed, scientific, restrained—and best'.[5]

Birks's grounding in Roman law was appropriate and significant. Classical
learning was an integral part of the world in which he was educated. For
someone who originally contemplated becoming a school Classics master, the
narrow Oxford course which he encountered as a student, with compulsory
Roman law, under John Kelly, a tutor who was himself a Roman law scholar,[6]
was likely to have a deep and lasting impression. It proved to be the foundation
for the reputation which Birks acquired as a Roman lawyer and legal historian.

---

[3] In the same decade, in *Morris v CW Martin & Sons Ltd* [1966] 1 QB 716, 730, Diplock LJ
began his judgment, agreeing with the conclusion reached in the first judgment, 'although the legal
route which has led me to this conclusion is not at all points identical with that traversed by [Lord
Denning MR]. After all, that is the beauty of the common law; it is a maze and not a motorway.'
Unfortunately, the attraction of mazes for leisure activities is less likely to appeal than a more
ordered, streamlined, and functional approach in everyday life.

[3a] He was admitted to the Middle Temple on 10th October 1966.

[4] There is a certain irony in the honour's being marked with initials shared with Quasi-Contract.

[5] PBH Birks, 'English and Roman Learning in *Moses v Macferlan*' (1984) 37 CLP 1 (the first
JAC Thomas lecture), 1.

[6] John Kelly became a Fellow of Trinity College, Oxford in 1961, the same year that Birks began
his legal studies there. Their time at Trinity was almost identical, Kelly leaving the year after Birks to
become Professor of Roman Law and Jurisprudence at University College Dublin from 1965–91.
In 1995, Birks delivered the second John Maurice Kelly Memorial lecture, 'Harrassment and Hubris:
The Right to an Equality of Respect' (1997) 32 Irish Jurist (NS) 1.

To a greater or lesser extent, this may seem to those who are more familiar with Birks's common law work as a parallel and largely unknown universe. But it had definite implications for all his work. Most obviously, he made a valuable contribution to, and reputation for, teaching and scholarship in Roman law and legal history as such, culminating in his election as Regius Professor of Civil Law at Oxford, in turn helping to assure that, while Roman law was steadily losing its place in the syllabus in other institutions, it remained a central part of an Oxford legal education. Furthermore, his expertise and contact with other prominent Roman law scholars was to pay dividends in connection with the development of his common law work. Most significantly perhaps, his learning of the Roman legal system gave him ideas about the ways in which the structure of the common law should be analysed and developed. Inevitably this would open him to criticism for trying to remould English law to fit a civilian pattern. But this was not the case. For many years, he consciously asserted the superiority of English law over Continental ways of doing things and it was only towards the end of his life that he became converted to a more civilian outlook on the English law of unjust enrichment. Indeed, in a world where older subjects such as Latin had to compete with newer subjects of study such as information technology, his emphasis was not on the study of subjects for their own sake but for what can be learnt from them and used in today's world.

It would have seemed natural, in the early 1960s, for Birks to have settled down immediately and exclusively into the life of an Oxford Roman law scholar. But Kelly encouraged him to learn from other places. After graduation, Birks went as a Teaching Associate to Northwestern University, Chicago. Familiarity with his subsequent reputation as an unjust enrichment scholar might raise the expectation that he was set upon this path in the land of the *Restatement on Restitution*. However, this happened not via the new world but the old world. For someone who was later to extol the virtues of the Oxford BCL course as the supreme method of education at Masters level, it may seem surprising that Birks did not become a BCL student but was persuaded by Kelly to go to University College London (UCL) to study Roman law under Tony Thomas[7] in the University of London LLM course, which was then taught on an intercollegiate basis.[8]

---

[7] Like Birks, JAC (Tony) Thomas became most widely known within the Common Law, as the co-author/editor with JC (later Sir John) Smith of the pioneering *A Casebook on Contract* (1st edn, 1957) (based on Smith's experience of Lon Fuller's course at Harvard). Also like Birks, Thomas was first a professor in Scotland (Douglas Professor of Civil Law at Glasgow, 1957–64), then in England (Professor of Roman Law in the University of London, at UCL, 1965–81).

[8] Until recently, it was a decision for a constituent law school whether or not it offered teaching (either individually or in association with another school) on the intercollegiate LLM. Thus, initially independent courses were run by the London School of Economics (LSE) and UCL; in the late 1970s the two courses merged for one year, then diverged again. In the late 1990s, a single course was taught by Charles Mitchell of King's College (KCL), Richard O'Dair (UCL), and Sarah Worthington of the LSE. UCL teaching ceased when O'Dair went into practice in 2002; and the LSE course ceased when the LSE withdrew from the intercollegiate course and set up its own LLM in 2003. The current London course (currently taught by Mitchell, from 2006 together with Robert Chambers) will be available only to its own students when KCL withdraws from the intercollegiate LLM in 2007.

The move was auspicious, for it was at UCL that Birks encountered George Webber. As a student of Roman law, Birks naturally learned the Roman law of unjust enrichment. With Webber, he embarked on his lifelong exploration of the English law of restitution of unjust enrichment. London can claim to be the cradle for the modern teaching of restitution in most of the common law world. But the story had in fact begun at Oxford.

There were early flutterings at Brasenose College. In 1947 Brasenose elected two new law fellows. One was Barry Nicholas,[9] a Roman and comparative law scholar who ultimately became principal of the college where Birks began his Oxford teaching career. The other was Ronald Maudsley,[10] who was ultimately to become best known for the revived *Hanbury & Maudsley's Modern Equity*.[11] As the college which has been home to the university's chair in comparative law, Brasenose has not surprisingly nurtured a comparative perspective on the law. Moreover, Maudsley studied at Harvard under Austin Scott[12] and maintained links with the USA, the place where the modern law of Restitution acquired a distinctive identity.

The gradual process of clustering groups of like cases into broad legal categories, generally regarded as brought to fruition by the creators of the textbooks of the nineteenth century, began with the more obvious areas of primary obligations, such as contract(s), tort(s) and trust(s), and left more problematic and controversial areas either by themselves or, more unhelpfully, tacked onto the initially established ones. Indeed, the associations within the names given to the major common law and equitable areas of the law of unjust enrichment, namely quasi-*contract*(s) and constructive *trust*(s), obstructed recognition of a unified body of law of unjust enrichment. A beacon for the future was then provided by the American Law Institute's inclusion of 'restitution and unjust enrichment' in its restatement of American law in the 1930s. The role of 'reporter' for this project was undertaken, symbolically, not by one person but two, the contributions of Warren Seavey on quasi-contracts and Austin Scott on constructive trusts being combined in what is formally entitled the *Restatement of the Law of RESTITUTION, Quasi Contracts and Constructive Trusts* but which is conventionally abbreviated to the pithier and therefore notably more memorable *Restatement of Restitution*.[13] However, the *Restatement* did not initiate the reception of unjust enrichment as a category of American law but confirmed a process that had been started half a century previously within its university law

---

[9] JKB(arry) M Nicholas: Fellow of Brasenose College, Oxford, 1947–78; All Souls Reader in Roman Law, 1949–71, Professor of Comparative Law, 1971–8, University of Oxford; Principal of Brasenose College, 1979–89. See P Birks (ed), *New Perspectives in the Roman Law of Property* (1989).
[10] Fellow of Brasenose College, Oxford, 1947–66; Professor of Law, University of London, at KCL, 1966–81.
[11] See RH Maudsley, *Hanbury's Modern Equity* (9th edn, 1969); *Hanbury & Maudsley's Modern Equity* (11th edn, 1981).   [12] On Scott, see the following paragraph.
[13] 1937.

schools.[14] As was to prove the case in the last quarter of a century in courts of the British Commonwealth, academic groundwork provided the basis for confirmation of the subject's existence by the more formal legal establishment and its subsequent more general acceptance.

Seavey and Scott brought their work to the attention of a wider, in particular English, audience[15] and it attracted the attention of a few, influential English lawyers.[16] Indeed, reviewing the *Restatement*, Lord Wright of Durley[17] wrote of the law of unjust enrichment that 'It will be impossible in the future to refuse to recognise its character and importance, or to speak of it as other than logically and precisely elaborated in case law and precedent'.[18] However, the American spark did not catch fire in the United Kingdom. The flame continued to burn brightly in practice and in university law courses across the Atlantic, yet it was to die down substantially by the time that it flared up in the United Kingdom.

The spark ignited in England in the summer of 1953. Robert Goff,[19] a Fellow of Lincoln College, Oxford, 'came to the conclusion that there was a huge gap in English law teaching and that Restitution was a wonderful subject waiting to be brought to light'. Soon afterwards, his colleague[20] Maudsley expressed an interest, particularly in the equity side, thereby complementing Goff's common law bias and mirroring the authorship of the *Restatement*, when, at Goff's suggestion, they decided to write a treatise on the subject. The process was repeated after Maudsley withdrew from the project[21] and[22] his place was taken by another academic with an equity background, Gareth Jones,[23] who had studied Restitution at

[14] See PH Winfield, 'The American Restatement of the Law of Restitution' (1938) 54 LQR 529; A Kull, 'James Barr Ames and the Early Modern History of Unjust Enrichment' (2005) 25 OJLS 297.   [15] WA Seavey and AW Scott, 'Restitution' (1938)54LQR 29.

[16] See Winfield, 'The American Restatement of the Law of Restitution' (1938) 54 LQR 529; Lord Wright, 'Book Review' (1937) 51 HLR 369. See also Sir AT Denning, 'The Recovery of Money' (1949) 65 LQR 37, 50; below, n 83.

[17] Lord of Appeal in Ordinary, 1932–47; Master of the Rolls, 1935–7. 'He understood the common law intuitively and had a feeling for the way it should develop. He was not content simply to decide an appeal; he wanted to establish general principles. This made him perhaps more completely admired in academic circles than among his colleagues': *DNB 1961–1970*, 1117 (Lord Devlin).

[18] (1937) 51 HLR 369, 383; reprinted as ch 2 of *Legal Essays and Addresses* (1939) 64–5.

[19] cr Lord Goff of Chieveley, 1986; Fellow of Lincoln College, Oxford, 1951–5; practising barrister, 1956–75; QC, 1967; Judge of the High Court, 1975–82; Lord Justice of Appeal, 1982–6; Lord of Appeal in Ordinary, 1986–98; Senior Law Lord, 1996–8. It is not uncommon for persons who have distinguished themselves in public life to have honorary degrees conferred upon them for their meritorious services. After he had done his best to identify the contribution which he personally had made to *Goff & Jones*, Goff received in 1972 from the University of Oxford the award of a (non-honorary) DCL: as Professor LCB Gower later quipped, for hard work—rather than on merit!

[20] Their colleges are adjacent and closely cooperated with each other at the time, the possibility of amalgamation even being considered when Lincoln's finances were at a low ebb.

[21] The only apparent fruit of Maudsley's interest in the subject which can be traced is 'Proprietary Remedies for the Recovery of Money' (1959) 75 LQR 234.

[22] At the suggestion of Brian Simpson, who succeeded Goff as the Lincoln law tutor when Goff entered full-time practice at the Bar. Simpson had previously introduced Jones to his future wife.

[23] Jones studied law at UCL (LLB 1951), Cambridge (LLB 1953) and Harvard (LLM 1954), then was a lecturer at Oriel and Exeter Colleges, Oxford (1956–8) and at KCL (1958–61; PhD 1961) before becoming a Fellow of Trinity College, Cambridge (1961–) and Downing Professor of the Laws of England, University of Cambridge (1975–98).

Harvard under Seavey and had began publishing in the area.[24] It is a criticism of contemporary academic life that those who oversee the universities require constant reassurance that work is being done and that this deters projects which require a long period of gestation and maturation. Such pressure is prone to strangle before birth a project which requires a survey of the whole of English law in order to identify, classify, and present an accurate and theoretically thought-out exposition of a hitherto inadequately recognized area of law.[25] In particular, this might have been the case on what was to prove an especially advantageous step for the advancement of the English law of Restitution, when Goff left full-time academic life to begin a career in practice at the bar.

This was, however, beneficial in at least four respects. First, any proper exposition of the law must combine both theoretical and practical perspectives; and Goff's practice inevitably enhanced both his understanding of the practical world and his appreciation of what those in practice require from a law book. Secondly, co-authorship by a practitioner enhances the receptiveness to a book and what it says by those in practice. Thirdly, Goff's steadily growing reputation at the bar and later on the bench gave his views on Restitution a stature which proved vital to the later integration of Restitution into the fabric of law and legal practice throughout the British Commonwealth. Fourthly, and paradoxically, it *initiated* the teaching of Restitution in English universities, without which the subsequent explosion of Restitution scholarship and case law would not have happened, at least in the way in which it did.

Before the more recent practice of involving established practitioners in university law teaching in order to contribute insights from their experience, there was a long practice of practitioners at the beginning of their career teaching part time, especially in London, with its ample pool of legal practitioners. Sometimes this is because of an established relationship between the institution and the teacher; but mainly it has been a source of cheap labour for the former and a means of finance for the latter.[26] For Goff, it was also an opportunity to test out developing ideas.[27] Restitution came therefore originally to be taught

---

[24] GH Jones, 'Change of Circumstances in Quasi-Contract' (1957) 73 LQR 48 may qualify as the first publication in the era of modern restitution scholarship. See also GH Jones, '*Per Quod Servitium Amisit*' (1958) 74 LQR 39.

[25] The major part of most research work is not apparent from its published results, for the core of a subject can only be properly identified by being able to distinguish it from what is less relevant or irrelevant. It is unlikely that a contemporary researcher would, like Goff and Jones, have, or be prepared to use, the time to read through every case in the *English Reports* in order to identify those which are important for his subject; or that, like Goff, he could pursue his academic career without publishing.

[26] Goff continued in the Oxford tradition of weekend teaching, for Lincoln, for a number of years after resigning his Fellowship.

[27] Indeed, if Jones has the credit for leading modern restitution publication by writing on change of circumstances in quasi-contract (see above, n 24), Goff took the next step, by contributing to a Law Reform Number of the law journal based at the LSE, an article under the more forward-looking title 'Reform of the Law of Restitution' (1961) 24 MLR 85. He identified five areas (mistake of law, apportionment, benefits conferred under illegal contracts, change of position, and compulsory discharge of liability), most of which were later subjected to judicial reform under his leadership.

within a course on Illegality and Restitution in the intercollegiate London LLM course,[28] by Aubrey Diamond and Goff[29] at the London School of Economics (LSE) and at UCL by Webber. It was while he was at UCL, first as a student and subsequently as a lecturer,[30] that Birks began his career in Restitution.[31] During that time, almost simultaneously, and symbolically, two books were published, in 1964 Samuel Stoljar's *Law of Quasi-Contract* and in 1966 Goff and Jones's *Law of Restitution*. The former appears to be the last book to be published under the heading of the old classification of the common law part of the law of unjust enrichment;[32] the latter was the first to be published outside the USA under the title under which the subject had become known there.

It is easier to teach a course in which the material is drawn together in a single book, not least because students tend to be unwilling to embark upon a course without the comfort of something comprehensive upon which to fall back. One advantage of *Goff & Jones*, therefore, was to make university courses on Restitution more viable. The subject was introduced by Jones into the Cambridge post-graduate course[33] in 1970 ('smuggled in as Restitution and Remedies') and in the same year into the Oxford BCL course by a combination of common law and equity scholars, principally by Guenter Treitel[34] and Derek Davies. The early years of Restitution teaching, in Oxford at least, were representative of a subject which was still seeking a recognized and coherent identity. Seminars and lectures originally focussed on topics within particular, established categories of law,[35] rather than within the more generalized structure and network of principles to which today's Restitution scholars and teachers have become acclimatized.

[28] Derived from a course on Illegality previously taught in the LLM by Sir David Hughes Parry at the LSE.   [29] In 1966, Diamond left and his place was taken by WR (Bill) Cornish.
[30] At UCL, while he was reading for the LLM, Birks became a part-time Assistant Lecturer (1966–7), then an Assistant Lecturer (1967–8), then a Lecturer in Roman Law (1968–71).
[31] Birks returned to UCL as a visiting professor in the late 1980s to early 1990s to resume teaching the course and, in consequence, to supervise the thesis which was the forerunner of Charles Mitchell's *The Law of Subrogation* (1995). One of his LLM students was Sonja Meier, whose work was later to influence Birks's final work: see below, n 76.
[32] Apart from Stoljar's second edition, in 1989.
[33] Though a Masters course, then called the LLB (the Cambridge undergraduate course being the BA), now the LLM.
[34] Treitel has subsequently claimed, however, that his greatest contribution to the subject was to encourage Birks to write his *Introduction to the Law of Restitution*. Birks would be amongst the first to emphasize also the amount of restitutionary learning in Treitel's *Law of Contract* (11th edn, 2003).
[35] In the 1972–3 session, the topics and seminar leaders were: (1) (A) Benefits conferred in an emergency (Treitel), (B) Expenditure on Property of Another (Davies); (2) Mistake: Estoppel and change of position (Donald Harris); (3) Incapacity (Birks); (4) Breach and other failure of performance (Treitel); (5) Duress, undue influence, and unconscionable bargains; Fraud and misrepresentation (Treitel); (6) Illegality (Birks); (7) Waiver of Tort (Treitel); (8) Discharge of Another's Obligation; Benefits Received under Anticipated Contracts (Birks). Lectures were given by Davies on Constructive Trusts. And Jeffrey Hackney gave lectures and a seminar on Remedies (primarily tracing) and Expenditure on Property of Another. To the modern restitution lawyer, question 8 of the first BCL examination paper, in 1971, appears to be rather odd: ' "It has been the policy of the law for over a hundred years to simplify and facilitate transactions in real property" (LORD UPJOHN). How far does the law relating to licences by estoppel illustrate this policy, and how far should it?'

Also, increasingly, and for a number of years, much time was spent on broad, general issues such as the implied contract theory and the imprecision of notions of 'unjust' enrichment,[36] and ultimately the question whether or not Restitution was a legitimate subject for independent study.[37] This has been criticized as the sort of pointless navel-gazing that gets universities a bad name, by those who believe that the function of universities is to expound the law precisely and certainly (presumably assuming that this is possible). As it transpired, these debates were to prove the testing ground for deeper understanding and better formulation of the law in both theory and practice. This impact was principally a consequence of Birks's return to Oxford, to a Fellowship at Brasenose, in 1971.

However, the impact of Birks's work on the wider legal world was not immediate. He became a typical old-style Oxbridge don, mainly concerned with wide and conscientious teaching and administration within his college but publishing little compared with the practices of today, and certainly by comparison with the extraordinarily prolific output of his later career. However, as with the slow gestation of *Goff & Jones*, the groundwork was being laboriously laid. And there were hurdles. In the early 1970s a new series of *Modern Legal Studies* began to appear, particularly with a view to encouraging publication of monographs by younger scholars. But the editors rejected Birks's proposal for a book on quasi-contract—in retrospect, perhaps not unfortunately, given the title. However, he found a more receptive response from the Clarendon Law Series, the highly successful series of illuminating short accounts of major areas of the law,[38] of which their leading author, Herbert Hart, was at the time Principal of Brasenose. The conciseness of Clarendons makes them ideal introductions to their subject-matter but, as Birks's *Introduction to the Law of Restitution*[39] forcefully demonstrated, Clarendon 'introductions' have never been superficial—and certainly not Birks's *Introduction*, which, though not a long book, outgrew the more concise requirements of the series. As one reviewer remarked, 'The book is intended to be, and is, seminal'.[40] The remarkable fact that the book has remained basic reading, despite enormous subsequent changes in the law, is attributable to the fact that, as another reviewer observed, 'its purpose is not to lay down definitive answers to the

---

[36] cf *Holt v Markham* [1923] 1 KB 504, 513, *per* Scrutton LJ ('well meaning sloppiness of thought').

[37] Such a general issue was in keeping with the nature of the opening question in many Oxford papers. Question 1 of the 1972 BCL paper was: 'Is there any point in treating the subject-matter of restitution as a unified body of law?' In the following year the coin was flipped and the paper began with: ' "Close study of the law of restitution reveals, as with contract and tort, a highly developed and reasonably systematic complex of rules" (GOFF and JONES). Discuss.'

[38] The first Clarendon was the *Introduction to the Law of Property* (1958) by FH(arry) Lawson, then Professor of Comparative Law and Fellow of Brasenose. In 1961, Hart published *The Concept of Law* and in 1962 Nicholas produced *An Introduction to Roman Law*.

[39] 1985. A revised edition was published in paperback in 1989 but the lightness of the revision (with updating endnotes) meant that it was essentially still the original work and not a second edition.

[40] JD Davies, Book Review [1986] LMCLQ 540, 541. These words were reproduced on the cover of the revised, paperback, edition, in 1989.

outstanding questions in Restitution but to provide the intellectual framework within which they can be debated and resolved'.[41] That framework was novel in more ways than one, being constructed in part with new, and memorable, language of unjust factors, interceptive subtraction, and the like.

The plan having been elaborated in book form, the stage was set for the ensuing campaign to implement it by a series of articles, lectures, seminars, and other activities, by Birks and others. The time was ripe. Restitutionary issues arise in most, if not all, areas of law; and, partly for that reason, Restitution is a difficult subject, so that those who successfully engage with it tend to be able and energetic disciples. Teaching had been firmly established in England's three main universities, in courses which attracted a wide international graduate student body.[42] The subject had two major texts and a growing volume of periodical literature and other books. Also, graduates who had studied Restitution were becoming established as university teachers and practitioners throughout the Commonwealth.[43]

Significantly, things were also changing in practice. In July 1977, Lord Diplock famously declared that 'there is no general doctrine of unjust enrichment recognised in English law'.[44] Yet, just over a fortnight later, Parliament had explicitly referred to, and therefore acknowledged, the notion of unjust enrichment, in the Torts (Interference with Goods) Act 1977.[45] More significantly, two years previously, the subject had acquired its most influential and sympathetic judicial medium with Goff's appointment to the High Court bench. In March 1979, he began delivery of a series of revolutionary judgments on the law of Restitution with the first English judgment interpreting the Law Reform (Frustrated Contracts) Act 1943, famously declaring that 'the fundamental principle underlying the Act . . . is prevention of the unjust enrichment of either party to the contract at the other's expense'.[46] However, characteristically

---

[41] Stephen Moriarty, Book Review [1986] CLJ 128, 131.

[42] The first LLB course was formally introduced into the syllabus of the University of Wales Institute for Science and Technology (now subsumed into Cardiff University) in 1975 by Rose but was never taught, as he left to join UCL, where he began teaching the first LLB Restitution course in 1984. Other undergraduate courses have been taught (eg by Mitchell and Donal Nolan at KCL from 1996–2001) but Restitution has generally not been successful in competing with other subjects for space in LLB syllabuses.

[43] eg one of Birks's London LLM students from the 1960s, now the President of the New South Wales Court of Appeal, was the lead author of the first Australian book, K Mason and JW Carter, *Restitution Law in Australia* (1995), the subject of the first Mansfield symposium: P Birks *et al*, 'The First Australian Textbook on Restitution' [1997] RLR 229.

[44] *Orakpo v Manson Developments Ltd* [1978] AC 95, 104.

[45] The Torts (Interference with Goods) Act 1977, s 7(4) and the ensuing example simply refer to a claimant's/finder's being 'unjustly enriched', without any apparent need to elaborate.

[46] *BP Exploration Co (Libya) Ltd v Hunt (No 2)* [1979] 1 WLR 783, 799A. The comprehensive, and therefore very long, nature of this important judgment initially discouraged the editor from reporting the case in the *Weekly Law Reports*. She was eventually persuaded to report a shortened version after the judge had taken her to lunch twice and agreed to draft the headnote. The first instance judgment was subsequently affirmed: [1981] 1 WLR 232 (CA); [1983] 2 AC 352. A comment ('Restitution after Frustration' (1981) 131 NLJ 955) was published with a view to emphasizing the area of law in a journal read by practitioners.

and in keeping with his office, he could not be expected to be a partisan crusader for the subject; and in the following month, in his second major judgment in the area, after hearing argument he delivered another leading judgment, in which he felt compelled to dissent from a proposition in *Goff & Jones*.[47] Nevertheless, Robert Goff's increasing stature and the delivery of judgments informed by academic research helped make Restitution more respectable in practice. Moreover, he famously encouraged the judiciary to be more willing to take account of academic writing.[48]

At this time, Birks moved not only from Oxford but also from the jurisdiction, to take up the Chair of Civil Law at Edinburgh. Shortly afterwards *Lloyd's Maritime and Commercial Law Quarterly* came under new editorship, with restitutionary sympathy, and so became a vehicle for publications on Restitution, particularly by Birks. Also the Society of Public Teachers of Law (SPTL), the professional association of British university law teachers, approved the formation of a Restitution Group. By a happy coincidence, the Society's next annual conference, and therefore the group's inaugural meeting, was held in Edinburgh, in September 1984.

The conference produced two notable contributions. First, Steven Hedley argued that the restitutionary elements in the law should be considered as they appeared to be in fact: not necessarily consistent or conforming to a neat theoretical framework, but as laid down by judicial decision. He established his position as a sceptic of Birks's rationalizing and reordering, helping to ensure that Birks's work would not be without its critics, and firing a continuing debate between the two positions.[49] Secondly, Birks seized the opportunity of his new location to write on the Scottish law of Restitution. The Roman, civil, law basis of Scottish law had made its law of unjustified enrichment more transparent than was the case south of the border but, like its southern cousin, it was in need of rejuvenating attention. Nicholas had performed such a service on a civil law system within a larger, more common law-based country, when he had written

---

[47] *Barclays Bank Ltd v WJ Simms Son & Cooke (Southern) Ltd* [1980] QB 677. See Jones, 'Lord Goff's Contribution to the Law of Restitution', ch 10 of W Swadling and G Jones, *The Search for Principle* (1999), 208.

[48] One of his first acts on elevation to the House of Lords was to initiate this revolution in memorable language: see *Spiliada Maritime Corp v Cansulex (The Spiliada)* [1987] AC 460, 488. For some, the high point of this practice occurred in *Kleinwort Benson Ltd v Lincoln City Council* [1999] 2 AC 349, 386, where Lord Goff phrased a question for consideration by reference to a footnote by Birks in 'No Consideration: Restitution after Void Contracts' (1993) 23 UWALR 195, 230 n 137. There have been occasions when judges may seem to have become overly zealous or selective in reference to certain academic literature: see eg *Kleinwort Benson Ltd v Birmingham City Council* [1997] QB 380, 384–385; *Royal Bank of Scotland Plc v Etridge (No 2)* [2001] UKHL 44; [2002] 2 AC 773, [82]. The instigator of this practice later spoke out against inappropriate citation, in *Hunter v Canary Wharf Ltd* [1997] AC 655, 694.

[49] Hedley's paper, 'Unjust Enrichment as the Basis of Restitution—An Overworked Concept' (1985) 15 LS 56, provoked an immediate response by Birks, 'Unjust Enrichment—A Reply to Mr Hedley' (1985) 5 LS 67.

on the Louisiana law of unjust enrichment two decades earlier,[50] not only providing a thorough re-examination of the law but providing the basic literature for its subsequent development in practice. Birks's work stimulated similar consequences in Scotland.[51]

A proactive campaign to attract Restitution scholars to participate in the meetings of the SPTL Restitution Group[52] helped to strengthen the community of Restitution scholars and the growth of periodical literature. The resolve to meet regularly whatever the circumstances was to have another important outcome. The 1988 SPTL conference was threatened by a dispute which provoked a call for a boycott of the host university, Hull. The conference, and certainly its smaller sub-meetings, were threatened with insufficient numbers. But it had become an article of faith with Restitution that the show had to go on.[53] If it had not, the convener would not have heard that the position of Honorary Secretary of the SPTL was about to fall vacant. It was with a view to nominating a successor of stature, who would energize the Society that, while returning over the Humber Bridge, he secured Birks's consent to stand. Pandora's box was opening further, and more than anticipated.

The previous year, Birks had moved to a chair at Southampton. But the Regius Chair of Civil Law at Oxford had recently fallen vacant and it was decided that the next holder should have expertise in both Roman law and English law. No one was more suited to the position than Birks, who took up the post, with a Fellowship at All Souls College, at the same time that he became Honorary Secretary of the SPTL, in 1989.

That summer was also pivotal in another way. A solicitor had abstracted funds from his firm's client account in order to fund his gambling addiction, and the firm was seeking payment of the missing amount from the Playboy Club. The claim was rejected by the trial judge and a majority of the Court of Appeal. The House of Lords was therefore presented with the opportunity of considering a claim of a restitutionary nature at the highest level. The claim was allowed, in

---

[50] B Nicholas, 'Unjustified Enrichment in the Civil Law and Louisiana Law' (1962) 36 Tulane LR 605 and (1963) 37 Tulane LR 49. The first collection of European materials on unjustified enrichment was dedicated to Nicholas's memory: J Beatson and E Schrage (eds), *Unjustified Enrichment* (2003).

[51] The convener of the Restitution group was at the time associate editor of *Current Legal Problems*, with the consequence that the Edinburgh paper was published there: 'Restitution: A View of the Scots Law' [1985] CLP 57. See also 'Six Questions in Search of a Subject—Unjust Enrichment in a Crisis of Identity' [1985] JR 227. See now M Hogg, 'Unjustified Enrichment in Scots Law Twenty Years On: Where Now?' [2006] RLR 1. See also H MacQueen, below Ch 21.

[52] The group provided the format for the current subject sections activities in the Society of Legal Scholars.

[53] The Restitution meeting was attended only by the four speakers, the convener, and Birks. On a later occasion, Birks claimed that Gareth Jones's attendance at his daughter Alison's wedding was an insufficient excuse for absence from an All Souls Restitution seminar. He also took a dim view of an overseas speaker's having to cancel an appearance during a boycott on flying caused by an international emergency.

Lipkin Gorman (a firm) v Karpnale Ltd.[54] The principal speech was delivered by the most junior member of the Appellate Committee, Lord Goff of Chieveley.[55] There remains a view that the firm's success hinged upon vindication of its proprietary rights and not on reversal of the club's unjust enrichment. But the House had emphasized the defendant's unjust enrichment and, moreover, had recognized change of position as a defence to claims based on unjust enrichment. The cat was now truly out of the bag.[56]

Seeds were also bearing fruit internationally. In Australia, Paul Finn, one of Birks's former pupils in the London LLM course,[57] had begun a series of seminars bringing together groups of judges, writers, practitioners, and academics who, in one role or another, had contributed to fostering an understanding of the subject-matter of the seminars. Unconventionally, Finn's rules were that a speaker did not deliver his paper in full and then take questions at the end; but the papers should be read in advance, and introduced briefly by another participant, with most time being devoted to a rigorous examination of the issues. Birks's participation in the seminar on Restitution, in 1989, was notable in a number of respects. The topic of his contribution, 'Restitution from the Executive: A Tercentenary Footnote to the Bill of Rights [1689]',[58] was timely in more ways than one.[59] And it was a forerunner of a subsequent decade and a half of international spreading of the restitutionary word and an encouragement to the development of the subject in other jurisdictions. It also had an influence on Birks's work for the SPTL.

Although the Society annually elects a president, who is the ship's figurehead, the honorary secretary remains in charge of the engine room. It was a time of great flux in legal education; and Birks set about the root and branch reorganization of the Society and the strong championship of its interests with outside bodies, becoming Secretary of the Lord Chancellor's Standing Conference on Legal Education[60] and advocating forcefully, particularly to professional bodies, the value of a thorough academic grounding for proper legal education.[61] Jones

---

[54] [1991] 2 AC 548.

[55] Lord Templeman also delivered a full speech. Lords Bridge of Harwich, Griffiths, and Ackner each delivered short speeches agreeing with both Lords Templeman and Goff. But Lord Goff's speech is clearly the main speech.

[56] 1989 was also the beginning of a decade in which Jack Beatson and Andrew Burrows, two of Birks's former pupils at Brasenose as well as students and colleagues in BCL seminars, successively held the post of the Commissioner heading the Law Commission's common law team. They were, in turn, the prime movers behind the Law Commission's reports *Restitution: Mistakes of Law and Ultra Vires Public Authority Receipts and Payments* (Law Com No 227, 1994) and *Aggravated, Exemplary and Restitutionary Damages* (Law Com No 247, 1997). Beatson later became the first person to be appointed directly from a full-time academic post to be a High Court judge.

[57] Finn became a Professor of Law at the Australian National University and then a judge of the Federal Court of Australia.   [58] ch 6 of PD Finn (ed), *Essays on Restitution* (1990).

[59] See below, n 65.   [60] 1991–4.

[61] The very real stress which was caused by the threat of potentially ruinous defamation proceedings if there were no retraction of and apology for a comment on the future of the Bar's vocational stage, and the courage with which the threat was resisted, should not be underestimated or forgotten. See 'The Empire Strikes Back' (1995) 10 SPTL Reporter 1.

has commented of the first of Finn's seminars that 'It is sad to reflect that such a gathering would be the rarest of events in this country, and a double-bill, held two years later, would be unthinkable'.[62] This was to change; with a vengeance. Birks innovated a substantial series of SPTL seminars, held at All Souls, and conducted in accordance with Finn rules, with a view to bringing together experts from academe, the professions, and the bench to discuss and so to solve major problems in legal education and the law. If it proved impossible to provide a final solution to such problems, it none the less produced a series of books as a contribution to their possible solution.

The organizational demands of the increased activities of the Honorary Secretaryship of the SPTL amounted to a full-time job. But it was one carried out in parallel with a full teaching load. This ensured that the BCL Restitution course was one of the most exciting and demanding[63] law courses in the world. It was complemented by a succession of doctoral students whom Birks supervised in producing an influential series of monographs on topics within Restitution and related areas. More remarkably, there was anything but a let-up in Birks's own publications. There will be those for whom it is a matter of regret that Birks did not spend more time in turning his research into leading books; and there have certainly been those who have thought that the sheer volume of his output in some way diminished his stature, or at least the stature which a more selective series of articles could have acquired. But Birks was a man with a mission, who was determined that every aspect of the restitutionary debate was properly and continually heard and that potential errors should be criticized and corrected.

This was in sympathy with the policy of the Lloyd's Maritime and Commercial Law Quarterly (LMCLQ), which was not merely to contribute to debate generally but, where possible, to influence it specifically. No one could have been more willing than Birks to prepare an article in time for publication for a House of Lords' hearing in a Restitution case. As on so many occasions, he burnt the midnight oil, delivering the article to the editor's house at 5.30 in the morning, in time for it to be edited and squeezed into the next issue at proof stage.[64]

---

[62] Review of PD Finn (ed), *Equity and Commercial Relationships* [1990] LMCLQ 128, 128.

[63] Given that there was nothing more important to compete for time, Birks had no qualms about instituting lectures for Restitution at 8.00 a.m. on a Monday morning.

[64] See 'The English Recognition of Unjust Enrichment' [1991] LMCLQ 473. The aim was that the article should be published prior to the hearing in *Woolwich Equitable Building Soc v IRC* [1993] AC 70. As it turned out, it was not Birks's LMCLQ article but his earlier Finn essay (above, n 58) which was cited in *Woolwich*, Lord Goff observing (ibid 166) that the Finn paper was foreshadowed by ' "Colour of Office": Restitutionary Redress against Public Authority' (1987) 14 JMCL 41, by Cornish. In *Woolwich* [1993] AC 70, 166, Lord Goff expressed 'little doubt that [the] essay by Professor Birks . . . provided the main inspiration for the argument of Woolwich, and the judgments of the majority of the Court of Appeal, in the present case'. Since this position prevailed, Birks can therefore be credited for a significant academic contribution to the development of the law and to the recovery by Woolwich of many millions of pounds from the public purse. Unfortunately, this assistance was not reciprocated when the then SPTL president attempted to apply his well-known fund-raising skills in trying to persuade Woolwich to provide some financial support for academic activities. See 'The Inequitable Woolwich, Meanest Bank in Town' (1996) 13 SPTL Reporter 45.

The nature of unjust enrichment, with restitutionary issues being spread over all areas of the law, the continuing recognition and explosion of restitutionary activity worldwide, and the particular affinity between developments throughout the British Commonwealth were making it increasingly difficult and necessary to identify and keep up with changes. Birks thought that some record ought to be kept of these developments. And so, in the early spring of 1993, he informed the editor of LMCLQ that the task should fall on him. What might in other circumstances have appeared a rather haughty approach was in fact then typical of Restitution scholars, who constituted a uniquely close community of ready collaborators. Once planted, the idea was transformed and a new journal, the *Restitution Law Review*, was created, with a core section digesting developments internationally, the usual sections for articles and notes, occasional sections highlighting law reform and legislation, book reviews and review articles, and materials which were not otherwise easily available.[65] The first article published[66] was, two months after publication of the first issue, cited by the Privy Council in *A-G for Hong Kong v Reid*,[67] possibly a record for citation of a new journal. Once again, the timing was right. The rapidity with which the RLR was first published was a consequence of the decision to publish (under the banner of the Mansfield Press)[68] as a private venture and the support of a leading firm of solicitors. They were involved in the 'swaps' litigation which was then set to revolutionize the English law of Restitution and therefore interested in research into it, for discovery and explanation of the relevant law.

Post Lipkin Gorman, and to highlight the relevance of restitutionary developments and the subject-matter of the RLR within the broader law of obligations, presentation of restitutionary writing in the *Review* became not so much a matter of emphasizing the importance of the law of unjust enrichment per se[69] as commissioning contributions from experts in other areas of the law of obligations and demonstrating the relevance of restitutionary topics to other areas. The experiment was extended with the publication of a series of books, mainly examining the relationship between Restitution and other areas of the law, in part derived from the Mansfield seminars instituted after Birks's retirement from

---

[65] eg O'Dair and Doran Lipshitz provided an English translation and report of the important case *Adras Building Material Ltd v Harlow & Jones GmbH* [1995] RLR 234, previously only available in Hebrew. In 1998, after attention was drawn to it by David Ibbetson, Sir William Evans's *Essay on the Action for Money Had and Received* was edited for a modern audience by Lionel Smith, Birks, and Rose and republished in [1998] RLR 3. Draft copies were rushed to counsel and the Appellate Committee of the House of Lords in time for the hearing in *Kleinwort Benson Ltd v Lincoln City Council* [1999] 2 AC 349. Cf ibid 368H.

[66] Sir Peter Millett, 'Bribes and Secret Commissions' [1993] RLR 7. The paper was initially delivered at an All Souls SPTL seminar: see 'Remedies: The Error in *Lister v Stubbs*', ch 5 of PBH Birks (ed), *The Frontiers of Liability* (1994).

[67] [1994] AC 324; [1994] 1 NZLR 1; [1995] RLR § 202.

[68] The name was drawn, more obviously, from Lord Mansfield's position as the judge in the seminal case of *Moses v Macferlan* (1760) 2 Burr 1005 and, the editor can now confess, his prominence in commercial law.   [69] See eg above, n 46.

the honorary secretaryship of the SPTL and the ending of the All Souls SPTL seminars.[70] In addition, a research resource was published in 1994,[71] an internet discussion group was set up in 1995,[72] and a website in 1998.[73] A basic problem with the law of Restitution, of finding the relevant material from a diverse range of sources, had altered to a more enduring problem, of how to manage the growing volume of accessible material.

Moreover, the process of rationalizing Restitution's place within the greater framework of the common law leads to greater questioning of that grander untidy scheme of principles, policies, and rules. Birks ventured into this wider arena alongside his work on Restitution itself, lecturing and writing on topics within the law of Restitution, in related areas, and also in unconnected areas. This culminated in the ambitious, if imperfectly realized, *English Private Law*.[74] Thus, his publications are as likely to be read by students of contract, property law, and trusts as by those specifically interested in Restitution. Whereas Restitution lawyers are still roughly categorized as either common lawyers or equity/property lawyers—a classification which cannot appeal to anyone interested in proper taxonomy—Birks uniquely transcended these divisions. He was an authoritative voice on wide areas of English law and recognized by many as the leading academic lawyer of his time.

Moreover, from his base at All Souls, he took the word out more frequently into the wider world, with increasing conference and teaching appearances throughout the common law world and beyond. In particular, and appropriately for an expert on Roman law, he regularly taught in Europe, especially in the Netherlands, and increased his contacts with civilian scholars. He had an important influence on the growth of research and publications (in English and other languages, especially German) on civilian aspects of the law of unjust enrichment and the growing awareness of English-speaking lawyers of Continental approaches. The expanded horizons produced by his comparative experience initially provided support for his strong conviction of the superiority

[70] The first book was Rose (ed), *Restitution and the Conflict of Laws* (1995). It was drawn to the attention of the judge in *Baring Bros & Co Ltd v Cunninghame DC* [1997] CLC 108, whose offer to counsel of time for further argument on the subject was declined! After 'The First Australian Text book on the Law of Restitution' (above, n 43), the Mansfield symposia produced Birks and Rose (eds), *Lessons of the Swaps Litigation* (2000) and Birks and Rose (eds), *Restitution and Equity: Volume 1: Resulting Trusts and Equitable Compensation* (2000). Also published were Rose (ed), *Restitution and Banking Law* (1998), A Skelton, *Restitution and Contract* (1998), A Jones, *Restitution and European Community Law* (2000), and Rose (ed), *Restitution and Insolvency* (2000). The final book from the Mansfield symposia (in answer to the question 'what's volume 2?') was Birks and Rose (eds), *Restitution and Equity: Volume 2: Breach of Trust*, which was published as Birks and Pretto, *Breach of Trust* (2002).

[71] P Birks and R Chambers, *The Restitution Research Resource 1994* (1994), followed by *The Restitution Research Resource 1997* (1997).

[72] The Restitution Discussion Group (rdg) was set up on 30 September 1995 by Smith, one of Birks's research students and subsequently the author of *The Law of Tracing* (1997).

[73] See http://www.ucc.ie/law/restitution/restitution.htm.

[74] 2000, with 2nd supp (2004).

of the common law treatment of issues of unjust enrichment, in particular its understood insistence on relatively clear 'unjust factors' to ground restitution. Yet, consistently with the spirit of continuing critical enquiry, he was always ready to cast aside the wrong answer, even if it was his own.[75]

The consequence, which he happily attributed to persuasion by the views of one of his former pupils,[76] was the publication in 2003—in the Clarendon Law Series, of which he had become the editor—of a new book.[77] The title now contained reference not to the response to the event upon which his subject was based (restitution) but to the event itself, explained generally by reference to receipt without basis: *Unjust Enrichment*.[78] In the month in which the book went to press, September 2003, the annual conference of the Society of Legal Studies (SLS, the renamed SPTL) was held in Oxford. Exactly half a century after Robert Goff had conceived the idea of a book on Restitution (and at the same time that Goff's innovative LSE Restitution course ceased),[79] the culmination of Birks's life's work on unjust enrichment[80] coincided with his presidency of the Society.

Birks's style was inspired, dramatic, and forceful. He has had a powerful influence on those who have been taught or lectured by him or who have read his works. He has led a generation of students, academics, practitioners, and judges along routes which he mapped out and constructed throughout the closing decades of the twentieth century. Then he experienced a Damascene conversion and declared that the promised land was in another direction. Inevitably, he provoked immediate scepticism and criticism—he could hardly complain, for these were qualities which he had encouraged. A symposium was organized at which the book was discussed.[81] Its proceedings fed into work which Birks had already begun. As any author realizes, particularly in a constantly changing area, the time at which he submits a book for publication is not when he has done all the work that could be done on it, but the time at which he is most conscious of how it could be improved. So, unusually, but characteristically, Birks had immediately begun writing the second edition of the new book, to reshape his new vision. The moment, as usual, was ripe. The new approach had its sceptics;

---

[75] Readers of his work became used to his call for previous expressions of superseded views to be called back and burnt. Inevitably, he opened himself to criticism for views which were prone to be unstable and unenduring.

[76] See esp Meier, *Irrtum und Zweckverfehlung* [Mistake and Failure of Purpose] (1999). See T Krebs, 'A German Contribution to English Enrichment Law' [1999] RLR 271.

[77] This was foreshadowed by the paper opening the conference to celebrate Jones's career: see P Birks, 'Misnomer', ch 1 of WR Cornish, R Nolan, J O'Sullivan, and G Virgo (eds), *Restitution: Past, Present and Future; Essays in Honour of Gareth Jones* (1998). For the annual conference during his presidency of the SLS, Birks requested subject section conveners to organize sessions discussing the most important article in the subject in the past decade. Mitchell McInnes responded to the invitation to address the Restitution section with 'Misnomer: A Classic' [2004] RLR 79.

[78] It was not the first book in the Commonwealth with this title. See G Klippert, *Unjust Enrichment* (1983), by a member of the 1972–3 BCL class and partly dedicated to Birks.

[79] See above, n 8. This followed the year after the cessation of teaching at UCL.

[80] See also above, n 77.

[81] For the proceedings, see Burrows *et al*, 'The New Birksian Approach to Unjust Enrichment' [2004] RLR 260.

but it was also attracting its converts. Initial reactions had to be taken account of and the map had to be quickly redrawn, so that the way was clear. A mere revision, as with the reissue of his *Introduction to the Law of Restitution*, would not do. The work, unfortunately, acquired a particular urgency but it was effectively completed when, on this threshold of the new world of unjust enrichment, its creator died.[82]

The book is a cliff-hanger. Only time will tell whether this new world has been correctly predicted or will be built along these lines. If it is not, we shall never know whether theory might have been turned into practice by the force of Birks's intellect and personality. What is certain is that Birks's career has had two major enduring effects. First, building on *Goff & Jones*, he has been the principal provider and driver of the scholarly framework for the advance of the law of Restitution of unjust enrichment in theory and practice over the last two decades. Secondly, more than anyone of his generation, he has demonstrated the value of scholarship in the legal world. He knew that he was lucky, to discover at an early stage in his career an exciting subject of tremendous importance, the significance of which was waiting to be expounded and exploited. The process involved going back to basics—and learning from the legal systems upon which modern civil and common law systems are based. It required a continually open mind, hard work, and thorough preparation, facing up to difficulties, seizing opportunities, clarity of expression and persistence, and not a little luck. Overall, it demonstrated the need for academics to know and understand the law and practice, and for all lawyers to realize that a proper understanding of principle and theory is necessary for the just operation and development of the law in the real world, to reconcile logic and experience. Whatever is the future for the law of unjust enrichment, these lessons will remain relevant for all law and lawyers.[83]

---

[82] On 6 July 2004. The second edition was published in 2005. See McInnes [2005] RLR 241.

[83] Much more work needs to be done in order to attempt a more thorough and balanced picture of the historical development of the law of Restitution than has been possible here. With that in mind, I shall be grateful to receive any information or stories about the evolution of the subject and those involved, whether in the classroom, in practice, or elsewhere. Then, no doubt, most of what I say here can be called back for burning.

Postscript: The process has begun. While this paper was in proof, William Swadling drew my attention to the following passage from the entry on Lord Denning in the *Oxford Dictionary of National Biography* (2004) 72037: 'One subject in which Denning was deeply interested was the development of a coherent law of restitution, to provide for adequate remedies in cases in which the defendant had been unjustly enriched at the expense of the plaintiff. At one time he started to gather together the relevant material with a view to writing a book on the subject but had to leave the task to others, warmly encouraged by him. Even so, some of his decisions betrayed his interest in, and knowledge of, this subject: in particular, *Nelson v Larholt* [1948] 1 KB 339 and *Larner v LCC* [1949] 2 KB 683.' The entry is signed 'Robert Goff'.

THE ENGLISH LAW OF UNJUST ENRICHMENT AND RESTITUTION

General Concepts

2

Absence of Basis: The New Birksian Scheme

*Andrew Burrows**

1. Introduction

For Peter the line between legal truth and falsehood was sharp and clear. His pictures of the law were painted with bold strokes that demanded the attention of the viewer. They left no room for the fuzzy outline of a middle course. So it was entirely in character that when, in *Unjust Enrichment*, he swung over to a civilian approach to the unjust question, he should portray his change of mind as a conversion of the most dramatic kind. Only he could have written that 'almost everything of mine now needs calling back for burning'.[1] It is the thesis of this essay that that was over-dramatic and that Peter had no need to condemn his earlier work. On close examination, the traditional 'common law approach'[2] and the new Birksian approach have advantages and disadvantages compared one with the other. The best way forward is not to abandon unjust factors in favour of 'absence of basis' but rather to see the latter as a helpful cross-check on the former in determining, in novel cases, whether an enrichment at the claimant's expense is unjust. In short, while Peter was correct to argue that one cannot mix the two approaches without risking chaos, the application of the common law unjust factors approach, cross-checked in difficult cases by his new civilian

* Norton Rose Professor of Commercial Law in the University of Oxford; Fellow of St Hugh's College. I am grateful to Robert Stevens, Fellow in Law at Lady Margaret Hall, for his comments.

[1] *Unjust Enrichment* (2nd edn, 2005) p xii (hereinafter referred to as Birks).

[2] This phrase is used throughout this essay to refer to the approach of requiring the claimant to establish an 'unjust factor', such as mistake or failure of consideration, and is reflected in the structure of *Goff & Jones, The Law of Restitution* (first published in 1966 and now in its sixth edition) and in all Birks's earlier writings, especially *An Introduction to the Law of Restitution* (rev edn, 1989). Although in *Unjust Enrichment* Birks claimed that English law has already adopted the civilian approach (so that there is now no distinctive common law approach) that claim is rejected in this chapter as an exaggerated view of the impact of the swaps cases.

approach, appears to give us the best of all worlds. At root, this is to say no more than that carefully constructed comparative insights can be of help in the development of the common law.

It is important to clarify at the outset that, while in developing his new 'absence of basis' scheme, Peter was heavily influenced by civil law systems, especially that in Germany, he did not see himself as embracing one particular civilian system. Rather he saw his scheme as 'an English version of the civilian "sine causa" approach'.[3] And it is clear that in some important respects his approach differs from any civilian system. So no attempt will here be made to analyse any particular civilian approach to the unjust question. Rather it is the Birksian system that will be carefully scrutinized and assessed on its own merits.[4]

2. The New Birksian Approach to the Unjust Question

On the new Birksian approach, the unjust question is ultimately answered by reference to one concept alone: absence of basis. In explaining in general terms what he meant by this, Birks divided unjust enrichments into two: participatory enrichments, which were then subdivided into obligatory and voluntary enrichments, and non-participatory enrichments. It is convenient to look at these in the following order: non-participatory enrichments, obligatory enrichments, voluntary enrichments.

Non-participatory enrichments (eg where the claimant is ignorant of the defendant being enriched at the claimant's expense) are, in general, straightforward. The non-participation means that, in general, there is no basis at all (not even a putative one) for the enrichment so that, prima facie,[5] restitution should be awarded.[6]

Obligatory enrichments are enrichments where the basis is a valid obligation. That is, the claimant pays (or renders a non-money benefit) to discharge an obligation. Restitution will prima facie follow if there was no valid obligation: that is, if the payment (or non-money benefit) was not due. Cases of payments made under a mistake as to liability, of money paid under void contracts, and of taxes demanded by a public authority ultra vires, are all examples within this

---

[3] Birks, p ix.

[4] For insights on the use of absence of basis in English law from the perspective of German law, see Chs 18–20 below. G Dannemann, in Ch 19, argues that changes would need to be made within English contract law and other neighbouring areas to accommodate properly an 'absence of basis' approach to unjust enrichment. T Krebs in Ch 20 argues that, especially if an absence of basis approach is to be followed, there are useful lessons to be drawn from the German law on 'non-participatory enrichments'. S Meier in Ch 18 suggests that, as has been shown in German law, in some areas absence of basis needs to be supplemented by additional requirements for restitution.

[5] 'Prima facie' restitution is used throughout to indicate that the unjust question has been resolved in the claimant's favour so that there will be restitution of an enrichment at the claimant's expense *subject to defences* (such as change of position).   [6] Birks, 129, 155.

category of where restitution is awarded: in each, the basis—that the money was due—was absent. In Birks's view, 'The vast majority of cases fall under this head'[7] by which he presumably meant that the vast majority of cases *where restitution is awarded* fall under this head.

The basis of voluntary enrichments is nearly always[8] a contract or trust (in both cases, without any supposed obligation) or a gift. So this covers where the claimant confers benefits on the basis that a contract will come into existence: the basis fails—and hence there is prima-facie restitution—where the anticipated contract does not eventuate. It also covers where benefits are conferred to constitute an express trust but the trust fails. But most significant of all to the Birksian scheme is that this head covers gifts. So restitution is granted where a gift is invalid. Moreover, 'gift' is used in a very wide sense so that the basis of an enrichment being a valid gift is relied on to explain the *denial* of restitution in very many situations. In particular, risk-takers are ruled out from restitution on the analysis that they are making gifts so that the basis of the enrichment is present not absent. So, for example, Birks wrote: 'The basis of an enrichment cannot be identified without an eye constantly on risk-taking. The busker wants to be paid but takes the risk of getting nothing. The basis of his offering is not reciprocal payment but gift.'[9] This also means that, in cases where at first sight the basis for a payment appears to be a valid obligation that is absent, one might, on closer inspection, have a gift where the person paying is taking the risk that the money is not due. And 'by-benefits'—that is, the incidental benefits to another of action taken in one's self-interest (eg heat rising from the claimant's flat to the defendant's)—are also treated as gifts (provided the actor was acting of his own free will) so that, as one would expect, there can be no restitution.[10]

A significant feature of the above scheme merits emphasis. The bases focussed on can, for shorthand, be said to be a *valid obligation (whether contractual, statutory, or otherwise)*[11] *or, if no obligation, a trust or gift or (anticipated) contract.* Viewed in that shorthand way, one can see clearly that the bases in mind correspond to categories of law that have been conventionally thought of as different from the law of unjust enrichment. Indeed the Canadian language of

[7] Birks, 130.
[8] Birks, 142. At 152–4 it was suggested that there might be other bases that might be absent but the examples given all seem to be covered by the basis being an obligation or a conditional gift. So, for example, an expected counter-performance under a contract is not seen as constituting the basis for an enrichment. Rather the basis is seen as the contractual obligation to render that counter-performance: the basis therefore fails only if the contractual obligation is invalid (see 119, 142). Outside contract, an expected counter-performance may be viewed as the condition of what is a gift. The basis would be absent when that condition fails, thereby rendering the gift invalid.
[9] Birks, 160: see also 130.
[10] Peculiarly Birks treated 'by-benefits' within his section on non-participatory enrichments. But his explanation in terms of gift surely means that where the actor was acting of his own free will (contrast 'legal compulsion', on which see Birks at 158–60) by-benefits should be seen as participatory voluntary enrichments. A gift cannot be non-participatory.
[11] Birks included only *legal* obligations as relevant bases; 'where a natural obligation survives the invalidity' was treated as a possible defence at Birks, 257–8.

'no *juristic* basis' may be thought especially apt.[12] An important point flowing from this is that one might naturally regard the details of the injustice in question as having already been decided outside the law of unjust enrichment. For example, in order to know whether a contractual obligation is valid or invalid one will need to turn to the law of contract. As a consequence one might regard the law of unjust enrichment as having little to say on the injustice question. So, for example, one can argue that it falls outside the law of unjust enrichment to examine when mistake or misrepresentation or duress or undue influence invalidates a contract or gift: it is sufficient simply to know that the contract or gift is invalid so that the basis is absent. Restitution (of an enrichment at the claimant's expense) is then prima facie triggered by that invalidity/absence of basis. Not surprisingly, Birks did not wish in this way to denude the law of unjust enrichment of its traditional content and he envisaged absence of basis as being at the head of a 'pyramid' that had, at its base—still apparently within the law of unjust enrichment—the details about invalidity.[13] But his scheme does lend itself to an interpretation that, in line with civilian thinking, pushes the details of the unjust question into categories of the law outside unjust enrichment.

3. Applying the Birksian Scheme to a Range of Cases

The last section examined the Birksian scheme at a general level. But to understand the scheme fully, it is an illuminating exercise to go through a range of situations, considered in leading common law cases on unjust enrichment, in order to clarify what the reasoning and decision would be under the Birksian scheme in comparison with that at common law.[14] This will also help us to determine which cases, if any, would be decided differently under the new scheme.

---

[12] This language was first used by Dickson J in *Rathwell v Rathwell* (1978) 83 DLR (3d) 289 and it was subsequently confirmed by a majority of the Supreme Court of Canada, including Dickson J, in *Pettkus v Becker* (1980) 117 DLR (3d) 257. For an excellent analysis of the Canadian approach to no juristic basis, arguing that it could be construed as consistent with what he argued was the preferable common law approach of looking for positive reasons for restitution, see Lionel Smith, 'The Mystery of "Juristic Reason"' (2000) 12 Supreme Court Law Review 211. More recently, the Supreme Court of Canada has more fully embraced the civilian approach while modifying it to find juristic bases (reasons for denying restitution) not only in existing categories but also by reference to the parties' expectations and public policy: see *Garland v Consumers Gas Co* (2004) 237 DLR (4th) 385; *Pacific National Investments v Victoria* (2004) 245 DLR (4th) 211. For analysis of these cases see eg M McInnes, 'Juristic Reasons and Unjust Factors in the Supreme Court of Canada' (2004) 120 LQR 554; R Grantham, 'Absence of Juristic Reason in the Supreme Court of Canada' [2005] RLR 102.   [13] Birks, 116.

[14] The nine situations dealt with are not intended to be comprehensive. To take one excluded example, non-contractual payments rendered by duress are not specifically discussed. But it would seem that the situations are representative in the sense that other situations fall to be dealt with under the Birksian scheme in an analogous way to that set out here. For example, non-contractual payments rendered by duress would be dealt with as a (voidable) gift (analogous to a voidable contract) or as being paid to discharge a liability (in an analogous way to a liability mistake of fact).

3.1. Payments Made under a Liability Mistake of Fact

In the leading case of *Kelly v Solari*[15] the claimant insurance company paid over money on a life insurance policy, apparently not realizing that the policy had lapsed because the deceased had failed to pay a premium. On the common law approach, the claimant was entitled to restitution assuming that it had paid by mistake. The decision of the court was to order a new trial and, according to the common law analysis, the purpose of that new trial was to ascertain whether the claimant had indeed paid by mistake. If it had, restitution would be ordered. But on the Birksian approach, it was not of central importance whether the claimant was mistaken or not. The crucial point was that the money was not due: that is, because the policy had lapsed, there was no obligation on the insurer to pay. In Birks's words, 'The mistake of the claimant has nothing to do with it'.[16] But that did not automatically mean that restitution should have been ordered because it might have been the case that the insurance company paid the money *ex gratia*, knowing that it was not due or thinking that it may not have been due. So on this analysis the purpose of the new trial was to ascertain what the basis of the payment had been: was it to discharge an obligation or as a gift? If the former, there would be restitution; if the latter, no restitution.

Similarly in *Barclays Bank Ltd v WJ Simms & Son*[17]—which established that mistakes causing payments count even if they are not mistakes as to liability to the payee—the Birksian approach would say that what triggered restitution was not the mistake but that the bank paid the money to discharge its obligation to its customer and yet there was no such obligation because the cheque had been stopped. The basis of the payment—the obligation to pay—was therefore absent.

What about *Kerrison v Glyn Mills Currie & Co*[18] where the claimant recovered money paid in anticipation of being liable to the payee but where that anticipated liability never accrued because the payee had become insolvent? On the common law approach, this has sometimes been thought to be a difficult case because there appears to have been a misprediction as to future liability rather than a mistake as to present liability (although one can still say that there was a causal mistake triggering restitution in that the payor mistakenly paid thinking that the payee was creditworthy).[19] On the Birksian approach, the restitution is explicable because the bank paid on the basis that the future obligation would eventuate and it did not: 'payment made on the basis of a liability to be met in the future is a perfectly good payment on a basis which may or may not hold good'.[20] So unless the bank was a risk-taker, and was therefore making the payment as a gift, there was an absence of basis to trigger restitution.

---

[15] (1841) 9 M & W 54.   [16] Birks, at 132.
[17] [1980] QB 677.   [18] (1911) 81 LJKB 465.
[19] A Burrows, *The Law of Restitution* (2nd edn, 2002) 133. Contra is Birks at 153, 'The result could not be reached through mistake'.   [20] Birks, 153.

3.2. Payments Made under Void Contracts

This area shot to the forefront of English judicial and academic thinking because
of the large number of cases in the 1990s dealing with payments made under
interest-rate swap contracts between banks and local authorities that were held to
be void as ultra vires the local authorities. Applying the common law approach
the correct analysis should have been that, leaving aside the possibility of local
authorities recovering because of their own incapacity, money paid under open
swaps (ie swaps that were not fully executed) was recoverable either for failure of
consideration (meaning failure of counter-performance)[21] or for mistake of law;
and money paid under closed swaps was recoverable for mistake of law.
Unfortunately, while the House of Lords in *Kleinwort Benson Ltd v Lincoln CC*[22]
accepted the mistake of law analysis, the failure of consideration analysis became
confused with a civilian absence of consideration approach. So it was that in
Westdeutsche Landesbank Girozentrale v Islington London BC[23] Hobhouse J at
first instance and the majority of the House of Lords (albeit as *obiter dicta*) saw
restitution as being triggered because the contract was void so that there was an
absence, or automatic failure, of consideration; and the same can be said of the
majority of the Court of Appeal in *Guinness Mahon & Co Ltd v Kensington and
Chelsea RLBC*.[24] It was the reasoning in those latter cases that led Birks to claim
that, as a matter of authority, English law had unequivocally rejected the unjust
factors approach and that there was no going back to it.[25] While this is an
exaggerated claim, not only because the courts in question never adverted to the
impact of their reasoning but also because it cannot be reconciled with the
reasoning in *Kleinwort Benson*, it is clear that on the Birksian scheme restitution
was straightforwardly recoverable (subject to defences) in the swaps cases,
whether under open or closed swaps, for absence of basis. The parties paid on the
basis that there was a valid obligation to pay. In fact the contract was void so that
there was no valid obligation. '[T]he swaps money had been paid to discharge a
contractual obligation and that obligation did not exist.'[26]

   While on the face of it, the Birksian approach has a surgical simplicity in
dealing with the swaps contracts, the position becomes more complex if one
alters the facts. What if one of the payors (let us assume the bank) knew that the
contract was void so that the money was not due? On the common law
approach, that payor could not recover for mistake because it was not mistaken.
While it could recover for failure of consideration in an open swap, there could

---

[21] This meaning of 'failure of consideration' was classically clarified, in the context of contracts
terminated for frustration, in *Fibrosa* [1943] AC 32. It also explains why one can sensibly talk of
total and partial failure of consideration. Birks's view that English law has, as a matter of authority,
abandoned the unjust factors approach would require one to accept that, without explicit reference
to this, the courts have abandoned that long-established understanding of 'failure of consideration'.

[22] [1999] 2 AC 349.   [23] [1994] 4 All ER 890 (Hobhouse J); [1996] AC 669.

[24] [1999] QB 215.   [25] Birks, 108–13.   [26] Birks, 113.

be no restitution—because no failure of consideration—if the bank had received full counter-performance. That is an intuitively appealing result. On the Birksian scheme, a bank that paid, knowing that the contract was void, would not be paying to discharge a valid obligation. Presumably one would say that the basis of the payment was therefore a gift. But would that mean that there could be no restitution in an open swap so that, for example, a bank that paid £1 million (knowing that the contract was void) and received no counter-payments would be denied restitution on the ground that its payment was a valid gift? Although this was not explored by him, Birks could presumably have reached the same result as at common law by going on to say that the gift was conditional on counter-payment, so that in a closed swap there would be no failure of that basis and hence no restitution, whereas in an open swap that basis (the condition of the gift) would fail so that there would be restitution.[27] But whether that use of the concept of a conditional gift is correct or not, the main point here is that by altering the facts we can see that it is misleading to regard the Birksian approach as leading to simple automatic restitution in all void contract cases.

One must add a further caveat to the simplicity of the Birksian scheme. He was at pains to emphasize that 'policy' defences have an important role to play in countering the automatic restitution that prima facie follows from an absence of basis approach to void (or other invalid) contracts. The best illustrations of this are in relation to illegal contracts and contracts entered into by minors (albeit that these are not void contracts as such). The policy behind invalidating a contract for illegality or minority may also mean that there should be no restitution of benefits conferred under it: that is, it may be that to allow restitution would contradict or 'stultify' the policy behind the contractual invalidity. So in the conclusion to his chapter on 'unjust-related defences' Birks wrote,

The 'absence of basis' method of deciding whether an enrichment at the expense of another is unjust can arouse anxieties . . . it worried commentators who foresaw and tried to prevent its coming victory in the swaps cases. Those anxieties would be well-founded if it seemed likely to degenerate into a dogma to the effect that invalidity entailed automatic restitution of value transferred . . . [But] the answer to the third of the five questions (unjust) establishes no more than a prima facie liability.[28]

3.3. Benefits Conferred under Terminated/Terminable or Avoided/Voidable Contracts

Birks's reasoning here is odd. One might have expected him to say in true civilian style that, once a contract has been terminated or been avoided, there is

---

[27] Although not directly adverted to in this context, in discussing *Re Cleadon Trust Ltd* [1939] Ch 286, Birks writes, '[T]here is nothing wrong with construing a payment for a voluntary reciprocation as a payment made on a basis which may or may not hold good'.

[28] Birks, 263.

an absence of basis triggering restitution: the benefits have been conferred to discharge a valid obligation and, once terminated or avoided, there is no valid obligation. Restitution is therefore not responding to duress or misrepresentation or undue influence or failure of counter-performance: it is rather responding to the invalidity of the contract where those factors have given a party the power to invalidate the contract. But he did not say that. Rather he reasoned that a terminable or voidable contract is invalid, and there is therefore an absence of basis, even though the contract has not yet been (and may never be) terminated or avoided. The power to terminate or rescind is itself a restitutionary right that responds to the absence of basis constituted by the (already present) invalidity. So Birks wrote,

> If we were to say that . . . the absence of valid basis only began from the termination or the rescission, we would not be able to explain the origin of the powers to terminate or to avoid, which are not granted by contract and cannot be said to arise from their own effects. These powers arise from the enrichment rendered unjust by the invalidity of the contract under which it was transferred.[29]

On the common law approach, restitution responds to the factor allowing rescission be it misrepresentation, duress, or undue influence or to a failure of consideration (where a contract has been terminated). The restitution of benefits conferred under an avoided (or terminated) contract can therefore be seen to turn on the same, or a similar, factor that rendered the contract invalid: although there are two stages, the same, or a similar, factor applies at each stage.[30] On this common law model, there is therefore no problem in treating rescission (or indeed termination) as a response to the unjust factors albeit that there has been a vigorous debate as to whether the rescission of a purely executory contract reverses any *enrichment* conferred on the defendant.[31]

It seems clear that Birks's surprising reasoning is a consequence of his desire to stick to his long-held view that the power to rescind (and to terminate) is a response to unjust enrichment while, at the same time, moving from the unjust factors to absence of basis. It was therefore necessary for him to treat those responses as triggered by an absence of basis that would more naturally be seen as occurring after rescission or termination not before.

A further difficulty with Birks's reasoning is that, by regarding there as being an absence of basis where a contract is terminable or voidable, it is not immediately obvious that it was open to him to distinguish the restitutionary consequences of a contract being terminated as opposed to being rescinded *ab initio*.

---

[29] Birks, 126.
[30] Hence the implied criticism by S Meier, 'Unjust Factors and Legal Grounds' in *Unjustified Enrichment* (eds D Johnston and R Zimmermann, 2002) 37, 70 that the common law approach produces an inelegant repetition of factors.
[31] Burrows, n 19 above, 56–9. Similarly one can strongly argue that, consequent on termination, the discharge of a future obligation to perform owed to the defendant does not reverse an enrichment of the defendant.

At common law it appears that not all the benefits conferred under a terminated, as opposed to an avoided, contract are recoverable in an action for unjust enrichment. Even if one moves away from the discredited rule that a failure of consideration needs to be total, it may be that an accrued right to payment remains contractually binding after termination so that it cannot be overriden by an unjust enrichment claim for failure of consideration. Conceivably, with some minor adjustment or clarification, these different restitutionary consequences can be accommodated within Birks's absence of basis scheme but certainly, when questioned,[32] he himself seemed to take the view (while not, apparently, regarding this as inconsistent with the best interpretation of the common law) that absence of basis entailed the same restitutionary consequences whether a contract was voidable or terminable.

3.4. Benefits Conferred under Unenforceable Contracts

The common law approach to benefits conferred under contracts unenforceable (by one or both parties) for want of formality is less clear-cut than may at first sight appear. This is for two reasons. First, the courts have not yet had to consider the impact on this area of the abrogation of the mistake of law bar in *Kleinwort Benson*. Secondly, the precise status of an unenforceable contract has not been addressed. One view is that it is merely another type of invalid contract, analogous to a void or avoided or terminated contract.[33] Restitution for mistake or failure of consideration can therefore be granted without infringing the normal rule that restitution cannot be granted where there is a valid contract. The second view is that an unenforceable contract is a valid contract but is simply unenforceable in the courts by one or both parties. Restitution should therefore only be granted where that contract is invalid for reasons other than unenforceability (most obviously where the defendant has failed to pay for work done so that the claimant can terminate for breach and be entitled to restitution for that work). The well-known leading cases of *Deglman v Guaranty Trust Co of Canada*[34] and *Pavey & Matthews Pty Ltd v Paul*[35] are consistent with either view because in each of them restitution for services was awarded in a situation where the recipient had refused to pay for those services—and hence would have been in breach allowing the claimant to terminate the contract—and yet the claimant could not bring a contractual claim for payment because the contract was

---

[32] In the symposium to review the first edition of Birks's book held in Oxford on 13 January 2004, the proceedings of which are published at [2004] RLR 260, he took the view, see 288, that a long-faithful but underpaid employee, who terminates for a repudiatory breach by his employer, is entitled to restitution for all the work he has done subject to the employer being given counter-restitution of payments made.

[33] A problem with this view is in marking out any real difference between a void and an unenforceable contract.   [34] [1954] 3 DLR 785.

[35] (1986) 162 CLR 221.

unenforceable. The choice between the two views would, in contrast, be put to the test if the unenforceable contract had been fully performed on both sides.

Similarly, the consequences of applying the Birksian scheme will here turn on which of the two views of an unenforceable contract one takes. If one treats an unenforceable contract as an invalid contract, the approach to restitution will be the same as for void contracts: that is, restitution will prima facie follow as a consequence of the absence of validity and hence absence of basis. But Birks himself took the second view. The basis will only fail, so as to trigger restitution, where the unenforceable contract was terminable or voidable on some other ground. He wrote,

> The word 'unenforceable' is by convention reserved for a good contract on which no action can be brought. Thus, if a contract is rendered unenforceable in the absence of a memorandum in writing, it must in addition be voidable or terminable on some other ground before value transferred under it can be regarded as having no basis and hence as an unjust enrichment.[36]

3.5. Benefits Conferred in Anticipation of a Contract that Does Not Materialize

In *William Lacey (Hounslow) Ltd v Davis*[37] restitution was granted in respect of building work done where the builder reasonably expected a contract to be concluded with the owner; and in *Chillingworth v Esche*,[38] restitution was ordered of a pre-contractual deposit paid 'subject to contract'. At common law the best explanation of these cases is that the benefits were rendered for a consideration that failed in that the reasonably expected counter-performance did not eventuate. On the other side of the line are cases (such as *Regalian Properties Ltd v London Docklands Development Corpn*[39] and *Rowe v Vale of White Horse DC*[40]) where restitution was denied because the claimant was a risk-taker who was unable to establish that the benefits had been conferred for a consideration that had failed.

On the Birksian approach, the first two cases are explained as ones where a benefit was conferred on the basis that a contract would eventuate so that there was an absence of basis where that contract did not come about. But Birks indicated that there is a thin line here between risk-takers and non-risk-takers. 'One eye has always to be kept on risk-taking. It is one thing to want a contract to come into existence and another to act solely on the basis that it will.'[41] The latter two cases denying restitution are ones where the claimants were risk-takers. The benefits were rendered as gifts so that they had a valid basis.[42]

---

[36] Birks, 126–7.   [37] [1957] 1 WLR 932.   [38] [1924] 1 Ch 97.
[39] [1995] 1 WLR 212.   [40] [2003] 1 Lloyd's Rep 418.   [41] Birks, 144.
[42] This would leave open the possibility that the gift was conditional so that if the condition failed the gift was invalidated: see above n 27.

3.6. Receipt of Misdirected Funds

Cases where money was transferred to the defendant without the 'owner's' consent, such as *Lipkin Gorman v Karpnale*[43] (at common law) and *Re Montagu's Settlement Trusts*[44] and *Ministry of Health v Simpson*[45] (in equity), have proved controversial and difficult to classify on the common law approach. It is submitted that the best explanation for them is that they illustrate the application of unjust factors such as ignorance and powerlessness. On Birks's new model these are 'non-participatory enrichments' and, as has been commented above,[46] they are explained straightforwardly as having no possible basis (not even a putative one). As there has been no participation, no possible obligation was being discharged and no contract, trust, or gift has been made.

3.7. Payments Consequent on an Ultra Vires Demand by a Public Authority

In *Woolwich Equitable Building Society v IRC*[47] it was held by the House of Lords that '... money paid by a citizen to a public authority in the form of taxes or other levies paid pursuant to an ultra vires demand by the authority is prima facie recoverable by the citizen as of right'.[48] On the common law approach, this *Woolwich* principle has been seen as a policy-motivated unjust factor. On the Birksian approach, restitution is straightforwardly explicable on the facts of *Woolwich* because the money was paid to discharge an obligation and there was no such obligation. Or put another way, it was paid on the basis that tax was due and it was not due. Birks also stressed that, because the payor had wanted to avoid payment, there was no question of the payor making a gift. 'There were no facts to suggest that it intended a gift or had knowingly taken a risk that the money was not due. All the evidence was that it had constantly contended that it was not liable to pay.'[49]

3.8. Compulsory Discharge of Another's Liability

At common law, the line of cases (exemplified by *Exall v Partridge*[50] and *Brook's Wharf and Bull Wharf Ltd v Goodman Bros*[51]) granting restitution to an unrequested and yet non-officious intervener against a person (the 'debtor') whose liability to another has been discharged has been explained as an application of the policy-based unjust factor of legal compulsion. On the Birksian scheme, restitution follows because, as between the intervener and the debtor, there is no basis for the debtor's enrichment. The intervener has not paid to discharge an obligation of the debtor and no gift is being made to the debtor. In Birks's

---

[43] [1991] 2 AC 548.   [44] [1987] Ch 264.   [45] [1951] AC 251.
[46] Above 34. See Birks, 154–8.   [47] [1993] AC 70.
[48] ibid at 177 (per Lord Goff of Chieveley).   [49] Birks, 134.
[50] (1799) 8 Term Rep 308.   [51] [1937] 1 KB 534.

words, 'It has no basis at all. The discharged debtor can offer no explanation at all as to why he should retain his enrichment. It is an enrichment without any explanatory basis...there was no reason at all why he should reap the by-benefit.'[52] Rather the basis that exists is as between the payor and the creditor with the payor paying in order to discharge the obligation that it owed to the creditor or to recover its property lawfully seized by the creditor.

3.9. By-Benefits of Acting Freely in One's Self-Interest

An important feature of the common law approach to unjust enrichment is that it provides an easy explanation for why benefits incidentally conferred by someone acting in self-interest do not trigger restitution. There is simply no unjust factor. So in *obiter dicta* in *Ruabon Steamship Co v The London Assurance*[53] Lord Halsbury thought it plainly unarguable that a person who cut down trees on his own land for his own benefit and thereby gave his neighbour the advantage of a better view could recover contribution from his neighbour. And in the United States case of *Ulmer v Farnsworth*[54] restitution was denied to the owner of a quarry who had pumped it dry thereby draining and rendering profitable his neighbour's quarry. On the face of it, this is a serious problem for the Birksian scheme because one might have thought that the conferral of such an incidental benefit (or 'by-benefit' as Birks called it) has no basis so that, alarmingly, there should be restitution. But in discussing the example of heat rising from one's flat, and thereby saving the upstairs neighbour heating expenses, Birks agreed that there should be no restitution. His explanation for this was that the basis of the by-benefit (provided the actor was acting of his own free will) is a gift 'albeit possibly not warmly wished'.[55]

3.10. Conclusion

So as to enhance our understanding of it, this section has explored the detailed workings of the Birksian scheme. Central to the theme of this essay, it has shown that that scheme does not necessarily lead to different results than those arrived at under the common law approach. On the contrary, in all the situations we have examined (with the possible exception of restitution after terminated contracts) it is likely that the Birksian approach would arrive at the same result, albeit by different reasoning, as the common law.[56] This is perhaps not entirely surprising: in seeking to provide an English version of the civilian approach, Birks was no doubt anxious to provide a scheme that would fit the English cases.

---

[52] Birks, 159.   [53] [1900] AC 6, 10.   [54] 15 A 65 (1888).

[55] Birks, 158: see also above 35. That the claimant is acting of his own free will is crucial in distinguishing this situation from compulsory discharge of another's liability (where, as we have seen in the last section, the Birksian reasoning is that no gift is being made to the debtor).

[56] It might be thought that *Deutsche Morgan Grenfell Group plc v IRC* [2005] EWCA Civ 78, [2006] 2 WLR 103 would be decided differently if one applied the Birksian scheme. But even if (contrary to

What about the burden of proof which is often put forward as a clear difference between the common law (burden on claimant) and civilian (burden on defendant) approaches to the unjust question? Birks did not directly address this[57] but there seems no reason why under his scheme the burden could not be placed on the claimant to establish the absence of basis (eg that it paid to discharge an obligation but there was no such obligation). In any event, it could only be in a very few cases that a difference in the burden of proof on the unjust question would lead to a difference in result.

An important conclusion, therefore, is that, in judging the merits of the Birksian scheme, one cannot straightforwardly point to particular results as being different and therefore better or worse than those reached at common law. Rather one must turn to other criteria for assessing the respective advantages and disadvantages of the two schemes.

The most obvious other criteria are elegance and ease of application. In explaining the results of particular cases, one may take the view that one scheme more elegantly and straightforwardly provides the answer than the other: and elegance and ease of application are important not only in enhancing understanding of the law but also in ensuring that courts do not go astray in deciding novel cases. So let us now turn to applying those criteria to assess the respective advantages or disadvantages of the two schemes.

4. The Elegance and Ease of Application of the Two Schemes

At first sight the Birksian scheme appears to win by a clear margin in terms of elegance. To have one single unifying concept of 'absence of basis' to determine the unjust question is neater than the common law's list of unjust factors and, in particular, its reliance on 'policy-motivated' factors.[58] Moreover, the inclusion of some unjust factors is controversial either because they have not been explicitly

---

the Court of Appeal) one accepted Park J's view that the advance corporation tax was due, Birks himself thought that there would be no difference between the common law and his approach: see Birks, 138–9. Another possible example of a case that would be decided differently is *CTN Cash and Carry Ltd v Gallaher Ltd* [1994] 4 All ER 714 which denied restitution for duress. Although not discussed by Birks, it would seem that, on an absence of basis approach, as the money was not owing and was not paid as a gift, it should have been recoverable. But, applying a common law approach, acceptance of a broader notion of duress in that context than that favoured by the Court of Appeal would also have resulted in the granting of restitution: for this argument, see G Dannemann, below 373–7.

[57] In civilian systems it appears that, once the claimant has shown that the defendant has been enriched at the claimant's expense, the burden of proof is on the defendant to establish a basis for the retention. But there is no discussion of this issue by Birks (although there is one reference, at 159, suggesting that the burden may be on the defendant).

[58] One might elaborate on this by saying that 'absence of basis' gives an added conceptual unity to the subject that a list of 'unjust factors' does not. This was perhaps especially a concern of Birks once he had moved to the position that there were other events that triggered restitution, apart from consent, wrongs, and unjust enrichment. On that approach, why should policy-motivated unjust factors triggering restitution be dealt with as part of unjust enrichment rather than 'others'?

accepted by the courts (eg ignorance) or because they are thought by some to lack explanatory power (eg legal compulsion). Even where there is a well-established unjust factor like mistake, the common law approach sets up a general causation test only for it then to be subjected to a major exception where there is a contract in play. Meier also points to the inelegant repetition of factors that render a contract voidable (and therefore belong within the law of contract) and yet which also are regarded as triggering restitution.[59] Moreover, as we have seen, some cases are much more easily dealt with under the Birksian scheme than at common law. The most obvious example is *Woolwich*. On the Birksian approach the payment in that case was recoverable because it was not due and was not made as a gift. In contrast to the common law approach, there is no need to agonize about whether the payment is, or is not, a tax or whether the payee is, or is not, a public authority.

Yet it is submitted that, for three main reasons,[60] that elegance is superficial and that the Birksian scheme is no easier to apply than the common law approach.

The first reason is that the Birksian scheme can only be made to fit the cases by a problematically wide use of the notion of gift. At several points in the examination of Birks's scheme above, we have seen that he had to fall back to relying on there having been a gift. All risk-takers are, for example, denied restitution because the valid basis of the enrichment is gift. The extreme example of this is Birks's treatment of 'by-benefits'. It is hard to see how someone, who may not be aware that he is conferring the by-benefit or may not want to benefit the defendant, can be said to be making a gift. As Peter Watts has written of Birks's treatment of by-benefits, 'Surely there is a gift here only because the law has already determined that there should be no claim. The better explanation is that enrichment per se does not need justification.'[61] That, of course, is to adopt the common law approach.

The second reason is that the scheme is elegant and straightforward only because it pushes out of sight many of the difficult questions of law that are dealt

---

[59] See n 30 above.

[60] A possible fourth reason (although I am not convinced by this argument or the examples referred to by those favouring it) is that the Birksian scheme cannot, without added complexity, cope with differentiations as between the unjust factors which, in contrast, the splitting up into unjust factors renders straightforward. Eg Buxton LJ in *Deutsche Morgan Grenfell Group plc v IRC* (n 56 above) thought it inappropriate to treat as if linked by the same injustice, claims for restitution from a private party and from a public authority; and Stevens [2004] RLR 271 has argued that a bona fide change of position may not be a defence in respect of all unjust factors.

[61] (2004) 121 LQR 163, 166 reviewing Birks, *Unjust Enrichment*. It is noteworthy that, while Birks uses a problematically wide notion of gift to stop absence of basis leading to unacceptable instances of restitution, the modified civilian approach recently adopted in Canada (see above n 12) has an inbuilt safety-net because the courts can find a juristic basis, outside established categories, by reference to the parties' expectations and public policy. Conceivably, a way of partly rescuing Birks from his overinclusive use of 'gift' might be to regard at least some risk-takers as conferring a benefit on the basis of the chance of being rewarded and to treat that 'chance of reward' as another category of basis within Birks's 'other bases' referred to in Birks, 152–4 (and see n 8 above).

with 'up front' under the common law approach. In other words, a scheme can be made to appear elegant if it no longer has to answer many difficult questions. Under the common law approach, the law of unjust enrichment has been the area in which it has been determined 'up front' whether gifts are recoverable on the grounds of, for example, mistake or duress or undue influence. On the Birksian scheme the difficult question as to the scope of those factors in the context of gifts goes to the submerged issue of whether the gift is invalid so that, at the elegant top of the pyramid, there is an absence of basis. Submerging the details does not help a judge faced with deciding, for example, whether there should, or should not, be restitution of a gift which the donor wishes to recover because he has made it mistakenly believing that the recipient was poor or shared his political views.[62] A linked point is that books and university courses organized on the Birksian model would look odd to common lawyers given that some of the law would presumably need to be covered in courses or books on 'The Law of Gifts'. One should also note that some of the difficult issues dealt with at the unjust factor stage in the common law approach (eg does minority trigger restitution?) re-emerge as difficulties at the defence stage in the Birksian scheme.[63]

The third, and more specific, reason is that the Birksian approach to restitution in respect of voidable and terminable contracts is unnatural and problematic. As we have seen,[64] it is odd to think of there being an absence of basis before termination or rescission; and, in so far as Birks is taking the view that the restitutionary consequences of termination and rescission are the same, it is not clear that that is acceptable.

One should also remind oneself here of the persuasive argument, previously put forward by Birks as being a virtue of the common law as opposed to the civil law, that most of the unjust factors are readily explicable to non-lawyers.[65] Putting to one side policy-motivated restitution, the 'I did not mean to give' scheme of unjust factors, broken down into 'no consent', 'vitiated consent', and 'qualified consent', is beautifully simple and clear. In contrast, an absence of basis approach is not readily understandable to the man on the Clapham omnibus because it immediately entails a legalistic explanation in order to understand what is meant by 'basis' and, in turn, 'invalidity'.

It is submitted, therefore, that one cannot say that the Birksian scheme is more elegant and easier to apply than the common law approach. Applying those criteria, both approaches have their advantages and disadvantages so that, taken in isolation, some cases are more easily decided on one than the other. It follows

---

[62] S Meier, at 53 of her article (n 30 above), in criticizing the width of the causative mistake test, argues that 'It is not possible to differentiate mistakes without resorting to a legal ground analysis'. But this does not seem correct. *If* one wished to differentiate the types of mistake that trigger restitution one could resort to saying that the root test is that the mistake is serious and that, while that test is always satisfied where one pays mistakenly believing that one is legally bound to do so, it may or may not be satisfied in respect of mistakenly rendered gifts.

[63] See p 39 above.   [64] See pp 39–41 above.

[65] See eg P Birks, *The Foundations of Unjust Enrichment: Six Centennial Lectures* (2002) 73–4.

from this that there is no good reason to abandon the common law approach. Contrary to Birks's claim, the courts have not done so[66] and it would require a very significant upheaval of precedent to do so.[67] As he is absolutely correct that mixing the two is a recipe for confusion and inconsistency, the best approach is to stick with what we know by continuing to apply the common law approach, while using the Birksian scheme as a cross-check in difficult or novel cases.

5. Conclusion

This essay has argued that Peter had no need to call back his earlier work for burning. Rather he could have presented his 'absence of basis' scheme alongside his earlier 'unjust factors' approach as an alternative line of reasoning to be used as a cross-check in difficult or novel cases. This would have been in keeping with a conventional use of comparative law. But Peter's dramatic mode of presentation was entirely in keeping with the passionate and charismatic person that I had known since I was 18 years old. Peter interviewed me for admission to Brasenose College where he was one of my two main tutors. Subsequently, as a colleague, I had the privilege of teaching Restitution with him on the BCL. By then he was a close friend and throughout was the main guide and influence in my academic career. As I have been thinking about, and writing, this essay, there have been glorious moments of suspended reality when I have half dreamt that I could pick up the phone, or send an e-mail, to ask Peter his views on my interpretation of his writings. Alas that cannot be. As for so many others, my academic life will for ever be poorer without him.

---

[66] See p 38 above.

[67] Although written in the context of the debate about the correct interpretation of 'no juristic basis' in Canada, the words of Lionel Smith at (2000) 12 SCLR 211, 244, are apt: 'We would effectively be starting from scratch in a fundamental field of the common law'.

3

Three Enrichment Issues

*Robert Stevens**

1. Peter

Having first attended the seminars as a student, I taught the Oxford Bachelor of Civil Law course with Peter Birks (and others) for ten years between 1994 and Peter's death in 2004. Teaching in seminars with Peter was, by some margin, the highlight of each week. I could not believe my good fortune in being paid money to do so. Sadly, at least in the early days, I suspect that many of the students could not believe my good fortune either. The final year was perhaps the most important, as week after week Peter was required to explain how his new re-drawing of the law worked.

Being young, I initially thought that the purpose of the seminars was to show where Peter's model of the law did not work. Peter was ferocious in debate. Although he had an unrivalled ability to see the principles and structure of the law, what is not always obvious from his published work, because it was not necessary for him to demonstrate this, was the depth of detailed knowledge of law that he carried with him. No development, in almost any jurisdiction which was accessible to him, passed him by. On detail you could rarely hope to win. Peter saw legal argument as concerned with the application of reason, like a game of chess. Occasionally I would have him in check. On one occasion he announced that I had swept all of his pieces from the board and that he only had a king and a pawn left. I sat back in triumph, only to find that this 'pawn' placed me in checkmate, as he carefully explained.

2. Introduction

In writing on enrichment one is presented with the frustrating task of trying to build bricks without straw. With few cases from which to build, when and how

* Fellow and Tutor in Law, Lady Margaret Hall, University of Oxford

the law determines that a defendant is enriched are extremely difficult questions to answer. Much of the pioneering work on these questions was done by Peter Birks and some of the terminology we now commonly use in the area, for example 'subjective devaluation', was coined by him. Enrichment was one of the few areas within the law of unjust enrichment where he did not radically alter his position between the publication of the Old Testament[1] and the New.[2] This essay is a conservative one and is by way of a gloss on Peter's work.

I will seek to address three issues. First, how is enrichment to be quantified? Secondly, how is an enrichment to be established where incomplete contractual performance has been received? Thirdly, can enrichment be established where title to an asset transferred does not pass?

3. Quantification

Suppose a window-cleaner gets into a muddle and confuses my house for the house next door. Whilst he has a contract to clean my neighbour's windows, he has no agreement with me. After the work, am I enriched by what has been done?[3]

Peter grew to hate the window-cleaner he created,[4] partly because of the powerful criticism of the concept of 'free acceptance' made by Professor Andrew Burrows.[5] But although he may be tired and battered, the window-cleaner still illustrates the concept of subjective devaluation which follows from the respect we must have for freedom of choice. Some people prefer dirty windows. Others wash their own windows and enjoy the warm water and suds. It cannot be said that the house owner is necessarily enriched by the cleaning; he is entitled to say he is not. Peter Birks identified five methods by which it is possible to overcome this argument from subjective devaluation. They form two groups. First, the defendant may have a sufficiently free choice so that he cannot appeal to subjective devaluation. This may be established where the very thing received can still be returned,[6] where an opportunity to reject the benefit has been foregone,[7] and where incomplete contractual performance has been received.[8] Secondly, the defendant may be incontrovertibly enriched. This may be established where an inevitable expense has been saved,[9] or the benefit has been realized as money.[10]

---

[1] P Birks, *An Introduction to the Law of Restitution* (rev edn, 1989) 109–32.
[2] P Birks, *Unjust Enrichment* (2nd edn, 2005) 49–72.   [3] Birks, (n 1) 316.
[4] ibid 266.
[5] A Burrows, 'Free Acceptance and the Law of Restitution' (1988) 104 LQR 576.
[6] eg McDonald v Coys of Kensington [2004] EWCA 47.
[7] eg *Weatherby v Banham* (1832) 5 C & P 228.
[8] eg *Planche v Colburn* (1831) 8 Bing 14.
[9] eg *Rowe v Vale of White Horse DC* [2003] 1 Lloyd's Rep 418.
[10] eg *Greenwood v Bennett* [1973] QB 195, CA.

If the house owner sits and watches the windows being washed, knowing that the window-cleaner expects to be paid and is consequently to be considered enriched by the work done, the quantum of the enrichment will be the market cost of the work. If free acceptance is sufficient, it debars the argument that he would have done the work himself or that he prefers dirty windows.[11] Similarly, where the defendant still has the asset received,[12] the quantification of a claim to its value will be determined by the market for it. However, where the claimant seeks to show that the defendant's enrichment is incontrovertible, more difficult questions of quantification arise. My purpose is not to address how enrichment is established but how it is to be quantified once it is.

An example:

> The defendant, a garage owner, entrusts one of his cars to a friend. The friend, whilst driving the car, is in a collision. He then fraudulently sells the car to the claimant. The claimant repairs the car. The defendant then recovers the car and sells it for far more than could have been realized had the repairs not been carried out.

Let us assume that the claimant has a claim in unjust enrichment. We know that the defendant is enriched because the repairs have been realized in money. There are, at least, six possible methods of quantifying the claim:

(a) the market cost of the work done;
(b) the realized sum, here the difference between the price which could have been obtained for the car without the repairs and the price actually obtained;
(c) the expenses the defendant would have incurred in having the car repaired;
(d) the expenses the claimant actually incurred in repairing the car;
(e) the fee the defendant would have charged another to repair the car;
(f) the fee the claimant would have charged another to repair the car.

Of these options, (e) and (f) can be dismissed. Neither is a measure of the defendant's enrichment, although both may be good evidence of the market value of the service. Similarly, (d) can be dismissed as it is a measure of loss, not gain.

(a), (b), and (c) are all plausible measures of gain, and they may not on the facts of the case differ. Further, it is difficult to think of any case where the expense the defendant would have incurred in having the car repaired would be *higher* than the market cost of doing so. Where the three measures do differ, which is the correct one?

The example is, of course, based on *Greenwood v Bennett*.[13] It was stated by counsel for the claimant that the defendant had sold the car for £400.[14]

---

[11] Birks, (n 2) 56. [12] *McDonald v Coys of Kensington* [2004] EWCA Civ 47.
[13] [1973] QB 195. See now Torts (Interference with Goods) Act 1977.
[14] [1973] QB 195, 198.

Assuming this to be correct, as the car had been worth £75 prior to repair, the defendant had £325 in his hands which he would not have had but for the claimant's work. The Court of Appeal awarded the claimant the lower sum of £226, which the court described as the claimant's costs of repairs[15] (measure (*d*)). However these costs appear to have been calculated according to the defendant's usual billing calculations, and so can be seen as either the claimant's usual fee, including his profit element (*e*), or the market cost of the repairs (*a*).

Why was the claimant not awarded the higher sum which had been realized? Four explanations are possible. These explanations are not mutually exclusive.

First, £226 was all that was claimed. However, there was no indication from any member of the court that the defendant could go further and claim the higher sum.

Secondly, it can be argued that in the law of unjust enrichment, in order for a claimant to establish that the enrichment was 'at his expense' he must establish a loss which corresponds with a gain.[16] The defendant may have been enriched to the tune of £325 but the claimant's loss was only £226 and this puts a 'cap' on recovery. Peter Birks in *Unjust Enrichment*[17] rejected this limitation, arguing that 'at the expense of' meant 'from' the claimant and did not require a loss which corresponded with a gain.

A detailed consideration of when it is possible to say that an enrichment is 'at the expense of' the claimant is beyond the scope of this essay. However, the issues of enrichment and 'at the expense of' are intertwined. In English law the evidence both for and against a requirement of corresponding loss is 'finely balanced'.[18] Peter Birks identified three examples from the case-law in support of his view that corresponding loss was unnecessary. None is free from difficulty. First, in *Hambly v Trott*[19] Lord Mansfield suggested that someone who uses another's horse without permission must pay a reasonable sum for its use even if the claimant would not have used it and the horse is better for the exercise. He stated that an action in trespass would not survive against an executor but that an action for the use value of the horse would. However, today the claim to the use value of the horse can be explained as a response to the wrong. It may be explained either as a gain-based remedy or because 'infringement of the right imports damage'[20] so that proof of loss or gain is irrelevant.[21] The addition of a claim in unjust enrichment seems unnecessary

---

[15] [1973] QB 195, 200 per Lord Denning MR.

[16] eg M McInnes, 'Interceptive Subtraction, Unjust Enrichment and Wrongs—A Reply to Professor Birks' [2003] CLJ 697.

[17] Birks, (n 2) 78–86; cf Birks, *An Introduction to the Law of Restitution*, rev 132.

[18] Birks, (n 2) 79.   [19] (1776) 1 Cowp 371; 98 ER 1136.

[20] *Ashby v White* (1703) 2 Ld Raym 938, 92 ER 126; rvsg (1703) 1 Sm LC (13th edn) 253, 1 ER 417, HL.

[21] cf *Watson Laidlaw & Co Ltd v Pott Cassells & Williamson* [1914] SC (HL) 18, 31 per Lord Shaw considering the same example.

now that tort claims survive the defendant's death. The second example is that the Court of Appeal has expressed the view that it is no defence to a claim in unjust enrichment for the restitution of money received, for the defendant to show that the claimant subsequently 'passed on' his initial loss to a third party.[22] This may be contrasted with the recognition of the defence of change of position. That the defendant's 'disenrichment' provides a defence whilst the claimant's 'disimpoverishment' does not might indicate that the law of unjust enrichment is concerned with gains but not losses. However, the absence of a defence of passing on may be explicable on the basis that it gives rise to serious evidential difficulties or that the making good of losses by third parties is to be ignored on the same basis as the collateral benefit of a first party insurance payout to a party carelessly injured is ignored in tort actions. The third example is that where a claimant brings a claim to an asset which has been substituted for his property, the claim is successful despite the fact that the substituted asset is worth far more than that which the claimant has lost.[23] However, several commentators deny that such claims are properly seen as explicable on the basis of unjust enrichment and the House of Lords has expressly said that they are not.[24]

A third explanation for the lower sum awarded in *Greenwood v Bennett* is that if the repairs had not been done, the defendant would have repaired the car at his own expense for £226. The defendant does not, therefore, have £325 in his hands which he would not otherwise have but for the claimant's work, but only £226. Professor Burrows describes this argument as the ability to 'subjectively devalue the incontrovertible benefit'.[25] This description is, however, unhelpful. It is impossible to controvert what is incontrovertible. Rather, even realized money is only an incontrovertible enrichment to the extent that the defendant has been saved expense in its acquisition.

On the facts found in *Greenwood v Bennett* it was never shown that the defendant could or would have had the same work done for £226, so that the third explanation cannot explain the result. However, applying a fourth explanation for the result demonstrates that this was unnecessary. Another example:

> The claimant repairs his neighbour's fences mistakenly believing that they are his own. His neighbour is away and could not do the work himself. The work costs, and could be bought, for £100. The repairs prevent the cattle of his neighbour (the defendant) from straying and being lost over a cliff. The cattle are subsequently sold for £1 million.

---

[22] *Kleinwort Benson v Birmingham City Council* [1997] QB 380, CA.
[23] eg *FC Jones (Trustee in Bankruptcy) v Jones* [1997] Ch 159, CA.
[24] *Foskett v McKeown* [2001] 1 AC 102, 127 per Lord Millett, 108–9 per Lord Browne-Wilkinson, 132 per Lord Hoffmann.   [25] A Burrows, *The Law of Restitution* (2nd edn, 2002) 20.

Even if we accept that the law of unjust enrichment does not require a correspondence between the claimant's loss and the defendant's gain, the claimant cannot claim £1million. This is because the full benefit of £1 million is not solely attributable to the repair of the fences; there is more than one necessary cause of this sum. It is true that 'but for' the repairs the defendant would not have had £1 million. However, another cause of this gain is the herd itself. 'But for' the cattle the sum would not have been realized. The hard work the defendant neighbour has put into the farm and building up the herd cannot be ignored. An apportionment must be made. The correct value of the enrichment which is causally attributable to the claimant's work is its market value of £100, not £1 million. No other attribution can be made other than an arbitrary one (eg 12 per cent of the sum realized).

In *Greenwood v Bennett* there were two causes of the gain of £325: the work and the car. The car's potential for improvement cannot be ignored in assessing the gain made from the work. If we attribute the potential for improvement to the car and not to the work, the market value (£226) gives a proper assessment of the defendant's enrichment from the work. It should be stressed that this argument is not the same as arguing that before a claim in unjust enrichment can be brought the claimant must have suffered a loss which corresponds with the defendant's gain. If the claimant had incurred far more expense in repairing the car than the market value for the work, he should still not be able to claim more than the market value, even where the realized gain is higher than this sum. Similarly, if the mistaken repairer of fences had incurred far higher costs than the market value of the work done, his claim cannot exceed its market value.

The argument presented here can be seen as the flipside of the view that unjust enrichment does not always require a correspondence between loss and gain. That the potential of property to be improved, exploited, or traded is to be attributed to the property owner is also seen in those cases where the owner is the claimant, rather than defendant.[26] Where the defendant's enrichment is a product of the claimant's property, the claimant is entitled to strip the defendant of the gains he has made.[27] Where the defendant's enrichment comes from the claimant's property, it is unnecessary for the claimant to show a correlative loss, but not in any other case.

Setting to one side the question of whether it is necessary for the claimant to identify a loss which corresponds with a gain, how is an incontrovertible enrichment to be quantified? In principle the claimant can recover the expense the defendant would have incurred in having the work carried out or, where it is no greater, the realized value of the work done, but never more than the market value of the work.

[26] Birks, (n 2) 82.
[27] eg, *Foskett v McKeown above; Edwards v Lee's Administrators* 96 SW 2d 1028 (Ky CA, 1936); cf *Beck v Northern Natural Gas Company* 170 F 3d 1018 (US Ct of Apps (10th Cir), 1999).

4. Incomplete Contractual Performance

Where a contract is unenforceable for failure to comply with a requirement of form and performance has been rendered which would otherwise entitle the claimant to claim payment, it is legitimate to treat the defendant as enriched. He has received what he bargained for.[28] However, it cannot be sufficient in order to establish enrichment that the defendant has received an incomplete contractual performance. If, for example, I bargain for a haircut with a barber, who dies two thirds of the way through performance, his estate neither should nor does have a claim for the value of the work done. An incomplete haircut may be worse than none at all and it will cost me just as much to have my haircut finished as if he had never started. Enrichment must be established in other ways. This can be done either by showing that the value of the work has been realized or, more commonly, that an expense has been saved because it will cost the defendant less to achieve the bargained for outcome because of the part performance.

Professor Burrows has suggested that incomplete performance should be rebuttably presumed to be an enrichment, and quantified by applying the contract price rateably to the proportion of the work completed.[29] This should be rejected. It is for the barber's estate to prove that I am enriched by the work done, not for me to disprove it. It may be that in many and possibly the majority of cases the claimant will be able to demonstrate enrichment. This does not justify a presumption in the claimant's favour, the doctrinal basis for which has not been articulated and which has not been adopted in the case-law. Indeed, it is very doubtful whether the rateable application of the contract price would give a correct quantification of the defendant's enrichment (or the claimant's loss) in the majority of cases in any event. In the common case of partially completed building work, the expense the defendant has been saved for the work to be completed will not be reflected in a rateable application of the contract price. The start-up expenses another builder would incur, and what he would conse-quently charge to complete the work, will mean that the enrichment is lower than a rateable application of the contract price would indicate. The start-up expenses the claimant builder has incurred means that the loss he has incurred will be higher than the rateable contract price. However, the claimant's expenses are irrelevant to a calculation of the defendant's enrichment.

The only substantive case on the quantification of enrichment in the context of frustration, indeed one of the very few cases addressing the issue of enrichment at all, is *BP Exploration Co (Libya) Ltd v Hunt (No 2)*.[30] The decision is unusual

---

[28] *Pavey & Matthews Pty Ltd v Paul* (1987) 162 CLR 221.
[29] Burrows, (n 25) 23–4, 344; cf G Jones, *Goff & Jones: The Law of Restitution* (6th edn, 2002) 20–35; M Garner 'The Role of Subjective Benefit in the Law of Unjust Enrichment' (1990) 10 OJLS 42, 53 'a fallacious jump'.   [30] [1979] 1 WLR 783 affirmed [1983] 2 AC 352, HL.

because despite going to the House of Lords, the only judge to give reasoned consideration of the issue was Robert Goff J at first instance. In order to bring a claim for the restitution of a benefit other than money under section 1(3) of the Law Reform (Frustrated Contracts) Act 1943, it is first necessary to identify the 'valuable benefit' conferred and then the 'just sum' to be awarded. Robert Goff J concluded that, on the wording of the section, the valuable benefit was not, ordinarily, the work itself. As the example of the barber demonstrates, as a matter of principle this is correct as part performance is not necessarily an enrichment in and of itself. He further concluded that it was usually necessary to identify an 'end product'.[31] If this is interpreted narrowly, so as to include only a benefit realized or realizable in money and not an expenditure saved, this appears incorrect.

Robert Goff J gave the following example:[32]

> The Claimant may have undertaken building work for a substantial sum which is, objectively speaking, of little or no value, for he may commence redecoration, to the defendant's execrable taste, of rooms which are in good decorative order. The contract is frustrated before the work is complete and the work is unaffected by the frustrating event.

Where payments under a contract have been earned prior to discharge by frustration, these remain payable.[33] However, in the example, the builder's estate cannot claim the agreed sum as it has not been earned. Is the defendant enriched? Robert Goff J argued that 'the partial work must be treated as a benefit to the defendant since he requested it, and valued it as such'.[34] However, if this were sufficient I would be enriched by the barber's incomplete haircut, which is not the case. Incomplete performance cannot be presumed, without more, to be an enrichment. Further, his conclusion that there is always a valuable benefit in such a case does not sit happily with the view that the valuable benefit for the purposes of the Act is the 'end product'. The end product, here the difference in value between the undecorated and decorated rooms, is zero.

In the case of the execrable redecoration, the correct quantification of enrichment is dependent on facts Robert Goff J does not discuss. Let us assume that the market price for the completed work is £5,000 but that the defendant has made a bad bargain so that the contract price is £10,000. If after the frustrating event the defendant has the work completed by another decorator for £1,000, there seems no doubt that he is enriched. He has received precisely what he bargained for. However, the quantification of the incontrovertible benefit is the market valuation of the decoration costs saved. The contract has nothing to say about the valuation to be placed on incomplete performance, any more than

---

[31] [1979] 1 WLR 783, 801. [32] [1979] 1 WLR 783, 803.
[33] Law Reform (Frustrated Contracts) Act 1943, s 2(4). [34] [1979] 1 WLR 783, 803.

my contract with the barber does. Further, it is not possible for the claimant to 'subjectively revalue'[35] and argue that the defendant valued the work at £10,000, that it has cost him £1,000 to complete, and thereby claim £9,000. The claimant's work has saved the defendant £4,000, but the frustrating event has saved him £5,000. This is apparent in the case where the claimant has barely commenced performance at the time of the frustrating event. It would not in such circumstances be possible to claim the difference between the contract price (£10,000) and the market cost of completion (£5,000). You cannot buck the market in this way.

Robert Goff J also gave the following example:

> If a prospector after some very simple prospecting discovers a large and unexpected deposit of valuable mineral, the benefit to the defendant (namely, the enhancement in the value of the land) may be enormous; it must be valued as such, always bearing in mind that the assessment of a just sum may very well lead to a much smaller amount being awarded to the claimant.[36]

This would be to place far too high a value on the work provided. There are, again, two causes of the enrichment of the defendant: the prospecting and the land's potential. To attribute the difference in value between the land with and without the discovery of the mineral deposit solely to the prospecting and not to the land appears incorrect. This would be so even if the cost of the prospecting work exceeded the value of the mineral deposits. Robert Goff J presumably intends this to be taken into account in assessing the 'just sum'.

BP v Hunt itself concerned work performed by BP in exploring and extracting oil on land, the oil concession to which Mr Hunt owned. BP took the risk of there being no oil but was to be generously remunerated if an oilfield was found. The exploration was a success, so that the concession was worth a vast sum. The concession was worked for a period but then expropriated by the Libyan government, frustrating the contract. Adopting the same approach to Mr Hunt's concession as to the hypothetical value of the mineral deposits, Robert Goff J valued Mr Hunt's realized enrichment, after the expropriation, at $170 million. He then assessed the 'valuable benefit' as half this sum, $85 million. The fifty-fifty split, which adopted the submissions of BP, was presumably to reflect the fact that there were two causes of the overall gain: BP's work and Hunt's concession. However, this judgment of Solomon, whilst not affecting the result in *BP v Hunt* itself, should not be adopted in future cases. If the same approach had been adopted in *Greenwood v Bennett* the claimant would have been confined to half the net realization (£187.50). This would not accurately reflect the fact in that case that the service was a more significant cause of the realized gain than the asset worked upon.

---

[35] cf Garner, 'The Role of Subjective Benefit' 42, 43; G Virgo, *The Principles of the Law of Restitution* (1999) 86–8. [36] [1979] 1 WLR 783, 803.

However, Robert Goff J did not award BP $85 million. BP were merely allowed to claim their fees incurred in exploring and extracting the oil plus the money and oil they had paid Mr Hunt, less the benefit conferred upon them by Mr Hunt prior to the frustrating event: $35 million. In confining the award to the expenses BP incurred in performing their side of the deal, *BP v Hunt* provides support to those who would argue that the law of unjust enrichment in England requires a correspondence between loss and gain before restitution can be awarded.[37]

An alternative, and preferable, explanation is that, as in *Greenwood v Bennett,* the only benefit attributable to the service provided by BP was the market value of the work they did. To an extent this was reflected in the price they charged for their services under the contract.[38] However, the contract was not a reliable guide. Under the contract BP accepted the risks of failure and had correspondingly greater rewards for success. If the exploration had proven unsuccessful they would have received less than the market rate for their work; when successful they received more than the market rate. Simply applying the contract formula to calculate the award would have been to make an award above the market rate for the work and this was correctly not done. Further, if BP's costs had exceeded the market value of their work, they should not have been entitled to claim the greater amount. The principled result was reached.

Robert Goff J has been criticized for his view that the time for assessing the valuable benefit is after the frustrating event. Let us suppose, as Robert Goff J did, that a contract for work on a building is frustrated by a fire which destroys the building and which also destroys the work which has been done.[39] In principle, should a claim be possible? If the building contract provides for payment upon completion of certain stages, any contractual entitlement to be paid will survive the fire, but in principle any claim based upon unjust enrichment should fail. In an unjust enrichment action, the enrichment should be quantified at the moment the claim arises, which is when the enrichment becomes unjust. In the case of mistaken car repairs, this is as the work is done, but where the claim arises from frustration of a contract any enrichment only becomes unjust after the frustrating event. In the language of 'unjust factors', there is only a failure of basis at that point. If a 'legal ground' analysis is preferred, the contract provides a legal ground for any enrichment up to the point when it is frustrated. After the fire, the value to the defendant of the work the claimant has done is zero. He has not received what he bargained for, no benefit has been realized, and the work done has not reduced the cost of achieving the bargained for result. In principle, the award should be nil.[40]

Does the language of the statute lead to the principled result? Professor Treitel has been critical of Robert Goff J's interpretation of the statutory text.[41] First, the

---

[37] Birks, 2nd (n 2) 80.   [38] [1979] 1 WLR 783, 822.
[39] cf *Appleby v Myers* (1867) LR 2 CP 651.
[40] See also *Parson Bros Ltd v Shea* (1965) 53 DLR (2d) 86.
[41] G Treitel, *The Law of Contract* (11th edn, 2003) 915.

wording of section 1(3) requires the assessment of the valuable benefit 'before the time of discharge', so, in the example, before not after the fire. Secondly, the effect of the circumstances giving rise to the frustrating event are to be taken into account at the second stage in assessing the just sum,[42] not in identifying the valuable benefit. Professor Treitel concludes that this gives the courts the discretion to make an award where this would 'promote justice' even in cases where after the frustrating event the defendant is not enriched at all.

Whilst Professor Treitel's textual criticism of Robert Goff J is unanswerable, the discretion he advocates should not be accepted. Where there is no enrichment, the doctrinal basis for making an award to compensate the claimant for his expenditure is unclear, and it is uncertain how the court is to exercise the discretion advocated.[43] The preferable approach is to reach the same conclusion as Robert Goff J, but to do so by saying that where after the frustrating event the defendant is not enriched, the 'just sum' is zero.

It would be unfortunate if the statutory language compelled a result which is different from that which would be reached by the application of principle. If a contract is entered into which, ten minutes after it is signed, is rendered impossible to perform by an unforeseeable event, the contract will be frustrated. If the same event has, unbeknownst to the parties, occurred ten minutes before the agreement is entered into, the contract will be void for common fundamental mistake. It would be unfortunate if different rules governed the right to the restitution of benefits conferred under the contract according to the accident of when the discharging event occurs. Interpretations should be adopted in order to minimize these differences. The English Law Reform (Frustrated Contracts) Act 1943 was a modest attempt to correct some anomalies in the common law's treatment of the consequences of frustration, for example the decision in *Chandler v Webster*.[44] The approach of some common law jurisdictions of introducing legislation to determine in novel ways the unwinding of frustrated contracts[45] but not the consequences of a contract being invalid for other reasons inevitably leads to like cases being treated differently.

In the examples given so far, the starting position has been that the correct valuation of the enrichment is that provided by the market and not by the contract. A difficult question arises where the claimant has made a bad bargain and seeks to escape that bargain through the law of unjust enrichment by claiming the market value of what has been done. The classic illustration of this problem is the decision of the Supreme Court of California in *Boomer v*

---

[42] Law Reform (Frustrated Contracts) Act 1943, s 1(3)(b).

[43] G Jones, *Goff & Jones The Law of Restitution* (6th edn, 2002) 558; cf E McKendrick, 'Frustration, Restitution and Loss Apportionment' in A Burrows (ed), *Essays on the Law of Restitution* (1991) 147.

[44] [1904] 1 KB 493 CA overruled *Fibrosa Spolka Akcjna v Fairbairn Lawson Combe Barbour Ltd* [1943] AC 32, HL.

[45] British Columbia Frustrated Contracts Act 1974, New South Wales Frustrated Contracts Act 1978, South Australian Frustrated Contracts Act 1988.

Muir.[46] The claimants constructed a dam on the defendant's land. Before the work was complete they were excluded from the site. Although only $20,000 remained payable under the contract if it had been completed, the claimants successfully claimed the much larger sum of $200,000, which reflected the market value of the work for which they had not been paid.

Seen as a claim in unjust enrichment, the result in *Boomer v Muir* appears incorrect. One way of arguing that this is so is by addressing the question of enrichment.[47] Not everyone wants a dam constructed on their land. In order to establish that the defendant was enriched by the work which was done, the claimants can rely upon the contract to show that the defendants had requested it. However, the terms of the contract only demonstrated that the defendants valued the completed work at $20,000. Beyond that sum the defendants could argue they were not enriched, and no claim could succeed.

What if, however, the claimants could establish enrichment without relying upon the terms of the contract? If the defendants had sold the land on which the dam had been built and it could be shown that $500,000 more was obtained as a result of the unpaid-for work, could this sum be claimed? As argued above, the most which can be attributed to the work is its market cost ($200,000); the rest of the gain is attributable to the potential of the property. Should the claimants be able to claim the market cost of the work where it exceeds the contract price?

The answer is no, but this conclusion cannot be obtained by focusing on the question of enrichment. Where the value of the work has been realized, the defendants are enriched to the extent that this does not exceed the market cost. However, is the enrichment unjust? The defendants are only unjustly enriched to the extent that they have not kept their side of the deal. If the defendants fully performed, here by paying all that could be earned under the contract, $20,000, it would be impossible to argue that any further enrichment was unjust. The defendants were only unjustly enriched to the extent that $20,000 has not been paid; no greater sum should be capable of being obtained through claiming in unjust enrichment. If the language of 'legal ground' is preferred, the payment of the outstanding $20,000 under the contract would provide a legal ground for any further enrichment. There is a 'contract ceiling' on recovery, not just a 'valuation ceiling'.[48]

Once it is accepted that incomplete performance of a contract does not necessarily establish enrichment, it becomes necessary to explain the classic case of *Planche v Colburn*.[49] The claimant was employed to write a book for a series entitled *The Juvenile Library*. After the claimant had done some of the work, the defendant decided to abandon the series. The defendant was saved no expense by

---

[46] 24 P 2d 570 (Cal Sup Ct, 1933); cf *Slowey v Lodder* (1900) 20 NZLR 321; affirmed sub nom *Lodder v Slowey* [1904] AC 442, PC.

[47] Burrows, (n 25) 346; Birks, 'In Defence of Free Acceptance' in Burrows, (n 43) 105, 136.

[48] Jones, (n 29) 513.   [49] (1831) 8 Bing 14.

what was done and obtained no realized benefit. The claimant was held to be entitled to a *quantum meruit*, reasonable remuneration, but this tells us nothing as to the doctrinal basis of recovery. If part performance of a contract is not a sufficient reason for establishing enrichment, it would be fictional to deem a defendant who prevents performance from being completed as enriched merely for that reason. If there was no enrichment, either *Planche v Colburn* is wrongly decided or there is an alternative explanation.

The first, and most obvious, alternative would be to treat the award in *Planche v Colburn* as today best explained as an award of damages for breach of contract. Either the defendant is entitled to be placed in the position he would have been in if the contract had been concluded, which would lead to the award of the difference between the contract price and the cost of completion, or if for some reason this was too uncertain to be calculated, the costs so far incurred.[50]

An alternative is to argue that the entitlement to reasonable remuneration does not depend upon unjust enrichment or breach of contract but rests on another doctrinal basis. This is the approach of Professors Treitel[51] and Beatson, the latter describing the claim as one based upon 'injurious reliance'.[52]

The two alternative explanations would not necessarily lead to the same result. Damages for breach of contract may not be awarded to allow 'escape from a bad bargain'.[53] Put another way, the highest sum which can be awarded as damages is the sum which would place the claimant in the position he would have been in if the contract had been performed. If damages are not claimed, but rather reasonable remuneration is sought for the work done which the defendant has wrongfully prevented from being completed, does this cap on recovery apply even though the claimant has conferred no benefit upon the defendant?

In the United States no such cap applies. In *Acme Process Equipment Company v United States*[54] the claimant was the manufacturer of rifles under a contract of supply with the government. The government repudiated the contract, no rifles were ever delivered, and the government consequently received no benefit from the work done prior to repudiation. The bargain was a bad one for the claimants but the court held that they were entitled to the reasonable value of the work they had done, despite the fact that this was far greater than the damages which would have been recoverable.

---

[50] Burrows, (n 25) 343.   [51] Treitel, (n 41) 822.

[52] J Beatson, *The Use and Abuse of Unjust Enrichment* (1991), 'Reliance and the Structure of Unjust Enrichment' 21, 49. Possible further examples of such a principle are said to include *Brewer Street Investments Ltd v Barclays Woollen Co Ltd* [1954] 1 QB 428 CA and *Sabemo Pty Ltd v North Sydney Municipal Council* [1977] 2 NSWLR 880; cf *Regalian Properties plc v London Dockland Development Corpn* [1995] 1 WLR 212.

[53] *C&P Haulage v Middleton* [1983] 1 WLR 1461. The same limitation applies in the United States.

[54] 347 F 2d 509 (Ct. Cl. 1965) reversed on other grounds 385 US 138 (1966). See also *Stephen v Camden & Philadelphia Soap Co* 68 A 69 (NJ, 1907); *Landmark Land Co v FDIC* 256 F 3d 135 (Fed Cir, 2001).

Regardless of whether the English courts proceed to recognize 'injurious reliance' as a separate ground for recovery, it is to be hoped that they will not follow the American example and permit the claimant to escape from a bad bargain in this way. The claimant has relied upon the expectation that he will be able to complete performance and obtain the contract price. He has no legitimate expectation of being able to claim more than he bargained for. The American 'paradox'[55] of permitting greater recovery for partial than full performance should not be introduced.

The contract price for full performance has three roles in determining the quantum of recovery in cases of incomplete performance. First, the contract price determines the ceiling of recovery. Secondly, the contract may provide evidence of the reduced market cost for the defendant in achieving the bargained for result after the partial performance. Thirdly, the contract may provide evidence of the market value of the work done and consequently the extent to which a realized enrichment is to be attributed to the work. However, it is the market, and not the contract, which provides the correct valuation of the enrichment from partial performance.

5. Where Title Does Not Pass

In theory, a difficult enrichment question arises where a claimant's asset is transferred into the hands of a defendant where no title to that asset passes. Is the claimant able to assert a claim in unjust enrichment or is no such claim possible because the defendant is never enriched or, which amounts to the same thing, the claimant cannot establish the 'at the expense of' element of the claim because the asset remains his?

Peter Birks argued, correctly in my view but contrary to the view of some commentators,[56] that the fact that pre-existing title persisted did not preclude a claim in unjust enrichment.[57] However, the problem is more easily short-circuited in the courtroom than in the classroom. An example:

> The claimant intending to make a gift of £50 to his brother hands over a £50 banknote to the defendant. The defendant bears a striking resemblance to the claimant's brother but is in fact a complete stranger.

The claimant's mistake is so extreme, a mistake as to the recipient's identity, that no title to the note will pass.[58] The claimant could bring a claim in conversion and recover the value of the note. However, let us assume that the claimant asserts a claim in unjust enrichment, relying upon *Kelly v Solari*[59] for

---

[55] G Treitel, *Remedies for Breach of Contract* (1988) 104.
[56] eg W Swadling, 'A Claim in Restitution' [1996] LMCLQ 63; Virgo, *Principles of the Law of Restitution*, 11–17.   [57] Birks, (n 2) 63–8.
[58] *R v Middleton* (1873) LR 2 CCR 38; *Cundy v Lindsay* (1878) 3 App Cas 459.
[59] (1841) 9 M&W 54.

the proposition that the recipient of a mistaken payment is obliged to make restitution. In order to make good his cause of action the claimant does not have to prove, any more than the insurance company in *Kelly v Solari*[60] did, that the defendant has obtained good title to the money. The receipt of money mistakenly paid is all that needs to be proven to establish prima facie liability. Can the defendant resist the claim by arguing that he is not enriched? No, he cannot. The claim cannot be resisted by the defendant arguing 'I am not enriched because this note is yours'. If the only possible means of resisting the claim in unjust enrichment is for the defendant to point to another, and superior, ground for recovery, the claim must succeed. Similarly if the defendant no longer has the note, perhaps because, delighted by his good fortune, he has given it away to charity, he would be foolish to attempt to argue that the note was still the claimant's at the time of receipt. The claim in unjust enrichment is subject to the defence of change of position; the claim in conversion is not.

It is theoretically possible that there may be an incidental rule which means that the claim in unjust enrichment is advantageous for the claimant when compared with a claim in conversion. It is conceivable, for example, that the limitation period could be longer. In practice, however, it is very difficult to think of any examples where this is in fact the case.

An analogy may be drawn with the criminal law. If a defendant is charged with necrophilia he would be exceptionally foolish to argue that he was not guilty on the basis that his victim, whilst unconscious, was still alive at the time of intercourse. Sexual intercourse with someone who is alive but unconscious, and consequently unable to give consent, is rape, a more serious offence.[61] Although in the abstract (or in a classroom) the defendant may not be guilty of necrophilia, in practice there is nothing he can argue to successfully resist the charge.

Another reason why the issue of passing of title in unjust enrichment excites more academic comment than litigation is that the simple case of the mistaken transfer of a banknote no longer represents the usual case in the area of misdirected funds, if it ever did. Another example:

> The claimant instructs his bank to make a transfer of funds into the account of the defendant whom he believes to be his brother and to whom he intends a gift. In fact the defendant is a complete stranger. The claimant's account with his bank is overdrawn and he has no contractual entitlement to further drawings, but the bank proceeds to make the payment. The defendant's account is also at all times overdrawn.

Although the mistake is the same in this example, in the case of bank transfers we cannot say that the claimant has 'retained title' to what has been transferred. The defendant has not received any asset of the claimant, although his liability to

---

[60] (1841) 11 LJ Ex 10.
[61] cf *R v Ladue* [1965] 4 CCC 264, 45 CR 287, 51 WWR 175.

his bank has been reduced. Similarly no asset has left the claimant, although his liability to his bank has increased. In the usual case of inter-bank transfers it is meaningless to speak of the claimant vindicating his pre-existing property rights.[62] It is not significant that no asset in the defendant's hands can be traceably attributed to an asset which left the claimant. Even where both accounts are in credit we cannot say that the money the defendant is owed by his bank is really owed to the claimant. This would come as something of a surprise to the defendant's bank. It is the defendant's 'abstract enrichment'[63] which is significant for the purposes of a personal claim in unjust enrichment, not whether we can identify any particular asset in the hands of the defendant which was once the claimant's.

6. Peter Again

Whether Peter would have thought any of the moves I have made in this essay are good ones, I do not know. I hope he would have accepted that some of them are. Peter Birks was the only great person I have ever known. In his writing he always tried to say something which would take our understanding of the law further. His work did not stop where the cases ended. However, he was not great because of his published work, although I think he was one of our most important English jurists. He was great because of his ability to inspire young scholars with his passion for the law, as generations of his students would testify. On one of the last occasions I saw him, I plucked up the courage to tell him as much. I now think that I told him more for my benefit than his.

---

[62] cf Virgo, *Principles of the Law of Restitution*, 11–17.   [63] Birks, (n 2) 69.

4

Some Thoughts on Change of Position

*Gareth Jones**

1. Introduction

This volume remembers Peter Birks, a scholar dedicated to the ideal that the law of restitution should be given a logical and coherent structure. Indeed, Peter was a *passionate* advocate of legal elegance. In the preface to the first supplement to the latest edition of Goff and Jones, I wrote that 'to achieve this goal he was prepared not only to rethink what he had previously written but to challenge what many had thought were entrenched legal principles'.[1] After reading his wonderfully stimulating *Unjust Enrichment*[2] I and no doubt others will tremble where we had firmly stood before.

Peter Birks had given much thought to the place of change of position in the law of restitution. In his *Unjust Enrichment*, so characteristically, he reflected again. And on reflection he preferred to describe the defence as 'disenrichment'.[3] This appropriately suggests that there must be a reduction in the assets of the recipient, although it is now accepted that it is unnecessary for the recipient 'to produce precise financial calculations quantifying the amount of the reduction'.[4]

---

[*] Downing Professor Emeritus of the Laws of England in the University of Cambridge; Fellow of Trinity College, Cambridge.

[1] First Supplement (2004) to Goff and Jones, *The Law of Restitution* (6th edn, 2002) (hereinafter referred to as Goff and Jones). In his early writings, Peter Birks urged scholars to 'look down to the cases'. But his legal epitaph is best captured in Williston's posthumous tribute to his mentor, Ames: 'Williston describes Ames as a "legal idealist" who saw it as his function to "weld from the decisions" a body of mutually consistent and coherent principles. To his mind there was but one right principle upon a given point, and if decisions failed to recognize it, so much the worse for the decisions': S Williston, 'James Barr Ames—His Services to Legal Education' (1916) 23 Harv LR 330–2, cited by Andrew Kull, 'James Barr Ames and the Early Modern History of Unjust Enrichment' (2005) 25 OJLS 297, 311. [2] (2nd edn, 2005).

[3] But he left open the possibility that there might be 'non-disenriching' changes of position: (n 2) 208–9 and 258–61.

[4] *Commerzbank AG v Jones* [2003] EWCA 1663, [2005] 1 Lloyd's Rep 298 at [39], per Mummery LJ.

There may be situations where the recipient does change his position but suffers no financial detriment[5] although as yet the cases provide few clues as to what these situations are likely to be.[6] In Birks's view, 'If valid examples are found they will be very rare indeed'.[7]

This essay, which seeks to explore some of the more contentious questions in the body of law relating to change of position (or disenrichment) and to suggest mildly radical conclusions, is offered as a modest tribute to the memory of a close and inspiring friend.

In the first edition of Goff and Jones, *The Law of Restitution* (published in 1966), the authors wrote:[8] 'The failure of the English courts to recognize a general defence of change of position to restitutionary claims is to be regretted'. It was not until 1991, in *Lipkin Gorman (a firm) v Karpnale Ltd*,[9] that the House of Lords accepted that there was such a defence. Indeed, passages in Lord Goff's speech explaining the nature and scope of the defence have been so influential that they have been interpreted as if they were statutory provisions.[10] *Lipkin Gorman* was bold law, for three reasons. First, there was relatively little authority to support the recognition of the defence. Secondly, the claim in *Lipkin Gorman* was arguably not a claim based on the unjust enrichment of the club, but a proprietary claim based on money had and received by the Club.[11] Third, Lord Goff distinguished, not perhaps convincingly, the speech of Lord Simonds in *Ministry of Health v Simpson*,[12] which appeared firmly to reject a general defence of change of position. However, the authority of *Ministry of Health* led Carnwath J to doubt, in *Gray v Richards Butler (a firm)*,[13] whether change of position is a defence to a claim against recipients of a legacy under a will.[14] It is predictable that this dictum will not be followed.

---

[5] In *Commerzbank AG v Jones* [2003] EWCA 1663, [2005] 1 Lloyd's Rep 298 at [65] Munby J went so far as to say that to require financial detriment or some detriment measurable in financial terms 'is completely unsound in principle'. But see n 7 below.

[6] The possible examples given by Mummery LJ and Munby J in *Commerzbank AG v Jones* [2003] EWCA 1663, [2005] 1 Lloyd's Rep 298 at [39] and [65]–[70] are not compelling for the recipient in them suffers financial hardship, albeit indirectly.   [7] (n 2) 261.

[8] At 486.   [9] [1991] 2 AC 540.

[10] As have his speeches in some other decisions: see *Woolwich Building Society v Inland Revenue Commissioners* [1993] AC 70 and *Kleinwort Benson Ltd v Lincoln City Council Ltd* [1999] 2 AC 349, as interpreted in *Deutsche Morgan Grenfell Group Plc v IRC* [2005] EWCA Civ 78, [2006] 2 WLR 103. See further below p 72 n 46.

[11] See Goff and Jones, 2–004 at 81; and, in particular, Lord Goff's statement in *Lipkin Gorman* [1991] 2 AC 548, 578 that the 'the plaintiff has to establish a basis on which he is entitled to the money. This (at least, as a general rule) he does by showing that the money is his legal property'. But his lordship also said (at 572) that the claim 'is not a proprietary claim, advanced on the basis that money remaining in the hands of the club is their property' and that it was 'founded upon the unjust enrichment of the club, and can succeed only if, in accordance with the principles of the law of restitution, the club was indeed unjustly enriched at the expense of the solicitors'.

[12] [1951] AC 251, 276. He agreed with Lord Simonds that the mere expenditure of money was not sufficient to establish the defence.

[13] *The Times*, 23 July 1996, but not reported on this point.

[14] The claim in *Ministry of Health v Simpson* arose out of the administration of the Diplock estate.

2. Change of Position and Public Policy

In principle only in exceptional circumstances should the court be persuaded that public policy defeats the defence of change of position. It has often been said that public policy is an unruly horse. But as the following examples demonstrate, public policy is also the Sea God Proteus, for it manifests itself in many different forms. In each situation the courts should identify the particular public policy and ask whether it is so dominant that it should trump the defence of change of position.

(a) Change of position is not a defence if the claimant lacked capacity to confer the benefit on the defendant even though the defendant acted in good faith (honestly)

Such were the facts of *Williams v Williams*.[15] The claimant, who suffered from significant intellectual impairment, sought a declaration that the deed of gift, whereby he had conveyed his house[16] to himself, his brother, and sister-in-law on trust for sale as tenants in common in the proportion of 50:25:25, was void. The Deputy Judge of the High Court, Kevin Garnett QC, granted the declaration. The claimant had not been provided with the 'kind of explanation which would have enabled him [the claimant] to understand the transaction ... simply because there is so little evidence about what [the claimant] was told'. Furthermore, the claimant 'was not given an adequate explanation and so did not have a proper understanding'.[17]

The Deputy Judge was sympathetic to the defendants' position; they had acted in perfect good faith. Their counsel relied on the 'general defence of change of position', citing 'Gough [[18]] and Jones (6th ed.) at paras 11–014 and 25–018', which, the Deputy Judge rightly pointed out, had 'nothing to do with the case of a gift which is void for want of capacity, and are not authority for that submission'.[19] It is conjectural whether the result would have been different if the court and counsel had read the relevant chapter, chapter 40, of Goff and Jones. But the decision is probably correct because the deed was void.[20] The defendant's change of position appears then not to be a defence, although, as the Judge implied, this may be harsh where the defendants acted honestly and in what they perceived to be the claimant's best interests.

---

[15] [2003] EWHC 742 (Ch).   [16] It was his only substantial asset.

[17] Following, on this point, *Re Beaney* [1978] 1 WLR 770, 774, per Martin Nourse QC, sitting as a Deputy Judge of the High Court: at [40] and [48].

[18] This is an unusual spelling of Lord Goff's surname.   [19] At [52]–[54].

[20] Furthermore, the defence would seemingly have failed on the facts; although the defendants had given up their secure council accommodation in reliance on the fact that they would have a share in the house as tenants in common with the claimant, they had not acted to their detriment. For as the Deputy Judge said, 'in any event', he would not have been 'inclined to make an order in the form which [counsel] suggested' because the defendants have had the benefit of rent-free accommodation for sixteen years: at [56].

(b) The defendant who has acted in good faith (honestly) should be able to
    rely on the defence of change of position even though he is presumed to
    have exercised undue influence over the claimant

In *Lipkin Gorman* Lord Goff held that the defence should not be open to a
wrongdoer; the action must not be founded on wrongdoing.[21] The defendant
who acted in good faith but was presumed to have exercised undue influence is
not a wrongdoer; his conduct is not reprehensible. It is true that undue influence
has often been characterized as an equitable wrong or even as a species of
equitable fraud.[22] But there is another characterization which is more persuasive.
As Mummery LJ has said,

the basis of the court's intervention is not the commission of a wrongful act by the
defendant, but that, *as a matter of public policy*, the presumed influence arising from the
relationship of trust and confidence should not operate to the disadvantage of the victim,
if the transaction is not satisfactorily explained by ordinary motives: *Allcard v Skinner*
(1887) 36 ChD 145, 171 . . . A transaction may be set aside by the court, even though the
actions and conduct of the person who benefits from it could not be criticised as
wrongful.[23]

If this explanation of the court's jurisdiction is endorsed, it should be open to the
court to hold that the good faith (honest) defendant who was presumed to have
exercised undue influence over the claimant should have the defence of change of
position. Indeed long before the defence of change of position was recognized by
name there was a notable dictum which so held. In *Allcard v Skinner*[24] Lindley LJ
accepted that the claimant, a novice in a religious order, would have been
entitled to recover from her Mother Superior, who was presumed to have unduly
influenced her, only so much of the sums gifted as 'had not been spent [on
charitable purposes] in accordance with the wishes of the plaintiff but remained
in the hands of the defendant'.[25]

(c) Change of position is not a defence, as the law now stands, if the
    defendant, acting in good faith (honestly), advanced money on a security
    proffered by a vulnerable surety who had been induced to do so because of
    another's undue influence or misrepresentation

---

[21] [1991] 2 AC 548, 558–9. For a further discussion of the meaning of wrongdoer in this
context, see below, p 79ff.
[22] See eg *Barclays Bank plc v O'Brien* [1994] AC 180, 189 and *CIBC Mortgages v Pitt* [1994] AC
200, 209.   [23] *Pesticcio v Hunt* [2004] EWCA Civ 372 at [20]. Emphasis added.
[24] (1887) 36 Ch D 145, 186. Lindley LJ did not suggest that the defendant would have
succeeded only if a reasonable person in the defendant's position would have realized that he was
exercising undue influence.
[25] The claimant's action failed because of her own laches in pursuing the suit. In *Williams v
Williams*, already discussed, the Deputy Judge was also prepared to hold that the deed was procured
by undue influence in which case the deed would have been voidable on terms. (*Allcard v Skinner*,
above, n 24, was not cited.) The question whether the defendants could have relied on the defence of
change of position did not arise for the deed was declared to be void for the claimant's lack of capacity.

The critical question is whether this manifestation of 'public policy', the protection of the vulnerable claimant, is so dominant that it should prevail over the interests of the good faith defendant. Take this familiar example. A wife, acting as a surety for her husband, borrows money, often a substantial amount, from a bank; the security for the loan is her matrimonial home. Can the security which she offered be subsequently set aside on the ground of her spouse's undue influence (or misrepresentation) or can the bank, the good faith secured creditor, successfully resist her claim, relying on its charge over the matrimonial home? It is received law that the courts have sought to solve this problem by asking whether the bank can be 'made liable under the doctrine of notice':[26] is the bank a purchaser in good faith for value without notice?[27] In *Royal Bank of Scotland v Etridge (No 2)*[28] the House of Lords accepted that the analogy of notice, including of course constructive notice, was not the 'conventional' one which relates primarily and traditionally to the priority of competing *property* rights. And yet it was not abandoned. Their lordships struggled to give meaning to the concept of 'notice' when required to resolve a dispute between *contracting* parties, one of whom was a vulnerable contractor who had placed her trust in a third party (misguidedly, as events turned out) and the other a good faith commercial lender. Courts of equity have for centuries protected the vulnerable person who had been 'forced, tricked or misled in any way';[29] on the other hand, commercial lenders should not be deterred from accepting the matrimonial home as security for the loan. To resolve this tension *Etridge (No 2)*, building on the existing case-law, held that the bank should be put 'on inquiry' in every case where the relationship between the surety and the principal debtor was non-commercial.[30] The yardstick is an objective one. So, for example, if the bank knew or ought to have known that the wife's solicitor had not duly and properly advised the wife, the 'bank will proceed at its own risk'.[31]

The defence of change of position was in its infancy when *Barclays Bank v O'Brien* was decided. Is it regrettable that no attempt was made in later case-law to solve the problem by allowing the third party, such as the bank, to plead the defence of change of position? Is there now any room for the defence of change of position? Does the silence of the courts suggest not?

In *Lipkin Gorman* Lord Goff was of the firm view that bona fide purchase and change of position were distinct defences.[32] In the *O'Brien* line of cases change of position was not invoked as a defence to an equitable proprietary claim. Bona fide purchase is, arguably, *one*, but not the exclusive, illustration of the defence of

---

[26] *Bainbrigge v Browne* (1881) 18 Ch D 188, *BCCI v Aboody* [1992] 4 All ER 955, 981, and *Barclays Bank v O'Brien* [1993] 4 All ER 417, 425, per Lord Browne-Wilkinson.

[27] See eg the judgment of Mummery LJ in *Barclays Bank plc v Boulter* [1997] 2 All ER 1002, CA.

[28] [2001] UKHL 44 at [38], per Lord Nicholls and [143], per Lord Scott. See also *Barclays Bank v Boulter* [1999] 4 All ER 513, 518, per Lord Hoffmann.

[29] *Allcard v Skinner* (1887) 36 Ch D 145, 183, per Lindley LJ.

[30] [2001] UKHL 44 at [87] per Lord Nicholls.   [31] At [55], per Lord Nicholls.

[32] [1991] 2 AC 448, 580–1.

change of position.[33] In *Niru Battery Manufacturing Co v Milestone Trading Co* Clarke LJ and Sedley LJ suggested that to defeat the defence of change of position 'something more' than mere negligence, for example, 'sharp practice', must be demonstrated.[34] The defendant who is merely negligent may invoke the defence. I would prefer to say, the *honest* defendant may do so.[35] If this is accepted it would appear that it is open to a court to conclude, on particular facts, that a defendant

    (i)   had acted throughout in good faith;
   (ii)   had *constructive notice* that the spouse acted under undue influence and was not therefore a 'bona fide purchaser';
  (iii) was not guilty of 'sharp practice'; but
  (iv) was merely negligent in not concluding that the spouse was acting under another's undue influence; and
   (v) had acted therefore honestly and to its detriment by reason of the fact that it made a loan in reliance on the security of the matrimonial home, a security which the claimant now seeks to avoid.

It is another question whether it is desirable to reach that conclusion. Many distinguished academic commentators, including Dr Bryan, Ms Chen-Wishart, and Professor Birks, fear that if the bank were allowed the defence of change of position the protection of the domestic security-giver would utterly be destroyed.[36] This would be the result if the bank, acting honestly but negligently, with 'notice' that the claimant was the victim of another's undue influence, could fall back on a more generous defence of change of position. But has too little weight been given to the fact that the loan was an arm's-length commercial transaction between the principal debtor and an honest creditor and that the creditor will suffer financial loss if it cannot look to the security offered by the surety? Have the courts been too paternalistic, too solicitous of the interests of the 'vulnerable' spouse, and too ready to protect her interests at the expense of the honest lender?[37]

---

[33] cf Sir Peter Millett who said that bona fide purchase was 'simply the paradigm change of position defence [to an equitable *proprietary* claim]': 'Tracing the Proceeds of Fraud' (1991) 107 LQR 71, 82.

[34] *Niru Battery Mfg Co v Milestone Trading Co* [2004] 1 All ER (Comm) 193 at [164], per Clarke LJ and at [190], per Sedley LJ, adopting the reasoning of Moore-Bick J in [2002] 2 All ER (Comm) 705 at [135]: below, p 79ff.   [35] See below, p 80.

[36] M Chen-Wishart, 'In Defence of Unjust Factors: A Study of Rescission for Duress, Fraud and Exploitation' in *Unjustified Enrichment* (eds D Johnston and R Zimmermann, 2002) 159, 170–3; M Bryan, 'Change of Position: Commentary' in *Restitution: Developments in Unjust Enrichment* (ed M McInnes) 79–80; Birks, (n 2) 218.

[37] Ms Chen-Wishart concedes that exceptionally change of position may be a defence if the defendant's expenditure, incurred in the attempted performance of the claimant's (ie surety's) purposes, has resulted in him suffering a loss: above, n 36. In support, she cites a dictum of Cotton LJ in *Allcard v Skinner* (1887) 36 ChD 145, 171 (the Mother Superior was not 'liable for money spent for the charitable purposes with which the Plaintiff and Defendant were at the time of the expenditure associated, and which the Plaintiff was at the time willing and anxious to promote') and *Cheese v Thomas* [1994] 1 WLR 129. It is not clear what are the 'the claimant's purposes'. Seemingly, in her view, the security sought by the bank would not fall within that exception.

There is the further consideration which the courts have not considered to be critical. The claimant surety may have enjoyed the benefit of the loan made to the principal debtor, often her husband,[38] and that the relationship between these parties may have been a harmonious one, at least at the time when she agreed to be surety. Neither the courts nor the media love banks, which seek to be recompensed by depriving the surety of the shelter of her home. Banks are rich and their sureties are poor, at least comparatively.

The defence of change of position may never have been fully argued. But the law is now most probably too entrenched for it to succeed. The spouse who is likely to be ejected from her home will always enlist great sympathy, even from lawyers.

(d) Change of position should be a defence if a transaction is illegal but the defendant has not been a party to the illegal act

It is trite law that a claimant cannot found a cause of action on an illegal or immoral act. Any defence, similarly founded, should fail. The application of this principle, which is one of policy, 'can lead to unfair consequences between the parties to the litigation'.[39] For that reason this principle should have no application if the defendant, acting honestly, had received stolen funds in pursuance of an illegal transaction and had paid them over to a third party on the instructions of the rogue. He should be allowed the defence of change of position. He is not seeking to found his defence on an illegal or immoral act. Regrettably in *Barros Mattos Jnr v MacDaniels Ltd*[40] Laddie J reached the opposite conclusion. He held that the claimants, assignees of the defrauded bank's right to sue, could recover the sums stolen by the rogue and paid by him to the defendants. He rejected the defence of change of position, namely, that the monies, some $8 million, had been paid to third parties on the rogue's instructions; although the defendants were not enriched, their detrimental change of position was illegal since it was made pursuant to a transaction which infringed Nigeria's foreign exchange regulations. It was harsh to hold on these facts that the defendant had engaged in illegal activities. The 'principle of international comity' properly prevents the enforcement of a *contract* expressly prohibited by Nigerian law.[41] But the defendants were not seeking to enforce such a contract. Quite the contrary; as agents they were simply relying on the instructions of their principal.

It is a distinct question, however, whether the defence of change of position should have failed on the inter-related ground which I consider in the following section of this essay.

---

[38] She may have agreed to be surety in order to finance her spouse's business venture which, both parties falsely hoped, would bring them prosperity.

[39] *Tinsley v Milligan* [1993] 3 All ER 65, 72, per Lord Goff.

[40] [2004] 3 All ER 299.   [41] *Foster v Driscoll* [1929] 1 KB 470.

(e) Change of position is not a defence if it stultifies the policy underlying a
    particular statutory provision or common law rule

There are many examples in the reports where a restitutionary *claim* has failed if
it would lead to the enforcement of a transaction which statute or common law
refuses to enforce.[42] *Barros Mattos*,[43] where the defendant was held to have
infringed statutory exchange regulations, is a rare example of a situation where
the *defence* of change of position failed on that ground. In my view, the
infraction of the Nigerian exchange control laws was a technical one. To deny
the honest defendants the benefit of the defence was an entirely disproportionate
response.[44] They had acted as a mere conduit pipe. Allowing the defence would
not have stultified the policy of the statutory regulations.

(f) The Revenue or a public authority which has received payments pursuant
    to an ultra vires demand should be able to rely on the defence of change of
    position

In the landmark decision of the House of Lords in *Woolwich Equitable Building
Society v Commissioners of Inland Revenue*[45] the House of Lords held that money
paid in consequence of an ultra vires demand was recoverable as of right. The
Court of Appeal has said that the House 'recognized, or created, a right and a
remedy that were specific to the particular circumstances of the demander and of
the payer, and which stood outside the mainstream of restitution as understood
in a private law context'.[46]

In *Woolwich* the House was not asked to consider what are the defences, if
any, to a claim to recover payments so demanded. Lord Goff found the reasoning of Wilson J, dissenting, in *Air Canada v British Columbia*,[47] 'most
attractive'.[48] Wilson J doubted whether it was appropriate for the courts to adopt
some kind of policy in order to protect the government against itself. If it should,
it 'should be one that distributes the loss fairly across the public. The loss should
not fall on the totally innocent taxpayer whose only fault is that it paid what the
legislature improperly said was due'.[49] Like Wilson J, Lord Goff doubted the
'advisability of imposing special limits on recovery in the case of "unconstitutional or ultra vires levies"'.[50] He did accept, however, that some limit may have
to be placed on the recovery of taxes paid pursuant to an unlawful demand.[51]

---

[42] See the examples cited in Goff and Jones, 1–085 ff.   [43] Above, n 40.
[44] A Tettenborn, 'Bank Fraud, Change of Position and Illegality: The Case of the Innocent
Money-Launderer' [2005] LMCLQ 6.   [45] [1993] AC 70.
[46] *Deutsche Morgan Grenfell Group plc v IRC* [2006] 2 WLR 103 at [272]. The Court of Appeal
also said that Lord Goff's speech in *Woolwich* 'set out the whole of the relevant law in effectively
canonical terms'.   [47] (1989) 59 DLR (4th) 161.
[48] [1993] AC 70, 175.
[49] (1989) 59 DLR (4th) 161, 169–70. She also rejected the defence of 'passing on' which the
majority of the Supreme Court had accepted.   [50] [1993] AC 70, 175–6.
[51] His lordship left open the question whether there should be a special defence 'in circumstances in which some very substantial sum of money may be held to have been exacted ultra vires
from a very large number of taxpayers': [1992] AC 70, 174. In *Waikato Regional Airport Ltd v The
Attorney-General (on behalf of the Director of Agriculture and Forestry)* [2003] UKPC 50 at [82] the

The traditional armoury of common law defences, such as that to prevent the recovery of money paid under a binding compromise, may be inadequate.[52] Lord Goff did not say that these common law defences had no part to play in this context.[53] But it is reasonable to conclude that his approval of Wilson J's dissent would have led him, if the issue had been before the House, to reject the common law defence, approved by the Supreme Court of Canada and some United States jurisdictions, that recovery should be denied if to allow it would cause 'fiscal chaos' (a defence which less pejoratively may be expressed by saying that there is an irrebuttable presumption that the public authority, having relied on the receipt of ultra vires payments, has changed its position to its detriment). To reject 'fiscal chaos' as a defence is not to deny that it may be difficult for a public authority to demonstrate a change of position. The Revenue, represented by the Commissioners of Inland Revenue, is not the only public authority.[54] There are 'lesser fry' with fewer resources, such as some local authorities. One such authority was Tower Hamlets Borough Council. Significantly, there are dicta of Lord Goff in the earlier decision of the House of Lords in *Tower Hamlets London Borough Council v Chetnik Developments Ltd*[55] which suggest that it is open to a court to hold that the public authority has changed its position,[56] although in that case it was held that to allow the defence of change of position would frustrate the intention of the legislature as embodied in the General Rate Act 1967.[57]

Certainly, the defence of change of position should not fail *in limine* on the ground that the public authority, having made an unlawful demand, was a wrongdoer. At the time it made its demand it acted in good faith, honestly.

Privy Council held that on the facts it was not necessary to decide whether there should be a special defence.

[52] Lord Goff accepted that it may be necessary for there to be other defences, in particular, a shorter limitation period although he did not suggest that it was open to the courts to make this change. Furthermore, neither Lord Goff nor Lord Slynn went so far as to say that a payment made with the intention of settling the Revenue's ultra vires claim was recoverable. Genuine compromises should not be set aside: cf *Brennan v Bolt Burdon* [2005] QB 303.

[53] In my view it is too great a claim to conclude from Lord Goff's approval of Wilson J's reasoning that he was much attracted by the argument that 'defences available to the recipient in a private law restitutionary claim should not be available to the revenue when it has collected under an ultra vires demand': *Commissioners of Inland Revenue v Deutsche Morgan Grenfell* [2005] EWCA Civ 78, [2005] STC 329 at [271] (iii), per Buxton LJ.

[54] cf eg, the Supreme Court of Ireland's decision in *Murphy v Attorney-General* [1982] IR 241 where the Court held that the State could rely on the defence of change of position against those who had already begun proceedings to recover unconstitutionally exacted taxes. Query whether the defence fails if it can be shown that a public authority can make restitution by levying higher taxes in later years, even though its coffers are now empty. The sparse dicta and the advice of an Advocate-General of the European Court are conflicting: see Gareth Jones, *Restitution in Public and Private Law* (1991) 44–5.   [55] [1988] 1 All ER 961, 974.

[56] The authority had 'employed a substantial part of its rate income to meet precepts by other authorities . . . Generally speaking I [Lord Goff] would have thought this to have been an appropriate ground for declining to make a refund . . .': at 974.

[57] However, the House of Lords granted judicial review of the local authority's decision not to grant a refund of rates. Its discretion had not been exercised in accordance with the statutory intent.

(g) It is doubtful whether change of position is a defence if the recipient has received a payment made out of the Consolidated Fund without Parliamentary authority for it has been said that the payment 'is simply illegal and ultra vires and may be recovered'

This quotation from the judgment of Viscount Haldane in *Auckland Harbour Board v R*,[58] suggests that there is no defence to a claim by the Crown for the return of monies so paid. And in Australia it has been confirmed that the recipient cannot rely on estoppel: 'public moneys disbursed contrary to statute can be recovered, despite representations by those who disbursed them'.[59] However, no English decision has authoritatively ruled out change of position.[60] In *R v Secretary of State for the Environment, ex parte London Borough of Camden*[61] Schiemann J thought that the arguments both for and against allowing the defences of change of position and estoppel are finely balanced: the detriment to the public, including the possible loss of revenue, must be weighed against the hardship to the individual who, having changed his position to his detriment, may nevertheless be compelled to make restitution. If it were to be held that the Revenue, having made an unlawful demand, can nevertheless rely on change of position as a defence,[62] is it not also just to allow the individual who is required to make restitution of ultra vires payments the benefit of the defence? The claim of the Crown for restitution of ultra vires payments is admittedly stronger than, and different in character from, its claim to retain monies it was never entitled to receive. But the difference is not so compelling as to override the equities of the individual's defence of change of position.

3. The Role of Change of Position in Relation to a Claim for Rescission[63]

In *Standard Bank London Ltd v Canara Bank*[64] counsel tentatively suggested that the claimant's obligation to make restitution in a claim for rescission 'may be tempered by a change of position on the part of the party seeking to rescind'.[65]

---

[58] [1924] AC 318, 326–7. Lord Haldane was giving the advice of the Privy Council. He went on to say that the payment may be recovered if 'it can . . . be traced'. This caveat, if it is a caveat, has puzzled later judges. The better view is that Lord Haldane was referring to '*tracing*' 'the identity of the recipient of the money'. For a full discussion, see Alison Jones, *Restitution and European Community Law* (2000) 122–4.   [59] *Attorney-General v Gray* [1977] 1 NSWLR 406, 409–10, per Hutley J.
[60] Indeed the defence succeeded in *Eastbourne Borough Council v Foster*, 20 December 2000, unreported. The point did not arise in the Court of Appeal [2002] ICR 1149: cited in A Burrows, *The Law of Restitution* (2nd edn, 2002) 422 n 14.
[61] 17 February 1995, unreported, cited by Alison Jones, (n 58) at 126 n 34.
[62] Above, p 73.
[63] See D Friedmann, 'Reversible Transfers—The Two Categories' [2003] RLR 1, 5.
[64] [2002] EWHC 1574 at [86].
[65] If this submission were accepted then the other party's change of position should also be a relevant factor.

Moore-Bick J's terse comment was that this submission directly conflicted with the 'principle hitherto accepted[66], namely that the ability to make restitution is a precondition of the exercise of that right [of rescission]'. A party to the contract may have received services or consumed property transferred or the property transferred may have changed its character. Her claim to rescind will then fail for she cannot return the benefit received.[67] Conversely, if the claimant has received no benefit she need not make restitution. But the other party may resist her claim for rescission by pleading that he has changed his position by conferring at her request a benefit on a third party. That defence may well fail. In *Mackenzie v Royal Bank of Scotland*[68] Mrs Mackenzie sought rescission of her contract guaranteeing a loan made by the bank to her husband's company. It was found that she had been induced to enter into it in consequence of the bank's innocent misrepresentation. In granting rescission Lord Atkin, giving the Privy Council's advice, said:

There is no difficulty as to restitutio in integrum. The mere fact that the party making the representation has treated the contract as binding and has acted on it does not preclude relief. Nor can it be said that the plaintiff received anything under the contract which she is unable to restore.[69]

Commentators are agreed that English law is unduly rigid and that rescission should be granted if a claimant is prepared to pay the value of the benefit received even though the particular benefit itself cannot be restored.[70] Even if the courts were to accept this principle, and there are some indications that they may well do so,[71] the problem posed by *Mackenzie's* case will remain.[72] The solution is this: change of position should be a bar to a claim for rescission if one party to the contract anticipates that the other contracting party will change her position by conferring a benefit on a third party and not on the other contracting party. The particular facts of *Mackenzie* are, however, troublesome because it was the bank's innocent misrepresentation which induced the claimant to give the guarantee. We return to this question later in this essay.[73]

---

[66] See eg *Erlanger v New Sombrero Phosphate Co* (1878) 3 App Cas 1218, 1278, per Lord Blackburn.

[67] *Clarke v Dickson* (1858) EB & E 148, 154–5, per Crompton J. See J Poole and A Keyser, 'Justifying Partial Rescission in English Law' (2005) 121 LQR 273.

[68] [1934] AC 468.

[69] At 476 cf *TSB Bank plc v Camfield* [1995] 1 WLR 430, where the wife had received no benefit for which she had to give credit.   [70] See Goff and Jones, 9–025.

[71] See eg the dictum of Lord Browne-Wilkinson in *Smith New Court Securities Ltd v Scrimegeour Vickers (Asset Management) Ltd* [1997] AC 254, 262; and cf *O'Sullivan v Management Agency and Music Ltd* [1985] QB 428.

[72] Above, n 68. In Ms Chen-Wishart's view *Mackenzie* can be explained as another illustration of the court's concern to protect the vulnerable claimant at the expense of the innocent defendant: see above, n 36 at 179 and accompanying text.   [73] See further below, p 81.

4. Exceptionally Change of Position May Be a Defence Even if the Claim Is Based on the Claimant's Title and Not Upon Another's Unjust Enrichment

4.1. At Common Law

Title to chattels is generously protected.[74] A person who converts another's chattel is strictly liable in tort and it matters not whether he acted in a genuine and reasonable belief that the goods were his.[75] As a general rule the injured party is entitled to damages, namely, the market value of the goods at the date of conversion. But the defendant may have benefited from the conversion. The injured party has then an alternative remedy. He may seek to recover the convertor's unjust enrichment.[76] But the convertor may have changed his position. For example, he may have converted a chattel, sold it, and given the proceeds to charity.[77] He who consciously converts another's chattel does not act honestly; he cannot shelter behind the defence of change of position. But can the honest (innocent) convertor rely on the defence of change of position? Is he deemed to be a wrongdoer? Does the answer depend on whether the injured party sues for loss suffered or in unjust enrichment for benefit gained? In his *Unjust Enrichment* Professor Birks gave this answer: 'A wrongdoer sued as such has no defence to change of position, but a wrongdoer sued in unjust enrichment will have the defence, unless disqualified by bad faith'.[78]

There are persuasive dicta that, if the injured party seeks the benefits gained from another's innocent infringement of his proprietary interests in a claim for unjust enrichment, that claim is subject to the defence of change of position.[79] In principle this must be correct. In Professor Milsom's view, the innocent convertor is 'a victim of history'.[80]

However, the injured party can effectively nip the defence of change of position in the bud by suing for loss suffered and not for the benefits gained. Whether the defence is available to the honest wrongdoer may then depend on

---

[74] As is title to land.

[75] *Kuwait Airways Corporation v Iraqi Airways Company (Nos 4 and 5)* [2002] AC 883 at [77]–[78], per Lord Nicholls.   [76] ibid at [79].

[77] cf above n 37.   [78] (2nd edn, 2005) at 213.

[79] *Kuwait Airways Corporation v Iraqi Airways Company (Nos 4 and 5)* [2002] AC 883 at [79], per Lord Nicholls. It is debatable whether *all* tortfeasors should make restitution. The case law does not give a clear answer. This knotty question is beyond the scope of this essay: see Goff and Jones, 36–002 ff.

[80] *Historical Foundations of the Common Law* (2nd edn, 1981) 378. The old cases hold that an innocent convertor is not a wrongdoer, even though his act is tortious—a strange paradox for the modern lawyer. In *Hambly v Trott* (1776) 1 Cowp 371 Lord Mansfield said that 'trover is in form a tort, but is in substance an action to try property', being 'merely a substitute of the old action of detinue . . .'. So, if we say that 'it is not now an action *ex maleficio*, though it is so in form', then the innocent convertor's deference of change of position should not fail.

the election of the injured party. This is not a happy conclusion. But it would take a bold court to hold that change of position is a defence to a claim for compensation for loss suffered.

Indeed, even if it accepted that the defence can apply to claims for compensation and that the innocent convertor is not a 'wrongdoer', the defence may fail for a further reason: change of position has been said not to be a defence to a claim based on the claimant's title to property in the defendant's hands.[81] At common law the claim that you have *my* money will rarely succeed for money has no earmark and will have passed into currency.[82] More frequently the question arises if a chattel is sold. The claimant claims the proceeds of that sale and is met by the defence of change of position. He cannot rely on his title to proceeds of the conversion; at law that money was never his. He will say that the money has been 'had and received to his use', to use the language of the old pleaders.[83] In principle, change of position should be a defence to this claim brought against the innocent convertor.

The question whether change of position is a defence to a proprietary claim will normally arise if the claimant relies on his equitable title.

4.2. In Equity

It is long established that the bona fide purchaser of the legal estate for value without notice of prior equitable interests takes free from those interests. Bona fide purchase is a complete defence to an equitable proprietary claim. There is no suggestion in the case-law that the good faith purchaser of the legal estate, who has constructive notice of prior equitable interests, should none the less be able to rely on the defence of change of position.[84]

A good faith donee of an equitable interest (often called a volunteer) is neither a purchaser for value nor does he purchase the legal estate. What defence, if any, does he have against the holder of an earlier equitable interest if he has no 'notice' of that prior equitable interest? There are the traditional equitable defences, such as fraud, accident or mistake, and laches. More radically, the Court of Appeal held in the well-known case of *Re Diplock*[85] that the next of kin's equitable proprietary claim would fail if it would be *inequitable* to allow them to trace. The Court of Appeal did not describe this defence as change of position. It would

---

[81] Below, § 4.2.

[82] For the case law, see Goff and Jones, 2–025. Only if the facts are exceptional, as they were in *Lipkin Gorman*, will a claimant succeed in establishing a proprietary claim. The honest recipient may then have the defence of change of position.

[83] But, as *Lipkin Gorman* demonstrates, it was the form of action which common lawyers could invoke to make a proprietary claim.

[84] This situation is different from that discussed earlier where it was tentatively suggested that the honest defendant may successfully plead change of position as a response to the surety's claim that she had acted under another's undue influence and that the honest defendant had 'notice' that she had so acted: above, 68ff.　　　　　　　　　　　　　　　　　　[85] [1948] Ch 465.

have been surprising if it had done so; it was another forty years or more before change of position was recognized as a defence. But the examples which the Court of Appeal gave of when it would be inequitable to allow the next of kin to trace their money were situations where innocent volunteers had changed their position, even though they were singularly unconvincing examples.[86] What was inequitable was the hardship which arose from the imposition of the charge.[87]

However, in *Re Diplock* the next of kin's personal claim against the innocent volunteers succeeded; it was no defence that the charities had spent the money.[88] In *Lipkin Gorman* the House of Lords restrictively distinguished *Re Diplock*. *Lipkin Gorman* is, arguably, authority for the principle that change of position is a defence to a personal claim based upon the claimant's legal title as distinct from a claim in unjust enrichment.[89] This argument gains even greater force if it is boldly said, with Professor Birks, that the *Lipkin Gorman* claim was, as was the claim in *Foskett v McKeown*,[90] a restitutionary proprietary claim, namely, that a proprietary claim to traceable assets 'must always arise from unjust enrichment'.[91] The decision of the House of Lords in *Foskett v McKeown* is, however, a formidable obstacle to the acceptance of this view.[92] The House of Lords affirmed that the claimants were vindicating their proprietary claim. However, their lordships did not quite go so far as to say that innocent volunteers, such as beneficiaries under a trust (the rogue's children in *Foskett*), could not rely on change of position as a defence to a claim based on title.[93] It has been argued that it is 'alien to the security of property interests that the conduct of a person who receives the plaintiff's asset should affect the plaintiff's right to enforce his property in it'.[94] *Re Diplock* suggests otherwise. To protect the innocent honest volunteer by allowing him the possibility that he can demonstrate a change of position—no easy task—is not to endanger the security of property interests.

It is not normally inequitable to require an honest defendant to return an identifiable asset which has been acquired with the claimants' (say the beneficiaries of a trust's) money. But on occasions it may. Such would be the case if the defendant on the receipt of the money acquires an asset but also spends other funds,

---

[86] It was inequitable because it would be a hardship to subrogate the next of kin to the rights of a creditor paid with the Diplock money and to grant them a lien over property improved with money received from the Diplock estate. For critical comments, see Goff and Jones, 2–042–2–043; and cf *Boscawen v Bajwa* [1995] 4 All ER 769, 779 ff.

[87] cf *Campden Hill Ltd v Chakrani* [2005] EWHC 911 (Ch), where it was held, on the facts before Hart J, that it was not inequitable to impose a charge over land bought with the claimant's money.

[88] Above, n 12.   [89] See above 66, n 11.   [90] [2001] 1 AC 102.

[91] This is Professor Birks's long-held position: see (n 2) 32 ff.

[92] But, in the view of Professor Burrows, the House of Lords' proprietary reasoning is based on the unsure foundation that the claimant's title 'continues' to enable him to claim the substituted asset: see A Burrows, 'Proprietary Restitution: Unmasking Unjust Enrichment' (2001) 117 LQR 412.

[93] Lord Millett was careful not to do so. His lordship said, at 122: '...a claim in unjust enrichment is subject to a change of position defence, which usually operates by reducing or extinguishing the element of enrichment. An action like the present is subject to the bona fide purchaser for value defence, which operates to clear the defendant's title.'

[94] D Fox, 'Legal Title as Ground of Restitutionary Liability' [2000] RLR 465, 488.

for example, on a vacation which he would not otherwise have taken but for the receipt of that money. His whole portfolio of wealth has then been diminished.

5. A Critical Question: When Is It 'Inequitable' to Require the Recipient to Make Restitution?

Lipkin Gorman has gained iconic status. Some judges have warned that Lord Goff's broad description of the defence should 'set nothing in stone' but should point 'Courts in the right direction for the future'.[95] But despite that injunction they have tended to interpret it as if it were indeed set in stone.[96] Lord Goff was wise enough not to define the scope of the defence 'in abstract terms' and emphasized that he did not wish 'to state the principle any less broadly than this: that the defence is available to a person whose position has so changed that it would be inequitable in all the circumstances to require him to make restitution, or alternatively to make restitution in full'.[97]

It is most unfortunate that the Court of Appeal in *Niru Battery Manufacturing Co v Milestone Trading Co*[98] should have interpreted Lord Goff's speech in *Lipkin Gorman* and his judgment, with Lord Bingham, in *Dextra Bank and Trust Company Ltd v Bank of Jamaica*,[99] as authority for the principle that the courts should be guided by the widest of principles. '[T]hey are not tied to a single rigid standard in deciding whether a defence of change of position succeeds. They are to decide whether it is *equitable* to uphold the defence'.[100]

When is it inequitable to require the defendant to make restitution?[101] Earlier cases will give no guidance if everything is said to turn on the particular facts. Future judges will have little help from being told that 'they are not tied to a single rigid standard in deciding whether a defence of change of position succeeds. They are to decide whether it is equitable to uphold the defence.'[102] Lord Goff invited future courts to build on his speech and to create principles from facts which could not necessarily be foreseen. In an earlier passage in his speech in *Lipkin Gorman* his lordship had emphasized that a defendant must not have changed his position 'in bad faith'; he must not be a 'wrongdoer'. But in *Niru Battery* the Court of Appeal

---

[95] *Niru Buttery Mfg Co v Milestone Trading Ltd* [2004] 1 All ER (Comm) 193 at [183], per Sedley LJ.
[96] Including Sedley LJ.   [97] [1991] 2 AC at 579–80.
[98] [2004] 2 All ER (Comm) 193. This decision is hereinafter referred to as *Niru Battery*.
[99] [2002] 1 All ER (Comm) 193 at [38] (PC).
[100] *Niru Battery* at [192], per Sedley LJ. Emphasis added.
[101] cf Clarke LJ at [149] : 'In short, as I read Lord Goff's speech the essential question is whether it would be inequitable or unconscionable, and thus unjust, to allow the recipient of money paid under a mistake of fact to deny restitution to the payer': and further at [152]. An extreme example of this 'broad-brush' analysis, which aroused Professor Birks's ire, is to be found in Munby J's judgment in *Commerzbank AG v Jones* [2003] EWCA 1663, [2005] 1 Lloyd's Rep 298 at [48] ff: 'This is an area of the law, it seems to me, in which technicality and black-letter law are to be avoided'. See also A Burrows, 'Clouding the Issues on Change of Position' [2004] CLJ 276.
[102] *Niru Battery* at [192], per Sedley LJ.

concluded that Lord Goff's emphasis was not upon whether the defendant was dishonest. For that reason the Court of Appeal refused 'to set up a good faith/bad faith dichotomy for the change of position defence'.

This is a highly debatable conclusion. In my view a more desirable principle is to affirm that the *honest* recipient should have the defence. I know what honesty means. But I do not know what *equitable* means. Much of the litigation which has arisen, and will arise, concerns payments made under mistake. The mistaken payer recovers his payment no matter that he is grossly negligent in failing to enquire into the facts. The other side of that coin should be that the honest, if naïve, recipient should have the opportunity to demonstrate that he has changed his position to his detriment. The burden of proof will be on him to demonstrate his honesty. The more naïve he was, the more unlikely it is that the court will accept that he was honest. But a person who engaged in 'sharp practice' is not honest. Moore-Bick J said, in *Niru Battery*,[103] that he did not think that 'a person who has, or thinks he has, good reason to believe that the payment was made by mistake will often be found to have acted in good faith if he pays money without first making enquiries of the person from whom he received it'.

This appears to be 'sharp practice'. This recipient consciously turns a blind eye to the fact that a person is mistaken. As the judge said, he is not simply acting negligently. Admittedly, to accept honesty as the hallmark of good faith helps to solve the problems, although the facts of *Niru Battery* vividly show that the line between 'turning a blind eye' and 'negligence' can be very thin.

Again, a situation may arise when no reasonable enquiry will resolve the doubts of the recipient. The payer may deny that he was mistaken even though the honest recipient asserted that he was. On these most unusual facts the New Zealand Court of Appeal held that he could rely on the defence of change of position.[104] The mere possibility of a restitutionary claim did not preclude the defence.[105] A more likely situation will arise if the recipient, believing that in law he is not bound to make restitution, changes his position. What if the precedents are against him at that time, but, having been warned, he is determined to take his case to an appellate court? Or, on more likely facts: is it material that he changes his position before or after the other party takes proceedings, formal or otherwise, to assert his ultimately successful claim? No firm answers can be given. The courts should interpret the defence most generously so as to protect the honest recipient who has changed his position on the receipt of the benefits conferred.

[103] [2002] 2 All ER (Comm) 705 at [135], endorsed by Clarke LJ and Sedley LJ: [2004] 1 All ER (Comm) 193 at [164] and [190]: see above, 70 n 34.
[104] *National Bank of New Zealand Ltd v Waitaki International Processing (NI) Ltd* [1999] 2 NZLR 211.
[105] In German law the recipient has the defence even if she consciously doubts that the payer is entitled to restitution: cited in Birks, 'Change of Position: The Nature of the Defence and its Relationship to Other Restitutionary Defences' in (ed, M McInnes, 1996), *Restitution: Developments in Unjust Enrichment*, 49, 58–9.

Finally, there is the question posed in *McKenzie v Royal Bank of Scotland*:[106] is change of position a defence if the claimant's mistake has been induced by the recipient's innocent or negligent (but not reckless) misrepresentation? Lord Denning LJ was of the opinion that if 'the recipient was at fault and the paymaster was not—as, for instance, if the mistake was due to an innocent misrepresentation or a breach of duty by the recipient—he clearly cannot escape liability saying that he has spent the money'.[107]

But the recipient in *Larner's* case had not simply made an innocent misrepresentation; he was under a moral obligation to provide information about his changed financial circumstances and that moral obligation would have been binding in any jurisdiction unfettered by the doctrine of consideration.[108] More important is the decision of the Privy Council in *Dextra Bank and Trust Company*.[109] The Privy Council's advice, given by Lord Bingham and Lord Goff, was quite clear: 'Their Lordship are . . . most reluctant to recognise the propriety of introducing the concept of relative fault into this branch of the common law, and indeed decline to do so'.[110]

The Privy Council emphasized that in *Lipkin Gorman* Lord Goff had not mentioned 'fault' in his description of the defence of change of position. Furthermore, the experience of the New Zealand courts was not encouraging, for the Privy Council saw its judges, in interpreting the New Zealand legislation,[111] 'struggling manfully to control and contain an alien concept'.[112]

Dextra Bank and Trust Company is most persuasive authority although not strictly binding on English courts. If the dicta of the Privy Council are followed, the negligent as well as the innocent misrepresentor will be able to rely on change of position. This is not a startling conclusion. Subject to that defence, the mistaken payer who is induced to contract will obtain restitution of his payment and may even recover damages for loss suffered.[113] Furthermore, the mere fact that the recipient is honest does not absolve him from demonstrating that he has acted to his detriment.[114]

---

[106] Above, n 68.   [107] *Larner v London County Council* [1949] 2 KB 683, 688–9.
[108] Goff and Jones, 4–017–4–018.   [109] [2002] 1 All ER (Comm) 193.
[110] [2002] 1 All ER (Comm) 193 at [45]. Cf the puzzling dicta of Sedley LJ in *Niru Battery* at [190]. The parties had not challenged the reasoning in *Dextra Bank*. But the Lord Justice said: 'It may fall for consideration on another occasion whether the balance of fault is to be ignored even where the claimant is blameless and the defendant solely at fault'. If the defendant is 'solely at fault' it is unlikely that he will be able to rely on the defence of change of position.
[111] Judicature Act, s 94B.   [112] At [45].
[113] The misrepresentee may have an action for damages if the misrepresentation was negligent and induced him to contract: even if the representation was innocent a court may award damages in lieu of rescission. See Misrepresentation Act 1967, ss 1, 2(1)(2). The representor may also be liable in tort at common law.
[114] As *Commerzbank AG v Jones* [2003] EWCA 1663, [2005] 1 Lloyd's Rep 298 demonstrates.

5

The Role of Fault in the Law of Restitution

*Graham Virgo**

In 1997 Peter Birks delivered his famous paper entitled 'Misnomer' at a conference in Cambridge in honour of Gareth Jones.[1] That paper has had a profound influence on the law of restitution subsequently. My own paper delivered at the same conference sought also to realign the subject in a 'multi-causal' way, by separating restitution and unjust enrichment, but whereas my paper was tentative, Peter's was forceful and significant. Since that lecture we discussed at length our approaches to the subject, whether at Peter's annual visit to lecture in Cambridge, at meetings in his rooms in All Souls or by regular email exchanges. Our ideas about the nature of the subject were often on the same track, but whereas Peter was an express train reaching his destination quickly and directly, I was rather more like the local train, often diverted and taking a much longer route. Sometimes our tracks ran together, but not always. Peter remained convinced that my approach to the vindication of property rights was incorrect. We had lengthy discussions about this. Sometimes he nearly persuaded me that he was right, but I remain unconvinced.

One thing Peter and I did agree on was that the future development of the subject required much more attention to be given to the significance of fault. That is what I want to investigate in this tribute to him. In 1999 he wrote a paper entitled 'The Role of Fault in the Law of Unjust Enrichment'[2] in which he argued that the unjust enrichment principle was founded on strict liability, with fault being relevant to defences and, exceptionally, to establish particular grounds of restitution. It is timely to revisit this topic for a number of reasons. First, despite Birks's subsequent reconstruction of the law of unjust enrichment as being founded on the notion of absence of basis,[3] he continued to emphasize the significance of strict liability as being at the heart of unjust enrichment. But it is important to consider whether the reasons for this strict liability approach are

---

* Reader in English Law in the University of Cambridge; Fellow of Downing College, Cambridge.

[1] *Restitution: Past, Present and Future* (eds W Cornish, R Nolan, J O'Sullivan, and G Virgo, 1998) ch 1.

[2] In *The Search for Principle: Essays in Honour of Lord Goff of Chieveley* (eds G Jones and W Swadling, 1999) 235–75.   [3] See P Birks, *Unjust Enrichment* (2nd edn, 2005).

satisfactory and whether this approach is reflected in the recent cases, especially considering the rapid development of the subject since 1999. Secondly, Birks confined his analysis to unjust enrichment, but the role of fault is significant to the whole of the law of restitution. Indeed, the issues of fault which underpin restitutionary claims founded on unjust enrichment, the commission of wrongs, and the vindication of property rights, are similar in terms of definition and ambit, so that the role of fault can be used to support the recognition of a unified law of restitution. Thirdly, and most importantly, the role of fault will undoubtedly be the key issue in the development of the law of restitution over the next decade. It is the role of fault which increasingly underpins the debate about the relationship between law and equity generally and the function of unconscionability specifically. It will be vital in the future to have a much clearer terminology relating to fault and to be aware that fault is actually endemic within the law of restitution.

1. Terminology

Despite Birks's consistent concern about precision of thought and language, the definition of fault was not examined in any detail in his 1999 paper. But subsequent events show that precision of language is required as regards the meaning of both strict liability and fault.

1.1. The Meaning of Strict Liability

It is generally recognized that claims in unjust enrichment are claims of strict liability. What this means is that the claimant is not required to show that the defendant was at fault in any way in order to establish his or her claim. For Birks the core case of unjust enrichment concerned a mistaken payment of a non-existent debt.[4] To establish such a claim it is sufficient for the claimant to show that the defendant was enriched at the claimant's expense and that the mistake satisfies the test of being a but for cause of the payment being made.[5] The defendant's conduct and thought process concerning the receipt of the payment are irrelevant as far as establishing the claim is concerned. It does not follow, however, that the defendant's conduct and thought process are of no significance at all, since the defendant has the opportunity to show that he changed his position following the receipt of the payment, but only if he had acted in good faith.[6]

---

[4] ibid 16.
[5] *Barclays Bank Ltd. v WJ Simms, Son and Cooke (Southern) Ltd* [1980] 1 QB 677. In *Unjust Enrichment* (2nd edn, 2005) Birks rejected the need to identify a causative mistake and preferred to emphasize the absence of basis for the payment, arising from the fact that there was no debt. This difference of approach has no effect on the analysis of the claim as being one of strict liability.
[6] *Lipkin Gorman (a firm) v Karpnale Ltd* [1991] 2 AC 548, 580 (Lord Goff).

Consequently, the burden is on the defendant to establish that he was not at fault in the sense of having acted in bad faith. This does not undermine the strict liability nature of the unjust enrichment claim, since the burden relating to fault is placed on the defendant and is not the concern of the claimant. It follows that the recognition of liability as strict means that the claimant's task in establishing unjust enrichment is much easier than it would be if the claimant had to establish fault. This is justified because the rationale of the unjust enrichment principle is not to make the defendant worse off, but to relocate an extant gain.[7]

1.2. The Range of Fault

Fault is properly defined as being concerned with the defendant's state of mind. This can be analysed at its most basic as involving either a subjective or an objective test. A subjective test involves assessing fault with reference to the defendant's own thought processes, whereas objective fault has regard to an external standard, namely the reasonable person's thought processes. This can still be described as relating to the defendant's state of mind in the sense that objective fault is concerned with what the defendant should have thought or known because the reasonable person would have thought or known it. Clearly an objective test is easier to prove since it is not concerned with determining what the defendant was thinking, although often it is necessary to consider the defendant's knowledge and then ask what the reasonable person would have concluded had he or she known the same as the defendant.

A more sophisticated analysis of fault involves the identification of a range of mental states, from the most subjective to the most objective. Where a particular type of fault is placed on this line depends on the precise definition of the fault element and such definitions are often lacking in the civil law, as compared with the criminal law.[8] But six key types of fault can be identified. These have proved to be especially important as regards accessorial liability in equity and also the meaning of bad faith for the defence of change of position. The language of good and bad faith is particularly uncertain and should be avoided, for, at its most basic, it is unclear whether bad faith should be determined with reference to a subjective or an objective test. It should also be emphasized that the language of fault does not necessarily connote blame or culpability.

Intention

Intention can only ever be analysed as a subjective state of mind. Its usual meaning is that of a desired consequence, but it can also be defined obliquely where the defendant desires one consequence but foresees another as a very high

---

[7] Birks, (n 3) 7.
[8] See Smith and Hogan, *Criminal Law* (ed Ormerod) (11th edn, 2005) chs 5 and 6.

possibility.[9] The function of both types of intention within the law of restitution is unclear, although intention certainly has a role even if it is primarily a negative one. So, for example, if the claimant intends to transfer an enrichment to the defendant this will constitute a voluntary transfer for which restitution is not available.

Knowledge

Whereas intention relates to consequences, knowledge relates to the existence of provable circumstances.[10] Knowledge has proved to be important in establishing accessorial liability for breach of trust, since a defendant who receives property knowing that it has been transferred in breach of trust will clearly be liable to make restitution.[11] Similarly, a defendant will not be able to rely on the defence of change of position if he or she consciously changed his or her position knowing of the facts which entitle the claimant to restitution.[12]

Dishonesty

In *Royal Brunei Airlines Sdn Bhd v Tan*[13] dishonesty was distinguished from knowledge and was equated with want of probity. In *Twinsectra v Yardley*[14] Lord Hutton appeared to have recognized a hybrid test of dishonesty, as adopted by the criminal law,[15] to determine liability for assisting a breach of trust or fiduciary duty. According to this test a defendant will be dishonest if his or her conduct is considered to be dishonest by the standards of reasonable people and the defendant realized that the conduct was dishonest by those standards. Lord Hutton concluded that this test had been recognized by Lord Nicholls in *Royal Brunei v Tan*, although Lord Nicholls actually adopted an objective test of dishonesty, albeit one which first requires the court to consider what the defendant knew or suspected and then to consider how the reasonable person would have characterized the defendant's conduct in the light of that knowledge.[16] This test of dishonesty has now been reasserted by the Privy Council in *Barlow Clowes International Ltd v Eurotrust International Ltd*,[17] another case involving dishonest assistance, where Lord Hoffmann, delivering the judgment of the Privy Council, interpreted Lord Hutton's judgment in *Twinsectra*, as well as his own, as being consistent with the objective test of dishonesty as recognized in *Tan*. Although not binding on the English courts, this is clearly a highly persuasive decision, albeit one which takes the notion of judicial re-interpretation to new heights. Lord Hutton's judgment was described as ambiguous, but it could

[9] Birks, (n 3) 158. In the criminal law oblique intent will exist where the defendant foresees a consequence as virtually certain: *R v Woollin* [1999] AC 82.
[10] cf belief which is more speculative.
[11] See eg *Carl-Zeiss Stiftung v Herbert Smith and Co (a firm) (No 2)* [1969] 2 Ch 276.
[12] See *McDonald v Coys of Kensington* [2004] EWCA Civ 47, [2004] 1 WLR 2775. See 99, below.   [13] [1995] 2 AC 378.
[14] [2002] UKHL 12, [2002] 2 AC 164.   [15] *R v Ghosh* [1982] QB 1053.
[16] See *Twinsectra Ltd v Yardley* [2002] 2 AC 164, 198 (Lord Millett).   [17] [2005] UKPC 37.

not have been clearer in its acceptance that the defendant had to be aware that his conduct could be characterized as dishonest.

Despite the best efforts of Lord Hoffmann in *Barlow Clowes* it appears that two distinct interpretations of dishonesty have emerged. The first, which was probably adopted in *Twinsectra*, is a hybrid test which is essentially subjective since, although it has regard to the standards of the reasonable person, this is filtered through the perception of the defendant as to what those standards are. Alternatively, the interpretation recognized in *Tan* and *Barlow Clowes* is an objective test which has regard to how the reasonable person would have characterized the standard of the defendant's conduct in the light of the defendant's knowledge of or suspicions about the facts; crucially it is irrelevant that the defendant would have judged his conduct by reference to different standards.

Even though there is clear disagreement as to how dishonesty should be interpreted, there is an additional issue which is even more important, namely why we need a test of dishonesty at all to establish civil liability. Indeed, as Lord Millett recognized in *Twinsectra v Yardley*,[18] it is not generally an appropriate condition of civil liability because such liability does not ordinarily require proof of a guilty mind. A guilty mind is significant for the criminal law, where culpability needs to be established to justify punishment, but it is unclear why it is felt necessary to incorporate this fault element in the civil law.

Unconscionability

Unconscionability was recognized by the Court of Appeal in *Bank of Credit and Commerce International (Overseas) Ltd v Akindele*[19] for the purposes of determining liability in equity for receiving property in breach of trust or fiduciary duty. Dishonesty was specifically rejected as the relevant fault element. It is not clear, however, how unconscionability is established, although the defendant's knowledge of the circumstances of the breach will clearly be a significant factor. Unconscionability as a test of fault was also recognized by the Court of Appeal in *Criterion Properties plc v Stratford UK Properties LLC*,[20] when determining whether the defendant could hold the claimant to an agreement which was unauthorized.[21] Whether enforcement of the agreement was unconscionable depended on a variety of factors, including:

(i) the fault of both parties to the agreement;[22]
(ii) the defendant's knowledge of the circumstances constituting the breach of duty in entering into the agreement in the first place;

[18] (n 16) 197.   [19] [2001] Ch 437.
[20] [2002] EWCA Civ 1783, [2003] 1 WLR 2108.
[21] The House of Lords decided the appeal on the basis of there being a prior question concerning whether the agreement was unauthorized, but their Lordships said nothing to undermine the Court of Appeal's interpretation of unconscionability. See 95, below.
[22] Compare the defence of change of position for which relative fault is not relevant. See 102, below.

(iii) whether the parties had obtained legal advice; and
(iv) the actions and knowledge of the defendant in the context of the commercial relationship as a whole.

This reference to knowledge suggests that 'unconscionable' is given a subjective interpretation, which would be consistent with a test which is concerned with the state of a party's conscience.

The significance of unconscionability has also been recognized in the context of the defence of change of position to determine whether the defendant had acted in bad faith. The proper interpretation of bad faith for these purposes was considered by Moore-Bick J in *Niru Battery Manufacturing Co v Milestone Trading Ltd*,[23] who held that it includes 'a failure to act in a commercially acceptable way and sharp practice that falls short of outright dishonesty'.[24] This suggests an objective standard of commercial acceptability which does not have regard to the defendant's perceptions of what that standard is. This approach was endorsed by the Court of Appeal,[25] yet, confusingly, that court went on to refer specifically to the unconscionability test as well.[26] This suggests that bad faith is to be interpreted subjectively, with regard to the defendant's own conscience.[27]

It remains unclear to what extent dishonesty and unconscionability differ. Indeed, Lord Millett equated the two types of fault in *Dubai Aluminium Co Ltd v Salaam*.[28] Technically they are distinct, since unconscionability does not seem to depend at all on the assessment of the reasonable person, but is only concerned with whether the defendant's conscience is affected. In *Criterion Properties* Carnwath LJ emphasized that the usefulness of the unconscionability test as a test of fault was that it would produce greater flexibility for the application of common sense in commercial situations.[29]

Risk-taking

Fault arising from the taking of risks is often described as recklessness, but risk-taking can also encompass other states of mind, notably suspicion. Risk-taking can be analysed either subjectively, with regard to the defendant's own perception of risk, or objectively, with regard to whether the defendant should have foreseen the risk because the reasonable person would have done so. It is the

[23] [2002] EWHC 1425 (Comm), [2002] 2 All ER (Comm) 705.   [24] ibid 741.
[25] [2003] EWCA 1446 (Civ).
[26] See also *Crown Dilmun, Dilmun Investments Ltd v Nicholas Sutton, Fulham River* [2004] EWHC 52, para [200] where Peter Smith J would have preferred to apply a test of knowledge rather than unconscionability, but he was bound by previous authority to apply the latter test. In *Lea v Roberts* (2005) 4 July, Deputy Judge Hazel Williams QC emphasized the significance of unconscionability to the defence.
[27] See also *Papamichael v National Westminster Bank plc* [2003] 1 Lloyd's Rep 341, 368 (Judge Chambers QC).   [28] [2002] UKHL 48, [2003] 2 AC 366, 391.
[29] [2003] 1 WLR 2108, 2119. Unconscionability was specifically rejected as a relevant test of fault in *Royal Brunei Airlines Sdn Bhd v Tan* [1995] 2 AC 378, 392 because it was not an expression used by non-lawyers.

subjective test of risk-taking which is adopted in the law of restitution. So, for example, the defence of change of position will be unavailable if the defendant was wilfully blind, by consciously failing to consider the implications of certain known facts,[30] or where he had grounds for suspecting that he was liable to make restitution to the claimant.[31]

Negligence

A defendant will be considered to have acted negligently where he failed to act as a reasonable person would have done. Such fault has sometimes been used to establish liability for receiving property in breach of trust or fiduciary duty,[32] but no longer.[33] Negligence has also sometimes been used to establish that the defendant was acting in bad faith for purposes of the defence of change of position,[34] but most cases recognize that a negligent defendant is not acting in bad faith.[35]

Conclusions

The recent cases concerning the interpretation of fault suggest, for the most part, that we are moving away from objective tests to notions of fault which are determined by reference to the defendant's own perceptions of the facts and of his or her own conduct. But with the growing emphasis on unconscionability the distinct categories of fault start to collapse, since all subjective tests can be described as involving unconscionability in some form. Consequently, it is increasingly difficult to define when the defendant can be considered to have been at fault. As Birks said, the word unconscionability 'covers all possibilities'.[36] The language of unconscionability, and dishonesty also, is peculiar since it relates to the evaluation of the nature of the defendant's conduct. Such tests are appropriate in the criminal context, where liability is often dependent, at least for serious crimes, on the defendant's guilty mind or culpability, but civil liability is not generally concerned with culpability or a guilty mind as such.[37] Instead, the language of intention, knowledge, belief, recklessness, and suspicion should be sufficient to determine whether or not a party was at fault for the purposes of

[30] *Lea v Roberts* (2005) 4 July, Deputy Judge Hazel Williams QC, para 80. See also *Manifest Shipping Co Ltd v Uni-Polaris Insurance Co Ltd* [2003] 1 AC 469. In *Barlow Clowes International Ltd v Eurotrust International Ltd* [2005] UKPC 37, para 12, this was considered to be a dishonest state of mind.
[31] *Niru Battery Manufacturing Co v Milestone Trading Ltd* [2002] 2 All ER (Comm) 705, 741 (Moore-Bick J).
[32] See eg *Belmont Finance Corp Ltd v Williams Furniture Ltd (No 2)* [1980] 1 All ER 393; *International Sales and Agencies Ltd v Marcus* [1982] 3 All ER 551.
[33] *BCCI v Akindele* [2001] Ch 437.
[34] *Papamichael v National Westminster Bank* [2003] Lloyd's Rep 341, 369 (Judge Chambers QC).
[35] *Dextra Bank & Trust Company Ltd v Bank of Jamaica* [2002] 1 All ER (Comm) 193; *Niru Battery Manufacturing Co v Milestone Trading Ltd* [2002] 2 All ER (Comm) 705, 738 (Moore-Bick J); *Maersk Air Ltd v Expeditors International (UK) Ltd* [2003] 1 Lloyd's Rep 491, 499.
[36] (n 3) 156.   [37] See *Twinsectra Ltd v Yardley* [2002] 2 AC 164, 197 (Lord Millett).

the law of restitution, for two reasons. First, because the meaning of these terms is much clearer and, secondly, because there should be no need to have regard to the defendant's evaluation of his conduct for the purposes of establishing restitutionary liability. Exceptionally tests of guilty mind may be relevant, but only where it is appropriate to impose liability specifically because of the defendant's culpability.

2. The Function of Fault in the Law of Restitution

Birks's 1999 paper focused specifically on the law of unjust enrichment rather than the law of restitution, but, in the light of subsequent events, it is today more useful to focus on the umbrella of the law of restitution, namely that body of law which is concerned with the award of gain-based remedies which arise by operation of law. On the view of the law of restitution which I have advocated[38] such restitutionary remedies will be awarded by reference to three distinct principles, namely the commission of wrongs, the vindication of property rights,[39] and the defendant's unjust enrichment. The role of fault differs depending on which particular principle is being considered. This is not just a matter of academic interest, involving taxonomy and policy; the function of fault is of vital practical importance too, because it affects what must be proved, by whom, and what the appropriate remedy should be.

Each of these three principles which underpin the law of restitution will be examined. It will be seen that fault has a variable role in establishing the claim, affecting the operation of defences and determining the type and extent of the appropriate remedy.

2.1. Wrongs

Establishing the Cause of Action

For restitutionary claims involving wrongdoing, the wrong constitutes the cause of action. All wrongs involve a breach of duty, whether the wrong be tort, breach of contract, or existing in equity. Fault is often required to establish the wrong, but it is certainly not essential. So, for example, certain torts involve strict liability, including the tort of conversion; a fiduciary will be liable in equity for breach of duty without proof of any fault;[40] and a defendant will be liable for an innocent breach of contract.

[38] *The Principles of the Law of Restitution* (2nd edn, 2006), 7. Birks did not object to the recognition of a law of restitution, as long as it was 'internally compartmentalised to distinguish between different causative events': (n 3) p x.
[39] As recognized in *Foskett v McKeown* [2001] 1 AC 102. For criticism of this approach see Andrew Burrows, *The Law of Restitution* (2nd edn, 2002); Birks, *Unjust Enrichment* (n 3).
[40] See eg *Boardman v Phipps* [1967] 2 AC 46.

Determining the Appropriate Remedy

A division is emerging between two key types of restitutionary remedy, as recognized by Edelman in his book *Gain-Based Damages*,[41] namely disgorgement remedies, which deprive the defendant of any gain made as a result of the commission of a wrong, and restitutionary remedies, which restore what the defendant has gained from the claimant as a result of the commission of a wrong. This distinction is particularly well illustrated by cases which have recognized gain-based remedies for breach of contract. These remedies may involve either disgorgement, as awarded in *Attorney-General v Blake*[42] where the defendant was required to give up all profits arising from the breach of contract, or restitution, as in *Experience Hendrix LLC v PPX Enterprises Inc*,[43] where the defendant was required to pay to the claimant an amount representing the sum saved by failing to pay the claimant a licence fee to use intellectual property rights. Once this differentiation between gain-based remedies is made, it is necessary to identify a rationale for making the distinction. For Edelman it usually turns on whether the defendant's breach of duty can be characterized as cynical.[44] If it is, disgorgement is appropriate; if it is not, the only appropriate gain-based remedy is restitutionary. But Edelman fails to define adequately what he means by a 'cynical' breach of duty and it is unhelpful to talk about such a breach without a clearer identification of what degree of fault it encompasses. It must require more than a deliberate breach of duty, because many breaches of duty are deliberate, especially in the context of breach of contract, and do not result in restitutionary relief. Perhaps cynical conduct should equate with bad faith, as defined for the purposes of the defence of change of position, which would incorporate dishonesty and unconscionability but not negligence. This might be justified on the basis that a disgorgement remedy should only be available where the defendant can be considered to be culpable in some way. That would certainly be consistent with the approach adopted by the House of Lords in *Blake* where the defendant was certainly culpable and so could be said to have acted unconscionably, however that test is defined.

Defences

Fault may also be relevant to restitutionary claims involving wrongdoing as regards the operation of the defence of change of position.[45] In *Lipkin Gorman v Karpnale*[46] Lord Goff stated that 'it is commonly accepted that the defence

---

[41] J Edelman, *Gain-Based Damages* (2002).   [42] [2001] 1 AC 268.

[43] [2003] EWCA Civ 323, [2003] 1 All ER (Comm) 830.

[44] (n 41) 111. Edelman also recognizes that disgorgement damages are available where the defendant breaches a fiduciary duty 'where the institution of trust and confidence requires additional protection by stripping even innocent wrongdoers of profits made'.

[45] Assuming that the defence is not confined in its operation to restitutionary claims founded on unjust enrichment.   [46] [1991] 2 AC 548, 580.

should not be available to a wrongdoer'.[47] It is not clear whether Lord Goff accepted this 'common' view. So, should the defence be available in respect of restitutionary claims founded on wrongdoing? Perhaps we should distinguish between degrees of wrongdoing, so that the defence should be available for an innocent wrongdoer but not a wrongdoer who committed the wrong with subjective fault. Indeed, there are *obiter dicta* which indicate that the defence might be available in a claim grounded on the tort of conversion, which does not require proof of fault.[48] But what about a fiduciary who has profited from his or her breach of duty? The denial of the defence in such a case could be justified by the strict approach which is adopted when imposing liability for breach of fiduciary duty and, especially, breach of trust.[49] There are, however, signs of a sea-change as regards this strict attitude, at least where the fiduciary acted in good faith.[50] If adopted more generally, this would indicate that change of position should be available in all cases where the wrongdoer has acted in good faith, in the sense of being without subjective fault.

2.2. Proprietary Restitutionary Claims

Where a restitutionary claim is founded on the vindication of proprietary rights, fault might be considered to be irrelevant since such claims are concerned with hard-nosed property rights[51] and, if the defendant has received the claimant's property or its traceable substitute, the strength of those property rights should justify restitutionary relief regardless of the defendant's fault. In fact, fault on the part of the defendant can be relevant in a number of different ways and the significance of fault has proved to be one of the most controversial matters concerning the development of the law relating to proprietary restitutionary claims in two contexts in particular.

Creation of the Proprietary Base

Proprietary interests can be created in a variety of ways, usually by agreement, but it has been recognized that they can be created in equity by virtue of the defendant's unconscionable conduct through the mechanism of the constructive trust. This results from the application of a very significant dictum of Lord Browne-Wilkinson in *Westdeutsche Landesbank Girozentrale v Islington LBC*[52] concerning the proper interpretation of *Chase Manhattan Bank NA v Israel-British Bank (London) Ltd*.[53] In *Chase Manhattan Bank* the claimant had

---

[47] In *Barros Mattos Junior v MacDaniels* [2004] EWHC 1188 (Ch), [2005] 1 WLR 247 this was interpreted as barring the defence where the very act of changing position was itself illegal.
[48] *Kuwait Airways Corpn v Iraqi Airways Co (Nos 4 and 5)* [2002] 2 AC 883, 1093 (Lord Nicholls).   [49] Edelman, (n 41) 111.
[50] See *Murad v Al-Saraj* [2005] EWCA Civ 959.
[51] *Foskett v McKeown* [2001] 1 AC 102, 109 (Lord Browne-Wilkinson).
[52] [1996] AC 669, 714–15.   [53] [1981] Ch 105.

mistakenly paid the defendant the same amount of money twice. Goulding J held that it was possible for the court to recognize that the claimant had an equitable proprietary interest in the money. Lord Browne-Wilkinson in *Westdeutsche Landesbank Girozentrale*[54] stated that, although Goulding J was wrong to conclude that the claimant had an equitable proprietary interest in the money from the moment that it had been received by the defendant, this equitable interest could have been created through the mechanism of a constructive trust which was triggered when the defendant knew, within two days of receiving the money, that the claimant had paid it by mistake. As Lord Browne-Wilkinson said: 'Although the mere receipt of the moneys, in ignorance of the mistake, gives rise to no trust, the retention of the moneys after the recipient bank learned of the mistake may well have given rise to a constructive trust . . . '.[55] In other words, the defendant's conscience had been affected by its knowledge of the mistake whilst it was in possession of the money which had been paid by the claimant. The defendant's subsequent failure to return the money once it was aware of the mistake constituted unconscionable conduct and it was this conduct which should be considered to have triggered the constructive trust.[56] This notion of the constructive trust being founded on the defendant's unconscionable conduct will arise in a variety of circumstances, but only where legal title has passed.[57] So, for example, a constructive trust will be recognized where the defendant has obtained property by fraud.[58] Similarly, if the defendant steals the claimant's money, the claimant will have an equitable proprietary interest in it because the defendant's conscience will have been affected at the time of receipt.[59]

This idea that the constructive trust can be triggered by the defendant's unconscionable conduct raises a number of difficult questions, particularly relating to how unconscionability should be defined for these purposes. If the claimant paid money by mistake or because the transaction was invalid, it is clear that the defendant's knowledge of the mistake or the invalidity of the transaction will be sufficient to characterize him or her as acting unconscionably. Presumably, it will also be sufficient that the defendant believes or suspects that the claimant was mistaken or that the transaction was invalid.[60] But what if the

---

[54] [1996] AC 669, 715.

[55] ibid. See also *Commerzbank AG v IMB Morgan plc* [2004] EWHC 2771 (Ch), [2004] All ER (D) 450 (Nov) at [36] (Lawrence Collins J).

[56] Followed in *Papamichael v National Westminster Bank plc* [2003] 1 Lloyd's Rep 341, 372 (Judge Chambers QC).   [57] *Shalson v Russo* [2003] EWHC 1637 (Ch), [2005] Ch 281.

[58] *Halley v The Law Society* [2003] EWCA Civ 97, para [48] Carnwath LJ; *Papamichael v National Westminster Bank plc* [2003] 1 Lloyd's Rep 341, 374 (Judge Chambers QC); *Commerzbank AG v IMB Morgan plc* [2004] EWHC 2771 (Ch), [2004] All ER (D) 450 (Nov) at [36] (Lawrence Collins J); *Sinclair Investment Holdings SA v Versailles Trade Finance Ltd* [2005] EWCA Civ 722.

[59] *Westdeutsche Landesbank Girozentrale v Islington LBC* [1996] AC 669, 716 (Lord Browne-Wilkinson).

[60] Although in *Papamichael v National Westminster Bank plc* [2003] 1 Lloyd's Rep 341, 373 Judge Chambers QC said that actual knowledge is required.

defendant ought to have known of the mistake or the invalidity? If this constitutes unconscionability it would dramatically widen the ambit of proprietary
restitutionary claims. But due to the policy of the law to restrict such claims, the
better view is that the rules for the imposition of constructive trusts should be
interpreted restrictively. Consequently, the defendant's conscience should only
be affected where he or she knew or suspected that the claimant had made a
mistake or that the transaction was invalid.[61] This is consistent with the subjective approach to fault which is generally recognized within the whole of the
law of restitution.[62]

Restitutionary Remedies to Vindicate Property Rights

Where the claimant has established that the defendant received property in
which the claimant has a proprietary interest, the claimant may claim a restitutionary remedy to vindicate this property right. Two types of restitutionary
claim are recognized. Where the defendant has retained property in which the
claimant has a proprietary interest the claimant may seek a proprietary restitutionary remedy to recover that property. Fault is irrelevant to both the claim and
the remedy. Questions of fault are also, largely, irrelevant to the defences to such
claims, primarily because the defence of change of position is not available where
a claimant seeks a proprietary restitutionary remedy.[63] This is because, where the
defendant has received and retained the claimant's property but, in reliance on
that receipt, the defendant changes his or her position by dissipating other
property, the defendant still retains the claimant's property and ought to make
restitution of it. However, there is another defence to such proprietary claims,
namely the defence of bona fide purchase of value. Clearly this defence is fault-
based in that it will only apply where the defendant acted in good faith.
However, good faith is interpreted differently for this defence than for change of
position. For the defence to operate at law good faith is equated with honesty.[64]
It is unclear how this test of culpability should be defined, especially as to
whether an objective or subjective assessment of the appropriate standard of
honesty should be adopted,[65] although it is clear that the defendant's knowledge
or suspicion that the transferor had defective title to the property which was
transferred is a significant consideration. In equity, however, an objective test of
negligence is adopted so that the defendant will not have acted in good faith if he
or she failed to make enquiries which would have been made by a reasonable
person in the defendant's position.[66] This inconsistency in the interpretation of

---

[61] In *Westdeutsche Landesbank Girozentrale v Islington LBC* [1996] AC 669, 705 Lord Browne-
Wilkinson appeared to accept that the defendant's conscience will only be affected where he or she
knew 'of the factors which are alleged to affect' his or her conscience.　　　　[62] See 89, above.
　[63] *Foskett v McKeown* [2001] 1 AC 102, 129 (Lord Millett).
　[64] *Nelson v Larholt* [1948] 1 KB 339.　　　[65] See 87, above.
　[66] *Nelson v Larholt* [1948] 1 KB 339. See also *Macmillan Inc v Bishopsgate Investment Trust plc*
[1995] 1 WLR 978, 1000 (Millett J).

fault, between common law and equity and change of position and bona fide purchase for value, is unacceptable. A test focusing on knowledge, belief, and suspicion, without regard to misleading expressions such as honesty, should be adopted for both defences in all contexts.

Where the defendant received the claimant's property but no longer retains it, the claimant will seek a personal restitutionary remedy to recover the value of the property received. Where the claim is founded on the vindication of a property right recognized at common law the liability of the defendant is strict.[67] This is illustrated by *Lipkin Gorman (a firm) v Karpnale Ltd*[68] where the defendant casino was liable to pay the value of money received from the dishonest partner of the claimant firm of solicitors, even though the defendant was unaware that the money had been stolen from the claimant. Where the claim is founded on the vindication of an equitable proprietary right, however, the liability of the defendant will depend on proof of fault to establish a claim in what is now called unconscionable receipt.[69] The fault requirement for the claim in unconscionable receipt has been criticized, most notably by Lord Nicholls of Birkenhead, writing extra-judicially.[70] If a strict liability claim is recognized at common law, why should such a claim not be recognized in equity as well? In fact, this type of strict liability restitutionary claim is already recognized in equity, in the particular context of the recovery of money by next-of-kin where that money had mistakenly been paid to charities by the personal representatives of the deceased's estate.[71] This should be developed to create a new strict liability action in equity, where the defendant has received but not retained property in which the claimant had a beneficial interest, which would be the mirror-image of the common law claim. The imposition of strict liability is justified both at law and in equity because, where a defendant received property in which the claimant has a proprietary interest, the strength of that proprietary interest requires the defendant to make restitution of its value.

Although it is still not possible to say that this represents the state of English law, in a very important dictum in *Criterion Properties plc v Stratford UK Properties LLC*[72] Lord Nicholls continued to point the law in the direction of recognizing a general receipt-based strict liability claim in equity. In *Criterion* Lord Nicholls considered the nature of the liability which would arise if an agreement, under which party B acquired benefits from party A, was set aside on

---

[67] See *Barros Mattos Jnr v MacDaniels Ltd* [2004] EWHC 1188 (Ch), [2005] 1 WLR 247, para 16 (Laddie J). [68] [1991] 2 AC 548.
[69] *BCCI v Akindele* [2001] Ch 437. See 87, above.
[70] 'Knowing Receipt: The Need for a New Landmark' in *Restitution: Past, Present and Future* (eds Cornish *et al*, 1998) 231–45. See also Birks (2000) King's College LJ 1, 10; *Twinsectra v Yardley* [2002] 2 AC 164, 194 (Lord Millett) and *Dubai Aluminium Co Ltd v Salaam* [2003] 2 AC 366, 391 (Lord Millett).
[71] *Ministry of Health v Simpson* [1951] AC 251. See also *GL Baker v Medway Building and Supplies Ltd* [1958] 2 All ER 532 where this strict liability personal claim was extended to *inter vivos* trusts. [72] [2004] 1 WLR 1846.

the ground that it had not been authorized. He said:[73]

> If, however, the agreement *is* set aside, B will be accountable for any benefits he may have received from A under the agreement. A will have a proprietary claim, if B still has the assets. Additionally, and irrespective of whether B still has the assets in question, A will have a personal claim against B for unjust enrichment, subject always to a defence of change of position. B's personal accountability will not be dependent upon proof of fault or 'unconscionable' conduct on his part. B's accountability, in this regard, will be strict.

This dictum raises a number of significant points. First, it is clearly *obiter*. It follows that the fault-based cause of action of unconscionable receipt continues to exist.[74] Secondly, the recognition of unjust enrichment as the principle which underpins the personal claim is significant but unfortunate. It is significant because it follows that Lord Nicholls expressly recognized a strict liability claim. But reliance on the unjust enrichment principle is surely irrelevant in this context. Where the defendant has received, but not retained, property in which the claimant has a proprietary interest, it should be sufficient to found the claim on the vindication of the claimant's property rights, in the same way as the common law claim in *Lipkin Gorman* is actually properly analysed as a proprietary claim for which personal remedies are available. But, despite this, the real significance of Lord Nicholls's approach is that, as he explicitly states, liability is strict. Finally, if this strict liability receipt-based claim in equity is recognized, does it follow that there is no longer any need to recognize the fault-based claim? Certainly there would be much less need to rely on the fault-based claim, because of the difficulties of establishing fault. But that claim would remain significant because the defence of change of position would not be available to it, whereas it would be available to the receipt-based claim. But this is significant to the analysis of the role of fault within the law of restitution. If a claimant relies on the receipt-based claim there is no need to prove fault, but the defendant can defeat that claim by relying on the defence of change of position. That defence is itself defeated if the defendant had acted in bad faith and, as has been seen, recent cases on the defence of change of position have relied on the notion of unconscionability to determine whether the defendant acted in bad faith. It follows that, even though Lord Nicholls recognized a strict liability claim, the same issue of fault is inevitably introduced through the back-door when considering whether or not the defence of change of position might be available to the defendant.

2.3. Unjust Enrichment

Defending Strict Liability

Many of the cases which have recognized the unjust enrichment principle implicitly assume that the cause of action is one of strict liability, and this has sometimes been recognized explicitly.[75] For Birks the strict liability nature of the

---

[73] ibid 1848.   [74] See 95, above.
[75] *OEM plc v Schneider* [2005] EWHC 1072 (Ch), para [33] (Peter Smith J).

unjust enrichment claim meant that it should be distinguished from a wrong. Indeed, he described it as a 'not-wrong'.[76] He emphasized that fault characterizes a wrong[77] which has a 'whiff of blameworthiness',[78] but crucially the essence of a wrong is that the defendant has breached a duty owed to the claimant.[79] Of course, it would be possible to convert liability for unjust enrichment into a wrong by identifying a breach of duty, but such a breach would only arise where the defendant was under an obligation to make restitution and, as Edelman has recognized,[80] this would be an extraordinary breach of duty since it would typically be passive. So, for example, if the claimant's money was mistakenly credited to the defendant's bank account without the defendant's knowledge, a breach of duty would be created from the failure of the defendant to make restitution. Even if it was accepted that such a breach could not arise until the defendant knew or suspected that the money should be repaid, the defendant would still be held liable without having done anything actively to constitute a breach of duty. Even the strict liability tort of conversion requires some positive act of interference by the defendant with the claimant's property. It follows that the unjust enrichment claim is properly characterized as not being founded on the commission of a wrong since it does not have the traits of wrongdoing. It does not depend on establishing a breach of duty by the defendant. Neither does it necessarily depend on the defendant being blameworthy in any way. Where the defendant has received an enrichment at the expense of the claimant within one of the recognized grounds of restitution, an obligation arises to correct the injustice by requiring the defendant to give up what should not have been received in the first place and that liability to make restitution is properly analysed as being strict.

Fault on the Part of the Defendant

Despite Birks's emphasis on the unjust enrichment claim being one of strict liability, he did recognize that there were certain exceptional situations where the defendant's fault was an essential part of the claim, because of a need to defer to some interest which competes with the interest in getting restitution.[81] In fact, fault is relevant in many different areas of the law of unjust enrichment. This is obvious as regards the interpretation of the change of position defence, which is not available where the defendant has acted in bad faith, the burden of proving lack of fault being placed on the defendant. Fault can also be relevant when identifying an enrichment. So, where the defendant has freely accepted a benefit he will not be able to establish that he did not value it. This principle of

---

[76] 'Rights, Wrongs and Remedies' (2000) OJLS 1, 25.

[77] ibid 27. Although, of course, he was well aware that there are a number of wrongs where liability is imposed regardless of fault eg liability for breach of fiduciary duty.   [78] ibid 31.

[79] See Edelman (n 41).

[80] ibid 34. See also Birks, 'The Role of Fault in the Law of Unjust Enrichment' in *The Search for Principle: Essays in Honour of Lord Goff of Chieveley* (ed Jones and Swadling, 1999) 238.

[81] Birks, (n 80) 258.

free acceptance applies where the defendant has consciously accepted an enrichment where he had an opportunity to reject it, knowing that the benefit was not provided gratuitously.[82] It appears that the rationale of the principle is that the defendant is prevented from subjectively devaluing a benefit by virtue of his or her unconscionable conduct. Here unconscionability must refer to the defendant knowing or, presumably, suspecting that the benefit had not been provided gratuitously.

The most controversial issue concerning the role of fault within unjust enrichment relates to its relevance to the grounds of restitution. It appears that the defendant's fault is relevant to grounds of restitution which arise in equity which are considered to be grounded on the defendant's unconscionable conduct. Probably the most significant ground is that of undue influence. In *National Commercial Bank (Jamaica) Ltd v Hew*[83] Lord Millett, delivering the opinion of the Privy Council, said that undue influence 'arises whenever one party has acted unconscionably by exploiting the influence to direct the conduct of another which he has obtained from the relationship between them'.

But what does unconscionability mean for these purposes? Surely it does not require proof that the defendant intended to influence the claimant unduly or considered the possibility of undue influence and continued regardless? This is inconsistent with the essential rationale of undue influence which affects the voluntariness of the claimant's actions.[84] The real danger of using the language of unconscionability in this context is that it may suggest that undue influence is a form of wrongdoing. Indeed, it is sometimes described as an equitable wrong.[85] Such a characterization is unfortunate and misleading, because it does not follow that a claimant, who has been unduly influenced by the defendant to transfer a benefit, can bring a restitutionary claim founded on wrongdoing; the claimant is confined to a restitutionary claim founded on unjust enrichment. But, even if undue influence is eventually treated as a form of wrongdoing for which compensatory remedies are awarded, there should continue to be a strict liability form of undue influence which triggers a restitutionary claim in unjust enrichment.[86] This could prove to be significant for, if two forms of undue influence are recognized, one fault-based and one involving strict liability, the success of the claim could depend on which form is used. Clearly the strict liability claim will be easier for the claimant to establish because no fault is involved, but it would be defeated by the defendant's innocent change of position. On the other

---

[82] *Rowe v Vale of White Horse DC* [2003] EWHC 388 (Admin), [2003] 1 Lloyd's Rep 418; *McDonald v Coys of Kensington* [2004] EWCA Civ 47, [2004] 1 WLR 2775. See below, 100, for discussion of free acceptance as ground of restitution.   [83] [2002] UKPC 51.

[84] *Royal Bank of Scotland plc v Etridge (No 2)* [2001] UKHL 44, [2002] 2 AC 773, 795 (Lord Nicholls of Birkenhead); *Daniels v Drew* [2005] EWCA Civ 507, para 36.

[85] *Yorkshire Bank plc v Tinsley* [2004] EWCA Civ 816, [2004] 1 WLR 2380, 2389 (Peter Gibson LJ). See Birks, 'Undue Influence as Wrongful Exploitation' (2004) 120 LQR 34.

[86] A useful analogy can be made with misrepresentation, which operates differently depending on whether it is the innocent version or the negligent or fraudulent version.

hand, the fault-based claim will be more difficult to establish but could not be defeated by the defendant's change of position because the proof of the defendant's unconscionable conduct will prevent reliance on the defence, assuming that the unconscionability to establish undue influence will equate with bad faith for change of position. Further, it might be thought unnecessary to differentiate between the strict liability and wrong-based versions of undue influence. But a similar differentiation was advocated for the receipt-based proprietary claim in equity.[87] It was seen in that context that the different types of receipt-based claim could be explained by reference to allocations of the different burden of proof depending on which type of claim is pursued. Precisely the same argument can be adopted as regards undue influence as well.

Another equitable ground of restitution which appears to involve fault arises from the general power of equity to relieve against transactions induced by unconscionable conduct where 'an unfair advantage has been gained by an unconscientious use of power by a stronger party against a weaker'.[88] This will operate where there is a degree of inequality between the parties, arising, for example, from the claimant's special disability, and the defendant's conduct is unconscionable.[89] In *Yorkshire Bank plc v Tinsley*[90] unconscionability was described as involving 'exploitation in a morally culpable manner'. If this ground of restitution is founded on unconscionability this should be interpreted subjectively so that the defendant will have acted unconscionably if he or she knew of the claimant's disability or disadvantage or, at the very least, was aware of the possibility of such characteristics.[91] This equitable ground of 'unconscionable conduct' may be an exceptional situation where fault is appropriate because of the need, as Birks recognized, to identify an additional reason to justify the intervention of equity,[92] namely the defendant's conduct in consciously exploiting the claimant justifies setting the transaction aside and restoring benefits which had been transferred to the claimant. This is consistent with the approach adopted in *Yorkshire Bank v Tinsley* where the court explicitly recognized that culpability must be established before the defendant is liable. But requiring a guilty mind goes too far. The focus on unconscionability is unnecessary; knowledge and suspicion are adequate fault elements to justify the intervention of equity.

Even in Birks's core case of restitution of mistaken payments, the liability to make restitution might not be as strict as is commonly thought. This is illustrated by the decision of the Court of Appeal in *McDonald v Coys of Kensington*.[93] Coys, a firm of auctioneers, sold a car to McDonald. It was an express

---

[87] See 96, above.   [88] *Lloyds Bank Ltd v Bundy* [1975] QB 326, 337 (Lord Denning MR).
[89] *Alec Lobb (Garages) Ltd v Total Oil Great Britain Ltd* [1985] 1 WLR 173, 182 (Dillon LJ).
[90] [2004] EWCA Civ 816, [2004] 1 WLR 2380. See also *Hart v O'Connor* [1985] AC 1000.
[91] See *Louth v Diprose* (1992) 175 CLR 621 where the High Court of Australia adopted a subjective test of fault; Bamforth, 'Unconscionability as a Vitiating Factor' [1995] LMCLQ 538, 550.
[92] Birks, (n 80) 266.   [93] [2004] EWCA Civ 47, [2004] 1 WLR 2775.

term of the contract of sale that the purchaser would not obtain the right to the personalized registration number, known as a mark, but the auctioneers failed to retain the right to the mark. Consequently, when the car was delivered to McDonald, he registered the mark in his name. The auctioneers sought restitution either of the right to the mark or its value. The key issue for the Court of Appeal was whether McDonald had been enriched. But the relevance of the case for present purposes is that, although the matter was not fully examined by the court, the fault of the defendant appears to have been a relevant consideration for the court in concluding that he had been unjustly enriched. The defendant's knowledge that the claimant wanted the mark to be returned was considered to be significant to the conclusion that the claimant's mistake was sufficient to ground a restitutionary claim.[94] This is a novel approach which appears to arise from a need to find an additional justification to explain why a claimant should obtain restitution on the ground of his or her own spontaneous mistake, which was not shared by the defendant at the time of receipt. The obligation to make restitution is easier to justify if the defendant was at fault in some way, albeit that this fault, in the sense of knowledge of the circumstances on which the claimant's restitutionary claim is founded, only arose subsequent to the receipt of the enrichment. Further, there is some evidence that the free acceptance principle, grounded on the defendant's unconscionable conduct, might operate as a ground of restitution in its own right, as recognized by Lightman J in *Rowe v Vale of White Horse DC*,[95] although it did not succeed on the facts.

This introduction of fault into the grounds of restitution has dangerous consequences, because it undermines the strict nature of liability for unjust enrichment and takes us perilously close to incorporating notions of unconscionability into the law of unjust enrichment.[96] Exceptionally this can be justified, but otherwise this trend must be resisted. Fault can be relevant to the defences, and exceptionally to the enrichment, but should generally be ignored when considering the ground of restitution. One particular dangerous consequence of incorporating unconscionability is that it confuses claims for unjust enrichment, for which personal restitutionary remedies only are available, with proprietary restitutionary claims where proprietary rights are created in equity by virtue of the defendant's unconscionable conduct,[97] with the consequence that it becomes ever more difficult to distinguish between the two types of claim. Where, however, fault is considered to be relevant to establish the ground of restitution, it should be interpreted subjectively, with regard to the defendant's knowledge or suspicion of relevant circumstances and without reference to unconscionability.

---

[94] [2004] 1 WLR 2775, paras 25 and 37 (Mance LJ).
[95] [2003] 1 Lloyd's Rep 418.
[96] See *Vedatech v Crystal Decisions (UK) Ltd* [2002] EWHC 818 where Jacobs J treated the action for money had and received as turning on the unconscionability of the defendant's conduct, with reference to justice and the equity of the case.   [97] See 92, above.

Fault on the Part of the Claimant

It is a generally recognized principle of the law of unjust enrichment that the fault of the claimant is not significant. This has been primarily recognized as regards claims to recover mistaken payments. The fact that the claimant may have been negligent in making the payment does not prevent restitution from being awarded. [98] Similarly, fault on the part of the claimant is not relevant to other significant grounds of restitution. So, for example, to establish total failure of consideration following a breach of contract, the fact that the claimant intentionally breached the contract does not defeat the restitutionary claim.[99]

But, despite this, the fault of the claimant may actually be significant to the restitutionary claim in a variety of ways. For example, the claimant's fault will be of direct relevance to determine whether he or she made a mistake. Knowledge of the true facts will certainly prevent the claimant from establishing a causative mistake, since knowledge is inconsistent with mistake.[100] Where the claimant transfers a benefit to the defendant being suspicious of the circumstances but prepared to take the risk that he or she is mistaken, he or she will have acted voluntarily and so will not be mistaken.[101] This is illustrated by *Rowe v Vale of White Horse DC*[102] where a council provided sewerage services deliberately without charge, because it was unclear whether it was able to demand payment for the provision of such services. It was held that the council could not bring a restitutionary claim founded on mistake, presumably because it had consciously taken the risk to continue to provide the service without charge until the legal position had been clarified. Where the claimant has made a mistake which would not have been made by a reasonable person, such negligence will not prevent the claimant from arguing that the mistake has caused him or her to transfer the benefit to the defendant.[103] However, in *Brennan v Bolt Burdon*[104] it was held that if a party ought to have known that a particular issue was about to be reconsidered on appeal then this would not constitute a mistake of law. This comes very close to saying that negligence on the part of the claimant will prevent reliance on the mistake. This is inconsistent with the interpretation of fault generally within the law of restitution, where the focus is on subjective notions of fault. Consequently, the traditional rule that the claimant's negligence

---

[98] *Kelly v Solari* (1841) 9 M and W 54, 59 (Parke B); *Scottish Equitable plc v Derby* [2001] 3 All ER 181.

[99] See especially *Dies v British and International Mining and Finance Co Ltd* [1939] 1 KB 724; *Rover International Ltd v Cannon Film Sales (No 3)* [1989] 1 WLR 912; *Item Software (UK) Ltd v Fassihi* [2004] EWCA Civ 1244, [2005] ICR 450.

[100] *Brisbane v Dacres* (1813) 5 Taunt 143, 159–60; 128 ER 641, 647–8 (Gibbs J); *Brennan v Bolt Burdon* [2004] EWCA Civ 1017, [2005] QB 303.   [101] See Birks, (n 3) 132.

[102] [2003] EWHC 388 (Admin), [2003] 1 Lloyd's Rep 418. See also *Brennan v Bolt Burdon* [2004] EWCA Civ 1017, [2005] QB 303 where it was held that a state of doubt concerning the interpretation of the law would not constitute a mistake of law.

[103] *Banque Financière de la Cité v Parc (Battersea) Ltd* [1999] 1 AC 221, 235 (Lord Hoffmann).

[104] [2004] EWCA Civ 1017, [2005] QB 303.

does not defeat a claim in unjust enrichment is justifiable since it is consistent with the general principles relating to fault within the law of restitution.

As regards the operation of the defence of change of position it has been clearly recognized that the fault of the claimant should not be taken into account when considering whether it is equitable for the defendant to rely on the defence.[105] But there is in fact some evidence that the fault of the claimant is being considered. In *Commerzbank AG v Gareth Price-Jones*[106] Munby J, whilst acknowledging that relative fault was irrelevant, was clearly influenced by the fact that the defendant changed his position as a result of his own negligent mistake, which was not shared or induced by the claimant, in reaching his conclusion that it was not equitable to allow the defendant to rely on the defence.[107] This is consistent with the interpretation of unconscionability by the Court of Appeal in *Criterion Properties*.[108] Indeed, in *Dextra Bank & Trust Co v Bank of Jamaica*,[109] although the Privy Council rejected the relevance of relative fault, it acknowledged that, if fault was to be taken into account at all, then it would be unjust to take into account the fault of the defendant and ignore the fault of the claimant. This is a perfectly logical conclusion. However, again, the reference to negligence is misplaced. Fault of the claimant is relevant, but only in a subjective sense. Negligence of the claimant in making a mistake should not be significant, precisely because it is not significant for the defendant either. Subjective fault of the claimant will be relevant but, where the claimant is seeking to establish a mistake, this subjective fault will negate the mistake and prevent the claimant from establishing unjust enrichment in the first place.

3. Conclusions

Much of Peter Birks's work involving the law of restitution and unjust enrichment was to identify principles and structure and, where necessary, impose order out of chaos. The question of fault within the law of restitution remains chaotic, but some order is gradually emerging. Analysis of the subject today reveals that fault does have a very important role, although that role is often hidden away. Within the law of unjust enrichment specifically, although it remains legitimate to describe the action as being usually one of strict liability, it is vital to be aware that this is not always the case. There are certainly situations where the defendant's fault is relevant for defences, to establish an enrichment, and, very exceptionally, even to establish a ground of restitution. Further, there is a growing tendency to identify fault as an additional justification for the award of

---

[105] *Dextra Bank & Trust Co v Bank of Jamaica* [2002] 1 All ER (Comm) 193; *Commerzbank AG v Gareth Price-Jones* [2003] EWCA Civ 1663, [2004] 1 P & CR D 15.   [106] ibid.
[107] See also *Niru Battery Manufacturing Co v Milestone Trading Ltd* (*No 2*) [2004] EWCA Civ 487, [2004] 2 Lloyd's Rep 319, para [33] (Clarke LJ).   [108] See 87, above.
[109] [2002] 1 All ER (Comm) 193.

restitutionary relief, where a finding of fault appears to provide a reassurance of liability. In the context of recovery of mistaken payments, for example, although the theoretical model might treat this as being an exemplar of strict liability, the reality is that fault has a function, either explicitly through the defences or implicitly to justify restitutionary relief. Establishing the defendant's fault in particular can get the law of restitution into those parts which it could not otherwise reach. Subjective fault on the part of the claimant is vital to claims for mistaken payments since it is inherent within the notion of mistake. Similarly, fault is relevant within the law of restitution to claims based on wrongs, both as regards defences and the nature of the remedy awarded, and also as regards claims to vindicate property rights, both to identify a proprietary right and to personal claims to vindicate such rights.

This is not an elegant picture. Fault has different roles in different parts of the law of restitution. Also, the very notion of fault is unclear. The language of unconscionability and dishonesty in particular are insecure and their relevance to restitutionary claims remains unproven, save perhaps to elucidate the notion of 'cynical' breach of duty for claims involving wrongs. The preferable language is that of intention, knowledge, belief, recklessness, and suspicion. But this survey of the law does reveal, at the very least, that objective notions of fault are, for the most part, consistently irrelevant to all restitutionary claims and so should be expunged.

Where do we go from here? We are at a crossroads. The direction we take will determine the future of the law of restitution generally and unjust enrichment specifically. But we can be guided by Birks's published works and, just as importantly, by his example in searching always for the right answer.

6

Subrogation: Persistent Misunderstandings

Charles Mitchell[*]

1. Introduction

In the autumn of 1988 I enrolled on the LLM degree course at University College London. The incoming students were addressed by Professor William Twining, who took a high line: 'Never again will you have this chance to stretch yourselves. Choose courses that you will find really challenging—like Peter Birks' Restitution course!' This sounded hard, but still with a few bold spirits I made my way to the class, and of course we found that he was right. Peter was a wonderfully stimulating teacher who fired us with enthusiasm. He gave us long, long reading lists and stunned us with tough questions each week, but his classes were indisputably the high point of the year. He taught without notes, off the top of his head, but his seminars were tightly structured and he had a formidable grasp of the case-law minutiae. 'How can he remember all this stuff?' we wondered. 'He must think about it all the time!' This later turned out to be close to the mark.

Afterwards, Peter supervised my doctoral thesis. He was brilliant, incisive, and demanding. He was also encouraging and supportive, and—as I can now perceive, ten years into my own teaching career—extraordinarily conscientious and generous with his time. Drafts of my work were covered with queries, objections, suggestions for better phrasing or stronger lines of argument. Postcards arrived from the other side of the world with the name of a just-remembered case which bore on the argument. Tutorials stretched from two hours to three, as we progressed from discussion of the questions in hand to range further afield. Often, Peter would think his way through a problem out loud, turning it this way and that, pulling back to recast it in some other form, sometimes taking a position *pro tem*, sometimes taking a firmer stand. This was the most valuable lesson which he taught me then: how to think. When my ideas finally came together, Peter was

[*] Professor of Law, King's College, London. I am grateful to Andrew Burrows and Stephen Watterson for their helpful comments on drafts of this essay.

quick to grasp them, and quick to see where they might lead. Conversations with Peter often felt like games with a chess grand master who was many moves ahead.

My thesis concerned the law of subrogation, and so I have taken this as the subject of my essay. Subrogation rights can be acquired by contract. Subrogation can also be awarded to claimants as a remedy to prevent or reverse unjust enrichment. Focussing on subrogation as a remedy, the central argument of my thesis was that there are two types of subrogation.[1] Both are awarded to claimants whose money has been paid to a creditor in respect of an obligation for which the defendant is liable. Both have traditionally been conceptualized as entailing a transfer of rights from the creditor to the claimant. But the means by which this transfer is accomplished, and the reasons why it may be appropriate, vary according to whether the creditor's rights have been extinguished by the claimant's payment. If so, then the purpose of the remedy is to reverse the benefit received by the defendant when his corresponding obligation to the creditor is discharged. If not, then the remedy has a dual prophylactic purpose: either to prevent the creditor from recovering twice over by enforcing his rights once he has been paid by the claimant, or to prevent the defendant from escaping his liability in the event that the creditor does not sue him. These differences are partly reflected in the pleading rules which govern subrogated claims, making it important for claimants to know whether the rights which they seek to acquire via subrogation have been extinguished by payment—something which can sometimes be hard to determine.[2]

In my thesis, I used the term 'simple subrogation' to describe the remedy awarded where the creditor's rights subsist notwithstanding the claimant's payment, and the term 'reviving subrogation' to describe the remedy awarded where the creditor's rights have been extinguished. The point of this terminology was to capture the idea running through the cases that where the creditor's rights have been extinguished, the courts must first 'revive' them, or 'keep them alive', before transferring them to the claimant; in contrast, where the creditor's rights subsist, this is unnecessary and they can simply be transferred. Developments over the past ten years have made the term 'reviving subrogation' seem rather less apt, but it remains useful provided that one stays alert to the fictional nature of the process of 'revival' and 'transfer' that the remedy entails. This is discussed further in Section 2 where it is explained that the courts have not always found this process easy to understand, essentially because they have taken too literally the metaphorical language which has often been used to describe a subrogated claimant's entitlement.

---

[1] C Mitchell, *The Law of Subrogation* (1994) 4–7, 8–12.

[2] As was spectacularly demonstrated by *Caledonia North Sea Ltd v London Bridge Engineering Ltd* 2000 SLT 1123 (Court of Session (Inner House)), affirmed sub nom *Caledonia North Sea Ltd v British Telecommunications plc* [2002] UKHL 4, [2002] 1 Lloyd's Rep 553, discussed in C Mitchell, *The Law of Contribution and Reimbursement* (2003) 179–82 and 280–2. This was a Scottish case but English law can present claimants with identical difficulties.

In subsequent sections, the discussion will turn to other misconceptions which have made it difficult to see clearly how reviving subrogation works and why it is awarded. In Section 3 it will be explained that in many cases where a creditor's extinguished personal rights have been 'transferred' via subrogation the courts could have produced the same outcome more rationally and more simply by allowing the claimant his own direct right of action in unjust enrichment. Section 4 will then consider the 'transfer' of extinguished proprietary rights via subrogation, and the argument will be made that the underlying basis for this remedy is unjust enrichment rather than a fictional presumption that the parties intended the 'transfer' to take place.

The discussion as a whole will demonstrate that although these various problems have persisted over the years, some important cases over the last decade have made it much easier for us to understand and avoid them. As we shall finally see in Section 5, however, these cases have raised some difficult questions in their turn.

2. 'Revival' and 'Transfer' of Extinguished Rights

A recurring worry for the English courts has been the thought that a right of action which has been extinguished by payment cannot be transferred to a claimant via subrogation, because it must have ceased to exist. For this reason subrogation was denied to sureties who had paid off secured debts, in a series of cases running from the 1750s to the 1850s.[3] Legislation was eventually thought necessary to overcome the difficulty: the Mercantile Law Amendment Act 1856, s 5, which remains in force, and which gives sureties and others who pay off a common liability the right to acquire the creditor's securities 'whether these shall or shall not be deemed at law to have been satisfied by the payment of the debt'. The inspiration for this section was the rule of Scots law, that a cautioner who pays a debt secured on the principal debtor's property can demand an assignation of the creditor's rights against the principal debtor, as his payment is deemed not to extinguish these rights, but to constitute the price of their sale to the cautioner.[4] This explains why the section states that a claimant 'shall be entitled to have [the creditor's securities] assigned to him', but in English law at least, it is clear that the claimant need not demand an express assignment from the creditor.[5]

---

[3] eg *Gammon v Stone* (1749) 1 Ves Sen 339, 27 ER 1068; *Woffington v Sparks* (1754) 2 Ves Sen 569, 28 ER 363; *Hodgson v Shaw* (1834) 3 My & K 183, 40 ER 70. Legal mortgages were not extinguished by the surety's payment 'as the mortgagor [could not] get back his estate again without a reconveyance'; *Copis v Middleton* (1823) T & R 224, 229; 37 ER 1083, 1085 (Lord Eldon LC).

[4] C Mitchell, 'Claims in Unjustified Enrichment to Recover Money Paid Pursuant to a Common Liability' (2001) 5 Edin LR 186, 214 n 130 and text.

[5] *Re M'Myn* (1886) 33 Ch D 575; *Re Lord Churchill* (1888) 39 Ch D 175; *Re Lamplugh Iron Ore Co* [1927] 1 Ch 308. This is consistent with the view expressed by Lord Hoffmann in *Banque*

In an independent development during the nineteenth century, the Chancery courts began to allow claimants with a limited interest in land who paid off a prior charge on the land to take the charge for themselves—and this right was subsequently extended to claimants with no interest in the land.⁶ It was said in these cases that the charge was 'kept alive' for the claimants' benefit. However, the extinction problem then resurfaced in *Re Diplock*.⁷ The executors of a will paid money out of the estate to various charities in the mistaken belief that the payments were authorized under the terms of the will. The money should have been paid to the testator's next-of-kin. Some of the charities used the money to pay off debts secured by mortgages on their property and so the next-of-kin sought to acquire the mortgages via subrogation to secure their claims for repayment. The Court of Appeal denied the claim, reasoning that once the securities had been extinguished there was nothing left to which the next-of-kin could be subrogated.⁸ However, this was to overlook the earlier Chancery cases which demonstrated that the extinction of secured rights is no bar to their transfer to a claimant in equity via subrogation. For this reason the Court of Appeal's analysis in *Re Diplock* was subsequently rejected by the Court of Appeal in *Boscawen v Bajwa*,⁹ Millett LJ stating that 'the discharge of a right is certainly not a bar to subrogation in equity, but is rather a pre-condition'.¹⁰ By this he meant that reviving subrogation, which he took to be a remedy for unjust enrichment, can be awarded only where the defendant's obligation to the creditor has been discharged, with the result that he has been enriched.

Further clarification followed in *Banque Financière de la Cité SA v Parc (Battersea) Ltd*.¹¹ In his leading speech Lord Hoffmann gave a rich and subtle account of the method by which subrogated claimants are deemed to have acquired extinguished rights under English law. He explained that the language of

---

Financière de la Cité SA v Parc (Battersea) Ltd [1999] 1 AC 221, 236 (quoted in the text to n 13), that reviving subrogation is a legal fiction which works by way of 'metaphor or analogy', and which entails no actual transfer of rights. Section 5 of the 1856 Act does not apply in Scotland, and the most recent Scottish authority to consider the point indicates that a deed of assignation is required to transfer the creditor's rights to a cautioner: *Villaswan Ltd (in rec) v Sheraton Caltrust (Blythswood) Ltd (in liq)* 1999 SCLR 199. However, this needs to be reappraised in the light of Lord Hoffmann's comments.

⁶ The origins and development of this line of authority are discussed in Section 4 below. Cases include: *Earl of Buckinghamshire v Hobart* (1818) 3 Swans 186, 202; 36 ER 824, 830; *Burrell v Earl of Egremont* (1844) 7 Beav 205, 232–3; 49 ER 1043, 1054; *Marson v Cox* (1879) 14 Ch D 140, 150; *Carlisle Banking Co v Thompson* (1884) 28 Ch D 398; *Patten v Bond* (1889) 60 LT 583; *Chetwynd v Allen* [1899] 1 Ch 353; *Crosbie-Hill v Sayer* [1908] 1 Ch 866; *Butler v Rice* [1910] 2 Ch 277; *Whiteley v Delaney* [1914] AC 132.   ⁷ [1948] Ch 465.
⁸ ibid 549: 'the effect of the payment to the bank was to extinguish the debt and the charge held by the bank ceased to exist. The case cannot . . . be regarded as one of subrogation.' These findings were followed in *Euroactividade AG v Mason Investments Ltd* unreported QBD 18 April 1994.
⁹ [1996] 1 WLR 328.
¹⁰ ibid 340, adding that the court in *Re Diplock* 'was probably doing no more than equate the remedy to the creation of a new charge for the purpose of considering whether this was justified'. Cf *Re Byfield* [1982] 1 Ch 267, 272; *Niru Battery Manufacturing Co v Milestone Trading Ltd (No 2)* [2004] EWCA Civ 487, [2004] 2 All ER (Comm) 289 [63].
¹¹ [1999] 1 AC 221 (hereafter '*BFC*').

'keeping rights alive' for the benefit of a subrogated claimant is wholly metaphorical, and that reviving subrogation entails no actual transfer of rights at all. In so holding, he drew on the insight in *An Introduction to the Law of Restitution* that 'the language and image of substitution' used in subrogation cases can obscure the fact that the courts need not give the claimant every advantage that was formerly enjoyed by the creditor: they can decide whether the claimant's position should be 'selectively or exactly' like the creditor's.[12] Lord Hoffmann said this:[13]

In my view, the phrase 'keeping the charge alive' needs to be handled with some care. It is not a literal truth but rather a metaphor or analogy.[14] In a case in which the whole of the secure debt is repaid, the charge is not kept alive at all. It is discharged and ceases to exist. In a case like the present, in which part of the secured debt is repaid, the charge remains alive only to secure the remainder of the debt for the benefit of the original chargee. Nothing can affect his rights and there is no question of competition between him and the party claiming subrogation. It is important to remember that, as Millett LJ pointed out in *Boscawen v Bajwa*,[15] subrogation is not a right or a cause of action but an equitable remedy against a party who would otherwise be unjustly enriched. It is a means by which the court regulates the legal relationships between a plaintiff and a defendant or defendants in order to prevent unjust enrichment. When judges say that the charge is 'kept alive' for the benefit of the plaintiff, what they mean is that his legal relations with a defendant who would otherwise be unjustly enriched are regulated as if the benefit of the charge had been assigned to him. It does not by any means follow that the plaintiff must for all purposes be treated as an actual assignee of the benefit of the charge and, in particular, that he would be so treated in relation to someone who would not [otherwise] be unjustly enriched.

Lord Hoffmann's analysis provides a satisfying answer to the extinction problem, while simultaneously recognizing that the courts have a far more sensitive discretion to adjust a subrogated claimant's relations with other parties than was previously realized. Following the *BFC* case we can now see that claimants can acquire extinguished rights via subrogation, not because the courts are able to 'revive' these and order the creditor to transfer them to the claimant, but because they can treat the claimant, by a legal fiction, *as though* he has acquired them, when making orders in the claimant's favour that bind the defendant and other parties. Moreover, when the courts exercise this power they can be selective in deciding which of the creditor's advantages should be deemed to have accrued to the claimant, and which other parties besides the defendant should be affected by the claimant's deemed enjoyment of these advantages. As Neuberger LJ stated in *Cheltenham & Gloucester plc v Appleyard*:[16]

the flexibility of the remedy is such that the court does not have to decide whether or not a [claimant] is generally subrogated to a particular security as against the world: it can, for instance, decide that a [claimant] is subrogated to a particular security as against some third parties, but not as against others.

---

[12] P Birks, *An Introduction to the Law of Restitution* (rev edn, 1989) 95.
[13] *BFC* (n 11) 236.   [14] Citing Birks, (n 12) 93–7.   [15] *Boscawen* (n 9) 335.
[16] [2004] EWCA Civ 291 [49].

The same point was also made by May LJ in *Filby v Mortgage Express (No 2) Ltd*:[17]

> The essence of the remedy is that the court declares the claimant to have a right having characteristics and content identical to that enjoyed [by the creditor] ... subject to any modification (for example as to rates of interest) necessary to ensure that the claimant does not get more than he bargained for.

In line with this analysis, we can now see clearly why a claimant who pays part of a defendant's secured debt cannot immediately acquire a proportionate share of the creditor's secured rights via subrogation and enforce these in competition with the creditor.[18] The reason is not that it is impossible for 'exactly the same right [to be] vested simultaneously in both creditor and in the person claiming subrogation', as was previously suggested in *Re T H Knitwear Ltd*.[19] It is, rather, that the court can decline to treat the claimant as though he has acquired any rights until it is satisfied that the creditor has been repaid in full. Again, we can now also understand why a claimant who acquires a mortgage via subrogation might be unable to enforce the foreclosure provisions in the mortgage deed, where he has been repaid more than the amount of the debt which was originally secured by the mortgage by the time of the claim.

These were the facts of *Halifax Mortgage Services Ltd v Muirhead*.[20] The defendant's husband borrowed £130,000 from the claimant, and used part of this sum to repay a £30,000 debt which was secured by a mortgage on the family home. He executed a new mortgage in the claimant's favour, but by an oversight no reference was made in the charging document to the defendant's beneficial interest in the property. Her husband defaulted on the loan, and the question arose whether the claimant could obtain an order for possession and sale against her, on the basis that it should be treated as though it had acquired the original mortgage, by which she had been bound, and under the terms of which her husband's default would have entitled the original mortgagee to such an order. At first instance the judge found in the claimant's favour on this issue. On appeal the defendant argued that the claimant should not be entitled to such treatment because by the time that her husband had defaulted on the loan he had already repaid the claimant more than would have been needed to extinguish the original mortgage. It followed that the claimant could not obtain an order against her for a default which took place after that date, if it were to be treated as though it stood in the shoes of the original mortgagee.

Evans LJ anticipated Lord Hoffmann's later comments in the *BFC* case, when he held that addressing this argument would be:[21]

---

[17] [2004] EWCA Civ 759 [63].
[18] A long-established rule: *Ewart v Latta* (1865) 4 Macq 983, 989; *ex parte Brett* (1871) LR 6 Ch App 838, 841; *Stothers v Borrowman* (1916) 33 DLR 179; *Rosenberg v Quan* (1958) 14 DLR (2d) 415.
[19] [1988] 1 Ch 275, 287.   [20] [1997] EWCA Civ 2901, (1997) 76 P & CR 418.
[21] ibid 428.

made easier if emphasis [were] placed on the existing equitable rights of the [claimant] re-mortgagee, rather than regarding them simply as rights which he has inherited from the original mortgagee.

Since the source of the claimant's rights against the defendant was unjust enrichment (mistake being the operative unjust factor[22]), the defendant's argument boiled down to this. She had been unjustly enriched when the claimant's money had been used to pay off the original mortgage because this had discharged her obligation to the mortgagee. If her husband had immediately broken the terms of his agreement with the claimant, a court could then have made a restitutionary order against her for account and payment. It could also have treated the claimant as though it possessed the same rights against the defendant as had previously been held by the original mortgagee, as a supplementary means of ensuring that she made restitution of the benefit which she had received. However, if an order for account and payment were made against her *now*, nothing would be found to be due on the taking of the account because the full amount of her enrichment had been repaid to the claimant by her husband, whose payments she now adopted as having been made on her behalf.

Evans LJ accepted this argument, but held that it turned on a question of fact which had not been decided at first instance. This was whether the parties had intended that the loan repayments made by the defendant's husband to the claimant should be applied first to discharge that portion of the loan which had been used to pay off the original mortgage. If so, then the defendant would have a complete defence; if not, then the money must have been applied to repay this and the rest of the loan in the ratio 3:10, and so the extent to which the defendant was still enriched would have to be calculated by reference to this figure.

3. 'Transfer' of Extinguished Personal Rights

As Neuberger LJ observed in the *Appleyard* case,[23] the 'classic case' of reviving subrogation involves a claimant 'who expected to receive security (in the proprietary sense—e.g. a mortgage) claiming subrogation to another security', but the remedy 'can also apply to personal rights'. Having said this, however, it must immediately be added that in most cases a claimant should not need to acquire a creditor's personal right against the defendant via subrogation because he ought to have a direct right of action against the defendant in any case.

Consider *Filby v Mortgage Express (No 2) Ltd*.[24] Here, the claimant lent money to the defendant's husband in the mistaken belief that she had signed a charging document creating a mortgage to secure repayment of the loan. In fact her

---

[22] ibid 425.
[23] *Appleyard* (n 16) [36], citing *Re Wrexham, Mold & Connah's Quay Railway Co* [1899] 1 Ch 440 (CA) 458; also noting that in *BFC* (n 11) the House of Lords resolved the case by treating the claimant as though it had acquired a personal right, what Lord Hoffmann called 'a negative form of protection . . . in the form of an undertaking': ibid 229.   [24] *Filby* (n 17).

signature was forged and the mortgage was a nullity against her. The husband used part of the money to pay off a prior mortgage, and she conceded that the claimant could acquire this security via subrogation. He also used some of the money to pay off part of the unsecured overdraft on their joint bank account, and the Court of Appeal held that the claimant could therefore acquire the bank's extinguished personal rights against the defendant via subrogation. There was nothing wrong with saying this, but it was an unnecessarily roundabout way of fixing her with liability. When her liability to the bank was discharged she was unjustly enriched at the claimant's expense, and so she was directly liable to the claimant in any case.

Again, in *Niru Battery Manufacturing Co v Milestone Trading Ltd (No 2)*,[25] two parties owed overlapping liabilities in tort and unjust enrichment to a third party, and the question arose whether a claim for contribution or reimbursement would lie between them when one paid the third party in full. Moore-Bick J held that no such claim would lie, either under the Civil Liability (Contribution) Act 1978 or at common law. However, he also held that the claimant could acquire the third party's extinguished personal rights against the defendant via reviving subrogation, and rely on these to recoup itself in full, in order to reverse the defendant's unjust enrichment at the claimant's expense. These findings were mutually inconsistent. If a defendant has been unjustly enriched at a claimant's expense, then the claimant has a direct personal claim against the defendant in his own right. It is self-contradictory to deny him such a claim, and then to give him someone else's personal claim via reviving subrogation, on the ground that the defendant would otherwise be unjustly enriched. On appeal,[26] the Court of Appeal upheld Moore-Bick J's finding that the claimant was entitled to subrogation, left open the question whether a claim lay under the 1978 Act, and reversed his finding that the claimant had no common law claim to reimbursement. For present purposes, the importance of this decision is that it eliminated the anomaly created by the judge's decision to allow recovery via subrogation while denying a direct claim.[27]

Anomalies of this sort are not new in English law. For at least 300 years the Chancery courts have allowed claimants to acquire a creditor's personal rights via reviving subrogation as a disguised means of allowing a direct personal claim that they thought would be caught by a policy bar: for example, in cases concerning loans to minors to purchase necessaries,[28] and ultra vires loans to companies to discharge their previously contracted intra vires debts.[29] An analogy can be

[25] [2003] EWHC 1032 (Comm), [2003] 2 All ER (Comm) 365.
[26] [2004] EWCA Civ 487, [2004] 2 All ER (Comm) 289.
[27] The decision is also important because it filled in a gap in the scheme of the 1978 Act by recognizing a common law claim to contribution and reimbursement between the parties: C Mitchell, 'Restitution' [2004] All ER Rev 320 [21.15]–[21.16].
[28] *James v Warren* (1706) Holt KB 104, 90 ER 956; *Marlow v Pitfeild* (1719) 1 P Wms 558, 24 ER 516; *Jenner v Morris* (1861) 3 De G F & J 45, 45 ER 795; *Lewis v Alleyene* (1888) 4 TLR 560.
[29] *Re German Mining Co* (1853) De G M & G 19, 43 ER 415; *Baroness Wenlock v River Dee Co* (1888) 38 Ch D 534; *Re Walter's Deed of Guarantee* [1933] 1 Ch 321.

drawn between cases of this sort and *Sinclair v Brougham*.[30] There the House of Lords imposed a trust as an indirect means of evading the policy bar against recovery on an ultra vires contract entered by a building society, believing that this bar would also have prevented the claimants from recovering on a 'quasi-contractual' action for money had and received. As the House of Lords subsequently held in *Westdeutsche Landesbank Girozentrale v Islington LBC*,[31] the court would have done better to allow a direct personal action in unjust enrichment on the basis that this did not conflict with the policy against recovery on the contract. One reason for thinking this was that the House of Lords had been mistaken in *Sinclair v Brougham* to equate 'quasi-contractual' claims with claims on an implied contract. Another, more pertinent to the present discussion, was that the courts should explain themselves clearly, and proceed directly, if they wish to allow a claim in unjust enrichment to recover benefits transferred under an invalid contract, notwithstanding a policy bar against enforcement of the agreement. They should not use roundabout reasoning which conceals their policy calculations and makes the law unnecessarily complex.

4. 'Transfer' of Extinguished Proprietary Rights

At common law a person entitled to an estate in land who acquires a charge over the land is thought to be unable to hold both interests, and so the charge is conclusively presumed to be merged in the estate.[32] In equity, this presumption can be rebutted by evidence that the parties intended to avoid a merger. Obviously it is easiest for a court to discover such an intention where the parties have expressly stated that the charge should be kept alive,[33] but an intention to avoid a merger can also be inferred from conduct.[34] This inference has been drawn where a person with a limited interest in land, such as a life tenant, acquires a charge over the land: the reason given is that otherwise the remainderman would derive an undue advantage from the extinction of the charge that would result from its merger with the limited interest.[35]

This rule was extended by Kay J in *Patten v Bond*.[36] Trust property held for the defendants was mortgaged to secure the repayment of £1,000 which had

---

[30] [1914] AC 398.   [31] [1996] AC 669, 709–14 (Lord Browne-Wilkinson).
[32] *Grice v Shaw* (1852) 10 Hare 76, 79; 68 ER 845, 847.
[33] *Adams v Angell* (1877) 5 Ch D 634.
[34] *Tyrwhitt v Tyrwhitt* (1863) 32 Beav 244, 55 ER 96; *Capital & Counties Bank Ltd v Rhodes* [1903] 1 Ch 631, 652; *Re Fletcher* [1917] 1 Ch 339; *St Mary's Parish Credit Union Ltd v T M Ball Lumber Co Ltd* [1961] SCR 310, 321; *Cinema Plus Ltd v ANZ Banking Group Ltd* (2000) 35 ACSR 1 [26]–[27]. Cf *Re Steele* (1979) 97 DLR (3d) 412, where the parties' conduct was inconsistent with an intention to keep the charge alive.
[35] *Forbes v Moffatt* (1811) 8 Ves Jun 384; 34 ER 362; *Burrell v Earl of Egremont* (1844) 7 Beav 205, 49 ER 1043; *Wilkes v Collin* (1869) LR 8 Eq 338; *Henderson v Wyborn* (1995) 143 NSR (2d) 362; *Kramer v Woodrow* (1997) OR (3d) 118.   [36] (1889) 60 LT 583.

been borrowed by the trustees. The mortgagee asked that £600 of the debt be repaid, but no trust funds were available for the purpose, and so the claimants paid this sum to the mortgagee at the trustees' request. Later, the defendants obtained a transfer of the balance of the mortgage debt, and purported to treat the mortgage as discharged. However, the claimants won a declaration that the mortgage had been kept alive for their benefit, to the extent of their £600 payment. In so holding, Kay J asserted that:[37]

> transactions of this kind are within the well-known rule of equity . . . that, where a person not interested in the equity of redemption pays off part of the mortgage, that is not a discharge; it is not the intention that there should be a complete discharge. . . . The court will assume that the mortgage is not discharged, even though the whole of the debt was paid off to the mortgagee, but considers it to be kept on in equity for the benefit of the person who paid.

In effect, Kay J held that even those without a present interest in land whose money is used to pay off a charge on the land are presumptively entitled to acquire the charge for their own benefit. However, there is a difference between a part-owner who pays off a charge on the land to protect his own interest, and a person who pays off a charge and who has no such interest. The part-owner is effectively compelled to pay to protect his position.[38] The other is not. Unless he can show a reason why he should be treated differently from any other claimant who has voluntarily paid off another person's debt, he should be denied a remedy, both for the technical reason that unrequested payments of debts do not discharge them, and for the more substantial reason that 'liabilities are not to be forced on people behind their backs'.[39]

Notwithstanding the anomalous nature of Kay J's finding, it was followed and approved in many cases during the twentieth century, where it was said that claimants whose money is used to pay off charges are entitled to acquire these charges via subrogation because they are presumed to have intended this at the time when they parted with their money.[40] This rule created some problems. The courts could see that it was too widely expressed and were driven to manufacture an exception which prevented a claimant from acquiring a security via subrogation where he had contracted to make an unsecured loan.[41] As Evans

---

[37] ibid 586.

[38] R Sutton, 'Payment of Debts Charged upon Property' in A Burrows (ed) *Essays on the Law of Restitution* (1991) 71.

[39] *Falcke v Scottish Imperial Insurance Co* (1886) 34 Ch D 234, 248. See too *Owen v Tate* [1976] 1 QB 402, and other cases cited in G Jones (ed), *Goff & Jones on the Law of Restitution* (6th edn, 2002) 18 n 17.

[40] eg *Chetwynd v Allen* [1899] 1 Ch 353; *Butler v Rice* [1910] 2 Ch 277; *Wilchynski v Williams* [1955] 1 DLR 845; *Ghana Commercial Bank v Chandiram* [1960] AC 732, 745; *Hill v ANZ Banking Group Ltd* [1974] 4 ALR 634; *Rogers v Resi-Statewide Corp Ltd* (1991) 105 ALR 145; *Roberts v National Guardian Mortgage Corp* unreported CA 8 November 1993.

[41] eg *Paul v Speirway Ltd (in liq)* [1976] Ch 220, 232; *Orakpo v Manson Investments Ltd* [1978] AC 95, 104–5; *Re Peake's Abattoirs Ltd* [1986] BCLC 73, 79.

LJ observed in the *Muirhead* case, the rule was also ill-adapted to resolve 'cases where the proceeds of a re-mortgage are used to discharge an existing mortgage, so that the maker of the new loan can obtain a first mortgage as his security'.[42] In such cases:[43]

the presumed intention to keep the original mortgage alive which is attributed to the re-mortgagee—the 'third party' who pays the sums due under it—cannot have been his intention in fact. He is concerned to ensure that the original mortgage is discharged rather than kept alive, so that he can obtain a first mortgage to secure his own advance. If he does have any actual intention to keep the original mortgage alive, this can only be conditional upon some failure of his own security, which he is unlikely to foresee or to recognise when the payment is made.

In the *BFC* case,[44] Lord Hoffmann reviewed this line of authority and held that it was misconceived—not because he disagreed with the results in the cases, but because he thought that the language in which they were expressed lacked explanatory force, and masked the true reason for the award of subrogation. In his view, a claimant whose money is used to pay off a charge over property may be entitled to acquire the charge if he has contracted for this. He may also be entitled to be treated as though he has acquired the charge via subrogation if the defendant and other parties with an interest in the property would otherwise be unjustly enriched at his expense. However, Lord Hoffmann insisted that a claimant must prove his entitlement in contract or unjust enrichment. If he cannot, then there is no reason to give him a remedy. The old language of presumptions of intention served a useful purpose prior to the full recognition of unjust enrichment as part of the English law of obligations in *Lipkin Gorman v Karpnale Ltd*.[45] But it is now:[46]

a mistake to regard the availability of subrogation as a remedy to prevent unjust enrichment as turning entirely upon the question of intention, whether common or unilateral. Such an analysis has inevitably to be propped up by presumptions which can verge on outright fictions, more appropriate to a less developed system than we now have. . . . [Outside of the case where the parties have contracted for subrogation, it] should be recognised that one is here concerned with a restitutionary remedy and that the appropriate questions are therefore, first, whether the defendant would be enriched at the plaintiff's expense; secondly, whether such enrichment would be unjust; and, thirdly, whether there are nonetheless reasons of policy for denying a remedy.

Old habits die hard. Since the *BFC* case was decided the Court of Appeal has revisited the law governing the acquisition of extinguished securities via subrogation on several occasions. Each time the court has found it difficult to take Lord Hoffmann at his word, and to move on from the old presumption-based analysis which he discarded in favour of an unjust enrichment analysis. In

---

[42] *Muirhead* (n 20) 425.   [43] ibid.   [44] *BFC* (n 11) 232–4.
[45] [1991] 2 AC 548.   [46] *BFC* (n 11) 234.

Halifax plc v Omar[47] and *Eagle Star Insurance plc v Karasiewicz*,[48] Jonathan Parker and Arden LJJ respectively held that a distinction should be drawn between claims to acquire extinguished personal rights via subrogation and claims to acquire extinguished proprietary rights via subrogation. In their view, the *BFC* case was concerned only with the former class of case, where subrogation is awarded as a remedy for unjust enrichment, and was not concerned with the latter class of case, to which the presumption-based analysis continues to apply.

This was a perverse misreading of Lord Hoffmann's speech. Since the presumption-based rule had only ever been invoked in cases where a claimant's money had been applied to pay off a security, he could only have been referring to these cases when he held that the rule had been superseded by unjust enrichment thinking. Moreover, the idea that there is a neat dichotomy between subrogation to personal rights and subrogation to secured rights misses the point of Lord Hoffmann's explanation of how the remedy works. As discussed in Section 2, he envisaged a much more finely graded spectrum of possibilities, ranging from subrogation to a security interest with its full original effect against the whole world, through subrogation to a security interest as against a more limited number of third parties, down to subrogation to a personal right effective against one other party.

In *Cheltenham & Gloucester plc v Appleyard*,[49] a third Court of Appeal expressed doubts about the reasoning in *Omar* and *Karasiewicz*,[50] and purported to accept Lord Hoffmann's account of subrogation to extinguished securities as a remedy for unjust enrichment.[51] But even in *Appleyard* the court hedged its bets, doubting 'if reference to [the *BFC* case] is likely to be of assistance in a conventional case' concerned with the acquisition of proprietary rights via subrogation,[52] and invoking the discredited principle that:[53]

where A's money is used to pay off the claim of B, who is a secured creditor, A is entitled to be regarded in equity as having had an assignment to him of B's rights as a secured creditor.

No doubt one reason for the courts' discomfort with the *BFC* case is the complexity of its facts and the worrying sense that something was not quite right with the order which was finally made.[54] No doubt, too, the reason why many practitioners and judges feel comfortable with the presumed intention formula is that it seems to offer a more pliable test than the law of unjust enrichment, with which they are unfamiliar. None the less Lord Hoffmann's exposition of the law is clear and cogent, and looking ahead, it seems likely that the presumed

---

[47] [2002] EWCA Civ 121, [2002] 2 P & CR 377.   [48] [2002] EWCA Civ 940.
[49] *Appleyard* (n 16).   [50] ibid [31].   [51] ibid [32] citing *BFC* (n 11) 231.
[52] ibid [49].
[53] ibid [25] quoting *Burston Finance Ltd v Speirway Ltd (in liq)* [1974] 1 WLR 1648, 1652.
[54] For the view that the HL's order created a circular priority system, see M Armstrong and A Cerfontaine, 'Subrogation, Unjust Enrichment and Insolvency: A French View of *Banque Financière de la Cité SA v Parc (Battersea) Ltd*' in FD Rose (ed), *Restitution and Insolvency* (2000) 77, 102–4; and cf M Bridge, 'Failed Contracts, Subrogation and Unjust Enrichment' [1999] JBL 323, 330–3.

intention formula will be trotted out less often as barristers and judges become more confident in their handling of restitutionary concepts.[55] How long this takes may depend in part upon the success with which the courts handle some of the questions to which the *BFC* case gives rise.

5. Outstanding Questions

When making an order which is designed to give effect to a claimant's restitutionary rights via reviving subrogation, the court should make it clear what transfers of value the order is meant to reverse. This should usually be obvious in the case of a defendant whose liability has been discharged by the claimant's payment to the creditor, but it may be less obvious in the case of third parties. So far as they are concerned, the most likely possibility is that their ability to recover a debt from the defendant is enhanced when the creditor's rights are extinguished, perhaps because they hold junior securities which are promoted on the extinction of the creditor's charge.[56] However, it remains to be decided by the English courts that this kind of benefit is sufficient for the purpose of making out a claim in unjust enrichment against third parties.[57]

The court should also explain why it would be unjust for the defendant and third parties to keep these benefits. A broadly conceived version of causative mistake has been identified as the operative unjust factor in some of the recent cases,[58] but the question arises whether it is appropriate for the courts to let arm's-length contracting parties resort to restitutionary claims founded on their own (possibly negligent) mistakes in order to escape the consequences of their commercial miscalculations.[59] Failure of consideration is another possibility on the facts of many cases, but here the question arises whether, and if so, why, the claim should be subject to a 'bargain ceiling' preventing a claimant from acquiring security where he has negotiated to make an unsecured loan,[60] particularly where the contract he negotiated is void or voidable;[61] or again, preventing a claimant who acquires a mortgage via reviving subrogation from

---

[55] A process which the *BFC* case has enabled by providing a clear four-step template for the pleading of claims in unjust enrichment: *BFC* (n 11) 227 (Lord Steyn) and 234 (Lord Hoffmann), followed in eg *Cressman v Coys of Kensington (Sales) Ltd* [2004] EWCA Civ 47, [2004] 1 WLR 2775 [22] (Mance LJ) and *Niru (No 2)* (n 29) [28] and [41] (Clarke LJ).

[56] As in eg *Appleyard* (n 16).

[57] A point considered in P Watts, 'Subrogation: A Step Too Far?' (1998) 114 LQR 341, 344; S Worthington, 'Subrogation Claims on Insolvency' in Rose (n 54) 66, 72–4. cf *Mutual Trust Co v Creditview Estate Homes Ltd* (1997) 149 OLR (4th) 385, 387; *Hong Kong Chinese Bank Ltd v Sky Phone Ltd* [2001] 1 HKC 50, 53.

[58] As in eg *Muirhead* (n 22) 425; *BFC* (n 11) 227 and 234; *Filby* (n 17) [48].

[59] For the view that it is not, see Bridge (n 54) 333.

[60] cf *Paul v Speirway* [1976] Ch 220, 232; *Boscawen* (n 9) 338; *Muirhead* (n 20) 426.

[61] cf *Re Wrexham, Mold and Connah's Quay Railway Co* [1899] 1 Ch 440; *Thurstan v Nottingham Permanent Building Soc* [1902] 1 Ch 1, affirmed on another point [1903] AC 6; *Orakpo v Manson Investments Ltd* [1978] AC 95.

enforcing the interest provisions in the mortgage deed where he has lent money to pay off the mortgage on terms that he will be repaid at a lower rate.[62]

Questions also arise about the form of orders which a court should make in reviving subrogation cases, and the effect which these may have on non-parties to the litigation. If the transfer of rights from the creditor to the claimant is wholly fictional, and is deemed to have taken place solely for the purposes of resolving the claimant's dispute with the defendant to his proceedings, then what effect does the court's order have on third parties who also have claims against the defendant and his property? Must they be joined to the proceedings and named in the court's order if they are to be affected by it? What of third parties who only come onto the scene and acquire securities over the defendant's property after the court's order has been made?[63] Where the court thinks it appropriate to treat a claimant as though he were the holder of a legal charge, does he actually obtain a legal charge? If so, does this take effect retrospectively, and what are the consequences of its non-registration between the time when the original charge was paid off and the time of the court's order?[64]

6. Conclusion

The English law of obligations has undergone a revolution over the past forty years, as unjust enrichment has emerged as an independent source of rights which 'ranks next to contract and tort'.[65] The place which reviving subrogation occupies within this area of the law, and the way in which the remedy works, have become significantly clearer in the past decade. Lord Hoffmann should take much of the credit for this, as his speech in the *BFC* case has laid some old misconceptions to rest. But as Peter wrote in his last book, the *BFC* case is 'both liberal and, perhaps disconcertingly, flexible'.[66] The implications of this flexibility remain to be fully explored.

---

[62] *Chetwynd v Allen* [1899] 1 Ch 353; *Western Trust & Savings Ltd v Rock* unreported CA 26 February 1993; *Muirhead* (n 20) 426, affirmed in *Appleyard* (n 16) [76].
[63] See eg *Ghana Commercial Bank v Chandiram* [1960] AC 732; *Boscawen* (n 9); *Omar* (n 47).
[64] cf *Castle Finance Ltd v Piddington* [1996] 1 FSCR 269; *Appleyard* (n 16).
[65] *BFC* (n 11) 227 (Lord Steyn).
[66] P Birks, *Unjust Enrichment* (2nd edn, 2005) 298 n 37.

7

Tracing

*Lionel Smith**

1. Introduction

I can still remember my first face-to-face meeting with Peter Birks, in 1992. I had just come to Oxford from Edmonton to begin my doctoral research with him. The business of the meeting was to decide what would be the subject of my research. As I arrived at Peter's rooms, someone else was just leaving; Peter described him as 'another restitution maniac'.[1] I soon learned that my initial plans, like those of most new doctoral students, were far too ambitious. I had, however, just written a rambling essay about *Lipkin Gorman*.[2] He was kinder about that essay than it deserved, and I think it was largely on the basis of my interest in that case that it was agreed that I would work on tracing.

When I discussed my research with other students, I encountered different responses. Some thought tracing was too hard; one was surprised that tracing could, by itself, justify doctoral research. But I always felt lucky in my topic. Even thirteen years later, however, I am still not sure that I understand it very well.

In this essay, I seek to trace, or follow, some strands in the evolution of Peter's thought regarding unjust enrichment and the law of tracing. Our law allows a claimant to assert rights in the traceable proceeds of an unauthorized disposition of the claimant's asset; Peter consistently argued that such claims arise to reverse unjust enrichment. I will argue that his understanding of tracing shaped his understanding of much of the law of unjust enrichment.

The plan of the essay is this. The next section sets out some of the new and controversial arguments made by Peter in *Unjust Enrichment*.[3] The section after

---

* James McGill Professor of Law, Faculty of Law, McGill University.

[1] I think Peter meant 'another' in addition to Peter, rather than in addition to me, although I have never been entirely sure.   [2] *Lipkin Gorman (a firm) v Karpnale Ltd* [1991] 2 AC 548, HL.
[3] P Birks, *Unjust Enrichment* (2nd edn, 2005). In some cases the argument appeared in other writing before the first edition of *Unjust Enrichment*, but none of the arguments appeared in print before 2000.

that will contend that all of these arguments were, to a greater or lesser degree, influenced by his understanding of the nature of claims to traceable proceeds.

2. New Claims in *Unjust Enrichment*

2.1. Enrichment by Relinquishment

There is an important distinction between *preventing* unjust enrichment and *reversing* it. The law of unjust enrichment identifies unjust enrichments and requires that they be reversed, but in some situations we might instead say that no unjust enrichment occurred; unjust enrichment was prevented by our rules on the transfer of rights. For example, assume that I transfer possession to you of a £50 note, but due to my mistake as to your identity, I remain the owner of the note.[4] On the dominant approach found in the civil law tradition, there is no claim in unjust enrichment.[5] None is needed, because there is no unjust enrichment, because there is no enrichment.[6] Any unjust enrichment is prevented from occurring by the law governing the transfer of rights, and so there is no need for a claim that operates to reverse unjust enrichments.

Peter had some sympathy for this approach to the relationship between unjust enrichment claims and the law governing the transfer of rights. That is, even though he was of the view that 'unjust enrichment law' could not be opposed to 'property law', because unjust enrichments are one source of property rights,[7] none the less he accepted that there is an important difference between the law's reversing unjust enrichment, by the creation of a new right (personal or proprietary), and the law's preventing unjust enrichment by deciding that the defendant is never legally enriched on the basis that the claimant's rights never passed to the defendant.[8] But he did not accept the civilian solution that treats these possibilities as mutually exclusive alternatives. Peter argued for a

---

[4] This assumes I was the owner at the start of the story, which may be difficult and indeed unnecessary to prove. Your possession will, of course, give you an interest in the note that will be protected against anyone who dispossessed you. Both of these points stem from the idea of relativity of title. But the problem raised in the text stands: as between you and me, my rights in the note (whatever they may be) have not passed to you.

[5] For discussion of some civilian approaches, see L Smith, 'Property, Subsidiarity and Unjust Enrichment' in D Johnston and R Zimmermann (eds), *Unjustified Enrichment: Key Issues in Comparative Perspective* (2002) 588, 593–96. See also the common law analysis of this issue in R Grantham and C Rickett, 'On the Subsidiarity of Unjust Enrichment' (2001) 117 LQR 273.

[6] Keeping in mind the relativity of title (n 4 above), we might say that you *were* enriched, inasmuch as you acquired a possessory title good against all the world except me. My rights, however, remain superior to yours, not only as against you, but as against anyone else. The claim that we are trying to explain is one that is measured by the value of my still-existing rights in the note, and which therefore exists as an alternative to (and not in addition to) the enforcement of those rights. See Birks (n 3 above) 64–8 (the new unjust enrichment claim is an alternative to the enforcement of surviving rights).   [7] Birks (n 3 above) 33, 68.

[8] Birks (n 3 above) 37; see also P Birks, *An Introduction to the Law of Restitution* (rev edn, 1989) 13–16, 25.

different view, in which they coexist. That is, there is no bar to a claim in unjust enrichment simply because there is in existence a right which, on its face, prevents any unjust enrichment from having arisen. On the facts presented above, Peter would contend that there can be a claim in unjust enrichment for £50. How does this occur? The claimant, in claiming that the defendant was enriched by £50, relinquishes to the defendant his rights in the note.[9]

Here we have to draw a distinction between claims for the value of use over time, and claims to capital value. Let us assume that I am out of possession of my £50 for six months. I might claim against you for the value of use over time; the value of use of £50 over six months is basically a claim for interest. Here I can say that you have been enriched by, and I have correspondingly been deprived of, the use of the £50 over that period of time. That claim might be for £2 or so, depending on interest rates. That is not our concern. That interest claim could be accepted, as a claim in unjust enrichment, even if there is no claim in unjust enrichment for £50. Our concern is with a claim for the capital value of £50. Peter's theory of elective relinquishment was deployed to show how that larger claim could be justified.

Why is this controversial? If it works, the relinquishment makes an enrichment, and also a corresponding deprivation. The reason most civilians would reject it is this. If I remain the owner of my £50 note, you are not enriched. There is no injustice for the law of unjust enrichment to rectify. Of course, we have the problem of one person being in possession of something that belongs to another person; that is a kind of injustice. But it is one that the law outside the law of unjust enrichment is competent to rectify. The law outside of unjust enrichment protects pre-existing property rights. In this regard, however, Peter argued that the claimant could have a choice. In his view, the retention of title was only a technicality;[10] since it existed for the claimant's benefit, the claimant could waive it. But the civilian approach has this reasoning in its favour. An unjust enrichment is a transfer of wealth that is defective or unjust according to the law. The idea of elective relinquishment arguably creates a loss of congruity between the transfer of wealth and the injustice. The injustice arises at the time of the mistaken transfer of possession, but there is as yet no enrichment. The enrichment occurs later, by the claimant's elective choice; but this in turn arguably extinguishes the injustice. How can the claimant simultaneously relinquish his title, and make a claim that the defendant has been unjustly enriched by the acquisition of that title? And if the claimant is allowed to relinquish, why should he be allowed to do so with retroactive effect?[11]

---

[9] Birks (n 3 above) 66–8. This view appeared earlier in P Birks, 'Receipt' in P Birks and A Pretto (eds), *Breach of Trust* (2002) 213, 232.

[10] Birks (n 9 above) 232; see also P Birks, 'Property and Unjust Enrichment: Categorical Truths' [1997] NZLJ 623, 654–6 (although the idea of relinquishment was not developed there).

[11] Peter's assumption was that the liability arose at the moment of receipt. This is clear from his discussion of the case of a subsequent expenditure by the defendant, in a way that benefited the

One analogy arises in the law of wrongs. If a defendant takes something belonging to the claimant, the claimant may get a judgment for compensation in money, measured by the value of the claimant's rights in the thing. As Peter noted, upon payment of the judgment, the claimant's rights are transferred by operation of law to the defendant.[12] We might say that here the claimant makes a choice, by asking for compensation in money rather than specific recovery; and, that the effect of this choice is the ultimate relinquishment of the claimant's rights. And we can observe that the principle can even have a retroactive effect. For example, the claimant's thing is taken by A and then sold to B. Both are liable to the claimant, but the claimant chooses to sue A and recovers the value of his rights in the thing. B committed a wrong against the claimant before the judgment against A was satisfied. Even so, B is now immune to any conversion claim by the claimant.[13]

So we do, in a sense, allow the claimant to abandon his rights in the thing in favour of a money award. Of course, it is not exactly a free choice; unlike in the civil law tradition, the money award is understood to be the claimant's primary recourse.[14] More importantly, this is not an elective relinquishment of title that establishes a cause of action. The cause of action is capable of explanation independently of the question of what kind of judgment the claimant seeks, or obtains, or collects. In other words, the cause of action does not depend upon any choice by the claimant; it is based on past facts, namely wrongful interference with the claimant's rights. Moreover, the claimant who chooses to ask for compensation in money does not *thereby* abandon his rights in the thing; they are lost only when the judgment is satisfied. This is a transfer of title by operation of law to prevent double recovery. The wrong is remediable by specific recovery or by a substitutive award in money, but it has to be one or the other. One cannot recover damages that have been calculated to make good the loss of one's rights, and keep those rights. The law *takes away* the claimant's rights in the thing when he has *received* the full value of those rights in money as compensation. By contrast, the theory of elective

---

defendant but did not count as a change of position (Birks (n 9 above) 236). His view was that unless liability arose at the moment of receipt, this person would not be liable. The implication is that elective relinquishment must be retroactive to the moment of receipt by the defendant. The case of subsequent enriching expenditure could alternatively be viewed as creating an unjust enrichment at the time of the enriching expenditure; at that time there is also a corresponding deprivation of the claimant.

[12] Birks (n 3 above) 66, citing the Torts (Interference with Goods) Act 1977, s 5, which codifies the common law rule.

[13] *Cooper v Shepherd* (1846) 3 CB 266, 136 ER 107, CP. See also LD Smith, *The Law of Tracing* (1997) 291–2, 378–9, where other cases are noted and the problem of partial recovery of compensation is discussed.

[14] If the claimant does seek specific recovery of the thing, it is in the discretion of the court whether to make such an order, or to deny it in favour of a money award, or indeed to give the *defendant* the choice. These alternatives are preserved by the Torts (Interference with Goods) Act 1977, s 3(2), but this is also the common law: *General and Finance Facilities Ltd v Cooks Cars (Romford) Ltd* [1963] 1 WLR 644, CA. The claimant's rights are lost when compensatory damages are paid, whether the claimant wanted money or specific recovery.

renunciation posits that the law permits the claimant to abandon those rights in order to create a new right to their value, by perfecting a cause of action that depends on their acquisition by the defendant.

Another possible analogy is the power to avoid a contract for misrepresentation. This gives the claimant a choice; it cannot be explained as arising through the claimant's consent; and it operates retroactively. The justification could be set out in the following way. If the claimant's consent to a contract was formed on the basis of a misrepresentation, that consent is flawed. The flaw exists at the moment of the agreement and in some sense vitiates it. It does not, however, destroy it so as to make the contract void, in the way that some very fundamental mistakes do destroy agreement. So the agreement is considered to be effective as such. Even so, the flaw generates a legal consequence: the claimant's power to avoid the contract. Since the flaw was in the claimant's consent, it is the claimant who has the choice whether or not to invoke it. If he does invoke it, he is invoking a flaw that vitiated his agreement; hence, the invocation of the flaw is treated as destroying the basis of the agreement, and so is given retroactive effect.[15]

Can this reasoning extend to the doctrine of elective renunciation? In the case in which I transfer possession to you of a £50 note, could we say that I have a power, arising at the moment of the transfer of possession, to transfer my rights in the note to you? As in the misrepresentation case, I did not fully consent to your enrichment. The difficulty is that my failure to consent has already been given the fullest possible effect by the law, in the decision that none of my rights passed to you. Now if I say I want to make you the owner (so as to constitute an unjust enrichment claim), I am hardly giving effect to the earlier defect of my consent. Rather, I am overriding it. If we continued with the contract analogy, this case is more like a mistake so fundamental that it negates the agreement. To allow retrospective election would be like allowing a person who has made such a mistake to waive it retroactively and bring a contract into existence.

It is the choice that must be explained. If the claimant has such a choice, then by exercising it, he can arguably bring about a situation in which the defendant

---

[15] There is also some analogy with the idea of subsequent failure of basis in the law of unjust enrichment. The basis (the mutually understood foundation for the transfer) must be in place at the time of enrichment and corresponding deprivation (eg 'I give you this gift in anticipation of your upcoming wedding'). When the basis fails (the wedding is called off), even if this occurs later, the conclusion is that the enrichment is now revealed to have been unjustified. In both cases, the power to rescind a contract and the case of failure of basis, a feature upon which the claimant now relies was present at the earlier time (the time of contracting or the time of enrichment). However, in the case of failure of basis, the failure of the basis does not have a retroactive effect; the claim is understood to arise only at the moment of failure, not at the earlier time of transfer: *Deglman v Guaranty Trust Co* [1954] SCR 725, [1954] 3 DLR 785; A Burrows, *The Law of Restitution* (2nd edn, 2002) 407–8. The reason is that although the basis must be in place at the time of the enrichment, the enrichment is not unjust until the basis fails. The basis, before it fails, does not amount to a flaw in the enrichment. But a mistake generated by a misrepresentation is a flaw in a contract or other legal act, a flaw that was fully formed at the time of the legal act.

has been unjustly enriched. But in that case, it cannot be the law of unjust enrichment that gives the claimant the choice, or else we would be in logical circle. Understanding the foundation of the choice would also help us to understand what facts create the choice.[16]

2.2. Claimant's Deprivation Unnecessary

The idea of elective relinquishment, if it worked, would not only establish an enrichment of the defendant, but also a corresponding deprivation of the claimant. But another controversial claim in *Unjust Enrichment* is that a claimant in unjust enrichment need not have suffered any deprivation. This is a move away from the pioneering distinction drawn in the *Introduction* between 'unjust enrichment by subtraction' and 'restitution for wrongs'.[17] The move was signalled in the paper he gave in 1999 at a conference in Cambridge on Comparative Unjust Enrichment.[18]

Why is this controversial? The law of unjust enrichment makes defendants liable even though they have not done anything wrong. This is unusual and requires careful normative justification. Wrongdoing by a defendant is usually a sufficient justification to shift losses. If a claimant has suffered loss caused by a defendant's wrong, the wrong explains why we can shift that loss from the claimant's shoulders to the defendant's shoulders; we require the payment of compensation. If a defendant has acquired a gain through an act that was wrongful against the claimant, the wrong provides a justification as to why we can shift that gain from the defendant to the claimant; we can require disgorgement of the gain.

Without any wrong, we are harder pressed to justify liability. *Unjust Enrichment* begins with a discussion of this feature, characteristic of the law of unjust enrichment, that civil liability arises without wrongdoing.[19] Peter used, as his core case, the example of a mistaken payment. He drew the conclusion that

---

[16] Peter thought that the choice would arise where the defendant found and kept the claimant's asset: he identified *Holiday v Sigil* (1826) 2 C & P 176, 172 ER 81, KB, in which the defendant found and kept the claimant's £500 note, as a case that is explicable as autonomous unjust enrichment: Birks (n 9 above) 231–2; Birks (n 3 above) 69, 73. It would be a question for the future whether the claimant could use this idea if the defendant's interaction with the asset was more fleeting (eg the defendant picked it up but immediately dropped it; the defendant merely touched it).   [17] Birks (n 8 above) 22–5.
[18] The conference paper, P Birks, ' "At The Expense of the Claimant": Direct and Indirect Enrichment in English Law', was published first online at the Oxford University Comparative Law Forum <http://ouclf.iuscomp.org> in 2000, and then in D Johnston and R Zimmermann (eds), *Unjustified Enrichment: Key Issues in Comparative Perspective* (2002) 493. Reactions include L Smith, 'Restitution: The Heart of Corrective Justice' (2001) 79 Tex L Rev 2115, especially 2146–8, 2156–9; R Grantham and C Rickett, 'Disgorgement for Unjust Enrichment?' (2003) 62 CLJ 159; M McInnes, 'Interceptive Subtraction, Unjust Enrichment and Wrongs—A Reply to Professor Birks' (2003) 62 CLJ 697.   [19] Birks (n 3 above) 1–9.

only 'slight facts' are needed to justify a liability in unjust enrichment.[20] He said on the first page of his book that 'The law of unjust enrichment is the law of all events materially identical to the mistaken payment of a non-existent debt'.[21] But a mistaken payment reveals both an enrichment of the defendant and a corresponding deprivation of the claimant. Part of Peter's argument, therefore, is aimed at proving that the corresponding deprivation is not a material feature of the mistaken payment case.

The law of unjust enrichment can be understood to be based on the same normative foundations as those that require a defendant in possession of a claimant's umbrella to return that umbrella to him. The obligation to return does not depend on consent or on wrongdoing. It depends on a pre-existing right, held by the claimant, to or in the umbrella. If the umbrella vanishes, so too does the claimant's existing right to it. After that, any claim would have to be justified in a different way. The mistaken payment case is different doctrinally, because the claimant's property rights are usually transferred to the defendant, despite the mistake.[22] But normatively, it is quite similar. The payment serves the same normative function as the umbrella. It is what has to be given back, without any allegation of wrongdoing.

On one view, this function can only be served if and to the extent that the claimant has suffered some kind of deprivation. Without that, and in the absence of wrongdoing, any gain acquired by the defendant lacks a sufficient link to the claimant.[23] The deprivation suffered in the mistaken payment case, on this view, is an essential feature of it, and no case is materially identical unless it shares that feature.

Peter took a wider view. For him, any gain which came from the claimant's rights was 'from' the claimant in the required sense.[24] So if the defendant had acquired a gain through the use of the claimant's property, there could be a claim in autonomous unjust enrichment to that full gain, regardless of the extent (if any) of any deprivation suffered by the claimant. Although he described Mitchell McInnes's rebuttal as 'very powerful',[25] Peter remained unpersuaded.

The result of the abandonment of any requirement of deprivation on the part of the claimant has been that the law of unjust enrichment, sometimes called 'autonomous unjust enrichment' to distinguish it carefully from the law of gain-based remedies for wrongful conduct, becomes conceptually much larger. Indeed it might be thought that it loses its autonomy. Almost every case of disgorgement

---

[20] ibid 7, 8, 9.   [21] ibid 1.

[22] In some situations (a mistake as to the identity of the payee, or as to the subject-matter delivered), a mistaken payment does not transfer the claimant's property rights to the defendant. This is discussed in the previous section. That case is the same as the umbrella case, both doctrinally and normatively.

[23] M McInnes, 'At the Plaintiff's Expense: Quantifying Restitutionary Relief' (1998) 57 CLJ 472.   [24] Birks (n 3 above) 79–82.

[25] ibid 81.

for wrongdoing, it seems, can be viewed as a case of unjust enrichment, because any wrong is an infringement of the claimant's entitlements.[26]

2.3. Abandonment of Reasons for Restitution

This is the most dramatic change in *Unjust Enrichment* from Peter's previous scholarship. Once there has been an enrichment at the claimant's expense, it must be determined whether it was an unjust enrichment. Traditionally the common law answered this question by elaborating a list of reasons for restitution.[27] Peter argued that we should move instead to a different approach, in which every enrichment will be seen as unjust unless a legal basis can be found to justify it. Canadian common law has started to move in this direction.[28] The implications are not entirely clear. My own view is that the change will ultimately be a change of emphasis. Under reasons for restitution, most cases of unjust enrichment were explicable either because the claimant did not really intend to enrich the defendant, or because there was a wider policy that required restitution even though the claimant did intend to enrich the defendant. The inquiry into legal bases will not be very different. It will seek to determine whether the claimant made a legally binding decision to enrich the defendant, or whether, even if she did not, some legal policy none the less requires that restitution be denied.

Be that as it may, the move to an approach based on absence of legal basis would on its face relieve us of any inquiry into reasons for restitution.

2.4. Dominance of the Abstract Conception of Wealth

Peter observed that our legal system knows two conceptions of wealth.[29] One is abstract and one is particular. The abstract approach is a balance-sheet approach to wealth, while the particular approach sees wealth as inhering in particular assets. The law of unjust enrichment typically takes the abstract approach. Its

---

[26] Birks (n 3 above) 81 indicated that he did not think that *Attorney-General v Blake* [2001] 1 AC 268, HL could be viewed as a case of unjust enrichment. That was a case of a gain made through the wrong of breach of contract. But if the principle is 'from my property, therefore sufficiently from me' (ibid 82), *Blake* seems like a good candidate. Blake made his gains through a violation of the claimant's contractual rights. The bulk of most people's wealth is today held in the form of contractual rights. Peter might have intended that 'property' in this principle be confined to its narrow sense of proprietary rights, and not its wide sense that includes all economic assets. That is the very distinction that was rejected in *Blake* itself with respect to the availability of gain-based awards for wrongdoing. A case of a gain acquired through the violation of a non-economic right (such as a paid beating) might be an example of a case that could support a claim for a gain-based remedy for the wrong, but was not within Peter's extended view of autonomous unjust enrichment.

[27] The list dates back to *Moses v Macferlan* (1760) 2 Burr 1005, 97 ER 676, KB.

[28] *Garland v Consumers' Gas Co* [2004] 1 SCR 629, 237 DLR (4th) 385.

[29] Birks (n 3 above) 69.

concern is with whether the defendant was enriched in that abstract sense. A defendant might be enriched because the claimant transported him in a vehicle, saving an inevitable expense; or, because the claimant paid the defendant's debt. In either case, we cannot point to a particular asset belonging to the defendant and say, 'there, that is the enrichment that came from the claimant'. Of course, in some cases, we can: if the claimant mistakenly transfers ownership of his car to the defendant, we can point to the enrichment in a particular form among all of the defendant's assets. The abstract conception is wider and includes the particular.

Peter said that the abstract conception had to be made dominant. He observed that this dominance must be achieved chiefly at the stage of defences. He said, '... the law is currently struggling, at the level of defences, to ensure that the discrete conception of wealth is always ultimately trumped by the abstract conception'.[30] The defence of change of position must be able to operate using the abstract conception; in other words, at least in some situations, a defendant can rely on his disenrichment, whether or not the wealth that he has dissipated in good faith has any specific or particular connection to the enrichment received from the claimant.[31]

Is this controversial? The identification of the two conceptions of wealth is not. The suggestion that one must dominate the other, however, makes sense only inasmuch as there is some conflict between them. Peter's argument was that the law ensures 'at the level of defences' that the abstract conception remains dominant. This implies that the conflict is between claims and defences, and that in some situations a claim is available that is based on the particular concept, and that this has to be corrected by the defences. A simple example will illustrate. The defendant acquires money in which the claimant has equitable rights under a trust. If the defendant uses that money to acquire a car, the car is the traceable product of the money. Prima facie, this means that the defendant now holds the car subject to the claimant's equitable rights. Now let us assume that further facts are established. First, the defendant shows that he was, in any event, going to acquire that car. Secondly, the defendant shows that, as a result of acquiring the money in which the claimant had an interest, the defendant set aside the money that he *would have* otherwise used to buy the car, and instead he donated this money to a charity. Let us assume that this charitable donation qualifies as a change of position. When Peter said that the law is struggling to ensure the dominance of the abstract approach *at the level of defences*, he meant that the defence of change of position must trump the claimant's assertion of rights in the car.[32]

---

[30] ibid 70.

[31] It must have some connection, but it is enough that it be by reliance, or perhaps merely by causation. It need not be the same particular thing, nor its traceable product.

[32] There could be some difficulty in reconciling this with the idea of a *numerus clausus* of property rights (Birks (n 3 above) 29), if the same property right is defeasible by change of position

Civilian legal systems also know both conceptions of wealth, but they are not necessarily in tension.[33] In the civilian perspective, each legal person has a 'patrimony', which is conceptually a wealth-container. A patrimony contains a person's assets, and also his or her liabilities.[34] The liabilities of any particular patrimony must be answered out of its assets; a patrimony is generally said to be indivisible, which means that one cannot shield any part of one's wealth, abstractly viewed, from the claims of creditors. As in the common law, the law of unjust enrichment uses a balance sheet or abstract approach; enrichment is judged by looking to the patrimony as a whole, rather than to particular assets. On the other hand, just as in the common law, property rights inhere in particular assets. In the civilian tradition, these two approaches are not seen to be in tension. This is probably because the law of unjust enrichment does not create property rights in this tradition.

The tension Peter identified is bound to arise if unjust enrichment, with its abstract approach, is understood to create property rights, which require a particular approach. On Peter's view, the law of unjust enrichment creates both obligations and property rights.[35] But he also accepted that property rights always have a particular subject-matter.[36] Property rights presuppose the particular approach, not the abstract approach.[37] In creating property rights, unjust enrichment is bound to create rights in particular assets. If the overall approach

in some cases (where it was generated by unjust enrichment) but not in others. This would be one argument in favour of concluding that unjust enrichment can never generate vested property rights but at the most, powers to vest property rights (see the discussion ibid 183–4). On this view the defence can be set up only against the power, and the *numerus clausus* of vested rights remains unaffected.

[33] Peter argued that English law had committed itself intuitively to the abstract approach, in that restitution has always been made by money awards, regardless of the form of enrichment. This practice can be understood historically, since the common counts were sub-species of *indebitatus assumpsit*, itself a sub-species of trespass. In other words, the claim was based historically on a damage claim for wrongdoing, and the award was therefore inevitably one made in money. The Chancery, for its part, frequently made orders based on the particular conception of wealth. But in any event all legal systems view enrichment as potentially abstract. In a case of particular enrichment (say by a property transfer), the civilian tradition may say that the defendant's primary obligation is to re-transfer the particular thing. But this is only a personal obligation, and does not give a real right in the thing. Furthermore, if specific re-transfer is unavailable, the defendant must make restitution in money; the obligation is not particular to the same extent as a real right, which stands or falls with its subject-matter. Finally, the acceptance of the abstract approach in civilian unjust enrichment law is evident from the availability of claims in cases of abstract enrichment, such as services or the discharge of the defendant's obligations.

[34] Although at any point in time it could have only one or the other, or, say at the moment of birth, neither. On this approach there are also extrapatrimonial rights, such as the right to vote. Patrimonial rights are those available for economic transactions.　　　　[35] Birks (n 3 above) 33, 68.

[36] ibid 180; P Birks (ed), *English Private Law*, 2 vols, vol 1 (2000) at pp xxxviii–xxxix.

[37] Even property rights in a 'fund' are no more than rights in each of the particular things that make up the fund at any point in time: RC Nolan, 'Property in a Fund' (2004) 120 LQR 108. To say that I own all the books in my library (as it changes from time to time) does not mean that 'library' is a word with a special meaning in property law.

of unjust enrichment must be abstract, then this particularity must be repaired at the level of defences.

3. Influence of the Law of Tracing

In this section, I will argue that in some measure, these new claims developed out of Peter's views regarding the law of tracing, broadly envisioned so as to include the rules of tracing as well as the kinds of claims that can be made upon the successful conclusion of the tracing exercise.

3.1. Personal Claims to Receipt of Trust Property

Not every case involving liability for receipt of trust property depends upon tracing, but a majority of them do, especially where the defendant has received money. It was in the context of these cases that Peter developed the theory of elective relinquishment. The problem that this theory solves does not arise, except theoretically, in the context of common law claims. The reason is that a defendant who defends a claim in unjust enrichment, by using the argument that the claimant remained the legal owner of the enrichment all along, has surely admitted wrongful interference with goods.[38] But it is more difficult where the claimant claims as a trust beneficiary. The defendant still in possession of trust property will be declared a trustee and consequential orders will be made. The defendant no longer in possession of trust property may be personally liable for the wrong of knowing receipt of trust property. But this will not be the case if he was innocent, in the sense that he neither was nor ought to have been aware of the claimant's rights. So here the question whether there is a claim in unjust enrichment is germane. Peter argued that there was such a claim, from the moment of receipt. The main need for it was in the case where the defendant had parted with the wealth in a way that enriched him, and that did not entitle him to the defence of change of position. Were he innocent all along, Peter argued, he would retain an enrichment for no good reason.[39]

The theory of elective relinquishment solved the problem of a lack of fit between unjust enrichment liability for receipt of trust property, and the core unjust enrichment cases of payments or services. Typically in unjust enrichment, the enrichment of the defendant is established by showing that the defendant is wealthier, in the abstract sense. The claimant's claim, so far from turning on a survival of the claimant's rights, is based on the loss of rights and the acquisition of a corresponding gain by the defendant. But the trust property cases are

---

[38] Robert Stevens is the most eloquent proponent of this point. See Ch 3 above.
[39] Birks (n 9 above) 236. Alternatively, such a person can be seen as enriched, not at the moment of receipt, but at the moment he disposes of the wealth in an enriching way: n 11 above; Smith (n 18 above) 2172–73.

different. If the claimant lost his equitable interest when the defendant acquired a legal interest in the property in question, there could be no claim in unjust enrichment, or else unjust enrichment would stultify the choices made for the protection of good faith recipients of trust property.[40] On the other hand, if the defendant has acquired property subject to the claimant's trust interest, then the enrichment upon which the claim is founded—the claimant's equitable interest—is exactly what has *not* been added to the defendant's wealth. The theory of elective relinquishment provides a way of finding the required enrichment on such facts.

3.2. Claims to the Proceeds of Unauthorized Disposition

Showing No Deprivation Needed

The evolution of Peter's thinking in this regard is quite plain. If the claimant owned something, and the defendant disposed of it, acquiring rights in some proceeds, then the claimant could assert rights in those proceeds. This does not depend on wrongdoing, nor does it depend on whether the defendant's disposal was legally effective to divest the claimant of his rights in the original asset. For Peter, the claimant's rights in relation to the proceeds arose to reverse an unjust enrichment.[41] Now take the case in which the defendant did not dispose entirely of the claimant's asset. Instead, he disposed of a half share in it, or of a time-limited interest in it, such as a lease for five years. What is true of the whole should be true also of a part: again, the claimant can lay claim to those proceeds. And if the first case is explained by unjust enrichment, so is the second.

But now suddenly see how close we are to the *Kentucky Caves* case.[42] The defendant Edwards invited strangers to trespass on the land of the claimant Lee. Indeed he charged them money for it, since the land in question included a beautiful cave, the entrance to which was on the defendant's land. He was forced to give up the relevant proportion of his gain. It is a classic case of a gain-based award for a wrong.[43] But it can also be viewed as a claim to traceable proceeds. It is a disposal by the defendant of part of the bundle of rights that make up the claimant's assets. The profits are a traceable product. And for Peter, if it was a claim to traceable proceeds, it was therefore a claim in subtractive unjust enrichment:

If investment of the whole value of another's asset—selling it—can later give that other the traceable substitute, exactly the same must apply to the investment of the user of another's asset—hiring it out. Mr. Edwards exploited the user of Mr. Lee's land and turned it into money. If the right of ownership attributes the earning opportunities of an

---

[40] It is different if the equitable rights are transferred directly to the defendant. That lines up with other property transfer cases.   [41] Birks (n 8 above) 377–85; Birks (n 3 above) 198–201.

[42] *Edwards v Lee's Administrators*, 96 SW2d 1028 (Ky CA, 1936).

[43] J Edelman, *Gain-Based Damages* (2002) 40.

asset to its owner, the same must be true of the earning opportunities inherent in the user of land. Hence, it must be true that Mr. Lee could have secured his award without relying on the facts in their character as a trespass but analysing them instead as an unjust enrichment at his expense in the subtractive sense.[44]

Not only should the claimant have a right to them, he should have a right *in* them; a proprietary right, as in the core case of claiming proceeds. Peter's approach also allows an unjust enrichment explanation for an *obiter dictum* of Lord Mansfield in *Hambly v Trott*.[45] Lord Mansfield suggested that there can be a claim in money had and received where the defendant uses the claimant's chattel without consent, and so derives a benefit, but without causing any loss.[46] This is perhaps a further step away from the core case of asset substitution, but it can be viewed in the same way. It is further than the *Kentucky Caves* case because now the gain is abstract and not particular; but that is not relevant in claims in unjust enrichment.[47] It is a gainful taking of part of what belongs to the claimant.

Peter also pointed to *Jones & Sons (Trustee) v Jones*.[48] In this case, the defendant acquired £11,700 belonging to the claimant and successfully invested it. She turned it into £50,760 sitting to her credit in a deposit account. The claimant, represented by the Official Receiver as insolvency officer, demanded this sum from the deposit account creditor. The creditor interpleaded and paid into court. The Court held that the claimant had a common law claim against the defendant in the amount of £50,760. Clearly, the value of the claim exceeded the claimant's deprivation.

It was in order to generalize across these cases, as cases of unjust enrichment, that Peter concluded that no deprivation need be shown by a claimant.

Relinquishment in Claims to Proceeds?

He might alternatively have brought them under the rubric of his doctrine of elective relinquishment. He deployed that doctrine to explain how a claimant could make a claim in unjust enrichment to the capital value of his asset, even if the claimant's rights never passed into the wealth of the defendant. Similarly, in making a claim to the exchange product of the claimant's asset, the claimant

---

[44] Birks (n 18 above) 510. This part of Peter's argument is also identified as a critical move by Grantham and Rickett (n 18 above) 173–4 and McInnes (n 18 above) 710–11. It appears in the online version of the article (n 18 above), which is essentially the same as the version published on paper. I have on file the draft of the paper given by Peter at the conference in 1999, and this argument does not appear in that text. The widening of Peter's conception of autonomous unjust enrichment can perhaps therefore be dated to between April 1999 (the date of the conference) and early 2000 (when the paper was published online).

[45] *Hambly v Trott* (1776) 1 Cowp 371, 98 ER 1136, KB, at 375, 1138.

[46] Compare Lord Shaw in *Watson, Laidlaw & Co Ltd v Pott, Cassels, and Williamson* (1914) 31 RPC 104, HL, at 119, contemplating a substantial award in such a case, but as a matter of 'recompense' for the infringement of the claimant's property right.

[47] Although it raises a difficulty about proprietary remedies, to which we will return.

[48] *Jones & Sons (Trustee) v Jones* [1997] Ch 159, CA.

could be seen to abandon his own rights in the original asset (and perhaps in the substitute as well, if he was claiming only the capital value of the substitute in money).[49] German law does something like this, in allowing personal claims measured by the value of traceable proceeds. If the defendant is in possession of something that belongs to the claimant, this in itself does not generate a claim in unjust enrichment; enrichment is legally prevented.[50] Assume that the defendant transfers possession of that asset of the claimant to a third party in exchange for proceeds. Now the defendant has acquired an enrichment that belongs to the defendant. Can the claimant sue the defendant in unjust enrichment? If (owing to the rules that protect good faith purchasers) the defendant's disposition was effective to divest the claimant of his original rights, then the enrichment of the defendant (by acquiring the proceeds) corresponds to the simultaneous deprivation of the claimant (by the loss of his original asset); a personal claim in unjust enrichment is available, to the proceeds or their value in money.[51] What if the defendant's disposition of the claimant's asset was legally ineffective? In this case, the defendant's enrichment (by acquiring the proceeds) does not correspond to a deprivation of the claimant; rather, it corresponds to a deprivation of the third party who transferred those proceeds and received no rights in return. The claimant in such a case retains his pre-existing rights, which can be asserted against the third party; unjust enrichment is legally prevented. But there is a further possibility. The General Part of the BGB (Civil Code) has a Title dealing generally with consent to legal transactions. §§ 184–5 provide in part:

184 [Retroactive effect of ratification] (1) Subsequent assent (ratification) operates from the moment when the legal transaction was entered into, unless otherwise provided . . .

185 [Disposal by unauthorized person] (1) A disposition affecting an object which is made by a person without title, if made with the approval of the person entitled, is effective.

(2) The disposition is valid if the person entitled ratifies it [and in two other cases].[52]

§ 185(2) means that an unauthorized and legally ineffective disposal of the claimant's asset can be authorized after the fact, even if there was no prior relationship between the claimant and the one making the disposal. If the claimant ratifies the defendant's disposition under § 185(2), then the defendant's

---

[49] If the claimant lost his rights in the original asset when the defendant disposed of it (say by a rule protecting bona fide purchasers), there is no need for any theory of renunciation. The claimant lost his rights at that moment, and at the same moment and in the same transaction, the defendant was enriched by the acquisition of the proceeds. This is a clear case of enrichment and corresponding deprivation, even though it occurs later than the time at which the defendant acquired the claimant's asset (nn 11, 39 above). The common law tradition, however, allows claims to proceeds whether or not the original rights have been lost, so the explanation must include the case where they have not been lost.   [50] Section 2.1 above.
[51] BS Markesinis, W Lorenz, and G Dannemann, *The Law of Contracts and Restitution: A Comparative Introduction*, ed BS Markesinis, vol I, *The German Law of Obligations* (1997) 747–8.
[52] This translation is in *The German Civil Code*, trans SL Goren (1994) 28.

enrichment (by the receipt of the proceeds) corresponds to the claimant's loss (by his own choice) of the original asset. German enrichment law will provide a personal claim to the proceeds or their value in money.[53]

The common law does not allow ratification, in the true sense, of such a transfer. If the disposition was made by an agent who was acting as an authorized agent, it is effective, even if the person with whom the agent dealt was unaware of the agency. If the disposition was made by someone purporting to act as an agent in dealings with the third party, but in reality lacking authority, ratification with retroactive effect by the principal is allowed. Here an authority is supplied that was absent, but that the agent purported and claimed to possess. But the common law draws a line where the agent neither had any authority, nor was purporting to have authority, to act as an agent. In that case there can be no ratification.[54] It would be fictional to use the consent-based concept of authority to regulate the effects of a transaction that had not a whiff of consent about it. At least one German writer describes the rule in BGB § 185 as fictional.[55] It would be fictional if the understanding was that the claimant's rights in the substitute are explicable on the basis of the claimant's consent to the substitution. The inherent difficulty of fictions is that they have no logical stopping place. Peter knew better than anyone that once you let slip the mooring line between a concept and its underlying factual reality, the concept, adrift, could go almost anywhere. But no one would want to explain the obligation to compensate for negligent personal injury on the basis that the claimant retroactively consents to the injury in exchange for a right to damages. Rights (and powers) arising by operation of law need to be explained without reference to consent.

The German principle is not fictional if it is understood as an election. The claimant, we assume, is still the owner of the original asset.[56] She is simply allowed to choose between taking the original or taking the proceeds.[57] In the common law, the cases support the idea that this is an election and not a true ratification.[58]

[53] Markesinis *et al* (n 51 above); R Zimmermann and J du Plessis, 'Basic Features of the German Law of Unjustified Enrichment' [1994] RLR 14, 28.
[54] *Falcke v Scottish Imperial Insurance Co* (1886), 34 ChD 234, CA, at 249–50; *Keighley, Maxsted & Co v Durant* [1901] AC 240, HL; Birks (n 8 above) 315.
[55] P Schlechtriem, 'Unjust Enrichment by Interference with Property Rights' in P Schlechtriem (ed), *Restitution—Unjust Enrichment and Negotiorum Gestio*, International Encyclopedia of Comparative Law, vol X (2001). [56] See n 49 above.
[57] In German law it seems that the choice to take the proceeds can be made conditional upon receipt of the proceeds, or can be delayed until the moment of receipt of the proceeds: Markesinis *et al* (n 51 above); Zimmermann and du Plessis (n 53 above). This underlines the character of the choice as an election between alternative recourses, and not as a substantive approval of or consent to the substitution. It recalls the rule discussed earlier (Section 2.1. above) that the payment of damages that compensate for the taking of the claimant's thing leads to the transfer of the claimant's rights in the thing to the defendant.
[58] *Taylor v Plumer* (1815) 3 M & S 562, 105 ER 721, KB, at 579–80, 724–5; *Marsh v Keating* (1834) 2 Cl & Fin 250, 6 ER 1149, 8 Bligh (NS) 651, 5 ER 1084, 1 Bing (NC) 198, 131 ER 1094, HL; *Lipkin Gorman (a firm) v Karpnale Ltd* [1991] 2 AC 548, HL, at 573; *Boscawen v Bajwa* [1996] 1 WLR 328, CA, at 341–2.

In this perspective, it is rather like obtaining a money award as compensation for the taking of a thing. When the money award is paid, the claimant's rights in the thing are lost. By abandoning the idea of true ratification based upon the claimant's consent to the substitution, we avoid fiction; but we leave ourselves still in need of an explanation. Why should the claimant have a choice to take the proceeds? The ability to claim the original asset is obvious. Why should the claimant be allowed to claim the proceeds? *If* the claimant is entitled to relinquish and abandon the original rights, with effect from the time of the substitution transaction, then the acquisition of the proceeds can certainly be seen as an unjust enrichment: the defendant is enriched (by the receipt of the proceeds) and the claimant has suffered a corresponding deprivation (by the loss of the original asset). But this brings us back to the original difficulty with the theory of elective relinquishment. Why should the claimant be allowed to relinquish the asset, in a way that perfects a cause of action that supposedly does not depend upon consent? In the original deployment of this idea, in the context of personal claims to the receipt of trust property, Peter envisioned a relinquishment that was retroactive to the moment of receipt by the defendant. If the same idea is to apply to substitutions, as in German law, it needs to be possible to relinquish retroactively, but not to the moment of receipt; only to the moment of the substitution. Although the exercise of such a power will create an unjust enrichment, what is needed is an explanation as to why such a power would arise. It seems that such an explanation must come from outside of unjust enrichment, in order to avoid a logical circle.

Geometric Multiplication

If one adopts the approach that deprivation of the claimant need not be shown, then the issue of how and when the claimant relinquishes its rights in the original asset seems less important. The defendant is enriched by the acquisition of the proceeds from a third party, and relinquishment might seem less important than in a two-party case, where it is essential to establish enrichment. In turn, however, this raises another issue. In the *Introduction*, Peter identified the problem he called 'geometric multiplication'.[59] A person cannot have his asset back, *and* the traceable product.[60] He proposed that the way to solve this was by the idea that a claimant does not have a vested right *in* traceable proceeds, but rather only a power to vest such rights in himself. In *Unjust Enrichment*, he continued to take the view that any other approach, even if combined with a requirement of election between inconsistent claims, would cause grave difficulties.[61]

This might seem inconsistent with the idea that no deprivation is required. On the view that any gain made from my property is 'from' me in the sense

---

[59] Birks (n 8 above) 393–4.
[60] In French, the equivalent to the English expression 'you cannot have your cake and eat it too' is 'you cannot have the butter and the money for the butter'.   [61] Birks (n 3 above) 198–9.

required to support a claim to that gain in unjust enrichment, it would appear that I should be allowed to claim both my original property, if my original rights subsist, *and* the traceable proceeds, in whatever generation of substitution, on the basis that they came 'from' me in the required sense. And yet Peter clearly thought that a claimant could not have both his asset and its proceeds. This is the converse of the point raised above. I have argued that the claimant's *ability* to choose the traceable proceeds needs an explanation from outside of the law of unjust enrichment. If unjust enrichment does not require any deprivation on the part of the claimant, then that explanation also needs to say why the claimant is *required* to choose between his asset and its proceeds, and is not allowed to have both.

Tracing Rules

In the previous sections, I have suggested that Peter's view of the structure of unjust enrichment law was shaped in large measure by his understanding of the law of tracing, broadly understood. This section makes a converse argument, that Peter's understanding of the law of unjust enrichment had implications for his view of the rules for tracing. The point, however, is ultimately the same: Peter's view that claims to traceable proceeds are claims in unjust enrichment meant that the two must be aligned.

We have seen that Peter observed that the law has two conceptions of wealth, the abstract (used by the law of unjust enrichment) and the particular (rights of property have a particular subject-matter). To the extent that rights of property come from unjust enrichment, there is inevitably a tension. In *Unjust Enrichment*, there is a suggestion that the dominance of the abstract conception should infiltrate the rules of tracing. 'The law relating to traceable substitutes of assets received also supposes that enrichment survives, not in the level of the abstract fund, but in particular assets in which the value of the original is re-invested.'[62] The text before and after this sentence makes it clear that he thought that in this regard, the law relating to traceable substitutes is barking up the wrong tree.[63] It operates in a way that is opposed to the dominance of the abstract view, which Peter viewed as the right approach for the law of unjust enrichment; and for the time being, the law was struggling to ensure the dominance of the abstract view via the defence of change of position.

The implication, on my reading, is that the rules of tracing need to be changed so that the dominance of the abstract approach is reflected there as well. This would mean that the dominance of the abstract approach would be in evidence,

---

[62] Birks (n 3 above) 70.

[63] Just before, he says that the common law of unjust enrichment has made an intuitive commitment to the abstract conception of wealth. Then there is the sentence in the text, along with a mention of the law of rescission. After the sentence in the text, he goes on to say that '. . . the law is currently struggling, at the level of defences, to ensure that the discrete conception of wealth is always ultimately trumped by the abstract conception'.

not just at the level of defences, but also at the level of claims that can be made. The traditional tracing rules are transactional: they look for exchange transactions, or their functional equivalent. This reflects the particular, and not the abstract, conception of wealth. Peter's arguments about the dominance of the abstract conception imply that the tracing rules should not be transactional, but causal. If those rules looked for causal outputs, rather than transactional outputs, they would reflect the dominance of the abstract approach.

Recall the example given above: the defendant acquires money in which the claimant has equitable rights under a trust. The defendant uses that money to acquire a car, but we know that the defendant was, in any event, going to acquire that car. We also know that the defendant, as a result of acquiring the money in which the claimant had an interest, set aside the money that he *would have* otherwise used to buy the car, and instead donated this money to a charity. Let us assume that this charitable donation qualifies as a change of position. Applying causal tracing rules, we would say that there is no traceable product held by the defendant; the causally traceable product was handed over to the charity. In this way, the defences would not have to do all the work. The dominance of the abstract approach would be present at the level of possible claims.

Peter knew that this would be a radical change to the law of tracing.[64] As we have observed, the difficulty arises because property rights always have a particular subject-matter. The law of unjust enrichment uses the abstract conception of wealth. If it creates property rights, it will create claims that have a particular subject-matter. The particularity of these claims will potentially conflict with the abstract conception of wealth used by unjust enrichment.

Consider the following case. A defendant is in possession of money in which the claimant has an equitable interest under a trust. The defendant uses it to pay his arrears of rent (the landlord being in good faith). Assume that the facts are such that the claimant would be able to assert equitable rights in any traceable proceeds. There are no traceable proceeds according to the traditional transactional tracing rules. Let it be assumed that we can identify the sum of money that the defendant *would have* used to pay his rent, had he not acquired the trust money. Causally speaking, this is the product of the claimant's trust money. If the abstract conception dominates, the claimant should be able to assert an equitable proprietary claim to the sum we have identified. In this way, the dominance of the abstract conception would be recognized at the level of claims.

---

[64] The disagreement in *Foskett v McKeown* [2001] 1 AC 102, HL was over exactly this point. The dissenters thought that the misappropriated trust money could not be traced into the life assurance payout because it was not a but-for cause of that payout. The majority, following the approach in the whole corpus of decisions across the common law world, applied a transactional approach. Others who have argued in favour of causal tracing rules include DA Oesterle, 'Deficiencies of the Restitutionary Right to Trace Misappropriated Property in Equity and in UCC § 9–306' (1983) 68 Cornell L Rev 172; C Rotherham, 'The Metaphysics of Tracing: Substituted Title and Property Rhetoric' (1996) 34 Osgoode Hall LJ 321; S Evans, 'Rethinking Tracing and the Law of Restitution' (1999) 115 LQR 469.

In other words, the abstract conception would be allowed to dominate, not only by denying claims in the right circumstances, but by allowing them as well.

But this will not be enough. It is conceivable that later still, the defendant makes some expenditure of *other* property in a way that should count as a change of position.[65] So even if the tracing rules were causal, it would not be enough. The grant of proprietary rights in some particular asset inevitably conflicts with the goal of making the abstract conception of wealth dominant. The dominance of the abstract conception would have to be guaranteed by allowing the defences to trump proprietary claims, even if the claims themselves were created according to causal tracing rules that reflect the abstract conception.

Consider one other example. It is the same as the last one, except that we cannot identify any asset as that which the defendant *would have* used to pay his rent, had he not been in possession of the claimant's assets. On the causal or abstract approach, the defendant has been enriched; there is an abstract increase in the defendant's net worth. Moreover, all the facts are in place that would allow the claimant to assert equitable proprietary rights in any proceeds that we could identify. Can the claimant assert equitable proprietary rights? One answer would be that he cannot, in the absence of being able to identify any particular subject-matter for those rights. But this would be to allow the particular approach to prevail over the abstract. It is only in the particular sense that we cannot identify any enrichment. Another approach would be to say that the claimant has a kind of floating interest over all the defendant's assets. This is a phenomenon that is known in consensual security, but not in property rights arising by operation of law. Even when granted consensually, it is in fact particular: it is a consensual grant of rights in all of the particular assets fitting a description.[66] Granted by the law, to give the effect of a proprietary right while implementing the abstract conception of wealth, it could not be tied to any particular asset or assets. It looks more like a preferential ordering of a debt than a proprietary right. But this is where we are seemingly led if we insist that (a) the law of unjust enrichment employs the abstract conception of wealth, *and* (b) the law of unjust enrichment sometimes grants proprietary rights. The end point is that the law of unjust enrichment has to grant 'abstract proprietary rights', proprietary rights without a subject-matter. Any other solution, including one that could accommodate the existing transactional tracing rules, would need to find the source of those proprietary rights in another principle. It would need to be a principle that was focused on the particular conception of wealth.

Reasons for Restitution

In this final section, I address one aspect of Peter's abandonment of reasons for restitution. Here I am not arguing that his views about unjust enrichment generally influenced his views about the law of claims to traceable proceeds, nor the reverse.

---

[65] Smith (n 13 above) 317–18.   [66] Nolan (n 37 above).

I only note that that the abandonment of reasons for restitution made it easier to sustain the view that claims to traceable proceeds are claims in unjust enrichment.

If a claim to the proceeds of an unauthorized disposition is a claim in unjust enrichment, then according to the traditional common law approach to such claims, a reason for restitution is required. For many years, Peter argued that 'ignorance' and 'powerlessness' must be reasons for restitution, even though they have not been recognized as such in the cases.[67] If a payment made by the claimant under a mistake constitutes an unjust enrichment, then even stronger is the case of an enrichment at the expense of the claimant that occurs without the claimant's awareness. This was Peter's *a fortiori* argument for ignorance as a reason for restitution. A similar argument could be made for powerlessness: if wealth is taken from a claimant who is aware but powerless to intervene, this is a stronger case for recovery than compulsion or mistake. Peter argued that the reason for restitution in cases of claims to traceable proceeds could be understood in these terms. In most cases it would be ignorance, since usually the claimant is not aware of the unauthorized disposition until later.

These arguments in favour of powerlessness and ignorance seem very strong as a matter of logic. At the same time, when they have allowed claims to traceable proceeds over the years, judges have never addressed the issue in these terms. There has never been any identification of a reason for restitution, or even a suggestion that one is needed. In this sense there was always a certain lack of fit between Peter's understanding of these cases and the reasons for judgment given by the judges. The abandonment of reasons for restitution goes some way towards resolving that. I do not suggest that Peter's decision to abandon reasons for restitution was motivated by a desire to address this lack of fit. I merely observe that the argument that claims to traceable proceeds are based on unjust enrichment does seem to be somewhat easier to sustain in a world where reasons for restitution do not need to be identified.

3.3. Unjust Enrichment and Tracing

Peter's insight that the process of tracing is analytically separate from the question of what claims can be made to or in respect of traceable proceeds had an enormous influence on my understanding of the law.[68] I had more difficulty in following the argument that all claims to the proceeds of unauthorized dispositions, or for their receipt, are claims in unjust enrichment. Those cases seemed to have features that did not line up with the core cases of unjust enrichment, cases like the mistaken

---

[67] See Birks (n 8 above) 140–6, under the heading 'ignorance' but including (at 141) powerlessness, on which see also 174; P Birks, 'Misdirected Funds: Restitution from the Recipient' [1989] LMCLQ 296, 305–10, 339; P Birks, 'The English Recognition of Unjust Enrichment' [1991] LMCLQ 473, 482–3; P Birks, *Restitution—The Future* (1992) 6, 27–8, 31, 40–1; P Birks, 'Unjust Enrichment and Wrongful Enrichment' (2001) 79 Tex L Rev 1767, 1793.

[68] Birks (n 8 above) 358.

payment. In claims for receipt of trust property, the claimant retains his original rights. This might also be true in claims to traceable proceeds; and in those claims, the subject-matter of the claim did not come from the claimant but from a third party. There did not seem to be any subtraction from the claimant's wealth, at least in the usual sense. Moreover, the transactional nature of the tracing rules did not seem to line up with the way in which enrichments are usually understood in unjust enrichment. Finally, in such claims there was no search for any reason for restitution. In Peter's final vision for the law of unjust enrichment, none of these objections is serious. A claimant can renounce his rights to satisfy the requirement of the defendant's enrichment. Claimants do not need to show any deprivation, nor any reason for restitution. And the transactional tracing rules appear to be out of place and in need of reform.

4. Conclusion

I also remember well my final meeting with Peter, in May 2004. After lunch we said goodbye outside Blackwell's. He disappeared into the crowd on Broad Street, in the heart of his beloved Oxford.

His scholarship leaves us many legacies. One of them is his openness to the lessons and experiences of other legal systems. 'Nationalism is always out of place in legal thought and argument. When it does push in, it always strikes a note which is either absurd or repulsive or both.'[69] His intellectual perseverance is another. Charles Darwin was one of Peter's intellectual models. I wonder if this was in part because when Darwin sailed from England on the *Beagle* in 1831, his plan was to become a country parson upon his return. It was by setting aside his preconceptions, and by following his observations to their logical conclusions, that Darwin developed his theory of natural selection and changed the course of human understanding. Peter also had the perseverance and the courage to follow his ideas where they led him.

Perhaps most strikingly of all, Peter aimed high. His scholarship was ambitious, although not in any personal sense. It was my honour to introduce Peter when he gave the Annual Lecture on Jurisprudence and Public Policy at McGill University in 2002. In my introduction I said that he was a master of Roman law and of the common law. As soon as he was on his feet, he said that he did not like to be called a master of anything. Of course, he was, but he had the humility of the genuine scholar. Peter's aspirations were not personal ones. His aspiration for private law was that it should be transparently rational. His aspiration for his own scholarship was that it should help the law to become so. Although our gifts may be less than Peter's, we can strive towards the same goals.

---

[69] Birks (n 3 above) 128.

8

Gain-Based Damages and Compensation

*James Edelman**

1. Introduction

I first met Peter on 20 June 1996. I was an undergraduate student at the University of Western Australia and Peter was visiting to deliver three lectures entitled 'Equity in the Modern Law: An Exercise in Taxonomy'.[1] I distinctly remember two things about his lectures. The first was his distinctive style. He held the audience completely captive from his first word until his last. Every word was carefully chosen. At the end of the first lecture the opening question was perceptive but aggressive. Peter was silent for almost a minute before politely delivering a carefully structured, devastating reply. Secondly, and more generally, I remember being struck by his courage. In a country where four of the finest judges, Justices Meagher, Gummow, Lehane, and Finn, were staunch defenders of the independence of equity, Peter advocated a taxonomy that integrated equitable rights, with their origins in the courts of Chancery, into categories to be treated alongside common law rights.

Over the seven years that I knew Peter as (consecutively) a lecturer, a supervisor, a mentor, and friend, I learned that my first impressions of him were an intractable part of his nature. I witnessed his attention to detail in supervisions which often involved long silences as he crafted a perfect answer; his passion for the law in his instant replies to emailed questions sent at 2 o'clock in the morning; and his courage in his pursuit of truth no matter what the cost. Indeed, Peter's courageous views on equity were the subject of the final conversation that I had with him in person more than seven years after I had first heard him speak. Over breakfast in Oxford, Peter spoke of a paper that he had agreed to give at a conference I was

---

* Fellow and Tutor in Law, Keble College, Oxford; Adjunct Professor, University of Western Australia. This essay benefited greatly from discussion with, and comments by, Andrew Burrows, Ralph Cunnington, Lionel Smith, and Robert Stevens.

[1] Published as P Birks, 'Equity in the Modern Law: An Exercise in Taxonomy' (1996) 26 UWA L Rev 1.

co-organizing at the end of the year. His title, which left little to the imagination, was 'The Curse of Duality'. He told me that provided he was well enough to fly he would deliver the paper to an audience that he expected to be particularly hostile. With a glint in his eye he said he would come in a Sherman tank.

In his preface to *Bracton's Note Book*,[2] Professor Maitland wrote that '[t]wice in the history of England has an Englishman had the motive, the courage, the power to write a reasonable book about English law as a whole'. Like Bracton and Blackstone, the ambition and effect of Peter's work on English law was motivated and powerful. But most of all, in challenging and refining their writings, and the great Roman jurists before them, Peter's work, like his life, was courageous. My contribution to this *gedenkschrift* seeks to honour that courage.

In this essay I deal with the issue upon which, for two years, I had the great privilege of Peter's supervision. I focus on three related themes. The first is a subject Peter addressed the first time that I heard him speak: 'damages' simply means a money award for a wrong. I did not have the courage to follow him unreservedly on this point in my doctoral thesis[3] although, later convinced, I did so in the book which developed from my thesis.[4] I will show that Peter's controversial view is correct from the point of view of precedent as well as principle.

The second theme uses this meaning of damages to explain the nature of gain-based damages in the law of wrongs. This theme was at the heart of my doctoral thesis: there is a fundamental difference between two different types of gain-based damages; one type aims to give back value wrongfully obtained from a claimant's assets or labour (*restitutionary* damages) whilst the other type aims to strip all profit wrongfully made irrespective of source (*disgorgement* damages). Recent cases have emphasized the distinction between these categories. In his final book, although still preferring a single label for the two measures, Peter wrote of the distinction between them as 'beyond contradiction . . . from the standpoint of both measure and rationale'.[5]

The final theme has emerged from a debate which takes as its premiss the separation of restitutionary damages from disgorgement damages. It relates to a fundamental question about the nature of awards of compensation and it considers the relationship between restitutionary damages and compensatory damages.

2. The Meaning of Damages

In the first sentence of the first English text on damages, Serjeant Joseph Sayer wrote that 'damages are a pecuniary recompense for an injury'.[6] Sayer did not

---

[2] FW Maitland (ed), *Bracton's Note Book: A Collection of Cases Decided in the King's Courts During the Reign of Henry the Third Annotated by a Lawyer of that Time, Seemingly by Henry of Bratton* (1887) 8.
[3] J Edelman, 'Gain-based *Awards* for Wrongdoing', unpublished DPhil thesis, University of Oxford, 2001 (emphasis added).   [4] J Edelman, *Gain-Based Damages* (2002).
[5] P Birks, *Unjust Enrichment* (2nd edn, 2005) 282.   [6] J Sayer, *The Law of Damages* (1760).

intend 'recompense' to mean 'compensation for loss'[7] because in a very early example he referred to a case in which it was 'laid down that in an action for account against a man as receiver of money to merchandize with, damages are recoverable for the profit which *has been made* or might have been made of the money'.[8]

An award of damages to strip a defendant of profit that has been made by the defendant is not compensation for the claimant's loss. We will see below that the developing trend is instead to describe these profit-stripping damages with the epithet 'disgorgement'. The word 'recompense', with its implied association with compensation, was not suitable nomenclature. A hundred years later, in the next English book on damages (which, in its seventeenth edition, is still the leading text on the subject today) Mayne avoided 'recompense' altogether.[9] Mayne defined damages as 'the pecuniary satisfaction which a plaintiff may obtain by success in an action'.[10] That definition was very nearly right. All difficulty would have been avoided if he had concluded the definition with the words 'for wrongdoing'. Without these words the definition did not distinguish between an action for a *secondary* right to damages and actions for enforcement of *primary* rights, such as a right to an agreed sum or an action for restitution of unjust enrichment.[11]

A further hundred years later, in 1962, the fifth editor of Mayne's classic text, Dr McGregor, spotted this deficiency. In an attempt to confine the definition of 'damages' to wrongdoing he defined them as 'the pecuniary compensation, obtainable by success in an action, for a wrong which is either a tort or a breach of contract'.[12] This introduced two major restrictions that had not existed previously. It confined damages to compensation and also to common law wrongdoing. In 2003, McGregor recognized that this definition was unworkable. In the first edition for almost 150 years to begin without a definition of damages, McGregor said that '[t]he impossible search for a clear-cut comprehensive definition is therefore abandoned'.[13] But, the two restrictions in McGregor's earlier definition, which correspond with prevailing understanding, could have still been abandoned by instead adopting a definition of damages as a money award for a wrong.

---

[7] Sir William Blackstone said that damages were an award 'given to a man by a jury, as a compensation and satisfaction for some injury sustained': W Blackstone, *Commentaries on the Law of England* (1766; 1979 facsimile University Chicago Press) vol 2 at 438.

[8] Citing 1 Rol Abr 575 Pl 27 (emphasis added).

[9] Possibly relying on the American text by Professor Sedgwick which had been published nine years earlier: T Sedgwick, *A Treatise of the Measure of Damages* (1874).

[10] J Mayne, *A Treatise on the Law of Damages: Comprising their Measure, the Mode in which they are Assessed and Reviewed, the Practice of Granting New Trials, and the Law of Set-off, and Compensation under the Land Clauses Act* (1856) 1.

[11] J Austin, *Lectures on Jurisprudence Vol II* (R Campbell (ed) 5th edn, 1885), Lecture XLV, 763; *Photo Production Ltd v Securicor Transport Ltd* [1980] AC 827 at 848–9.

[12] H McGregor, *Mayne and McGregor on Damages* (12th edn, 1961) at 3. This definition was adopted by Lord Hailsham LC in *Broome v Cassell & Co* [1972] AC 1027 at 1070.

[13] H McGregor, *McGregor on Damages* (17th edn, 2003) at 6 [1-008].

The two usual objections commonly brought to such a definition of damages correspond with the two restrictions in McGregor's earlier definition. Neither of them can be sustained. The first objection—that damages are synonymous with compensation—is usually accompanied by a reference to the classic judicial statement of the nature of compensatory damages by Lord Blackburn's in *Livingstone v Rawyards Coal Company.*[14] Yet, as we will see below, in *Livingstone v Rawyards Coal Company* itself, all of the Law Lords recognized that damages might be non-compensatory. Further, although the etymology of 'damages' is ambiguous,[15] the earliest legal usages of 'damages' included money awards of three times the loss suffered by the defendant which was plainly not a compensatory award.[16] Today we still have numerous species of non-compensatory damages: exemplary damages, nominal damages, contemptuous damages, and, as we will see below, restitutionary damages and disgorgement damages. The different descriptive epithets for damages correspond with different purposes or goals. As Lord Steyn said in *Smith New Court Securities Ltd v Scrimgeour Vickers (Asset Management) Ltd,*[17] the goals of tort law are not confined to compensation but extend to appeasement, deterrence, and justice.

The second objection to a definition of damages as a money award for wrongdoing is that such a definition is not confined to wrongdoing at *common law.*[18] This reflects the tradition of cautious use of the word 'damages' in equity. The first edition of Sir Arthur Underhill's *Underhill's Concise Guide to Equity,*[19] did not even acknowledge a jurisdiction to award damages in equity. Although other leading authors recognized this jurisdiction it was narrowly confined. Thus, the first edition of Edmund Snell's *The Principles of Equity*[20] and the first English edition of Joseph Story's classic American work on equity,[21] said that it was 'settled' that there can be no relief where *only* damages are sought in equity.[22]

---

[14] (1880) 5 App Cas 25 at 39. See *British Westinghouse Electric and Manufacturing Co Ltd v Underground Electric Railways Co of London Ltd* [1912] AC 673 at 689; *Tai Hing Cotton Mill Ltd v Kamsing Knitting Factory* [1979] AC 91 at 104; *Ruxley Electronics and Construction Ltd v Forsyth* [1996] AC 344 at 355, 365–6; *Dodd Properties (Kent) Ltd v Canterbury City Council* [1980] 1 WLR 433 at 451.

[15] Deriving perhaps from the Latin *damnum* or the French *domage*, which might suggest an association with loss: J Simpson and E Weiner (eds), *Oxford English Dictionary* (2nd edn, 1989) 224.

[16] *Act 8 Hen. VI*, c 9 (1430) 'Le pleyntif recovera ses damages au treble vers le defendant'. See also Statute of Gloucester, 1278, 6 Edw I, c 5 (treble damages for waste). The author of Note (1957) 70 HLR 517 observes that an even earlier example of multiple damages is Exodus 22: 9.

[17] [1997] AC 254.

[18] Most prominently H McGregor, *McGregor on Damages* (17th edn, 2003) at [1-008]; RP Meagher, JD Heydon, and MJ Leeming, *Equity Doctrines and Remedies* (4th edn, 2002) at 831 (in a chapter headed 'Damages in Equity').

[19] A Underhill, *A Concise Guide to Modern Equity* (1885).

[20] E Snell, *The Principles of Equity* (1868) at 475.

[21] W Grigsby (ed), *Commentaries on Equity Jurisprudence by Mr Justice Story* (1884) at 534–5.

[22] Snell cited for this curious proposition a case where damages *were* awarded in lieu of specific performance of an obligation to repair and install a spirit vault: *Middleton v Greenwood* (1864) 2 De G J and Sm 142 at 145; 46 ER 329 at 330. In 1880, the editor of the 5th edn took the step of removing 'damages' from the index.

It is true that equity had such a jurisdiction to award damages incidental to other equitable relief. Although there were doubts about the scope of that jurisdiction,[23] it was put beyond doubt in 1858 by Sir Hugh Cairns's Act.[24] It is now accepted that damages in equity pursuant to that Act are to be measured in the same way as they are at common law.[25] But this was not the limit of equity's jurisdiction to award damages.[26] In 1870, Sir John Stuart VC referred to a long line of authority which recognized damages in equity against negligent solicitors.[27] He said that 'although an action at law may be sustained and damages recovered against a solicitor for loss occasioned by the negligence in the discharge of his duty, this court in a proper case would give relief without sending the injured client to a court of law'.[28] The same was true in suits to recover damages for fraud. In *Peek v Gurney*,[29] Lord Chelmsford said that loss suffered as a result of fraudulent misrepresentations could be recovered by a suit in chancery; the proceeding in equity 'is precisely analogous to the common law action for deceit' and 'is a suit instituted to recover damages'.[30]

On many occasions equity courts would also make awards of compensatory damages without explicitly describing the award as such. For instance, when an action was brought by a beneficiary against a negligent trustee for loss suffered, equity courts usually ordered the trustee to account on the basis of wilful default.[31] Dr Elliott has shown that this process of accounting, which surcharged the account by the amount of loss arising from the trustee's negligence, is just compensatory damages by another name.[32] Other equitable labels for damages were 'equitable debt' or 'restitution'. In *Ex p Adamson*,[33]

---

[23] See *Cleaton v Gower* (1674) Fin 164; 23 ER 90; *Denton v Stewart* (1786) 17 Ves 280; 34 ER 108 and *Greenaway v Adams* (1806) 12 Ves 395; 33 ER 149, cut down by *Todd v Gee* (1810) 17 Ves 273; 34 ER 106 and *Jenkins v Parkinson* (1833) 2 My & K 5; 39 ER 846.

[24] *Chancery Amendment Act* 1858, 21 and 22 Vict c 27.

[25] *Johnson v Agnew* [1980] AC 367.

[26] cf *Corporation of Ludlow v Greenhouse* (1827) 1 Bligh (NS) 18 at 57–8; 4 ER 780 at 795 in which Lord Redesdale said that he was not aware of any case in which a court of Chancery had awarded damages for a breach of trust.

[27] See eg *Floyd v Nangle* (1747) 3 Atk 567; 26 ER 1127; *Dixon v Wilkinson* (1859) 4 De G & J 508 at 523; 45 ER 198 at 203. This negligence jurisdiction in equity was thought to have been abandoned by the late nineteenth century by Viscount Haldane LC in *Nocton v Lord Ashburton* [1914] AC 932 at 956. See further JD Heydon, 'Are the Duties of Company Directors to Exercise Skill and Care Fiduciary?' in S Degeling and J Edelman, *Equity in Commercial Law* (2005) ch 10.　　[28] *Chapman v Chapman* (1870) LR 9 Eq 276 at 294.

[29] (1873) LR 6 HL 377. Cf *Newham v May* (1824) 13 Price 749 at 752; 147 ER 1142 at 1143–4; *Ranelaugh v Hayes* (1683) 1 Vern 189 at 190; 23 ER 405 at 406.

[30] *Peek v Gurney* (1873) LR 6 HL 377, 390 at 393. See also *Ramshire v Bolton* (1869) 8 LR Eq 294; *Slim v Croucher* (1860) 1 De G F & J 518 at 524; 45 ER 462 at 466.

[31] D Yale, *Lord Nottingham's Chancery Cases* (vol 2 1961 Selden Soc) at 141.

[32] SB Elliott, 'Compensation Claims against Trustees' Oxford DPhil thesis, 2002; S Elliott and C Mitchell, 'Remedies for Dishonest Assistance' (2004) 67 MLR 16.

[33] (1878) 8 Ch D 807.

the defrauded claimant paid money to a partnership for a cotton venture which did not exist. James and Bagallay LJJ held that the individual partners and the firm were liable to the claimant for the amount of his payment: 'it has always been held in the Court of Chancery that for a fraud, as for a breach of trust, each participator is liable'.[34] But to meet the (misconceived and ahistorical) argument by counsel that the Court of Chancery had no jurisdiction to award damages for fraud, they said that the order was 'for an equitable debt or liability in the nature of a debt. It was a suit for the restitution of the actual money or thing, or value of the thing.' This is mere sophistry. It would have made things far clearer for the majority to have rejected the argument that equity did not make awards of damages and to have said, as Brightman LJ did in *Bartlett v Barclays Bank Trust Co Ltd*,[35] that 'the so-called restitution which the defendant must now make... is in reality compensation for loss... not readily distinguishable from damages except with the aid of a powerful legal microscope'.[36]

Although the modern trend is to refer to compensatory awards in equity as 'equitable compensation' rather than 'compensatory damages',[37] some recent English cases have referred to compensatory money awards in equity as 'damages'.[38] This is a more coherent approach, consistent with a meaning of damages simply as a money award for wrongdoing. Indeed, the only justification ever advanced for withholding the label damages from the varied types of *equitable* wrongdoing was that money awards in equity were determined by judges rather than juries.[39] But juries rarely determine damages at common law and the label 'damages' survives.

With neither principle nor authority to prevent recognition that (1) damages include money awards for wrongdoing in equity and (2) damages are not limited to compensation, we then arrive at a definition very close to that used 250 years ago: damages are a money award for wrongdoing.

---

[34] (1878) 8 Ch D 807 at 819.

[35] *Bartlett v Barclays Bank Trust Co Ltd (No 2)* [1980] Ch 515.

[36] ibid at 545.

[37] It has been observed by some judges that this is a 'distinction without a difference'. See *Acquaculture Corporation v New Zealand Green Mussel Co Ltd* [1990] 3 NZLR 299 at 301 (Cooke P); *Bristol & West Building Society v Mothew* [1998] Ch 1 at 17 (Millett LJ); *Base Metal Trading Ltd v Shamurin* [2004] EWCA (Civ) 1316 at [19] (Tuckey LJ).

[38] *Personal Representatives of Tang Man Sit v Capacious Investments Ltd* [1996] AC 514 at 520; *Bristol & West Building Society v Mothew* [1998] Ch 1 at 17; *Cia de Seguros Imperiod v Heath (REBX) Ltd* [2001] 1 WLR 112 (CA) at 125; *Walsh v Deloitte & Touche Inc* [2001] UKPC 37 at [7]. See also *Re Lake* [1903] 1 KB 439 at 443; *Brickenden v London Loan & Savings Co* [1934] 3 DLR 465 at 469–70; *Ahmed Angullia bin Hadjee Mohamed Salleh Angullia v Estate and Trust Agencies (1927) Limited* [1938] AC 624 at 637.

[39] W Grigsby (ed), *Commentaries on Equity Jurisprudence by Mr Justice Story* (1884) 534. E Coke, *Institutes of the Laws of England* (1642) s 257a; W Blackstone, *Commentaries on the Law of England* (1766) vol 2 at 438. See *Clifford v Brooke* 13 Ves 130, 131, 134; *Blore v Sutton* (1817) 3 Meriv 237 at 248; 36 ER 91 at 95; *Newham v May* (1824) 13 Price 749 at 752; 147 ER 1142 at 1144.

3. Disgorgement Damages and Restitutionary Damages

3.1. Disgorgement Damages

We saw above that the common law has long recognized awards of damages with non-compensatory purposes. We also saw, as Sayer observed, that common law damages were sometimes awarded to disgorge profits from a wrongdoing defendant. This principle has a long history. Although the award of damages was usually left to the jury, as Bracton observed in relation to novel disseisin in the thirteenth century, judges could increase the damages given by the jury to ensure that a wrongdoer did not profit from the wrong.[40]

A classic illustration of disgorgement damages is *Livingstone v Rawyards Coal Company*[41] which, we saw above, also contains the classic statement of how compensatory damages are measured in tort. The defendant had mined for coal under the claimant's land, mistakenly thinking that it had a right to do so. When the claimant realized that the defendant had no such right he sought disgorgement of the value of the coal obtained by the defendant. Although the claim was refused, all the Law Lords in that case said that if the defendant had acted dishonestly (with 'bad faith or sinister intention'[42]) the defendant would have been ordered to disgorge the market value of the coal in the defendant's hands less expenses (in other words, the profit from the tort).

These profit-stripping damages are not confined to the tort of trespass to land. They are well recognized for torts of trademark infringement or passing off[43] where the infringement is wilful.[44] The broad proposition is put concisely in the United States *Restatement of Restitution*: 'If [the defendant] was consciously tortious in acquiring the benefit, he is also deprived of any profit derived from his subsequent dealing with it'.[45] Judging by the most recent tentative draft, it is very likely that the same position will be taken in the forthcoming United States *Restatement on Restitution (Third)*.[46]

---

[40] G Woodbine and S Thorne (trans), *Bracton on the Laws and Customs of England* (vol 3, 1977) 76: '*Quod quidem non expedit ut praedictum est si disseisitor de damno alieno lucrum reportaret.*'

[41] (1880) 5 App Cas 25 at 39. See *British Westinghouse Electric and Manufacturing Co Ltd v Underground Electric Railways Co of London Ltd* [1912] AC 673 at 689; *Tai Hing Cotton Mill Ltd v Kamsing Knitting Factory* [1979] AC 91 at 104; *Ruxley Electronics and Construction Ltd v Forsyth* [1996] AC 344 at 355, 365–6; *Dodd Properties (Kent) Ltd v Canterbury City Council* [1980] 1 WLR 433 at 451.

[42] (1880) 5 App Cas 25 at 31 (Earl Cairns LC), 34 (Lord Hatherley), 39 (Lord Blackburn).

[43] *Edelsten v Edelsten* (1862) 31 Beav 292 at 298; 54 ER 1151 at 1153; *Hall v Barrows* (1863) 1 De G J & S 150; 46 ER 873.

[44] *Moet v Couston* (1864) 33 Beav 578; 55 ER 493; *AG Spalding & Bros v AW Gamage Ltd* (1915) 32 RPC 273 at 283.

[45] American Law Institute, *Restatement of the Law of Restitution: Quasi Contracts and Constructive Trusts* (1937) Introductory note to ch 8, 595–6. See eg *Olwell v Nye & Nissen Co* 173 P 2d 652 (1946) 654.

[46] American Law Institute, *Restatement of the Law of Restitution and Unjust Enrichment*, Tentative Draft No 4 (April 2005) 41 'profits gained through conscious interference with protected rights are manifestly inequitable'.

Like *Livingstone,* older trespass cases described this profit-stripping measure simply as 'damages'[47] although others have used the language of the common count of 'money had and received'.[48] Fortunately, a more descriptive epithet is now emerging as judges and commentators begin to describe profit-stripping damages as 'disgorgement'[49] or, as a complete term, 'disgorgement damages'.[50]

Although disgorgement damages at common law have a strong historical footing, the lack of a descriptive epithet such as 'disgorgement' contrasts with the distinctive label 'account of profits' in equity[51] where disgorgement of profits is awarded for conscious or cynical wrongdoing such as breaches of confidence,[52] dishonest participation in a breach of fiduciary duty,[53] and even innocent breaches of fiduciary duty.[54] The lack of a distinctive nomenclature has sometimes led judges to consider that profit-stripping awards are not available for tortious wrongdoing at common law.[55] In *Halifax Building Society v Thomas,*[56] in *obiter dicta,* on a matter conceded by counsel, Peter Gibson LJ said that 'there is no decided authority that comes anywhere near allowing disgorgement of profits for the tort of deceit or fraud'. This is not correct. There is considerable authority at common law as well as in equity for the disgorgement of profits of

---

[47] *Powell v Aiken* (1858) 4 K & J 343, 351; 70 ER 144 at 147 (the award of 'damages' for trespass effected 'an account of profit realised . . . by the working of coal to give relief in respect of wrongs attended with profit to the wrongdoer' (Sir William Page Wood V-C); *Jegon v Vivian* (1871) LR 6 Ch App 742, 762 (The 'damages' award stripped profits because 'this Court never allows a man to make a profit by a wrong' (Lord Hatherley LC). See also *Attorney General v Blake* [2001] 1 AC 268 at 284 citing cases including *British Motor Trade Association v Gilbert* [1951] 2 All ER 641 for other awards of 'damages' which operated to strip profits.

[48] *Reading v Attorney General* [1951] AC 507; *Mahesan S/O Thambiah v Malaysian Government Officers Co-operative Housing Society* [1979] AC 374 at 376; *Armagas Ltd v Mundogas SA* [1986] AC 717 at 742–3 (Robert Goff LJ); decision aff'd [1986] 1 AC 717; *Petrotrade Inc v Smith* [2000] 1 Lloyds Rep 486 at 490; *Federal Sugar Refining Co v US Sugar Equalization Board Inc* (1920) 268 F 575 (DCNY).

[49] *Attorney General v Blake* [2001] 1 AC 268 at 291, 292; *United Pan-Europe Communications NV v Deutsche Bank AG* [2000] 2 BCLC 461 at [44]; *Kuwait Airways Corp v Iraqi Airways Co* [2004] EWHC 2603 at [387]; *Westminster City Council v Porter* [2002] EWHC 2179 (Ch) at [3]; *Mahonia Ltd v J P Morgan Chase Bank* [2004] EWHC 1938 at [223]; *Harris v Digital Pulse Pty Ltd* (2003) 56 NSWLR 298 at [362], [380], [404], [407]; *Dubai Aluminium Co Ltd v Salaam* [2003] 2 AC 366 at [50], [53], [62] (Lord Nicholls), [80], [81], [151]–[167] (Lord Millett). For examples of earlier usages of 'disgorgement' see L Smith, 'The Province of the Law of Restitution' (1992) 71 Canadian Bar Rev 672 at 696 n 99.

[50] Lord Millett, 'Book Review: Gain-Based Damages' [2003] 4 OUCLJ 55; *Hospitality Group Pty Ltd v Australian Rugby Union Ltd* [2001] FCA 1040; (2001) 110 FCR 157 at 196 [159] (Hill and Finkelstein JJ).

[51] This common reference to an 'account of profits' is misleading as the process of accounting is distinct from the disgorgement order stripping the profits: *Glazier v Australian Men's Health (No 2)* [2001] NSWSC 6 (22 January 2001) at [36].

[52] *Attorney General v Guardian Newspapers (No 2)* ('*Spycatcher*') [1990] 1 AC 19.

[53] *Cook v Deeks* [1916] AC 554.

[54] *Boardman v Phipps* [1967] 2 AC 46; *Regal (Hastings) Ltd v Gulliver* [1967] 2 AC 134.

[55] *Hospitality Group Pty Ltd v Australian Rugby Union Ltd* (2001) 110 FCR 157 at 197 [162] 'it is not possible to slot an account of profits into the general framework of remedies that are available in tort'.   [56] [1996] Ch 217 at 227.

deceit or fraud. As Lord Millett said in *Dubai Aluminium Company Ltd v Salaam*,[57] 'it is increasingly recognised today that the ends of justice sometimes go beyond compensating a plaintiff for his loss and may extend to stripping a defendant of his profits'. The common law authorities usually involved the fraudulent receipt of bribes by an agent purchasing goods for his principal. The courts often described these disgorgement damages as 'money had and received' to disgorge profits tortiously made by the agent.[58] Although some judges said that the basis of the award was an (irrebuttable) presumption that the money secretly paid to the agent was in reduction of the contract price, this was an obvious fiction because the claimant could still recover from the agent even if he had already recovered his loss from the vendor.[59] One recent case explicitly affirmed the availability of disgorgement of profits as a remedy for the tort of deceit (distinguishing the decision and remarks of Peter Gibson LJ),[60] although in the Court of Appeal it was said that the trial judge had intended to confine his remarks to breach of fiduciary duty.[61]

What all the cases of disgorgement damages have in common, whether at common law or in equity, is a goal of deterrence of wrongdoing. When the defendant's wrongful act is committed knowingly or cynically, disgorgement provides a measure of deterrence, both specific (to the wrongdoer) and generally (to others). Application of a rule that cynical wrongdoers must disgorge profits is one deterrent factor that the wrongdoer before the court (as well as others like him) will consider if the opportunity arises to profit from wrongdoing again. There are only three instances in which the law qualifies the broad rule that cynical wrongdoers must disgorge profits. The first is a statutory exception which has been interpreted to allow disgorgement of profits from a breach of copyright or design rights even where the breach is innocent.[62] The history of this statutory provision is based upon a now-rejected fiction that the profits of the defendant were 'owned' by the claimant and the provision is inconsistent with all other common law torts including all other intellectual property wrongs.[63] Deterrence of innocent breaches of copyright is not needed and is an anomaly that should be abolished. The second qualification is that disgorgement of profits is ordered for a breach of fiduciary duty even if the breach is innocent. This is not an anomaly. The order is justified in these cases because the trust and vulnerability inherent in the fiduciary relationship requires greater protection of the rights of the principal

---

[57] [2002] UKHL 48 at [164]; See also *Paragon Finance v D B Thackerar & Co* [1999] 1 All ER 400 at 409 (Millett LJ).
[58] eg *Hovenden v Millhoff* (1900) 83 LT 41 at 42. See also *Mahesan S/O Thambiah v Malaysian Government Officers Co-operative Housing Society* [1979] AC 374; *Petrotrade Inc v Smith* [2000] 1 Lloyds Rep 486; *Fyffes Group Ltd v Templeman* [2000] 2 Lloyds Rep 643.
[59] *Mayor, Aldermen and Burgesses of the Borough of Salford v Lever* [1891] 1 QB 168; *Grant v Gold Exploration and Development Syndicate* [1900] 1 QB 233 at 244 (AL Smith LJ).
[60] *Murad v Al Saraj* [2004] EWHC 1235.   [61] *Murad v Al Saraj* [2005] EWCA Civ 959.
[62] *Copyrights, Designs and Patents Act* 1988, s 97. See *Wienerworld Ltd v Vision Video Ltd* [1998] FSR 832.   [63] Edelman (n 4 above) 233–4.

by a higher degree of deterrence from breach. Fiduciaries must know that they cannot profit from any breach of their duties of loyalty, however innocent. The final qualification is in cases of breach of contract. Here, it seems that a cynical breach is not enough to justify disgorgement. Recent cases have insisted upon a 'legitimate interest' in preventing the defendant from profiting from the breach.[64] Whilst the meaning of 'legitimate interest' is not yet settled, the existence of a further limitation contrasts the wrong of breach of contract with breach of fiduciary duty. Whilst a higher level of deterrence for fiduciaries requires disgorgement even for innocent breaches, a lower level of deterrence for contracting parties means that even a cynical breach is not enough to require the deterrent order of disgorgement.

3.2. Restitutionary Damages

In 1998, Peter Birks explained that 'restitution' is a multi-causal response.[65] In other words, restitution is not confined to unjust enrichment but is also a response to other legal events. One of those is wrongdoing. When restitution is awarded for a wrong it has nothing to do with unjust enrichment.[66] The addition of the label 'damages' to 'restitution' signifies that restitutionary damages are a response to a legal or equitable wrong and not to unjust enrichment although in both cases restitution is made of a benefit that the defendant has obtained from the claimant's assets or labour. The goal of this award is not deterrence of wrongdoing (indeed, the wrongdoer in some strict liability wrongs may be wholly innocent) nor is it compensation for financial losses. In *Gain-Based Damages*[67] I described the rationale as Aristotelian corrective justice: reversing a transfer of value from the claimant to the defendant. As Lord Goff said, restitution operates to 'restore [both of] the parties to the position they were in before they entered the transaction . . . that is of course, the function of the law of restitution'.[68]

A good example of a decision on restitutionary damages is *Gondal v Dillon Newsagents Ltd*.[69] The Gondals acquired a sub-post office from Post Office Counters Ltd (POCL) and entered a three year sub-lease of premises (with a fifteen-year continuation lease) with Dillons Newsagents Ltd. After six months, an audit of the business showed a shortfall of £20,000. Mr Gondal was suspended as postmaster and POCL began running the business on his behalf

---

[64] *Attorney General v Blake* [2001] 1 AC 268; *Esso Petroleum Co Ltd v Niad* [2001] All ER (D) 324; *Experience Hendrix LLC v PPX Enterprises Inc* [2003] EWCA Civ 323; [2003] 1 All ER (Comm) 830.

[65] P Birks, 'Misnomer' in W Cornish, R Nolan, J O'Sullivan, and G Virgo, *Restitution: Past Present and Future* (1998) at 1.   [66] Birks (above, n 5) 13.

[67] Edelman (above, n 4) at 80, quoting L Fuller and W Perdue, 'The Reliance Interest in Contract Damages' (1936) 46 Yale LJ 52 at 56.

[68] *Westdeutsche Landesbank Girozentrale v Islington LBC* [1996] AC 669 at 681 (Lord Goff).

[69] [2001] RLR 221.

while the business was for sale. A prospective purchaser, Postal Management Services, offered £5,000 but the Gondals rejected this, seeking an entirely unrealistic £125,000. Dillons notified the Gondals that they were in breach of their lease by having parted with possession of the premises without consent and Dillons then retook possession and installed Mr Moore from Postal Management Services as postmaster. But due to defects in service of their notice, when Dillons retook possession the lease was still on foot. The Gondals sued Dillons and Mr Moore (the new postmaster) for trespass. The Gondals sought restitutionary damages. The trial judge held that the defendants had wrongfully (although innocently) obtained the benefit of the use of the premises during their period of occupation but had not obtained the benefit of use during the Gondals' reversionary lease. The value of the benefit during their occupation was £10,000. In the Court of Appeal, Simon Brown LJ (with whom Pill LJ and Sir John Vinelott agreed) upheld this decision and said:[70] 'a restitutionary award, ie damages calculated according to the value of the benefit received by the occupier, is rightly decided not by reference to what subjectively the landlord would have otherwise done with his property, but rather by an objective determination of what the wrongful occupation was worth to the trespasser'.

Historically this award for trespass would have been described as 'mesne profits'.[71] But its focus on benefit to the defendant was clear: if no evidence were given as to the length of time that the defendant has been in possession, no more than nominal damages could be awarded.[72] The focus of the award is on the value of the use made by the defendant.[73] Other labels were used at common law and in equity to describe these money awards for wrongdoing which were also based on the value of the benefit the defendant obtained from the claimant's assets or labour: wayleaves, reasonable royalties, rescissory damages, user damages.[74]

Although some have argued that a more restrictive approach should be applied to restitutionary damages for breach of contract,[75] recent cases appear to be treating them in the same way as restitutionary damages for torts and equitable wrongs.[76] A deliberate or cynical breach of duty is not required. The strength of the principle of corrective justice underlying restitution of a benefit gained from the assets or labour of the claimant is at least as powerful as the principle of compensation. It requires restitution of benefits wrongfully derived from the claimant's assets or labour no matter how innocent the wrongdoing.

---

[70] [2001] RLR 221 at 228. See also *Ministry of Defence v Ashman* [1993] 2 EGLR 102 at 105 (Hoffmann LJ). See also *Ministry of Defence v Thompson* [1993] 2 EGLR 107.

[71] In *Ministry of Defence v Ashman* [1993] 2 EGLR 102 at 106, Hoffmann LJ said that it is time to recognize that the claim is one for restitution and to 'call a spade a spade'.

[72] *Ive v Scott* (1841) 9 Dowl 993 at 994 (Wightman J).

[73] *Horsford v Bird & Ors (Jamaica)* [2006] UKPC 3 at [15].

[74] Edelman (above, n 4) at 68–9, 207–11, 224–33.

[75] See A Burrows, *The Law of Restitution* (2nd edn, 2002) 462.

[76] See esp *O'Brien Homes Ltd v Lane* [2004] EWHC 303. See also *Experience Hendrix LLC v PPX Enterprises* Inc [2003] EWCA Civ 323; [2003] 1 All ER 830 (Comm); *Esso Petroleum Co Ltd v Niad Ltd* [2001] AER (D) 324.

James Edelman

3.3. Do We Need Two Different Labels?

It is clear that it is essential to draw a distinction between restitutionary damages and disgorgement damages. One of the most obvious reasons is because in many situations of cynical breach a claimant will have a *choice* between them and the quantum of each may be very different; the award which is preferred will depend upon the amount of profit actually made by the defendant (disgorgement) compared with the objective value of the benefit received by the defendant from the claimant's assets or labour (restitution). Courts and commentators have also acknowledged that 'a clear distinction should be drawn'[77] between these two measures of damages. As Heydon JA said in *Harris v Digital Pulse Pty Ltd*[78] 'the rules relating to an account of profits are not restitutionary in the sense that they do not rest on giving back something which the plaintiff once had . . .'.

In his final book, Peter argued that although the difference between these two measures was 'beyond contradiction . . . from the standpoint of both measure and rationale', they still could both be described by the same label 'restitution' as they were both gain-based measures.[79] Likewise, in *Bloor (Measham) Ltd v Calcott*[80] Hart J contrasted 'the benefit' and 'the loss' measures, explaining that the word 'restitutionary' could be used to describe a disgorgement measure provided it is clearly understood that it is describing an award used to disgorge benefits.[81] The difficulty with this approach is that it confuses different levels of generality. At the broadest level of generality both of these gain-based measures, as well as compensation and punishment for wrongdoing, can be called 'damages'. At a greater level of particularity, restitution and disgorgement awards for wrongdoing could be called gain-based damages. The problem with using 'restitutionary damages' as a synonym for 'gain-based damages' is that at the most meaningful level of particularity, where the awards are differentiated by purpose, 'restitutionary damages' and 'restitution' (which have no deterrent goal) must be kept distinct from 'disgorgement damages' (which has a central goal of deterrence).

---

[77] *Kuwait Airways Corp v Iraqi Airways Co* [2004] EWHC 2603 at [462] (Cresswell J). See also *Esso Petroleum v Niad* [2001] All ER (D) 324; *Experience Hendrix LLC v PPX Enterprises Inc* [2003] EWCA Civ 323; [2003] 1 All ER (Comm) 830; *Hospitality Group Pty Ltd v Australian Rugby Union Ltd* (2001) 110 FCR 157 at 196–7 [160]–[162]; R Cunnington, 'Rock, Restitution and Disgorgement' (2004) Journal of Obligations and Remedies 46; H Dagan *The Law and Ethics of Restitution* (2004) 214; D Friedmann, 'Restitution for Wrongs: The Measure of Recovery' (2001) 79 Texas Law Rev 1879 at 1880–3; American Law Institute, *Restatement of the Law of Restitution and Unjust Enrichment*, Tentative Draft No 4 (April 2005) 41 'the distinction is fundamental . . .' (although the latter three consider the law of wrongs as operating on a principle of unjust enrichment whilst the premise of this essay is that unjust enrichment and wrongdoing are wholly independent categories).
[78] *Harris v Digital Pulse Pty Ltd* (2003) 56 NSWLR 298 at [414].
[79] Birks (above, n 5) 282.   [80] [2001] EWHC Ch 467; [2002] 1 EGLR 1.
[81] See also *Westminster City Council v Porter* [2002] EWHC 2179 (Ch);[2003] Ch 436 at [3].

4. Restitutionary Damages and the Nature of Compensation

4.1. Restitutionary Damages and a Rights-Based Thesis of Compensation

We have seen that restitutionary damages are not concerned with financial loss to the claimant. In *Gondal v Dillon,* the Court of Appeal held that no bargain would have been struck but restitutionary damages were still awarded. Some commentators argue that such an award is nevertheless compensatory for financial loss because of an irrebuttable presumption that a bargain would have been struck.[82] But this is a fiction. In a case where the claimant would never have agreed to a bargain, he suffers no financial loss.[83] Lord Nicholls has said that such a characterization of damages is a 'strained and artificial meaning. The injured person's rights were invaded but, in financial terms, he suffered no loss.'[84]

However, there is another, more subtle, argument that would allow many of these cases to be explained as *compensatory* damages. Professor McInnes has recently argued that where a claimant's right has been violated, this necessarily entails a loss because it is a subtraction from the claimant's *dominium.* An award of compensation can be made, irrespective of financial loss, of the value of the right violated; the award stands in the place of the right that has been infringed.[85] Support for McInnes's thesis can be found in those cases in which the judges speak of 'compensation' and 'loss' as measured by the value of the right infringed rather than by the claimant's financial position: 'the plaintiff has suffered a loss in that the defendant has taken without paying for it . . . the right to do the act . . . that is what the plaintiff has lost'.[86] With its emphasis on the value of the right infringed, McInnes's approach can be described as a rights-based approach to compensation. Taking a rights-based approach, an award of compensatory damages will be based on the same principles whether it is given for breach of contract or for a tort or for an equitable wrong. In all cases, the money award is for the value of the claimant's right that has been infringed. For torts and equitable wrongs it is the value of the claimant's right (eg, to integrity of the person or property or reputation) and for breach of contract the award is of

---

[82] RJ Sharpe and SM Waddams, 'Damages for Lost Opportunity to Bargain' (1982) 2 OJLS 290 at 296–7.　　　　　　　　　　　　　　　　　　　[83] [2001] RLR 221 at 228.

[84] *Attorney General v Blake* [2001] 1 AC 268 (HL) 279. See also *Lane v O'Brien Homes Ltd* [2004] EWHC 303 at [22].

[85] M McInnes, 'Account of Profits for Common Law Wrongs' in S Degeling and J Edelman, *Equity in Commercial Law* (2005) 416. At various points, the argument of Sharpe and Waddams tends toward this view: Sharpe and Waddams (n 82 above) at 296.

[86] *Tito v Waddell (No 2)* [1977] Ch 106, 335; *Jaggard v Sawyer* [1995] 1 WLR 269, 282. See also *Wrotham Park Estate Co v Parkside Homes* [1974] 1 WLR 798 at 812, 813; *Livingstone v Rawyards Coal Company* (1880) 5 App Cas 25 at 41 (Lord Blackburn).

the value of the infringed right to performance of a promised duty. In each case consequential losses that are not too remote will also be recoverable.[87]

If applied to all cases, this rights-based compensation approach would subsume most cases of restitutionary damages. Restitutionary damages require that a benefit is received by the defendant wrongfully from the assets or labour of the claimant. In other words, they require an infringement of the rights of the claimant and a corresponding benefit to the defendant. But a rights-based measure of compensation will apply in cases where a claimant's right is infringed even if the defendant obtains no corresponding benefit.[88] For instance, the claimant in *Gondal v Dillon* would only have needed to show that he was wrongfully evicted from the premises without needing to show that the defendant had been in possession. Indeed, this observation was made by Simon Brown LJ, who observed that a rights-based measure of compensation (which he described as 'the objective approach') might also have resulted in recovery of £10,000, although not the further £5,000 because the Gondals had not lost their right to sell the remaining reversionary lease.[89]

4.2. Cases which Reject a Rights-Based Measure of Compensation

This rights-based compensation thesis is controversial. There are many cases in which such an 'objective' award of the value of the infringed right has been refused and a lesser award of financial compensation made. Almost all these cases involve instances in which the infringed right is held for commercial purposes. A good example is the Australian decision in *Butler v Egg and Egg Pulp Marketing Board*.[90] The appellants were producers of eggs. Legislation in Victoria vested the ownership of eggs laid by the appellants' hens in the Board. Upon sale of the eggs by the Board, at heavily reduced rates, the Board would pay a portion of the price to the appellants and retain the rest. In violation of their duty to deliver the eggs to the Board, the appellants sold eggs at market rates. The Board sued the appellants for conversion arguing that its loss was the market value of the eggs. The appellants argued that compensatory damages should be measured by the financial loss suffered by the Board and not by the objective value (the market value) of the Board's right to the eggs. The High Court of Australia accepted the argument of the appellants and assessed the financial loss of the Board at £1,100, being the difference between the price for which it would have sold the eggs and

---

[87] The remoteness test for contract and non-intentional torts converge to a test of what is within the reasonable contemplation of the parties: cf *Jackson v Royal Bank of Scotland* [2005] UKHL 3; [2005] 1 WLR 377 at [48] (Lord Walker) and *Cambridge Water Co v Eastern Counties Leather Plc* [1994] 2 AC 264 (HL).

[88] *Rees v Darlington Memorial Hospital NHS Trust* [2003] UKHL 52; [2004] 1 AC 309 (loss of a right to determine the size of the claimant's family); *Ruxley Electronics and Construction Ltd v Forsyth* [1996] AC 344 (loss of a right to a swimming pool of a particular depth); *Johnson v Unisys* [2003] 1 AC 518 (loss of a right to a fair dismissal).   [89] [2001] RLR 221 at 228–9.

[90] (1966) 114 CLR 185. See also *Douglas v Hello! Ltd (No 3)* [2005] EWCA Civ 595; [2006] QB 125 at [247] where compensation was refused because the claimants had 'exhausted their relevant commercial interest'.

the amount which it would have had to pay to the appellants. Justices Taylor and Owen held that[91] 'the statement which appears so often in the books that the general rule is that the plaintiff in an action of conversion is entitled to recover the full value of the goods converted ... should not be allowed to obscure the broad principle that damages are awarded by way of compensation [for financial loss]'. This result was referred to with approval by Lord Nicholls in the leading speech in *Kuwait Airways Corporation v Iraqi Airways Company*.[92] Of course, in *Butler* the claimant Board had sought only compensation. If it had sought restitutionary damages it could have recovered the objective value of the opportunity to sell the eggs which the appellants wrongfully obtained by infringement of the claimant's right to sell the eggs.[93] A claim for disgorgement damages for this cynical wrongdoing would have been even greater—the full profit made by the appellants from sale of the eggs.

At first glance, the decision of the Privy Council in *Solloway v McLaughlin*[94] appears to contradict such an argument and appears to be a decision which allows compensation for the value of an infringed right which is held for commercial purposes. In that case, in October 1929, at the start of the great depression, McLaughlin instructed a stockbroking company (of which the appellants were directors) to buy 7,000 shares in a mining company at $7 each on margin (credit). McLaughlin deposited 3,500 of the same shares as security. The stockbrokers told him that the shares had been purchased. The shares declined in value and on a margin call he provided 10,500 further shares as security and $8,000 cash. McLaughlin closed his account in January 1930 and the stockbroking company transferred 21,000 shares to him (the 7,000 purchased and 14,000 given as security). He later discovered that the stockbroking company had engaged in a fraudulent scheme. First, they had not purchased the 7,000 shares in October 1929 as he had requested but purchased them on the falling market in January 1930 after McLaughlin closed his account. Secondly, they sold the 14,000 shares that McLaughlin deposited as security which they also repurchased in January 1930 at lower prices. McLaughlin brought an action against the company seeking (1) $49,000 that he had paid for the 7,000 shares purchased in October 1929 (giving credit for the value of the shares delivered to him in January 1930), and (2) the profit made by the company from selling and repurchasing the shares given as security. Delivering the advice of the Privy Council, Lord Atkin upheld the first claim explaining that the payments from McLaughlin were 'in respect of transactions which form part of the fraud' so he was 'entitled to recover back the money paid on the footing of an honest

---

[91] (1966) 114 CLR 185 at 191. See also at 192 (Menzies J). See also *Chinery v Viall* (1860) 5 H & N 288; 157 ER 1192 (Bramwell B): 'it is not an absolute rule that the value of the goods is to be taken as the measure of damage'.

[92] [2002] UKHL 19, [2002] 2 AC 883 at [66] (Lord Nicholls; Lords Steyn, Hoffmann and Hope agreeing).

[93] Which would probably have been less than the full market value of the eggs as a reasonable vendor of such rights would not insist on a price equal to the full market value of the eggs.

[94] [1938] AC 247.

transaction'.[95] In other words, although McLaughlin had ultimately suffered no financial loss he was entitled to damages for money he paid as a result of the tort of deceit. As to the second head of recovery, Lord Atkin advised that the disposal of McLaughlin's shares 'amounted to nothing short of conversion'[96] and damages for the conversion should be measured by the value of the shares at the date of the conversion even though there had been no financial loss.

If *Solloway v McLaughlin* were a case of compensation for loss then the compensation could only be explained as the value of the commercial right and it would be inconsistent with many other cases like *Butler*.[97] But Lord Nicholls observed in *Kuwait Airways Corporation v Iraqi Airways Company*[98] that it should not be understood as an award of compensation at all. It is an award of restitutionary damages. The $49,000 McLaughlin paid as well as the money received from the sale of his security represented the objective value of *benefits* wrongfully (by deceit) obtained by the stockbrokers from McLaughlin's assets. Indeed both awards are also explicable as disgorgement damages because they were also the actual profit made from the deceit.

4.3. Cases which Award a Rights-Based Measure of Compensation

In support of the rights-based compensation thesis, there are many cases involving infringement of rights held for non-commercial purposes where the awards made are explicable only as the value of the right and not for financial loss. In *Clydebank Engineering and Shipbuilding Co Ltd v Don Jose Ramos Yzquierdo Y Castaneda*[99] the claimant's late delivery of a vessel meant that it was not sunk together with the rest of the Spanish fleet. The House of Lords held that the claimant was required to pay compensation of the agreed value of £500 per week for late delivery notwithstanding that no financial loss was suffered because the delay was to the claimant's advantage by saving the vessel. The same result can be seen in relation to the sale of defective goods for non-commercial purposes[100] as well as cases involving negligent infringement of a non-commercial right to use a chattel where compensation for infringement of the valuable right has been awarded despite the absence of financial loss.[101] Another example is an award of the cost of curing a breach of contract (if cure is

---

[95] [1938] AC 247 at 257.   [96] [1938] AC 247 at 257.
[97] *Hiort v London and North Western Railway Co* 4 Exch Div 188, 199; *Williams v Peel River Land and Mineral Co Ltd* (1886) 55 LT 689, 692–3; *Wickham Holdings v Brooke House Motors Ltd* [1967] 1 WLR 295, 299–300; *Brandeis Goldschmidt & Co Ltd v Western Transport Ltd* [1981] QB 864, 870; *IBL Ltd v Coussens* [1991] 2 All ER 133, 139, and 142.
[98] [2002] 2 AC 883 at [63]–[66] (Lord Nicholls; Lords Steyn, Hoffmann, and Hope agreeing).   [99] [1905] AC 6 (HL).
[100] In relation to goods see s 53(3) of the Sale of Goods Act 1979 which provides that the difference in value of goods (*not* the financial loss) is the prima facie measure of loss. Cp *British Motor Trade Association v Gilbert* [1951] 2 All ER 641 (non-commercial right) with *Bence Graphics Ltd v Fasson Ltd* [1998] QB 87 (commercial right).
[101] *The Greta Holme* [1897] AC 596; *The Mediana* [1900] AC 113; *The Marpessa* [1907] AC 241; *Admiralty Commissioners v SS Chekiang* [1926] AC 637; *Admiralty Commissioners v SS*

reasonable) in non-commercial contracts where no financial loss has been suffered.¹⁰²

In all these cases, the award represents the value of the infringed right rather than compensation for financial loss, although any additional claim for further consequential loss must still be a proved financial loss¹⁰³ or a proved consequential personal loss (such as consequential awards for additional pain and suffering, loss of enjoyment, or consumer surplus).

4.4. Reconciliation: Rights-Based Compensation Measure for Infringement of Rights Held for Non-commercial Purposes

By accepting a rights-based approach to compensation, but limiting its application, *at least,* to infringement of rights held for non-commercial purposes, it is possible to reconcile these two long lines of authority. Although this will sometimes require a difficult line to be drawn between rights held for commercial purposes and those held for non-commercial purposes, it is no more difficult a dividing line than the more general governing limitation separating cases where it is 'reasonable' to require compensation of the value of the infringed right and cases where it is 'unreasonable' to do so.¹⁰⁴

However, the distinction is not without controversy. *Target Holdings Ltd v Redferns (a firm)*¹⁰⁵ involved a breach of duty by trustees for a purchaser of property in paying the purchase price before they received the security. This led to a financial loss that the beneficiaries would probably have suffered in any event. A compensatory damages award was sought for the value of the beneficiaries' violated right not to have an unauthorized disposition of their purchase price. In the leading speech in the House of Lords, Lord Browne-Wilkinson refused the claim because no financial loss had been caused by the wrongdoing. His lordship applied the distinction advocated in this essay saying that there could be no recovery because it is 'wrong to lift wholesale the detailed rules developed in the context of traditional trusts and then seek to apply them to trusts . . . in commercial and financial dealings'.¹⁰⁶ However, Lord Millett has extrajudicially disagreed with the suggestion that such a rights-based award for breach of trust should be confined to non-commercial cases.¹⁰⁷ On the other

---

Susquehanna [1926] AC 655; *The Hebridean Coast* [1961] AC 545. See also *Dimond v Lovell* [2002] 1 AC 384 at 406 (Lord Hobhouse insisting that the chattel be 'non-profit earning').

¹⁰² *Ruxley Electronics and Construction Ltd v Forsyth* [1996] AC 344 (*obiter dicta*) and *Radford v De Froberville* [1977] 1 WLR 1262 at 1285.

¹⁰³ 'When we are speaking of general damages no such principle [of rights-based compensation] applies at all': *The Mediana* [1900] AC 113 at 118, approved in *Admiralty Commissioners v SS Chekiang* [1926] AC 637 at 644.

¹⁰⁴ *Ruxley Electronics and Construction Ltd v Forsyth* [1996] AC 344 (HL).

¹⁰⁵ [1996] 1 AC 421.   ¹⁰⁶ [1996] 1 AC 421 at 435 (Lord Browne-Wilkinson).

¹⁰⁷ P Millett, 'Equity's Place in the Law of Commerce' (1998) 114 LQR 214. See also S Elliott, 'Remoteness Criteria in Equity' (2002) 65 MLR 588; P Birks, 'Equity in the Modern Law: An Exercise in Taxonomy' (1996) 26 UWAL Rev 1; *Bairstow v Queen's Moat Houses plc* [2001] 2

hand, Lord Millett himself rejected a rights-based approach in a case involving a breach of an equitable duty of care causing infringement of commercial rights.[108] In another recent decision, *Alfred McAlpine Construction Ltd v Panatown Ltd*,[109] one issue was whether a defendant that had breached a commercial contract with the claimant was required to pay compensation of the value of the claimant's commercial right to non-defective performance. The claimant had suffered no financial loss because it had contracted for the building work to be done for a third party. Although Lords Clyde and Jauncey held that financial loss was essential to recovery, Lords Goff and Millett thought that the claimant was entitled to the value of the commercial right infringed even though the contract was a commercial one.[110]

Although such a distinction between rights held for commercial and non-commercial purposes will be controversial, there is a powerful policy reason in support of it. A claimant that holds a commercial right is in a better position than the defendant (who may be entirely unaware of the right) to assess (and insure) financial risk and also to reduce or mitigate an initial financial loss. If a rights-based measure of compensation were allowed in such cases it would provide a disincentive for a claimant to reduce a loss which might flow from the infringement of those commercial rights. However, this policy does not prevent a claim for restitutionary damages—which will also represent the value of the commercial right infringed—if the defendant obtains a benefit from the wrong. Even if the claimant has suffered no financial loss, restitutionary damages (of the value gained by the defendant from the claimant) present a more compelling case because they also require a co-relative benefit to be wrongfully obtained from the claimant so that efficiency concerns about reducing a claimant's loss are irrelevant.[111]

5. Conclusion

The meaning of damages advocated in this essay will be unattractive to some, perhaps many, because it is not limited to compensation nor is it coterminous with common law. In these ways it challenges a prevailing paradigm that damages means compensation at common law. The first time I heard Peter speak he said, of damages, that 'we are talking about only one thing, namely money

---

BCLC 531 at 549 (Robert Walker LJ). See also *Youyang Pty Ltd v Minter Ellison Morris Fletcher* (2003) 212 CLR 484 at 502.

[108] *Bristol and West Building Society v Mothew* [1998] Ch 1.   [109] [2001] 1 AC 518.

[110] [2001] 1 AC 518 at 548 (Lord Goff). See also 587 (Lord Millett). Lord Browne-Wilkinson was prepared to assume this to be true because he considered that he did not need to decide the point in any event: [2001] 1 AC 518 at 577.

[111] L Fuller and W Perdue, 'The Reliance Interest in Contract Damages' (1936) 46 Yale LJ 52.

awards for wrongs' which are breaches of a duty whether at law or in equity.[112] Under Peter's supervision, this bold nomenclature of damages was the beginning of my intellectual journey in this area. The first theme of this essay was to show that although it may not be a popular definition, this meaning of damages is supported by both legal history and principle.

With damages as a description of a genus of money awards for wrongs, the identification and clarification of its different species is essential to intellectual order. Differentiation between two different awards of gain-based damages (restitutionary damages and disgorgement damages) permits an understanding of their different purposes and when each should be awarded. This was the primary point of the second theme of this essay.

The third theme engages with the latest development in this debate. Recent work by Professor McInnes, building upon a differentiation between disgorgement damages and restitutionary damages, has now raised the question of the relationship between restitutionary damages and compensatory damages by suggesting a broader understanding of the operation of compensation. He has suggested that compensation is based upon the value of a right that has been infringed (as well as any consequential loss) rather than an award which is solely reparative for financial and (exceptionally) other personal losses. It was argued in the third section of this essay that this stricter, rights-based compensation model only applies in cases involving interference with rights held for non-commercial purposes[113] and that policy supports such a limitation. In such non-commercial cases, restitutionary damages will usually be superfluous because they require proof of an additional element, namely that the defendant has obtained a corresponding benefit as a result of the wrongful infringement of the claimant's right. However, in cases involving infringement of rights held for commercial purposes, or if it is otherwise unreasonable to award a rights-based measure of compensation, restitutionary damages will be essential to restore to the claimant the corresponding benefit obtained by the defendant from infringement of the claimant's right. As Lord Millett has said comparing a rights-based approach to compensatory damages with restitutionary damages, 'there is room for both approaches'.[114]

The three themes in this essay have sought to contribute to Peter's lifelong academic quest for the beauty and grace of a transparent and ordered law. The very first time I heard Peter speak, he referred to disorderly law as no more than an alibi for illegitimate power.[115] And in the opening pages of his final book, Peter described order with the metaphor of a beautiful butterfly emerging from a

---

[112] P Birks, 'Equity in the Modern Law: An Exercise in Taxonomy' (1996) 26 UWA L Rev 1 at 29. See also P Birks, *Restitution—The Future* (1992) at 18 and P Birks, *Civil Wrongs: A New World* (1992) at 71; P Birks, 'The Concept of a Civil Wrong' in D Owen, *Philosophical Foundations of Tort Law* (1995) 31 at 51.

[113] And subject to other limitations such as 'reasonableness' of the award.

[114] *Alfred McAlpine Construction Ltd v Panatown Ltd* [2001] 1 AC 518 at 586.

[115] Published in Birks (above, n 112) at 99.

chrysalis.[116] To borrow from Coke's description of the writing of Littleton, Peter's quest, and the work he produced, was an 'ornament' of the common law.[117] Ornament is descriptive of beauty, grace, and honour.[118] The ornament of Peter's work lay in the beauty and grace it brought to the law. The honour came from his courage in the pursuit of truth in the face of strong opposition.

---

[116] Birks (above, n 5) p xii.
[117] E Coke, *Institutes of the Laws of England* (15th edn, 1894, vol 1) at p xxxv.
[118] J Simpson and E Weiner (eds), *Oxford English Dictionary* (2nd edn, 1989) 939.

THE ENGLISH LAW OF
UNJUST ENRICHMENT
AND RESTITUTION

Some Particular Unjust Factors

9

Unlawful Statutes and Mistake of Law: Is There a Smile on the Face of Schrödinger's Cat?

*Jack Beatson**

1. Introduction

Peter Birks was a good friend, a charismatic teacher, and an extraordinarily creative scholar, whose death has deprived British law schools and English law of one of its most fertile minds.[1] He coupled the clarity and certainty with which he advanced his ideas with a willingness to reconsider and even radically alter his position. The most dramatic example is the re-conceptualization of the law of restitution advocated in his *Unjust Enrichment*, the second edition of which was published posthumously. In the note he sent me with a copy of the first edition he said: 'you will see that I have gone right down the snake. Back to square one. I must throw a treble to restart'. He argued that 'in the swaps cases English law changed direction' so that the juridical foundation of claims in unjust enrichment is the absence of a basis for the benefit transferred rather than, as English common lawyers have been brought up to believe, the establishment by the claimant of a ground of restitution.[2] If this is so, the fundamental structure of the English law of restitution no longer rests on a number of grounds for restitution, such as mistake, duress, necessity, and failure or absence of consideration, which Birks described as 'unjust factors', but has become similar to the law in many civilian jurisdictions. That this would be a revolutionary change is clear from the

---

* One of Her Majesty's Judges, formerly Rouse Ball Professor of English Law, University of Cambridge.

[1] For my general assessment of his contribution, see the *Guardian*, 16 July 2004.

[2] Chapters 5–6. See R Stevens [2004] RTR 270–3 and 288 and Chs 2, 18–20 in this volume. By 'the swaps cases' we mean *Westdeutsche Landesbank Girozentrale v Islington LBC* [1999] AC 669 and its progeny: see P Birks, *Unjust Enrichment* (2nd edn, 2005) 108–13; A Burrows, *The Law of Restitution* (2nd edn, 2002) 386–8, 397–401.

statement by Lord Goff in *Woolwich Building Society v IRC* (*No 2*) in 1992 that English law 'might have developed so as to recognise a condictio indebitii—an action for the recovery of money on the ground that it was not due. But it did not do so'.[3]

Birks's advocacy of a principled law of restitution was perhaps most effective in the case of the restitution of sums paid to the executive as a result of an ultra vires demand. In 1990 in what Lord Goff described as a 'powerful essay' he argued for the recognition of a right to the restitution of such payments.[4] The right was recognized soon afterwards in the *Woolwich* case in which the Court of Appeal and the House of Lords, by bare majorities, allowed a claim by the Building Society to recover sums paid to the Inland Revenue in respect of interest paid to its members. In his speech Lord Goff said he had little doubt Birks's essay 'provided the main inspiration for the argument of Woolwich, and the judgments of the majority of the Court of Appeal'.[5]

Birks's views did not, however, prevail in *Kleinwort Benson plc v Lincoln CC*.[6] The House of Lords, also by a bare majority, stated that it was not necessary to maintain the rule barring the recovery of money paid under a mistake of law. Birks had long taken a narrower approach to what constitutes a mistake than other commentators, excluding what he termed 'mispredictions',[7] and was less hostile than others to the bar on the recovery of payments made under mistake of law.[8] He considered that the decision in *Kleinwort Benson* extended an already over-stretched notion of mistake by its endorsement of the declaratory theory of common law decision-making.[9] It was held that where a payment is made prior to a judicial change in the law, because the law is regarded as having always been what the judicial decision has stated it to be, the pre-decision payment must be regarded as mistaken.[10] Birks agreed with the Law Commission's 1994 Report,[11] and with Lord Browne-Wilkinson and Lord Lloyd who dissented. Such a payment was not made under a mistake because, in Lord Browne-Wilkinson's words, where a decision of a court has in fact changed the law 'retrospectivity cannot falsify history'.[12] Birks considered that in such a case the claimant is no more mistaken than the person who gets soaked because he mispredicted the weather.[13] He

---

[3] [1993] AC 70, at 172D.
[4] 'Restitution from the Executive: A Tercentenary Footnote to the Bill of Rights' in P Finn (ed), *Essays on Restitution* (1990) 164–205.
[5] [1993] AC 70, 166. Lord Goff also cited WR Cornish's earlier Sultan Azlan Shah lecture, ' "Colour of Office": Restitutionary Redress Against Public Authority' (1987) 14 Jo Malaysian and Comp Law 41.   [6] [1999] 2 AC 349.
[7] *An Introduction to the Law of Restitution* (rev edn, 1989) 147–8.
[8] ibid 165. See also 'Mistakes of Law' [2000] CLP 205, 216.
[9] Birks (above, n 2) 112, 239–40.
[10] [1999] 2 AC 349, 379, 399, 410 (Lord Goff, Lord Hoffmann, and Lord Hope). See J Finnis, 'The Fairy Tale's Moral' (1999) 115 LQR 170; L Smith, 'Restitution for Mistake of Law' [1999] RLR 148.   [11] Law Com No 227, §§ 5.3, 5.13.
[12] [1999] 2 AC 349 at 358. See Lord Lloyd at 393.
[13] Birks (above, n 2) 239; 'Mistakes of Law' [2000] CLP 205, 223–4.

maintained that a claim can only be based on mistake if the mistake is one based on data that can be verified or falsified at the time of the payment, and that until the law was stated in the later decision there was no such data.[14]

This essay concerns the relationship between the *Woolwich* principle and other common law grounds for restitution, in particular mistake of law. This relationship was considered by the Court of Appeal in *Deutsche Morgan Grenfell Group plc v IRC*,[15] a decision handed down almost seven months after Peter Birks died, and now on appeal to the House of Lords. At the time of writing the appeal has not been heard. Despite the obvious disadvantages of writing about the case at this stage, I decided to do so because the issues it raises go to the core of Birks's conception of restitution. The case is of fundamental importance not only to the scope and impact of the *Woolwich* case but also because it will give their lordships the opportunity to decide whether or not the English law of restitution is to be re-conceptualized or, given the declaratory theory, has been re-conceptualized in the way suggested by Birks. I hardly touch on the second of these issues because it is considered by other contributors to this volume.[16]

2. *Deutsche Morgan Grenfell Group plc v IRC*

The *Deutsche Morgan Grenfell* case arose out of a successful challenge by *Metallgesellschaft Ltd*, the United Kingdom subsidiary of a German company, to legislation which precluded a subsidiary of a parent company not resident in the UK from making a group income election enabling it to avoid paying advance corporation tax. The challenge was launched in 1993 but not resolved until 8 March 2001. On 12 September 2000 Advocate-General Fennelly published an opinion supporting *Metallgesellschaft's* claim and on 8 March 2001 the ECJ (European Court of Justice), adopting his opinion, held that the UK's statutory regime contravened EC law in discriminating between companies with parent companies resident in the UK (which could make a group income election) and those with parent companies resident in other EU states.[17] *Deutsche Morgan Grenfell* was aware of *Metallgesellschaft's* claim and by early July 1995 understood that it had merit but the evidence of its head of taxation was that pending the

---

[14] Burrows (above, n 2) 155, thus summarizes Birks's position in [2000] CLP 205, 224–30. See also Law Com No 227 (1994), §§ 5.2–5.3; S Meier and R Zimmermann, 'Judicial Development of the Law, *Error Iuris* and the Law of Unjustified Enrichment—A View from Germany' (1999) 115 LQR 556. But cf Lord Hope in *Kleinwort Benson v Lincoln CC* at 411E, 178 below.

[15] [2005] EWCA Civ 78, [2006] 2 WLR 103, allowing an appeal by the IRC from Park J, [2003] 4 All ER 645. For commentary on the Court of Appeal, see A Burrows, 'Restitution in Respect of Mistakenly Paid Tax' (2005) 121 LQR 540; J Edelman, 'Limitation Periods and the Theory of Unjust Enrichment' (2005) 68 MLR 848; R Stevens, 'Justified Enrichment' (2005) 5 OUCLJ 141. I am grateful to the authors for sending me copies prior to their publication.

[16] See Chs 2, 18–20.

[17] C-397/98 and C–410/98 *Metallgesellschaft Ltd v IRC* and *Hoechst v IRC* [2001] Ch 620.

outcome of the litigation it was bound to pay advance corporation tax in accordance with the UK statute. On 13 October 2000, before the ECJ's decision, *Deutsche Morgan Grenfell* instituted proceedings to recover interest in respect of advance corporation tax it had paid in 1993, 1995, and 1996, relying on both the *Woolwich* principle and on the fact that it paid the tax under a mistake of law. It is one of many claims (totalling some £20 billion)[18] brought by UK subsidiaries of parent companies based in other member states in the light of the ECJ's decision and managed by a group litigation order.

Park J had held that there is a right at common law to the repayment of tax paid under a mistake of law, that the bank's claim was based on its mistake as to the entitlement of the Inland Revenue to advance corporation tax, which it did not discover until the ECJ's decision, and that the extended limitation period for relief from the consequences of mistake in section 32(1)(c) of the Limitation Act 1980 applied so that time only ran from the date of the ECJ's decision.

The bank was only partially successful in the Court of Appeal. In a careful and closely reasoned decision, it held that a taxpayer who has made an overpayment of tax under a mistake of law can only recover that payment under the *Woolwich* principle or one of the statutory regimes governing the recovery of tax paid which is not due. The effect of the decision is that in the case of tax not due but paid under a mistake, the extended limitation period for relief from the consequences of mistake in section 32(1)(c) of the Limitation Act 1980 cannot apply. The bank's claim to recover the 1993 payment was thus based on the unlawfulness of the demand and became statute-barred six years after the payment was made, so that the claim failed.[19] The Court held that tax paid under a mistake is also recoverable in those cases, notably section 33 of the Taxes Management Act 1970,[20] where such a right is granted by statute. On the facts of *Deutsche Morgan Grenfell* none of the statutory regimes was applicable. Moreover, Buxton and Rix LJJ considered that it was difficult to say the bank was mistaken with respect to at least some of the payments because they were made when the bank knew of the challenge by *Metallgesellschaft*, understood it to have merit, and thus knew that there was a ground to contest liability.[21]

While the Court, especially Buxton LJ, saw difficulties in fitting the concept of mistake into the context of an unlawful demand,[22] it is not fanciful to suggest

---

[18] *The Times* 22 June 2005, 38. See also *Autologic Holdings plc v IRC* [2005] UKHL 54, [2005] 3 WLR 339; *Sempra Metals Ltd v IRC* [2005] EWCA Civ 389.

[19] This essay does not address the question whether (as Buxton LJ dissenting held) amendments made to the pleadings on 19 August 2002 to include particulars of the 1995 and 1996 payments had the effect of adding new claims which were also time–barred, or whether the original claim was made in respect of all payments of advanced corporation tax by *Deutsche Morgan Grenfell*: see paras [238–47], [253–60], [292–7].

[20] See Law Commission Report No 227 (1994), paras 9.21 ff. There are also statutory rights in the case of inheritance tax, stamp duty, VAT, excise duties, insurance premium tax, national insurance, and council tax: see Law Com No 227, paras 13.7 ff, 13.17 ff, 14.14 ff, 15.4 ff, and 15.24 ff.   [21] See 177–179 below.

[22] Buxton LJ paras [279–84]. See also Jonathan Parker LJ, Transcript 18 November 2004, p 139.

that the disadvantages seen in the application of that extended limitation period to payments of tax mistakenly believed to be due played a part in its approach to the determination of the content of the substantive law.[23] The House of Lords may also consider that it would be unattractive to apply the extended limitation period to a claimant who, knowing of a challenge to a liability to which it is also subject, nevertheless decides to pay. This essay, however, argues that unless the House of Lords adopts Birks's re-conceptualization of the law of restitution, or decides that on the facts the bank was not mistaken, they will find it difficult to uphold the decision of the Court of Appeal without significant modifications to the decisions in the *Woolwich* and *Kleinwort Benson* cases. For this reason *Deutsche Morgan Grenfell* may turn out to be as important to the architecture of the law of restitution as the decisions in *Lipkin Gorman v Karpnale*[24] and the swaps cases.[25]

Not surprisingly, although Buxton LJ, in what he described as a footnote, indicated that he saw difficulties in the argument that restitutionary claims all rest on the single ground of 'absence of basis',[26] neither Park J nor the Court of Appeal was concerned with the broad question of whether the effect of the swaps cases was to re-conceptualize the law of restitution. They were concerned with the precise effect of the decisions in the *Woolwich* and *Kleinwort Benson* cases.

What would Peter Birks have made of their decisions, and how would he want the House of Lords to approach the case? We know what he thought of Park J's decision. The second edition of *Unjust Enrichment* states[27] that Park J's decision 'came to an indefensible result' because, 'although it came after the swaps cases, it followed the old method of looking for unjust factors'. It was also Birks's view that, even on the old method of looking for unjust factors, the bank could not have succeeded on the ground of mistake. He would have considered that the bank could not properly found its claim on mistake because, until the decision of the ECJ (or possibly the opinion of the Advocate-General), no data that could be verified as true or false existed.[28] Moreover, the tax which *Deutsche Bank* paid 'had been paid under a valid obligation' because, until a group election was made, the bank, like every company, was bound to pay advance corporation tax. They 'had abstained from doing [the things necessary to earn an exemption] in the belief, later falsified, that they were not entitled to'.[29] It seems reasonably clear that Birks would have argued that the House of Lords should dismiss the bank's appeal in respect of the interest on the 1993 payment, preferably on the ground that when the payments were made there was a legal basis for them, but alternatively on the ground that the bank had not paid under a mistake.[30] But what would he have made of the ruling that within the 'old' approach, mistake

---

[23] Paras [2], [207], and [283]. See also the exchange between Buxton LJ and Mr Laurence Rabinowitz QC counsel for the bank, transcript 18 November 2004, p 144 lines 16 ff.
[24] [1991] 2 AC 548.   [25] See n 2 above.   [26] para [274].   [27] (2005) 138.
[28] See 164–5 above.   [29] Birks (above, n 2) 139.   [30] See 177ff below.

was not a ground for the restitution of tax paid to the executive and that the only common law ground for recovery was the *Woolwich* principle?

3. The Key to the Court of Appeal's Conclusion

In *Kleinwort Benson plc v Lincoln CC* Lord Goff stated that:

. . . in our law of restitution we now find two separate and distinct regimes in respect of the repayment of money paid under a mistake of law. These are (1) cases concerned with the repayment of taxes and other similar charges which, when exacted ultra vires, are recoverable as of right at common law under the principle in *Woolwich*, and otherwise are the subject of statutory regimes regulating recovery; and (2) other cases, which may broadly be described as concerned with repayment of money paid under private transactions, and which are governed by the common law.[31]

In *Deutsche Morgan Grenfell* these sentences were subjected to minute analysis.[32] In his reply counsel for the Revenue warned against reading Lord Goff's speech as if it was a statute, but Rix LJ's response, no doubt in the light of the way the argument had proceeded, was that it was a bit too late to make that submission.[33] Buxton LJ stated that, while he had warned himself against treating Lord Goff's speeches in *Kleinwort Benson* and *Woolwich* as if they were statutes, they were no ordinary judgments because 'the leading authority in a particular area of the law set himself to explain developments in that law which were acknowledged to be of general significance' and did so 'by a detailed and careful analysis which is plainly intended to set out the whole of the relevant law in effectively canonical terms'.[34] Without in any way devaluing the enormity of Lord Goff's contribution to *Kleinwort Benson* and to the decision in the *Woolwich* case, it is submitted that an assessment of what precisely was decided in the cases requires consideration of all the majority speeches. The concentration on this passage in his speech in *Kleinwort Benson* and on individual passages in his speech in *Woolwich* may have deflected attention from the overall effect of the majority speeches in the two cases.

Jonathan Parker LJ stated that the first of the two regimes which Lord Goff identifies 'is a comprehensive and complete regime in relation to overpayments of tax made under a mistake of law' and the second regime 'is a comprehensive and complete regime in relation to all payments made under a mistake of law *other* than payments of tax'.[35] He had earlier referred to Lord Goff's statement in the *Woolwich* case[36] that if there is a right of recovery in respect of taxes exacted by the revenue it is irrelevant to consider whether the rule barring recovery of money paid under a

---

[31] [1999] 2 AC 349 at 382.   [32] para [93], per Jonathan Parker LJ.
[33] Transcript 18 November 2004, p 166.
[34] [265]. See also Jonathan Parker LJ at para [192].   [35] [205].
[36] Discussing Wilson J's dissenting judgment in *Air Canada v British Columbia* [1989] 1 SCR 1161.

mistake of law should be abolished 'for that rule can have no application where the remedy arises not from error on the part of the taxpayer, but from the unlawful nature of the demand by the revenue'.[37] Jonathan Parker LJ stated that Lord Goff was plainly referring to cases in which there is an unlawful demand *and* a mistake of law. He also relied on the importance attached by Lord Goff to the fact that an ultra vires demand falls outside the various statutory regimes, that Woolwich was neither enabled nor required to seek its remedy through the statutory framework, and that most cases will be regulated by the various statutory regimes in force.[38] He concluded that the result is that, in cases where the demand is lawful, recovery will be regulated by the statutory regimes.[39] Rix LJ agreed.[40] Buxton LJ's formulation is narrower. He considered that this passage shows that *Woolwich* provides a complete code to address recovery of payments under ultra vires demands and that issues of mistake are irrelevant in such cases.[41] He did not refer to the statutory regimes.

Buxton LJ emphasized that the development of the law in the *Woolwich* case was based on constitutional principle and not on any deduction from or development of the existing rules of restitution. The new remedy 'perhaps' drew on ordinary principles of restitution but did not directly apply them. The basis of recovery and the defences available meant that it stood outside the main stream of restitution as understood in a private law context.[42] He stated that Lord Goff did not only think 'that *Woolwich* recovery was the only remedy for ultra vires payments; but also . . . that such payments were amenable only to recovery under the *Woolwich* rule and not under the rubric of payments under a mistake'.[43] It is, with respect, submitted that there are a number of difficulties with the Court of Appeal's approach to the decisions in *Woolwich* and *Kleinwort Benson* which put into question the court's conclusion.

4. The Court of Appeal's Approach to the Decision in *Woolwich*

Before *Woolwich*, it was accepted that payments received by a public authority were susceptible to restitution on the basis of the standard grounds for restitution, notably duress[44] and mistake of fact.[45] Lord Goff's statement that the rule

---

[37] [1993] AC 70, 176D–E. See also Lord Slynn at 205A 'I do not agree that this [the *Woolwich*] principle cannot apply where there is a mistake of law. That is the situation where the relief is most likely to be needed and if it [is] excluded not much is left'.
[38] ibid 169H and 176G–H.   [39] paras [200], [207].   [40] paras [250], [261].
[41] paras [273], [279].   [42] paras [271–2], citing [1993] AC 70, 172B–G and 173E, 174C–E.
[43] [267].
[44] *Morgan v Palmer* (1824) 2 B & C 729; *Brocklebank Ltd v R* [1925] 1 KB 52; *Mason v New South Wales* (1959) 102 CLR 108.
[45] *Meadows v Grand Junction Waterworks Co* 1905 21 TLR 538. In *National Pari Mutuel Association Ltd v R* (1930) 46 TLR 594 (betting tax) and *Green v Portsmouth Stadium* [1953] 2 QB 190, 195 (statutory admission charges) it was assumed that had the money been paid under a mistake of fact it would have been recoverable.

barring recovery of money paid under a mistake of law 'can have no application' where the remedy arises not from error on the part of the taxpayer but from the unlawfulness of the demand, should not be understood to mean that where the right of recovery is based on the unlawfulness of the demand that is the only ground of recovery. The more natural meaning is that he believed there was no need to consider the bar that then existed for payments made under a mistake of law because that bar has no application where there is another ground for recovery.[46] At that time, as Hobhouse J stated in *Westdeutsche Landesbank Girozentrale v Islington LBC*,[47] the position was that 'the essence of mistake of law is that it does not provide a basis of recovery: it is not that, without more, it provides a defence to a claim for money had and received'. The Law Commission's 1994 report considered that Lord Goff's statement did not mean he saw the recovery of sums demanded ultra vires as trumping any right to recovery of sums paid under a mistake of law and stated that 'several grounds for restitution can coexist in one set of factual circumstances'.[48]

That this is so is supported by what Lord Goff said in the *Kleinwort Benson* case about a statement by Mason CJ in *Commissioner for State Revenue v Royal Insurance*. Mason CJ stated that in *Woolwich* the House of Lords was 'unwilling to acknowledge that causative mistake of law is a basis of recovery'[49] but Lord Goff said '. . . with respect, no question of recovery on the ground of mistake arose in that case, because the Woolwich Building Society throughout asserted that the money was not due'.[50] This is difficult to reconcile with the view that in *Woolwich* Lord Goff excluded causative mistake of law as a ground of recovery for taxes. If Lord Goff regarded the new ground for recovery in *Woolwich* as a replacement for any right to recover on the ground of mistake and indeed the other common law grounds for restitution, Mason CJ would have been substantially correct, and surely Lord Goff would have said so rather than giving the impression that, as there was no mistake in *Woolwich*, the question remained open. If it is suggested that, whatever the decision in *Woolwich*, in *Kleinwort Benson*, Lord Goff intended to hold that the recovery of taxes and similar charges lay outside the right to recover payments made under a mistake of law enunciated in that case, it is also submitted that he would not have corrected Mason CJ in the way he did.

Some further support is obtained from what Lord Goff said in *Kleinwort Benson* about Birks's view that mistake cannot be relied upon as a ground for recovery in the case of closed swaps.[51] Lord Goff said that the only possible basis for this thesis is that failure of consideration should be allowed to trump mistake of law as a ground for recovery of benefits conferred, but that an equally strong argument could be made in favour of mistake of law trumping failure of

---

[46] See also the way Lord Goff expressed his conclusion at 177F.
[47] [1994] 4 All ER 890, 933.   [48] Law Com No 227 (1994) § 10.2 n 1.
[49] (1994) 182 CLR 51, 57 (High Court of Australia).   [50] [1999] 2 AC 349, 375.
[51] (1993) 23 UWALR 195, 230 n.

consideration, and, significantly, that 'either approach is antagonistic to the usual preference of English law to allow either of two alternative remedies to be available, leaving any possible conflict to be solved by election at a later stage'.[52] Lord Goff has been a firm proponent of English law's traditional preference for concurrent liability, under which, if the facts give rise to more than one cause of action, a person can advance his claim as he wishes and no doubt will do so on the basis of the cause of action which is most advantageous to him.[53] If in *Woolwich* Lord Goff intended to depart from the usual preference of English law, surely he would have said so.

Buxton LJ's assessment of the distance between the *Woolwich* principle and what he called 'the ordinary principles of restitution' undoubtedly gains some support from Lord Goff's rejection of a development of the common law concepts of compulsion or mistake as the basis of the new ground of recovery[54] and the fact that the reasons given by Lord Goff for enunciating a new restitutionary right are all based on the special position of the State and other public authorities.[55] That support is, however, it is submitted, limited because, even if it is correct to regard the right recognized in *Woolwich* as one which stands 'outside the main stream of restitution as understood in a private law context',[56] it does not follow that the new ground for restitution is to be a substitute for and to replace the common law grounds for restitution. There is, moreover, no indication in *Woolwich* that the development in that case was to have that effect as opposed to supplementing the common law grounds with an additional ground. Indeed there are clear indications to the contrary. Lord Goff and Lord Slynn stated that the building society would have been able to recover if it had paid under a mistake of fact.[57] The authorities from which the *Woolwich* principle was derived include cases of compulsion, and Lord Browne Wilkinson also relied on the analogy of total failure of consideration, a standard ground of restitution.[58] The majority speeches accepted that if there had been duress, or the conditions of *colore officii* were met, there would have been recovery.[59]

Buxton LJ also relied on what Lord Goff said about defences, stating that Lord Goff was 'strongly attracted' to the argument that defences available to a private payee should not be available to the revenue when it has collected tax under an

---

[52] [1999] 2 AC 349, 387B–C. Cf Buxton LJ in *Deutsche Morgan Grenfell* at para [289].

[53] See *Coupland v Arabian Gulf Petroleum Co* [1983] 1 WLR 1136; *Attorney-General v Guardian Newspapers (No 2)* [1990] 1 AC 109; *Henderson v Merrett Syndicates Ltd* [1995] 2 AC 145, 193–4. While the position may appear to be different in the case of overlapping claims in contract and restitution (*The Evia Luck* [1992] 2 AC 152, 165; *The Trident Beauty* [1994] 1 WLR 161, 164), this is so only until the contract is discharged and thereafter only where the contract expressly or impliedly excludes what would otherwise be a restitutionary obligation.

[54] [1993] 1 AC 70, 173F.

[55] See also J Beatson, 'Restitution of Taxes, Levies and Other Imports: Defining the Extent of the *Woolwich* Principle' (1993) 109 LQR 401, 409; Law Com No 227 (1994) § 6.41.

[56] Buxton LJ at para [272].   [57] [1993] AC 70, 164D–E, 201B.

[58] [1993] AC 70, 197.

[59] [1993] AC 70, 164–5, 197–8, 200–1. See Beatson (1993) 109 LQR 401, 406.

ultra vires demand.[60] The disapplication of general restitutionary defences and the provision of additional statutory limitations on any restitutionary right against the revenue, such as short time limits, would certainly give the *Woolwich* claim a different flavour from other restitutionary claims but it is submitted that the position is more complicated than Buxton LJ's statement suggests.

Lord Goff did recognize that 'the armoury of common law defences, such as those which prevent recovery under a binding compromise or to avoid a threat of litigation, may be either inapposite or inadequate' in the context of modern taxation law[61] so that it may be necessary to have recourse to other defences. The only additional bar he mentioned is a short time limit which would have to be introduced by legislation,[62] but he also doubted the advantage of special limits on the recovery of ultra vires levies.[63] He also stated he found the reasoning of Wilson J in rejecting a defence of 'passing on' 'most attractive'[64] but 'passing on' is not in fact a common law defence to a restitutionary claim.[65] There is no indication that Lord Goff favoured the disapplication of other common law defences such as change of position. Since it will, as a general rule, be factually difficult for a public authority to establish a change of position,[66] it is in any event probably unnecessary to disapply it in the case of ultra vires receipts. So the only defence unequivocally questioned is that of compromise or payment to avoid threatened litigation and this was because a demand for payment by a public authority is implicitly backed up by the coercive power of the state.[67]

5. The Court of Appeal's Approach to the Decision in *Kleinwort Benson plc v Lincoln*

Before the decision in *Bilbie v Lumlie*,[68] often seen as the origin of the rule precluding recovery of money paid under a mistake of law, no distinction was made between mistaken payments made to public authorities and such payments made to private individuals or entities. The justifications given for the rule—the greater prevalence of doubtful questions of law and the policy favouring security of receipts and certainty in commercial dealings[69]—apply to both public and

---

[60] para [271(ii)].   [61] [1993] AC 70, 174 C–D.   [62] ibid 176–7.
[63] ibid 176E.   [64] ibid 176D.
[65] *Kleinwort Benson Ltd v Birmingham CC* [1997] QB 380; A Burrows, *The Law of Restitution* (2nd edn, 2002) 593–6.
[66] Save one with modest assets: see *Waikato Regional Airport v Attorney-General* [2003] UKPC 50; R Goff and G Jones, *The Law of Restitution* (6th edn, 2002) 676; J Beatson and W Bishop, 'Mistaken Payments in the Law of Restitution' (1986) 36 U of Tor LJ 149, 156.
[67] [1993] AC 70, 172F.   [68] (1802) 2 East 469.
[69] Birks (above, n 7) 165. See also Sutton 'Kelly v Solari: The Justification of the Ignorantia Iuris Rule' (1966) 2 NZLR 173, 174–5; *Kleinwort Benson v Lincoln CC* [1999] 2 AC 349, 384F–G.In *Hydro Electric Commission of the Township of Nepean v Ontario Hydro* [1982] 1 SCR 347, 412 Estey J stated that the rule resulted in 'certainty in commerce and in public transactions [which] is an

private payees and do not justify a distinction between them. In the section of his speech dealing with its abrogation, Lord Goff stated that the rule 'should no longer be maintained as part of English law, and that English law should now recognise that there is *a general right to recover money paid under a mistake*, whether of fact or law subject to the defences available in the law of restitution' (emphasis added).[70] There is nothing in this section or in the other majority speeches to indicate that a distinction was being drawn between the effect of causative mistake of law on payments to private individuals or entities and payments of tax or similar charges to public authorities. His lordship did address the fears which formerly appeared to require a blanket exclusion of recovery but said that to cater for them 'the law must evolve appropriate defences which can, together with the defence of change of position, provide protection where appropriate for recipients of money paid under a mistake of law in those cases in which justice or policy does not require them to refund the money'.[71]

The reference to 'two separate and distinct regimes' which was relied on by the Inland Revenue and accepted by the Court of Appeal in *Deutsche Morgan Grenfell* was not in the section of Lord Goff's speech dealing with the abrogation of the mistake of law rule but in the section dealing with possible defences, and in particular a defence barring recovery of payments made in accordance with a settled understanding of the law. Park J considered that if Lord Goff intended to state that, although money paid under a mistake of law was generally recoverable at common law, there was no common law right to recover tax paid under a mistake of law, he would have done so in the section of the speech dealing with the abrogation of the rule and not when considering possible defences.[72] The Court of Appeal did not agree. Jonathan Parker LJ considered that it was 'natural' to refer to the different regimes in that context.[73] Buxton LJ stated that the language and structure of this part of Lord Goff's judgment demonstrated that his analysis of the two separate streams of relief was regarded by him as setting out the substantive law that pointed to a particular solution to the issue of the settled understanding of the law defence.[74] With respect, these explanations do not square with Lord Goff's express statement that what was being done was to create *a general right of recovery* which would need to be qualified by the development of *appropriate defences*. If the general right of recovery does not apply to payments of tax and similar charges, this would surely have been stated in the discussion of that general right.

This last point is underlined by the fact that in *Kleinwort Benson*, in the part of his speech dealing with the abrogation of the rule, Lord Goff cited three decisions of final courts of appeal in Canada, South Africa, and Australia involving

---

essential element of the well being of the community' and the 'consequential freedom from disruptive undoing of past transactions'.

[70] [1999] 2 AC 349, 375   [71] ibid 373D–E.

[72] [2003] 4 All ER 646, para [18(ii)]. See also *Mallusk Cold Storage Ltd v Dept Finance and Personnel* [2003] QBD (NI) 370, para [25].   [73] para [210].

[74] para [278].

overpayments of tax made under a mistake of law, without indicating that the general common law right enunciated does not apply to tax paid under such a mistake. The natural inference from the citation of these cases together with 'private law' cases from other jurisdictions in which money paid under a mistake of law was held to be recoverable[75] is, as Park J stated in respect of one of them,[76] that Lord Goff saw no objection to a similar result forming part of English common law in the case of tax paid under such a mistake.

The Court of Appeal, however, stated that Lord Goff's references to these cases did not support the bank's case. Only Jonathan Parker LJ considered the Supreme Court of Canada's decision in *Air Canada v British Columbia*.[77] He stated that Lord Goff's reference to that case did not assist *Deutsche Morgan Grenfell* because it was made in the general context of the abrogation of the mistake of law rule and in the particular context of the concession in *Kleinwort Benson* that the rule required some modification.[78]

The second case referred to, *Willis Faber Enthoven (Pty) Ltd v Receiver of Taxes*,[79] was a restitutionary claim for the recovery of tax paid that succeeded. Jonathan Parker LJ considered it was referred to 'merely as an example of a decision in a civil law jurisdiction in which the mistake of law rule was rejected' and that 'it mattered not for the purpose of that reference that *Willis Faber* involved an overpayment of tax'.[80] Notwithstanding his view that Lord Goff 'plainly intended to set out the whole of the relevant law in effectively canonical terms',[81] Buxton LJ said that Lord Goff did not subject *Willis Faber* to any detailed analysis, and the case concerned South African law, a system based on the *conditio indebiti*, which as Lord Goff had explained in *Woolwich*, England had decided not to adopt.[82] He concluded that it was impossible to spell out of his passing reference to it a conclusion that conflicts with the specific language used 'everywhere else in his speech'.[83] The third case referred to was the decision of the High Court of Australia in *Commissioner for State Revenue v Royal Insurance*.[84] Jonathan Parker and Buxton LJJ stated that the reference to that case was only to correct a dictum of Mason CJ about what had been decided in *Woolwich* and did not assist.

With respect to these reasons, again, it can be asked, if the general right of recovery does not apply to payments of tax and similar charges, why did Lord Goff, acknowledged to be the leading authority in this area of the law, cite these

[75] *David Securities Pty Ltd v Commonwealth Bank of Australia* (1992) 175 CLR 353; *Morgan Guaranty Trust Co of New York v Lothian RC* 1995 SC 151.
[76] [2003] 4 All ER 645, 656, said of *Willis Faber Enthoven (Pty) Ltd v Receiver of Taxes* (1992) (4) SA 202.   [77] [1989] 1 SCR 1161.
[78] para [221].   [79] (1992) (4) SA 202 (South African Appellate Division).
[80] para [220].   [81] para [265].   [82] para [286].
[83] para [286]. It would seem from his lordship's judgment that he is primarily referring to the reference to 'separate and distinct regimes' in *Kleinwort Benson* and to his conclusion ([279]) that in *Woolwich* Lord Goff held that 'issues of mistake are irrelevant in ultra vires cases'.
[84] (1994) 182 CLR 51.

three cases alongside 'private law' cases from other jurisdictions? If this was so, surely he would have stated or at least indicated that, while what these cases had to say about the mistake of law rule in general was helpful, their particular context—overpayment of tax—meant they were not of assistance because, either as a result of the *Woolwich* case or of *Kleinwort Benson*, there is no common law right based on mistake to recover tax in English law? The way the Court of Appeal put aside Lord Goff's reference to the *Royal Insurance* case is, for the reasons given above,[85] particularly puzzling.

Finally, as Professor Burrows has shown,[86] the Court of Appeal's position on 'separate and distinct regimes' produces an inconsistency without a clear justification between the treatment of taxes and similar charges and other payments made to public authorities which are subject to the *Woolwich* principle.[87] Such a distinction has the potential to create a body of law as complicated as that created by *O'Reilly v Mackman's*[88] principle of procedural exclusivity.[89]

6. The Impact of the Statutory Regimes for the Recovery of Taxes and Similar Charges

One obvious distinction between taxes on the one hand and similar charges and other payments to public authorities on the other hand is that, in the case of the former, Parliament is more likely to have enacted provisions regulating recovery. It is, however, submitted that one cannot use the existence of the statutory regimes to justify the non-applicability of the *Kleinwort Benson* principle to payments of tax and similar charges falling outside the scope of those regimes, as Jonathan Parker and Rix LJJ did.[90] Why should a decision to legislate for one tax or public charge carry with it the implication that Parliament intended there to be no right of recovery whatsoever for other taxes and charges in respect of which there is legislative silence and no statutory regulation of the recovery of the sums overpaid?

Support for the proposition that no such legislative intention can be discerned is to be found in the statements in *Woolwich* that the building society would have been able to recover if it had paid under a mistake of fact, duress, or *colore officii*.[91] What was significant there was that none of the statutory regimes regulating the recovery of tax paid but not due, including section 33 of the Taxes Management Act 1970, were engaged either in the sense of founding a right to recover or in providing statutory limitations to any such right,

---

[85] See 170 above.   [86] (2005) 121 LQR 540, 542.
[87] J Beatson (1993) 109 LQR 401, 417.   [88] [1983] 2 AC 237.
[89] On the rise and fall of the exclusivity principle, see Law Com No 226 § 3.8 ff.
[90] See 169 above.   [91] See 169, 171 above.

whether arising under statute or under the common law.[92] So also, as none of those statutory regimes were engaged in *Deutsche Morgan Grenfell*, if the advance corporation tax had been paid under duress or mistake, whether of fact or of law, in principle it should have been recoverable under the ordinary rules of the law of restitution.[93]

Tangential support that no such legislative intention should be discerned can be found in the decision of the House of Lords in *Autologic plc v Inland Revenue Commissioners*.[94] This considered when a taxpayer is required to have recourse to the specialist tax tribunals and when there may be recourse to the High Court. In situations where the tribunals have jurisdiction, it was held that High Court proceedings would be an abuse of process. Where the tribunals do not have jurisdiction,[95] it was held to be proper to proceed in the High Court. Within their jurisdiction the statutory tribunals have exclusive jurisdiction but that does not mean that where they have no jurisdiction there is no alternative remedial route.

The acceptance by the Court of Appeal of the Revenue's argument that the only routes for the recovery of tax and similar charges are the *Woolwich* principle and statute means that, if affirmed, in some cases in which, before *Woolwich*, there was a right to restitution, there will now be no remedy. It is not difficult to envisage facts in which none of the statutory regimes are engaged, as they were not in *Deutsche Morgan Grenfell*. The existing statutory regimes do not cover all taxes and they are subject to conditions. For instance, if the payment is not made pursuant to an assessment, section 33 of the Taxes Management Act will not be engaged. Tax or a similar charge not due may also be paid in circumstances which do not give rise to a claim under the *Woolwich* principle because there is no ultra vires demand. One example is where a person pays income tax twice because he forgets he has already paid.[96] Another, based on the facts in *Willis Faber*, is where a person pays after receiving erroneous legal advice which leads him to believe he is under a legal obligation to pay when he is not.

The difficulties do not entirely disappear even where one of the statutory regimes is engaged. A statutory regime regulating the recovery of overpaid tax can be interpreted as excluding common law claims *which were known to exist at the time it was enacted*; for example, in the case of section 33 of the Taxes

---

[92] [1993] AC 70 at 169–70, 199–200. Lord Goff and Lord Slynn referred to two reasons for s 33 not applying in that case apart from the fundamental one that s 33 did not apply to an ultra vires demand; first, it was doubtful that s 33 applied to composite rate tax, and secondly, that s 33 only applied to charges under an assessment and no assessment was raised on *Woolwich* because the money was paid, though under protest.

[93] See also Lord Goff at 169–70 (while the statutes may overlay and replace the common law principles where they apply, they become neutral in their effect when the development of those principles is considered by the courts).

[94] [2005] UKHL 54; [2005] 3 WLR 339.

[95] Including claims for restitutionary and other relief in respect of the UK's failure to give proper effect to Community law: ibid, para [41].

[96] A Burrows (2005) 121 LQR 540, 542.

Management Act, a claim to recover a payment made under a mistake of fact. But the regimes enacted before 1999 assumed that there was no common law right to recover tax paid under a mistake of law. So, to this extent, they were not based on an exclusion or limitation of a common law right, but on a perceived extension of the rights of taxpayers. It is possible that this was done to mitigate what the legislature perceived, as it turns out wrongly, to be an unfair common law rule.

Although, when interpreting a statute, what is relevant is Parliament's understanding of the law, rather than the law in an abstract juridical correctitude,[97] there is a difference between legislation passed under a misapprehension as to the law and an amending Act.[98] The fact that the statutory regimes governing tax not due were in this way enacted on a mistaken basis should not logically affect the underlying common law position. So, for example, in *Prichard v Briggs*[99] the Court of Appeal held that the fact that the 1925 property statutes were clearly framed on the mistaken assumption that a right of preemption creates an interest in land did not change the underlying law. The position may be different where it is clear that Parliament intended to lay down a comprehensive and exclusive statutory code,[100] but the decision in *Woolwich* shows this is not so in the case of payments of tax not due.[101] Moreover, in the case of statutes excluding or limiting the rights of citizens against the state, including common law rights to the recovery of taxes not due which have been seen as 'constitutional',[102] there is a particular need for clarity and care. Such rights should not be removed as a result merely of an assumption or an allusion in a statute passed under a misapprehension as to the existing law.

7. Was the Bank in *Deutsche Morgan Grenfell* Mistaken?

In *Kleinwort Benson* Lord Hoffmann stated that the decision left open 'what may be difficult evidential questions over whether a person making a payment has made a mistake or not' and that 'there is room for a spectrum of states of mind between genuine belief in [the] validity [of the obligation to pay], founding a claim based on mistake and a clear acceptance of the risk'[103] but those were not

---

[97] *Black Clawson International Ltd v Papierwerke Waldhof-Aschaffenberg AG* [1975] AC 591, 614 (Lord Simon of Glaisdale). See generally *Bennion's Statutory Interpretation* (4th edn, 2002) 590–1, 602–3.

[98] *Marcic v Thames Water Utilities Ltd* [2004] 2 AC 42, relied on by the Revenue, is distinguishable because there was no such legislative mistake.

[99] [1980] 1 All ER 294, 312–13, 329 (Goff and Templeman LJJ). See also *Radwan v Radwan (No 2)* [1972] 3 All ER 1026, 1039 per Cumming Bruce J.

[100] See *Billson v Residential Apartments Ltd* [1991] 3 All ER 265, at 281 (Browne-Wilkinson V-C); *Bennion* (above, n 97) 591.

[101] *British Steel plc v Commissioners of Customs & Excise* [1997] 2 All ER 366, 376, 382.

[102] See 169 above. See by analogy *R v Secretary of State for the Home Department, ex p Simms* [2000] 2 AC 115, 131 (Lord Hoffmann).   [103] [1999] 2 AC 349, 401.

before the House. It has been noted that in *Deutsche Morgan Grenfell* Buxton and
Rix LJJ doubted that the bank had paid under a mistake because by the time
some of the payments were made, the bank's understanding was that *Metallgesellschaft's* claim had merit.[104] They referred to Lord Hope's statements that
'cases where the payer was aware that there was an issue of law which was relevant
but, being in doubt as to what the law was, paid without waiting to resolve
that doubt' were not cases of mistake because 'a state of doubt is different to a
mistake'[105] and 'a payment made in the knowledge that there was a ground to
controvert liability is irrecoverable'.[106] But Lord Hope also said that the critical
question is 'whether the payer would have made the payment if he had known
what he is now being told was the law' and that it is 'the state of mind of the
payer at the time of the payment which will determine whether he paid under a
mistake'.[107]

Any tension between what is said about the state of mind of the payer being the
critical question and what is said about knowledge that there was a ground to
controvert liability is apparent and not real. The position of a person who would
not have made the payment if he had known what he is now being told was the
law, but who knows at the time of the payment that there is a ground to controvert
liability, will depend on his precise state of mind. If he 'knows' that there is a
ground upon which liability can successfully be controverted, it would seem that
he 'knows' the law and is not mistaken. If what he 'knows' is that there is a ground
upon which it can legitimately be argued that liability can be controverted, but the
outcome is uncertain, he may be found to have accepted the risk and be unable to
recover. What if, as was the case in *Deutsche Morgan Grenfell*, notwithstanding that
he knows there is a ground upon which it can legitimately be argued that liability
can be controverted, he believes that until the outcome is determined he is liable to
pay? The uncontroverted evidence of the bank's head of taxation was that, notwithstanding its understanding about *Metallgesellschaft's* claim, the bank considered that because of the statutory position it was liable to pay the tax pending
the outcome of the litigation. The bank thus believed that advance corporation tax
was payable when on the true state of the law it was not. Since the vital issue is
whether the payer had doubts as to his liability to pay, given this evidence, it is
submitted Jonathan Parker LJ correctly concluded the bank was mistaken. He
stated that this 'was plainly a mistake of law' which fell fairly and squarely within
the *Kleinwort Benson* principle.[108]

[104] paras [262] and [281–3]. See 166 above. Note that what constitutes an operative mistake is
broader in restitution than in contract (*Midland Bank plc v Brown Shipley & Co Ltd* [1991] 2 All ER
690, 700–1; Burrows, (above, n 65) 143) so that contract cases (such as *Brennan v Bolt Burdon*
[2004] EWCA Civ 1017, [2004] 3 WLR 1321) should be treated with caution.
[105] [1999] 2 AC 349, 410B–C. The Law Commission considered that recovery on the ground
of mistake was precluded when the payer (*a*) has doubts as to his liability but pays nevertheless or
(*b*) assumes the risk of any mistake: Law Com No 227 (1994) §§ 2.33–2.34.
[106] ibid 412C.   [107] ibid at 411C–D.
[108] paras [232–3]. Cf R Stevens (2005) 5 OUCLJ 141.

Peter Birks's view that a claim based on mistake must be based on data that can be verified as true or false at the time of the payment was rejected by the House of Lords in *Kleinwort Benson*.[109] It is, however, submitted that his view provides the only clear path to a conclusion that in *Deutsche Morgan Grenfell* the bank was not mistaken. Unless the House wishes to revisit that question, adapting Lord Goff's words, when the bank paid the money it believed it was bound in law to do so. It is now told that, on the law as held to be applicable at the date of the payment, he was not bound to pay it. Plainly, therefore, it paid the money under a mistake of law.[110]

8. Birks's Re-conceptualization

If the argument above is correct, it appears that the only way for the decision of the Court of Appeal to be affirmed may be on the basis of Birks's re-conceptualization of the law of restitution. This is because if the claim is based on the absence of a basis for the payment, it will not be based on mistake and the extended limitation period cannot apply.[111] A re-conceptualization of this area of the law does not seem to have been the intention of Lord Goff and the other judges who decided the swaps cases. They considered they were adding a new ground for restitution. Re-conceptualization on this scale does not, moreover, fit comfortably into the normal process of common law change.[112] It would mean that whenever a person paid another money that was not due he would prima facie be able to recover it subject to defences. This seems unlikely, but the question is whether, as Birks maintained, the necessary consequence of the decisions in the swaps cases is that the kaleidoscope that is the common law has been turned and now has a new pattern. The consequence would be an upheaval of much settled doctrine, but what a triumph it would be for his powerful analysis.

Whatever the outcome, it is arguable that the undoubted difficulties that confronted the Court of Appeal are ones that only arise because of the combined effect of the emphatic endorsement in *Kleinwort Benson* of the declaratory theory of judicial decision-making[113] and subsequent failure to address the problem legislatively. Legislation might address the problem, either, as the Law Commission originally recommended, by excluding payments made in accordance with a settled view of the law which was departed from by a subsequent judicial

---

[109] [1999] 2 AC 349, 380–1, 382H, 399–400, 411D–E.

[110] See [1999] 2 AC 349 at 379G–H.

[111] See *Phillips-Higgins v Harper* [1954] 1 QB 411; A Burrows (2005) 121 LQR 540, 544. Cf J Edelman (2005) 68 MLR 848, 851–3.

[112] See Lord Goff in *Kleinwort Benson v Lincoln CC* [1999] 2 AC 349, 378; 'The Search for Principle' (1983) 69 Proc Brit Academy 170.

[113] For another difficulty, see *Brennan v Bolt Burdon* [2004] EWCA 1017, para [63] per Sedley LJ.

decision,[114] or as the Commission later recommended by an appropriate limitation period for such cases,[115] or as was done after the decision of Park J on 18 July 2003, by enacting that (with effect from 8 September 2003) the extended limitation period does not apply in relation to a mistake of law relating to a taxation matter[116] although that might itself be vulnerable under EU Law.[117] But legislation was only needed because of the application of the declaratory theory. On this, one can imagine Peter Birks, with his penchant for zoological analogies, asking whether the refusal of the House of Lords to accept the indeterminacy of a question of law that is subsequently changed meant that they could tell us not only whether Schrödinger's cat is alive,[118] but also whether it is smiling at the consequences of *Kleinwort Benson's* adherence to abstract juridical correctitude.[119]

---

[114] Law Com No 227 (1994) §§ 5.5, 5.13. The Scottish Law Commission disagreed with this proposal (DP No 95 § 2.125, and DP No 99 § 3.51) and it was criticized in *Kleinwort Benson:* [1999] AC 349, at 381–4 and 414–15. See also Brooke LJ in *Eagerpath Ltd v Edwards* (1999) 73 TC 427, paras [35–6].   [115] Law Com No 270 (2001) § 4.76 ff.

[116] Finance Act 2004, s 320.

[117] M Chowdry, 'The Revenue's Response: A Time Bar on Claims' (2005) 121 LQR 546.

[118] See Lord Hoffmann in *Kleinwort Benson v Lincoln CC* [1999] 2 AC 349, 399E–F.

[119] See Lord Simon of Glaisdale in *Black Clawson International Ltd v Papierwerke Waldhof-Aschaffenberg AG* [1975] AC 591, 614.

10

The Further Travails of Duress

*Ewan McKendrick**

In 1990 Peter Birks wrote an extended case-note entitled 'The Travails of Duress'.[1] The aims of the case note were to reduce the uncertainty in the law of duress, to challenge the role given to the 'coercion of the will test', and to reduce, if not eliminate, the concealed discretion which the law had conferred on the courts when deciding cases concerned with duress. His note focussed on three leading decisions of the period: *Crescendo Management Pty Ltd v Westpac Banking Corp*,[2] *Williams v Roffey Bros & Nicholls (Contractors) Ltd*,[3] and *Dimskal Shipping Co SA v International Transport Workers Federation (The Evia Luck (No 2))*.[4] While duress did not feature prominently in Birks's subsequent writings,[5] his note, written in his characteristically lucid style, makes an important contribution to the identification of the critical issues that must be addressed in the development of the law relating to duress. It would be gratifying to be able to report that the law has indeed developed since Birks completed his case-note, that the uncertainties which he identified have disappeared, and that the law has been put on a more coherent basis. Unfortunately, it is not possible to do so. Uncertainties continue to exist in the law and the concealed discretion which the courts enjoy has not been entirely eliminated.

The aim of this essay is to examine three issues. The first is the circumstances in which duress will suffice to entitle a party to set aside a contract and recover a benefit which has been conferred on the other party to the contract. The second aim is to examine the entitlement of a party to recover a benefit which it has conferred on another party as a result of the application of duress but there is no contract between the parties. The third is to examine the circumstances in which the application of duress will give to the party subject to the duress a claim for compensatory damages.

---

* Professor of English Private Law in the University of Oxford; Fellow of Lady Margaret Hall, Oxford.

[1] P Birks, 'The Travails of Duress' [1990] LMCLQ 342.   [2] (1988) 19 NSWLR 40.
[3] [1991] 1 QB 1.
[4] [1990] 1 Lloyd's Rep 319. A subsequent appeal to the House of Lords was dismissed: [1992] 2 AC 152.
[5] It makes the occasional appearance in his last book, *Unjust Enrichment* (2nd edn, 2005) under the label of 'illegitimate pressure': see eg pp 106 and 135. It also featured, largely by way of contrast

1. Duress and the Avoidance of a Contract

Turning now to our first question, when will duress suffice to entitle a party to set aside a contract and recover a benefit which has been conferred on the other party to the contract? Lord Hoffmann in *R v Attorney-General for England and Wales*[6] summarized the law relating to duress in the following passage:

In *Universe Tankships Inc of Monrovia v International Transport Workers Federation* [1983] 1 AC 366, 400 Lord Scarman said that there were two elements in the wrong of duress. One was pressure amounting to compulsion of the will of the victim and the second was the illegitimacy of the pressure. R says that to offer him the alternative of being returned to unit, which was regarded in the SAS as a public humiliation, was compulsion of his will. It left him no practical alternative. Their lordships are content to assume that this was the case. But, as Lord Wilberforce and Lord Simon of Glaisdale said in *Barton* v *Armstrong* [1976] AC 104, 121:

'in life . . . many acts are done under pressure, sometimes overwhelming pressure, so that one can say that the actor had no choice but to act. Absence of choice in this sense does not negate consent in law: for this the pressure must be one of a kind which the law does not regard as legitimate.'

The legitimacy of the pressure must be examined from two aspects: first, the nature of the pressure and secondly, the nature of the demand which the pressure is applied to support: see Lord Scarman in the *Universe Tankships* case, at p 401. Generally speaking, the threat of any form of unlawful action will be regarded as illegitimate. On the other hand, the fact that the threat is lawful does not necessarily make the pressure legitimate. As Lord Atkin said in *Thorne* v *Motor Trade Association* [1937] AC 797, 806:

'The ordinary blackmailer normally threatens to do what he has a perfect right to do— namely, communicate some compromising conduct to a person whose knowledge is likely to affect the person threatened . . . What he has to justify is not the threat, but the demand of money.'[7]

This passage is illuminating for a number of reasons. The first is the reference to the 'wrong of duress'. The second is the acceptance of the fact that duress consists of 'two elements'. The third is that these two elements are not seen as alternatives: in order to establish a claim of duress a claimant must prove *both* a 'compulsion of the will' and the application by the defendant of 'illegitimate pressure'. The final point to note is that Lord Hoffmann appeared to favour a two-stage approach to the illegitimacy of the pressure applied. The first of these issues will be examined in a later section of this essay. The remaining issues will be examined in the following sections.

---

to undue influence, in P Birks and N Chin, 'On the Nature of Undue Influence' in J Beatson and D Friedmann (eds), *Good Faith and Fault in Contract Law* (1995) 68.

   [6] [2003] UKPC 22.   [7] ibid at [15]–[16].

1.1. Compulsion of the Will

The 'compulsion of the will' element of the test has had a chequered history. The phrase used to denote this element of the test has varied slightly over time. Initially the phrase which found favour with the courts was that there must have been a 'coercion of the will so as to vitiate consent'[8] or that the will of the victim must have been 'overborne'.[9] It was one of the principal aims of Birks's case-note to repudiate those tests. He asserted that the 'coercion of the will test' was a 'plausible-sounding but inscrutable test' and that it amounted to a 'false step'[10] and, indeed, was a 'heresy'.[11] He found support for his argument in the judgment of McHugh JA (as he then was) in *Crescendo Management Pty Ltd v Westpac Banking Corp*[12] when he stated:

the overbearing of the will theory of duress should be rejected. A person who is the subject of duress usually knows only too well what he is doing. But he chooses to submit to the demand or pressure rather than take an alternative course of action. The proper approach in my opinion is to ask whether any applied pressure induced the victim to enter into the contract and then ask whether that pressure went beyond what the law is prepared to countenance as legitimate.[13]

The demise of the 'coercion of the will' test seemed to be confirmed by the speech of Lord Goff in *Dimskal Shipping Co SA v International Transport Workers Federation* (*The Evia Luck* (*No. 2*))[14] when, drawing on the case-note written by Birks and the work of Professors Atiyah[15] and Beatson,[16] he expressed his agreement with McHugh JA and stated that he doubted whether it was 'helpful in this context to speak of the plaintiff's will having been coerced'.[17] References to the 'coercion of the will' have declined in more recent cases. While it is true that Lord Hoffmann in *R* referred to the 'compulsion' of the will of the victim, it should be noted that this element was not in issue on the facts of the case. The Privy Council was content to assume that there had been the requisite compulsion of R's will. Does Lord Hoffmann's reference to the 'compulsion' of the will of the victim amount to an attempt to reintroduce the 'overborne will' theory into the law of duress and, if it does, is this a desirable step to take?

It is suggested that it is not an attempt to reintroduce the 'overborne will' theory and, further, that any attempt to do so would be undesirable. The principal objection to the overborne will theory was the suggestion that the person subject to the duress had no choice at all. As McHugh JA observed in *Crescendo Management*, the person subject to the duress does make a choice and

---

[8] *Pao On v Lau Yiu Long* [1980] AC 614, 635–6.
[9] *Occidental Worldwide Investment Corporation v Skibs A/S Avanti* (*The Siboen and The Sibotre*) [1976] 1 Lloyd's Rep 293, 336.   [10] Birks (above, n 1) 342.
[11] ibid at 344.   [12] (1988) 19 NSWLR 40.   [13] ibid at 45–6.
[14] [1992] 2 AC 152.
[15] 'Economic Duress and the "Overborne Will"' (1982) 98 LQR 197.
[16] *The Use and Abuse of Unjust Enrichment* (1991) 113–17.   [17] [1992] AC 152, 166.

does know what she is doing. However it does not follow from this that the nature of the consent given by the claimant is an irrelevant factor. Her consent is relevant for the purpose of establishing that there is a sufficient causal link between the pressure applied by the defendant and the decision of the claimant to enter into the contract.

However, the rejection of the 'overborne will' test will not bring an end to our difficulties. The identification of the test to be applied when determining whether or not there is a sufficient connection between the pressure applied and the decision of the claimant to enter into the contract has given rise to difficulty and appears likely to continue to do so. Perhaps this should not occasion surprise given that causation has proved to be a difficult issue in other areas of private law, most notably in the context of the tort of negligence.[18] The starting point for any discussion of this issue must be the decision of the Privy Council in *Barton v Armstrong*.[19] *Barton* was a case of physical duress where it was held that it sufficed for the claimant to prove that the threats made by the defendant were 'a' reason for him entering into the contract and that the claimant was entitled to set aside the contract even though he might have entered into the contract if the defendant had uttered no threats to induce him to do so.[20] Further, it was stated that it was for the defendant to prove that there was no causal link between his threats and the decision of the claimant to enter into the contract. In the words of the majority judgment:

it was for Armstrong [the defendant] to establish, if he could, that the threats which he was making and the unlawful pressure which he was exerting for the purpose of inducing Barton [the claimant] to sign the agreement and which Barton knew were being made and exerted for this purpose in fact contributed nothing to Barton's decision to sign.[21]

This is an extremely pro-claimant stance. It is one thing to conclude that the claimant need not prove that the illegitimate pressure was 'the' reason, the 'predominant' reason, or the 'clinching' reason for the decision to enter into the contract.[22] It is quite another to place upon the defendant the onus of proving the absence of a causal link. It is likely to be extremely difficult if not impossible for a defendant to prove that his threats 'contributed nothing' to the claimant's decision to enter into the contract. What is the justification for this reversal of the onus of proof? The answer would appear to lie in the court's disapproval of the defendant's conduct. Support for the proposition that the court was influenced by the reprehensible nature of the defendant's conduct can be derived

[18] See *Fairchild v Glenhaven Funeral Services Ltd* [2002] UKHL 22; [2003] 1 AC 32; *Chester v Afshar* [2004] UKHL 41; [2005] 1 AC 134; *Barker v Corus UK Ltd* [2006] UKHL 20; *White v Paul Davidson & Taylor* [2004] EWCA Civ 1511; *Beary v Pall Mall Investments (a firm)* [2005] EWCA Civ 415.   [19] [1976] AC 104.
[20] ibid at 120.   [21] ibid at 120.
[22] ibid at 121. These tests were all rejected by the minority, Lords Wilberforce and Simon of Glaisdale, but their dissent was based on the application of the law to the facts of the case rather than the formulation of the legal rule itself.

from the fact that the Privy Council drew an analogy with the case of fraud where the conduct of the defendant is also morally reprehensible. This conclusion is not without its attractions in so far as it denies to defendants who have behaved particularly badly the opportunity to hide behind the evidential difficulties which a claimant may face. However it may be that this departure from the normal rules of proof will create more problems than it solves. In the first place, the reversal of the onus of proof is likely to be of critical importance only in very unusual circumstances[23] and the benefit likely to be derived from it is therefore small. In the vast majority of cases it will be obvious that a threat of the gravity of a threat to murder caused the claimant to enter into the contract. In the case where it is not clear on the evidence whether the threat did contribute to the claimant's decision to enter into the contract, one would have thought that the task of the court should be to examine the facts of the case with great care and not to resort to a switch in the onus of proof in order to make it easier for them to decide the case and thus absolve them from their duty to examine the facts with the utmost care. Secondly, once the courts create a special rule for a particular case, the difficulty which then tends to follow is one of discerning the circumstances in which the special rule is to operate. And this is exactly the difficulty which the courts have got themselves into in subsequent duress cases.

Cases post-*Barton* have displayed a marked reluctance to follow the liberal approach to causation taken in *Barton*. Instead, the courts have inclined towards a test which requires the establishment of a greater link between the pressure applied by the defendant and the claimant's decision to enter into the contract. In *Dimskal Shipping Co SA v International Transport Workers Federation (The Evia Luck (No 2))*[24] Lord Goff stated, in the context of an economic duress claim, that the illegitimate pressure must have constituted 'a significant cause inducing the plaintiff to enter into the relevant contract'.[25] The addition of the word 'significant' is important. But it is an addition which may prove to be troublesome. In the first place, it is not at all clear what meaning is to be given to 'significant' in this context. Secondly, it may be that this additional requirement is confined to cases of economic duress. If this is correct, it will require us to draw a distinction between cases of economic duress and cases of duress of the person (with cases of duress of goods possibly languishing uncertainly somewhere in between). However, it is unlikely that Lord Goff intended to draw any such distinction. He purported to derive his 'significant' cause requirement from a passage in the minority judgment in *Barton*. This reliance on the minority judgment is rather odd because it is extremely difficult to extract a 'significant' cause requirement from the passage cited. But the fact that Lord Goff purported to derive his test from *Barton* makes it extremely difficult if not impossible to conclude that he was intending to apply a different test in the context of economic duress from that applicable in the case of duress of the person.

---

[23] ibid at 119.   [24] [1992] 2 AC 152.   [25] ibid at 165.

However support for a more stringent approach than that taken in *Barton* can be found in the judgment of Mance J (as he then was) in *Huyton SA v Peter Cremer GmbH & Co*[26] He expressly distinguished between cases of duress of the person and cases of economic duress and suggested that the

relaxed view of causation in the special context of duress to the person cannot prevail in the less serious context of economic duress. The minimum basic test of subjective causation in economic duress ought, it appears to me, to be a 'but for' test. The illegitimate pressure must have been such as actually caused the making of the agreement, in the sense that it would not otherwise have been made either at all or, at least, in the terms in which it was made. In that sense, the pressure must have been decisive or clinching.[27]

While Mance J accepted that the 'but for' test was a 'minimum basic test' he later went on to express the concern that, in the context of economic duress, 'a simple "but for" test of subjective causation in conjunction with a requirement of actual or threatened breach of duty could lead too readily to relief being granted'.[28] Such a test did not, in his view, require a claimant to establish that there had been the 'hallmark of deflection of will'.[29] He therefore inclined towards a more stringent test (from the perspective of the claimant) in which the test for causation was linked to the degree of the illegitimacy of the pressure applied by the defendant.[30]

The picture which emerges from the case-law is one of unnecessary complexity. The test for causation in the law of unjust enrichment is generally the usual 'but for' test.[31] Applied to the case of duress, this would require a claimant to prove that she would not have entered into the contract but for the application of the illegitimate pressure. It is clear that this was not the test applied in *Barton*. It sufficed for the claimant to prove that the illegitimate pressure was 'a' reason for his entry into the contract; that is to say, the claimant had only to show that the pressure contributed to his decision to enter into the contract. However it would appear that this test is not applied in all cases of duress. In some cases a more stringent test is applied, while in others the test applied is a more liberal one. It is more liberal in those duress of the person cases where the onus of proof is reversed and it is more stringent in cases of economic duress where, at a minimum, the claimant must establish a 'significant' causal link between the duress and his decision to enter into the contract and may have to go further and satisfy the usual 'but for' test. This patchwork is less than satisfactory.

There are two principal issues to be resolved. The first relates to the test to be applied when deciding whether or not there is a sufficient connection between the duress and the decision of the claimant to enter into the contract. It is suggested that it should generally suffice for the claimant to prove that the duress contributed to her decision to enter into the contract, in the sense that it was 'a'

---

[26] [1999] 1 Lloyd's Rep 620.
[27] ibid at 636.   [28] ibid.   [29] ibid at 638.   [30] ibid at 637.
[31] See generally A Burrows, *The Law of Restitution* (2nd edn, 2002) 44–8.

reason for her decision to enter into the contract. This approach is consistent with that taken in the analogous area of misrepresentation.[32] It does not require the claimant positively to prove that the duress caused her to enter into the contract. Rather it is a 'softer' test which requires only that the claimant prove that the duress contributed positively to the decision to enter into the contract, in the sense that it was actively present to her mind when she decided to enter into the contract.[33]

The second and more difficult issue is whether the law should countenance departures from this rule and apply different rules to cases of duress of the person from those applicable in economic duress cases. It is suggested that no hard and fast line should be drawn between cases of duress of the person and economic duress. A threat to a claimant's economic position may be more coercive to her than a threat to her person and, as cases such as *Barton* demonstrate, a defendant may threaten both a claimant's physical and his economic well-being. In the latter case it would seem odd to apply one test in the context of duress of the person and another in the context of economic duress. An alternative analysis might be to adopt a 'sliding scale' approach which depends upon the degree of the illegitimacy of the pressure applied. At one end of the spectrum would be the pro-claimant test for cases of duress of the person as set out in the majority judgment in *Barton* and, at the other end, the more stringent approach taken in economic duress cases such as *Huyton* and *The Evia Luck (No 2)*. The difficulty with the sliding scale approach is not only the distinction which it draws between duress of the person and economic duress but the fact that it is likely to be productive of uncertainty and may give to the courts what Birks termed an 'inarticulate discretion'.[34] This is especially so in relation to the 'significant' cause test. This bristles with uncertainty and should be avoided. The preferable approach is to adhere to a uniform test for the sufficiency of the connection between the duress and the decision of the claimant to enter into the contract.

1.2. 'Illegitimate' Pressure

As has been noted, the Privy Council in *R* appeared to envisage a two-stage approach to illegitimacy. First, if the threat is of unlawful action, it will generally be illegitimate. Secondly, where the threat is of lawful action, it is not necessarily legitimate and so may be illegitimate. We shall take each case in turn.

The case where the threat is of unlawful action is the more straightforward of the two categories. Thus unlawful threats, such as a threat to commit a crime or a tort, will generally amount to the application of illegitimate pressure.[35] The more difficult case is the one in which the pressure takes the form of a threatened breach of contract. Here the cases do not speak with one voice. Two principal

---

[32] See eg *Edgington v Fitzmaurice* (1880) 25 Ch D 459.
[33] ibid at 483. See also *Barton v Armstrong* [1976] AC 104, 122.
[34] Birks (above, n 1) 347.   [35] See eg *Barton v Armstrong* [1974] AC 104.

views are possible. The first is that every threatened breach of contract is in principle illegitimate. There is much to be said for this view. English law does not generally distinguish between a good faith and a bad faith breach of contract: a breach is a breach and all breaches are unlawful in the eyes of the law. Further, cases can be found in which the courts have concluded that a threatened breach of contract was illegitimate without finding it necessary to discuss whether the threatened breach of contract was in good faith or in bad faith.[36] The second view is that not all breaches of contract should be regarded as illegitimate and that the courts should distinguish in this context between a defendant who acts in bad faith and one who acts in good faith.[37] Birks inclined to the latter view in that he indicated a preference for the view that 'a threatened breach of contract is not for these purposes illegitimate unless accompanied by bad faith or malice— the deliberate exploitation of difficulties of the other party'.[38] A similar view has been taken, albeit with qualifications, by Professor Burrows.[39]

The case of the breach of contract that is threatened in bad faith does not present a difficulty; such a threat is in principle illegitimate. The difficult case is the breach of contract that is threatened in good faith. Should such a threat always be classified as the application of illegitimate pressure? As we have seen, the cases do not provide us with a conclusive answer to this question. The question must therefore be answered as one of principle. The view that a good faith breach of contract should not inevitably be regarded as 'illegitimate' derives support from the wish to keep the doctrine of economic duress within relatively narrow limits and the desire to uphold agreements which have been renegotiated in good faith by the contracting parties.[40] The argument to the contrary is based on the fact that English law does not generally distinguish between good faith and bad faith breaches of contract, that it is not entirely clear where the line is to be drawn in this context between 'good faith' and 'bad faith', that the courts should strive to uphold the integrity of the initial contract concluded between the parties and that the renegotiation of a contract should not be regarded as inevitably beneficial and therefore deserving of protection. It is suggested that the latter view is the better one. Given that English law does not generally distinguish between good faith and bad faith breaches of contract, it is suggested that it should not create the distinction here in the absence of a compelling reason to do so. No such compelling case has, as yet, been produced. The principal factor

---

[36] See eg *North Ocean Shipping Co Ltd v Hyundai Construction Co Ltd* (*The Atlantic Baron*) [1979] QB 705 and *Atlas Express Ltd v Kafco* (*Importers and Distributors*) *Ltd* [1989] QB 833.

[37] Support for this view can be gleaned from cases such as *DSDN Subsea Ltd v Petroleum Geo–Services ASA* [2000] BLR 530 and *Huyton SA v Peter Cremer GmbH & Co* [1999] 1 Lloyd's Rep 620.

[38] Birks (above, n 1) 346.

[39] Above, n 31, 230–4. His 'qualifications' are that a threat should not be regarded as illegitimate 'if the threat is a reaction to circumstances that almost constitute frustration' or if the threat 'merely corrects what was always clearly a bad bargain'.

[40] Many of the cases in which economic duress has been invoked are cases concerned with the renegotiation of contracts.

which appears to have led many commentators to resort to the 'bad faith' analysis is the fear of too much restitution. In particular, there is a concern to uphold the integrity of 'an apparent compromise made in good faith on both sides'.[41] This is a legitimate concern. But it does not mandate a rule to the effect that a threat made in bad faith is a prerequisite to an economic duress claim.

More difficult still is the case where the pressure is not in itself unlawful. There is a temptation to conclude that the defendant cannot be acting illegitimately if the threat itself is lawful. But illegitimacy is not the same thing as unlawfulness. A threat can be illegitimate even if it is not unlawful.[42] As Lord Hoffmann observed in *R*, it is necessary to extend the category of illegitimacy to catch the case of blackmail, where the threat itself is lawful but is used to attain a goal which is unlawful.[43] Blackmail is, however, the exception, not the rule. The general rule is that a defendant who threatens to do what he is entitled to do will not be held to have applied illegitimate pressure upon the claimant.[44] Thus a refusal to contract does not constitute the application of illegitimate pressure, at least in the absence of bad faith on the part of the person who refuses to enter into the contract.[45] A refusal to waive an existing contractual obligation does not amount to the application of illegitimate pressure[46] nor is it illegitimate for an owner of goods let on hire-purchase to threaten to repossess the goods when the hirer is in default and has not attempted to obtain relief against forfeiture.[47] Similarly, a threat to resort to law does not generally constitute duress. For example, there is nothing improper in threatening to sue someone for a debt in the case where there is a bona fide belief that the debt is owed. Matters are otherwise where the legal process is used for an improper purpose, for example to extract a promise of payment in return for not initiating a prosecution against someone. In the latter case the agreement may be set aside on the ground of duress.[48]

---

[41] *Huyton SA v Peter Cremer GmbH & Co* [1999] 1 Lloyd's Rep 620, 637.

[42] The distinction between 'illegitimacy' and 'unlawfulness' is of particular importance when discussing whether or not duress can give rise to a claim for compensatory damages, on which see further pp 195–7 below.

[43] See to similar effect the speech of Lord Scarman in *Universe Tankships of Monrovia v International Transport Workers' Federation ('The Universe Sentinel')* [1983] 1 AC 366, 401.

[44] See eg *R v Attorney-General for England and Wales* [2003] UKPC 22 which was a case where the threat was one which the Crown was entitled to make and it was held not to be illegitimate.

[45] *CTN Cash and Carry Ltd v Gallaher* [1994] 4 All ER 714; *Smith v William Charlick Ltd* (1924) 34 CLR 38. *CTN Cash and Carry* does not stand for the proposition that a bad faith refusal to contract will constitute the application of illegitimate pressure. What the court did was to leave the question open: it did not purport to answer it. However both Steyn and Nicholls LJJ were careful to state that they were not deciding that a refusal to contract can 'never' constitute duress. In exceptional cases it may possibly do so.

[46] *Alec Lobb (Garages) Ltd v Total Oil (Great Britain) Ltd* [1983] 1 WLR 87, 94.

[47] *Alf Vaughan & Co Ltd v Royscot Trust plc* [1999] 1 All ER (Comm) 856.

[48] *Mutual Finance Ltd v John Wetton & Sons Ltd* [1937] 2 KB 389. Claimants in these cases have often relied on actual undue influence rather than duress but it would appear that the doctrine of duress is in principle capable of encompassing these cases.

While the cases are not entirely easy to reconcile, the areas of disagreement can be identified with some clarity. The difficulties lie in discerning when a threatened breach of contract is illegitimate and in identifying the circumstances in which a threat to do that which is lawful can be held to be illegitimate. There is a danger that the courts, faced by such difficulties, will resort to the language of discretion in order to preserve for themselves a degree of flexibility. An example of this phenomenon may be found in the judgment of Dyson J in *DSDN Subsea Ltd v Petroleum Geo-Services ASA*[49] when he stated that:

In determining whether there has been illegitimate pressure, the court takes into account a range of factors. These include whether there has been an actual or threatened breach of contract; whether the person allegedly exerting the pressure has acted in good or bad faith; whether the victim had any realistic practical alternative but to submit to the pressure; whether the victim protested at the time; and whether he affirmed and sought to rely on the contract. These are all relevant factors. Illegitimate pressure must be distinguished from the rough and tumble of the pressures of normal commercial bargaining.[50]

The difficulty with this approach is that it tends to generate uncertainty because it collapses issues that are best kept separate and distinct. For example, the question whether or not the victim had 'any realistic practical alternative' does not seem to be of any relevance to the question whether the pressure which has been applied is illegitimate. A preferable approach to this flexible, discretionary approach is to seek to identify the meaning of 'illegitimacy' with greater precision.

1.3. No Reasonable Alternative

Lord Hoffmann in *R* also refers to the fact that R alleged that he had 'no practical alternative' but to submit to the threat made on behalf of the Crown. Emphasis on the relevance of the lack of a (reasonable) alternative is apparent in some of the earlier cases, mostly notably the decision of the Court of Appeal in *B & S Contracts and Design Ltd v Victor Green Publications Ltd*[51] and the judgment of Dyson J in *DSDN Subsea Ltd v Petroleum Geo-Services ASA.*[52] Thus far this element has been given a role principally in cases of economic duress. In the case of duress of the person the victim of the duress may not have any realistic alternatives open to her; she can either submit to the threat or face the consequences. But in the case of economic duress, the claimant may have other alternatives open to her. For example, she may be able to seek injunctive relief through the courts or may be able to locate an alternative source of supply.

It is difficult to deny the potential relevance of the presence or absence of a reasonable alternative in some duress cases. The real issue is whether or not it should

---

[49] [2000] BLR 530.   [50] ibid at [131].
[51] [1984] ICR 419. Other examples include *Hennessy v Craigmile and Co Ltd* [1986] ICR 461 and *The Alev* [1989] 1 Lloyd's Rep 138.   [52] [2000] BLR 530.

be regarded as a separate, essential ingredient of a duress claim. This is a difficult issue. Take the case where a vendor of goods threatens to break her contract with the purchaser unless the purchaser agrees to pay a significantly higher price for the goods which the vendor had already contracted to sell to the purchaser.[53] Assume further that the goods are available in the market place at a price which is close to the original contract price. In such a case, if the purchaser chooses not to purchase alternative goods in the market but to pay the inflated sum demanded by the vendor, she should not be entitled to invoke the doctrine of duress in order to deny her liability to pay the inflated price demanded by the vendor.

The difficulty lies in explaining why it is that the purchaser may not be entitled to deny her liability to pay the higher price. One possible ground is the lack of a sufficient causal link between the demand by the vendor and the decision of the purchaser to pay the higher sum. However, as we have noted, the test to be used when determining whether or not there is a sufficient link between the pressure and the decision to enter into the contract is disputed. If the test is whether the pressure contributed towards the decision to enter into the contract then the purchaser is likely to be able to satisfy this test. Alternatively, if the test requires the purchaser to prove that the pressure was a 'significant' cause of her decision to enter into the contract or was the 'but for' cause, she may not be able to satisfy the test. It is perhaps this type of case that has led courts and commentators not to apply a test which requires a claimant simply to show that the pressure contributed to her decision to enter into the contract. But there may be other ways of handling this type of case. One is to conclude that the lack of a reasonable alternative is an essential ingredient in a duress claim. The difficulty with this proposition is that the availability or otherwise of a reasonable alternative appears to be largely if not entirely irrelevant in cases of duress of the person and duress of goods.[54] This takes us back to the issue, discussed above, whether a distinction should be drawn between cases of duress of the person and cases of economic duress. Given the view expressed above that such a distinction should not be drawn, the lack of a reasonable alternative should not be seen as an inevitable feature of a duress claim, given its apparent irrelevance in cases of duress of the person and duress of goods. This was, in essence, the approach taken by Mance J in *Huyton SA v Peter Cremer GmbH & Co.*[55] While he recognized that it was not necessary to go so far as to recognize the existence of 'an inflexible third essential ingredient of economic duress that there should be no or no practical alternative course open to the innocent party'[56] he stated that it 'seems . . . self-evident that relief may not be appropriate, if an innocent party

[53] It is of course possible that there might be a problem in such a case in identifying the existence of consideration for the purchaser's promise. But let us assume for the purposes of this example that the consideration requirement has been satisfied. The reduced significance of consideration in the context of the renegotiation of contracts is noted at 194 below.

[54] See eg *Astley v Reynolds* (1731) 2 Stra 915, 916 where no significance was attached to the possibility that there was an alternative claim in trover.   [55] [1999] 1 Lloyd's Rep 620.

[56] ibid at 638.

decides, as a matter of choice, not to pursue an alternative remedy which any and possibly some other reasonable persons in his circumstances would have pursued'.[57] The difficulty lies in finding the most appropriate label to give effect to this notion. It has sometimes operated under the title of 'submission to an honest claim'[58] but the notion of a non-contractual submission to an honest claim has been criticized on the ground that it is unhelpful.[59] It is suggested that the essence of what should be seen as a defence lies in the notion of a 'choice' between reasonable alternatives; namely that the purchaser, faced with a choice between reasonable alternatives, chose to agree to the terms put forward by the defendant rather than pursue the alternative course of action. The law frequently requires the innocent party to act reasonably, the most obvious example being the doctrine of mitigation. A similar principle is in issue here. In other words the defendant is entitled to raise, as a defence, the fact that the claimant had a choice between different possible courses of action, that the choice was a choice between reasonable alternatives, and that the claimant did have the ability to make a choice between these alternatives. But the important point to note is that the existence of a reasonable alternative is not part of the definition of the cause of action; rather it is an element in a defence which may be invoked by a defendant.[60]

1.4. The Absence of Consent

Thus far it has been assumed that the absence of consent on the part of the claimant will not suffice of itself to establish a claim of duress. This is confirmed by the judgment of Lord Hoffmann in *R* in that he concluded that there were 'two elements' to the 'wrong of duress'. 'Compulsion of the will' is one of these elements but it will not suffice, of itself, to make out a claim of duress. This view has been challenged by Professor Stephen Smith.[61] He asserts that there are 'two distinct grounds upon which the impugned contract might be invalidated, one plaintiff-based and the other defendant-based'.[62] The 'plaintiff-based' ground is that 'the person denying the contract's validity . . . did not consent to the contract'.[63] This view is not without its attractions. In the first place, given that contract is generally regarded as an obligation which arises from consent or from agreement, the claim that the

---

[57] ibid.
[58] See eg Goff and Jones *The Law of Restitution* (6th edn, 2002). An example of the defence in operation may be found in *Maskell v Horner* [1915] 3 KB 106.
[59] Burrows (above, n 31) 559.
[60] There are other defences to a duress claim. One of the principal defences is affirmation: see *North Ocean Shipping Co Ltd v Hyundai Construction Co Ltd (The Atlantic Baron)* [1979] QB 705.
[61] His view was first set out in his article 'Contracting under Pressure: A Theory of Duress' [1997] CLJ 343 and has since been restated, in slightly modified form, in his book *Contract Theory* (2004) 316–40.   [62] ibid at 344.
[63] ibid.

absence of consent negates the existence of a contract has a strong intuitive appeal. Secondly, in so far as there are statements in some early cases to the effect that duress renders a contract 'void',[64] this lends some support to the claim that absence of consent is the basis of duress. However, this explanation encounters two difficulties. The first is the objection, already noted, that the person subject to duress does in fact consent in so far as she does make a choice. True, that choice was constrained by the pressure applied to the claimant, but it was a choice nevertheless. This line of argument does, however, encounter problems. It can be argued that the question whether there has been 'consent' for the purposes of the law of contract is a legal question so that the presence of a choice, as a matter of fact, cannot be a definitive answer to the question whether, as a matter of law, there is sufficient consent to satisfy the requirements of the law of contract. The second difficulty is that it is now clearly established in the case-law that duress renders a contract voidable, not void. Although the Privy Council in *Barton v Armstrong* was content to accept the submission of counsel for Barton that the effect of duress was to render the deed 'void' as far as he was concerned, the view which has been accepted in the case-law post-*Barton* is that duress renders a contract voidable and not void.[65]

In the final analysis Smith concedes that 'the label "duress" should be reserved to claims based on the wrongdoing principle';[66] that is to say that the court should not enforce a contract which has been obtained by wrongdoing. He does not abandon his 'consent principle' but he concedes that it should not be subsumed within the law of duress.[67]

1.5. Substantive Unfairness

There is one further basis for duress which should be mentioned, only to be dismissed, and that is the unfairness of the terms of the contract. While substantive unfairness is a common feature of duress cases, it does not constitute the foundation of the doctrine. The reason for this is that the presence of substantive fairness is not, of itself, sufficient to constitute duress, nor is its absence sufficient to negative the existence of duress. For example, if I am compelled by circumstances to sell my house quickly and forced to lower the price, the unfairness of the price will not of itself suffice to demonstrate the existence of duress. On the other hand, if a robber forces me at gunpoint to sell my house for a fair price, the fairness of the price will not prevent me from setting aside the contract on the ground of duress. What is wrong with the contract is not the fairness or the unfairness of the terms of the contract, but the nature of the threats that have been used in order to induce me to enter into it. In other words, duress is an example of 'procedural unfairness' not 'substantive unfairness'.

---

[64] See eg *Barton v Armstrong* [1976] AC 104.
[65] See eg *Pao On v Lau Yiu Long* [1980] AC 614.
[66] SA Smith, *Contract Theory* (2004) 339.   [67] ibid.

2. Non-contractual Payments Made under Duress

Having considered the circumstances in which a contract can be set aside on the ground of duress, it is now time to consider the entitlement of a claimant to recover a non-contractual payment made or a benefit conferred under duress. At the outset it must be noted that the utility of distinguishing in this context between contractual and non-contractual payments has been doubted. For example, Professor Burrows argues that it is 'unhelpful to treat separately payments made under contracts entered into under duress'.[68] He offers three reasons for not distinguishing between contracts entered into under duress and non-contractual payments made under duress.

The first is that for some categories of duress, such as economic duress, 'there are few cases dealing with the restitution of non-contractual as opposed to contractual payments'.[69] This may be so. But the fact that there are few illustrative cases does not mean that, in the few cases in which they do arise, the law should not recognize that there is a distinction between contractual and non-contractual payments. In the case of benefits conferred under mistake, we do distinguish between mistaken payments, on the one hand, and contracts entered into under a mistake. And, if we draw the distinction in the case of mistake and have no doubt that the distinction has validity in that context,[70] why not also draw the same distinction in the case of duress?

The second objection is that 'the line between contractual and non-contractual payments, which (leaving aside deeds) turns on whether there is consideration for the payment, can be problematic where one is paying to remove a threat, especially a threat to break a contract'.[71] Many duress cases arise out of the renegotiation of an existing contract. Where money is paid on the variation or the renegotiation of a contract, it can sometimes be difficult to tell whether or not the payment was a contractual one (because the variation was supported by consideration) or non-contractual (because the variation was not supported by consideration). The modern tendency, post-*Williams v Roffey Bros & Nicholls (Contractors) Ltd*,[72] is to find the existence of consideration in the context of the re-negotiation of contracts with the result that the vast majority of cases of alleged duress in the context of the renegotiation of a contract will fall into the contractual rather than the non-contractual category.[73] But the fact that it can sometimes be difficult to distinguish between contractual and non-contractual cases and that the category of contractual cases has expanded post-*Williams* does

---

[68] Burrows (above, n 31) 215.   [69] ibid.   [70] ibid at 143.   [71] ibid at 215.

[72] [1991] 1 QB 1. But it cannot be assumed that consideration is now an irrelevance. There is still life left in the doctrine: *South Caribbean Trading Ltd v Trafigura Beheer BV* [2004] EWHC 2676 (Comm); [2005] 1 Lloyd's Rep 128 at [107]–[108].

[73] See eg *North Ocean Shipping Co Ltd v Hyundai Construction Co Ltd* (*The Atlantic Baron*) [1979] QB 705 and *Pao On v Lau Yiu Long* [1980] AC 614.

not mean that we should abandon all attempts to draw the distinction or to deal separately with the case where it is clear that there is no contract between the parties. Take the case of a payment of £1,000 made under duress and there is no promised counter-performance. In this instance, there is in substance a promise to confer a gift on another party. There is no contract to set aside and so why should the claimant have to satisfy the standard that would be applicable had a contract been concluded? The concern to uphold the stability of commercial transactions, apparent in many economic duress cases, is not applicable in this instance and so should not trouble the courts.

The third objection is that 'it may be that there is no difference between the scope of duress for contractual and non-contractual payments'.[74] This is the heart of the matter. Burrows notes that *Skeate v Beale*[75] did draw such a distinction in so far as it was held that, 'while duress of goods might well be a ground of restitution for non-contractual payments, it was not a ground for invalidating a contract and recovering payments made under it'.[76] He then continues by pointing out, correctly, that the *Skeate v Beale* restriction has since been abandoned by English law and that 'the courts have not sought to distinguish in any way the ambit of duress for contractual and non-contractual payments'.[77] However, as he notes, there has been 'virtually no direct judicial discussion of whether there should be any difference'[78] and, further, that the absence of any such distinction 'would represent a marked difference between restitution for duress and for mistake; because for mistake it is clear that a more stringent test has to be satisfied before a contractual, as opposed to a non-contractual payment, can be recovered'.[79] In the absence of any direct judicial discussion of the issue, one must treat with caution claims that the distinction between contractual and non-contractual payments does not exist.[80] Given that in other contexts the law differentiates between a contract and a mere payment, it is suggested that the same distinction ought to be drawn in the present context. This being the case, the threshold for non-contractual payments ought to be set at a lower level than that applicable to contractual payments. This is unlikely to lead to a radical difference in the substantive content of the applicable rules. In order to bring a claim a claimant will have to prove that the application by the defendant of illegitimate pressure contributed to her decision to confer a benefit upon the defendant. However, in so far as the defences are aimed at preserving the stability of commercial contracts, these considerations are not applicable to non-contractual payments and, to this extent, the right to recover non-contractual payments ought to be wider.

One additional reason for distinguishing between contractual and non-contractual payments is that it is important to emphasize that a restitutionary

---

[74] Burrows (above, n 31) 216.   [75] (1841) 11 Ad & El 983.
[76] Burrows (above, n 31) 216.   [77] ibid.   [78] ibid at 217.   [79] ibid.
[80] Although support for the claim that the distinction is irrelevant may be gained from the law of misrepresentation, which does not distinguish between contractual and non-contractual claims.

right to recover a payment allegedly made under duress cannot arise in the case where the payment was made pursuant to a contract and that contract has not been set aside. In a recent article, the claim has been made that it may be 'more beneficial' for a victim of duress to 'rely upon restitution' than to invoke the doctrine of economic duress.[81] Restitution was perceived to be more attractive to a claimant than attempting to set aside a contract on the ground of economic duress because restitution is 'not dependent upon making contracts voidable and so "freedom of contract" theory should not be such an obstacle'.[82] In the words of the author, the victim 'should seek restitution rather than rescission of a contract'.[83] The fundamental flaw in this analysis is that, unless and until the contract is set aside, it is not possible to resort to the law of restitution for the purpose of recovering benefits conferred in the performance of that contract. It is not the case that the claimant has an unrestricted choice between 'rescission' and 'restitution': unless and until it is set aside, it is the contract which governs the rights and obligations of the parties. This being the case, a claimant who is party to a contract with the defendant cannot obtain an advantage by resorting to the law of restitution in order to recover any benefit conferred. She must show that the duress is sufficient to set aside the contract and, once she has established that, then benefits conferred upon the other party to the contract will be recovered as part of the process of rescission of the contract.[84] But she cannot recover the benefit simply by ignoring the contract and bringing a claim based solely on the law of restitution.

3. Duress and the Claim for Compensatory Damages

Lord Hoffmann in *R* refers to the 'wrong of duress'. The description of duress as a 'wrong' is potentially dangerous in so far as the use of the word 'wrong' suggests that duress can give rise to a claim for compensatory damages. It is necessary to proceed with caution here. Thus far we have been discussing the circumstances in which the application of duress creates a right to recover the value of a benefit conferred upon the defendant. That question is analytically distinct from the question whether or not duress gives rise to a claim for compensatory damages[85] and therefore must be treated separately.

---

[81] H Lal, 'Commercial Exploitation in Construction Contracts: The Role of Economic Duress and Unjust Enrichment' [2005] *International Construction Law Review* 466.

[82] ibid at 475.   [83] ibid.

[84] It is possible that some confusion has been caused here by *North Ocean Shipping Co Ltd v Hyundai Construction Co Ltd (The Atlantic Baron)* [1979] QB 705 where Mocatta J (at 714) referred both to rescission of the contract and the availability of an action for money had and received. However, it is extremely unlikely that he intended to imply that money could be recovered in an action for money had and received if the contract had not been set aside. Normally, any order for the recovery of payments made is part of the process of rescission and is not the subject of a separate claim for money had and received.   [85] See Burrows (above, n 31) 212–3.

There are in fact a number of references to the existence of a 'tort' of economic duress. In *Universe Tankships of Monrovia v International Transport Workers' Federation* ('*The Universe Sentinel*')[86] Lord Scarman stated that 'duress, if proved, not only renders voidable a transaction into which a person has entered under its compulsion but is actionable as a tort, if it causes damage or loss'.[87] By contrast, Lord Diplock in the same case was more circumspect. He stated that 'the use of economic duress to induce another person to part with property or money is not a tort per se: the form that the duress takes may, or may not, be tortious'.[88] The conflict between Lord Scarman and Lord Diplock has not been resolved in subsequent cases.[89] While passing references can be found to the 'tort of economic duress'[90] these references cannot be regarded as conclusive either as to the existence of the tort or its scope.

In his case-note Birks anticipated the problems that may lie ahead. Thus he stated that the 'temptation studiously to be resisted is the robust generalization which would equate restitution-yielding pressure with tortious pressure'.[91] The two cannot automatically be equated. When considering whether duress gives rise to a claim for compensatory damages it is necessary to take account of the economic torts. The distinction generally drawn in the economic torts is not between the legitimate and the illegitimate use of economic power but between the use of lawful and unlawful means.[92] It is the presence of unlawful means which is the critical element in most of the economic torts, with the obvious exception of the anomalous tort of conspiracy.[93] It is at this point that the distinction between 'unlawfulness' and 'illegitimacy' becomes important. Given the general requirement for the presence of unlawful means in the economic torts, economic duress should not be actionable in tort in the case where the duress consists of the application of pressure which is 'illegitimate' but does not involve the use of unlawful means.[94] More difficult, and more likely to be of practical concern, is the question whether a threatened breach of contract can constitute unlawful means for the purpose of giving rise to a liability in tort. English law has clearly recognized this form of liability in three-party cases in the form of the tort of intimidation.[95] The question whether liability can also be

---

[86] [1983] 1 AC 366.   [87] ibid at 400.   [88] ibid at 385.

[89] In *Dimskal Shipping Co SA v International Transport Workers Federation* (*The Evia Luck (No 2)*) [1992] 2 AC 152, 166 Lord Goff cited the passage from the speech of Lord Diplock with approval but it cannot be said that this approval conclusively resolves the issue.

[90] *Alec Lobb (Garages) Ltd v Total Oil (Great Britain) Ltd* [1985] 1 WLR 173, 178; *Circuit Systems Ltd (in liq) v Zuken-Redac (UK) Ltd* [1997] 1 WLR 721, 739; *Huyton SA v Peter Cremer GmbH & Co* [1999] 1 Lloyd's Rep 620, 638; *Kyrri-Royle v Burger King Ltd* [2005] EWHC 303 (Ch) at [75].   [91] Birks (above, n 1) 349.

[92] *Allen v Flood* [1898] AC 1.

[93] *Quinn v Leatham* [1901] AC 495; *Crofter Hand Woven Harris Tweed Co v Veitch* [1942] AC 435.

[94] Of course much here depends on the meaning to be given to the word 'illegitimate', on which see pp 187–90 above. A case in point might be a refusal to contract. If a refusal to contract can be illegitimate for the purpose of setting aside a contract, it should not give rise to a liability for compensatory damages because a refusal to contract, while it may in certain circumstances be 'illegitimate', is not unlawful.   [95] *Rookes v Barnard* [1964] AC 1129.

imposed in a case of two-party intimidation is more controversial. Lord Reid expressly doubted the appropriateness of the analogy between three-party and two-party cases[96] but other commentators have argued that there is no difference in principle between the two cases.[97] If a threatened breach of contract does constitute unlawful means for the purposes of two-party intimidation, then every threatened breach of contract has the potential simultaneously to create liability in the tort of intimidation. Given that a claimant who is faced by a threatened breach of contract has her contractual remedies in respect of the threatened breach and may also be able to set aside any agreement entered into as a result of the threat, is there any real need to confer upon her an additional right of action to recover compensatory damages? Some commentators have concluded that there is no justification for creating such an additional right of action,[98] while others have taken the view that, the law having taken the step of holding that a breach of contract can constitute unlawful means, there is no logical justification for concluding that it cannot constitute unlawful means in a two-party case.[99] The latter view appears to be the stronger of the two. Assume in *Barton* that the defendant had inflicted physical violence upon the claimant in order to induce the claimant to enter into the contract. In such a case the physical violence would constitute the tort of battery and, as such, would confer upon the claimant an entitlement to recover compensatory damages in addition to the right to set aside the contract and recover any benefits conferred thereunder. Should matters really be so very different when the threat is not of physical violence but of economic ruin? However, it is not necessary to resolve this issue here. All that is being said is that the question whether duress can constitute a tort and give rise to a claim for compensatory damages is an analytically distinct issue and therefore requires separate consideration from the question whether duress gives rise to a right to set aside a contract and to recover benefits conferred upon the other party to the contract. The bald assertion of Lord Hoffmann that duress is a 'wrong' will require careful handling.

4. Conclusion

The travails that afflict the law of duress seem destined to continue. While the Privy Council in *R* has gone some way towards putting the law on a secure basis, in other respects the decision creates the potential for further confusion, particularly in regard to the classification of duress as a wrong. The task of putting the law on a secure conceptual basis will undoubtedly be more difficult in the absence of Peter Birks. His formidable powers of analysis, his concern for

[96] *JT Stratford & Son Ltd v Lindley* [1965] AC 269, 325.
[97] *Clerk and Lindsell on Torts* (19th edn, 2006) 25–85.
[98] H Carty, *Economic Torts* (2001) 94–7.
[99] *Clerk and Lindsell* (above, n 97) 25–85.

classification, and his passion for his subject will be difficult if not impossible to replace.

In October 2004 I assumed the role of Chair of the Board of the Faculty of Law in Oxford and, acting in that capacity, I have been acutely aware of the enormous hole left in the life of the Faculty by Peter's sudden and untimely death. In my own case, Peter had an enormous influence on the early years of my academic life, particularly between 1988 and 1991 when we taught together on the LLM in the University of London. It was a privilege to know him and to work with him. He is greatly missed.

11

Undue Influence: *Beyond* Impaired Consent and Wrongdoing towards a Relational Analysis

*Mindy Chen-Wishart**

When I accepted Jack Beatson's kind invitation to 'help' with his conference on *Good Faith and Fault in Contract Law* I realized too late that he did not mean with the photocopying. But there, I first encountered Peter 'On the Nature of Undue Influence'.[1] Looking back, I can only think that I was delirious from surviving my first conference paper and believed I would soon abscond the jurisdiction, for I said to Peter over the conference dinner 'You're wrong, of course'. He met this impertinence with openness, curiosity, and respect. It has taken over a decade to start a proper reply. In the intervening years, I had the privilege of being his colleague and observing close up his passion and brilliance for the law and for legal education. He threw his all into both; they were his work and his fun—unjust enrichment law never featured so largely in my Christmases as the four our families shared. His students were in awe of him. They were admitted into a world where the law was exciting and personal—images of squirrels, seahorses, and platypuses helped to stress the importance of classification; discussion of judgments barely freed from embargo, often citing Birks, had us all in the thick of the action. And always, there was his enormously charismatic personality. He replied to his resounding defeat in an impromptu class vote on 'free acceptance' with: 'No wonder the ancient Greeks never

* Fellow and Tutor in Law, Merton College, Oxford.
   I am grateful to Professor Richard Sutton for discussions on undue influence over many years; the influence of his email correspondence will be clear to him. My thanks also to Professor Jane Stapleton whose critical ear (walking to the Trout Inn and back) and comments on a draft helped to crystallize my thinking. Laura Hoyano and Jennifer Payne allowed me to think out loud and the seminar discussions in Philosophical Foundations of Contract Law prompted a different perspective.

[1] P Birks and NY Chin, 'On the Nature of Undue Influence' in J Beatson and D Friedman (eds), *Good Faith and Fault in Contract Law* (1995) 57, (hereafter 'Birks and Chin'). And see P Birks, *Unjust Enrichment* (2nd edn, 2005) 135–6, 148–50, P Birks, 'Undue Influence as Wrongful Exploitation' (2004) 120 LQR 35.

developed great law'. Peter and Jackie's warm friendship sustained me in my first years in Oxford.

1. Introduction

Transactions made between parties in relationships involving high levels of trust and confidence are regulated by the doctrine of undue influence. Restitution must be made of any enrichment obtained thereby because it is unjust or unjustified. But to know that the exercise of undue influence is 'bad' tells us nothing useful when it comes to pinpointing its precise pathology or mapping its boundaries. Lord Chelmsford LC observed that 'the Courts have always been careful not to fetter this useful jurisdiction by defining the exact limits of its exercise'.[2] Their 'remarkable success'[3] in this is assisted by the intangible nature of 'influence' (to have, or be subject to it, is not to possess or concede anything visible), by the infinite manifestations of its 'exercise' (which may appear quite innocuous—flattery, helpful advice, insistent urging—or not appear at all, the influenced person simply conforms with the known preference of the trusted person), by the fact that 'influence' and the 'undue-ness' of its exercise are matters of degree and not of kind, and by the mingling of undue influence and related doctrines on the same facts (eg misrepresentation, lawful act duress, unconscionable dealing, or breach of fiduciary duty).

But, perhaps the main source of confusion over the nature of undue influence is one of language; its key concepts do not mean what they appear to mean. Thus, Courts have *deemed* the *claimant's consent to be defective*, but only because the *defendant's conduct* has fallen short of the standard required.[4] To raise the inference of undue influence it is necessary to show a transaction which '*calls for an explanation*', yet the expression is applied to transactions which are *objectively unacceptable*, albeit perfectly explicable.[5] Most problematically, the language of defendant unconscientiousness (eg 'impropriety', 'abuse', 'betrayal', 'wrongdoing', 'stigma', 'reprehensible', 'fault') *implies the need for bad conduct or bad faith*, when *neither is required*.[6] In reality, the claimant's consent may not be defective, the transaction may be quite explicable and the defendant's fraud may be 'constructive', his abuse 'passive', and his liability to make restitution strict.

The language of impaired consent and abuse of trust has obscured the search for the basis of undue influence. Unsurprisingly, the debate has ossified in

---

[2] *Tate v Williamson* (1866) L Rep, Appeal Cases (2nd series) 55, 61.

[3] Birks and Chin 57.

[4] *Royal Bank of Scotland v Etridge (No 2)* [2001] 4 All ER 449, para 7. Hereafter '*Etridge*'. In the context of duress see *Universe Tankships Inc of Monrovia v International Transport Workers Federation (the Universe Sentinel)* [1983] 1 AC 366, 384. And see text accompanying nn 13–16 below.

[5] See text accompanying nn 65–75 below.

[6] eg *Re the Estate of Brocklehurst* [1978] 1 Ch 14, 19 and see text accompanying nn 79–91 below.

bipolar form:[7] is the doctrine concerned with the claimant's impaired consent to the challenged transaction (and so 'claimant-sided'), or with the trusted party's reprehensible use of his influence in procuring the claimant's consent (and so 'defendant-sided')? This 'either or' approach has the attraction of conceptual simplicity, clarity, and easy marketability, but it misses the target when simply superimposed on the subtle and complex dynamics of trusting relationships. Moreover, the dichotomy is, in a sense, false. Since the defendant-sided version is concerned with the defendant's role in distorting the *claimant's consent*, it is reducible to the same rationale as the claimant-sided version. The difference between the two versions lies merely in the *source* of the claimant's impairment (either the defendant's conduct or the claimant's own judgment). The fact that both versions require *causation* (ie that each must have caused the claimant's decision to transact) means that both versions can be presented in terms of the claimant's impaired consent.[8] This explains why Birks and Chin regard even duress, which requires the undoubtedly defendant-sided finding of illegitimate pressure, as claimant-sided.[9]

This essay represents the first stage in the development of a new theory of undue influence. It argues that any one-dimensional view of undue influence fails and that any credible theory of undue influence must accommodate a multi-dimensional approach. It should be no surprise that a doctrine regulating transactions between parties in a relationship of trust and confidence should be concerned with the conduct and motivation of *both* participants *and* with the outcome of the transaction, all judged against the *norms* of the *relationship* between the parties. A new fully developed relational theory of undue influence must be left to a later stage, but its contours can be briefly outlined here. There is nothing wrong (pathological) with the claimant's trust in, dependence on, or allegiance to a defendant with whom she shares a caring relationship (a relationship of influence). Trust, dependence, or allegiance is constitutive of close relationships, which, in turn, facilitate human flourishing and characterize a good life. To uphold the integrity of such valuable relationships, the law requires the defendant to have due regard for the *substantive and procedural norms implicit in the relationship of influence* he shares with the claimant when he transacts with her. If he violates these norms, he cannot enforce or retain the benefits of the transaction even if he has done nothing illegitimate to procure the claimant's

---

[7] Birks and Chin, R Bigwood 'Undue Influence: "Impaired Consent" or "Wicked Exploitation"' (1996) 16 OJLS 503, *Exploitative Contracts* (2003), 'Contracts by Unfair Advantage: From Exploitation to Transactional Neglect' (2005) 23 OJLS 65.

[8] This focus on causation or inducement (ie whether the defendant's conduct caused the claimant's consent) means that even misrepresentation and unconscionable conduct can be described as 'claimant-sided'.

[9] Birks and Chin 88–9 argue that free consent is impaired only when it is distorted by an alien (illegitimate) pressure, so that although pressure must be illegitimate, duress is a 'claimant-sided phenomenon, so that relief flows from the impairment of the claimant's decision-making capacity, not from unconscientiousness on the part of the other'.

consent and even if he has not consciously set out to exploit the claimant. In the context of a relationship of influence, the defendant cannot always accept a transaction just because the claimant would agree and even if she offers; he certainly cannot do so if the transaction is grossly improvident to the claimant unless, and sometimes *even if,* he takes additional steps to protect the claimant. This multi-dimensional relational theory of undue influence is consistent with: (i) a proper regard for the value of trusting relationships, (ii) the richness of the Common Law, (iii) the stated burden of proof for undue influence, (iv) the recent House of Lords pronouncements in *Royal Bank of Scotland v Etridge* (*No 2*),[10] and (v) the classical but curious case of *Allcard v Skinner*.[11] The focus of this essay is the poverty and lack of fit of both the claimant and the defendant-sided accounts of undue influence.

2. What Hart Can Teach Us

A claimant-sided focus on the *absence of proper consent* in determining the voidability (and so recoverability) of any transfer is understandable. In a liberal democracy, an individual's autonomy (sovereign will) takes pre-eminent place in explaining her transactional *liability*. However, it is a mistake to then assume that the law governing the *vitiation* of transactions is straightforwardly explicable by a negation of the positive conditions of liability, namely by that party's *absence* of consent.

In 'The Ascription of Responsibility and Right'[12] HLA Hart describes such an approach as 'a disastrous over-simplification and distortion'. He notes the temptation to reason that 'cases where contracts are held not to exist "must" be cases where some necessary condition, required in the definition of contract, is absent'.[13] But he warns that this line of reasoning (which applies equally to non-contractual transactions) fails to recognize: (i) that consent is a *necessary but not sufficient,* condition of transactional liability, and (ii) that the validity of a transaction is a *two-stage* inquiry, so that even when the language of consent is used in determining both the formation and vitiation stages, they deal with *qualitatively different* concerns. He writes:[14]

When the student has learned that in English law there are positive conditions required for the existence of a valid contract . . . his understanding of the legal concept of a contract is still incomplete. . . . For these conditions, although necessary, are not always sufficient and he has still to learn what can *defeat* the claim that there is a valid contract, even

[10] [2001] 4 All ER 449.
[11] (1887) 36 Chancery Division (2nd series) 145.
[12] HLA Hart, 'The Ascription of Responsibility and Rights' Proceedings of the Aristotelian Society (1948) 49, also in AGN Flew (ed), *Logic and Language: First Series* (1960) 145, 173.
[13] ibid 183.   [14] ibid 174–6 (emphasis in the original).

though all these conditions are satisfied. That is the student still has to learn what can follow on the word 'unless' which should accompany the statement of these conditions . . . the law has a word which with some hesitation I borrow and extend: This is the word '*defeasible*' used of a legal interest in property which is subject to termination or '*defeat*' in a number of different contingencies but remains intact if no such contingencies mature. In this sense then, contract is a defeasible concept.

Hart surveys the range of vitiating factors and concludes that they are 'irreducibly defeasible in character and to ignore this is to misrepresent' them. This is obscured by the theorist who takes the *language of impaired consent* in relation to vitiation as suggesting 'that there are certain psychological elements required by the law as necessary conditions of contract and that the defences are merely admitted as negative *evidence* of these', rather than as 'a compendious reference to the defences with which claims in contract may be weakened or met'.[15]

This distinction between factual (psychological) and legal (in the eye of the law) consent[16] is supported by Lord Nicholls's statement in *Etridge* that whenever the defendant's procurement of the claimant's consent is judged improper, that consent will not be *deemed* an expression of the claimant's will.[17] Thus, talk of consent here is *conclusory*, not explanatory; it is merely shorthand for the variety of factors which can render the transaction defeasible. It is wrong to reason from the vitiating factors that:[18]

the definition of contract requires as necessary conditions that the mind of the parties should be 'fully informed' and their wills 'free' . . . the defence, *e.g.*, that B entered into a contract with A as a result of the undue influence exerted upon him by A is not evidence of the absence of a factor called true 'consent'. . . . And the practice of the law (in which general phrases such as true consent are of little importance) as distinct from the theoretical statement of it by jurists (in which general terms bulk largely) makes this clear; for no party attempting to enforce a contract is required to give evidence that there was 'true, full and free consent'. . . . Of course, the theorist could make his theory that there are psychological elements ('full and free consent') required as necessary conditions of contract, irrefutable by ascribing the actual procedure of the courts to the practical difficulties of proving 'mental facts'; and it is sometimes said that it is merely a matter of practical convenience . . . that the onus of proof is usually upon the defendant to prove the non-existence of these necessary elements. . . . But to insist on this as the real explanation of the actual procedure of the courts in applying the defeasible concept of a contract would merely be to express an obstinate loyalty to the persuasive but misleading

---

[15] ibid 177. At 180, Hart explains that 'the logical character of words like "voluntary" is anomalous and ill-understood. They are treated in such definitions as words having positive force, yet, as can be seen from Aristotle's discussion in *Book III of the Nicomachean Ethics*, the word "voluntary" in fact serves to exclude a heterogeneous range of cases such as physical compulsion, coercion by threats, accidents, the stakes, etc, and not to designate a mental element or state; nor does "involuntary" signify the absence of this mental element or state.'

[16] The analogy is to *factual* and *legal* benefit in the context of the consideration doctrine.

[17] *Etridge* para 7.

[18] Hart (n 12 above) 177–8.

logical ideal that all concepts must be capable of definition through a set of necessary and sufficient conditions.

Hart's counsel allows us to *detach* the basis for *vitiating* transactions from the basis for *enforcing* them. Space is then opened up to consider values at work *other than consent*. The question is whether, in view of the relevant circumstances bringing the case within a recognized head of exception, a claimant should be *relieved of responsibility* for the transaction, *despite her consent* to it.[19]

This resonates with rejection of the 'overborne will' explanation of duress. Lord Scarman said:[20] 'The classic case of duress is ... not the lack of will to submit but the victim's intentional submission arising from the realisation that there is no practical choice open to him'. Where this results from the defendant's illegitimate pressure, the law does not ascribe the normal responsibility it would to the victim's consent; that consent is *deemed* to be vitiated.[21] This view avoids the fiction that the claimant gave no effective consent despite acting knowingly and intentionally. Rather, it takes the realistic and respectful view that the claimant engages with reason in consenting to the transaction, but should nevertheless be excused from responsibility in the circumstances. A similar analysis of undue influence would avoid the unrealistic and somewhat insulting characterization of a claimant who chooses to trust the defendant's judgment as thereby 'impaired'.

The first step in building a new vision of undue influence is to clear the ground of unfruitful lines of inquiry and accurately describe the phenomenon that we are trying to explain. Peter Cane gives us a starting point:[22]

The 'top-downer' (it seems) dons theoretical spectacles before looking at the map, whereas the ('pragmatic') middle-leveller first picks out the topological high spots and then chooses a conceptual lens to bring them into theoretical focus. The middle-leveller is, we might think, more likely than the top-downer to produce a convincing theory *of* law, as opposed to a theory *about* law. But if that were the aim, an approach that started 'at the bottom'—in the messy detail of the law and legal phenomena—might be even more promising.

3. No Defendant Wickedness Required

The classic case of *Allcard v Skinner*[23] is consistent with neither the unconscientious conduct nor the impaired consent rationales. A young woman associated herself

---

[19] ibid 174.
[20] *Universe Tankships Inc of Monrovia v International Transport Workers Federation* (*The Universe Sentinel*) [1983] 1 AC 366, 400.   [21] ibid 384.
[22] P Cane, 'The Anatomy of Private Law Theory: A 25th Anniversary Essay' (2005) 25 OJLS 203, 207, referring to J Coleman, *Risks and Wrongs* (1992) 8–9; *The Practice of Principle* (1998) 5–6.
[23] (1887) 36 Chancery Division (2nd series) 145 (hereafter '*Allcard v Skinner*').

with an Anglican sisterhood, taking a vow of poverty, chastity, and obedience. Eighteen months later, she joined the convent as a full member. Thereafter, she received a substantial bequest from her father's estate, which she gave over to the Mother Superior of the convent. The rules of the convent imposed the most absolute submission by the nuns to the Mother Superior who was to be regarded as the 'voice of God'; they could not seek outside advice without her permission. The nun eventually left the sisterhood and sought the return of what remained of her gifts. The Court found presumed undue influence although it acquitted the Mother Superior of any wrongdoing or selfish motive. Indeed, true to the aspirations of the Order, she would have regarded it as in the nun's own best interest to divest herself of her worldly trappings. The conclusion that undue influence does not necessitate the defendant's bad faith or bad conduct is expressly confirmed in several recent cases.[24]

4. Impaired Consent

However, such rejection of a defendant-sided (reprehensible conduct) view does not inexorably vindicate the claimant-sided (impaired consent) view. Five difficulties can be identified.

4.1. Contrary to Authority

Allcard v Skinner itself cannot support the impaired consent view. Lindley LJ said that everything the nun did was 'referable to her own willing submission to the vows she took and to the rules which she approved, and to her own enthusiastic devotion to the life and work of the sisterhood'.[25] She 'chose it as the best for herself; she devoted herself to it, heart and soul.... But though infatuated, there is no evidence to shew that she was in such a state of mental imbecility as to justify the inference that she was unable to take care of herself or to manage her own affairs'.[26] Bowen LJ agreed that:[27]

persons who are under the most complete influence of religious feeling are perfectly free to act upon it in the disposition of their property, and not the less free because they are enthusiasts. Persons of this kind are not dead in law. They are dead indeed to the world so far as their own wishes and feelings about the things of the world are concerned; but such indifference to things external does not prevent them in law from being free agents. In the present instance there was no duress, no incompetency, no want of mental power on the

---

[24] eg *Cheese v Thomas* [1994] 1 All ER 35, *Hammond v Osborn* [2002] EWCA Civ 885, para 32 and *Jennings v Cairns, In the Estate of Davidge* [2003] EWCA Civ 1935, para 33, *Randall v Randall* (Chancery Div 28 May 2004), paras 36–9.   [25] *Allcard v Skinner* 184.
[26] ibid 178, and at 181 'although the Plaintiff was a religious enthusiast, no one could treat her as in point of law *non compos mentis*'.   [27] ibid 189.

part of the donor. It seems to me that, so far as regards to her rights she had the absolute power to deal with the property as she chose.

4.2. Trusting is Not Pathological

Undue influence claimants (like the nun) may appear naïve, romantic, or idealistic, too trusting and selfless, but are they thereby legally 'subnormal'? Birks and Chin answer in the affirmative: Such claimants are 'impaired in their judgmental capacity . . . arising from their morbid dependence on another'.[28] 'The relevant weakness . . . is that, within the relationship, by reason of excessive dependence on the other person, he or she lacks the capacity for self-management which the law attributes to the generality of adults'.[29] Her 'autonomy' or the 'integrity of [her] judgment' is 'markedly sub-standard' or 'impaired to an exceptional degree'.[30]

An alternative view is that when the nun gave away her worldly possessions she did not lack autonomy—she *exercised* it. There is nothing intrinsically wrong with the existence or even the use of influence. Indeed Isaacs J recognized that 'influence may be used wisely, judiciously and helpfully'[31] for the benefit or advantage of the person influenced. Just as Birks and Chin stress that relational submission, religious zeal, or sexual fixation is merely the way of life for some people and does not connote wrongdoing by the defendant,[32] so it should be recognized that they imply no pathological impairment on the claimant's part. As Kekewich J said at trial in *Allcard v Skinner*:[33]

The law does not exclude influence. Nay, it recognises influence as natural and right. Few, if any, men are gifted with characters enabling them to act, or even think, with complete independence of others, which could not largely exist without destroying the foundations of society. But the law requires that influence, however natural and however right, shall not be unduly exercised.

4.3. Breadth and Uncertainty

A further difficulty with the impaired consent view is the impossibility (and oddness) of constructing a workable distinction between appropriate and inappropriate levels of trust, dependency, or allegiance. Moreover, while Birks and Chin suggest that 'the law relieves only an extreme loss of autonomy',[34] something beyond the 99th percentile,[35] since adults of 'widely differing intelligence and personality come under all sorts of different influences, and must be presumed able to cope', the cases do not impose such a high threshold. In *Tate v Williamson* Lord Chelmsford LC said:[36]

---

[28] Birks and Chin 85.   [29] Birks and Chin 67.   [30] Birks and Chin 67, 68, 81, 87.
[31] *Watkins v Combes* (1922) 30 Commonwealth L Rep 180, 193–4.
[32] Birks and Chin 77–9.   [33] *Allcard v Skinner* 157–8.   [34] Birks and Chin 87.
[35] Professor Birks made this point in the BCL Restitution seminars on undue influence.
[36] (1866) LR 2 Ch App 55, 61, see also *Etridge*, para 8.

Wherever two persons stand in such a relation that, while it continues, confidence is necessarily reposed by one, and the influence which naturally grows out of that confidence is possessed by the other, and this confidence is abused, or the influence is exerted to obtain an advantage at the expense of the confiding party, the person so availing himself of his position will not be permitted to retain the advantage, although the transaction could not have been impeached if no such confidential relation had existed.

In truth, a legally relevant relationship of influence is a broad notion and potentially encompasses relationships with anyone one loves, likes, respects, works with, or can be said to have common cause with. It is more *ordinary* than extraordinary. Moreover, influence can go both ways and vary with the context of the parties' interaction. Thus, relational ascendancy has been accepted in husbands over their wives,[37] adult children over their parents[38] and vice versa,[39] between other family members,[40] employers over employees[41] and vice versa,[42] banks over customers,[43] between friends,[44] and even between those in a pre-existing contractual relationship.[45] Proof of 'blind, unquestioning trust' or a 'dominating influence' is unnecessary. It is enough that in instances of past dealing the claimant generally reposed trust and confidence in the other party in matters affecting the management of the claimant's affairs.[46] But *Tufton v Sperni*[47] shows that it may arise even in one-off dealings. Moreover, where direct evidence of the relevant relationship is absent or, usually, ambiguous, the Court

---

[37] eg *Bank of Credit & Commerce International SA v Aboody* [1990] 1 QB 923 and the numerous wife guarantee cases where undue influence was found.

[38] eg *Humphreys v Humphreys* [2004] EWHC (Ch) 2201, [2005] Family Court Rep 712, *Mortgage Agency Services Number Two Ltd v Chater* [2003] EWCA Civ 490, *Greene King plc v Stanley and others* [2001] EWCA Civ 1966, *Wright v Cherrytree Finance Ltd and others* [2001] EWCA Civ 449, *Meredith v Lackschewitz-Martin and another* [2002] EWHC (Ch) 1462.

[39] The parent–child relationship is accepted as generating an automatic presumption of a relationship of influence under the old class 2A.

[40] eg *Vale v Armstrong and another* [2004] EWHC (Ch) 1160 (nephew over aunt), *Cheese v Thomas* [1994] 1 All ER 35 (great-nephew over great-uncle), *Williams v Williams* [2003] EWHC (Ch) 742 (brothers), *Watson v Huber* Chancery Div 9 March 2005 (half-sisters), *Pesticcio v Niersmans* [2003] 2 Planning & Compensation Rep D22 (sister over brother), *Randall v Randall* [2004] EWHC 2258, 7 Int Trusts & Estates L Rep 340 (nephew over aunt), *Jennings v Cairns* [2003] EWCA Civ 1935 (niece over aunt).

[41] *Crédit Lyonnais Bank Nederland NV v Burch* [1997] 1 All ER 144, *Steeples v Lee* [1998] 1 FLR 138.

[42] *Re Craig* [1971] Ch 95 (a companion-housekeeper), *Re Morris (deceased)*, *Special Trustees for Great Ormond Street Hospital for Children v Rushin and others* [2000] All ER (D) 598 (housekeeper), *Goldsworthy v Brickell* [1987] Ch 378 (farm manager), *O'Sullivan v Management Agency and Music Ltd* [1985] QB 428 (manager of a pop singer).

[43] *Lloyds Bank Ltd v Bundy* [1975] QB 326.

[44] *Hammond v Osborn* [2002] EWCA Civ 885, *Wright v Hodgkinson* [2004] EWHC (Ch) 3091, [2004] All ER (D) 427.

[45] *Macklin v Dowset* [2003] EWHC (Ch) 2812, [2003] All ER (D) 304.

[46] *Goldsworthy v Brickell* [1987] Ch 378, 404.

[47] [1952] 2 Times L Rep 516, a Muslim convert with no business experience wanted to set up a centre for Muslim culture. Another Muslim with business expertise, brought onto the committee overseeing the project, sold the claimant his own house for the project at more than twice the market value and reserved numerous privileges. Presumed undue influence was found.

may infer it from the unusual nature (ie gross improvidence) of the transaction for the claimant,[48] thus broadening the class even further.

4.4. Strained Meaning and Odd Fit with the Burden of Proof

To say that a transaction resulting from the 'exercise of undue influence' (implying a defendant-focus) really means one 'caused by [the claimant's] excessive dependence'[49] is strained. Birks and Chin go on to say that the old class 1 'actual' undue influence (once shorn of the non-relational pressure cases)[50] really designates transactions *caused*[51] by morbid dependence, while the old class 2 'presumed' undue influence really designates transactions *presumed to be caused*[52] by morbid dependence. This fits awkwardly with the restatement in *Etridge* that the traditional categories represent *different* ways of proving undue influence since, on the Birks and Chin scheme, both ways of proving undue influence rest on proof of the *same* relationship of influence[53] from which excessive dependence (their stated reason for relief) is found.

4.5. Misleading Demotion of Other Elements

The claimant-sided view of undue influence elevates the impact of the relationship of influence on the claimant, while minimizing the Court's clear concern with the resulting transaction and the propriety of the defendant's behaviour. In *Etridge* Lord Nicholls explains that:[54]

Proof that the complainant placed trust and confidence in the other party in relation to the management of the complainant's financial affairs, coupled with *a transaction which calls for explanation,* will normally be sufficient . . . for the Court to infer that . . . the transaction can only have been procured by undue influence. In other words . . . that *the defendant abused the influence he acquired* in the parties' relationship. He preferred his own interests. *He did not behave fairly to the other.* So the evidential burden then shifts to him . . . to counter the inference which otherwise should be drawn. (Emphasis added.)

---

[48] eg in *Crédit Lyonnais Bank Nederland NV v Burch Crédit Lyonnais v Burch* [1997] 1 All ER 144 a junior employee guaranteed her employer's debts. Direct evidence of a relationship of influence was flimsy: she had worked for him for ten years and sometimes baby-sat and visited his family in London and Italy. Millett LJ said at 154–5: '[T]he mere fact that a transaction is improvident or manifestly disadvantageous to one party is not sufficient by itself to give rise to a presumption that it has been obtained by the exercise of undue influence; but where it is obtained by a party between whom and the complainant there is a relationship like that of employer and junior employee which is easily capable of developing into a relationship of trust and confidence, the nature of the transaction may be sufficient to justify the inference that such a development has taken place; and where the transaction is so extravagantly improvident that it is virtually inexplicable on any other basis, the inference will be readily drawn.'

[49] Birks and Chin 85–8.   [50] See text accompanying nn 92–110 below.
[51] Birks and Chin 76–7, 87–8.   [52] Birks and Chin 87–8.
[53] See text accompanying nn 97–104 below.
[54] *Etridge*, para 14, and see paras 16, 17, 93, 104–7, 156, 161.

That is, proof of 'excessive dependence', even if extreme, is *insufficient* to raise an inference of undue influence. There must *also* be something untoward about the resulting transaction and the defendant's behaviour.

5. The Role of Transactional Outcome

5.1. Birks and Chin

Birks and Chin offer two explanations for the Court's concern with the resulting transaction:[55] (a) that it is a *pragmatic restrictor* of 'relief for impaired autonomy, meeting the fear that otherwise too many transactions might be unsettled' and; (b) it is *evidence* supporting the presumption that the transaction was *caused by the claimant's excessive dependence*. The problem is that this sort of argument can equally be made in support of an unconscientious exploitation version of undue influence (an unfair outcome is evidence, and relational dependence is a pragmatic restrictor to prevent 'too much restitution'), or even of a substantive unfairness version (the unfair outcome is of the essence, while the claimant's relational dependence and the defendant's behaviour are corroborative evidence of that unfairness, or are pragmatic restrictors).

5.2. What *Etridge* Says

In *Etridge*[56] Lord Nicholls confirms the role of transactional outcome as a restrictor, but one which is *vital* to a defendant-sided view of undue influence. A relationship of influence does not bar transactions between parties to it; to presume undue influence by the trusted party without more would be 'too far-reaching'. It would taint 'every Christmas or birthday gift by a child to a parent', 'every transaction between a client and his solicitor or between a patient and his doctor' and that would be 'absurd'. So 'something more is needed before the law reverses the burden of proof, something which calls for an explanation'. While Lord Nicholls notes without disagreement that *CIBC Mortgages Plc v Pitt*[57] dispenses with an improvident transaction as essential to undue influence, he stresses its indispensability where undue influence is inferred and observes that, anyway, it will invariably feature even in proved (actual) undue influence cases.[58]

5.3. Essence or Evidence?

In practice, the line between treating an improvident transaction as *of the essence* of undue influence, and treating it merely as *evidence* of something amiss in the

[55] Birks and Chin 82. [56] *Etridge*, para 24.
[57] [1994] 1 AC 200. [58] *Etridge*, para 12.

claimant's judgment or the defendant's conduct (neither of which is anchored by well-defined criteria) will always be a hazy one. If we diminish the importance of the unfair outcome in the story of undue influence, we run the risk of distorting the judicial decisional process, and losing (rather than gaining) a degree of consistency. Indeed, far from pragmatically restricting the scope of claimant-sided relief, as Birks and Chin claim, the cases show how resulting unfairness can *broaden* the reach of the doctrine whether conceived of in claimant or defendant-sided terms. Where evidence is otherwise scarce or absent, it can justify the inference that the claimant was sufficiently trusting of or dependent on the defendant,[59] that the defendant must have improperly procured the claimant's consent to the transaction,[60] or that the claimant could not have been emancipated from the defendant's influence (whether by independent advice or otherwise).[61] Conversely, absence of clear unfairness to the claimant (or the acceptable explicability of any apparent unfairness)[62] leads to the reverse inferences: that the claimant acted without impairment,[63] that the defendant's conduct was unobjectionable,[64] or that any independent advice did successfully emancipate the claimant.[65]

5.4. Terminology

The expression 'manifest disadvantage' was criticized in *Etridge*. While the label is usually unproblematic (when applied to substantial gifts or sales at undervalue), it can be misapplied in the non-commercial guarantee situation where, typically, the wife guarantees a bank's loan to her husband but later claims that it resulted from her husband's undue influence.[66] The error identified by Lord Nicholls is in going to either extreme, of treating such transactions as *always* bad for her (because she undertakes an onerous obligation while personally obtaining nothing in return), or of treating such transactions as *never* bad for her (because the fortunes of husband and wife are merged, particularly if his business is the source of the family income). *Etridge* lays down the correct approach in *all* cases: the question is whether the transaction '*calls for an explanation*' in the sense that it is 'not to be reasonably

---

[59] eg *Crédit Lyonnaise v Burch* [1997] 1 All ER 144, see n 48 above.
[60] eg *Re Craig* [1971] Ch 95 where actual influence was inferred, see n 104 below.
[61] eg *Hammond v Osborn* [2002] EWCA Civ 885.
[62] eg No undue influence found in *Portman Building Society v Dusangh* [2000] 2 All ER (Comm) 221 father guaranteeing son's debt, *Campbell v Campbell* (Chancery Div 21 February 1996) mother gifting house to son who she believed had been unjustly imprisoned, and *Davies v Dobson* (Chancery Div 7 July 2000) grandmother gifting house to granddaughter who she brought up as her daughter. Compare the unacceptable reason in *Crédit Lyonnais Bank Nederland NV v Burch* [1997] 1 All ER 144. *Re The Estate of Brocklehurst* [1978] 1 Ch 14 seems on the borderline, see text accompanying n 125 below.   [63] eg *Hughes v Hughes* [2005] EWHC (Ch) 469.
[64] eg *Glanville v Glanville* [2002] EWHC 1271, *Popowski v Popowski* [2004] EWHC (Ch) 668, *Turkey v Awadh* [2005] EWCA Civ 382, [2005] 2 FCR 7.
[65] eg *Papouis v West* [2004] EWHC (Ch) 396 see text accompanying n 126 below.
[66] *Etridge*, paras 26–7.

accounted for on the ground of friendship, relationship, charity, or on the ordinary motives on which ordinary men act' and so, is presumed to have resulted from the defendant's undue influence.[67]

However, Lord Nicholls's warning about misconstruing labels applies equally to the new formulation of 'calls for an explanation'. Its tendency to inhibit inferences of undue influence in wife guarantee cases is noted in *Chitty*,[68] since it would be 'unrealistically blinkered' not to recognize that '[o]rdinarily, the fortunes of husband and wife are bound up together . . . [and that a] wife's affection and self-interest run hand-in-hand'.[69] But, care must be taken lest the shorthand of 'calls for an explanation' misleads the Court into denying relief simply because a gift appears to be perfectly explicable by the claimant's commitment or allegiance to the defendant.[70] Examples are readily found. Lord Scott said in *Etridge*[71] that a wife's willingness to guarantee her husband's debts is 'a natural and admirable consequence of the relationship of a mutually loyal married couple. . . . To regard the husband in such a case as a presumed "wrongdoer" . . . [is not] consistent with the relationship of trust and confidence that is a part of every healthy marriage'. In the same sense, there is nothing inexplicable about the nun's decision in *Allcard v Skinner* to give her worldly possessions, as she has given herself, to the service of God.

On the claimant-sided view, the simple sole test should be the claimant's consent. Evidence of that consent drawn from the resulting transaction should be detached from the standard of the ordinary motive of the hypothetical ordinary person where the evidence shows the claimant to be an *extra*ordinary person. It is true that we see the Court admitting evidence of the claimant's personality and circumstance as indicative of the unlikelihood that she freely consented to the transaction,[72] or alternatively, that she *did* in fact consent for extraordinary but acceptable reasons.[73] But *Allcard v Skinner* shows that consent cannot be the sole test. A nun is, almost by definition, extraordinary because so few women are. The fact that her perfectly understandable gift was nevertheless held to 'call for an explanation' shows that the new formulation masks an implicit judgment about the *objective acceptability* of the transaction in the context of the parties' relationship. Here, as elsewhere,[74] it is not so much a genuine search for a party's

---

[67] *Etridge*, paras 22, 24, 28–9. [68] *Chitty's Law of Contract* (29th edn, 2004) para 7–075.
[69] *Etridge*, para 28.
[70] 'the relationship between the donor and the donee . . . is something of a two-edged sword. On one side, it helps to explain the gift. On the other, it provides the opportunity to take unfair advantage', *Randall v Randall* (Chancery Div 28 May 2004) para 42.
[71] *Etridge*, para 159.
[72] eg *Randall v Randall* (Chancery Div 28 May 2004) para 71 the donor was 'not the sort of person to engage in spontaneous acts of charity or generosity at all'. Moreover, her gift 'prejudiced the position of the donkeys' she so loved. See also *Meredith v Lackschewitz-Martin* [2002] EWHC (Ch) 1462 and *Padgham v Rochelle* [2002] All ER (D).
[73] eg *Re The Estate of Brocklehurst* [1978] 1 Ch 14 see text accompanying n 126 below, and *Portman Building Society v Dusangh* [2000] 2 All ER (Comm) 221.
[74] *Davis v Fareham Urban UDC* [1956] AC 696, 728.

consent as the imposition of objective standards (of the reasonable person) against which abnormality (indicating undue influence) is judged. The nun's gift was explicable and was not induced by any bad behaviour or exploitative intention of the Mother Superior, and yet the gift was inappropriate, objectively judged. The reason is that it failed to provide for the contingency that she may later choose a different life.[75] The gift substantially curtailed her future autonomy, her future freedom.

   This discussion shows how malleable and difficult to stabilize a consent-based view of undue influence is. It also begs the question of the role of transactional outcome in so far as it goes beyond the inquiry into the claimant's consent. The answer given by *Etridge* is that it suggests 'that the defendant abused the influence he acquired in the parties' relationship. He preferred his own interests. He did not behave fairly to the other.'[76] However, an analysis of this defendant-sided view reveals its inadequacy and need for very substantial qualification.

6. What *Has* the Defendant Done?

The dominant view, subscribed to by *Etridge* and other recent leading cases,[77] is that undue influence targets the defendant's conduct in procuring the transaction. The doctrine seeks to:[78]

ensure that the influence of one person over another is not abused. In everyday life people constantly seek to . . . persuade those with whom they are dealing to enter into transactions, whether great or small. The law has set limits to the means properly employable for this purpose. . . . If the intention was produced by an unacceptable means, the law will not permit the transaction to stand. The means used is regarded as an exercise of improper or 'undue' influence, and hence unacceptable.

But, what, exactly, is objectionable about the defendant's behaviour?

6.1. No Wickedness Required: Birks and Chin

Birks and Chin's work helps to stake out the area in three ways. First, we have noted recent judicial support for their observation that undue influence requires neither bad faith nor bad conduct.[79] This is underscored by the nature of the rebuttal. Since it is insufficient for a defendant to rebut any *inference* of undue influence by showing his good faith and irreproachable conduct, the

---

[75] *Allcard v Skinner* 179; she did not consider 'the consequences to herself . . . it never occurred to her that she should ever wish to leave the sisterhood or desire to have her money back'.
[76] *Etridge*, para 14.
[77] eg *R v Attorney-General for England and Wales* [2003] UKPC 22 and *National Commercial Bank (Jamaica) Ltd v Hew* [2003] UKPC 51.   [78] *Etridge*, paras 6–7.
[79] See n 24 above.

inference raised *cannot* be that the defendant has acted wrongly or in bad faith.[80] The Mother Superior was the 'model of rectitude'[81] and yet undue influence was found.

Secondly, they disentangle defendant unconscientiousness *at the time of the transaction* (in procuring the claimant's consent to the transaction or transfer) from defendant unconscientiousness *ex post* (solely in retention of the benefit received). The latter is conclusory and not explanatory; 'the only substantial reason why [the defendant's] behaviour is described as bad is that there is some other and antecedent reason why he should forego the benefit in question'.[82]

Thirdly, they explain where the Court of Appeal went wrong in *BCCI v Aboody*.[83] Despite the finding that Mrs Aboody's mind was in effect 'only a channel through which the will of [Mr Aboody] operated',[84] relief was denied because the Court found no causal link between Mr Aboody's bullying conduct[85] and Mrs Aboody's willingness to guarantee his debt. She would have signed even if he had acted conscientiously and insured that she fully understood the risks she was undertaking, whether via his own disclosure or independent advice. The flaw in this reasoning is that 'it obstructs the finding of undue influence in the most extreme case', where the claimant's deference to the defendant is 'systematic and unchallenged',[86] as in *Allcard v Skinner*. The correct approach is instanced by *Bank of Montréal v Stuart*[87] where it was said of the wife, who was 'absolutely cleaned out' by acting as surety for her husband: 'She says she acted of her own free will . . . and that she would have scorned to consult anyone. . . . Her declarations . . . shew how deeprooted and how lasting the influence of her husband was.'

6.2. Objective Impropriety

These three lines drawn by Birks and Chin narrow but do not extinguish the space which can be occupied by a defendant (or other)-sided view of undue influence. Direct proof of bad intention has never been required and it is entirely sensible to detach the jurisdiction from the sensitivity of the defendant's (subjective) conscience. The standard is *objective*; the relevant conscience is that of the Court of Equity. As Lord Eldon said in *Huguenin v Baseley*:[88] 'The question is, not, whether she knew, what she was doing, had done, or proposed to do, but how the intention was produced: whether all that care and providence was placed round her' that should have been. Bridge LJ also puts the issue in normative

---

[80] Birks and Chin 67–76.   [81] Birks and Chin 79.
[82] Birks and Chin 60.   [83] [1990] 1 QB 923.   [84] ibid 969.
[85] When the adviser (insisted on by the bank) tried to suggest ways of limiting Mrs Aboody's liability her husband burst into the room and said 'why the hell do not you get on with what you are paid to do and witness her signature?' A scene followed which reduced Mrs Aboody to tears. The solicitor wrote in his attendance note 'husband is a bully. Under pressure and she wants peace.'
[86] Birks and Chin 76–9.   [87] [1911] AC 120, 137.   [88] 14 Ves 273, 299.

terms: what had the defendant 'left undone which he ought to have done or . . . done which he ought not to have done'?[89] Judged *objectively,* the Mother Superior *failed to do all that she should have to protect the nun's interests.* Her conduct was above reproach, but she still failed to meet the high standards of Equity (expressing the implicit norms of the relationship of influence). Subject to the bars to rescission, her liability to make restitution is *strict.*

This is consistent with the view in *Etridge* that undue influence need not be active but may be *passive.*[90] Lord Nicholls's statement also gives us clues about the pathology masked by the defendant-sided talk of 'abuse' and 'betrayal':[91]

[T]he influence one person has over another provides scope for misuse without any specific overt acts of persuasion. The relationship between two individuals may be such that, without more, one of them is disposed to agree a course of action proposed by the other. Typically this occurs when one person places trust in another to look after his affairs and interests, and the latter betrays this trust *by preferring his own interests.* He abuses the influence he has acquired. (Emphasis added)

It is implicit in the passage that there is nothing intrinsically wrong with the claimant's decision to go along with the defendant's judgment. Moreover, where the transaction is *not* manifestly improvident to the claimant, there is nothing suspicious. There is only talk of betrayal when the transaction *is* so improvident for it raises the inference that the defendant *has* preferred his self-interest *thereby* abusing his influence. Thus, undue influence has a clear substantive dimension (a concern with outcomes). But, it also has a procedural dimension, although that requires more unpacking.

6.3. 'Actual' Undue Influence

What are we to make of the old class 1 'actual' undue influence cases premised on the defendant's coercive procurement of the claimant's consent to the transaction? Birks and Chin argue that 'all cases of pressure should be treated as duress'.[92] Exporting out the defendant-sided cases advances their argument that undue influence is (or really should be) reserved for claimant-sided 'relational' cases.[93] This view is unconvincing; I make four observations.

First, the implicit 'relational'/'non-relational' distinction is subject to the caveat that even the 'non-relational' cases involve exploitation of the claimant's known *relationship* of love and affection, albeit with a third party rather than with the defendant. The relationship makes the claimant vulnerable to the defendant's threat to harm the third party by prosecution[94] or disclosure. For

---

[89] *Re The Estate of Brocklehurst* [1978] 1 Ch 14, 39.
[90] See text accompanying n 79 and see n 24 above.   [91] *Etridge*, para 9.
[92] Birks and Chin 63.   [93] Birks and Chin 67.
[94] *Williams v Bayley* (1866) LR 1 LH 200, threat to prosecute the claimant's son.

example, in *Mutual Finance Ltd v John Wetton & Sons Ltd*[95] Joseph Wetton forged the signatures of his father and his brother Percy in guaranteeing his friend's debt to Mutual Finance. On the friend's default, Mutual Finance impliedly threatened to prosecute Joseph unless Percy agreed to honour the guarantee. The agreement was set aside for actual undue influence because Mutual Finance knew that Percy only agreed out of fear that the shock of his brother's prosecution would endanger his invalid father's life. The analogy with 'duress to the person' is relatively clear. A looser analogy can be drawn with the 'three-party non-commercial guarantee' cases: the creditor's implicit threat to 'harm' the debtor (by controlling the flow of the debtor's finance), with whom the claimant shares a caring relationship, is practically relievable only by the claimant's willingness to act as guarantor. Of course, considerations of administrative convenience have radically lowered the threshold for potential relief (ie a non-commercial guarantor receiving no direct benefit from the lender) *and* the creditor's obligation to safeguard the enforceability of the guarantee (ie to make minimal disclosure and ensure certification of legal advice to the guarantor). 'Equity, it is said, is not past the age of child-bearing.'[96]

Secondly, even if it makes sense to export the non-relational cases from undue influence to duress, this does not rid undue influence of all pressure cases. Where *pressure* occurs in the context of *a relationship of influence*, the case should continue to be litigated under undue influence rather than under duress, as even Birks and Chin concede. This is not because, as they argue,[97] the defendant's pressure is subsidiary to the claimant's 'impairment', but rather, because the defendant's 'bad conduct', while *unnecessary*, may nevertheless be *sufficient* for undue influence. It violates *an implicit procedural norm* of the relationship of influence.

Thirdly, it is an error to trivialize the sort of defendant conduct impugned by the Courts—'excessive pressure, emotional blackmail or bullying'.[98] Such conduct may[99] seem 'relatively innocuous',[100] insufficient to register on the radar of duress,[101] but its legal significance must be understood *in the context of the parties' relationship of influence*. In that context, the law imposes a procedural disability

---

[95] [1937] 2 KB 389.   [96] *Etridge*, para 89.   [97] Birks and Chin 77, 95.
[98] *Etridge*, para 160. Other behaviour castigated includes isolation of the plaintiff from others and attempts at 'cover up' once questions are asked.
[99] The conduct may be more serious as in *Bank of Credit and Commerce International SA (in liquidation) v Hussain and another* [1999] All ER (D) 1442, where the husband often subjected his wife to public humiliation verbally and physically (slapping her and pulling her hair) and coerced her guarantee of his debt by putting her head in a sink and turning on the hot water. In *Langton v Langton* [1995] 2 FLR 890, the son and daughter-in-law of a man imprisoned for murdering his wife moved in with him on his release. They knew he feared further institutionalization and threatened to stop caring for him as his health deteriorated if he did not turn over his property to them. In *Woolwich plc v Gomm* (2000) 79 P & CR 61 (CA) the husband coerced his wife, who was 'vulnerable, dependant and impressionable' and from whom he had long separated, to guarantee his debt by threatening not to pay her maintenance.
[100] *Chitty's Law of Contract* (29th edn, 2004) para 7–049.   [101] Birks and Chin 77.

on the defendant: he cannot behave as he might towards an arm's-length stranger (on whom, anyway, such relatively innocuous pressures would have minimal impact) because the effect of such conduct is magnified when directed towards someone over whom the defendant has abnormal influence. For example, in *Bank of Scotland v Bennett*[102] the husband used wounding and insulting words to compare his wife's disloyalty to the loyalty of his relatives and to imply her irrelevance if she refused to agree. The judge found 'moral blackmail amounting to coercion and victimization'. In *Clarke v Prus*[103] an elderly man, befriended by a younger woman, gave her gifts totaling £1.9 million over some twenty years. The Court concluded that 'what started out as Mr Clarke's folly . . . finished up as Mrs Prus' victimization at the end of his life' when her requests turned into increasingly vehement demands made through verbal onslaughts and oppressive harassment. The Court has even been prepared to infer such overt improper procurement.[104]

Fourthly, to retain relational pressure cases within undue influence (rather than hiving them off into duress) is consistent with the position in *Etridge* that there is only *one* class of undue influence[105] but *two* ways of committing (or proving) it. Undue influence 'may be an overt wrong, such as oppression; or it may be the *failure to perform an equitable duty*, such as a failure by one in whom trust and confidence is reposed not to abuse that trust by *failing to deal fairly with her and have proper regard to her interests*'[106] (emphasis added). *Whenever* undue influence is alleged, the Court's inquiry inevitably gravitates around *the same three* features, namely:[107] (a) the motivation of the *claimant* in view of her personality, her relationship with the defendant, and any independent advice she received; (b) the *defendant*'s conduct in view of his relationship with the claimant, and; (c) the *resulting transaction*. As Lord Clyde explains, '[a]t the end of the day, after trial, there will either be proof of undue influence or that proof will fail and it will be found that there was no undue influence. In the former case, whatever the relationship of the parties and however the influence was exerted, there will be found to have been an actual case of undue influence. In the latter there will be none.'[108] It would, therefore, be illogical to deny the existence of actual undue influence but find presumed undue influence.[109]

While it is now conventional to say that the claimant proves undue influence either actually or with the benefit of an evidential inference which remains un-rebutted, it is more precise to say that undue influence may be exercised by

[102] [1997] 1 FLR 801.   [103] Chancery Div 8 March 1995.

[104] In *Re Craig* [1971] Ch 95 an old man gave or spent on his companion-housekeeper three-quarters of his wealth over six years. Absent direct evidence of pressure the court still found active undue influence because of the amount of the gifts, the claimant's vulnerability to pressure by the defendant, the evidence of the direct exercise of that pressure on other occasions and for other purposes, the parties' knowledge of the claimant's utter dependence on the defendant, and the whole history of the relationship.   [105] *Etridge*, paras 16, 93.

[106] *Etridge*, para 107.   [107] *Etridge*, para 13.   [108] *Etridge*, para 93.

[109] *Etridge*, para 219.

acts (actively, by overt unfair persuasion) or by *omissions* (passively, by failure to inform, advise, or otherwise safeguard the claimant's interests). *Both* are manifestations of the essence of undue influence; namely, the defendant's *failure to safeguard the claimant's interests* in view of their relationship.[110] *Both* represent the implicit norms of the relationship of influence. The traditional categories are merely points on a spectrum.

7. What is the Inference to be Rebutted?

7.1. Not Impaired Consent

Identifying the nature of the *rebuttal* informs the nature of the undue influence being inferred. Birks and Chin argue that the rebuttal meets (negates) the pathology of impaired consent, usually via independent advice. They cite *Allcard v Skinner*: the transaction must be shown to be 'the spontaneous act of the donor under circumstances which enabled him to exercise an independent will'.[111] However, this is susceptible of explanations other than a straightforward concern with consent (whether ultimately rooted in the claimant's dependency or the defendant's reprehensible procurement). We are reminded of Hart's counsel.[112] And, again, a closer look at *Allcard v Skinner* is instructive. Even where there is ample finding that the donor knew what was expected of her before she joined the sisterhood (when advice from her barrister brother was available) and that her actions were entirely referable to her assessment of her best interest, the inference of undue influence was not rebutted; this undermines the view that the rebuttal is about negating impaired consent. In undue influence, Bowen LJ distinguishes 'the rights of the donor' to make the transfer, which are unrestricted, from 'the obligations which are imposed upon the conscience of the donee by the principles of this Court' arising from 'public policy and fair play'.[113]

7.2. Not Wrongful Procurement

At the same time, Cotton LJ states that: 'the Court interferes, not on the ground that any wrongful act has in fact been committed by the donee, but... to prevent the relations which existed between the parties and the influence arising therefrom being abused'.[114] Indeed, it may be impossible to rebut the inference of undue influence even if the defendant (who has not actively exercised his influence) does all he realistically can to emancipate the plaintiff. In *Allcard v Skinner*,[115] Kekewich J

---

[110] *Etridge*, paras 9, 14, 107.   [111] *Allcard v Skinner* 171.
[112] See text accompanying nn 12–19 above.   [113] *Allcard v Skinner* 189–90.
[114] *Allcard v Skinner* 171.
[115] At 159; at 184 Lindley LJ required proof that the nun knew 'she would have been allowed to obtain [outside] advice if she had desired to do so... [and that] she was free to act on the advice

concluded that any advice against the gift 'however plainly and strongly given, would in all probability be disregarded . . . she would have put from her the advice received as a temptation of the evil one'. *Bank of Montréal v Stuart*,[116] and *Crédit Lyonnais v Burch*[117] are analogous. What will suffice to rebut the presumption depends on the weight of the presumption,[118] 'the greater the disadvantage to the vulnerable person, the more cogent must be the explanation before the presumption will be regarded as rebutted'.[119]

7.3. 'Public Policy', 'Failure to Protect'

That leaves the 'public policy' rationale of preventing 'relations which existed between the parties and the influence arising therefrom being abused'. The resonance with the *Etridge* reasoning of 'failure to protect'[120] is clear. However, such an answer needs a great deal more explaining for it implies an *obligation to protect* which begs two further questions: the *source* of the obligation and the *contents* of the obligation. A fully developed and justified theory must await a later airing,[121] but some markers can be put down.

8. Towards a Relational Theory of Undue Influence

Since there is no general obligation to protect one's transactional partner, the *source* of the defendant's obligation towards the claimant must lie in the normative expectations arising from their relationship of trust and confidence, a relationship in which the defendant participates. Here, we may look to the rationale and framework of fiduciary law. Far from being 'superfluous' and 'confusing',[122] it may inform the substantive and procedural limits imposed by undue influence law on the defendant's dealing with the claimant. The law on terms implied by law into certain relationships such as tenancy and employment may also assist. Additionally, the scholarship emphasizing the *relational* dimension of contracting, characterized by cooperation, trust, flexibility, and altruism[123] (contrasted with the '*discrete* and self-interested' paradigm of

---

which might be given to her', but any suggestion that the nun would have done something different had she been better advised seems quite fictional on the evidence before the court.

[116] [1911] AC 120.
[117] [1997] 1 All ER 144, see M Chen-Wishart, 'The *O'Brien* Principle and Substantive Unfairness' (1997) 56 CLJ 60.   [118] *Etridge*, para 20.
[119] *Etridge*, para 24.   [120] *Etridge*, paras 9, 107, see text accompanying nn 54, 91 above.
[121] 'Undue Influence: Vindicating Relationships of Influence' forthcoming CLP in autumn 2006.
[122] Birks and Chin 91–2.
[123] eg I Macneil, 'Contracts: Adjustments of Long-Term Economic Relations under Classical, Neoclassical and Relational Contract Law' (1978) 192 Northwestern U L Rev 854; 'Relational Contract: What We Do and Do Not Know'(1985) 3 Wisconsin L Rev 483; D Campbell, H Collins, and J Wightman (eds), *Implicit Dimensions of Contract: Discrete, Relational, and Network Contracts* (2003).

contracting), may also colour our thinking about the implicit procedural and substantive norms governing the ultimate of relational transaction.

The second question relates to the *content* of the defendant's obligation (or the claimant's interests to be safeguarded). Here, the two remaining areas of the undue influence inquiry (the defendant's behaviour and the resulting transaction) reveal the procedural and substantive content of the implicit norms of a relationship of influence. The defendant must not *actively* abuse his influence by exerting, even modest, pressure on a claimant who attempts to exercise her judgment to assess the specific transaction; this is the old class 1 'actual' undue influence. But he may have to go further (than merely refraining from active abuse); in order to retain the benefit of a transaction which is *grossly improvident* to the claimant, he must show that he has positively empowered the claimant to exercise her *specific* transactional judgment (as opposed to her *general* transactional judgment to trust the defendant); this explains the rebuttal in the old class 2 'presumed' undue influence.

That is, the defendant must *either* protect the claimant's welfare interest (if he does, there would be no improvidence to raise the inference of undue influence) *or*, successfully emancipate the claimant to protect her own welfare interest (if he does, he can rebut any inference of undue influence). Accordingly, evidence of the claimant's 'full, free and informed'[124] consent (the rebuttal) can show that, despite first appearances: (a) the claimant *did* have an acceptable explanation for the transaction, and so the defendant did not fail to (ie *did*) protect the claimant's *welfare interest*, or (b) the claimant *did* actively exercise her judgment in relation to the transaction (rather than simply choosing to trust the defendant), so that the defendant either owes her no obligation to start with, or has successfully shifted that obligation to another (the independent adviser), leaving the defendant free to deal at arm's-length (self-interestedly) with her.

In practice the claimant's welfare interest and her specific transactional autonomy interest are difficult to separate. Moreover, the courts have sometimes merged two analytically separate issues: the raising of the inference and its rebuttal. For example, in *Re Brocklehurst's Estate*[125] an elderly aristocrat, without independent advice, gave a garage proprietor a 99-year lease of the shooting rights over his estate. The court found no relationship of trust and confidence between the parties and that, anyway, any presumption was rebutted since the gift was a 'spontaneous and independent act', explicable by the parties' friendship *and* by the donor's desire to deliberately reduce the estate's value before it was inherited by a detested nephew after his death. Similarly, in *Papouis v West*[126] an elderly woman exercised her right to buy her council house at a substantial discount with a 50 per cent contribution from her niece. She then executed a deed of trust in favour of her niece on the understanding that she (the aunt) could live there rent-free for life. The Court rejected undue influence on the basis

---

[124] *Zamet v Hyman* [1961] 3 All ER 933, 1446.   [125] [1978] 1 Ch 14.

[126] [2004] EWHC (Ch) 396.

222 Mindy Chen-Wishart

of the aunt's robustness and independence of mind, the lack of improvidence to her, and the adequacy of the advice she received.

This accords with one of the key messages of *Etridge*, namely that we should not be distracted by talk of presumptions; *it is all a matter of evidence.*[127] This begs the question of what undue influence looks like stripped of its protective clothing—the paraphernalia of images and presumptions which serve to obscure rather than clarify its meaning. From that perspective, what is needed is an explanation which accommodates all three key elements: the appropriateness of the transaction, the claimant's motivation, and the defendant's behaviour *in the context of the parties' relationship.*

The relational theory briefly outlined promises a better fit than either the claimant or defendant-sided theories. It can explain how the structure of undue influence encompasses instances of both active (albeit modest) pressure and passive acceptance by the defendant: active procurement is the extreme and visible tip of the iceberg; passive undue influence describes ascendancy which operates continuously and invisibly unless its effect is supplanted (the influence is 'on' unless and until it is *successfully* 'switched off', eg by independent advice). Most importantly, the relational theory goes beyond the single factor explanation of a complex phenomenon. It accommodates all three areas of inquiry triggered by a claim of undue influence; no factor in the burden of proof needs demoting or discounting. This is consonant with Hart's thesis that the vitiating (defeasibility) factors express distinct ideas and values which excuse a claimant from responsibility despite the presence of consent. The parties' relationship of influence bars the defendant from transacting with the claimant as if at arm's-length. Instead, he must meet the standards of Equity in his positive (affirmative) regard for the claimant's welfare interest or specific transactional autonomy interest in the transaction (he must look after her or emancipate her to look after herself). The relational theory explains the inextricable link between the parties' relationship and the defendant's substantive and procedural 'obligations'. The nature of that relationship determines what transactions 'call for an explanation',[128] and what 'counts' as improper active pressure and as adequate rebuttal.[129]

---

[127] *Etridge*, paras 17, 92, 107, 158.   [128] See text accompanying nn 67–76 above.

[129] eg in *Etridge*, para 32, Lord Nicholls cautions against being too ready to find undue influence in *husband and wife cases*: 'Statements or conduct by a husband which do not pass beyond the bounds of what may be expected of a reasonable husband in the circumstances should not, without more, be castigated as undue influence. Similarly, when a husband is forecasting the future of his business, and expressing his hopes or fears, a degree of hyperbole may be only natural. Courts should not too readily treat such exaggerations as misstatements.' In contrast, *Allcard v Skinner* 157–8 'the law requires that influence, however natural and however right, shall not be unduly exercised, that is, shall be exercised only in due proportion to the surrounding circumstances and the strength of the person submitted to it. The more powerful influence or the weaker patient alike evokes a stronger application of the safeguard'; 183 'of all influences religious influence is the most dangerous and the most powerful'.

12

Unjust Enrichment, Discharge for Breach, and the Primacy of Contract

Gerard McMeel*

I went up to Brasenose in 1987 where I was a beneficiary of Peter's tutorials in three subjects, whilst remarkably he held successively three chairs. First, Roman Law, whilst he was Professor at Edinburgh. The first Saturday morning tutorial somehow turned to a recently unearthed fragment which provided new insights on Roman civil procedure: in one of those electrifying sessions for which Peter was famous any fear that law was a dry subject was quickly banished. Then Contract; Peter at Southampton. Lastly, BCL Restitution, with Peter now gracing the Regius Chair of Civil Law at Oxford. For him to be giving tutorials at Brasenose, whilst a Professor, let alone at institutions many miles from Oxford, speaks volumes of his industry and loyalty both to Brasenose and Oxford. Peter was a legend in Roman Law and Restitution. He was a formidable Contract lawyer too, but it could be sensed that Peter considered the subject more settled, with the dynamic developments just over the horizon. Nevertheless I shall suggest that contractual principles have continued to develop (albeit not as dramatically as unjust enrichment), especially in relation to construction and remedies. Accordingly contracts, even discharged contracts, continue to have a profound impact on the terrain where unjust enrichment operates. There is no

---

* Professor of Law, University of Bristol.
   The following abbreviations for principal works cited are employed in this chapter: K Barker, 'Unjust Enrichment: Containing the Beast' (1995) 15 OJLS 457 ('Barker'); J Beatson, 'The Temptation of Elegance: Concurrence of Restitutionary and Contractual Claims' in W Swadling and G Jones (eds), *The Search for Principle—Essays in Honour of Lord Goff of Chieveley* (1999) 143 ('Beatson') (also published in revised form as J Beatson, 'Restitution and Contract: Non-Cumul?' (2000) 1 Theoretical Inquiries in Law 83); P Birks, 'Failure of Consideration' in F Rose (ed), *Consensus ad Idem—Essays on the Law of Contract—In Honour of Guenter Treitel* (1996), 179 ('Birks, *Failure of Consideration*'); P Birks, Unjust Enrichment (2nd edn, 2005) ('Birks, *Unjust Enrichment*'); G Jones, *Goff and Jones on the Law of Restitution* (6th edn, 2002) ('*Goff and Jones*'); R Grantham and C Rickett, 'On the Subsidiarity of Unjust Enrichment' (2001) 117 LQR 273 ('Grantham and Rickett'); S Smith, 'Concurrent Liability in Contract and Unjust Enrichment: The Fundamental Breach Requirement' (1999) 115 LQR 245 ('Smith'); A Tettenborn, 'Subsisting Contracts and Failure of Consideration—A Little Scepticism' [2002] *Restitution Law* Review 1 ('Tettenborn').

logical or conceptual limit to the impact which contractual arrangements may have on claims in unjust enrichment as the potential source of defences or limitations on recovery. A continuing intense relationship between the two sources of obligation is inevitable.

1. The Varieties of Contractual Failure

Birks recently revisited the question of the differing degrees of invalidity of contracts.[1] One must tread carefully because the different species of contractual ineffectiveness do not necessarily entail identical consequences in the law of restitution. The textbooks proclaim that where a valid and subsisting contract makes provision (expressly or impliedly) for the transfer of a benefit, the contract governs and it cannot be circumvented by a claim in unjust enrichment.[2] Obviously this rule does not apply directly to void contracts which give rise to their own special problems and lie outside our enquiry.[3] Where the contract is initially valid, restitution is unwelcome unless the contract is discharged or avoided. Authoritative judicial pronouncements in the context of voidable contracts emphatically constrain the province of restitution in this way.[4] If an apparently valid contract is tainted by a vice during negotiations, the victim may set the contract aside if he acts promptly to rescind or avoid it. Such relief is commonplace for misrepresentation and compulsion,[5] is retrospective in its effect, and most commentators accept that (at least where the contract was partially performed) it is restitutionary. The rationale is that one party's consent was obtained by improper means and it is unjust that the other should be entitled to retain the benefit acquired thereby, namely the benefit of a binding contract.[6] Mutual restitution is entirely apt. In contrast, my principal contention in this essay is that where an initially valid contract is discharged in response to breach[7] a fully retrospective regime of mutual

---

[1] Birks, *Unjust Enrichment*, 125–7.

[2] H Beale (ed), *Chitty on Contracts* (29th edn, 2004) paras 29–019 and 29–058; *Goff and Jones*, para 1–063.

[3] It should not be too readily assumed that restitutionary relief is the automatic response to contractual voidness. The public policy underlying the statutory or common law rule which entails voidness is critical: *Guinness Mahon & Co Ltd v Kensington & Chelsea Royal London Borough Council* [1999] QB 215, 231–3 (Waller LJ).

[4] *Dimskal Shipping Co SA v International Transport Workers' Federation, The Evia Luck (No 2)* [1992] 2 AC 152, 165 (Lord Goff: duress); *Portman Building Society v Hamlyn Taylor Neck* [1998] 4 All ER 202, 208 (Millett LJ: mistake or misrepresentation). See also *Criterion Properties plc v Stratford UK Properties LLC* [2004] UKHL 28; [2004] 1 WLR 1846 (want of authority).

[5] Subject to bars of affirmation, lapse of time, impossibility of restitution, intervening third-party rights, and s 2(2) of the Misrepresentation Act 1967, which embodies a policy that on occasion wiping out the entire contract is too draconian a response to a non-fraudulent misrepresentation.

[6] Compare *Whittaker v Campbell* [1983] 3 All ER 582, 586 (Robert Goff LJ).

[7] For over sixty years the principal species of discharge by operation of law—ineffectiveness as a result of impossibility of performance or other frustrating event—has been hived off to a special regime under the Law Reform (Frustrated Contracts) Act 1943.

restitution of benefits may be an unprincipled and disproportionate response. As regards the restitutionary consequences, one cannot simply align contracts discharged for breach with other species of failed contracts. Discharged contracts necessarily have their own distinctive regime under which the terms of the contract, properly construed, may continue to play an important role.

In contrast, Birks ultimately thought there was a failure of basis (and therefore a prima-facie right to restitution) if a contract was merely 'terminable for repudiatory breach'.[8] He accepted that where a contract was initially valid, the need for an election by the innocent party entailed that the other party could not claim in unjust enrichment unless and until the other exercised its right to rescind or terminate (but only election distinguished those remedies from voidness). Moreover, Birks was content that the restitutionary consequences for broken contracts were no different to the regime for frustrated contracts or those avoided for misrepresentation or compulsion. He therefore underplayed the distinctiveness of rescission from termination. Most controversially, he sought to explain *both* as responses to unjust enrichment.

If we were to say that terminability and voidability were insufficient in themselves and that the absence of valid basis only began from the termination or the rescission, we would not be able to explain the origin of the powers to terminate or to avoid, which are not granted by contract and cannot be said to arise from their own effects. These powers arise from the enrichment rendered unjust by the invalidity of the contract under which it was transferred. [9]

This, with respect, is circular: the enrichment is unjust because repudiatory breach renders the initially valid contract terminable, and therefore unjust enrichment is the source of the power which renders contracts terminable. This is misconceived because termination for breach does not arise from unjust enrichment. The power to terminate is premised on wrongdoing: the repudiatory breach[10] of contract.[11] Contracts depend on at least some degree of mutual cooperation. Where trust and confidence is undermined, the victim of breach

---

[8] Birks, *Unjust Enrichment*, 120, 125, 141–2.   [9] Birks, *Unjust Enrichment*, 126.

[10] 'Repudiatory breach' comprises (1) breach of condition; (2) a sufficiently serious breach of an 'intermediate term' as recognized in *Hong Kong Fir Shipping Co Ltd v Kawaski Kisen Kaisha Ltd* [1962] 2 QB 28; (3) evincing an intention not to perform, often called 'repudiation' or 'renunciation'.

[11] Repudiatory breach, including renunciations (both actual and anticipatory) are all present breaches of contract and generate the innocent party's power to terminate. With regard to the third species of repudiatory breach, it is necessary to treat with caution the beguiling (but misleading) metaphor that 'an unaccepted repudiation is a thing writ in water' (compare Tettenborn, 2) which simply means that if the innocent party affirms the contract stands, but it does not negate wrongdoing. The authorities do not speak with a single voice on the 'wrongfulness' of renunciation, but the more modern view is that it is a wrong. Contrast older authorities such as *Johnstone v Milling* (1886) 16 QBD 460, 467 (Lord Esher MR: 'renunciation . . . does not, by itself, amount to a breach of contract') with the more modern view in *Moschi v Lep Air Services* [1973] AC 331, 350 (Lord Diplock: describing 'repudiation' as 'wrongful' and treating the innocent party as 'exercising a right conferred upon him by law of which the sole source is the original contract').

may wish to withhold future cooperation. That is the basis of termination, and lies behind the frequent inclusion of express termination provisions in written contracts.[12] When an employee is dismissed for stealing, the reason for the dismissal is the breakdown in trust, not the benefit of the stolen items or the wages earned whilst dishonest. Unjust enrichment cannot explain the source of the power or its prospectivity.

2. Three Contexts where Contract may Restrict Restitution

An applicable contract, that is one which as a matter of construction allocates rights, duties, and risks between persons, may preclude or limit a restitutionary claim, whether or not it is subsisting, and indeed whether or not there is any direct link between claimant and defendant. Just as there is no theoretical limit to the types of contract parties can enter into, so there is no logical or conceptual limit to the way in which an applicable contract can exclude or modify an otherwise arguable restitutionary claim. The question is always: does an initially valid contract (whether discharged or not) as a matter of construction govern the transfer of the disputed benefit? It has been too readily assumed that discharge (without further ado) permits restitutionary claims to be formulated in the wake of a broken contract. I propose to sketch three contexts in which the provisions of a contract may afford defences to a restitutionary claim. The second of these— contracts discharged for breach—lies at the heart of our concern. Nevertheless the first and third reveal the wider implications of my suggested 'construction' approach.

First, where there is a *subsisting contract* it is a matter of construction whether its terms govern the transfer of the disputed benefit. If it does the contractual regime applies and a claimant will be confined to contractual remedies, such as enforcing its primary obligations as in a debt claim, or in seeking substitutionary relief as in a damages claim.[13]

Secondly, even where a contract is *discharged* the court's primary task is to examine the contract to determine whether its terms govern the transfer of the disputed benefit. If as a matter of construction a contractual provision provides the solution there can ordinarily be no recourse to restitutionary relief.[14]

---

[12] The power to terminate pursuant to an express clause arises from consent, not wrongdoing or unjust enrichment. The triggering event does not have to be a breach of contract. It may be the expiry of period of notice.

[13] Propelled by restitution scholarship, damages for breach of contract are no longer necessarily loss-based. Instead they can be benefit-based, which opens up a whole new range of ways of formulating a claim by the innocent party. See *Experience Hendrix LLC v PPX Enterprises Inc* [2003] EWCA Civ 323; [2003] 1 All ER (Comm) 830.

[14] The common law approach grounded on construction is codified by a statutory provision in the context of frustrated contracts (which applies whether the contract is discharged or not): s 2(3) of the Law Reform (Frustrated Contracts) Act 1943. See Beatson, 159.

In both these contexts certain policy-based doctrines may override the contractual provisions, including the jurisdictions over penalties and to grant relief against forfeiture. These are exceptional and limited remedies which limit freedom of contract and are based on public policy (and not failure of consideration).

Thirdly, even if there is no contract directly linking the claimant and the defendant there may be in any event a *contractual setting* relevant to the contested benefit which may render it inappropriate to permit a restitutionary claim.

Before developing my suggested approach in greater detail, it is necessary to consider the traditional limitations on restitution in these contexts, the roles of discharge and construction, and recent academic debate on the primacy (or otherwise) of contract.

3. Two Hurdles: Total Failure and Discharge

Every breach of contract entitles the victim to damages. English law traditionally insists on two further preconditions before restitution has a role.[15] First, the contract must be legitimately terminated, which requires either repudiatory breach or the operation of an express termination clause. Secondly, where the claimant makes a payment he is only entitled to recover on the ground of failure of consideration (in the sense of a failure of the recipient's counter-performance[16]), if the failure has been *total*.[17] The latter restriction has long been a target for those desirous of liberating the grounds for restitution by excising unprincipled restrictions on the availability of the cause of action.[18] Given the unanimous academic view that the 'totality' requirement is indefensible I shall not discuss it further and assume it has had its day.[19] Modern accounts favour a

[15] These two preconditions are only clearly spelt out in relation to money claims, whether by the innocent party, or more recently by the party in breach. The earliest example of acceptance of a claim based explicitly on failure of consideration by a party in breach appears to be as recent as *Rover International Ltd v Cannon Film Sales Ltd (No 3)* [1989] 1 WLR 912, 932 (Kerr LJ) and 936 (Dillon LJ). Non-money claims have traditionally been obscured by the language of *quantum meruit* and hampered by the doctrine of 'entire obligation'. Following Birks it is widely thought that (enrichment difficulties aside) symmetry should prevail. See P Birks, 'Restitution after Ineffective Contracts: Issues for the 1990s' (1990) 2 JCL 227. This discussion focuses on money claims.

[16] *Fibrosa Spolka Akcyjna v Fairbairn Lawson Combe Barbour Ltd* [1943] AC 32, 48 (Viscount Simon LC).

[17] The rule dates back to at least *Hunt v Silk* (1804) 5 East 449, 102 ER 1142 (KB).

[18] An early example was Goff's discussion in 1961, which suggested that where the payee was in breach in practice the rule caused no injustice as the payer could recoup in respect of any benefits conferred (presumably as a head of loss) in a claim for damages for breach of contract. This did not avail the party in breach: 'The simple solution appears to be to grant a general right of recovery to the extent that the consideration for the payment has failed, subject always to the payee's right to recover damages in respect of any breach of which the payer has been guilty'. See R Goff, 'Reform of the Law of Restitution' (1961) 24 MLR 85, 90.

[19] See Lord Goff in *Westdeusche Landesbank Girozentrale v Islington London Borough Council* [1996] AC 669, 682 (HL). For evidence of that development: *David Securities Pty Ltd v*

generous approach to restitution where there can be counter-restitution,[20] and advocate that failure of consideration should be a cause of action, whether the failure is total or partial (and I shall assume that is correct as a starting point). Our focus is the modern relevance of the first rule.

4. The Primacy of Contract Debate

The respective role of contractual and restitutionary techniques where contracts fail through breach has provoked a lively academic debate over the last ten years, which has not to date been reflected in the case-law.[21] The issue is formulated in a number of ways. Can there be concurrent liability in contract and unjust enrichment?[22] Should claims in restitution be subsidiary to claims in contract? Should restitution recognize the primacy of contract and defer to it in its legitimate sphere of influence? The arguments in favour (of some degree) of contractual primacy are various (and overlapping). There are: arguments from inconsistency or contradiction, and the related argument from circularity;[23] arguments based on the interstitial or supplementary nature of restitution;[24] arguments based on the contractual allocation of risk;[25] and arguments from policy.[26]

In his classic discussion of failure of consideration[27] Birks succeeded in moving the debate on from indefensible restrictions on claims to a more focussed discussion of the relationship between the two subjects. He insisted on the excision of 'total' from the cause of action, pleading the general trend favouring mutual restitution.[28] Trenchantly he insisted that the only tenable defence of the

---

Commonwealth Bank of Australia (1992) 175 CLR 353, 383 (HCA); *Goss v Chilcott* [1996] AC 788, 798 (PC: Lord Goff).

[20] Restitution may already follow where the consideration can be readily apportioned or where counter-restituion is straightforward: *David Securities Pty Ltd v Commonwealth Bank of Australia* (1992) 175 CLR 353.

[21] The two principal textbooks each accordingly contain a pregnant footnote digesting this literature: *Goff and Jones*, para 1–061 n 78; A Burrows, *The Law of Restitution* (2nd edn, 2002) 323 n 1.

[22] This is an incomplete way of posing the problem as it overlooks the position of the party in breach.

[23] eg A Burrows, 'Solving the Problem of Concurrent Liability' in A Burrows, *Understanding the Law of Obligations—Essays on Contract, Tort and Restitution* (1998) 16, 20–4; Beatson, 146.

[24] eg Grantham and Rickett, 274, 289.   [25] eg Beatson, 169.

[26] eg P Birks, *An Introduction to the Law of Restitution* (1989) 46–7: not subverting bargains.

[27] Birks, 'Failure of Consideration', 179. Compare E McKendrick, 'Total Failure of Consideration and Counter-Restitution: Two Issues or One?' in P Birks (ed), *Laundering and Tracing* (1995) 217 for a more cautious assessment.

[28] In respect of voidable, frustrated, and (some) void contracts. Obviously this records Birks's earlier view that recovery for failure of consideration could be total or partial. His final view was that recovery should be on the ground of failure of basis, which could either fail or not: 'There is no such thing as a partial failure of basis' (Birks, *Unjust Enrichment*, 121). Given that terminability for repudiatory breach was a failure of basis, and restitution subject to counter-restitution could follow, in practice the outcome would be the same.

totality hurdle was that it was a 'blunt instrument to reduce the incidence of conflict' between causes of action in contract and in unjust enrichment. Even this was 'intellectually disreputable'. Adherents of contractual primacy should instead articulate an explicit, coherent argument based on that principle. They should advocate either 'systematic subsidiarity' in the form of a total bar on unjust enrichment claims where an action for breach was available, or at least for a 'cap' or ceiling on recovery in restitution.[29] This certainly threw down the gauntlet. However, disappointingly, Birks resisted any firm conclusion on the merits of the primacy of contract argument, accepting (for present purposes) that an undischarged contract should regulate those matters governed by it, but ending on a strong hint that when the question was squarely addressed (with the unrelated distraction of 'totality' deleted) the law would ultimately favour concurrency.[30]

Simultaneously Barker articulated the most trenchant rejection of contractual primacy. He regretted that restitution has been 'born into an almost stifling culture of contractual protectionism'. Barker preferred the modern environment in which claims in unjust enrichment 'have (quite rightly) been set free to explore the territory logically available to them'.[31] He rejected any continuing undue deference to a 'dead arrangement's terms'.[32] Ineffectiveness of a contract should lead to a 'decline' in that deference, but Barker is not convinced this always follows.[33] Barker is particularly critical of judicial over-enthusiasm in identifying implied ouster of restitutionary claims: 'Whilst parties should naturally be free to limit the rights provided them by law, we cannot and should not presume them to have done so in all cases where contracts fail'.[34]

Barker's eloquent defence of a wholly independent law of restitution not doffing its cap to neighbouring subjects is vigorously drawn. Nevertheless I shall suggest below that the law does indeed deploy presumptions of the sort identified (albeit critically) by Barker.

In his characteristically sensitive discussion[35] Beatson eschewed any rigid rule but insisted that 'before discharge in nearly all cases and after discharge in some

---

[29] Birks, 'Failure of Consideration', 189. A 'contract ceiling' argument is a sub-species of argument for contractual primacy, which permits a concurrent restitutionary claim but caps recovery at the contractual level. For book-length discussion see A Skelton, *Restitution and Contract* (1998), which takes a generally sceptical view of 'contract ceiling' arguments. He is more sympathetic to 'valuation ceilings' for measuring enrichment. For a recent example of both contractual primacy and contractual ceiling arguments pointing in the same direction, see *Taylor v Motability Finance Ltd* [2004] EWHC 2619 (Comm) (unreported).

[30] Birks, 'Failure of Consideration', 192, 201–2.   [31] Barker, 459.

[32] Barker, 462: in particular taking to task Robert Goff J's acceptance of the validity of a valuation ceiling in the context of s 1(3) of the Law Reform (Frustrated Contracts) Act 1943 in respect of contracts discharged by frustration in *BP Exploration (Libya) Ltd v Hunt (No 2)* [1979] 1 WLR 783.

[33] Barker, 460: 'If contract law itself perceives there never to have been a binding allocation of risk, or has identified a reason why that allocation should no longer be respected, there no longer seems to be a good "contractual" reason for inhibiting restitutionary rights'.   [34] Barker, 462.

[35] Beatson, 143.

cases, allowing concurrence of claims would involve inconsistency and circularity'. Accordingly, insisting on a blunt rule barring restitutionary claims 'may neglect a small but theoretically important category of case'. Beatson rightly stressed the importance of construction issues including both the terms of the contract and 'its nature',[36] or what I would describe as the characterization of contractual species. Beatson's crucial insight was that previous writers have too readily assumed that pre-discharge restitution will necessarily subvert the contractual allocation of risk and conversely have too readily assumed that post-discharge restitution will not subvert such arrangements. In the latter context the question is, whether as a matter of construction, accrued rights are conditional or unconditional. However, Beatson also suggests, incorrectly in my view, that in long-term contracts 'there is more likely to be a gap in the allocation of risks'.[37]

   Grantham and Rickett picked up the gauntlet thrown down by Birks five years earlier, and have trumpeted contractual primacy.[38] Their account of subsidiarity is highly theoretical, although they are explicit that the underlying normative principle is the importance of 'individual autonomy and choice'.[39] However the structure for private law which they erect (in which unjust enrichment plays a bit part) is one based on the beguilingly neat assertion that contract and property are concerned with the appearance of consent, objectively ascertained,[40] whereas their four sub-categories of unjust enrichment[41] are concerned with identifying 'defective subjective consent'.[42] This broad assertion is not justified by the case-law on formation of contracts cited.[43] General private law takes subjective understandings into account when it is appropriate to do so. Within this elegant (albeit precarious) superstructure, Grantham and Rickett conclude that unjust enrichment is a supplementary doctrine to both contract and property law. Unjust enrichment is a subsidiary doctrine: it is 'interstitial'[44] and a 'gap-filler'.[45]

   The abstraction of Grantham and Rickett's argument undermines its potency. What really matters is that in the hierarchy of normative force English law accords primacy to contract because it records the intentions of the parties themselves, which is the whole purpose of the facilitative enterprise of private

---

[36] Beatson, 146.   [37] Beatson, 154.   [38] Grantham and Rickett, 273.

[39] Grantham and Rickett, 274.

[40] 'Private law is largely concerned only with the objective manifestation of consent' (Grantham and Rickett, 285).

[41] Lack of capacity, mistake, compulsion, failure of condition.

[42] Grantham and Rickett, 281.

[43] The two leading discussions of Blackburn J in *Smith v Hughes* (1871) LR 6 QB 597 and the House of Lords in *Paal Wilson & Co A/S v Partenreederei Hannah Blumenthal, The Hannah Blumenthal* [1983] AC 854 both insist that a binding contract only results if the objective construction of the offer and the offeree's subjective understanding when giving his assent coincide. See *Shogun Finance Ltd v Hudson* [2003] UKHL 62, [2004] 1 AC 919, para [185] per Lord Phillips: 'the task of ascertaining whether the parties have reached agreement as to the terms of the contract can involve a quite complex amalgam of the objective and the subjective and involve the application of a principle that bears close comparison with the doctrine of estoppel'.

[44] Grantham and Rickett, 274.   [45] Grantham and Rickett, 298.

law. Even the most ill-defined of exchanges is likely to provide more clues as to how the parties envisaged their relationship (and therefore material for resolving the concrete dispute) than the comparatively blunt principle against unjust enrichment.

Similarly abstract, but diametrically opposed in orientation, Stephen Smith's discussion[46] has a feel of 'blue skies' thinking about it. He quickly assumes (as I have) that the totality rule has been or will be quietly dropped. His discussion is incomplete, because by focussing on 'concurrent liability' he ignores the more poignant situation of the party in breach who has no cause of action if he is shut out from restitution.[47] Smith's argument is devastatingly simple (echoing Barker): 'an obligation should be allowed to cover its natural field'. The usual three-stage test for unjust enrichment is satisfied, even in cases of partial failure of consideration. He sees contract defences as unprincipled because the only 'proper defence' to a claim in unjust enrichment is a ' "defence" of no unjust enrichment'.[48] Smith does not regard the 'contract governs' objection as relevant: it is 'an apparent article of faith amongst restitution lawyers', but is dismissed on the peremptory basis that it is not fundamental breach but rather the other's decision to terminate which renders the contract inoperative.[49] The only problems which Smith envisages with unrestricted claims for partial failure of consideration in respect of both discharged and undischarged contracts are evidential and quantification difficulties.

In my view Smith gives insufficient weight to contractual limitations. People are enriched daily in situations in which it is not unjust for them to retain that benefit, and the most common explanation is the contractual context in which that transfer occurred. One can factor in the 'contract governs' principle at a number of stages in the traditional three- or four-stage tests for restitution.[50] Most obviously an applicable contract may entail that there is no injustice (third question) or constitutes an injustice-related defence (fourth question). Smith must be wrong to assert that restitutionary defences must be purely concerned with 'unjust enrichment'. The policy-based defence of good faith purchase refutes that assertion.

---

[46] Smith, 245.

[47] Somewhat misleadingly he re-characterizes the discharge hurdle into a 'fundamental breach' requirement, which even he has to admit does not fit squarely with two aspects of doctrine. First, the innocent party normally has an election to terminate or keep the contract alive. Secondly, the existence of conditions means a party can terminate in such cases even for a trivial breach. Smith, 247.   [48] Smith, 248–9.

[49] Smith, 252–3.

[50] Goff and Jones speak of 'limits' to restitutionary claims as opposed to defences: para 1–061. One solution is to insert a third question after 'enrichment' and 'at the expense of' enquiring whether there is an applicable contractual regime, before going on (if at all) to 'injustice' as suggested in G McMeel, *The Modern Law of Restitution* (2000) 6, 8–9. Support for this approach may be garnered from the recent decision of the House of Lords in *Criterion Properties plc v Stratford UK Properties LLC* [2004] UKHL 28; [2004] 1 WLR 1846, and in particular Lord Nicholls at para [4].

Lastly, Tettenborn is sceptical of statements by commentators of the 'subsisting contract principle'.[51] One concern is post-termination obligations, such as employees' duties of confidentiality. This misunderstands the nature of termination (to which we shall return). He also expresses concerns about adjustments under long-term contracts. However these will often be more easily achieved through the techniques of construction and implication than by recourse to the blunt tool of unjust enrichment. As a matter of principle Tettenborn instead favours a narrower rule that contract trumps restitution where 'on their proper interpretation, the terms of a contract between the parties are inconsistent with the existence of a claim to restitution for failure of consideration'.[52] It is difficult to quarrel with this formulation. Attention shifts from the existence of a contract to its construction. Except where the contract expressly or impliedly ousts restitution, claims may lie.

Three interim conclusions can be drawn from this survey of the recent literature. First, it has been suggested that discharge is a 'red herring' for drawing the line between the respective provinces of contract and restitution.[53] I will suggest that this overstates the case, and it remains necessary to distinguish discharged and undischarged contracts. Pre-discharge claims for restitution are bound to fail. Nevertheless it is right to point out that in the post-discharge environment restitution will also often be inappropriate. Secondly, attention is now focussed on whether or not a particular transfer is regulated by the contract's provisions and whether there is a binding allocation of risk ascertained through the techniques of construction (whether the contract is discharged or not). Thirdly, the most significant area of future contention is likely to be the extent to which courts and commentators are willing to identify an implicit allocation of risk, where the contract is not explicit. It is understandable, given the subject's history, that any whiff of fiction will be closely examined. However, I will suggest the courts will in practice be keen to discern implicit intentions in the interstices of contracts in appropriate cases.

5. The Significance of the Prospectivity of Discharge

Any restitutionary intervention in the wake of a contract discharged for repudiatory breach must be sensitive to contract law's policy choices. First, discharge is *prospective* only, in obvious contrast to rescission. This is critical, but the rule

---

[51] Tettenborn, 1. As a matter of authority Tettenborn surveys the case-law from the eighteenth to the twentieth century and rejecting Burrows's label of 'sparse' for the authorities supporting the subsisting contract principle, concludes rather that the case-law in favour is 'decidedly weak'. Tettenborn, 1 and 5–8. See A Burrows, *The Law of Restitution* (2nd edn, 2002) 323 n 1: 'This principle is not as explicitly spelt out in any case as one would have expected'.

[52] Tettenborn, 3.   [53] Principally Beatson and Tettenborn.

only obtained canonical status just a quarter of a century ago.[54] Secondly, a party who terminates may claim damages for both past and future (post-discharge) loss. This is because discharge excuses the innocent party from further performance altogether, but does not similarly excuse the party in breach who must still provide redress for lost future performance. In contrast, the party in breach may only claim damages for any losses caused by any breaches by the terminating party prior to discharge.[55] When termination is pursuant to an express clause usually (unless the contract provides otherwise) the contract comes to an end prospectively, often from a date specified by the contractual machinery. In contrast to discharge for repudiatory breach, a party who exercises a power conferred by a clause may have damages for loss limited to breaches up to the date of termination, and therefore not recover future losses.[56] The theory is that the contract has provided a facility for one or both parties to bring it to an end in certain events and therefore the party so electing is giving up its right to insist on future performance and accordingly any substitutionary relief in lieu thereof.

Prospective discharge is a proportionate response. The injustice lies in the other party's conduct in breaching a fundamental term or committing a serious breach such that it would be unjust to require further performance from the victim. However, superimposing on this a retrospective regime of mutual restitution may be inapt. Whilst such a response may appear apt for one-off exchanges, such as sale of goods, it is not necessarily a desirable exercise in a long-term relationship. If the Vice-Chancellor of the University of Bristol wrongfully dismisses me in repudiatory breach of my employment contract, would anyone think it proportionate to revisit a dozen years of mutual benefit rendering? In reality each month's salary and corresponding performance will be treated as severable[57] and the parties held to have intended that these instalments of performance should be provided for by the contract's terms and the money earned.[58] The same is true of other contracts which are more long term or relational in their nature, including hire, joint ventures, and many commercial supply arrangements. Failure of consideration (even partial failure) will rarely be arguable. In contrast, the early cases and juristic examples tend to focus on sale

---

[54] See the two House of Lords cases in the 1980 volume of the *Appeal Cases*: *Johnson v Agnew* [1980] AC 367, 392–3 (Lord Wilberforce) and *Photo Productions Ltd v Securicor* [1980] AC 827; see also *Hyundai Heavy Industries Co Ltd v Papadoupoulous* [1980] 1 WLR 1129 and the classic analysis of Dixon J in the High Court of Australia in *Macdonald v Denys Lascelles Ltd* (1933) 48 CLR 457.   [55] *Gill & Duffus SA v Berger & Co Inc* [1984] AC 382.

[56] *Financings Ltd v Baldock* [1963] 2 QB 104. Contrast the position where the clause is construed as being a condition, and therefore both termination and damages for future losses are recoverable: *Lombard North Central v Butterworth* [1987] QB 527.

[57] The Apportionment Act 1870, ss 2 and 5 (modifying the common law 'entire' obligation rule) apportions on a day-to-day basis certain periodical payments including salaries and pensions. There is some debate as to whether it also applies to wages. See *Goff and Jones*, para 20–049.

[58] s 2(4) of the Law Reform (Frustrated Contracts) Act 1943 makes similar provision for frustrated contracts.

of goods and land. It is only in respect of such discrete bargains that full-on restitution with its retrospective edge appears defensible.

The prospective nature of termination requires careful analysis, especially with long-term contracts. Discharge entails the release of the innocent party from future unperformed primary obligations, but the party in breach remains accountable for future lost performance by substitutionary relief in the form of damages. Retrospective readjustment of prior performances does not sit comfortably with this contractual remedy. Prospectivity of discharge may entail that there is no failure of consideration (total or partial) for pre-discharge performance. Rather, especially in more long-term arrangements, the assumption tends to be that the right to keep the benefit of prior performances has been earned. Adapting Birks's terminology: there remains a legal basis for such performance. Any adjustments for discrepancies may be more easily explicable on the basis of implicit provisions of the parties' contractual relationship.[59]

Furthermore in the post-discharge hinterland the contract's provisions may continue to determine the parties' relationship. That contracts may continue to regulate the relationship is taken for granted in drafting provisions.[60] For example, key employees will usually find in their service contracts extensive provision for non-competition and respect for trade secrets explicitly continuing beyond termination of the employment relationship.[61] The terms may have plenty to say about benefits which have been or ought to have been transferred

---

[59] eg in *DO Ferguson & Associates v Sohl* (1992) 62 Build LR 95 the contractor's claim for a reasonable sum for work done but not paid for prior to termination (which failed on the facts) is more readily explicable on the basis that an express or implied term entitled it to payment for services rendered on a (contractual) *quantum meruit* basis.

[60] It first became obvious in the context of arbitration clauses that certain contractual provisions must have been intended to govern both pre- and post-discharge. It is no accident that *Heyman v Darwins Ltd* [1942] AC 356 (HL) is a *locus classicus* of prospectivity. Could a party which alleged that the other was in repudiatory breach ignore an arbitration clause which governed disputes 'in respect of this agreement' and instead issue a writ? No. The House of Lords unanimously upheld the operation of the arbitration clause and sidelined prior authority to the contrary. Whether discharged for breach or automatically by frustration, an appropriately drafted clause still applied to the determination of those issues. See Viscount Simon LC (at 367), Lord Macmillan (at 374), and, most emphatically, Lord Porter: 'To say that the contract is rescinded or has come to an end or has ceased to exist may in individual cases convey the truth with sufficient accuracy, but the fuller expression that the injured party is thereby absolved from future performance of his obligations under the contract is a more exact description of the position' (at 399).

[61] Numerous clauses are dormant or of limited impact whilst a contract is successful. Many only spring to life when the evil day descends. First, the dispute resolution terms: arbitration, jurisdiction, and choice of law clauses. Secondly, clauses seeking (so far as public policy allows) to protect a firm's business by imposing restrictions on competitive economic activity, on the use of trade secrets or other confidential information, and to protect interests in intellectual property (especially post-termination). Another cluster creates or modifies contractual and other legal remedies: express termination, exemption, retention of title, accelerated payment clauses, and clauses to restrict set-off. Finally, there is a cluster to protect the integrity of the written instrument itself by restricting its easy modification and the parties' recourse to extra-contractual remedies: clauses requiring variations or waivers to be in writing, negating reliance on statements during negotiations and entire agreement clauses. See generally J Carter, *Breach of Contract* (2nd edn, 1991) ch 12.

and their location post-termination. Accelerated payment provisions, liquidated damages, and forfeiture clauses are obvious examples. Legal intervention on the ground of failure of consideration may be difficult to justify as there will be a clear contractual basis for the (claim to) payments or transfers. Restitutionary intervention is more likely to be policy-motivated, and entails rewriting the parties' bargain. For these reasons contracts discharged by breach or otherwise terminated cannot simply be aligned with void, voidable, and frustrated contracts so far as the law of restitution is concerned. Fully retrospective restitution and counter-restitution will usually be too blunt a response for this sophisticated environment.

6. The Fundamental Importance of Construction

Construction may appear a poor candidate to patrol this highly contested border between contract and restitution. Nevertheless in the very nature of things this conclusion is inescapable. Construction encompasses both the interpretation of the express terms and the neighbouring technique of the *implication*.[62] Its importance arises from the common law's default commitment to freedom of contract. Parties are free (subject to public policy) to set their own rules for future cooperative behaviour. Once the deal is struck, *pacta sunt servanda*. Parties to an exchange are rarely unacquainted and will have exchanged information through some medium of communication. Even the most basic arrangements will yield some desultory correspondence evidencing the parties' intentions or ways of doing business. More commonly standard terms or integrated contracts are incorporated in the relationship. A high degree of specification usually attends the deal. In contrast, both the tort of negligence and unjust enrichment are blunt instruments, with comparatively abstract conceptual structures apt for resolving disputes between strangers. Therefore when there is an exchange relationship at the heart of the interaction between claimant and defendant it is unsurprising that a court would wish to acquaint itself with the bargaining that has taken place.

Everybody accepts that it is possible to contract out of restitution. Even Barker grudgingly accepts: 'that the existence of a valid contract between A and B should exclude restitutionary rights between them, thereby encouraging full contractual specification and excluding any interstitial, gap-filling role for unjust enrichment inside existing contractual relationships'.[63] What tends to differ is the degree of each commentator's appetite for accepting construction arguments where the parties have not been explicit. Again Barker is the most sceptical: 'Whilst there is no objection to denying a restitutionary remedy to a plaintiff who has in fact so

---

[62] *Equitable Life Assurance Society v Hyman* [2002] 1 AC 408, 458–9 (Lord Steyn).
[63] Barker, 459. See A Skelton, *Restitution and Contract* (1998) 22.

agreed, it is questionable, to my mind, to presume an agreement of this kind where none has been expressed'.

Barker would prefer 'very clear evidence'[64] of such abandonment. In my view Barker has demonstrated that the courts (albeit not explicitly) do deploy presumptions about the availability or otherwise of restitutionary remedies. These appear to be the exact opposite of the principles applicable to contractual remedies.[65]

In practice judges are keen to discern both explicit and implicit intentions. Contracts often contain machinery for the repayment of sums overpaid by one party in respect of performance not received, invariably described by practitioners as 'clawback' provisions. In *The Trident Beauty* a time charter stipulated for hire to be paid in advance. The contract provided that 'any overpaid hire . . . [is] to be returned at once'. However, Lord Goff intimated that: 'even in the absence of any such express contractual provision, advance hire which proves to be paid in respect of the period during which the vessel was rendered off-hire under a term of the contract must ordinarily be repaid, and if necessary a term will be implied into the contract to that effect'.[66]

This is suggestive of a significant role for implication in dealing with contractual overpayments, especially in ongoing relationships. Construction, including gap-filling by implication, gives effect to the parties' agreed relationship. Non-consensual bases of legal obligation should defer to these.

Despite recent restatements on contractual construction,[67] the courts continue to deploy various presumptions about the parties' likely intentions. First, there is a well-established rule of construction that it is presumed that a party to a contract is not entitled to take advantage of his own wrong as against the other party to the contract.[68] Secondly, there is said to be a presumption that clear

---

[64] Barker, 462. Barker draws instructive parallels with tort claims in contractual settings. Compare also Robert Goff J's rejection of a submission that s 2(3) of the Law Reform (Frustrated Contracts) Act 1943 only applied where a provision was *clearly* intended to operate in the event of frustration in *BP Exploration (Libya) Ltd v Hunt (No 2)* [1979] 1 WLR 783, 806.

[65] In curious contrast to Barker's scepticism about implicit intentions, Smith, drawing on Wittgenstein's famous 'Show the children a game' discussion (L Wittgenstein, *Philosophical Investigations* (1953; trans G Anscombe, 1958) 33) rejects the reductionist view that intentions can only be discerned from explicit statements and that any gap-filling is fictional. However, he does not apply this insight to the role played by applicable contracts, and shields his broadly permissive attitude to concurrency from the implications of this insight. See Smith, 259.

[66] *Pan Ocean Shipping Co Ltd v Creditcorp Ltd, The Trident Beauty* [1994] 1 WLR 161, 164. See also *Cargill International v Bangladesh Sugar & Food* [1996] 4 All ER 563 (QBD), [1998] 1 WLR 461 (CA); *Comdel Commodities Ltd v Siporex Trade SN* [1997] 1 Lloyd's Rep 424; *Tradigrain SA v State Trading Corp of India* [2005] EWHC 2206 (Comm), [2006] 1 Lloyd's Rep 216.

[67] Most famously *Investors Compensation Scheme Ltd v West Bromwich Building Society* [1998] 1 WLR 892, 912–13 where Lord Hoffmann's five-paragraph account was prefaced by the (perhaps too reductionist) statement that 'Almost all the old intellectual baggage of "legal" interpretation has been discarded'.

[68] This is related to the rule that repudiatory breach does not generally bring the contract to an end, rather the innocent party's election does, and the rule against so-called 'self-induced' frustration: *Alghussein Establishment v Eton College* [1988] 1 WLR 587; *Cheall v Association of Professional Executive Clerical and Computer Staff* [1983] 2 AC 180, 189–90.

words are required to exclude or modify contractual remedies.[69] It is clear that what are preserved are 'contractual remedies' such as accrued rights in debt and for damages for prior breaches. It does not seem that the same approach is deployed for non-contractual remedies arising by operation of law. Indeed (following Barker's insight) the opposite presumption is deployed (albeit silently and perhaps unconsciously) in that restitutionary rights are in general held to be excluded by an applicable contractual regime.

We can now return to the three contexts where an applicable contract may restrict restitution. In each, I suggest that a 'construction' approach is appropriate.

7. The Subsisting Contract Regime

This should be uncontroversial.[70] In *The Trident Beauty*, where there was an express clawback regime, Lord Goff asserted:

as between shipowner and charterer there is a contractual regime which legislates for the recovery of overpaid hire. It follows that, as a general rule, the law of restitution has no part to play in the matter; the existence of the agreed regime renders the imposition by the law of a remedy in restitution both unnecessary and inappropriate.[71]

That this was a contractual, rather than a restitutionary, means of recovery was reinforced by the fact that recovery could comprise partial failure in respect of advance hire, illustrating the greater sensitivity of a contractual regime of repayment.

There is no room for unjust enrichment where a contract is on foot.[72] This is the simple matter of the construction of a valid contract. Even if there is a repudiatory breach the victim may elect to keep the contract alive leaving no role for restitution.[73] An issue which has troubled commentators[74] is the plight of a party in breach who has made a substantial advance payment, but cannot raise the funds for the balance of the price. Is the innocent party entitled to keep the contract open indefinitely and therefore the money paid in advance? It is

---

[69] The classical statement of the rule was the speech of Lord Diplock in *Gilbert-Ash* (*Northern*) *Ltd v Modern Engineering* (*Bristol*) *Ltd* [1974] AC 689, 717: 'in construing such a contract one starts with the presumption that neither party intends to abandon any remedies for its breach arising by operation of law, and clear express words must be used in order to rebut that presumption'.

[70] Contrast *Miles v Wakefield Metropolitan District Council* [1987] AC 539 (HL) where the rule was overlooked in *obiter dicta* by Lord Brightman (at 553) and Lord Templeman (at 561). Contrast Lord Bridge (at 552). Lords Brandon and Oliver reserved their opinion.

[71] *Pan Ocean Shipping Co Ltd v Creditcorp Ltd, The Trident Beauty* [1994] 1 WLR 161, 164.

[72] See Birks, *Unjust Enrichment*, 126: 'no claim in unjust enrichment is possible if and so long as the contract remains in being. The work has been incompletely done in discharge of a contractual obligation and that obligation which is its basis still stands' (at 125).

[73] Most commentators agree with this, although Beatson prefers to say 'hardly ever' room for restitution rather than 'never'. Beatson, 146.   [74] eg Tettenborn, 2.

illustrated by a variation on the facts of *Dies v British and International Mining and Finance Corporation Ltd*[75] where a buyer made an advance payment of a third of the price, but later wrongfully failed to accept delivery. The seller terminated and the buyer recovered the advance payment. What would happen if the seller elected to keep the contract open?

Birks's original solution remains persuasive.[76] By analogy with developments where the innocent party is precluded from keeping the contract alive just to earn a debt,[77] Birks suggested that an innocent party may not have a legitimate interest in keeping the contract open. Presumably the court could deem the contract discharged, and restitution may follow. The courts may eventually adopt a power to override the innocent party's election in appropriate cases, and, in effect, 'deem discharge', where there has been no cooperative behaviour for a substantial period, probably by judicial development of the 'legitimate interest' principle as suggested by Birks. Until that happens the party in breach has no recourse outside the contract.

Despite this orthodoxy in *Roxborough v Rothmans of Pall Mall Australia Ltd*[78] the majority of the High Court of Australia still managed to reach an unprincipled result. The dispute was a test case concerning a contract between a wholesaler and a retailer of tobacco products. An attempt by the State of New South Wales to dress up a tobacco tax as a licence fee was ruled unconstitutional by the High Court in earlier proceedings because the Constitution reserved excise matters to the federal authorities.[79] Many contracts were concluded on the basis that the fee was payable by the wholesaler and would be passed down the chain to end-customers. Between wholesaler and retailer the 'licence fee' was invoiced as a separate amount. The majority held that the licence fee element was severable and the retailers were entitled to recover that portion of the price from the wholesalers on the ground of total failure of consideration. The fact that these were fully performed valid contracts was largely ignored in the majority judgments.[80] The dissenting judgment of Kirby J stating that the claim based on total failure was 'impossible' to assert and upholding the contractual regime is far more persuasive: 'The individual contracts...were uncontestably valid.

---

[75] [1939] 1 KB 724.
[76] P Birks, *An Introduction to the Law of Restitution* (rev edn, 1989) 235–6 n 48. Interestingly it is a contractual solution.
[77] *Clea Shipping Corp v Bulk Oil International Ltd, The Alaskan Trader (No 2)* [1984] 1 All ER 129. Tettenborn (at 2 n 10) criticizes Birks's reliance on this authority by pointing out that Lloyd J (at 137) thought the contract remained alive but the remedies were restricted. More recent authority on termination proceeds pragmatically by recognizing the importance of cooperation and holds that a continuing failure to perform can indicate acceptance of repudiatory breach: *Vitol SA v Norelf Ltd, The Santa Clara* [1996] AC 800, 811 (Lord Steyn).
[78] [2001] HCA 516, (2001) 208 CLR 516.
[79] *Ha v New South Wales* (1997) 189 CLR 465.
[80] Gleeson CJ, Gaudron and Hayne JJ delivered a joint judgment where the issue is at best considered *en passant* (at para [21]; similarly Gummow J at para [65]) despite the fact that counsel for the respondents (Mr Walker SC and Mr Jackman) argued that: 'The payments were made in

They were not ineffective. Nor were they terminated.'[81] His Honour's careful reasoning should prevail in other common law countries.[82]

8. The Discharged Contract Regime

The traditional account states that once the contract is discharged restitution may follow, albeit in practice this has been largely hampered by the insistence on total failure of consideration. In contrast, more recently commentators[83] have insisted that discharge is not the end of the story. *Dies* properly belongs here as the contract was discharged. Even if the courts develop 'deemed discharge' (as suggested in the preceding section) it will still be a matter of construction whether restitution is appropriate.[84] In *Dies* Stable J observed that 'to enable the seller to keep [the money] he must be able to point to some language in the contract from which the inference to be drawn is that the parties intended and agreed that he should'.[85] Stable J determined that the payment was not a deposit. Therefore once the contract was discharged the seller had no contractual or other right to retain it. The seller had not earned the money in accordance with any contractual provision.[86] If it had been a deposit, as a matter of public

discharge of contractual obligations. The contract has not been discharged for breach or frustration or otherwise become avoided or unenforceable. Hence there was no total failure of consideration' ((2001) 208 CLR 516, 520). That may run together the two classic preconditions, but nevertheless put the argument squarely to the Court. The reasoning of Callinan J (at para [197]) that bringing proceedings for restitution is effectively a termination is implausible.

[81] para [166]. Kirby J acknowledged there may be exceptional cases where restitution may operate in an 'effective contract' (citing J Beatson, 'Restitution and Contract: Non-Cumul?' (2000) 1 *Theoretical Inquiries in Law* 83) but was not prepared to hold this was one of them. See for the discussion paras [165–73], and in particular the observations on policy at [173]. He also rejected the only faintly arguable basis for recovery, namely an implied contractual term (at paras [156–64]). Only Callinan J of the majority accepted this argument (at para [204]).

[82] The case is discussed in P Birks, 'Failure of Consideration and its Place on the Map' (2002) 2 Ox Commonwealth Law J 1 and J Beatson and G Virgo, 'Contract, Unjust Enrichment and Unconscionability' (2002) 118 LQR 352. Beatson and Virgo rightly applaud Kirby J and stress the 'fundamental principle' that restitution is 'subordinate to the law of contract'. In contrast, Birks accepts that the result is defensible because the licence fee payments were non-negotiable and could be severed. He further suggests that the result in the English case of *Orphanos v Queen Mary College* [1985] AC 761 needs to be revisited. However the House of Lords' conclusion on construction of the individual contract in that case, emphasizing that the student had agreed he would be admitted as an overseas student, seems correct.   [83] Beatson, 169-70; Tettenborn, 1.

[84] B MacFarlane and R Stevens, 'In Defence of *Sumpter v Hedges*' (2002) 118 LQR 569, 585 are right in their discussion of *Dies* to point out the importance of construction. However, discharge, whether elective or deemed, remains critical otherwise the contract is contradictory with an express term saying 'pay up' and an implied term saying that the buyer can have his money back if he cannot perform.   [85] [1939] 1 KB 724, 743.

[86] Similarly in *DO Ferguson & Associates v Sohl* (1992) 62 Build LR 95 the contractor had no right to overpayments by the employer in respect of services which it had not rendered. Nothing in the contract or elsewhere entitled him to those overpayments. Restitution on the ground of partial failure of consideration (not total failure as implausibly held by the Court of Appeal) or failure of basis was appropriate.

policy it would probably have been recoverable as an unreasonable deposit.[87] The contract governs subject to policy-motivated interventions.

The seminal case is *Hyundai Heavy Industries Co Ltd v Papadopoulos*[88] where a shipbuilder agreed to build a vessel for a sum payable in five instalments, but the second instalment of 2.5 per cent of the price was not paid. The shipbuilder cancelled under an express clause. The buyer's guarantors were liable: cancellation did not wipe out the accrued right to the second instalment. Shipbuilding was not simply a sale, but more resembled a building contract. Beatson explains this approach as principally construction-based. The payee's reliance expenditure is protected, albeit in a broad-brush fashion, by holding that where expenditure was envisaged as part of the contract price, any advance payment is irrecoverable in restitution or remains due in contract. However he also suggests that this can be supplemented by restitutionary principles to ensure that the party incurring expenditure does not thereby receive a windfall.[89] At present there is no sign that English law has followed that latter suggestion. Developments analogous to the jurisdictions to relieve against forfeiture or against unreasonable deposits cannot be ruled out, but the courts' instinct is to hold commercial parties to their bargains.

This was confirmed by *Stocznia Gdanska SA v Latvian Shipping Co*[90] where the House of Lords revisited the issue. The case concerned payments under two shipbuilding contracts. Again second instalments of 20 per cent fell due, but were not forthcoming. The shipyard terminated both contracts. The House of Lords awarded summary judgment, expressly applying *Hyundai*. The Court of Appeal had been attracted to an argument based on express terms which entitled the yard, in the event of termination, to retain instalments already paid, and that accordingly any common law rights were displaced by express contractual machinery. In contrast the House of Lords applied the presumption of construction that a party does not intend to abandon any remedies for breach of contract arising by operation of law.[91] Characterization was also an issue. What species of contract was the court dealing with? As in *Hyundai* these were not sales, but contracts for work and materials. This was logically prior to any discussion of failure of consideration. Lord Goff was clear that 'payment of instalments for the price was geared to progress in the construction of the vessel'.[92] Having identified the contract as one for work and materials with a predetermined scheme of instalments, the restitutionary notion of failure of consideration was inapplicable.

---

[87] *Workers' Trust & Merchant Bank Ltd v Dojap Investments Ltd* [1993] AC 573 (PC: recognizing a 10 per cent rule); Beale (1993) 109 LQR 524.   [88] [1980] 1 WLR 1129.
[89] J Beatson, *The Use and Abuse of Unjust Enrichment* (1991), 45–77; based on J Beatson, 'Discharge for Breach: The Position of Instalments, Deposits and Other Payments Due before Completion' (1981) 97 LQR 389.   [90] [1998] 1 WLR 574, noted [1998] LMCLQ 308.
[91] *Gilbert-Ash (Northern) Ltd v Modern Engineering (Bristol) Ltd* [1974] AC 689.
[92] [1998] 1 WLR 574, 588.

Two crucial points. First, termination was pursuant to express termination clauses so the shipbuilders may not have been able to claim damages for future lost profit in addition to termination. Secondly, construction determined the outcome even for the post-termination hinterland. It is possible to overplay the importance of characterization: were they sales as in *Dies* or contracts for work and materials as in *Hyundai*? The better view is that the latter case was a clear example of a modern commercial contract for a substantial duration with detailed provisions apt for both operative and terminated contracts. Similarly many long-term contracts for the supply of goods will resemble *Hyundai* and will be equally unsuitable for a restitutionary response if terminated. Identifying what species of contract one is dealing with may help orientate the court, but it is only a precursor to the more detailed exercise in construction which is necessitated if one party seeks to raise a restitutionary claim in the wake of the contract's failure.

9. The Contractual Setting Regime

Strikingly English law also recognizes that the contractual setting to the transfer of a disputed benefit will often oust any recourse to restitutionary relief even though there is no direct contractual relationship between claimant and defendant.[93] The critical example is the sub-contractor who undertakes work on the property of the employer but is not paid because of the insolvency of the main contractor. Can he seek direct restitutionary relief for a *quantum meruit* against the employer (whose property has benefited from his efforts) effectively bypassing the main- and sub-contract regime which indirectly links them. The answer appears to be no.

Brown & Davis Ltd v Galbraith[94] is instructive, although it predates modern recognition of restitution. An insured driver took his car to the plaintiff repairer following a collision and they provided a quotation. Subsequently the insurer's assessor agreed a revised figure with the repairer and then authorized the work to be carried out, with the excess figure of £25 to be collected from the insured. An invoice less the excess was sent to the insurer, but before it was paid the insurer became insolvent. The Court of Appeal reversed the decision of the judge who had held that the insured driver was liable on an implied contract for the total cost. Cairns LJ accepted that in addition to the express contract between insurer

---

[93] By analogy with principles by which the tort of negligence is excluded or limited by the contractual setting: *Norwich City Council v Harvey* [1989] 1 WLR 828, *Simaan General Contracting Co v Pilkington Glass Ltd (No 2)* [1988] QB 758, 781 (Bingham LJ) and *Henderson v Merrett Syndicates Ltd* [1995] 2 AC 145, 195-5 (Lord Goff). A similar exercise in contractual construction is required by the Contracts (Rights of Third Parties) Act 1999, s 1: see Law Commission Report, *Privity of Contract: Contracts for the Benefit of Third Parties* (Law Com No 242 (1996) para 7.18.
[94] [1972] 1 WLR 997.

and repairer under which the insurer agreed to pay for the repairs less the excess, there was also an implied contract between repairer and insured whereby the former agreed to take reasonable care and skill in carrying out the repairs and the latter agreed to pay, but in no greater amount than the excess.[95] Sachs LJ stressed that the primary liability was on the insurer. For the repairer to succeed required him to 'assert some form of secondary or collateral liability on the part of the owner'.[96] Both the agency or guarantee routes were unrealistic: it would involve the insured either standing as principal behind, or guaranteeing the liabilities of, a major insurance company. The guarantee route also faced the obstacle of section 4 of the Statute of Frauds 1677. Whilst the insured had a collateral primary obligation, the evidence pointed against any liability for the whole of the account.

It seems clear that the court was identifying a genuine implied contract in fact, rather than engaging in any restitutionary analysis.[97] Nevertheless the reasoning leaves no room for any liability on the driver for a *quantum meruit*. The repairer contracted on the basis of payment from the insurer. To impose a legal obligation on the driver without more would subvert the law on guarantee which protects those who may be tempted to answer for the debts of another. In fact the scenario is *a fortiori* from the surety scenario in that insured drivers often deposit their cars with garages on the understanding that the insurer will pay, in situations where the amount involved is well beyond their budget.[98]

In *The Trident Beauty*[99] a shipowner had assigned its right to hire under a charterparty to the defendant bank. An advance payment of hire was paid by the charterer to the bank. The vessel was off-hire for the relevant period. The shipowner became insolvent. The charterer terminated and sought restitution from the bank. Both hurdles of termination and total failure appeared to be cleared. Nevertheless the House of Lords rejected the claim against the assignee. Lord Goff stressed the importance of the entire contractual setting between both charterer and shipowner and between shipowner and assignee. It was not conclusive that there was no direct contractual link between charterer and bank. Whilst the debt had been assigned to the bank, the burden of performing the contract remained on the shipowner. Lord Goff insisted that the charterer's only remedy was its contractual right to recover against the shipowner (albeit now worthless), and observed that 'serious difficulties arise if the law seeks to expand

---

[95] [1972] 1 WLR 997, 1006. Buckley LJ agreed that the evidence indicated: 'the arrangement between the parties was that the repairers would look to the insurance company for payment for the repairs, except to the extent of the excess'.   [96] [1972] 1 WLR 997, 1008.

[97] Or what might once have been called an implied contract in law.

[98] cf Sachs LJ weighing as a contextual factor that it was 'well known that many repairs involve the payment of large sums well beyond the means of the owners': [1972] 1 WLR 997, 1008. cf 'The garage has taken the risk of the insolvency of the insurance company' (Birks, *Unjust Enrichment*, 91).

[99] *Pan Ocean Shipping Co Ltd v Creditcorp Ltd, The Trident Beauty* [1994] 1 WLR 161.

the law of restitution to redistribute risks for which provision has been made under an applicable contract'.[100]

There was no failure of the bargained-for counter-performance. The contract between charterer and shipowner entitled the charterer to use of the vessel, or in the event of that primary obligation not being performed, an express secondary right to overpaid hire from the shipowner. Prior to termination a debt had accrued. Therefore there was no failure of consideration in that the charterer had got exactly what it bargained for. Equally the law of restitution was ousted by the financing contract between the shipowner and its bankers, which had provided facilities to the shipowner in return for its covenant to repay and associated security, including the assignment of hire. Lord Goff observed that the bank 'is not the mere recipient of a windfall but is an assignee who has purchased from [the shipowner] the right to receive a contractual debt'.[101]

Barker attacks the case on numerous fronts, and in particular with regard to risk allocation he questions whether there was in reality an implied provision for the events which happened. The decision led 'to damaging presumptions: that if one specifies contractual rights, one is confined to them; and that if plaintiffs want restitution from a third party, they must bargain for it'.[102] In my view the first suggested presumption is clearly established (but the second is too widely stated) and I would question the word 'damaging'. There was no injustice. The charterer bargained for and got two valuable rights against the shipowner. If the shipowner had made a partial repayment to the charterer (ignoring totality) would the charterer have been able to recover in full or only the balance from the bank? In effect the charterer was seeking to make the assignee a guarantor of the assignor's performance to the debtor. Parties generally cannot accumulate potential recoveries unless they expressly bargain for them. It is exactly the same issue as in *Brown & Davis*. Parties do not commonly contract for a range of persons to be jointly and severally liable for the price of their contractual performance, albeit they are perfectly free to enter into such arrangements. Persons may stand as sureties if they comply with the form required. Ordinarily one person is primarily liable under the contractual arrangements. If Barker's approach were to be adopted there would be no need to make such arrangements as the law would deem it to be usual that (regardless of who had promised to pay) one could in any event always look to recoup from the actual beneficiary of the performance. If the law was so established such claims would be routine in the fall-out of insolvency. Contrary to Barker, the available 'breathing space' for unjust enrichment is often circumscribed by the

---

[100] [1994] 1 WLR 161, 166.

[101] [1994] 1 WLR 161, 166. cf Neill LJ in the Court of Appeal:'[The bank was] in a position analogous to that of a bona fide purchaser for value' [1993] 1 Lloyd's Rep 443, 449.

[102] [1994] LMCLQ 305, 310. See also A Burrows 'Restitution from Assignees' [1994] RLR 52, P Watts, 'Does a Subcontractor have Restitutionary Rights against the Employer?' [1995] LMCLQ 398 and G Tolhurst 'Asssignment, Equities, *The Trident Beauty* and Restitution' [1999] CLJ 546.

contractual regime, even in the absence of privity between claimant and defendant.[103]

10. Conclusion

Propelled by Birks, the debate has moved from an arid insistence on totality as a precondition to recovery on the ground of failure of consideration to a vigorous debate about the respective provinces of contract and unjust enrichment. There will never be an outright victor in this battle of ideas, but whilst the common law remains committed to freedom of contract, contractual terms will often oust or modify an apparently arguable claim in unjust enrichment. The prospective nature of discharge and the post-discharge operation of provisions may also affect such claims. Taking the parties' intentions seriously, through the techniques of construction, will often entail the primacy of contract over unjust enrichment, whether or not the contract is still subsisting, and whether or not there is any direct contractual privity between claimant and defendant.

---

[103] The account of the law which I have normatively grounded in the policies of contract law coincides with Birks's ultimate view, albeit characteristically (but unconvincingly) he grounds it in the language of unjust enrichment in the context of 'at the expense of' (second question): Birks, *Unjust Enrichment*, 89–93. 'Leapfrogging out of an initially valid contract is not allowed. One may never attack one's contractual counter-party's immediate enrichee.' However, Birks more convincingly goes on to articulate a policy-based reason for the same conclusion: 'Contracts entail the risk of insolvency' (at 90).

THE ENGLISH LAW OF UNJUST ENRICHMENT AND RESTITUTION

Property, Insolvency, and Restitution

13

Resulting Trusts

*Robert Chambers**

1. Introduction

I met Peter Birks in 1992, but felt his influence several years earlier when I first read *An Introduction to the Law of Restitution*.[1] I had never before encountered a book like it. Although I had received a good basic legal education, it was on a minor scale: an understanding of particular rules in particular contexts. No one had asked the big questions about the organization of law as a whole and the relationships among its constituent parts. No one had analysed the law with such clarity and logic.

It was my great fortune and joy to become Peter's DPhil student, with a proposal to explore the relationship between constructive trusts and unjust enrichment. After a term spent reading and attending the BCL restitution seminars, I was no closer to refining my thesis topic. Peter asked me to read his recently published essay, 'Restitution and Resulting Trusts',[2] over the Christmas vacation. The penny dropped. I had not been asking the right question or had not been asking a big enough question. Perhaps 'the resulting trust, not the constructive trust, is equity's principal contribution to the independent law of unjust enrichment'.[3]

It was typical of Peter's supervision that he did not press the topic on me, but asked whether I thought it would make a good thesis topic and whether I would be happy doing it. Of course, I could not be happier. My only worry was doing justice to an important topic that he could do better and faster himself. I did not then appreciate how difficult it can be for supervisors to entrust precious cargo to student drivers. Peter generously and patiently saw me through that process and

* Professor of Law, King's College London.

[1] P Birks, *An Introduction to the Law of Restitution* (rev edn, 1989).
[2] P Birks, 'Restitution and Resulting Trusts' in S Goldstein (ed), *Equity and Contemporary Legal Developments* (1992) 335.
[3] ibid 372.

into an academic career. I cannot imagine a kinder or wiser supervisor, mentor, or friend. I still ask when writing, 'What would Peter think of this?'

Not everyone shared my enthusiasm for Peter's essay on resulting trusts. Lord Goff's famous response was:

Professor Birks has argued for a wider role for the resulting trust in the field of restitution, and specifically for its availability in cases of mistake and failure of consideration. His thesis is avowedly experimental, written to test the temperature of the water. I feel bound to respond that the temperature of the water must be regarded as decidedly cold.[4]

However cold, the water must be braved. The pressing problem addressed by Peter's essay in 1992 was not just the proper role of the resulting trust, but the broader issue of property rights to restitution of unjust enrichment. When does the claimant have a property right to the enrichment itself rather than (or in addition to) a personal right to its value? That question is still difficult to answer. As Andrew Burrows has said, 'Proprietary restitution is the most complex area within the law of restitution'.[5] According to Peter, 'The law as to the incidence of rights *in rem* in response to unjust enrichment is in a very poor state'.[6] It is a problem that remains unsolved despite great strides in other areas of the law of unjust enrichment and law of restitution. If the resulting trust is not part of the solution, then some other way must be found.

Like Peter, I believe the answer lies in the resulting trust. I agree with Lord Millett's extra-judicial assessment that 'the development of a coherent doctrine of proprietary restitution for subtractive unjust enrichment is impossible unless it is based on the resulting trust as traditionally understood'.[7] This does not mean that the resulting trust should be the only form of proprietary restitution or even its predominant form. Rather, the resulting trust in its traditional categories provides the basis for developing the law by analogy. All property rights to restitution of unjust enrichment should arise in accordance with the same basic principles on which resulting trusts are based.

Ten years ago, this bold claim would have been much more difficult to sustain. Working by analogy to 'the resulting trust as traditionally understood' requires a consensus regarding that understanding, which has emerged only in recent years. Despite some vigorous opposition,[8] the now prevailing view is that which Lord Millett expressed in *Air Jamaica Ltd v Charlton*:

Like a constructive trust, a resulting trust arises by operation of law, though unlike a constructive trust it gives effect to intention. But it arises whether or not the transferor

---

[4] *Westdeutsche Landesbank Girozentrale v Islington LBC* [1996] AC 669 (HL) 689.
[5] A Burrows, 'The English Law of Restitution: A Ten-Year Review' in JW Neyers, M McInnes, and SGA Pitel (eds), *Understanding Unjust Enrichment* (2004) 11, 23.
[6] P Birks, *Unjust Enrichment* (2nd edn, 2005) 180.
[7] P Millett, 'Restitution and Constructive Trusts' (1998) 114 LQR 399, 410.
[8] Most notably W Swadling, 'A New Role for Resulting Trusts?' (1996) 16 Legal Studies 110; W Swadling, 'A Hard Look at *Hodgson v Marks*' in P Birks and F Rose (eds), *Restitution and Equity* (2000) 61.

intended to retain a beneficial interest—he almost always does not—since it responds to the absence of any intention on his part to pass a beneficial interest to the recipient.[9]

The real controversy is no longer about the operation of the resulting trust in its traditional categories, but whether that can be described as restitution of unjust enrichment. The main differences relate to terminology, not substance. There is no room in this short essay to refute the arguments against the understanding of the resulting trust expressed by Lord Millett. That has been done elsewhere.[10] This essay outlines the argument that resulting trusts always arise to effect restitution of unjust enrichment. It then explains how that understanding of the resulting trust in its traditional categories can provide the paradigm for understanding all property rights to restitution of unjust enrichment.

2. The Traditional Categories

Most resulting trusts fall into two main categories, which can be labelled 'failed express trusts' and 'apparent gifts'.[11] In the first category, the claimant transferred an asset to the defendant in trust, but failed to dispose of the entire beneficial ownership of that asset. The defendant will hold the surplus on resulting trust for the claimant unless it is proven that the claimant intended to give it to the defendant. In the second category, it appears that the defendant received a gift at the claimant's expense, either directly from the claimant or purchased from a third party by the claimant. The defendant will hold that asset on resulting trust for the claimant unless it is proven or presumed that the claimant intended to make a gift.

The two traditional categories do not account for all resulting trusts, which can arise even when there is no failed express trust and no apparent gift. The trusts that fall outside the traditional categories are not recent innovations. For example, in *Ryall v Ryall*,[12] money in a deceased person's estate was misappropriated by the executor and used to buy land for himself. That land was held on resulting trust for the legatees of the estate (provided they could trace the value of the money to the purchase of the land). There was no failed express trust and no apparent gift, but an orthodox resulting trust none the less, arising in response to a similar event. There is nothing wrong with the traditional categories. This case shows only that we need at least one more category of resulting

---

[9] [1999] 1 WLR 1399 (PC) 1412.

[10] R Chambers, *Resulting Trusts* (1997) 11–67; R Chambers, 'Resulting Trusts in Canada' (2000) 38 Alberta L Rev 378, 382–96; reprinted (2002) 16 Trust L Int 104, 108–20.

[11] See P Millett, 'Pension Schemes and the Law of Trusts' (2000) 14 Trust L Int 66, 73; D Hayton and C Mitchell, *Hayton & Marshall Commentary and Cases on the Law of Trusts and Equitable Remedies* (12th edn, 2005) 293.   [12] (1739) 1 Atk 59, 26 ER 39.

trusts created by other events. It confirms Peter's wise and long-standing advice that no taxonomy is complete without a category of others.

2.1. Restitution

The assertion that resulting trusts are restitutionary is controversial primarily because of uncertainty or disagreements over the use of the term restitution. It is sometimes used to mean compensation, that is, reparation for the claimant's loss, but has become a term of art in modern private law meaning recovery of the defendant's gain. I use a modified version of the definition Peter used in 1985: 'Restitution is the response which consists in causing one person to give up to another an enrichment received *at his expense* or its value in money'.[13]

Peter would no longer approve of this definition unless it was modified by removing the italicized words 'at his expense'. When it was published, he believed in the 'perfect quadration between restitution and unjust enrichment',[14] which meant that restitution was the only response to unjust enrichment and unjust enrichment was the only source of rights to restitution. He later abandoned that view. Restitution remains the only response to unjust enrichment, but also responds to consent, wrongs, and other events.[15] Expense to the claimant is a necessary element of unjust enrichment, but not for restitution-yielding events in the other categories.

No doubt this modification is controversial. Several prominent legal scholars still believe that restitution quadrates with unjust enrichment.[16] However, this controversy does not affect resulting trusts or property rights to restitution of unjust enrichment. The unmodified definition would suffice for present purposes. All resulting trusts cause 'one person to give up to another an enrichment received at his expense'. However, this is merely an explanation of what resulting trusts do and not why they arise. One can accept this proposition and still reject the proposition below that resulting trusts are created by unjust enrichment.

Peter's definition of restitution emphasizes two points that are particularly important for resulting trusts and proprietary restitution as a whole. First, it says 'give up' instead of 'give back'. Restitution is giving up an enrichment or its value, although some scholars would restrict restitution to mean 'give back' and

---

[13] Birks (n 1 above) 13 (emphasis added or, more accurately, emphasis removed, since the entire definition appears in italics in the original).   [14] ibid 18.

[15] P Birks, 'Misnomer' in WR Cornish, R Nolan, J O'Sullivan, and G Virgo (eds), *Restitution Past, Present and Future: Essays in Honour of Gareth Jones* (1998) 1; Birks (n 6 above) 11–13, 25–8, 278–80.

[16] A Burrows, 'Quadrating Restitution and Unjust Enrichment: A Matter of Principle?' [2000] Restitution L Rev 257; A Burrows, *The Law of Restitution* (2nd edn, 2002) 5–7; R Goff and G Jones, *The Law of Restitution* (6th edn, 2002) 3 (but see 12); M McInnes, 'Restitution, Unjust Enrichment and the Perfect Quadration Thesis' [1999] Restitution L Rev 118; L Smith, 'The Province of the Law of Restitution' (1992) 71 Canadian Bar Rev 672, 698; A Tettenborn, *Law of Restitution in England and Ireland* (3rd edn, 2002) 1–2, 36–42.

prefer to use a different word, 'disgorgement', to mean 'give up'.[17] Secondly, the definition clearly distinguishes between restitution of an enrichment and restitution of its value in money.

The term 'resulting trust' implies giving back. As Peter wrote:

The name is a concealed synonym of 'restitutionary' in the unextended sense in which it was confined to giving *back*... The two Latin verbs for 'jumping back' are '*resilio*' and '*resulto*'. In Latinate English 'resulting' meant, and here still means, 'jumping back'.[18]

The resulting trust is the descendant of the resulting use, which arose when land was transferred without apparent consideration. The natural assumption was that the transferor intended to create a use for himself, since this was a popular method of estate planning before the Statute of Uses 1535.[19] That assumption evolved into the presumption of resulting use and ultimately the presumption of resulting trust. The resulting use always carried the beneficial use of land back to the transferor and its name is an accurate reflection of what it did. However, the modern resulting trust is not confined to giving back, but often operates to cause the resulting trustee to give up an enrichment that did not previously belong to the claimant.

For example, a settlor may create an express trust that gives the trustee the authority to buy, sell, and exchange trust assets. If the trust later fails and the trustee holds the surplus trust assets on resulting trust for the settlor, the subject of the resulting trust might not be the assets originally settled in trust, but the traceable proceeds of those assets. In that case, the trustee is not giving back assets that used to belong to the settlor, but giving up assets acquired at the settlor's expense.

In cases where the claimant made an apparent gift by purchasing an asset for the defendant, the subject of the resulting trust is always something that did not previously belong to the claimant. These resulting trusts do not cause something to be given back, but cause something to be given up which was acquired from a third party at the claimant's expense. Although they are often called 'purchase money resulting trusts', the expense to the claimant need not be money paid, but can be anything accepted by the vendor in exchange for the transfer, including an assortment of farm animals or right to a discount.[20]

In modern private law, restitution was artificially extended to mean giving up and not just giving back an enrichment or its value. The term resulting trust has been extended in the same way. What originally meant 'give back' has come to mean 'give up'. All resulting trusts cause the defendant to give up an enrichment received at the claimant's expense, but only some of them cause the defendant to give back an enrichment.

---

[17] M McInnes, 'The Measure of Restitution' (2002) 52 U Toronto LJ 163, 185; Smith (n 16 above) 696.   [18] Birks (n 6 above) 304.
[19] JH Baker, *An Introduction to English Legal History* (4th edn, 2002) 249–51.
[20] *Mumpower v Castle* 104 SE 706 (Virginia CA 1920); *Springette v Defoe* (1992) 24 HLR 552 (CA).

2.2. Unjust Enrichment

The description of a trust as resulting indicates that it causes the defendant to give up an enrichment received at the claimant's expense, but does not reveal why it arises. There are four categories of events which might conceivably give rise to resulting trusts: manifestations of consent, wrongs, unjust enrichment, or other causative events.[21] Since this classification is exhaustive of all possible sources of legal rights, resulting trusts must arise in response to events found in at least one of these categories. Resulting trusts, like restitution, might be 'multi-causal',[22] that is, they might be created by events found in more than one category. However, it turns out that resulting trusts are 'mono-causal', at least within the traditional categories of failed express trusts and apparent gifts. They all arise in response to unjust enrichment.

A trust can have the same effect as a resulting trust without actually being a resulting trust. As Peter noted, express trusts and constructive trusts can also be 'resulting in pattern' by causing beneficial ownership of an asset to 'jump back' to the settlor or claimant.[23] The category of resulting trusts does not cut across other categories and remove those express, constructive, or statutory trusts that happen to be resulting in pattern. It lines up with the others as a category of trusts based on the events that create them. While all resulting trusts are restitutionary, restitutionary trusts are not always resulting.

In the beginning, the resulting use probably was created by consent. As mentioned above, when land was transferred without apparent consideration, the natural assumption was that the transferor intended to create a use for himself. Since writing was not required to create a use of land, that intention (whether proven or presumed) would be sufficient to create the intended use. However, this changed as the resulting use evolved to become the resulting trust. The modern resulting trust arises not because the claimant intended to create a trust, but because the claimant did not intend to benefit the defendant.

There are numerous cases in which a resulting trust arose although it was clear that the claimant did not intend to create that trust.[24] Even in those cases where claimants did intend to create trusts for themselves, that intention was not the direct source of the resulting trust. It was relevant because it meant that the claimant did not intend to benefit the defendant. For example, in *Hodgson v Marks*,[25] a widow transferred her home to her lodger intending to create an express trust for herself. The express trust was invalid because it was not made in writing as required by section 53 of the Law of Property Act 1925 and the lodger

---

[21] Birks (n 6 above) 24.

[22] ibid 25; W Swadling 'The Multi–causality of Resulting Trusts' presented at the Society of Legal Scholars Sheffield Conference, 14 September 2004.   [23] Birks (n 1 above) 60.

[24] *Vandervell v Inland Revenue Commissioners* [1967] 2 AC 291 (HL); *Brown v Brown* (1993) 31 NSWLR 582 (CA); *Goodfellow v Robertson* (1871) 18 Gr 572 (Ont Ch).

[25] [1971] Ch 892 (CA).

held the home on resulting trust for her. If she had intended to create a trust for her nephew instead of a trust for herself, the outcome would have been the same. Either way, her intention to create a trust would fail, but show that she did not intend to make a gift to her lodger. That lack of intention is, in Peter's words, 'a fact which, along with others, calls for the creation of rights by operation of law'.[26]

In their traditional categories, resulting trusts do not respond to wrongs. The resulting trust that arises on the failure of an express trust has nothing to do with breach of trust. Express trustees who have properly performed all the duties of their office will hold any surplus on resulting trust for the settlor unless it is proven that the settlor intended to give it to them. The resulting trust of an apparent gift will arise even though the defendant is wholly innocent and unaware of the existence of the trust assets or the transaction giving rise to the trust.[27] The defendant's conduct is not relevant.

Outside the traditional categories, resulting trusts can arise when assets are misappropriated from the claimant and used without the claimant's consent to buy assets for the defendant.[28] It may be possible to analyse these cases as restitution for wrongs, with the trust arising to compel the defendant to give up an asset acquired by breach of fiduciary duty, fraud, or theft.[29] However, it seems much more likely that the resulting trust operates on the same principles outside its traditional categories as it does within them. It responds not directly to the wrong, but to the enrichment of the defendant at the claimant's expense without the claimant's consent. In addition to the remedies the claimant has in respect of the wrong, the claimant also has a property right to restitution of the enrichment which depends not on the defendant's wrongful conduct but on the claimant's lack of intention to benefit the defendant. This analysis has the advantage of explaining why the trust arises regardless of whether the defendant was actively involved in the misappropriation or just passively and honestly received assets purchased with misappropriated value.[30]

Since resulting trusts are not created by manifestations of consent or wrongs, they must be created by unjust enrichment or some other event. The last category is simply a catch-all, which includes all right-creating events that do not belong in the three nominate categories. The category of unjust enrichment was recognized relatively late in the development of the common law. It was carved out of the catch-all category and still seems somewhat residual in nature. It

---

[26] Birks (n 1 above) 65.
[27] *Birch v Blagrave* (1755) Amb 264, 27 ER 176; *Childers v Childers* (1857) 1 De G & J 482, 44 ER 810; *Re Vinogradoff* [1935] WN 68.
[28] *Ryall v Ryall* (1739) 1 Atk 59, 26 ER 39; *Merchants Express Co v Morton* (1868) 15 Gr 274 (Ont Ch); *El Ajou v Dollar Land Holdings plc* [1993] 3 All ER 717 (Ch D) 734; reversed [1994] 2 All ER 685 (CA).
[29] In *Re Kolari* (1981) 36 OR (2d) 473 (Ont DC) 478, Stortini DCJ said that a 'resulting trust arises where property is obtained by fraud or theft'.
[30] *Sharp v McNeil* (1913) 15 DLR 73 (NSSCAD); affirmed (1915) 70 DLR 740 (SCC).

includes those cases in which the defendant was enriched at the expense of the claimant and must make restitution of that enrichment or its value, but excludes cases in which the right to restitution was created by consent, wrongdoing, statute, or a judgment of the court.[31] The definition of unjust enrichment still relies in part on the exclusion of other categories.

Defining something in terms of what it is not may seem unwieldy or unsatisfactory. Fortunately, Peter provided a most useful and succinct definition of unjust enrichment in positive terms, based on its 'core case': 'The law of unjust enrichment is the law of all events materially identical to the mistaken payment of a non-existent debt'.[32]

By generalizing from this core case, it is possible to work out the existence and ambit of the category of unjust enrichment.[33] Payment can be generalized to enrichment at the expense of another and mistake can be generalized to reasons why the enrichment is unjust. The events that give rise to resulting trusts belong in the same category as mistaken payment. The asset subject to the trust is always an enrichment received by the defendant at the claimant's expense and the claimant's lack of intention to benefit the defendant is the reason why that enrichment is unjust and must be given up.

Ross Grantham and Charles Rickett object to this analysis and argue that the resulting trust is merely a 'default rule' of property law:

Our contention is that the resulting trust and its foundational presumptions operate as part of the law of property, simply as a series of default rules to locate the beneficial interest in property when the transfer of the property is itself either ambiguous as to the location of that interest, or ineffective to dispose of the interest.[34]

Calling something a default rule is merely an observation of what usually occurs and not an explanation of why it occurs. The default colour of the sky is blue, but that does not answer a child's question why the sky is blue. In most situations, it is enough to know the default rule. That usually satisfies a client or a lawyer working in a different area of law, but the proper development of the law always requires explanation as well as observation. There are many default rules in the law and many of them concern the creation of legal rights and duties. For example, the payment of a bribe usually creates a constructive trust,[35] while a payment by mistake usually creates a debt.[36] We are now able to explain why those rules exist and the resulting trust is no greater mystery.

Calling the resulting trust a default rule of property law says nothing of the events that create it and, in particular, does not remove it from the category of rights created by unjust enrichment. Despite suggestions to the contrary from

---

[31] Birks (n 6 above) 8–9, 11, 25–6.   [32] ibid 3.   [33] ibid 9–11.
[34] C Rickett and R Grantham 'Resulting Trusts—A Rather Limited Doctrine' in P Birks and F Rose (eds), *Restitution and Equity: Resulting Trusts and Equitable Compensation* (2000) 39, 48.
[35] *AG Hong Kong v Reid* [1994] 1 AC 324, [1994] 1 NZLR 1 (PC).
[36] *Kleinwort Benson Ltd v Lincoln CC* [1999] 2 AC 349 (HL).

the highest authority,[37] property and unjust enrichment are not opposing categories. Property is a kind of right, while unjust enrichment is a source of rights. Unjust enrichment sometimes creates property rights and property rights are sometimes created by unjust enrichment.[38] The law of property and law of unjust enrichment intersect and resulting trusts exist in the place where they meet.

3. Restitution of Unjust Enrichment

The description of the resulting trust as restitution of unjust enrichment does not change what it does or why it arises. It merely describes the orthodox resulting trust in modern and more general terms. As Peter said, 'The generic conception of the event which triggers restitution adds nothing to the existing law and effects no change except what comes from better understanding of what is there already'.[39] It helps us better understand the operation of the resulting trust within its traditional categories. It also invites comparisons. Generalizing from failed express trusts and apparent (but unintended) gifts to unjust enrichment at the claimant's expense makes it easier to compare the events that create resulting trusts with events that create other rights to restitution. Generalizing from resulting trust to restitution makes it easier to compare resulting trusts with other restitutionary rights.

3.1. A Core Case

Peter began *Unjust Enrichment* with *Kelly v Solari*,[40] which he described as the 'classical English illustration of mistaken payment of a non-existent debt'.[41] He chose it because it was unequivocally a case of unjust enrichment. The recipient was an honest widow. Her obligation to repay cannot be explained by consent, wrongdoing, or any event other than her unjust enrichment at the payer's expense. Although the case was decided 150 years before the law of unjust enrichment was formally recognized in England,[42] it proves that restitution of unjust enrichment has long been part of English law, even if only with respect to mistaken payments. It also provides the paradigm for understanding all other cases of unjust enrichment.

---

[37] *Foskett v McKeown* [2001] 1 AC 102 (HL) 127.
[38] Birks (n 6 above) 32–8; A Burrows, *The Law of Restitution* (2nd edn, 2002) 64–7; A Burrows, 'The English Law of Restitution: A Ten–Year Review' in J Neyers, M McInnes, and S Pitel (eds), *Understanding Unjust Enrichment* (2004) 11, 23–9; R Chambers, 'Tracing and Unjust Enrichment' in J Neyers, M McInnes, and S Pitel (eds), *Understanding Unjust Enrichment* (2004) 263, 264–5.
[39] Birks (n 1 above) 27.   [40] (1841) 9 M & W 54, 152 ER 24.
[41] Birks (n 6 above) 5.   [42] *Lipkin Gorman v Karpnale Ltd* [1991] 2 AC 548 (HL).

Ryall v Ryall, discussed above,[43] might be regarded as the *Kelly v Solari* of proprietary restitution. It is the first of many cases of resulting trust which prove that English law has long provided property rights to the enrichment itself and not merely personal rights to its value. These cases also provide the paradigm for understanding other cases of proprietary restitution. Working by analogy to the orthodox resulting trust may help solve the pressing problems in this area of law.

3.2. Two Kinds of Restitution

There are two possible kinds of responses to unjust enrichment: restitution of the enrichment or restitution of its value. The right to restitution of the enrichment itself is a property right to a specific thing. It cannot arise unless the enrichment is something which can be subject to property rights. The value of that thing in the market or to the defendant is irrelevant.[44] What matters most is its location and continued existence. The right to restitution of it can be enforced against anyone who has it, subject to defences protecting honest buyers (such as bona fide purchase, indefeasible title, and the exceptions to *nemo dat*). There are several different ways to achieve restitution of the enrichment itself, including resulting and constructive trusts, rescission, and rectification. They provide the claimant with beneficial ownership of the enrichment or the power to obtain it.

In contrast, the right to restitution of the value of an enrichment is not a right to any particular thing, but a right to payment from a specific person. What matters is not the form of enrichment, but its value to the defendant who received it. If its subjective value to that defendant is less than full market value (eg because that defendant could have obtained the same enrichment elsewhere at a discounted price), the right to restitution is reduced accordingly.[45] Restitution of the value of an enrichment is always a debt, although it may be described in different ways, such as the action for money had and received, *quantum meruit*, or liability for knowing receipt.[46]

Restitution of the value of enrichment is sometimes achieved with the help of an equitable lien, which secures the defendant's obligation to pay for that value and arises to facilitate payment of that debt. Since the lien can attach to assets other than the enrichment, it can arise even though the enrichment is a service that cannot be given up.[47] If the lien does attach to the enrichment, it does not compel the defendant to give it up. The defendant is free to use other resources

---

[43] (1739) 1 Atk 59, 26 ER 39; see text at n 12.
[44] A Burrows, *The Law of Restitution* (2nd edn, 2002) 16.
[45] *Ministry of Defence v Ashman* [1993] 2 EGLR 102, 66 P & CR 195 (CA). Peter coined the term 'subjective devaluation' to explain why the defendant is not liable for the full market value of an enrichment in cases where the enrichment has less or no value to the defendant in the circumstances: Birks (n 1 above) 109; Burrows (n 44 above) 18.   [46] Birks (n 6 above) 284–95.
[47] A right to restitution of the value of preserving or improving land might be secured by a lien on the estate even though that estate is not the enrichment. A purchaser's lien secures the right to restitution of the purchase price, but attaches to the estate sold rather than the money paid.

to meet that obligation and is not required to surrender the enrichment itself (unless the failure to pay leads to a forced sale).

The largest and most pressing problem in proprietary restitution is uncertainty over the kind of restitution available in response to unjust enrichment. Is the claimant entitled to restitution of the enrichment itself, restitution of its value, or both? Often there is no clear answer. Most cases of resulting trust were claims only to the enrichment itself, while most other cases of unjust enrichment were claims only to payment of its value. The few English cases that dealt with claims for both kinds of restitution are flawed or controversial. While they may reach the correct result, the reasons for judgment do not adequately explain the choices made.

For example, in *Sinclair v Brougham*,[48] the claimants had only property rights to restitution of money paid under void loan contracts, but the rejection of their personal claims was based on the now discredited implied contract theory of restitution. In *Westdeutsche Landesbank Girozentrale v Islington LBC*,[49] the claimant had only a personal right to restitution of the value of money paid under a void loan contract, but the only issue on appeal was the claimant's right to interest. With no examination of the underlying unjust enrichment, the case reveals little about why proprietary restitution was unavailable. In *Chase Manhattan Bank NA v Israel-British Bank* (*London*) *Ltd*[50] the claimant had both a property right to restitution of a mistaken payment and a personal right to its value. While the outcome seems correct (to me), the judgment relies on *Sinclair v Brougham* and an unnecessary appeal to fiduciary duties.

There is no easy solution to this problem, but the first step towards a solution is consideration of the resulting trust, which proves that English law does provide property rights to restitution of the enrichment itself and provides the paradigm for all rights created for the same purpose. The principles that govern proprietary restitution generally cannot be inconsistent with its core case. In every case of resulting trust, the enrichment was an asset received by the defendant at the claimant's expense and the defendant did not acquire unrestricted beneficial ownership of that asset before the trust arose. While a resulting trust does not arise every time these conditions are satisfied, it cannot arise unless they are. This should be true of all rights to restitution of the enrichment itself.

The resulting trust does not tell us much about the relevance of unjust factors, which are the reasons why enrichments are unjust. The unjust factor may dictate the particular method of restitution (such as a power to rescind rather than a trust), but not the kind of restitution available. The resulting trust suggests (albeit weakly) that the right to restitution of the enrichment itself should be possible for all unjust factors.

---

[48] [1914] AC 398 (HL).   [49] [1996] AC 669 (HL).   [50] [1981] Ch 105.

3.3. Enrichment

There are cases in which only one kind of restitution is possible. If the enrichment has value to the defendant, but cannot be given up *in specie*, then restitution will be restricted to payment of its value. This occurs when the enrichment consists of services performed, expenses saved, or assets that no longer exist (such as goods consumed or a lease expired). Conversely, if the enrichment can be given up *in specie*, but has no value to the defendant, then restitution will be restricted to surrender of the enrichment itself. For example, the claimant might rescind a gift of something that has only sentimental value or rescind the sale of an asset for which the defendant paid full market value or more. In such cases, the claimant can obtain restitution of the enrichment itself, but has no claim for its value.[51]

The resulting trust is equitable beneficial ownership of the enrichment itself and cannot arise unless the enrichment is an asset that can be the subject-matter of a trust. Also, the enrichment must be an asset *received* by the defendant. A resulting trust will not arise if the enrichment is merely the improvement or preservation of an asset already owned by the defendant.[52] In that case, the enrichment is not the asset, but the performance of a service or payment of a debt which had the effect of increasing or preserving its value. Restitution will be limited to payment of that value, although that personal claim might be secured by a lien over the asset.[53]

It has been suggested that the claimant should have a property right to restitution only if the enrichment is a rare or unique asset.[54] In other cases, the payment of money would enable the claimant to purchase an adequate replacement from another source. This would treat the restitution claimant like a purchaser under a contract of sale, who is entitled to specific performance of the contract only when damages are inadequate.[55] Lord Millett said that the recovery of assets through rescission might be 'a form of specific performance (or "specific unperformance")' which equity makes available because a money judgment is an inadequate remedy'.[56]

---

[51] *Soulos v Korkontzilas* [1997] 2 SCR 217, 146 DLR (4th) 214, was similar. The claimant had a property right to restitution of a wrongful enrichment, but no personal claim for its value, because the defendant had acquired land in breach of fiduciary duty, but paid more than its market value.

[52] According to J Mee, *The Property Rights of Cohabitees* (2002) 76–92, indirect contributions to the repayment of a mortgage may give rise to an 'extended resulting trust' in Ireland, but these are not true resulting trusts and are called constructive trusts in other jurisdictions.

[53] *Calverley v Green* (1984) 155 CLR 242 (HCA). The improved or preserved asset might be held on constructive trust for the claimant, particularly in cases involving the division of family property, but those trusts are not restitutionary. Although Canadian courts routinely call this restitution of unjust enrichment, the constructive trust of family property is created in part by the claimant's expectation of sharing the asset and is perfectionary: G Elias, *Explaining Constructive Trusts* (1990) 157; R Chambers, 'Constructive Trusts in Canada' (1999) 37 Alberta L Rev 173, 197–207; reprinted (2002) 16 Trust L Int 2, 2–10.

[54] M Cope, *Constructive Trusts* (1992) 487; P Millett, 'Restitution and Constructive Trusts' (1998) 114 LQR 399, 416.   [55] *Adderley v Dixon* (1824) 1 Sim & St 607, 57 ER 239, 240.

[56] P Millett, 'Restitution and Constructive Trusts' (1998) 114 LQR 399, 416.

This suggestion is not without merit, but its adoption would substantially change the law. There are many cases of resulting trusts involving ordinary, replaceable assets, such as bank accounts. Also, many resulting trusts arise over assets that did not previously belong to the claimant. The defendant is not giving back something that may have special significance to the claimant, but giving up something the claimant never owned before. Unlike purchasers under a contract of sale, many resulting trust beneficiaries did not choose to invest in the asset subject to the trust. Many of them never wanted or expected to get that asset and it is difficult to understand why the ability to purchase its replacement would matter to them or be relevant to their claim.

There is another reason why the comparison with the contract of sale is inapt. Damages for breach of contract are measured by the loss to the claimant and would compensate the claimant fully for the cost of acquiring a replacement from another source. In contrast, the personal right to restitution of unjust enrichment is always measured by the value of that enrichment to that particular defendant. With subjective devaluation, the claimant's personal right may be less than the market value of the asset. Also, it would not include the transaction costs of acquiring a replacement. Even if courts were willing to compel defendants to give up the realizable value of the enrichment,[57] the net proceeds of its sale would often be less than the full market price that the claimant would have to pay for its replacement. Restitution of the enrichment itself avoids difficult issues of subjective and net value.

3.4. Unjust Factors

Unjust factors can affect the particular method of proprietary restitution. For example, rights to rescission may be legal or equitable depending on the reason for rescission. Transactions induced by fraud or duress may be rescinded at common law, while transactions induced by innocent misrepresentations or undue influence may be rescinded only in equity. Although specific rights to restitution may vary with the unjust factor, the kind of restitution does not. If the claimant can rescind the transaction (for whatever reason) and thereby recover an asset transferred to the defendant, the claimant has a right to restitution of the enrichment itself and not just a right to its value.

If the unjust enrichment is an asset received by the defendant, the essence of the claim to restitution is that the defendant should not have received that asset or should not retain it for her or his own benefit. This is true regardless of the particular reason why the enrichment is unjust. The unjust factor does not provide a good reason for preferring one kind of restitution over another.

---

[57] The defendant is clearly enriched by the value of goods or land once they have been exchanged for money, but it is controversial whether that is true before the sale: see Birks (n 6 above) 61–2; Burrows (n 44 above) 18–19.

It cannot explain why some defendants must give up the enrichment itself, while others may keep it and pay for its value.

There is no clear limit to the unjust factors which may give rise to resulting trusts. Some resulting trusts respond to the misappropriation of assets without the claimant's knowledge. Peter said the unjust factor in such cases was the claimant's ignorance.[58] The failed express trust cases involve failure of consideration (which 'means that the state of affairs contemplated as the basis or reason for the payment has failed').[59] Assets were transferred to the intended trustee subject to a condition regarding their use and the resulting trust arose when it became impossible to fulfil that condition. The resulting trust might also arise in response to other unjust factors, such as mistake, duress, or undue influence, but there is no clear authority for that proposition.[60]

Resulting trusts do not prove whether proprietary restitution should be available for every unjust factor. However, they do provide two indications that the type of unjust factor is not relevant to this issue. First, while some failures of consideration give rise to resulting trusts, most others produce only personal rights to restitution of the value of the enrichment. These cases cannot be separated on the basis of unjust factor. As Peter said:

> It is difficult to see how a difference could be drawn between one failure of consideration and another. It would, for example, be impossible to argue that in some cases the proprietary base is preserved by reason of an especially clear or intense qualification of the transferor's intent to enrich the recipient. For the truth is that failure of consideration always depends on a clear manifestation of that qualified intent.[61]

Secondly, many resulting trusts are not linked to any particular unjust factor, but respond to an absence of consideration, which Peter preferred to call absence of basis.[62] In the apparent gift cases, the trust arises because the claimant was under no obligation to provide the enrichment and it was proven or presumed that it was not a gift. In Peter's words, 'if the gift is thus knocked out, the transfer is left without any explanation. The transferee is enriched *sine causa*'.[63] This looks like a civilian model of unjust enrichment, which focuses on the defendant's entitlement to the enrichment rather than the claimant's reason for restitution.

Unjust factors and absence of basis are not unrelated. An unjust factor will not entitle a claimant to restitution unless it removes the defendant's entitlement to the enrichment. Conversely, the absence of basis for an enrichment often occurs because its intended basis was invalidated by an unjust factor. However, absence of basis is not a kind of unjust factor, nor is it linked to any particular unjust factors. As Peter said, 'absence of basis cuts across the list of unjust factors'.[64]

---

[58] Birks (n 1 above) 140–2.   [59] ibid 223.
[60] R Chambers, *Resulting Trusts* (1997) 125–37.
[61] Birks (n 1 above) 387.   [62] Birks (n 6 above) 117–19.   [63] ibid 306.
[64] ibid 114.

By responding to absence of basis, resulting trusts indicate that proprietary restitution also cuts across that list.

3.5. Restrictions on Ownership

If the enrichment is an asset received by the defendant, then restitution of the enrichment itself is possible, but not always available. Some other factor is also relevant and it is not the unjust factor. A study of the resulting trust suggests that the defendant's right to the enrichment is the other factor. Restitution will be limited to a personal claim for value if the defendant obtains unrestricted beneficial ownership of the enrichment before the claimant's right to restitution arises.[65]

Rights to restitution usually arise at the moment the defendant receives the enrichment. If the enrichment is an asset that can be given up *in specie*, then the claimant should have a right to restitution of that asset, since the defendant was never free to use it for her or his own benefit. The resulting trust of an apparent gift always arises at the moment of receipt. The same is true of trusts of mis-appropriated assets. Even in cases where the claimant must first rescind a contract or other transaction to recover ownership of an asset, the right to restitution arises at the outset when the defendant receives the asset. Before rescission, the claimant has a power to obtain ownership of the asset, which can be enforced against the defendant and others, subject to defences protecting honest buyers.[66]

When the unjust factor is failure of consideration, the enrichment may be unjust at the moment of receipt (in cases of initial failure) or become unjust at some later date (in cases of subsequent failure). If the consideration has already failed when the defendant receives the enrichment, a right to restitution of the enrichment itself is possible.[67] If the consideration fails after receipt, there is a period of time in which the enrichment of the defendant is not unjust. Whether the claimant is entitled to restitution of the enrichment itself depends on the defendant's right to the enrichment during that time.

In the failed express trust cases, it does not matter whether the trust failed at the outset or only subsequently, because the trustees were never free to use the trust assets for their own benefit. In either case, the resulting trust arises to compel the trustees to give up the enrichment itself. In cases where money was paid as a deposit and the purchase could not be completed, the claimant had a property right to restitution of the deposit itself when the defendants agreed to keep it in a separate account,[68] but not when the defendants were free to use it as they pleased.[69]

---

[65] ibid 182; Burrows (n 44 above) 67–9; Chambers (n 60 above) 148–53.
[66] Birks (n 6 above) 183–4; R Chambers, 'Tracing and Unjust Enrichment' in J Neyers, M McInnes, and S Pitel (eds) *Understanding Unjust Enrichment* (2004) 263, 299–302.
[67] *Neste Oy v Lloyds Bank plc* [1983] 2 Lloyds LR 658.
[68] *Re Nanwa Goldmines Ltd* [1955] 1 WLR 1080.
[69] *Moseley v Cressey's Co* (1865) LR 1 Eq 405; *Re Goldcorp Exchange Ltd* [1994] 3 NZLR 385, [1995] 1 AC 74 (PC) 103–4.

If the defendant acquires unrestricted beneficial ownership of the enrichment before it becomes unjust, there is no justification for compelling the defendant to give up that enrichment, even if it continues to exist as an asset identifiable among the defendant's assets. The defendant was free to expend or destroy the enrichment before the right to restitution arose and its continued existence is merely fortuitous. As Lord Millett said, 'the mere fact that the moneys are still identifiable . . . does not of itself form a basis for any proprietary claim'.[70]

The focus on the defendant's right to the enrichment is similar to the concept of a 'proprietary base', which Peter once used to explain the availability of proprietary restitution:

> The phrase 'proprietary base' is used to capture this idea: if he wishes to assert a right *in rem* in the surviving enrichment, the plaintiff must show that at the beginning of the story he had a proprietary right in the subject-matter, and that nothing other than substitutions or intermixtures happened to deprive him of that right *in rem*.[71]

This concept leads to the correct result in most cases, but has the potential to mislead in two respects. First, it focuses attention on the claimant's right to the enrichment rather than the defendant's right to it. Normally, these are two sides of the same coin because the defendant's right to use the asset is restricted by the claimant's right to it. However, the claimant's right to restitution of the enrichment itself does not depend on the continuation of the claimant's proprietary base from the time of enrichment to the time it becomes unjust. It is necessary only that the defendant does not acquire unrestricted beneficial ownership of the enrichment before the claimant's right arises. When an express trust fails, a resulting trust for the settlor can arise regardless of whether the settlor had any interest in the trust assets between the creation of the express trust and its failure.[72] This is because the trustees' right to the trust assets was restricted from the outset and they were never free to use the enrichment for their own benefit.

Secondly, the concept of proprietary base is easily misunderstood to mean that the expense to the claimant must be the loss of a property right. It implies that the claimant's property right to the enrichment is justified because it used to belong to the claimant or is the traceable proceeds of assets that used to belong to the claimant. The resulting trust shows this to be false. In cases where the enrichment is an asset purchased for the defendant by the claimant, the expense to the claimant need not be the loss of an asset. A resulting trust can arise even if the claimant's only contribution to the purchase price is acceptance of a liability.[73] The defendant's receipt of the enrichment is 'the beginning of the story' to which Peter referred above.

---

[70] *Eldan Services Ltd v Chandag Motors Ltd* [1990] 3 All ER 459 (Millett J) 461.

[71] Birks (n 1 above) 379. Also see R Goode, 'Ownership and Obligation in Commercial Transactions' (1987) 103 LQR 433, 433; R Goode, 'Property and Unjust Enrichment' in Burrows (ed) *Essays on the Law of Restitution* (1991) 215, 219.

[72] *Re Ames' Settlement* [1946] Ch 217.   [73] *Calverley v Green* (1984) 155 CLR 242.

An example may help. Suppose the defendant misappropriated money from two bank accounts and used it to buy land. One misappropriation reduced the positive balance of claimant A's account, while the other increased the existing overdraft of claimant B's account.[74] The expense to each claimant is different: A lost an asset (the bank's debt to A) while B incurred a liability (B's debt to the bank). However, the defendant received the same enrichment at each claimant's expense and both claimants have property rights to restitution of the enrichment itself. Although B did not lose an asset, A and B had the same 'proprietary base' because 'the beginning of the story' was the defendant's receipt of money at their expense. The case is materially identical to a purchase money resulting trust, which depends on the nature of the defendant's enrichment at the claimant's expense, without regard to the nature of that expense.

4. Conclusion

When I encounter an area of uncertainty in the law of restitution of unjust enrichment, I often find it helpful to compare it to the resulting trust. The basic principles that guide the availability and various forms of proprietary restitution should not be inconsistent with its core case, at least not without sufficient justification. While this will not answer questions of fine detail, it is a useful way to check whether a basic premise is sound.

The traditional categories of resulting trust provide a sound basis for 'the development of a coherent doctrine of proprietary restitution for subtractive unjust enrichment',[75] even if the resulting trust is confined to those categories. However, the proper development of the law would be aided by one further and simple step. We should label as resulting every trust that effects restitution of unjust enrichment. Currently, we use two different labels for these trusts: resulting and constructive. This invites confusion for two reasons. First, it suggests falsely that there is a meaningful difference between resulting trusts and those constructive trusts that do respond to unjust enrichment. Secondly, constructive trusts also arise to effect restitution of wrongful enrichment and to perfect intentions to benefit others.[76] As courts have found (especially in Canada), it is easy to confuse these three functions and make categorical mistakes, such as assuming that wrongful enrichment requires expense to the claimant[77] or that unjust enrichment depends on the claimant's legitimate expectations.[78]

---

[74] I thank Robert Stevens for this example.

[75] P Millett, 'Restitution and Constructive Trusts' (1998) 114 LQR 399, 410.

[76] G Elias, *Explaining Constructive Trusts* (1990) 4–6; R Chambers, 'Constructive Trusts in Canada' (1999) 37 Alberta L Rev 173; reprinted (2001) 15 Trust L Int 214, (2002) 16 Trust L Int 2.

[77] *Lac Minerals Ltd v International Corona Resources Ltd* [1989] 2 SCR 574, 61 DLR (4th) 14 (SCC) 45. [78] *Pettkus v Becker* [1980] 2 SCR 834, 117 DLR (3d) 257 (SCC) 274.

So, what would Peter think of this essay? First, he would disagree with some points and eagerly await the chance to debate them. He believed that theories of law should be tested by public academic debate. It did not matter to him who won so long as the truth came out. Secondly, he would probably repeat what he said of my DPhil thesis: 'Far too much of this Birks fellow'. I think he worried that his students might have trouble emerging from his shadow if they agreed with him too often. Then, I struggled to find points of disagreement. On this occasion, I hope I will be forgiven for including as much Birks as I please.

Finally, Peter would think that this essay ends on a timid note. Redrawing the lines between resulting and constructive trusts is a very small step, using terminology that is not very helpful. Those categories appear to overlap and their labels are mismatched: while 'resulting' directs our attention to the effect of the trust, 'constructive' indicates only that the trust was not created directly by intention.[79] They are flawed categories and, as Peter said, 'Flawed classification is a source and symptom of intellectual disorder'.[80] He would want us to take a bolder step:

'Unjust enrichment trust' says what needs saying . . . There is also no point within the law of unjust enrichment in distinguishing between constructive and resulting trusts . . . It is the unity of the causative event that matters, not the labels used during the time when that causative event could not be named.'[81]

---

[79] Birks (n 6 above) 302–5.   [80] ibid 20.   [81] ibid 304, 307.

14

Jones v Jones: Property or Unjust Enrichment?

*Peter Millett**

My subtitle for this contribution, for reasons that will become obvious, is 'Dear Peter'. Peter Birks was a giant among restitution lawyers. True, he was not responsible for the disentanglement of restitution from the law of contract and its establishment as a separate branch of the common law based on the principle of unjust enrichment. This was the work of Professors Warren Seavey and Austin Scott, the authors of the *Restatement of the Law of Restitution* published by the American Law Institute in 1937. Its introduction into English and Common-wealth law had to await the publication of *The Law of Restitution* by Goff and Jones in 1966. This gathered together all the old cases and gave a conceptual unity to what had previously been a rag-bag of diverse rules. It showed that they were founded on a single, unifying principle of unjust enrichment. It introduced a new subject into English law to take its place alongside contract and tort.

But it was Peter Birks who gave the subject its formal structure. In his book, modestly entitled *An Introduction to the Law of Restitution*,[1] he clarified that there are three questions which arise in every case of unjust enrichment: (i) has the defendant been enriched? (ii) is his enrichment at the expense of the claimant? (iii) is his enrichment unjust? In his later writings,[2] he added two further questions to his conceptual structure for the subject: (iv) what kind of restitu-tionary right (personal or proprietary) is triggered by the unjust enrichment?; and (v) has the defendant any defence to the claim?

Peter possessed a brilliant analytical mind as well as a profound knowledge of both English and Roman law, and an easy familiarity with the enormous volume of English case-law. He was exceptionally well placed to undertake the ration-alization of the new branch of the law and give it its proper place in the law. In his later years he became obsessed with taxonomy and recanted many of the

---

* Former Lord of Appeal in Ordinary.
[1] (1985, rev paperback edn, 1989).
[2] See eg his last work *Unjust Enrichment* (2nd edn, 2005) 39.

propositions which he had previously pronounced. He advanced his revised opinions as forcefully as he had propounded the earlier; but they were not always as well received, for now he had to contend with those like me whom he had previously persuaded.

Above all Peter was a superb teacher. It was a revelation to hear him deliver a lecture, usually without notes, and to an audience whom he held in thrall. His influence on the development of the law of restitution can be seen not only in his own writings but in those of his former pupils. Under his guidance many of them published expanded versions of their doctoral theses, and it is to them, and so indirectly to Peter, that we owe a range of monographs on important aspects of restitution or equity such as subrogation, tracing, resulting trusts, and gain-based damages.

While academic lawyers have led the way in developing a coherent structure for the law of restitution, the judges have played their part not only in their judgments but also in extra-curial debate where they are free from the constraints of precedent and able to change their minds with the same freedom that Peter enjoyed. His disciples were not confined to students and former students, for he was generous with his advice. Judges sought his help when confronted by a difficult or controversial problem in his field, and he never withheld it, or complained when his opinion was not followed or, more frequently, adopted without acknowledgment.

I count myself as one of Peter's disciples, though a somewhat wayward one. I once accused him of convincing me of a proposition of law and then, no sooner than I had adopted it in a reported judgment, of changing his mind and leaving me stranded. 'Oh no', he replied, 'You are eclectic'. I like to think that this was meant as praise; but I am not entirely sure that it was.

I sought his help while preparing my judgment in *Agip (Africa) Ltd v Jackson*,[3] where the claimants had traced funds embezzled by their chief accountant into and through the hands of the defendants. The case was argued in the traditional terms of 'knowing assistance' and 'knowing receipt', but I realized that the latter claim was restitutionary and wanted to bridge the linguistic divide by adopting the language of unjust enrichment as well as that of equity. The trouble was that I could not find a satisfactory 'unjust factor'. In their writings Peter and Professor Andrew Burrows had identified 'ignorance' or 'powerlessness'; but neither really fitted the bill. I thought that it was 'want of authority'; but this led to the defendants' want of title rather than their unjust enrichment. So I wrote to Peter and asked him, in all innocence, just where was the dividing line between the law of unjust enrichment and the law of property. He took the trouble to reply by a long letter in which, while admitting that I had put my finger on one of the most difficult and controversial issues in the law of restitution, he patiently explained that the law of property applied only to the original thing: any claim to its

---

[3] [1990] Ch 265, affirmed [1991] Ch 547, CA.

traceable proceeds lay in the law of unjust enrichment. It is an explanation which I have never been able to accept. But the identification of the claim in knowing receipt as a claim in unjust enrichment was a great simplification. It meant that liability was strict but subject to the change of position defence. As a puisne judge, however, I could not say so in *Agip*; that would have to wait until later.

Once I had reached the House of Lords, Peter suggested that he and I, with one or two others, should hold a public debate, or possibly a series of debates, on issues in the law of restitution. I was keen to do this; but Peter died before we could arrange it. At the time of his death we were carrying on a debate by correspondence. The trigger was the Court of Appeal's decision in *FC Jones v Jones*,[4] which Peter had welcomed. Mr Jones had been made bankrupt. Before his trustee in bankruptcy could act, he withdrew some £11,000 from his bank account and gave it to his wife, who invested the money in potato futures and turned it into £50,000. When her husband's trustee in bankruptcy began to make enquiries, she closed the dealing account and placed the money on deposit with a bank. The trustee in bankruptcy claimed payment from the bank, and the bank interpleaded. The trustee in bankruptcy won.

Peter described the case as an 'unequivocal example' of unjust enrichment by interceptive subtraction.[5] I regarded it (and still do) as a rare example of the tracing exercise giving rise to a proprietary claim at common law. I began the correspondence by writing to Peter; he replied inviting my criticism of his approach, which I duly supplied. I have no doubt that my response would have produced a work of demolition from him, but alas! he became too ill to write it.

The result is that there are two letters of mine to only one of his, which distorts the balance of the argument and might be thought inappropriate in a book intended to honour Peter and not me. But his letter demonstrates the clarity and precision of his scholarship. It deserves a wider readership for his contribution and not mine.

House of Lords,
30th November 2003

Dear Peter,

I have just read your most recent analysis of *Jones v Jones* as 'an unequivocal example' of unjust enrichment by interceptive subtraction. It is an analysis with which I have to say that I am in profound disagreement. Since you are (and I mean this by way of tribute) always prepared to change your mind and retreat from a previously held position, may I try to persuade you that this analysis is untenable? It certainly does not represent the basis of my own judgment, nor that of Beldam LJ.

---

[4] [1997] Ch 159.
[5] Birks, 'Personal Property: Proprietary Rights and Remedies' (2000) 11 King's College Law Journal 1, 14; *Unjust Enrichment* (1st edn, 2003) 68–71. See also *Unjust Enrichment* (2nd edn, 2005) 82–6.

Neither of us decided the case on the ground of unjust enrichment. I went out of my way to say that Mr. Jones' trustee in bankruptcy was not suing Mrs. Jones for money had and received (the old common claim for unjust enrichment): see p. 164 G–H. In fact he was not suing her at all: see p. 170 F. He demanded payment from the bank where Mrs. Jones held an account into which she had paid the money which was the subject of his claim. When the bank refused his demand he brought an action *against the bank*. The cause of action was in debt. The bank naturally interpleaded. It did not care whether it paid the money to Mrs. Jones or her husband's trustee, so long as it did not have to pay twice. Mrs. Jones was joined as defendant to the interpleader, and issue was joined between her and the trustee. As between them the question was which of them could give a good receipt to the bank. That depended on which of them had the legal title to the chose in action represented by the debt which was due from the bank: see p. 170 F–G. The trustee claimed the money from the bank because it belonged to him or represented profits made by the use of money which belonged to him: see p. 168 D. This was a question of title, not unjust enrichment. Beldam LJ and I upheld his claim on this basis: see p. l71 H, l72 A–B.

Neither of us accepted the deputy judge's conclusion that Mrs. Jones was a constructive trustee of the debt; we held that she never had any title to it at all: see p. 164 E–F, 167 D–E, and 172 A–B. Mr. Jones had been divested of all title, both legal and equitable, by statute, which had vested legal title in the trustee to the debt and its traceable proceeds.

If the trustee's claim had been based in unjust enrichment, then the orthodox view has hitherto been that the claimant can recover only the first measure of restitution, ie. the value actually received by the defendant. He would not have been able to claim the profits which Mrs. Jones made by investing in potato futures. I understand that you have now found a way of circumventing this rule by including in the description of the money had and received the opportunity to make a profit by investing it. I am not wholly convinced by an insight which has never been considered by the courts and which seems to introduce concepts of property while disclaiming any such thing; but it merits further thought. But I suggest that two considerations point strongly against accepting your analysis.

First, it is clear that, had Mrs. Jones become bankrupt, so that the dispute on the interpleader was whether the bank should pay Mr. Jones' trustee or Mrs. Jones' trustee, the former would have succeeded (and rightly so). It is quite impossible to read the judgment as giving Mrs. Jones' trustee any prospect of success. She had no title to the chose in action in dispute, which would therefore not have vested in her trustee in bankruptcy. But a claim in unjust enrichment is a personal claim. Had the trustee brought an action for money had and received (or unjust enrichment) against Mrs. Jones, then (i) contrary to our decision, the bank would not have obtained a good receipt by paying Mr. Jones' trustee;

(ii) it would have obtained a good receipt by paying Mrs. Jones' trustee; and (iii) Mr. Jones' trustee would have had to prove in her bankruptcy.

Secondly, as many commentators have observed, the actual result of the case was very unfair to Mrs. Jones. If she had not withdrawn the money in the first place, the trustee would never have obtained more than the original sum. He benefited from the astuteness (or luck) with which Mrs. Jones invested the money; yet she got no recognition for this.

The reason, however, is that no such claim was ever made by Mrs. Jones. The only question which the court was asked to decide was: to whom should the bank pay the money? If Mrs. Jones had made a claim to an allowance for her investment skill, it might well have succeeded. A court of equity would direct an enquiry to enable it to order payment of 'all just allowances' for the skill and effort of an innocent recipient of trust property in enhancing its value. Applying this to a case where the defendant was not a trustee because she had no title but only possession may require an extension of the law; but it is hardly a major step and it may well be taken in a future case. But it would surely be a major and, to my mind, very difficult step to extend it to a case where the claim was a personal claim for money had and received (or unjust enrichment). On the present state of the authorities the claimant is entitled to the first measure of restitution and nothing more; the defendant is entitled to retain the whole of the profit which he made by the skilful use of the money *unless* it was made by the use of money which belonged throughout to the claimant, in which case he may be awarded a just allowance for his services in making the profit and must pay the balance to the claimant.

This seems to me to be a fair, coherent and logical framework. I do not think that it is affected by distinguishing between unjust enrichment and interceptive unjust enrichment. Traditionally the latter has always been circumscribed by the requirement that the money, if not intercepted, would 'certainly' have been paid to the claimant (which effectively treats the claim as a property claim) or would 'probably' have been received by him (which has its own problems). But in *Jones v Jones* we can say for a certainty that the money *would not have been invested in potato futures or at all*. It would have been used to pay Mr. Jones' creditors. This would justify awarding Mrs. Jones a 'just allowance' equal to 100% of the profits or, in more traditional usage, confining the claimant to the first measure of restitution. But he got the lot.

The real question may be whether a claim which is question-beggingly described as 'interceptive unjust enrichment' is really a claim in unjust enrichment at all (ie. a personal claim); or whether, like the tracing rules, it forms part of the law of property. The whole subject of the line between the law of unjust enrichment and the law of property needs rationalisation. I know you regard my own position (as adopted by the House of Lords in *Foskett v McKeown*)[6] as 'unstable'. I have come

---

[6] [2001] 1 AC 102 (reference inserted by the editors).

to regard yours as indefensible and contrary to both authority and principle. Now I am about to retire, we should debate it sometime...

With all best wishes,
Yours,
Peter

All Souls College,
Oxford
8th December 2003

Dear Peter,

I am sure it is a relief of some kind to you, but for the rest of us it is a tragedy that you are going. I hope you will at least continue to sit from time to time.

I have written down a set of numbered propositions which are meant to reveal the stages towards the conclusion with which you disagree. If we care to debate this, it would be very helpful to me to know with which of my propositions you disagree.

There is an article in this week's Cambridge Law Journal by Mitchell McInnes which, in insisting on 'corresponding loss' as an essential component in the identification of the claimant, also rules out my explanation of *Jones*. There is one thing which I concede to McInnes at once, namely that this has nothing whatever to do with interceptive subtraction. An interception presupposes corresponding loss, he rightly says. The questions must be separated: when is there an interceptive subtraction? And is 'from my property' sufficiently 'from me' for the law of unjust enrichment? The implication of my numbered points is that, if the answer to the latter is 'no', we have no satisfactory explanation for some of the things which we regularly do...

Yours ever,
Peter

A. What kind of debt?

(1) Debt is and always has been multi-causal. There is a debt when one person owes another a sum certain. The cause may be contract, wrong, unjust enrichment, or other event.

(2) The action for money had and received was an action in debt: 'Whereas the defendant was indebted to the plaintiff in [£10] as so much money before that time had and received to the plaintiff's use and, being so indebted, in consideration thereof...'

(3) For centuries the law has allowed claims in debt for money had and received against defendants holding money belonging to the claimant.

(4) If the *Jones* action is contemplated as an action of debt by the trustee competing with another action of debt by Mrs Jones, the latter is a contractual debt but the former cannot be.

(5) The trustee's action in debt might have been said to have arisen from a wrong (on *United Australia* reasoning)[7] but was not. And just as well, for the only wrong in sight was conversion of two cheques, and one would not want a solution which could not possibly apply to electronic transfers.

(6) The trustee's debt, not being contract-based or wrongs-based, arose from the fact that the bank had money which belonged to the trustee (No.3 above). While the forms of action lived, that was contemplated as debt from money had and received.

(7) Although it is a mistake to say that every debt which used to be contemplated as arising from the receipt of money to another's use arises in modern terms from unjust enrichment, there is no reason to transfer this example from unjust enrichment to miscellaneous other events, which is the only other category available since contract and wrongs have been eliminated already.

(8) It follows that the trustee's action of debt against the bank was an action for a debt which arose from unjust enrichment.

(9) The conclusion in No 8 holds good whatever the correct explanation of the trustee's entitlement to the money (or the account). But in fact it also happens that the best explanation of his entitlement is that, in the hands of Mrs Jones, it was an unjust enrichment at his expense.

B. Why was it the trustee's money?

(1) The law of property is the law of property rights (rights in rem) just as the law of obligations is the law of rights in personam. All rights arise from events.

(2) *A-G for Hong Kong v Reid*[8] belongs in the law of property because the claimant acquired a property right and in the law of wrongs because that property right arose from a wrong. *Chase Manhattan Bank NA v Israel British Bank (London) Ltd*[9] (as decided) belongs in the law of property because the claimant had a property right, and in the law of unjust enrichment because that property right arose from a mistaken payment, the central example of an unjust enrichment.

(3) When without *C*'s knowledge *D* exchanges *C*'s money for a car, *C* acquires a property right in the car. The case belongs in the law of property because all

---

[7] *United Australia Ltd v Barclays Bank Ltd* [1941] AC 1 (reference inserted by the editors).
[8] [1994] 1 AC 324 (reference inserted by the editors).
[9] [1981] Ch 105 (reference inserted by the editors).

property rights belong there. But it also belongs in the law of non-consensual substitution, that being the event from which the property right arose.

(4) An alternative view is that *C*'s right in the car arose from whatever event earlier gave him his property in the money, so that to identify the source of the right in the car we would have to ask whether *C*'s right in the money arose from contract, wrong, unjust enrichment or other event. That view, which is supported by the continental metaphor 'real subrogation', is untenable because the right in the car will often not be identical to the right in the money and because, even if that were not so, it would be offensive to common sense to affirm that in the acquisition of the money *C* also acquired whatever might in the future be obtained with it.

(5) If the analysis in No 4 is abandoned, we have to ask what kind of event non-consensual substitution is. It is manifestly not a contract or other indication of consent. The word non-consensual says as much. It is often a wrong but not always, and the *Jones* case says nothing of any wrong.

(6) It follows that non-consensual substitution is either an unjust enrichment or a miscellaneous other event.

(7) A good account can be given of it as an unjust enrichment. *D* is enriched by the car, the enrichment is from *C* in the sense that it is from *C's* property, and there is no consent or other explanation for the enrichment.

(8) By contrast no account at all of the operation of non-consensual substitution can be given in the category of miscellaneous other events. Its companions there, such as accession, specification and occupation of a *res nullius*, are all explicable on the basis that the law cannot tolerate a vacuum in the entitlement to valuable things. There is no vacuum in relation to substitutes. If the substitute is not an unjust enrichment there is no need whatever for the law to respond to non-consensual substitution.

(9) The preferable solution is to regard rights arising from non-consensual substitution as arising from unjust enrichment.

House of Lords
20th December 2003

Dear Peter,
   Thank you for your kind letter...

   You asked me with which of your propositions I disagreed.
   I agree with your first three propositions in Section A, while bearing in mind (because this is what matters) that the action for money had and received was a personal claim, formerly for breach of an implied promise to pay and nowadays for breach of an obligation to pay imposed by law; and gave rise to a personal remedy consisting of an order to pay a sum equal to the amount of the debt and not to restore the property itself, let alone any profits made by its use. It is true

that the action lay, not only where the defendant owed the plaintiff money, but also where he had the plaintiff's money in his possession; but it nonetheless lay to enforce a personal obligation. Property rights generate personal as well as proprietary claims and remedies... (I think that this may be the point of disagreement between us; though it seems a truism to me).

My point of departure is with the last five words in A4. The trustee's action for debt *was* in respect of a contractual debt. The bank's liability arose out of its receipt of the money deposited by Mrs. Jones and was exclusively contractual. There was only one debt, which was contractual; and the question was: who owned the right to enforce it? This was a dispute about the ownership of property between Mrs. Jones and the trustee; it was not a dispute with the bank.

This kind of tripartite situation is a familiar one. The commonest case is where A lends money to B and afterwards assigns the debt to C. C gives notice of the assignment to B and demands payment of the debt owed to A. A disputes the validity of the assignment and demands payment to himself. B cannot safely pay either of them once he has notice of the alleged assignment. Issue is joined between A and C. The outcome depends on the validity of the assignment, and must be sought in the law of property, which governs the creation, acquisition, disposal and transmission of property rights. There is only one debt; its source is contractual; unjust enrichment has nothing to do with it. Whether A or C succeeds in his claim to own the debt, he is bound by the terms of the contract between A and B. Likewise in *Jones v Jones* the bank would have been entitled to the same notice of withdrawal and liable to the same rate of interest whether Mrs. Jones or the trustee succeeded.

Authorised substitution provides another example. A, a trustee, deposits the proceeds of an authorised sale of trust investments in a bank. The debt is a contractual one which the bank owes to A; but it belongs in equity to the beneficiaries who can take steps to enforce it. Or C authorises A to deposit his (C's) money in a bank. The debt is contractual and is owed to A; but C can take steps to enforce it.

Jones v Jones was concerned with an unauthorised substitution; but the position is the same. The trustee did not complain of the unauthorised investment; ie. he did not treat it as a wrong (as he could have done). This would have given him a personal claim for the loss and confined his recovery to the amount originally taken from him. Instead he sought to profit from the investment Mrs. Jones had made with his money; ie. *he treated it as if it were an authorised investment.* Tracing is part of the law of property because it is concerned with the transmission of property rights. (Another point of disagreement between us.)

The issue between the trustee and Mrs. Jones was: which of us can give a good receipt to the bank? ie. *as between us,* which of us owns the debt, including that part which represented the profits from the dealings? As between creditor and debtor, the creditor is *owed* the debt, he does not *own* it: but as between the creditor and third parties, he *owns* it. The dispute was as to the *ownership* of a personal claim against the bank. When the trustee won, his claim against the bank as the party with the right to enforce a contractual debt succeeded.

The solution to a dispute about the ownership of an asset, be it land, or chattels, or a chose in action, is located in the law of property, not in the law of unjust enrichment. The law of property is not only multi-causal; it is indifferent as to its cause. The claimant who can establish that the asset in dispute is his property has the same rights however his property was acquired, whether by purchase, sale, inheritance, or (as in *Jones v Jones*) by force of statute. Indeed, it may be and usually is unnecessary for him to establish ownership; possession will do. Even a finder may bring a proprietary claim and will succeed against anyone except the true owner.

In my opinion the trustee succeeded because (i) the money which Mrs. Jones deposited with the bank was money in her possession which belonged in law to him; and accordingly (ii) as between him and Mrs. Jones he was entitled in law to the debt due from the bank which represented the money which she had deposited. He could compel her to withdraw the money and pay it over to him, because title prevails over possession. The Court simply short-circuited this by authorising the bank to pay the money direct to the trustee.

Property, like debt, is multi-causal, but once acquired, the classification of the event which resulted in its acquisition is simply irrelevant. The only question for the court is whether the event did result in the acquisition of property by the claimant. That is because the law's response to an invasion of property is more far-reaching than its response to a breach of a personal obligation. Entitlement to property generates both personal and proprietary claims and remedies. Absent a proprietary title then the claimant is confined to a personal claim and, save (possibly) in rare circumstances which have yet to be defined, only personal remedies.

I profoundly disagree with B2. *AG for Hong Kong v Reid* belongs exclusively in the law of property. It does *not* belong in the law of wrongs at all. The claimant was entitled to the money because it belonged to him. The *ratio* of the case is that Reid was bound to pay the money over *in specie* as soon as he received it. This can only be because it belonged to the claimant.

Unfortunately no one explained *why* he owned it, though I did in my article 'Bribes and Secret Commissions'.[10] It cannot have been because it was wrong for Reid to accept the money. The claimant did not complain of this wrong (without which the claim must have failed!); but of his failure to pay the money over. In other words, he sought to take advantage of the receipt by treating it as an authorised receipt. Reid's failure to pay it over *in specie* to the claimant was not wrong at all unless it already belonged to the claimant. One cannot say: he should have paid it to the claimant because it belonged to him; and it belonged to him because Reid ought to have paid it to him.

[10] [1993] RLR 1.

The point was that Reid could not have obtained the money *legitimately* unless he obtained it for and on behalf of the claimant; and the law does not permit a person to retain property for himself which he could have obtained legitimately only if he did so for the benefit of another by asserting that he obtained it illegitimately for himself.

This is a theme which runs through the law of property, especially (though not exclusively) that part of the law of property which is equity. A person who obtains property illegitimately must account for it in exactly the same way as if he had obtained it legitimately. The trustee who invests trust money in his own name in an unauthorised investment cannot keep it by saying that it was a breach of trust if the beneficiary is willing to treat the investment as authorised. See too my explanation of *Walker v Webb*[11] in *Lonhro v Fayed (No 2)*.[12] The only legitimate basis on which Webb could have obtained the grant of a Crown lease was if he were acting on behalf of Walker. He was not, but he was not allowed to deny it. So he held the lease in trust for Walker.

Reid's liability did not, therefore, arise from a wrong. His possession of the money arose from a wrong, but he could not justify his retention of the money by saying so. His liability to pay it over to the claimant arose from the fact that, had he obtained it legitimately, which he was not allowed to deny, he would have been bound to pay it over to the claimant. In the same manner Mrs. Jones was accountable to the trustee to the same extent as if he had authorised her to withdraw the money and invest it in potato futures on his behalf.

My main quarrel with your jurisprudence is that it does not help the County Court Judge. What he wants to know is: to what remedies is the claimant entitled? Or more likely: what must the claimant prove in order to obtain the relief he is asking for? He needs a map; and your physical event/legal response doesn't provide him with one. I prefer a scheme based on the traditional right/claim/remedy. Proprietary remedies are founded on the ownership of an asset; personal remedies on an obligation to pay. If the claimant can establish a proprietary right he may bring proprietary or personal claims and obtain proprietary or personal remedies. If he cannot establish a proprietary right, he is (save in exceptional circumstances) confined to personal claims and remedies.

Where do I go wrong?

Merry Christmas!

Regards,

Peter

---

[11] (1845) Res & Eq 19.   [12] [1992] 1 WLR 1.

15

Unjust Delivery

*William Swadling**

Peter Birks always insisted on teaching the law through the cases. The first seminar on the BCL Restitution course, which I taught with him over many years, always started with a detailed discussion of *Kelly v Solari*,[1] in which an insurance company paid out to a widow on her husband's lapsed policy. Assuming the company was mistaken in making the payment, the widow was liable to repay the sum received. But what triggered that liability? Until shortly before his tragic and untimely death, Peter would have said that it was because the company's 'judgment was vitiated in the matter of the transfer of wealth to the defendant'.[2]

On this view, the law of unjust enrichment, at least in the areas of mistake and other factors going to consent,[3] can be seen as concerned with protecting claimant autonomy.[4] Cases in which a decision to transfer value was mistaken generate a liability to repay that value because the claimant's consent to the transfer was defective.[5] However, the question then arises: given that the claimant's consent to the transfer in *Kelly v Solari* was defective, why did title to the money still pass? Is autonomy not also a value in the law of property? Assuming a payment in cash,[6] why could the company not also bring conversion in respect of the widow's receipt of the notes?

The answer is that the company's mistake, though generating a claim in unjust enrichment, was not such as to prevent title passing. As Robert Goff J (as he then was) said in *Barclays Bank Ltd v W J Simms & Son and Cooke (Southern) Ltd*:[7] '[W]here an action is brought to recover money paid under a mistake of fact,

---

* Fellow and Tutor in Law, Brasenose College, Oxford.

[1] (1841) 9 M & W 54.

[2] P Birks, *An Introduction to the Law of Restitution* (rev edn, 1989) 147.

[3] There are some 'unjust factors', eg payment pursuant to an ultra vires demand of the executive, which arguably have nothing to do with any vitiation or qualification of consent.

[4] Not all would agree. Smith, for example, argues that it is simply an application of the principles of corrective justice: L Smith, 'Restitution: The Heart of Corrective Justice' (2001) 79 Texas LR 2115, though even he is ultimately forced into an explanation based on lack of consent: ibid at 2140.

[5] Peter's later explanation of cases such as *Kelly v Solari* was that there was an 'absence of basis' for the payment: Birks (above, n 2) 101–28.   [6] She was in fact paid by cheque.

[7] [1980] QB 677.

property will almost invariably have passed to the defendant, the effect of the action, if successful, being simply to impose on the defendant a personal obligation to repay the money'.[8] But this will not always be so. Some mistakes, said Robert Goff J, were such as to 'vitiate an intention to transfer property';[9] it is with this latter type of mistake that this essay is concerned.

The question then becomes: What sort of mistakes stop title passing? Is it simply a matter of degree, that there are some mistakes so serious that title does not pass? And moving beyond mistake, are there also some acts of duress or undue influence so serious that title will not pass? And can the same be said of certain failures of basis?[10] Unfortunately, once we leave the central case of mistake, these issues are rarely addressed.[11] And even within mistake, cases where the mistake is such as to prevent title passing are few and far between. The orthodoxy, however, is that such mistakes do exist.[12] These so-called 'fundamental' mistakes[13] are said to be threefold: mistakes as to the identity of the transferee;[14] mistakes as to the identity of the goods;[15] and mistakes as to the quantity of goods.[16] Where such a mistake exists, the claim will be no longer one in unjust enrichment but in tort, in respect of what we might call an 'unjust delivery'.[17]

The distinction between an unjust enrichment and an unjust delivery is vitally important for many reasons. One, at least until the enactment of the Theft Act 1968, was that a person who dishonestly appropriated goods delivered to him by mistake could not be convicted of theft if title to the goods had passed by the act of delivery.[18] Secondly, while a defence of change of position is potentially available to a defendant sued in unjust enrichment, no such defence will avail a

---

[8] ibid, at 689.   [9] [1980] QB 677, 689.

[10] It might be objected that this is not a valid question, for the failure will, *ex hypothesi*, be subsequent to the act of delivery, in which case the most that could happen would be that the failure causes the title to revest.

[11] Exceptions are D Fox, 'The Transfer of Legal Title to Money' [1996] RLR 60, and G Virgo, *The Principles of the Law of Restitution* (1999) 602–16.

[12] See eg AS Burrows, *The Law of Restitution* (2nd edn, 2002) 67 n 2 and 144. A detailed examination is made by G Williams, 'Mistake in the Law of Theft' [1977] CLJ 62; Fox (above, n 11); Virgo (above, n 11) 607–10.

[13] The use of the term 'fundamental' is unfortunate, not only because its meaning is unstable (see eg the comments of Brennan J in *David Securities v Commonwealth Bank of Australia* (1992) 175 CLR 353, 395), but because it is sometimes proposed as an alternative to the supposed liability test in the recovery of mistaken payments: see eg the dictum of Lord Wright in *Norwich Union Fire Insurance Society Ltd v Wm H Prince Ltd* [1934] AC 455, 463. This dual usage can lead to confusion. Thus, Glanville Williams, in an otherwise excellent article, sees the Court of Appeal in *Morgan v Ashcroft* [1938] 1 KB 49 as falling into error over the passing of title to money, when in fact all that was being discussed was the availability of a personal claim in unjust enrichment: (above, n 12) 67–8.   [14] Virgo (above, n 11) 607.

[15] ibid 608.   [16] ibid 608–10.

[17] cf the argument that where title does not pass the claimant can renounce his title and thereafter bring a claim in unjust enrichment: P Birks, *Unjust Enrichment* (2nd edn, 2005) 66–7. For consideration of this argument, see the essays by Robert Stevens and Lionel Smith in this volume.

[18] The law was changed by the Theft Act 1968, s 5(4), so that such a person might now be guilty of theft, though even this is doubtful: Williams (above, n 12) 71.

tortfeasor,[19] and where we are dealing with an unjust delivery, the deliveree's receipt will of necessity be tortious. Thirdly, if title passed to the deliveree, that title will be available to be sold and the proceeds used to pay the deliveree's debts where he is insolvent. By contrast, where title remains with the deliveror, the insolvency official will commit conversion, and thus render himself personally liable, should he sell the goods received. Finally, there may be issues in the conflict of laws and in the law of limitation.

This essay examines the three main authorities[20] usually cited for the proposition that mistakes as to identity, subject-matter, and quantity prevent title passing, *R v Middleton* (mistake as to identity), *R v Ashwell* (mistake as to subject-matter), and *Ilich v R* (mistake as to quantity). The question which needs to be asked is why these mistakes, but no others, prevent title passing. One explanation advanced is that mistakes as to identity, subject-matter, and quantity show that title was not intended to pass, whereas mistakes such as that in *Kelly v Solari* show only that there was no intention to benefit the recipient.[21] But it is impossible to distinguish between title and 'benefit' in this regard, for the way in which Mrs Solari was intended to be benefited, again assuming a payment in money, was by receipt of the claimant's title to the money. A more coherent approach is to ask whether the mistake negatives one of the constituent elements of a valid delivery.[22] To that end, we need to know the requirements of a 'just' delivery. But we cannot leave it there, for titles to goods are protected through the law of torts and through the law of torts alone. We therefore need to ask whether the deliveror has any claim against the deliveree in respect of the goods themselves, for if he does not, the conclusion must be that his title either passed or was destroyed. With these two points in mind, this essay finds that the cases of *Middleton, Ashwell,* and *Ilich* were wrongly decided, thus casting doubt on the proposition that there is any such thing as an unjust delivery, at least where the unjust factor is mistake.

1. Terminology

We need to first say a word about terminology, more specifically, about the terms 'property', 'title', and 'money'.

1.1. Property

The term 'property' is ambiguous. In common parlance, it is used to refer to the thing which is the subject-matter of the right, as, for example, when a person says, 'That car is my property'. But though this is how a layman might use the

---

[19] *Lipkin Gorman (a firm) v Karpnale Ltd* [1991] 2 AC 548, 580 (Lord Goff).
[20] Constraints of space preclude an examination of every possible case.
[21] Virgo (above, n 11) 610.   [22] This is the approach of Fox (above, n 11).

term, it should never be the language of the lawyer. The word 'property' in the mouth of a lawyer should only be used as an adjective, not a noun, for it distinguishes one type of right from another, *scil* a personal right from a property right. To the lawyer, the word property describes a peculiar feature of a right, not a particular thing.[23] And the peculiar feature it describes is the exigibility of that right against strangers to its creation. Thus, a property right, unless for some reason destroyed, will bind a third party, whereas a personal right will not. If, for example, I lease a parcel of land to you, your rights under that lease bind any person to whom I convey my own right to the land. But if I instead grant you only a licence to use that land, your rights bind no one but me.[24] The reason is that in the first case I gave you a property right to the use of the land, while in the second you have only a personal right to do the same.[25] In both cases, however, the thing, the land, is the same. The lesson this teaches is that we must never talk about things as property, but only use the term to describe certain rights over things.

1.2. Title

The word 'title' is also difficult, for no regard is generally given to its content, it being very often used simply as a synonym for 'right'. At other times, it is seen as connected with a particular type of right, the right to possession, though separate from it. Thus, *Clerk and Lindsell on Torts*, when speaking of the tort of conversion, says that 'unlike trespass, it covers not merely an interference with the claimant's possessory interest in his chattels but also an injury to his right or title in them'.[26]

Both these senses, however, are wrong. Etymologically, the word title derives from 'entitlement'. But that only raises the question, entitlement to what? The answer is, possession. Title, in other words, means a right to possession. Thus, if I have a title to land, I have a right to possession of that land. Likewise, if I have a title to a book, I have a right to possession of that book.[27] It is for that reason that the statement in *Clerk and Lindsell* is flawed, for it is not possible to interfere with my title to a parcel of land or a book without at the same time interfering with my right to possession of the same.

[23] Thus, the Sale of Goods Act 1979, in ss 2, 17, 18, 19, and 20, talks of the 'property in the goods', by which is presumably meant 'property *rights* in the goods'. In this respect, the word 'ownership' might be thought to have an advantage over 'property', for it clearly denotes something different from the thing itself. However, as we shall see, English law has no concept of ownership: below, text to n 36.   [24] *Ashburn Anstalt v Arnold* [1989] Ch 1.
[25] Examples are *Hill v Tupper* (1863) 2 H & C 121 (exclusive right to put pleasure boats on a canal does not bind third parties) and *King v David Allen & Sons (Billposting) Ltd* [1916] 2 AC 54 (right to affix advertising material to a building for a fixed period does not bind third parties).
[26] *Clerk & Lindsell on Torts* (19th edn, 2006) para 17-02.
[27] See eg the usage of Auld LJ in *Waverley Borough Council v Fletcher* [1996] QB 334, 346, 350, a case of a contest between a finder of a medieval brooch and a fee simple holder of the land in which the brooch was found.

It must never be forgotten that titles are relative. If I have a right to possession of a book, it does not thereby follow that my title is the strongest there is, for I may have only found it in the street. But though my right to possession may not be as strong as that of the loser of the book, it does not follow that I have no title at all. In the same way that a squatter on land acquires *a* fee simple title to that land,[28] though not immediately the *best* fee simple title,[29] I have *a* title to the book, though not the best title there might be.

And the reason I have a title to the book is that rights to possession arise, *inter alia*, from the fact of taking possession. The leading case is *Armory v Delamirie*,[30] where a chimney-sweeper's boy famously found a jewel contained in a ring in a chimney. The jeweller to whom the boy took it to be valued handed him back the empty socket, and the boy successfully sued him in conversion. The court held that the fact of the boy's possession of the jewel was enough to give him a right to sue.[31] More recently, the Court of Appeal in *Costelloe v Chief Constable of Derbyshire*[32] held that a person who received a stolen car in bad faith could sue the police for refusing to return it to him once their statutory power to detain it for the purposes of criminal proceedings had expired.[33] Lightman J said that:

> ... possession means the same thing and is entitled to the same legal protection whether or not it has been obtained lawfully or by theft or by other unlawful means. It vests in the possessor a possessory title[34] which is good against the world save as against anyone setting up or claiming under a better title.[35]

A further point to note is that it is title and not ownership which English law protects. Despite what the layman might think, there is no concept of ownership in English law. The proof of that proposition lies in the fact that English law provides no form of protection to anyone we might wish to describe as the 'owner' of goods greater than that provided to someone who simply finds them in the street. As we will see below,[36] all who sue in respect of interferences with

---

[28] *Rosenberg v Cook* (1881) LR 8 QBD 162.

[29] The squatter's title will be 'upgraded', so to speak, if his wrongful possession is not challenged by the person he has dispossessed for the duration of the limitation period. However, he does not at the expiry of the limitation period acquire the title of the person dispossessed—there is no 'Parliamentary conveyance': *Tichbourne v Weir* (1892) 67 LT 735. The position is, of course, different where titles are registered. [30] (1722) 1 Str 505.

[31] '... the finder of a jewel, though he does not by such finding acquire an absolute property or ownership, yet he has such a property as will enable him to keep it against all but the rightful owner, and consequently may maintain trover': (1722) 1 Str 505 (Pratt CJ).

[32] [2001] 1 WLR 1437.

[33] A limited power of seizure and detention is conferred by the Police and Criminal Evidence Act 1984, ss 19 and 22.

[34] The statement of Lord Cairns LC in *Cundy v Lindsay* (1878) 3 App Cas 459, 464, that a purchaser from a thief acquires no title, must be read as meaning 'no title good against the victim of the theft'.

[35] [2001] 1 WLR 1437, 1450. Lightman J's use of the term 'possessory title' might be seen as tautologous, for it translates as a possessory right to possession. But 'possessory' here indicates the origin of the right, and says nothing of its content. [36] Below, text to nn 49–76.

goods have to bring their claims within the ambit of certain torts, and the only thing which those torts protect is the right to possession.

The final point to note is that title is sometimes used to describe the interest of a beneficiary under a trust. Some commentators, and occasionally even judges, talk of an absolutely entitled trust beneficiary having an 'equitable title' to the thing the rights over which form the subject-matter of the trust.[37] But this is inaccurate, for the beneficiary of a trust has no right to possession of anything, certainly not at law,[38] nor even in equity.[39] And since this essay is concerned with the passing of title, it is by definition not concerned with any rules of equity.

1.3. Money

The final term we need to examine is 'money'. By money, is meant coins and banknotes.[40] Money, in other words, means cash. It does not include choses in action or debts. Though a layman might talk of having 'money in the bank', it is not the case that banks maintain individual piggy banks for their customers containing the very notes deposited.[41] That has never been the case, even before the age of electronic banking. When I pay a £10 note into my bank account, my title to that note passes to the bank. There is no relationship of bailor and bailee. Nor does the bank hold the title for me as trustee; it is theirs absolutely.[42] What in fact happens is that I exchange my title for a right to sue the bank for the payment of £10. But that right is a personal one, binding no one but the bank. Money, on the other hand, is a thing which can form the subject-matter of a property right. Thus, I can sue in conversion someone who takes a £10 note from my pocket without my consent. In this regard, money is just one type of good, no different from a car or a television set. The only distinction between money and other things is the wider

---

[37] See eg *Chinn v Collins* [1981] AC 533, 548 (Lord Wilberforce); *MCC Proceeds Inc v Lehman Bros Int (Europe) Ltd* [1998] 4 All ER 675, 691 (Mummery LJ); *Westdeutsche Landesbank Girozentrale v Islington LBC* [1996] AC 669, 706–7 (Lord Browne-Wilkinson); J Penner, *The Law of Trusts* (4th edn, 2004) 17–18.

[38] *Leigh & Sillavan Ltd v Aliakmon Shipping Co Ltd, The Aliakmon* [1986] AC 785, 812 (Lord Brandon). The position is different where the beneficiary is physically in possession, for the fact of possession will itself generate a common law right to possession, thus enabling the beneficiary to bring conversion: *Healey v Healey* [1915] 1 KB 938. In *International Factors Ltd v Rodriguez* [1979] QB 351, the Court of Appeal misread *Healey* as giving all trust beneficiaries a right to sue in conversion. For this reason, Mummery LJ in *MCC Proceeds Inc v Lehman Bros International (Europe)* [1998] 4 All ER 675, 690, rightly said that the *dictum* was 'not good law'.

[39] *City of London BS v Flegg* [1988] AC 54, 81–4 (Lord Oliver).

[40] Banknotes carry on their face a promise to pay, and so are technically personal rights good only against the promisor. But they are treated in English law as chattels: 'the representation of money which is made transferable by delivery only, must be subject to the same rules as the money which it represents': *Wookey v Pole* (1820) 4 B & Ad 1, 7 (Best J).

[41] As Staughton J said in *Libyan Arab Foreign Bank v Bankers Trust* [1989] QB 728, 748, 'Students are taught at an early stage of their studies in the law that it is incorrect to speak of "all my money in the bank"'.   [42] *Foley v Hill* (1848) 2 HLC 28.

extent of the destructive effect of *bona fide* purchase[43] when money is used as currency;[44] but this of itself does not make money fundamentally different from any other type of good. Thus, in *Clarke v Shee and Johnson*,[45] the claimant's employee gambled away money with the defendant which he had received on his employer's behalf, and which he was bound to hand over to him *in specie*. The gaming contract being rendered unlawful by statute, this was not a situation in which the defence of *bona fide* purchase could avail the defendant.[46] Lord Mansfield CJ consequently allowed the claimant to recover for the defendant's wrong,[47] for the money was 'in the nature of specific property'.[48]

2. The Protection of Titles to Goods

We cannot begin to understand the law of personal property unless we first know how titles to goods are protected.[49] The common law has no equivalent of the Roman *vindicatio*. There is no action by which a claimant can say, 'That cow is mine'. What is protected is title, not ownership, and it is protected indirectly, through the law of wrongs, not by the direct assertion of a right.[50] Indeed, so important are the various torts which protect title that their abolition would mean we no longer had a law of personal property.

This area is highly complex, for two reasons. First, there are many different ways in which a defendant might interfere with a claimant's title. Throwing a rock through the windscreen of a car to which he has a right of possession, for example, is a vastly different thing to taking the car out of his possession altogether. Secondly, a number of different actions, which often overlapped and which were introduced at different stages of our legal history, have been provided by the common law with respect to the protection of titles to goods: detinue, trespass, conversion, and negligence. The rights a title-holder has are only those he can assert through these torts. Each must therefore be examined in turn.

2.1. Detinue

Detinue was abolished in England in 1978, although its contents were transferred to conversion.[51] Detinue was the oldest common law action concerned

---

[43] Details in W Swadling, 'Restitution and *Bona Fide* Purchase' in W Swadling (ed), *The Limits of Restitutionary Claims: A Comparative Analysis* (1997) 79–105.

[44] *Moss v Hancock* [1899] 2 QB 211.   [45] (1773) 1 Cowp 197.

[46] cf *Lipkin Gorman* (*a firm*) *v Karpnale Ltd* [1991] 2 AC 548, where the House of Lords held that payment pursuant to a 'contract' of gaming rendered void by statute did not amount to a payment for value, and so did not entitle the payee to plead the defence.

[47] The plaintiff's argument at (1773) 1 Cowp 197, 198, unequivocally shows that the claim was brought in wrongs.   [48] (1773) 1 Cowp 197, 200.

[49] The account which follows is necessarily only an outline. For a detailed exposition, see *Clerk & Lindsell on Torts* (19th edn, 2005) ch 17.

[50] Discussion in P Birks, 'Personal Property: Proprietary Rights and Remedies' (2000) 11 KCLJ 1.   [51] Torts (Interference with Goods) Act 1977, s 2.

with the protection of title to goods, and consisted in the defendant's refusal to deliver goods on demand to one having a better right to them. The complaint was that the defendant 'unjustly detained' the goods; there was no requirement that the claimant assert 'ownership'. The defendant had the option of delivering the goods to the claimant or paying him their value.[52] Although detinue was primarily the action of a bailor against his bailee, there was no requirement that the possession of the defendant be initially with the consent of the claimant: one to whom the bailee had given the goods could be sued in detinue; and the action could even be brought against a finder.

The mere possession of goods to which another had a better right to possession was not, however, detinue. The actions of the defendant had to be adverse to the title of the claimant. So, a bailee who held over after the termination of a bailment did not by that act alone make himself liable in detinue. Only a later refusal to redeliver on demand would cause the action to lie. Moreover, a finder did not commit detinue by the mere act of taking a thing into his possession, for he may have only had the intention of keeping it safe for the loser.

One drawback of detinue was that it would generally only lie where the defendant still had the goods in question.[53] A far bigger problem, however, was that until 1833 it was an action to which the defendant could wage his law.[54] For that reason, two newer forms of action, trespass and conversion, both of which involved proof by jury trial, took over much of the work of detinue.

2.2. Trespass to Goods

Trespass originally meant simply 'wrong', so that defamation was as much a trespass as a physical assault on a person.[55] Only later did it harden into the form it has today, that of a direct physical interference with either a person or goods. So far as goods are concerned, there are two forms of trespass: trespass *de bonis asportatis* and trespass on the case. Both require a direct rather than indirect act. The former requires a forcible non-consensual taking, while the latter is available for non-consensual physical damage short of a taking, for example, the

---

[52] From 1854, courts of common law were able to compel the defendant in certain circumstances to hand over the goods themselves: Common Law Procedure Act 1854, s 78. This jurisdiction had long been available in equity.

[53] Exceptionally, a bailee was liable where he no longer had the goods unless he could show that their loss, destruction, or transfer had occurred without fault on his part.

[54] Wager of law was a method of proof in which a defendant made out the truth of his defence simply by enlisting the aid of eleven other people to swear that he was honest. The difficulty was that there were professional oath-swearers, whose services could be obtained at a relatively low cost: details in J Baker, *An Introduction to English Legal History* (4th edn, 2002) 5–6, 74. Wager of law was abolished by statute in 1833.

[55] As Milsom wrote: '. . . had there been a medieval *Salmond* or *Winfield* trespass would have been the title, not of a chapter, but of the book': (1958) 74 LQR 195, 407. The older usage is still present in the Lord's Prayer (forgive us our trespasses).

scratching of a car. Damages are measured by the loss to the claimant, not by the value of the goods. It would seem, however, that though an accidental taking will sound in trespass, accidental physical damage to the goods, even when direct, will only sound in negligence.[56]

2.3. Conversion (Trover)

The tort of conversion started as a species of trespass on the case, but eventually evolved into a free-standing tort. The claimant alleged that he had 'casually lost a chattel out of his possession, that it afterwards came into the defendant's possession by finding, and the defendant, well knowing it to be the plaintiff's property, yet refused to return it to the plaintiff and converted and disposed of it to his own use'. It was originally known as 'trover',[57] from the allegation of finding[58] contained in the writ. The allegation, however, was a fiction and could not be traversed. The substance of the claim was the defendant's conversion of the goods. 'Conversion' was a word in ordinary parlance, and simply meant a 'change' or 'alteration'. So, for example, a bailee who appropriated bailed goods to himself converted or changed their possession. Thus, a consumption of the goods by the bailee was a conversion, as was an unauthorized delivery to a third hand. When in the nineteenth century the necessity of pleading the fictitious finding was abolished,[59] the tort was eventually renamed conversion.

The chief difficulty standing in the path of formulating a comprehensive definition of conversion is the myriad ways in which a defendant might convert or change the possession of goods to his own use. The essential thing is to distinguish conversion from trespass.[60] Though any touching of goods without the consent of a person with a better title will be a trespass, not every unauthorized touching will be a conversion, for it is not every touching which 'converts' the possession of the thing to the defendant's own use. If, for example, you drop a watch in the street which I then pick up, I no doubt commit the tort of trespass. But whether I commit conversion depends on other factors. If I pick it up with the intention of treating it as my own, then that is clearly a conversion, for I am holding it for me, not for you. But if I pick it up with the intention of running after you to return it, in the same way that it was not detinue,[61] it is not conversion. The reason the distinction between the torts of trespass and conversion is important is because success in an action of conversion results in the defendant having to pay the claimant the full value of the goods, whereas in trespass it will subject him only to a claim for their diminution in value. The

---

[56] *National Coal Board v Evans* [1951] 2 KB 861.
[57] Or less often 'trover and conversion'.   [58] From the French, *trouver*.
[59] By the Common Law Procedure Act 1852, s 49.
[60] This is the approach of J Fleming, *The Law of Torts* (9th edn, 1998) 58–82.
[61] Above, text to nn 51–4.

point is illustrated by *Fouldes v Willoughy*.[62] The claimant brought himself and his horses on board the defendant's ferry. Not wishing to carry the claimant, and for the purpose of encouraging him to disembark, the defendant put the horses ashore. The claimant nevertheless stayed on the ferry and the horses were lost. The defendant, though he committed trespass, was held not liable for the value of the horses, only for the diminution in value which was the direct result of his act.

The following acts have been held to be conversions: the taking of a chattel out of the possession of a person with the intention of exercising a permanent or temporary dominion over it;[63] the detention of a chattel in circumstances adverse to the person entitled to possession;[64] the wrongful delivery by a carrier of a chattel to a third person;[65] the wrongful receipt of a chattel;[66] the wrongful disposition of a chattel;[67] the wrongful use of a chattel;[68] and the deliberate[69] wrongful destruction of a chattel.[70] Mere loss by a bailee was not at common law a conversion, though, as we have seen, it did sound in detinue.[71]

2.4. Negligence

Where the act of the defendant is indirect and does not amount to a denial of the claimant's title, the only possible claim will be in negligence. Moreover, even where the act is direct, unless it was done deliberately, it will only sound in negligence. Thus, while the deliberate scratching of a car is trespass, its accidental scratching, provided the constituent elements of the cause of action are present, is only negligence.[72]

2.5. The Relevance of Fault

Negligence apart, none of the torts protecting title to goods require fault on the part of the defendant. Detinue, trespass, and conversion are all torts of strict liability. A purely innocent detention, trespass, or conversion is just as actionable as one accompanied by a guilty state of mind. As Cleasby B said in *Fowler v Hollins*,[73] we deal with property in chattels at our peril.[74] Thus, in the case itself,

---

[62] (1841) 8 M & W 540.
[63] *Lancashire & Yorkshire Rly v MacNicoll* (1919) 88 LJKB 601.
[64] *Howard E Perry & Co Ltd v British Railways Board* [1980] 1 WLR 1375.
[65] *Devereux v Barclay* (1819) 2 B & A 702.   [66] *Farrant v Farrant* (1822) 3 Stark 130.
[67] *Martindale v Smith* (1841) 1 QB 389.
[68] *Kuwait Airways Corpn v Iraqi Airways Co (Nos 4 & 5)* [2002] 2 AC 883.
[69] Accidental destruction is not conversion: *Simmons v Lillystone* (1853) 8 Exch 431, 442.
[70] *Heald v Carey* (1852) 11 CB 977.
[71] By s 2(2) of the Torts (Interference with Goods) Act 1977 such facts now amount to a conversion.   [72] *National Coal Board v Evans* [1951] 2 KB 861.
[73] (1872) LR 7 QB 616.
[74] ibid at 639. In *Kuwait Airways Corpn v Iraqi Airways Co (Nos 4 & 5)* [2002] 2 AC 883, 1093, Lord Nichols said: 'Consistently with its purpose of providing a remedy for the misappropriation of

a broker who innocently sold goods to which the claimant had a better title was liable in conversion, even though he had accounted to the rogue for the price he received. And in *Farquharson Bros & Co v King*,[75] an innocent purchaser for value of timber from an employee of the claimant was held liable in conversion.

The only time fault is ever relevant is where the defendant seeks to take advantage of the sporadically available defence of *bona fide* purchase to say that the title of the claimant was destroyed *vis-à-vis* him by his act of purchase.[76] Where such a defence is potentially available, the presence of fault on the part of the purchaser will disqualify him from its protection. At no point, however, does fault ever form part of the cause of action itself.

3. Just Delivery

We now turn to the passing of title. At first, the only way in which title to goods could pass was by delivery. Only later did it become possible to transfer title by deed. And at around the same time, it was also provided that where there was a contract of sale, title would pass when the parties intended it to pass, irrespective of whether there was any deed or delivery.[77] However, since in the vast majority of unjust enrichment cases involving goods the relevant device for the passage of title is delivery, we will confine our discussion to that. There are two elements of a valid or 'just' delivery: a physical handing over of possession of the thing or its equivalent, and an intention that the deliveror's title should pass to the deliveree.

It should be noted, however, that most textbook and judicial accounts of the passing of title divide up the topic according to the context of the transfer,[78] and then assume that only two contexts, gift and sale, cover the field. But a moment's reflection will show that this cannot be so. Contexts beyond gift and sale which also involve a passing of title include: payments for a service; payments of taxes; satisfaction of judgment debts; exchanges of goods; repayments of loans of money or other fungibles; conveyances to mortgagees; transfers to trustees;[79] and, payments to bookmakers. In respect of the latter, it is interesting to see how in *Lipkin Gorman v Karpnale Ltd*,[80] by assuming that gift and sale covered the whole field, Lords Templeman and Goff were forced to categorize such a

---

goods, liability [in conversion] is strict. . . . [It does not] matter whether the defendant was a thief or acted in the genuine and reasonable belief that the goods were his'.

[75] [1902] AC 325.   [76] Details in Swadling, 'Restitution', (above n 43).
[77] Details in *Cochrane v Moore* (1890) 25 QBD 57, 60–73 (Bowen & Fry LJJ).
[78] *Crossley Vaines*, for example, has chapters on Sale and Gift, but no chapters on Delivery, Deed, or Intent Pursuant to a Contract of Sale: ELG Tyler and NE Palmer, *Crossley Vaines' Personal Property* (5th edn, 1973).
[79] The creation of a trust in favour of another is sometimes talked about as a species of gift. But it is clearly different from an outright transfer of title, and it is in any case difficult to describe a transfer of rights to a trustee on trust for the transferor as a gift at all.   [80] [1991] 2 AC 548.

payment as a gift.[81] But that is manifestly false, and, as we will see below,[82] a similar exercise led the court into error in *R v Middleton*.[83]

3.1. Handing Over of Possession or Equivalent

The gist of a just delivery is a change in the possession of the goods. One way in which the possession can change is where there is a physical handing over of the thing to another. So, if I want to make a gift to you of my title to a watch or money, the easiest thing for me to do is to simply hand you the watch or money. But this is not the only way in which possession can change.[84] I might, for example, tell you of the location of the watch or money and leave you to pick it up yourself. Thus, in *Thomas v Times Book Co Ltd*,[85] Plowman J held that a gift of the manuscript of *Under Milk Wood* was perfect because the donor had told the donee of its probable whereabouts[86] and the donee had then taken it into his possession with the consent of the donor.[87]

It is essential, however, that the possession of the goods be changed by a voluntary act of the deliveror. There will, for example, be no just delivery where you take a £10 note out of my jacket pocket without my consent. Nor is there a just delivery where I hand over my jacket not knowing that it contains a £10 note, for I cannot form an intent to deliver something the existence of which I am ignorant. In *Cartwright v Green*[88] a bureau was delivered to the defendant for repair. In a secret drawer, the defendant found some money, which he appropriated to his own use. The question was whether this could be larceny, the forerunner of theft. The argument that it could not, for there was a delivery of the money, and larceny required a felonious taking, was rejected. There was no delivery because there had been no intent to hand over the money to the repairer.[89] The same result obtained in *Merry v Green*,[90] where title to a purse and money contained in a hidden compartment of a secretary was held not to have passed on the sale of the secretary:

. . . though there was a delivery of the secretary, and a lawful property in it thereby vested in the plaintiff, there was no delivery so as to give a lawful possession of the purse and money. The vendor had no intention to deliver it, nor the vendee to receive it; both were ignorant of its existence: and when the plaintiff discovered that there was a secret drawer containing the purse and money, it was simply a case of finding . . . .[91]

---

[81] ibid at 562 (Lord Templeman), 575 (Lord Goff).   [82] Below, text to nn 116–20.
[83] (1873) LR 2 CCC 38.
[84] There is much learning on constructive delivery, 'symbolic' delivery, and delivery between spouses which need not concern us here: details in *Crossley Vaines* (above, n 78) 305–10.
[85] [1966] 1 WLR 911.
[86] Dylan Thomas thought that he had left it in one of a number of public houses in Soho or in a taxi.   [87] [1966] 1 WLR 911, at 919.
[88] (1803) 8 Ves 405.   [89] ibid at 409.   [90] (1841) 7 M & W 623.
[91] ibid at 631 (Parke B).

3.2. Intent to Pass Title

But a voluntary handing over of possession cannot suffice, for otherwise every bailment would involve a passing of title. If I lend you a book, though I voluntarily hand you possession of the book, there is no intent on my part that my right to possession vest in you.[92] For title to pass, there must additionally be an accompanying intent that the title of the deliveror passes to the deliveree.

Crucially for our purposes, the fact that the deliveror is mistaken as to his liability to transfer the goods will not prevent there being a just delivery. In *Chambers v Miller*[93] a bank instructed its staff not to honour the cheques of a particular customer. Forgetting the instruction, a clerk cashed a cheque drawn on the customer's account in favour of the claimant and handed him the notes. When, almost immediately, the clerk discovered his mistake, he and the bank manager detained the claimant and forced him to return the money. The claimant sued in trespass to the person, and the issue turned on whether or not title to the notes remained in the bank. It was held that, despite the clerk's mistake, title had passed, with the result that the defendants had committed trespass to the person in detaining the claimant. Erle CJ said that the moment the clerk laid down the notes on the counter, the banker's property in the money passed and could not be lawfully retaken. That must be right, for, despite the clerk's mistake, there was still present all the elements of a just delivery. His mistake was simply as to the bank's liability to pay,[94] and it could not be said that the claimant committed conversion or any other tort when he took up the notes with the consent of all concerned.[95]

---

[92] It is of course different with the loan of a fungible, such as money or a cup of sugar, for there I do not expect to get the very thing back. The thing is instead meant to be consumed, and title is intended to pass.   [93] (1862) 3 F & F 202.

[94] For that reason, it is difficult to see how Goulding J in *Chase Manhattan v Israel-British Bank* [1981] Ch 105 could come to a different conclusion about the passing of rights in equity. He there held that a liability mistake prevented the payor's equitable right in a chose in action passing to the payee. Apart from the obvious objection that the payor had no separate equitable interest prior to the payment (*Westdeutsche Landesbank Girozentrale v Islington LBC* [1996] AC 669, 706), there is no logical reason why courts of equity should take a different view of the matter. If the intent to pass the right was there, it was there both at common law and in equity, for it exists regardless of the system judging it, a view recently accepted as correct in respect of the agreement required for the formation of a contract in *Great Peace Shipping Ltd v Tsavliris Salvage (Int) Ltd* [2003] QB 679.

[95] In this respect, *Moynes v Coopper* [1956] 1 QB 439 presents a difficulty. The defendant had received an advance on his weekly wages. Forgetting that fact, he was paid his full wages at the end of the week. He only discovered the mistake when he later opened his pay packet, at which point he appropriated the money to his own use. His conviction for theft was quashed by the Divisional Court on the ground that, since he had been handed the money by his employer, the trespassory taking necessary for the crime of larceny (below, text to nn 103–6) was not present. The court seems to have assumed, however, that title to the money had not passed, for there would otherwise be no possibility of the defendant committing larceny at all. Yet, since the employer's mistake was only as to its liability to pay, this assumption must be wrong.

Moreover, the same rule applies even where the deliveror's liability mistake is fraudulently induced by the deliveree. In *R v Prince*,[96] a wife forged and cashed a cheque for £900 on her husband's account. Her lover, to whom she gave one of the notes received, was acquitted of handling stolen goods. Title to the notes had passed despite the clerk's mistake. The wife had not, therefore, committed larceny, and her lover could not be convicted of handling stolen property. Blackburn J said: '. . . if the owner intended the property to pass, though he would not so have intended had he known the real facts, that is sufficient to prevent the offence of obtaining another's property from amounting to larceny'.[97]

That must also be right. Whether title passes is a matter of the intent of the person making the delivery. If a mistake as to liability spontaneously made, as in *Chambers v Miller*, does not stop title passing, then the same mistake induced by fraud cannot logically have any different effect, for the state of mind of the deliveree is entirely separate from that of the deliveror. In this respect, it is simply the converse of the rule that liability in unjust enrichment is independent of the defendant's fault.[98]

The final point to note is that delivery pursuant to a void contract of sale will not prevent title passing. Though under the law of sales of goods, title can pass by intent alone, it is clearly not the only way in which it can happen. Thus, in *Singh v Ali*,[99] an agreement was made for the sale of a lorry, which sale was illegal as contravening certain licensing regulations. The lorry was delivered but later seized by the vendor. He was sued in detinue. His argument that 'the contract was illegal and void, and therefore it could have no consequences in law and no property could pass to the plaintiff'[100] was rejected by the Privy Council. According to Lord Denning: 'Although the transaction between the plaintiff and the defendant was illegal, nevertheless it was fully executed and carried out: and on that account it was effective to pass the property in the lorry to the plaintiff'.[101] There was, in other words, a just delivery, and the fact that the contract pursuant to which it was made was void in no way contradicted this.[102]

4. Three Cases of Unjust Delivery

We now come to the three cases which are the focus of this essay, cases where, despite a physical handing over of the goods, title was held not to pass. As none concerned bailments, they can only be cases of 'unjust' delivery. The purpose of this section is to ask whether they were correctly decided, for if they were not, doubt is cast on the proposition that there can be such a thing as a fundamental mistake.

---

[96] (1868) LR 1 CCR 150.
[97] ibid at 154.
[98] *Kelly v Solari* (1841) 9 M & W 54, 58 (Parke B), 59 (Rolfe B).   [99] [1960] AC 167.
[100] ibid, at 173.   [101] ibid at 176.
[102] cf in the context of a chose in action, *Westdeutsche Landesbank Gironzentrale v Islington LBC* [1996] AC 669, 689–90 (Lord Goff).

Two of the three cases involve the old offence of larceny.[103] The *actus reus* of larceny required a taking (*cepit*) and a carrying away (*asportavit*) without the consent of the prior possessor (*invito domino*). Most importantly, the taking had to amount to a trespass. Thus, if the thing alleged to have been stolen was handed over with the consent of the prior possessor, there could be no larceny, for there was then no trespass.[104] As a consequence, there could be no larceny where the goods were consensually in the possession of the accused before he formed the intent to deprive the prior possessor of them. A further rule was that it was not possible to commit larceny if title to the thing alleged to have been stolen had passed to the accused. As Scrutton LJ said in *Folkes v King*,[105] 'it is clear that if the legal property passes, dealing with it is not larceny'.[106]

Before we start, it should be noted that there is a line of cases, which includes *Cundy v Lindsay*,[107] *King's Norton Metal Co Ltd v Edridge Merrett & Co Ltd*,[108] *Phillips v Brooks*,[109] *Ingram v Little*,[110] *Lewis v Averay*,[111] and *Shogun Finance Ltd v Hudson*,[112] that at first sight appears relevant to our inquiry. All involved fraudulently induced contracts of sale, and the question in each was whether the vendor's mistake made the contract void or only voidable. This was important, for in each case the goods had been sold on, and if the initial contract of sale was void, the subsequent purchaser's act of taking the goods would be a conversion, whereas if the initial contract was merely voidable, there would be no liability as against the fraudulently induced vendor provided only that the second purchase preceded the latter's act of rescission.[113] However, none of these cases are relevant to our enquiry for they all proceed on the hypothesis that title passed by virtue of the contract or not at all,[114] an assumption plainly at odds with the illegality cases examined above.[115] Unfortunately, the issue whether title might have passed in some other way, most notably by delivery, was never addressed.

---

[103] Larceny was abolished in England by the Theft Act 1968 and replaced by the more wide-ranging offence of theft.

[104] Exceptions were made in the case of bailees and those who obtained possession by a 'trick'.

[105] [1923] 1 KB 282, 307.

[106] It might be thought that the same would be true of the statutory offence of theft. However, a majority of the House of Lords came to the remarkable conclusion in *R v Hinks* [2001] 2 AC 241 that it is possible to commit theft in respect of things to which title had passed to the defendant. The dissent of Lord Hobhouse, who said that a criminal law should not fall out of step with the civil law, is compelling.   [107] (1878) 3 App Cas 459.

[108] (1897) 14 TLR 98.   [109] [1919] 2 KB 243.   [110] [1961] 1 QB 31.

[111] [1972] 1 QB 198.   [112] [2004] 1 AC 919.

[113] The question was relevant in *Shogun Finance Ltd v Hudson* [2004] 1 AC 919 for a slightly different reason. In the absence of a contract of sale, a third-party purchaser would not obtain the protection of the Hire-Purchase Act 1964, s 27(1)(2).

[114] 'If property in the goods in question passed, it could only pass by way of contract; there is nothing else which could have passed property': *Cundy v Lindsay* (1878) 3 App Cas 549, 464 (Lord Cairns LC).

[115] Above, text to nn 99–102. Discussed at greater length in Swadling, 'Rescission, Property, and the Common Law' (2005) 121 LQR 123.

4.1. Mistakes as to Identity: *R v Middleton*[116]

R v Middleton is the leading authority for the proposition that a mistake as to the identity of the deliveree is a fundamental mistake and therefore one which prevents title passing.[117] Middleton applied for and was given a warrant to withdraw 10 shillings from his Post Office account. When paying out on the warrant, the clerk looked at a warrant for a different person and paid out £8/16/10 instead. He nevertheless recorded the withdrawal of £8/16/10 in Middleton's passbook. Middleton realized the clerk's mistake, but took the money regardless. His conviction for larceny was upheld by a majority of a fifteen member Court for Crown Cases Reserved.

The immediate problem is in reconciling this result with *R v Prince*.[118] The only mistake the clerk made was as to the Post Office's liability to pay, and, as *R v Prince* shows, a mistake as to liability, even when fraudulently induced, does not prevent title passing.[119] How then did the majority find Middleton guilty? Cockburn CJ, Blackburn, Mellor, Lush, Grove, Denman, and Archibald JJ held that title did not pass because the payment to Middleton could not be classified as either a sale or a gift. It was true that where a sale had been induced by fraud, the vendor could rescind and revest title, but in the present case:

> ... the property still remains that of the Postmaster-General, and never did vest in the prisoner at all. There was no contract to render it his which required to be rescinded; there was no gift of it to him, for there was no intention to give it to him or to any one. It was simply a handing it over by a pure mistake, and no property passed.[120]

But that cannot be right. As we have seen, gift and sale do not cover the whole field. Indeed, if the judges were right, then even if the clerk had paid Middleton the correct amount, title would not have passed, for there would still have been no gift or sale. Moreover, in *R v Prince* there was neither a gift nor a sale yet title still passed.

Bovill CJ and Keating J upheld the conviction on the narrow ground that the clerk only had authority to part with 10 shillings, and not £8/16/10. However, such a conclusion is itself difficult to reconcile with both *Chambers v Miller* and *R v Prince*, and leads to the ridiculous result that the defendant would have been innocent if the mistake had been made by the Postmaster-General himself, but guilty when made by an employee.[121] Crucially for our purposes, a

---

[116] (1873) LR 2 CCR 38.   [117] Virgo (above, n 11) 607–8.
[118] As Martin B said in dissent: '... the act of the accused in *Reg v Prince* was a grosser act, and more akin to larceny than that of the prisoner in this case; yet it was held not larceny. I defy any man to explain to any one not a lawyer the difference between the two cases. The distinction seems to me worthy of an ancient casuist': (1873) LR 2 CCC, 38, 53. For a devastating critique of the case from the perspective of the criminal law, see JWC Turner, 'Two Cases of Larceny' in L Radzinowicz and JWC Turner (eds), *The Modern Approach to Criminal Law* (1945) 356–74.
[119] Text to nn 95–8.   [120] (1873) LR 2 CCR 38, 44.
[121] A fact acknowledged by Kelly CB, who nevertheless upheld the conviction: (1873) LR 2 CCR 38, 49.

further reason for the failure of title to pass was also given. This was because the clerk:

... never intended to part with the £8/16/10 to the person who presented an order for only 10s, and he placed the money on the counter by mistake, though at the time he (by mistake) intended that the prisoner should take it up, and by mistake entered the amount in the prisoner's book.[122]

The difficulty with this reasoning, however, is that it assumes that the mere fact that the clerk was mistaken prevented title passing; yet, as we have seen, the one thing in this area which is certain is that not all mistakes have this effect. If the clerk intended Middleton to have the money, then title passed, despite the fact that his intent was mistakenly formed.[123]

These difficulties have led some commentators to seize on the alternative reasoning of Bovill CJ and Keating J to reinterpret *Middleton* as a case concerned with a mistake as to identity rather than liability.[124] But this is hardly a representation of the reasoning of the majority of those in favour of upholding the conviction. And it is in any case a strained interpretation of the case. Although the clerk looked at a warrant which referred to a different person, he did not intend to pay the money to anyone other than Middleton, as is evidenced by the fact that he recorded the transaction in Middleton's pass-book.

But even if we could say that *Middleton* was a mistaken identity case, it is not immediately clear how that would have prevented title passing to Middleton. Suppose you have an identical twin. Mistaking him or her for you, I hand them a £10 note as a birthday present. They realize my mistake, but take the money nevertheless. Can it be said that title does not pass? How can my act be described as a non-voluntary act? I intended to give the £10 to the person I thought was you. But the fact that they were not you and I was mistaken as to their identity does not mean that I did not intend them to have it. The issue is addressed in the dissent of Bramwell B,[125] whose reasoning on this point, it is submitted, is unanswerable. He said:

No doubt the clerk did not intend to do an act of the sort described and give to Middleton what did not belong to him, yet he intended to do the act he did. What he did

---

[122] (1873) LR 2 CCR 38, 48.

[123] The two other judges in the majority were Kelly CB and Pigott B. Kelly CB also found the defendant guilty on the ground that the clerk had no authority to pay over the sum which he did. Pigott B, by contrast, upheld the conviction on the ground that the prisoner's dishonest intent was formed before he took the money off the counter. The case was therefore analogous to a finding. The difficulty here, of course, is that until he took possession of the notes and coins, Middleton could not commit larceny, for until then there was not the required taking of the money. And when he did take the money, the act of delivery was complete and title passed, with the result that he could not be guilty of the crime. The analogy with finding is obviously misplaced, for in that case there is no delivery with intent to pass title. We will see below (text to nn 128–39) that a similarly flawed analogy with finding was used in *R v Ashwell* (1885) LR 16 QBD 190.

[124] Williams (above, n 13) 67 n 13; Fox (above, n 11) 65 n 29; Virgo (above, n 11) 607–8.

[125] The other dissentients were Martin B, Brett J, and Cleasby B.

he did not do involuntarily nor accidentally, but on purpose. . . . If the reasoning as to not intending to give this money is correct, then, as it is certain that the . . . clerk did not intend to give Middleton 10s, it follows that he intended to give him nothing. That cannot be. In truth, he intended to give him what he gave, *because he made the mistake*. This matter may be tested in this way: A tells B that he has ordered a wine merchant to give B a dozen of wine, B goes to the wine merchant, bona fide receives, and drinks a dozen of wine. After it is consumed, the wine merchant discovers he gave B the wrong dozen, and demands it of B, who, having consumed it, cannot return it. It is clear the wine merchant can maintain no action against B, as B could plead the wine merchant's leave and licence.[126]

That must be right. A delivery of possession accompanied by an intent that the deliveror's right to possession be vested in the deliveree is all that is needed to pass title, and both these elements were present in *Middleton*.[127] Though the delivery was caused by mistake, the delivery itself contained no element of mistake. So too with the example of your twin. I intended them to have my title to the £10 note precisely because I was mistaken, not otherwise.

4.2. Mistakes as to Subject-Matter: *R v Ashwell*[128]

The second case, *R v Ashwell*, is generally cited as authority for the proposition that a mistake as to the subject-matter of the delivery is a fundamental mistake and therefore prevents title passing. However, it too is open to criticism. The facts were these. Ashwell asked Keogh for the loan of a shilling. In the dark, Keogh mistakenly handed him a sovereign. Upon discovering the error, Ashwell, who initially shared the mistake, appropriated the sovereign to his own use. The Court for Crown Cases Reserved was evenly divided as to the correctness of his conviction for larceny, with the result that it stood.[129] Crucially, counsel for the defendant did not take his stand on the passing of title,[130] and all fourteen judges simply assumed that title in the sovereign had not passed.

Those in favour of quashing the conviction held that since the taking by Ashwell was with the consent of Keogh, it was not a felonious taking, and one of the constituent elements of the crime was therefore missing.[131] Those in favour

---

[126] (1873) LR 2 CCR 38, 55–6 (emphasis added).
[127] For this reason, *Middleton* was not followed by a majority of the Supreme Court of South Australia in *R v Potsik* (1973) 6 SASR 389.   [128] (1885) 16 QBD 190.
[129] Those in favour of upholding the conviction were Lord Coleridge CJ, with whom Grove, Pollock, and Huddleston JJ concurred, Cave J, with whom Hawkins J agreed, and Denman J. Those in favour of acquittal were Smith J, Mathew J, Stephen J, with whom Day and Wills JJ agreed, Manisty J, and Field J.
[130] This is not surprising, for in *Middleton* an example was discussed in argument of a cabman who is handed a sovereign in mistake for a shilling. All the judges seemed to agree that the cabman would only commit larceny if he was aware of the mistake at the moment he received the coin.
[131] 'Keogh . . . intended to deliver the coin to the prisoner, and the prisoner to receive it': (1886) LR 16 QBD 190, 197, per Smith J.

of upholding the conviction said that Keogh's mistake prevented there being any delivery of the sovereign at the time of the handing over,[132] with the result that the case was no different from that of a person who found a sovereign in the street and who dishonestly appropriated it to his own use. Reliance for this proposition was placed on *Cartwright v Green*[133] and *Merry v Green*,[134] decisions which Lord Coleridge CJ said would have to be overruled if the conviction was quashed.[135] It is difficult, however, to see that this is correct. Both cases, as we have already seen,[136] were concerned with the question whether there had been a delivery of goods where, unknown to the person handing them over, they were contained in a larger thing. *Ashwell* was not such a case, for Keogh knew that he was handing over the particular coin; the only thing he did not know was its value. The point is well made by Smith J in dissent:

No intention to deliver the chattel (namely, the purse and the money) *at all* ever existed [in *Cartwright v Green* and *Merry v Green*], whereas in the present case there was every intention to deliver the chattel (namely, the coin), and it was delivered and honestly received.[137]

Lord Coleridge CJ's answer to this, that the sovereign was also a container, a container of 20 shillings,[138] is unconvincing, for it confuses the physical and the metaphysical. Moreover, it is difficult to see how the defendant could not be said to be in possession of the sovereign until he knew its value, for if that were true, we would be left with the absurd result that he would be unable to maintain conversion against a pickpocket who immediately took it from him.

But what of the assumption of all the judges concerned that the prosecutor's mistake had the effect of preventing title to the sovereign passing? It is difficult to see how this could be so, especially in light of the statement of Smith J set out above. There was an intent to pass the coin to the defendant, there being only a mistake as to its value. In that respect, it seems an even clearer case than the example of the wine merchant given by Bramwell B in *Middleton*. In fact, because all fourteen judges were of the opinion that the defendant was not a trespasser at the moment he received the coin from Keogh, it must follow that Keogh's consent to the prisoner having the coin was not vitiated by his mistake as to its value. For if Keogh's consent would have provided a good defence to a claim in trespass, it must also have done so if Keogh had instead brought conversion, for, despite his mistake, Keogh clearly intended his title to the coin to vest in the prisoner. And if there was no claim in either trespass or conversion,

---

[132] '... there was no delivery of the sovereign to the prisoner ..., because there was no intention to deliver...': (1885) LR 16 QBD 190, 225, per Lord Coleridge CJ.

[133] (1803) 8 Ves 405.   [134] (1841) 7 M & W 623.

[135] (1885) LR 16 QBD 190, 225.   [136] Above, text to nn 88–91.

[137] (1885) LR 16 QBD 190, 198 (emphasis in original).

[138] 'I can see no sensible or intelligible distinction between the delivery of a bureau not known to contain a sum of money or a purse and the delivery of a piece of metal not known to contain in it 20s....': (1885) LR 16 QBD 190, 225.

then title to the coin must have passed, for, as we have seen,[139] there is no other way in English law to assert title to goods.

4.3. Mistakes as to Quantity: *Ilich v R*[140]

The third and final type of fundamental mistake is a mistake as to the quantity of goods delivered. An example of such a case is said to be *R v Ilich*.[141] Ilich was working in Western Australia as a locum veterinary surgeon for a man called Brighton. He was owed $1,176 for his work, but Brighton, being much agitated because of the disorder in which Ilich had left the surgery, mistakenly handed him an envelope containing an excess of $530. Ilich did not immediately realize Brighton's mistake, though when he did, he appropriated the money to his own use. His conviction for stealing[142] the excess was quashed by a majority of the High Court of Australia,[143] though not on the ground that title had passed despite Brighton's mistake. Instead, the court reasoned that title 'passed' only because the money had passed into currency by virtue of Ilich being a good faith purchaser for value.[144] It has to be immediately said that this reasoning is flawed. The defence of *bona fide* purchase is only relevant in the context of a transfer of a title to a thing to which some third party has a better right. A thief, for example, might spend money stolen from you in buying a car from an innocent vendor. Your claim for conversion of the money against the vendor of the car will be met by a defence of good faith purchase. The defence has no application, however, to what we might call a 'two-party' dispute, where there is no contest between titles.

In *Barclay's Bank plc v Boulter*,[145] a wife was induced to grant a mortgage to a bank because of an alleged misrepresentation by her husband. She sought to set it aside on the alleged ground the bank had constructive notice of the husband's misrepresentation. The issue for the court was the location of the burden of proof of the constructive notice. The Court of Appeal had held,[146] by analogy with the defence of bona fide purchase,[147] that the burden was on the mortgagee. This was rejected by the House of Lords. The bona fide purchase rule enabled a purchaser to defeat a prior interest which burdened the title he bought, whereas the mortgagee here took the charge directly from the wife. The defence could

---

[139] Above, text to nn 49–76.   [140] (1987) 162 CLR 110.

[141] Virgo (above, n 11) 608–9.

[142] The offence of stealing is defined in s 371 of the Western Australian Criminal Code. It includes both a fraudulent taking and a fraudulent conversion of goods, and for that reason cases such as *R v Ashwell* (1885) 16 QBD 190 (above, text to nn 128–39) and *Moynes v Coopper* [1956] 1 QB 439 (above, n 97) were not considered relevant by the court.

[143] Wilson, Brennan, Deane, and Dawson JJ, Gibbs CJ dissenting.

[144] (1987) 162 CLR 110, 128–30 (Wilson and Dawson JJ) 138–9 (Brennan J) 142–3 (Deane J).   [145] [1999] 1 WLR 1919.

[146] [1998] 1 WLR 1, 10–11 (Mummery LJ).

[147] There is no doubt that where this defence applies, the burden of proof is on the person relying on it: *Pilcher v Rawlins* (1872) 7 Ch App 259, 268–9 (James LJ).

have no application, for the wife 'had the necessary title to grant [the mortgage]. There was no prior interest, which the bank needed to defeat.'[148]

This was also the position in *Ilich*. The only question was whether Brighton's title to the money had passed to Ilich. There was no third party claiming a better title than Brighton. It was not therefore open to the majority to invoke the *bona fide* purchase defence. The question instead should have been whether Brighton's mistake was sufficient to prevent title in all the notes in the envelope passing to Ilich. All members of the High Court assumed that it was, for there would have otherwise been no need to invoke the bona fide purchase defence.[149] But it is difficult to see how title to the money failed to pass. Although Brighton did indeed make a mistake when counting out the notes, he meant to put the particular bundle in the envelope he handed to Ilich. It was not like *Cartwright v Green* or *Merry v Green*, where the deliveror had no knowledge that there was anything in the cabinets. Moreover, it is difficult to see in respect of which particular notes Brighton could have brought conversion. Gibbs CJ, who would have upheld the conviction,[150] said that it was 'not material that Mr Brighton could not have sued for conversion of the $530'.[151] But it is submitted that this fact is crucial, for without a claim in either conversion or trespass, Brighton had no way of asserting title. And if Brighton no longer had a title at the point of receipt, Ilich could not be guilty of stealing money belonging to another.

5. Conclusion

To decide whether a delivery is an unjust delivery it must be asked both whether the requirements of a just delivery have been satisfied and whether the claimant can maintain an action in tort against the deliveree. Applying that thinking, none of the three cases discussed were correctly decided, which in turn throws doubt on the notion that there are mistakes so fundamental as to prevent title passing by delivery. *R v Middleton* is incorrect because it both wrongly distinguished between a fraudulently induced mistake and a spontaneous mistake, and because it assumed that gift and sale cover the whole territory of delivery. Nor can it be rehabilitated as a case concerned with a mistake as to identity, both because that was not how the majority of the court reasoned, and because a mistake of identity can have no different effect than a liability mistake. *R v Ashwell* is also a weak authority. The point that title had not passed when the sovereign was

---

[148] [1999] 1 WLR 1919, 1924 (Lord Hoffmann). See generally, Swadling, 'Restitution', n 43, 92–5; Sir Peter Millett, 'Restitution and Constructive Trusts' (1998) 114 LQR 399, 409.

[149] Reliance on the rule also leads to the unacceptable result that Ilich would have been rightly convicted if he had been paid in kind rather than in cash, for in that situation the *bona fide* purchase defence would have had no application.

[150] Gibbs CJ alone saw that the *bona fide* purchase defence could have no application on the facts of the case: (1987) 162 CLR 110, 118.   [151] (1987) 162 CLR 110, 118.

mistakenly handed over instead of a shilling was not tested in argument. The only issue for the court was whether the taking by the defendant was trespassory, and the majority only found it was by putting him in the position of the finder in *Cartwright v Green* and *Merry v Green*. This analogy, however, was misplaced. Our final case was *Ilich v R*, where the court, though this time reaching the correct result, did so by the prohibited route of applying the defence of *bona fide* purchase to a 'two-party' rather than a 'three-party' case. The assumption by all concerned that title did not otherwise pass was false, for Brighton did intend to transfer his title to the very notes he handed to Ilich. Nor was it true, as Gibbs CJ said, that the absence of a claim in conversion was irrelevant to the question of title. Titles to goods are protected through the law of wrongs, and through the law of wrongs alone. The unavailability of a claim in tort meant that there was no longer any title to goods belonging to another, and no possibility, therefore, of a conviction for stealing those goods.

Peter Birks often bemoaned the lack of teaching of personal property in English law schools,[152] and was instrumental in setting up such a course in Oxford. The point of this essay has been to show how unjust enrichment lawyers need to know their personal property law, for they will otherwise be unable to distinguish an unjust enrichment from an unjust delivery. That said, the indications are that an unjust delivery will be a very rare thing indeed. And though this essay has done no more than scratch the surface of the problem, it is of interest to note that in none of the cases discussed could it be said that the vitiation of the deliveror's intent had any effect on the passing of title. This question needs pursuing, for it may well turn out that there are in fact no cases where the unjust factor, though rendering the enrichment unjust, has the same effect in respect of the act of delivery. There may, in other words, be no such thing as an 'unjust delivery'.

---

[152] See eg his review of A Bell, *The Modern Law of Personal Property in England and Ireland* (1989) in (2001) *SPTL Reporter* 31.

16

The Avoidance of Transactions in Insolvency Proceedings and Restitutionary Defences

*Roy Goode**

1. Introduction

As a general commercial lawyer I came late to the discovery of Peter Birks's ground-breaking book, *An Introduction to the Law of Restitution*, and was overwhelmed by its power and originality and by the lucidity which has been the hallmark of Peter's writings. Later I came to know him better as a friend and colleague passionately devoted to legal education, ever willing to help others, always respectful of opinions that differed from his own, and very ready (perhaps too ready) to accept that he was in error. His great ambition, he once told me, was to write a comprehensive textbook on the law of restitution, a task which sadly he did not live to accomplish. But he will long be remembered both for his scholarship and for his personal qualities. It is a privilege, for one whose field is not the law of restitution, to be invited to contribute to these essays in his memory.

1.1. Nature of the Enquiry

The Insolvency Act 1986 contains a number of provisions for the avoidance of transactions on the insolvency of a company, to which must be added section 395 of the Companies Act 1985 dealing with the avoidance of unregistered

* Emeritus Professor of Law in the University of Oxford, Emeritus Fellow of St John's College, Oxford. I am indebted to Professor Andrew Burrows, who has once again beguiled me into straying from my normal patch, for his detailed comments on the draft of this essay and for his generous help in illuminating a number of issues arising in the law of restitution which were unclear to me. I should also like to thank Robert Stevens of Lady Margaret Hall, Oxford, for an instructive discussion. Neither has any responsibility for any errors this essay may contain.

charges.[1] In an instructive paper[2] Dr Simone Degeling has tested the proposition advanced by the present writer and others that several of these provisions are designed to reverse an unjust enrichment, and has concluded that this is indeed the case. The purpose of this essay is to examine the validity and significance of that conclusion in relation to each of the avoidance provisions and to discuss two questions in particular. The first is whether the restitutionary purpose of a particular statutory provision attracts the common law defences of estoppel, change of position, or bona fide purchase in answer to a claim in unjust enrichment. The second is the extent to which a defendant to such a claim who has a cross-claim for unjust enrichment against the insolvent company is entitled to have it satisfied, whether by payment, set-off, or otherwise, instead of being left to prove in the liquidation as an unsecured creditor.

1.2. Pure Defences, Transaction-Related Cross-Claims and Unrelated Cross-Claims

As we shall see,[3] in the context of the avoidance provisions a fundamental distinction is to be drawn (1) between pure defences and cross-claims the defendant may have against the insolvent company for unjust enrichment, and (2) between cross-claims which are so related to the offending transaction or the property transferred under it that if they were not satisfied the company would be better off than if it had not entered into the offending transaction in the first place, and cross-claims that are not of this nature. The former, which include cross-claims for the purchase price paid by the defendant under the transaction and value subsequently added to the transferred property by improvements he has made, will be referred to hereafter as 'transaction-related cross-claims' and the latter as 'unrelated cross-claims'.[4] The significance of the distinction between these categories lies in the fact that, if it be the case that the statutory provisions are designed to restore the company to the position in which it would have been if it had not entered into the offending transaction, it is not consistent with that policy to allow pure defences that would ordinarily be available in the law of restitution or to give the defendant a right to payment of unrelated cross-claims. It is only if the cross-claim is a transaction-related cross-claim that the

---

[1] 'Avoidance' is here used in an extended sense to cover not only cases where the transaction is void or voidable but those where, though the transaction itself is valid, its effects may be reversed. For a detailed treatment of the statutory provisions see Roy Goode, *Principles of Corporate Insolvency Law* (3rd edn, 2005) ch 11, and John Armour and Howard Bennett (eds), *Vulnerable Transactions in Corporate Insolvency* (2003), an excellent collection of papers on the different statutory provisions. For an illuminating analysis of the rationale of the avoidance provisions, see Andrew Keay, *Avoidance Provisions in Insolvency Law* (1997) ch 3.

[2] Simone Degeling, 'Restitution for Vulnerable Transactions' in *Vulnerable Transactions in Corporate Insolvency* (above, n 1) ch 9.   [3] Below, 316.

[4] A claim for value added by improvements to property transferred is transaction-related not in the sense of forming part of the consideration for the transfer but in the sense that it enhances the subject-matter of the transfer.

liquidator's satisfaction of it is consistent with restoration of the status quo and, indeed, is necessary to avoid unjust enrichment of the insolvent company. By contrast, to allow a pure defence is to leave the value of the company's assets diminished by the offending transaction, while to pay an unrelated cross-claim is to reduce its assets to the detriment of the general body of creditors, in either case in breach of the statutory policy. Again, the issue of bad faith, which defeats a pure defence such as change of position, is irrelevant to a transaction-related cross-claim. So where a contract is rescinded for fraudulent misrepresentation, the defendant, in giving back what he has received under the contract, is entitled to have what he gave in return restored to him, despite his fraud.

> Though the defendant has been fraudulent, he must not be robbed, nor must the plaintiff be unjustly enriched, as he would be if he both got back what he had parted with and kept what he had received in return. The purpose of the relief is not punishment, but compensation.[5]

1.3. Pure Property Claims and Restitutionary Claims

It is further necessary to distinguish from the outset a pure property claim from a claim based on subtractive unjust enrichment. In the case of the former the claimant recovers his asset not because of any unjust enrichment of the defendant[6] but because the asset belonged to him prior to the subtraction and still belongs to him. The effect of the controversial decision of the House of Lords in *Foskett v McKeown*[7] that a proprietary claim to proceeds of the claimant's asset is itself a pure property claim, not a claim based on unjust enrichment,[8] imposes a further restriction on the scope of proprietary restitutionary claims, though some such

---

[5] *Spence v Crawford* [1939] 3 All ER 271, per Lord Wright at 288–9.

[6] Whether by subtractive enrichment, that is, enrichment by transfer from the claimant's estate, or by enrichment through a wrong, where the claim is not for the value lost by the claimant but for the giving up of benefits derived by an improper act in relation to the claimant, whether affecting his pre-existing property (as in the case of abuse of the claimant's intellectual property rights) or not, as where a company director procures for himself a benefit from a business opportunity which he ought, if he pursued it at all, to have pursued for his company. The distinction was first identified by Birks, *An Introduction to the Law of Restitution* (rev edn, 1989), forming a central plank of his taxonomy of restitution, though towards the end of his life he abandoned it, taking the position that restitution for wrongs did not belong to the law of unjust enrichment at all. See Birks, *Unjust Enrichment* (2nd edn, 2005) 21 ff, and the discussion by Andrew Burrows, *The Law of Restitution* (2nd edn, 2002) 25 ff, adhering to Birks's original position. For the purposes of this essay it is unnecessary to come down on one side or the other. For brevity the term 'unjust enrichment' is used to encompass both categories of restitution.   [7] [2001] 1 AC 102.

[8] The decision is controversial because it had been thought by many scholars that the idea that proceeds of the claimant's property are simply the property itself in a new form had been effectively exploded in Professor Lionel Smith's ground-breaking work *The Law of Tracing* (1997) in which he pointed out (at 15) that it is misleading to suggest that the subject of a tracing claim is the original asset in a new form, and that what is traced is not the thing itself but the value it represents. Strangely, though the idea was borrowed by Lord Millett in *Foskett v McKeown* [2001] 1 AC 102 at 128 in the course of a speech in which he referred on a different point to Professor Smith's monograph, he did not follow the logic of it.

claims remain, for example, proprietary restitution of profits derived from a wrong to the claimant, such as abuse of a fiduciary position, which is an equitable wrong. On the other hand, the claimant may be unable to pursue a proprietary claim, because the defendant no longer has the claimant's asset or its proceeds, or may choose to restrict himself to a purely personal claim requiring the defendant to give back or give up the money value of benefits which should have been received for the claimant. Such personal claims may be based either on subtractive unjust enrichment or on a wrong.[9] The distinction between pure property claims and claims based on subtractive unjust enrichment is significant because to the extent that defences such as estoppel, change of position, and bona fide purchase are peculiar to subtractive unjust enrichment claims[10] they are not available against a pure property claim,[11] though they are available against personal claims for subtractive unjust enrichment arising from improper receipts of or dealings in property.[12] It is doubtful, however, whether change of position is a defence to a claim for restitution for a wrong.[13]

This essay is concerned primarily with claims against and defences by the company's counterparty, not claims against and defences by third parties to whom that counterparty may have paid or transferred what he received from the company. However, the defence of bona fide purchase is concerned with indirect recipients, not with the original transferee.[14] An indirect recipient who is a bona fide purchaser for value will usually be protected, either under section 241(2) of the Insolvency Act 1986 or, in the case of a transfer of land or payment of money in cash or by transfer of funds to a bank account in his name, by virtue of an overriding legal title at common law[15] or even, where the claim against him is based on unjust enrichment rather than property, an equitable title.[16]

2. The Character of the Statutory Avoidance Provisions

The avoidance provisions of the Insolvency Act vary widely in scope and effect. Four different categories can be identified.

---

[9] See n 7 above. In some situations the claimant has a choice between basing his claim on subtractive enrichment, in which the defendant is required to give *back* what he received from the claimant, or on a wrong, in which he has to give *up* a benefit which is not necessarily derived from the claimant's pre-existing property right and which may be greater than the claimant's loss, on the basis that a wrongdoer ought not to profit from his wrongdoing. For the purpose of this essay, nothing turns on the distinction.

[10] Estoppel is a defence which may arise outside the law of unjust enrichment, for example, in contractual relations (promissory estoppel) or property (proprietary estoppel). Bona fide purchase appears to have a more extended meaning as a defence to a claim for unjust enrichment than it does as a defence to a property claim, where it is confined to a bona fide purchase of the legal title. See below, 314.   [11] *Foskett v McKeown* (above, n 7), per Lord Millett at 129.

[12] A point emphasized by Lord Millett extra-judicially in 'Proprietary Restitution' in S Degeling and J Edelman (eds), *Equity in Commercial Law* (2005) ch 12.

[13] Burrows (above, n 6) 524–7.   [14] Burrows (above, n 6) 91.   [15] See below, 314–5.

[16] See below, 314.

2.1. Provisions for Reversal of the Effect of the Transaction

In these cases the offending transaction is not itself made void; the court is simply given the power to reverse its effect so as to restore the company to the position in which it would have been if the transaction had not been made.[17] Into this category fall sections 238, 239, and 423 of the Act dealing respectively with transactions at an undervalue,[18] preferences,[19] and transactions defrauding creditors.[20] The statutory provisions are not self-executing; nothing happens unless the office-holder (liquidator or administrator) applies to the court for an order.[21] On application by the office-holder (ie liquidator or administrator), the court must 'make such order as it thinks fit for restoring the position to what it would have been if the company had not entered into that transaction'.[22] This general power is reinforced by a wide range of specific powers, including the power to order the vesting or revesting of property in the company, the payment of money to the company, the release or discharge of any security it has given and the revival of the obligations of a surety released or discharged by the transaction under review.[23] Here all the ingredients of a claim based on subtractive unjust enrichment are present. The recipient has made a gain, the gain has come about by subtraction from the company's assets, and it is 'unjust' in the sense that it offends against a policy of insolvency law that when a company has become

[17] Where the transaction involved the payment of money, the order will usually be for repayment; where it involved the transfer of property, the court may order either its retransfer or payment of its value at the time of the original transfer. In the latter case the proprietary effects of the original transaction remain undisturbed.

[18] In essence, cases where the company makes a gift or enters into a no-consideration transaction or one in which it pays significantly more than the value of what it receives or receives significantly less than the value of what it supplies.

[19] A company gives a preference to a person if that person is a creditor, a surety, or a guarantor and the company does anything or suffers anything to be done which has the effect of putting that person into a position which, in the event of the company going into insolvent liquidation, will be better than the position he would have been in if that thing had not been done. But the section does not apply unless, in giving the preference, the company was influenced by the desire to produce the above effect.

A payment by way of preference, unlike a transaction at an undervalue, does not reduce the net asset value of the company, for it reduces *pro tanto* the company's liabilities, leaving the net asset position unchanged. Its effect is simply to give one creditor more than his fair share of the assets at the expense of other creditors. But the statutory remedy is the same, namely to restore the status quo in order to ensure that all unsecured creditors share in the sum recovered.

[20] In contrast to the other provisions, s 423 applies whether or not the company is in liquidation and if it is not it may be invoked by the particular creditor deprived of access to the debtor company's assets.

[21] The provisions as to transactions at an undervalue and preferences apply only if the company enters into the transaction or gives the preference within a specified period ending with the onset of insolvency and was unable to pay its debts at the time of or in consequence of the transaction in question, neither of which conditions applies to the avoidance of transactions defrauding creditors.

[22] Insolvency Act 1986, s 238(3).

[23] ibid, s 241(1). The provisions of ss 238–41 apply without prejudice to the availability of any other remedy, even in relation to a transaction or preference which the company had no power to enter into or give (s 241(4)).

insolvent its assets should be preserved for the benefit of its creditors at large.[24] The statutory remedy is to restore the company's position to what it would have been if it had not entered into the transaction, and even if the court orders revesting of the identical property originally transferred this is by way of conferment of a new property right, not simply the vindication of the original title, so that the claim is not a pure property claim but reverses an unjust enrichment.

2.2. Provisions Rendering the Transaction Irretrievably Void

In other cases, the transaction is made void automatically without any action on the part of the office-holder but the consequences of invalidity are not spelled out and are left to rules of the common law, no power of validation being conferred on the court. Grounds of avoidance falling within this category are provided by section 245 of the Insolvency Act relating to the grant of a floating charge given otherwise than for a specified form of new value and within the relevant period prior to liquidation or administration[25] and section 395 of the Companies Act dealing with the failure to register a registrable charge. Where no steps have been taken to enforce the charge after the commencement of winding-up or administration[26] the question of remedies does not arise; the charge is invalidated and the erstwhile chargee is converted into an unsecured creditor. It is only if the chargee enforces the charge, for example, by repossession or realization, after it has become void, that the liquidator or administrator needs to pursue any claim, and this will usually be a pure property claim, not one based on unjust enrichment. Such a situation is in practice likely to be rare, so that these two provisions need not be further considered.

2.3. Post-petition Dispositions

Section 127 of the Insolvency Act invalidates any disposition of the company's property made after the commencement of a compulsory winding-up[27]unless the

---

[24] Peter Birks and Charles Mitchell, 'Unjust Enrichment' in Birks (ed), *English Private Law* (2000), vol II, para 15.173.

[25] The policy appears to be to ensure that the holder of the floating charge gives contemporaneous or subsequent value either in cash or in a form of benefit to the company which arises from day to day trading and has a readily ascertainable value (see Roy Goode, *Principles of Corporate Insolvency Law* (3rd edn, 2005) para 11–114). Since the relevant fact in the case of a permitted consideration is not the consideration itself but its value, the effect of s 245 is to require that the giving of the charge does not involve any reduction in the value of the assets available to the creditors at large.

[26] Until winding-up or administration, the charge remains valid against the company, and to the extent that it is enforced before one of these procedures intervenes, it ceases to be a security, so that its invalidity is of no consequence. See *Re Row Dal Construction Pty Ltd* [1966] VR 249, applied in *NV Slavenburg's Bank Ltd v Intercontinental Natural Resources Ltd* [1980] 1 All ER 955, a decision on what is now s 395 of the Companies Act 1985; *Mace Builders (Glasgow) Ltd v Lunn* [1987] Ch 191, a decision to similar effect on what is now s 245 of the Insolvency Act 1986. Where a charge is rendered void under s 395 the sum secured becomes immediately due and payable. It is not generally appreciated that this applies not only where the company goes into winding-up or administration but also where it grants a subsequent charge.

[27] Which in the case of a winding-up order relates back to the time of the petition on which the order was made (Insolvency Act 1986, s 129(2)).

disposition was authorized in advance or validated subsequently by the court. The purpose of the statutory provisions is to ensure that the creditors are paid *pari passu*[28] and to that end to prevent a diminution of the company's assets pending the hearing of the petition. Accordingly, while the section draws no distinction between dispositions made for full value and in the ordinary course of business and other dispositions and, indeed, gives no guidance of any kind as to the way in which the court should exercise its discretion, the courts have exercised the power of validation to ensure that transactions for full value are protected and that the defendant is not penalized further than is necessary to restore to the fund of assets available in the liquidation the amount of any loss.[29] So section 127 has in practice been applied to produce results very similar to those arising from orders under sections 238 and 239. In *Re Hollicourt (Contracts) Ltd v Bank of Ireland*[30] it was common ground that where section 127 applied the company's claim was 'restitutionary' in character[31] and in *Rose v AIB Group (UK)plc*[32] the judge, though holding that the defence of change of position was not available on the facts, did not rule out its application in principle.

Nevertheless section 127 is different in kind from sections 238 and 239 in two respects. First, it is not based on unjust enrichment but on preservation of assets. Unless the transaction is authorized or validated by the court, the defendant acquires no title under the disposition and has to give back the asset he received regardless of whether he was enriched by the transaction or gave full value, though in practice full-value transactions will usually be approved. Secondly, in contrast to the position under section 127, transactions caught by sections 238 and 239 sections are not void; it is left to the court to decide what measures are appropriate to reverse their detrimental effect. So orders under the latter sections are essentially restitutionary in character, whereas claims for the recovery of assets transferred under a disposition that is void under section 127 are pure property claims and are not based in unjust enrichment, though the position is otherwise where the liquidator pursues a purely personal remedy, for example, for repayment of money paid as a preference. Finally, whereas sections 238 and 241 together lay down in detail the court's remedial powers, section 127 merely renders the offending disposition void and says nothing about the consequences of the court's refusal to validate the disposition, these being left to be dealt with in accordance with common law rules. It is therefore necessary to deal separately with these two sets of provisions when we come to consider the availability of restitutionary defences.

---

[28] *Re Gray's Inn Construction Co Ltd* [1980] 1 All ER 814, per Buckley LJ at 819, 820; *Re J Leslie Engineers Co Ltd* [1976] 1 WLR 292, per Oliver J at 304.
[29] *Re Gray's Inn Construction Co Ltd*, above, per Buckley LJ at 822.   [30] [2001] Ch 555.
[31] See the judgment of Mummery LJ at para 22.
[32] [2003] 1 WLR 2791, *sub nom Re Tain Construction Ltd* discussed below, 312.

2.4. Extortionate Credit Transactions

A further category, distinctive in character, is the extortionate credit transaction.[33] This is neither invalid nor necessarily wholly reversible but may be set aside, wholly or in part, or simply varied, as the justice of the case requires.[34] It is a special case which needs no further consideration.

2.5. Conclusions on the Characterization of Claims under the Avoidance Provisions

It will be apparent from what has been said above that there is a sharp division between sections 238, 239, and 423 (relating respectively to transactions at an undervalue, preferences, and transactions defrauding creditors) on the one hand and section 127 (relating to post-petition dispositions)[35] on the other. The former do not nullify the offending transfer so as to vindicate an existing property right but merely empower the court to order return of the property, thereby creating a new property right, or to make a selection from a wide range of alternative forms of relief, including the payment of money, and in every case the objective is to restore the position to what it would have been if the company had not entered into the offending transaction. These provisions therefore fit into the unjust enrichment framework. By contrast, in the absence of validation by the court, section 127 applies even to dispositions for full value and simply renders the offending transfer void, leaving the consequences to be dealt with by the common law. While personal claims by the company, acting through the liquidator—for example for money had and received—may be analysed as reversing unjust enrichment, the recovery *in specie* of a transferred asset or its proceeds is a pure property claim not based on unjust enrichment.

These conclusions take us only so far. We still need to know whether and why it matters that claims under sections 238, 239, and 423 have the character of unjust enrichment claims while claims for the recovery of property disposed of in breach of section 127 do not. In particular we need the answers to two questions. Does the characterization affect the remedies available for breach of the statutory provisions? And does it influence the defences and cross-claims that are available to the defendant? Before answering these questions we need to examine the way in which the courts have approached the applicability of common law defences to claims based on statute.

---

[33] ibid, s 244.

[34] In addition to these provisions, ss 213 and 214 of the Insolvency Act empower the court to order directors of a company in liquidation who have caused it loss by fraudulent or improper trading to make such contribution (if any) to the company's assets as the court thinks proper. Since the measure of recovery is based on loss to the company, not benefit to the directors, ss 213 and 214 are not restitutionary and are not discussed.

[35] And to floating charges, but for the reason given above these will not be discussed further.

3. The General Approach to Common Law Defences to a Statutory Claim

Whether common law defences can be set up in answer to a statutory claim is a question that has arisen primarily in the context of the defences of estoppel and change of position, though it is also necessary to consider the defence of bona fide purchase, which has been held to be a defence distinct from that of change of position.[36] Estoppel is of little importance in the law of restitution, for the facts necessary to support it are rarely present and it has anyway been largely superseded by the broader defence of change of position. It is retained here only as a vehicle for a discussion of cases in which it has been invoked as a defence to a statutory claim.

In asserting a defence such as estoppel, change of position, or bona fide purchase in answer to a statutory claim, whether restitutionary or otherwise, there are at least three obstacles to be overcome. First, it might be said that where statute provides a remedy a party cannot be precluded from invoking it by some common law principle. For example, it might be argued that there can be no estoppel against a statute. Put in this way, the proposition is clearly too broad.[37] The question is 'whether the law that confronts the estoppel can be seen to represent a social policy to which the court must give effect in the interests of the public generally or some section of the public, despite any rules of evidence as between themselves that the parties may have created by their conduct or otherwise'.[38] Thus it has been held that a party cannot be estopped from relying on a provision of moneylending legislation to invalidate a transaction[39] but might be precluded by estoppel from asserting that a disposition of an interest in land is void for want of writing, since the requirement of writing 'does not have such an obviously social aim as statutory provisions relating to moneylenders . . .'.[40]

The other two obstacles are more formidable. The first is that whilst common law defences against a statute may be available in litigation between private parties where no others have an interest, it is quite another matter where the statutory provisions in question are concerned to protect the wider interests of the public or

---

[36] *Lipkin Gorman v Karpnale Ltd* [1991] 2 AC 548, per Lord Goff at 580–1.

[37] See generally J Andrews, 'Estoppels Against Statutes' (1996) 29 MLR 1.

[38] *Kok Hoong v Leong Cheong Kweng Mines Ltd* [1964] AC 993 at 1016.

[39] ibid. The most recent case in which estoppel against a statute was rejected is *Evans v Amicus Healthcare Ltd* [2005] Fam 1.

[40] *Yaxley v Gotts* [2000] Ch 162, per Robert Walker LJ at 175, applied in *Shah v Shah* [2002] QB 35. In the former case the judge at first instance applied the doctrine of proprietary estoppel to uphold a disposition not in writing, contrary to s 2 of the Law of Property (Miscellaneous Provisions) Act 1989. The Court of Appeal upheld the appeal on the ground of a constructive trust, applying s 2(5) of the Act, but considered that the judge was entitled to rely on proprietary estoppel as an alternative ground. See also *Actionstrength Ltd v International Glass Engineering IN.GL.EN. SpA* [2003] 2 AC 541.

a section of the public. In such cases neither estoppel nor change of position should be available as a defence. The court's task is to implement the policy of the statute. As we have seen, the insolvency avoidance provisions are designed to ensure *pari passu* distribution. To allow a defence such as estoppel or change of position would be to promote the interests of a particular party who had received a benefit to which he was not entitled over those of the general body of creditors whom the statute is designed to protect. The second objection is that where the statute itself contains detailed remedial provisions it is not open to the court to invoke common law rules to bypass the limitations which the statute embodies. This may be described as a particular application of the Occam's razor principle.[41]

3.1. Statutes Serving a Wider Public Policy[42]

The root decision precluding common law defences against a statute designed to promote a public interest rather than purely private rights between two parties is that of the Privy Council in *Maritime Electric Co Ltd v General Dairies Ltd*,[43] in which the appellants, a private company with a duty under the New Brunswick Public Utilities Act to make supplies of electricity at rates controlled by the statute, charged the respondents only one-tenth of the amount due from them because of an error in the meter-reading and sought to recover the balance due. The respondents pleaded estoppel in that they had acted in reliance on the correctness of the bills but this defence was rejected by the Privy Council, which held that estoppel did not avail against a statute enacted for the benefit of a section of the public and imposing a duty to that end—in the instant case, a duty to collect and receive payment in accordance with the law.

   And just as a duty of performance imposed by a statute enacted for the public interest cannot be excluded by estoppel, so also a body invested with a discretion under such a statute cannot be estopped from exercising it.[44]

   The public interest principle was similarly applied in *Kok Hoong v Leong Chong Kweng Mines Ltd*,[45] where it was held that a borrower could not be estopped *per rem judicatem* from invoking the provisions of the Malaysian Moneylenders Ordinance 1951 rendering the loan made to him irrecoverable.

---

[41] The so-called principle of parsimony that in explaining a phenomenon entities must not be needlessly multiplied.

[42] See generally Gareth Jones, Ch 4, this volume; Goff and Jones, *The Law of Restitution* (6th edn, 2002) paras 1–085 ff.

[43] [1937] AC 610. On very similar facts a contrary conclusion was reached by a majority of the Supreme Court of Canada in *Hydro Electric Commission of Kenora v Vacationland Dairy Co-operative Ltd* [1994] 1 SCR 80, a case on the differently worded Ontario Public Utilities Act. See also the decision of the Supreme Court of Newfoundland in *Social Services Appeal Board v Butler* (1996) 139 Nfld and PEIR 282, upholding a defence of change of circumstances in answer to a claim by the Department of Social Security for repayment of amounts overpaid in respect of social security benefits. Rather surprisingly, no reference was made to any of the above decisions.

[44] *Southend-on-Sea Corp v Hodgson (Wickford) Ltd* [1962] 1 QB 416.

[45] [1964] AC 993.

Delivering the opinion of the Privy Council, Viscount Radcliffe dealt with the estoppel plea in the following terms:

In their Lordships' opinion a more direct test to apply in any case such as the present, where the laws of moneylending or monetary security are involved, is to ask whether the law that confronts the estoppel can be seen to represent a social policy to which the court must give effect in the interests of the public generally or some section of the public, despite any rules of evidence as between themselves that the parties may have created by their conduct or otherwise. Thus the laws of gaming or usury ... override an estoppel: so do the provisions of the Rent Restriction Acts with regard to orders for possession of controlled tenancies ...

General social policy does from time to time require the denial of legal validity to certain transactions by certain persons. This may be for their own protection, as in the case of the infant or other category of persons enjoying what is to some extent a protected status, or for the protection of others who may come to be engaged in dealings with them, *as, for instance, the creditors of a bankrupt*. In all such cases there is no room for the application of another general and familiar principle of the law that a man may, if he wishes, disclaim a statutory provision enacted for his benefit, for what is for a man's benefit and what is for his protection are not synonymous terms. Nor is it open to the court to give its sanction to departures from any law that reflects such a policy, even though the party concerned has himself behaved in such a way as would otherwise tie his hands. (Emphasis added.)[46]

3.2. Statutes Containing Detailed Remedial Provisions

A separate ground for rejecting restitutionary defences at common law is that the relevant statute itself provides for the detailed working out of the consequences of an infringement of its provisions. This has been adverted to in several cases[47] and applies with particular force to sections 238, 239, and 423 of the Insolvency Act.[48] Against this background I turn to consider how the policies underlying the avoidance provisions of the Insolvency Act impact on the availability of common law defences to a restitutionary claim. Cross-claims based on unjust enrichment, even if asserted by way of defence, raise different considerations and are discussed in Section 4.

4. Are There Common Law Defences to Claims under the Insolvency Avoidance Provisions?

We have seen that sections 238, 239, and 423 of the Insolvency Act are distinct in character from section 127 in that they do not nullify offending transactions

---

[46] [1964] AC 993 at 1016–17.

[47] eg *Principal Group Ltd v Anderson*, below, n 54, para 8 ('part of a very detailed, closely interwoven statutory scheme'); *Rose v AIB Group (UK) plc*, above, n 57, para 41, contrasting s 127 with ss 238 and 239 ('Those sections provide express remedies to which the liquidator is entitled if certain conditions are satisfied; in the case of section 127, in contrast, no remedy is provided for recovery (where a validation order is not made) and the matter is left to the general law').

[48] See below, 310.

but provide for their reversal in order to restore the insolvent company to the status quo, whereas section 127 simply renders void dispositions made after the commencement of a compulsory winding-up unless authorized or validated by the court and says nothing about the consequences of invalidity, leaving these to be determined by the common law. These two sets of provisions therefore need to be considered separately.

4.1. Sections 238, 239, and 423

There has been no reported case dealing with the availability of common law restitutionary defences to applications by a liquidator under sections 238, 239, or 423. The question therefore has to be answered by reference to the policy underlying those provisions, which is clearly expressed in sections 238(3) and 423(2)(a) as 'restoring the position to what it would have been if the company had not entered into that transaction'. The purpose is, of course, to protect the creditors from the effects of a transaction which would be damaging to their interests, and the court has at its disposal a wide range of powers to achieve that objective. To allow a defence of estoppel or change of position would be to advantage one party, the defendant, at the expense of the creditors, in violation of the policy of the statute. Such defences cannot, therefore, be entertained. The defence of bona fide purchase stands in a somewhat different position because it is expressly provided for by sections 241(2) and 425(2), which, however, does not protect the counterparty to the transaction with the company, only a subsequent transferee in good faith and for value.[49] It is clear that in view of section 241(2) there is no scope for the common law defence of bona fide purchase, even if one were to assume that in the absence of section 241(2) there might have been circumstances in which the court could have applied it consistently with the policy of restoration of the company to the status quo.

Incompatibility with the policy of the statute is not the only ground for disallowing common law restitutionary defences. A further ground is that the court has not only a general power to order restoration to the status quo but specific powers providing for no fewer than seven different kinds of order. There is thus no place for, and no need to resort to, common law restitutionary defences to a claim under the above sections for restoration of value to the company. So defences such as estoppel and change of position cannot come into play, nor is there any scope for the common law defence of bona fide purchase for value, because section 241(2) lays down in detail the conditions in which a bona fide purchaser for value is protected.[50]

---

[49] There is a presumption against good faith in the circumstances set out in s 241(2A)–(3C).

[50] Counter-restitution, though sometimes described as a defence, is best viewed as a cross-claim which may in certain circumstances be asserted defensively. It is discussed in the next section.

4.2. Section 127

As we have seen, section 127 is merely an invalidating provision and does not prescribe any remedies consequent upon avoidance. These are left to the common law and typically take the form either of an order for recovery of the property that is the subject of the offending disposition or its proceeds[51] or, where money was paid over and has been spent, an order for repayment in a claim for money had and received. To what extent are purely passive defences[52] available to a claim for recovery of property disposed of in breach of section 127? We consider first the defence of change of position. Bona fide purchase raises distinct considerations which need to be addressed separately. Estoppel, which in this context is of little significance, is governed by the same considerations as apply to change of position and is not further discussed.

Change of Position

The reference to creditors of a bankrupt in the decision of the Privy Council in *Kok Hoong v Leong Chong Kweng Mines Ltd*[53] presaged two Canadian cases directly on the issue. In *Principal Group Ltd v Anderson*[54] the facts were as follows. Almost six years after the Principal Group became bankrupt, the trustee in bankruptcy brought proceedings for the recovery of payments made to the company's former employees on the ground that these constituted fraudulent preferences and were void under section 95(1) of the Canadian Bankruptcy and Insolvency Act 1985. The defendants did not dispute this but contended that they had changed their position in reliance on the payments for spending the money on poor investments or other forms of expenditure which they would not have incurred but for the payments to them. This defence was rejected by the Alberta Court of Appeal in Bankruptcy, which, applying the *Maritime Electric* decision, held that the duty of the trustee was to treat all creditors equally and pay them pro rata, and for that purpose to collect in money paid and property transferred under transactions that sought to avoid the statute. There was accordingly no place for the defence of change of position. The point was succinctly made in the following passage of the court's judgment:

... it cannot be doubted that the Act imposes in the clearest and most express and elaborate terms duties upon a trustee in bankruptcy of treating all the creditors equally and seeing that they are all paid pro rata. All the provisions of that Act interlock closely. Section 95 and similar anti-avoidance sections are very detailed backstops to that scheme.

---

[51] Alternatively the liquidator could ask for an account and payment of profits made by the defendant from the use or investment of an asset which *ex hypothesi* did not belong to him.

[52] That is, defences which do not involve the assertion of a cross-claim for unjust enrichment used defensively. The latter are considered in the next section.

[53] [1964] AC 993 at 1016. See above, 309.

[54] (1997) 147 DLR (4th) 229, also *sub nom Re Ernst and Young Inc.*

The Act does more than forbid preferences and allow a suit to recover them. It makes
such payments fraudulent and void: s. 95(1). If they are void, then no property passed,
and the payees are in possession of some of the bankrupt's property. The duty of the
trustee to collect the property of the bankrupt is elementary . . . The whole idea of the
defence of change of position is that the equity lies with the payee and not with the payor
who wants to get back his payment. But where a trustee in bankruptcy carries out a duty
to undo a fraudulent payment, it is difficult to say that change of position makes the
trustee's suit inequitable.[55]

A similar decision was given by the Alberta Court of Queen's Bench in *Re Titan
Investments Ltd Partnership*.[56] These cases are directly relevant to claims by the
liquidator for recovery of assets transferred in breach of section 127 because they
involved statutory rules as to preference which, like section 127 but unlike
section 239, rendered the offending transaction wholly void.

However, in England there has been a more equivocal approach to change
of position as a defence in the context of insolvency. *Rose v AIB Group (UK)
plc*[57] is a case in point. The liquidator of Tain Construction Ltd sought a
declaration that a payment made to the defendant bank was void under section
127 of the Act. The bank pleaded change of position resulting from reliance
on the liquidator's conduct and argued that the court should make a validation
order, since to refuse it would be pointless as it would simply give rise to a
claim for restitution by the liquidator to which change of position was a
defence. Mr Nicholas Warren QC, sitting as a Deputy High Court Judge, held
that the defence was not available to the bank, first, because section 127 was
there to validate transactions which are or may be for the benefit of the
creditors generally, not to provide a remedy for errors on the part of the
liquidator; and, secondly, because the bank was aware, at the time it received
the payment, that it risked being vulnerable to a claim under section 127.

Significantly, however, the judge did not accept the argument advanced on
behalf of the liquidator that as a matter of principle there was no room for the
defence of change of position in the context of section 127. After noting the wide
terms in which the change of position defence had been articulated by Lord Goff
in *Lipkin Gorman v Karpnale Ltd*[58] he made the following comment on the
decision in *Principal Group Ltd v Anderson*:

I find that case of little help. It concerns a provision significantly different from section
127, that section containing as it does the power for the court to validate transactions.
Further, there is no discussion of the relevant restitutionary principles, nor did the court
even refer to the *Lipkin Gorman* case . . .

---

[55] ibid at 233–4.   [56] [2005] AJ No 141, 2005 ABQB 637.
[57] [2003] 1 WLR 2791, *sub nom Re Tain Construction Ltd* [2003] 2 BCLC 374.
[58] [1991] 2 AC 548 at 580: '. . . I do not wish to state the principle any less broadly than this: that
the defence is available to a person whose position has so changed that it would be inequitable in all
the circumstances to require him to make restitution, or alternatively to make restitution in full'.

Attractively as the argument was presented by Mr Prentis, I do not consider that change of position can be entirely ruled out as a possible way of resisting a claim for repayment by a liquidator. It seems to me that the question of validation of a disposition is distinct from the question of actual recovery if the disposition is not validated. I do not see why the defence should not be available where, for instance, a creditor did not know and could not have known (because it had not yet been advertised) of the existence of the petition. After all, in other cases where payments can be treated as void or ultra vires, it is commonplace that restitution is available subject to restitutionary defences. The purpose behind the discretion conferred on the court to validate a disposition is not the same as the purpose of the change of position defence, albeit that both are based on an over-arching concept of fairness. The former is directed principally at achieving a pari passu distribution of assets whilst permitting transactions which are, or are likely to be, of benefit to the company to take place; the latter is an inherent qualification to the right of restitution and which, in its very nature, will be detrimental to the company and distort the pari passu distribution of assets.

It is not easy to follow this reasoning, which seems to lead to a diametrically opposite conclusion that supports the Canadian decisions. One would have thought that if the defence of change of position was unavailable even in relation to a statutory provision which gave the court no power of validation or adjustment, then *a fortiori* it should not be available where the court is given a power to validate the offending transaction, for if, as the judge rightly said, the change of position defence is one which in its very nature is detrimental to the company and distorts the *pari passu* distribution of assets, that is surely a compelling ground for rejecting it. Indeed, it serves only to emphasize the point that the policy underlying the court's power of validation under section 127 has nothing to do with the factors relevant to restitutionary defences; the question in each case is whether the transaction under attack was reasonably conceived as being for the company's benefit.[59] The point has been succinctly made in relation to the avoidance provisions generally by Dr Duncan Sheehan:

However, if the integrity of the insolvency regime is not to be undermined it must itself provide for the circumstances when dispositions are effective. Rules outside the regime should have no effect. The insolvency regime does provide a means for deciding when payments cannot be recovered, one which generally requires a benefit to all creditors. To introduce change of position is to bypass this statutory scheme and to benefit one party over others—precisely what insolvency regimes lean against. That it is hard on the recipient is unfortunately irrelevant.[60]

So change of position not adding value to the company or its property—for example, the gift of money to a charity which was only made possible because of the disposition—cannot be entertained as a defence, because it undermines the policy of section 127, which is to protect creditors by restoring lost value to the

---

[59] *Re Park Ward & Co* [1926] Ch 828.
[60] Duncan Sheehan, 'Change of position in insolvency' [2004] CLJ 41 at 43.

insolvent company. Change of position is in any event a defence peculiar to a claim in unjust enrichment; it is not available as an answer to a pure property claim,[61] which must be determined by ordinary rules of property law.

Bona Fide Purchase

What of the defence of bona fide purchase? The first point to note is that in relation to section 127, as under section 241 and under the general law of unjust enrichment, this defence does not avail the party to the offending transaction with the company. Even if the legal title is transferred by the company to a bona fide purchaser for value, this is not a defence; it has been held that while the disposition is effective to convey the legal title, the purchaser takes it as bare trustee for the company, which in the absence of a validation order is entitled to have it retransferred and to call for an account of any profit derived from it,[62] albeit with a countervailing duty to repay the price paid by the purchaser.

What is the position of a bona fide purchaser from the company's transferee? It is unfortunate that in most of the literature and case-law in which the defence of bona fide purchase is discussed, it is not made clear whether *any* bona fide purchase for value suffices or whether, in accordance with general principles of property law, it must be a purchase of the legal title. In other words, is there a defence of bona fide purchase which is peculiar to the law of unjust enrichment and which protects a purchaser of an equitable interest? That would appear to be the unspoken assumption among restitution lawyers.[63] If this be correct the nature of the claim for return of property disposed of in breach of section 127 is highly relevant. Since it is a pure property claim, not a claim in unjust enrichment, it would violate a fundamental priority rule in the law of property if a purchaser from the company's transferee acquiring only an equitable interest[64] were allowed to assert that interest as displacing the legal title of the company. A bona fide purchaser for value of the legal title from the company's transferee *would* acquire an overriding title, not, however, because of the restitutionary

---

[61] See above, 301.

[62] *Re French's (Wine Bar) Ltd* [1987] BCLC 499, per Vinelott J at 505. Despite this decision it is thought that in general legal title even to land cannot pass under a void disposition. For a comprehensive survey of the cases on the effect of the relation back doctrine in bankruptcy see the judgment of Millett LJ in *Re Dennis* [1996] Ch 80, and see in particular *Re Gunsbourg* [1920] 2 KB 426, where it was held that on invalidation the trustee in bankruptcy could sue a person in possession of the property under the transfer in trover or detinue, which can only be because the possessor was retrospectively divested of legal title in favour of the trustee, and *Doe d Lloyd v Powell* (1826) 5 B & C 308, in which a conveyance by the debtor of all real and personal property for the benefit of his creditors was held to be an act of bankruptcy which on bankruptcy supervening became retrospectively null and void. It would be otherwise in the case of a statutory provision which merely declared the *contract* void, because this would not affect the transfer later carried out by the independent act of conveyance. The key factor in the *French's (Wine Bar)* case appears to have been that the assignee of the lease had been registered as the proprietor in the Land Registry.

[63] This is the view of Burrows (above, n 6, at 590 n 15), one of the few authors to discuss the question.

[64] eg because the interest acquired by the company's transferee was only equitable.

defence of bona fide purchase but because of the priority rules of the law of property.[65] Similarly the nullity of the disposition under section 127 does not affect the operation of other exceptions to the *nemo dat* rule. Money, for example, has always been regarded as a special case because of its character as currency, which means that once it reaches the hands of a bona fide recipient for value he acquires title even if the money was originally stolen.[66] Likewise if a negotiable instrument is issued to a creditor by the company after the commencement of winding-up and is then negotiated to one who takes as a holder in due course under section 29 of the Bills of Exchange Act 1882, the holder acquires a good title despite the fact that his transferor had no title to convey.[67]

Thus while exceptions to the *nemo dat* rule, whether at common law or by statute, continue to be available even where a disposition has been avoided under section 127, in other cases the title of the company must be respected in order to avoid the undermining of established priority rules in the law of property. But in these cases there is a still more important reason for rejecting bona fide purchase as a defence to a claim under section 127, namely that, as in the case of change of position, no value is given back by the defendant to the company, so that to allow the defence would leave the company to continue to suffer the very detriment which section 127 is designed to negate.

5. Cross-Claims Based on Unjust Enrichment of the Company

We have seen that merely passive restitutionary defences that would be available at common law cannot be asserted in answer to a claim by the liquidator under the statutory provisions, either because those provisions themselves lay down the circumstances in which the court is precluded from making an order on the liquidator's application, as is the case with sections 238, 239, and 423 of the Insolvency Act, or because to allow the defence would be to deprive the company of an asset to the detriment of creditors, whom the provisions are designed to protect.

Cross-claims for unjust enrichment, on the other hand, raise different considerations because they are based on the giving of value to the company.

[65] In *Foskett v McKeown* [2001] 1 AC 102 Lord Millett, after observing that a claim to trace into proceeds was a pure property claim, contrasted this with a claim in unjust enrichment and stated (at 129): 'Furthermore, a claim in unjust enrichment is subject to a change of position defence, which usually operates by reducing or extinguishing the element of enrichment. An action like the present is subject to the bona fide purchaser for value defence, which operates to clear the defendant's title.' It is thought that his lordship must have meant a bona fide purchaser of the legal title, for in property law one who acquires merely an equitable interest is usually subordinate both to the holder of a legal title and to the holder of a prior equitable interest.
[66] *Miller v Race* (1758) 1 Burr 452, per Lord Mansfield at 457. See generally *Mann on the Legal Aspect of Money* (ed C Proctor) (6th edn, 2005).
[67] Bills of Exchange Act 1882, s 54.

Cross-claims may be asserted defensively by way of set-off, where both claims are in money or are reducible to money or, where they are not, may be made as counterclaims.

The defendant is, of course, a creditor as regards such cross-claims and is entitled to lodge a proof for them in the winding-up, but given the fact that ordinary unsecured creditors almost invariably fare badly in the distribution stakes, the ability to lodge a proof is likely to be of little comfort to him. The essential question is whether he can bypass competition from other creditors by having his cross-claim satisfied by the liquidator, whether by payment, set-off, or as a condition of the liquidator's right to an order under the statutory provisions in question, instead of being left to prove as an unsecured creditor. It is here that the distinction previously drawn between transaction-related and unrelated cross-claims[68] becomes of crucial importance.

It will be recalled that a transaction-related cross-claim is one so related to the transaction or to the property acquired under it that its satisfaction by the liquidation is necessary if the insolvent company is not to be unjustly enriched by recoveries under the statutory provisions. Two types of claim fall within this category. First, there is the value of any benefits conferred on the company by the defendant as consideration for the property and other rights acquired under the offending transaction. Examples are the purchase price paid for the property and the grant of a loan or the discharge of liabilities of the company which were assumed by the defendant as part of the deal. The second type of transaction-related cross-claim is for the value added to the property transferred by improvements made by the defendant.[69] If the court is asked to make an order under section 238 revesting property in the company *in specie* and the defendant has increased its value by making improvements, then in exercise of its general power under section 238(3) the court can either order payment of the unimproved value of the property or order its retransfer as it stands but direct the liquidator to pay the defendant the amount of value added by the improvement. The same considerations apply to orders in respect of property transferred by way of preference.[70]

In all these cases the application of common law principles of restitution follows the policy of the statute, which is to preserve the value of the assets as it

---

[68] Above, 300.
[69] *Greenwood v Bennett* [1973] QB 195. The benefit necessary to establish a claim or cross-claim for unjust enrichment is assumed where the defendant's acts were requested by the company or bargained for or possibly if, though they were not, they were freely accepted, though the principle of free acceptance is controversial, see Burrows, (n 6 above, 20, 402). None of these cases will usually apply in the situation under discussion; instead, the defendant may show that the benefit is 'incontrovertible', which in the case of value added to property generally means that the value has been realized, eg by sale of the property, or that it is otherwise indisputable. See generally Burrows (above, n 6) 18–20.
[70] See Andrew Keay, 'The Recovery of Voidable Preferences: Aspects of Restoration' in Francis Rose (ed) *Restitution and Insolvency*, ch 13.

was at the time of the winding-up petition, not to put the company in a better position than it would have been if it had not entered into the offending transaction. The statutory provisions are no bar to such a claim, which is outside the statute altogether.[71] Where, for example, securities are transferred under a disposition that is void under section 127, the purchaser must give up the securities, which do not belong to him, but is entitled to counterclaim[72] for repayment of the price as paid on a total failure of consideration, and the fact that the claim against him is a pure property claim is irrelevant. The same is true of other value he has furnished, for example the discharge of the company's liabilities pursuant to the void transaction or expenditure he has incurred in improving the property, to the extent of the value added by such expenditure. Payment of his claim in these cases does not reduce the value of the company's assets below what they were immediately prior to the offending disposition, it merely prevents the company from unjustly retaining a benefit which but for the transaction it would never have received.

To be contrasted with transaction-related cross-claims are cross-claims which are not related either to the transaction or to the property. For example, if the defendant made a loan to the company prior to his entry into the transaction and not as part of it or made a loan subsequent to the transaction but independently of it rather than as part of the agreed consideration, he is not entitled to repayment ahead of other creditors but must prove in competition with them in the winding-up. To pay his claim would unfairly promote him over other creditors. This is true even of unrelated cross-claims which are themselves based on unjust enrichment. For example, if the defendant, prior to the making of the offending transaction, had bought goods from the company to which, as he later discovered, it had no title, he has a personal claim for money paid on a total failure of consideration, but though this is based on unjust enrichment it does not qualify for payment, for again this would be to the detriment of other creditors. The acid test is whether the benefit received by the company is one which it would not have received but for its entry into the offending transaction. If this is the case, it must pay or give credit for the value of the benefit in order to achieve the statutory objective of restoring the status quo. The position is otherwise if it received the benefit independently of the transaction.

---

[71] See *North Central Wagon and Finance Co Ltd v Brailsford* [1962] 1 All ER 502, applying *Davies v Rees* (1886) 17 QBD 408 and *Bradford Advance Co Ltd v Ayers* [1924] WN 152, in which it was held that where a bill of sale securing a loan of money was void under the Bills of Sale Acts, not only as to the security but also as to the personal covenants for payment contained in it, the lender was nevertheless entitled to recover the money lent with reasonable interest as money had and received.

[72] Where the liquidator's claim is a money claim, the defendant may also use his cross-claim as a set-off. But set-off is not available against a proprietary claim. See Goode (above, n 1) paras 8.24, 8.27–8.28.; Rory Derham, *The Law of Set-Off* (3rd edn, 2003) ch 9.

The working out of these principles varies according to whether the liquidator's claim is based on sections 238, 239, or 423 on the one hand or section 127 on the other.

5.1. Claims under Sections 238, 239, and 423

In relation to claims by the liquidator under sections 238, 239, and 423, transaction-related cross-claims are automatically accommodated by the statutory requirement that the order should be such as the court thinks fit for restoring the position to what it would have been if the company had not entered into the transaction. So in _Phillips v Brewin Dolphin Bell Lawrie Ltd_[73] the House of Lords, varying the order made by the High Court and Court of Appeal, directed that where the defendant who had received the benefit of a transaction at an undervalue had made a loan to the company which it would not have made but for its entry into the transaction, the court, in reversing the effect of the transaction and ordering return of the value of benefits received from the company, should exercise its power under section 238(3) to order the liquidator to give credit for the amount of the loan with interest.[74] Thus the cross-claim in cases within sections 238, 239, and 423 owes nothing to the common law of unjust enrichment; it is inherent in the court's duty to exercise its powers in furtherance of the statutory objective of restoring the status quo.

5.2. Claims under Section 127

The position here is somewhat different. As we have seen, section 127 says nothing about the consequences of the invalidity of a disposition not authorized or ratified by the court. These are left to the common law. It follows that cross-claims for recovery of the price or other consideration for the disposition and for the value added by improvements to the property transferred fall fairly and squarely within the law of unjust enrichment. There is, however, at least one qualification of the normal rules. Just as change of position cannot be invoked by the transferee as a defence to the company's claim based on invalidity of the disposition, so also a cross-claim by the transferee for repayment of money paid as consideration for the transfer or for the value added to the property transferred cannot be defeated by a plea of change of position by the company, for this would leave the company with both the property and the price paid for it. This would not only be inequitable but would undermine the policy of section 127, which is to ensure that the company is neither worse off nor better off than it would have been if the disposition had not been made.

[73] [2001] 1 WLR 143.
[74] In calculating the amount of undervalue, the judge at first instance had given credit for the amount of redundancy payments discharged by the defendant as part of the transaction and this was not in dispute on appeal.

6. Conclusions

From the foregoing analysis the following conclusions may be drawn:

(1) The statutory avoidance provisions embodied in sections 238, 239, and 423 of the Insolvency Act 1986 are designed to reverse unjust enrichment, but they are driven by a specific policy, namely the restoration of value to the company for the benefit of its creditors, that overrides the standard rules governing unjust enrichment. So defences such as estoppel and change of position that might be available against a solvent company cannot be utilized, because this would be to give the defendant an advantage to the detriment of other creditors, contrary to the policy of the Act. Moreover, those provisions confer on the court wide powers as to the orders it can make to restore the company to the position existing before the making of the offending transaction, and also have special rules for the protection of indirect purchasers, so that they leave no scope for common law defences or cross-claims.

(2) By contrast with sections 238, 239, and 423, section 127 is concerned with the preservation of the company's assets as they existed at the time of presentation of the winding-up petition and says nothing about what is to happen if the court refuses to validate a disposition made in breach of the section. That is left to the common law and paves the way for a proprietary claim by the liquidator for recovery *in specie* of the asset disposed of in breach of the section or its proceeds or alternatively a personal claim (1) for the value of the asset where its proceeds have been dissipated or (2) where the asset was money paid as a preference, for repayment, or (3) for an account and payment of profits derived from wrongdoing, for example, use or investment of assets which *ex hypothesi* never belonged to the defendant. Defences such as estoppel, change of position, or bona fide purchase, which might be available against a solvent company, cannot be invoked, for their application would give an advantage to the disponee at the expense of creditors, contrary to the policy of the statute. Where the liquidator pursues a proprietary claim, restitutionary defences are barred on the additional ground that they may not be invoked against a claim which is based on property rather than unjust enrichment. Any defence must therefore be based on some common law or statutory exception to the *nemo dat* rule.

(3) In sum, the common law rules of unjust enrichment have no role to play in relation to the avoidance provisions of the Insolvency Act except as regards transaction-related cross-claims by the defendant, that is, claims for (1) the value of any consideration furnished by him under the offending transaction, whether in the form of payment of a price or the assumption and discharge of liabilities of the insolvent company or the making of any other payments on its behalf, or any combination of these or (2) the value added by the defendant's improvements to property of which the liquidator seeks recovery. The defendant is entitled to have

such cross-claims satisfied, whether by way of payment, set-off, or otherwise, and is not restricted to proving in the winding-up in competition with other creditors. This is because the satisfaction of such cross-claims accords with the policy of the avoidance provisions of the Insolvency Act, which is to restore the status quo existing immediately prior to the offending transaction, leaving the insolvent company neither worse off nor better off than it would have been if it had not entered into the transaction in the first place, whereas failure to satisfy the defendant's cross-claim would result in unjust enrichment of the company.

PART II

THE COMPARATIVE LAW OF UNJUST ENRICHMENT AND RESTITUTION

17

Restitution after Termination for Breach of Contract: German Law after the Reform of 2002

Reinhard Zimmermann[*]

1. Introduction

Peter Birks was very interested in German law and legal culture. He often came to Freiburg, Regensburg, and other German universities for lectures, seminars, and study visits. He inspired countless German postgraduates to engage in comparative work, and he welcomed their contributions to his famous restitution courses in Oxford and London. A few years ago, he asked me to address his students on the topic of restitution after termination for breach of contract in German law. That lecture was subsequently published in the Restitution Law Review.[1] The BGB's set of rules entitled 'termination', but effectively dealing with the consequences of termination (§§ 346 ff BGB), used to be one of the most unsatisfactory parts of the German law of obligations.[2] Just about everybody writing on the subject has quoted Ernst von Caemmerer's indictment that the respective rules were bungled, from the point of view of legal drafting, and highly questionable, as far as legal policy is concerned: with the result that they had given rise to an almost impenetrable jungle of disputes.[3] A fundamental reform was very widely regarded

---

[*] Director, Max Planck Institute of Comparative and International Private Law, Hamburg.

[1] 'Restitution after Termination for Breach of Contract in German Law', 1997 Restitution LR 13 ff. The same topic has been dealt with by G Dannemann, 'Restitution for Termination of Contract in German Law', in F Rose (ed), *Failure of Contracts* (1997), 129 ff, and T Krebs, *Restitution at the Crossroads: A Comparative Study* (2001) 89 ff.

[2] See eg Bundesminister der Justiz (ed), *Abschlußbericht der Kommission zur Überarbeitung des Schuldrechts* (1992) 178.

[3] '. . . gesetzestechnisch so mißglückt und in zentralen Fragen auch rechtspolitisch so fragwürdig und umstritten, daß ein für Theorie und Praxis kaum noch zu durchdringendes Dickicht von Streitfragen und Thesen entstanden ist': E von Caemmerer, ' "Mortuus redhibetur": Bemerkungen zu den Urteilen BGHZ 53, 144 und 57, 137' in *Festschrift für Karl Larenz* (1973) 625.

as necessary. It was eventually effected as part and parcel of the so-called Modernization of the German Law of Obligations and became law on 1 January 2002.[4] Since Peter would almost certainly have wanted me to report, and comment, on the new rules on restitution after termination for breach of contract, I will use the present opportunity to do so. This essay, therefore, constitutes no more than a sequel to the earlier one. At the same time, for me, it revives the memory of an old and treasured friendship.[5]

2. The Shadow of History

That the rules on termination for breach of contract (including the pertinent restitution regime) in the BGB of 1896/1900 were so unsatisfactory, appears to have much to do with the fact that they were of very recent origin. Nineteenth century pandectist legal doctrine still adhered to the principle of Roman law that a contract could not unilaterally be brought to a premature end, even in cases of breach of contract.[6] The aggrieved party was limited to a claim for damages. If one party was to be granted a right of termination, a specific provision to that effect had to be included in the contract. In the case of *mora debitoris*, a narrowly circumscribed exception came to be recognized in the course of the nineteenth century,[7] but it was only the draftsmen of the BGB who made the fundamental break with traditional doctrine.[8] Conceptually, it was the *lex commissoria* that stood at the cradle of this development.[9] As a result, the BGB of 1896/1900 used to refer to its provisions on the *conventional* right of termination when it dealt with the (newly recognized) *statutory* right of termination.[10] The Code, in a way, still looked at a statutory right of termination as if it had been tacitly agreed upon. This created a number of difficulties in that it was never quite clear to what extent the rules on the conventional right of termination were really suitable for application to statutory rights of termination. Thus, to mention but

---

[4] 'Gesetz zur Modernisierung des Schuldrechts of 26 November 2001' (2001) I *Bundesgesetzblatt* 3138. As a result, the German Civil Code (BGB) was re-promulgated on 2 January 2002: *Bundesgesetzblatt* (2002) I, 42. The text of the new provisions with a parallel English translation is available in the German Law Archive, http://www.iuscomp.org./gla/. For a discussion, see R Zimmermann, *The New German Law of Obligations: Historical and Comparative Perspectives* (2005).

[5] R Zimmermann, 'Peter Birks und die Privatrechtswissenschaft in England' (2004) *Juristenzeitung* 1064 ff.

[6] See eg B Windscheid and T Kipp, *Lehrbuch des Pandektenrechts* (9th edn, 1906) § 321, 2; and see now A Thier, in M Schmoeckel, J Rückert, and R Zimmermann (eds), *Historisch-kritischer Kommentar zum BGB* (vol II, in preparation) §§ 346–59: 'Rücktritt und Widerruf', n 24.

[7] Windscheid and Kipp (n 6) § 280 n 1; *HKK*/Thier (n 6) n 24. On the development in nineteenth century commercial law, see KO Scherner, *Rücktrittsrecht wegen Nichterfüllung: Untersuchungen zur deutschen Privatrechtslehre der Neuzeit* (1965) 157 ff; *HKK*/Thier (n 6) n 26.

[8] For a detailed discussion, see HG Leser, *Der Rücktritt vom Vertrag* (1975) 26 ff; *HKK*/Thier (n 6) nn 27 ff.   [9] Leser (n 8) 16 ff; *HKK*/Thier (n 6) nn 24, 26, 27 ff.

[10] § 327 BGB (old version). On the problems associated with this rule, see [1997] RLR 15 f (with references).

one example, § 351 I BGB (old version) used to exclude the right of termination if the party who was entitled to terminate was to blame for the destruction, significant deterioration, or impossibility of returning what he had received. 'Is to blame' (*verschuldet hat*) refers to the two general modes of fault specified in § 276 I BGB, that is, deliberate and negligent behaviour. The attribution of fault is not particularly difficult in situations involving a conventional right of termination. Admittedly, the recipient is dealing with an object that has been transferred to him on the basis of a valid contract. But that contract was concluded subject to a right of termination and he should have realized that a situation might arise where he would have to return what he had received. It is scarcely remarkable if the law requires him to be diligent. Matters are different, however, when we look at statutory rights of termination. Here the party terminating can hardly anticipate the breach of contract committed by the other party, and no one can therefore blame him if he deals with the object received as any owner is entitled to deal with his property: he may even intentionally destroy it. Fault, therefore, appears to be an awkward criterion for determining whether or not the right to termination is excluded.[11]

German courts and legal writers also had to operate in the long shadow cast by legal history in another respect. The provisions contained in §§ 346 ff BGB of 1896/1900 were based on an amalgamation of the rules concerning the *lex commissoria* and the *actio redhibitoria*.[12] The *actio redhibitoria* was a remedy available to purchasers of defective slaves or cattle in order to demand repayment of the price against the return of what they had bought.[13] Strangely, however, they were even able to claim back the purchase price if the slave or animal had died. *Mortuus redhibetur* is the famous tag extracted from the sources.[14] It is a fiction with which the Roman jurists operated in cases of restitution under the *actio redhibitoria*.[15] The situation had to be treated *as if* the purchaser had been able to return the (living) slave or animal. On that supposition, however, he was able to claim back his purchase price even though the slave had in fact died and could not be returned. Effectively, therefore, the risk that the object of the sale has perished was placed on the shoulders of the seller. The question why the Roman lawyers employed this fiction, and with it the strange risk regime, has not

[11] For an overview of how the notion of 'fault' was interpreted in terms of § 351 BGB (old version), see K Larenz, *Lehrbuch des Schuldrechts* (vol I, 14th edn, 1987) 408 ff; F Janßen, in *Münchener Kommentar zum Bürgerlichen Gesetzbuch* (vol II, 4th edn, 2001) § 351, nn 5 ff; H Heinrichs, in *Palandt, Bürgerliches Gesetzbuch* (61st edn, 2002) § 351, nn 3 f; and see K Herold, *Das Rückabwicklungsschuldverhältnis aufgrund vertraglichen oder gesetzlichen Rücktritts* (2001) 96 ff; P Hellwege, *Die Rückabwicklung gegenseitiger Verträge als einheitliches Problem* (2004) 25 f; *HKK*/Thier (n 6) n 39.

[12] See the analysis by Leser (n 8) 26 ff, 286 ff (summary); *HKK*/Thier (n 6) nn 27 ff.

[13] For details, see R Zimmermann, *The Law of Obligations: Roman Foundations of the Civilian Tradition* (paperback edn 1996) 311 ff.

[14] See Paul, D.21.1.47; Pomponius, D.21.1.48 pr.; Ulpian, D.21.1.31.5 and 6; Ulpian, D.21.1.31.24; Ulpian, D.21.1.38.3.

[15] For a more detailed discussion, see *Law of Obligations* (n 13) 330 ff; *HKK*/Thier (n 6) nn 13 ff.

yet found a satisfactory answer.[16] None the less, it was perpetuated, in a generalized form, in § 350 BGB of 1896/1900. This rule was destined to become one of the main areas of contention under the old law.[17]

3. Foundations

Under the new 2002 law, some very basic propositions concerning termination after breach of contract remain unchanged. Termination is effected by informal, unilateral declaration to the other party.[18] Unlike rescission (*Anfechtung*), termination (*Rücktritt*)[19] does not lead to a situation where the contract is treated as never having been made.[20] The contract merely undergoes a transformation. No longer does it aim at implementing what was contractually agreed; it aims, instead, at unwinding the relationship between the parties.[21] Since this winding-up relationship is conceived to be of a contractual nature, §§ 346 ff BGB are regarded as restitution rules *sui generis* rather than as modified enrichment claims.[22] For the law of unjustified enrichment can only be resorted to if a transfer has been made 'without legal ground'[23]—which would mean, in the

---

[16] It has been suggested that *mortuus redhibetur* was restricted, in classical law, to cases where the purchaser lost the slave due to the defect which gave rise to the *actio redhibitoria*; see H Honsell, 'Von den ädilizischen Rechtsbehelfen zum modernen Sachmängelrecht' in *Gedächtnisschrift für Wolfgang Kunkel* (1984) 61; P Mader, 'Mortuus redhibetur?' (1984) 101 ZSS 206 ff. This is the position adopted, *mutatis mutandis*, in the French and Italian codes (Article 1647 *Code civil*; Article 1492(3) *Codice civile*). It would certainly be attractive to attribute it to the Roman jurists. The problem is, however, that we find no indication in the sources for such a restrictive interpretation.

[17] See the references in Leser (n 8) 192; *Abschlußbericht* (n 2) 179; Herold (n 11) 74 ff; *HKK/* Thier (n 6) nn 38 ff.

[18] § 349 BGB (old and new). The right to terminate, therefore, is what is usually referred to in German law as 'Gestaltungsrecht' (ie the right unilaterally to shape, or transform, a legal relationship). *Wandelung* (ie the modernized statutory version of the Roman *actio redhibitoria*), on the other hand, was not a *Gestaltungsrecht* under the old law, but a claim; for details see [1997] RLR 20. As a result of the reform, the claim to effect *Wandelung* has been replaced by a right to terminate.

[19] On the terminology see, in comparative perspective, *HKK/*Thier (n 6) n 2.

[20] As far as rescission is concerned, see § 142 I BGB: 'If a legal transaction which is liable to be rescinded is rescinded, it is deemed to have been void from the outset'. The BGB permits rescission in cases of 'defects of will' (mistake, fraud, threat): §§ 119, 123 BGB; cf also Dannemann (n 1) 129.

[21] See eg J Hager, in B Dauner-Lieb, T Heidel, M Lepa, and G Ring (eds), *Anwaltkommentar Schuldrecht* (2002) § 346 n 13; D Kaiser, in *J von Staudingers Kommentar zum Bürgerlichen Gesetzbuch* (rev edn, 2004) § 346 n 67; Helmut Heinrichs, in *Palandt, Bürgerliches Gesetzbuch* (64th edn, 2005) Einf v § 346 n 6; A Stadler, in O Jauernig (ed) *Bürgerliches Gesetzbuch* (11th edn, 2004) Vor §§ 346–54 n 3; from the point of view of Swiss law see, most recently, W Wiegand, 'Zur Rückabwicklung gescheiterter Verträge' in *Gauchs Welt: Festschrift für Peter Gauch* (2004) 710 ff. For the practical implications of the fact that the contract is seen to survive termination, see Dannemann (n 1) 149 f; R Zimmermann, 'Restitutio in integrum' in *Privatrecht und Methode: Festschrift für Ernst A. Kramer* (2004) 747; Hellwege (n 11) 29 f, 352.

[22] R Gaier, in *Münchener Kommentar zum Bürgerlichen Gesetzbuch* (vol 2a, 4th edn, 2003) Vor § 346 n 8.

[23] § 812 I 1 BGB; for the centrality of this requirement in the German law of unjustified enrichment, see R Zimmermann, 'Unjustified Enrichment: The Modern Civilian Approach' (1995) 15 OJLS 406 f.

present situation, on the basis of a contract that turns out to be invalid, or to have fallen away. Here, however, the contract continues to exist, though in a state of transformation. Like many other questions of a doctrinal nature, this is not expressly stated in the BGB itself; nor was it stated in it before the reform. But it was a view that had been gaining ground from the 1920s onwards[24] until it eventually came to enjoy overwhelming support.[25]

Under the new law, as well as under the old, on termination, the parties are obliged to return to each other whatever performance they have received and to surrender the benefits derived from that performance.[26] Similarly, where a return is excluded because of the nature of what has been received (in particular, services rendered and the use of an object), the value has to be made good.[27] Another principle that has remained unchanged is that the obligations arising as a result of termination (such as to return whatever performance the parties have received) have to be performed concurrently.[28]

One of the major changes effected by the reform lies in the fact that §§ 346 ff BGB are now directly applicable both to conventional and to statutory rights of termination. As a result, it is no longer necessary to determine to what extent and with which modifications provisions devised for the conventional right of termination may be applied to the statutory right of termination. The decision

[24] Originally, it had been held that termination brings to an end, rather than merely transforms, the contract; and §§ 346 ff had therefore indeed been regarded as modified enrichment rules: see RGZ 50, 255 (266 f); RGZ 107, 345 (348); Leser (n 8) 154 ff (with copious references). The decisive swing of opinion started with H Stoll, *Die Wirkungen des vertragsmäßigen Rücktritts* (Dr jur thesis, Bonn, 1921); idem, 'Rücktritt und Schadensersatz' (1929) 131 AcP 141 ff; see the analysis by Leser (n 8) 157 ff; *HKK*/Thier (n 6) nn 35 ff; Hellwege (n 11) 467 ff.

[25] BGHZ 88, 46 ff; BGH, 1990 NJW 2068 f; BGH, 1994 NJW 1161 f; H Kaduk, in *J von Staudingers Kommentar zum Bürgerlichen Gesetzbuch* (12th edn, 1994) Vorbem zu §§ 346 ff, nn 12 ff; *Palandt*/Heinrichs (n 11) Einf v § 346 n 2; Larenz (n 11) 404 ff; and see *HKK*/Thier (n 6) n 37.

[26] § 346 I BGB. For the old law, see §§ 346 I 1 and 347, 2 BGB (old version, the latter rule applying to benefits derived from the performance); for comment, see *Staudinger*/Kaiser (n 21) § 346 n 2. As far as concerns benefits which the recipient has failed to derive, contrary to the rules of proper management, see § 347 I BGB: he has to make good their value. Concerning statutory rights of termination, the standard of *diligentia quam in suis* applies; in this respect, the position of the recipient is the same as under § 346 III 1 no 3 BGB; see below, text to nn 67–9. For a comparison of § 347 I BGB with the old law, see *Staudinger*/Kaiser (n 21) § 347, nn 4 ff. § 347 I BGB expressly states that it must have been possible for the recipient to derive the benefits; this is redundant in view of the fact that a person cannot be obliged, according to the rules of proper management, to derive benefits which it is impossible for him to derive from the object; see F Faust, in P Huber and F Faust, *Schuldrechtsmodernisierung* (2002) 259. The (official) heading of § 347 BGB ('Nutzungen und Verwendungen nach Rücktritt') is misleading in that it insinuates that the rule only applies to benefits which the recipient has failed to derive after termination.

[27] § 346 II no 1 BGB. From a systematic standpoint, this rule has been wrongly located: it should have been part of § 346 I (which deals with the duty to return) rather than § 346 II (covering situations where the return of what has been transferred subsequently becomes impossible). See *Münchener Kommentar*/Gaier (n 22) § 346 n 21 and *Staudinger*/Kaiser (n 21) § 346 n 98. The new rule generalizes the idea underlying the old (§ 346, 2 BGB (old version)); this is in accordance with what used to be recognized under the old law: see *Münchener Kommentar*/Gaier (n 22) § 346 n 21; *Staudinger*/Kaiser (n 21) § 346 n 98.

[28] § 348 BGB (both old and new). The German term is *Leistung Zug um Zug*.

about how a reasonable restitution regime should look has now been taken by the draftsmen of the Code themselves and is no longer hidden behind the cryptic words of awkward reference rules.[29] In addition, the special remedy of redhibition in sales law (ie the modernized version of the Roman *actio redhibitoria*, as embodied in §§ 459, 462, 465, 467 BGB (old version)) has been replaced by a statutory right of termination to which §§ 346 ff BGB are directly applicable.[30] Taken together, these two steps have led to a considerable, and entirely welcome, streamlining of the law.[31]

4. The Allocation of Risk

The great substantive question to be settled with regard to termination is: what happens if one of the parties is unable to return the performance received by him? The paradigm is the defective car that has been bought and transferred to the purchaser and that has subsequently been destroyed or seriously damaged in a road accident, or while standing in the purchaser's garage.[32] Can the purchaser terminate the contract and claim back the purchase price, once the defect has been discovered?[33] The BGB in its original form attempted to deal with this type of situation by excluding the right of termination if the party entitled to terminate was to blame for the destruction, significant deterioration, or impossibility, for any other reason, of returning the object received.[34] However, if that object had been accidentally destroyed, the right of termination was not excluded.[35] Essentially, the problem is one of risk allocation. This raises two questions. How is the risk of destruction or deterioration to be allocated? And which device is to be used in order to effect whatever risk allocation is regarded as equitable or appropriate?

As to the first question, the risk of accidental destruction was placed on the seller under the old law. For, as a result of being able to terminate, the purchaser was able to claim back his purchase price without having to render restitution himself. This risk distribution, however, is odd, particularly if the general risk

[29] See, for the old law, § 327 BGB (old version); cf also § 467 BGB (old version) concerning the *actio redhibitoria*.

[30] § 437 no 2 BGB; see Zimmermann, *New German Law* (n 4), ch 3, VII.

[31] For a more detailed analysis of the improvements brought about by the new law, as compared with the old, see Faust, in Huber/Faust (n 26) 238 f; cf also *Staudinger*/Kaiser (n 21) Vorbem zu §§ 346–54 nn 19 ff.

[32] See von Caemmerer, *(First) Festschrift Larenz* 621 ff; G Wagner, 'Mortuus Redhibetur im neuen Schuldrecht?' in *Festschrift für Ulrich Huber* (2006) 592ff. The discussion tends to focus on liability for non-conformity, since with regard to many other types of breach of a contractual duty (default, impossibility of performance) the problem of one party being unable to return the object received under the contract can only arise in exceptional situations.

[33] Termination can be effected either before or after the car has been destroyed, or seriously damaged. In the former situation, the normal rules concerning breach of a contractual duty apply; see below, text to n 70.   [34] § 351 BGB (old version).

[35] § 350 BGB (old version).

rule governing contracts of sale is kept in mind: the risk of accidental destruction passes to the purchaser 'on delivery of the object sold'.[36] It is easy to see the reason underlying this general rule: the object of the sale is in the purchaser's sphere: he is in charge of it, and he can control, guard, and protect it from any interference.[37] It is only equitable that, as a corollary, he also has to bear the risk. § 350 BGB (old version), in case of termination, made the risk 'jump back' to the seller, and it is difficult to find a justification for this sudden reversal of fortunes.[38] There is only one type of situation where this 'jumping back' of the risk appears to be appropriate, and that is where *the defect itself* has led to the destruction or significant deterioration of the object. For, where the defect is the cause of destruction and where, therefore, it is the seller who creates the risk which has to be distributed, he cannot reasonably complain if he finds himself burdened with it. Thus, while § 350 BGB was unanimously regarded as entirely appropriate to regulate this type of situation,[39] it was the object of constant criticism in all other respects.[40] This, incidentally, was also the reason why many commentators found it attractive to extend the range of application of § 351 BGB (ie the rule excluding termination where the party entitled to terminate 'is to blame' for the impossibility of returning the object received)[41] as far as possible: it leaves the risk with the purchaser. This extension, in turn, was facilitated by the unsuitability of the fault criterion in the present context.[42] The real reason for excluding the right of termination was said to be the prohibition of *venire contra factum proprium*:[43] a person unable to render restitution can be seen to act inconsistently if he brings about a situation which obliges him to render restitution. Yet, under which circumstances exactly such inconsistency has to be attributed to the party terminating was difficult to say. Thus, for instance, it was proposed to enquire whether the impossibility of returning the object received was due to 'excessive use'[44] or to 'behaviour creating increased risks'.[45]

---

[36] § 446 BGB.

[37] U Huber, in *Soergel, Kommentar zum Bürgerlichen Gesetzbuch* (vol III, 12th edn, 1991) Vor § 446 nn 15 ff; RM Beckmann, in *J von Staudingers Kommentar zum Bürgerlichen Gesetzbuch* (rev edn, 2004) § 446 n 7; G Hager, *Die Gefahrtragung beim Kauf* (1982) 176 ff; Larenz (n 11) 408.

[38] This has been emphasized, particularly clearly, by von Caemmerer, *(First) Festschrift Larenz* 621 ff, 631 ff.

[39] von Caemmerer, *(First) Festschrift Larenz* 628; *Soergel*/U Huber (n 37) § 467 n 10; H Honsell, 1970 *Monatsschrift für Deutsches Recht* 719.

[40] See the references in *Abschlußbericht* (n 2) 179 f.; Leser (n 8) 192 f; Hellwege (n 11) 23 ff. For a defence of § 350 BGB, see J Kohler, *Die gestörte Rückabwicklung gescheiterter Austauschverträge* (1989) 339 ff, 356 ff; Herold (n 11) 82 ff. [41] Above, text before n 11.

[42] Above, text to n 11.

[43] *Staudinger*/Kaduk (n 25) § 351 n 2; *Münchener Kommentar*/Janßen (n 11) § 351 n 4; *Palandt*/Heinrichs (n 11) § 351 n 1; but see R Singer, *Das Verbot widersprüchlichen Verhaltens* (1993) 36 f. The prohibition of *venire contra factum proprium*, in turn, derives from the general duty to act in accordance with the principle of good faith; see *Palandt*/Heinrichs (n 21) § 242 nn 55 ff; GH Roth, in *Münchener Kommentar zum Bürgerlichen Gesetzbuch* (vol 2a, 4th edn, 2003) § 242 nn 255 ff; H-P Mansel, in O Jauernig (ed), *Bürgerliches Gesetzbuch* (11th edn, 2004) § 242, nn 48 ff.

[44] HP Westermann, in *Münchener Kommentar zum Bürgerlichen Gesetzbuch* (vol III, 3rd edn, 1995) § 467 n 4. [45] Larenz (n 11) 409.

Others considered § 351 BGB (old version) to be applicable if the impossibility resulted from a 'voluntary' or 'free' action,[46] or even simply from any kind of use on the part of the person terminating the contract.[47] It had even been suggested that § 351 should be applied to all cases other than those where the impossibility to return resulted from the latent defect.[48]

5. Implementation of the Risk Regime

This was an untidy, and altogether unsatisfactory, situation.[49] Equally unsatisfactory was the answer given to the question as to how best to implement whatever policy decision is regarded as appropriate.

Essentially, two options are available to the draftsmen of a restitution regime. First, they can exclude the right to termination wherever the person who wants to terminate the contract is supposed to carry the risk of the impossibility of returning what he has given. For, since he is not allowed to terminate, he will not be able to reclaim whatever he has given (in our example, the purchase price). Alternatively, the law can still allow him to terminate, and thus to reclaim the purchase price, but at the same time impose a liability on him to make good the value of the object received. The main difference is this: if the right to termination is excluded, the values remain as exchanged, say, under the contract of sale; but if restitution in kind is simply replaced with a liability to make good the value received, the values are retransferred to the *status quo ante*. In other words: under the restitution-of-value regime the purchaser can escape from a bad bargain.[50] This may be regarded as an undeserved windfall. More compelling, however, is another consideration: as long as a legal system is prepared to grant a right of termination on account of breach of contract, and as long as it imposes duties to make restitution consequent upon termination, it accepts that there has to be a retransfer of values.[51] The situation should not be different merely as a result of the fact that one party is unable to render restitution in kind.

It is widely agreed that, as between the two possible solutions, the imposition of a liability to make good the value is more subtle than an exclusion of the

[46] von Caemmerer, (*First*) *Festschrift Larenz* 632; H Honsell, in *J von Staudingers Kommentar zum Bürgerlichen Gesetzbuch* (13th edn, 1995) § 467 n 8. This view was inspired, partly, by Art 82 II a CISG.
[47] HJ Wieling, 'Synallagma bei Nichtigkeit und gesetzlichem Rücktritt' (1973) *Juristische Schulung* 399.   [48] Honsell, 1970 *Monatsschrift für Deutsches Recht* 719.
[49] See the references in Hellwege (n 11) 25 f; *HKK*/Thier (n 6) n 39.
[50] This applies, as long as the value of the object received by the purchaser is assessed 'objectively', ie not on the basis of the counter-performance agreed upon by the parties. For the position of the BGB, in this respect, and for criticism of that position, see below, text to nn 60–2 and 78–81.
[51] In other words: a purchaser who has received a flawless car worth €8,000 for a price of €10,000 is stuck with his bargain; but if the car turns out to be defective, he is able to claim back his price as long as he is willing to give up the car in return.

right of termination.[52] Thus, in particular, it would hardly be appropriate to exclude the right of termination in all cases of deterioration of the object received. That is why it was limited, according to § 351 BGB (old version), to instances of 'significant deterioration'. However, it is not always easy to determine when a deterioration is significant.[53] Nor does there appear to be good reason to draw a sharp, and necessarily arbitrary, line in order to attribute the risk either the one way or the other. But the right to terminate can only either be excluded or not excluded. It must be all or nothing. The purchaser's liability, on the one hand, can be flexibly adjusted depending on the extent to which there has been a deterioration. It may not, of course, always be easy, after the destruction or deterioration of the defective object, to determine its value before the destruction or deterioration.[54] But this is hardly a convincing reason for rejecting the restitution-of-value approach; after all, exactly the same valuation has to be made in terms of the law of unjustified enrichment when a contract of sale that has been executed is subsequently rescinded. If the object of the sale has been destroyed, it cannot be retransferred. But if the purchaser wants to reclaim his purchase price, he has to deduct the value of the object received and this means, of course, the value of the object before its destruction.[55] For cars, which appear to be the most important commodity involved in this type of situation, extensive tables are available to simplify the process of valuation.[56] Comparison with the law of unjustified enrichment, therefore, provides another reason for imposing a liability to make good the value of the object received on the party terminating the contract, rather than to exclude his right of termination; for the law of unjustified enrichment also does not use the

[52] *Abschlußbericht* (n 2) 185; *Staudinger*/Kaiser (n 21) § 346 n 131; Hellwege (n 11) 564 ff; Wagner, *Festschrift Huber* 606. Restitution of value was a device previously used with regard to regulating the consequences of revocation of consumer transactions; see § 361 a BGB (old version) and, previous to the introduction of § 361 a BGB, the rules contained in § 3 Revocation of Doorstep Contracts Act and § 7 IV Consumer Credit Act. For details, see Hellwege (n 11) 61 ff; *HKK*/Thier (n 6) n 43. The same approach had been adopted, in nineteenth century pandectist doctrine, for effecting restitution under the *actio redhibitoria*; see Windscheid/Kipp (n 6) § 394, 2; G Hanausek, *Die Haftung des Verkäufers für die Beschaffenheit der Ware nach römischem und gemeinem Recht mit besonderer Berücksichtigung des Handelsrechts* (1883) 143 ff; *Staudinger*/Kaiser (n 21) Vorbem zu §§ 346–54 n 7; Hellwege (n 11) 450 f; *HKK*/Thier (n 6) n 25.

[53] See the discussion in *Staudinger*/Kaduk (n 25) § 351 n 21 ff; and the criticism by J Kohler, 'Bemerkungen zur vorgeschlagenen Überarbeitung des Rücktrittsrechts' (1993) *Wertpapier Mitteilungen* 49 f.

[54] This was the reason prompting the draftsmen of the BGB of 1900 to reject the restitution-of-value model of the *ius commune*; see *Motive zu dem Entwurfe eines Bürgerlichen Gesetzbuches für das Deutsche Reich* (vol II, 1888) 231 = Bennno Mugdan, *Die gesammten Materialien zum Bürgerlichen Gesetzbuch für das Deutsche Reich* (vol II, 1899) 128; *Staudinger*/Kaiser (n 21) Vorbem zu §§ 346–54 n 11; for criticism, see Herold (n 11) 112; Hellwege (n 11) 565 f.

[55] §§ 812 I 1, 818 II BGB in conjunction with the so-called *Saldotheorie*; see below text to n 107.

[56] *SchwackeListe Autokatalog*; see eg H Oetker, in *Münchener Kommentar zum Bürgerlichen Gesetzbuch* (vol 2a, 4th edn, 2003) § 251 n 24. The *SchwackeListe* is regularly used by the courts; for a recent example, see *Bundesfinanzhof*, 2005 *Deutsches Steuerrecht* 1437 ff.

latter device when it places the risk of destruction of the object received on the shoulders of the purchaser.[57]

6. The Details of the New Regime

Unsurprisingly, in view of what has been said, the new law deviates from the old, so far as concerns both the question of risk allocation and the means of implementing it. The new law no longer excludes a party's right to terminate on account of his inability to render restitution, not even if he has intentionally destroyed the object that he has received.[58] According to the new § 346 II 1 no 3 BGB, that party (ie, in our example, the purchaser) has to make good the value, to the extent that the object received has deteriorated, or has been destroyed. However, any deterioration resulting from the proper use of the object for its intended purpose has to be disregarded. The latter limitation is intended to avoid an overcompensation of the seller who is already entitled, under § 346 I BGB, to recover whatever benefits the purchaser has derived from his (the seller's) performance.[59] If the contract specifies a counter-performance, the calculation of the value of the object received is to be based on that counter-performance.[60] This rule is supposed to leave the parties' decision as to how to rate the performance (ie what price to put on the object of the sale) unaffected by the termination.[61] If, therefore, the purchaser has bought a car worth €8,000 for €10,000, he will, if he cannot return the car, have to pay €10,000 to the seller, ie exactly as much as he is able to claim from the latter. There is one case, however, where the counter-performance does not determine the value of the performance; this is, where the value of the object received is reduced as a result of a defect. For the counter-performance fixed by the parties merely reflects the value of an object free from defects, not of the defective object. The value of the object therefore has to be determined by the price, as reduced in accordance with §§

---

[57] It is widely agreed that restitution under §§ 812 ff BGB has to be coordinated, as far as possible, with restitution after termination of contract; see eg von Caemmerer, (*First*) *Festschrift Larenz* 638; *Abschlußbericht* (n 2) 185; K Larenz and C-W Canaris, *Lehrbuch des Schuldrechts* (vol II/2, 13th edn, 1994) 324 ff; W Lorenz, *J von Staudingers Kommentar zum Bürgerlichen Gesetzbuch* (rev edn, 1999) § 818 n 41 ff; J Hager, 'Das geplante Recht des Rücktritts und des Widerrufs' in W Ernst and R Zimmermann (eds), *Zivilrechtswissenschaft und Schuldrechtsreform* (2001) 441 ff; *HKK*/Thier (n 6) n 41.

[58] In particularly blatant cases the purchaser may be barred from terminating the contract in terms of § 242 BGB (abusive exercise of a right—*mißbräuchliche Rechtsausübung*): see *Abschlußbericht* (n 2) 185; Faust, in Huber/Faust (n 26) 242; but see *Münchener Kommentar*/Gaier (n 22) § 346 n 14. On *mißbräuchliche Rechtsausübung*, see *Münchener Kommentar*/Roth (n 43) § 242 nn 211 ff; *Palandt*/Heinrichs (n 21) § 242 nn 38 ff; Jauernig/Mansel (n 43) nn 37 ff.

[59] See *Münchener Kommentar*/Gaier (n 22) § 346 n 43; *Staudinger*/Kaiser (n 21) § 346 n 141; Faust, in Huber/Faust (n 26) 245. On the restitution of benefits under § 346 I BGB (see above, n 26). If these benefits cannot be surrendered because of their nature, their value has to be made good according to § 346 II 1 no 1 BGB.

[60] § 346 II 2 BGB. Cf also § 346, 2 BGB (old version).   [61] *Abschlußbericht* (n 2) 185.

441 III, 638 III BGB.[62] This can be reconciled with the wording of § 346 II 2 BGB which merely determines that the calculation of the value 'has to be based' on the counter-performance.[63]

§ 346 III 1 nos 2 and 3 BGB establish three important exceptions to the general principle that the purchaser must make good the value: in so far as the seller is responsible for the deterioration or destruction (i), if the damage would also have occurred, had the object still been with the seller (ii), and, with regard to statutory rights of termination, if the deterioration or destruction has occurred even though the purchaser had taken the same care which he usually takes with regard to his own affairs (iii).[64] The justification for rule (i) is self-evident. The rule under (ii)[65] appears to be based on the consideration that the deterioration or destruction is not intrinsically related to the fact that the object, as a result of the executed contract of sale, has been in the purchaser's sphere of influence.[66] Thus, there is no specific reason to burden the purchaser with the risk of deterioration or destruction by imposing an obligation on him to make good the value. Finally, rule (iii). Here the draftsmen of the new law attempted to obviate the problems previously associated with the criterion of fault.[67] Fault, in the form of negligent behaviour, is a normative standard which is hardly workable with regard to property belonging to the debtor himself. For what is the generally accepted standard of care which a person has to display with regard to his own car, or bicycle, or soccer ball? This is why the normative standard has been replaced by an empirical one:[68] it has to be determined whether the debtor

---

[62] *Münchener Kommentar*/Gaier (n 22) § 346 n 47; *Staudinger*/Kaiser (n 21) § 346 n 156; Faust, in Huber/Faust (n 26) 252 f; Wagner, *Festschrift Huber*, 603f.

[63] Faust, in Huber/Faust (n 26) 252. The draft of the Commission charged with the revision of the German law of obligations, on the other hand, had determined that the counter-performance 'takes the place' of the value of the object; see § 346 II 2 *Kommissionsentwurf: Abschlußbericht* (n 2) 175. On that Commission and the development of the reform process in general, see Zimmermann, *New German Law* (n 4) ch 1, XII. Generally, concerning the effects of termination of contract, the draftsmen of the new law have closely followed the recommendations of the Commission and have very largely taken over their draft. This has not happened in other areas of the law, such as breach of contract and extinctive prescription.

[64] The terms 'purchaser' and 'seller' are used here to illustrate the most common type of situation (see text to n 32). The BGB refers, more generally, to 'the party terminating' and 'the other party'.

[65] It covers cases such as the following. A holiday house has been sold and transferred to the purchaser; it is subsequently destroyed by a violent thunderstorm. The purchaser terminates the contract because of a defect attaching to the house. Or: A garage has been sold and transferred to the purchaser; it is subsequently disfigured by graffiti. Again, the purchaser terminates the contract because of a defect attaching to the garage.

[66] *Anwaltkommentar*/Hager (n 21) § 346 n 47; *Münchener Kommentar*/Gaier (n 22) § 346 n 54; *Staudinger*/Kaiser (n 21) § 346 nn 175 ff; Faust, in Huber/Faust (n 26) 248. Cf also § 287, 2 BGB, dealing with a similar problem (though in the context of a damages rather than restitution claim).

[67] Above, text to n 11.

[68] S Grundmann, in *Münchener Kommentar zum Bürgerlichen Gesetzbuch* (vol 2a, 4th edn, 2003) § 277 n 1. This empirical standard, however, has its limits. On the one hand, liability for *diligentia quam in suis* cannot be stricter than liability according to the normal standard of negligence ('A person who is liable *only* for failure to display the standard of care that he displays in his own

has been less careful with regard to the object received under the contract of sale than with other, similar, objects belonging to him. This type of enquiry is certainly more workable. It does, however, lead to the result that the seller has to carry the risk not only of accidental deterioration, or destruction, but also of a deterioration or destruction resulting from lack of care on the part of the purchaser, as long as such lack of care is characteristic of the purchaser. The justification provided for this risk regime is that the seller, after all, has not properly performed (the object of the sale is defective) and has not therefore been able reasonably to rely on the fact that the risk of deterioration or destruction has definitively passed to the purchaser.[69]

7. Liability for Breach of Duty

If the deterioration or destruction occurs after the contract has been terminated, the party terminating is liable under the general rules concerning breach of duty.[70] In particular, therefore, the other party can claim damages in terms of §§ 280 I, III, 283 BGB.[71] This follows from the fact that termination leads to a contractual (winding-up) relationship, imposing upon both parties duties to return what they have received.[72] Therefore § 346 IV BGB (the creditor may claim damages, in accordance with §§ 280–3 BGB, for the infringement of a duty under § 346 I BGB) is merely of a declaratory nature.[73] The claim for damages, under the old as much as under the new law of obligations, is based on fault.[74] The question thus arises whether continuing to use the object after termination can be regarded as behaviour that does not meet the generally accepted standard of care. This is not the case if the party who terminates the contract (ie, in our example, the purchaser) has a reasonable interest in continuing to use the object which also deserves to be protected *vis-à-vis* the seller. A typical example would be the continued use of a car in view of the fact that (i) it is more advantageous for the purchaser than having to procure a substitute and (ii) the seller has a claim for the benefits resulting from the transfer of the car to the purchaser.[75] Damages for delay in performing the duty to restore the car after termination of the contract can be claimed in terms of §§ 280 I, II, 286 BGB.

affairs . . . '); on the other hand, it does not relieve the debtor of liability for grossly negligent behaviour (§ 277 BGB).

[69] *Abschlußbericht* (n 2) 188.

[70] See eg *Staudinger*/Kaiser (n 21) § 348 nn 19 ff; cf also *Münchener Kommentar*/Gaier (n 22) § 346 n 68; Faust, in Huber/Faust (n 26) 256.

[71] For details, see Zimmermann, *New German Law* (n 4) ch 2, III.

[72] Above, text following n 20.

[73] *Münchener Kommentar*/Gaier (n 22) § 346 n 66; *Staudinger*/Kaiser (n 21) § 348 n 8; Faust, in Huber/Faust (n 26) 256.   [74] § 280 I 2 BGB.

[75] H Heinrichs, 'Schadensersatzansprüche wegen Pflichtverletzung gegen den nach § 346 BGB zur Rückgewähr verpflichteten Schuldner', in *Liber Amicorum Eike Schmidt* (2004) 182; Wagner, *Festschrift Huber* 614ff.

8. Evaluation

The new regime contains a number of welcome features in comparison with the old. In particular, it removes unnecessary complications[76] and has brought about the transition to a model based on restitution of value rather than on excluding the right to terminate.[77] At the same time, however, the new rules are open to criticism on several counts. I mention only the two most important.

(i) The decision to base the calculation of the value of the object received on the counter-performance agreed upon by the parties is in fundamental contradiction to the aim of termination—acknowledged also by the draftsmen of the new law[78]—to restore the situation as it existed before conclusion of the contract (or, one may say, to effect *restitutio in integrum*). There can be no justification for being guided, with regard to restitution, by the parties' ideas as to the value of the seller's performance.[79] For, effectively, the parties are stuck with a contract from which they want to escape. This is as unacceptable in cases where the object that has been sold cannot be returned as it would be in cases where it can still be returned. If, for example, a car worth €10,000 is sold for €12,000, and the contract is subsequently terminated, it is accepted, as a matter of course, that the purchaser may claim back €12,000 while only having to return a car worth €10,000.[80] There is no reason why the seller should be better off (ie receive €12,000) merely as a result of the fact that the car has been destroyed. It is also, incidentally, impossible to explain why someone who has received a performance that can be returned should be treated differently (better or worse, depending on whether he has made a good or bad bargain) from the person who has received a performance which, by its nature, cannot be returned (with the result that he has to make good the value).[81]

---

[76] Such as the ones associated with the fact that the rules concerning restitution after termination for breach of contract used to be tailored to conventional rights of termination and were applicable to statutory rights of termination only *mutatis mutandis*; above, text following n 10.

[77] This is the most important change effected by the reform; see *HKK*/Thier (n 6) n 46; Wagner, *Festschrift Huber* 606. It also applies to situations where the debtor has consumed, transferred, encumbered, processed, or transformed the object received, for, according to § 346 II 1 no 2 BGB, he has to make good the value (to the extent that he has consumed, transferred, etc the object). There is no duty to make good the value if the defect which gives rise to the right to termination becomes apparent only in the course of processing or transforming the object: § 346 III 1 no 1 BGB. For the old law, see §§ 352, 353 BGB (old version), § 467, 1 BGB (old version). On these provisions, see *Abschlußbericht* (n 2) 183 ff; Faust, in Huber/Faust (n 26) 243 f; *Münchener Kommentar*/Gaier (n 22) § 346 nn 40 ff, 51 f; *Staudinger*/Kaiser (n 21) § 346 nn 133 ff, 165 ff.

[78] *Abschlußbericht* (n 2) 175; and see *Staudinger*/Kaiser (n 21) § 346 Vorbem zu §§ 346–54 n 1; Hellwege (n 11) 28 f; *Münchener Kommentar*/Gaier (n 22) Vor § 346 n 5.

[79] For criticism, see Herold (n 11) 112 ff; Hager, in Ernst/Zimmermann (n 57) 450 f; *Anwaltkommentar*/Hager (n 66) § 346 n 40; *Staudinger*/Kaiser (n 21) § 346 n 155 ff; Faust, in Huber/Faust (n 26) 241, 251 f; Hellwege (n 11) 567 ff; R Gaier, 'Das Rücktritts(folgen)recht nach dem Schuldrechtsmodernisierungsgesetz' (2002) 56 *Wertpapier Mitteilungen* 9 f.

[80] See the examples provided by *Staudinger*/Kaiser (n 21) § 346 n 155 and Faust, in Faust/Huber (n 26) 251 f. [81] § 346 II 1 no 1, read with § 346 II 2 BGB.

(ii) Strangely, and in spite of the criticism levelled against the old risk rule embodied in § 350 BGB,[82] the draftsmen of the new law, as far as statutory rights of termination are concerned, decided not only to retain it, but also to extend it. For, under the new law, the risk jumps back to the seller not only if the object has been accidentally destroyed, but also if it has not been carefully kept, handled, or looked after, as long as this was how the purchaser would usually treat his own property. This entails, *inter alia*, that the risk of the purchaser being a careless person has to be borne by the seller. The new German solution, in that respect, ventures beyond the range of internationally accepted, reasonable solutions to the difficult question of risk allocation, and it does so without good reason.[83] The fact that it is the seller who has not performed properly and has thus given rise to the purchaser's right to terminate is irrelevant, so long as the defect is not intrinsically related to the deterioration or destruction of the object sold. Of course, where the seller knows of the defect inherent in the object, he cannot reasonably rely on the fact that the risk has definitely passed to the purchaser. Usually, however, he does not know about it. Termination no longer requires fault on the part of 'the other party'.[84] Thus, it would appear to be more appropriate to be guided by what position the purchaser, unaware of the defect, could reasonably anticipate: he would have lost his purchase price and the object handed over to him would have been at his own risk.[85] He should not now be in a more favourable position merely because that object turns out to be defective. The existence of the defect would then be a lucky coincidence, and chance is hardly a convincing criterion for allocating risk. This applies to cases of accidental deterioration or destruction; and *a fortiori* to the privileged position granted to the purchaser under § 346 III no 3 BGB also in cases where he fails to observe the generally accepted degree of care. The standard of *diligentia quam in suis* is normally reserved for situations where a close personal relationship exists between the two parties involved[86]—which is not normally the case between sellers and purchasers of motor-cars or other commodities.

9. Sidestepping the New Rules

It is hardly surprising, therefore, that a number of ways have been suggested for sidestepping, at least in part, the risk regime laid down in § 346 III 1 no 3 BGB.[87]

---

[82] Above, text to n 40.

[83] This is emphasized particularly clearly by Wagner, *Festschrift Huber* 608ff.

[84] Under the old law, this used to be different. The statutory version of the *actio redhibitoria* (*Wandlung*) could be brought irrespective of fault. For details, see Zimmermann, *New German Law* (n 4) ch 2, VII.   [85] For a related situation, see Larenz/Canaris (n 57) 323 ff.

[86] See §§ 708 (partners), 1359 (spouses), 1664 (parents and children), 2131 (provisional and reversionary heir); cf also § 690 BGB (a case of one person gratuitously acting in another person's interest). See Herold (n 11) 122; Wagner, *Festschrift Huber* 610. Wagner also draws attention to the fact that even here the application of the (milder) standard of *diligentia quam in suis* is rejected in cases of traffic accidents (teleological restriction).

[87] For what follows, see the analysis by Wagner, *Festschrift Huber* 610ff.

Thus, a complex argument has been developed, in terms of which, via §§ 437 no 2 and 326 V BGB, the rule of § 323 VI BGB may be held to be applicable:[88] termination is excluded if the creditor is solely, or overwhelmingly, responsible for the circumstance which would entitle him to terminate; and the circumstance which would entitle (in this case, the purchaser) to terminate the contract is not simply the defect in the object but, in addition, the impossibility of rendering supplementary performance.[89] Effectively, this constitutes a revival of § 351 BGB (old version) which, for very good reasons, the draftsmen of the new law have decided to abolish.[90] Others have advocated an extensive application of § 346 IV BGB:[91] the creditor may claim damages, in accordance with §§ 280–3 BGB, for the infringement of a duty under § 346 I BGB.[92] In terms of § 346 I BGB, the purchaser is obliged to return what he has received. If he is unable to do so, or if he can only give the object back in a deteriorated condition, he commits a breach of duty. Thus, he is liable for damages, unless he can show that he has not been responsible for the breach of duty. This is the case if he did not know, and could not have known, about his right to terminate. In other cases it applies only if the purchaser has observed the generally accepted standards of care with regard to the object which he has received. Once again, this is hard to reconcile with the intention of the draftsmen of the new law, since allowing a claim for damages would render the restitution-of-value regime, as laid down in § 346 II BGB, largely nugatory.[93] And, just like the view mentioned above, it would revive the awkward enquiry as to which standard of care a person is obliged to observe with regard to his own property. Others again have argued for a teleological restriction of § 346 III 1 no 3 BGB to those cases where the person entitled to terminate did not know about this right when the object had deteriorated or was destroyed.[94] This argument, however, leads to implausible distinctions.[95]

[88] S Lorenz, 'Rücktritt, Minderung und Schadensersatz wegen Sachmängeln im neuen Kaufrecht: Was hat der Verkäufer zu vertreten?' (2002) NJW 2498 f; J Kohler, 'Rücktrittsausschluß im Gewährleistungsrecht bei nachträglicher Nacherfüllungsunmöglichkeit—Wiederkehr der §§ 350, 351 BGB a.F.?', (2003) 203 AcP 539 ff; F Faust, in HG Bamberger and H Roth, *Kommentar zum Bürgerlichen Gesetzbuch* (vol I, 2003) § 437 n 33, § 439 n 56.
[89] Under the new German sales law, the primary right of the purchaser, in case of non-conformity, is the right to supplementary performance: § 437, no 1 BGB; and see Zimmermann, *New German Law* (n 4) ch 3, V. Destruction of the object transferred renders supplementary performance impossible and thus gives rise to a right to terminate (§ 326 V BGB): a right which is excluded if the purchaser was responsible for the destruction.
[90] B Dauner-Lieb and A Arnold, 'Kein Rücktrittsrecht des Käufers bei von ihm verschuldeter Unmöglichkeit der Nacherfüllung?' in *Festschrift für Walther Hadding* (2004) 25 ff; Heinrichs, *Liber Amicorum Schmidt* 163; Wagner, *Festschrift Huber* 611.
[91] Gaier, 2002 *Wertpapier Mitteilungen* 12 ff; *Münchener Kommentar*/Gaier (n 22) § 346 nn 61 ff; Heinrichs, *Liber Amicorum Schmidt* 164 ff; *Palandt*/Heinrichs (n 21) § 346 nn 15 ff.
[92] Above, text following n 71.   [93] Wagner, *Festschrift Huber* 616ff.
[94] *Anwaltkommentar*/Hager (n 66) § 346 n 50; Thier, *Festschrift Heldrich* 446 f.
[95] An example provided by G Wagner, *Festschrift Huber* 620 makes this clear: The purchaser of a defective car uses the car for a holiday trip to Italy. In an Italian garage the defect is discovered and the purchaser informed accordingly. The defect, however, does not prevent the car from being used for the homeward journey. Why should the car now be at the purchaser's risk whereas for the journey to Italy the purchaser enjoyed the privilege of § 346 III 1 no 3 BGB?

These are not the only aspects of the new law which are open to criticism. Thus, the rule contained in § 346 III 1 no 2, second alternative,[96] appears to be based on a *petitio principii*. For, if it is said that there is no specific reason to burden the purchaser with the risk of an accidental deterioration or destruction, if the damage would also have occurred if the object had still been with the seller, it might equally, or more plausibly, be argued that there is no specific reason to burden the seller with that very risk (by shifting it back to him from the purchaser). After all, the object was in fact with the purchaser when it was destroyed or deteriorated, for the contract of sale had not only been concluded but had also been fully executed.[97] Another criticism is that, while § 346 III 1 no 2 BGB deals with the situation where the seller is responsible for the destruction or deterioration of the object, it fails to provide a rule for cases where the destruction or deterioration results from the defect inherent in the object. For a seller is liable for a defect in the object sold even where he is not responsible (ie cannot be blamed) for that defect. Since, however, it is generally agreed that in the latter situation too the risk should be on the seller, it has been suggested that § 346 III 1 no 2 BGB should be applied *per analogiam*.[98]

10. The Dichotomy of Restitution Regimes

Two further points may be mentioned, both of them relating to structural aspects of the German rules. On the one hand, they appear to be unnecessarily complex and badly arranged.[99] On the other hand, just as under the old law, they merely relate to termination of contract. It is true that they have gained in importance as a result of the much broader range of application of the right to terminate.[100] That right is no longer dependent on whether or not the other party has been responsible for the defective performance.[101] The old right of redhibition has been replaced by a right to terminate.[102] Change of circumstances can also, sometimes, give rise to a right to terminate with the result that §§ 346 ff BGB are applicable (as opposed to the law of unjustified enrichment).[103] And according to § 357 I

---

[96] Above, text to n 65. This rule is new. The introduction of a similar rule had been proposed, but rejected, in the course of preparing the BGB of 1900; for details, see Herold (n 11) 118 f.

[97] For criticism of § 346 III 1 no 2, second alternative, see *Staudinger*/Kaiser (n 21) nn 176 ff.

[98] C-W Canaris, *Schuldrechtsreform 2002* (2002), xl. G Wagner comments that it can hardly be regarded as evidence of a high degree of legislative skill if the most obvious situation where the risk has to 'jump back' to the seller is not specifically regulated and has to be dealt with, laboriously, by means of an *argumentum per analogiam*: *Festschrift Huber* 607f. Cf also Faust in Huber/Faust (n 26) 247 f; Hager, in Ernst/Zimmermann (n 57) 440; *Anwaltkommentar*/Hager (n 66) § 346 n 45; *Staudinger*/Kaiser (n 21) § 346 n 170; *Palandt*/Heinrichs, (n 21) § 346 n 12.

[99] See eg the criticism by Faust in Huber/Faust (n 26) 243 and *Staudinger*/Kaiser (n 21) § 346 n 132 concerning the structure of § 346 II and III BGB.

[100] For details, see Faust, in Huber/Faust (n 26) 240; *Staudinger*/Kaiser (n 21) § 346 nn 4 ff

[101] Above, text to n 84.   [102] Above, text to n 30.

[103] § 313 III 1 BGB. It has been argued that § 346 III 1 no 3 BGB should not be applied to termination as a result of change of circumstances since its rationale—it is more equitable for the

BGB, the provisions on statutory termination apply with comparatively minor modifications to the right of revocation and return in consumer contracts.[104] All of this entails a considerable streamlining of the law. At the same time, however, it is also true that the traditional dichotomy of restitution regimes continues to persist: if the contract has been rescinded as a result of mistake, fraud, or duress, or if it is void because of illegality, immorality, or for any other reason, the restitution of performances exchanged has to be effected under the rules of unjustified enrichment;[105] but if the contract has been terminated, the contractual restitution rules of §§ 346 ff BGB have to be applied. Yet, the considerations on which the relevant rules have to be based are essentially the same in both cases. That is why, under the old law, the so-called *Saldotheorie*[106] was the subject of so much dispute and criticism;[107] for by placing the risk of accidental destruction or deterioration on the shoulders of the purchaser (his claim for the retransfer of the purchase price has to be reduced to the extent that he himself is unable to render restitution), it ran counter to what used to be recognized with regard to termination under § 350 BGB. Even under the old law, therefore, efforts were made to adjust restitution, in terms of §§ 812 ff BGB, and §§ 346 ff BGB to each other[108]—which, essentially, meant the transfer of the evaluations underlying §§ 350 f BGB, unsatisfactory as they were, into the law of unjustified enrichment.

The draftsmen of the new law, too, were inspired by a desire to ensure the maximum degree of harmony between the two restitution regimes.[109] This means that, in so far as, under the rules relating to termination of contract, the purchaser has to make good the value of what he has received, the *Saldotheorie* governs the determination of restitution claims under the law of unjustified enrichment:[110] to the extent that the purchaser is no longer able himself to make restitution, the purchaser cannot claim back the purchase price. He cannot, in other words, plead cessation of enrichment (§ 818 III BGB) in that respect. On the other hand, he can claim back the purchase price even though he is unable himself to make restitution where, in terms of § 346 III 1 nos 2 and 3 BGB, the

---

seller to have to carry the risk of destruction or deterioration in view of the fact that, by not properly performing, he has provided the cause for the purchaser's right to terminate—does not apply to this situation (teleological restriction). See Canaris (n 98) p xlv; *Münchener Kommentar*/Gaier (n 22) § 346 n 56.

[104] On which see Zimmermann, *New German Law* (n 4) ch 5, IV 3 and VI 2 b.
[105] Above, text to n 23.
[106] For an overview in English, see R Zimmermann and J du Plessis, 'Basic Features of the German Law of Unjustified Enrichment' [1994] RLR 40 ff (also, incidentally, a contribution stimulated by Peter Birks).
[107] For all details, see *Staudinger*/W Lorenz (n 57) § 818 nn 41 ff; Hellwege (n 11) 106 ff.
[108] See eg von Caemmerer, *(First) Festschrift Larenz* 638; Larenz/Canaris (n 57) 327; C-W Canaris, 'Die Gegenleistungskondiktion' in *Festschrift für Werner Lorenz* (1991) 19, 26; U Huber, 'Leistungsstörungen' in Bundesminister der Justiz (ed), *Gutachten und Vorschläge zur Überarbeitung des Schuldrechts* (vol I, 1981) 647, 735 f, 853 f; *Staudinger*/W Lorenz (n 57) § 818, nn 42 ff; Hager, in Ernst/Zimmermann (n 57) 441.   [109] *Abschlußbericht* (n 2) 185.
[110] For the details, see Hellwege (n 11) 152 ff; Thier, *Festschrift Heldrich* 450 ff.

seller would have to carry the risk of destruction or deterioration. None the less, there is no perfect correspondence. The value of the seller's performance is not to be assessed on the basis of the counter-performance.[111] Nor does the *Saldotheorie* provide the basis for an independent claim; it only operates to reduce the purchaser's claim.[112] Perfect harmony can only be achieved by devising a uniform set of restitution rules covering all types of failure of bilateral contracts. While there is much to be said for such a uniform regime,[113] the idea would run counter to a deeply established pattern of thinking in German law according to which any transfer made without legal ground has to be restored under the rules of the law of unjustified enrichment. A performance rendered in order to discharge a contract that subsequently turns out to be invalid is thus governed by the same rules as a payment made to the wrong recipient.

11. The European Perspective

Matters, however, look different when it comes to drafting a model regulation on a European level. The Principles of European Contract Law, prepared by the so-called Lando-Commission, constitute the most advanced attempt to devise such model regulation.[114] Here we find rules, dealing with the restitution of benefits exchanged, in no less than three different places.[115] Article 4:114 PECL refers to situations where a contract has been avoided, Articles 9:305 ff PECL deal with the consequences of termination of contract in cases of non-performance, and Art 15:104 PECL covers the restitution of benefits received under a contract that has turned out to be invalid because of illegality.[116] The first and the third of these provisions are largely (but not completely!) identical, whereas the second is based on an entirely different approach.[117] This discrepancy is unjustifiable. In addition,

[111] Hellwege (n 11) 158.
[112] Hellwege (n 11) 153 ff. This feature of the *Saldotheorie* had already been criticized before the reform of the German law of obligations in view of the problems it causes when only one party has executed his performance. Flume and Canaris, in particular, have therefore argued that the seller should be granted an independent claim against the purchaser and that the purchaser should not be able to raise the defence of change of position (§ 818 III BGB); see W Flume, 'Der Wegfall der Bereicherung in der Entwicklung vom römischen zum geltenden Recht' in *Festschrift für Hans Niedermeyer* (1953) 103 ff; Canaris, *Festschrift W Lorenz* 19 ff.
[113] Hellwege (n 11) 520 ff; Zimmermann, *Festschrift Kramer* 735 ff; C Wendehorst, 'Die Leistungskondiktion und ihre Binnenstruktur in rechtsvergleichender Perspektive' in R Zimmermann (ed), *Grundstrukturen eines Europäischen Bereicherungsrechts* (2005) 68 ff.
[114] On the Principles of European Contract Law, see R Zimmermann, 'The Principles of European Contract Law: Contemporary Manifestation of the Old, and Possible Foundation for a New, European Scholarship of Private Law' in *Essays in Honour of Hein Kötz* (in preparation).
[115] For details of what follows, see C Coen, *Vertragsscheitern und Rückabwicklung* (2003) 253 ff; Hellwege (n 11) 576 ff; Zimmermann, *Festschrift Kramer* 735 ff.
[116] 'Illegality' is the general term chosen for situations where contracts are contrary to principles recognized as fundamental in the laws of the Member States of the European Union (Art 15:101 PECL) or where they infringe mandatory rules of law (Art 15:102 PECL).
[117] See Zimmermann, *Festschrift Kramer* 739 ff.

in the one case the draftsmen of the Principles have not dealt with important issues, such as the distribution of risk, whereas in the other case they have drawn their inspiration from a model devised in English law (restitution as a result of failure of consideration) that has, in the meantime, been discredited even in its country of origin.[118] Also, by dealing with three specific instances of restitution, the draftsmen of the Principles have left a number of other situations unregulated even though they can also give rise to problems concerning the restitution of benefits (eg termination of the contract as a result of change of circumstances).[119] Obviously, this will still have to be tidied up, and the most appropriate solution appears to be a uniform regime which would cover all instances of restitution of benefits received under a contract that has, for whatever reason, failed to provide a basis for the transfer of these benefits.[120] Whether the contract is rescinded (avoided), or whether it is terminated cannot make a difference. As far as *restitutio in integrum* is concerned, this is a mere technicality.[121]

12. Conclusion

German law, after the reform of 2002, contains the most recent set of rules concerning restitution after termination for breach of contract. Inevitably, therefore, it will attract the attention of other lawyers in Europe, particularly those with an interest in the development of European private law on a comparative basis. And indeed, the experience gained in the course of a long and tortuous process of discussion justifies that attention. Nevertheless, it has not led to a set of rules that is distinguished by its clarity and plausibility. For, while the new §§ 346 ff BGB have finally emerged from the long shadow of the *lex commissoria*, they are still wedded to the idea of *mortuus redhibetur*. Moreover, the new rules are not consistently geared towards the aim of *restitutio in integrum*. And they only deal with termination of contract, not with all other instances of failure of contract. They thus preserve a split in the treatment of this area of the law, which is as inconvenient as it is unnecessary.

---

[118] S Meier, *Irrtum und Zweckverfehlung* (1999) 253 ff; G Virgo, 'Failure of Consideration: Myth and Meaning in the English Law of Restitution' in D Johnston and R Zimmermann (eds), *Unjustified Enrichment: Key Issues in Comparative Perspective* (2002) 103 ff; P Birks, *Unjust Enrichment* (2nd edn, 2005) 101 ff.   [119] Art 6:111 (3) (a) PECL.

[120] For a suggestion, see Hellwege (n 11) 537 ff; cf also Zimmermann, *Festschrift Kramer* 753 f; Wendehorst (n 113) 82 f.

[121] Along the same lines, from the point of view of Swiss law, see B Schmidlin, in *Berner Kommentar* (vol VI, part I/2/1b, *Mängel des Vertragsabschlusses, Kommentar zu* Art 23–31 OR, 1995), Art 31 nn 45 ff, 97 ff; Wiegand, *Festschrift Gauch* 717 ff.

18

No Basis: A Comparative View

*Sonja Meier**

1. Introduction

When I came to London to study for an LLM in 1990, I wanted to do core subjects of English private law. To my disappointment, contract and tort were not taught at postgraduate level. But there was a mysterious course called 'restitution', which, after some investigation, turned out to resemble the law of unjustified enrichment. Although I had not yet heard of Peter Birks, who came from Oxford each week to teach the course together with Ewan McKendrick, I decided to take the course.

What followed was probably the most stimulating experience in my academic life. I am still grateful for having had the opportunity of encountering such a fascinating teacher in a small group of about eleven students. Questions of restitution law continued to absorb much of my attention after my return to Germany. The friendly contact with Peter also continued. When he eventually switched to a no basis approach, his acknowledgement of my contribution was far too generous. I would dearly have wished that discussion with him could have gone on.

In this chapter, I look at Peter's absence of basis approach from a comparative, mainly German, point of view. I argue that he was right in basing recovery on a failure of basis in transfer cases—even though criticisms have been advanced against it (Section 2). I also look at the application of a no basis test in other cases of unjust enrichment and warn against approaches which try to generalize too much (Section 3).

* Max Planck Institute for Comparative and International Private Law, Hamburg. I am grateful to Jacques du Plessis for valuable comments.

2. Failure of Basis in Transfer Cases

The claimant C makes a transfer to the defendant D in order to fulfil an obligation, or in view of some other legal relationship with D. The obligation or relationship turns out not to exist or to have fallen away. All civilian legal systems regard these cases as a special sub-category under the head of unjust enrichment, calling the obligation or relationship a 'legal ground'. Restitution is based on the absence of this legal ground.[1] It can be explained more specifically by a failure of C's purpose in making the transfer, which was directed to the legal ground. In short, restitution can in these cases be said to rest on a failure of the basis of the transfer. Birks's new approach[2] conforms to this model. It rejects the unjust-factor approach, which does not primarily focus on the basis of the transfer and thereby, arguably, loses the link to the question whether and why the underlying basis does not exist.

2.1. Breach and Frustration

Where a performance made under a valid contract is recovered, it is usually[3] due to a failed or at least materially deficient counter-performance. It is certainly possible to found restitution directly on the failure of the counter-performance, by stating that the purpose of a contractual performance is the receipt of the counter-performance. An alternative approach is to regard the receipt of the counter-performance as the purpose, not of performing, but of incurring a contractual liability. Failure of the counter-performance then leads (either automatically or after termination) to a falling away of the obligation to perform, which in return results in a failure of basis triggering restitution. The second approach does not depend to any greater extent on a fiction, but merely adds an additional intellectual step.

There has always been the problem of determining what exactly happens to the obligation to perform in cases of frustration or termination for breach. The original view that the contract is invalidated *ab initio* was given up in both England and Germany, in order to keep alive arbitration and exemption clauses, or claims for damages which had already accrued. But restitution can still be explained by a failure of basis, if termination or frustration is seen as destroying, not the entire contract, but the contractual obligations to perform.

---

[1] For comparative accounts see I Englard, *Restitution of Benefits Conferred Without Obligation* (International Encyclopedia of Comparative Law, vol X, ch 5, 1991) no 8; P Schlechtriem, *Restitution und Bereicherungsausgleich in Europa*, vol I (2000) no 2/1 (cf in English, P Schlechtriem, C Coen, and R Hornung, 'Restitution and Unjust Enrichment in Europe' [2001] European Review of Private Law 377); C Wendehorst, 'Die Leistungskondiktion und ihre Binnenstruktur in rechtsvergleichender Perspektive' in R Zimmermann (ed), *Grundstrukturen eines Europäischen Bereicherungsrechts* (2005) 47, 58 ff; for the historical background R Zimmermann, *The Law of Obligations: Roman Foundations of the Civilian Tradition* (1990) 834 ff.

[2] *Unjust Enrichment* (2nd edn, 2005) 101 ff.

[3] There may be exceptional cases of contract violations that do not concern the performance but give a right to termination; for German law see BGB § 324.

The German solution, however, was shaped by the fact that the Code contains, outside enrichment law, special rules for restitution after termination.[4] This was due to the draftsmen's view that enrichment law could not cope with the special problems of unwinding mutual performances, in particular if one performance could not be returned. They failed to notice that enrichment law had in any event to deal with these problems in cases where performances under void or avoided contracts had been exchanged. In the result, German law has two sets of rules for dealing with the special problems of unwinding mutual contractual performances. This is unsatisfactory and has always caused problems of synchronization. In a second step, the realization that a contract is not invalidated by termination, together with the existence of special rules for termination in the Code, led to the view that restitution after termination is a contractual remedy: termination is seen as changing the contract into an 'unwinding relationship'. This (now predominant) view has further widened the gap between restitution after termination (contract) and restitution in cases of void or avoided contracts (unjustified enrichment). Comparative research suggests that a better solution is a unified scheme for unwinding mutual contracts, irrespective of whether the contract is invalid or merely terminated, and providing for appropriate modifications where necessary.[5]

The initial English reaction to the realization that a contract is not invalidated by frustration was to regard it as destroying only those contractual obligations that are due after frustration. In *Chandler v Webster*,[6] the full £141 was due before the frustrating event. The obligation to pay was not invalidated. Therefore, the tenant could not recover the £100 which he had already paid and was still liable for the balance of £41. The problem with this outcome was not a restitutionary one: there is nothing wrong in denying recovery of performances under obligations that have not been invalidated. The difficulty lay, rather, in contract law—more precisely, in the proposition that an obligation is not affected by the fact that counter-performance has become impossible or senseless.

This contractual wound was healed in *Fibrosa*,[7] but in restitution, which is, arguably, in the wrong place. The judges left open the question whether the claimant's obligation had been invalidated by the frustrating event, but allowed a claim

---

[4] §§ 346 ff BGB. For accounts in English, see R Zimmermann, 'Restitution after Termination for Breach of Contract in German Law' [1997] RLR 13; G Dannemann, 'Restitution for Termination of Contract in German Law' in F Rose (ed), *Failure of Contracts* (1997) 129; T Krebs, *Restitution at the Crossroads: A Comparative Study* (2001) 91 ff; for the new law after the 2001 reform see R Zimmermann, Essay 17 in this volume.

[5] P Hellwege, *Die Rückabwicklung gegenseitiger Verträge als einheitliches Problem* (2004) 526–31 (comparing German, English, and Scots law; cf, in English, P Hellwege, 'Unwinding Mutual Contracts: *Restitutio in Integrum* v the Defence of Change of Position' in D Johnston and R Zimmermann (eds) *Unjustified Enrichment* (2002) 243, 263); Wendehorst (n 1) 82–3; see also C Coen, *Vertragsscheitern und Rückabwicklung* (2003) 49 ff (comparing German law, English law, CISG, PICC, and PECL); Schlechtriem (n 1) no 3/1–5; Schlechtriem *et al* (n 1) 391–4.

[6] [1904] 1 KB 493, CA.

[7] *Fibrosa Spolka Akcyjna v Fairbairn Lawson Combe Barbour Ltd* [1943] AC 32, HL.

to recover on the basis of total failure of consideration.[8] Today frustration is governed by statute, but the *Fibrosa* model can still be found in the law of breach of contract. On the one hand, termination is said to leave intact obligations which were due to be performed before termination. On the other hand, recovery is possible if the counter-performance fails.[9] The fate of unpaid obligations, like the balance of £41 in *Chandler v Webster*,[10] is somewhat unclear. It is said not to be affected by termination as such. But if the tenant paid the £41, he could recover for failure of consideration. It seems to follow that he should be relieved from paying in the first place.[11] This explanation of the claimant's release from liability turns things upside down, creating unnecessary complexity. If, because of the total failure of counter-performance, the claimant can recover if he had already paid, and ceases to be liable if he had not yet done so, one can no longer speak of a valid obligation. In these cases, termination works retrospectively, invalidating the obligation to perform. This is a failure of basis.

Given that termination requires a substantial failure of the counter-performance,[12] the additional requirement of a (total) failure of consideration for purposes of obtaining restitution seems to play only a limited role. First, it has been used by the courts to avoid problems of valuation of minor benefits which the claimant had received. But, increasingly, this approach is rejected. Secondly, recovery has sometimes to be prevented where partial performances and corresponding counter-performances have been exchanged before termination.[13] But this can also be achieved by a failure of basis approach, by acknowledging that termination does not invalidate obligations under previous 'part exchanges'.[14] This approach has the

[8] cf the comparative analysis in R Evans–Jones and K Kruse, 'Failure of Consideration' in Johnston and Zimmermann (n 5) 128.
[9] G Treitel, *The Law of Contract* (10th edn, 1999) 789.
[10] As where the tenant could not see the procession due to the landlord's breach of contract.
[11] cf Treitel (n 9) 789, 848.   [12] Treitel (n 9) 714 ff.
[13] This mainly concerns contracts for lease or employment contracts, as well as contracts to build a ship where part payments are due after certain stages of construction, as in *Hyundai Heavy Industries Ltd v Papadopoulos* [1980] 1 WLR 1129, HL; and *Stocznia Gdanska SA v Latvian Shipping Co* [1998] 1 WLR 574, HL. Cf H MacQueen, 'Contract, Unjustified Enrichment and Concurrent Liability: A Scots Perspective' in F Rose (ed), *Failure of Contracts* (1997) 199, 217 ff.
[14] cf J Beatson, 'Discharge for Breach: Instalments, Deposits, and Other Payments Due Before Completion' in J Beatson, *The Use and Abuse of Unjust Enrichment* (1991) 45, arguing in favour of treating paid and unpaid prepayments symmetrically by asking whether the right to prepayment is conditional or unconditional. This approach rightly focuses on the basis of the prepayment.
In German law, the usual form of termination invalidating all contractual obligations to perform (*Rücktritt*) is not applied to long-term contracts like lease, employment, or partnership. Instead, there is a right to terminate *in futuro* (*Kündigung*) that does not affect past obligations or performances at all; see K Larenz, *Lehrbuch des Schuldrechts*, vol I, *Allgemeiner Teil* (14th edn, 1987) 415–17; BS Markesinis, W Lorenz, and G Dannemann, *The German Law of Obligations*, vol I, *The Law of Contracts and Restitution: A Comparative Introduction* (1997) 649. The Unidroit Principles, Art 7.3.6, provide for a basic rule of restitution after termination and an exception for divisible contracts where performance has extended over a period of time. Thus the drafters have consciously rejected the solution of the Principles of European Contract Law (which follow the failure of consideration model, Art 9.305–9), regarding it as too complicated. For comparative analysis see Coen (n 5) 246–7, 281 ff; R Zimmermann, 'Restitutio in Integrum. Die Rückabwicklung fehlgeschlagener Verträge nach den

advantage of not focusing exclusively on recovery. If C rents a car in January and terminates the contract in July because the car broke down in July, he should not only be unable to recover the rent paid for the period up to June, but should, equally, remain liable to pay the rent for that period if he has not already done so.

The general problem with the unjust-factor approach is that it focuses on the question of recovery, separating it from the question of liability to perform outstanding obligations. But these questions 'do I have to perform?' and 'can I recover in a case where I have already performed?' are connected. It does not make sense to apply unjust factors to the second question in the framework of the law of restitution, while leaving the first question (without unjust factors) somewhere in the law of contract.

The new approach by Birks offers a more straightforward solution. Restitution rests on the failure of basis, which is the contractual obligation. Actual termination destroys a contractual obligation to perform.[15] However, Birks's proposition that even mere terminability is enough to destroy the basis looks somewhat odd, since it requires an exception for the party in breach.[16] The reason for including terminability seems to be[17] a property question: it is to justify the decision in *Neste Oy v Lloyds Bank*,[18] that a contractual payment turns the recipient into a trustee if, at the time of payment, it is certain that there will be no counter-performance. For Birks this proprietary response requires an initial failure of basis.[19] Therefore, mere terminability must be a failure of basis. In this essay we cannot pursue the question of whether it is appropriate to give a property right to a contracting party who, after all, assumed the risk of the insolvency of the other party. If it is not appropriate, the model could be streamlined by saying that, even in cases of terminability, there continues to be a basis so long as there has been no termination.

2.2. Defective Contracts

Both in English and German law some contractual defects give rise to a claim in restitution while others do not (the first group, I would argue, being the majority). In English law, even a contract labelled 'void' need not necessarily trigger restitution. After the swaps cases, it has been argued that one has to look for the reason why a contract is void or defective in order to decide whether restitution should be

---

Principles of European Contract Law, den Unidroit Principles und dem Avant-projet eines Code Européen des Contrats' in H Honsell, R Zäch, F Hasenböhler, F Harrer, and R Rhinow (eds), *Privatrecht und Methode: Festschrift für Ernst A Kramer* (2004) 735.

[15] Birks (n 2) 140–2.   [16] Birks (n 2) 126, 142.

[17] The reason cannot be that termination itself is regarded as a restitutionary remedy. Even if invalidating contracts belonged to the law of restitution, the test for 'unjust' is not the same as for benefits conferred (cf D Friedmann, 'Reversible Transfers—The Two Categories' [2003] RLR 1). Contracts cannot be invalidated for 'no basis', nor for any causal mistake. Termination cannot and need not be explained by 'no basis'.   [18] [1983] 2 Lloyd's Rep 658.

[19] Birks (n 2) 187.

possible even after full execution.[20] That must be right. But this is to look to the basis of the transfer, not to the unjust factor. An approach founding restitution on the failure of legal ground, or basis, does not dictate any specific result. It must be for English judges to decide whether restitution should follow after a void swap. The no basis approach merely requires the court to look for the underlying basis (the obligation under the defective contract) and to decide whether this basis holds good so as to allow the recipient to keep the benefit.

The unjust-factor approach does not primarily focus on the underlying contract. It is a mistake to assume that unjust factors necessarily mirror the reason why the contract is defective.[21] A mistake by the transferor may relate to the validity of the contract which is defective for other reasons, as in *Kleinwort Benson v Lincoln.*[22] In other cases, the mistake may be a 'purely causal mistake' relating to the transferor's motives and should not necessarily matter at all. If restitution under void executed swaps by parties knowing of the invalidity is not desired, this result should not be affected by the fact that one party mistakenly assumed that the swap would be advantageous to him from the point of view of his tax liability. Legal certainty would be better served if, instead of focusing on some diffuse elements of the transferor's state of mind, we were to look at the underlying defective contract and to decide, on a case by case basis, which kind of defects lead to restitution and which do not.

Unenforceable contracts clearly do not give a right to restitution. Although unenforceable, they form a basis. More difficult are those cases where the contract is labelled invalid or void but restitution is not warranted, for example, in cases of non-compliance with formal requirements[23] or minor illegality.[24] As

---

[20] E McKendrick, 'The Reason for Restitution' in P Birks and F Rose (eds), *Lessons of the Swaps Litigation* (2000) 84, 108; Krebs (n 4) 263; G Virgo, 'Failure of Consideration: Myth and Meaning in the English Law of Restitution' in Johnston and Zimmermann (n 5) 103, 121; D Sheehan, 'Natural Obligations in English Law' [2004] LMCLQ 172, 186–7.

[21] For the same reason, the unjust factors cannot be defended by arguing that they determine the details of the restitutionary response (cf M Chen–Wishart, 'In Defence of Unjust Factors: A Study of Rescission for Duress, Fraud and Exploitation' in Johnston and Zimmermann (n 5) 159; R Stevens, 'The New Birksian Approach to Unjust Enrichment' [2004] RLR 271). It is certainly true that the measure of recovery, the defences, and other remedial aspects are dependent on the reason why the contract is invalid (and other circumstances of the case), but this reason is not necessarily reflected by the unjust factor. The defendant's liability is, in both England and Germany, stricter if he knew he was not entitled to the benefit, and generally more lenient if he is a minor, independently of the unjust factor. The defence of change of position may be appropriate in some cases of mistake (wrong recipient) or failure of consideration (payment subject to contract), but not in others (in particular the exchange of performances under valid and void contracts, where several unjust factors are conceivable). Cf Krebs (n 4) 297–300.

[22] *Kleinwort Benson Ltd v Lincoln City Council* [1999] 2 AC 349, HL. This is not to say that the mistake is not important: its existence shows that the claimant did not take the risk that the basis does not exist. See Section 2.5 below.

[23] eg *Tootal Clothing Ltd v Guinea Properties Ltd* (1992) 64 P & CR 452, CA. For a comparative account see England (n 1) no 102–111.

[24] Cases of serious illegality cannot be used as an argument for or against a no basis approach. No legal system working with a legal ground model has been forced to grant automatic restitution

Krebs has rightly pointed out, German law works with a technical notion of voidness, which is used only if restitution is to follow, whereas in English law 'void' has no such meaning.[25] I have argued elsewhere that 'void contract' need not necessarily mean 'no basis'.[26] The non-technical use of the word 'void' may permit us to conclude that the purported contract, although not enforceable, may provide a reason for retaining benefits transferred under it. Others have suggested that we should work with 'just factors' or natural obligations.[27] Birks's solution is to use the defence of stultification. His argument is that there cannot be a basis when a statute says there is no contract.[28] Whether to locate the solution under 'unjust' or under the defences may still be a matter of debate. Saying that a contract, though void, can nevertheless provide a basis has the advantage that the underlying obligation and the reason for its invalidity are investigated together at one stage. On the other hand, saying that there is no basis but a defence has the advantage of making for a simpler notion of 'basis'.

Sometimes the validity of the contract depends on the decision of one party. For Birks, mere rescindability (eg for misrepresentation) is enough to show a failure of basis.[29] Again, I would regard it as more natural to say that the basis falls away (retrospectively) only after rescission—which obviates the need to make special exceptions for the other party's right to recover. The same can be said of contracts with minors. The adult cannot recover his performance if the minor wants to stick to the contract. For Birks, the contract provides no basis and therefore the bar to restitution by the adult has to be explained by the defence of stultification.[30] But it can be argued that, today, minors' contracts are not void, but usually simply not binding on the minor, and, more importantly, that the minor in these cases has a claim for money performance (albeit not specific performance) against the adult.[31] If the adult is obliged to pay, there must be a basis. Therefore, a contract by a minor could be said to form a basis until the minor 'abandons' the contract.[32]

---

in these cases. The results of the cases in German and English law cannot be explained by mere reference to 'no basis' or to unjust factors, but only with reference to a defence of turpitude/illegality, which both laws apply in a similar way. The problem is rather when to apply the defence and when not. See the comparative analyses by K Zweigert and H Kötz, *An Introduction to Comparative Law* (T Weir (tr), 3rd edn, 1998) 575–82; H van Kooten, 'Illegality and Restitution as a Matter of Policy Considerations' [2001] RLR 67; G Dannemann, 'Illegality as Defence against Unjust Enrichment Claims' in Johnston and Zimmermann (n 5) 310.

[25] Krebs (n 4) 88, 179 ff, 247–8.
[26] S Meier, 'Restitution after Executed Void Contracts' in Birks and Rose (n 20) 168, 182, 201–2.
[27] Krebs (n 4) 263–70; Sheehan (n 20) 185–93.   [28] Birks (n 2) 257.
[29] Birks (n 2) 126.   [30] Birks (n 2) 116–17, 254–5.   [31] Treitel (n 9) 508.
[32] In special cases this would require a formal repudiation, but usually an indication that he does not feel himself bound would be enough, like non-performance or a claim to recover his performance.

2.3. Other Bases

The (purported) basis underlying a transfer and, if existing, justifying the retention of the benefit, need not be a contractual, or even any other obligation. It can be a kind of legal relationship between the claimant and defendant which comes into existence only with the transfer (as in the case of contracts, trusts, and gifts),[33] or even after the transfer.[34]

The Civil Law recognizes as legal grounds obligations which are not enforceable but which nevertheless provide a reason for the recipient to retain the benefit—most notably time-barred claims.[35] They exclude recovery even if the transferor mistakenly assumed that the obligation was legally enforceable. Such 'natural' obligations seem to have been recognized also in England before the mistake of law bar was introduced.[36] Now, after its abolition, even proponents of the unjust-factor approach argue for their renaissance.[37] In Birks's scheme natural obligations are recognized not as bases but as defences.[38] Again, there is a certain unresolved tension between the notion of basis and those defences which Birks calls 'unjust related'.[39] Quite a number of them (*res iudicata*, contract for finality, informality, natural obligations) relate to what civilians call a legal ground. The question whether they are better regarded as bases or as defences may also depend on the burden of proof.

2.4. The Burden of Proof

Founding restitution on the absence of a legal ground does not mean that the defendant has to show and prove a justification in order to keep the benefit. At least from a German point of view, that would be regarded as monstrous. Unjust enrichment law follows the general rule that a claimant has to show the necessary elements of his claim. German law has the following rules for enrichments by transfers.[40] The claimant has to show that he transferred a benefit to the defendant on a particular basis that does not exist. If the existence of this basis is a matter of dispute between the claimant and the defendant, the burden of proof

[33] As pointed out by Birks (n 2) 143–52.
[34] I shall discuss this subject separately below; see Section 2.6.
[35] For a comparative account, see England (n 1) no 21–9; for German law Krebs (n 4) 267–8. Other candidates are moral obligations like that in *Larner v London County Council* [1949] 2 KB 683, CA, or obligations discharged by an insolvency agreement, cf the Scottish case *Moore's Executors v M'Dermid* 1913 1 SLT 278. [36] Sheehan (n 20).
[37] Krebs (n 4) 269; Sheehan (n 20) 184 ff. [38] Birks (n 2) 257–8.
[39] Birks (n 2) 224–64. *Res iudicata* appears both as a basis and in the chapter on defences, ibid 140, 233.
[40] See Bundesgerichtshof (BGH), 1983 Neue Juristische Wochenschrift (NJW) 626; BGH 1990 NJW 392, 393; W Lorenz, in *J von Staudingers Kommentar zum Bürgerlichen Gesetzbuch*, §§ 812–22 (1999) § 812 no 92; M Lieb, in *Münchener Kommentar zum Bürgerlichen Gesetzbuch*, Vol V (4th edn, 2004) § 812 no 393; and D König, *Ungerechtfertigte Bereicherung* (1985) 33 ff, translated in J Beatson and E Schrage (eds), *Cases, Materials and Texts on Unjustified Enrichment* (2003) 6 G 41.

is on the claimant. If the basis named by the claimant does not exist, the defendant may argue that there is instead (or in truth) another basis justifying the transfer. It is for the defendant to point to a particular basis, but when the existence of this second basis is disputed, the burden of proof is once again on the claimant.

It should be noted that a strict application of the unjust-factor approach requires that, where a transfer has been made under a potentially invalid contract and the claimant can show some kind of causal mistake (eg the mistake about tax consequences referred to above), the burden of proof regarding the validity of the contract seems to shift to the defendant, because the contractual claim is merely a defence. This is at least a doubtful result.

The burden of proof might be an argument for regarding natural obligations and the other unjust-related defences mentioned above as bases rather than as defences: if the existence of an underlying time-barred obligation, judgment, or informal contract is disputed, the burden of proof should be on the claimant.

2.5. Additional Requirements Besides no Basis

Comparative experience shows that there have been various ways of denying recovery to a transferor who asserts a failure of basis if he knew perfectly well that the basis did not exist or would not come into existence.[41] Some countries work with an error requirement, which differs from the unjust-factor mistake in that it is only a secondary element in addition to the absence of basis and the mistake always relates to the existence of the legal ground. The German Code provides a defence if the claimant knows that the legal ground does not exist.[42] Other countries do without a special requirement or defence, preventing recovery by undeserving claimants by recourse to a presumption of donation or to the prohibition of *venire contra factum proprium*. Comparative research suggests that there has been a shift of focus away from considering the transferor's state of mind and towards an inquiry into whether it is worth protecting the recipient's reliance on retaining the benefit.[43]

For Birks, a claimant who pays under an obligation, knowing that it does not exist or not caring whether it exists, can be denied recovery by the argument that the basis of his transfer is a gift, which did not fail.[44] More generally, a claimant must not knowingly take the risk that the basis does not exist.[45] The denial of recovery seems to be by way of establishing a basis for the transfer rather than by way of a defence. In any case, the bar does not apply to the *Woolwich* claim[46]

---

[41] Schlechtriem (n 1) no 2/72–119, 2/142–77, 2/548; Wendehorst (n 1) 74, 98–9; in English: England (n 1) no 13, 17–20; J du Plessis, 'Towards a Rational Structure of Liability for Unjustified Enrichment: Thoughts from Two Mixed Jurisdictions' in R Zimmermann, *Grundstrukturen* (n 1) 175, 191–2, 204–9.   [42] BGB § 814; cf also § 815 for future bases.
[43] Du Plessis (n 41) 204–9.   [44] Birks (n 2) 103–4.   [45] Birks (n 2) 130, 142.
[46] *Woolwich Equitable Building Society v Inland Revenue Commissioners* [1993] AC 70, HL.

(which Birks now regards as a normal case of transfer without basis, not being restricted to ultra vires receipts).[47] It would follow that knowledge by the transferor that the obligation does not exist does not bar recovery if the transferor (i) communicated his intention to recover to the defendant and (ii) instituted legal proceedings in order to establish the non-existence of the obligation. Such a rule would not only provide a more satisfactory explanation for the outcomes in the *Sebel Products* and *Nurdin & Peacock* cases,[48] but would also shift the focus to the defendant, whose reliance in these cases may not be worth protecting.

2.6. Future Bases and Bases Not Known to the Recipient

One of the major problems of a failure of basis approach is to determine what constitutes a basis. Both German and English law sometimes allow recovery in cases of a failure of a future basis[49] or a basis unknown to the recipient.[50] But if every present or future fact contemplated by the transferor, but not necessarily communicated to the recipient, counts as a basis, there is the danger of an uncontrollable flood of restitution claims.

The solution of the unjust-factor approach is to differentiate between present and future.[51] If the fact which the claimant wrongly assumes concerns the present, the unjust factor is mistake, triggering recovery. If the fact concerns the future, the unjust factor can only be failure of consideration. Recovery then requires that the basis of the transfer had been communicated to the recipient. Whereas the transferor does not bear the risk that his assumptions about the present are wrong, he carries the risk concerning assumptions about the future, which he can, however, shift to the transferee by communication.

This has a certain intuitive appeal. However, a transferor may also be a risk-taker as to the present, even if he is mistaken: C cleans D's windows in the hope of being remunerated afterwards, not knowing that D is on holiday. Vice versa, it can be argued that sometimes a transferor should not be regarded as a risk-taker even with regard to future events, for example, where A pays in order to discharge a future liability that he reasonably expects to come into existence. If we assume that in *Kerrison v Glyn*[52] the basis, in the form of the future liability, was not communicated, the unjust-factor approach can explain recovery only

---

[47] Birks (n 2) 134.

[48] *Sebel Products Ltd v Commissioners of Customs and Excise* [1949] Ch 409; *Nurdin & Peacock v Ramsden* [1999] 1 WLR 1249.

[49] An English example is *Kerrison v Glyn, Mills, Currie & Co* (1911) 81 LJKB 465, HL, where the basis was a liability which the claimant expected to accrue in the future.

[50] eg a transfer to the wrong recipient, or cases like *RE Jones Ltd v Waring and Gillow Ltd* [1926] AC 670, HL, where the claimant and defendant are fraudulently induced by a third party to believe in different bases of the transfer.

[51] P Birks, *An Introduction to the Law of Restitution* (1985) 147–8, 219; P Birks, 'Restitution after Ineffective Contracts' (1990) 2 JCL 227, 235; A Burrows, *The Law of Restitution* (2nd edn, 2002) 146, 408; McKendrick (n 20) 105. 'Present' includes past facts.

[52] *Kerrison v Glyn, Mills, Currie & Co* (1911) 81 LJKB 465, HL.

by relying on the fact that the act of bankruptcy had occurred before the payment, so that there was a causal mistake. If it had occurred shortly after payment, recovery had to be denied. I do not find this supposed differentiation convincing. A more promising approach is to focus on the kind of purpose which the transferor had in mind. If it related to an established sub-species of basis, like obligation or trust, the transferor probably does not take the risk that it does not exist or will not come into existence. On the other hand, if it is the hope of remuneration, the transferor should always be regarded as a risk-taker unless he communicated his intention to the transferee.

German law, in this regard, basically distinguishes between transfers under an assumed present obligation, where communication is not needed for recovery,[53] and transfers in order to elicit a future counter-performance (outside contract), where recovery requires that the purpose is communicated to the transferee.[54] Thus, we find here both the contrast 'present–future' and the contrast 'obligation–remuneration' at work. A transfer under an assumed future obligation lies in-between; it is therefore disputed whether it belongs to the first or second group.[55]

Rightly, in my view, in his new approach Birks abandons the fundamental differentiation between present and future facts. The test for (assumed) present and future bases is the same: the claimant must not knowingly take the risk that the basis does not exist or will not come into existence. He does not take the risk if his intention is impaired, or if he communicated the basis to the defendant, or if he can reasonably expect the defendant to know the basis.[56] There seems to be no problem with this approach as long as the basis is a contract, other obligation, trust, or gift. However, it may be dangerous to view the notion of 'basis' too broadly.[57] A transferor intending to qualify the transfer with regard to any circumstances outside the established bases should arguably be required to communicate his qualification.

---

[53] This is the *condictio indebiti*, to be found in BGB § 812 I 1, 1st alternative.

[54] § 812 I 2, 2nd alternative, the *condictio causa data causa non secuta* (or *condictio ob rem*). It resembles recovery for non-contractual failure of consideration in England. The basis is, however, not seen in the counter-performance, but in a kind of agreement between transferor and transferee. It comes into existence when the transferee takes the benefit knowing the transferor's purpose, and justifies the retention by the transferee. Failure of counter-performance extinguishes this conventional right to retain. The analysis is similar to that presented above for contractual performances. See D Reuter and M Martinek, *Ungerechtfertigte Bereicherung* (1983) 148–54; K Larenz and CW Canaris, *Lehrbuch des Schuldrechts*, vol II/2, *Besonderer Teil* (13th edn, 1994) 152–3; Lieb (n 40) § 812 no 196, 200–2.

[55] cf Reichsgericht, (1909) 71 Entscheidungen in Zivilsachen (RGZ) 316; Reuter/Martinek (n 54) 152–3; Lieb (n 40) § 812 no 212; Lorenz (n 40) § 814 no 8.

[56] Birks (n 2) 142 ff; cf F Maher, 'A New Conception of Failure of Basis' [2004] RLR 96, 100–4.

[57] cf Birks (n 2) 152–4, in particular Birks's discussion of *Re Cleadon Trust Ltd* [1939] Ch 286, CA.

3. 'No Basis' in Other Cases

Comparative experience shows that a failure of basis approach faces no serious obstacles in the transfer cases discussed above.[58] It is different with other cases of unjust enrichment. If there is no transfer aimed at a specific purpose, it is difficult to conceive wherein such a failure could lie. At best, the legal ground or basis for the enrichment is simply absent. If the notion of 'no legal ground' were simply a label used to describe situations where enrichment claims are granted, it would not mean much. The question is, rather, whether 'no legal ground' or 'no basis' has a more specific meaning which can be used to give a better explanation of the law.[59]

3.1. Benefits Taken Away

English authors have distinguished between the following two groups of cases.

(a) D receives an asset that has been taken away from C. This is enrichment by subtraction. D need not be a wrongdoer. In practice, D is usually a third party. The link between C and D is established by the fact that the asset belonged (at law or in equity) to C when D received it. The reason for restitution (ignorance, C's property right) has proved to be controversial.[60]

(b) The enrichment of D is a result of a wrong committed by D. There is no subtraction, that is, the asset D received has never been part of C's patrimony. It has been disputed whether these cases belong to the law of unjust enrichment, to a unified law of restitution, or to the law of wrongs.[61] Some of them probably cannot be explained in terms of enrichment at the claimant's expense.[62] But

---

[58] cf the comparative analysis by Wendehorst (n 1) 81 and du Plessis (n 41) 202 ff who both come out in favour of the *sine causa* model rather than the unjust-factor approach; also N Whitty, 'Rationality, Nationality and the Taxonomy of Unjustified Enrichment' in Johnston and Zimmermann (n 5) 658, 680 ff; F Schäfer, *Das Bereicherungsrecht in Europa* (2001) 680–1.

[59] cf du Plessis (n 41) 175 ff, distinguishing a wide and a narrow meaning of 'without legal cause'.

[60] cf Birks, *An Introduction to the Law of Restitution* (1985) 140–6; W Swadling, 'A Claim in Restitution?' [1996] LMCLQ 63; RB Grantham and CEF Rickett, 'Restitution, Property and Ignorance—A Reply to Mr Swadling' [1996] LMCLQ 463; Burrows (n 51) 182 ff; G Virgo, *The Principles of the Law of Restitution* (1999) 11–16, 591 ff; Lord Goff of Chieveley and G Jones, *The Law of Restitution* (6th edn, 2002) para 4-002; P Jaffey, *The Nature and Scope of Restitution* (2000) 160–2; L Smith, 'Unjust Enrichment, Property, and the Structure of Trusts' (2000) 116 LQR 412.

[61] See eg P Birks, 'Misnomer' in WR Cornish, R Nolan, J O'Sullivan and G Virgo (eds), *Restitution: Past, Present and Future* (1998) 1; Burrows (n 51) 25–31, 455–62; Virgo (n 60) 10, 445 ff; M McInnes, 'Restitution, Unjust Enrichment and the Perfect Quadration Thesis' [1999] RLR 118, 120–2.

[62] 'Disgorgement cases' like *AG v Blake* [2001] 1 AC 268, HL, or cases where fiduciaries have to give up gains made in breach of duty, like *Boardman v Phipps* [1967] 2 AC 46, HL; cf P Schlechtriem, *Restitution und Bereicherungsausgleich in Europa*, vol II (2001) no 6/150–1. German law has a number of scattered gain-based claims against fiduciaries outside unjust enrichment law; see, comparing German and English law, K Rusch, *Gewinnhaftung bei Verletzung von Treuepflichten* (2003). See also T Krebs, Essay 20 in this volume.

others could be so explained, for example, where D sells or uses C's car without C's consent. For such an analysis it had to be acknowledged that (i) unjust enrichment claims require neither a loss by the claimant[63] nor a direct shift of wealth and (ii) the use or the proceeds of the sale of a thing are benefits attributed by law to its owner and so D's enrichment is at C's expense.[64] Birks now favours a dual analysis in these cases.[65] C's claim to recover the benefit can then be explained both by D's unjust enrichment and by the wrong.[66]

A common feature of the cases in group (a) and of those in group (b) that are regarded as instances of unjust enrichment is that D appropriates a right which the law attributes to C. This is either C's property, or a right arising from C's property, or another right which the law attributes exclusively to C. The invasion of such a right could then be regarded as the reason for restitution. But one might equally well locate these considerations under 'at the expense of' and then explain restitution by the absence of a basis in the form of C's consent.[67] This is what Birks now does by joining both groups of cases as 'non-participatory enrichments' and saying that in these cases there is normally no basis.[68] There seems to be no particular difficulty with this approach.

3.2. Incidental Benefits

Things get more difficult if the enrichment has been caused by the claimant (but did not involve a failed transfer, as dealt with at Section 2 above). One of the problems which German authors faced after the Code introduced a general enrichment action was to explain why not every incidental benefit can be

[63] Burrows (n 51) 28; Birks (n 2) 78–86.

[64] cf J Beatson, 'The Nature of Waiver of Tort' in J Beatson, *The Use and Abuse of Unjust Enrichment* (1991) 206, 208, 230–4; D Friedmann, 'Restitution for Wrongs: The Basis of Liability' in Cornish *et al* (n 61) 133; T Krebs, 'Eingriffskondiktion und Restitution for Wrongs im englischen Recht' in Zimmermann, *Grundstrukturen* (n 1) 141 ff; S Swann, 'The Structure of Liability for Unjustified Enrichment: First Proposals of the Study Group on a European Civil Code', ibid 265, 270–1. The claim may, however, be directed to the reasonable value, not to the profits.

[65] Birks (n 2) 15, 83–5.

[66] cf Goff and Jones (n 60) para 32–002. For comparative accounts dealing with the appropriate description of restitution after wrongs, see C von Bar, *The Common European Law of Torts*, vol I (1998), no 519–25; Schlechtriem (n 62) no 6/3–47; see also P Schlechtriem, *Unjust Enrichment by Interference with Property Rights* (International Encyclopedia of Comparative Law, vol X, ch 8, 2001) no 1–12. In German law, the only remedy in delict is compensation; therefore the claim has to be in unjust enrichment. But there is a similar controversy whether the reason for the claim in these cases is the law's attribution of the benefit to C or the unlawful interference by D: Reuter and Martinek (n 54) 234–48; Larenz and Canaris (n 54) 168–72; Lieb (n 40) § 812 no 234–52; D Medicus, *Bürgerliches Recht* (19th edn, 2002) no 704–12; see also Markesinis/Lorenz/Dannemann (n 4) 744–6; and D Visser, 'Wohin führt der Weg von Damaskus? Peter Birks: Unjust Enrichment' [2005] Zeitschrift für Europäisches Privatrecht 118, 124–5 (criticizing Birks's approach in this regard). It may be that these are two sides of the same coin, see Schlechtriem (n 62) no 6/8.

[67] In German law it is debated whether the fact that the benefit is attributed to C belongs to 'at the expense of' or to 'unjustified'; cf Lieb (n 40) § 812 no 234; Reuter and Martinek (n 54) 240–1.

[68] Birks (n 2) 129, 155.

recovered as being without legal ground.[69] It seems that Birks's no basis approach faces similar problems. There is no right to restitution if C's central heating cuts the fuel bills of his upstairs neighbour D. But the suggested explanation that C's principal activity was freely intended[70] is not entirely convincing. Presumably C will not be entitled to restitution if he was obliged to heat his flat under a contract with his landlord, which turns out to be void, or where a third party forced him to do so. This means that another explanation has to be found, even if we work with unjust factors.

The best explanation seems to be that D's enrichment is not at C's expense. Causation alone is not enough. Instead, one can ask whether the law attributes the benefit to the claimant. Heat which escapes a flat is not attributed to the owner of the flat or to the person generating it; it belongs to no one. The same holds true if I switch on the light in my flat which shines into my neighbour's room with the result that she can read a book without having to turn her light on, thereby saving her having to spend money on electricity. I am allowed to prevent the light or the heat from escaping from my flat, but as soon as it does, any resulting benefits are no longer attributed to me.

3.3. Improvements

A general enrichment action, basing restitution on the absence of legal ground, has always encountered difficulties when applied to claims of 'improvers', that is, claimants improving the property of another without intending to discharge an obligation or to make an unqualified gift.[71]

In some cases the improver C acts on an understanding shared by or known to the owner D, for example, that C and D will live together in the improved house, or that C will inherit the property. In German law, it is disputed whether in these cases the *condictio ob rem* (a claim based on making a transfer) or the general enrichment action for enrichments outside transfers will apply. However, the German courts and also some authors apply the same test, no matter which action is used, namely, whether C's expectation is shared by or communicated to D, and whether it has failed.[72] Secret expectations do not lead to restitution. The basis for retaining the enrichment would then be a gift. Similar results can be

---

[69] See eg Larenz and Canaris (n 54) 134–6; Lorenz (n 40) § 812 no 23; and Bundesgerichtshof, (1989) 107 Entscheidungen in Zivilsachen (BGHZ) 117, translated in Markesinis *et al* (n 14) case 137; and in Beatson and Schrage (n 40) 4 G7. Cf, for English law, A Tettenborn, *Law of Restitution in England and Ireland* (3rd edn, 2002) para 1–42.   [70] Birks (n 2) 158–9.

[71] Where the claimant so intends, restitution should depend on a failure of this basis. Cf P Schlechtriem, C Coen, and R Hornung, 'Restitution and Unjust Enrichment in Europe' [2001] European Review of Private Law 377, 396.

[72] Bundesgerichtshof (1961) 35 BGHZ 356; (1965) 44 BGHZ 321; 1970 NJW 136; (1989) 108 BGHZ 256, 263, 265; 2001 NJW 3118; Reuter and Martinek (n 54) 169–71; Lorenz (n 40) § 812 no 112; Larenz and Canaris (n 54) 150, 154; Lieb (n 40) § 812 no 199, 207.

reached by the unjust factor failure of consideration or by the absence of basis approach.[73]

More difficult are cases where C improves D's property because he believes that he is the owner (the *bona fide* improver) or because, although not mistaken, he intends to enjoy the improved property since the owner is absent (the *mala fide* improver).

Civil law countries have inherited from Roman law specific rules for cases where the improvement (of land or of chattels) is made by a possessor.[74] Recovery depends, *inter alia*, on whether C believed he was the owner; the kind of improvement; whether the expenses were necessary, merely useful, or only of a luxurious nature; whether the improvement was in D's interest; and whether C's claim is a counter-claim against D vindicating the property or an independent claim. These rules do not entirely fit the 'enrichment without legal ground' model: the measure of recovery is usually the expenses, not the enrichment. In some cases expenses can be recovered without enrichment, whereas the *mala fide* improver can sometimes not recover, despite an incontrovertible benefit to the owner. The rules are not pure unjust enrichment law, but balance the interests of the owner and the possessor, thereby partly allocating losses.[75] The lack of a legal ground alone is not enough.[76]

In German law, however, these are statutory rules which apply in special cases. Those improvement cases which are not governed by them fall under general enrichment law—which founds restitution on the absence of legal ground.[77] As 'no legal ground' means 'no contract, agreement, obligation, gift etc', even a *mala fide* improver can, in principle, recover. This raises the question why the owner should be required to pay for a benefit which he never asked for when the improver was not mistaken. Whereas some authors favour excluding restitution altogether in such cases by special defences, the majority (in line with most Civil Law systems) grant even the *mala fide* improver a

---

[73] Birks (n 2) 150.

[74] For comparative accounts see D Verse, *Verwendungen im Eigentümer-Besitzer-Verhältnis* (1999) (German, French, and English law); Schlechtriem (n 62) no 5/1–143; for Scots law J Wolffe, 'Enrichment by Improvements in Scots Law' in Johnston and Zimmermann (n 5) 384–430.

[75] A similar point is made for American law by A Kull, 'Mistaken Improvements and the Restitution Calculus' in Johnston and Zimmermann (n 5) 369–83.

[76] This has brought a comparatist to the conclusion that regarding improvements, the unjust-factor approach is more workable than the *sine causa* approach: Wendehorst (n 1) 127–8. It may also explain Lord Rodger's reference to a 'relevant factor' causing an enrichment to be unjust in *Shilliday v Smith* 1998 SC 725, 731: he referred to improvement cases.

[77] See Verse (n 74) 43 ff, 157 ff, comparing the law of unjustified enrichment (§§ 812 ff BGB), as applied to improvements, with the statutory rules on improvements by possessors (§§ 987 ff BGB), arguing that the existence of two sets of rules is both unnecessary and confusing; cf also, in English, R Zimmermann and J du Plessis, 'Basic Features of the German Law of Unjustified Enrichment' [1994] RLR 14, 30; R Zimmermann, *Roman Law, Contemporary Law, European Law* (2001) 115–18; MJ Schermaier, 'Current Questions in the German Law of Enrichment' in EJH Schrage (ed), *Unjust Enrichment and the Law of Contract* (2001) 115, 117–21; Markesinis *et al* (n 4) 749–50; Beatson and Schrage (n 40) 44–6, 441–3, 448–9.

claim, but protect the owner by an extremely subjective test of enrichment.[78] Thus, restitution may indeed be based on an absence of legal ground. But the use of defences or of different tests of enrichment, according to whether the improver was mistaken or not, shows that this is only the starting point for the inquiry.

In England improvement claims are more restricted. There seems to be no restitution for improvements to another's land unless the owner acquiesced. Improvements to chattels may give rise to a claim if the improver thought that he was owner. The legal writers seem to favour a general rule granting restitution to mistaken improvers.[79] A *mala fide* improver is denied recovery. Founding restitution on the absence of a legal ground in the German sense (no contract, gift etc) seems, therefore, not to work.

Birks does not explicitly discuss the case of a mistaken improver. Probably he would see it as a case of non-participatory enrichment, the enrichment being a by-product of the improvement. The test would then be whether the improvement was freely intended, in which case the basis is a gift. The mistaken improver can recover because his intention was impaired. In the end, this approach seems to come close to the unjust-factors approach: there is a basis if no vitiating factors are present. The meaning of 'basis' is different from the meaning of legal ground in the Civil Law.

In English law it seems indeed to be more natural to say that restitution by an improver requires an additional element like mistake. But it is probably not every kind of mistake that can found restitution. Negligence by the improver may play a role. Restitution may be uncontroversial if the improver regarded himself as owner. But someone who consciously improves another's property, while being mistaken about his own financial means or the character of the owner[80] may be denied recovery—at least if the English hostility against officious intermeddlers is taken seriously.

The results in the improvement cases can, therefore, be explained neither by the absence of a legal ground in the narrow sense, nor by an unjust-factor approach that uses the 'causal mistake' test for all kinds of enrichment constellations. There are mistaken transfers and mistaken improvers, but the function and scope of mistake are arguably different.[81]

---

[78] Larenz and Canaris (n 54) 286–91; Lieb (n 40) § 812 no 307–14; Verse (n 74) 119 ff; for accounts in English see T Krebs, 'Unrequested Benefits in German Law', in JW Neyers, M McInnes, and SGA Pitel (eds), *Understanding Unjust Enrichment* (2004) 247; D Verse, 'Improvements and Enrichment: A Comparative Analysis' [1998] RLR 85.

[79] Burrows (n 51) 162–6; Goff and Jones (n 60) paras 6–001, 6–011.

[80] Or wrongly assuming that enrichment law will provide a remedy, cf *Nurdin & Peacock v Ramsden* [1999] 1 WLR 1249.

[81] cf, commenting on *Shilliday v Smith* (n 76), P Hellwege, 'Rationalising the Scottish Law of Unjustified Enrichment' (2000) 11 Stellenbosch Law Review 50, 62–3; du Plessis (n 41) 199–200.

3.4. Payment of Another's Debt: Restitution Against the Debtor

Civilian legal systems allow a stranger C to discharge another's debt.[82] Restitution against the debtor D is sometimes based on the law of *negotiorum gestio*, if the discharge was in D's interest. Otherwise, C has a claim in unjustified enrichment. In view of the free assignability of debts, the fact that C makes himself a creditor of D is not regarded as a problem.[83] D may, however, not have been enriched when the original claim was subject to defences or counter-claims. The solution of modern German law is to allow D to raise all the defences which he had against his creditor as defences against C's restitution claim, in order to ensure that he is not made worse off by C's payment.[84] Under these circumstances restitution is awarded liberally. 'No legal ground' here merely means that no contract or other legal relationship existed between C and D. Unlike the 'transfer cases' (above, Section 2), restitution cannot be explained by a failure of basis. C has achieved his primary purpose of discharging D's debt, and he knew that D had not agreed to remunerate him. The reason for restitution is that the burden of discharging the debt rests on D rather than on C. As the claim is not founded upon a failure of basis, knowledge that there is no legal ground *vis-à-vis* D is no defence. Because of these differences, German law regards payments of another's debt as a special sub-category of unjustified enrichment.

The first problem in English law is that a stranger is not simply entitled to discharge another's debt. For present purposes it will be assumed that the debt has been discharged or, as Birks has suggested,[85] that an imperfect discharge can found a restitution claim by way of subrogation. Restitution against the debtor is then not granted automatically but seems to require a specific reason. This makes the unjust-factor approach attractive. Birks's new approach is similar. The discharge is a by-product of the payment. If C pays voluntarily, he freely intends the discharge; the basis is a gift. If C's intention to pay is vitiated by what amounts to an unjust-factor, for example, legal compulsion, there is no basis for the discharge.[86]

---

[82] For comparative accounts see D Friedmann and N Cohen, *Payment of Another's Debt* (International Encyclopedia of Comparative Law, vol X, ch 10, 1991); Schlechtriem (n 62) no 7/154-205; S Whittaker, 'Performance of another's obligation: French and English law contrasted' in Johnston and Zimmermann (n 5) 433–57; H MacQueen, 'Payment of Another's Debt' ibid 458–89 (focusing on Scots law).

[83] Extreme cases can be taken care of by the good faith requirement in Germany or a 'no fault' requirement in France; see Friedmann and Cohen (n 82) no 14–15; Whittaker (n 82) 444.

[84] Larenz and Canaris (n 54) 192; Reuter and Martinek (n 54) 189–92, 471–3; Lieb (n 40) § 812 no 124–5; Medicus (n 66) no 952; cf Friedmann and Cohen (n 82) no 23. Nevertheless, it is not perceived as subrogation. The claim against D is not the (secured) creditor's claim but C's (unsecured) claim in unjustified enrichment.

[85] Birks (n 2) 61, 159–60, 170–1; following C Mitchell, *The Law of Subrogation* (1994) 5–6, 9–10.

[86] Birks (n 2) 55, 158–60.

In the light of English law's hostility against intermeddlers, it is no surprise that restitution against the debtor requires additional elements apart from discharge. It is, however, questionable whether these elements can be fitted into a general system of unjust factors. A volunteer who willingly discharges another's debt will presumably not be granted restitution if his motive for doing so was impaired by a mistake, for example, about his own financial abilities or the character of the debtor.

More importantly, the unjust factor 'legal compulsion'[87] (used for restitution claims against the principal debtor by sureties, co-debtors, or owners of goods which have been seized by the creditor) does not fit the other unjust factors of impaired intention. Prima facie, it distinguishes the deserving compelled claimant from the intermeddler. The consequence would be to exclude from restitution claimants who voluntarily brought themselves into the situation of legal compulsion,[88] like 'officious sureties'. This was done in *Owen v Tate*,[89] but it is arguably wrong. Moreover, legal compulsion is applied only in three-party cases, and here only in cases of discharge of another's debt, not in improvement situations. If C, having contracted with T to renovate D's house, only starts working because T threatened to go to court, he cannot recover from D. He worked under a contract with T and should look to T for his remuneration.[90] But the surety, contractual co-debtor, or insurer can have restitution—despite having paid under a contract with the creditor. All this means that, in cases of discharge of another's debt, legal compulsion may be able to indicate when there is restitution, but not explain why there is restitution.

The real reason why the surety or co-debtor is allowed to recoup his payment from the principal debtor seems to be neither legal compulsion nor an absence of basis but the fact that there is a plurality of debtors. Without apportionment, the creditor would be allowed to decide who bears the final burden, which would be neither just nor efficient.[91] This may be the reason why the Mercantile Law

---

[87] Burrows (n 51) 273 ff; Virgo (n 60) 223 ff; Mitchell, ibid 51 ff.; Tettenborn (n 69) no 8/1, 8/7–8/10.

[88] Similar arguments in C Mitchell, *The Law of Contribution and Reimbursement* (2003) no 3.27; MP Gergen, 'Self-Interested Intervention in the Law of Unjust Enrichment' in Zimmermann (ed), *Grundstrukturen* (n 1) 243, 255; cf also Jaffey (n 60) 95–6.

[89] [1976] 1 QB 402, CA.

[90] cf Goff and Jones (n 60) no 1–074; Birks (n 2) 89–92.

[91] cf Friedmann and Cohen (n 82) no 13; D Friedmann and N Cohen, *Adjustment among Multiple Debtors* (International Encyclopedia of Comparative Law, vol X, ch 11, 1991) no 9; J Dieckmann, *Der Derivativregreß des Bürgen gegen den Hauptschuldner im englischen und deutschen Recht* (2003) 99–102, 123–7, 289–91. It is, therefore, questionable whether subrogation in these cases is a matter of unjust enrichment at all, cf R Williams, 'Preventing Unjust Enrichment' [2000] RLR 492; S Hedley, *Restitution: Its Division and Ordering* (2001) 119–48; J Hilliard, 'A Case for the Abolition of Legal Compulsion as a Ground of Restitution' [2002] CLJ 551; from a historical and comparative point of view, focusing on the surety's right to subrogation, Dieckmann, ibid 245–314, 446–63, 515–24; cf in English J Dieckmann, 'Scots Law Influence on English Law: The Guarantor's Right to Derivative Recourse (Subrogation)' (2004) 8 Edin LR 329, 343–9.

Amendment Act, granting subrogation to sureties and co-debtors, does not distinguish between officious and deserving sureties.

Although restitution after discharge of another's debt requires more than the discharge, it does not seem to be possible to explain the outcomes simply by using the same test as in other constellations of unjust enrichment.[92]

4. Conclusion

The German experience with its general enrichment action in § 812 BGB was initially not a happy one.[93] The uncertainty created by the formula 'enrichment without legal ground' was dissipated only slowly by academic writers who distinguished between different sub-groups of unjust enrichment, each with its own test for 'no legal ground'.[94] English law, as Krebs has rightly pointed out, would face the same difficulties if it introduced a general enrichment action that was to be applied indiscriminately in the various enrichment constellations.[95] But an equally indiscriminate application of a general system of unjust factors cannot cope with the peculiarities of the different constellations either. There may be specific reasons for restitution, but they are not the same everywhere. A more promising way forward is not to start with a general test (whether it is no basis or an unjust factor system), but to inquire into the specific problems of each enrichment constellation, finding out what the reason for restitution really is.

For the large group of cases where the claimant who benefits the defendant has a particular basis (contract, other obligation, etc) in mind, the failure of basis approach now suggested by Peter Birks seems to offer the clearest and most convincing analysis. In other cases, the absence of a basis (in the narrow sense) is a necessary element for restitution, but it need not be a sufficient one. There are often additional requirements for recovery which need to be specified. By taking into account the material differences between the various case constellations, English law can avoid the problems which German law had to grapple with for so long. The conceptual unity of all unjust enrichment claims does not require that the same test of 'unjust' should be applied to each sub-group.

---

[92] For a similar argument MacQueen (n 82) 488; cf also Whitty (n 58) 710–11.

[93] For accounts in English, see Zimmermann, *The Law of Obligations* (n 1) 887–91; R Zimmermann and J du Plessis, 'Basic Features of the German Law of Unjustified Enrichment' [1994] RLR 14; Krebs (n 4) 201 ff.

[94] Larenz and Canaris (n 54) 142–5; Lorenz (n 40) § 812 no 1–2. Additionally, the test for 'at the expense of' is different in cases of transfers and in other cases of enrichment.

[95] Krebs (n 4) 237, 249–50, 253.

19

Unjust Enrichment as Absence of Basis: Can English Law Cope?

*Gerhard Dannemann**

Peter Birks asked me in 1994, when I joined the Oxford Law Faculty, to teach German unjust enrichment law within his Restitution course. At that time he insisted that unjust enrichment in English law was based on individual unjust factors such as mistake or failure of consideration, but he thought it important for his students to be familiar with the main alternative adopted by, among others, the German Civil Code (BGB) in § 812, that is, a general clause whereby a shift of wealth is to be reversed if there is no legal basis for this enrichment.

Perhaps he had half-expected me to propagate the same approach for English law. However, as a result of many seminar discussions, I came to the conclusion that several of those elements of German contract law which had been put into the BGB in order to make an absence of basis approach dovetail with contract law were either lacking or unclear in English law.[1] And while I thought that there were some gaps in English unjust enrichment law which did not exist in German law because of its general clause,[2] my conclusion at the time was that these gaps were about to be, or at least could be, closed from within the unjust factor approach. We therefore never explored just how well English law could cope with an absence of basis approach.

In *Unjust Enrichment*, Peter Birks abandoned unjust factors in favour of an approach which generally calls for the reversal of enrichments which lack a legal basis.[3] If this approach were to be adopted in English law, it would significantly change the way in which unjust enrichment interacts with other areas of law, and contract law in particular. German law can point us to some of the issues which

---

[*] Professor of British Legal, Economic, and Social Structures, Humboldt University, Berlin.

[1] BS Markesinis, W Lorenz, and G Dannemann, *The German Law of Obligations, Vol I: The Law of Contracts and Restitution* (1997) 726–8.

[2] ibid 770: mistake of law as bar to recovery, the requirement of failure of consideration to be total, and an all too narrow construction of compulsion outside contracts (see below section 3).

[3] P Birks, *Unjust Enrichment* (2nd ed, 2005) ch 5.

English law would need to address. The present article will focus on the following three situations:

- enrichment through execution of non-contractual agreements (section 1);
- enrichment through execution of non-enforceable contracts (section 2);
- enrichment through execution of ill-founded disputed claims (section 3).

1. Execution of Non-contractual Agreements

There are many situations in which one party has knowingly enriched the other in order to execute an agreement which is not a contract under English law, notably because one of the parties is not to provide any consideration. No unjust factor has hitherto called for the restitution of such a benefit if everything goes according to plan, and this result is usually right. An absence of basis approach, though, might struggle to find the right basis which allows recipients to keep their enrichments.

1.1. Gifts and Trusts

Birks is well aware that English law, with its comparatively narrow understanding of contract, must venture further and include other agreements, in particular gifts and trusts, both of which he considers provide a legal basis which justifies enrichment.[4] However, the German experience shows that there are many other agreements under which one party is to receive something for nothing, and that these should also be 'unjust enrichment-proof', that is, considered as providing a legal basis.

1.2. Gratuitous Use

A person may give money, chattels, or real property to another person not for keeping, but for using:

- A asks Z: 'Can you lend me £100 until the end of the month?'
- B, who needs to pick up a friend at the airport, is offered the use of her neighbour Y's car.
- C is allowed to use the flat of his acquaintance X while X is away on holiday.

A, B, and C duly return what has been given to them. Can Z, Y, and X claim in unjust enrichment for the value of this use? There can be no doubt that A, B, and C have been enriched by being allowed to use Z's, Y's, or X's money, car, or flat at their expense. Z, Y, and X could try to find some unjust factor, but this would be an uphill struggle if the circumstances indicate that the use was to be gratuitous.

---

[4] ibid 148 ff. It is an altogether different matter that gifts can be more easily revoked than contracts on the ground of mistake.

How could an absence of basis approach defeat such claims? Such a basis can be provided by agreements between the parties involved. German law knows several agreements which fit this bill, all of which are considered to be contracts.

Gratuitous use of money is covered in German law by §§ 488–98 BGB on contracts of loan. Parties are free to stipulate that no interest should be paid. So a contract for a gratuitous loan explains why, under German law, Z cannot sue A in unjust enrichment for interest on the amount lent to A.

In English law, it is uncertain whether this can be a contract before the loan is paid over, because the promise of a loan is not supported by any consideration, except perhaps the promise to pay the money back. In *Chitty on Contracts* Guest notes that 'there appears to be no authority on this question'.[5] Peter Birks takes the view that the loan is paid over voluntarily, but with the purpose of imposing a contractual obligation of repayment on the recipient.[6] Once we have a valid contract of loan, this provides the basis on which A is entitled to the free use of Z's money. Gratuitous loans are therefore unproblematic for an absence of basis approach.

§§ 598–606 BGB on *Leihe* cover gratuitous lending of chattels or real property. The agreement by which Y allows B to use his car is such a contract of *Leihe*, and provides a basis for her enrichment. The closest English equivalent, gratuitous bailment in the form of a *commodatum*,[7] is not a contract, but situated somewhere between contract, tort, and property law—an agreement made in connection with the transfer of possession of a chattel under which the bailee is allowed to use the chattel without charge.

Can bailment be the basis for this shift of value which would prevent Y from subsequently charging B for the use of his car? This is largely uncharted territory. The preferable view is to see the bailment agreement as a basis for this enrichment, with the result that there is nothing unjust about the enrichment from the outset. This view is most consistent with the main characteristic of the absence of basis approach, which simply leaves it to other areas of the law (such as contract, tort, or property) to find out whether a shift of wealth is justified or not. Bailment explains this enrichment just as well as a car rental contract would, because both agreements allow B to use Y's car.

Whereas the German *Leihe* covers both chattels and real property, bailment is limited to the former. It offers no help for explaining why X should not be allowed to sue C for the value of the use of his flat. The classification of this type of agreement under English law is not straightforward—perhaps a gratuitous licence,[8]

---

[5] H Beale (gen ed), *Chitty on Contracts* (29th edn, 2004), vol I 38–223 n 1103.

[6] Birks (n 3) 144 f.

[7] *Coggs v Barnard* (1703) 2 Ld Raym 909, 916, per Holt CJ; *Chitty on Contracts* (n 5) para 33–041. This is not to be confused with deposit, an agreement for gratuitous safekeeping (*Coggs v Barnard* 913), to which the closest German equivalent is *Verwahrung*, §§ 688–700 BGB.

[8] See *Ramnarace v Lutchman* [2001] UKPC 25; [2001] 1 WLR 1651, 1656; *Manchester Airport Plc v Dutton* [2000] 1 QB 133 (CA).

which could explain C's entitlement to possession not only for the purpose of property law, but also in terms of enrichment.

1.3. Gratuitous Services

An absence of basis approach would also force English law to look more closely at agreements whereby one person is to provide gratuitous services to another.

- D, who lives in London, has been offered a job in Carlisle and asks W, her cousin who lives locally, to find and rent for her a two bedroom flat.
- E asks his friend V: 'I wonder whether you could look after my children this evening. I have to go to a parents' meeting.'
- F, who is painting her house, is pleased when her neighbour U offers help and spends hours doing the fiddly bits.

D, E, and F are enriched by services or work provided by W, V, and U. Under German law, both contracts for services (§§ 611–30 BGB) and contracts for works (§§ 631–51 BGB) can be entered into as gratuitous agreements. There is also a contract entitled *Auftrag* or mandate (from the Roman *mandatum* whereby one party agrees to carry out somebody else's business gratuitously (§§ 662–74 BGB)).[9] All three contacts provide a legal basis for the enrichment which occurs when these contracts are performed.

Can English law provide similar bases? Gifts, being limited to gratuitous transfer of property,[10] are not an option. Much of what German law covers with *Auftrag* can be understood in English law as an agency agreement, which can also be made outside contract law.[11] Again, this appears to have been little explored in terms of unjust enrichment, but I suggest that the agreement provides the basis which entitles the principal to keep the benefit of the agent's work without having to pay for the value of this service in unjust enrichment. For this reason, in our example, W should not be allowed to claim in unjust enrichment a fee for having acted as D's agent.

English law will find it more difficult to cover the gratuitous provision of other services, or of works. For a rather limited range of cases, one particular form of bailment, that is, mandate (also derived from the Roman *mandatum*), can help, as mandate is characterized by the undertaking of the bailee to perform a gratuitous act, normally some service to be performed in relation with the bailed chattel.[12] However, mandate can provide no explanation if possession in the

---

[9] Remuneration would make this a *Geschäftsbesorgungsvertrag* under §§ 675–6 BGB.

[10] *Halsbury's Laws of England*, 4th edn. Reissue, vol 20, 16. But see Lord Goff of Chieveley and G Jones, *The Law of Restitution* (6th edn, 2002) para 1–062, who appear to treat gratuitous services as gifts.   [11] *Chitty on Contracts* (n 5) para 31–020.

[12] *Coggs v Bernard* (1703) 2 Ld Raym 909, 918, per Holt CJ, drawing on Bracton; *Chitty on Contracts* (n 5) para 33–040. The case concerned the gratuitous keeping of a consignment of brandy; the defendant was held liable for his negligence. It is noteworthy that Holt CJ, at 920, found consideration in the bailor having entrusted his goods to the bailee.

chattel does not pass, or in the large majority of cases where the gratuitous service is not related to any chattel, as in our example of V babysitting for E.

It may become necessary to resort to a general notion of agreements outside contract law, going beyond those which are presently recognized in English law, such as gifts, express trusts, bailment, and certain forms of agency.[13] Gifts are unenforceable because of the lack of consideration but, once executed, they provide a legal basis for an enrichment. We have seen above that there are many other agreements which are also not enforceable for lack of consideration, but which can just as well explain a shift of wealth. An absence of basis approach towards unjust enrichment is best served by treating all such agreements alike, regardless of whether or not they fall within recognized categories of non-contractual agreements.

2. Execution of Unenforceable Contractual Claims

The second group of cases on which an absence of basis approach needs to focus concerns claims which are based on contract, but which nevertheless cannot be enforced. Birks distinguishes unenforceable contracts from those which are void, voidable, terminated, or terminable. Whereas the latter cannot provide a basis for keeping an enrichment, an unenforceable contract as 'a good contract on which no action can be brought' can do so.[14] This must be right and, by definition, an agreement should be labelled as 'unenforceable' rather than 'void', etc, if what has been performed under such an agreement cannot be claimed back.

In *Moses v Macferlan*, Lord Mansfield presented not only the well-known positive list of what are now understood to be unjust factors, but also a negative list composed of unenforceable claims. We are told that a claim in unjust enrichment

does not lie for money paid by the plaintiff, which is claimed of him as payable in point of honor and honesty, although it could not have been recovered from him by any course of law; as in payment of a debt barred by the Statute of limitations, or contracted during his infancy, or to the extent of principal and legal interest upon an usurious contract, or, for money fairly lost at play: because in all these cases, the defendant may retain it with a safe conscience, though by positive law he was barred from recovering.[15]

For many years the negative list was neglected in English law because in most of these situations no unjust factor could be detected. This changed, however, when in *Kleinwort Benson v Lincoln City Council* the House of Lords abolished the rule

---

[13] It is noteworthy that G McMeel, 'On the Redundancy of the Concept of Bailment' in A Hudson (ed), *New Perspectives on Property Law, Obligations and Restitution* (2004) 247, has recently argued that 'bailment has no autonomous legal content' and should be dissolved into 'concepts of consent, wrongdoing, unjust enrichment or property'.   [14] Birks (n 3) 126.
[15] *Moses v Macferlan* (1760) 2 Burr 1005 (KB).

that mistake of law could not justify a claim for restitution.[16] Now, every item on Lord Mansfield's negative list can be described in terms of mistake.[17] For example, the payer may have mistakenly believed that a claim was not time-barred. Regardless of whether one follows an unjust factor approach, or an absence of basis approach, the time has come to take a fresh look at reasons which could justify the retention of such enrichments.

Sonja Meier and Thomas Krebs have illuminated this issue from an Anglo-German perspective.[18] More recently, Duncan Sheehan has taken a closer look at Lord Mansfield's negative list, providing powerful arguments to show that English law still recognizes natural obligations which, although unenforceable, can explain why no claim will lie in unjust enrichment if they have been performed.[19]

Birks agrees that, under an absence of basis approach, English law can no longer afford to ignore the issue of natural obligations.[20] Where no legally enforceable claim exists, natural obligations give a legal face to moral obligations. In his view, they operate in the form of a defence against a claim which would otherwise lie in unjust enrichment.

Classifying natural obligations, or reclassifying Lord Mansfield's negative list under defences, makes sense for an unjust factor approach. The claimant has paid a debt which was time-barred under the mistaken assumption that it was not; the existence of the debt as a natural obligation provides a defence. I suggest, however, that on an absence of basis approach, most of Lord Mansfield's negative list, and most natural obligations, should feature not as a defence, but rather as justification for the enrichment. The enrichment is not unjust, but can be explained by an obligation which, although not enforceable, allows the defendant to keep the enrichment once the claimant has performed.

I have argued above that, just as gifts can explain enrichment, the same should apply to many other gratuitous and unenforceable agreements. This argument is now carried one step further. Just as the doctrine of consideration is directed against the enforcement of a gratuitous promise but not against its voluntary execution, so the rules on limitation of claims are directed against the enforcement of obligations after a certain time has passed, not against the voluntary execution of such obligations. In both situations the unenforceable obligation provides the basis which allows the recipient to keep the enrichment.

By contrast, the rules on illegality are directed not only against the enforcement of, for example, agreements to launder money or to conceal assets from creditors,

---

[16] *Kleinwort Benson Ltd v Lincoln City Council* [1999] 2 AC 349 (HL).

[17] See G Dannemann, 'Unjust Enrichment by Transfer: Some Comparative Remarks' (2001) 79 Texas L Rev 1837, 1844 f.

[18] S Meier, *Irrtum und Zweckverfehlung* (1999) 301–53; T Krebs, *Restitution at the Crossroads* (2001) ch 14.

[19] D Sheehan, 'Natural Obligations in English Law' [2004] LMCLQ 172 ff. Sheehan, 196, distinguishes three types, of which only the first serves as a defence against a claim in unjust enrichment. See also Krebs (n 18) 267 ff.   [20] Birks (n 3) 258.

but equally against the execution of such agreements. Such void obligations cannot form a basis on which the recipient may keep the enrichment.[21]

What does the above imply for Lord Mansfield's negative list, or Sheehan's list of natural obligations? We now take a closer look at the most important examples: (1) limitation of actions, (2) requirements of form, and (3) contracts beyond the capacity of minors. Gambling agreements would have been included in this list until section 335 of the Gambling Act 2005 made all lawful gambling agreements enforceable, so that they now provide the same basis for an enrichment as, say, a contract of sale.

2.1. Limitation of Claims

Limitation features on the lists of both Lord Mansfield and Dr Sheehan.[22] Time-barred claims, while not enforceable, nevertheless provide a basis for an enrichment once they have been honoured. Limitation rules aim to protect defendants by offering finality after a certain time has lapsed,[23] but do not strike at the payment of time-barred debts. The German Civil Code states the consequence explicitly in § 214(2) BGB: 'Performance made in satisfaction of a claim that has become time-barred may not be reclaimed, even if made without knowledge of the time-bar'.[24]

2.2. Requirements of Form

It is interesting to note that Lord Mansfield's negative list does not mention requirements of form, even though the Statute of Frauds preceded *Moses v Macferlan* by 87 years. On the other hand, Sheehan counts contracts which are void for lack of formality amongst natural obligations.[25]

Section 4 of the Statute of Frauds provides that certain agreements are not actionable unless they are evidenced in writing; in its present version, the section applies to guarantees.[26] Although unenforceable, an oral guarantee can nevertheless provide a basis for the guarantor's payment. No one has suggested that a guarantor who has paid up should be able to recover on the ground that the

---

[21] Recovery may nevertheless be refused because illegality may be available as a defence. See Birks (n 3) 247; G Dannemann, 'Illegality as a Defence against Unjust Enrichment Claims' (2000) Oxford U Comparative L Forum No. 4 at http://ouclf.iuscomp.org.

[22] Sheehan (n 19) 188, who, however, views time-barred claims as 'anomalous natural obligations when seen against other examples'.   [23] *Chitty on Contracts* (n 5) para 28–001.

[24] Translation by G Thomas and G Dannemann, 'German Civil Code—Bürgerliches Gesetzbuch. Bilingual edition of the provisions amended by the Law of Obligations Reform Act' *German Law Archive* (2002), http://www.iuscomp.org/gla/statutes/BGB.htm.

[25] Sheehan (n 19) 188. See also Krebs (n 18) 263 ff.

[26] See *Actionstrength Ltd v International Glass Engineering Ltd* [2003] UKHL 17; [2003] 2 AC 541, where the House of Lords refused to override the requirement of writing in equity on the ground that the recipients had relied on an oral guarantee.

guarantee agreement was not evidenced in writing; strong authority suggests that no such action should lie.[27] The same is true for contracts which are caught by section 2(1) Law of Property (Miscellaneous Provisions) Act 1989. This Act has gone beyond the 'evidenced in writing' requirement established by its predecessors[28] and provides in section 2(1): 'A contract for the sale or other disposition of an interest in land can only be made in writing and only by incorporating all the terms which the parties have expressly agreed in one document or, where contracts are exchanged, in each'.

In *Tootal Clothing v Guinea Properties*, the Court of Appeal limited the effects of this section to contracts prior to their performance.[29] Scott LJ stated:

However, section 2 is of relevance only to executory contracts. It has no relevance to contracts which have been completed. If parties choose to complete an oral land contract or a land contract that does not in some respect or other comply with section 2, they are at liberty to do so. Once they have done so, it becomes irrelevant that the contract they have completed may not have been in accordance with section 2.

It is unlikely that Scott LJ intended this dictum to dovetail with an absence of basis approach, but if he had, he could hardly have formulated it better. The form requirement lapses once the oral contract has been completed, and the contract stands as a basis which defeats a claim in unjust enrichment.

There are, however, some statutory requirements of form which provide for a different solution. The recent case of *Wilson v First County Trust Ltd* involved as defendant a pawnbroker who had lent the claimant borrower a sum of money for six months on the security of her car.[30] The agreement did not state the total amount of credit as required by section 61(1) Consumer Credit Act, with the consequence that, under sections 65(1) and 127(3), the agreement could not be enforced against the debtor. So the borrower was allowed to keep the money and did not have to pay interest. Furthermore, the pawnbroker had no defence against the borrower's claim for recovery of the car.

This makes it clear that section 127(3) of the Consumer Credit Act is not limited to executory contracts and that it is unlikely that an agreement which falls short of the requirements of sections 65(1) and 127(3) can provide any basis for the mutual enrichments exchanged under such a contract.[30a] This is best understood as a baseless enrichment, and the result—which provides a windfall to the borrower, and appears somewhat harsh on the lender—as a policy-motivated defence which is given to the borrower only, not for the individual

[27] *Thomas v Brown* (1876) 1 QBD 714. The High Court (Quain J) rejected an action for recovery of a deposit under a contract for the sale of land which was void under section 4 of the Statute of Frauds because it did not disclose the vendor.

[28] Section 40 of the Law of Property Act 1925; Section 4 of the Statute of Frauds.

[29] *Tootal Clothing v Guinea Properties* (1992) 64 P & CR 452; see also Goff and Jones (n 10) para 21–001; Sheehan (n 19) 189.

[30] *Wilson v First County Trust Ltd* [2003] UKHL 40; [2004] 1 AC 816.

[30a] Section 127(3) was repealed by section 15 of the Consumer Credit Act 2006.

borrower's benefit but in order to provide a strong incentive for lenders to observe the requirement of form. Lord Nicholls put the point in this way:[31]

But when legislation renders the entire agreement inoperative, to use a neutral word, for failure to comply with prescribed formalities the legislation itself is the primary source of guidance on what are the legal consequences. Here the intention of Parliament is clear.

Other statutory requirements of form must be examined in the same way to discover whether they too aim to make executed contracts void.[32] The wording of the provisions in question may often offer no more than limited guidance. For example, section 18 of the Gambling Act 1845 (now repealed by section 334 of the Gambling Act 2005) made gambling agreements 'null and void', yet at the same time prohibited the recovery of any deposit made for that purpose. *Lipkin Gorman* confirmed that parties could not recover what they had paid under a null and void agreement of that kind.[33] Similarly, although section 1 of the Infants Relief Act 1874 made certain contracts entered into by minors 'absolutely void', this did not mean that infants could recover what they had performed.[34] On the other hand, even where a statute provides that lack of form will render a contract 'unenforceable', the recipient of performance under such a contract may be liable in unjust enrichment, as the Australian case of *Pavey and Matthews v Paul* shows.[35]

In German law, invalidating provisions are usually written with unjust enrichment in mind. Some provisions which impose a certain form state expressly that once the contract has been executed, the lack of form is healed and the agreement becomes valid. This is for example what the German Civil Code provides for guarantees in § 766 sentence 3.[36] On the other hand, that provision is one of several exceptions to the general rule in § 125 BGB, which simply renders agreements void if they lack the required form.[37] The *Bundesgerichtshof* (BGH, Federal Court of Justice) has refused to elevate those express exceptions into a general principle of healing by way of execution.[38] In consequence, agreements which lack a required form generally remain void even if they have

---

[31] ibid at para 49.
[32] Similarly Krebs (n 18) 263, also arguing from an Anglo-German perspective; see also Meier (n 18) 301 ff.   [33] *Lipkin Gorman v Karpnale Ltd* [1991] 2 AC 548, 577.
[34] *Pearce v Brain* [1929] 2 KB 310, see below section 2.3. This category of 'absolutely void' contracts was abolished by section 1 of the Minors' Contracts Act 1987. See *Chitty on Contracts* (n 5) para 8–005.
[35] *Pavey and Matthews Proprietary Ltd v Paul* (1987) 162 CLR 221 (HCA). A builder was entitled to a *quantum meruit* (not the contractual rate) for work provided under a building contract which was 'unenforceable' for lack of written form required by section 45 of the Builders Licensing Act 1971 (NSW). Birks (n 3) 127 appears to take a different view as he treats Mrs Paul's refusal to pay as repudiation. But can one-sided performance suffice for making the contract enforceable *vis-à-vis* the other party?
[36] No form is required for commercial guarantees under § 350 *Handelsgesetzbuch* (Commercial Code).
[37] Others exceptions include contracts for dispositions of land, § 311b, and gifts, § 518(2) BGB.
[38] BGH 2.2.1967 NJW 1967, 1128.

been fully executed. Whatever has been performed can be claimed back in unjust enrichment, as the void agreement provides no basis for the enrichment. Illegality may or may not be available as a defence.[39]

I doubt, however, whether any similar, or even opposing, general rule can be extracted from English law. For an absence of basis approach in English law, this implies that only careful statutory interpretation will reveal whether a contract which lacks a required form can provide a basis that entitles the recipient to keep the enrichment.

2.3. Contracts beyond the Capacity of Minors

Under English law, minors are capable of entering into contracts, in particular those which provide them with 'necessaries'. Additionally, contracts involving the acquisition of a permanent interest in property are binding on a minor unless they are repudiated. Furthermore, on attaining full age, a person may ratify contracts which had previously not been binding for lack of capacity.[40] All three types of valid contracts are of no further interest in the present context. But what about contracts which go beyond necessaries and which are either repudiated or not ratified?

Such contracts figure on Lord Mansfield's negative list, whereas Sheehan argues that they will often be unable to produce a natural obligation, because this would frequently undermine the protective purpose of provisions on capacity.[41]

These different views indicate that it can be difficult to reconcile existing rules on personal incapacity of minors with general rules of unjust enrichment law, regardless of whether one follows an unjust factor approach, or an absence of basis approach. At the risk of considerable oversimplification, the following general patterns can be observed:

(1) Minors are not liable to return any performance made under an agreement which is unenforceable against them for lack of capacity,[42] even if there has been failure of consideration or a mistake about the minor's age. This common law rule is modified by a statutory provision which allows courts to order restitution of property acquired by a minor on a discretionary basis.[43]

(2) On the other hand, a minor can in principle recover what he or she has performed under an agreement which is not subsequently ratified, or after it has been repudiated. It appears, however, that this is possible only where failure of consideration has been total, which will frequently not

---

[39] See generally Dannemann (n 21).
[40] See *Chitty on Contracts* (n 5) paras 8-002 to 8-044.   [41] Sheehan (n 19) 191.
[42] *Chitty on Contracts* (n 5) para 8-049.
[43] Under section 3 of the Minors' Contracts Act 1987 it is in the discretion of the courts whether the minor should return to the other party any property acquired under such an invalid agreement, but subsection (2) also states that '[n]othing in this section shall be taken to prejudice any other remedy available to the [other party]'.

be the case. The main authorities for this view date from the 1920s, namely *Steinberg v Scala (Leeds) Ltd,* for contracts which were repudiated,[44] and *Pearce v Brain* for contracts which were not ratified.[45]

Some writers have criticized this view. Andrew Burrows has argued forcefully that greater prominence should be given to the protective policy of rules on contractual capacity of minors, so that the requirement of total failure must be reconsidered.[46] Sheehan believes that recovery would now be possible in the case of a minor's mistaken belief that the contract was enforceable (mistake of law).[47] Meier, who points out that there are other situations in which minors will more easily obtain restitution, is critical of the general inconsistency.[48] Be that as it may, both of the above restrictions—which, incidentally, are unknown to German law [49]—are not easily squared with the modern understanding of failure of consideration as an unjust factor, where the 'total' requirement has otherwise been substantially eroded.[50] Nor could they be reconciled with an absence of basis approach. Whereas the first restriction can be formulated as a policy-based defence aimed at the protection of minors, it is difficult to find any explanation for the second.

3. Execution of Ill-founded Disputed Claims

A shift towards an absence of basis approach could help to close what I believe to be the only remaining substantial gap within the unjust factor approach, a gap which generally produces highly unsatisfactory results, and exceptionally produces satisfactory results, but at the expense of consistency and clarity. A string of English cases are variations of the following standard situation:[51]

- G makes a *bona fide* request for payment from T. T disputes the claim, but pays under protest in order to avert grave consequences threatened by G. Later, it transpires that G's demand was not justified.

---

[44] *Steinberg v Scala (Leeds) Ltd* [1923] 2 Ch 452 (CA). A minor who had bought shares in a company was not allowed to have her name removed from the register, and to receive her money back, on the ground that there had not been a total failure of consideration. Whittaker sees this as part of a general rule whereby restitution is not allowed for performance made prior to repudiation: *Chitty on Contracts* (n 5) para 8–040.

[45] *Pearce v Brain* [1929] 2 KB 310. A minor had exchanged a motorcycle and sidecar worth £30 for a car worth £15; the rear axle of the car broke after the minor had driven some 70 miles. Recovery was disallowed because failure of consideration had not been total.

[46] A Burrows, *The Law of Restitution* (2nd edn, 2002) 415.   [47] Sheehan (n 19) 191.

[48] Meier (n 18) 323 f. She points out that minors can generally claim back what they have performed, as long as the other party has not performed, even if the other party is willing to do so: *Corpe v Overton* (1833) 10 Bing 252, last cited and distinguished in *Steinberg v Scala (Leeds) Ltd* [1923] 2 Ch 452, 460 f.

[49] For an account of German rules on the contractual capacity of minors from an unjust enrichment perspective, see Krebs (n 18) 180 ff.   [50] See Burrows (n 46) 333 ff.

[51] *CTN Cash and Carry Ltd v Gallaher Ltd* [1994] 4 All ER 714 (CA): in order to avert the threatened withdrawal of a voluntary credit facility, the claimants paid for goods which had been

The basic rule in English law is that T cannot recover. While the unjust enrichment interpretations of 'mistake' and 'failure of consideration' are far more generous than the corresponding doctrines in contract law, 'compulsion' as an unjust factor coincides with (ie is as narrow as) the contractual doctrines of duress and undue influence.[52] That makes sense if there is a contractual basis for the demand, which is then destroyed by duress or undue influence, but not if the claim was baseless to begin with. If, due to a stupid mistake, I pay what I do not owe, I can recover. If I make the same unwarranted payment under pressure to my economic livelihood, I generally cannot.

CTN Cash & Carry v Gallaher shows that English judges will shake their heads in disbelief that reputable companies such as G should refuse to pay back what they were not owed, and regret that they cannot order them to do so.[53] Sometimes, though, a shining knight will come to the rescue. It appeared in the form of an ingenious and circular mistake of law in *Nurdin & Peacock v DB Ramsden*.[54] Under the threat of forfeiture of lease and repossession, claimants had overpaid their rent. Neuberger J allowed them to recover on the ground that they had mistakenly believed that they were entitled to do so—with the effect that they had not been mistaken at all. Shining knights may save the day, but they come at a certain price.

More interesting in the present context is *Woolwich v Inland Revenue*.[55] The claimants had paid an ultra vires tax demand under protest, in order not to be branded as tax cheats and ultimately exposed to the enforcement mechanisms of the Inland Revenue. The House of Lords allowed recovery by introducing the absence of basis approach into a particular area of the English law of unjust enrichment, namely demands by public authorities.

Woolwich shows what would happen to other cases of execution of ill-founded disputed claims if an absence of basis approach were to be adopted for the entire English law of unjust enrichment. In all the above situations, T could claim back what was paid under protest, because no basis could be found on which G would

---

destroyed before the risk had passed. *Maskell v Horner* [1915] 3 KB 106 (CA): the claimant was forced to pay unjustified market tolls by defendant seizing his goods or threatening to do so. *Twyford v Manchester Corporation* [1946] Ch 236: the unsuccessful claimant had paid under protest a fee unlawfully charged for the permission to 're-cut, re-paint or re-guild' inscriptions on gravestones within their cemetery. Similarly, *Still v Equitable Life Assurance Society of United States* 54 SW 2d 947 (SCt Tenn 1932): the insured claimant was not allowed to recover the premiums which he had paid under protest in order to avert the lapse of his policy, after the insurer had wrongly, but in good faith, refused a contractually stipulated waiver of premiums on the ground of the insured's total disability. See the following text for two more examples.

[52] For this reason, recovery was allowed in *Maskell v Horner* [1915] 3 KB 106 because the compulsion would have been strong enough to set aside a contract on the ground of duress to goods. There was, of course, no such contract in that case.

[53] *CTN Cash and Carry Ltd v Gallaher Ltd* [1994] 4 All ER 714, 719 (Steyn LJ) and 720 (Sir Donald Nicholls VC).

[54] *Nurdin & Peacock v DB Ramsden & Co Ltd* [1999] 1 All ER 941.

[55] *Woolwich Equitable Building Society v Inland Revenue Commissioners* [1993] AC 70 (HL).

be allowed to keep the enrichment.[56] *CTN Cash & Carry* would therefore need to be overruled, and *Nurdin & Peacock v DB Ramsden* would find a much more satisfactory explanation.

For the same reason, English law would need to take a fresh look at what Goff and Jones have called 'assumption of risk' and 'submission to an honest claim'.[57] In the present unjust factor landscape, these are usually seen as two separate issues which are located partly within mistake (assumption of risk) and partly within compulsion (submission to an honest claim).[58]

This is less problematic for mistake, where one can indeed wonder how substantial doubts must be in order to have the same effect as a straightforward mistake.[59] To say 'you were not mistaken, because you only had some doubts' can make sense. On the other hand, it makes no sense to say 'you were not compelled, because you submitted to the demand'. Without submission, no compulsion is complete. A necessary element of compulsion cannot at the same time give rise to a defence against compulsion. And an unjustified demand cannot become just merely because the person making the claim honestly believed it to exist. Therefore, none of the elements of 'submission to an honest claim' can provide a justification for the recipient being entitled to keep the enrichment.

Having said this, both assumption of risk and submission to an honest claim can prevent restitution if discussions between the parties have resulted in a contract of compromise, whereby parties resolve their dispute somewhere in the middle. This compromise provides the basis for the enrichment, and parties cannot rely on mistake of law, or on compulsion, in order to reclaim what they have performed under the compromise[60]—unless, of course, mistake or compulsion makes that compromise void or voidable under the rules of contract law.[61]

Non-contractual submissions should be treated differently. If the payer eventually agrees to make a full payment, there is no consideration, and hence no contract of settlement[62] (and even German law would not recognize such

---

[56] In *Maskell v Horner* [1915] 3 KB 106, 118, Lord Reading CJ held *obiter* that if a person voluntarily and knowingly pays a disputed claim in order to close a transaction, this is to be treated as a gift. This should, however, not apply to payment under protest.

[57] Goff and Jones (n 10) paras 4–030 to 4–032; and paras 10–052 to 10–056.

[58] However, in *Kleinwort Benson Ltd v Lincoln City Council* [1999] 2 AC 349, 382G, Lord Goff recognized, in addition to change of position, 'settlement of an honest claim (the scope of which is a matter of debate)' as a defence against unjust enrichment claims.

[59] This issue is not fully resolved. Lord Hope stated in *Kleinwort Benson Ltd v Lincoln City Council* [1999] 2 AC 349, 410, that a 'person who pays when in doubt takes the risk that he may be wrong' but, within a few months, recovery was allowed in such a case: *Nurdin & Peacock v DB Ramsden & Co Ltd* [1999] 1 All ER 941, an inconsistency pointed out by P Schlechtriem, *Restitution und Bereicherungsausgleich in Europa* vol I (2000) 141 f n 429. I would argue that *Nurdin Peacock* is primarily a case of involuntary, rather than mistaken, payment.

[60] See *Brennan v Burdon and others* [2004] EWCA Civ 1017; [2005] QB 303: a compromise cannot be set aside on the ground that it was entered into under a mistake of law (that a claim was time-barred).

[61] Goff and Jones (n 10) para 4–032 say the same about mistake of law.

[62] See Burrows (n 46) 139.

a 'gratuitous settlement').[63] Furthermore, there is often no agreement, just reluctant payment.

For an absence of basis approach, these are straightforward cases of enrichments made without basis. Only if the claimant knowingly and voluntarily paid what was not due, will this give rise to a defence, as § 814 BGB provides for German law.[64]

The most important practical difference between an English unjust factor approach, and a German absence of basis approach, concerns payments made under an express reservation. While reservations generally exclude the defence under § 814 BGB,[65] English law will give effect to a reservation only if the recipient has accepted it.[66] This view, whereby a contract is needed to justify restitution, rather than to justify enrichment, is diametrically opposed to an absence of basis approach. There can be no hope of reconciliation. The acceptance requirement for reservations must therefore figure on the casualty list if English law shifts to an absence of basis approach.[67]

4. Conclusions

Adopting an absence of basis approach cannot be confined to the unjust enrichment taxonomy. It creates strong incentives for further development not only within English unjust enrichment law, but also within contract law and other neighbouring areas.

(1) A hitherto somewhat rudimentary and piecemeal English law of agreements outside contract law would need to be developed from a number of particular gratuitous agreements—such as gifts, express trusts, certain forms of agency or bailment—into a more general notion of agreements. Those agreements, although unenforceable mainly for lack of consideration, provide a basis which allows recipients to keep what they have received in their execution.

(2) English law would have to distinguish more consistently and clearly between contracts which are unenforceable (which can provide a basis for an enrichment) and contracts which are void (which cannot).

[63] Under § 779 BGB, a contract of compromise requires both parties to give in, whereas a mere recognition of a debt under § 781 BGB can be claimed back in unjust enrichment (§ 812(2) BGB) if the recognition is not supported by an existing claim.

[64] See Markesinis *et al* (n 1) 736. Knowledge of lack of basis amounts to a defence under the wording of § 814 BGB. Cases such as BGH 17.2.1982, BGHZ 83, 278, 282 have extended this defence to involuntary performance. Voluntary and knowing payment of what is not due could also be understood as a gift, which would then provide a basis for this enrichment.

[65] Except for reservations made as standard procedure rather than on the circumstances of the individual case: OLG Koblenz 20.9.1983, NJW 1984, 135.

[66] *Nurdin & Peacock v DB Ramsden & Co Ltd* [1999] 1 All ER 941, 957 f.

[67] For an argument as to why it makes commercial sense to give effect to such reservations, see Dannemann (2001) 79 Texas L Rev 1858–9.

(3)   English law might have to rethink the restitutionary consequences of the execution of contracts which exceed the personal capacity of minors, and in particular allow a minor to recover even where failure of consideration was not total.

(4)   English law would have to allow restitution where ill-founded claims were performed under protest. This would require some cases to be overruled.

In my view, consequences (3) and (4) are thoroughly desirable, and should therefore be considered as an advantage of the absence of basis approach. However, it should also be mentioned that both changes can be brought about within an unjust factor approach. In the case of (3), dropping or eroding the total failure requirement for minors would even lead to greater consistency within the unjust factor approach. As far as (4) is concerned, I have argued elsewhere in greater detail why there is nothing in the unjust factor approach which would force English law to be so parsimonious with 'compulsion' as a factor (by limiting this to compulsion which is strong enough to set a contract aside even where no such contract exists in the first place), and so generous with 'mistake' (by not limiting this to mistakes which make contracts void or voidable).[68]

In the case of (2), a clear and consistent distinction between unenforceable and void contracts is beneficial not only for an absence of basis approach, but also for an approach which recognizes mistake of law as unjust factor. Mistakes about enforceability will generally be irrelevant, whereas mistakes about validity will generally give rise to a claim for restitution.

There remains consequence (1), some pressure towards developing a more general notion of gratuitous agreements. I can see neither any particular harm nor any great difficulty in this, but it would not be necessary under an unjust factor approach.

As I mentioned at the outset, this article takes up where discussions in Peter's Restitution course ended some years ago. Contrary to my doubts at the time, I now believe that English law can cope with an absence of basis approach. And while I still think that change from within could close the major remaining gap in the unjust factor approach, a shift towards absence of basis could apply some welcome pressure to overcome this flaw and accelerate the process by a decade or two. Perhaps this evaluation is a somewhat English pragmatic response to a somewhat German concern, namely the consistency and clarity of classification, which made Peter eventually believe that English law must shift to an absence of basis approach.[69]

---

[68] (2001) 79 Texas L Rev 1854–9.   [69] Most clearly at Birks (n 3) 114 ff.

20

The Fallacy of 'Restitution for Wrongs'

*Thomas Krebs**

When I was in the final stages of preparing my doctoral thesis for publication, Peter Birks, who had been my supervisor, warned me to scale down my defence of the English system of unjust factors: 'I'm afraid this is one we're going to lose'. I now know that, even then, he was contemplating changing sides. He had finally been convinced that the German approach, which founded restitution on the absence of legal basis, was, in fact, the 'better method'.[1] My own attempt to defend his original taxonomy by pointing out the structural differences between English and German law only seemed to harden his resolve. I am still grateful to have had some small part in the evolution of his thought, even if only as Watson to his Holmes.

My original plan had been to devote just one half of my DPhil thesis to a defence of the unjust factors approach, intending to deal in the second half with 'restitution for wrongs' and the phenomenon of alternative analysis.[2] Here, I actually thought the Germans had got it right: although restitution often followed a wrong, this did not mean that it was based on the wrong. In other words, I planned to back up the theories of Jack Beatson[3] and Daniel Friedmann[4] using

* Fellow and Tutor in Law, Brasenose College, Oxford. I would like to thank Birke Häcker and Andrew Scott, both of All Souls College, Oxford, for their valuable comments on an earlier draft of this essay.

[1] P Birks, *Unjust Enrichment* (2nd edn, 2005) p xiii.

[2] The label 'alternative analysis' was first used by P Birks, *An Introduction to the Law of Restitution* (reprinted 1993), 44 (still referring to 'alternative analyses'), 314. Burrows has summed the phenomenon up as follows: 'To recognise alternative analysis is to accept that, on a given set of facts, it may be to the claimant's advantage or disadvantage to formulate the restitutionary claim in unjust enrichment by subtraction as opposed to basing it on the wrong. The possibility of alternative analysis also means that, in interpreting past decisions, one cannot assume that restitution has been triggered by the wrong just because, on facts involving a gain caused by a wrong, restitution has been granted: the true explanation for the restitution may be unjust enrichment by subtraction not that the wrong has triggered restitution.' A Burrows, *The Law of Restitution* (2nd edn, 2002) 456. The expression is now used throughout the literature on restitution, if not as a term of art, then as a convenient shorthand.

[3] J Beatson, 'The Nature of Waiver of Tort' in J Beatson, *The Use and Abuse of Unjust Enrichment* (1991) 206.

[4] D Friedmann, 'Restitution of Benefits Obtained through the Appropriation of Property or the Commission of a Wrong' (1980) Col LR 504; 'Restitution for Wrongs: The Basis of Liability' in WR Cornish, R Nolan, J O'Sullivan, and G Virgo (eds), *Restitution: Past Present and Future* (1998) 133.

comparative material. When I put this idea to Peter, back in 1996, he shook his head gravely. 'You're biting off more than you can chew. Concentrate on one question at a time. Besides, you're just wrong. Absolutely wrong.'

1. Non-participatory Enrichments in German Law

The main provision of German unjust enrichment law, § 812 I BGB, reads: 'Wer durch die Leistung eines anderen oder in sonstiger Weise auf dessen Kosten etwas ohne rechtlichen Grund erlangt, ist ihm zur Herausgabe verpflichtet. . . .'[5]

This general provision on unjust enrichment has since been divided up by writers and courts. A bright line is drawn between restitution of enrichments by performance ('*Leistungskondiktion*') and enrichments 'in another way' ('*Eingriffskondiktion*'). This essay is concerned with this latter category. The dichotomy looks rather similar to the distinction between 'subtractive' unjust enrichment and restitution for wrongs. The similarity is deceptive. In German law, even although the requirements of the two claims may be different, the cause of action remains 'unjust enrichment'.

To understand the modern German position, it is necessary to give a brief historical overview. The modern version of the *Eingriffskondiktion*, that is, the claim to restitution based on a non-participatory enrichment, will then be analysed. We will finally turn to English law.

1.1. A Brief History of the *Eingriffskondiktion*

The Corresponding Loss Requirement

The foundations of the modern German law of unjust enrichment were laid by Friedrich Carl von Savigny in his seminal work *System des heutigen römischen Rechts*. He rejects any suggestion that enrichment law is some kind of 'higher order' law based upon discretionary justice. Savigny seeks to put all enrichment claims on a common foundation: the absence of a legal ground for the enrichment.[6] The restitutionary claim is kept in check by insisting that an asset of the defendant's has moved to the claimant. In German, this is referred to as '*Vermögensverschiebung*' ('shift of wealth'). This was later interpreted to mean that a claim in unjust enrichment could lie only where the claimant had suffered a loss corresponding to the defendant's enrichment. If this restriction is strictly observed, it excludes unjust enrichment claims in all cases in which the

---

[5] 'He who obtains something through somebody else's performance or in another way at his expense without a legal cause, is obliged to make restitution to the other.' References to German provisions will be to the BGB unless otherwise indicated.

[6] *FC v Savigny, System des heutigen römischen Rechts* (1840–9), vol V, Beylage XIV, 525.

unauthorized use of corporeal things is in issue. More seriously still, the law of unjust enrichment would not protect intellectual property rights.[7]

The German courts responded to this limitation in two ways. For infringement of intellectual property, they awarded 'compensation' that was really restitutionary, giving the claimant the option to choose between his actual loss, the amount of a reasonable licence fee, and the actual profits obtained by the defendant as a result of the infringement.[8] In other words, the courts awarded 'restitution for wrongs', because the law of unjust enrichment was too narrow. In user cases, they often simply ignored the 'shift of wealth' requirement. In a case decided by the *Reichsgericht* in 1919 the claimant had contractually agreed to allow the defendant to supply its factory by means of trains that ran over a railway track across the claimant's land. The defendant later built a second factory on an adjacent plot of land and proceeded to use the railway track to supply this. This use of the track was not authorized and the claimant sued in contract and unjust enrichment. The latter claim failed before the appeal court because the claimant was contractually responsible for the maintenance of the railway track and had thus not suffered a loss. The *Reichsgericht* allowed the enrichment claim. The 'shift of wealth' requirement or the words 'at the expense of' are not even mentioned in the judgment. Instead, the court's language focuses on the defendant's behaviour, expressing its disapproval of the defendant's 'unlawful', 'unauthorized', and 'selfish' conduct.[9] The language of the court echoes ideas expressed some ten years earlier by Fritz Schulz.

Quasi-Delict[10]

Schulz's contribution is sometimes referred to as a turning point in the law of unjust enrichment. This is an exaggeration. His ambitious scheme, put forward in an essay comprising an entire volume of a journal,[11] never got close to being accepted. One of his ideas was influential: to base restitution on the wrongfulness ('*Rechtswidrigkeit*') of the defendant's action. His focal point is unlawful acquisition rather than a shift of wealth without legal ground.[12] It is therefore characteristic of his system that it does not require the claimant to suffer a loss.[13] This enables Schulz to apply his system to intellectual property and user cases.[14] He goes further still. Businesses have a right not to be unfairly competed with. If that right is infringed they should be entitled to the gains made by their competitors.[15] Finally, 90 years before *Attorney General v Blake*,[16] Schulz advocated gain-based awards following breach of contract.[17]

---

[7] cf R Ellger, *Bereicherung durch Eingriff* (2002), 58.   [8] ibid 67 ff.
[9] RG 20.12.1919, RGZ 97, 312.   [10] cf Ellger (n 7 above) 89.
[11] F Schulz, 'System der Rechte auf den Eingriffserwerb', AcP 105, 1.
[12] cf R Zimmermann and J Du Plessis, 'Basic Features of the German Law of Unjustified Enrichment' [1994] RLR 14.   [13] Schulz (n 11 above) 440.
[14] Schulz (n 11 above) 49–190.   [15] Schulz (n 11 above) 218 ff.
[16] [2001] 1 AC 268.   [17] Schulz (n 11 above) 5 ff.

Wilburg and von Caemmerer

The real turning point came in 1934, when Walter Wilburg wrote a seminal book reassessing the whole of enrichment law.[18] Wilburg's most significant insight is that the *sine causa* approach only functions adequately where the claimant consciously and purposively enriches the defendant pursuant to a supposed underlying obligation. Outside those cases, which have since been referred to as *Leistungkondiktion*, the absence of a legal basis for the enrichment cannot be sufficient to show whether it is unjust or not. This, to Wilburg, is the main problem with German enrichment law.[19] The claimant's loss is seen as a 'merely symptomatic' phenomenon.[20]

Wilburg sees Schulz's achievement as lying in his recognition of the significance of the infringement of a right. Where Schulz goes wrong is in focusing on the wrongfulness of that infringement. Wrongfulness does not represent a useful criterion where the law of unjust enrichment is concerned. While to Schulz the wrongfulness of the infringement is the focal point of the inquiry, Wilburg focuses on the infringed right.[21] Restitution is thus not a response to wrongfulness but a means of vindicating a right. The nature and ambit of the right need to be analysed in order to decide whether or not an infringement of the right by another will trigger a restitutionary response.[22]

It was only after the war, when Ernst von Caemmerer turned his attention to enrichment law, that Wilburg's ideas were recognized as valuable.[23] Like Wilburg, he identifies the reason for restitution, in cases of non-participatory enrichments, in the purpose of the infringed right. The paradigm is, again, property. Von Caemmerer argues that it is in the nature of property to attribute a certain benefit to the owner. At the same time, property rights exclude others from the benefit. If, therefore, somebody uses another's property, he obtains something which the property right attributes to the owner. The property right attributes to him the '*uti, frui, abuti*' of the thing in question.[24]

---

[18] W Wilburg, *Die Lehre von der ungerechtfertigten Bereicherung nach österreichischem und deutschem Recht* (1934).

[19] 'Gesetz und Lehre übertragen den Gedanken des fehlenden Grundes auf die sonstigen Fälle der ungerechtfertigten Bereicherung. Diese Übertragung verdunkelt das ganze Bereicherungsrecht.' ('The code and legal writers have taken the "absence of ground" concept and applied it across the board. This overshadows the whole law of unjustified enrichment.') Wilburg (n 18 above) 12.   [20] ibid.

[21] 'Nicht die außerhalb des Rechtes liegende Idee einer Vorteilsentziehung als strafende Reaktion gegen unrechtes Handeln, sondern der rein sachliche Zweck des verkürzten Rechtes, bestimmte Güter und deren Nutzen dem Berechtigten zuzuweisen, scheint das Geheimnis der Ungerechtfertigtheit fremden Erwerbes zu enthalten.' ('The secret of when an enrichment at the expense of another is unjust seems to be the purely objective purpose of the infringed right to attribute certain things and their use to the right holder, rather than the idea of stripping someone of a benefit as a sanction of unlawful conduct, wholly independently of the underlying right.') Wilburg (n 18 above) 27.

[22] For a more detailed account of the Wilburg/von Caemmerer taxonomy of the German law of unjust enrichment, see T Krebs, *Restitution at the Crossroads* (2001) 207–17.

[23] E von Caemmerer, 'Bereicherung und unerlaubte Handlung' in *Festschrift für Rabel*, vol I (1954), 333.   [24] ibid 353.

The division between enrichments by performance and enrichments 'in another way' is today fundamental to German enrichment law, thanks to Wilburg's original idea and von Caemmerer's elegant and persuasive development of it. Where the *Eingriffskondiktion* is concerned, the attribution doctrine represents a significant advance in comparison with previous attempts to limit the scope of enrichment law. The requirement of a direct shift of wealth was simply not suitable to modern conditions. The scope of enrichment law was thus unduly and unjustifiably restricted. On the other hand, arguably, the wrongfulness approach advocated by Schulz expanded restitutionary liability rather too far.

A Revival of the Wrongfulness Doctrine?

Wolfgang Ernst, in an illuminating biography of Schulz, writes that the *Rechtswidrigkeitstheorie* 'can be said to be the doctrinal proposition most often refuted or "proved wrong" in Germany's twentieth-century civilian scholarship'.[25] The critics of the attribution doctrine nevertheless drew on Schulz's wrongfulness approach in formulating an alternative theory, tying a claim in unjust enrichment to a wrongful act on the part of the defendant. Any approach based on wrongfulness tends to favour restitution in a greater number of cases than the attribution doctrine. What is striking, however, is that, in limiting the *Eingriffskondiktion*, the proponents of the modern wrongfulness theory draw on criteria that are not all that different from the attribution doctrine itself. Thus, Horst Jakobs,[26] probably the most influential representative of the wrongfulness school, argues that it is a requirement of the claim that the relevant gain should have 'touched' the claimant's estate and that the gain should be 'the consequence of an action which conflicts with the right of another'.[27] Jakobs is here moving very close to the attribution doctrine. Hartmut Haines,[28] another of its ardent critics, is closer still. To him, not all unlawful acts trigger restitution, but only those which violate a rule designed to protect individual interests.[29] To determine whether an enrichment is unjust it is therefore necessary to look to the purpose of the infringed rule. Again, the similarities with the attribution doctrine are obvious.

1.2. The Dominant View in Modern German Enrichment Law

The renaissance of the wrongfulness theory was relatively short-lived. The dominant German view today is that it is not possible to reach sensible results without examining the nature and scope of the infringed rights. The attribution

---

[25] W Ernst, 'Fritz Schulz (1879–1957)', in J Beatson and R Zimmermann (eds), *Jurists Uprooted—German-Speaking Émigré Lawyers in Twentieth-Century Britain* (2004) 105, 114.
[26] HH Jakobs, *Eingriffserwerb und Vermögensverschiebung in der Lehre von der ungerechtfertigten Bereicherung* (1964).   [27] ibid 64.
[28] H Haines, *Bereicherungsansprüche bei Warenzeichenverletzungen und unlauterem Wettbewerb* (1970).   [29] ibid 93 ff.

doctrine has been adopted both in the literature and in the cases.[30] Different writers, however, have suggested different ways of determining whether a right has attributive content. On the dominant view it is necessary to ask whether the claimant would have been able to legitimize the gain made by the defendant.[31] Some writers ask whether the claimant was deprived of the possibility of charging the defendant a fee for allowing him to exploit the claimant's right.[32] Others aim at the marketability of the infringed right.[33] What follows is a short overview[34] of the different rights that have, or have not, been found to have attributive content.

Property Rights

Property rights are central. Their attributive content is beyond question. The modern German approach thus has no problems with cases such as the old railway case decided by the *Reichsgericht* in 1919.[35]

Intellectual Property

The German courts continue to award 'compensatory' damages calculable in three ways: actual loss, licence fee, and infringer's profits. These awards depend on some degree of fault on the part of the infringer. It was argued above that the only reason why the courts opted for the wrong as the cause of action was the supposed unavailability of an enrichment claim for lack of a corresponding loss on the part of the claimant. More recently, the BGH has held that an unjust enrichment claim will be available even in cases of innocent infringement.[36] The court has thus recognized the 'attributive content' of these rights.

Unfair Competition

Unfair competition ('*unlauterer Wettbewerb*') is the main battleground between the attribution and wrongfulness doctrines. It includes elements of passing off and breach of confidence as well as rules against concerted practices and abuse of dominant positions.[37] Does a breach of these rules have restitutionary

---

[30] BGHZ 82, 299, 306. The BGH does seem to assume that it is necessary that the enrichment be unlawful. This has been criticized in the literature (eg H-G Koppensteiner and EH Kramer, *Ungerechtfertigte Bereicherung* (1988) 75). It is clear, however, that the BGH does not consider wrongfulness to be a sufficient criterion.   [31] cf Koppensteiner and Kramer (n 30 above) 76.

[32] MünchKomm-Lieb, § 812 no 208; J Esser and HL Weyers, *Schuldrecht II, Besonderer Teil* (7th edn, 1991) 400.

[33] D Reuter and M Martinek, *Ungerechtfertigte Bereicherung* (1983) 256.

[34] The discussion owes much to the excellent summary in Koppensteiner and Kramer (n 30 above) 79 ff.   [35] cf text to n 9 above.

[36] BGHZ 68, 90. See further BGHZ 77, 16; BGHZ 82, 299.

[37] Abuse of a dominant position and concerted practices are in fact dealt with in the *Gesetz gegen Wettbewerbsbeschränkungen* (*GWB*). The *Gesetz gegen den unlauteren Wettbewerb* (*UWG*) was recently reformed quite comprehensively in order to implement Council Directive 97/55/EC of 6 October 1997. The general clause in § 3, proscribing unfair competition liable to disadvantage competitors or consumers, is now backed by examples outlined in § 4. In most cases these merely

consequences under § 812 I? Generally proponents of the wrongfulness theory tend to allow such claims to a greater or lesser extent,[38] whereas those who advocate the now-dominant attribution doctrine are more cautious. They ask whether the different rules protect individuals by giving them enforceable rights or are more in the nature of 'rules of the game'.[39] Thus, there is clearly no right 'not to be disadvantaged by a competitor's misleading advertising',[40] or 'not to be exposed to a competitor's abuse of his dominant position'.[41] These do not favour individual competitors, nor can individual competitors grant permission to infringe these rules.[42]

Personality Rights

German law protects 'personality rights', such as the right to one's image and name, and the right to privacy.[43] To what extent can these rights be said to have attributive content? In the late 1950s and early 1960s some writers strongly held the view that such rights were simply not commercial rights and so did not carry any attributive content.[44] As commercial exploitation of specific personality rights by way of 'character-merchandizing' became commonplace, this stance became less and less tenable.

The BGH never had any qualms about recognizing the commercial value of the right to one's image. In 1956 it decided the famous 'Paul Dahlke' case.[45] A well-known German actor had, with his consent, been photographed sitting on the photographer's moped. The photographer sold these photos to the manufacturer of the moped who used them in an advertising campaign. Dahlke sued the manufacturer. The BGH held the defendant liable in the law of unjust enrichment. The court accepted that the right to the image of a celebrity has a commercial value and, as such, attributive content. The case can be contrasted with the so-called 'gentleman rider' case, decided barely two years later.[46] A man widely respected in society, but not quite in the 'celebrity' class,

reflect the jurisprudence of the German courts interpreting the old general clause in § 1 UWG. Acts of intimidation, the taking advantage of inexperienced younger customers, subliminal advertising, and slavish imitation of the products of a competitor are thereby all prohibited. §§ 5 and 6 are concerned with comparative and misleading advertising. §§ 16–18 provide for criminal sanctions for some forms of deceptive advertising and for the betrayal of trade secrets.

[38] cf Schulz (n 11 above) 218 ff.; Jakobs (n 26 above) 117; Haines (n 28 above) 93 ff.
[39] The term *'Spielregeln'* was first used in this context by L Raiser, 'Der Stand der Lehre vom subjektiven Recht im deutschen Zivilrecht' JZ 1961, 469. [40] § 5 UWG.
[41] § 19 GWB.
[42] Interestingly, the reform of German competition law in 2004 introduced a new sanction—disgorgement *to the state* of profits caused by unfair competition, provided the violation of the UWG was deliberate (§ 10 UWG). The legislator recognizes the potency of a profit-stripping sanction ('unfair competition does not pay'), while acknowledging that giving these profits to an individual competitor would be impractical and, in fact, unjust.
[43] BGH 25.5.1954, BGHZ 13, 334.
[44] cf E-J Mestmäcker, 'Eingriffserwerb und Rechtsverletzung in der ungerechtfertigten Bereicherung' JZ 1958, 525; Raiser (n 39 above) 471. [45] BGH 8.5.1956, BGHZ 20, 345.
[46] BGH 14.2.1958, BGHZ 26, 349.

was photographed on his horse. The photograph was used in an advertising campaign for a virility drug. The slogan read: 'He rides again for Germany'. The court did not even consider the possibility of an *Eingriffskondiktion*: it was obvious that no *commercial* right of the claimant's had been usurped. A non-celebrity's right to his image did not, in other words, have any attributive content.

Contractual Rights

German law is generally hostile to restitutionary remedies for breach of contract. There is one exception: where the defendant is no longer able to perform the contract, § 285 allows the other party to claim whatever the defendant has obtained as a substitute. For instance, under a double sale, the first buyer can claim the price achieved by the defendant seller under the second sale contract. In effect, the defendant is stripped of the profits of his breach.[47] Some writers have argued that the idea behind this provision should be taken to inform § 812 I by giving some contractual rights attributive content.[48] So far, these attempts have not been successful. To Wilburg, for example, one of the most powerful arguments against the 'unlawfulness' idea put forward by Schulz was that this would lead to restitution of gains made in breach of contract. He relies on the following example:[49] a blacksmith lives next door to a composer. He has entered into a contract with the composer under which he agrees not to make any noise during certain times of the day. If he breaches that contract, says Wilburg, he will surely not be exposed to a claim stripping him of the profits made during the hours in question.

1.3. The Measure of Restitution

It will be remembered that § 812 I provides that the defendant has to give up that which he has obtained. In so far as this is possible, this requires restitution *in specie*, in line with a general preference in German private law for specific remedies. Under § 818 II, if such specific restitution is not possible, the defendant has to pay to the claimant the monetary value of what he obtained. This provision will, of course, apply in all user and intellectual property cases.

　　Can the claimant strip the defendant of causally connected profits or is he limited to the objective value of what the defendant obtained directly? In this debate the proponents of the wrongfulness theory generally favour the former[50]

---

[47] In English law a similar result could be achieved without resorting to restitution for breach of contract, of course. By the first contract of sale property would normally pass to the buyer who would then have the choice between two defendants in conversion.

[48] Schulz (n 11 above) 7 ff; J Köndgen, 'Immaterialschadensersatz, Gewinnabschöpfung oder Privatstrafen als Sanktion für Vertragsbruch? Eine rechtsvergleichend-ökonomische Analyse' (1992) 56 RabelsZ 696; R Bollenberger, *Das stellvertretende Commodum* (1999) 160 f.

[49] Wilburg (n 18 above) 105, citing Staudinger-Werner, § 281 no. 3.

[50] Schulz (n 11 above) 428 f, C Kellmann, *Grundsätze der* Gewinnhaftung (1969) 110 ff, Jakobs (n 26 above) 136 ff.

whereas those who follow the attribution doctrine generally prefer limiting the claimant to the latter.[51] There are nevertheless some adherents of the attribution doctrine who favour stripping the defendant of his profits, arguing that, on the basis of the attribution theory, this gain should be attributed to the holder of the right and not to the person who has exploited a right that was not his.[52] In addition, given the very strong change of position defence in § 818 III, the claimant bears the risk that the defendant will be able to argue that he has not been enriched at all or, at any rate, not to the extent of the objective value of the infringed right. In these circumstances it is seen as only fair to give the claimant the benefit of any additional profits realized by the defendant. If the claimant bears a risk of loss, he should also have the chance of gain.[53]

The question is whether the *innocent* defendant can be made to disgorge his profits—the cynical defendant will, wherever he infringes a right carrying attributive content, be required to give up 'all he obtained' in any event: § 687 II 1.[54] The scope of application of this provision is generally agreed to include all cases that would otherwise be covered by the *Eingriffskondiktion*. This provides the strongest argument against a general profit-stripping response in cases of innocent infringement.[55]

1.4. Summary of the German Experience

Before we turn our attention to English law, we may pause for a moment and summarize the main insights to be gained from this account of the development of the present German law:

1. In order to avoid discretionary justice, early German enrichment law narrowed the claim artificially by insisting on a direct shift of wealth or at least a corresponding loss to the claimant. This requirement proved too narrow in intellectual property and user cases.

2. It was first sought to overcome these problems by focusing on the wrongfulness of the enriching act. Wrongfulness was taken to be a requirement of a claim in unjust enrichment, although the cause of action remained the unjust enrichment rather than the wrong. While influential, these attempts were ultimately unsuccessful, mainly because they led to a much increased scope for enrichment law.

---

[51] von Caemmerer (n 23 above) 356; RH Weber, 'Gewinnherausgabe—Rechtsfigur zwischen Schadensersatz-, Geschäftsführungs- und Bereicherungsrecht' ZSR 1992, 333, 362; P Schlechtriem, 'Bereicherung aus fremdem Persönlichkeitsrecht' *Festschrift für Hefermehl* (1976) 445, 458 ff; Ellger (n 7 above) 906 ff.

[52] See especially H Brandner, 'Die Herausgabe von Verletzervorteilen im Patentrecht und im Recht gegen den unlauteren Wettbewerb' GRUR 1980, 359, 360; Wilburg (n 18 above) 128 ff.

[53] Koppensteiner and Kramer (n 30 above) 156; Esser and Weyers (n 32 above) § 51 I 1 f

[54] Nor will he be able to rely on the disenrichment defence to a claim under §812: see §§ 818 IV, 292.

[55] von Caemmerer (n 23 above) 359.

3. The now-dominant view in Germany bases the *Eingriffskondiktion* on the nature and scope of the infringed right. An analysis of that right is meant to answer the question whether the legal order attributes the benefit in question exclusively to the holder of the right.

2. Restitution for Wrongs and Unjust Enrichment— Can the Divide Be Bridged?

There are currently two competing explanations in English law for restitution of non-participatory enrichments. One bases restitution on unjust enrichment, the other on a wrong committed by the defendant 'against' the claimant. Yet we still need to ask why restitution, and restitution to the claimant, is indeed the correct response to a wrong. If the wrong is truly the correct basis for restitution in these cases, the logical consequence is said to be that restitution should be available for *all* wrongs,[56] for, surely, 'nobody should profit from his own wrong'. That is not the law and we need to be able to explain why not.

Where non-participatory unjust enrichments are concerned, we encounter similar problems. The German experience has shown that 'absence of basis' is simply not an adequate explanation for the availability of restitution in such cases. Where the claimant has made a conscious transfer, we have everything we need to link him to the enrichment. In other cases, the words 'at the expense of' are creaking under the strain. If we have not noticed this, then it is because we have always focused on comparatively 'easy' cases, foremost among them cases involving infringements of property. Once we leave that safe ground, the problems begin: how do we link the enrichment to this claimant? Strangely enough, this is exactly the question we have to ask under the heading 'restitution for wrongs'. This is because the problems are, in truth, the same.

2.1. Alternative Analysis?

There is nothing wrong with alternative analysis[57] or concurrent liability. It is something our law accepts. A bus driver owes his passengers a duty to drive carefully because the law imposes this duty on bus drivers. He also owes the same duty in contract, because passengers expect bus drivers to be careful and will therefore only agree to be carried if the bus driver agrees to fulfil that expectation. Alternative analysis in unjust enrichment and wrongs is different. The law of wrongs is about the protection of rights. So is the law of unjust enrichment. If a right is infringed, this can give rise to a liability in the law of wrongs to make

---

[56] J Edelman, *Gain-Based Damages* (2002) 81.
[57] For an explanation of the term, cf n 2 above.

good any loss suffered by the holder of the right. This is what the law of wrongs is primarily concerned with.[58] The law of unjust enrichment, too, can react to the infringement of a right. Whether it does so depends on the scope and nature of the right. The point is that both tort and unjust enrichment respond to the infringement of the same right.[59] Once the focus shifts from the wrong to the right, it becomes clear that the underlying issue is the same.[60] Alternative analysis is no longer alternative. It becomes cumulative. The law ends up asking different, inconsistent, questions in response to the same problem.

So if the choice is not to be made by the claimant, it must be made by the law. Should the focus be on the wrong or the right? The wrongfulness theory in German law was ultimately unsuccessful. In its modern version, it would still provide a palatable approach in English law. The essence of the modern version is that wrongfulness is a necessary, but not a sufficient, reason for restitution.[61] An analysis of the right infringed by the defendant cannot be avoided when deciding whether restitution should follow. Once it becomes clear that wrongfulness alone is not enough, does it have any role left? Edelman suggests that the measure of restitution should differ according to the degree of wrongfulness of the defendant's actions. Only a 'cynical' wrongdoer should be stripped of all the profits causally connected to the commission of a wrong.[62] As the German experience shows, this is indeed a valuable insight. There is, however, no reason why the law of unjust enrichment should not be able to sanction cynical behaviour by stripping the defendant of all his profits, just as it protects the innocent defendant by allowing him the defence of change of position. That defence privileges the innocent. The flip-side may well be a more severe measure of restitution for the guilty.

2.2. Three Bad Reasons for Restitution for Wrongs

We saw above how in Germany the 'shift of wealth' requirement long prevented the law of unjust enrichment from adequately dealing with user and intellectual property cases. In English law, there were two additional reasons: the idea that restitution was based on an implied contract and, even when that heresy had been overcome, the relative underdevelopment of the law of unjust enrichment. Along with the supposed requirement of a corresponding loss, these induced the courts to deal with user cases, in particular, under the heading 'waiver of tort'.

---

[58] I do not dispute that, sometimes, the law of wrongs has additional responses in its armoury, such as exemplary damages: cf Edelman, (n 56 above) 7–21. Yet it would be difficult to deny that compensation for harm is the *primary* function of the law of wrongs, and restitution of gain the *primary* function of unjust enrichment.

[59] This has recently been forcefully argued by D Friedmann, 'The Protection of Entitlements via the Law of Restitution—Expectancies and Privacy' (2005) 121 LQR 400, 406.

[60] The same point can be made in relation to the leading case on concurrent liability in contract and tort, *Henderson v Merrett Syndicates* [1995] 2 AC 145: both the contractual and the tortious duties in that case were based on the defendants' voluntary assumption of responsibility (at 182, Lord Goff). The House of Lords was therefore arguably wrong in allowing the claimants to rely both on tort and contract claims. [61] Ellger (n 7 above) 125.

[62] Edelman (n 56 above) 65–111.

Implied Contracts and Waived Torts

'Waiver of tort' was later interpreted to mean 'restitution for a tort'.[63] This seems strained. The natural meaning suggests the opposite, namely that the tort is being ignored and the claim brought in unjust enrichment. When lawyers first referred to 'waiving a tort' they would also have talked about 'implying a contract'. This was the heyday of the implied contract heresy. In the case of wrongfully acquired benefits, the fiction of the implied contract was stretched to breaking point. How could it possibly be said, for example, that a thief, when taking goods belonging to the claimant, impliedly promised to return them? To 'waive' the tort meant that the claimant ignored it, making the fiction available once more and, with it, the restitutionary remedy.[64]

Originally it was thought that the claimant had to make that choice once and for all. That was wrong. In *United Australia v Barclays Bank*[65] the claimant company had fallen victim to a fraud. One of its employees had endorsed a cheque payable to the claimant to another company ('M') involved in the fraud. M paid the cheque into its account with Barclays Bank. The claimant first brought an action for money had and received against M. When M went into liquidation, it brought a claim against Barclays in conversion. Barclays argued that, by bringing the claim in money had and received, the claimant had 'waived' the tort of conversion and could no longer rely on it. The House of Lords held that this was a misunderstanding of the term 'waiver of tort'. Bringing the action did not constitute a once and for all election. Only by suing M to judgment could the claimant lose its right to sue in conversion. The case is therefore authority for the proposition that bringing an action for money had and received does not extinguish a tort claim. There are, however, some dicta in the speech by Viscount Simon LC which have been relied upon as authority for the proposition that the original claim against M had been a claim based on the tort of deceit and/or conversion, although the form of action had been money had and received.[66] These dicta indeed suggest two things which do not fit with the view here put forward, namely that the tort is a *sine qua non* of the restitutionary claim and that the claimant chooses between remedies, not causes of action. The conclusion that can be drawn from this is that 'waiver of tort' in fact means 'restitution for a tort'.[67] The context of the passage is important, however.

---

[63] Burrows (n 2 above) 463.   [64] Edelman (n 56 above) 121.   [65] [1941] AC 1.

[66] 'When the plaintiff "waived the tort" and brought assumpsit he did not thereby elect to be treated from that time forward on the basis that no tort had been committed; indeed, if it were to be understood that no tort had been committed, how could an action in assumpsit lie? It lies only because the acquisition of the defendant is wrongful and there is thus an obligation to make restitution . . . The substance of the matter is that on certain facts he is claiming redress either in the form of compensation, ie damages as for a tort, or in the form of restitution of money to which he is entitled, but which the defendant has wrongfully received. The same set of facts entitles the plaintiff to claim either form of redress. At some stage of the proceedings the plaintiff must elect which remedy he will have.' [1941] AC 1, 18–19.   [67] Burrows (n 2 above) 463.

The point of the judgment is that the conversion claim for compensation survives and that compensation and restitution are not incompatible. Viscount Simon is at pains to point out that the same facts, which can lead to a claim for compensation, can also be relied on to found a claim to restitution, namely the violation of a legally protected interest, in this case, the claimant's property in the cheque.

Corresponding Loss Requirement

The question of whether a claim in unjust enrichment is available where the claimant has not suffered a loss is hotly debated in the common law. Canada, in opting for a *sine causa* model of unjust enrichment liability, has opted for a 'disenrichment' requirement.[68] Birks, in putting forward his own version of restitution for 'absence of basis', refuses to follow the Canadian lead. Although he describes the argument as 'finely balanced',[69] he comes down firmly against any such requirement. Some commentators have argued against this precisely because it would lead to the virtual abolition of restitution for wrongs.[70] This is indeed correct, but it is not necessarily an argument in favour of the loss requirement. Birks's analysis of *Trustee of Jones v Jones*[71] makes this point extremely well. In that case Mr Jones had drawn cheques on his firm's account. These were paid into his wife's bank account during the 'twilight period' of her husband's bankruptcy. She used the money to deal in potato futures. Her dealings were extremely successful and she multiplied the original money. Her husband's trustee in bankruptcy was able to recover her entire profits for the estate. The Court of Appeal did not base this result on any wrong. Birks argues that pushing the case into restitution for wrongs is not possible:

The wife in that case received the trustee's money by two cheques. To explain the outcome in the law of wrongs, one must, as the court did not, tie it to conversion of the cheques. But that would mean that, if the transfer had been paperless, the result would have been completely different.[72]

Again, it becomes clear that the wrong is not really the issue. It is the infringement of the underlying property right. To the law of unjust enrichment, it matters not how that property right was infringed. It does matter to the law of wrongs.

The opponents of the disenrichment requirement have another powerful ally in Lord Mansfield himself. In *Hambly v Trott*,[73] he said, *obiter*, but quite unambiguously, that riding a horse without the owner's permission would trigger an unjust enrichment claim, a claim which, unlike trespass, would not be affected by the *actio personalis* rule.[74] The later refusal by the Court of Appeal in

[68] See the excellent account by L Smith, 'The Mystery of Juristic Reason' (2000) 12 SCLR (2d) 211.
[69] Birks (n 1 above) 79.
[70] RB Grantham and CEF Rickett, 'Disgorgement for Unjust Enrichment' [2003] CLJ 159.
[71] [1997] Ch 159.   [72] Birks (n 1 above) 85.   [73] (1776) 1 Cowp 371, 98 ER 1136.
[74] *'Actio personalis moritur cum persona'* ('A personal action dies with the person'). This now defunct rule meant that a claim in tort could not be brought against a deceased tortfeasor's estate.

Phillips v Homfray[75] to accept that the saving of expense by using another's property amounts to an enrichment is inconsistent with Lord Mansfield's view. Surely Lord Mansfield, unconstrained by the implied contract heresy (in which he never believed) and unconcerned about the lack of a corresponding loss on the part of the claimant, got it right. So did Peter Birks.

If the disenrichment requirement is jettisoned, this also means that the measure of restitution is open to reconsideration. Rather like privileging the innocent defendant through change of position, the cynical defendant could be subjected to much stricter and more far-reaching unjust enrichment liability.

Unjust Enrichment Underdeveloped

'Ignorance' has always been a problematic ground for restitution. Goff and Jones have never accepted Birks's argument that a legal system which allows restitution of a mistaken payment must *a fortiori* allow restitution where the claimant's will was never exercised at all. They write:

If we turn from the case of transfer by the plaintiff to the case where an asset of the plaintiff comes into the hands of the defendant without any transfer by or on behalf of the plaintiff, the fact of the plaintiff's ignorance of the event (if that be the case) may or may not be relevant, but it cannot in our opinion constitute of itself a ground of recovery. For even where the plaintiff is ignorant of what is happening, recovery of the asset or its value must depend upon some specific ground of recovery, relating the plaintiff to the asset and rendering it unjust for the defendant to retain it.[76]

This passage reveals the weakness of 'ignorance'. It is reminiscent of Wilburg's attack on the unified understanding of § 812 I BGB. Ignorance alone is not enough. We need to look closely at the nature of the underlying right.

Unfortunately, Birks's new model of unjust enrichment liability does not solve this problem. He writes: 'In general, an absolutely involuntary enrichment will have no explanatory basis at all'.[77] The *sine causa* approach is thus applied whether the enrichment came about by performance or not. The danger of restitutionary overkill becomes clear when one considers cases of incidental benefits. Birks himself deals with the case in which the heat from my flat rises to the flat above, reducing my upstairs neighbour's fuel bills. He is worried about this case.[78] Clearly, my neighbour has been enriched. His enrichment is 'at my expense',[79] and there is no legal basis for it. That my neighbour does not incur restitutionary liability is tentatively explained on the basis of some form of involuntary gift on my part. Birks writes:

Matters must be judged at the commencement of the principal activity. If the principal activity is freely intended, in the way that I intend to heat my flat, the incidents of that

---

[75] (1883) 24 Ch D 439.   [76] R Goff and G Jones, *The Law of Restitution* (2002), 180.
[77] Birks (n 1 above) 155.   [78] ibid 158.
[79] It will be remembered that Birks rejects the 'corresponding loss' requirement.

activity are also intended, however little they may be wanted. A terrorist who plants a bomb in a shopping centre may not want to kill the shoppers but obliquely intends their death.[80]

Even if that explanation is accepted, it cannot explain all cases of incidental benefits. A classic German example involves the construction of a new railway line. This causes one property to go up, another to go down in value.[81] Both appreciation and devaluation are caused by the same event, they are causally connected. Therefore, it is possible to say that the first owner's gain has been 'at the expense' of another.[82] The first owner's enrichment has no legal basis: the second owner owed him nothing. Finally, Birks's gift analysis does not work here: the principal activity is *not* freely intended and the enrichor can do nothing to prevent it. In fact, 'ignorance' faces the same problems in explaining cases of this kind. Just because the enrichor is 'ignorant' of what is happening to the value of his property (and the value of the enrichee's) does not mean that the enrichee should be compelled to make restitution.

Therefore, neither 'ignorance' as an unjust factor nor the undifferentiated *sine causa* approach put forward in Birks's late work deals with these cases adequately. This area of the law of unjust enrichment is still 'under construction'. Judges and commentators feel on much safer ground in the law of wrongs. The flight into wrongs can therefore be readily understood. But, as was argued above, basing restitution on wrongs brings its own problems of restitutionary overkill.

It is cruel that Peter Birks died before he could develop his thinking on the participatory/non-participatory division. He was, of course, fully aware of the German law. He took a first step in the direction of what he saw to be the more rational system. If the law follows him, or has, as he thought, already irrevocably moved towards a *sine causa* approach, others will have to take the next step.

2.3. Unjust Enrichment and Attribution of Rights

In rethinking cases hitherto categorized as belonging to the category 'restitution for wrongs', it makes sense to focus on the rights in issue in those cases. The aim is to demonstrate that the attribution theory can be used to account for the majority of them.

Property Rights

Deprivation of Property
In *Lamine v Dorrell*,[83] a case frequently cited as an example of restitution for wrongs, the defendant had stolen and sold negotiable instruments belonging

---

[80] ibid.   [81] Wilburg (n 18 above) 14 ff.
[82] The only way round this would be to insist that loss and gain must 'correspond'—we have seen that this immediately excludes user and intellectual property cases: cf the discussion above, pp 380f.
[83] (1701) 2 Ld Raym 1216.

to the claimant, who successfully sued him for restitution of the sale price. Similarly, in *Chesworth v Farrar*,[84] a landlord had sold antiques belonging to his tenant. The tenant was entitled to the sale price.[85] It is generally accepted that all these cases, along with many others in the same vein,[86] are amenable to alternative analysis. They can be explained easily by resorting to the German attribution doctrine: the infringed rights attributed the benefit in question to the claimant. The cause of action is unjust enrichment.

User Cases

User cases are the same.[87] An unjust enrichment account of them only works, however, if Birks's view is accepted that English law does not require a corresponding deprivation.

Disturbance

In English law, my interest in the quiet enjoyment of my land is protected by the tort of nuisance. A nightclub opens in a mainly residential area. Loud music at night disturbs the residents. If the court decides that the interference is unreasonable, will the nightclub owner be required to pay a licence fee to the residents? Or will he, given that he knew about the residents' complaints, be liable to hand over all his profits? The answer must be 'no'. This is because no individual resident would have been able to grant the nightclub a licence to play loud music at night in a residential neighbourhood.[88]

Nuisance protects other rights, too. In *Carr-Saunders v Dick McNeil*[89] the claimant had acquired a prescriptive right to light. The defendant's new building obscured that light. Although he analysed the award as compensatory, Millett J awarded the value of a licence to deprive the claimant of this right. This is in line with the attribution doctrine in German law. Had the parties negotiated prior to the erection of the building, the claimant would have been able to permit it subject to being paid a reasonable sum. The right can thus be analysed as attributing the benefit of light to the claimant. In this it differs from the general interest which a person has in the quiet enjoyment of his land.

Nuisance can also lie to protect rights of a different nature altogether. In *Stoke-on-Trent City Council v Wass*[90] the claimant local authority owned the market rights within its area. Nuisance lay to enforce this right. When the defendant

---

[84] [1967] 1 QB 407.

[85] Beatson has shown that *Chesworth v Farrar,* contrary to *obiter dicta* in the case, is in fact authority that the restitutionary claim is non-parasitic: Beatson, *The Use and Abuse of Unjust Enrichment* (1991) 218.

[86] eg *Oughton v Seppings* (1830) 1 B & Ad 241, *Powell v Rees* (1837) 7 Ad & El 427.

[87] *Strand Electric and Engineering Co v Brisford Entertainments Ltd* [1952] 2 QB 246; *Penarth Dock Engineering Co Ltd v Pounds* [1963] 1 Lloyd's Rep 359.

[88] Goff and Jones agree with the result, but seem to base this on the impracticality of calculating awards rather than on principle: Goff and Jones (n 76 above) 788.

[89] [1986] 1 WLR 922.   [90] [1988] 1 WLR 1406.

operated an unauthorized market, the claimant sued. It succeeded in stopping the unlawful market by injunctive relief, but failed to obtain restitutionary damages. Edelman says that this case must now be regarded as wrong.[91] His main argument is that in the *Carr-Saunders* case restitutionary damages had been awarded for the tort of nuisance. If the case is re-analysed under the German attribution doctrine, however, the decision makes perfect sense. The Council did not own the market right for profit; it owned it in order to make sure the market was conducted in an orderly manner. It was given the market right so that it could enforce the 'rules of the game'. The court instinctively stumbled on the correct result.

Nuisance is thus a very good example of what happens if a blanket rule is adopted that wrongful acts, or even certain wrongs, will *always* lead to a restitutionary remedy. Nuisance protects different rights and interests—these need to be analysed carefully in order to decide when their infringement will appropriately trigger restitution of gains.

Intellectual Property

The concept of intellectual property developed in England well before the law of unjust enrichment was fully recognized, and certainly before the implied contract heresy had been overcome.[92] As in Germany, the law of wrongs was thus mainly responsible for the vindication of intellectual property rights and—given that compensatory awards in this area were frequently inadequate—restitution, whether by way of an account of profits or otherwise, was granted as a remedy for a wrong.[93] This should not have systemic implications now that the law of unjust enrichment has (almost) caught up. The parallel with the German law of intellectual property, and the pseudo-compensation awarded by the German courts in these cases, is quite striking.[94]

Competition Rights

In *Garden Cottage Foods v Milk Marketing Board*[95] Lord Diplock suggested that an infringement of Articles 81 and 82 of the EC Treaty could give rise to an action for breach of statutory duty in the English courts. This has since been confirmed by the Court of Appeal in *Crehan v Inntrepreneur Pub Company*,[96] even though it was recognized that the tort of breach of statutory duty was being stretched to breaking point in order to give effect to Community legislation. If Edelman is right in saying that *all* civil wrongs should give rise to restitutionary claims, this must be true of breach of statutory duty and hence of breaches of

[91] Edelman (n 56 above) 135.
[92] The Statute of Anne (8 Anne c 19), first introducing a kind of copyright, was passed as early as 1709.
[93] cf s 61(1)(d) Patents Act 1977; s 96(2) Copyright, Designs and Patents Act 1988.
[94] cf text to n 8, above.   [95] [1984] AC 130.   [96] [2004] EWCA Civ 637.

Arts 81 and 82 of the EC Treaty. Surely this cannot be right. These Articles lay down 'rules of the game'. Their effectiveness is greatly increased if, in accordance with the express wish of the European Court of Justice, individual companies are given the right to sue for damages in situations where they feel that they have been the victim of the abuse of a dominant position or concerted practices. It is clear, however, that an individual competitor, or even a group of competitors, cannot grant a company or a group of companies a 'licence' to breach Arts 81 and 82. The rights conferred on them are not of that nature. The application of the 'attribution doctrine' thus clearly dictates that no restitutionary claim should be available. This is not because it would be difficult to calculate such an award. It is because the underlying right does not attribute an exclusive legal position to any one 'victim' of the wrong.

The Right to Privacy

Article 8 of the European Convention on Human Rights provides that '[e]veryone has the right to respect for his private and family life, his home and his correspondence'. Now that the Human Rights Act 1998 has incorporated the Convention into domestic law, English law has to answer the question whether a breach of this right to privacy will give rise to a restitutionary response. Friedmann has recently argued that English law has rather jumped the gun on this question. The decision against recognizing a general tort of breach of privacy and in favour of a more piecemeal form of protection through the equitable wrong of breach of confidence has led to a restitutionary response, simply because breach of confidence is a wrong for which an account of profits is available. Friedmann would prefer a careful analysis of the right before deciding whether a restitutionary response is appropriate.[97] Essentially, he is putting forward a version of the attribution theory. The remedial response to a breach of the right to privacy should not be determined by jurisdictional accident. Friedmann rightly points out that defamation is generally thought to be a tort that cannot be 'waived' so that, had the courts decided to create a new tort of breach of privacy, it is unlikely that restitution would have been available for it.[98] In Germany there has been a passionate debate about privacy and related rights—these are regarded by some as rights of a higher order which should not be commercialized.[99] Although these arguments did not prevail in the end, the debate should nevertheless take place, the question should be asked.

Fiduciary Duties

Explaining restitution following a breach of fiduciary duty in terms of the attribution doctrine seems rather strained. German writers commenting on English

---

[97] D Friedmann, 'Protection of Entitlements via the Law of Restitution—Expectancies and Privacy' [2005] 121 LQR 400, 415.   [98] ibid 417.
[99] See pp 385f, above.

law seem to agree that there are different forces at work in this area.[100] For example, the opportunity to accept bribes is not a benefit which the beneficiary enjoys to the exclusion of the fiduciary.[101] Thus, Peter Schlechtriem comments on *Reading v Attorney-General*,[102] which concerned a soldier using his uniform to assist smugglers, that the defendant had to give up his profits, 'not because he encroached on an exclusive commercial sphere attributed to the State, but because disgorgement of profits of disgraceful behaviour is meant to sanction and deter'.[103]

Fiduciary duties are very strict. It may be that the focus here is (rightly) on the duty rather than on any right underlying it, precisely because the beneficiary is, to an extent, at the fiduciary's mercy. Regulation of conduct rather than protection of rights is at issue. As long as the concept of the fiduciary duty is well defined and kept within predictable bounds, this is unlikely to lead to too much restitution. It would, however, be wrong to draw the conclusion that, because the fiduciary has to give up the profits of a breach of his fiduciary duties to the beneficiary, there must exist a category called 'restitution for wrongs', making restitution available for all kinds of wrong.

Contractual Rights

There is no reason why the attribution doctrine as advocated here should be confined to absolute interests. The main difference between an absolute right and a contractual right is that the former protects an interest against the whole world whereas the latter does so only against the other contractual party. If that other party violates the contractual right there is no reason why an unjust enrichment claim should be ruled out from the start. The problem with basing restitution on the wrong of the breach is that this method fails to provide appropriate mechanisms for deciding what breaches should give rise to a restitutionary claim. The leading case, *Attorney-General v Blake*,[104] thus does not tell us very much about the circumstances in which restitution should be available, confining it to 'exceptional' circumstances, with the decisive question being whether 'the plaintiff had a legitimate interest in preventing the defendant's profit-making activity'.[105] If the law were to focus on the contractual right instead of the wrong of breaching it, one useful criterion, based on the attribution doctrine, would be to ask whether the contractual right reserves to the claimant a sphere of economic activity from which the defendant is excluded. In our discussion of the German law, we came across the example of a blacksmith who has entered into a contract with a neighbouring composer not to hammer at certain times of the day.[106] This contract, it could be argued, lays down a rule of

---

[100] See K Rusch, *Gewinnhaftung bei Verletzung von Treuepflichten* (2003) 252; P Schlechtriem, 'Güterschutz durch Eingriffskondiktionen' in Institut für ausländisches und internationales Privat- und Wirtschaftsrecht Universität Heidelberg (ed), *Ungerechtfertigte Bereicherung* (1984) 57.
[101] Rusch (n 100 above) 252.   [102] [1951] AC 507.
[103] Schlechtriem (n 100 above) 61.   [104] [2001] 1 AC 268.
[105] ibid 285, per Lord Nicholls.   [106] cf text to n 49, above.

behaviour which the blacksmith needs to observe in order to make it possible for him to coexist harmoniously with his neighbour. It does not reserve to the composer a sphere of economic activity (hammering for profit). In contrast, if the blacksmith sold his smithy and signed a non-competition agreement, breach of that agreement might lead to a restitutionary award. Here, the contract attributes to the claimant a sphere of economic activity from which he can exclude the defendant.[107]

Blake itself does not sit well with the attribution doctrine formulated in this way. An infamous convicted spy and double agent had published his reminiscences. The Crown claimed his royalties. It faced the problem that, when Blake published his book, the information contained in it was no longer confidential. He was therefore held liable to account for his royalties on the basis that publishing his memoirs without the Crown's consent breached a confidentiality agreement he had signed on entering the secret service. It would be difficult to argue that this agreement attributed to the Crown the right to control whether, and how, Blake's experiences in the secret service would be exploited commercially. The House of Lords stressed that the duty of confidentiality imposed on Blake by the agreement was closely akin to a fiduciary duty.[108] It may well be that this is the proper explanation of why the Crown's claim was allowed: their lordships were not concerned to protect a profit-making opportunity reserved to the Crown, but to sanction behaviour falling short of what should be expected of members of the intelligence services.

The lesson that can be learned from Germany in this context is that not all contractual rights are the same. Once we focus on the contractual right rather than on its breach, we may be a step nearer to answering the difficult question as to when the claimant has a legitimate interest in restitution.

3. Conclusion

Peter Birks maintained throughout his scholarly life that the distinction between autonomous unjust enrichment and restitution for wrongs was fundamental. In his later work, there are some signs that he was reconsidering this position.[109] In the light of his adoption of a *sine causa* approach, this is hardly surprising. He knew the German law well and was always keenly aware of the danger of 'too much restitution'.

[107] cf Bollenberger (n 48 above) 160 ff.

[108] *Blake*, 285, per Lord Nicholls. It should be noted that it had been held at first instance that Blake was not a fiduciary, and that there had been no appeal against this. Otherwise, the House might well have been able to find for the Crown on the basis of breach of fiduciary duty.

[109] It is striking, for instance, that he acknowledged in the preface to the first edition of *Unjust Enrichment* that Daniel Friedmann and Jack Beatson, the two most prominent critics of 'restitution for wrongs' may well have been 'one jump ahead' of him at times: Birks (n 1 above) p xiii, having just stated that 'by assuming without proving, and in fact almost certainly incorrectly, that the

It has been argued in this short essay that the English law of unjust enrichment needs to think again about non-participatory enrichments in general. What needs to be realized is that both the law of wrongs and the law of unjust enrichment are really concerned with rights. Both should therefore be using the same criteria to decide in what circumstances restitution will be available following the infringement of a right. As a result, restitution for wrongs may collapse into autonomous unjust enrichment or vice versa.

I am not arguing for a wholesale adoption of the German law on this subject. I only draw attention to more than a hundred years of German learning which may well be useful, particularly if English law decides to follow Peter Birks down a more civilian path.

claimant in unjust enrichment must have suffered a loss corresponding to the defendant's gain, I adopted a much too narrow view of the extent to which cases of restitution for wrongs are susceptible of alternative analysis in unjust enrichment' (p xii). In a footnote to his essay 'Misnomer' in Cornish *et al* (n 4 above) 18 n 38 he refers to *Trustee of Jones v Jones* [1996] 3 WLR 703 and continues that the case 'makes it obvious that more can be achieved than might have been thought without relying on any wrong'. Thus, he concludes: 'The view of J. Beatson that "waiver of tort" must be explained in "non-parasitic" terms, independently of the tort in question, may yet be proved right, not in the sense of explaining or displacing restitution for wrongs, but in identifying the larger scope of autonomous unjust enrichment'.

21

Peter Birks and Scots Enrichment Law

*Hector MacQueen**

'A bad case, I fear, of fools rush in': so Peter Birks endorsed the offprint he gave me of his 1985 *Current Legal Problems* article, 'Restitution: A View of the Scots Law'.[1] But in reality, that paper, together with an article published almost simultaneously in the *Juridical Review* and entitled 'Six Questions in Search of an Answer: Unjust Enrichment in a Crisis of Identity',[2] represented the beginning of the modern academic analysis of Scots enrichment law, and indeed the first serious discussion of the subject since the days of Kames and Hume.[3] Giving his seminal opinion in *Shilliday v Smith* in 1998, Lord President Rodger observed: 'Anyone who wants to glimpse something of the underlying realities must start from the work of Professor Peter Birks'.[4] This essay will attempt to assess Birks's role in the major reconstruction of Scots enrichment law that followed his initial contributions. It will also touch on his use of Scots law as a comparative example, not only in his work on the English law of restitution, but also in his crusade for the more systematic analysis, teaching, and presentation of English law in general.

The state of Scots enrichment law at the time of Birks's 1981 appointment to the Chair of Civil Law in Edinburgh is most readily gleaned from the five-page exposition in the relevant chapter of the eighth edition of the standard introductory text on private law, *Gloag and Henderson*, published in 1980 and entitled 'Quasi-Contract'.[5] It dealt with obligations said to resemble contractual ones in

* Professor of Private Law, University of Edinburgh. I am grateful to my Edinburgh colleagues, Martin Hogg and Niall Whitty, for helpful discussion of an earlier draft of this essay.

[1] (1985) 38 CLP 57 (henceforth 'View').

[2] 1985 JR 227 (henceforth 'Six Questions').

[3] For Kames and Hume, see HL MacQueen and WDH Sellar, 'Unjust Enrichment in Scots Law' in EJH Schrage (ed), *Unjust Enrichment: The Comparative Legal History of the Law of Restitution* (1995) 289, 298–9.

[4] 1998 SC 725, 727. See further Lord Rodger's extra-judicial elaboration in 'Developing the Law Today: National and International Influences' 2002 *Tydskrif vir die Suid-Afrikaanse Reg* 1, 7; also references to Birks's writing in the opinion of Lord President Hope in *Morgan Guaranty Trust Co of New York v Lothian Regional Council* 1995 SC 151, 157, and in his speech in *Dollar Land (Cumbernauld) Ltd v CIN Properties Ltd* 1998 SC (HL) 90, 98 (each cited below, at respectively text to nn 69, 75).

[5] WA Wilson and AB Wilkinson (eds), *Gloag and Henderson's Introduction to the Law of Scotland* (8th edn, 1980) ch XIV.

requiring payment or performance rather than reparation of loss caused by something done or omitted; but the obligations were imposed by law, not by the consent of the party obliged. There were two main heads, restitution and recompense. Restitution was about the return of goods by a possessor to their true owner or, in the case of goods consumed, to pay their value. The principle also extended to the plea of repetition, under which money might be recovered, either because it had been paid by mistake (*condictio indebiti*) or because it had been paid in advance for a consideration not received (*condictio causa data causa non secuta*). The other main head, recompense, received a longer treatment. The principle had been defined by the institutional writer Bell: 'Where one has gained by the lawful act of another, done without any intention of donation, he is bound to recompense or indemnify that other to the extent of the gain'.[6] This was too widely stated, however, since it could reach merely incidental benefits arising without loss to the party conferring the benefit.[7] Recompense properly applied where there was no contract, or work had been done in circumstances precluding any contractual claim. Typical cases were *bona fide* improvements to another's property in the mistaken belief that it was one's own; work done under a contract but so disconform to the contract that a claim for the price was precluded; and goods supplied or work done under a contract where the recipient could plead incapacity, or that statute made the contract void. Recompense was subsidiary in being inapplicable if another remedy was available.

The first hint that Birks's Edinburgh appointment had led him to explore Scots law came in his Thomas Memorial Lecture,[8] which analysed Lord Mansfield's use of Roman law in *Moses v Macferlan* (1760).[9] In the course of a characteristically wide-ranging discussion, Birks referred to Bankton's *Institute of the Law of Scotland*, published nine years before *Moses v Macferlan*, as anticipating Mansfield in putting the action for money had and received on an enrichment rather than a contractual basis.[10] Bankton compared Scots and English law to show that the action for money had and received appeared to cover the same ground as the Roman *condictio* already long received in Scotland. So, 'Bankton, in 1751, thought that the cases in which Roman *condictio* was restitutionary in operation provided the model for both Scottish and English law'.[11]

This observation provided the platform from which the more detailed discussion of Scots law in the *Current Legal Problems* paper began.[12] English law

---

[6] GJ Bell, *Principles of the Law of Scotland* (10th edn, by W Guthrie, 1899) § 538.
[7] *Edinburgh Tramways Co v Courtenay* 1909 SC 99, 105 (Lord President Dunedin).
[8] 'English and Roman Learning in *Moses v Macferlan*' (1984) 37 CLP 1.
[9] (1760) 2 Burr 1005; 97 ER 676.
[10] The suggestion of MacQueen and Sellar (n 3) 314–16 that Mansfield may also have been influenced by Kames has won support in JA Dieckmann, 'Scots Influence on English Law: The Guarantor's Right to Derivative Recourse (Subrogation)' (2004) 8 Edinburgh LR 329, 349–54.
[11] 'English and Roman Learning' (n 8) 16.
[12] The paper was given at the first meeting of the then-SPTL Restitution Law section, held in Edinburgh in 1984.

could learn from Civilian systems in the effort to give restitution shape and
system: 'analytically, all systems wrestle with the same restitutionary problems;
and, historically, English law does here share the civilian root'.[13] He went on:
'Aversion from comparison is most obviously impoverishing in relation to Scots
law whose materials are both rich and accessible'.[14] Scots law manifested a systematic and structured approach in which enrichment law, divided into two
major sub-categories of 'restitution' and 'recompense', was long established and
clearly distinguished from contract; moreover, it did not suffer from the 'curse
of English restitution...the dualism which has been inherited from the
institutional separation of law and equity'.[15]

Both the *Current Legal Problems* and *Juridical* papers criticized the Scottish
division of restitution and recompense, however. Restitution (including repetition) was given primacy of place in expositions of the law, so that recompense,
which otherwise was so defined to be, '*prima facie*, wide enough to cover every
case of unjust enrichment at the expense of another',[16] was actually 'in some
sense a residual category of unjust enrichment'.[17] The division was, Birks
argued,[18] based on the nature of the benefit received (property and money in the
case of restitution, services in recompense). But this led to 'very curious questions...such as whether a mistake is necessary in order to perfect a claim in
respect of work done non-contractually';[19] and about the division between
enrichment recovery and the vindication of property.[20] In an important passage
pointing firmly towards the future direction of the law, Birks wrote:

The worst consequence of division by benefit received is the impression given that the
causes of action actually differ depending on the form in which an enrichment is received,
when a moment's reflection reveals that the form in which value is received . . . is merely
contingent: morally and legally neutral. . . . The only cure is to unify the subject by
confining the benefit-based division within the one issue to which it matters, namely
whether the recipient has been enriched to an extent expressible in money.[21]

Further, the use of 'restitution' as a specific term of art within the field also
meant that it could not be the name of the whole field. This tended to encourage
instead the unhelpful label of quasi-contract, hinting that implied contracts were
the basis of recovery. A system talking mainly in terms of contract and delict,
however, ought to use unjust enrichment.[22] The survival of the *condictiones* and
their Latin names (*indebiti, causa data causa non secuta*, and so on) obscured what
was actually going on: the case for modernization of language was overwhelming.[23] The subject suffered from a lack of detailed literature, and needed

---

[13] 'View' (n 1) 57.   [14] ibid 57.   [15] ibid 61.   [16] 'Six Questions' (n 2) 234.
[17] 'Six Questions' (n 2) 234.   [18] 'View' (n 1) 62–3; 'Six Questions' (n 2) 234.
[19] ibid 61–3 (quotation at 62). See also 'Six Questions' (n 2) 233–8.
[20] 'View' (n 1) 75–8; 'Six Questions' (n 2) 235–8, 241.   [21] 'View' (n 1) 63.
[22] 'View' (n 1) 58–61; 'Six Questions' (n 2) 230–3.
[23] 'View' (n 1) 64; 'Six Questions' (n 2) 238–41.

an 'agreed map', 'an intelligible modern typology of the facts which constitute the reasons for making the defender disgorge an enrichment'.[24]

The map or typology which Birks offered to Scots law for a generalized approach to enrichment was the one recently published for English law in his *Introduction to the Law of Restitution*.[25] Just as this sought to provide the skeleton of principle on which the material in *Goff and Jones* could hang,[26] so his *Current Legal Problems* paper sketched out how the major Scottish cases could be arranged in a system which can be labelled for short as one of 'unjust factors'.[27] A defender (D) was enriched either by subtraction from the pursuer (P) or by doing wrong to P, and such enrichment fell to be reversed when in addition there was an unjust factor. In the case of enrichment by subtraction, the unjust factors either affected the voluntariness of the enrichment (eg mistake or coercion), or qualified it with a condition such as a contractual reciprocation (in English terms, failure of consideration; in Roman-Scots ones, *causa data causa non secuta*). D was also enriched by and liable to make restitution after 'free acceptance', that is, by choosing to accept value in the knowledge that it was not being offered gratuitously. Finally restitution might be required in other cases by policy considerations.[28] Scots enrichment law appeared not to have admitted claims of enrichment for wrongs but this ignored the many cases in which fiduciaries such as trustees, partners, agents, and company directors had been compelled to give up the profits made from breach of their duty to avoid conflicts of interest. While the origins of Scots law in this area might be different from English law, the two had grown together.[29]

Within this overall structure, Birks noted a number of features of Scots law of interest to the common lawyer. In general it took an objective approach to enrichments, especially non-money ones, and hence was able to recognize much more readily liability in cases of improvement to another's property and in cases of contractual part-performance.[30] Further, failure of consideration did not have to be total for recovery to take place.[31] But the objective approach also meant that little recognition had been accorded to free acceptance, or to 'subjective devaluation' as a ground for reducing or denying a claim (value depending on choice, unchosen benefits cannot be valued). Thus pursuers unable to negative voluntariness might have succeeded on the alternative of free acceptance.[32]

Mistake (or, in Scots terms, error) dominated Scots law thinking about enrichment, but, in the *condictio indebiti* was limited, thanks to the civilian root, to liability mistakes—that is, the mistaken belief that payment or performance was legally due. The danger that non-liability mistakes or mispredictions would not ground any claim for recovery was lessened, however, by the availability of claims

---

[24] 'View' (n 1) 65; 'Six Questions' (n 2) 240.
[25] 1985 (henceforth *Restitution*).   [26] *Restitution* 1, 3.
[27] The phrase is used in 'View' (n 1) 65.   [28] For all this see 'View' (n 1) 65–74.
[29] 'View' (n 1) 74–5; 'Six Questions' (n 2) 242–5.
[30] 'View' (n 1) 67–8; 'Six Questions' (n 2) 241.   [31] 'View' (n 1) 71.
[32] ibid 72–3.

under the *condictiones sine causa* and *causa data causa non secuta*. It had been accepted, but without enthusiasm, that mistake of law precluded recovery.[33] There had been little discussion of coercion as a factor negativing voluntariness.[34]

A final distinction which Birks found in Scots as in English law lay in measures of recovery. In the usual case, the measure was the value received by D, always converted into money, whether or not the benefit originally conferred had been money. The second measure was, in Birks's shorthand, 'value surviving'[35] what D still held of what he had received, or where he held something representing what he had received ('as a car bought with the £5,000'[36]). The Scots law category of restitution operated in this area, but with 'a complicating and somewhat alarming twist': the basis was a personal obligation to restore rather than property. Thus Scots law seemed to avoid the question of whether a restitutionary claim could ever have proprietary effects, despite its importance in, for example, cases where D was bankrupt when the claim was made. It did however seem to have rules on tracing (the identification of assets representing what was originally conferred on D) which, whatever their roots, were now the same as in English law, so that 'no possible good could come from dividing it'.[37]

In sum, Birks's 1985 articles pointed up the incoherence and uncertainty in which Scots enrichment law stood as a result of its terminology, structure, and lack of commitment to any overall principle. He proposed a unified approach to the subject, based around the simple idea of liability to make restitution of an unjust enrichment to the person at whose expense it was made. That should be developed with the structure for which he was also arguing in English law, using a division of two kinds of enrichment (by subtraction and wrongs), and a list of unjust factors to determine when an enrichment would be reversible.

The most obvious result of Birks's articles was the publication, in 1992, of the first book on Scots enrichment law, by Bill Stewart of Strathclyde University.[38] Stewart thus sought to fill the gap in the literature identified by Birks. Further, he accepted the model delineated in the *Current Legal Problems* paper, with a General Part setting out 'the Birksian analysis' of unjust enrichment, and the following Special Part examining the Scots authorities in the light of that analysis. Stewart's book is certainly valuable for its coverage, not only of the Scottish cases but also of other writings; and throughout he is mindful of the Civilian tradition in Scotland and the value of comparison with legal systems beyond Britain. But it is difficult not to feel in retrospect that the book was premature (a feeling reinforced by its non-citation in the major cases re-orienting the law between 1995 and 1998, and the lack of further editions despite those cases[39]).

---

[33] ibid 68–70.   [34] ibid 70; 'Six Questions' (n 2) 245–7.   [35] 'View' (n 1) 65.
[36] ibid 75.   [37] ibid 76–8.
[38] WJ Stewart, *The Law of Restitution in Scotland: Being Mainly a Study of the Personal Obligation to Redress Unjust Enrichment* (1992).
[39] A supplement was published in 1995 after the *Morgan Guaranty* case; and Stewart has been the Scottish correspondent of the *Restitution Law Review* since its inception in 1993, providing an

An immediate awkwardness is its title: *Restitution*, despite Birks's own recommendation of unjust enrichment as the subject name in Scotland. Then, the (admittedly small) Scottish literature since 1985 had not suggested that Birks's analysis was uncontroversial or without difficulties.[40] Indeed, it was not uncontroversial for English law either, as witness a debate about free acceptance which began in 1988.[41] Further, Stewart's argument that the Birksian analysis was 'applicable to the law in any jurisdiction'[42] was not really tested against the comparative material. The extent to which Birks's *Current Legal Problems* paper was affected by being addressed primarily to English lawyers, to persuade them of the utility of his analysis, may have been underestimated. And finally the Special Part was rooted, not in general enrichment principles, but in the familiar categories of restitution, repetition, and recompense, so that the self-imposed task was not actually quite complete. The difficulty of accomplishing it might have suggested that the Scottish material could not readily be made to sit under the Birksian analysis.

The first significant writing after the 1985 articles had come from Ross Macdonald of Dundee University, in papers which carefully masked their disagreement with at least some aspects of Birks's contributions. In 1988 Macdonald argued that, contrary to the *Chase Manhattan* case in England,[43] Scots law did not recognize proprietary restitutionary remedies in cases where money had been paid under mistake. Tracing permitted no more than identification of the sum to which a personal claim of restitution might be made. Proprietary claims were only allowed in fiduciary relationships where a constructive trust arose, and this was not an automatic consequence of a mistaken payment. The courts did not appear inclined to extend the law, and they should not do so.[44] Two cases reported shortly after the article's publication were decided in line with Macdonald's analysis. In the first, cattle were sold in breach of a hire purchase agreement, with the proceeds of the sale ending up in the hands of a firm subsequently sequestrated. It was held that the original owner of the cattle had no preferential claim to these proceeds in the sequestration, in part because there was still a claim to recover the cattle themselves from the third party purchaser.[45] In the second case, A obtained £50,000 from B by fraud and applied the funds to the purchase of a house in the name of his mistress C. B being unable to recover from A claimed from C and was held entitled to repayment of the £50,000, on the basis that no one was entitled to profit from the fraud of another. B's claim

---

annual opportunity for updating annotation and comment. But the lack of a second edition remains a little surprising.

[40] See further below, text to nn 43–8.

[41] The state of the debate by the early 1990s is most readily seen from A Burrows, *The Law of Restitution* (1st edn, 1993) 11–14, 315–20.

[42] Stewart, *Restitution* (n 38) para 1.4.

[43] *Chase Manhattan Bank NA Ltd v Israel-British Bank (London) Ltd* [1981] Ch 105.

[44] 'Restitution and Property Law' 1988 SLT (News) 81–6.

[45] *Raymond Harrison & Co's Trustee v North-West Securities Ltd* 1989 SLT 718.

was however clearly personal only, not a proprietary one to the house bought with the fraudulently procured funds.[46]

In 1989 Macdonald produced an elegant analysis of mistaken payments in Scots law which, while briefly acknowledging Birks's contribution, again took a rather different approach. He stressed instead the Civilian roots of Scots law, with the *condictio indebiti* as the central point of departure, and argued for its development potential:

By 1800 the idea had clearly emerged—even if it was not universally followed—that unjust, 'inequitable' enrichment was the unifying basis of the various remedies within restitution and recompense. Scots law never went on to recognize a generalized enrichment action, but the intellectual framework for that development was—and is—in place.[47]

Macdonald also criticized the law's narrow conceptualization of liability mistakes as the only basis for recovery in restitution and repetition; drew on historical sources to show that in the eighteenth century no distinction was drawn between errors of fact and law; and discussed in some detail defences available to the recipient of a mistaken payment: the payer's knowledge that the payment was not due, the payer's negligence, and the recipient's change of position. The law was hamstrung by its dependence on Roman law classifications: 'ultimately a new synthesis in terms of unjust enrichment must come'.[48] In other words, Macdonald supported Birks's argument in favour of a more general and principled enrichment liability; but his route to that goal was by way of a less conservative approach to the sources left in Scots law by its civilian tradition, rather than through the adoption of a wholly new framework.

The first significant case to raise issues relevant to this second article was *Royal Bank of Scotland v Watt*,[49] decided by the Second Division of the Court of Session in 1990. The case involved a fraudulently altered cheque which the innocent W received from a rogue and paid into his bank account. He then withdrew the equivalent amount of cash from his account and gave it to the rogue. The bank, being unable to recover the amount of the cheque from the account on which it was drawn, claimed repetition of the whole sum from W. At first instance, W successfully pleaded that since he no longer had the money he was no longer enriched and so could not be liable. On appeal, however, it was held that this argument confused repetition and recompense. Enrichment was only relevant to the latter. With repetition the questions were whether it was equitable that the defender retain the money *and* inequitable that return should be required. Here W should have been more on his guard and had not acted reasonably in the circumstances; the equities were against him.

---

[46] *M & I Instrument Engineers Ltd v Varsada and Beattie* 1991 SLT 106.
[47] DR Macdonald, 'Mistaken Payments in Scots Law' 1989 JR 49, 52–3.
[48] ibid 68.   [49] 1991 SC 48.

Watt seemed to confirm the conservatism of the Scottish judiciary and their reluctance to develop enrichment principles with which to link up and perhaps eliminate some of the confusion surrounding restitution, repetition, and recompense. Nor did the court appear to take the correct approach to the principles of the *condictio indebiti*: the bank had by mistake paid W a sum that was not due to him, thus incontrovertibly enriching him, and the question thereafter should have been whether W's subsequent change of position made it inequitable to require him to make repayment, rather than a double inquiry balancing the equity of retention against the inequity of return.[50]

What really began to change the picture in Scotland was neither a Scottish case nor a piece of Scottish writing. The catalyst was rather the *Woolwich* case in England.[51] The plaintiff building society (W) had paid £57 million to the Inland Revenue to meet a supposed tax liability disputed by W. Payment was made under reservation to avoid commercial difficulties for W. W was later successful in establishing the absence of liability and sued for interest of £7 million on the payment which the Revenue had returned *ex gratia*. No right to interest existed unless there was a preceding right to restitution of the payment. Initially unsuccessful, W prevailed by majorities, first in the Court of Appeal (2–1) in 1991 and then, in 1992, in the House of Lords (3–2; the two dissentients being the Scottish Law Lords, Keith and Jauncey). From an English perspective, the importance of the case was its recognition of a new 'unjust factor' leading to reversal of enrichment, namely, the recovery from a public body of a payment made after an *ultra vires* demand. This factor was founded on the constitutional principle that taxes should not be levied without the authority of Parliament. The need for the new unjust factor arose because the existing ones did not fit: W had not made a mistake (although the Inland Revenue had of course made a mistake of law); nor had W been coerced, having made the payment to protect their commercial interests rather than because the Revenue compelled it. The scenario had been prefigured as a possible example for 'policy-motivated' restitution in Birks's *Restitution*;[52] but its formulation as a specific unjust factor owed much to a powerful further article published in 1990.[53] That such an innovation was required showed none the less that the original system was not after all complete.

---

[50] On change of position see *Crédit Lyonnais v George Stevenson & Co Ltd* (1901) 9 SLT 93, 95; GC Borland, 'Change of Position in Scots Law' 1996 SLT (News) 139; P Hellwege, 'The Scope of Application of Change of Position in the Law of Unjust Enrichment: A Comparative Study' [1999] RLR 92. For contemporary reaction to *Watt* see GL Gretton, 'Unjust Enrichment in Scotland' [1992] JBL 108; HL MacQueen, 'Unjustified Enrichment in Scots Law' [1992] JBL 333; R Evans-Jones, 'Identifying the Enriched: Some Complex Relationships Involving the Condictio Indebiti' 1992 SLT (News) 25–9; Stewart, *Restitution* (n 38) paras 4.46–4.55.

[51] *Woolwich Building Society v Inland Revenue* [1993] AC 70 (CA and HL) reversing [1989] 1 WLR 137.

[52] Birks, *Restitution* 294–9 (and n 22 in rev paperback edn, 1989).

[53] 'Restitution from the Executive: A Tercentenary Footnote to the Bill of Rights' in PD Finn (ed), *Essays on Restitution* (1990) 164.

The question for Scots lawyers now increasingly emphasizing the civilian heritage in enrichment law[54] was how the *Woolwich* situation would be treated in the Scottish courts. Could restitution and repetition be extended on Civilian lines to achieve the same result as the House of Lords, or was a new ground of recovery on Birksian lines required? Was legislation a better answer, assuming that the *Woolwich* result was correct as a matter of policy? From the point of view of the existing law, *Woolwich* had not only the dissenting contributions of the Scottish judges, but also reference to two Scottish precedents. In *Glasgow Corporation v Lord Advocate*[55] the Court of Session had held that constitutional principle did not require the repayment of purchase tax mistakenly demanded by and paid to the public authorities, and that the *condictio indebiti* did not lie for recovery of payments made subject to an error of law in interpreting a statute. This narrow approach was justified on policy grounds, namely the risks and uncertainty arising if on every occasion a taxing statute received a new interpretation in the courts adversely affected taxpayers had a right to restitution of mistakenly paid moneys. The error of law bar was adopted to give effect to this policy consideration. On the other hand, in *British Oxygen Co Ltd v South of Scotland Electricity Board*[56] the House of Lords had ordered repetition of overpayments made by the pursuer as the result of the defender's charges for electricity supply being higher than they should have been under statute. The basis for this decision was the pursuer's absence of choice in the situation, since the defender was a monopolist, that is, the case was one of compulsion rather than error, since the pursuer knew that the charge was not legally justified.

The basic issues were as follows. Could W have used the *condictio indebiti*? If that *condictio* was limited in Scots law to cases where the payer had made a liability error, then the answer had to be no. The *British Oxygen* case might suggest that the *condictio* reached other cases of undue payments such as forced ones; or it might fall under another of the *condictiones* received in Scots law: for example, the *condictio ob turpem vel injustam causam* (the action for recovery of a transfer made for an illegal or immoral purpose, here relief from improper compulsion) or the residual *condictio sine causa* (the action for recovery of a transfer retained without any legal justification for doing so, such as a valid indebtedness). But neither of these *condictiones* was much explored in the case itself or in previous Scots law. In any event the *Woolwich* judges had been unsympathetic to the idea that W had been the victim of compulsion in making payment to the Revenue; that had rather been an act of rational calculation and risk assessment. A further possibility was that the *condictio indebiti* was not limited (in an unjust factor-like way) by requirements such as error and compulsion; rather it lay wherever a payment was undue or lacked a legal

---

[54] eg R Evans-Jones, 'Unjust Enrichment, Contract and the Third Reception of Roman Law in Scotland' (1993) 109 LQR 663.

[55] 1959 SC 203 (also discussed in Birks, 'Tercentenary Footnote' (n 53) 184–5).

[56] 1959 SC (HL) 17; [1959] 1 WLR 587 (HL).

justification. Then the only question would be whether the Revenue's defence arising from W's knowledge that the payment was not due could be overcome by the equity in the latter's favour resulting from making the payment subject to a sufficient reservation.[57]

Another possible response to *Woolwich* was legislation, which the dissenting Scots Law Lords had thought was the only way forward. The Law Commission of England and Wales published a consultation paper on the matter in 1991, also tackling the mistake of law bar to restitution as part of that exercise.[58] Given that the issues were as likely to affect Scottish as English taxpayers; that the House of Lords in *Woolwich* overruled the policy as well as some English cases relied upon in the leading Scots authority of *Glasgow Corporation v Lord Advocate*; and that the Scottish error of law rule had been borrowed from English law, it was inevitable that the Scottish Law Commission would also become involved in consideration of the problem. The Commission, led by Niall Whitty, began with a two-volume Discussion Paper on error of law published in September 1993,[59] and not quite three years later produced two further Discussion Papers, the first on the same subject, the other on the *Woolwich* question specifically.[60] In the end, the Commission made no recommendation for legislative action, being content to leave development of the law to the courts;[61] but its Papers had a powerful effect, not only on the academic literature, but also on the 1994 decision in *Morgan Guaranty of New York Co Ltd v Lothian Regional Council*[62] to overrule *Glasgow Corporation v Lord Advocate* and bring to an end the error of law bar to recovery.

Here, however, the importance of these Discussion Papers is the critique developed by the first of them in relation to Birks's contribution to the analysis of Scots enrichment law. Having had relatively little difficulty in proposing the abolition of the error of law rule in repetition and the *condictio indebiti*, the

---

[57] R Evans-Jones, 'Payments in Mistake of Law—Full Circle?' (1992) 37 Journal of the Law Society of Scotland 92; Stewart, *Restitution* (n 38) paras 5.53, 7.23; JE du Plessis and H Wicke, '*Woolwich Equitable v IRC* and the Condictio Indebiti in Scots Law' 1992 SLT (News) 303; R Evans-Jones, 'Some Reflections on the Condictio Indebiti in a Mixed Legal System' (1994) 111 SALJ 759. A reservation accepted by the recipient as the basis of the payment might give rise to a contractual claim for repayment. Not explored in the literature, so far as I have seen, is the possibility that a payment made subject to a clear reservation might be recoverable under the *condictio causa data causa non secuta*, or the *condictio ob causam finitam*, regardless of whether or not the reservation was accepted by the recipient.

[58] Law Commission, *Restitution of Payments Made Under a Mistake of Law* (Law Com CP No 120 July 1991).

[59] Scottish Law Commission, *Recovery of Benefits Conferred under Error of Law* (Scot Law Com DP No 95 September 1993).

[60] Scottish Law Commission, *Judicial Abolition of the Error of Law Rule and its Aftermath* (Scot Law Com DP No 99 February 1996); Scottish Law Commission, *Recovery of Ultra Vires Public Authority Receipts and Disbursements* (Scot Law Com DP No 100 February 1996).

[61] Scottish Law Commission, *Unjustified Enrichment: Error of Law and Public Authority Receipts and Disbursements* (Scot Law Com Report No 169 February 1999).

[62] 1995 SC 151; see further below, text to nn 68–71.

Commission turned to consider the rule in other parts of enrichment law, since a merely partial abolition would make little sense. In this stage of the exercise, a need was felt for a suitable overall taxonomy, which the traditional taxonomy certainly did not provide, the scope and reach of recompense being particularly obscure. But Birks's reorientation was not appropriate either. First, the division of restitution, repetition, and recompense was mistakenly understood to depend upon the benefit conferred, whereas it actually depended upon the redress being sought. Further, recompense was not a residual remedy but dealt with distinct (albeit diverse) groups of cases.[63] Scots law did not fit easily into a framework developed to explain English law. So, for example, a standard recompense case was that of mistaken improvements of another's property by a *bona fide* possessor, while English law generally denied recovery in such cases. '[T]he Scottish terrain must be fully surveyed before it can be known how far a map of English law will serve as a reliable guide to it', wrote the Commission. 'Otherwise there is a risk that the terrain will be inappropriately and even inadvertently changed to fit the English map.'[64] The Commission went on to propose instead the use of a taxonomy based upon the German model developed by the jurists Walter Wilburg and Ernst von Caemmerer, the essence of which was a fourfold typology of claims as follows: (1) those arising from the pursuer's intentional or conscious conferral of a benefit in money, good, or services upon the defender; (2) those arising from the pursuer's unauthorized improvements of another's property; (3) those arising from the pursuer's performance of another's obligation; and (4) those arising from the defender's unauthorized interference with the pursuer's property rights enriching the defender.[65]

Such arguments were not advanced only in print. In the autumns of 1993 and 1994 the Commission sponsored seminars in Edinburgh at which the reform and possible codification of enrichment law was discussed by academics from Scotland, England (including Birks), Germany, and South Africa, along with Scottish practitioners, judges, and Law Commissioners.[66] By the conclusion of these events, participants were pretty clear about the fundamental differences between the Civilian (or, more specifically, German) and the English

[63] Niall Whitty later developed from this point a criticism of the view that recompense was a subsidiary 'general enrichment action' akin to that found in French law and systems derived therefrom. See for the view MacQueen and Sellar (n 3) 294–6, 305–14, and WDH Sellar, 'Unjust Enrichment' in *Laws of Scotland: Stair Memorial Encyclopaedia* vol 15 (1996) paras 73–86; and for Whitty's initial criticism, 'Some Trends and Issues in Scots Enrichment Law' 1994 JR 127.
[64] Scot Law Com DP No 95 (n 59) vol 1 118.
[65] See ibid 98–123 for the foregoing. The argument was much influenced by R Zimmermann, 'A Road through the Enrichment-Forest? Experiences with a General Enrichment Action' (1985) 18 Comparative & International LJ of Southern Africa 1.
[66] For the proceedings of the 1993 seminar see 1994 JR 127–99 (contributions of Whitty, MacQueen, and Reid) and Evans-Jones (above n 57). The 1994 seminar, on codification, had papers from Reinhard Zimmermann (published as 'Unjustified Enrichment: The Modern Civilian Approach' (1995) 15 OJLS 403), Danie Visser and Eric Clive, as well as Peter Birks (Scot Law Com DP No 100 (n 60) para 1.31 n 15).

(or Birksian) approach to the identification of reversible enrichment. Where the Civilian approach was to regard enrichments as unjustified unless shown to have a legal basis or justification, such as a gift or contract, the English view took enrichments to be justified and required reasons—the unjust factors—to reverse them. In other words, almost polar differences existed between the two starting points for analysis. A key issue was the void contract, especially if fully performed: was restitution an automatic consequence of the nullity (the Civilian view), or was an inquiry required using autonomous restitutionary grounds of invalidity (the Common Law view)?[67] With it being clear that Scots law had started from a Civilian basis, the wholesale adoption of an unjust factors approach would indeed be a radical step. On the other hand, the importance of error in so much of Scots enrichment law showed that a role was already played by at least one autonomous unjust factor.

This clarification of the debate was achieved just before a Court of Five Judges (many of whom had attended the Scottish Law Commission seminars) decided in the 'swaps' case of *Morgan Guaranty of New York v Lothian Regional Council*[68] that the error of law bar to recovery should be abolished, and that there should be repetition under the *condictio indebiti* of payments made under a contract void because it was ultra vires of one of the parties, a local authority in Scotland. The case is notable in many respects, in particular Lord President Hope's tribute to Birks's work along with other academic lawyers 'whose detailed research and vigorous criticism has already had a marked influence on debate among the judiciary'.[69] In sharp contrast to the *Watt* case just four years before, Lord Hope emphasized the need for a unified, enrichment-based approach: '[t]he important point is that these actions [of repetition, restitution, and recompense] are all means to the same end, which is to redress an unjustified enrichment upon the broad equitable principle *nemo debet locupletari aliena jactura*'.[70] This helped overcome arguments that recompense was more appropriate in the case than repetition.[71] The court also held, however, that a liability error, whether of fact or law, had to be shown by the party seeking recovery under the *condictio indebiti*, albeit that the error did not also have to be excusable, that being a factor which would go to the equity or otherwise of retention and which would have to be raised by the defender. So there was an element of the 'unjustified if' or unjust factor approach in the decision; the voidness of the contract was not enough by itself. Finally the Lord President observed that a result of the decision was that Scots law could

---

[67] Zimmermann (n 66) 405–12; P Birks, 'No Consideration: Restitution after Void Contracts' (1993) 23 University of Western Australia LR 195.

[68] 1995 SC 151. On 'swaps' see E McKendrick, 'Local Authorities and Swaps: Undermining the Market?' in R Cranston (ed), *Making Commercial Law: Essays in Honour of Roy Goode* (1997) 201.

[69] 1995 SC 151, 155.   [70] ibid.

[71] For the issue, see NR Whitty, 'Ultra Vires Swap Contracts and Unjustified Enrichment' 1994 SLT (News) 337; A Rodger, 'Recovering Payments under Void Contracts in Scots Law' in W Swadling and G Jones (eds), *The Search for Principle: Essays in Honour of Lord Goff of Chieveley* (2000) 1.

provide a remedy in the *Woolwich*-type case: a puzzling comment, given the survival of the requirement of error.[72]

The next critical case in Scots law was *Shilliday v Smith*,[73] from which Lord Rodger's testimony to Birks's contribution has already been quoted. *Shilliday* was then approved by Lord Hope of Craighead in the House of Lords case of *Dollar Land (Cumbernauld) Ltd v CIN Properties Ltd*,[74] where he again spoke of the need to unify unjustified enrichment, finding support in the relevant passage already quoted from Birks's *Current Legal Problems* article.[75] The outcome of these two decisions was the relegation of repetition, restitution, and recompense to the status of mere remedies, which the court can grant once it has decided that an enrichment is unjustified. In principle an enrichment is unjustified and falls to be reversed if its retention is supported by no legal ground. The general starting point is, however, that enrichments will remain where they are unless a reason can be shown for their reversal. It is for the person who wants to reclaim an enrichment to show reasons why that should be allowed. In particular, this is the role now to be played by the *condictiones* in cases of enrichment by conferral, as descriptions of type-situations in which an enrichment of any kind would be seen as unjustified. In this way Scots law seeks to evade the reproach of uncertainty often levelled at the Canadian Supreme Court's parallel 'absence of juristic reason' approach to restitution.[76]

Some commentators have celebrated the apparent commitment in all this to 'absence of legal ground' as the basis of Scots enrichment law;[77] others have seen in Lord Rodger's praise for Birks and his use of the *condictiones* as guidance to when enrichments are unjustified a version of the 'unjust factors' approach.[78] Perhaps, however, a 'third way' has been created in Scots law, in which it is not enough to show either absence of a legal ground or the presence of a factor (such as error) making retention of the enrichment unjustified; both must be present in some shape or form.[79] Certainly absence of a legal ground can only be a necessary rather than a sufficient basis for identifying reversible enrichment: incidental enrichments, where one incurred expenditure for one's own purposes (*in suo*, in Scots law terms) and, as it were by a side-wind, benefited another, have

---

[72] R Evans-Jones, 'From Undue Transfer Back to Retention without a Legal Basis' in R Evans-Jones (ed), *The Civil Law Tradition in Scotland* (Stair Society 1995) 213; R Evans-Jones and P Hellwege, 'Swaps, Error of Law and Unjust Enrichment' (1996) 1 Scottish Law & Practice Quarterly 1.   [73] 1998 SC 725.

[74] 1998 SC (HL) 90.   [75] ibid 98.

[76] NR Whitty, 'The Scottish Enrichment Revolution' (2001) 6 Scottish Law & Practice Q 167; HL MacQueen, 'Unjustified Enrichment in Mixed Legal Systems' (2005) 13 RLR 21.

[77] P Hellwege, 'Rationalising the Scottish Law of Unjustified Enrichment' (2000) 11 Stellenbosch LR 50.   [78] WJ Stewart, 'Scotland' (1998) 6 RLR 261.

[79] NR Whitty and D Visser, 'Unjustified Enrichment' in R Zimmermann, D Visser, and K Reid (eds), *Mixed Legal Systems in Comparative Perspective: Property and Obligations in Scotland and South Africa* (2004) 399, 412. A recent sheriff court case referring to both 'absence of legal ground' and 'unjust factors' is *Moggach v Milne* 2005 GWD 8-107 (full text at http://www.scotcourts.gov.uk/opinions/A451.html).

to be excluded from recovery, as does knowing imposition of a benefit without contract or intention to donate.[80] In conventional Scots law thinking, this explains the requirement of an error in property improvement cases, the improver's error being that the property is his or hers; but when the case of intervention to perform another's non-money obligation will give rise to unjustified enrichment of that other, rather than being seen as the intervener's own risk, remains somewhat unclear.[81]

The revision of Scots enrichment law is far from complete. The trilogy of leading cases deals only with enrichment by transfer, as does the first and so far only volume of Robin Evans-Jones's textbook, published in 2003.[82] There it is argued that the Scots law solution to *Woolwich* is provided by the *condictio sine causa*, to which the defence of knowledge is not applicable.[83] Ghosts from the past, such as the subsidiarity of recompense, still haunt the courts.[84] For the time being the law in relation to other kinds of enrichment—as for example by improvements of another's property in the erroneous belief that it is one's own, by performance of another's obligations, or by unauthorized use, taking, or interference with another's property—is being developed mainly by academic writing, the basically German typology having commanded increasing acceptance.[85] A category of 'restitution for wrongs' has not developed; instead the question is whether the established category of enrichment by unauthorized appropriation of another's property can or should extend to embrace breach of fiduciary and contractual obligations.[86] The relationship between fiduciary obligations, constructive trusts and property effects in enrichment cases remains obscure, although it seems unlikely that Scots law will ever go very far down this particular avenue.[87]

It might then seem that the effects of Birks's 1985 articles were mixed. He persuaded Scots lawyers to take a fresh look at their enrichment law, to base it much more clearly upon a general enrichment principle, and to use that principle to eliminate much confusion and obfuscation. The outcome, the map whose drawing at least in the literature has now progressed very far, is, however, clearly not the one Birks originally proposed. But then, following his assertion that after all unjust enrichment did not quadrate with every case where

---

[80] EM Clive, Appendix to Scot Law Com DP No 99 (n 60) 50–6.

[81] HL MacQueen, *Unjustified Enrichment Law Basics* (2004) 14–16, 42–3; *Transco plc v Glasgow City Council* 2005 SCLR 733 (noted in NR Whitty '*Transco v Glasgow City Council*: Developing Enrichment Law after *Shilliday*' (2006) 10 Edinburgh LR 113).

[82] R Evans-Jones *Unjustified Enrichment Volume 1: Enrichment by Deliberate Conferral: Condictio* (2003).   [83] ibid, paras 6.27–6.49.

[84] *Transco plc v Glasgow City Council* 2005 SCLR 733.

[85] See in particular the Scottish contributions to D Johnston and R Zimmermann (eds), *Unjustified Enrichment: Key Issues in Comparative Perspective* (2002); Evans-Jones, *Unjustified Enrichment* (n 82) paras 1.67–1.101; MA Hogg, *Obligations* (2nd edn, 2006).

[86] J Blackie and I Farlam, 'Enrichment by Act of the Party Enriched' in Zimmermann *et al* (n 79) 469; MacQueen, *Unjustified Enrichment* (n 81) 17–18, 43–4.

[87] GL Gretton, 'Constructive Trusts' (1997) 1 Edinburgh LR 281 and 408; P Hood, 'What is So Special about Being a Fiduciary?' (2000) 4 Edinburgh LR 308.

restitution was granted, his consequent rejection of restitution for wrongs, and his final abandonment of unjust factors for 'absence of basis' in the analysis of English law,[88] it seems certain that his Scots law articles would have joined others called back for burning given the opportunity.[89]

Any influence the Scottish debates may have had on Birks's *volte face* is unclear, however. He could not sympathize if Scottish rejection of an unjust factors system was based upon the view that it was too English. 'Nationalism is always out of place in legal thought and argument. When it does push in, it always strikes a note which is either absurd or repulsive or both.'[90] Certainly, the writings in which Birks's changes of mind slowly became apparent make almost no reference to Scots law. But an indirect Scottish effect cannot be ruled out. The Scottish writing was not so much anti-English as, like Birks himself, pro-German. What had first drawn him to the study of Scots law was its search for order, principle, and scientific underpinnings.[91] He admired the tradition of systematic overview literature, going back to the institutional writers (and in particular Stair), and continuing down to the present in the (albeit debased) form of *Gloag & Henderson*.[92] *English Private Law* was first conceived in avowed imitation of *Gloag & Henderson*.[93] It was thanks to Birks that in 1990 a Scottish contribution was procured for a comparative history of enrichment law eventually published in 1995.[94] Occasional comments in other writings showed him still wrestling from time to time with Scottish difficulties.[95] At an Oxford meeting in 1998 Birks gave me my first sight of the *Shilliday* opinion, just received from Lord Rodger. At a comparative conference in Cambridge in April 1999 where six Scots lawyers also contributed some critical views of the 'Birksian analysis' from their post-*Shilliday* world, Birks and others heatedly contested the possible abandonment of unjust factors and the appropriateness of the 'absence of basis' approach for English law after *Kleinwort Benson Ltd v Lincoln City Council*.[96]

---

[88] 'Misnomer' in WR Cornish, R Nolan, J O'Sullivan, and G Virgo (eds), *Restitution Past, Present and Future: Essays in Honour of Gareth Jones* (1998) 1; 'Mistakes of Law' (2000) 53 CLP 205; 'Comparative Unjust Enrichment' in P Birks and A Pretto (eds), *Themes in Comparative Law in Honour of Bernard Rudden* (2002) 139; 'A Letter to America: the New Restatement of Restitution' (2003) 3 Global Jurist Frontiers issue 2 article 2. See also P Birks, *The Foundations of Unjust Enrichment: Six Centennial Lectures* (2002) 72–4, 146 (lectures given in 1999).

[89] Birks, *Unjust Enrichment* (1st edn, 2003) p xiv; (2nd edn, 2005) p xii.

[90] ibid 128. I recall a similar oral comment during discussion at an Aberdeen conference in 1995.

[91] 'View' (n 1) 58 (citing Lord President Dunedin's dictum about 'marks or notes of the situation in which recompense is due' in *Edinburgh & District Tramways v Courtenay* 1909 SC 99, 106).

[92] See P Birks and G McLeod, 'The Implied Contract Theory of Quasi-Contract: Civilian Opinion Current in the Century before Blackstone' (1986) 6 OJLS 46 (discussion of Stair 56–8); P Birks, 'Definition and Division: A Meditation on *Institutes* 3.13' in P Birks (ed), *The Classification of Obligations* (1997) 1 (discussion of Stair 28–9); P Birks, 'More Logic and Less Experience: The Difference between Scots Law and English Law' in DL Carey Miller and R Zimmermann (eds), *The Civilian Tradition and Scots Law: Aberdeen Quincentenary Essays* (1997) 167–90.

[93] P Birks (ed), *English Private Law* (2000), vol 1 p xxx.

[94] MacQueen and Sellar (n 3).   [95] eg *Restitution—The Future* (1992) 102–5.

[96] [1999] 2 AC 349. The conference proceedings were subsequently published: Johnston and Zimmermann (n 85).

Birks's later writings do make reference to one Scots lawyer: Lord Hope of Craighead and his speech in *Kleinwort Benson*, in particular a passage where distinctions between Common Law and Civilian approaches are downplayed and it is suggested that, since both depend on unjust enrichment, each also relies on absence of legal ground, but from different angles.[97] Initially in support of continuing an unjust factors approach, because it said more directly and clearly when an enrichment would be unjust and reversible,[98] but eventually in favour of the absence of basis approach,[99] Birks declared that such integration was impossible. However, he conceded some limited possibilities for reconciliation, deploying the metaphor of a pyramid with absence of basis at the pinnacle and unjust factors forming the base through which enrichment claims have to work to show the lack of legal justification. But the unjust factors have no independent enrichment or restitution law content; their exposition can be left to the books on contract, trusts, tax, public law, and so on. So, for example, the *Woolwich* case is simply an instance of recovery of a payment which was not due under tax law, making its retention by the Revenue without a legal basis.[100] Policy-motivated restitution disappears from amongst the unjust factors and finds its place instead as a consideration in the defences. This is not so very far from the 'third way' of Scots enrichment law, especially its continuing use of a broad concept of 'equity' in the development of defences.

An apt conclusion is to return to the six questions Birks asked Scots lawyers in 1985, this time with close at hand the latest edition of *Gloag and Henderson*,[101] the Obligations volume of the *Stair Memorial Encyclopaedia*, and Evans-Jones's textbook. These make it safe to affirm that Scots law distinguishes enrichment from contract, and that the name for this body of law is unjustified or unjust enrichment, not quasi-contract or restitution. The subject's internal divisions have been comprehensively redrawn, and a new analytical vocabulary is emerging, albeit with Latin still in place by way of the *condictiones*. Their reliance on the concept of *causa*, barely used or known in general Scots law since the seventeenth century, may still pose difficulties even for the Scots lawyer in Parliament House, never mind the lay person on the Morningside bus.[102] Perhaps Birks's language of initial failure of basis (the undue transfer) and subsequent failure (roughly the *condictio causa data causa non secuta*) will help a little here.[103] Scots lawyers need to decide, however, whether within a basically 'absence of legal ground' system, having a narrow *condictio indebiti* based upon liability error

---

97 [1999] 2 AC 409.

98 'Mistakes of Law' (n 88) 230–6; 'Comparative Unjust Enrichment' (n 88) 149–51.

99 *Unjust Enrichment* (n 89) (1st edn) 99–102; (2nd edn) 113–16.

100 ibid 133–4. Compare the statement in the 1st edn 118 ('within the law of unjust enrichment in the post-swaps world [*Woolwich*] cuts a very ordinary figure'), dropped from the 2nd edn. Cf for Scots law text accompanying n 83 above.

101 HL MacQueen *et al* (eds) *Gloag and Henderson's Law of Scotland* (11th edn, 2001), ch 28.

102 Evans-Jones *Unjustified Enrichment* (n 82) paras 2.03–2.14.

103 *Unjust Enrichment* (n 89) (2nd edn) 129–60.

makes sense alongside a residual *condictio sine causa*, since it means that 'absence of legal ground' appears twice in the overall taxonomy but at different levels.[104] On Birks's two final questions about the content of the law, uncertainty (but possibly not very much) continues to exist at the borders between enrichment, property, and 'wrongs';[105] but *negotiorum gestio* has been the subject of detailed research clearly placing it outside enrichment law.[106] Perhaps the last word can be left to a paraphrase of Peter Birks: the attention paid to his six questions has indeed helped avoid tiresome confusions and laid the foundations of an efficient, intelligible, and independent law of unjustified enrichment.[107]

[104] J du Plessis, 'Towards a Rational Structure of Liability for Unjustified Enrichment: Thoughts from Two Mixed Jurisdictions' in R Zimmermann (ed), *Grundstrukturen eines Europäischen Bereicherungsrechts* (2005) 175.   [105] See above text to nn 81–7.
[106] NR Whitty, 'Negotiorum Gestio' in *Laws of Scotland: Stair Memorial Encyclopaedia* vol 15 (1996) paras 87–143.   [107] 'Six Questions' (n 2) 227.

PART III
ROMAN LAW

22

What did *Damnum Iniuria* Actually Mean?

*Alan Rodger**

Admittedly, it may seem rather late in the day to be raising this question when the lex Aquilia[1] was passed at least 2,200 years ago and when, according to Ulpian, it modified all the previous laws that had referred to *damnum iniuria*: *quae ante se de damno iniuria locutae sunt.*[2] Nevertheless, the question is worth asking, if only because scholars have shown a curious reluctance to mention it, far less to answer it.

Students are taught that the wrong for which the lex Aquilia supplied the remedy was *damnum iniuria datum.*[3] The great authorities such as Karlowa,[4] Girard,[5] Bonfante,[6] Buckland,[7] Kunkel,[8] Arangio-Ruiz,[9] and Kaser[10] all say the same. But if, for instance, you had asked Gaius or Ulpian or even Justinian himself, they would not have agreed. They would all have said that the wrong

* A Lord of Appeal in Ordinary. I am grateful to David Ibbetson for his comments which saved me from a number of errors. A version of this essay was delivered as a lecture to the Institut du droit romain, Université Panthéon-Assas Paris II, on 9 December 2005. I made a number of changes in response to comments on that occasion, especially from Michel Humbert and Pierre Andreau.

[1] M Crawford (ed), *Roman Statutes* vol II (1996) 723 contains an attempted reconstruction of the text under the aegis of John Crook. For ancient concern about establishing an authentic text of laws and other official decrees, see C Williamson, *The Laws of the Roman People* (2005) 394–7. In this essay I refer to three works in an abbreviated form: A Pernice, *Die Lehre von den Sachbeschädigungen nach römischem Rechte* (1867) = *Lehre*; O Lenel, *Das Edictum Perpetuum* (3rd edn, 1927) = *EP* and O Lenel, *Palingenesia Iuris Civilis* (1889, reprinted 1960) = *Palingenesia*.

[2] D.9.2.1 pr, Ulpian 18 *ad edictum*.

[3] eg B Nicholas, *An Introduction to Roman Law* (1962) 218, R Zimmermann, *The Law of Obligations: Roman Foundations of the Civilian Tradition* (1990) 969 and M Kaser and R Knütel, *Römisches Privatrecht* (17th edn, 2003) 319. Similarly, the only 'technical term' which students will find in the glossary in BW Frier, *A Casebook on the Roman Law of Delict* (1989) 246 is *damnum iniuria datum*.

[4] O Karlowa, *Römische Rechtsgeschichte* (1901) 793.

[5] PF Girard, *Manuel élémentaire de droit romain* (8th edn, by F Senn, 1929, reprinted 2003) 440.

[6] P Bonfante, *Istituzioni di diritto romano* (10th edn, 1934, reprinted 1957) 523.

[7] WW Buckland, *A Textbook of Roman Law* (3rd edn, by PG Stein 1963, reprinted 1975) 585.

[8] P Jörs and W Kunkel, *Römisches Privatrecht* (3rd edn, 1949) 256; now H Honsell, T Mayer-Maly, and W Selb, *Römisches Privatrecht* (4th edn, 1987) 383 (Honsell).

[9] V Arangio-Ruiz, *Istituzioni di diritto romano* (14th edn, 1968) 373.

[10] M Kaser, *Das Römische Privatrecht* vol I (2nd edn, 1971) 619.

was *damnum iniuria*. That is how Ulpian put the matter in the sentence which I
have quoted from the introduction to the relevant section of his commentary on
the Praetor's Edict.[11] In Institutes 3.210 Gaius, for his part, says that the action
for *damnum iniuria* is established by the lex Aquilia: *damni iniuriae actio con-
stituitur per legem Aquiliam*.[12] Justinian repeats this in his Institutes 4.3 pr.
Elsewhere, like Gaius and Ulpian, other classical jurists refer to the action based
on the lex Aquilia as the 'action for *damnum iniuria*': *damni iniuriae actio*—an
expression which Buckland nevertheless condemns as 'meaningless'.[13] Cicero
also uses *damnum iniuria* in connexion with the lex Aquilia in two passages in
his speech *pro Tullio*[14] but, unfortunately, neither the text nor the context is
sufficiently clear to make it safe to base any conclusions on them.

Of course, the expression *damnum iniuria datum* is not a modern coinage. As
Mommsen points out,[15] however, *damnum iniuria* is the predominant form in
the texts, *damnum iniuria datum* being found comparatively infrequently.[16] But,
to take perhaps the best example, in Institutes 3.217 Gaius says that, in the case
of all non-pecus animals and inanimate objects, loss which has been caused
unlawfully, *damnum iniuria datum*, is redressed under chapter 3 of the lex
Aquilia. In his Institutes 4.3.13 Justinian repeats this passage. In D.9.2.11.7,
from book 18 of his edictal commentary, Ulpian reports Julian's opinion on the
situation where loss had been caused unlawfully (*damnum iniuria datum esset*) in
the case of a slave whom a purchaser had been going to return to the seller.

[11] Nothing daunted, JC Hasse, *Die Culpa des Römischen Rechts* (2nd edn, by DA Bethmann-
Hollweg, 1838) 17 refers to Ulpian as saying that the lex Aquilia did away with all earlier laws which
had dealt with *damnum iniuria datum*.   [12] See also Gaius, Institutes 4.76 and 112.
[13] WW Buckland, *The Main Institutions of Roman Private Law* (1931) 336. For examples of the
usage from a variety of authors, however, see D.19.2.57 (Iavolenus); 24.3.18.1 (Pomponius);
9.2.32 pr (Gaius) and Gaius, Institutes 4.76 and 112; D.35.2.30 pr (Maecianus); 20.1.27 (*quasi*)
(Marcianus); 9.2.27 pr and 9.3.1.4 (implied) (Ulpian) and 4.9.6.4 (Paul). The expression was
condemned by a youthful Kaser as 'always suspect'—though the text he was discussing actually
referred to *damni iniuria agere*. See M Kaser, *Quanti ea res est* (1935) 10 n 4. By progressive stages
he abandoned that position: *Das Römische Privatrecht* (n 10) vol I (1st edn, 1955) 518 n 3; vol I
(2nd edn) 620 n 6.
[14] *pro Tullio* 5.11 and 16.41. Cicero is explaining why the praetor M Terentius Varro Lucullus
introduced the *actio vi bonorum raptorum*. See *EP* 391 and E Costa, *Cicerone Giureconsulto* vol 1
(1927, reprinted 1964), 149–51 and the literature cited in Honsell *et al*, *Römisches Privatrecht* (n 8)
363 n 40 and BW Frier, *The Rise of the Roman Jurists* (1985) 52 n 39 and 79–80. The praetor who
granted the action was probably L Caecilius Metellus: TRS Broughton, *The Magistrates of the
Roman Republic* vol II (1952, reprinted 1984) 122 and 128–9; MC Alexander, *Trials in the Late
Roman Republic 149 BC to 50 BC* (1990) 86.
[15] T Mommsen, *Römisches Strafrecht* (1899, reprinted 1955) 826 n 1.
[16] In addition to Gaius, Institutes 3.217 and Justinian, Institutes 4.3.13, the phrase occurs three
times in D.9.2, in 11.7, 27.17 (but not in the corresponding passage in Collatio 2.4.1 (see below at
n 53)) and 49.1. Quintilian, *declamationes maiores* 13.1 has *damnum per iniuriam datum*. The
expression *damnum iniuria dare* is, of course, also found in various other forms in relation to the lex
Aquilia: see eg D.4.4.9.2 (Ulpian); 9.2.5.3 (Ulpian); ht 7.3 (Proculus reported by Ulpian); ht 29.7
(Ulpian); ht 30.2 (Paul); ht 52.1 and 52.2 (Alfenus). Cf also Cicero, *pro Tullio* 5.12 and Quintilian,
declamationes minores 13.7: *in duas enim, quantum animadvertere potui, quaestiones dividit causam:
an damnum sit, et an iniuria datum*.

Presumably because it is comparatively unusual and because of the way it is used in the texts, Mommsen made the plausible suggestion that *damnum iniuria datum* was not a technical term. Despite this, modern scholars seem comfortable with it and prefer to use it, rather than *damnum iniuria*,[17] to describe the harm remedied by the lex Aquilia. This is undoubtedly because the grammar and meaning of *damnum iniuria datum* are easy to grasp. The noun *iniuria*[18] is in the ablative ('by unlawfulness') and is used adverbially. The meaning of the phrase is therefore 'loss caused unlawfully'.[19]

Though one word shorter, the phrase *damnum iniuria* appears that much harder to understand and translate.[20] In the texts which I have mentioned both the nouns *damnum* and *iniuria* are in the same grammatical case. In Gaius' Institutes 3.210 and Justinian's Institutes 4.3 pr, they are both in the genitive, as they are in the other texts referring to the action for *damnum iniuria*.[21] Equally clearly, in D.9.2.1 pr both nouns are in the ablative. So, in the nominative, the phrase would be *damnum iniuria*. It is this expression that we must try to understand, since it is the one that came most readily to the lips of the Roman jurists.

Iniuria in *damnum iniuria*

The obvious temptation is to start from *damnum iniuria datum* and to try to see how that phrase, with *damnum* in the nominative and *iniuria* in the ablative, could somehow have given rise to the expression *damnum iniuria* with both nouns in the same case. The supposed route begins with the idea that the relevant action was originally called the *actio damni iniuria dati*.[22] This became shortened to *actio damni iniuria*[23] and then, because the ablative *iniuria* made no real sense in the shortened version, it became attracted into the same case as *damni* so as to

---

[17] Mommsen himself thought that the technical term for damage to property in Roman law was *damnum iniuria*, but his explanation of this expression was misconceived. See D Daube, 'On the Use of the Term *damnum*' in V Arangio-Ruiz (ed), *Studi in onore di Siro Solazzi* (1948) 93, 98 n 35 = D Cohen and D Simon (eds), *David Daube: Collected Studies in Roman Law* (1991) 279, 284 n 35.

[18] *Iniuria* is, of course, one of the key concepts for the understanding of the lex Aquilia. Much of the vast and, for present purposes, often strangely unhelpful literature is surveyed in F La Rosa, 'Il valore originario di "iniuria" nella "Lex Aquilia"' (1998) 44 Labeo 366.

[19] See, however, n 53 below.

[20] In a short note, 'Actio damni iniuriae' (1927) 6 RHD 120, Buckland draws attention to the curious fact that, when completing the text of Collatio 2.5.1 by reference to Justinian' Institutes 4.4 pr, modern editors write *damnum iniuriae* where the text of the Institutes gives *damnum iniuria*. In D.47.2.31 pr *damno* appears to be in the ablative: if so, this would be an example of *damnum iniuriae*. Cf PS 2.31.23.   [21] See nn 13 and 26.

[22] Quintilian, *declamationes maiores* XIII 1 begins: *damni per iniuriam dati sit actio*—let there be an action for loss (*damnum*) caused by wrongdoing (*per iniuriam*).

[23] This term seems to appear only once in the Digest in D.4.9.6.1 (Paul): *quamquam et furti actio et damni iniuria mecum sit*. Cicero, *pro Roscio comoedo* 32 has *iudicium damni iniuria*.

give the *actio damni iniuriae*.[24] It may be—we need not decide—that an ellipse of this kind lies behind such phrases as *damni iniuria agere* or *damni iniuria teneri*, which are found[25] alongside *damni iniuriae agere* or *teneri*.[26] But the supposed development from the (unattested and non-technical) expression *actio damni iniuria dati* seems a strangely elaborate and methodologically questionable way to explain the emergence of the free-standing technical expression, *damnum iniuria*, which Roman authors apparently regard as entirely straightforward. More particularly, it is worth noting that when Ulpian uses *damnum iniuria* in D.9.2.1 pr he is not giving the name of an action but of the harm to which he thought the lex Aquilia referred. Doubtless, it is because modern scholars feel that they have somehow not got to the bottom of *damnum iniuria* that they opt instead for *damnum iniuria datum*.

Birks, on the other hand, thought that the chapter of the Praetor's Edict containing the formula or formulae of the actions on the lex Aquilia was entitled *de damno iniuria*, 'about *damnum iniuria*'.[27] We shall encounter that theory again but at present need only note that, in his view, the two words *damnum iniuria* are in apposition.[28] It is better, however, to see the phrase as an example of the kind of asyndeton that was common in legal texts and terminology from an early period.[29] But, even if the grammatical form of the expression is identified in this way, the same questions still have to be answered. What do the words mean? What does the expression formed by the two words mean? Daube

---

[24] W Kalb, *Wegweiser in die römische Rechtssprache* (1912, reprinted 1984) 15 n 1. Cf HJ Roby, *An Introduction to the Study of Justinian's Digest* (1884, reprinted 2000) ccxix–ccxx and CH Monro, *Digest IX 2* (1898) 43–4.

[25] *agere* or *agi*: D.9.2.29.1 and 29.3 (Ulpian); 43.24.7.4 (twice) (Ulpian); 47.2.23 (Ulpian); 47.8.2.26 (Ulpian). *argui*: D.40.12.24.4 (Paul). *conveniri*: D.12.2.28.6 (Paul). *defendi*: 12.2.28.7 (Paul). *teneri*: D.9.2.27.10, 11, and 29 (Ulpian); and ht 45.5 (Paul).

[26] *agere* or *agi*: Gaius, Institutes 4.37 and 171; Justinian, Institutes 4.16.1; D.24.1.37 (Julian); 9.1.1.4 (Ulpian); 19.5.14.3 (including an intrusive *de*) (Ulpian reporting Aristo); 39.4.1.4 (Ulpian); 47.8.2.26 (Ulpian); 47.10.15.46 (Ulpian). *exigere*: D.9.3.1.4 (Ulpian). *teneri*: D.41.1.54.2 (Modestinus); 9.2.41.1 (Ulpian).

[27] P Birks, 'The Edictal Rubric "ad legem Aquiliam"' in R Pérez-Bustamante (ed), *Estudios de Historia del Derecho Europeo: Homenaje al Professor G Martínez Díez* (1994) vol 1 81, 83. See also P Birks, 'Ulpian 18 *ad edictum*: Introducing *damnum iniuria*' in R Feenstra, AS Hartkamp, JE Spruit, PJ Sijpestein, and LC Winkel (eds), *Collatio Iuris Romani: Etudes dédiées à Hans Ankum à l'occasion de son 65e anniversaire* vol 1 (1995) 17, esp 23–4.

[28] Buckland (n 20) 6 RHD 120, 121 reminisces about Cambridge in the 1880s when Monro used to teach, in Buckland's view correctly, that the use of *damnum iniuria* without *datum* led the jurists unconsciously to use the words as if they were in apposition. See also Buckland, *A Textbook of Roman Law* (n 7) 585 n 8. For apposition see R Kühner and C Stegmann, *Ausführliche Grammatik der lateinischen Sprache* (5th edn, by A Thierfelder, 1976) vol II 1 243–51. Buckland himself believed, however, that in *damnum iniuria*, the second word is in the ablative: *The Main Institutions* (n 13) 336. That is implausible, to say the least.

[29] W Kalb, *Das Juristenlatein* (2nd edn, 1888, reprinted 1984) 37–41; C de Meo, *Lingue tecniche del latino* (2nd edn, 1986) 116; Kühner and Stegmann, *Ausführliche Grammatik* (n 28) II 2 149–50 (for nouns); M Leumann, JB Hofmann, and A Szantyr, *Lateinische Grammatik* vol II (1965) 828; JHW Penney, 'Connections in Archaic Latin Prose' in T Reinhardt, M Lapidge, and JN Adams (eds), *Aspects of the Language of Latin Prose* (2005) 37.

proposed to translate them as 'a loss caused to another by injuring his beast or slave',[30] but it is impossible to derive all that content from these two words: for instance, the restriction to injury to a beast or slave depends on Daube's wider thesis that chapter 3 originally applied only to such injuries.[31] Birks suggests[32] that the words might be translated literally by the ugly 'loss-wrong'. Of course, he does not actually go on to use that expression himself. He speaks, instead, of 'the action for unlawful loss'. So it looks as though he takes the view that in *damnum iniuria* the word *iniuria* refers to the fact that the defendant's conduct which causes the loss is wrongful. Basically, he too sees the phrase as a shorthand way of saying that the action lies for loss that is caused wrongfully—*damnum iniuria datum*.[33] So we are not much further forward.

But perhaps a bit. If the two words *damnum iniuria* were indeed to be translated as 'loss-wrong', each of them would be referring to a very different aspect of the situation—that there should be loss and that the loss should be caused unlawfully. But where we find other legal expressions in the form of an asyndeton, for example, *ruta caesa* (quarried and cut), *sarta tecta* (repaired and covered), *usus fructus* (use and enjoyment), *pactum conventum* (promised and agreed), *emptum venditum* (bought and sold), *locatum conductum* (let and hired), the two words tend to complement one another.[34] On the strength of that pattern, we should expect *iniuria* to complement *damnum*. In other words, we should expect that in this phrase *iniuria* would mean something akin to *damnum* so that the pair of words *damnum iniuria* would describe the kind of loss or injury for which the lex Aquilia provided a remedy.

In fact, as we shall see, it is well recognized—though curiously often over-looked—that in legal texts, including texts on the lex Aquilia, *iniuria* not infrequently means unlawful 'injury' or 'harm' or 'detriment'.[35] Unless con-strained by something in the relevant text, we are therefore free to translate *iniuria* in *damnum iniuria* as, say, 'unlawful injury'—injury being used generally and not confined, of course, to physical injury.[36] Then we see that, when Ulpian

---

[30] *Studi in onore di Siro Solazzi* (n 17) 98 n 35 = *Collected Studies in Roman Law* (n 17) 284 n 35.

[31] D Daube, 'On the Third Chapter of the *Lex Aquilia*' (1936) 52 LQR 253 = *Collected Studies in Roman Law* (n 17) 3.

[32] *Estudios de Historia del Derecho Europeo: Homenaje al Profesor G Martínez Díez* (n 27) vol 1 81, 83.

[33] This is confirmed by the fact that he kept open the possibility that the Edictal heading was *de damno iniuria dato*. He would scarcely have done so, at least without further argument, if he had seen much to choose between them.

[34] Kühner and Stegmann, *Ausführliche Grammatik* (n 28) vol II 2 149 says, referring to asyndeta in general, that the two words most often express synonymous, more rarely opposing, ideas.

[35] In non-legal contexts the word *iniuria* was used more generally of wrongs in the sense of socially unfair acts and injustices, as P Birks, 'The Early History of Iniuria' (1969) 37 TvR 163, 171 n 13 stressed with particular reference to Plautus and Terence.

[36] On the whole, this is the translation which I adopt, but there are cases where another equivalent such as harm or detriment seems more appropriate. The exact nuances of the term in particular texts are not my concern on this occasion.

said in D.9.2.1 pr that the lex Aquilia modified all the previous laws which dealt with *damnum iniuria*, he meant all the previous laws which dealt with 'loss and unlawful injury'. Similarly, for Gaius in Institutes 3.210 and Justinian in Institutes 4.3 pr 'the action for loss and unlawful injury' was established by the lex Aquilia. More generally, in legal shorthand an action based on the lex Aquilia was called an 'action for loss and unlawful injury' and parties sued and were sued for 'loss and unlawful injury'. On this approach, the phrase *damnum iniuria* does indeed comprise two nouns which complement one another so as to describe the harm for which the lex Aquilia supplied a remedy.

From D.9.2.1 pr we know that Ulpian considered that the lex Aquilia referred to *damnum iniuria*. It is possible, though not provable,[37] that the statute had an official title which indicated its subject-matter. If so, the text of Ulpian might suggest *lex Aquilia de damno iniuria* rather than *lex Aquilia de damno*.[38] For present purposes, however, what matters is that jurists and others thought of the statute as providing a remedy for *damnum iniuria*, loss and unlawful injury. If they were right, it is not surprising that chapters 1 and 3 were framed to catch defendants who had acted 'unlawfully', *iniuria*. What, in practice, counted as *damnum iniuria* would alter over time, reflecting changes in the jurists' thinking about the terms of the statute (especially *iniuria*, 'unlawfully') and about the scope of the available remedies.[39]

There is, it must be stressed, nothing new in the point that the various meanings of the Latin word *iniuria* include 'loss', 'injury', 'harm', or 'detriment'. That can be seen from the entries for *iniuria* in the recognized dictionaries.[40] Indeed, Pernice long ago made the point that the use of *iniuria* in the sense of economic damage (*Vermögensschaden*) is quite usual.[41] What is new, therefore, is simply the suggestion that unlawful injury, rather than unlawfulness, is the meaning of *iniuria*[42] in the phrase *damnum iniuria*. Nevertheless, before returning to that phrase, I propose to vouch the more general point by looking

---

[37] *Roman Statutes* (n 1) 723.

[38] Favoured by G Rotondi, *Leges Publicae Populi Romani* (1912) 241 and M Elster, *Die Gesetze der mittleren römischen Republik* (2003) 127. Presumably, they have, for example, Cicero, *pro Tullio* 4.9 (*cum sciret de damno legem esse Aquiliam*) in mind. To judge by the title of his book, von Lübtow thought that the lex Aquilia was *de damno iniuria dato*: U von Lübtow, *Untersuchungen zur lex Aquilia de damno iniuria dato* (1971).

[39] I return to these matters briefly below, in discussing D.47.10.1 pr and 9.2.5.1. For a discussion of *iniuria* with citation of the literature see Zimmermann (n 3) 998–1013.

[40] *Thesaurus Linguae Latinae* vol VII 1 (1934–64), article on *iniuria*, col 1671, lines 57–68 'de damno ipso'; *Oxford Latin Dictionary* (1982), entry on *iniuria*, 5, 'loss or detriment inflicted on or sustained by a person in respect of his estate, rights etc'; E Seckel, *Heumanns Handlexicon zu den Quellen des römischen Rechts* (9th edn, 1914), entry on *iniuria*, c) 'widerrechtlicher Schaden, Nachteil'. Unfortunately the article on *iniuria* in the *Vocabularium Iurisprudentiae Romanae* vol III/1 (1979) does not analyse the meanings.

[41] *Lehre* 28. See also A Pernice, *Labeo* vol 2 1 (1878, reprinted 1963) 10 at n 13.

[42] It is unnecessary to try to determine whether *iniuria* relating to the unlawfulness of the defendant's act emerged before *iniuria* relating to the unlawful result of such an act. Cf D Daube, *Roman Law: Linguistic, Social and Philosophical Aspects* (1969) 57–9 (referring to action nouns).

briefly at some legal texts which make the position clear and then, in more detail, at D.9.2.27.25.

Texts where *Iniuria* means Injury, Harm, Prejudice, etc

The lex Junia gave free status to Junian Latins but, according to Gaius' Institutes 3.56, this was not to affect their patrons' right to succeed to their estate, lest the benefit conferred on them turn into a harm to their patrons: *ne beneficium istis datum in iniuriam patronorum converteretur.* In D.43.8.2.10, from book 68 of his edictal commentary, Ulpian discusses the wording of the interdict *ne quid in loco publico*, forbidding the defendant from doing anything in a public place *qua ex re quid illi damni detur.* Ulpian sees this provision, that what is done should cause no *damnum* to the plaintiff, as meaning that it should be permitted only if it can be done without *iniuria* to anyone: *ita oportet permitti ut sine iniuria cuiusquam fiat.* He really treats *damnum* and *iniuria* as synonymous in this context.[43] Similarly, at Urso and Irni a duumvir or, at Urso, an aedile was entitled to construct whatever roads, ditches, or drains he wished, provided it could be done without harm to private individuals, *sine iniuria privatorum.*[44] In Urso the councillors could allow a colonist to take overflow water which he was then entitled to use, in so far as this did not harm any private individual, *sine privati iniuria.*[45]

Moving on to the lex Aquilia, in D.43.24.7.4, Ulpian 71 *ad edictum*, Ulpian reports the decision of Servius that if, in order to create a fire-break, someone destroys a house which would have burned down anyway, there is no liability under the lex Aquilia *quoniam nullam iniuriam aut damnum dare videtur*—since he is regarded as causing no unlawful injury (*iniuria*) or loss (*damnum*). Again, the two terms are used in close parallel. So interpreted, the statement is readily understandable. By contrast, if *iniuria* is translated (incorrectly) as 'unlawfulness', not only is the idea of 'causing unlawfulness' rather odd, but Servius seems unable to choose between two completely different reasons for holding that there is no liability under the statute. Making this mistake, Kaser describes the alternative *nullam iniuriam aut damnum* as 'grossly unclear'.[46] When the words

---

[43] P Birks, 'Other Men's Meat: Aquilian Liability for Proper User' (1981) 16 Irish Jurist 141, 156 n 67 does not give *iniuria* its appropriate meaning in this text and so is driven to adopting a very strained interpretation.

[44] Lex Coloniae Genetivae ch 77: *Roman Statutes* (n 1) vol I 393, 404; Lex Irnitana ch 82: J González, 'The *Lex Irnitana*: A New Copy of the Flavian Municipal Law' (1986) 76 JRS 147, 175. The slight difference between the provisions is immaterial for present purposes. The Lex Tarentina col 1, line 40 was doubtless in the same terms, but the engraver has omitted *privatorum* in the clause *quod eius sine iniuria fiat*: *Roman Statutes* (n 1) 301, 305 with the comment at 311. See also Frontinus, *de aquaeductis* 125. S Schipani, *Responsabilità 'ex lege Aquilia': Criteri di Imputazione e Problema della 'Culpa'* (1969) 70–3 says that understanding the use of *iniuria* in such passages is 'more delicate' but rather fails to come to grips with it.

[45] Lex Coloniae Genetivae ch 100: *Roman Statutes* vol I, 393, 408. The bronze has *privatim*—clearly an error by the engraver. [46] Kaser, *Quanti ea res est* (n 13) 10 n 4.

are translated correctly, the supposed lack of clarity disappears and the slur is lifted from Servius' reputation.[47]

The Meaning of *Iniuria* in D.9.2.27.25

I now consider a text where a mistake in the translation of *iniuria* appears to have contributed to an error by Lenel in reading the map of book 18 of Ulpian's edictal commentary. Unfortunately, in due course, Birks relied on Lenel's mistaken view as support for a rather wider thesis on the nature of *iniuria* in chapter 3 of the lex Aquilia.[48] Properly understood, however, the text is a useful illustration of a decision, relating to the lex Aquilia, which turns on *iniuria*, meaning unlawful injury or loss.

The text in question is D.9.2.27.25, Ulpian 18 *ad edictum*:

si olivam immaturam decerpserit vel segetem desecuerit immaturam vel vineas crudas, Aquilia tenebitur: quod si iam maturas, cessat Aquilia: nulla enim iniuria est, cum tibi etiam impensas donaverit, quae in collectionem huiusmodi fructuum impenduntur: sed si collecta haec interceperit, furti tenetur. Octavenus in uvis adicit, nisi, inquit, in terram uvas proiecit, ut effunderentur.

Although I would translate the text differently in a number of respects, it is convenient to set out Kolbert's version in the standard English translation:

If someone harvests olives before their due season or cuts down green corn or unripe grapes, he is liable under the *lex Aquilia*; but if they are ripe for harvest, the Aquilian action does not lie, as no wrongful harm has been done; rather, he has made you a gift of the costs involved in harvesting a crop of this nature. But if he makes off with a crop after collecting it, he is liable for theft, unless, Octavenus adds in the case of the grapes, he threw them down on the ground so that they were a dead loss.[49]

In order to see the true context in which Ulpian made these remarks, we must go back a little way in his commentary.

Palingenesia of D.9.2.27.17–28

In 27.13 Ulpian turns to comment on the verb *ruperit* in chapter 3 of the lex Aquilia.[50] In 27.14–16 he explains, with examples, that the term has been given a wide interpretation, making it the equivalent of *corruperit*. But then in 27.17

---

[47] This is not to suggest, of course, that merely correcting the translation solves all the problems of the text. See J-F Gerkens, '*Aeque perituris . . .*': *Une approche de la causalité dépassante en droit romain classique* (1997) 33–84 for an exhaustive discussion.

[48] Birks (n 43) 16 Irish Jurist 141, 153–60.

[49] A Watson (ed), *The Digest of Justinian* (1985) vol I. The translation of the part giving Octavenus' opinion on the grapes, though following a generally accepted line, is quite mistaken.

[50] In the articles cited in n 27 Birks argued that Ulpian's edictal commentary was written on the wording of the formula or formulae in the praetor's Edict rather than on the wording of the lex

he gives a rather more abstract definition of the term as it has been developed. He says, first, that it covers the defendant who wounds his victim with various implements so as to cut or bruise him but, secondly, only if this causes loss unlawfully: *sed ita demum si damnum iniuria datum sit*. So, if the slave is not made less valuable or worse in some way, the lex Aquilia does not apply. The statute applies to *ruptiones* which cause loss. This second aspect of the interpretation of the term *ruperit* presumably derived, not from any quality of the word itself, but from the fact that, according to 27.5, chapter 3 applies only *si quis alteri damnum faxit*.[51]

The Digest text of 27.17 speaks of the defendant being liable only if his act caused the plaintiff loss 'unlawfully' (*iniuria*). As the remainder of the text shows, and as his commentary goes on to make clear, however, the point Ulpian is making is that the act must cause the plaintiff loss. In that context *iniuria*, 'unlawfully', is, strictly speaking, superfluous.[52] It may therefore be that the text in Collatio 2.4.1, where *iniuria* does not appear, is to be preferred.[53]

In the texts which follow, Ulpian gives examples illustrating these two aspects of the definition. Dealing with the first aspect, in 27.18–24 he refers to cases involving different, more or less direct, ways in which things are damaged. All of them had been held to fall within the term *ruperit*. Then, in 27.25–28, Ulpian explores the second aspect, the requirement that the defendant' act should have caused the plaintiff loss. So in 27.25 Ulpian is giving examples of cases where the defendant' act does not cause loss to the plaintiff and where, accordingly, it does not fall within the scope of the term *ruperit*. Hence the lex Aquilia does not apply.

It is important to stress that Ulpian' remarks in 27.25–8 are properly to be regarded as part of his commentary on *ruperit* because Lenel suggested that his commentary on that term finished at 27.24 and that 27.25–8 formed part of his commentary on *damnum faxit iniuria*.[54] Although Lenel maintained this

Aquilia itself. While I have derived much benefit from his observations on individual texts, I remain firmly of the view that, in the main, the commentary followed the wording of the statute.

[51] A diamond-cutter who 'broke' (*fregerit*) someone else's stone and thereby maximized its value would likewise not be liable under the statute, since he did not cause the owner of the stone any loss—indeed, on the contrary, he would have brought the owner a positive gain.

[52] Pernice, *Lehre* 28 n 4 makes this point, but it is obscured by a wrong reference to 27.15 instead of 27.17.

[53] The Digest text might be interpreted as saying that there is liability only si '*damnum iniuria' datum sit*—only if 'loss and injury' has been caused. This would involve taking the two words as a phrase, with the participle being in accord with the more remote, but dominant, *damnum*. Cf Kühner and Stegmann, *Ausführliche Grammatik* (n 28) vol II 1 53. It is not impossible that this would also be the appropriate translation, say, in Gaius' Institutes 3.217 and D.9.2.11.7. The formulation in 43.24.7.4 points to *damnum iniuriam dare* as a possible usage. On the other hand, if the intention were merely to refer to *damnum iniuria*, it is hard to see why *datum* would be inserted. So I would be inclined to reject that approach.

[54] *EP* 203 n 9; *Palingenesia* vol II 530 n 1. Lenel's approach was the basis for the mistaken suggestion in A Rodger, 'Labeo, Proculus and the Ones that Got Away' (1972) 88 LQR 402, 403 n 7 that Ulpian started his commentary on *iniuria* in 27.25.

analysis through all the editions of his *Edictum Perpetuum*, he was not altogether confident about his scheme since he commented that, at this point, the sections of the commentary were not to be identified with complete certainty.[55] His doubts are scarcely surprising since he really has to say that after commenting on *ruperit* Ulpian went back to comment on words, *si quis alteri damnum faxit*, which came before that term in the statute. In fact, Lenel's suggestion is even more problematical since the phrase (*si damnum faxit iniuria*) which he envisages as the lemma for Ulpian's comment is not actually found in the statute: according to 27.5, the words *damnum faxit* and *iniuria* were unconnected and occurred, far apart, in different clauses of chapter 3. Lenel may have included *iniuria* partly because it appears in 27.17[56] and partly because he saw that the decision in 27.25 turned on there being *nulla iniuria*, but mistook the meaning of *iniuria* in that passage. As is plain from 27.17, however, Ulpian built the requirement that the defendant should have caused loss into his interpretation of *ruperit*. So far as 27.25–8 are concerned, therefore, although they deal with that requirement, they do so as part of Ulpian's commentary on *ruperit*.

   For present purposes it is unnecessary to decide how Ulpian's commentary proceeded after 27.28.[57] What matters is that in 27.25–8 he was concerned with the requirement that the defendant's act should have caused the plaintiff loss, not with the requirement that he should have acted unlawfully, *iniuria*. An interpretation of 27.25 which makes the decision turn on the lawfulness of the defendant's act is accordingly inconsistent with its place in the commentary.

Iniuria Meaning 'Unlawful Injury' in D.9.2.27.25

Unfortunately, Birks approached 27.25 in the belief, derived from Lenel, that it formed part of Ulpian's commentary on *iniuria* in chapter 3.[58] Since, on this view, by the time he reached 27.25 Ulpian had already completed his commentary on *ruperit*, Birks excluded the possibility that Ulpian was raising new issues as to *rumpere* or *corrumpere*. But he thought that, in asides, Ulpian might refer to factors, such as the absence of *damnum*, which might negative liability even where the defendant's act was unlawful. The main focus of the text would, however, be on the need for the defendant to have acted unlawfully, *iniuria*.

   While there may be quibbles about some of the wording, the thrust of the first part of 27.25 is clear. If someone picks another's olives or cuts his corn or picks his grapes when they are still unripe, he is liable under the lex Aquilia. From the

---

[55] *EP* 203 n 9.

[56] Significantly, he failed to record that it does not appear in the Collatio text: *Palingenesia* vol II 529. The lapse is the more telling since Lenel was usually meticulously accurate in such matters.

[57] The matter is by no means straightforward. In 29 pr–29.5, however, it looks as if Ulpian is indeed discussing the requirement that the defendant should have acted unlawfully, *iniuria*—as Lenel thought: *EP* 203 n 9; *Palingenesia* vol II 531.   [58] 16 Irish Jurist 141 (n 43) 152.

context, the basis of the defendant's liability must be that he *ruperit* the olives, corn, or grapes while they were still unripe. But, the text goes on, if the crops were already ripe when he harvested them, the lex Aquilia does not apply. Again, we can be sure from the context not just that this is because the defendant *non ruperit* the crops in terms of the statute but, more particularly, because any *ruptio* that there was did not involve loss to their owner and, as explained in 27.17, the statute applies only to *ruptiones* which cause loss.

That explanation is to be found in the text itself. For the moment we pass over Ulpian's statement, *nulla enim iniuria est*, and note his explanation, in the clauses *cum tibi... impenduntur*, that the person who harvests the crop makes you a gift of the costs involved in harvesting fruits of this kind. Pringsheim[59] rejects these clauses and the reasoning they contain as interpolated, principally on the ground that it is not actually the case that there was an intention to make a gift. This seems hypercritical: if someone harvests another's crop, so long as he does not make off with it or consume it, the owner has the advantage of the work done in harvesting it and, in that respect, the harvester confers a free benefit as opposed to inflicting a loss.

These clauses contain the reasoning for Ulpian's conclusion that the lex Aquilia does not apply to this situation because—*nulla enim iniuria est*—there is no *iniuria*. Von Lübtow proceeds on the basis that 27.25 comes from Ulpian's commentary on *damnum faxit*.[60] For him, the decision must have been based on the idea that the owner of the crop does not suffer *damnum*. He therefore rewrites this part of the text so that Ulpian says that the lex Aquilia does not apply because no loss (*damnum*) has been caused—*nullum enim damnum datum est*. But, as Birks points out,[61] if the text had been in that form, the explanation in *cum... impenduntur* would have so clearly fitted that no one would have dreamed of changing it to read *nulla enim iniuria est*.

For his part, Birks thinks that in this text Ulpian is discussing whether the person who harvested the crops acted unlawfully, *iniuria*.[62] In his view, Ulpian thought that, when the crops were ripe, the person concerned did not act unlawfully, *iniuria*, by harvesting them, since they were ready for the kind of *ruptio* by harvesting which their nature destined them to suffer.[63] As Birks recognizes, however, if this was indeed the reason why there was no *iniuria* and the lex Aquilia did not apply in such a case, then the further explanation given in the clauses *cum... impenduntur* is necessarily false. So Birks too felt obliged to condemn it as interpolated.[64]

---

[59] F Pringsheim, 'Animus donandi' (1921) 42 ZSS 273, 321 = *Gesammelte Abhandlungen* vol I (1961) 252, 285; followed by von Lübtow, *Untersuchungen* (n 38) 133.   [60] ibid 132.
[61] 16 Irish Jurist 141, 157.
[62] ibid 157–60. In his *Casebook* (n 3) 60 Frier translates the text in the same way and sees it as important for Ulpian's view of what counts as wrongful within the context of the lex Aquilia.
[63] This is, of course, part of a much larger thesis based, in particular, on a scholion of Hagiotheodoretos in Basilica 60.3.30, which cannot be explored here.
[64] 16 Irish Jurist 141, 158.

The arguments of von Lübtow and Birks are mistaken. Although they come to radically different conclusions, both scholars go wrong because they mistranslate *iniuria*. This is actually rather strange since Pernice had pointed out[65] that 27.25 is one of the texts where *iniuria* is used to refer not to the unlawfulness of the defendant's action, but to damage to the plaintiff's estate (*Vermögensschaden*).[66] While Kolbert correctly translates *iniuria* as 'wrongful harm', by referring to 'wrongful conduct' ('*onrechtmatig handelen*' and '*widerrechtliche Handlung*'), the more recent Dutch and German translations[67] completely miss the point. Happily, when we give *iniuria* its proper meaning of, say, 'unlawful injury', the supposed problems which von Lübtow and Birks detected in the text melt away.

Von Lübtow went to all the trouble of deleting *iniuria* and replacing it with *damnum* so that Ulpian would say that the lex Aquilia did not apply because the owner of the crop suffered no loss, *damnum*. But, once we realize that Ulpian is using *iniuria* as a virtual synonym for *damnum*, the alteration is plainly unnecessary. When he says that the lex Aquilia does not apply because there is no *iniuria*, Ulpian is indeed saying that it does not apply because the owner of the crop suffers no unlawful injury—which can be equiparated with loss. Whatever one may think of the invocation of gift, the further explanation which then follows is a justification for this view. The reasoning is coherent.

Similarly, once the correct meaning of *iniuria* is identified, it becomes plain that Ulpian was not saying that the person who harvested the crop escaped liability because he did not act unlawfully, *iniuria*. In particular, there is no basis for the view that he was not liable because the *ruptio* was simply part of the natural destiny of the crop. On the contrary—and somewhat less interestingly—the defendant is not liable simply because the owner does not suffer any unlawful injury, in the sense of loss. The tension which Birks thought he detected between *nulla enim iniuria est* and the further justification in *cum . . . impenduntur* does not exist.

Pernice obviously found it slightly surprising that Ulpian used *iniuria* in the sense of 'unlawful injury' in 27.25 and other texts where he discusses the lex Aquilia, even though the same word was used with the different meaning of 'unlawfulness' in chapters 1 and 3 of the statute.[68] But there would be nothing at all strange in Ulpian using *iniuria* in this sense if that was its meaning in the phrase *damnum iniuria*, which described the kind of harm for which the statute provided remedies. Indeed, it then becomes clearer why—as Birks noticed—in 27.28 Ulpian first justifies his decision by reference to the absence of *iniuria* and then, in effect, explains that justification.

[65] *Lehre* 28. Birks was aware of the passage since he refers to it.
[66] He also referred to D.9.2.30.1 (Paul), 37 pr (Iavolenus), and 54 (Papinian). On *damnum* see further Pernice, *Lehre* 93.
[67] JE Spruit, R Feenstra, and KEM Bongenaar, *Corpus Iuris Civilis: Tekst en Vertaling* vol II *Digesten 1–10* (1994) 726; O Behrends, R Knütel, B Kupisch, and HH Seiler, *Corpus Iuris Civilis: Text und Übersetzung* vol II *Digesten 1–10* (1995) 750. [68] *Lehre* 28.

Next, we must consider two texts where, it is suggested, Ulpian is explaining this meaning of *iniuria* in *damnum iniuria*.

D.47.10.1 pr

The first is 47.10.1 pr, Ulpian 56 *ad edictum*:

iniuria ex eo dicta est, quod non iure fiat: omne enim, quod non iure fit, iniuria fieri dicitur. hoc generaliter. specialiter autem iniuria dicitur contumelia. interdum iniuriae appellatione damnum culpa datum significatur, ut in lege Aquilia dicere solemus...

Thomas[69] translates:

Wrong is so called from that which happens not rightly; for everything which does not come about rightly is said to occur wrongfully. This in general. But, specifically, 'wrong' is the designation for contumely. Sometimes again, by the term 'wrong' there is indicated damage occasioned by fault, as we say in respect of the *lex Aquilia*.

The text[70] comes from Ulpian's introduction to the Edictal title *de iniuriis* where he is distinguishing between the meanings which *iniuria* has in different contexts.[71]

Ulpian begins by saying that *iniuria* derives from *quod non iure fit*, what is done 'not lawfully'. For everything which is done *non iure* (unlawfully) is said to be done *iniuria*. That is the general position. In a special sense, he goes on, *iniuria* is defined as *contumelia* (insult). Clearly, Ulpian has in mind the delict relating to insult. Then he says that sometimes by the term *iniuria* is meant *damnum culpa datum*, 'as we are accustomed to say[72] in the case of the lex Aquilia'.[73]

Note what Ulpian does and does not say. He does *not* say that in the case of the lex Aquilia something is considered as being done *iniuria* (unlawfully) if it is done by *culpa* (fault). Rather, he says that in the case of the lex Aquilia the jurists are accustomed to say that *damnum culpa datum* is meant by *iniuria*. In other words, *iniuria* (unlawful injury) means 'loss' (*damnum*), more particularly loss caused by the defendant's fault (*damnum culpa datum*)—because that is the loss which is recoverable under the statute.

---

[69] Watson (ed), *The Digest of Justinian* (n 49) vol IV. My disagreements with Thomas's translation can be seen from the discussion.

[70] It is one of the texts which the *Thesaurus Linguae Latinae* (n 40) vol VII 1 1671, ll 57–68 gives for *iniuria* meaning *damnum*.

[71] *EP* 397 n 2; *Palingenesia* vol II 766, fragment 1335. See A Rodger, 'Introducing Iniuria' (1991) 51 TvR 1. F Schulz, *History of Roman Legal Science* (1946, reprinted 1953) 200–1 (= *Geschichte der Römischen Rechtswissenschaft* (1961) 249) considers that in Ulpian's commentary many of the introductions to Edictal titles are later interpolations.

[72] The phrase is favoured by Ulpian: T Honoré, *Ulpian: Pioneer of Human Rights* (2nd edn, 2002) 58 n 275.

[73] So, correctly, JE Spruit and PJ Verdam in *Corpus iuris civilis: Tekst en Vertaling* vol VI (2001) 513: 'Soms wordt met de aanduiding *iniuria* door schuld toegebrachte schade bedoeld, zoals wij dat plegen te zeggen bij de Lex Aquilia'.

This unequivocal statement about the way that *iniuria* is usually interpreted in the case of the lex Aquilia cannot refer to the meaning of that word in chapter 1 or chapter 3. In neither context does *iniuria* mean loss of any kind. In both it refers to the unlawful way in which the defendant acted—and so caused loss to the plaintiff. This is no reason, however, to reject what Ulpian says as inappropriate and therefore interpolated.[74] In effect, by his time, the terms *damnum* and *iniuria* in *damnum iniuria* have fused, with *damnum* becoming dominant—because it occurs in chapter 3. With that in mind, Ulpian is explaining what counts as *iniuria* (unlawful injury) in *damnum iniuria*, the harm remedied by the lex Aquilia, just as he explains what counts as *iniuria* (insult), the harm that is remedied by the edicts relating to insult. This is precisely the kind of explanation that one would expect to find in an introductory passage of this kind.

D.9.2.5.1

The other text which tends to confirm that *iniuria*, unlawful injury, was used as one element in the description of the harm remedied by the statute is D.9.2.5.1, which has elements in common with D.47.10.1 pr. At the start of the excerpts from Ulpian's commentary on chapter 1 of the statute, in D.9.2.3, he remarks that the lex Aquilia applies where a slave man or woman has been killed unlawfully, *iniuria*.[75] He regards this as an appropriate qualification of the defendant's liability. Ulpian then explores this qualification in more detail. In 5 pr he says that a defendant who kills someone who attacks him with a weapon is not regarded as having killed unlawfully, *iniuria*, but that if he chose to kill his attacker when he could have captured him, then he is considered to have acted unlawfully (*iniuria fecisse*) and so he will also be liable under the lex Cornelia.

In 5.1, from book 18 *ad edictum*, Ulpian continues:

> iniuriam autem hic accipere nos oportet non quemadmodum circa iniuriarum actionem contumeliam quandam, sed quod non iure factum est, hoc est contra ius, id est si culpa quis occiderit: et ideo interdum utraque actio concurrit et legis Aquiliae et iniuriarum, sed duae erunt aestimationes, alia damni, alia contumeliae. igitur iniuriam hic damnum accipiemus culpa datum etiam ab eo qui nocere noluit.

Kolbert[76] translates:

> We must here, of course, not take *injuria* as meaning some sort of insult, as it indicates in the action for insult, but as indicating something done illegally, that is, contrary to the laws—as, for example, if one kills wrongfully. Thus, although from time to time the action under the *lex Aquilia* and the action for insult concur, there will in such a case be

[74] See *Index Interpolationum*.   [75] *EP* 199 n 1; *Palingenesia* vol II 522 n 4, para 613.
[76] Watson (ed), *The Digest of Justinian* (n 49) vol I. Again, any slight disagreements with Kolbert's translation can be seen from the discussion.

two assessed heads of damages, one for wrongful harm and one for insult. Therefore, we interpret *iniuria* for present purposes as including damage caused in a blameworthy fashion, even by one who did not intend the harm.

The opening words are plainly based on the use of the term *iniuria* in chapter 1, as shown in the examples of lawful and unlawful killing which Ulpian has just given. Ulpian points out that in this context the word *iniuria* is not to be interpreted as a kind of insult, as in the case of the *actio iniuriarum*, but as what is done unlawfully, that is contrary to the law, that is if someone has killed *culpa*, by fault. Even supposing that this part of the text might have been reworked,[77] its basic character as a comment on *iniuria*, meaning 'unlawfully', is clear. The text goes on to point out that it follows from the different meanings which *iniuria* has in the case of the *actio iniuriarum* and the lex Aquilia that sometimes both actions are available together, the difference being in the damages, which are calculated in the one case on the basis of loss and in the other on the basis of insult.

Up to this point the discussion relates to *iniuria* in the sense of 'unlawfully'. But then comes a change.[78] Ulpian says: 'therefore we shall treat[79] *iniuria* here as loss which has been caused by fault, even by someone who did not want to cause harm'.[80] Ulpian is not repeating what he has just said,[81] but is making a different point. Again, it is important to see exactly what he says: we treat as *iniuria* loss caused by fault even where there was no intention to cause harm. In other words here, just as in D.47.10.1 pr, Ulpian is using *iniuria* (unlawful injury) as a synonym for loss (*damnum*) and, because in the lex Aquilia there is liability for loss which has been caused by any kind of fault (*culpa*), he says that in this context *iniuria* is to be interpreted as meaning *damnum* which the defendant

---

[77] A tricky assumption, given that much of the text is also preserved in Collatio 7.3.4. For far-reaching suggestions of interpolation, which I would regard as unacceptable, see W Kunkel, 'Exegetische Studien zur aquilischen Haftung' (1929) 49 ZSS 158, 168–71 and F Wieacker, *Textstufen klassischer Juristen* (1960) 237–8. Honsell in *Römisches Privatrecht* (n 8) 231 n 6 considers that there is no longer any dispute that these aspects of the text are genuine.

[78] This is rightly recognized by some at least of the scholars who treat this part of the text as interpolated. See *Index Interpolationum*. Unfortunately, those scholars who regard the sentence as genuine tend not to acknowledge what Ulpian is actually saying and treat it as if he were saying that a person acted *iniuria* for the purposes of the lex Aquilia if he acted *culpa*. See eg U Wesel, *Rhetorische Statuslehre und Gesetzesauslegung der römischen Juristen* (1967) 48–9.

[79] Honoré, *Ulpian* (n 72) 60 n 322 points out that *accipiemus* is characteristic of Ulpian's style.

[80] Perhaps because *iniuria* is left in Latin, the passage is correctly translated in H Hausmanninger, *Das Schadenersatzrecht der lex Aquilia* (3rd edn, 1987) 43: 'Unter *iniuria* verstehen wir also hier einen Schaden, der schuldhaft zugefügt worden ist, selbst durch jemanden, der keine Absicht hatte zu schaden'. Less happy is Behrends *et al*, *Corpus Iuris Civilis: Text und Übersetzung* vol II (n 67) 734: 'Wir verstehen daher unter Widerrechtlichkeit in der lex Aquilia auch die schuldhafte Schädigung, die jemand zufügt, der nicht schädigen will'. Here too the Dutch translators misconstrue *iniuria* as 'onrechtmatig handelen' and so are forced to introduce the idea of the defendant bringing about loss, which is not to be found in the original Latin: 'Wij verstaan dus hier onder onrechtmatig handelen het toebrengen van schade met schuld, ook indien dat geschied is door iemand die niet de bedoeling had schade aan te richten.': Spruit *et al*, *Corpus Iuris Civilis: Tekst en Vertaling* vol II (n 67) 711.   [81] *Pace* Birks, in *Collatio Iuris Romani* (n 27) vol 1 17, 27.

causes by fault even when he did not intend to cause harm.[82] Again, it is obvious that Ulpian cannot be commenting on *iniuria* in chapter 1, or indeed chapter 3, of the statute since the term does not mean loss of any kind in either context. Presumably this is why Beseler says that a glance at the surrounding context shows that this sentence must be a marginal gloss.[83] But the similarity with D.47.10.1 pr suggests that the more likely explanation for the fact that Ulpian is not commenting on *iniuria* as used in either chapter is that, here too, he is explaining, more generally, what the term means when used in the phrase *damnum iniuria*, describing the harm to which the statute applies. His point is that, when the terms of chapter 1—interpreted as meaning that the slave or animal should have been killed by *culpa*—are taken into account, it becomes clear that the *iniuria* or unlawful injury which the statute covers is loss that is inflicted by the fault, *culpa*, of the defendant, even if he does not intend to cause harm.

An Introductory Passage?

Birks considered that the heading of the section of the Praetor's Edict dealing with the lex Aquilia was *de damno iniuria*. That seems entirely possible, not least because—as he points out—Lenel's chosen rubric, *ad legem Aquiliam*, is unique, among the rubrics recorded or reconstructed by him, in taking its name from a statute.[84] Even if one just assumed that in 5.1 Ulpian was discussing *iniuria* in *damnum iniuria*, the expression used to describe the harm for which the statute provided a remedy, Birks would still have made the same point. In either event, he would have protested, we should expect to find Ulpian discussing *iniuria* as part of the concept of *damnum iniuria* in a general introductory passage rather than in a comment on *iniuria*, meaning 'unlawfully', in chapter 1. So he would have insisted that, even supposing that the meaning put forward here for *iniuria* in *damnum iniuria* were correct, we should still infer that this bit of 5.1 had originally formed part of an introductory passage and had been moved by the compilers to its present position where it appears to be part of a comment on *iniuria* in chapter 1.[85]

---

[82] His failure to grasp the meaning of *iniuria* here leads E Grueber, *The Lex Aquilia* (1886) 11 into a mistranslation of this sentence which is too painful to repeat. Similarly, P Ziliotto, *L'imputazione del danno aquiliano tra iniuria e damnum corpore datum* (2000) 43 completely misses the point when she says that in this passage Ulpian is treating loss *iniuria datum* as the same as loss *culpa datum* even where the defendant did not want to cause harm.

[83] G Beseler, *Beiträge zur Kritik der römischen Rechtsquellen* vol III (1913) 105, in a study of texts with *igitur* as first word in the clause.

[84] *Estudios de Historia del Derecho Europeo: Homenaje al Professor G Martínez Díez* (n 27) vol 1 81, 83; *Collatio Iuris Romani* (n 27) vol 1 17, 23–4. He also makes the acute point, at 84 and 24 n 29 respectively, that *eadem lex Aquilia* in 27.5 does not really fit if the commentary was on a title devoted exclusively to the lex Aquilia.

[85] *Collatio Iuris Romani* (n 27) vol 1 17, 24–8 gives his later thoughts on the point.

As Birks was the first to acknowledge, by its very nature a shift of this kind would be difficult to detect. The hypothesis is therefore likely to remain conjectural. There are two particular reasons for caution.

First, perhaps because of his special interest in the delict of *iniuria*, Birks concentrates on the likelihood of an introduction containing the comments on *iniuria*. So he plots the possible shifts for texts dealing with *iniuria*. But any introduction would have had to deal with both *damnum* and *iniuria*. Like the comments on *iniuria*, however, any comments on *damnum* which have been preserved seem to occur in the course of Ulpian's commentary on the provisions of the statute—in D.9.2.21 and 23 pr—23.7 (chapter 1) and 27.25–8 (chapter 3). Birks does not—and really could not—suggest that these passages on *damnum* were originally to be found in an introduction.

Secondly, this aspect of the structure of the commentary is actually not surprising. While Ulpian may well have said something about *damnum iniuria* in his introduction to this chapter in the Praetor's Edict, he could not have exhausted the topic. After all, as a practical matter, the scope of the words could be gauged only from looking at the provisions of the statute and the way that they were interpreted and applied. What counted as *damnum iniuria* was the loss and unlawful injury for which a plaintiff could recover damages under the statute. So the 'meaning' of *damnum iniuria* could not really be explored in advance, in isolation from the rest of the commentary on the statute. In that situation, it would not be so surprising if Ulpian had left any real discussion of the scope of *damnum* until he reached the relevant part of his commentary on damages under chapter 1. Similarly, Ulpian might well have chosen to investigate the different meanings of *iniuria* at the first point in his commentary where that concept came up and where he was then in a position to explain how *iniuria*, in the context of *damnum iniuria*, fell to be interpreted, having regard to the decisions on the role of *iniuria* in chapter 1. I therefore see insufficient reason to suppose that the part of 5.1 dealing with this aspect of *iniuria* did not originally form part of Ulpian's commentary on chapter 1.

Conclusion

What did *damnum iniuria* actually mean? Loss and unlawful injury.

The phrase *damnum iniuria* comprises two nouns in the nominative and in asyndeton. They are used to describe the loss and unlawful injury (or harm or detriment) for which the lex Aquilia gave remedies. Ultimately, therefore, the scope of *damnum iniuria* depended on the way the jurists interpreted the provisions of the statute. As Ulpian explains in D.47.10.1 pr and 9.2.5.1, by his time *iniuria* in *damnum iniuria* had come to mean *damnum*, more particularly loss caused by fault, even though unintentional. But that was the result of a development that had taken place over the best part of 500 years. The course of that development needs to be explored. For instance, how were *damnum* and *iniuria* originally to be distinguished? What, if anything, did *damnum* originally add to *iniuria* and vice versa? Is it relevant that *damnum* finds no place in chapter 1? What did Servius mean by saying in D.43.24.7.4 that a defendant who pulled down a building that was going to be destroyed *nullam iniuriam aut damnum dare videtur*? What is the force of *aut* in that sentence? Why did *damnum* apparently become the dominant term? Space precludes any further investigation of these and similar matters on this occasion: happily, the instructive mysteries of the lex Aquilia are far from exhausted.

One hesitates to imagine what Peter would have thought of all this. Almost certainly, he would have disagreed—or even disapproved. But discussion of *iniuria* always interested him. The first time I met him, at a conference in Amsterdam in September 1969, Peter had the proofs of his forthcoming article on *iniuria*[86] with him. And his last email to me, a few weeks before he died, said that he had been planning to write a Milsomian version of the Roman law of delict but 'that won't be possible'. In the thirty-five years that we were friends, Peter was a source of inspiration and encouragement for me and countless others, not only in Roman law and modern law but, indeed, more generally. Generous to a fault with his time, he was ready to argue points with passion and humour—and then to follow up with letters, postcards, or emails. Among his many passions, perhaps the greatest, however, was for teaching, which he saw as stimulating rather than stifling research. The present essay grew out of teaching I did at Oxford as a result of his death. That, at least, would have appealed to Peter.

---

[86] 'The Early History of Iniuria' (1969) 37 TvR 163. The influence of the (then) recent work of Milsom on his approach in this, one of his very first articles, is obvious.

23

The Romanization of Spain: The Contribution of City Laws in the Light of the *Lex Irnitana*

Joseph Georg Wolf *

I

In his recent book on the relationship between speech and meaning, *Was wir sagen, wenn wir reden* (2004), Hans-Martin Gauger includes some observations on the Latin language. Indeed one of his chapters is headed 'Nothing is more useful than Latin'—and not just because it gives access to other languages, especially the Romance languages, Italian, Spanish, Portuguese, and French, whose vocabulary remains largely Latinate. This community of language is due to the fact that such a wide variety of peoples and places in the Western half of the Roman Empire were Romanized. To be more specific, as Walter von Wartburg described,[1] the West was Romanized by language, though it is not easy to distinguish the linguistic from the other cultural, social, economic, and legal aspects of the process.

The German word *Romanisieren* is of relatively common usage—the Duden dictionary gives its meaning as 'making Roman' or 'making Romanistic'—but it is also, as one would expect, a technical term, used in particular by ancient historians. German adopted it from the French *Romaniser*; and since in Italian it is *Romanizzare* and in Spanish *Romanizar*, one might infer that there was a Latin word *Romanisare*. But, though in Greek we find ῥωμαΐζειν, to speak Latin (and ἑλληνίζειν, to speak Greek) there is nothing of the sort in Latin itself. The words in the Romance languages are later formations, which may help to explain why even in technical writing the word *Romanisieren* is rather imprecise.

The imprecision of the word has often been regretted, and there has even been a proposal to abandon it altogether. If we are to use it properly we need to

---

* Emeritus Professor of Roman Law, Albert Ludwigs University Freiburg-im-Breisgau. The author and editors are very grateful to Tony Weir, Fellow of Trinity College, Cambridge, for the translation of this essay from German into English.

[1] See W von Wartburg, *Die Entstehung der Romanischen Völker* (1939) 34.

identify the distinctive features of Romanization instead of including all the possible ways in which Rome had an impact on other peoples. Thus one could say that the presence of imported Italian pottery was an indication of Romanization. But if that were a sufficient test, one would have to credit the Germans on the far side of the Rhine with being Romanized. The granting of *civitas Romana* has often been held to be an indication of advanced Romanization. To take it as the critical test leads one, however, into difficulties: after all, in 212 AD Caracalla conferred Roman citizenship on all the non-Roman inhabitants of the Empire, but one can hardly speak of the hellenic East as Romanized, at any rate without major qualifications.

Since it is the Latin language which forms the primary distinction between the Romanized West and the Hellenized East one can really speak of Romanization only with regard to the Latin Western Empire. Latin was not only the language of the military and the administration: it was also the everyday language of businessmen and tradesmen and not just of the upper classes but also, as countless inscriptions testify, of ordinary citizens as well. Rome never forced those it conquered to speak Latin but constantly encouraged them to adopt it. The adoption did not happen at a stroke, of course: the speed of the process varied greatly from place to place, depending on many factors, some intrinsic, such as ethnicity and culture, some external, such as immigration by Romans or recruitment into the army. These factors naturally made for differences in the kind of Latin adopted in different regions. A further role was played by the relative density of population. Even in the late second century AD the Bishop of Lyons, a Greek by the name of Irenaios, had to preach in Celtic in order to be understood by his Gallic flock, a fact which confirms the natural assumption that local languages survived alongside Latin, at any rate outside the cities, and disappeared only gradually, as the Romance languages began to develop. Finally, one must remember that the spread of the Latin language, like Romanization itself, occurred at very different times in the Western provinces. Dacia had not even been conquered at a time when Spain had already made its mark on Latin literature thanks to Columella, Seneca, Lucan, Quintilian, and Martial. And it was from Spain that Trajan, the conqueror of Dacia and the first non-Italian emperor, came, from a place called Italica, near the Seville of today, then Hispalis.

The reception of the Latin language was a process of adaptation by the subject peoples of the West. Doubtless they realized that in view of the conquerors' superior strength the only way they could survive was by assimilating themselves to the Romans as models. The adoption of the language of the Romans was at the heart of this process of adaptation, but of course there were other features as well.

In the 60s or 70s of the first century AD Pliny the Elder said that Gaul was more like Italy than a province,[2] and even earlier than that, in AD 48, barely a

---

[2] *Natural History*, 3.4.31.

century after the bloody conquest of Gaul, the Emperor Claudius, in requiring the senate to award the province the *ius honorum*, the right of access to official positions, stated that the inhabitants of Gaul were quite the equals of the Romans *moribus artibus*, that is, as regards conduct and mode of thinking, in practical efficiency and intellectual quality.[3] Pliny may have exaggerated and Claudius may have been extrapolating from the local elites in Gaul, but they do tell us what we should understand by 'Romanization'—namely the adoption of the Roman way of life.

The Romans no more forced their way of life than their language on the subject peoples, but they did promote its adoption. Indeed they regarded this as not only their function but their duty. This is put beyond doubt by the famous lines in which Virgil summed up the role of Rome in the *Aeneid* 6.851–3, the epic published after the poet's death by the express order of the Emperor Augustus:

> Tu regere imperio populos, Romane, memento—
> hae tibi erunt artes—pacique imponere morem,
> parcere subiectis et debellare superbos.

> Remember, you Romans, that your role is to rule, pacify and civilize,
> to be forbearing with those who submit and severe with those who are insolent.

In this pregnant formula Virgil was saying nothing new: he was merely reflecting the belief and conviction of his time.

The poet is speaking to his own people—'Remember, you Romans . . . —your role is to rule over other peoples'. *Regere imperio populos* was to be the theme of Roman power politics, to deal severely with those who refuse to submit (*debellare superbos*) but to treat gently those who do, not to kill or enslave them (*parcere subiectis*). Cicero had already stated this as a maxim of Roman political morality[4] which is to be found also in Livy[5] and Horace.[6] It is the principle on which Caesar acted in Gaul. Again, Rome's mission was to make peace and see that it was maintained, not only peace between Rome and the subject peoples, but also, and perhaps principally, peace among the subject peoples themselves, for in Gaul and Spain the different tribes had often been at each others' throats. But after pacification the Romans were to instil good conduct, to civilise (*paci inponere morem*).[7]

In his biography of his father-in-law, Agricola, Tacitus shows how, after pacifying the conquered, Rome sought to civilize them.[8] When Agricola was the governor of Britain as Vespasian's nominee from 77 to 84 AD, he personally

---

[3] Tacitus, *Annals* 11.24.   [4] *de Officiis* 1.34–5.   [5] 42.17.
[6] *Carmen saeculare* 51.
[7] *Mos* is a word with a wide range of meanings, not just morality, but including law and orderliness, the proper way of living and thinking. The jurists themselves give us many examples of the way Rome remained true to its mission, especially Ulpian's *de officio proconsulis*, a kind of handbook for provincial governors, written during the reign of Caracalla.   [8] *Agricola* 21.

encouraged the Britons, then living in scattered villages, to build temples, forums, and houses. He helped them with public funding and founded schools for the education in the *artes liberales* of the sons of the leaders. He was successful in these endeavours: those who had been reluctant to learn Latin were now eager to speak it, and even began to favour Roman dress and to wear the toga. Finally—and all this is in Tacitus—the natives yielded to the temptations of leisure, dallying in colonnades, taking hot baths, and dining on festive fare.

As has been suggested, the factors which led to Romanization in the different areas of the Empire were very various in origin and operation as regards both the subject peoples and the conquerors, but there was *one* invariable and ubiquitous precondition—the form of urban life.

The city was the focus of life in the ancient world, and the city state was its form of political organization. People had been living in cities by the Tigris and Euphrates for millennia when urban living was adopted by the Phoenicians and then by the Greeks and Etruscans, especially in the coastal areas of the Western Mediterranean. Founded by the Etruscans, Rome remained attached to its constitution as a city state well into imperial times—that is, long after it had become a territorial power in 89 BC with the incorporation of the Italians, long after Caesar had put paid to the republic and Augustus had inaugurated the monarchy, and long after the city on the Tiber had come to rule the world.

For the Romans, as for the Greeks, Etruscans, and Phoenicians, the city was the epitome of the way to live, regarded as superior to all other forms of life, which must accordingly give way to it. Only in an urban world with transparent political and social relationships could there be order and peace in one's daily doings and dealings. Thus for the Roman administrators the city was the prime provider, the only means of providing the institutions which met the needs of the conquerors, especially as regards taxation and military recruitment.

In the centuries before the First Punic War when Italy was being conquered, many cities, large and small, were founded on the model of the hill towns of the Etruscans and the coastal colonies of the Greeks. It was no different when Rome expanded outside Italy and found that in the conquered territories of the West people were not traditionally urbanized, as they were in the East. To speak only of Spain, Gaul, and Britain, the Celtic and Iberian peoples were not grouped in cities but by tribes. Their *oppida* were open loose congeries of huts, sometimes behind an earthen wall, but not institutional centres with any political role. They were therefore not fitted to undertake the administrative roles required by the Roman rulers, at any rate not to their satisfaction for, as we have seen, the Roman system of administration depended on capable city institutions.

One of the things that never ceases to surprise us about the Roman state is that its administration got by for centuries, both at home and in the provinces, with very little in the way of bureaucracy.[9] Even in imperial times this changed only

---

[9] W. Liebenam, *Städteverwaltung im römischen Kaiserreiche* (1900, reprinted 1967) 312.

gradually. Since administrative functions were by and large handed over to the cities, provincial governors needed only a small staff: the provinces, like Italy, were divided into urban areas which administered themselves under the supervision of the governor. From the administrative point of view the Roman world empire was a union of urban communities;[10] the city was the foundation on which imperial administration rested.

If by 'Romanization' we understand the adoption of the Roman way of life, its primary precondition in the West was the urbanization of the Celtic and Iberian settlements. Urbanization is indeed in itself the best instance of Romanization.

Urbanization took many different legal forms and occurred in different ways. We shall focus on Spain, about which we are quite well informed by Pliny. Here cities fell into two principal categories: there were peregrine cities, whose status might vary but which never had a constitution granted to them by Rome, and the so-called privileged cities, which did have a Roman legal constitution. The great majority of peregrine cities were 'stipendiary', bound to pay tribute, subject cities in the broader or narrower sense, and subject to Roman authority.[11] A few peregrine cities were *civitates foederatae*[12] or *liberae*,[13] and had received limited sovereignty, such as having their own laws of administration and jurisdiction, the former by treaty, the latter by revocable law. The 'privileged' cities were *coloniae* or *municipia*, the latter usually being native communities, while the former were settled by Roman colonists. The members of either could be Roman citizens or subject to Latin law, the *ius Latinum*, a kind of lesser citizenship whereby the citizens were equated to Romans in matters of private law and the magistrates were granted *civitas Romana* at the end of their period of office.

Rome's engagement with Spain began in 218 BC, at the start of the Second Punic War, but it took all of two centuries for the conquest to be completed. It is true that in 206 BC the Carthaginians were chased out of Spain and the east coast as well as the Ebro basin in the north-east and the interior in the south up to the River Guadalquivir (the Roman Baetis) were brought under control. In that year Spain was divided into two provinces. Gadir, the venerable Phoenician port which the Romans called Gades, became a *civitas foederata*, while Italica, already mentioned as the birthplace of Trajan and his successor Hadrian, was founded as a *colonia civium Romanorum* for the disbanded legionaries of P Cornelius Scipio, the conquering general. To judge by the impressive numbers reported at the time of Augustus, the governors of the new provinces must have begun urbanizing the newly pacified areas right away.

Augustus divided the Iberian peninsula into three new provinces. The smallest and most southerly, more or less equivalent to present day Andalusia, was Baetica, named after the river.[14] It was by far the richest of the three provinces in

---

[10] Liebenam (n 9) 452; further references in von Wartburg (n 1)

[11] J Marquardt, *Römische Staatsverwaltung* vol I (2nd edn, 1884, reprinted 1957) 80 ff.

[12] Marquardt (n 11) 73 ff.   [13] Marquardt (n 11) 76 ff.

[14] Pliny, *Natural History* 3.7.9.

terms of cities, of which there were 175. These included 129 peregrine cities, 120 of which paid tribute.[15] Pliny gives the names of many of them, often adding what they were called in Latin, thus *Segida, quae Augurina cognominatur, Ulia, quae Fidentia, Urgago quae Alba*, and so on. These secondary names show that by Roman standards even the peregrine cities were really *civitates* emerging from native settlements, for it was rare for an entirely new city to be created on strategic grounds by resettling displaced persons. As to the layout of the cities, we must take it that this was imposed from above; the land was measured, the city plan drafted, the streets laid out, the forum put in place, the temple erected, perhaps also an encircling wall built, all under the supervision of Roman experts and possibly funded by the governor. According to Tacitus this was what happened in Britain under Agricola.

Urbanization involved no automatic privilege. The peregrine inhabitants remained peregrines, but the status of the city and that of its inhabitants could change—and indeed often did so. In Spain this happened to all the unprivileged cities, even before the end of the first century AD: without exception they became *municipia* and were equipped with a constitution, a 'city law', and so became cities as defined in Roman public law. Normally they became *municipia iuris Latini* and thereby, as we shall shortly see, acquired considerable independence in terms of administration and jurisdiction.

This process of municipalization in Spain was begun by Caesar[16] and energetically promoted by Augustus, but it was ignored by his successors until Vespasian accorded the *ius Latinum* to 'the whole of Spain': *universae Hispaniae Vespasianus imperator Augustus iactatum procellis rei publicae Latium tribuit.*[17] By 'universae Hispaniae' Pliny must be referring to all the communities not yet privileged, that is, all those remaining peregrine,[18] and must mean that throughout Spain the *ius Latinum* was 'accorded' by promoting the peregrine

[15] Pliny, *Natural History* 3.7; in addition to the 120 cities which paid tribute there were six free and three federated cities, and of the 46 privileged cities nine were colonies, ten were *municipia civium Romanorum*, and 27 *municipia iuris Latini*.

[16] There are only a few known foundations during the republic. See H Galsterer, *Untersuchungen zum römischen Städtewesen auf der iberischen Halbinsel* (1971) 7 ff. Apart from Italica already mentioned, the following are significant examples. In 171 BC the Roman Senate caused the establishment in the Greek or Phoenician community of Carteia, near the Straits of Gibraltar, of a *colonia iuris Latini* for 4,000 sons of Roman legionaries and Spanish women. Since legionaries could not marry, their children took the status of their mother, and thus were peregrines. By joining the colony they did not become Roman citizens but were granted a lesser civic status, the *ius Latinum*, to be further discussed below. In 45 BC in Urso, nowadays Osuna, about 30 kilometres east of Seville, Caesar founded a colony of *libertini*, freedmen from the urban proletariat of Rome; this was to punish the Iberi for the vigorous resistance they had made to him in the town which Pompey had fortified.

[17] Pliny, *Natural History* 3.30. On the problems of the text see eg T Mommsen, 'Die Stadtrechte der lateinischen Gemeinden Salpensa und Malaca in der Provinz Baetica' in *Gesammelte Schriften* vol I (1904, reprinted 1965) 272, 293 n 22.

[18] Gaius, Institutes 1.95. . . . *quod ius quibusdam peregrinis civitatibus datum est vel a populo Romano vel a senatu vel a Caesare.* See T Mommsen, *Römisches Staatsrecht* (3rd edn, 1887, reprinted 1952) vol II 888 ff.

cities to the status of *municipia*.[19] We have no further information about how this was done, but it certainly took some time for the imperial edict to be implemented. I give a few examples of cities which we shall meet with later: Sabora, near Arunda, the Ronda of today, became a *municipium* before AD 78;[20] Salpensa, overlooking Hispalis (our Seville), at the beginning of the 80s; shortly thereafter came the flourishing Malaca (now Malaga); and not until the early 90s Irni, the Irni now known to us, to which we can finally turn our attention.

II

Until 1981 it was not known that a city called Irni had ever existed or that its city law, the *Lex Irnitana*, had been engraved on ten bronze tablets, 90 centimetres in width and 57 centimetres in height. In the spring of that year, however, some persons unknown, using a metal detector, discovered six of these tablets and forthwith sold them in two lots. The story came out and before long the whereabouts of the tablets became known. They are now to be found, excellently preserved, in the Archaeological Museum in Seville.

The six tablets are numbers 3, 5, 7, 8, 9, and 10 of the *Lex Irnitana*. The text of Tablet 3 is verbally identical with what we have of the city law of Salpensa, extensive fragments of which, as of the city law of Malaca, have been known since 1861. The text of Tablet 7 is identical with a large part of the text which we have from Malaca. It is therefore beyond doubt that the city laws of Salpensa, Malaca, and Irni were all based on a common model. The names of these three cities include the word *Flavium*—*municipium Flavium Salpensanum, Flavium Malacitanum, Flavium Irnitanum*— recalling that it was Vespasian who granted them Latinity. Since many other municipalities in Spain also include *Flavium* in their name, we can infer that the city laws of all these places were taken, word for word, from one and the same original. This hypothesis is confirmed by fragments of the city laws of three other *municipia*. Thus it is not just the law of a single city that we have in the *Lex Irnitana*: it acquaints us with all the Flavian city laws of Spain and the organization of all the municipalities that were promoted to the status of *municipia* under Vespasian's decree.

The text which we have of the *Lex Irnitana* is not complete, but if we add the part of the *Lex Malacitana* which does not appear on the six tables of the *Lex Irnitana*, it amounts, amazingly enough, to two-thirds of the Flavian city

---

[19] On these questions see Galsterer (n 16) 37 ff.

[20] In his *epistula* dated 25 July 78 (CIL 2, 195 no 1423; Bruns, *Fontes* 255 no 81; FIRA vol I 422 no 74) Vespasian gave permission to the people of Sabora, who wanted to relocate their city, *sub nomine meo ... in planum exstruere*. The Saborans were evidently concerned about retaining their city's identity, and wanted to be sure that the city to be built in the plain would be recognized as a *municipium Flavianum*. Contra, Galsterer (n 16) 41 f.

laws—much more than we knew of all the previous city laws of the Roman Empire taken together.[21]

As we have said, the Flavian city laws follow a common model word for word, differing only as regards quantities, such as the financial limit of jurisdiction: it is lower in the *Lex Irnitana* than in the *Lex Malacitana*.

Such deviations were doubtless attributable to differences in the size and importance of the cities. Geza Alföldy therefore concludes that Irni, which is otherwise completely unknown, must have been 'a third-class city'.[22] Now Irni lay between Seville and Malaga, admittedly not on the highway leading from the ancient port to the interior, which went by Urso (now Osuna), a colony of Roman citizens set up on the order of Caesar. But it was by no means distant from the through traffic and lay in a good strategic position, about 20 kilometres south of Urso on the road to Sabora and Arunda (now Ronda). In any case, Irni could not have been a very small town, for its town council numbered 63 *decuriones* or councillors, a number which bespeaks a population of several thousand inhabitants.[23]

The Flavian municipal legislation is like all the Roman city laws known to us in having the three institutions characteristic of the city of Rome itself, namely (a) the meeting of the citizens, (b) the city council, and (c) the annual officials. The meetings of the citizens reflected the *comitia* of the Roman city and were even named after them. The city council, where the *decuriones* met, was like the Senate. The annual officials, that is, the *duumviri*, the *aediles*, and the *quaestores*, were the equivalent of the magistrates in Rome.

(a) The first chapter of the Law of Irni, which dealt with the *comitia*, is lost to us,[24] but we can infer from later provisions that the citizens were put into *curiae* for voting purposes, as in the ancient Roman *comitia curiata*.[25] The *curiae*, not more than 11 in number by law or such lesser number as the council ordained, were to be established within a given period by the *duumviri*, the highest magistrates of the city.[26] We do not know how the voting units were composed.[27] The *comitia*, so far as we know, had no role other than in the election or by-election of magistrates.[28] The details of the election itself were very precisely regulated. The electoral *comitia* were summoned and led by the older of the two *duumviri*.[29] Only those candidates whom he had nominated and whose

---

[21] An English version by Michael Crawford of the *Lex Irnitana* and of the supplementary parts of the *Lex Malacitana* may be found in J González, 'The *Lex Irnitana*: A New Copy of the Flavian Municipal Law' (1986) 76 JRS 147, 182. The *Lex Irnitana* is cited hereafter as 'LI' and the *Lex Malacitana* as 'LM'.   [22] *Römisches Städtewesen auf der neukastilischen Hochebene* (1987) 109.

[23] And not impecunious either, for it must have cost a lot to engrave the city law on ten bronze tablets, each with three columns of dense lettering—a cost which the law itself placed on the city.

[24] See LM Ch 52, I 35–7: *utique ea distributione curiarum, de qua supra conprehensum est, suffragia ferri debebunt, ita per tabellam ferantur facito.*

[25] LM Ch 52, I 35–7, and see n 24.   [26] LI Ch 50, 5C 46–51.

[27] See T Spitzl, *Lex municipii Malacitani* (1984) 38 f.

[28] LM Ch 52, I 33–5. Cf Mommsen, *Gesammelte Schriften* vol I (n 17) 304.

[29] LM Ch 52, I 29–35.

qualifications he had verified could be elected.[30] The *curiae* assembled, on his command, in separate enclosures, voted simultaneously,[31] and reported their votes to the leader.[32] The order in which the decisions of the *curiae* were given was determined by lot, but as soon as any candidate had obtained a majority of the *curiae*, the count was abandoned and the successful party was proclaimed *duumvir*, aedile, or quaestor.[33] Voting was in writing on tablets (*per tabellam*),[34] which permitted secrecy. In the event of an equality of votes, there were detailed regulations to produce a result based on the respective marital and paternal status of the candidates.[35] Supervisors (*custodes*) were appointed to guard against fraud and forgery. Each *curia* had a basket in which the tablets were placed, and the voting was observed by three persons nominated and sworn in by the electoral officer. They had to be local citizens belonging to some other *curia*, and they were allowed to vote at their place of observation rather than in their own *curia* since they must not let the baskets out of their sight. In addition each candidate could appoint a *custos* of his own for each voting basket.[36] It was especially important to guard against manipulation of the vote because people could be forced to stand for election, as I now explain.

The *duumvir* was required to put forward at least as many candidates as there were official posts to fill, thus at least two for the highest post, that of the duumvirate itself. If there was only one applicant or none at all, he had to designate as candidates one or two of the citizens entitled to vote. The candidates so designated could in their turn nominate a candidate each, and each of these could nominate another, but all of them were presented to the *comitia* by the *duumvir* as if they had submitted their candidature voluntarily and in due time, so that the question whether a candidate was acting under compulsion or not played no part in the election.[37] A citizen entitled to vote could neither decline to be a candidate nor refuse to serve if elected: these were civic duties, the *munera* of the citizen, as indeed the word *municeps* implies.

The fact that citizens could be forced to be candidates suggests that legislators realized that, despite the lasting benefits accorded to those who served, office might not be regarded as an unqualified bonus. A person who had served as a magistrate could count on being elected town councillor at the next opportunity and, if he was already a town councillor when elected *duumvir*, aedile, or quaestor, he acquired Roman citizenship at the end of his period in office—not just for himself, but also for his parents, his wife, and the legitimate children of both himself and his sons.[38] Roman citizenship did not affect his rights as a

---

[30] LM Ch 54, I 60–II 3.   [31] LM Ch 55, II 4–9. Cf Spitzl (n 27) 46 f.
[32] LM Ch 57, II 49–50.   [33] LM Ch 57, II 49–59. Cf Spitzl (n 27) 53 ff.
[34] LM Ch 55, II 8–9.
[35] For the procedure in the various *curiae*: LM Ch 56, II 32–47; in the *comitia* Ch 57, II 59–65.
[36] LM Ch 55, II 9–25.   [37] LM Ch 51, I 1–27; Mommsen (n 17) 316.
[38] In LI Ch 21, 3A 39–45: *Qui ex senatoribus decurionibus . . . conscriptisve municipii Flavi Irnitani magistrates . . . creati sunt erunt, ii, cum eo honore abierint . . . cives Romani sunto . . .* H Galsterer, '*Municipium Flavium Irnitanum*: A Latin Town in Spain' (1988) 78 JRS 78, 90 n 66 and

citizen of the *municipium* and afforded no exemption from the duties of a *municeps*, but it did enhance his social standing, a provision perhaps designed to create a civic patriciate.

(b) The *Lex Irnitana* provided for a town council of 63 members. We have no information about how it was constituted, the rules doubtless being contained in the parts of the law that are lost to us. It was kept up to strength by co-option, annually if need be. Any free-born citizen of Irni who was at least 25 years old and had a fortune of at least 5,000 sesterces was eligible.[39]

The town council was the most important institution of the community, for it had a wide competence and its decision had to be sought on many matters. It was convened by the *duumviri*,[40] who managed its sittings in accordance with rules laid down by the law itself. At the start of the official year the council had to vote the funds required for religious observances, games, and public feasts,[41] fix the dates of official and court holidays,[42] state what tasks each of the communal slaves should perform,[43] and much more besides. Only if authorized by the council could the *duumviri* incur expenditure[44] and borrow money.[45] Its decision was required before any house in the city could be pulled down unless it was to be rebuilt within a year.[46] It had to advise on, and recommend, the construction of streets and paths, ditches and drains.[47] The council alone could require citizens and inhabitants to perform services either by themselves or with their beasts, within the narrow limits laid down by the law itself.[48] The council decided on the appointment of city clerks as archivists and accountants,[49] as well as on their pay and that of other members of the staff.[50] It also decided on the manumission of communal slaves.[51] A person who had been fined (*multa*) could complain to the town council,[52] which could exceptionally act as a court at the request of a citizen or inhabitant who was bringing a claim against the city.[53] For most decisions the legal quorum was two-thirds of the members,[54] and for many a two-thirds majority of the votes cast was required.[55] Voting was sometimes by voting tablets (*per tabellam*) and occasionally, as when the council was acting as a court, on an oath sworn by the *decuriones* immediately before the vote was taken.[56]

González (n 21) 215 infer from the text that it was a general condition of eligibility for the magistrature that one be a *decurio* and at least 25 years old. To the contrary is F Lamberti, *Tabulae Irnitanae* (1993) 33. See Mommsen (n 17) 298 ff.

[39] This can be inferred from LI Ch 86, 9B 49–54. At about the same time the financial qualification for the decurionate in Como was 100,000 sesterces. In his *Letters* 1.19.2 Pliny the Younger states: *esse autem tibi centum milium censum satis indicat, quod apud nos decurio es.*

[40] LI Ch 49, 5C 34–5.   [41] LI Ch 77, 8C 21–8.   [42] LI Ch 49, 5C 24–32.
[43] LI Ch 78, 8C 29–36.   [44] LI Ch 79, 8C 37–58.   [45] LI Ch 80, 9A 14–21.
[46] LI Ch 62, 7A 37–47.   [47] LI Ch 82, 9A 29–34.   [48] LI Ch 83, 9A 35–51.
[49] LI Ch 73, 8B 32–5.   [50] LI Ch 73, 8B 43–4.   [51] LI Ch 72, 8B 6–30.
[52] LI Ch 66, 7C 14–17.   [53] LI Ch 69, 8A 10–24.
[54] Exceptionally three-quarters: LI Ch 79, 8C 50–1.
[55] LI Ch 45, 5B 26–30; a majority of three-quarters was required to overturn a prior decision: LI Ch 42, 5A 36–41.   [56] LI Ch 69, 8A 10–24.

(c) It was for the *duumviri* to procure the necessary decisions of the council, which they and the other magistrates, the aediles and the quaestors, then executed. But their functions went further than this. The aediles[57] were responsible for the supply of corn, for the state of the baths and drains, and for quiet and good order in the city, They supervised the temples, places of worship, and the market, and they controlled weights and measures. They exercised jurisdiction in minor matters and could impose fines and exact security for their payment. The quaestors managed the city's moneys. They guarded and managed the treasury, effected authorized disbursements, as for games or religious purposes, and collected any arrears.[58]

We do not have the chapter on the competence and tasks of the *duumviri*, but we have seen that they summoned the meetings of the citizens and convened the town council, that they presented the right number of candidates for election and had to charge the town council with numerous tasks. Either of the *duumviri*, as the highest power in the city, could, with minor limitations, obstruct any proposal of his colleague or lower officials and take over any matter, even if it fell within the competence of the aediles or quaestors. By reason of their position, the *duumviri*, like the consuls in the city of Rome, were, so to speak, plenipotentiaries. Two of the roles expressly reserved to them deserve to be described in a little more detail.

(1) As was noted above, the Roman state got by, until well into imperial times, without much in the way of a bureaucracy. The staff of the provincial cities themselves, on which much of the administration devolved, was likewise quite modest. Like the state itself, the cities had their business done by private citizens, individuals, or groups. Tax farming is a well-known instance: *publicani* leased the taxing power from the state, paying a lump sum for the right to collect and keep any taxes due to the state. Tax farming was the principal feature of economic management throughout the ancient world, and the wide extent to which it was used by the Romans is demonstrated by a bronze tablet found in Southern Portugal, known as the Mining Ordinance of Vipasca.[59] The fragment provides for the administrators of the mine to lease out the trades of auctioneers, bath-house managers, cobblers, barbers, fullers, and schoolteachers. So it is clear that the state claimed all kinds of trading activity as its own. We do not know whether Irni went as far as this, but the *Lex Irnitana* certainly obliged the *duumviri* to lease out the collection of *vectigalia et ultro tributa*—taxes and other tributes—as well as anything else that should be leased out—*sive quid aliut ... locari oportebit*—and required them to publish, *in tabulas communes*, where all could read them, all such contracts and the price paid.[60] Elsewhere the law strictly forbids magistrates, their sons and grandchildren, their brothers,

---

[57] LI Ch 19, 3A 5–16.   [58] LI Ch 20, 3A 28–30.
[59] CIL 2 788 no 5181; Bruns, *Fontes* 289 no 112; FIRA vol I 502 no 105.
[60] LI Ch 63, 7B 3–13.

fathers and grandfathers to act as tax-farmers or to take any part in a tax-farming partnership, and anyone who infringed this provision was liable to be prosecuted by any citizen and held liable to the city for double his interest in the matter.[61] The drawbacks of the tax-farming system were plainly well-known to the legislator.

(2) The other competence of the *duumviri* which calls for attention is their jurisdiction, from which, indeed, they took their title—in full *duumviri qui iure dicundo praesunt* or *duumviri iure dicundo* for short. The jurisdiction accorded to them by city law was purely civil: criminal jurisdiction was reserved to the governor. Civil jurisdiction, the true hallmark of city autonomy, takes up nine chapters (84–92) of the *Lex Irnitana*, more than any other area of administration, and its 217 lines occupy four of the 30 columns of the law.[62] These chapters are devoted exclusively to the constitution and procedure of the court. As to the substantive law to be applied, there was a brief global reference to the Roman *ius civile*,[63] which was naturally applicable to the citizens and inhabitants of Latin *municipia*. As to civil procedure, by contrast, the basic Roman principles were simply taken for granted.

The structure of the chapters is self-explanatory and the sequence of the essential rules is quite clear.

Chapter 84 deals with the attribution and definition of jurisdiction itself.[64] The jurisdiction accorded to the *duumviri* is substantively extensive, but limited in amount. Extensive though the jurisdiction *ratione materiae* is, the law does make some exceptions: some are defined in abstract terms, some named individually, while some are subject to the proviso that the parties may agree to have the matter treated locally. The financial limit to the jurisdiction was surprisingly low, and it was absolute, not subject to waiver by the parties: complaints worth more than a thousand sesterces were always reserved to the governor. Let us take an example. Claims based on agency (mandatum) were removed from the jurisdiction of the *duumviri* because of the very serious consequences of the *infamia* which affected the defendant if he was held liable. If the claim was for 1,200 sesterces, the *duumvir* could not hear it since it was over the financial limit, but even if it was for 800 sesterces he still could not hear it, since claims based on mandate fell outside his jurisdiction. In the latter case, however, unlike the former, the parties could agree that he should hear it—such is the fine tuning of the jurisdictional rules, contained in a single sentence, grammatically taut but so complex that for years important aspects of the rule were misunderstood by modern scholars.

The following chapter (85) of the law obliges the *duumvir* to publish and abide by the jurisdictional edict of the governor, a sort of register of writs listing all the kinds of claims which could be heard; the edict had to be posted publicly

[61] LI Ch J, 5C 10–18. [62] LI Ch 84, 9A 51 to Ch 92, 10B 51.
[63] LI Ch 93, 10B 52 to 10C 4. [64] JG Wolf, '*Iurisdictio Irnitana*' (2000) 66 SDHI 29–61.

for the greater part of every day in a manner visible to all[65]—a provision which assumes that literacy was widespread.

In the next section[66] we find rules on the preparation and publication of the list of judges, the selection of the particular judge, and his nomination by the magistrate. Among his many other achievements, Peter Birks was one of the first to appreciate the fundamental significance of these provisions.[67] The structure of Roman adjudication and courts strikes the modern observer as very strange. The procedure was divided into two parts, separated in both time and place: an introductory proceeding before the magistrate, in Irni the *duumvir*, was followed by another before the *iudex*, a private citizen nominated by the magistrate and instructed to hear the case and pronounce judgment. The issue between the parties was identified by the magistrate after hearing the plaintiff's demand and the defendant's reply, and it was communicated to the *iudex* who was bound to proceed and give judgment in accordance with the magistrate's instruction. The first stage of the proceedings was concluded by the nomination of the *iudex* and the magistrate's instruction to him. It is the way the *iudex* was chosen which is of present interest to us.

If the parties in Irni were able to agree that a particular citizen should judge the case, the *duumvir* was bound to appoint him as *iudex*, and the person agreed on by the parties could excuse himself only on grounds of illness or age. If the parties could not agree on a nominee, there ensued a complex procedure of resort to the list of potential judges.

Chapter 86 of the law obliged the *duumviri* in their first five days in office to draw up a list of judges and to display this list *in tabulis scripta*, legibly written on wooden tablets, *aput tribunal suum*, outside the court. The number of judges on the list, some of whom must be councillors and some not, was determined by the governor. Like the councillors the judges freely chosen must be free-born citizens at least 25 years old, possessed of at least 5,000 sesterces, and thought by the *duumviri* to be suitable for a judicial function. Finally the candidates were to be placed in three *curiae*, ideally of equal strength.

If the parties could not agree on a particular judge, the judge would be selected from the list in accordance with the procedure which is laid down in chapter 87. Each party could eliminate one of the *curiae*, the claimant choosing first, thereby reducing the choice for the defendant to two: the judge had to come from the sole remaining *curia*. The selection of the eventual *iudex* followed the same pattern, with the parties taking it in turn to eliminate names until only one was left, who was then nominated by the magistrate. Here too the law determined who should start. If there was an odd number of candidates, the claimant started but if the number was even, the defendant started. This provision ensured that in all cases the defendant had the final choice since, at the end, when there were

---

[65] LI Ch 85, 9B 28–42.   [66] LI Ch 86, 9B 42 to Ch 89, 10A 25.
[67] P Birks, 'New Light on the Roman Legal System: The Appointment of Judges' [1988] CLJ 36–60.

only two candidates to choose between, he decided which of them should judge the matter. This was a minor benefit to the defendant who could not avoid the lawsuit.

After this report on the *Lex Irnitana*, let me attempt briefly to sum up the way in which the city laws contributed to the Romanization of Spain.

III

1. One objection must be dealt with first. We have the law, but do we know whether it was implemented and applied? After all, implementation and application of such detailed and demanding provisions, especially in conjunction with mandatory Roman private law, must have called for a highly developed legal system at this early stage. In order to answer the question we must distinguish between the constitutional law of the city and the private law applicable between citizens.

For the city constitution we can find the answer in the *Lex Irnitana* itself. In the first place, it provides for a significant monetary sanction if any of its provisions is ignored or its measures obstructed, for example, if the elected magistrate refuses to take the oath of office properly or at all[68] or seeks to affect or obstruct the electoral committees.[69] But, in addition, in chapter 96, its final chapter, the *Lex Irnitana* provides for an enormous fine, no less than 100,000 sesterces, to be imposed on anyone who deliberately evades or infringes the law. Like any other fine, it can be claimed by any citizen on behalf of the city. Such sanctions make it clear that the constitution of the city was in fact applied and fully implemented.

But the answer must be different when we turn to the application of Roman private law. It is true that the *Lex Irnitana* expressly obliges the citizens of Irni to fashion and manage their legal relationships according to the Roman *ius civile*,[70] and requires the *duumviri* to publish and follow the edict of the governor listing all the available claims, a sort of a register of writs.[71] It is also clear that Roman jurisdiction and procedure were introduced forthwith and that the citizens could claim their rights only before the Roman court of the *duumvir*. Yet it is difficult to believe that, however docile they might be, the Iberian citizens of Irni overnight abandoned their traditional ways and followed the new law, which must have seemed very strange, in view of the power it gave the *paterfamilias*, in view of its layers of succession rights, of its neighbourhood law, or even of the rights of the buyer of defective goods. It must have taken many years, a generation or so, perhaps more, before people actually regulated their daily affairs in accordance

---

[68] LI Ch 26, 3B 49–52.   [69] LM Ch 58, Col II 66 to Col III 5.
[70] LI Ch 93, 10B 52 to 10C 4.   [71] LI Ch 85, 9B 28–42.

with this law. But the fact that the Code which the Visigoths promulgated in AD 506 for the Roman inhabitants of their empire was based on imperial constitutions and juristic writings of the second and third centuries[72] shows that, in the long run, it did irradiate life in Spain, and doubtless in Irni as well.

2. But the city laws did more to Romanize Spain than merely introduce and implement a Roman constitution for the community as well as the Roman private law which was surely more important for daily life. These are the objective indicia of the transformation, but what was of lasting significance was what people subjectively learned from their experience of them.

This is a matter for thoughtful speculation rather than for drawing conclusions from what is probable or even possible. We know the aims which the introduction of the city laws and the granting of *civitas Latina* were intended to achieve, and we can assume that efforts were made to achieve them, but we need to know to what extent the efforts were actually successful. In Irni itself there is no evidence of this, and elsewhere there are only inscriptions testifying to the careers of officials in the hierarchy. Subject to this reservation, however, we can ask what the people expected, gained, and retained from the new legal order.[73]

First there would be independence and personal responsibility in the forming of their legal relationships. The freedom of contracting inherent in the *ius civile* ensured and promoted responsible independence—as we have seen, the law let the parties themselves choose the judge who would resolve their disputes.

Related to this sense of individual responsibility is the sense of solidarity, in that the individual was responsible for the community which guaranteed his personal power of self-determination. The city law provides us with many examples, especially the way people participated in the administration of their community. This they might do by serving on the town council as a *decurio*, or as a *duumvir*, an aedile, or a quaestor in office for a year, or as a candidate in the list of judges or as a nominated judge, or perhaps even as an ambassador sent by the town council[74] to the governor of the province or to the Emperor in Rome. Another citizen might act as a sworn supervisor (*custos*) of the election of magistrates or, last but not least, as a prosecutor in respect of fines due to the city. The fact that a citizen might be compelled to serve as magistrate, judge, or ambassador merely underlines his duties to the community.

Again, the people would inevitably realize that the law laid down particular procedures for every event of legal relevance in the life of the community. One need only think of the election of magistrates in the *comitia*: the proclamation of candidature, the publication of the list of candidates, the enforced nomination of

---

[72] On the *Lex Romana Visigothorum* see L Wenger, *Die Quellen des römischen Rechts* (1953) 555 ff; HF Jolowicz and B Nicholas, *Historical Introduction to the Study of Roman Law* (3rd edn, 1972) 466–7.

[73] On what follows see F Wieacker, *Voraussetzungen europäischer Rechtskultur* (1985) 20 = F Wieacker, 'Foundations of European Legal Culture' (translated and annotated by E Bodenheimer) (1990) 38 Am J Comp L 19.   [74] LI Ch 45, 5B 10–45.

candidates whenever necessary, the summoning of the electors, the role of the presiding officer, the details regarding the election, the counting of the votes right up to the publication of the outcome. There was no detail which the *Lex Irnitana* left unregulated. Or one might adduce the procedure which I have described for choosing a judge from the lists.

3. The procedural rules of the *Lex Irnitana* are highly legalistic, and such legalism was characteristic of Roman law as a whole, not just of the law of procedure. It is the product of dissociating law from the values and aims of those living in society, the isolation of the rules of law from purely social rules sanctioned by moral codes, ethics, usage, or convention. This differentiation permits the rules of law to reign supreme, and law becomes autonomous, not part of generally accepted social morality or revealed in sacred texts, as in Jewry and Islam. To state the matter more clearly: the 'exclusive superiority of the rules of law' entails the resolution of disputes and conflicts arising from social relationships by means of a general legal rule, recognized as valid and independent of values or aims external to it, be they social, moral, or political.

The final question is how this remarkable peculiarity of Roman law was made known to its new subjects, such as the citizens of Irni. How could they come to appreciate the autonomous nature of the legal system which was now their own? Perhaps its recognition and acceptance in Irni and elsewhere in Spain were promoted by consciousness of the benefits of the new legal order, in that the exclusive superiority of legal rules involved the juridification of social relations and thereby liberated social conflicts from emotion, self-interest, and prejudice. It also sidestepped the capricious use of irrational modes of proof and law-finding and rationalized the resolution of conflicts in a manner which better secured the rights of the citizen. For the Romans, whose jurists had created this law, it was the basis of the civilization which, following Virgil, they were to bring to the subject peoples once peace was achieved in an effort to make them in their own image. It is hard to say how far they succeeded and so we must leave aside the question whether the Iberians and Celts in Spain ever became, as Claudius had alleged of the people in Gaul, the equals of the Romans *moribus et artibus*. Only one thing is sure: learning Latin was almost the most useful thing they could do.

24

Absent Parties and Bloody-Minded Judges

*Ernest Metzger**

Teachers of Roman law in Britain often ask their new students on arrival to write an essay on the liability of Roman judges. I wrote one for Peter, but it was not a success. I will try again. What I give below is nothing like the traditional exegesis I attempted before. I use instead a method of argument I could not have appreciated with my first effort, but that with Peter's help I now value very much.

Modern romanists sometimes use classification as a tool for making sense of their evidence: they presume that a rule occupies a certain place in the development of the law because it is classified in such-and-such a way. To outsiders this may seem obviously back-to-front, but as a historical method it is respected, and even romanists with no sympathy for Savigny and his successors may silently assume that there is an inherent order in the rules they study,[1] and that a rule's place in the overall order is a useful and important piece of historical evidence. Those who knew Peter through his work on taxonomy might expect him to be one of this number, but in fact he does not belong at all. The same person who wanted the law to develop on clear lines knew perfectly well that it tended not to do so. Of course, Roman-law rules do have intrinsic qualities that help to reveal their development, but human actors are evident everywhere, if one takes the time to consider the rules from their point of view. They leave 'footprints' on the rules and on the texts that transmit them, and to spot the footprint and describe the human actor who produced it is, at once, an act of imagination and interpretation.[2] The human actors in Roman litigation leave very deep footprints on the rules and the texts, and Peter made their footprints a favourite object of study from the very start. In 1969, when he wrote on the use of formulae and their

* Douglas Professor of Civil Law, University of Glasgow.

[1] See S Vogenauer, 'An Empire of Light? Learning and Lawmaking in the History of German Law' (2005) 64 CLJ 481, 499; F Wieacker, *A History of Private Law in Europe* (translated by T Weir, 1995) 293–4, 296–7; M Reimann, 'Nineteenth Century German Legal Science' (1990) 31 Boston College Law Review 837, 854–5.

[2] See E Metzger, '*Quare?* Argument in David Daube, After Karl Popper' in E Metzger (ed), *Law for All Times: Essays in Memory of David Daube* [= 2 Roman Legal Tradition] (2004) 27, and especially 50–8.

introduction into litigation, the general view was that, from the late republic onwards, civil procedure had become less formal, but that it had developed in this direction in a 'piecemeal fashion' for reasons that were hard to explain. Peter pointed out that there were significant players in the story—advocates—for whom the categories 'formal' and 'informal' were relatively unimportant compared to gaining victory for their clients. The presence of these advocates and their particular mind-set, he argued, helped to explain the piecemeal nature of the reform.[3] A second example: in 1976, he argued that the edict *Ne quid infamandi causa fiat*[4] was about to be introduced when Seneca presented an imaginary *controversia* that seemed, in the opinion of some scholars, to assume that the edict already existed.[5] It is not an easy job to discover the state of the law from imaginary speeches (and some would probably say it should not be attempted at all with this material[6]), but Peter was able to build a remarkable argument largely from the tenor and emphasis of the speeches. Reconstructing a plaintiff's charge from a defendant's response was of course child's play: Peter also indicated places where a defendant would not have failed to show restraint but none the less did, thus revealing a charge *not* brought against him; where a plaintiff would never have passed up an argument, had it been known; and where a defendant would not have fired over his opponent's head. Here again, Peter found a way into the meaning of the material by considering first how we would expect the advocates to behave. A third example: in 1994, he discussed how chapter two of the lex Aquilia fell out of use, arguing that Gaius' explanation (the availability of the action on mandate) could not be right, since an advocate would continue to covet the advantages of the delictual action whenever they offered themselves. This led him to reconsider what prompted the enactment of chapter two in the first place: he concluded that chapter two was killed off by events, not by new rules.[7]

These are typical examples. What Peter is doing in each example is appealing to the reader's own knowledge and experience. He is saying to the reader: if you accept for the sake of argument that the players in these lawsuits acted on these motives, you will discover that you are reading exactly the text you would expect to read. He addressed the reader in just this way when he wrote on the liability of Roman judges, my subject here.[8] His argument was that judges typically gave no reasons for their judgments, and though the argument was

---

[3] P Birks, 'From *Legis Actio* to *Formula*' (1969) 4 Irish Jurist (ns) 356, 363–7. Peter's view was quickly cited with approval in HF Jolowicz and B Nicholas, *Historical Introduction to the Study of Roman Law* (3rd edn, 1972) 224–5.

[4] O Lenel, *Das Edictum Perpetuum* (3rd edn, 1927) s 193.

[5] Seneca, *Controversiae* 10.1; P Birks, '*Infamandi causa facta* in Disguise?' in *Essays in Honour of Ben Beinart* (1978) 1.83–104, and again briefly, in 'Harassment and Hubris. The Right to an Equality of Respect' (1997) 32 Irish Jurist 1, 12–13.

[6] JA Crook, *Legal Advocacy in the Roman World* (1995) 163–7.

[7] P Birks, 'Wrongful Loss by Co–Promisees' (1994) 22 Index 181, 181–2.

[8] P Birks, 'A New Argument for a Narrow View of *litem suam facere*' (1984) 52 Tijdschrift voor Rechtsgeschiedenis 373, 381–3.

supported by evidence, his first appeal was to the proposition that judges would not willingly give weapons to their opponents. In similar fashion, I begin with the players and leave the evidence to the end.[9]

1. Serious Misbehaviour by the Judge

In the Roman formulary procedure, the magistrate composed a statement of the issues and charged the judge to decide the lawsuit according to that statement in a so-called 'formula'. In doing so the magistrate set clear boundaries to the conduct of the trial, and it would not be difficult for the judge to stay within the boundaries. The formula stated precisely the conditions for condemnation, so that if a judge, for example, got his sums wrong[10] or revisited a fact he was instructed to accept as given,[11] the error would be obvious to all. But careful instructions do not cure everything. What if a judge decides not to sit? What if he decides to sit when he is not supposed to? This is a special category of misconduct, and it is hard to put right. A judge who acts in this way is not ignoring this or that instruction, but in a sense flouting all of the rules—substantive, procedural, administrative—at the same time.[12] The problem is not special to Roman law. In the modern law, an ordinary appeal does not readily cure this kind of misconduct, because by its nature the misconduct creates delay and expense before an appeal can even be taken.[13] More generally, an appeal is a clumsy way to treat a complaint that is directed not against a particular error by the judge, but against the way the judge is performing the duties of his office over a span of time. In short, it is difficult to frame 'the judge is bloody-minded' as a point of appeal, and an impatient litigant may instead

---

[9] The following was not available to me at the time of writing: R Scevola, *La responsabilità del iudex privatus* (2004).

[10] G.4.52: *Debet autem iudex attendere ut, cum certae pecuniae condemnatio posita sit, neque maioris neque minoris summa posita condemnet; alioquin litem suam facit. Item si taxatio posita sit, ne pluris condemnet quam taxatum sit; alias enim similiter litem suam facit.* Similarly, when a plaintiff has claimed too high a sum in the *intentio* of the formula, the judge is not free simply to ignore the overclaim and award a lesser amount: G.4.53–53a. Compare the later procedure: D.49.8.1.1, Macer 2 *de appellationibus*.

[11] On formulae with a fiction, directing the judge to accept a fact as true, see G.4.34–8 (eg the judge could not ignore the direction *si civis romanus esset* (G.4.37) and absolve a defendant because the plaintiff was a peregrine). Similarly, a plaintiff could elicit an admission from the defendant by *interrogatio in iure* that he (the defendant) was in some respect the proper party to be sued; this bound the judge: M Kaser and K Hackl, *Das römische Zivilprozessrecht* (2nd edn, 1996) 251–3. In contrast, facts set forth in the *demonstratio* of the formula were not necessarily 'established' for trial: G.4.58.   [12] See the quotation from *Roche v Evaporated Milk Ass'n* in n 14 below.

[13] Even an interlocutory appeal: see *In Re Hood* No 05–60470 (US Ct of Apps (5th Cir), 21 June 2005) (unpublished). In this unremarkable mandamus action, the district judge had denied the defendant's motion for summary judgment, but seven months later had still not entered an appealable order on the motion. The plaintiff petitioned the court of appeals for mandamus; the defendant, wishing to appeal the denial of summary judgment but unable to do so, did not oppose the petition. The court of appeals found mandamus to be justified.

need a special remedy, typically mandamus or prohibition, an order to the judge to get on with it, or to stop doing what he is doing.[14] Remedies like these, however, presume a hierarchy of judicial authority that the classical law did not have, and we find instead that the Romans responded to problems like these by threatening the judge with personal liability in a wholly separate action. This is where the counterparts to mandamus and prohibition may be found.

Generally speaking, a judge became personally liable[15] if he committed certain basic procedural errors.[16] Possibly none of these errors was too difficult for him to avoid,[17] but there were nevertheless specific events that he negotiated at his peril. One of these events is *adjournment*. On its face, the act of 'adjourning wrongly' or 'failing to adjourn' is too innocent to justify holding a judge personally liable, but if we bear in mind that adjournment (self-evidently) affects when a judge sits, then we can understand why a Roman judge had to pay attention to adjournment: the rules of adjournment told the judge when he should or should not sit, and if he followed these rules under threat of personal liability, then they will have accomplished the same results as mandamus and prohibition accomplish in the modern law. Thus a Roman judge who adjourns without returning puts any potential judgment in jeopardy, and the rules of adjournment may have encouraged him to finish the job in the same way that the threat of a writ of mandamus would.[18] So also with the writ of prohibition: there

---

[14] 'The traditional use of [the extraordinary writs of mandamus and prohibition] in aid of appellate jurisdiction both at common law and in the federal courts has been to confine an inferior court to a lawful exercise of its prescribed jurisdiction or to compel it to exercise its authority when it is its duty to do so.' *Roche v Evaporated Milk Ass'n* 319 US 21, 26 (1943). Until 1996, writs of mandamus and prohibition in the United States courts of appeals were directed against the lower court judge *as respondent*. (Notes of Advisory Committee on Rules, 1996 Amendment to Federal Rule of Appellate Procedure 21.) In England and Wales, these remedies are now subsumed under judicial review (CPR 54.2). In the United States, they are undifferentiated in the enabling legislation (All Writs Act, 28 USC § 1651) but distinct remedies in court practice (Federal Rules of Appellate Procedure 21; Rules of the Supreme Court of the United States 20(3)). In Scotland, a litigant who waits on a Sheriff to act will tend either to weather the delay, or to wait for judgment and then appeal, or to write a plaintive letter to the Sheriff Principal.

[15] The judge was famously liable under the edict (see Lenel, *Edictum Perpetuum* (n 4) s 59, but positioned with some hesitation), but also by statute, perhaps specifically the *lex Iulia de iudiciis privatis* (see *lex Irnitana* c 91, tab 10B, l 15, and n 45 below).

[16] See, most recently, OF Robinson, 'Justinian and the Compilers' View of the *iudex qui litem suam fecerit*' in H–G Knothe and J Kohler (eds), *Status Familiae: Festschrift für Andreas Wacke zum 65 Geburtstag* (2001) 389; 'The "iudex qui litem suam fecerit" Explained' (1999) 116 ZSS 195. Other literature is cited in Metzger, *A New Outline of the Roman Civil Trial* (1998) 152–3. Opinion has turned very much against the kind of view taken by Kelly, that the *substance* of the judge's decision came under review, a view that takes as its point of departure the reference to 'licet per imprudentiam' in D.50.13.6, Gaius 3 *rerum cottidianarum*, D.44.7.5.4, Gaius 3 *aureorum*, and Institutes 4.5 pr: JM Kelly, *Roman Litigation* (1966) 102–17. Some modern opinion nevertheless accepts liability for acts other than basic procedural breaches, eg an intentionally wrong judgment: DN MacCormick, 'Iudex qui litem suam facit' 1977 Acta Juridica 149, 155–7; Birks, 'A New Argument' (n 8) 383–587.

[17] 'Any reasonable judge, even a beginner, could avoid such lapses.' Birks, 'A New Argument' (n 8) 384.

[18] If the act of adjourning properly required the judge to return on another day, then a 'failure to adjourn' would include a failure to return, and a rule that imposed liability for failure to adjourn

are situations in which a Roman judge must adjourn whether he wishes to or not, and this is transparently an 'injunction not to sit'.

In the classical sources there is one outstanding example of the second kind. When a party is *absent for a good reason*, the law appears to have made a special effort to force the judge to adjourn and thus enjoin him from sitting. To us, this is a familiar rule of due process. In Roman law, the rule has always been discernible in the classical sources, though it is only recently that new evidence has brought to light what is very nearly a statement of the rule itself: in the principal text below, chapter 91 of the *lex Irnitana*, absent parties are protected by means of mandatory adjournments. Unfortunately, the point is easily missed, because adjournment is not our own instrument of choice for enforcing rules of due process. We are apt to take 'adjournment' at face value and read the *lex Irnitana* to mean simply 'the judge shall adjourn in just the right way'. But the drafter has left a different footprint: he wanted the judge to hear both sides of the case, and he has highlighted the rules of adjournment so that this basic principle of fairness will be observed.[19]

2. Sitting When a Party is Absent

The Roman formulary procedure usually allowed both sides to be heard before a decision was taken, and this was true of both phases of the lawsuit.[20] For the trial phase, it was not a hard-and-fast rule: a party was given the opportunity to be

would be helping to ensure that judgment was given. On the possibility that the particular form of adjournment discusssed below included an obligation to return, see Metzger, *New Outline* (n 16) 137–9, 147–8; D Mantovani, 'La "diei diffissio" nella "lex Irnitana"' in *Iuris Vincula: Studi in onore di Mario Talamanca* (2001) 242–3; JG Wolf, '*Diem diffindere*: Die Vertagung im Urteils-termin nach der *Lex Irnitana*' in P McKechnie (ed), *Thinking Like a Lawyer* (2002) 28, 37–8. However, one crucial piece of evidence on this point must be re-examined: P Ant 22 (*recto*): see CH Roberts, *The Antinoopolis Papyrus* (1950) vol 1, no 22; Metzger, *New Outline* (n 16) ch 11 (with literature); and most recently, Mantovani, 'La "diei diffissio" nella "lex Irnitana"' 254–9. Since I first wrote about this text, I have edited the *verso* of the same parchment, and found it to have been unreliably edited by the same person who edited the *recto*: see E Metzger, 'A Fragment of Ulpian on *intertium* and *acceptilatio*' 2006 SDHI (forthcoming). But this text aside, it is self-evident that a judge who adjourns and never returns puts the judgment in jeopardy: see D.50.5.13 pr, 2–3, Ulpian 23 *ad edictum*.

[19] I should make clear at the outset that this essay does not argue that the rules of adjournment are concerned *solely* with protecting absent parties. It happens that the events which force judges to adjourn appear to be the kinds of events which also force parties to be absent: see n 40 below and accompanying text. But this could easily be due to the accidental survival of certain texts, and there is in fact one text, P Ant 22 (n 18), which suggests that a mandatory adjournment might take place in utterly different circumstances.

[20] A Wacke, '*Audiatur et altera pars*. Zum rechtlichen Gehörs im römischen Zivil- und Strafprozeß' in MJ Schermaier and Z Végh (eds), *Ars Boni et Aequi: Festschrift für Wolfgang Waldstein zum 65 Geburtstag* (1993) 378; Kaser and Hackl, *Das römische Zivilprozessrecht* (n 11) 359. See also the more general treatments in J Kelly, 'Audi alteram partem' (1964) 9 Natural Law Forum 103; D Asser, 'Audi et alteram partem: A Limit to Judicial Activity' in ADE Lewis and DJ Ibbetson (eds), *The Roman Law Tradition* (1994) 209. No Roman text expresses it as a

present at trial, but it was up to him to use that opportunity.[21] Admittedly the
sources for this are few; this may be because the formulary procedure found a
way to ensure that (1) the defendant was present at *litis contestatio,* and (2) the
trial phase began immediately afterwards.[22] Thus the presence of the (willing[23])
defendant at the beginning of trial could virtually be taken for granted. However,
if there was an interruption and a time was set for reconvening, a party might not
appear at the appointed time (it is in the nature of things that whatever provokes
the absence is often unforeseen when the first proceeding adjourns[24]). Or, a party
might appear at the appointed time, but leave before judgment was given. In
either case an absent party risks having a judgment ordered against him. This is
where the law steps in to protect the absent party. If he has a good reason for
being absent, then the trial must be adjourned, and any judgment ordered in his
absence will be a nullity.[25]

'principle', but it is sometimes expressed indirectly (Kelly cites D.48.8.2, Ulpian 1 *de adulteriis*, as a
rare example), and of course it was silently observed in many rules of procedure (we think of the
various events *in iure* that require the cooperation of the parties: Wacke, 'Audiatur et altera pars'
378). There are also instances in which the idea is ignored: E Metzger, 'Roman Judges, Case Law,
and Principles of Procedure' (2004) 22 Law and History Review 243, 263 n 97).

[21] H Apelt, *Die Urteilsnichtigkeit im römischen Prozeß* (1936); Wacke, 'Audiatur et altera pars'
(n 20) 378, 397; on the lack of an explicit statement of the 'opportunity' idea, see especially 397–8.
Some express the view that both parties must be present at a trial in order to give the judge the most
vivid impression of the case. See Kaser and Hackl, *Das römische Zivilprozessrecht* (n 11) 359. But the
desire to preserve vivid impressions is probably a nineteenth century preoccupation, projected onto
Roman sources: Metzger, 'Roman Judges' (n 20) 265–70. On the other hand, whether the Romans
observed the idea out of a desire to give the judge all pertinent information, or a desire to be fair, is
debatable: Kelly, 'Audi alteram partem' (n 20) 105–7.

[22] See E Metzger, *Roman Litigation* (2005) 114–22. This is a summary of my examination of the
lex Irnitana, particularly chs 90–2, which reveal in unmatched detail how parties are brought
together for *litis contestatio* and trial in a *iudicia legitima.* See also Apelt, *Die Urteilsnichtigkeit* (n 21)
73: 'Gewiß kann kein judicium privatum der klassischen Zeit ohne Anwesenheit beider Parteien
begründet werden. Selbst wenn der Prozeß durch einen cognitor geführt werden soll, ist zur
Bestellung dieses Vertreters ein Gegenübertreten der Parteien erforderlich, und wer für den
Abwesenden als procurator auftreten will, muß diesem die Parteirolle abnehmen.'

[23] There must have been defendants, perhaps many, who were indifferent about appearing at
trial because the only defences they could offer were those they presented to the magistrate to
oppose the granting of the formula. For all practical purposes these defendants would have lost their
case at stage one, would have no hope of resisting a judgment against them, and would have no
appetite for going through the motions of a trial. The existence of such defendants is all the more
reason why we would expect the Roman rules on absences from trial to be framed in terms of
'opportunity to be present', and not absence alone.

[24] See Metzger, *New Outline* (n 16) 145; text accompanying nn 59–60 below.

[25] D Medicus, 'Zur Urteilsberichtigung in der actio iudicati des Formularprozesses' (1964) 81
ZSS 233, 275 and n 169; Apelt, *Die Urteilsnichtigkeit* (n 21) 74–5; Kaser and Hackl, *Das römische
Zivilprozessrecht* (n 11) 374. In the translation accompanying this text, I have given 'definite and
legitimate' for *sonticus.* This follows the suggestion of the Twelve Tables' most recent editors, who
have reconstructed XII Tab 2.2 partly on the basis of the quoted passage: M Crawford (ed), *Roman
Statutes* (London) 623. One wonders nevertheless if there can be any real difference, in its
application, between this and, eg, my 'serious' (Metzger, *New Outline* (n 16) 93), Wacke's
'schwerwiegend' (Wacke, 'Audiatur et altera pars' (n 20) 381 n 59), or Mantovani's 'vera'
(Mantovani, 'La "diei diffissio" nella "lex Irnitana"' (n 18) 248).

D.42.1.60, Julian 5 *digestorum*. Quaesitum est, cum alter ex litigatoribus febricitans discessisset et iudex absente eo pronuntiasset, an iure videretur pronuntiasse. Respondit: morbus sonticus etiam invitis litigatoribus ac iudice diem differt. Sonticus autem existimandus est, qui cuiusque rei agendae impedimento est. Litiganti porro quid magis impedimento est, quam motus corporis contra naturam, quem febrem appellant? Igitur si rei iudicandae tempore alter ex litigatoribus febrem habuit, res non videtur iudicata. Potest tamen dici esse aliquam et febrium differentiam: nam si quis sanus alias ac robustus tempore iudicandi levissima febre correptus fuerit, aut si quis tam veterem quartanam habeat ut in ea omnibus negotiis superesse soleat, poterit dici morbum sonticum non habere.

It was asked whether judgment is deemed to have been lawfully given when either of the litigants left in a fever and the judge gave judgment in his absence. The answer was that a definite and legitimate illness effects an adjournment, even if the litigants and judge are unwilling. It is, moreover, regarded as 'definite and legitimate' if it hinders the transaction of any business. And what hinders a litigant more than the aberrant shaking of the body called fever? So if either of the litigants takes a fever at the time the matter is adjudged, the matter is not regarded as adjudged. Even fevers, however, can be distinguished one from another: so if a person who is otherwise well and strong is hit with a fairly light fever at the time of judging, or if he suffers the kind of chronic quartan fever that he can usually surmount in all his affairs, one could say he does not have a 'definite and legitimate illness'.

In spite of some interpolation[26] the meaning of the text is clear.[27] A judge can give judgment in the absence of either party, but in some circumstances he should not, and when those circumstances arise, they effect an automatic adjournment. We are told specifically that there is an automatic adjournment

---

[26] The *Index Interpolationum* records Mommsen's suggestion: *respondit* interpolated for *respondi* (see Mommsen and Krueger's Digest, at 42.1.60; cf *quaesitum est ... respondit* at D.14.4.12, Julian 12 *digestorum,* unamended). On my reading, Julian's own views begin further on, with *Potest tamen dici* ('but let me point out ...'); on this reading he has cited the unnamed jurist as a lead-in to his own views on the nuance of 'fever'. Also, the *Index Interpolationum* restores *diem differt* to *diem diffindit* (the more usual term); this is possible but perhaps unnecessary: see Metzger, *New Outline* (n 16) 139; cf Mantovani, 'La "diei diffissio" nella "lex Irnitana"' (n 18) 250–1 and n 103. The most suspect part of the fragment is *sonticus autem ... appellant*. As I discuss immediately below, Julian is not giving an opinion on when, generally speaking, *morbus sonticus* forces an adjournment, but on when one particular kind of illness-episode does so. This is therefore emphatically not the place to discuss what 'morbus sonticus' means: the example assumes that *morbus sonticus* is a valid excuse, the only question being whether the excuse remains valid in this kind of case. It is true that Beseler omits much more than this as interpolation: not only *sonticus autem ... appellant*, but *Igitur ... iudicata*. G von Beseler, *Beiträge zur Kritik der römischen Rechtsquellen* vol 4 (1920) 206. He omits the whole of the latter sentence, however, because he sees what he believes is a sure sign of interpolation: '*igitur* vorgestellt': G von Beseler, 'Romanistische Studien' (1930) 10 Tijdschrift voor Rechtsgeschiedenis 161, 169. But this means that the opening question *an iure videretur pronuntiasse* is never answered. If we ignore the two interpolated sentences, we might expect the text originally to have read: ' ... diem differt. Si igitur rei iudicandae ...', with *igitur* after *si* (as in D.41.4.7.7, Julian 44 *digestorum*). Even if *igitur* was moved in the editing, it is the right word and should be retained. Two pieces of evidence, discovered since Beseler wrote, confirm that a 'failure to adjourn' sometimes leads to 'no judgment'. See n 41 below.

[27] Medicus, 'Urteilsberichtigung' (n 25) 275 n 169: 'sachlich unverdächtig'.

when a party leaves mid-trial in a fever. If the judge gives judgment none the less, the judgment is of no effect.[28]

Must the judge adjourn whenever a litigant is seriously ill, or only when the litigant's serious illness suddenly manifests itself mid-trial? Some read Julian as supporting only the latter,[29] but here we should take our lead from Daube: Julian is unlikely to be citing another jurist unless there is 'some element of special interest',[30] and if there is already a recognized rule on mid-trial illnesses, there is no element of special interest. If we assume, however, that any serious illness justifies an absence,[31] it becomes a nice question whether a litigant who leaves mid-trial should be treated in the same way as one who never appeared at all. And we notice that Julian answers with a general rule that is somewhat broader than the question put to him: *morbus sonticus etiam invitis litigatoribus ac iudice diem differt.* If (as it appears) the gist of his answer is 'the general rule stands', then Julian has indeed given us the general rule, one that has apparently not changed since the Twelve Tables. Ulpian says:[32]

D.2.11.2.3, Ulpian 74 *ad edictum.* Et ideo etiam lex duodecim tabularum, si iudex vel alteruter ex litigatoribus morbo sontico impediatur, iubet diem iudicii esse diffissum.

And so even the law of the Twelve Tables demands that the day of trial be postponed if the judge or either of the litigants is hindered by a definite and legitimate illness.

[28] Of course to say that a judgment is of no effect is a shorthand for saying that that judgment has no force in specific circumstances where other judgments do have force, eg appeal, contempt proceedings, *actio iudicati, revocatio in duplum.* See A Steinwenter, *Studien zum römischen Versäumnisverfahren* (1914) 66–8; Apelt, *Die Urteilsnichtigkeit* (n 21) 71–7; Kaser and Hackl, *Das römische Zivilprozessrecht* (n 11) 375–6. Virtually all of the sources on absence of parties and nullity of judgment are concerned with *cognitio* and not the formulary procedure (on D.42.1.47 pr, Paul 5 *sententiarum* (= PS 5.5a.5a) see Apelt, *Die Urteilsnichtigkeit* (n 21) 72–3; on D.5.1.75, Julian 36 *digestorum*, see Steinwenter, *Studien* 66, 67 and n 2). Hence the importance of Julian in D.42.1.60 for establishing the relationship between nullity of judgment and the judge's liability in the classical law. One also wonders whether there are clues on liability in D.5.1.46, Paul 2 *quaestionum*: *Iudex datus in eodem officio permanet, licet furere coeperit, qui recte ab initio iudex addictus est. Sed iudicandi necessitatem morbus sonticus remittit. Ergo mutari debet.* One inference is that on these facts alone the judge would not be liable for failure to give judgment; another, that his replacement must be ordered first (see D.5.1.18 pr, Ulpian 23 *ad edictum*). Siems believes that this text of Paul contradicts the rule that mandates adjournment (not *mutatio iudicis*) when the judge is sick. H Siems, 'Bemerkungen zu sunnis und morbus sonticus' (1986) 103 ZSS 409, 419. But there is no inconsistency: the mandatory adjournment relieves the judge of his duty to give judgment for a time, but nothing in the text of Julian prevents the judge from returning to give judgment later, or not, as his health permits.

[29] Medicus, 'Urteilsberichtigung' (n 25) 275; Apelt, *Die Urteilsnichtigkeit* (n 21) 75.

[30] D Daube, 'Turpitude in Digest 12.5.5' in RS Bagnall and WV Harris (eds), *Studies in Roman Law in Memory of A. Arthur Schiller* (1986) 33–4 = D Cohen and D Simon (eds), *David Daube Collected Studies in Roman Law* (1991) 1403–4.

[31] As in the case of an appearance *in iure*: D.2.11.2.3, Ulpian 74 *ad edictum*.

[32] The quoted statement, apparently dealing with appearances before judges, falls in the middle of a discussion of appearances *in iure*, and specifically just after a reference to appearances *in iure* missed on account of illness (see O Lenel, *Palingenesia Iuris Civilis* (1889) vol 2 855 (Ulpian, fragment 1653)). Could the quoted statement also be dealing with persons who fail to appear *in iure* (see O Behrends, *Das Zwölftafelprozess* (1974) 76)? The term 'diem diffindere' virtually always refers to adjournment of trial (see nn 36–9 below and accompanying text; cf Livy 9.38.15, on the

The cited rule of the Twelve Tables is reconstructed by its most recent editors more or less like this:[33]

XII Tab. 2.2. Morbus sonticus aut status dies cum hoste, quid eorum fuit, iudici arbitrove reove is dies diffissus esto.

A definite and legitimate illness or a (trial) day set with a foreigner, whichever has happened, the trial day is to be postponed for the judge, arbiter, or litigant.

Julian has therefore given us one instance in which the classical law would not recognize a judgment that was given in a party's absence.[34] The rule he gives is one application of a wider rule that forced judges to adjourn when a party was absent on account of illness. Julian uses *diem differre* ('putting off the day') where the usual term is *diem diffindere* ('divide the day'), but the institution appears to be the same.[35]

The practice of adjourning by 'dividing the day' is reasonably well understood, particularly since the discovery of the *lex Irnitana* twenty years ago.[36] It is a form of adjournment used in the trial phase, in cases tried before a single judge,[37] and was one of the subjects of the emperor Augustus' procedural reforms in the *lex Iulia de iudiciis privatis*.[38] We refer to it as 'adjournment', though to accomplish it properly, the judge might also have been obliged to return at a later time.[39]

Morbus sonticus is an event that prevented parties from appearing and brought about an automatic adjournment: on this the sources are secure. But it may be

adjournment of a republican assembly) and this form of adjournment was not used in the later law: it would therefore be difficult to explain why the compilers showed an interest in preserving a reference to the oldest of Roman laws, only to alter the text with a term that is (1) inapplicable to postponements *in iure*, and (2) not even of their own time. Even Beseler found nothing more suspicious in this text than *et ideo* for *nam*: G von Beseler, [Miszellen] (1925) 45 ZSS 396, 458. See Mantovani, 'La "diei diffissio" nella "lex Irnitana"' (n 18) 252 n 106: 'Il richiamo alla norma decemvirale, all'evidenza, è effettuato per analogia, per mostrare cioè che anche le XII Tavole, in un caso analogo, giustificavano l'assenza determinata da motivi di salute.'

[33] *Roman Statutes* (n 25) 623. The translation follows the editors in taking *iudici arbitrove reove* to depend on *esto* (perhaps following Julian: *invitis litigatoribus ac iudice*), though equally probably these words could depend on *morbus sonticus*.

[34] The nuance of *morbus sonticus* is not relevant to this essay. For other sources on *morbus sonticus*, see C Lanza, 'Impedimenti del giudice' (1987) 90 Bullettino dell'Istituto di Diritto Romano 467, 467–99; Siems, 'Bemerkungen zu sunnis und morbus sonticus' (n 28).

[35] And the discrepancy may be due to interpolation: see n 26 above.

[36] The modern literature often refers to this institution as 'diffissio' or 'dierum diffissio', which is the form found in Aulus Gellius, *NA* 14.2.1. Perhaps this form should be avoided: in the cited text Gellius speaks of being advised on *dierum diffissionibus comperendinationibusque*, and one suspects that he invented 'diffissio' because he needed a substantive in order to use *-que* and produce 'comperendinationibusque', a word he clearly relishes. See Metzger, *New Outline* (n 16) 91–2. No other source uses 'diffissio' in this context; the legal sources use 'diem diffindere'.

[37] Metzger, *New Outline* (n 16) 94–5.

[38] Aulus Gellius, *NA* 14.2.1; *lex Irnitana*, c 91, tab 10B, l 15; D Johnston, 'Three Thoughts on Roman Private Law and the *lex Irnitana*' (1987) 77 JRS 62, 62–3.

[39] Metzger, *New Outline* (n 16) 137–41; Mantovani, 'La "diei diffissio" nella "lex Irnitana"' (n 18) 242–3.

possible to add other events that, like *morbus sonticus*, prevented parties from appearing. The *lex Coloniae Genetivae Iuliae* contains what appears to be a list of excuses for non-appearance, *morbus sonticus* among them.[40] The context in which these arise is not adjournment nor even private lawsuits, but some have suggested that the list is relevant to *diem diffindere*, and reveals either the original grounds allowed in the Twelve Tables, or a later extension of those grounds. Several of these grounds show (if we accept that they are relevant) that the law was sensitive to a party's other public commitments: *vadimonium, iudicium, magistratus potestasve populi Romani*. None of these events is perhaps as slippery for the judge to determine as *morbus sonticus*, but like *morbus sonticus*, they are the sorts of solid excuses which ought to stop proceedings and vitiate any judgment given in a party's absence.

3. *Lex Irnitana*, Chapter 91

The discovery of the *lex Irnitana* in 1981 brought to light new information on both judges' liability and adjournment.[41] The *lex Irnitana* is a first-century 'town charter' for a small town in southwestern Spain, and though it is not properly a Roman law for Roman citizens, it directs the residents of the town to use the civil procedure of Rome in local lawsuits. For us, this is where its value lies: even where it does not directly reproduce Roman rules of civil procedure, it refers to them indirectly, and this gives away some of their underlying features.

On the whole the provisions on the administration of justice are not difficult to read and understand, but adjournment by 'dividing the day' is treated in a certain part of the statute exceptionally marked by difficult syntax, abrupt insertions, and painstakingly careful legal terminology. The explanation for this change of style is in the text itself:[42] there are certain matters that the statute does

---

[40] *Lex Coloniae Genetivae*, tab c, col 2, ll 21–5, 32–5 (ch 95): *Roman Statutes* (n 25) 407. Also perhaps relevant is the similar list of grounds included in a soldier's oath and recited by Gellius, *NA* 16.4.3–4. For the literature see Metzger, *New Outline* (n 16) 97–100; Mantovani, 'La "diei diffissio" nella "lex Irnitana"' (n 18) 249 n 98.

[41] The main editions of the *lex Irnitana* are F Lamberti, *Tabulae Irnitanae: municipalità e 'ius Romanorum'* (1993); J González, 'A New Copy of the Flavian Municipal Law' (1986) 76 Journal of Roman Studies 147. There are in fact two principal sources on the subject of adjournment and judgment: the provision of the *lex Irnitana* discussed below, and P Ant 22 (*recto*), cited in n 18 above. The two sources recite remarkably similar language, and have been the subject of much discussion: A d'Ors, 'Litem suam facere' (1982) 48 SDHI 368, 377; I Cremades and J Paricio, 'La responsibilidad del juez en el derecho romano clasico' (1984) 54 Anuario de historia del derecho Español 179, 182; F de Martino, 'Litem suam facere' (1988) 91 Bullettino dell'Istituto di Diritto Romano 1, 17–20; F Lamberti, 'Riflessioni in tema di "litem suam facere"' (1990) 36 Labeo 218, 228–36; Mantovani, 'La "diei diffissio" nella "lex Irnitana"' (n 18) 254–9; C de Koninck, '*Iudex qui litem suam facere*. La responsabilité quasi-delictuelle du iudex privatus dans la procédure formulaire' in L de Ligt, J de Ruiter, E Slob, JM Tevel, M van de Vrugt, and LC Winkel (eds), *Viva Vox Iuris Romani: Essays in Honour of Johannes Emil Spruit* (2002) 82–3.

[42] Overviews of this part of the *lex Irnitana* are given in Metzger, *New Outline* (n 16) 13–16; Wolf, '*Diem diffindere*' (n 18) 22–6; Mantovani, 'La "diei diffissio" nella "lex Irnitana"' (n 18)

not deal with directly, and on which it refers the reader to other sources of law. This requires the text to include all manner of qualification. The relevant part dealing with adjournment and judgment is below:[43]

Lex Irni., c. 91, tab. 10B, ll 10–21. Itaque ... [12] diem diffindendi, iudicandi in foro [13] eius municipi aut ubi pacti erunt dum intra fines eius munici- [14] pi, utique ex isdem causis dies diffindatur diffissus sit, [15] utique si neque diffissum e lege neque iudicatum sit per quos di- [16] es quoque loco ex hac lege iudicari licebit oportebit iudici arbitrove [16] lis damni sit, utique si intra it tempus quod supra conprehensum [18] est iudicatum non sit, res in iudicio non sit, siremps lex ius causaque esto atque uti si praetor populi Romani inter cives Ro- [19] manos iudicari iussisset ibique de ea re iudicium fieri oporteret ex [20] quacumque lege rogatione quocumque [21] plebis scito iudicia privata in urbe Roma fieri oportebit. ...

Accordingly, for dividing the day, [and] for judging in the forum of the *municipium* or where they agree, so long as it is within the boundaries of the *municipium*, the law, right, and case shall be the same as if the *praetor* of the Roman people had ordered the matter adjudged between Roman citizens and it was proper for the trial to take place there in that matter, according to whatever law, *rogatio*, or plebiscite it is proper for private trials to take place in the city of Rome, so that the day may be divided or may have been divided for the same reasons [as would obtain in Rome[44]], [and] so that, if [the day] is not divided according to the statute[45] and the case is not adjudged during the days and in the place that adjudication is lawful and proper under this statute, the judge or arbiter shall face liability, and so that, if there is no judgment within the period of time indicated above,[46] the case shall not be *in iudicio*. ...

This passage is less opaque than it might seem on the first reading. The thrust of the passage is that, so far as adjournment and judgment are concerned, persons should act as if they were engaged in a *iudicium legitimum* in Rome. This much is straightforward. But local variations, even relatively trifling ones, are spelled out in the text, and this interrupts the general flow. So for instance because the little town of Irni, for which the statute was written, is not literally the 'Rome' of a *iudicium legitimum*, the drafter reminds the reader by various

216–34. Wolf's comments deserve special mention. Chapter 91 is divided into two halves which to some degree repeat one another. Wolf suggests that the second half can be interpreted as 'correcting' the first half by providing information specific to Irni that could not be conveyed by the kind of blanket reference to the practice at Rome contained in the first half. On this basis Wolf suggests persuasively that the two halves were not drafted at the same time. Wolf, '*Diem diffindere*' (n 18) 22–6. Compare the very different 'two versions' explanation of A d'Ors, 'Nuevos datos de la ley Irnitana sobre jurisdicción municipal' (1983) 49 SDHI 18, 40–4.

[43] The text of González, 'A New Copy of the Flavian Municipal Law' (n 41) 179.

[44] ibid 236.

[45] Possibly the *lex Iulia* alone (see n 38 above), or possibly *lex* generally, including the Twelve Tables: Mantovani, 'La "diei diffissio" nella "lex Irnitana"' (n 18) 245–8.

[46] This is a reference to an earlier part of the same chapter: tab 10A, l 53–tab 10B, l 3. There, the text points out that if judgment does not take place within the time period set down in the *lex Iulia de iudiciis privatis* and certain accompanying *senatus consulta*, the suit is no longer under the power of the judge. We know from Gaius (*Institutes* 4.104) that a *iudicium legitimum* expired if eighteen months passed without judgment; this was popularly called 'the death of the lawsuit' (*mors litis*).

means that he should substitute Irni for Rome (*iudicandi . . . municipi*, ll 12–14; *quoque loco*, l 16). There are similar accommodations to the local calendar (*per quos dies*, l 16).[47]

The drafter has adopted another practice that interrupts the general flow: instead of leaving the parties and judge either to learn Roman procedure or struggle in the dark, he includes several result clauses (ie 'following Roman procedure means *this*'). Here he selects certain matters from among the rules of Roman procedure and brings them to the attention of the parties and judge.[48] The matters the drafter selects for inclusion are presumably those he wants to ensure the locals do not miss. It is important for them to know that a judge who fails to give judgment will face an action (*iudici lis damni sit*), but that after eighteen months[49] the principal lawsuit dies and the matter is closed, judgment or no (ll 15–18). It is also important for them to know that *the judge must adjourn properly*, and that if he does not, he may become personally liable.

A reader who understands 'adjourn' to mean simply 'rise for the day' will find it anomalous that adjournment receives special mention in these result clauses. He will find it particularly anomalous to see [*non*] *diffissum* alongside [*non*] *iudicatum* (ll 15–17) as a basis for the judge's liability. But we know that some adjournments are mandatory, and that when a judge gives judgment notwithstanding a mandatory adjournment, *his judgment is a nullity*.[50] This is the state of affairs the *lex Irnitana* guards against. It directs the judge to adjourn when a *causa* arises (l 14); he is not free to continue sitting and to give judgment. If the judge does continue to sit (*si neque diffissum e lege*, l 15) and gives a specious judgment, then he will become liable (*iudici lis damni sit*, ll 16–17), unless he redeems himself by giving a proper judgment (*neque iudicatum sit*, l 15).[51]

Thus the judge who improperly continues to sit does not become liable on that fact alone. This is precisely what the realities of litigation require: the existence of a *causa* can be subtle, and a judge has no immediate way of knowing whether an absent party is absent for a good reason or not. We know from Julian that even a party who leaves mid-trial on account of illness is not necessarily excused, and there is considerable room in Julian's example for an honest judge simply to make a mistake. But since the judge's liability is conditioned on both 'non diffissum' and 'non iudicatum', an honest mistake can be put right by giving a proper judgment. Only the judge who *stands by* his specious judgment faces an action, and the *causa* which (it is claimed) ought to have divided the day becomes the subject of that action.[52] In the end, a judge will either give

---

[47] Wolf, '*Diem diffindere*' (n 18) 25; Mantovani, 'La "diei diffissio" nella "lex Irnitana"' (n 18) 230.

[48] My translation above puts all of these result clauses at the very end, to make this clear.

[49] See n 46.   [50] Above, nn 25–8 and accompanying text.

[51] For the sake of keeping this discussion within limits, I am omitting to discuss another aspect of *diem diffindere*: the case of a judge who leaves but does not return. See Metzger, *New Outline* (n 16) 137–9 and n 18 above. It is possible that this judge is also within the scope of the words *neque diffissum e lege* (l 15).   [52] Apparently a civil law action under the *lex Iulia*.

judgment, or be called to account by a party for not doing so, or hold out for eighteen months and obtain a kind of amnesty: this is what the drafter of the *lex Irnitana* brings to the attention of the locals.

This is one view of *diem diffindere* in the *lex Irnitana*: that there were reasons that prevented judges from sitting lawfully. The opposing view is that when a judge wished to adjourn, he needed to give a reason.[53] It is perfectly true, and is widely accepted, that the sources distinguish adjournments performed by judges and adjournments brought about automatically by events.[54] This does not mean, however, that both forms of adjournment were based on *causae*.

(1) There is a current of opinion[55] that holds that where *diem diffindere* appears in the double, present/perfect form (as in 1 14 quoted above), the present form expresses an adjournment ordered by a judge, while the perfect form expresses an 'automatic' adjournment, brought about by operation of law (as with *morbus sonticus*). Thus (on this view) when the *lex Irnitana* says *utique ex isdem causis dies diffindatur diffissus sit*, it is suggesting that judge-ordered adjournments, like automatic adjournments, were 'for cause'.[56] Yet in a passage of Gellius we have an example of a judge-ordered adjournment that, to all appearances, took place for no reason at all,[57] and we have no examples (so far as I am aware) of a judge voluntarily adjourning for a given cause.[58] I have suggested elsewhere that the double, present/perfect form of *diem diffindere* is not a technical distinction based on 'type of adjournment', but was prompted by

---

[53] See A Burdese [Recensiones Librorum] (1991) 57 SDHI 449, 451–2; G Zanon, 'De intertium dando' (1992) 58 SDHI 309, 317 n 38; Wolf, '*Diem diffindere*' (n 18) 31; Mantovani, 'La "diei diffissio" nella "lex Irnitana"' (n 18) 248 n 96. Recently, this view has found support in a supposed law requiring a judge to finish the case in one day; adjournment therefore would need justification. But as I discuss below, this is not a 'law' but a nineteenth-century *Märchen* with no support in the sources.

[54] See Mantovani, 'La "diei diffissio" nella "lex Irnitana"' (n 18) 250–1 (comparing D.42.1.60 with Gell *NA* 14.2.11).

[55] See Mantovani, 'La "diei diffissio" nella "lex Irnitana"' (n 18) 250; Zanon, 'De intertium dando' (n 53) 317 n 38; Burdese (n 53) 452; González, 'A New Copy of the Flavian Municipal Law' (n 41) 235.

[56] When Mantovani says that the *lex Irnitana* attests 'indirettamente' that judge-ordered adjournments were based on *causae*, I assume this is based on the observation that *ex isdem causis* precedes *diffindatur* as well as *diffissus* at 1 14: Mantovani, 'La "diei diffissio" nella "lex Irnitana"' (n 18) 248.

[57] Gell *NA* 14.2.11. Gellius relates that he was uncertain about the verdict he should reach in a case he was trying, and adjourned to seek the advice of a philosopher. Cf Wolf, '*Diem diffindere*' (n 18) 31–2, who suggests that 'uncertainty' was a ground for adjournment, citing also Cicero, *pro Caecina* 6 (a recuperatorial trial postponed because the judges were uncertain about the correct decision). Mantovani prefers the evidence of the *lex Irnitana*, which he believes indirectly (see n 56 above) attests that adjournments were based on particular causes. He also speculates that Gellius may have withheld from the reader the cause of his adjournment, and finally, that a judge-ordered adjournment, in the absence of specific grounds, might be given 'discrezionalmente', which seems to give the point away. Mantovani, 'La "diei diffissio" nella "lex Irnitana"' (n 18) 248 and n 96.

[58] The principal sources for *diem diffindere* are cited and discussed in Metzger, *New Outline* (n 16) 150–1. The sources tend to speak as if an event, not a judge, is the instrument of division.

careful drafting and the unpredictable nature of *causae*.[59] Some *causae* arise mid-trial (eg Julian's mid-trial fever; another court appointment[60]), and these would force the judge to divide the day on the spot. But other *causae*, for instance *morbus sonticus*, will simply prevent a party or the judge from ever turning up. In the latter case there can be no adjournment on the spot, but only a retrospective acknowledgement, at a later time, that the earlier proceeding never took place. The distinction between anticipated and unanticipated *causae* is unavoidable, and is adequate to explain why the drafter of the *lex Irnitana* would speak of adjournment in both the present and perfect tenses.[61] Hence the words *utique ex ... causis dies diffindatur diffissus sit* need not include judge-ordered adjournments. When the parties and judge wish to go home for the day, they do not need to give a reason.

(2) Some writers who hold that all adjournments are for cause are perhaps silently taking their cue from the 'liability clause' quoted above (c 91, tab 10B, ll 15–17). Immediately before the liability clause, the statute has directed adjournments to take place for cause. Then the liability clause declares that 'failure to adjourn' is a condition for liability (*neque diffissum e lege*). If a judge could adjourn without giving a reason, then (on this argument) he deprives the clause *neque diffissum e lege* of its force; therefore, the logic goes, he is allowed to adjourn only for certain permitted reasons. But the real effect of reading the liability clause this way is to forgive each and every 'unjustified adjournment' so long as judgment is given, and this makes one wonder why judge-ordered adjournments have to be justified in the first place. The act of giving judgment does indeed forgive a judge's failure to adjourn, but it does so only because the judge, having given a specious judgment instead of adjourning as he was supposed to, has not yet finished the job. These are the judges the 'liability clause' speaks of: only the most stubborn and defiant of them could, and should, face liability.

This would be nothing more than a disagreement about how Roman judges adjourned, but for the fact that the *lex Irnitana*, on the reading suggested here, is outstanding evidence that the Roman formulary procedure observed a basic principle of fairness and due process. When the *lex Irnitana* says (in paraphrase) 'the day shall be divided on the occasions named in the *lex Iulia*, and if it is not, the judge may be liable', it is expressing the principle of *audi et alteram partem* with exceptional clarity; it is expressing the principle for the classical law; and it is telling us that the principle was included in the emperor Augustus' great 'judicature act'. For the first time we have very nearly a statement of the principle itself, together with the rules on how and when the principle was enforced.

---

[59] Metzger, *New Outline* (n 16) 142–6.   [60] See n 40 above.
[61] This view should therefore be sharply distinguished from the view of Burdese and those who follow him: cf the treatment of this view in Mantovani, 'La "diei diffissio" nella "lex Irnitana"' (n 18) 250 n 100; Wolf, '*Diem diffindere*' (n 18) 28 n 54.

4. Due Process of Another Kind

Some have interpreted the rules of adjournment in the *lex Irnitana* to express an entirely different principle of due process. Under a supposed rule of the Twelve Tables, a trial could not last longer than one day. This served the 'principle of immediacy', a familiar principle of procedure in continental jurisprudence. A rule that serves the principle of immediacy is one that helps to put matters before the judge in the most direct manner possible, thus helping to ensure a more accurate judgment. Wolf is the most recent writer to bring the 'one-day rule' and *diem diffindere* together.[62] He argues that a judge must divide the day, or give judgment, before the end of the day was reached, or incur liability.[63] This explanation of adjournment rivals the explanation based on the principle of 'hearing both sides', and incidentally supports the idea of voluntary adjournment for cause.[64] It therefore needs discussion.

The one-day rule is not discussed in ancient sources but was first noticed only in the nineteenth century, when it was held up as a model of due process and good sense.[65] Its discoverer was Philip Eduard Huschke,[66] in one of his earliest publications, a commentary on Cicero's *pro Tullio*.[67] Cicero had referred to his opponent Quinctius' long-windedness, noting that at the previous session Quinctius had not brought his defence to a proper close, and had stopped speaking only because night-time had arrived.[68] Huschke set out to explain the words 'nox tibi finem dicendi fecit'. He believed he had found the right explanation in the Twelve Tables, specifically in a provision that described sunset as 'the latest time'. In the most recent edition of the Twelve Tables, this provision and those that immediately precede it read as follows:

XII Tab 1.6. Ubi pacunt, orato. 7. Ni pacunt, in comitio aut in foro ante meridem causam conici<un>to. *Comperoranto ambo praesentes. 8. Post meridiem praesenti litem addicito. 9. Si ambo praesentes, sol occasus suprema tempestas esto.

[62] Others: FL von Keller, *Der römische Civilprozess und die Actionen* (7th edn, 1883) 337 and n 779; M von Bethmann-Hollweg, *Der römische Civilprozeß* (1885) vol 2 591; J Crook, DEL Johnston, and P Stein, 'Intertiumjagd and the Lex Irnitana: A Colloquium' (1987) 70 Zeitschrift für Papyrologie und Epigraphik 173, 179 (P Birks).

[63] Wolf, '*Diem diffindere*' (n 18) 33–6.　　　[64] See n 53 above.

[65] I have written on other aspects of the supposed one-day rule at *New Outline* (n 16) 101–22 (ancient sources for the supposed rule), and 'Roman Judges' (n 20) 265–75 (the supposed rule in the context of German law reform). Here I write on the rule's origin.

[66] This is my best judgment: Huschke is the earliest source cited in Keller's textbook (F von Keller, *Der römische Civilprocess und die Actionen* (1852) 283–4); Huschke himself cites no modern authority; and if the rule had ever existed before Huschke, it would have deserved some mention in either Heffter or Dirksen, published immediately before Huschke: HE Dirksen, *Uebersicht der bisherigen Versuche zur Kritik und Herstellung des Textes der Zwölftafelfragmente* (1824); AW Heffter, *Institutionen des römischen und teutschen Civilprozesses* (1825).

[67] *M. Tullii Ciceronis orationis pro M. Tullio quae exstant cum commentariis et excursibus Ph. Eduardi Huschke* in IG Huschke (ed), *Analecta Litteraria* (1826) 106–7 (to Cicero, *pro Tullio* 6: 'finem dicendi').　　　[68] Cicero, *pro Tullio* 6.

6. He (the plaintiff) is to plead, where they agree. 7. If they do not agree, they are to present their case in the Comitium or the Forum before midday. They are to finish bringing action together, both present. 8. After midday he is to confirm the suit to the one present. 9. If both are present, sunset is to be the last time.

The editors persuasively suggest that table 1.6–7 describes the sequence of events in the ordinary case: when both parties appear, they present their arguments. Table 1.8 describes a different track, when one party does not appear. In that event judgment is given in favour of the party who is present. Table 1.9 recognizes that when both parties are present, they may have to wait for the magistrate until sunset, but proceedings will not take place after that time.[69] It is in this last provision that Huschke believed he had found a rule limiting trials to one day.

Huschke's argument was based on a text of table 1.7–9 drawn solely from Aulus Gellius, *Noctes Atticae* 17.2. This is the text[70] Huschke gives:

Ante meridiem causam conscito, quom perorant ambo praesentes: post meridiem praesenti stlitem addicito. Sol occasus suprema tempestas esto.

which he understands to mean something like the following:

[The *iudex*] shall entertain the suit before midday, at which time they shall plead their case, both parties being present: after midday he shall give judgment in favour of the one who is present. Sunset shall be the latest time.

Then follows Huschke's analysis. What we notice straight away is that he never properly interprets the text, but relies instead on a literary conceit.[71]

Note how the *decemviri* in their great wisdom were, for the most part, unwilling to allow a lawsuit to live longer than the day it began and, at the same time, in a rough approximation to nature, accommodated the progress of a suit to the course of the sun. As the sun first appeared, everyone would assemble; as it rose a little, they would briefly describe the controversy; as it surged towards midday, the suit warmed with speeches; as

---

[69] *Roman Statutes* (n 25) 594–6.
[70] The quoted text is not Dirksen's (then recently published; see n 66), but is taken from Gellius alone.
[71] Huschke's commentary in full, at 106–7, reads as follows: 'Nota est ex Gell. N.A. 17, 2. lex duodecim tabularum, dicens: *Ante meridiem causam conscito, quom perorant ambo praesentes: post meridiem praesenti stlitem addicito. Sol occasus suprema tempestas esto.* Quibus verbis lex non praetorem, quod plerique omnes autumant, sed iudicem alloquitur.... Vides igitur decemviros, sapientissimos viros, plerumque <107> noluisse litem ei diei, qua coepta erat, supervivere, simulque naturam quodammodo imitantes, litis processum solis cursui accommodasse; quo excoriente conveniebatur, paulum se tollente, caussa breviter demonstrabatur, ad meridiem assurgente, lis peroratione fervescebat, inclinante, iudex secum reputabat, occidente, litem addicebat. Ceterum etiam si vigentior esset lis, quam quae eodem die mori posset, certe cum sole interim occidere et sopiri iusserunt: *Sol occasus suprema tempestas esto,* quae verba etiam referuntur a Festo v. Supremum, Varrone de L.L. 5, 2 et 6, 3. Macrob. Saturn. 1, 3. Censorin. de die nat. c. ult. Plin. H.N. 7, 60. Haec igitur lex etiam Ciceronis aevo observatur; certe lex Plaetoria (Varr. l.c. Censorin. l.c.) eam non abrogavit, sed adiecit tantum, ut id quoque tempus esset supremum, quo praetor in comitio supremam pronuntiasset.... Denique animadvertendum est h.l. quod ait Cicero *nox tibi finem dicendum fecit.*'

it descended, the judge would think the matter over; as it set, he gave judgment. However, even if the suit had too much life in it to die on the same day, the *decemviri* demanded at the very least that the case should, for the time being, set with the sun, and be put to rest: *Sol occasus suprema tempestas esto*.

From this strange beginning an entire tradition grew: subsequent writers, interpreting the rule more strictly than Huschke had done, discovered in Roman procedure an affection for short, uninterrupted, and 'vivid' trials, followed immediately by judgment.[72] What is most important to note, for our purposes, is that the tradition begins with one very shaky assumption. The 'sunset rule' probably had nothing to do with *iudices* and trials at all, but referred instead to the first phase of a lawsuit, before the magistrate.[73] To his credit Huschke considers the issue, though he comes down on the side of *iudices*. Yet the words *stlitem addicito* (better: *litem addicito*) are against him because, as the most recent editors of the Twelve Tables say, *addicere*, at least in the later law, is 'quintessentially the act of a magistrate', and the only hallmark of the trial phase here, *lis*, is ambiguous at best.[74] These words immediately precede the sunset rule, and the better view, as just discussed, is that from *post meridiem* onwards the text is speaking of parties who await the *magistrate*: if after midday only one party appears, victory goes to him; if both appear, they may have to wait until sunset for the magistrate.[75]

Also against Huschke is the *lex Plaetoria* (post 241 BC) which, among other things, attempted to regulate precisely how long the *praetor urbanus* should administer justice on a given day.[76]

Praetor urbanus qui nunc est quique posthac factus erit duo lictores apud se habeto iusque per supremam ad solem occasum usque inter cives dicito.

Whoever is now urban praetor and whoever shall be appointed hereafter is to have two lictors with him and he is to have jurisdiction between citizens through the last hour right down to sunset.

This is one reconstruction of a difficult text. From Varro (*De lingua latina* 6.5) we understand that the *lex Plaetoria* 'redefined' the *suprema tempestas* of the Twelve Tables by allowing the *praetor urbanus* to declare a certain time as 'suprema' on a particular day.[77] The quoted text, reconstructed from Censorinus

---

[72] Metzger, 'Roman Judges' (n 20) 265–9.

[73] cf Metzger, *New Outline* (n 16) 112–17. Formerly I followed Kaser and assumed that the sunset rule was speaking about trials. I had not yet taken in the commentary on the Twelve Tables and *lex Plaetoria* provided by *Roman Statutes* (n 25), then only just published.

[74] *Roman Statutes* (n 25) 594. Cf M Kaser, 'Prätor und Judex im römischen Zivilprozess' (1964) 32 Tijdschrift voor Rechtsgeschiedenis 329, 352: 'Das Problem löst sich, wenn man annimt, daß bei Ausbleiben einer Partei vor dem Judex die Entscheidung vor den Prätor kam, der nun das litem addicere vornahm'.   [75] Above, text accompanying n 69.

[76] *Roman Statutes* (n 25) no 44 (text and translation of JA Crook). Cf JA Crook, 'Lex Plaetoria (FIRA no 3)' (1984) 62 Athenaeum (ns) 586.

[77] Crook suggests that by allowing the *praetor* to declare *suprema* himself, the *lex Plaetoria* solved the problem of determining the close of the judicial day when sunset was not easily observable. 'Lex Plaetoria' (n 76) 592.

(*De die natali* 24), would permit the *praetor* to administer justice up to sunset, presumably because 'suprema' is now redefined and would fall, or could fall, before sunset. Others offer different reconstructions, and in fact an earlier one by the same editor had a very different emphasis.[78] But whichever is best, we know that the *lex Plaetoria* had effected a change in what the *praetor* was required to do under the sunset rule of table 1.9, and this suggests he, and not the judge, was the subject of that rule. This is not the only possible explanation; one could argue that the sunset rule applied to *praetor* and judge alike. But the fact remains that the sunset rule is directly attested for the *praetor* in texts on the *lex Plaetoria*, whereas one must strain very hard to see even a trace of the rule applied to a judge.[79]

In short, the evidence is poor that a one-day rule ever existed, and there is therefore no reason to believe that the practice of dividing the day served such a rule.

5. Conclusion

The Romans sought to give both sides an opportunity to be heard at trial. The means they used to achieve this were peculiarly their own: they used rules of adjournment to force the judge to rise; enforcement was not by writ or appeal, but by a separate action; and the onus of looking after the interests of the absent party fell heavily on the judge. In cases like this, where the ends are achieved by unexpected means, it is easy to miss what the text is trying to say. We are liable to pass over the real ends and supply instead the ends we more habitually associate with the means. We can avoid this by looking out for apparent anomalies in the

---

[78] ibid: ... *iusque ad supremam aut solem occasum usque inter cives dicito*. This would have discouraged a *praetor* from administering justice beyond sunset.

[79] Metzger, 'Roman Judges' (n 20) 268–9. Wolf also disagrees with me on the *substance* of the sunset rule. I had argued that the rule prohibited proceedings from taking place at night (Metzger, *New Outline* (n 16) 112–18; expressing the same view is *Roman Statutes* (n 25) 596; G Pugliese, *Il processo formulare* (1963) vol 1 405; H Lévy-Bruhl, *Recherches sur les actions de la loi* (1960) 207; JA Crook [Book Reviews] (1998) 57 CLJ 413, 414). My argument was that the ancient authors who serve as sources for the rule speak of 'suprema tempestas' as a *time of day*, which is utterly different from the alternative meaning, *point of demarcation* or *instant*. On the understanding of these authors, table 1.9 was declaring sunsets (plural) as 'the latest time of day' for proceedings generally, rather than sunset (singular) as 'the latest instant' for particular proceedings on a particular day. In response, Wolf agreed that the sources for this provision of the Twelve Tables do speak of *suprema* as a time of day, but argued that sunset (like 'midday') is nevertheless a 'moment' (*Zeitpunkt*), and is not transformed into a 'period of time' (*Zeitabschnitt*) simply because certain ancient authors have chosen to discuss it that way: Wolf, 'Diem diffindere' (n 18) 34–6. I suspect this is a misunderstanding, caused by myself. In my discussion I had spoken of *Zeitpunkt* and *Tageszeit* as alternatives for *tempestas*. I did so because a German edition of the Twelve Tables had translated *tempestas* as *Zeitpunkt* (R Düll, *Das Zwölftafelgesetz* (1944) 27), and I regarded that as an inappropriate gloss ('point of demarcation' or 'instant', where the better meaning was 'time of day'). I now appreciate from Wolf's discussion that a *Zeitpunkt* may also be an English 'moment', which is to say a *Tageszeit* that is nevertheless not a *Zeitabschnitt*, but that was not meaning of *Zeitpunkt* I was after.

text, and then showing how the motives and the circumstances of the ancient actors explain why the text is expressed just so. Particularly in matters of litigation, the ancient actors did not behave so differently from the way they behave today, and they often leave footprints in the texts that are immediately familiar to us. If we have the imagination to see their footprints, we have interpreted the text. Peter taught me this.

25

'You Never Can Tell with Bees': Good Advice from Pooh for Students of the *Lex Aquilia*

*Arianna Pretto-Sakmann**

1. The Birksian Fauna

Animals of all shapes and sizes feature very prominently in Peter Birks's writing. Seemingly, his taxonomy of events—the well-known sequence of consent, wrongs, unjust enrichment, and miscellaneous others[1]—giving rise to restitutionary entitlements, could not do without analogies with all kinds of animals 'herbivores, carnivores, or eaters of other things'.[2] The difficulties in the characterization of certain causative events typically moved from some naturalistic inquiry as to whether, for example, a barnacle was a crustacean or a mollusc, and ended with a reminder that it was, 'from its larval stage', the former.[3] He invited his readers to persevere in legal taxonomy and warned against surrendering to its difficulties:

Few enough of us will ever have given much thought to the dugong. Those few who contemplated shrews will probably have fallen for their superficial resemblance to mice. Every one of us will have assumed, until instructed otherwise, that fishiness consisted in finny locomotion through an aquatic habitat. No sooner had one learned that the whale was more closely related to the shrew than to the trout, than one's notion of a mammal

*Associate-in-Law, Columbia Law School, New York; formerly Fellow and Tutor in Law, Brasenose College, Oxford. I would like to thank Alessandro Spina, formerly an MJur student at St Catherine's College, Oxford, and currently *dottorando di ricerca* at the University of Siena, Italy, for valuable discussion and for drawing my attention to the reform of the Italian law on apiaries.

[1] In support of the so-called multicausalist approach and against the quadrationist one, see eg P Birks 'Unjust Enrichment and Wrongful Enrichment' (2001) 79 Texas L Rev 1769.

[2] P Birks, 'Annual Miegunyah Lecture: Equity, Conscience, and Unjust Enrichment' (1999) 23 Melb UL Rev 1, 1.

[3] ibid 9.

was severely tested by Ornithorhynchus Anatinus, the egg-laying, milk-feeding, duck-billed platypus.[4]

The bewilderment of his audience, especially of those innocent supervisees who, being completely unfamiliar with the notion of the platypus, put their ignorance down to their not being native English speakers, would be brushed aside with the somewhat condescending remark that '[l]awyers understand that kind of dispute very well'.[5]

The same confidence led the former Regius Professor to experiment with more daring analogies. Having fully explored the taxonomical potential of 'labradors, dogs, and canines' as an illustration of the ascending scale of 'loan, contract, consent',[6] his scholarship began to feature a more diverse taxo-fauna comprising all orders of creatures, ranging from cetaceans to leeches. From the latter he derived the 'leech theory of the behaviour of proprietary rights in and through substitutions', for there is a certain right which, 'detached from the original *res*, will wait to sink its head in any passing substitute'.[7] However, it is widely believed that the epitome of this Darwinism for lawyers came with the study of *myrmecophaga tridactyla* and *phataginus tricuspis*, which showed how, respectively, the giant anteater and the tree pangolin could be at once terrestrial and insectivorous. This in turn showed—to him, at least, very clearly—how there was no logical opposition between the category of property and that of unjust enrichment.[8]

Animals were not confined to the taxonomy of restitutionary obligations. A cow called Buttercup was ever present in his teaching of Roman law, often as the subject of eloquent explanations, complete with gestures, of how a *vindicatio*, the prototype of a proprietary action, was brought. Standing on the podium in the Gulbenkian Theatre, where he lectured on Roman law to the under-graduates, he would punch the air with his fist and cry out 'This cow is mine!'.[9] Likewise, no advanced course on the Roman law of delict was complete without the sacrifice of a 'bleating' sheep being mentioned with affectionate respect.

Sometimes these animal associations would stretch even more widely: a draft chapter of this writer's doctoral dissertation came back annotated with a comment disapproving of one particular author as 'the killer whale', from which one 'may nonetheless leap Jonah-like to safety'. As a Director of Graduate Studies for Research, Birks described his keen interest in postgraduate matters as the 'clucking of an irritating hen worried for the chicks'. As a senior

---

[4] ibid 23.   [5] ibid 9.
[6] Birks, 'Unjust Enrichment and Wrongful Enrichment' (n 1) 1778–9.
[7] P Birks, 'Property, Unjust Enrichment, and Tracing' (2001) 54 CLP 231, 244.
[8] ibid 238–9.
[9] Buttercup, still present in P Birks, 'Personal Property: Proprietary Rights and Remedies' (2000) 11 King's College LJ 1, 6, was inexplicably replaced by a car, a note, and a picture in the recent P Birks, *Unjust Enrichment* (2nd edn, 2005) 64–5. It took three objects to match her powers of evocation.

colleague, he worried about newly elected fellows over-teaching under-graduates—the well-known Oxonian problem of teaching 'over stint'—lest they might come to behave like 'the pelican who in extremis will pluck the flesh of its own breast to feed its young'. Of course, he never followed that recommendation himself, for he was unfailingly—and at times overly—generous with his own time.

2. A Wealth of Wisdom in Bees

Amidst this abundance of animals, it is no surprise that Peter took on board my suggestion that an exploration of the wondrous world of bees might yield some interesting findings. After all, according to the *Encyclopaedia Britannica* of 1910, a wealth of wisdom is to be learnt from them:

[T]he members of [the bee commonwealth] are in all respects equally well endowed. They are in turn skilled scientists, architects, builders, artisans, labourers and even scavengers; but collectively they are the rulers on whom the colony depends for the wonderful condition of law and order which has made the bee-community a model of good government for all mankind. . . . All [the well-read and intelligent bee-keeper] needs is good bee weather and an apiary free from disease to make him appreciate bee-craft as one of the most remunerative of rural industries; affording a wholesome open-air life conducive to good health and yielding an abundance of contentment.[10]

The study of bee law did not disappoint. A meeting of the London Roman Law Group in March 2002 supplied the occasion to present some parallel but independent conclusions. Peter addressed the topic of 'Bees, Pearls, and Aqueducts: A Palingenetic Problem in Ulpian *18 ad edictum*', focusing on the rules concerning entitlement to sue under the *lex Aquilia*.[11] Under the title 'De Apibus Semper Dubitandum' ('you never can tell with bees'), I spoke of the need to make good the neglect of natural history when assessing the place of bees in the Roman law of property. The warning which I adopted as my title came from a pronouncement by Pu Ursus, the Latin *alter ego* of Winnie the Pooh in Lenard's translation of Milne's books. In one of his adventures, having planned to ascend to the top of a tree with a balloon (*cum folliculo*) to steal honey from a resident group of bees, Pu Ursus discusses with his friend Christophorus Robinus the idea of employing a green balloon, rather than a blue one, in the enterprise, so as to increase his chances of concealment. Bees would thus see him as an appendix to the green tree and accept his presence around them. Christopher Robin

---

[10] WB Carr, entry 'Bee', in *Encyclopaedia Britannica* (11th edn, 1910/11) vol 3 (1910), 635, 635–7. Cf Pliny the Elder, *Natural History* 11.59: 'Apes sunt et rusticae silvestresque, horridae aspectu, multo iracundiores, sed opere ac labore praestantes'.

[11] The contents of Peter's paper have not been used in this chapter.

expresses doubts as to whether some smart bee will not detect Pooh under the balloon:[12]

'Nonne te sub folliculo [apes] animadvertent?' rogavisti.
'Fortasse animadvertent me, fortasse autem minime,' dixit Winnie ille Pu.
'De apibus semper dubitandum est.' Ac paulisper meditatus subjunxit:
'Conabor nubelula parva et nigra videri. Id eos decipiet.'[13]

In deepening that preliminary study, this tribute to Peter looks at bees with Birksian, that is, dual curiosity: both for their own sake, out of genuine interest in them, and as tools for deepening our understanding of the law.

3. Roman Bees: No Smoke without a Fire

Bees punctuate Roman law. They are discussed in conjunction with, and offer insights into, a number of important legal issues: the classification of the nature of animals into wild and tamed, the acquisition of the title of ownership in animals, and various Aquilian developments of relationships between neighbours. Some of these legal implications are described in a *locus classicus* by Celsus which presents a puzzling, at least at first sight, association between bees and fire:

Collatio 12.7.10, Ulpian 18 *ad edictum.* item Celsus libro XXVII Digestorum scribit: si cum apes meae ad tuas advolassent, tu eas exusseris, quosdam negare competere legis Aquiliae actionem, inter quos et Proculum, quasi apes dominii mei non fuerint. sed id falsum esse Celsus ait, cum apes revenire soleant et fructui mihi sint. sed Proculus eo movetur, quod nec mansuetae nec ita clausae fuerint. ipse autem Celsus ait nihil inter has et columbas interesse, quae, si manum refugiunt, domi tamen fugiunt.[14]

The translation by Bruce Frier reads as follows:[15]

Likewise Celsus, in the twenty-seventh book of his Digests, writes that if my bees fly over onto your (property) and you burn them up, some jurists deny that the action under the Lex Aquilia lies; among them is Proculus, on the theory that the bees are not my property. But Celsus says this is false, since the bees are accustomed to return and are a source of profit for me. But Proculus was swayed by the fact that they are neither

---

[12] AA Milne, *Winnie-the-Pooh* (1926) 11, translated into Latin by A Lenard with the title of AA Milnei, *Winnie Ille Pu* (1960) 6–7.

[13] 'Wouldn't they notice you underneath the balloon?', asked Christopher Robin. 'They might or they might not,' said Winnie-the-Pooh. 'You never can tell with bees.' He thought for a moment and said: 'I shall try to look like a small black cloud. That will deceive them.'

[14] *Collatio,* 12.7.10. Frier has suggested changes to the text which include the insertion of *aedes* after *tuas* (in BW Frier, 'Bees and Lawyers' (1982/3) 78 Classical Journal 105, 108) and the replacement of the final *fugiunt* with *remanent* (in BW Frier, 'Why Did the Jurists Change Roman Law? Bees and Lawyers Revisited' in *Omaggio a Peter Stein* (1994) 22 Index 135, 135).

[15] BW Frier, *A Casebook on the Roman Law of Delict* (1989) 110. The casebook specifies that the question in the text 'revolves around whether a beekeeper retains ownership of bees when they are not enclosed in a hive, but flying off in search of pollen'.

domesticated nor sufficiently enclosed. Still, Celsus himself says that there is no difference between them and doves, which, if they escape the hand, still fly home.

The text also survives in a well-known Digest excerpt from Ulpian. That the abbreviated text bears no trace of the controversy which the *Collatio* indicates had developed between Proculus and Celsus is, according to Frier, true to the compilers' aim of distilling classical juristic writings by eliminating antiquated controversies concerning long-settled legal rules:[16]

D.9.2.27.12, Ulpian 18 *ad edictum.* si cum apes meae ad tuas advolassent, tu eas exusseris, legis Aquiliae actionem competere Celsus ait.

As translated by Kolbert:[17]

If, when my bees had flown off to join yours, you burn them out, Celsus says the action on the *lex Aquilia* lies.

The modest claim of this essay is that a more attractive interpretation of these texts than has hitherto been achieved is possible if closer attention is paid to the behaviour of the bees featuring in them. We will therefore postpone the study of the two excerpts till after we have defined the place of bees and honey in history and examined important elements of the natural history of bees, to do, respectively, with their attitude to smoke and with their habit of swarming. That should facilitate the translation of the passages and spare us a few otherwise unavoidable errors.

4. Brief History of Bees and Honey

The main species of honey-bee, or *apis mellifera*, is widely distributed over the earth and was well known in the ancient world. The first honey-collecting scene, the illustration of a man extracting honey from a hive at the top of a tree, was painted on rock in eastern Spain around 6,000 BC.[18] Progress came when man supplied bees with appliances which helped them to store more surplus honey for him. However,

the character and work of the bees remain[ed] the same, and we can never describe them as really domesticated animals; they often, as beekeepers know to their cost, display independence of character; it has been truly said that 'Bees never do anything invariably'.[19]

The earliest certain evidence of bee-keeping and honey handling and packing was found in Egypt around 2,400 BC.[20] The use of hives of all shapes and

---

[16] Frier, 'Bees and Lawyers Revisited' (n 14 above) 137.
[17] In A Watson, T Mommsen, and P Krüger (eds), *The Digest of Justinian* (1985) vol I 284–5.
[18] E Crane, *Archeology of Beekeeping* (1983) 22.
[19] H Ransome, *The Sacred Bee* (1937) 21.   [20] Crane (n 18) 36.

materials is documented from Ancient Greece onwards, archaeological excavation yielding terracotta hives from the mid-fifteenth century BC.[21] In Roman times, hives made from logs, cork bark, wooden boards, woven wicker, fennel, dung, or bricks were described by Varro (116–28 BC), Virgil (70–19 BC), Columella (AD 1–68), Pliny the Elder (AD 23–79), Celsus (early second century AD), and the pseudo-Quintilian.[22] Virgil, who is said to have kept bees, praises them in his *Georgics* as endowed 'with a share of the divine intelligence' (*esse apibus partem divinae mentis*).[23]

In Roman Egypt, a recognized corporation of bee-keepers was probably in place in Ptolemaic times. A source of considerable profit to the government, the art of bee-keeping was protected from exactions and unnecessary interference. Papyri have been found bearing petitions of bee-keepers to the strategus of their town, lamenting, for instance, damage caused to their hives during night-raids.[24] Separate papyri distinguish the case of an impending loss of hives caused by the action of others from that of harm to the hives done though neglect, showing that loss was thought of as a serious matter which had been the subject of analysis.[25] Evidence suggests that after Diocletian bee-keeping was a guild activity.

The significance of honey in a pre-sugar society cannot be recaptured in our sugared one. Many a recipe in the Roman cookbook by Apicius,[26] whose name seems suddenly significant, made use of honey. In the classical world it was not uncommon for the corpse of a general dying on a distant battlefield to be preserved in a sealed coffin filled with honey till its return to his native land.[27]

Honey is not all that bees are good for.[28] Beeswax, secreted by worker honey-bees from wax glands on the underside of their abdomen, was used for countless ancient artefacts, many of which survive to this day thanks to the wax being inert and retaining its shape at most atmospheric temperatures.[29] Surrounded by a religious aura, bees used to be celebrated on Holy Saturday in the blessing of the taper (*In Sabbato Sancto: Benedictio Cerei*) sung by the Deacon to the paschal candle as he asperged it and inserted in it five grains

---

[21] ibid 45.   [22] ibid 52.

[23] Virgil, *Georgics* 4.219 ff. Cf Ransome (n 19) 19: 'Beekeepers feel that they belong to a fraternity which reckons Vergil among their number'.

[24] RD Sullivan and RA Coles (eds), P Oxy LXVII 4582 'Petition from Beekeepers' (14–27 September AD 16, published 2001, now in Sackler Library, Oxford) http://www.papyrology.ox.-ac.uk (accessed 31 December 2005).

[25] RD Sullivan, 'A Petition of Beekeepers at Oxyrhynchus' (1973) 10 Bulletin of the American Society of Papyrologists 5, 11–12.

[26] Apicius, *De Re Coquinaria* (*A Cookbook*). See eg *dulcia domestica* (home-made sweets, ibid 7.13.1), *ova sfongia ex lacte* (roughly, pancakes with milk, ibid 7.13.8), *tiropatinam* (a kind of soufflé, ibid 7.13.7).

[27] Crane (n 18) 240 reports Strabo as recounting that the body of Alexander the Great was placed in a golden coffin filled with white honey.

[28] According to recent data, about 60 per cent of all food consumed in America has a bee connection. Without bees, the country would lose about $20 billion in crops—almonds, citrus fruits, pears, cucumbers, and apples—from plants which are not self-pollinating: 'To Bee or Not to Bee' *The Economist*, 4 June 2005, 55.   [29] Crane (n 18) 240–6.

of incense in the shape of a cross. One of these so-called *exultet* songs, part of a missal used in the Cathedral of Exeter in the eleventh century, reads like an ode to the 'truly blessed and wonderful bee', maker of the taper, who surpasses all other creatures subject to man, 'for though it be small in body (*minima corporis paruitate*) and feeble in strength (*uiribus imbecillis*), it is strong in ability (*fortis ingenio*)'. The *exultet*, not unlike similar manuscripts found in Italian monasteries, ends with a daring analogy between the Virgin Mary and the bee, 'who produces posterity, rejoices in offspring, yet retains her virginity':[30]

O uere beata et mirabilis apis. O uere beata et mirabilis apis, cuius nec sexum masculi uiolant, fetus non quassant, nec filii destruunt castitatem. Sicut sancta concepit uirgo maria, uirgo peperit, et uirgo permansit.

The simile did not survive Vatican II, probably due to the perception of a certain pagan character inherent in all bee affairs.[31]

Leaving the production of honey and wax far behind, an aspect of the instinctive behaviour of bees may help to further electronic communication in the near future. The nectar-collecting bee zips back and forth to flower patches and, upon returning to the hive, transfers its takings to a stay-at-home bee, who stashes the nectar in a honeycomb. The forager decides whether its patch is worthwhile by the number of food-storer bees ready to take the nectar: the higher the number, the more successful the run it will have had. Successful patches are then signalled to fellow foragers through the famous waggle dance, whose length is in direct proportion to how profitable the patch is going to be. Mysteriously, the observation of this procedure has been found of help in solving the problem of the unpredictability of Internet traffic and of the changing levels of customer demand for access to certain websites, which requires Internet providers to allocate varying numbers of server computers to a particular application, just as bee colonies allocate varying numbers of foragers to each flower patch depending on its profitability.[32] A 'honey-bee algorithm' has been developed and is being tested.

5. Elements of Bees' Natural History

The socio-economic importance of bees, as described in the previous section, justifies the repeated attempts throughout history to establish control over these animals. In that process, the function of smoke and the mechanisms governing

[30] Tenth-century English *exultet*, in FE Warren (ed) *Leofric Missal* (1883) 97. The missal was used in Exeter Cathedral during the episcopate of its first bishop, AD 1050–72. I thank Professor Bernard Rudden for drawing my attention to this text. Some twenty illuminated manuscripts, known as the *Exultet* Rolls, also survive in the Italian monasteries of Capua, Gaeta, Montecassino, and Pisa: Crane (n 18) 53.
[31] Interestingly, the only mention of a bee from the blessing of the taper which survived in the Roman rite approved by the Council of Trent was the phrase, here omitted, 'apis mater eduxit' ([wax] brought forth by the mother bee).   [32] 'The Internest' *The Economist*, 17 April 2004, 86–7.

swarming are of the utmost importance. Each of these topics must be examined in turn.

5.1. Smoke

Modern bee-keeping benefits from having mastered the knowledge of smoke. It is deemed to be one of the greatest discoveries in bee-keeping that honey bees are subdued by smoke.[33] The need to subdue them arises when bees are bad-tempered—which they are apt to be if they are being robbed of their harvest, or if they are queenless, or during a period when food is short. At other times too they can become fractious unless they are handled quietly and with consideration.

The soothing effect is exploited by bee-keepers when extracting honey from hives, since bees are understandably reluctant to give it up. Nowadays smoke is produced artificially with the aid of smokers.[34] A puff or two of smoke at the entrance to a hive and a two-minute wait for it to take effect do the trick. Once the hive is opened, a further puff at the top will help to make the harvesting of the honey easier. The practice is to use only enough smoke to keep the bees from getting out of hand. Some strains are more docile than others but in all cases the colony undergoes a serious disruption when their honey is taken.[35]

The best smoke is cool smoke. The fuels that give the coolest smoke, and produce less of the undesirable tar which fouls the smoker, are dry decayed wood and stringy bark. When these cannot be obtained, old corduroy, cotton rag, old soft sacking, dried grass cuttings, and old hay are good substitutes. Corrugated paper has the disadvantage that it produces a considerable deposit. A little tobacco smoke can be effective in the case of minor inspections of the hives made without a veil, provided one is dealing with quiet bees.[36]

The soothing effect of smoke was well known to ancient beekeepers. Nearly a whole book in Columella's *De Re Rustica*, or *Agriculture*, is devoted to bees, and within it is an agreeably detailed account of the use of smoke, both for cleaning the hives from the filth which has accumulated during the winter season—an operation ideally performed, we learn, during the forty-eight days which follow the March equinox[37]—and for removing the honey. For the removal, the morning should generally be chosen; for it is not advisable that the bees should be provoked when they are already exasperated by the midday heat (*neque enim convenit aestu medio exasperatas apes lacessi*). Smoke made from galbanum or from dried dung (*fumum ... factum galbano vel arido fimo*), mixed with live coals in an earthenware vessel, is applied to the hive. The smoke is blown towards the bees with a puff of breath. The bees, unable to endure the smell of burning, immediately move to the

---

[33] EB Wedmore, *A Manual of Bee-Keeping for English-Speaking Bee-Keepers* (3rd edn, 12th reprint, 1988) [853], [1571], [1573].   [34] ibid [857]–[860].
[35] ibid [854]–[856].   [36] ibid [857]–[860].
[37] Columella, *De Re Rustica* (*On Agriculture*) 9.14.1–2; cf 9.14.7.

front part of their abode and sometimes outside the porch:

talis olla cum est alveari obiecta, spiritu admoto fumus ad apes promovetur. quae confestim nidoris impatientes in priorem partem domicilii et interdum extra vestibulum se conferunt.[38]

Before the invention of smokers the making of the smoke required great care, since in the process one could cause a conflagration. There was a risk of smoking the bees to death, or of burning them up. Recurrent episodes of bee-burning described here and there in the law probably mean that an attempt at bee pacification has gone wrong, although it is not impossible that the burning-up could be deliberate—a lazy and wasteful way of getting at the honey. One interesting consequence is that honey had a special value when taken from the hive without the use of smoke, for it would then be obtained at greater risk from unpacified bees. This was the famous unsmoked (*akapniston*) honey, found in the country of the silver mines, near mount Hymettus, of which we hear in Strabo's *Geography*.[39]

Despite the examples of Columella and Strabo, however, it cannot be assumed that the effect of smoke was always understood. In the *Aeneid*, for example, irritated bees feature in the picture of the foundation of Rome. Dreadful wars loom, which will lead to the bloodthirsty battle scenes in the last book. In the moment of the final defeat of the Latins, as Aeneas and the Dardans drive forward to the walls of the city of King Latinus, the following allegory is offered:

> inclusas ut cum latebroso in pumice pastor
> vestigavit apes fumoque implevit amaro;
> illae intus trepidae rerum per cerea castra
> discurrunt magnisque acuunt stridoribus iras;
> volvitur ater odor tectis, tum murmure caeco
> intus saxa sonant, vacuasque it fumus ad auras.[40]

Which can be translated:

[A]s when a shepherd has tracked down bees within concealing rocks and has filled their space with bitter smoke, and the bees inside rush hither and thither through their wax fortress alarmed for their property and intensify their rage in buzzing, the black smell swirls to their roofs, the rocks amplify the blind murmur, and the smoke is carried off on the empty winds.[41]

Here the shepherd is after the honey in a wild hive on the rocks. Smoke can be used even in the open, to recover a swarm which has gone astray and to take it

---

[38] ibid 9.15.4–6.

[39] Strabo, *Geography* 9.1.23. Alongside especially good honey there was also particularly bad stuff, although not on smoke-related grounds. Pliny alludes to poisonous honey, which produced madness, found in the district of the Sanni in Pontus, as also in Persia and Mauretania (Pliny, *Natural History* 21.77). The people of these regions paid a wax tax to the Romans, but not a honey tax, on account of its poisonous qualities: Ransome (n 19) 86.

[40] Virgil, *Aeneid* 12.586–90.   [41] My translation, as agreed with Peter Birks.

484Arianna Pretto-Sakmann

back to the hive or apiary. Here the smoke alarms the bees and makes them *trepidae*, that is, 'restless, agitated, disturbed, alarmed'. *Rerum* is difficult.[42] It could allude to the bees' worry for their property, or their society. The soothing effect of the smoke is absent from the Latin text.[43] If Virgil really did keep bees, the image of the commotion produced by the smoke is inexplicable on other than poetic grounds. Natural history was probably sacrificed to literary effect.

5.2. Swarming

Bees are in the habit of coming and going to and from their hive. The Romans thought of them as endowed with an 'intent to return', or *animus revertendi*.[44] There is one qualification to this instinct for returning home. Bees lose their *animus revertendi* when they create new colonies by swarming. In spring, the rearing of young increases rapidly. Towards the summer, the colony is likely to rear drones (males) and several queens (females). When the new queens are nearly adult, the old queen leaves the hive in a swarm with half of the adult workers. A day or two before a swarm issues, scout bees fly off to locate a new nesting place, generally in the vicinity of the hive (20 to 100 feet away). If the scouts are satisfied, shortly afterwards a swarm will be found occupying the place. In the colony left in the hive, generally, only one new queen survives. When she is sufficiently developed, she flies out and mates with a dozen drones in the air, returns to the hive, and lays eggs for the colony to continue. By providing hives, the bee-keeper makes good the deficiency of nesting sites and tries to keep colonies together in an apiary, thus also managing to limit the loss of honey which would ensue if bees were left free to fly off.[45]

It is now time to revert to the law. Only one element is now missing before proceeding to the interpretation of the excerpts—a word on ownership.

6. Ownership in Bees

It is essential to establish who owns the bees in *Collatio* 12.7.10. The plaintiff is seeking to bring an action for wrongful loss (*damnum iniuria datum*) under chapter three of the *lex Aquilia*. To sue under the statute, the plaintiff must be

[42] cf Livy, *History* 5.11, 36.31: *trepidi rerum suarum*.
[43] Interestingly, the translation by John Dryden recovers that effect by playing down the commotion and speaking of bees who are 'disus'd to flight, and shoot their sleepy stings' as they try 'to shun the bitter fumes in vain'. Theodore C Williams's translation has the shepherd 'stir up the nested bees with plenteous fume'. His rendering of bees flying 'desperate round the waxen citadel' with 'buzzing fury' is more true to the text, though less to natural history.
[44] For the classification of animals, see below Section 6.1.
[45] Wedmore (n 33) [1075]–[1085]; Crane (n 18). A picturesque, if slightly less accurate, account of swarming is in Varro, *Rerum Rusticarum* (*On Agriculture*) 3.16.29–31. Especially entertaining is the remark that a swarm occurs when many young have been born and the bees want to send them out as a colony, 'just as the Sabines used to do frequently on account of the number of their children' (*ut olim crebro Sabini factitaverunt propter multitudinem liberorum*).

owner.[46] The defendant, with whom the early classical jurist Proculus sides, denies liability because the plaintiff did not own the bees at the time when they were killed. Celsus advocates the opposite solution: ownership in the bees is said to continue in the plaintiff. The strengths of the competing arguments can only be assessed by looking at the rules for establishing ownership.

6.1. Bees in the Classification of Animals

The classification of animals in Roman law contemplates at least two well-defined categories: that of wild or undomesticated animals (*animalia ferae naturae*), and that of tamed animals (*animalia mansuetae naturae*). Wildness (*feritas*) is a characteristic of the species and not of the individual animal.[47] A tamed lion is still an animal *ferae naturae* and the most savage of dogs is *mansuetae naturae*. Animals *ferae naturae* are *res nullius*, or nobody's thing, so long as they remain in their wild state. The owner of the land on which they are has no special title to them. Ownership in them can be acquired by taking (*occupatio*), provided that the taking is effective and leads to retention. Seizure appears to have been necessary. It is not certain that killing or trapping was enough to possess an animal. Severe wounding seems to have sufficed in the late Republic, but classical jurists insisted on seizing, for 'in a hunt much can go wrong'.[48]

Ownership lasted only so long as the animal was effectively held. In the event of escape, ownership is retained only if recapture is reasonably probable. Thus, an animal was held to have recovered its natural freedom when it was out of sight or when, though still in sight, it was difficult for the owner to reach it. If your lion jumps over your wall and wanders off, he becomes a *res nullius* again. Likewise, if my lion, imported from Africa for the gladiators' show in the arena, escapes while being off-loaded at the port of Ostia, and eats your slave, I am not responsible: he was mine for a time only and has now reverted to his natural state of liberty.[49] On the other hand, the animal was not lost so long as the owner was pursuing him. The rule seems to have been along the following lines: if the probability of recovering the animal was no greater than that of catching a different one, that would amount to having lost the first animal.

---

[46] D.9.2.11.6, Ulpian 18 *ad edictum*. Actions *in factum* relax this requirement, but still at least require that someone own the object when the loss is inflicted; eg D.41.1.55, Proculus 2 *epistularum* (action *in factum* when a wild boar is released from a hunter's net): Frier, 'Bees and Lawyers Revisited' (n 14) 146 n 10.

[47] A point made by many, eg B Nicholas, *An Introduction to Roman Law* (1962) 131; JAC Thomas, *Textbook of Roman Law* (1976) 167; G McLeod, 'Wild and Tame Animals in Roman Law' in P Birks (ed), *New Perspectives in the Roman Law of Property—Essays for Barry Nicholas* (1989) 169, 171. [48] Gaius, *Institutes* 2.66–9; Justinian, *Institutes* 2.1.12–13.

[49] It is not certain whether a return to natural freedom involved a reversion to the animal's natural habitat, which central Italy could hardly be said to be for lions.

Bees were a special case. Gaius observes that, 'as regards animals as habitually haunt some place (*quae ex consuetudine abire et redire solent*), for instance pigeons and bees, . . . there is a traditional rule (*talem habemus regulam traditam*) that they cease to be ours and belong to the first taker, if they have ceased to have the disposition to return. They are considered to have ceased to have this disposition when they have abandoned the habit of returning (*revertendi autem animum videntur desinere habere cum revertendi consuetudinem deseruerint*)'.[50] The debate about whether it was the intent to return, rather than the habit, which mattered, is rather academic and need not worry us: the two concepts merge, intent being determined and judged on the basis of behaviour.[51]

Justinian says of bees:

If they swarm in your tree they are not yours till you manage to contain them in a hive (*antequam a te alveo includantur*). They are in the same position as birds nesting in the same tree. If another person hives them he becomes their owner. Also, anyone can take their honey (*favos . . . quilibet eximere potest*), if they have made any. If you see someone coming on to your land, you can obviously stop him before anything is done.[52] A swarm which leaves your hive remains yours while it is within your sight and can be followed without difficulty (*examen, quod ex alveo tuo evolaverit, eo usque tuum esse intellegitur, donec in conspectu tuo est nec difficilis eius persecutio est*). Otherwise someone else can take it.

However, Justinian confirms the existence of the special rule for animals which come and go.[53] Bees, therefore, are owned even when at liberty so long as they have the *animus revertendi*. When they lose it and clear off, they reassert their original condition as *res nullius*. Under that rule a swarm would become ownerless.

6.2. The Metaphor of Taming

The observation that the wild character of bees was qualified by a will to return to their original location led to them being assimilated to doves. Another way of expressing this aspect of the life of the bee, whereby it goes to and fro, was by employing the metaphor of taming. Daube thought of doves as '*mansuetae*, tamed, ie, induced to lay aside their wildness'.[54] Even in the case of doves,

[50] Gaius, *Institutes* 2.68, in F de Zulueta (ed and tr), *The Institutes of Gaius* (1946); cf D.41.1.3, Gaius 2 *rerum cottidianarum sive aureorum* and ht 4, Florentinus 6 *institutionum*. For comment, see D Daube, 'Doves and Bees' in D Cohen and D Simon (eds), *David Daube: Collected Studies in Roman Law* (1991) 899, originally in *Mélanges Lévy-Bruhl* (1959) 63; WW Buckland *A Textbook of Roman Law from Augustus to Justinian* (3rd edn by PG Stein, 1963) 205–6; Thomas (n 47) 166–7. The loss of ownership is described in the same terms in BGB § 960 Abs 3: 'Ein gezähmtes Tier wird herrenlos, wenn es die Gewohnheit ablegt, an den ihm bestimmten Ort zurückzukehren'.

[51] See eg Daube (n 50) 912.

[52] Justinian, *Institutes*, 2.1.14–16, cf D.41.1.5.2–4, Gaius 2 *rerum cottidianarum sive aureorum*.

[53] Justinian, *Institutes* 2.1.14–16, cf D.41.1.5.5, Gaius 2 *rerum cottidianarum sive aureorum*.

[54] Daube (n 50) 901.

however, the metaphor of taming was incorrect and inappropriate. Although Daube thought that doves had to be 'trained to return'[55] and other scholars have spoken of a 'habit of returning in psychologically domesticated wild animals'[56]—almost a contradiction in terms—birds belonging to the family of 'rock doves' or 'homing pigeons' possess a natural homing instinct. Not all pigeons possess this ability. Wild pigeons do not. But from early times the homing pigeon's instinctive ability to find its way home from great distances has been harnessed in a number of ways, such as for communication in times of war and, with the advent of the railway, for pigeon races, where the pigeons return to the competitors' lofts. However, the talent to return does not, in itself, derive from domestication.[57]

Daube firmly believed that the rule for the ownership of bees became settled by analogy with doves.[58] He wrote:

This rule was first established for doves and the like—peacocks, for instance—and then extended to bees. For one thing, in all relevant texts [in G.2.68; in D.10.2.8.1, where Ulpian refers to an application of the rule by Pomponius; in D.41.2.3.16, where Paul discusses possession of such animals] the doves precede the bees. Indeed . . . the way the bees are brought in—'the same may be said of bees', 'also bees'—provides a clear indication of how the law grew up. For another thing, there is the direct evidence of Ulpian's report in *Collatio* 12.7.10 (shorn of its historical details in D.9.2.27.12). Proculus, we are told, did not regard me as the owner of bees which, having flown from me to you, had been destroyed by you. By Celsus's time this view still found defenders, but he decided against it—one of his arguments being that there was no difference between bees and doves. So there was no dispute against the latter: they had always come under the rule.

Thus, Daube thought, the similar habit of bees—clearly not tamed—was invoked to justify a re-classification of doves, the price of which was a 'blurring of the distinction between "wild" and "tamed" ':

There were now animals, such as doves accustomed to return, which were at the same time of *natura fera*—they belonged to that species, they were essentially, naturally wild—and *mansuetae*—as individuals, so to speak.[59]

And he concluded:

To recapitulate. In Varro's time, doves as well as bees, while flying about, are *res nullius*; they are wild and therefore not owned except when shut up. By the beginning of the

---

[55] ibid 901.

[56] U von Lübtow, *Untersuchungen zur lex Aquilia de damno iniuria dato* (1971) 184–5 speaks, with regard to doves, of 'Gewohnheit der Rückkehr bei den gezähmten, . . . psychisch beherrschten, wilden Tieren'.

[57] Amongst the countless websites, see that of the International Federation of American Homing Pigeon Fanciers http://www.ifpigeon.com (accessed 30 November 2005), or that of British Homing World, 'Britain's premier pigeon-racing weekly' http://www.pigeonracing.com (accessed on the same date).   [58] Daube (n 50) 899.

[59] ibid 901.

classical period, doves, peacocks etc. which habitually come back—but not bees—count as tamed, not wild. They are owned, therefore, like geese, even while flying about, though, as laid down in a *regula*, ownership terminates on their losing *animus revertendi*, when they become wild again. *Animus revertendi* is interpreted as shewing itself in *consuetudo revertendi*. Celsus decides that bees, also in the habit of coming back, are to be treated like doves. Doves are now re-assigned to the same class as bees: both are of wild nature, and even doves tamed so as to be faithful to a place remain essentially wild. The *regula* is adjusted to the new state of things; in its expanded form—known to Pomponius—the principal, opening part ordains that animals habitually coming back, doves and bees, though of a wild nature are owned so long as they have *animus revertendi*. In order to harmonize the law with the general principle concerning ownership of *ferae*, possession of animals habitually coming back is considered intact even while they are absent.[60]

The reconstruction does not seem wholly convincing. Although it is difficult to know for certain what the rules were before the assimilation of bees and doves, the considerable importance of bees as a source of nutrition, and the frequency of controversies about their ownership, make it plausible to suppose that bees would have been regarded as owned in an 'ordinary way', and not by way of exception. The argument is easily supported through the extensive coverage of bees in literature and in works on agriculture. Columella devotes almost a whole book to bees in his *Agriculture*, but gives much less attention to doves. Hence it cannot be right to think of bees as being unprovided for until the analogy with doves came along. It must be that they were, so to speak, *more* provided for and that the analogy with doves was a demotion, necessitated by the true facts.

6.3. Bees as Fruit

Celsus' opinion in the *Collatio* excerpt may be taken to indicate a distinct and possibly older way of inferring continued bee ownership—distinct, that is, from the presence of *animus revertendi*. Reference to *fructus* could signify that bees were regarded as a crop and owned according to the rules laid down for fruit, that is, through harvesting (*fructuum separatio*) from the fruit-bearing thing, that is, presumably, the colony from which the swarm departs.[61]

A subsidiary point in favour of the hypothesis that bees were first placed under the ordinary rules (as for *fructus*, not wild animals) is the widespread, albeit erroneous, view that bees could be 'grown', in much the same way as plants. That view is documented, for instance, in Virgil's *Georgics* 4.295–314, which contains a 'recipe for bees':

> How often in the past the putrid blood
> Of slaughtered cattle has engendered bees . . .

---

[60] ibid 912. For further discussion of the two versions of the *regula*, as reported by Gaius, respectively, in *Institutes* 2.68 (as *regula tradita* or long–established) and D.41.1.5.5, 2 *rerum cottidianarum* (as *regula comprobata* or agreed upon by jurists), see P Stein, *Regulae Iuris—From Juristic Rules to Legal Maxims* (1966) 99–101.   [61] Justinian, *Institutes* 2.1.35.

A bullock with two years' growth of curving horns.
Both nostrils and the life-breath of his mouth
Are plugged, for all his struggles . . .
They abandon him shut up, with broken branches
Under his flanks and thyme and fresh-picked cassia . . .
Meanwhile the moisture in those softened bones
Warms and ferments, and little animals,
An amazing sight, first limbless, then with wings
Whirring, begin to swarm, and gradually
Try the thin air, till suddenly, like rain
Shed from a cloud in the summer, out they burst . . . [62]

The generation of bees at a certain time of year—after the solstice and until the rising of the dog-star—from a slain bullock (*iuvenco perempto*) or from the bellies of oxen (*ventribus bubulis*) is also described in Columella, who attributes the recording of this discovery to Democritus, Mago, and Virgil.[63] The same Columella, in his study of the uses of smoke, notes that the hives are best fumigated with smoke produced by burning ox-dung (*incenso bubulo fimo*), for this smoke is 'particularly well-suited to bees as if some affinity existed between it and them' (*hic enim quasi quadam cognatione generis maxime est apibus aptus*).[64] The latter remark is also found in Pliny.[65]

The belief is ancient. In the Bible, in Judges, book 14, Samson resolves to take his wife amongst the daughters of the uncircumcised Philistines. That greatly displeases his parents. On his first visit to the vineyards of Timnath, a young lion roars against him and he kills it.

[7] And he went down, and talked with the woman; and she pleased Samson well.

[8] And after a time he returned to take her, and he turned aside to see the carcase of the lion: and, behold, *there was* a swarm of bees and honey in the carcase of the lion.[66]

[9] And he took thereof in his hands, and went on eating, and came to his father and

---

[62] Virgil, *Georgics* 4.295–314; the translation is in G Anderson-Dargatz, *A Recipe for Bees* (2000) 252. Selected lines from Virgil's original read as follows:

> Interea teneris tepefactus in ossibus umor
> aestuat et visenda modis animalia miris,
> trunca pedum primo, mox et stridentia pennis,
> miscentur tenuemque magis magis aera carpunt,
> donec, ut aestivis effusus nubibus imber,
> erupere aut ut nervo pulsante sagittae,
> prima leves ineunt si quando proelia Parthi . . .

[63] Columella, *On Agriculture* 9.14.6–7.   [64] ibid 9.14.1–2.

[65] Pliny the Elder, *Natural History* 21.80, discussed in Ransome (n 19 above) 89. The Romans used to throw 'dust or honey-water' on the bees to quieten them if fighting, and cow-dung smoke when taking honey.

[66] M Black and HH Rowley (eds), *Peake's Commentary on the Bible* (1962) 313 note that verse 8 contains a misrepresentation: 'Bees would only nest there if the carcass had dried, but there was an ancient belief that bees bred from rotting animal matter'.

mother, and he gave them, and they did eat: but he told not them that he had taken the honey out of the carcase of the lion.

There follows the well-known posing of the riddle by Samson to his companions:

[12] And Samson said unto them, I will now put forth a riddle unto you: if ye can certainly declare it me within the seven days of the feast, and find *it* out, then I will give you thirty sheets and thirty changes of garments:
[13] But if ye cannot declare *it* me, then shall *ye* give me thirty sheets and thirty changes of garments. And they said unto him, Put forth thy riddle, that we may hear it.
[14] And he said unto them, Out of the eater came forth meat, and out of the strong came forth sweetness. And they could not in three days expound the riddle. . . . [67]

The Philistines cannot solve the riddle. Samson tells his wife, and she tells her people. The answer, a riddle within a riddle, reads: 'What is sweeter than honey? And what is stronger than a lion?'[68]

The importance of Celsus' argument *'cum apes . . . mihi fructui s<i>nt'* in *Collatio* 12.7.10 is repeatedly played down by Daube, who calls it a 'motive', on which one should not place too much reliance given that there is 'much textual corruption in this section' and 'the possibility, suggested by the indicative *sunt* which clashes with *cum soleant*, of the words being a gloss'.[69] Frier, by contrast, without arriving at the conclusion which we favour—that ownership in bees was probably originally acquired much in the same way as fruits were harvested— translates *fructui* as 'a source of profit' and applauds Celsus' use of juristic casuistry to 'promote the overall social adequacy of Roman law'.[70] Proculus' opinion—to the effect that bees were still regarded as wild and not owned unless they were shut up in the hive—is irreconcilable with that strategy for the protection of wealth. In Frier's words:

A beekeeper must allow his bees to fly free if they are to return a profit to him; and if the legal 'cost' of continued ownership is keeping them constantly enclosed, that 'cost' is too high. But if his bees fly out onto another's land, law should protect them in their flight, by granting to the beekeeper a continuing ownership. This is so not just because the bees still 'belong' (in one sense or another) to their owner, but *because their owner is a beekeeper*, and beekeeping is a desirable and productive activity, one that law should foster and protect. Through this argument, Celsus grounds his rule in economic reality and 'public policy'. . . . [H]is decision that a subcategory [of animals which come and go] is required rests ultimately upon two judgments: first, that law will become more socially adequate if this subcategory is summoned into existence; second (and more significant), that it is in fact desirable to increase law's social adequacy. The difference in legal quality between Proculus' holding, and that of Celsus, is not a small or casual one: it is the difference between law caught in a conceptual straitjacket, and law liberated by a perception of its underlying social purposes.[71]

---

[67] Judges 14.5–14.   [68] ibid 14.17.   [69] Daube (n 50) 910.
[70] Frier, 'Bees and Lawyers Revisited' (n 14) 144.
[71] ibid 135–7.

While this social analysis is plausible and unproblematic, it ignores the technical legal meaning of the word 'fruit', thus offering a reading of the text which, from a semantic standpoint, does not fit with the way we interpret other texts dealing with fruits.

7. Bees and Neighbours

7.1. Tension in the Neighbourhood

We must now attempt an interpretation of *Collatio* 12.7.10. In the background of both texts are relations between neighbours. As we all know, these can deteriorate. The presence of bees may well exacerbate them further. The reasons for the bad feeling can vary: bees making a nuisance of themselves with their buzzing; nectar-collecting bees viewed as a danger because of their potential for stinging; an unwelcome swarm; or a bee-keeper trespassing on neighbouring land in the process of going to collect a swarm. The *Encyclopedia Britannica*, the wisdom of whose 'Bee' entry we have invoked before, warns:

The great majority of apiaries owned by British bee-keepers are located in close proximity to neighbours; consequently a serious upset among the bees would in many cases involve an amount of trouble which should if possible be avoided; therefore quietness and the exercise of care when manipulating are always recommended by teachers, and practiced by those who wisely take their lessons to heart.[72]

Such is the extent of the problem that, in the same spirit, recent Italian legislation (*Legge* 24 dicembre 2004 no 313), whilst mindful of the need to recognize bee-keeping as an activity of national interest and to preserve 'bee diversity' (art 1) and 'the purity of the Italian bee (*Apis mellifera ligustica Spinola* and *Apis mellifera sicula Montagano*)' (art 5), amended the 1942 Civil Code through the introduction of article 896-*bis*, entitled 'Minimum distances between apiaries'. The new provision acknowledges that bee-keeping can qualify as a dangerous activity.[73]

7.2. The Alleged Relationship between Disturbance and Burning

Why are the bees in the excerpts by Ulpian making a nuisance of themselves? Frier insists that the bees at issue are 'individual bees' who 'left [the plaintiff's]

---

[72] Entry 'Bee' (n 10) 636.

[73] Legge 24 dicembre 2004 no 313, art 8; cf Civil Code art 896–*bis*, 'Distanze minime per gli apiari'. The statute terminates a line of cases (notably, Cassazione 26 marzo 1974 no 837 and 16 ottobre 1991 no 10912) which had denied that beekeeping could be classed as an *attività pericolosa*. Previously, when faced with dangerous bees, courts would invoke general principles of extra-contractual liability as set out in art 2043. Art 896–*bis* CC now provides that apiaries must be located at a distance of no less than ten metres from streets where there is a right of public passage, five metres from the boundaries of public or private property, and one kilometre from factories and plants where sugar is produced. These limitations may be waived by agreement of the parties.

hive presumably in search of pollen; they crossed onto a neighbor's land, and the neighbor "burned them up"'.[74] The underlying assumption is that the burning is one way, not unlike the poisoning of flowers, to 'destroy irritating insects',[75] for sometimes there is indeed 'a "good" reason to exterminate the bees (eg, an allergy to bee stings)'.[76] Nörr has argued that burning as a method of exterminating bees is chosen by Celsus in order to avoid the problems of causal directness[77] which seem to arise, for example, in D.9.2.49 pr, Ulpian 9 *disputationum.* This text has been explained by Nörr as a case of using smoke to chase swarms of bees away (*durch 'Ausräuchern' zu vertreiben*). When death ensues accidentally, the situation qualifies 'as supplying the cause of death' rather than 'killing':

Si quis fumo facto apes alienas fugaverit vel etiam necaverit, magis causam mortis praestitisse videtur quam occidisse, et ideo in factum actione tenebitur.

If someone drives away, or even kills, another's bees by making smoke, he seems rather to have provided the cause of their death rather than directly to have killed them, and so he will be liable to an action *in factum.*[78]

Nörr appears to have correctly understood the effect of smoke since he remarks that, in moderation, it can calm bees. He adds that stronger smoke causes them to fly off (*fugare*).[79] For our purposes pacification is more interesting and better documented than flight, but the excerpt is none the less worth a mention because it shows that conflagration is often contemplated as an undesired effect of the application of smoke which was intended for other purposes.

Still, with reference to *Collatio* 12.7.10, Frier believes that the burning is intentional. Although seemingly aware that ' "burning up" individual bees seems either surreal or bookish',[80] he insists that 'swarms are not at issue in this text',[81] for 'swarms are governed by wholly different rules' and 'it is unintelligible to

---

[74] Frier, 'Bees and Lawyers Revisited' (n 14) 135.

[75] cf Quintilian's thirteenth *Declamatio Maior*, discussed ibid 140 and 143, where irritating bees belonging to a poor plaintiff are poisoned by the rich neighbour defendant. The latter is held to be *reus damni iniuria dati.*   [76] Frier, 'Bees and Lawyers Revisited' (n 14) 146 n 14.

[77] D Nörr, *Causa mortis—Auf den Spuren einer Redewendung* (1986) 193: 'Ging man gegen die Bienen durch "Verbrennen" vor (s Cels bei Ulp Coll 12.7.10), so scheint die *"iniuria"* des Täters nicht problematisch gewesen zu sein . . . Mit starkem Rauch kann man Bienen verjagen; wenn der Nachbar dieses Mittel wählt, so konnten die Bienen durch Ersticken oder mittelbar durch den Tod des Weisels umkommen. In diesem Falle war die unmittelbare Anwendung des 3. Kapitels (trotz der Uminterpretation von *"rumpere"* in *"corrumpere"*) fragwürdig.'

[78] Watson *et al, Digest* (n 17) 291.

[79] Nörr (n 77) 192–3: 'Mäßiger Rauch beruhigt Bienen; mit seiner Hilfe kann man Bienenschwärme fangen und sich beim Zeideln der Bienen erwehren. . . . Mit starkem Rauch kann man Bienen verjagen . . .'. I have found less evidence of the latter in books on bee-keeping.

[80] Frier, 'Bees and Lawyers Revisited' (n 14) 148–9 n 45 attributes this remark to Brian Simpson. Cf also D Nörr, 'Texte zur Lex Aquilia', in HP Benöhr, K Hackl, R Knütel, and A Wacke (eds), *Iuris Professio: Festgabe für M. Kaser zum 80. Geburtstag* (1986) 211 = TJ Chiusi, W Kaiser, and H-D Spengler (eds), *Dieter Nörr: Historiae Iuris Antiqui: Gesammelte Schriften* (2003) vol III 1701.   [81] Frier (n 80) 143.

ascribe an *animus revertendi* to a swarm'.[82] Scholars have often attempted to distinguish between texts dealing with swarms and those dealing with individual bees.[83] The purpose of relating some excerpts to individual bees is evidently to get round the loss of *animus revertendi*, thus preserving the plaintiff's ownership and his standing under the *lex Aquilia*. Frier's interpretation is not entirely plausible in that it tries to make the bees' nature square with the law. In the paragraphs which follow we argue for an alternative reading of the text.

7.3. An Alternative Reading 1: *ad tuas*, Swarms, Smoke, and Fire

When swarms fly off, they do not fly far. The likelihood of a swarm choosing the neighbour's land as its new residence is high. In *Collatio* 12.7.10 my bees are said to have flown '*ad tuas*'. The phrase is difficult. If Ulpian knew about bees, he could not have meant that my bees flew to your bees, '*ad tuas apes*', as a prelude to a fusion of the ownership of the two swarms which had hitherto belonged to different owners, for swarms do not normally merge. It is in the nature of swarming bees to find a separate place in which to establish themselves. In order to prevent a loss of a source of honey through swarming, the ingenuity of bee-keepers has devised artificial mechanisms to make swarms merge. These always entail the destruction of one queen.[84] But that happens for the convenience of the bee-keepers, not of the bees.[85] Frier inserts *arbores* after *ad tuas*. But, in truth, that addition is unnecessary given his reading of the text which, he claims, is concerned with single bees rather than with swarms. Bee-keepers' manuals routinely explain that the admission of new individuals to the hive, when nectar-loaded or very young, is possible. Ones and twos, which may have deserted their own colony or gone astray, may become integrated into a new one.[86] In such a case, the interpretation of *apes meae* flying *ad tuas* (*apes*) would be acceptable. But, nevertheless, it cannot be right. For one thing, the owner would never know about the odd deserting bee flying off to join the neighbour's swarm. Missing ones and twos go unnoticed. For another, as Frier himself acknowledges, ones and twos could hardly be targeted for selective burning.

---

[82] ibid 145 n 7.

[83] See eg Frier, who distinguishes texts concerned with swarms—such as Gaius, D.41.1.5.4, and Justinian, *Institutes* 2.1.14—from those concerned with individual bees—such as Ulpian, D.9.2.49 pr (liability for wrongful damage if smoke is used to drive away or kill bees), and D.10.2.8.1 (liability for theft if bees or doves are stolen). In reality, the distinction is difficult to justify.

[84] Wedmore (n 33) [1404]–[1423].

[85] In view of this, the significance of BGB § 963 is difficult to grasp. The section deals with the situation of co-ownership ensuing from the merger of swarms belonging to different owners: 'Vereinigen sich ausgezogene Bienenschwärme mehrerer Eigentümer, so werden die Eigentümer, welche ihre Schwärme verfolgt haben, Miteigentümer des eingefangenen Gesamtschwarmes; die Anteile bestimmen sich nach der Zahl der verfolgten Schwärme'. The provision can only plausibly refer to artificial mergers carried out by bee-keepers.   [86] Wedmore (n 33) [1405].

Alternative translations for *ad tuas* must be thought of. It is almost certain that the feminine plural cannot mean the same as the neuter plural *ad tua* (*loca*), hence my bees cannot simply have flown 'onto your property'. The neuter singular would be more appropriate if this were the writer's intended meaning.[87] Frier translates 'onto your (property)', but that is unlikely without something more in the wording. It is equally unlikely that they will have flown *ad tuas* (*arbores*), as he suggests, since at least one preceding mention of trees would be necessary to sustain a possessive pronoun. We suggest that *ad tuas* could better be explained as a metonymy: a mention of bees for where bees reside, and thereby a reference to 'land' or 'property'.

In all probability, the *ad tuas* text is a case of a swarm taking off, thus losing its *animus revertendi*. A neighbour rather inaptly tries to use smoke to pacify the swarm and capture it, or take the honey. The attempt at pacification fails. Fire and destruction ensue.

7.4. An Alternative Reading 2: *fructus* and Aquilian Entitlement

The entitlement to sue under the *lex Aquilia* is co-terminous with ownership. If the bees have lost their habit of returning, they are no longer owned under either of the two versions of the *regula*, set out by Gaius and described by Daube, for wild animals which come and go. That proposition, advocated by Proculus, is disturbing, in that a precious store of wealth might be subject to wasteful loss without a remedy.

There are only two paths conducive to the preservation of ownership—and therefore of entitlement to sue—in the owner. One is the attempt to read the text as referring to single bees which come and go, and which have therefore not lost their habit of returning. That is the solution which Frier attributes to Celsus, conveniently reinforced by considerations of the social adequacy of the law. But both arguments are objectionable. The owner of five or six individual bees which had gone astray would hardly sue in respect of their killing, for he would scarcely even realize that they had gone missing. Besides, in themselves, single bees are not capable of producing any significant quantity of honey. Hence their value as a source of profit would be negligible, not least for purposes of calculating the measure of damages under chapter 3, which looks at thirty days' worth in the bee's life. Finally, it is difficult to believe that the misappropriation of a bee or two could have engaged Ulpian's attention on more than one occasion. Swarms must be what is at stake here.

The other path leading to ownership must therefore rely on some mode of acquisition other than, and possibly anterior to, the *regula* for wild animals which come and go. We can only think of the separation of *fructus* as a crop.

---

[87] eg the Pseudo-Quintilian, *Declamationes Maiores*, 13.4 has *in meo* for 'on my land'.

A swarm leaves my garden. It separates from the originating bee mass. I am the owner of both.[88] There are two consequences to that. First, I am probably allowed to enter the neighbour's land, without fear of trespassing, in order to recover the swarm.[89] Secondly, in the event of destruction of my bees through a conflagration, my standing under the *lex Aquilia* will not be disputed. I shall be able to bring an *actio directa*.[90]

8. Conclusion

Peter Birks looked at animals with interest both because the peculiar nature of some of them held many surprises, and because they exemplified the problems of legal classification. His vision of Roman law was complex. When it came to advocating the importance of continuing to teach the subject to Oxford undergraduates, his notion of it was 'forward-looking': he viewed it as 'a historico-comparative introduction to law' and 'a platform for entry into the language and structure of all modern civilian systems'. Abandoning the subject, he once said, 'would in my view be roughly the equivalent of poking out one's own eyes'.[91] However, in his own research, he favoured a 'backward-looking' approach to Roman law: he took delight, as he put it, in understanding 'how things really worked in 100 AD'. This contribution has sought to look at both bees and their law in a suitably curious manner. The natural history of bees suggests that, with regard to *Collatio* 12.10.7, the rule of thumb of preferring the

[88] A different conclusion is reached by BGB 964 in the event that the bees might have occupied a hive already belonging to other bees: 'Ist ein Bienenschwarm in eine fremde besetzte Bienenwohnung eingezogen, so erstrecken sich das Eigentum und die sonstigen Rechte an den Bienen, mit denen die Wohnung besetzt war, auf den eingezogenen Schwarm. Das Eigentum und die sonstigen Rechte an dem Schwarme erlöschen'. A detailed commentary is in S Schulz, *Die historische Entwicklung des Rechts an Bienen* (§§ 961–964 BGB) (1990), reviewed T Drosdeck, 'Der wilde Wurm ist tot!' (1991) 10 Rechtshistorisches Journal 96.

[89] In this sense, EJ Cohn, 'Bees and the Law' (1939) 55 LQR 289, 293. Consistently, he reads Gaius' statement in D.41.1.5.3, denying a right of entry, as referring solely to ownerless bees. However, he concludes that the owner could still enter a neighbour's land by analogy either with D.10.4.15, in search of treasure, or with the *interdictum de glande legenda*, which, in later law, came to be extended to all kinds of fruit. Cf § 962 BGB: 'Der Eigentümer des Bienenschwarmes darf bei der Verfolgung fremde Grundstücke betreten. Ist der Schwarm in eine fremde nicht besetzte Bienenwohnung eingezogen, so darf der Eigentümer des Schwarmes zum Zwecke des Einfangens die Wohnung öffnen und die Waben herausnehmen oder herausbrechen. Er hat den entstehenden Schaden zu ersetzen.'

[90] von Lübtow (n 56) 184–5 contrasts the case of *Vertreiben fremder Bienen durch Rauch* (chasing away of bees by smoke, in D.9.2.49 pr), which is a case of *actio in factum* (except that the occupier of the land, having behaved lawfully, is not responsible) with the case of *Vernichtung zugeflogener Bienen* (destruction of bees which have gathered together by a conflagration), against which one may bring an *actio directa*. According to Nörr, *Causa mortis* (n 77) 192–3, the effect of chasing away (*vertreiben* or *verscheuchen*), as opposed to pacifying bees, is obtained through stronger smoke (or perhaps, a more vigorous application of smoke: it is not entirely clear which Nörr means by *stark*). [91] From Peter Birks's last email to the Faculty mailing list, 24 May 2004.

lectio difficilior might prove right. For one thing, their natural history indicates that burning should be viewed, not as an antidote to disturbance, but as the result of some failure in applying smoke to capture a swarm. For another, bees might turn out to have been fruits, not in our efficiency-driven sense of 'sources of wealth', but in a more ancient and, back then, more plausible way, as crops.

26

Late Arrivals: The Appendix in Justinian's Digest Reconsidered

Tony Honoré*

Peter Birks owed much to John Kelly, who taught him Roman law, and to Herbert Hart, who commissioned the book on Restitution for the Clarendon Law Series and made, he told me, some 500 comments on Peter's first draft. As time went on, Peter's historical and analytical interests dovetailed. He appreciated how Roman texts and classifications could be used not merely as a teaching tool but to build up a branch of modern law. His commitment to the value of law as an intellectual discipline was total.

We were mutually supportive. But the paths of the 26th and 27th holders of the Regius Chair of Civil Law in Oxford ran parallel rather than converged. Peter's Roman-related modern interest was Restitution/Unjust Enrichment, to which he made a fundamental contribution. Mine concerned Trusts in the civil law. His classical focus was on early Roman law and the institutional tradition, mine on palingenetic studies and the later Empire. He had, before his sudden exodus, found my renewed attack on the compilation of Justinian's Digest exciting,[1] and the present tribute to the genius of Justinian's minister Tribonian will not come as a surprise.

In the course of a complex enterprise such as the compilation of Justinian's Digest in AD 530–3 changes of plan, to meet unexpected snags, are inevitable. This essay deals with a change of plan on the part of Tribonian, who was in charge of the operation, to deal with the fact that there were more works to be read and excerpted by the Digest commission than originally envisaged. It concerns the works known as the Appendix and proposes a new theory as to their character.

The term Appendix refers to a group of writings that fall outside the three main groups of work, termed the Sabinian, edictal, and Papinian masses,

* Emeritus Fellow of All Souls College, Oxford; formerly Regius Professor of Civil Law, University of Oxford.

[1] P Birks, 'Roman Law in Twentieth-Century Britain' in J Beatson and R Zimmermann (eds), *Jurists Uprooted. German-speaking Émigré Lawyers in Twentieth-Century Britain* (2004) 257 n 20.

detected by Bluhme in 1820.[2] Like the main masses, these writings appear in the Digest titles in a regular sequence and in that sense constitute a fourth mass.[3] But the number of works,[4] books,[5] and excerpts[6] in this group is less than for the other masses. In over three-quarters of the titles in which texts from them occur they come at the end of the title.[7] Hence the term 'Appendix'.

I argue that the Appendix is a composite mass, drawn from all three main masses. It consists, as Bluhme thought,[8] of works that became available to Justinian's compilers after the reading of the main masses had begun. These late arrivals were each allotted to their appropriate main mass.[9] The committees charged with reading the main masses were however told to read these books only after they had finished reading the works originally assigned to them. Through pressure of time, the three committees had made only a modest start on the late arrivals. Tribonian then decided to collect the unread works from all three masses and entrust them to an ad hoc committee. Simultaneously other commissioners began to edit the Digest titles from book 1 onwards, title by title (50 books and 431 titles in all), combining texts from all three masses. When the ad hoc committee had finished reading the Appendix, the editors of the Digest titles inserted the excerpts from them in each title at a point that depended on the progress that had been made in editing that title.[10] In the first half of the Digest, which had by then been fully edited, they inserted the Appendix excerpts at the end of each title. From about the middle, when the editors had settled the order of masses but had not decided how to end each title, they put the Appendix texts in the penultimate position, before whatever texts were chosen to end it. From book 40 onwards the Appendix was treated as a fourth mass on a level with the other three. The editors could then place it wherever seemed best, not necessarily at or near the end of a title.

Some problems emerge. What works make up the Appendix and in what order do they come? What is their common feature? How do they relate to the main masses? Whereabouts in each title have the editors put the Appendix texts?

---

[2] F Bluhme (1820) 4 ZGR 257, reprinted in (1960) 6 Labeo 50, 235, 368.

[3] G Hugo, 'Der von Bluhme entdeckten Reihen sind vier' (1837) 6 Civilistisches Magazin 512, 514–15; contra D Mantovani, *Digesto e masse Bluhmiane* (1987) 1–3, 16–9, 109–124; 'Le masse Bluhmiane sono tre' (1993) 4 Seminarios Complutenses de Derecho Romano 87. I refer to these works as Mantovani (1987) and Mantovani (1993) respectively.

[4] At least 11 or 12, listed below at nn 15–17.

[5] Of a Digest total of 1,522 at least 101 or 110, depending on the view taken of the two series of inscriptions for Labeo's *posteriora*, belong to the Appendix: see below nn 15–17.

[6] About 299 out of a Digest total of 9,133 (3.27 per cent).

[7] On my count, in 102 out of 127 titles in which there are Appendix texts. There are also 10 to 13 titles in which the Appendix is the last mass but is succeeded by codal texts: see below nn 119–26.

[8] Bluhme (n 2) 317.

[9] The works of Pomponius to the edictal committee, to which his works were in principle assigned; those of Scaevola to the Papinian committee for the same reason; those of Venuleius to the Sabinian committee; see below nn 102–5.

[10] What follows essentially adopts the theory proposed by Mantovani (1987) 114–16, 123.

1. What Works Constitute the Appendix and in What Order Do They Come?

The Bluhme–Krueger *Ordo librorum* (BK Ordo)[11] lists 13 Appendix works, which Krueger put after the Sabinian, edictal, and Papinian masses and numbered from 263 to 275. Two should be removed because their listing rests on a single text with a false inscription.[12] These are no 266 (*Idem = <Proculus> libri III ex posterioribus Labeonis*) and no 272 (*Valens libri VII actionum*). That leaves 11 works, about four of which Mantovani expresses doubt.[13] All four can, however, be defended. In the table that follows this list of 11 (or, if the two versions of Labeo's *posteriora* are treated as separate works, 12) defensible works are set out along with the number of books,[14] texts, and lines[15] from each that appear in the Digest. They are in the order in which I think they were presented for incorporation in the Digest, with the BK number in brackets.

Scaevola's *Digesta*, it may be noted, provides over half the lines from these works: 3,072 out of 5,002 (61.4 per cent).

		Work and number of books	Texts	Lines
1	(BK 263)	Paul, *Imperiales sententiae* 2 (out of 6)	6	27
2	(BK 265)	Labeo, *Posteriora a Iavoleno epitomata* books 2–10 (1–2 in Sabinian mass)	25	328
	(BK 94)	Iavolenus, *Ex posterioribus Labeonis* books 2–10 (1–2 in Sabinian mass)	38	419
3	(BK 264)	Quintus Mucius Scaevola, ὅρων 1	4	20
4	(BK 267)	Scaevola, *Digesta* books 3–40 (1–2 in Papinian mass)	120	3072
5	(BK 268)	Labeo, *Pithana a Paulo epitomata* 8	34	299
6	(BK 269)	Pomponius, *Epistulae* 20[16]	24	258
7	(BK 270)	Pomponius, *Senatusconsulta* 5	9	103
8	(BK 271)	Scaevola, *Quaestiones publice tractatae* 1	9	158
9	(BK 273)	Venuleius Saturninus, *Actiones* 10	7	57
10	(BK 274)	Venuleius Saturninus, *De interdictis* 6	20	246
11	(BK 275)	Furius Anthianus, *Ad edictum* 1	3	15

I deal first with the four works (items 1, 3, 10, and 11) doubted by Mantovani[17] and then with two (items 2 and 4), the early books of which were read by the Sabinian and Papinian committees respectively.

[11] T Mommsen and P Krueger (eds), *Corpus Iuris Civilis* (stereotype ed) vol 1 927–31.
[12] Mantovani (1987) 109.   [13] Mantovani (1987) 109–12.
[14] 101 or 110 books out of 1522.
[15] As printed in O Lenel, *Palingenesia Iuris Civilis* (1889).
[16] Of the texts inscribed Pomponius, *Epistulae et variae lectiones* instead of just *Epistulae*, some seem to belong to the edictal mass, where his *variae lectiones* come at BK 155. I have not attempted to assign all of them to the correct mass, but see Mantovani (1993) 112–13.
[17] The position of the first two is also doubted by H Krüger, 'Römische Juristen und ihre Werke' in *Studi in onore di Pietro Bonfante nel XL anno d'insegnamento* (1930) vol 2 234 f.

The first suspect work is Paul's *Imperiales sententiae in cognitionibus prolatae*, an account of cases heard by the emperor Severus.[18] Of the six books attributed to this work the Digest has only an epitome in two books. It can be assumed that only this epitome was available to Justinian's compilers.[19]

Mantovani doubts whether this work belongs to the Appendix because, of the six texts from it in the Digest, three come at the end of the Papinian mass.[20] Two texts are at the end of the Appendix mass.[21] But Kaiser points out[22] that one of these last two appears in a series of texts that are plainly out of order, and there is reason to suppose that this text is not really the last in the title but was followed by two others the source of which is unknown.[23] The conflict between the remaining text that comes at the end of the Appendix, D.35.1.113, and D.50.16.240, which comes at the beginning, should be solved, he argues, in favour of D.50.16.240. The title 50.16 *De Verborum Significatione* has suffered little editorial intervention, whereas 35.1 has about 20 texts displaced by the editors. The sixth text from *Imperiales sententiae* (D.40.1.10) seems more likely to be an insertion in an earlier mass than to constitute the Appendix, since in the title in question there is another Appendix text in its normal position at the end of the title.[24] The case for moving *Imperiales sententiae* to the Papinian mass is therefore weak.[25]

In any case it is closely related to Paul's *Decreta* in three books, which was excerpted as part of the Papinian mass (BK no 222). There were evidently two summaries of Paul's original six-book collection of cases.[26] Had both been available from the outset, they would have been read together as a group rather than widely separated. That they were not read together shows that the second summary, *Imperiales sententiae*, became available only later. It is a late arrival and, if assigned to the Papinian committee, was not to be read until the works originally assigned to that committee, including the *Decreta,* had been read.

The next suspect work is Quintus Mucius Scaevola's one book of ὅρων ('definitions'),[27] from which four texts survive. One of these ends a title after the Papinian mass.[28] Another follows the Papinian mass but precedes a text from Labeo's *Pithana*, no 5 in the Appendix list.[29] A third comes after the text from Paul's *Imperiales sententiae* in D.50.16 just discussed and is followed by five Appendix texts.[30] The fourth[31] comes from the most regular of all the titles, D.50.17, after a text from Iavolenus, *Ex posterioribus Labeonis*, a work which is for

---

[18] Mantovani (1987) 109–10; (1993) 103.

[19] D Liebs in K Sallman (ed), *Handbuch der Lateinischen Literatur der Antike* vol 4 (1997) § 423 no 79.   [20] D.28.5.93; 37.14.24; 50.16.240.

[21] D.35.1.113; 36.1.83.

[22] W Kaiser, 'Digestenentstehung und Digestenüberlieferung' (1991) 108 ZSS 330, 339–40.

[23] D.36.1.84, 85 (Basilica 35.1.84,85).

[24] D.40.1.26 (Iav 4 *post Lab*) is the final text in the title.

[25] So also Kaiser (n 22) 339–40. D Osler thinks that the texts are consistent with the work coming either at the end of the Papinian mass or at the beginning of the Appendix: 'Following Bluhme: a note on Dario Mantovani, "Digesto e masse Bluhmiane" ': (1988) 38 IVRA 137, 147.

[26] Liebs (n 19).   [27] Mantovani (1987) 110; (1993) 103–4.   [28] D.43.20.8.

[29] D.41.1.64.   [30] D.50.16.241.   [31] D.50.17.73.

good reason listed in the Appendix table.[32] There is little doubt that Quintus Mucius' monograph belongs to the Appendix.[33] Osler, on the basis of this fourth text, would place it after Labeo's *Posteriora*.[34] This involves holding that the third text, D.50.16.241, is displaced within the Appendix mass, since it comes before 50.16.242 from Iavolenus, *Ex posterioribus Labeonis*. With some hesitation I have assumed that he is correct.

Mantovani also doubts Venuleius' six books, *De interdictis*,[35] but his scepticism is not persuasive. Of the texts from this work D.41.2.52 and 53 come after a text from Iavolenus' *Posteriora Labeonis* book 5. D.41.1.66 comes after a text from Quintus Mucius' ὅρων and two from Labeo's *Pithana*; D.44.3.15 after a text from Scaevola's *Quaestiones publice tractatae*; D.43.26.22 after one from Venuleius' *Actiones*. Together these texts point to a position for Venuleius' *Interdicta* after items 2, 3, 4, 5, and 8 in the Appendix table.

Mantovani points out that excerpts from Venuleius' work are found only in books 41 to 44 of the Digest, whereas one might expect the 20 texts from it to be more widely distributed. Thirteen texts come in book 43, which concerns interdicts.[36] Seven appear in neighbouring Digest books.[37] At this late stage in the process of reading when, on Mantovani's view, the editors had already finished their work up to about book 40,[38] the committee reading this work may have confined its attention to titles in the last 10 books of the Digest. Mantovani also points to texts interwoven with excerpts from Ulpian's books 70,[39] 71,[40] and 73[41] *Ad edictum*, or which come at the end of a title after an Ulpian text from these books.[42] Given that the Appendix excerpts were now available to the editors before they edited each title, they could easily interweave the Appendix texts with texts from other masses. When they did not, it was normal to place Appendix texts at the end of a title. In sum, I see no reason to doubt that Venuleius' *De interdictis* was read towards the end of the Appendix mass, but that the commissioners reading it took account of its place near the end of the long-drawn-out process of reading for, and editing, the Digest.

The last work listed in the Appendix is Furius Anthianus's one book *Ad edictum*, the only one of five to which the compilers had access.[43] From it we have three fragments, which come at the end of their respective titles.[44] Mantovani doubts whether this work can be securely attributed to the Appendix.[45] But one text comes after two Appendix texts from Labeo's *Pithana*.[46] Moreover the texts

---

[32] Below nn 64–71. [33] Kaiser (n 22) 340. [34] Osler (n 25) 149–50.
[35] Mantovani (1987) 111–12.
[36] D.43.19.4; 21.4; 23.2; 24.2, 4, 8, 10, 12, 22; 26.7, 22; 29.2, 4; 30.5.
[37] D.41.2.52, 53; 41.1.66; 42.8.8, 11, 25; 44.3.15.
[38] Mantovani (1987); below nn 127–31. [39] D.43.19.4.
[40] D.43.24.2, 4, 8, 10, 12; 43.26.7; 43.29.2. [41] D.42.8.11.
[42] D.43.21.4; 43.23.2; 43.29.4.
[43] Index auctorum XXXVI Ἄνθου ἤτοι Φωρίου Ανθιανοῦ μέρος edictu βιβλία πέντε: D Liebs, 'Lectio difficilior' in *Studi in onore di Edoardo Volterra* (1971) vol 5 65 n 59 in fine.
[44] D.2.14.62; 4.3.40; 6.1.80. [45] Mantovani (1987) 112. [46] D.6.1.80.

that Mantovani cites from the second book of Scaevola's *Digesta* in titles 2.14[47] and 4.3[48] have been shown by Osler to belong to the Papinian mass.[49] In that case there is no reason why the Furius Anthianus texts (D.2.14.47 and 4.3.32) should not belong to the Appendix, the end being the usual position for Appendix texts. It is likely that Furius Anthianus' book comes at or near the end of the Appendix.[50]

2. What Is the Common Feature of the Appendix Works?

H Krüger thought that the Appendix consisted of works destined for students to read in the fifth year of study, a 'constitution-mass'.[51] But the works are by no means confined to constitutions. I adhere to the traditional view that these works were late arrivals. As they arrived they were assigned to the mass to which the works of the author in question were in principle assigned, but were to be read by each committee after its main assignment. Mantovani challenges the assumption that the Appendix works were late arrivals.[52] He thinks that they were mainly parallel editions of works forming part of the main masses. Thus Pomponius' *epistulae* in the Appendix (BK 269) were parallel to his *Variae lectiones* in the edictal mass (BK 153). The parallel works were left on one side until, if ever, there was time for them to be read. But would this be a sensible arrangement? At least in the Sabinian mass similar works by an author could be read together as part of a group. Papinian's *Libri 2 de adulteriis* and his *Liber singularis* on the same subject were read together (BK 31). Reading similar works by the same author was essential if the best texts were to be discovered and excerpted for the Digest. On the other hand if works not previously available arrived after the committees had begun reading those already available, the prescribed order of reading could not be constantly altered in the light of the new arrivals. It was rational to postpone reading late arrivals until the original programme was complete. Instead, Mantovani's observation explains why, when these parallel works arrived, they were not incorporated in the existing reading programme but were put at the end of each mass. This happened in the case of Scaevola's *Digesta,* of which the first two books were read towards the end of the Papinian mass rather than along with his other works, which come near the beginning of the mass (BK 184, 187, 189, 191, 193).[53]

3. How Do the Appendix Works Relate to the Main Masses?

Bluhme assigned the Appendix works to the Papinian committee, since the Appendix normally follows the Papinian mass.[54] Mantovani rightly disputes this

---

[47] D.2.14.47.   [48] D.4.3.32.   [49] Osler (n 25) 154–7.
[50] Kaiser (n 22) 338 n 53.
[51] H Krüger, *Die Herstellung der Digesten Justinians und der Gang der Exzerption* (1922).
[52] Mantovani (1993) 114–19.   [53] Below nn 84–93.   [54] Bluhme (n 2) 309 f.

assignment.[55] For one thing, the Appendix does not always follow the Papinian mass. The titles were edited in a way that took account of the character and bulk of the materials provided by each mass, and particularly of the convenience of treating Ulpian, whose work mainly falls in the Sabinian mass, as the lead author for most topics.[56] In the upshot, the Sabinian mass is chosen as the first mass in 249 of the 431 titles, the edictal in 163, and the Papinian in 19.[57] The Papinian mass usually comes in the third position because it is less bulky and consists largely of case-law.

Although the Appendix usually follows the Papinian mass, there are 20 titles with both a Papinian mass and an Appendix where the Appendix comes at the end of the title but after another mass.[58] There are also eight titles where the Appendix precedes another mass. In seven of these it precedes the Papinian mass; in the eighth it follows it.[59] We can disregard six titles where the only Appendix text is inserted in another mass[60] and 14 where there is no Papinian mass.[61] In the upshot the Appendix follows the Sabinian mass in 15 titles, the edictal mass in 12.[62] That leaves 80 titles in which the Appendix follows the Papinian mass, including 10 or 12 where it is in turn followed by one or more codal texts.[63]

The Appendix often follows the Papinian mass because it was editorially sensible to put the general material first and to leave the *Quaestiones* and *Responsa* of Papinian, Scaevola and Paul, essentially case law, to the end. The normal position of the Appendix, which contains less material than the other masses, is at the end of a title, either because it was not available to the editors earlier or, if it was, because of its slender character. It is found there in 102 of the 127 titles in which it occurs. So it is not surprising that it often comes straight after the Papinian mass. This does not make it part of the Papinian mass, or indeed of any of the main masses.

---

[55] Mantovani (1987) 112, 116, 123–4. cf Osler (n 25) 144–6.

[56] T Honoré, 'How Tribonian Organised the Compilation of Justinian's Digest' (2004) 121 ZSS 1, 21.

[57] The order of the masses in a title, and whether a text counts as part of a mass or as a detached text, is sometimes debatable. I have generally followed Krueger's views except where, as discussed above, he seems to have placed texts in the wrong mass.

[58] D.2.14 (after Sab), 4.4 (after Sab), 5.3 (after Sab), 6.1 (after ed), 9.4 (after Sab), 13.5 (after ed), 14.2 (after Sab), 14.6 (after ed), 22.1 (after ed), 22.3 (after Sab), 23.5 (after ed), 24.3 (after ed), 34.5 (after ed), 35.2 (after Sab), 36.3 (after Sab), 36.4 (after ed), 42.1 (after Sab), 44.7 (after ed), 46.5 (after Sab), 49.15 (after Sab). My list does not entirely coincide with Osler's list of titles in which the Papinian mass does not appear in the third position: Osler (n 25) 145–6 n 31. In my view, in D.15.3 the Appendix (15.3.21) follows the Papinian mass (15.3.19–20). In D.43.30 there is no Papinian mass, only a displaced text (43.30.2). Osler rightly doubts D.33.4 and he was not bound to list D.50.1, since Scaevola's *Digesta* books 1 and 2 belong to the Papinian mass. Mantovani (1987) 114 n 43 lists 19 titles to which I would add eight (D.2.14, 4.4, 9.4, 13.5, 14.6, 22.3, 35.2, 36.3).

[59] D.40.5 (after ed), 40.14 (after Sab), 44.1 (after Sab), 46.1 (after ed), 46.3 (after ed), 49.14 (after Sab), and 50.17 (after Sab). The only exception is D.48.10, where it comes between the Papinian and edictal masses.

[60] D.3.5 (Sab); 4.8 (ed); 7.4 (ed); 40.13 (between ed and Pap); 43.19 (ed), 45.1 (Pap).

[61] D.4.3, 8.5, 12.2, 25.4, 28.8, 33.6, 41.9, 43.21, 43.23, 43.24, 43.26, 43.29, 43.30, 50.12.

[62] Above nn 58–9.   [63] Below nn 119–26.

There was, however, a connection between the Appendix and the main masses. Two works that belong mainly to the Appendix were read in part by one of the main committees. The first books in Labeo's *Posteriora* and Scaevola's *Digesta* were read as part of the Sabinian and Papinian masses respectively.

Labeo's *Posteriora* appears in the Digest in two sets of texts, one inscribed Iavolenus, *Ex posterioribus Labeonis*, the other Labeo, *Posteriora a Iavoleno epitomata*. Both refer to a summary of Labeo's posthumous works in 10 books. The two series of inscriptions occur in both the Sabinian and the Appendix masses. Neither is confined to a particular book or books. To Bluhme the different inscriptions represented separate works[64] and the BK Ordo accordingly puts the Iavolenus texts at the end of the Sabinian mass at no 94 and the Labeo texts in the Appendix at no 265. The *Index auctorum* VII.2, however, attributes 10 books of *Posteriora* to Labeo and nothing comparable to Iavolenus. Had the compilers regarded the *Posteriora* as a single work by Iavolenus, it should have been assigned to the edictal mass, to which Iavolenus' 15 books *Ex Cassio*, 14 of *Epistulae*, and five *Ex Plautio* belong.[65] But if the compilers considered that there were two different summaries of Labeo's manuscripts by Iavolenus, one predominantly of Labeo texts, the other in the nature of a commentary by Iavolenus, the two had obviously to be read together as a group. In that case, if they assigned the works of Labeo to the Sabinian committee, the Iavolenus work was grouped with it in the Sabinian rather than the edictal mass.[66] This is what the compilers did with Paul's *Epitomarum Alfeni Digestorum libri VIII*, when two summaries of Alfenus' work were available.[67] Though the *Index auctorum* is sometimes unreliable, it suggests that to the compilers the *Posteriora* was a single work of Labeo. Lenel treated it as a single work but assigned it to Iavolenus.[68]

Even if there were separate works, the BK assignment of the Iavolenus work to the Sabinian mass and the Labeo work to the Appendix was a mistake. The excerpts from book 1 and some from book 2 of the *Posteriora*, in both the Labeo and the Iavolenus series of inscriptions, belong to the end of the Sabinian mass, while a larger number of excerpts from book 2, and all those from books 3 to 10 from both series, belong to the Appendix.[69] This conclusion is well established.[70] In this case what began as part of the Sabinian mass ended up as an item in the Appendix. Mantovani has plausibly suggested that the transfer occurred because at a certain stage, in the interests of speed, the Digest commissioners began assembling the texts already excerpted from the three main masses into titles and books without waiting until the reading of the remaining works was complete.[71]

[64] Bluhme (n 2) 320–3.   [65] BK Ordo 152, 153.
[66] T Honoré, 'Labeo's *Posteriora* and the Digest Commission', in A Watson (ed), *Daube Noster* (1974) 162.   [67] BK 16, following Alfenus Varus, libri XL <=7> digestorum at BK 15.
[68] Lenel, *Palingenesia Iuris Civilis* vol 1 299 n 1.
[69] Honoré (n 66) 161–81; Mantovani (1987) 117 n 48.
[70] Mantovani (1987) 116–20; Kaiser (n 22) 338; Osler (n 25) 150–3.
[71] Mantovani (1987) 115–23.

The Appendix consists of the works that had not yet been read when that decision was taken. Mantovani goes on to suggest that the Appendix is a continuation of the Sabinian mass and that the *Posteriora* were consequently read without interruption by the Sabinian committee.[72] This last conclusion has been rejected by some scholars[73] and is in my view mistaken.

It is true that if the summary of Paul's *Imperiales sententiae* really belongs to the Papinian mass, and if Quintus Mucius' ὅρων comes after Labeo's *Posteriora* in the Appendix table, Labeo's *Posteriora* from book 2 to book 10 could have been the first work in the Appendix list and could have been read by the Sabinian committee without interruption. But Osler has pointed to an objection.[74] In the article that first highlighted the different masses in which texts from the early and later books of the *Posteriora* occurred, I suggested that the five texts from book 2 that form part of the Sabinian mass, however inscribed, come from the first part of that book, but the 14 in the Appendix position come from the later part of that book.[75] Does the subject-matter of these texts fit that hypothesis? The five texts in the Sabinian position come from titles 28.7 (*De condicionibus institutionum*),[76] 29.2 (*De acquirenda vel omittenda hereditate*),[77] 33.4 (*De dote praelegata*),[78] 34.2 (*De auro argento etc. legatis*),[79] and 35.1 (*De condicionibus et demonstrationibus*).[80] The 14 texts in the Appendix position come from books 32, 33, 34, 36, and 50 of the Digest, [81] so that there is a good deal of overlap with the first five. Title 34.2, admittedly a title in which the various masses appear twice, has one text from book 2 of the *Posteriora* in the Sabinian, another in the Appendix position.[82] It may be that further analysis will show that the fragments in the two masses relate respectively to topics that came earlier or later in that book.[83] Or may the committee charged with reading the Appendix works have read book 2 again and taken a more copious series of excerpts from it than the Sabinian committee had done: 14 texts against the previous five? In that case the Appendix committee cannot have consisted of the same commissioners as the Sabinian committee, and the Appendix cannot be a continuation of the Sabinian mass. Moreover, the *Posteriora* was probably not the first work to be read by the Appendix committee. Paul's *Imperiales sententiae* may perhaps have been the first.

---

[72] Mantovani (1987) 121, 124; (1993) 98–100, 107–8.

[73] Osler (n 25) 146; Kaiser (n 22) 341, citing the adding of codal texts to the Sabinian mass in 35.1.41–2 following on the excerpts from Labeo's *Posteriora* books 1 and 2 at 39–40. This shows that the Sabinian mass was edited as a mass after the reading of these two books. It is inconsistent with *uninterrupted* reading of the *Posteriora* but not necessarily with continued reading after an interval of time.

[74] Osler (n 25) 153–4. Mantovani (1993) 106 points out that Lenel, *Palingenesia Iuris Civilis* vol 1 299 f simply arranged the fragments of this work in the order in which they appear in the Digest.

[75] Above n 69.   [76] D.28.7.20.   [77] D.29.2.64.   [78] D.33.4.6.

[79] D.34.2.31.   [80] D.35.1.40.

[81] D.32.29, 30, 100; 33.1.17; 33.2.30; 33.2.31; 33.2.41; 33.5.20; 33.7.4, 25; 33.8.22; 34.2.39; 36.4.14; 50.16.242.   [82] D.34.2.31, 39.

[83] Mantovani (1987) 120 n 55; Mantovani (1993) 106, 107.

Another objection to the supposed continuity between the Sabinian mass and the Appendix is Osler's thesis that the texts from Scaevola's *Digesta*, like those from Labeo's *Posteriora*, belong partly to the Papinian mass and partly to the Appendix.[84] Those from the first two books, he argues, belong to the Papinian mass, the rest to the Appendix. From the first two books we have eight fragments. In D.2.14.47 (1 *dig*) the Scaevola text comes near the end of the Papinian mass after a text from Tryphoninus' *Disputationes*. It is followed by another text from the Papinian mass, 2.14.48 from Gaius *Ad legem XII tabularum*. Then, after the Sabinian mass from 2.14.49 onwards, the title ends with an Appendix text, 2.14.62, from Furius Anthianus.[85] D.4.3 is similar in that 4.3.32 (2 *dig*) follows the edictal mass and is followed by the Sabinian mass. The final text of the title, 4.3.40, presumably constituting the Appendix, again comes from Furius Anthianus.[86] There are no other texts from the Papinian mass in this title apart from one insertion in the edictal mass.[87] Much the same is true of D.4.4.39 (2 *dig*) where the preceding Papinian mass text is from Paul's *Decreta*, and, after the Sabinian mass from 4.4.40 onwards, the title ends with an Appendix text, 4.4.50, from Pomponius' *Epistulae*.[88] In D.4.8.44 the Scaevola text from 2 *dig* comes between the Papinian and Sabinian masses. At this early stage of the editorial process it would be unique for the Appendix to appear before another mass, something that does not happen until book 40,[89] whereas the position of the text fits the end of the Papinian mass. D.50.1 and 50.7 are less strong cases, because here, though the Scaevola texts (50.1.24 and 50.7.13) come between the Papinian and edictal masses, at this stage in the editorial process the editors were free to put the Appendix in whatever position they thought best.[90] But since in both titles the Scaevola texts come at the end of the Papinian mass, after texts from Hermogenianus, *Iuris epitomae* (BK no 206) and Paul, *De iure libellorum* (BK no 250) respectively, and are not followed by Appendix texts, they are inconclusive. In D.2.15 the Scaevola text (2.15.3) is part of a trio of introductory texts, all of which are displaced from their normal position. In D.50.9 the Scaevola text (50.9.6) comes at the end of the title but, as there is no other text from either the Papinian mass or the Appendix, we cannot tell to which mass it belongs.

In all eight cases the position of the text from books 1 and 2 of Scaevola's *Digesta* is consistent with its coming near the end of the Papinian mass and in the first four listed it fits that position better than the Appendix. But D.2.14.48 (Gai 3 *Ad legem XII tabularum* = BK 247), which comes after 2.14.47 (Scae 1 *dig*) shows that the first two books of the *Digesta* may not have been read as the last item of the Papinian mass but shortly before the last, since a number of one-book monographs come after Gaius on the XII Tables.[91] On the other hand

---

84 Osler (n 25) 154–8; Mantovani (1993) 104.   85 D.2.14.62.   86 D.4.3.40.
87 D.4.3.19 (Pap 37 *quaest*).   88 D.4.4.50.   89 Below n 126.
90 Below nn 126–30.   91 Mantovani (1993) 108.

Scaevola's *Digesta* must have been read after BK 221 (Tryphoninus 12 *disp*) in view of D.2.14.46, which precedes 2.14.47 (Scae 1 *dig*). One can argue that it was read after Paul 1 *de iure libellorum* (BK 250) in view of D.50.7.12 from that work which precedes 50.7.13 (Scae 1 *dig*). The exact position of Paul's *De iure libellorum* in the Papinian mass is uncertain,[92] but in general one-book monographs come towards the end of that mass, at any rate after the Tryphoninus group at BK 219–22.[93] If we suppose that the first two books were read a week or two before the end and that the remainder were left to be read later, that would show that the idea of detaching Appendix works from the main masses was planned in advance.

Osler makes the further point about the relation of the Appendix to the Papinian mass that, in the 32 titles he lists where both the Papinian mass and the Appendix appear but the Papinian mass is not in the third position,[94] the Appendix comes immediately after it in only seven or eight cases. These at first sight include the six titles 2.14, 4.3, 4.4, 4.8, 50.1, and 50.7 just discussed, in all of which the Appendix does not in fact follow the Papinian mass if the first two books of Scaevola are taken to belong to the Papinian mass rather than the Appendix.[95] This is another argument against the view that the Appendix forms part of the Papinian mass. It would be odd if the Appendix followed the Papinian mass in just those few cases in which the Appendix text came from these two books of Scaevola's *Digesta*.

We may safely assign the first two books of Scaevola's *Digesta* to the Papinian mass and the remaining 38 to the Appendix. This has important implications. The Appendix cannot both be part of the Sabinian mass, because Labeo's *Posteriora* formed part of that mass, and also part of the Papinian mass, because Scaevola's *Digesta* formed part of the Papinian mass. The Appendix cannot, in fact, be part of either, but must be a collection of books drawn from both and also, probably, from the edictal mass. The case of Scaevola's *Digesta* is particularly revealing, if we assume that it was treated as part of the Papinian mass before its transfer to the Appendix. For it cannot have been available to the compilers at the outset of their work. Such a substantial work, in 40 books, would in that case have been read earlier in the operations of the Papinian committee. From the BK Ordo it is clear that the programme of all three main committees required them to read the most substantial works first. In all three masses the number of lines per book declines towards the end.[96] In the Sabinian (BK 69–92) and Papinian (BK 224–61) masses there is a long list of

[92] Mantovani (1987) 101.

[93] Mantovani (1987) 101 places Paul, *De iure singulari* after BK 219 and Paul, *De officio adsessorum* after BK 220.   [94] Osler (n 25) 145–6 n 31.

[95] Only in D.47.10.24 does the Appendix follow the Papinian mass when the latter is in the second position in the title. D.33.4 is not an exception, because there the text from Labeo's *posteriora* at 33.4.6 is part of the Sabinian mass, and the Appendix at 33.4.13–14 appears after the Papinian mass at 33.4.11–12, but is followed by three displaced texts at 33.4.15–17.

[96] Honoré (n 56) 7 n 38.

minor works read towards the end of the mass. Many of these are one-book monographs of Paul, of which the compilers read 60, none of which can be confirmed as part of the edictal mass.[97] Although it is often doubtful whether a one-book monograph should be assigned to the Sabinian or Papinian mass and whereabouts within the mass it should be placed, there are enough whose position is secure to show that the general scheme was for the minor works to be read towards the end of these two masses.[98] The *Posteriora* of Labeo and the *Digesta* of Scaevola do not fit this scheme. That is a reason for regarding them, and also Paul's *Imperiales sententiae*,[99] as late arrivals that had to be fitted in after the initial assignment of works to the three committees had been made. Mantovani's scepticism about whether the Appendix consists of late arrivals, and whether the *Digesta* of Scaevola was a late arrival,[100] is therefore weakened.

How was it decided to which committee to assign each work? The system by which Tribonian allotted works to the committees has been explained elsewhere.[101] Each author was assigned to a particular mass, but some of his works could be hived off to another mass to form an interrelated group, for example a group of works on adultery. How does this apply to the Appendix works? In the case of Labeo's *Posteriora* there was no previous Labeo work to go by. The choice of committee was open and the Sabinian was selected. In the case of Scaevola, however, his *Quaestiones* and *Responsa* had already been assigned to the Papinian mass, his four books of *Regulae* to the *Regulae* group in the Sabinian mass.[102] The Papinian mass was therefore the appropriate one for his *Digesta* unless this work was to be allocated to a group of works similar in point of subject-matter or genre. The *Digesta*, had they been available from the start, might (but would not necessarily) have been combined with the *Digesta* of Celsus and Marcellus in the edictal mass. In fact, as Osler shows,[103] it went to the Papinian mass. Applying the same principles to the other Appendix works, Venuleius' *Actiones* and *Interdicta* went to the Papinian committee, given his 19 books of *Stipulationes* at BK 216. Pomponius' *Epistulae* and *Senatusconsulta* went to the edictal committee in view of his books *Ad Quintum Mucium* and *Variae lectiones* at BK 154 and 156. The summary of Paul's *Imperiales sententiae* went to the Papinian committee, not because Paul's works were assigned to this committee (on the contrary, they were divided more or less equally between the three masses) but because the other summary, Paul's *Decreta*, had already been assigned to that mass at BK 222. The *Quaestiones publice tractatae* of Scaevola, assuming the compilers mistakenly regarded this as a work of Cervidius Scaevola, would also

[97] Paul, *ad legem Cinciam* is his only *liber singularis* allotted to the edictal mass (BK 170) but its real mass is uncertain (Mantovani (1987) 97).

[98] Mantovani's analysis ((1987) 90–103) confirms the existence of 17 *libri singulares* of Paul in the Sabinian mass and 17 in the Papinian mass but leaves 26 doubtful, including 11 which have left no excerpts in the Digest.   [99] Above nn 18–25.

[100] Mantovani (1987) 116.   [101] Honoré (n 96) 18–25.

[102] BK 36–46. One ought probably to add to this group, as 46 *bis*, Marcellus, *responsorum* 1 (BK 59): Mantovani (1987) 104–5.   [103] Above nn 84–93.

go to the Papinian committee. Given the allocation to the Sabinian committee of Labeo's *posteriora*, his *Pithana* would also be allotted to it. The monographs by Quintus Mucius, and the only available part of the commentary by Furius Anthianus, might have been placed in any of the masses, since these were the only works of theirs available to the compilers.

The extra works, especially Scaevola's *Digesta*, would impose a heavier burden on the Papinian committee (57 books) than on the other committees (17 or 26 for the Sabinian committee, 25 for the edictal). This may have been one reason for reorganizing the programme of reading and excerpting.

We do not know how the Appendix committee was composed. It is not likely to have consisted of any of the committees charged with reading the original three masses. The Sabinian and Papinian committees were the two senior committees and must have been headed by Tribonian and Constantine,[104] who would be needed for the editorial work which, as Mantovani convincingly argues, went on at the same time. The same is, I think, true of Theophilus who, as the senior law professor, must have been in charge of the edictal committee.[105] Those charged with reading and excerpting the Appendix are likely to have been chosen from among the three more junior law professors, Dorotheus, Anatolius, and Cratinus.

4. In What Position Did the Editors Place the Appendix Texts in the Digest Titles?

On the basis of the works identified above as belonging to the Appendix, an Appendix text or texts appears in 127 titles of the Digest.[106] Their position in these titles supports Mantovani's analysis. In the early books the titles seem to have been fully edited before the Appendix texts became available. The editors had already added codal texts when appropriate.[107] By a codal text is meant one either chosen as suitable to end a mass or title or one that has become detached from the main mass to which it originally belonged and is then added at the end, in a sort of tidying-up operation. At least up to D.22.3 the Appendix excerpts were added at the end, if necessary after the codal texts.[108] There were very few insertions of Appendix texts in the first four books of the Digest.[109]

---

[104] Honoré (n 96) 12–13.   [105] ibid.

[106] Mantovani (1987) lists 131 titles. D.28.7 should be removed because of the assignment to the Sabinian mass of Labeo's *Posteriora* in the Labeo inscribed series book 1 and some texts from book 2. The assignment of Scaevola's *Digesta* books 1 and 2 to the Papinian mass leads to the removal of D.2.15, 50.1, 50.7, and 50.9. In my view, D.40.13 should be added.

[107] Mantovani (1987) 104–6.

[108] The Appendix comes after one or more codal texts in eight titles: D.2.14, 4.4, 11.1, 12.6, 13.5, 16.3, 21.1, and 22.3: Mantovani (1987) 115 n 47. I do not share Mantovani's doubts about 2.14 and 4.4.   [109] Mantovani (1993) 110–13 argues that there were none.

Five titles present difficulties: D.3.5, 4.8, 7.4, 19.2, and 23.3. In the first three a single Appendix text is inserted in the Sabinian or edictal mass. How was this possible if these titles had been fully edited? In D.4.8 the apparent insertion, inscribed Pomponius 17 *Epistularum et variarum lectionum*, may be not an Appendix text but, as treated by Krueger,[110] one from Pomponius' *Variae lectiones* in the edictal mass (BK 156), but displaced within that mass. In D.3.5 and 7.4 the insertions in the Sabinian mass, both relevant, come from Labeo's *Posteriora* books 6 and 3.[111] Was the editor of these titles keeping track of how the excerpting of the *Posteriora*, read early on in the Appendix operation,[112] was progressing? Since the work was taking place in the imperial palace and the excerpted texts had to be assigned to a title, presumably at once, this would have been possible. The title editor could then discover which Appendix texts were marked for his title and perhaps pre-empt a relevant text. In D.19.2 an apposite text from Labeo's *Posteriora* book 4 [113] is again inserted in the Sabinian mass, though the bulk of the Appendix consists of six texts at the end of the title. In D.23.3 there are five Appendix texts at the end of the title, the first two separated from the last three by two insertions, a text of Papinian from the Papinian mass[114] and one of Proculus from the edictal mass.[115] Neither insertion really fits the position in which it occurs and they seem more like texts that have become detached. But, as Kaiser suggests,[116] in that case the last two Appendix texts in this title, which invert the order of Scaevola's *Digesta* and Labeo's *Pithana*,[117] may form part, not of the regular Appendix, but of a detached group of codal texts. It might follow that the phase of the editorial process in which the Appendix comes in principle before the codal texts had already begun at D.23.3. Whatever the truth about D.23.3, the conclusion is that Mantovani's theory about the placing of the Appendix in the earlier books of the Digest is sound, but that texts from Labeo's *Posteriora* in both series of inscriptions seem to have been available before the process of reading and excerpting the Appendix works was complete.

From D 33.1, and perhaps as early as 23.3, a change in editing takes place.[118] In some titles Appendix texts appear in a penultimate position, before the codal texts that end the title. The title editors apparently had access to the Appendix texts after they had settled the order of the three main masses but before they had finished editing the title. This is true in D.33.1, 33.4, 33.8, 33.10, 34.1, 34.3, 35.1 and perhaps 29.5, 36.1, and 36.4.[119] In most of these titles the codal texts

---

[110] *Corpus Iuris* (Stereotype ed) vol 1 96 n 14; also Mantovani (1993) 112.
[111] D.3.5.42 (Lab 6 *post*); 7.4.24 (Iav 3 *post Lab*).   [112] Above nn 15–17, 64–83.
[113] D.19.2.28 (Lab 4 *post*).   [114] D.23.2.81 (Pap 8 *quaest*).
[115] D.23.2.82 (Proc 5 *epist*).   [116] Kaiser (n 22) 340 n 60.
[117] D.23.3.84 (Lab 6 *pith*), 23.3.85 (Scae 8 *dig*).
[118] Mantovani (1987) 115; (1993) 104–6.
[119] It continues in the later titles 44.3, 47.2, 47.10, and 50.12: below n 126. Mantovani (1993) 115 n 47 regards 7.4 as an exception but there the Appendix text is an insertion in the edictal mass. D.35.2 really is an exception (below n 122). D.29.5 may not contain any codal text but merely end with two Appendix texts (n 118). D.23.3 (nn 114–18 above) perhaps belongs to a transitional phase and shows that the change in editing took place earlier than book 33.

look as if they had become detached from the main mass or masses.[120] D.29.5, where the codal text has been chosen to end the title, presents a problem. There, although in the Florentine manuscript the apparent codal text follows the Appendix,[121] Kaiser stresses that it has been shifted by the Florentine editor from the end of D.29.6, where the text he was copying had mistakenly placed it.[122] Hence in 29.5 the Appendix text originally ended the title. But it may be that 29.5.27 (Call 1 *iur fisc*) is not really a codal text but part of the Appendix. In D.35.2 three Appendix texts end the title but come after a codal text from the Papinian mass. Here the title editor seems to have inserted before the Appendix a detached Papinian text that either did not fit the main Papinian mass or had been overlooked.[123] Editorial practice was evidently not entirely uniform. The Appendix texts were now available to be inserted after the main masses and before any codal texts. Most editors seem to have put the Appendix before the codal texts but perhaps some left them to the end where they would previously have gone.

In these books where the Appendix appears before the codal texts there are also titles in which the Appendix ends the title, as before, and follows directly on one of the three main masses.[124] Moreover some Appendix texts are inserted in other masses. D.30.46 (Pomp 9 *epist*) is inserted in the Sabinian mass at a relevant point. The same is true of D.38.4.2 and 4 (Pomp 4 *SCC*), also in the Sabinian mass. But D.35.1.105 (Pomp 5 *epist*) comes after a series of Papinian mass texts that are out of order, and before two Sabinian mass texts, also out of order. There is no obvious reason why it should come where it does. It seems to belong to a group of texts which are detached from their masses. In D.40.1 an Appendix text comes at the end of the title and another Appendix text is inserted between the Sabinian and edictal masses. In 40.4 three Appendix texts come at the end but one is inserted between the Sabinian and edictal masses. In neither case is the reason for the insertion obvious.

The pattern detected by Mantovani for these books in the 30s of the Digest is convincing, but allowance must be made for some editorial discretion when there are both codal and Appendix texts.

Towards the end of book 40 a fresh approach to editing is seen.[125] In D.40.5, for the first time, the Appendix comes before the Sabinian and Papinian masses. This pattern is repeated in 40.14, 44.1, 46.1, 46.3, and 49.14, in all of which the

[120] D.33.1.22–4 (from the Sabinian mass); 33.4.15–17 (from all three masses); 33.8.24–6 (all three masses); 33.10.13–14 (edictal mass); 34.1.20–3 (Papinian mass); 34.3.29–31 (edictal and Papinian masses); 35.1.105–7 (perhaps from all three masses).
[121] D.29.5.26 (Scae 4 *dig*), 29.5.27 (Call 1 *iur fisc*).
[122] Kaiser (n 22) 340–1; Mantovani (1993) 105.
[123] Kaiser (n 22) 340; Mantovani (1993) 105. There is an earlier text from the same book of Papinian at D.35.2.10 (Pap 20 *quaest*).
[124] D.32 (two cycles); 33.5; 33.6 (two cycles); 33.7 (two cycles); 34.2 (two cycles); 34.4; 34.5; 34.9; 35.1; 35.2; 36.2; 36.3; 37.14; 38.2; 38.4; 38.17; 39.5; 40.1; 40.4.
[125] Mantovani (1987) 115–16.

Appendix precedes the Papinian mass and in 48.10, where the single Appendix text precedes the edictal mass. In 50.17 the Appendix comes before both the Papinian and edictal masses. It has become possible, as Mantovani stresses, for the Appendix to be treated like the other masses and to come before another mass when the title editors think it convenient. Editing is now more flexible. There are three titles (44.3, 47.2, 47.10) in which the Appendix comes before a carefully chosen codal text[126] and one (50.12) in which it precedes a detached Sabinian text that has been put at the end of the title because it does not cohere with the first text in the title.[127] There are also titles in which, as before, Appendix texts have been inserted in other masses.[128] In some cases the Appendix both appears as a mass of its own and an Appendix text is inserted in another mass.[129]

If I have reconstructed the story correctly, it testifies to Tribonian's steady ingenuity in seeing the Digest project through on time without neglecting any source that might yield valuable texts. In this respect Tribonian was a true Roman. So was Peter Birks.

---

[126] D.44.3.16 (Paul 3 *Sab*); 47.2.92 (Ulp 38 *ed*); 47.10.45 (Herm 5 *epit*).
[127] D.50.12.1, 15 (Ulp 1 *de off cur reip*).
[128] D.43.19.4 (in the edictal mass); 45.1.122 (one text in the Papinian mass).
[129] D.42.8.23–5 but also 42.8.8, 11; 43.24.22 but also 43.24.2, 4, 8, 10, 12; 43.26, 21–2 but also 43.26.7; 43.29.4 but also 43.29.2. All these instances involve Venuleius' *de interdictis*, but in principle the technique is not confined to this work. It occurred earlier in D.19.2.

27

Logic and Experience in Roman Law

*David Johnston**

I first met Peter Birks just before I began research in Roman law. At the time he was a professor in Edinburgh. We had a short conversation during which he impressed on me that while in Edinburgh I would be better to spend time in discussion not with him but with a real Roman lawyer. He pointed me in the direction of one of the editors of this volume. Over the next years (not least in the viva for my doctorate) I had plenty of opportunities to satisfy myself that Peter Birks was undoubtedly a real Roman lawyer—a jurist in the proper sense of the word. This essay explores some general themes that interest me in his work.

Logic and experience are recurring themes in the essays of Peter Birks. More than once he refers to Oliver Wendell Holmes's well-known aphorism: 'The life of the law has not been logic: it has been experience'.[1] Sometimes this theme is explicit, as in the title of the essay 'More Logic and Less Experience: The Difference between Scots Law and English Law'.[2] On other occasions Birks's focus is more on the importance of a logical structure for the law and on the value of the institutional scheme for understanding and developing the law and for training lawyers to do so.[3] Peter Birks undoubtedly agreed with another distinguished Regius Professor of Civil Law, Sir Henry Maine, that one of the principal benefits in studying Roman law is 'to clear up obscurity surrounding fundamental conceptions of jurisprudence'.[4]

Birks's work emphasizes the importance of logical analysis. Yet in looking at legal history it also recognizes that there is a tension between logic and experience.[5]

* QC, formerly Regius Professor of Civil Law, University of Cambridge.

[1] OW Holmes, *The Common Law* (1881) 1.

[2] Essay in DL Carey Miller and R Zimmermann (eds), *The Civilian Tradition and Scots Law* (1997) 167.

[3] eg in 'Fictions Ancient and Modern' in N MacCormick and P Birks (eds), *The Legal Mind* (1986) 82, 85; 'The Foundation of Legal Rationality in Scotland', in R Evans-Jones (ed), *The Civil Law Tradition in Scotland* (1995) 81.

[4] H Maine, 'Roman Law and Legal Education' reprinted in Maine, *Village Communities in the East and West* (7th edn, 1895) 330, 376.

[5] eg in 'An Unacceptable Face of Human Property' in P Birks (ed), *New Perspectives in the Roman Law of Property* (1989) 61.

Reality is untidy; the interests at play in the development and evolution of law are multifarious. This view is not universally held: one influential view is that legal change has almost nothing to do with the demands of the real world but is embarked upon purely by lawyers and jurists seeking to make their legal system technically better: in other words, it is a matter of internal logic, not experience.[6]

Since a good deal has been written about legal change, it may be necessary to advance a reason for mentioning it again. Here is one: history is written by the victors. Little is heard of those who fell by the wayside as history marched on. Much the same seems to be true of legal change. Ideas, concepts, or institutions which were superseded or suppressed get little attention. But they too may illuminate the questions how and why law develops and changes. This essay considers some examples that bear on this theme, and the roles played by logic on the one hand and experience on the other. At the doctrinal extremes perhaps without undue exaggeration it may be said that there are two possible views, both with respectable pedigrees. One is that change amounts to a sort of natural selection, so the interpretation or approach which wins through can be viewed as doing so on the principle of the survival of the fittest. This view is of course associated at least for matters of natural history with Darwin. An alternative view is that every change is for the worse. This view in some form goes back as far as Plato, reappears during the Renaissance among the humanists, and resurfaces periodically when the highest courts issue judgments that meet with the disapproval of academics or practitioners.[7] So far as change in the law is concerned, the question arises whether logic or experience favours either of these two views.

1. Good Faith in Contract

A rapid paraphrase of the structure of the Roman law of obligations provides the necessary background to the first example. Within the fourfold division of obligations set out in Justinian's *Institutes*, contractual obligations are themselves subdivided, again into four (real, verbal, literal, consensual).[8] Roman law had two types (*genera*) of contract: strict law contracts and *bonae fidei* or good faith contracts. The main example of a strict law contract was the unilateral promise or *stipulatio* concluded by oral question and answer, which had to be in formal terms and had to correspond with one another. So long as there was the necessary formal correspondence of question and answer, there was no restriction on the possible content of the promise—apart from the fact that an illegal or immoral promise would be unenforceable. *Stipulatio* could therefore be used to give legal force to an agreement of any kind. It was a formal contract but an extremely

[6] A Watson, *The Evolution of Law* (1985) 119, and in many other works by the same author.
[7] eg in Scotland the decision of the House of Lords in *Sharp v Thomson* 1997 SC (HL) 66.
[8] Justinian, *Institutes* 3.13.2; cf M Kaser, *Das römische Privatrecht* vol I (2nd edn, 1971) 522; R Zimmermann, *The Law of Obligations* (1990) 10.

flexible one. It was interpreted strictly, without regard to flexible standards such as good faith but simply according to its plain meaning.

The second genus of contract was precisely the opposite: entirely free of form and based on the notion of good faith. But each species within this genus was applicable in only one specific situation. The various species variously came into being when an object was delivered (as for instance in deposit or pledge) or by simple agreement (as for example in the case of sale, hire, and partnership). In neither case was there any need for any set form. But the enforceability of the contract depended on its meeting the precise legal definition for that particular contract. If it did not, there was no contract.

The emergence of the consensual contract of sale (*emptio venditio*) at latest in the second century BC was a critical moment in the history of Roman commerce.[9] Previously sale must have depended on an exchange of stipulations, in which the seller promised to deliver the object of sale, and the buyer promised to pay the price. That had various drawbacks: formality; the fact that routine terms (eg warranties about the quality of the goods sold) had each individually to be spelled out and formally promised in every contract; and the fact that the buyer and seller (or their slaves on their behalf) must meet face to face in order to make the contract by oral exchange of question and answer. The development of the consensual contract of sale overcame all of these disadvantages. The contract of sale automatically implied warranties on the part of the seller about his or her title to the goods and about their quality. The law already set out the essentials which applied to a contract: the whole point of the contract was that without need for express stipulation certain legal effects were automatically produced.

To say that sale is a 'good faith' contract means that the parties' dealings with one another were assessed in any eventual litigation on the basis of what good faith demanded.[10] So, without any need for adding further express promises or undertakings, the law on sale kept pace with the customs of trade and commerce. It was open to a judge to find that the failure of a party to act in accordance with ordinary commercial standards was not consonant with good faith and therefore amounted to a breach of contract. The standard of good faith therefore gave the contract extraordinary vitality and flexibility. Any damages would also be assessed by the court according to what good faith, in the view of the judge, demanded.

In view of the advantages of the good faith contract of sale it would be easy to assume that the movement in Roman law was from rigid formality to a new improved system of contracts interpreted according to good faith: an evolution in favour of fairness and good faith as a universal standard, much as exists in Germany today.[11] But this does not fit with the evidence, as some examples show.

---

[9] cf Kaser (n 8) 545.

[10] M Kaser and R Hackl, *Das römische Zivilprozessrecht* (2nd edn, 1996) 326, 334 with further refs.

[11] § 242 BGB.

The first is the so-called *lex de Gallia Cisalpina* of 42 BC. One of its provisions is concerned with the case where a person seeks security from his neighbour because he is concerned that the dilapidated state of his neighbour's house is going to inflict damage on his own property (*damnum infectum*). The provisions of the *lex* are complex and raise a number of issues; for present purposes it is enough to paraphrase the formula that it sets out: 'If, before the raising of the present action, Quintus Licinius had entered into a stipulation in favour of Lucius Seius in respect of threatened loss, in terms of the stipulation which the peregrine praetor at Rome has set out in his edict, then whatever Quintus Licinius ought, according to that stipulation, to give to or do for Lucius Seius as a matter of good faith up to the sum of [. . .], let the judge condemn him for that . . . '.[12]

These are model pleadings for litigation arising out of a stipulation, drafted using stock names. The point of interest is that the pleadings are based on a formal contract of stipulation. But the stipulation is not in the normal form. Instead it includes a reference to good faith. In conventional legal terms, that is an oxymoron, since the whole point of stipulation was that it was a contract governed by strict law and not mitigated by the fluid demands of good faith. This is our oldest evidence of the formula, or pleadings, for any Roman action. The origin and purpose of this reference to good faith are disputed; perhaps most likely is that it has something to do with good faith as being the basis of juris-diction over foreigners.[13] What may safely be said, however, is that this is an extinct species. In classical law stipulation is the archetype of an agreement which is interpreted according to strict law. Here then we seem to have a fossil, a relic of the past. Why did this type of stipulation die out? A provisional answer may be that, to subject a formal and strict-law contract such as stipulation to a requirement of good faith simply undermined its purpose. There are places in which legal certainty is more important than flexibility or good faith.

Some of the surviving documents of later legal practice provide a different perspective on the same issue. One typical example is the sale of a slave docu-mented by a Greek papyrus of AD 151.[14] The slave is warranted to be healthy in accordance with the standard required by the magistrates in charge of the market-place, the aediles; payment of double the price is also promised if the

[12] Text, translation, and commentary in M Crawford (ed), Roman Statutes vol I (1996) no 28, ch 20, ll 22–31: 's(ei) ant<e>quam id iudicium q(ua) d(e) r(e) a(gitur) eam stipulationem quam is quei Romae inter peregreinos ius deicet in albo propositam habet L. Seio repromeississet: tum quicquid eum Q. Licinium ex ea stipulatione L. Seio d(are) f(acere) opert<e>ret ex f(ide) b(ona) d(um) t(axat) (sestertium), e(ius) i(udex) Q. Licinium L. Seio, sei ex decreto IIvir(ei) IIIIvir(ei) praefec(tei)ve Mutinensis, quod eius <is> IIvir IIIIvir praefect(tus)ve ex lege Rubria, seive id pl(ebei){ve}sc(itum) est decreverit, Q. Licinius eo nomine qua d(e) r(e) agitur L. Seio damnei infectei repromittere noluit, c(ondemnato); s(ei) n(on) p(arret), a(bsolvito).'
[13] Kaser and Hackl (n 10) 155 with further refs.
[14] V Arangio-Ruiz (ed), *Fontes Iuris Romani Antejustiniani* vol III (1943) no 133; cf also nos 87–9 and 132.

buyer is evicted from possession. Both of these warranties are given by a form of stipulation, *fideiussio*; particularly interesting is the fact that the stipulation incorporates by reference the aediles' edict and its list of diseases and defects in respect of which warranty is given. It would be surprising if by this date these warranties were not already implied in the contract of sale. It seems therefore most likely that the buyer was reluctant to rely on implied terms and good faith and preferred the certainty of a stipulation.[15] A further example may be found in a Dacian document of AD 167.[16] This sets out terms for a partnership between moneylenders in—so far as its fragmentary state reveals—some detail. Provision is made for the shares to be contributed by the partners and their shares in profit and loss. Partnership is a good faith contract, and the relations between the partners would therefore ordinarily be judged by that standard. For that reason it is unusual that this document goes on to confirm the terms of the partnership by means of a stipulation. Since the document contains only a stipulation made by one of the partners undertaking obligations to the other, it seems likely that another, reciprocal version of the document would also have been produced.

It is common to think of 'good faith' contracts as having the advantage of simplicity. But what practice seems to show beyond question is the continuing vitality and importance of the formal contract of stipulation. Time and again what we find in practice is a detailed 'good faith' contract which is then executed by one party or each party taking a stipulation from the other, so that the promisor is bound in terms of a formal promise to the promisee. This is true of the examples mentioned, sale and partnership, but it is not confined to them. The consequence seems to be that the parties gave up the apparent benefits of the good faith contract—ease of formation, implied terms, a less rigid procedural regime—in favour of a contract which required to be entered into formally by the parties (or their representatives) face to face, and which would be interpreted strictly. The message is not unambiguous. In these documents it is always possible that the parties simply misunderstood the law. But it does at least seem possible that to the Romans the archetype of contract remained the formal promise, and the strictness with which it was interpreted offered the welcome benefit of certainty. This fits with the demise of the stipulation in accordance with good faith.

Combined, this evidence suggests that the good-faith stipulation represented an evolutionary dead end. It was one which could be pursued no further because it undermined the very value of the stipulation itself. The law provided a range of different types of contract for different purposes. What was valuable about the stipulation was that, in spite of the fact that strict interpretation might work injustice in the individual case, it offered certainty. Sometimes even those who

---

[15] Drafting to the same effect may be found in some of the tablets from Herculaneum: see TH 59–62 (mid-first century AD) as newly re-edited by G Camodeca in U Manthe and C Krampe (eds), *Quaestiones iuris: Festschrift für Joseph Georg Wolf zum 70 Geburtstag* (2000) 53.

[16] Arangio-Ruiz (n 14) no 157.

were entering into contracts which were typically governed by good faith, such as sale or partnership or a building contract, wanted certainty above all. For them the route of choice was stipulation. To water it down with good faith was to dilute it to the point of unpalatability.

2. Damages for Personal Injuries

In Roman law damages for personal injuries were not normally awarded: the law dealt for the most part only with damage to property, and so the only personal injuries which routinely concerned it were injuries to human items of property, slaves.[17]

It is true that there are a few hints even in the Digest that damages could go further. So, for instance, in the case of harm caused by animals, *pauperies*, we are told that the physical harm done to a free person cannot be assessed in damages, since a free body cannot be valued. But account can be taken of medical expenses and of past and future loss of earnings (*operae*, an *opera* being a day's work) owing to the victim's incapacity.[18]

So far as concerns the general Roman remedy for loss wrongfully caused, the lex Aquilia, again there are only the faintest traces of any remedy in connexion with injury caused to free persons. The best-known example is the passage in which Ulpian and Paul discuss Julian's views on how to deal with damages for the case of a boy who, while apprenticed to an over-excitable cobbler, lost an eye after being struck by him on the head with a shoe last. There is no claim for the physical harm, but the boy's father is given a claim for medical expenses and also for the loss he will sustain as a result of the decrease in the son's earnings as a result of the injury.[19]

In a modern incident of this sort, it is clear that the main element in the claim would not be solatium or general damages for the eye but the loss of future earnings, which for a person who was expected to have a bright future might be considerable. But nothing more is said about this in the Roman texts. There are probably two main reasons for this. First, the measure of damages which the lex Aquilia provided for injury short of death was based on the loss of value of the injured thing in the nearest thirty days.[20] This formulation in terms of loss of value of an object within a short period provided no obvious basis for including in the damages an assessment of loss of earnings in future years. So when

[17] Zimmermann (n 8) 1014.
[18] D.9.1.3, Gaius 7 *ad edictum*: '... scilicet ut non deformitatis ratio habeatur, cum liberum corpus aestimationem non recipiat, sed impensarum in curationem factarum et operarum amissarum quasque amissurus quis esset inutilis factus'; cf D.9.2.13, Ulpian 18 *ad edictum*.
[19] D.9.2.7 pr, Ulpian 18 *ad edictum*: 'Qua actione patrem consecuturum ait quod minus ex operis filii sui propter vitiatum oculum sit habiturus et impendia quae pro eius curatione fecerit'.
[20] cf Zimmermann (n 8) 962.

damages were assessed for that, they must have been assessed in some other way. What that was we do not hear. Secondly, the Roman view was that an action based on the lex Aquilia was partly concerned with compensation but also in part aimed at recovering a penalty for the harm done. It is true that the texts show that the Roman jurists attempted to quantify damages precisely (a matter of importance particularly where damages might be doubled). But to make an elaborate quantification of damages might be thought unnecessary, since there was no notion that the proper role of the law of delict was, so far as possible, to put the victim in the same position as if the delict had not occurred. It did not matter if the victim was over-compensated by that standard, because any excess over actual loss could simply be regarded as a penalty. For these reasons the Roman texts are very unhelpful when it comes to assessing future loss of earnings. But matters moved on in later centuries.

When the study of the Roman texts revived in Bologna around 1100, most of the scholars who worked on them—the glossators—followed the few hints in the texts and accepted that there could be an action of damages for injury done to a free person. Some also allowed an action for damages following the death of a free person. All adhered to the principle that a free person could not be valued, so there was no claim for solatium or general damages. What they did, however, for the most part allow was a claim for medical expenses and a claim for loss of earnings. Some of them certainly doubted whether they should. The doubters doubted this kind of claim on the rational ground that it was hard to know how to quantify future loss of earnings.[21] This was not least because a method for doing so was not spelled out in the Digest. But there were a few hints to be found in other contexts.

The main one was to be found in a text in the Digest containing a table attributed to Ulpian which was used to calculate the value of a legacy of *alimenta*, that is, an annual sum intended as a grant or allowance to maintain the recipient, usually a former slave or retainer. Owing to the legislation about the maximum amounts which a testator was entitled to leave in legacies (in particular the *lex Falcidia*), the law of succession did give rise to the need to be able to quantify the value of legacies of this sort. Since the legacy would typically be paid for the recipient's lifetime, it was necessary to estimate how long he or she would live. That is precisely what this table does.[22]

---

[21] Gloss 'habet actionem' on D.9.2.13 pr.

[22] D.35.2.68 pr, Aemilius Macer 2 *ad legem vicesimam hereditatem*: 'computationi in alimentis faciendae hanc formam esse Ulpianus scribit, ut a prima aetate usque ad annum vicesimum quantitas alimentorum triginta annorum computetur eiusque quantitatis Falcidia praestetur, ab annis vero viginti usque ad annum vicesimum quintum annorum viginti octo, ab annis viginti quinque usque ad annos triginta annorum viginti quinque, ab annis triginta usque ad annos triginta quinque annorum viginti duo, ab annis triginta quinque usque ad annos quadraginta annorum viginti, ab annis quadraginta usque ad annos quinquaginta tot annorum computatio fit quot aetati eius ad annum sexagesimum deerit remisso uno anno. Ab anno vero quinquagesimo usque ad

For the computation of maintenance (*alimenta*), Ulpian gives this formula: from birth to twenty, the amount of thirty years' maintenance will be assessed, and the Falcidian will be applied to that amount; between twenty and twenty-five, twenty-eight years; between twenty-five and thirty, twenty-five years; between thirty and thirty-five, twenty-two years; between thirty-five and forty, twenty years; between forty and fifty there will be a computation of as many years as are lacking to sixty, with a deduction of one year; between fifty and fifty-five, nine years; between fifty-five and sixty, seven years; for any age over sixty, five years. Ulpian says that we observe this rule also for the computation of a usufruct. Still, it has been the practice for the computation from birth to thirty to be of thirty years, and from thirty of as many years as are lacking to sixty. The computation never goes beyond thirty.

The basic rule is that where the beneficiary of the legacy was aged under twenty, the legacy would be valued as a legacy of thirty annual instalments of maintenance. From age twenty up to sixty, there was a sliding scale which slid in nine points from a valuation of twenty-eight years down to a low of five years. Modern studies indicate that the figures set out in the table are remarkably close to probable life expectancy in a pre-industrial society such as Rome.[23] It is interesting to note, however, that this table evidently seemed too complicated to some, and the text concludes with a simplified version which, we are told, is in normal use. Under this simplified approach, for a beneficiary aged up to thirty, the valuation is of thirty years; and for a beneficiary over thirty, the valuation is of the difference between actual age and age sixty. The valuation never goes beyond thirty.

This was the text on which some of the glossators seized as the solution to quantifying loss of earnings caused by wrongfully inflicted injury.[24] The standard edition of the gloss notes on the main Roman texts that a claim for loss of future earnings should be valued in accordance with the table.[25] This view goes back as far as the jurist Azo at the beginning of the thirteenth century, so far as claims for injury are concerned. He suggested that in determining how long the loss of earnings would last, the simpler version of the table should be used, so producing a figure between zero and a possible maximum of thirty, in modern terms a

annum quinquagesimum quintum annorum novem, ab annis quinquaginta quinque usque ad annum sexagesimum annorum septem, ab annis sexaginta cuiuscumque aetatis sit annorum quinque. Eoque nos iure uti Ulpianus ait et circa computationem usus fructus faciendam. Solitum est tamen a prima aetate usque ad annum trigesimum computationem annorum triginta fieri, ab annis vero triginta tot annorum computationem inire quot ad annum sexagesimum deesse videntur. Numquam ergo amplius quam triginta annorum computatio initur.'

[23] B Frier, 'Roman Life Expectancy: Ulpian's Evidence' (1982) 86 Harvard Studies in Classical Philology 213.

[24] For detailed discussion of these points, see R Feenstra, 'L'actio legis Aquiliae en cas d'homicide chez les Glossateurs' in JE Spruit, *Maior viginti quinque annis* (1979) 45; also H Lange, *Schadenersatz und Privatstrafe in der mittelalterlichen Rechtstheorie* (1955); H Kaufmann, *Rezeption und usus modernus der actio legis Aquiliae* (1958).

[25] Gloss 'Impensarum' to D.9.1.3: 'Operarum autem amittendarum fit computatio secundum [D.35.2.68 pr]'; Azo, *Summa institutionum, title de obligationibus quae quasi ex delicto nascuntur.*

multiplier. The actual value of the recurrent *operae* or earnings (the multiplicand) was to be found by taking the injured person's daily earnings, and deducting holidays and other days in which he would not work. If his earnings were variable, then the amount he most often earned was to be taken. Azo's pupil Roffredus[26] took over this scheme and extended it to apply also in the case of valuing the claims of dependants arising from the death of a free person.

This is just one example of the glossators' normal procedure: as ever, they sought to justify their views by authority, by reference to texts in the Digest. The adoption of this table shows considerable ingenuity in resolving a thorny problem about how many years' worth of earnings ought to be included in the damages. Technically sophisticated though this approach clearly was, it seems doubtful whether it was much employed in practice. There are three reasons for thinking this. First, even the glossators admitted that a different approach to valuation might be used. Azo suggested that an alternative to the use of the table was that the judge should simply pronounce judgment 'for the amount of earnings he will lose'.[27] This seems to suggest an approach with a broader brush. Secondly, the glossators still took the view that the purpose of an action under the lex Aquilia was the recovery of a penalty. Although some of them tried to limit this principle, there was not much scope, given what the authoritative Roman texts said, for doing so. Since the action was aimed at a penalty, it remained unnecessary to quantify exactly what it was that the victim had lost in order to justify the level of damages. Thirdly, in the glossators' day Lombard law still worked on a much more ancient basis: there were fixed penalties for injuries caused; there was also a procedure for making composition, or buying peace, with the victim's family. For the Lombards, the lost earnings would be included in the global reckoning. In general it seems probable that the table of calculations was used not as a mechanical means of assessing damages, but perhaps at best as a cross-check or as providing a justification for the sum to be paid in composition.[28]

A provisional conclusion from this material is that, although in the twelfth and thirteenth centuries a technically sophisticated method for assessing future loss by taking account of life expectancy was available, none the less it does not appear to have displaced a more rough and ready approach to quantification of damages.[29] Four centuries later, a similar pattern can be detected in the work of two seventeenth-century jurists, Hugo Grotius and Johannes Voet.

In his *Introduction to the Jurisprudence of Holland*, written in 1620, Grotius deals with compensation payable for wrongfully causing death. He explains that compensation is due to those 'who were maintained by the dead man's labour,

---

[26] FC von Savigny, *Geschichte des römischen Rechts im Mittelalter* (2nd edn, 1834–51) vol V 189.

[27] *Summa* (n 25 above): '*condemno te in operis quibus hic cariturus est*'.

[28] Feenstra (n 24) 229–30.

[29] The late Spanish scholastics also preferred a broader approach to quantification of loss: see eg L Lessius (d 1623), *De iustitia et iure* 2.9 d 20.

for loss sustained and profit missed calculated on the basis of an annuity'.[30] Although he does not explain how precisely this calculation is made, it seems likely that it is along the same lines as set out in the table already considered. Twenty-five years later, however, in the last edition of *De iure belli ac pacis* he revised before his death in 1645, Grotius says that the liability is to pay to those the deceased had a duty to support the value of their expectation of support, regard being had to the age of the deceased.[31] Where a person has simply been injured, the liability is for medical expenses plus the loss of earnings arising from the injury.[32] There seems to be a departure here from the annuity method in favour of a somewhat broader approach. Now there is no suggestion that, once the victim' age is known, all that is needed is a calculation. Instead, what Grotius says is rather different: account is to be taken of the age of the deceased. That implies a greater degree of flexibility.

Half a century later, in 1698, Johannes Voet stated that on a man's death his widow and children have an action for the amount which, in the conscience of the judge, seems fair, having regard to the support which the deceased was able and accustomed to provide from his earnings.[33] This, he emphasizes, is not a penalty but reparation of actual loss;[34] in the course of the seventeenth century the view that the lex Aquilia was directed not at a penalty but at compensation had become widely accepted.[35] In working out the compensation, however, Voet is concerned purely with what seems fair to the judge. He does not even mention annuities or calculations. No doubt it is possible that a judge, in deciding what was fair, might take account of the result reached by using tables or calculations of annuities. But he would appear to be under no obligation to do so. From 1620 to 1698 there therefore seems to have been a gradual drift away from the annuity approach towards more flexibility, and towards leaving the matter in the discretion of the judge.

This material illustrates at two different historical moments—in the thirteenth and seventeenth centuries—the emergence of technical methods, based on tables or valuations of annuities, for calculating future loss of earnings. But in each case

[30] *Inleidinghe tot de Hollandsche Rechts-gheleertheydt* 3.33.2; also 3.34.2 on injuries short of death. The translation is by RW Lee, *The Jurisprudence of Holland* (1926).
[31] *De iure belli ac pacis* 2.17.13: 'Homicida injustus tenetur solvere impensas si quae factae sunt in medicos, et iis quos occisus alere ex officio solebat, puta parentibus, uxoribus, liberis dare tantum quantum illa spes alimentorum, ratione habita aetatis occisi, valebat'.
[32] 2.17.14 '. . . tenebitur . . . ad aestimationem ejus quod jam qui mutilatus est minus poterit lucrari.'
[33] *Commentarius ad Pandectas* 9.2.11: 'Nec dubium, quin ex usu hodierno latius illa agendi potestas extensa sit: in quantum ob hominem liberum culpa occisum uxori et liberis actio datur in id quod religioni judicantis aequum videbitur, habita ratione victus, quem occisus uxori liberisque suis aut aliis propinquis ex operis potuisset ac solitus esset subministrare'.
[34] Voet (n 33): '. . . unicuique in id quanti sua interesse docet actio danda; tum quia singuli non de poena sed damno sibi illato reparando contendunt'.
[35] G Rotondi, 'Dalla *lex Aquilia* all'art 1151 Cod Civ: ricerche storico-dogmatiche' (1916–17) in V Arangio-Ruiz, E Albertario, and P de Francisci (eds), *Scritti Giuridici* vol II (1922) 465, 517–18; H Coing, *Europäisches Privatrecht* vol I (1985) 510.

the technical approach seems to have failed to take firm hold. Since history keeps repeating itself, it is not surprising that we find much the same considerations in play nowadays. For many years the courts assessed such things as claims for future loss of earnings by deciding on a figure representing the annual loss (or in the case of a claim arising from a death the annual extent of dependency upon the deceased). They then applied a multiplier to it, based on the age of the person injured, the number of years for which the loss of earnings would be expected to last, but adjusted to reflect the present payment of a lump sum, the contingencies of life, and likely variation in the level of earnings. The method currently in use in the courts in the United Kingdom involves the employment of figures derived from life tables, but these still need to be adjusted for the individual case in order to take account of numerous contingencies.[36] This is more or less what Azo advocated in the thirteenth century. In the seventeenth century, Voet would have described this process as arriving at a figure which seems in the conscience of the judge to be fair.

3. Epilogue

One conclusion that may be drawn from these historical examples is that it is too simple to suppose that law evolves from simple broad-brush techniques in the direction of technical superiority. Technical, logical, or rigid methods have their place, but they do not always serve best where what is needed is justice between the parties. It is obvious that there are various possible grounds for legal change: change in favour of the technical superiority of a rule or institution; change for social or economic reasons; change on grounds of fairness or equity. How do the examples considered fit into these categories?

The first example was concerned with the extinct species of the stipulation in good faith. It would be possible to say that the triumph of the strict stipulation was due to its technical superiority as a matter of law, filling a gap in the legal system which would otherwise exist. But it seems more plausible to say that the strict stipulation was simply more useful in practice, because for at least some transactions what was needed was certainty above all. The second example showed that some societies in some periods have shown a preference for a flexible, broad-brush means of quantifying damages, even when they had more sophisticated methods at their disposal. Here the explanation for the success and resilience of simpler methods seems most likely to lie in the perception that they were an adequately fair way of doing justice between the parties.

If therefore we can view legal change as a kind of natural selection, which involves the survival of the fittest, 'fittest' has to be understood in a wide sense. As the examples illustrate, in one context what is most fit may be an adaptable

---

[36] cf *Wells v Wells* [1999] AC 345.

institution; in another it may be a rigid and fixed one. What is required is justice and the flexibility to achieve it. In a given society the fittest rule or institution may therefore appear rough and ready but, if it is fitter for the task, then there is every reason why it rather than a sophisticated newcomer should survive or even prevail. Similarly, if experience has led to the development of rules that are regarded as fair, albeit imperfectly logical, there is little reason why an application of strict logic should lead to their replacement with something else. The importance of logic and rationality in law cannot be doubted. But experience also teaches that there is more to life than logic.

28

Unjust Enrichment: The Tenant's Tale

*Eltjo Schrage**

1. Introduction

It has often been said that since, as a matter of history, restitution in the common law has its origin in the courts, it is a law of remedies rather than of rights. Even the term 'restitution' looks to the remedy sought, irrespective of the nature of the claim. On the other hand, in Civil Law systems, the term 'unjust' (or 'unjustified') enrichment looks to the ground for seeking a remedy. This is the basis on which the rights that can be claimed in court are formulated. Civilian systems, however, confine the operation of unjust enrichment to the law of obligations. Fundamental to the Civil Law's conception of unjust enrichment is the strict boundary between property and obligations, between owning and owing. It is a given of Civil Law systems that unjust enrichment generates only personal claims. The main effect is that for civilian systems claimants in unjust enrichment are unsecured creditors. No one ever put the point better than Peter Birks: 'As against an insolvent enrichee, [these unsecured creditors] have to join the crowd waiting to share *pro rata* the scraps left over after the secured creditors have been satisfied'.[1]

Undoubtedly, the sharp distinction between the realms of property and obligations is part of the inheritance of Civil Law from Roman law. Birks took note of Bill Swadling's argument that English law ought to make the same choice and move as quickly as possible to the position where unjust enrichment generates only personal claims.[2] Clearly, that is not the present position in common law systems. Indeed, in his answer to Graham Virgo,[3] Birks stated explicitly that nothing prevents a legal system, which chooses to do so, from reversing an enrichment by conferring a new and different proprietary right which arises from

---

* Professor of Law, University of Amsterdam.
[1] P Birks, *Unjust Enrichment* (2nd edition, 2005) 32.   [2] *Unjust Enrichment* (n 1) 32 n 17.
[3] G Virgo, *The Principles of the Law of Restitution* (1999) 15–17, 592–601.

Eltjo Schrage

the unjust enrichment and in order to reverse it.[4] More than anyone, Birks was aware of the differences between the histories of the common law and the Civil Law in this respect. This helps explain why he was one of the protagonists of the view that the project on comparative legal history should begin with the volume on unjust enrichment.[5] A few years later he also contributed to the volume on negligence.[6] In the spring of 2004 he excused himself from a conference for the preparation of a third volume, on the comparative history of contracts in favour of third parties. We could not have foreseen that he would die so soon afterwards.

2. The Problem

One of the direct consequences of the strict boundary between property and obligations in the Civil Law is the fact that transfer of title is a realm of its own, into which restitutionary principles are allowed to penetrate only very hesitatingly. Unlike in several modern systems such as French law, in Roman law contracts themselves did not pass title: for title to pass, in addition to the contract there had to be a separate act of conveyance.[7] According to Roman law, by itself neither the contract of sale nor the contract of lease transferred any property rights. In the case of the sale of a *res mancipi*, there had to be a *mancipatio* while for *res nec mancipi* there had to be *traditio*. Alternatively, *in iure cessio* could be used for both.[8] But, by the time of Justinian, *in iure cessio* and *mancipatio* had both fallen into disuse. In the Digest, therefore, *traditio* is the only way of transferring ownership. In Roman times the contract of lease never transferred a property right. The *locatio ad longum tempus*, which differs in this respect from an ordinary lease, was a medieval invention of the *ius commune*.

According to Roman law, lease had no effects on the property position. The owner remained the owner and possessor; in return for an obligation to make periodical payments, the lessee acquired the right to make use of the property and to gather the fruits. This was definitely a right *in personam*. At the end of the agreed period, the lessee was obliged to return the property in the state in which he had received it. If the lessee had made alterations, or even improvements, to the subjects, these additions were regulated by the law of property. If something was fixed to the object of the lease and so lost its independent existence and, in effect, became part of the leased object, then the title to the improvement passed to the owner of the leased object. This type of acquisition of ownership is known

---

[4] *Unjust Enrichment* (n 1) 37.
[5] EJH Schrage (ed), *Unjust Enrichment: The Comparative Legal History of the Law of Restitution* (2nd edn, 1999).
[6] EJH Schrage (ed), *Negligence: The Comparative Legal History of the Law of Torts* (2001).
[7] R Zimmermann, *The Law of Obligations: Roman Foundations of the Civilian Tradition* (1996) ch 9.
[8] M Kaser, *Das Römische Privatrecht* (2nd edn, 1971) vol 1, 416 ff.

as *accessio*.[9] Where, on the other hand, the attachment could be removed without damaging the leased object, ownership remained vested in the original owner of the attachment and, when the lease came to an end, he was entitled to remove it. For example, the lessee could remove paintings which he had brought into the house since he was still their lawful owner. But the property rights in pictures which the lessee had painted on the walls passed to the owner of the house. The tenant could take away the paintings only if he could remove them without damaging the house. The usual term for this right of removal was the *ius tollendi*. The underlying principle is very simple: give the owner what belongs to him. Under such a system the lessee must carefully consider the improvements he wants to make since he loses ownership of the fixtures. A sensible lessee would make improvements of this kind only if he regarded the investment as profitable, given the unexpired portion of the lease.

As so often, however, practice turned out to be more complicated than theory. What is to happen if the owner reasserts his title to the house and seeks to have the premises vacated sooner than the lessee had anticipated, having regard to the terms of the contract? Or, to put the matter even more broadly: what is the legal position if the lessor prevents the lessee from removing his additions to the leased premises? The Roman jurists gave an amusing example.[10] A tenant had installed a bronze chest in the house. Subsequently, the owner narrowed the entrance to the house and so made it impossible for the tenant to remove the chest. This problem attracted a rich and diverse literature in medieval times, but all that we need notice for present purposes is that, even in this instructive case, the lessee cannot bring an action for unjust enrichment, but has to avail himself of a remedy in property (an *actio ad exhibendum*) or in contract (an *action ex conducto*).

Justinian summarizes the position which we have described in his Institutes 2.1.30:[11]

Ex diverso si quis in alieno solo sua materia domum aedificaverit, illius fit domus, cuius et solum est. Sed hoc casu materiae dominus proprietatem eius amittit, quia voluntate eius alienata intelligitur, utique si non ignorabat in alieno solo se aedificare: et ideo, licet diruta sit domus, vindicare materiam non possit, certe illud constat, si in possessione

---

[9] D.34.2.19.13, Ulpian 20 *ad Sabinum*: semper enim cum quaerimus, quid cui cedat, illud spectamus, quid cuius rei ornandae causa adhibetur, ut accessio cedat principali. cedent igitur gemmae fialis vel lancibus inclusae, auro argentove. Cf D.33.8.2, Gaius 18 *ad edictum*. *Accessio* as opposed to *fructus* or *partus* refers to its independent origin: D.21.1.31.24, Ulpian 1 *ad edictum aedilium curulium*; D.47.2.62.2, Africanus 8 *quaestionum*. David Daube focused attention on the fact that the Romans themselves used the verb rather than the substantive: D Daube, *Roman Law, Linguistic, Social and Philosophical Aspects* (1969) 16 ff. Kaser was also of the view that in Roman times the substantive did not have a technical meaning: *Das Römische Privatrecht* (n 8) vol 1, 428. Referring *inter alia* to D.22.1.3 pr, the gloss *foeneretur* to D.6.1.62, Papinian 12 *quaestionum*, distinguishes between *accessio civilis* and *accessio naturalis*.

[10] D.19.2.19.5, Ulpian 32 *ad edictum*.

[11] I deal with the medieval and later interpretations of this text, which served as the *sedes materiae* for the present problem, in EJH Schrage, 'Scienti alienum esse solum potest culpa obici (Inst 2.1.30). Sachenrecht oder Bereicherungsrecht?' (2001) 47 RIDA (3rd series) 403.

constituto aedificatore soli dominus petat domum suam esse nec solvat pretium materiae et mercedes fabrorum, posse eum per exceptionem doli mali repelli, utique si bonae fidei possessor fuit qui aedificasset: nam scienti alienum esse solum potest culpa obici, quod temere aedificaverit in eo solo, quod intellegeret alienum esse.

Birks and McLeod[12] translate:

Conversely if someone builds a house with his own materials on another's land, the landowner still becomes owner of the house. Here the owner of the materials does lose his ownership because he is taken to have parted with them voluntarily. That assumes he knew he was building in another's land. In that case, even if the house comes down he cannot vindicate the materials. Suppose the builder is in possession and the owner of the land vindicates. He asserts the house is his but will not pay the cost of labour and materials. His action can be defeated by the plea of deceit. That assumes, though, that the builder acquired possession in good faith. Where he knew the land was not his, it can be replied that it was his fault for taking the risk of building on land which he knew was not his.

The (initially strict) division between property and contract means that in such situations the lessee loses his property without any right to compensation. In fact that is still the system under articles 1723 and 1730 of the French Civil Code and was the position under article 1603 of the Dutch Civil Code of 1838 which was modelled on the French Code. Over the last few decades, however, by applying the principles of unjust enrichment, several jurisdictions have tried to change the position by giving the lessee a right, albeit a limited right, to compensation in certain circumstances. We honour the memory of Peter Birks by analysing this development.

3. The Lessee as a Possessor with a Proprietary Right

The importance for society of the contract of lease increased during the medieval period. In the course of the twelfth and thirteenth centuries leases proved useful in two spheres. First, they provided a means by which the nobility and the Church could allow their faithful subjects to enjoy an area of land in return for payment of a fixed sum of money. Secondly, the new cities which had grown up needed housing for their inhabitants. Owners of land found it advantageous to be able to lease out dwelling-houses, for a fixed or indefinite period, provided that they could increase the rent from time to time, or even repossess the property. In short, the rapid growth of the cities led to an increase in the use of contracts of lease.[13] Naturally, in that situation, the law went in search of possible ways of satisfying the needs of lessees. Surprisingly,

---

[12] P Birks and G McLeod, *Justinian's Institutes* (1987) 59.
[13] P Godding, 'Le Droit privé dans les Pays-Bas méridionaux du 12ᵉ au 18ᵉ siècle' Académie Royale de Belgique: Mémoires de la Classe des Lettres, 2nd series, vol 14 (1987) 459 (with bibliography).

the common law and the continental *ius commune* each underwent a similar development, although the two developments occurred independently of one other.

On the continent the legal position of one particular class of tenants, lessees in perpetuity, was assimilated to the position of those having rights in property such as *emphyteusis* or usufruct. From the time of the Glossators onwards, the learned law distinguished between a lease for a limited period and a long lease, a *locatio ad longum tempus*. The formal basis of this distinction was to be found in the *Corpus Iuris*. In D.6.3.1.pr Justinian incorporated a text of Paul, book 21 *ad edictum*, which describes *emphyteusis* as relating to lands which were to be let out in perpetuity (*in perpetuum*). In Institutes 3.24.3 Justinian interpreted this as meaning that the tenure related to *praedia quae perpetuo quibusdam fruenda traduntur* and which no one could take away from the tenant so long as he paid the owner the rent or other return, *quamdiu pensio sive reditus pro his domino praestetur*. Similar reasoning is to be found in D.17.2.1, where in book 32 of his edictal commentary Paul states that a partnership can be entered into *in perpetuum*, that is, for life (*dum vivunt*). In his gloss Accursius identified the perpetual lease with the long lease and, with the definition of *emphyteusis* in mind, he accepted that the holder of a long lease should have an *actio in rem*. In consequence, he stated that this type of lessee had a real right in the property, a *ius in re*.[14] It follows directly from the text of D.6.3.1.1 (*quamvis non efficiantur domini*), however, that these lessees do not acquire ownership. On this basis Johannes Bassianus denied that the lessee acquired *dominium utile*, but Accursius said that it was arguable that he did.[15] Consequently, the tenant under a long lease, unlike the tenant under a short lease, can bring an *actio in rem*. According to classical Roman law, the tenant under a short lease may be in physical possession of the leased object but he is not the formal possessor. As a result of the medieval development of the law, however, the tenant under a long lease, the *conductor ad longum tempus*, comes to enjoy the same legal protection as a *bona fide* possessor. On eviction by the genuine owner, the *bona fide* possessor is entitled to compensation for the improvements he has made to the property during his time in possession.[16] The same protection was now extended to the tenant under a long lease.

---

[14] EJH Schrage, 'Colonia partiaria: Zum Rechtsbegriff der Teilpacht aus der Sicht der Glossatoren' in JA Ankum, JE Spruit, and FBJ Wubbe (eds), *Satura Roberto Feenstra . . . oblata* (1985) 393; EJH Schrage, 'Sale Breaks Hire—Or Does It? Medieval Foundations of the Roman-Dutch Concept' in (1986) 54 TvR 287, extended version in German: 'Zur mittelalterlichen Geschichte des Grundsatzes "Kauf bricht nicht Miete"', in EJH Schrage (ed), *Das römische Recht im Mittelalter* (1987) 281; 'Koop breekt geen huur' (1997) 3 Fundamina 58.

[15] Gl. *In rem* ad D.6.1.3: Et nota secundum Io[annem Bassianum] quod non dicit hic, quod etiam utile habeat dominium, sed satis potest dici.

[16] For the Roman law see WW Buckland, *A Textbook of Roman Law* (3rd edn, by PG Stein 1963, reprinted 1975) 215.

In southern France, in particular, quite a few scholars followed this line of thinking—and for obvious reasons.[17] In doing so, they did not adhere to the doctrine of the Bologna school relating to the method and title for transferring ownership, the *modus et titulus dominii transferendi*, but pursued another line of thought. According to the medieval French jurisprudence, the contract of sale itself transferred ownership of an object. A separate delivery of the object was not needed for title to pass. In article 1583 of the Civil Code, French law still adheres to this system. Similarly, it was argued, a contract of lease itself could potentially transfer a real right in the property to the lessee. Two objections to this approach were soon raised, however. First, it remained unclear why the mere lapse of a long period of time could change the right of the lessee from a personal right, a right *in personam*, into a property right. Secondly, on a more practical level, the recognition of the long lease as a separate institution opened the way to the avoidance of taxes which were generally charged on the disposal of immovable property. These two objections to the attempts to enhance the legal position of the lessee spelled the end of the lease being considered as a property right.

But attempts to give the lessee compensation for improvements continued.[18] Since the law of property was blocked as a way of obtaining compensation, scholars turned their attention to the law of contract and quasi-contract. At a time when different actions all had their own individual fixed schemes of pre-conditions to their availability and of implied effects, the action given to someone who had managed another's affairs, the *actio negotiorum gestorum contraria*, seemed to be an obvious tool for this purpose—at least if it were given a broad interpretation. The action usually served as a kind of unjust enrichment action. More particularly, it lay for the costs which the plaintiff had incurred while enriching the defendant, for example, by doing work on his property. The action presupposed, however, that the plaintiff had intended to manage the defendant's affairs—that he had had an *animus negotii alieni gerendi*. Therefore, the action was available only if the interests of the defendant had really been in the plaintiff's mind when he improved the property. So the action would lie against a lessor for the costs which the lessee had incurred while improving the lessor's property, but only if the lessee had indeed had the lessor's interests in mind at the time. But, in reality, a tenant will hardly ever have the interests of the landlord in mind when he decides to improve the property. It is his own interests which induce him to incur the expenditure: he intends to enhance his own enjoyment. So the lessor will be able to defend any proceedings on the ground

---

[17] EJH Schrage, 'Traditionibus et usucapionibus, non nudis pactis dominia rerum transferuntur: Die Wahl zwischen dem Konsens- und dem Traditionsprinzip in der Geschichte' in M Ascheri, F Ebel, M Heckel, A Padoa-Schioppa, W Pöggeler, F Ranieri, and W Rütten (eds), '*Ins Wasser geworfen und Ozeane durchquert*': *Festschrift für Knut Wolfgang Nörr* (2003) 813.

[18] EJH Schrage, 'Qui in fundo alieno aedificavit. Die actio negotiorum gestorum als Vorstufe einer allgemeinen Bereicherungsklage' (1989) 36 RIDA (3rd series) 401.

that one of the prerequisites of an *actio negotiorum gestorum contraria* is not met. A claim was often dismissed on these grounds.[19]

Consequently, from the Middle Ages onwards, continental scholars (among whom Martinus Gosia[20] deserves special mention) tried to read the *Corpus Iuris Civilis* in such a way as to discover in its pages a general remedy for unjust enrichment which would solve the problems arising out of the conflicting interests of the landlord and the tenant. If the tenant's improvements had been of such a nature that they served not only his own interests but also those of the landlord or of subsequent tenants, then the tenant should be allowed to claim the amount of the enrichment accruing to the landlord. An easily accessible survey of the whole debate is to be found in the collection of controversies that Andreas Fachinaeus published from the early seventeenth century onwards under the title *Controversiarum iuris libri tredecim*.[21]

4. The Dutch Civil Code of 1838

The late Advocate General to the Dutch Supreme Court, GE Langemeijer, once remarked that Dutch nineteenth century private law could be regarded as extremely just, provided that one accepted its underlying presuppositions. The most important of these presuppositions was the primary importance of private ownership which had been acquired in a legally correct way or in accordance with the law of prescription.[22] However paradoxical it may sound, even the law of landlord and tenant came to be shaped by this notion of the primacy of the landlord's ownership of the property. This had a direct impact on the tenant's obligation to return the property at the end of the contract, either in the state which the parties had described[23] or, if they had omitted any description, in a good condition.[24] If the tenant failed to comply with his obligations, he was immediately and directly in default and liable in damages. The Dutch Supreme Court summarized the state of the law concisely:

The tenant is obliged to return the leased property in good condition. This obligation cannot be split up into an obligation to return and a conditional obligation to bring the leased object back up to a good condition. Consequently the obligation can only be fulfilled at the end of the contract. If it is not, the tenant is directly and by operation of law in default. Further notice is not required, since such a notice purports to give an

---

[19] EJH Schrage, 'Europese Klassiekers: Der Erbensucher' (2004) 21 Nederlands Tijdschrift voor Burgerlijk Recht (NTBR) 44.

[20] See JJ Hallebeek, 'Developments in Medieval Roman Law' in EJH Schrage (ed), *Unjust Enrichment: The Comparative Legal History of the Law of Restitution* (1999) 59.

[21] A Fachinaeus, *Controversiarum iuris libri tredecim. Editio postrema ab authore multis additionibus et emendationibus illustrata* (1626) I LXXV.

[22] GE Langemeijer, *De gerechtigheid in ons burgerlijk vermogensrecht* (1994) 14.

[23] Article 1598 of the Civil Code of 1838.   [24] Article 1599 of the Civil Code of 1838.

additional period of time for the performance and thus to limit the term of compliance without default.[25]

In principle, the burden of proving the termination of the contract lay on the landlord who claimed damages.[26]

The assessment of damages under the old law often produced surprising results—for the most part because, if calculated in the abstract, the amount of the financial loss might differ substantially from the plaintiff's actual loss. This proved to be so in the case of a landlord who had leased an apartment building in the centre of The Hague to the State.[27] The lease was for the State to use the building as offices. In the written contract the tenant had agreed to restore the building to a state fit for habitation on the expiry of the lease. But the State refused to do so and the subsequent negotiations about the damages which the State should pay for its breach of contract started in a very bad atmosphere. So, in an attempt to limit the damages, the landlord leased the building to Shell. Shell agreed to refurbish and modernize the building so as to turn it into an office block which met their needs. The State then argued that its breach of contract had not caused the landlord any loss because the building was going to be used for offices anyway. On that basis it refused to pay any damages. The Supreme Court ruled that the State was not deprived of this defence merely because it had been in default. There was no breach of the requirements of good faith just because a debtor gained when his creditor did not suffer any loss and, as a result, the debtor can raise the defence of lack of damage or lack of interest on the part of the creditor.

In short, no damages if there is no harm. This decision put an end to a practice which some property-owning companies had adopted. As owners of blocks of flats, they had been in the habit of making claims for compensation whenever a tenant failed to put his flat back into its original condition at the end of the lease. Although the practice of making these claims was long-standing and widespread, it was far from reasonable—certainly in cases where the contracts of lease had run for decades and the tenants had, at their own expense, altered the houses so as to meet modern standards. The High Court[28] set a good example by holding that a tenant who laid fitted carpets throughout the house was not in breach either of the clause in the lease which forbade him to make any alterations to the house or of the equivalent statutory provision.[29] Even the fact that the tenant had left the carpet behind at the end of the lease did not automatically entitle the landlord to

---

[25] *Van der Meer v Woningbouwvereniging Beter Wonen*, Hoge Raad, 27 November 1998, Nederlandse Jurisprudentie (NJ) 1999, 380 with a note by PA Stein; Advocatenblad 1999, 99, with a note by C Schouten; Nederlands Tijdschrift voor Burgerlijk Recht 1999, with a note by P Abas.

[26] *Braam v Stichting Standvast Wonen*, Hoge Raad, 5 December 2003, NJ 2004, 75.

[27] *Flatgebouw 'Van Hogenhoucklaan' v Staat der Nederlanden*, Hoge Raad, 23 March 1979, NJ 1979, 482 with a note by AR Bloembergen.

[28] *Sociale Woningbouw v Van der Breggen*, Rechtbank 's-Hertogenbosch, 29 January 1982, NJ 1983, 141.   [29] Article 1596 of the Civil Code of 1838.

damages. A breach of the contractual obligation of the tenant to return the dwelling in its original state arose only where, on the facts, there had been some deterioration in the state of the immovable property. The Supreme Court held that as a general rule the landlord's claim for damages should not succeed if he did not actually undertake any repairs but, instead, sold the property after the termination of the contract. The action for damages should lie only if the changes made by the tenant had the effect of reducing the price.[30] In short, in such cases damages should not be calculated on an abstract basis, but on the basis of the actual facts of the case.[31]

The amount of the damages to be paid is limited by the requirements of good faith. The Supreme Court so held in the *Van Ulzen* case.[32] There the landlord, who had not inspected the premises before the termination of the contract, suddenly, out of the blue, presented the tenant with a substantial bill for the costs which he claimed to have incurred in putting the dwelling into good order. In these circumstances the Court did not consider that the landlord had waived his entire claim for damages, but nevertheless held that he could not claim more than the tenant would have spent on the repairs if he had undertaken them himself.

Under the old law the tenant was responsible for the costs necessarily incurred in restoring the premises to the agreed state or (in the absence of an agreement) to a good state. The relationship between the landlord and the tenant was certainly not symmetrical, however. The landlord was not liable to pay for improvements to the property. Although the tenant had the right to take them away, as in Roman law, he had—in the absence of any agreement for financial compensation—no pecuniary claim against the landlord. The Supreme Court confirmed this in *Reimes v Constandse qq*:[33]

According to pre-1992 law (which applies to this case) the co-owner of the leased property, who is enriched by the improvements made by the tenant, is in principle not obliged to make good the expenses incurred by the tenant while improving the immovable. In accordance with article 1603 of the Civil Code of 1838, the tenant has the right to remove the improvements on his departure, but he has no claim for his expenses, except in extraordinary circumstances.

The reference to 'extraordinary circumstances' is not found in the text of the statute; it is an additional remark by the Supreme Court, which opened the door to a claim for financial compensation by a tenant who had, for one reason or another, left the improvements behind when he vacated the premises.

The actual case before the court was indeed a very special one. The defendant, Mr Reimes, combined two roles. On the one hand, he was the owner and lessor of certain immovable property. On the other, he was the only shareholder and

[30] *Van Ulzen v Goolkate*, Hoge Raad 10 June 1988, NJ 1988, 965.
[31] So, Advocate General Huydecoper in his conclusions in *Staat der Nederlanden v De Nieuwe Woning*, Hoge Raad, 3 October 2003, NJ 2004, 50.　　[32] See n 30.
[33] Hoge Raad, 17 September 1993, NJ 1993, 740.

chief executive of a limited company. In the former capacity he leased out the
property to himself in the latter capacity. As tenant, he refurbished the
immovable property at the expense of the limited company and he made quite
extensive fixed improvements to the property. But he failed to pay the suppliers'
bills and, as a result, the limited company went into bankruptcy. Because of that,
Reimes gave the company notice of termination of the lease. The company
vacated the premises without exercising its right to remove the improvements. So
Reimes, as owner, was enriched by the value of the improvements. This enabled
him to restart the business under another name. The receiver, however, tried to
retain the improvements for the benefit of the estate of the insolvent company
and raised an action for unjust enrichment against Reimes. In the very special
circumstances of the case the Supreme Court held in favour of the receiver. Thus
the statutory rule remained in place, but the gates were opened to a number of
exceptions. These exceptions cried out for statutory recognition.

5. Exceptions come to Replace the Statutory Rule

At the termination of the lease the landlord used to have a right to have the
property restored to its original state or to an agreed state; the tenant used to have
the right to take away his improvements, but he did not have a pecuniary claim
for the value of his improvements if he left them behind. This was the general
rule in the Civil Law jurisdictions. Eventually, however, two developments took
place: one was on a social level, the other on a technical legal level.

The social development came about because the tenants' organizations and
the professional landlords' organizations joined forces to increase the degree of
reciprocity in the contractual relations between the parties.

In the Netherlands an association of residents of leased property and the trade
organization of companies owning buildings, *Aedes*, jointly formulated standard
contractual clauses on improvements made by tenants. The starting point for
this work was the mutual interest of the tenant and the landlord in having the
dwelling in a proper condition. By implication, the landlord should recognize a
sort of right of the tenant to do odd jobs. Such a right did not form part of the
rules on leases of dwellings under the old Civil Code: it was left to the discretion
of the parties. But landlords should not refuse permission for alterations which
the tenant wanted to make unless they would harm the prospects of leasing the
property and lead to a decrease in its value. On the other hand, a considerable
number of requirements were imposed on the tenant. Any work had to comply
with the public building regulations and with the requirements of the fire
authorities or the regulations of the municipal energy or water companies and
similar bodies. Provided that the tenant met these requirements, the landlord
should not insist on the removal of the fixed improvements at the end of the

lease. Moreover, it was recognized that the tenant should have a contractual right to compensation for the improvements which he left behind. Compensation should be based on the real value of the improvements and on how long they might be expected to last. By these proposals both associations did their utmost to bring the tenant's interest in his living space into equilibrium with the landlord's financial interest in the property.

In the meantime, however, a development along similar lines took place in the relevant law. In *Quint v te Poel*[34] the Dutch Supreme Court had unequivocally ruled that the Civil Code of 1838 did not contain a general remedy for unjust enrichment, but only a limited number of rather strictly limited remedies which applied in specific situations. It was not necessary to enumerate them exhaustively: analogous remedies could be recognized, provided that they fitted into the legal system. That limited range of remedies belongs to the past, however. The position was radically altered by article 6:212 of the New Dutch Civil Code of 1992 which introduced a general remedy for unjust enrichment:

1. A person who has been unjustifiably enriched at the expense of another is obliged, so far as reasonable, to make good the other's loss, up to the amount of his enrichment.
2. An enrichment shall be discounted to the extent that it is decreased by reason of circumstances for which the person enriched is not answerable.
3. An enrichment shall be discounted to the extent that it is decreased during a time in which the person enriched could not as a reasonable person be expected to take into consideration the existence of an obligation to make good the other's loss. The calculation of this decrease must include expenses which would not have been incurred but for the enrichment.

The combination of these two developments—the reconsideration of the equilibrium between the interests of the tenant and of the landlord and the introduction of the general remedy for unjust enrichment—necessitated a rethink of the statutory provisions on the law of leases. The new codification, which took effect on 1 August 2004, gave ample opportunity for examining the borderline between the law of property and the law of obligations. Article 7:215, paragraph 3, is one result: 'within the limits of article 6:212 the tenant will have a claim for the value of the legitimate alterations and additions which cannot be undone at the end of the contract of lease'.

Under the new law it remains the case that the primary obligations of the tenant are, first, the regular payment of the rent and, secondly, the maintenance of the property in good condition. If he fails to maintain the property, he is liable in damages. Under this new provision, however, the lessee can bring a claim for compensation for improvements he has made, but subject to the restrictions that

---

[34] *Quint v te Poel*, Hoge Raad, 30 January 1959, NJ 1959, 548, with a note by DJ Veegens.

apply to the general claim for unjust enrichment in article 6.212. Unfortunately, one of the best-known features of that general claim for unjust enrichment is that its limits are hard to define. In that situation, are the limits to the tenant's right to compensation for improvements actually ascertainable? In a recent decision the Dutch Supreme Court had to deal with a number of important questions raised by the new provisions.[35]

6. *Dupomex v Duijvelaar*

The mother of the Duijvelaar brothers and sisters was the owner of a factory which she had leased to the predecessor of Dupomex Ltd in 1975. In 1978—under the old Civil Code—the parties agreed a written contract of lease in which they stipulated that the tenant was entitled to make drastic alterations to the subjects at its own expense, provided that they were in keeping with the development as a whole and the commercial value of the building was not reduced thereby. At the end of the contractual period, the tenant was entitled either to remove any improvements without damaging the subjects, or to leave the improvements in the building. Dupomex made extensive use of these provisions. They added a second storey to the office accommodation and considerably enlarged the workshop. This extension to the workshop scarcely featured in the subsequent proceedings between the parties, however, since Dupomex had removed it at the end of the contract. More importantly, in 1990 Dupomex raised the roof of the original workshop.

According to Dupomex, the rent under the contract was relatively high because it was intended to act as a pension for the mother. She died on 11 July 1999 and Dupomex then felt free to give notice to terminate the contract. The mother had four heirs. The first heir was entitled to half the estate, the second—who was the chief executive and main shareholder in Dupomex—to a quarter and the remaining two heirs were entitled to a one-eighth share each. In their notice of termination Dupomex claimed compensation for their improvements to the building, including the extension to the workshop, the raising of the roof, and an extension to the office accommodation. Having regard to the terms of the contract, the heirs refused to pay any compensation. Dupomex then served them with a writ seeking payment of €220,000 plus interest and costs. The district court decided that, in principle, Dupomex had a right to compensation and held that, in the circumstances, it was up to the defendants to establish what the appropriate sum should be. On appeal, however, the High Court quashed the judgment of the District Court and dismissed the claim entirely. Dupomex appealed to the Supreme Court which confirmed the decision of the High Court and dismissed the appeal.

---

[35] *Dupomex v Duijvelaar*, Hoge Raad, 25 June 2004, NJ 2005, 338.

Making the leap from a system with a limited number of remedies for well-defined cases of unjust enrichment (the position under the 1838 code) to an open-textured system consisting of one general remedy (the position under the new Civil Code) is one thing; formulating the limits of this new remedy is quite another. Although he did not seem particularly sympathetic to the point, even under the old law Advocate General Langemeijer had voiced the feelings of all those who feared that 'the principle of unjust enrichment, which had for thousands of years remained a hothouse plant, would suddenly grow into a giant tree whose roots would wrench the foundations of the legal system out of their joints'.[36] Consequently, Langemeijer considered that it was necessary to stem the flood of possible enrichment remedies by invoking the principles of good faith and reason.

And indeed there is every reason for caution and restraint at the borderline between the law of landlord and tenant and the law of unjust enrichment. On that borderline lurks the problem of the enrichment which is forced on a defendant—the problem which is the litmus test of every enrichment action. The tenant should not be able to impose on the landlord an unexpected, unwanted, and, in principle, unlimited liability for unjustified enrichment. The author of the provision in the New Code tried to solve this problem. The Explanatory Memorandum—the Dutch equivalent of Hansard—formulates two criteria which are intended to serve as useful tools for assessing the tenant's claim for compensation.[37] The first is whether the tenant incurred expenses which were useful, but which were not yet fully profitable at the termination of the lease and for which he had received no compensation from the succeeding tenant. The Memorandum gives the example of the costs of installing insulation or a new heating system, which would eventually lead to lower energy bills. The second criterion is whether the landlord is objectively enriched and will profit from that enrichment, for example, by an increase in the rent he can demand or by savings in respect of the maintenance of the building. In summary, having regard to the requirements of the general enrichment action in article 6:212, monetary compensation for the tenant who did not exercise his right to take away his improvements is due only when (1) the tenant is impoverished; (2) the landlord is objectively enriched; (3) there is a causal relationship between the impoverishment and the enrichment; and (4) restitution is reasonable in the circumstances.

In their decision the Supreme Court stressed the independent existence of the final requirement. Under both the old and the new law, the right of the tenant to take away the improvements prejudices his claim that the landlord has been unjustly enriched at his expense. The counterpart of this right of the tenant is the

---

[36] GE Langemeijer, 'Prognostica over Ongerechtvaardigde Verrijking' in *Op de Grenzen van Komend Recht: Opstellen aangeboden aan Prof JH Beekhuis* (1969) 163.

[37] De Memorie van Toelichting , Kamerstukken II, 26 089, no 3, p 27; the Minister, Mr Korthals, on the occasion of the examination of the draft law, Kamerstukken II 2000–2001, 26 089, no 19, p 25.

landlord's right to demand that the leased subjects should be restored to their original condition or to the condition that had been agreed with the tenant. For their own practical or other reasons, both parties may quite legitimately decide to waive these rights. But waiver does not automatically, or by operation of law, create a right to compensation. The fact that the tenant waives his right to remove the improvements does not mean that he can therefore claim the value of the improvements from the landlord. Equally, the fact that the landlord waives his right to have the building restored to its original or agreed condition does not automatically imply that the tenant is obliged to pay the landlord compensation in a case where he does not realize any significant savings by not removing the improvements. In their judgment in the *Dupomex* case the Supreme Court stated at para 3.3:

With reference to the question whether a tenant has a claim on the basis of unjust enrichment for the value of the improvements which he has not removed on the termination of the lease, it should be emphasised that this question should only be answered in the affirmative in so far as the specific circumstances justify it. In that connexion, it might be important, inter alia, to see: what emerges from the contract of lease, or from collateral agreements of the parties, about making alterations to the subjects of the lease; to what extent the tenant has been able to recover the expenditure which he incurred in making the alterations, or has been able to bring it into account with any subsequent tenant; to what extent the expenditure concerns alterations which might have been regarded as written off; and whether the landlord has in fact profited from the improvements, eg because he can sell the subjects for a higher price or can demand a higher rent from a subsequent tenant than would have been the case if the alterations had not been made.

In applying these principles to the case, it is important to recall that in the lease Dupomex had contracted that they should have the power to make alterations to the property at their own expense and that, at the end of the lease, they were to have a choice of either undoing the alterations or leaving them in the property—but the contract did not envisage a right to compensation if Dupomex left the alterations in the property. *Ex nihilo sequitur quodlibet*: something can be deduced from nothing. The fact that the contract was silent on the matter did not necessarily imply that the claim of the tenant should be dismissed. Should the parties have agreed on such a clause? On a reasonable interpretation of the contract, did the parties assume that there was an obligation on the landlord to pay compensation in those circumstances? Was there anything in any remarks, statements, or actions to indicate that the parties had intended to agree on a certain form of compensation?

At the time when the parties signed the deed constituting the lease, Dutch law did not recognize a general remedy for unjust enrichment. The relevant law was to be found in *Quint v Te Poel,* decided in 1959.[38] There the Supreme Court

---

[38] Hoge Raad, 30 January 1959, NJ 1959, 548 with a note by DJ Veegens. See text accompanying n 34.

held that the law recognized only a limited number of well-defined remedies, which should fit into the overall scheme of the legal system. Furthermore, by that time there had been no social developments which would have justified the view that the parties would have assumed that the tenant would have a right to compensation if, like Dupomex, he refrained from exercising his contractual right to remove the alterations. In these circumstances it is certainly not obvious that the parties to the contract could reasonably have deduced from their respective statements and actions that the contract dealt with compensation. Moreover, although the Supreme Court does not lay much stress on the point, in the lower courts the parties had emphasized that the large sums which had to be paid periodically as rent were intended to serve as the mother's pension and, for that reason, exceeded the normal market rent. If this interpretation is right, then it certainly would have been strange for the parties to agree expressly on a relatively high rent, while supposedly agreeing impliedly that the mother, as landlord, would pay compensation for improvements left behind at the termination of the contract. They would have been acting inconsistently—*venire contra factum proprium*, as the *Veteres* would call it. The two propositions are certainly difficult to reconcile.

The position would be no different if (part of) the fixed improvements turned out to be unfit for removal, either by their very nature or otherwise. In that case also there is room for a right to compensation only to a very limited extent and in special circumstances. In this case Dupomex had failed to demonstrate any such special circumstances.

7. Subsidiarity of the Enrichment Action?

In the past, French scholars tended to adopt the position that the general remedy for unjust enrichment in the *Boudier* case[39] was like a Trojan horse which, if once admitted into the fine building of the patrimonial law, would destroy its foundations from within.[40] In order to prevent this destruction, by the beginning of the twentieth century France had developed the concept of the subsidiarity of the general remedy for unjust enrichment. The enrichment action lies only when other remedies are not available.[41] We may leave aside the question whether this is really a useful concept for defining the limits of the general remedy for unjust

---

[39] *Julien Patureau c Boudier* Cour de Cassation 15 June 1892, DP 92.1.596, S 93.1.281, note Labbé; H Capitant, *Les Grands Arrêts de la jurisprudence civile* (11th edn, 2000) no 145.

[40] EJH Schrage, 'Over de verbintenis uit ongerechtvaardigde verrijking' in SCJ Kortmann and others (eds), *Onderneming en 10 jaar Nieuw Burgerlijk Recht* (2002) 621–58.

[41] 'L'Action fondée sur l'enrichissement sans cause ne peut être admise qu'à défaut de toute autre action ouverte au demandeur': Cour de Cassation, third chamber, *Dame Masselin c Decaens* 29 April 1971, Bull civ III no 277.

enrichment.[42] In the various Civil Law jurisdictions its importance varies. In France in recent times the concept of subsidiarity as such has been severely criticized; nevertheless it crops up regularly in decisions of the Cour de Cassation, notably as an argument for dismissing the claim.[43] Italy still considers it to be the best defence against what would otherwise be an uncontrolled flood of actions, but in the Netherlands the notion of the subsidiarity of the enrichment action has never received much attention since the waiver of an action generally has different effects.[44] The Explanatory Memorandum, however, devoted a few paragraphs to the concept.

The question whether any particular enrichment should be regarded as unjustified depends largely on the content of the contract—in the *Dupomex* case the contract of lease. Whether an action for unjust enrichment lies depends on the contract, since in it the parties themselves define which enrichment of a party flows from the operation of the contract and is therefore not unjustified. The agreement between the parties is decisive on this point,[45] and also on whether compensation for the impoverished party is reasonable. The Supreme Court does not say much about this, but that is not surprising since the interpretation of contracts is generally treated as an issue of fact rather than of law, with the result that it is not a matter for the Supreme Court.

The opinion of the Advocate General to the Supreme Court does, however, clarify another aspect of the facts. While devoting considerable attention to the relatively high rent which Dupomex paid as a pension to the mother, he also recalls a further important fact. Dupomex made use of its contractual right to alter and enlarge the building drastically. Immediately after completing the building works, Dupomex leased out a large part of the property to a sub-tenant—no doubt in an effort to obtain some return on their expenditure. That road led nowhere, however, since the sub-tenant went bankrupt shortly afterwards. Therefore Dupomex missed out on any return on their investment. It was not long after the sub-tenant's bankruptcy that the mother died and Dupomex gave notice of termination of the contract. In these circumstances should the claim of Dupomex for unjust enrichment be granted or dismissed? On the facts it appears that Dupomex was impoverished not so much by the enrichment of the estate of the mother as by the bankruptcy of the sub-tenant. Neither the

---

[42] At the invitation of Peter Birks and Frank Rose I discussed this question at a conference of the Society of Public Teachers of Law in Cambridge: 'Contract and Restitution: A Few Comparative Remarks' in FD Rose, *Failure of Contracts: Contractual, Restitutionary and Proprietary Consequences* (1997) 231.

[43] The Cour de Cassation held that an unpaid subcontractor, MTB, could not bring an enrichment action against the defendants, who were the clients of the insolvent main contractor, because the subcontractor 'avait disposé de l'action directe à l'encontre des époux Bréband, qu'elle n'avait pu excercer qu'en raison de son absence d'agrément par ces derniers': Cour de Cassation, third chamber, *Société Menuiseries et Toitures de Brenne c Époux Bréband* 4 December 2002, Bull civ III no 247.

[44] EJH Schrage, 'Europese Klassiekers: De Zaak Boudier' (2004) 21 NTBR 138.

[45] Kamerstukken II 1997–8, 26 089, no 3, 27, end of para 5.

general action for unjust enrichment in article 6:212, nor the specific action in article 7:215 of the New Code is intended to apply to losses of that kind. In other words, the causal relationship between the impoverishment of Dupomex and the enrichment of the Duijvelaar heirs was too weak to found the action for unjust enrichment, since the main cause of the impoverishment lay in the bankruptcy of the sub-tenant.

8. Conclusion

The general remedy for unjust enrichment is apparently not the Trojan horse that some scholars thought they had spotted within the structure of the law. Neither is it a floodgate which, when once opened, causes the waters to rush in. Nevertheless this horse or floodgate is worth keeping under close observation—as Peter Birks saw very clearly. Enrichment that is forced upon the recipient should not give a right to compensation.

PART IV
LEGAL HISTORY

29

Bezoar-Stones, Gall-Stones, and Gem-Stones: A Chapter in the History of the Tort of Deceit

John Baker

*John Baker**

Peter Birks was the leading academic jurist of our generation. We do not use the term 'jurist' very often in this country, and I am not sure I have used it before. But no other word catches so exactly Peter's dedication to abstract legal scholarship and his leadership in promoting it as an enterprise of supreme worth. We began our careers together as assistant lecturers at University College London in the mid-1960s, seduced by the £1,000 a year which seemed just enough to divert us from practice. For each of us it turned out to be a permanent diversion, as in Peter's case might well have been guessed at the time. His evident excitement about legal ideas at once infected me, and—since it never dimmed—it continued to affect me whenever we met over the next forty years. As young lecturers we were keen to share our little discoveries, both intellectual and mundane: in one mad vacation we even set up our own bindery in the basement of what is now Bentham House in order to restore a heap of decaying books rescued from a colleague's chambers in Lincoln's Inn. Re-covering the outsides of old law books was one thing; recovering what was inside them was the greater challenge, and certainly more agreeable to our colleagues. What united us especially in beginning that greater task was the teaching of Professor Milsom, by which we had both been fired with enthusiasm—Peter was taking the LLM course in his spare time, while I had been an undergraduate student. Every week Peter would return to Endsleigh Gardens from the Aldwych freighted with new ideas and already turning in his mind the possibilities for applying the new insights[1] to the history of Roman law. The experience shaped his thinking, as it did mine, for the rest of his life. Only two years ago he wrote that:[2]

---

* Downing Professor of the Laws of England in the University of Cambridge; Fellow of St Catharine's College, Cambridge.

[1] This was in the dim days before the publication of *Historical Foundations of the Common Law* in 1969. [2] *Jurists Uprooted*, ed J Beatson and R Zimmermann (2004) 258, 259.

Those who stand in the tradition of Maitland [and] Milsom . . . come to Roman law with one great advantage. They know what it is to have had no law library at all, to have started, so to say, from scratch . . . Milsom's illuminating work shows that without a library law is qualitatively different and that the library builds up very slowly. The principle of uncertainty dominates outside the law of actions. The law of succession comes nearest to being an exception, where a finite set of questions constantly has to be answered. The dominant principle tells us that without a library there are no answers to the questions which only a library can answer. The periphery of every proposition retains the natural uncertainty of everyday lay discourse.

In that recent essay, Peter went on to express the hope for a 'marriage' between the history of the common law and that of Roman law, combining the insights of Milsom with those of Lenel. He believed passionately—another term I do not use often—that each discipline had much to learn from the other. I hope he would have enjoyed the puzzles explored in this essay. The development of the action on the case for deceit was certainly uninfluenced by libraries. It seems to modern eyes to have belonged both to the law of tort and to the law of contract, chiefly because—in the absence of books in the library labelled *Contracts* or *Torts*[3]— neither existed as a distinct entity during the formative period. And there is reason to believe that the story has surprisingly close parallels in the history of Roman law.[4]

The writ of trespass on the case for deceit, as distinct from the older writ of deceit—which was also a species of trespass but limited to fraudulent conduct in the course of litigation—seems to have been formulated by the Chancery in 1382 for use against the vendor of a blind horse,[5] though there was nothing new in 1382 about the underlying concept.[6] The formula was:

cum idem JA barganizasset cum prefato JW ad emendum quondam equum ab eo, idem JW sciens equum in morbo cecitatis collapsum eundem equum warantisando eum sanum oculis et membris prefato JA pro magna pecunie summa falso et fraudulenter vendidit . . . ['whereas *P* had bargained with *D* to buy from him a certain horse, *D*, knowing the horse to be blind, falsely and fraudulently sold the same horse to *P* for a great sum of money by warranting it sound in eye and limb'].

---

[3] The appearance of such books in nineteenth-century England may well be partly attributable to the 'silent influence of Gaius and Justinian': P Birks (ed), *English Private Law* (2000) p xlvi.

[4] See the four papers by B Nicholas, P Stein, A Rogerson, and A Honoré, in D Daube (ed), *Studies in the Roman Law of Sale*, (1959) chs 7–10.

[5] *Aylesbury v Wattes* (1382) YB Mich 6 Ric II (Ames Fdn) 119 pl 27; CP 40/987, m 561; 103 Selden Soc 447. It was approved again, after challenge, in *Rempston v Morley* (1383) YB Trin 7 Ric II (Ames Fdn) 30 pl 11; Fitz Abr, *Ley*, 41.

[6] See the city case of *Shoreditch v Lane* (1300) in AH Thomas (ed) *Calendar of Early Mayor's Court Rolls 1298–1307* [*CEMCR*] (1924), 68; *Lacer v Canterbury* (1304) ibid 154 (described as a plea of trespass). As for the king's courts, there is a prototype of 1307 in 58 Selden Soc 179; AKR Kiralfy, *A Source Book of English Law* (1957) 145 (warranty on the sale of a horse, where the plaintiff was a royal officer requiring the horse for military purposes). There is a less clear precedent in *Adam Browne's Case* (1368) YB 42 Lib Ass 8; Kiralfy (above) 144 (described as an appeal, it is a bill seeking damages against the vendor for eviction of the goods, which had been stolen from someone else and sold to the plaintiff without good title; it seems to be an action for deceit in selling stolen goods as his own, but there is no mention in the report of knowledge or warranty).

Although there was no need for actions on the case to be tied to certain forms, and we shall come across some variations later, this remained the standard formula for the next few centuries.[7] There were three main elements in the formula: (i) a prior bargain for a sale (or, less commonly, a hiring) of goods, set in the pluperfect tense; (ii) knowledge by the seller of some defect or quality in the goods (the *sciens* clause); and (iii) a sale of the goods with a warranty that they were free from the defect or possessed some quality other than that known to the seller.[8] The words *falso et fraudulenter*, sometimes elaborated into a *machinans decipere* clause, probably did not add anything further of substance, though they might take on a more substantive meaning in other actions on the case for fraud outside the realms of sale.

Assuming for the present that this was the only formula available for those who found they had bought something other than what they thought they had bargained for, how far can we take the words at face value as an indication of what had to be proved? The answer, of course, is that we cannot know. But we can make some sensible guesses by looking at the pleadings in such actions. Professor Milsom has pointed out that the *sciens* was never traversed, which makes it very likely that, provided a warranty could be proved, the seller's state of mind was not regarded as material.[9] If so, this was a remedy not only for fraud but for any false warranty which induced a buyer to complete the sale. The element of inducement, or reliance on the warranty, is obliquely hinted at in the formula, since the phrase *warantizando vendidit* was presumably intended to convey that the sale was effected by means of the warranty. If the buyer did not rely on the warranty—or if he should not have done so, for instance where the subject-matter of the warranty was evident to his own senses[10]—he could not bring the action. The most important word in the formula seems, therefore, to be this *warantizando*. What, then, was a warranty?

---

[7] eg *Emson v Daxe* (1495) CP 40/931, m 293): 'cum idem R cum prefato B ad emendum quoddam dolium vini vocati claret apud L barganizasset, predictus B, sciens vinum predictum corruptum et insalubre, vinum illud incorruptum et salubre warrantizando vinum predictum pro magna pecunie summa prefato Ricardo falso et fraudulenter ibidem vendidit . . .'. The plaintiff is Richard Emson (or Empson), presumably the Middle Templar and later infamous minister of Henry VII.

[8] The action was not confined to defects, but was also available (for instance) where a seller misrepresented the length of a bale of cloth.

[9] SFC Milsom, 'Sale of Goods in the Fifteenth Century' (1961) 77 LQR 257–84, 280; *Historical Foundations of the Common Law* (2nd edn, 1981) 364 ('If the defendant had given a warranty, it was immaterial whether he had in fact been deceitful'). We have noticed a traverse in the sixteenth century, but it resulted in a demurrer: *Woode v Rutter* (1538) CP 40/1096, m 412; 6 *Oxford History of the Laws of England* [hereafter *OHLE*] 772 n 33.

[10] *Drew Barantine's Case* (1411) in JH Baker and SFC Milsom, *Sources of English Legal History: Private Law to 1750* (1986) [hereafter B&M] 509; *Anon* (1471) B&M 511, 513, per Bryan CJ; *Grete v Lane* (1496) KB 27/934, m 30; *Monyton v Wylson* (1517) KB 27/1024, m 23d; 6 *OHLE* 772 n 35; James Hales's reading in Gray's Inn (1532) B&M 349 (misdated).

That is a surprisingly difficult question. The word had an earlier history in the context of feudal tenure and grants of land; and in that context, although it has a contractual ring, and was described as a 'covenant real', it took on a special meaning infused with ideas of lordship, and the defence of title, and was commonly implied without any express agreement.[11] At any rate, an express warranty of land, according to Littleton and Coke, was such a technical matter that it could only be effected by using the verb *warantizare* or its English equivalent.[12] In the ordinary contractual context, by the end of the eighteenth century, a warranty would become a species of promise, so that *assumpsit* would lie upon it;[13] and to English lawyers from the nineteenth century until the present a warranty is simply a term in a contract, a species of term less important than a condition. Maybe that is, as Williston remarked, the 'natural' meaning of warranty.[14] In the first reported cases (1382–3), counsel argued that the action did not lie without a deed because a warranty was a covenant.[15] The argument did not succeed, but it must at least have made sense; and this is borne out by the records of local courts in which sellers 'promise' that goods have certain qualities.[16] There are other cases in Tudor times in which we can detect some confusion or overlapping between warranty and promise.[17] Yet the action on the case for deceit was devised in the 1380s, a generation later than the action of *assumpsit*. If a warranty was simply a promise or undertaking, there would have been no need to invent the deceit formula; *assumpsit* would have done the job. The new writ must have been devised to meet a specific problem; and the nature of the difficulty may be hinted at in some fifteenth-century cases. Promises relate to the future, warranties to present fact.[18] A promise that a blind horse has good

---

[11] Co Litt 365–6. Coke said that 'the learning of warranties is one of the most curious and cunning learnings of our law'.

[12] T Littleton, *Tenures* [1481], sec 733 (from Co Litt: 'cest parol et verbe warrantizo fait le garrantie . . . et nul auter verbe en nostre ley'); Co Litt 384a.

[13] The origin of this development may have been, not that the warranty was itself seen as a promise, but that a promise had been made to deliver the goods with the quality warranted: 6 *OHLE* 772–3. For an unsuccessful attempt to combine such a count with a count for deceit, see *Denison v Ralphson* (1682) 1 Vent 365, sub nom *Bevingsay v Ralston*, Skin 66.

[14] S Williston, *The Law of Contracts* (1920) 1297, para 673. He nevertheless contended that *assumpsit* to enforce a warranty was essentially a quasi-contractual action: id, 2676, para 1505.

[15] See n 5 above; and also *Garrok v Heytesbury* (1387) B&M 507; *Anon* (1452) Statham, *Actions sur le Cas*, 26; Simpson, *History of Contract*, 244–5. In *Anon* (1471) B&M 511, 512, Choke J said that an action of covenant would lie on a warranty of goods made by a third party, if there was a deed.

[16] eg *Waderove v Oxford* (1275) 2 Selden Soc 140 ('promisit in venditione' that wool weighed 8½ lb); *Dunstable v Bal* (1278) 46 Selden Soc 2 ('promisit' that wool equal to sample); *Mauncestre v Bolom* (1305) in *CEMCR*, p 262 (promise that wine good, and also declaring it good and merchantable); *Stanton v Honing* (1317) 23 Selden Soc 102 ('promisit' that herring equal to sample). See also Milsom, 'Sale of Goods' (n 9 above) 278.

[17] 6 *OHLE* 772–3; *Andrew v Boughey* (1552) 1 Dyer 75.

[18] *Anon* (1471) B&M 511, 513, per Choke J ('one may not warrant something yet to come'). cf *Kinge v Braine* (1596) B&M 517, where the same argument was rejected by Clench and Fenner JJ; they drew attention to the common clause in marine insurance contracts whereby a merchant warranted the safe return of a ship. But there is a reversion to the older approach in *Matrevers v Aland* (1651) 1 Rolle Abr 97.

eyesight, or that bad wine is good, is a promise impossible to be performed.[19] The new remedy is not for failing to make good a promise which could never have been performed, but for misleading someone into making a detrimental but valid (and now executed) contract.[20] If that is the true explanation for the innovation, it might be supposed that 'warranty' was equated with a misrepresentation or misstatement of fact. But that seems not to be correct either. The cases to be examined presently draw a clear distinction between a warranty and a mere affirmation; and it is the latter, we may suppose, which is synonymous with a representation of fact. What was it then, which elevated an affirmation to the level of a warranty? It seems unlikely that, as with land, it depended on using the magic word 'warrant'.[21] Presumably something tantamount would have been sufficient, such as 'assure' or 'pledge'.[22] By the end of the seventeenth century, Holt CJ is supposed to have ruled that any affirmation by a seller was a warranty, if the buyer relied on it.[23] According to other versions of what he said, the distinction depended on whether the statement was made at the time of sale;[24] and that may have expressed older learning.[25] But Holt CJ did not on either view mean to provide an exclusive definition, and his dicta do not bring out the special character of the warranty. Presumably the essence of a warranty is a guarantee—which is the French version of the same word.[26] For this we have good modern authority. 'Everyone knows what a man means when he says, "I guarantee it", or "I warrant it", or "I give you my word on it". He means that he binds himself to it.'[27] Lord Denning was not a historian, but we are inclined to think that in this instance a medieval lawyer would have agreed with him. In Roman terms, to warrant is *praestare* or *adseverare* rather than mere *adfirmare*.[28] The words used by the seller, and the timing of his statement, were evidence as to

---

[19] Note, however, that impossibility was no defence to an action on a penal bond: 6 *OHLE* 828.

[20] Simpson goes so far as to say that this analysis was 'the source of much that is unintelligible in modern law': *History of the Common Law of Contract* (1975), 243.

[21] Williston assumed it had been so in the early seventeenth century: S Williston, 'What Constitutes an Express Warranty in the Law of Sales' (1908) 21 Harvard Law Rev 555–82, 556.

[22] cf Customs of Exeter (c1282) 21 Selden Soc 182 (sale 'en plevine' without defects); *Dyer v Grantham* (1317) 23 Selden Soc 105–6 ('plevina' that goods equal to sample).

[23] *Crosse v Gardner* (1689) Comb 142, 143; Holt 5; Carth 90; 3 Mod Rep 261; 1 Show KB 68; *Medina v Stoughton* (1700) 1 Salk 210; 1 Ld Raym 593. cf the (American) Uniform Sales Act 1906, s 12: 'an affirmation of fact or any promise by the seller relating to the goods is an express warranty if the natural tendency of such affirmation or promise is to induce the buyer to purchase the goods, and if the buyer purchases the goods relying thereon'.

[24] This proposition, though famous, does not appear in the reports but is a gloss upon those cases by Buller J: *Pasley v Freeman* (1789) 3 TR 51, 57; reporter's note in [1957] 1 All ER 328.

[25] In *Lopus v Chandeler* (1606) B&M 518, 521, Tanfield J seems to have understood an affirmation as a pre-contractual statement, what we now call a 'mere representation', whilst a warranty was a contractual term.

[26] In law French, indeed, there is no distinction between warranty and guarantee. The seller is said to 'garrante' his goods.

[27] *Oscar Chess Ltd v Williams* [1957] 1 All ER 325, 327, per Denning LJ.

[28] D.19.1.6.4, Pomponius 9 *ad Sabinum*; 19.1.13.3, Ulpian 32 *ad edictum*.

the existence of a warranty but not conclusive.[29] Like all questions of fact, the precise meaning lay with the jury; and that is why we do not find it elucidated in the books.

We have noted the probability that the action on the case lay where there was a false warranty but no knowledge of its falsity. What, however, if there was knowledge—and therefore, presumably, an intention to deceive—but the deceiving statement was not a warranty? If *warantizando* was the key word, there could hardly be liability without any warranty at all. Fitzherbert was of that view in 1534, referring to a sale of wine: in the absence of a warranty, the buyer 'must buy at his own risk, and his eyes and taste should be his judges'.[30] The default rule was *caveat emptor*,[31] or (in homely Lancashire speech) 'Let your eye be your chapman'.[32] Although Fitzherbert did not accept it, there was nevertheless generally held to be an exception in the case of wine and food; no warranty was in that case necessary.[33] But Fitzherbert was writing about forms, and the year-book doctrine could be applied in practice without changing the forms, by resort to implication or fiction: a warranty was in fact usually alleged in the case of victuals, although it was not legally necessary to prove one.[34] Some have supposed the explanation for the exception to be that the liability of the seller of victuals was essentially statutory.[35] Perhaps in origin it was. But there was another exception which had no statutory basis. A seller of goods without title could be sued in an action on the case without a warranty, and perhaps without proof of knowledge either.[36] No doubt that was another special case, since there cannot be a sale without a thing to sell.

---

[29] eg a warranty made before the sale could still qualify as a warranty: *Goldsmith v Preston* (1605) 1 Rolle Abr 96.

[30] A Fitzherbert, *La Novel Natura Brevium* (1534) fo 94; B&M 344.

[31] The maxim was in use by Elizabethan times: *Kenrick v Burges* (1583) Moo KB 126 (referring to the case where the buyer made an offer to buy and the seller merely agreed). It seems to have been popularized by Coke CJ, in the context of sales of land: 4 Co Rep 26; 5 Co Rep 84 (cited in 3 Buls 216, 1 Rolle Rep 195), 3 Buls 116.

[32] Lancaster custumal (1562) 21 Selden Soc 183 ('Also they which bye any malte . . . lette their eye be their chapman, and yf it prove nought, thei shall have no remedie for it afterwards except thei can prove the seller thereof dyd warrand the same to be good').

[33] YB Pas 7 Hen IV fo 14 pl 19; Mich 9 Hen VI fo 53 pl 37 (B&M 510); Trin 11 Edw IV fo 6 pl 10 (B&M 511, 513); Milsom 'Sale of Goods' (n 9 above) 279; *Anon* (1491) Caryll's reports, 115 Selden Soc 73; B&M 515; James Hales's reading in Gray's Inn (1532) B&M 350 (misdated).

[34] Milsom 'Sale of Goods' (n 9 above) 279 (for the earlier fifteenth century); *Thurgo v Sabrichesworth* (1493) KB 27/929, m 16 (rotten malt); *Constable v Potter* (1497) KB 27/945, m 49 (unwholesome herring); *Howe v Olyver* (1498) KB 27/946, m 50d (insufficient malt); *Fresby v Fereby* (1512) CP 40/999, m 117 (bad salmon); *Predyaux v Tute* (1521) CP 40/1032A, m 121 (sixteen pipes of beer warranted drinkable but made plaintiff ill; pleads he delivered sufficient beer and not that mentioned in declaration); *Emson v Daxe* (1495) CP 40/931, m 293 (n 7 above).

[35] *Anon* (1430) B&M 509, 510; *Anon* (1491) Caryll's reports, 115 Selden Soc 73; B&M 515; *Burnby v Bollett* (1847) 16 M&W 644, 654, per Parke B; DJ Ibbetson, *Historical Introduction to the Law of Obligations* (1999) 85.

[36] 77 LQR 282 (precedent of 1444); James Hales's reading of 1532 (above n 33), semble; *Kenrick v Burges* (1583) Moo KB 126 (*sciens* and assertion, but no warranty); *Kettle v Miller* (1585) CP 40/1444, m 406d; cited in J Herne, *The Pleader* (1657) 102, margin ('machinans defraudare' clause, but no *sciens*, warranty, or even affirmation); perhaps the same as *Dale's Case* (1585) Cro Eliz

But it is not obvious why the exceptions should have ended there. If it was possible to bring an action on the case for non-contractual forms of deceit, such as winning money with false dice,[37] or obtaining money by false pretences,[38] or perhaps even for giving a false character-reference on which the plaintiff relied,[39] it is difficult to see why it should not have lain for tricking someone into a bad bargain by means falling short of a warranty.

There was indeed a theory that any seller who knew of a concealed defect and misrepresented the facts was liable to an action. Serjeant Godered said that this had been decided by the King's Bench before 1430 in the case of badly fulled cloth,[40] and in 1442 Paston J said it had been so decided by the Common Pleas in the case of a horse with an internal illness.[41] Both dicta were somewhat weak, and the propositions were doubted by the reporters; but there were other precedents,[42] and in about 1506 Frowyk CJ asserted that, 'if someone sells me cloth or something else which he knows to be bad, now I am deceived by his own knowledge, and in this case—inasmuch as he was aware (*sciens*) and sold it, albeit the sale was without warranty—he shall nevertheless be punished by a writ on my case'.[43] That was directly contrary to Fitzherbert's view; but the remark

---

44, CP (*sciens* required, though Anderson CJ said it could be presumed); *Berye v Lone* (1595) CP 40/1552, m 1333; British Library [hereafter BL] MS Add 37321, fo 21, margin; Herne (above) 102, 224 (sale of gelding which he affirmed was his own; no *sciens* or warranty); *PJ v WE* (undated) in JHB MS 109, fo 48 (*sciens*, but no warranty or affirmation); *Lopus v Chandeler* (1606) B&M 518, 522, 523, per Popham CJ obiter (knowledge required, but not warranty); *Furnis v Leicester* (1618) Cro Jac 474 ('falso et deceptive' sold sheep, affirming them to be his own, without warranty; judgment for plaintiff); sub nom *Lister v Furnace*, 1 Rolle Abr 90; *Warner v Tallerd* (1650) 1 Rolle Abr 91 (affirmation, but no *sciens* or warranty); *Harding v Freeman* (1651–2) Style 310, 1 Rolle Abr 91 (similar). cf *Roswel v Vaughan* (1607) Cro Jac 196, Exch (warranty necessary); *Sprigwell v Allen* (1648) Aleyn 91; BL MS cit 2 East 448n, KB (actual knowledge necessary).

[37] Even Fitzherbert accepted this (*Novel Natura Brevium* (1534) fo 95; B&M 344), citing a precedent of 1465; it was also sanctioned by the Register (*Registrum Omnium Brevium*, fo 290). Later precedents: B&M 345 n 16; *Cryer v Feversham* (*c*1573) BL MS Harley 664, fo 63v; *Burbage v Eltock* (1637) CUL MS Gg.2.20, fo 991.

[38] eg *Bonfester v Reynold* (1510) CP 40/992, m 354 (selling tithes as servant of vicar who was in fact dead); *Thompson v Gardner* (1597) Moo KB 538; AKR Kiralfy, *The Action on the Case* (1949) 82; *Tracy v Veal* (1609) Cro Jac 223; *Cavendish v Lady Midleton* (1628) B&M 523.

[39] The two cases in 6 *OHLE* 773 rest primarily on negligence; but cf *Fromond v Derk* (1426) in *Calendar of Plea and Memoranda Rolls of the City of London 1413–37*, ed AH Thomas (1943) 201.

[40] *Anon* (1430) B&M 509, 510. It was pointed out that this was irrelevant to the case in hand, where a warranty was alleged.

[41] *Doige's Case* (1442) B&M 391, 394. Here the reporter questioned Paston J's precedent, suggesting that a warranty had been alleged, and advised recourse to the record.

[42] eg *Ellesmere v Whytbred* (1467) CP 40/823, m 283 ('cum P cum D ad quendam crateram de argento ab eo emendam apud L barganizasset, D, sciens argentum crateris predicti cum stanno mixtum, craterem illum de argento puro et cum stanno minime [mixtum] ibidem vendidit'). The plaintiff, Robert Ellesmere, was a goldsmith (CP 40/824, m 23), but this is not disclosed in the writ. (cf 6 *OHLE* 772 n 28, where the text contains an error; in the cases cited there, a warranty was alleged.)

[43] *Note* (*c*1506) Keil 91; translated in Caryll's reports, 116 Selden Soc 552; B&M 516. Frowyk CJ nevertheless mentioned victuals as a special case, perhaps implying that even *sciens* was not necessary there.

remained in the safe obscurity of manuscript until it was printed in 'Keilwey', and it may be that Fitzherbert's *caveat emptor* position was received as the sixteenth-century orthodoxy. If that is so, it seems very likely that it was the publication of 'Keilwey' in 1602 which prompted a renewal of interest in the subject during the first two decades of the seventeenth century.

The first of the Jacobean cases is well known, though only from the unsatisfactory printed reports. Geronimo Lopez, a Portuguese merchant,[44] had in 1597 given a diamond ring worth £100 to a London goldsmith called Robert Chandeler in exchange for a stone falsely asserted (but not warranted) to be a 'beazer' or 'bezoar' stone. Everyone in 1597 knew what a bezoar stone was, though few had seen one.[45] The word 'bezoar' is said to have come—via Arabic, and then Spanish—from a Persian word denoting an antidote against poison.[46] The stones in question were calculus concretions found in the stomachs of animals, and also said to occur in dragons and sea-serpents; they were brought from the far ends of the earth and retailed at a high price, because they were believed to cure many diseases.[47] They seem to have become all the rage in the late sixteenth century, probably as a result of Spanish imports from the New World. The Spanish court was using them in the late 1580s;[48] Queen Elizabeth I had two as part of her crown jewels; and in 1597 Lord Cobham presented one to Lord Buckhurst, which was considered a fine and rare gift.[49] So highly were they esteemed that elaborate openwork cases were made for them in precious metals; several examples of these bezoar-stone holders may be seen in museums, and two were sold in London recently.[50]

---

[44] He was implicated in 1594 in the treason of Dr Lopez, Queen Elizabeth's physician, to whom he may have been related, but was eventually discharged: *Calendar of State Papers (Domestic) 1591–4*, 379, 416 (said to be a great friend of Dr Lopez), 418 (one of three persons with custody of Dr Lopez), 443 (released and going to Flanders). He is perhaps the Geronimo Lopez Sapayo who reported Francis Drake's departure to the king of Spain in 1587: *Calendar of State Papers (Spanish) 1587–1603*, 75. His surname is given as 'Lopus' in the records.

[45] The knowledge is far from defunct today, especially to followers of Harry Potter. A search for bezoar stones on Yahoo produced 63,000 hits.

[46] 2 *OED* 163, where the first example is from 1580.

[47] Further information is available on the Internet from *http://www.bezoarstones.com*, which currently offers such a stone taken from a dragon or sea-serpent for $3,500, and a wide range of less choice specimens for as little as $150. They are said not only to have medicinal properties but to improve luck, prosperity, and love. The site also offers guidance on how to detect counterfeit bezoar stones, the principal clue being that they do not work.

[48] *Calendar of State Papers (Venetian) 1581–91* (several references).

[49] *Calendar of State Papers (Domestic) 1595–7*, 485. Note also *Calendar of State Papers (Domestic) 1601–3*, 300 (letter to correspondent in Venice, 1603, asking him to send one, since he had found them useful in curing colds).

[50] Bonham's on 16 October 2003; article in *The Daily Telegraph*, 13 October 2003. Another, said to be English, was sold at Christies, 19 November 2003, lot 136. One of them (dated *c*1680) was subsequently offered for sale by Wartski, the London jewellers. These may have been meant for man-made 'Goa stones' rather than bezoar stones. Goa stones were artificial bezoars manufactured by Portuguese Jesuits in Goa, and many were exported to Europe in the later seventeenth century.

Lopez presumably became aware of the inefficacy of his purchase soon after the event, but he did not bring his action until the next century, about a year after the publication of 'Keilwey'. In fact, contrary to what was once thought, he brought at least four actions.[51] The record of the first action has not yet been found, and we do not have a report of the arguments at the initial stage; but we know from Croke's report that Lopez obtained judgment in the King's Bench, only to have it reversed in the Exchequer Chamber in 1604 on the ground that a mere assertion (or 'affirmation') was not actionable without a warranty.[52] The court said, 'and although[53] he knew it to be no bezoar stone, it is not material; for everyone in selling his wares will affirm that his wares are good, or the horse which he sells is sound, yet if he does not warrant them to be so it is no cause of action'. It seems from a citation of the case by the same George Croke, in 1618,[54] that knowledge had not been pleaded correctly: it was not stated that the defendant knew of the falsity of the stone at the time of the sale, and any knowledge thereafter was irrelevant. But the decision to reverse was in any case not unanimous. Anderson CJ dissented, saying, 'the deceit in selling it for a bezoar stone, whereas it is not so, is a cause of action'. He thus adopted the view of his predecessor Frowyk CJ, and it may have been this weighty dissent which encouraged Lopez to pursue the matter further.

In 1603 he brought a second action, this time in the Common Pleas (Anderson CJ's court), and the record shows that the count was in the following form:[55] whereas (i) the defendant is and for twelve years past has been a goldsmith with expertise in precious stones ('habuit scienciam et cognitionem de naturis et qualitatibus geminarum et lapidum preciosorum') and with the ability to distinguish between them and assess their prices, and gained his living thereby, (ii) on 1 October 1597 he asserted and affirmed ('asseruit et affirmavit') to the plaintiff that he had a true and perfect bezoar stone ('verum et perfectum lapidum preciosum vocatum a Beazers stone ac de vera natura et qualitate inde'), and (iii) the plaintiff was possessed of a diamond ring worth £100, the plaintiff bargained with the defendant to buy the stone asserted to be a bezoar stone, and the defendant, knowing the stone not to be a bezoar stone, 'sed falsum et fictum Anglice a false and counterfeit beazers stone', affirmed it to be a bezoar stone, and, the plaintiff being wholly unaware ('penitus ignaro') whether it was or not, but relying ('fidem adhibens') on the defendant, the defendant falsely and fraudulently sold him the stone in return for the diamond ring. The defendant

---

[51] cf Simpson, *History of Contract*, 536 n 2 ('I do not accept the view that here were two actions between the parties').

[52] Sub nom *Chandelor v Lopus* (1604) Cro Jac 4; B&M 518.

[53] This probably represents *coment que* in law French, the language in which Croke's reports were written (autograph in the Hertford Record Office, not examined for present purposes). If it does, the true sense may be 'even if'.

[54] *Southern v Howe* (1618) 2 Rolle Rep 4.

[55] CP 40/1705, m 1767 (Trinity term 1603). There is no reason to think this differed materially from the first (KB) action.

pleaded Not guilty, but nothing more is known beyond the writ summoning the jury. Note that it was not a case of passive concealment—to which *caveat emptor* clearly applied—but of an affirmation, falling short of a warranty, made in the knowledge that it was false: a deceitful misrepresentation. Whether or not the pleading was the same in the first action, Lopez had evidently been advised that the point was still not finally decided and that it deserved another airing. The inclusion of the declaration in at least two contemporary books of entries suggests there was some professional opinion in his favour;[56] but it must be supposed that Lopez was nonsuited, because in the following year he started again. In the third suit, also in the Common Pleas, the defendant demurred to the declaration; the proceedings were adjourned for advisement until Easter term 1604, but no judgment was entered.[57] Again, we must suppose that the plaintiff abandoned the suit.

Lopez seems not, however, to have been the kind of plaintiff who gives up easily. In 1606 he brought a fourth action, returning this time to the King's Bench. This action is known to us not only from the record,[58] but from a manuscript report discovered at Harvard by Beale in the 1890s and since found in at least four other manuscripts.[59] The count was exactly the same as in the Common Pleas actions, and again the defendant demurred to the declaration. Popham CJ, adopting the procedure he had used in *Slade's Case*, 'thought it good that it should be considered by all the justices of England; for if it were found in favour of the plaintiff it would affect all the contracts in England, which would be dangerous. Therefore he would procure all the justices to consider it.' There is no evidence that that happened, though we have fairly full reports of the arguments in the King's Bench. Counsel for the plaintiff relied on Frowyk, as reported in 'Keilwey', and even argued that 'asserted and affirmed' was tantamount to a warranty if the assertion was made knowing that it was false. The defendant argued that 'when someone is selling wares it is lawful for him to speak the best of them that he can, in order to raise the price' and that an action did not lie in the absence of a warranty or reliance. The reliance as pleaded here, he said, was irrelevant, because expertise in bezoar stones belonged to apothecaries and not to goldsmiths; moreover, the plaintiff had himself inspected the stone before buying it. The principle of *caveat emptor* should apply. Popham CJ's prima-facie opinion was favourable to the plaintiff. He agreed that a mere

[56] BL MS Add 37321, fo 21, margin; Herne (n 36 above) 102 (reference only). The citation suggests it was a sale of a sapphire for a diamond.

[57] Record: CP 40/1710/2, m 1252 (second part of Hilary term 1604; very fragile bundle). This is also cited by Herne.

[58] KB 27/1391, m 265; 1 Dyer (1688 edn) 75 n; Kiralfy, *Action on the Case* (n 38 above) 85–6; B&M 518–20. The entry ends with the joinder in demurrer.

[59] 8 Harvard Law Rev 283; B&M 520–3 (collating five MSS of the same report). This anonymous note was something of a landmark, in so far as it was the first time a legal historian had shown how our understanding of an early-modern reported case could be substantially revised by recourse to manuscripts.

affirmation was not actionable—there must be either a warranty or knowledge of the untruth of the affirmation, and an intention of deceiving. But in the instant case there *was* knowledge, and it was immaterial (according to Popham CJ) whether the seller was a druggist or a goldsmith, if he knew he was selling something false. On the other hand, Popham CJ thought it a 'dangerous case' of widespread importance which required further consideration. Evidently it was not the current understanding in 1606 that deceitful affirmations were generally actionable: the fear about letting in new claims shows that the law was still unclear. The only other judge to speak in the King's Bench was Tanfield J, who said he would reserve his opinion. No trace of a final decision has been found, and no judgment is entered on the roll; only the first decision, therefore, was transmitted to posterity. Everyone agreed that the action lay without a warranty in the case of victuals, or a sale without title. But the effect of a fraudulent misrepresentation, short of warranty, was left in the air.

The citation in 1618 is instructive as to the extent of the uncertainty at the time. Croke's contention was that the ground for reversal of the first judgment in the Exchequer Chamber was merely that knowledge had not been pleaded at the time of the sale: a verdict that the defendant knew the stone to be false might therefore refer to knowledge gained later, and that would not entitle the plaintiff to succeed. The implication is that Croke thought an action would have lain without a warranty, if knowledge had been correctly pleaded and proved. He made no mention of the second, third, or fourth actions—perhaps because they were never decided—and appears to have argued that the point was determined by the King's Bench judgment at first instance: since the reversal was only on the pleading point, it did not affect the substance of the decision. Against him, however, Serjeant Bridgman argued that no action lay for deceit without a warranty, except in the case of victuals, because the rule was *caveat emptor*. Bridgman's view, it seems, was that the reversal of the judgment restored what he took to be the old (pre-Frowyk) law, whereas Croke's view was that the reversal on a pleading point left intact the *ratio decidendi* of the King's Bench in 1604 (ie the Frowyk position). Dodderidge J seems to have sided with Croke, but the 1618 case itself—as we shall see—was decided on a different point.

Lopus v Chandeler has been regarded as a leading case in the common law.[60] Yet it was a leading case which did not settle anything—save in the sense that, by not clearly resolving the question either way, it left *caveat emptor* in place as the basic principle for another 400 years, albeit with a growing encrustation of exceptions. As far as the printed reports were concerned, there could be no

---

[60] RC McMurtie, 'Chandelor v. Lopus' (1887) 1 Harvard Law Rev 191–5, 192 (criticizing the dismissal of the case by MM Bigelow, *The Law of Fraud* (1877) p iii); JW Smith, *A Selection of Leading Cases in the Common Law*, 13th edn by TW Chitty, AT Denning, and CP Harvey, vol 2 (1929) 57–8; *Heilbut, Symons & Co v Buckleton* [1913] AC 30, 38, per Lord Haldane LC; *Oscar Chess Ltd v Williams* [1957] 1 All ER 325, 327–8, per Denning LJ (former editor of *Smith's Leading Cases*, above).

remedy for a false misrepresentation, even (at first) a fraudulent misrepresentation, unless there had been a firm warranty as opposed to a mere affirmation. According to the traditional learning, it was not until 1789 that the courts recognized a remedy for a fraudulent misstatement independently of warranty.[61] It is very doubtful, however, whether contemporaries saw matters so clearly. Some of the judges in 1606 evidently thought that there was already liability for a fraudulent, or knowing, affirmation of something false: not because the law was moving forward, but because the indecision in Lopez's cases had left Frowyk CJ's recently unearthed doctrine in place and displaced Fitzherbert's extrajudicial opinion. Which view prevailed in practice could only be established by combing through the miles of unread plea rolls from the seventeenth century.

One clue is provided by an unreported case of 1609 concerning a more painful kind of stone. John Guy, an attorney of the Common Pleas, brought an action on the case against an amateur doctor called Robert Lane.[62] His complaint was that, whereas the plaintiff had a stone in his bladder,[63] by reason whereof he sought a cure by dissolving the stone, the defendant, knowing all this, and being a person unskilled in curing that illness ('homo imperitus et ignarus in curatione infirmitatis predicte'), scheming and fraudulently intending to deceive and defraud the plaintiff, asserted and affirmed himself to have the necessary skill ('fore peritum et habere scienciam et peritiam dissolvendi calculum in vesica'); and the plaintiff, trusting in that affirmation, retained him; whereupon the defendant, for £6 13s. 4d. paid in hand and 20 marks to be paid upon 'the finishinge cure', undertook the cure, whereas in truth the defendant did not have the knowledge claimed and was never a qualified doctor or surgeon in the city of London or elsewhere; and by reason thereof the defendant so negligently treated the plaintiff and applied such unsuitable medicines that for want of knowledge the stone was not dissolved but became daily more and more dangerous and harmful to the plaintiff, to the great deception, prejudice, and impoverishment of the plaintiff. All we know of what happened next is that the defendant pleaded Not guilty, and that a jury was summoned; but some thought the pleading precedent worth preserving in books of entries.[64] This was not a sale of goods, and it might perhaps have been framed differently in *assumpsit* for negligence, or even as an action for negligence *per se*;[65] but the plaintiff's pleader evidently thought that an action lay for the deceit, which would have had the advantage of

---

[61] *Pasley v Freeman* (1789) 3 TR 51. This case is stated by all the textbooks on tort to have been a new departure, but it was really just a clarification.   [62] CP 40/1826/2, m 1118.

[63] Also excoriation in the bladder, but repetition of this is omitted here to save space.

[64] BL MS Add 37321, fo 19 (Latin text); Herne (n 36 above) 135 (English text, from an entry the previous term, citing Trin 7 Jac I, m 211 or 1211). There is a remote precedent in *Taylour v Trerice* (1511) B&M 516, where the defendant was allowed to choose wine for the plaintiff in reliance on his assertion that he was a connoisseur ('in cognitione bonitatis vinorum valde sciens').

[65] cf *Wild v Hall* (12 Car I or Car II, c1636 or 1660) in Girdler's book of entries, CUL MS Add 9430(3), fo 108: the plaintiff accidentally put out the instep of his tibia; the defendant affirmed himself to be skilled in the art of bone-setting, and affirmed that the tibia was broken when in truth

obviating the need to prove negligence. Here, then, within five years of *Lopus v Chandeler*, is a precedent for bringing an action on a misrepresentation where there was knowledge of the falsity of an assertion of fact, but no warranty.

In *Baily v Merrell* (1615) the action for deceit seems at first sight to have taken a step back, but the facts were unusual.[66] The consignor of a bale of woad affirmed that it weighed 800 lb when in fact it was 2,000 lb, and the carrier relied on this misrepresentation with the result that his horses died of fatigue. In an action on the case for deceit, the defendant argued that (i) it was foolish of the plaintiff to rely on the statement when he could (and should) have weighed the cargo himself,[67] and (ii) there was only an affirmation, not a warranty. The judges of the King's Bench, in the absence of Coke CJ, seem at first to have been divided on both points; but the case was adjourned with a strong indication that the action would not lie without a warranty, and it is said that the plaintiff did not think it worth moving again. The outcome seems understandable enough on the facts, especially since there is no mention in the reports of fraud. This particular indecision, therefore, did not carry the matter further in any direction. But the fact that the plaintiff was advised to bring the action, and its support in principle by some of the judges, may indicate a continuing body of professional opinion in favour of deceit without warranty.

Our third case concerning stones is *Southern v Howe* (1618).[68] The facts were found by a special verdict in the King's Bench in an action on the case for deceit. The plaintiff had been asked by the defendant's factor in Barbary[69] to sell some counterfeit jewels for him; not knowing that they were counterfeit, he sold them to the king of Barbary for £800, when they were worth only £100, and delivered the money to the defendant; the king, on discovering the facts, committed the plaintiff to prison until he repaid the purchase price, which he had to do from his own funds. The plaintiff contended that this was an actionable deceit, even though there was no warranty, and his counsel appears (from Croke's report) to have relied on *Lopus v Chandeler*. The discussion is confused by questions of agency, and by speculation as to whether the king had imprisoned Southern lawfully. The best argument, which seems to have been decisive, was that, if the stones were worth £100, they must have been real jewels of some kind and could not be called counterfeit; unlike silver, which had a certain value, the worth of jewels was purely a matter of personal taste. For good measure, however, it was argued that there could be no liability without a warranty. On this point, according to Rolle's report, Mountagu CJ agreed with the defendant that the action only lay without a warranty if someone sold another's goods as his own, or

---

it was only the instep; he undertook to cure the tibia and set it in plaster, and later received £6 10s. for the cure; nevertheless he so negligently applied the cure to the instep that the plaintiff suffered 'magna dolores et gravamina', and the instep became lame and incurable.

[66] 3 Buls 95; Cro Jac 386; 1 Rolle Rep 275; 1 Rolle Abr 96–7.

[67] cf *Drew Barantine's Case* (1411) B&M 509.

[68] 2 Rolle Rep 5, 26; Cro Jac 468; Poph 143.   [69] The north coast of Africa.

sold unwholesome wine or victual. It would not lie if someone sold wine which
was drinkable though not very good, or something which was not worth as much
as the buyer was led to believe. Judgment was given for the defendant. The real
issue here was the distinction between matters of opinion and statements of
fact;[70] and it is not clear from the report precisely what the defendant had told
the plaintiff that was untrue. In so far as Mountagu CJ appeared to hold that an
action would not lie for a knowing misrepresentation of fact, falling short of a
warranty, it was not only unnecessary for the decision of the case in hand but was
not generally accepted in subsequent seventeenth-century cases. At any rate, in
1652 and 1663 the courts sanctioned actions of deceit where there was *sciens* but
no warranty.[71]

   To end with confusion or uncertainty would not be untypical of a common-
law story; but this is not quite the end. English legal historians, like Roman
lawyers, know well enough that the formal position is not always the whole truth
and nothing but the truth. Sales of victuals and sales without title were indeed
special cases, in that it was apparently not necessary for the buyer even to allege a
warranty. But suppose the plaintiff did allege a warranty, which required only
the single word *warantizando*. That would be enough to protect him against a
motion in arrest of judgment. And yet, as we noted in starting, we do not know
what had to be proved to win the verdict.[72] When Holt CJ said that every
affirmation at the time of the sale was a warranty, if relied upon, there was no
great stir; it was doubtless no more than many juries had assumed in practice.
But it took much of the force out of the formal proposition that there had to be a
warranty rather than a mere affirmation of fact. And might we not suppose that,
even when there was no explicit affirmation, a reasonable jury could imply a
warranty from surrounding circumstances, if it was something so obvious that it
went without saying? It was clear that an undertaking could be so implied in
assumpsit—for instance, an undertaking to pay for goods bought, even when
there was no explicit promise to do so.[73] If you sold food, it was obvious that you
were purporting to sell something edible (though not necessarily palatable), and
indeed that you had good title to what you were selling. No doubt in those
particular cases it is otiose to speak of implied warranties, because the action lay
without any warranty at all; but Rolle, at any rate, thought it right to speak of

---

[70] This distinction was explicitly made in *Ekins v Tresham* (1663) below, explaining *Harvey v
Young* (1597) Yelv 20 (affirmation that property worth £150 not actionable).

[71] *Fowke v Boyle* (1652) Style 343, 348 (selling false bills of public faith to the value of £800,
affirming them to be true but knowing them to be false, with intent to deceive him); *Ekins v
Tresham* (1663) 1 Lev 102, sub nom *Leakins v Clissel*, 1 Sid 146 (falsely and fraudulently affirming
that property was let for £42, so that the plaintiff, relying on this, gave £500 for it, when in truth it
was only let for £32).

[72] cf Simpson, *History of Contract,* 246 ('it seems futile to attempt to discover what counted as a
warranty; what counted as a warranty was simply a jury matter').

[73] *Norwood v Rede* (1557) B&M 448, 449 ('every contract executory is an undertaking in itself');
Slade v Morley (1602) B&M 420, 429, 439–40.

warranties 'in law'.[74] Suppose, however, that you bought a piece of meat for your hound, a transaction not covered by the victuals legislation, and there was no express guarantee that it was edible; could it be implied not only that you would get good title to the meat but also, if you made the purpose known, that it would be fit for canine consumption (or, at least, not fatal to dogs)? There is reason to think that warranties were indeed implied in suitable cases long before the practice was brought into the light of day by the circuit reports printed at the end of the Georgian period.[75] But that is another story, and one which needs further exploration.

---

[74] 1 Rolle Abr 90 (P1–3), glossing YB Mich 9 Hen VI fo 53 pl 37 (B&M 510).
[75] JH Baker, *Introduction to English Legal History* (4th edn, 2002) 358.

30

Denials Ancient and Modern, with some Roman Footnotes

*Jeffrey Hackney**

Littleton in his chapter of Rents saith that a denyer shall make a disseisin[1]

News of our Peter's illness provoked instinctive denial, and for many of us, the awfulness of his premature death still leaves the void which denial seeks to fill. So here is a bit of common law denial as a humble memorial to my old pal. This essay deals with the three areas of law which Peter and I have discussed over the years—Roman law and the medieval and contemporary common law. Sadly the medieval common law had not figured in our discussion in recent times and if I may assert a negative, I doubt if there will ever again, in the history of the world, be a time when two men are both late home for supper (one of them more unusually than the other, I suspect) because they have been stuck at a road junction on their bikes trying to satisfy the seemingly insatiable desire of one of them to know just how exactly *escambium* actually worked in title to land cases at common law in the thirteenth century. It would have been good fun discussing some of the following nonsense with him.[2]

This essay looks at the way denial of title has operated in two areas of the common law, not usually seen as having much in common. In the law of leases, a

---

* Fellow and Tutor in Law, Wadham College, Oxford.

[1] *Isaack v Clarke* (1615) 2 Bulstr 306, 311 (Croke J).

[2] In particular, he would without doubt have fairly rapidly solved a mystery which unduly held me up while reading for this. One of Coke CJ's less irritating habits is that of making up quotations. At the end of the *Case of the Marshalsea* (1612) 10 Co Rep 68b, after some unctuous observations on bringing unity between the courts, he finishes as follows: 'So that our successors, as I believe, may take up the saying of the prince of poets

> *Haud unquam neque concio nos neque curia dictis*
> *Audivit pugnare, animo sed semper eodem*
> *Et sentire eadem, atque eadem decernere vellet'.*

What prince of poets would that be then? A non-poetic version (reading *velle*): 'Never did a meeting or a court hear us fighting against what had previously been said [or perhaps just "in words"], but always with the same mind wanting to think and decide the same things'.

specially vicious landlord-oriented rule has recently been weakened by a judicious use of contract reasoning. What is less well known is that the common law's protection of chattel interests may have been helped into its classical 'metaphysical'[3] tort of conversion form by an injudicious misuse of the leasehold rule. Whatever else may be said of the Romans and their classicism, it must be said they dealt better with these problems.[4]

I

In *British Telecommunications Plc v The Department of the Environment*,[5] BT was, on the face of it, tenant of the Department, and the parties were in dispute. Two issues arose for decision. The first, a construction point, centred around BT's claim that it was the freeholder. If BT succeeded on this point, the matter was effectively over. But if it failed, BT had prepared a case to argue the action as tenant. The Department replied that BT's claim to the freehold was a denial of its title and that by this denial BT had put an end to the tenancy and the Department was entitled to possession. The second issue could not therefore, in its view, arise. Lindsay J found himself in the depths of a feudal doctrine for which he showed no evident enthusiasm.

It was admitted by BT, at least as far as the High Court was concerned, that a sufficient denial of his landlord's title by a tenant might allow a landlord to put an end to the tenancy and then either take or be awarded possession of the premises. Disapproval of this 'medieval law' had been expressed in the Court of Appeal in *Warner v Sampson*.[6] That court had not taken the opportunity, however, to ditch the old law but had merely clipped its wings and held that so long as the pleading in question was not an affirmative setting-up by the tenant of a title adverse to the landlord, there was no sufficient denial to put his tenancy in jeopardy. So if a pleaded general denial meant no more than that the defendant was in possession, no harm would ensue. But in the present case, BT expressly claimed that it had title. This brought it squarely inside the one example which the Court of Appeal had reserved as the remaining vestige of the old law. Lord Denning had said ' . . . it is plain that a disclaimer by a tenant in a Court of Record does not give rise to a forfeiture unless it amounts, expressly or impliedly, to an assertion or affirmance by the tenant of title in himself or a stranger'.[7] It was clear that BT had done just this, despite warnings of the consequences, and the Department pressed its claim to forfeiture. BT thus had

---

[3] SFC Milsom, *Historical Foundations of the Common Law* (2nd edn, 1981) 377, the beginning of all wisdom on this topic.

[4] As Maitland saw: FW Maitland, *The Forms of Action at Common Law* (1909–54) 75.

[5] [1996] NPC 148 (20 October, Chancery Division—transcript from LEXIS-NEXIS).

[6] [1959] 1 QB 297, 316 where Lord Denning could not pass by the opportunity to cite Lord Atkin's 'mediaeval chains' passage: *United Australia Ltd v Barclays Bank Ltd* [1941] AC 1, 29.

[7] [1959] 1 QB 297, 335.

to challenge the old law virtually head-on. It asked the judge to look at the contractual aspects of a lease and to see if a different result could be reached by analogizing the case to that of contractual repudiation, where the conduct of the party had to be judged in all the circumstances.[8] So viewed, it argued, BT was not just denying the title: its pleadings on the second point expressly accepted that the Department might indeed be landlord. To the Department's argument that the record was the best and most unambiguous evidence of the tenant's acts and that there was no suggestion in this case to suggest an entrapment by the landlord, BT countered that if the tenant wished to go outside it, it was wrong to prevent him, and it was possible to envisage cases where the record alone would give no true view of the tenant's position. Where the denial was not on the record, the court clearly had to look at all the circumstances surrounding the challenge.[9] BT's denial did not, it argued, have the unequivocal character required by the rule. And there was authority allowing the court not to confine itself to the record.

The judge resisted the Department's invitation to be blinkered and took the view that while he would not accept that it was appropriate for a wholesale importation of contract rules into leaseholds, it would be odd if a tenant should lose the roof over his head by some term less exacting than that governing a long-term contract for his heating oil. A reference to the court in good faith by a party putting questions for the court's decision where there are properly arguable points at issue, might not amount to a sufficient repudiation. So if despite the pleading, nothing showed that BT, should the construction point go against it, was even so minded to persist in its denial of the Department's title, and if on the contrary if it lost that point, it would accept the landlord's position as such, the denial on the pleading would lack the unequivocal character needed to invoke the forfeiture rule. The judge accepted that the contract analogy was valid, and since BT's denial did not have the necessary unequivocal character required by the rule, the court was able to proceed to the second point.

This is a fairly substantial and welcome re-tuning of the rule as it was left in *Warner v Sampson*. The denial rule was conceived in circumstances so different from those of the present day that it is impossible to think it could today have been invented.[10] The decision is also a contribution to the ongoing debate about whether leases are predominantly contracts or estates. Leases did not begin their lives as part of the tenurial structure of freehold land, and as 'mere' contracts did not have the benefit of the real actions until the late middle ages.[11] But feudal theory found its way into their nature and this rule is a good illustration of that

---

[8] *Woodar v Wimpey* [1980] 1 WLR 277; *Spettabile Consorzio v Northumberland Shipbuilding Co Ltd* (1919) 121 LT 628.

[9] *Wisbech St Mary Parish Council v Lilly* [1956] 1 WLR 121.

[10] See P Baker, 'Inadvertent Forfeiture: the End of a Heresy' (1959) 75 LQR 310, which contains many of the old authorities.

[11] See AWB Simpson, *A History of the Land Law* (2nd edn, 1986) 92–3, 247–56.

tendency. The contract-property dilemma in leases has other manifestations to which this case may be added. On one view it is the happy chance that the earlier history of leases as contracts allowed the courts in the late nineteenth century to treat a lease void for informality as a contract for a lease, and on the back of that, allowing a grant of a fee simple void for informality to be treated as a contract for a fee simple.[12] But the judge's alluring analogy with the heating oil contract and the oddity of two different regimes tends to ignore for instance the contemporary horrors of forfeiture law and the seemingly unresolved question of whether an assignee-tenant who is not liable for a breach of covenant of a non-continuous nature is still vulnerable to a forfeiture.[13]

II

The early basis of the rule may not be as clear as the judgments in *Warner v Sampson* suggest and the reported arguments of counsel suggest that Lord Denning's historical account of it, going back to Glanvill, may even have been the result of a little private research. How, if that is indeed what happened, the disclaimer or denial by freehold tenants was transposed into the very different law governing the new estate of the lease in the later Middle Ages still awaits its historian.[14] The modern cases look back to Coke's treatment and through him to Littleton. But there are two stories in those accounts, which the quotation at the head of this essay may, in its context, creatively confuse. These were denial of the landlord's title and denial of rent.

The denial of title point was most clearly raised in the late sixteenth century in *Dicksey v Spencer*,[15] where a tenant, sued for rent by his landlord, claimed that he had purchased the freehold from the same landlord. The court was clear that a denial of a landlord's title in a pleading produced a forfeiture even if the landlord joined issue by traversing it. Coke picked the matter up in a more limited way in the Institutes.[16] A forfeiture may arise by record where a tenant claims a greater right than he ought. This might arise expressly where a tenant for life in a court of record expressly claims the fee or where a lessee who had been ousted (presumably by his landlord) brought an assize of novel disseisin, a remedy limited to the freeholder. Whether the termor's claiming the fee as a defence in an action by the landlord also triggered the rule is unclear: Coke's example of an implied

[12] J Hackney, 'Usucapio and the Law of Trusts' in J Getzler (ed), *Rationalising Property, Equity and Trusts: Essays in Honour of Edward Burn* (2003) 28–9.
[13] *Kataria v Safeland plc* [1998] 1 EGLR 39: forfeiture is a 'proprietary' remedy. This was a case of an assignee landlord suing a tenant in breach, but the language if unrestrained by the facts would go much wider.
[14] For an account of the law centring upon the Statute of Westminster II, 1285, c. 2, see Professor SFC Milsom's introduction to *Novae Narrationes*, 80 Selden Society (1963).
[15] (1587) 3 Leo 169; Gouldsborough 40; Godbolt 105; Moore 211.
[16] Coke upon Littleton f 251a–b sect 416.

claim is limited to a lessee being sued in a writ of right and joining issue and thereby claiming to be the freeholder. We are not given an example of a tenant making such a claim in the course of routine litigation in which the landlord is seeking to enforce the tenant's duties under the lease. Coke follows this by an example of forfeiture where the tenant affirms the reversion or remainder to be in a third party. This account lacks the precision and certainty of the report in *Dicksey v Spencer*.

But there is another element in the account by Littleton which Coke is glossing. This is denial of rent by a tenant. There are three kinds of rent; rent service, rent charge, and rent seck. A rent service arose where a tenant held land of a lord at a rent; a rent charge where a tenant in fee simple had made a grant of the fee and reserved a rent with the express provision that if the rent were not paid, he should have power to distrain; a rent seck arose in circumstances similar to those which created a rent charge, but where the grantor did not provide for a power to distrain, there being no such power granted by the general law.[17] Denial of rent in the last two cases amounted to a disseisin, a wrongful dispossession,[18] of the rent, in the hands of the chargee. In the case of a rent seck, where there was no power to distrain for rent, this was an essential remedy, but in the case of a rent charge, where distress was available, it looked like an illogical luxury. In neither of these cases would the disseisin be of the land, since the disseisee was not seised of the land at the moment of denial, but only of the rent. But the illogicality did not extend to the situation where there was a rent service, as would be due under a term of years. Denial of rent by such a tenant was no disseisin.[19] Coke's gloss of these sections accepts Littleton's analysis.[20] It had been applied in the case of a rent seck in *Maund's Case*[21] where it was held that one who had such a rent could bring an assize of novel disseisin to recover his rent, arrears, costs, and damages.

III

The outline of the common law's 'private law' protection of chattels was well established by the end of the thirteenth century by a series of forms of action[22] which were to be a hallmark of the pre-nineteenth-century common law. The action of debt lay to recover fungibles as well as money, and a form of it which

---

[17] Littleton sects 213, 217.

[18] Coke contrasts disseisin which is wrongful with ejectment or dispossessing, which may be by right or by wrong. Co Litt sect 233.

[19] Littleton chapter XII Rents: sects 213, 233, 237, 238. TE Tomlins (ed), *Lyttleton, his Treatise of Tenures* (1978).   [20] Co Litt: sects 213, 233.

[21] (1601) 7 Co Rep 28b.

[22] 'Actions' not 'writs'. The Common Pleas had an extensive writ jurisdiction but the King's Bench was able to handle a similar range of material by the use of bills. Even in areas where the King's Bench did have writ jurisdiction, plaintiffs would still use bills. *Isaack v Clark* (n 1) is such an action.

came to be known as detinue lay for non-fungibles. Replevin lay for the recovery of chattels distrained by a lord, and account would lie against one who had held chattels to the use of another either as bailiff or receiver, whether with a duty to hand them to the principal or a third party. Even the action of covenant could be used to protect agreements where chattels were the subject-matter. Interference with goods could be protected by trespass or the action (of trespass) on the case when it came to be seen as a distinct action and, later, actions.[23] These forms were not created on any conceptual grid such as was the case in classical Roman law, but seem to have emerged according to the capacity of plaintiffs to persuade judges and/or chancery officials to accept or issue them. This was neither classical English nor English classical law.[24] Until the modern period it also had a number of procedural vices which affected the formation of doctrine.

The first was its failure in the thirteenth century to update its methods of proof. This has had a permanent effect on the law protecting chattel interests. In trespass and the action on the case, trial by jury was the only available mode. Unlike the modern jury, it was selected from amongst those likely to be familiar with the issue and when the Westminster courts established themselves in the thirteenth century, actions were split into three elements. A first stage established the issue; if it was appropriate for a jury, the action was adjourned and a trial before a jury took place in the county (the *nisi prius* stage); the verdict of the jury was then returned to Westminster where judgment would be entered. In this way the common law was able to have a fully equipped headquarters at Westminster and allow jurors to remain in their counties.[25] Jury trial was also available in informal debt[26] and detinue but a defendant in these actions could choose proof by wager of law. Where a defendant waged his law, he swore to the truth of his case, and if he was supported by sufficient oath helpers,[27] that was it. One articulated justification for it, quite apart from letting God decide (in the best Christian sense) was that deals made and performed in private were not rationally triable by strangers, and it must always have been hard in a small community[28] to get eleven people to risk either their eternal soul or their standing in the community for a neighbour's horse. But wager of law was never

---

[23] A short account of the application of these forms to chattel protection is in JH Baker, *An Introduction to English Legal History* (4th edn, 2002) 363–5 and ch 22.

[24] *Non obstante* Professor Ibbetson's seductively titled *A Historical Introduction to the Law of Obligations* (1999).

[25] Regularized by the Statute of Westminster II 1285 c. 30. Judges swung between thinking juries ought to decide some difficult issues, by encouraging the pleading of a general issue, which would leave much discretion in their hands and realizing, as commercial litigants (eg gasoline companies) do today in the USA, that in some cases, if you have to go to trial by jury, you may as well give in. See eg *Hill v Hanks* (1614) 2 Bulstrode 201, 205 per Coke CJ—'countrey jurors will not find for the customer' (one levying a charge by custom) and contrast *Gibbons v Pepper* (1695) 1 Ld Raymond 38 where a judge appears to encourage a defendant in a difficult area to throw himself on the discretion of the jury.   [26] Excluding debt on an obligation—on a sealed instrument.

[27] Regularly eleven in royal courts.

[28] England was unusual in Europe, in being large-town free in the Middle Ages. C Platt, *The English Medieval Town* (1976) 15.

reformed, as the jury was, to adapt it to trial at headquarters by requiring oath helpers to be from the community local to the dispute. They could be complete strangers, doing it for money. Royal judges expressed distaste for wager from the early fourteenth century,[29] and by the seventeenth century the judicial determination to avoid it was overt.[30] This particular defect seems to have punched above its weight, since few who were entitled to wage their law actually did so, but the risk of a wager may just have been too great for plaintiffs. From the beginning it was simply assumed that there would be for instance no debt or detinue on the case, bringing with it jury trial, and apart from seeking to limit the fact situations where wager would lie,[31] the principal way in which judges colluded with plaintiffs seeking to deprive defendants of their birthright, was to allow plaintiffs to recharacterize their causes of action into torts—trespass and case.

This was not as easy as it might have been. Judges in England had the power to reject forms which they thought ill chosen after they had been selected (and paid for) by plaintiffs. So a plaintiff, forced to experiment by the failure of the system to update itself by legislation, was in a difficult position. The Chancery, which issued writs, despite some limited early muscle flexing, did not claim this power,[32] and even writ-plaintiffs were consigned to an expensive lottery where the issue might be not whether anyone thought you should win on the substance but whether they thought you should win on the form you had chosen and whether, if not, you could get free from the clutches of the court with a non-suit[33] rather than be condemned to fail and find that the inappropriate action you had brought had proceeded so far that it had consumed your chance of bringing the correct one. This disgraceful system—protecting the forms—was to continue to blot the common law until the nineteenth century. There were two further complications. The first was the so-called 'double remedies rule'. From the beginning the judges had a list of 'general' and 'special' actions. Debt/detinue was included in the former list and the latter were the actions on the case, and it was an early axiom that you could not use a special action if a general action would do,[34] though in the sixteenth century an open conflict arose between the King's Bench, which was willing to treat this more as a paper rule and the

---

[29] *Anon* (1315) YB 2 & 3 Edw II, 19 Selden Soc 195; JH Baker and SFC Milsom, *Sources of English Legal History* (hereafter B&M) (1986) 265. But in typical common law fashion did not confront the problem head-on.

[30] See Coke CJ in *Slade's Case* (1602) 4 Co Rep 92b, 95b: 'Also it is good in these days in as many cases as may be done by law, to oust the defendant of his law, and to try it by the country [the jury], for otherwise it would be occasion of much perjury'.

[31] See the fifteenth-century Lecture on Wager of Law in B&M 214.

[32] J Biancalana, *The Fee Tail and the Common Recovery in Medieval England* (2001) 92–8; *Devereux v Tuchet* (1310) YB 3 Ed II, 20 Selden Soc 16.

[33] B&M 221 n 15.

[34] 'And where a general action lies, a special action on the case does not' per Kingsmill J in *Orwell v Mortoft* (1505) YB Mich 20 Hen VII, fo 8, p 118 (B&M 406). The language of *Bishop v Viscountess Montague* (1601) Cro Eliz 824 treats trespass as a general writ.

Common Pleas which defended it as a rule they could not change at will.[35] So in the Common Pleas overlapping forms were anathema. And just to make life that bit more intolerable, the common law stuck to its early view that all pleadings had to lead to a single, certain issue, seriously hampering plaintiffs' ability to experiment with alternative formulations.[36]

IV

The debt/detinue form(s) suffered from these pressures. Informal debt for money and fungibles, in order to avoid the undesirable features of that form[37] was replaced by a species of the action on the case—assumpsit—by recharacterizing agreements as exchanged promises.[38] In detinue the form of the action required the defendant to restore a chattel which he unjustly detained. By the mid-fifteenth century it was being pleaded in two forms only: either upon a bailment[39] by the plaintiff to the defendant or upon a loss by the plaintiff and a finding by the defendant.[40] It seems that if the defendant returned the object, in whatever condition, he would go quit; if not, or if after judgment he declined to deliver it, the sheriff would distrain for its value.[41] The plaintiff was unable to secure compensation in detinue therefore for damage to his goods. While this rule made some sense in the case of the finder, in the case of the bailee it appears

[35] *Anon* (1576) KU Ms (B&M 529) (CP); *Anon* (1579) LI MS Misc 488, 64 (B&M 533) (KB); *Anon* (1582) HLS MS Acc 704755 fo 106 (B&M 534) (CP). Coke's report of *Slade's case* (n 30) misleadingly suggests at various places that the conflict was over, eg at 95a. In the late fifteenth century there were even those who thought that a plaintiff might choose amongst the insufficiently closely defined general actions: see eg the judicial dissent in *Calwodelegh v John* (1479) YB Hil 18 Ed IV, fo 23, pl 5 (B&M 526).

[36] William Blackstone, *Commentaries on the Laws of England*, 1765–9 (reprinted 1979), vol 3 308, 311. Blackstone points out that Queen Anne had allowed some 'duplicity' in pleading and cites 4 & 5 Ann c 16. This is c 3 in the Statutes of the Realm edition.

[37] Some of which were also substantive.   [38] The story culminating in *Slade's Case* (n 30).

[39] Whatever that was: in 1473 Laken J [KB] was seeking to draw a distinction between a bailment of, and a bargain to take and carry goods. This seems a very Roman distinction and Bryan CJ [CP] would have none of it: the *Carrier's Case* (1473) in *Select Cases in the Exchequer Chamber*, 64 Selden Soc 30, 33. Counts on bailments are also used in sale where the vendor continues to hold the goods but this story develops differently.

[40] This latter seemingly to raise the bare issue between the parties as to which of them had the property, preventing the defendant raising irrelevant issues about how he had come into possession. It is tempting to see it as a simple civilian 'property' formulation but the 'unjustly' element sits uncomfortably with such a concept where justice and injustice are kept apart from questions of ownership. It is also an obstacle to seeing it simply as a primary duty form in Pothier's classification and reflects the early common law's habit of mixing elements of property and tort: see eg SFC Milsom, 'Trespass from Henry III to Edward III' (1958) 74 LQR 573 n 68 and RJ Pothier, *A Treatise on Obligations Considered in a Moral and Legal View* (tr F–X Martin, 1999) 111–12.

[41] *Paler v Bartlett* (1605) Yelverton 71. Whether he could legitimately distrain for more than the value in order to coerce the defendant into handing over the goods if he still had them is unknown. At all events chattels, even if property, are not real property: there are no real actions to guarantee recovery.

to be nonsense, but the authorities seem to assume it.[42] But if the possessor had damaged the object, or used it without the plaintiff's consent, he would be liable independently in trespass or case.[43] There were difficulties with trespass in that it required a *vi et armis* wrong and this led to problems with whether an initially lawful acquisition of possession could be made trespassory by subsequent bad behaviour.[44] In bailment the problem was that the bailee having taken delivery at the hand of the plaintiff could hardly be said to have taken it forcibly. There was some fictitious pleading of violence in the early fourteenth century[45] though it is possible that we have overstated the fictions and missed some subtlety.[46] And the common lawyers saw that if I had hired a horse to ride to York, and rode it to Carlisle I could, presumably because the horse was in some way fatigued or harmed, be made liable in tort.[47] By the 1470s a new use[48] of an old concept emerged to unify the multifarious strands which the story contained and which assisted the flight from wager. This was the concept of conversion. In the *Carrier's Case*[49] (1473) the charge of felony against a bailee was that he had agreed to carry bales of woad to Southampton but had taken them elsewhere, broken open the bales, taken the goods, and converted them to his own use. Quite what you had to do to convert someone else's property is not clear. It is hard to see the influence of the Roman law *specificatio* doctrine, as some have; certainly there is no discussion in the very full report of the *Carrier's case* to suggest that he had made a new thing from the woad. The cases resemble those on what amounts to the annexation of chattels to land—a combination of degree and purpose[50] and

[42] It is regrettable that this calumny against the common law judges continues to be made without a case where a bailor had refused to accept damaged goods when offered and then failed in detinue, but the conclusion seems to be assumed by the cases.
[43] According to Popham J in *Anon* (1601) Goulds 155 pl 183, a defendant who had used the plaintiff's chattel without his consent could not escape liability in case if he had returned it to the plaintiff even before action was brought. [44] *Six Carpenters Case* (1610) 8 Co Rep 146a.
[45] Story classically told in Milsom, 'Trespass from Henry III to Edward III' (1958) 74 LQR 195–224, 407–36, 561–90 and 'Not Doing is No Trespass, A View of the Boundaries of Case' [1954] CLJ 105–17.
[46] *Rattlesdene v Grunestone* (1317) YB 10 Ed II, 54 Selden Soc 141 (B&M 300) is seen as a good example of a fictitious action. The plaintiff had bought a tun of wine from the defendants and left it with the vendors pending delivery. The vendors had, he said, with force and arms drawn off part of the wine and refilled it with salt water. In the *Carriers Case* (n 39), which introduced the notion of breaking bulk into the law of felony, the case seems to be seen as an early example of such a concept. Choke J says that a bailee to whom a vat is bailed commits no trespass if he sells the vat, but if he withdraws twenty pints, it is felony, since the twenty pints were not given to him. Bryan CJ appears to agree and cites the 1317 case (mis-cited) in support.
[47] *Calwodelegh v John* (1505) YB Hil 18 Ed IV fo 23 pl 5 (B&M 526).
[48] SFC Milsom, 'Sale of Goods in the Fifteenth Century' (1961) 77 LQR 257, 278 n 42. Conversion continues to be used to describe the legitimate practice of executors in selling to pay their deceased's debts in this period: *Anon* (1514) 1 Dyer 1b 'if then they do not waste the goods, but convert and apply them to the best advantage of their testator...'. And in 1505 a vendor who failed to deliver quarters of barley to his purchaser was charged in an action on the case that he had not delivered them within the time agreed, but had converted them to his own use: the dispute is as to whether he should have sued in Debt: *Orwell v Mortoft* (1505) YB Mich 20 Hen VII fo 8 p118 (B&M 406).
[49] n 39. [50] *Holland v Hodgson* (1872) LR 7 CP 328 at 335.

the line between converting and not converting may be no easier than that
between a section of the community and a fluctuating body of private individuals
in charity law.[51] At all events the next century saw a list of cases where plaintiffs
sought to drive defaulting bailees out of the substantive and procedural protection of detinue. Where the bailee had actually done something, the invention
of a tort was the kind of ingenious game we had seen with the remoulding of
contract cases into tort cases in the early sixteenth century. But where nothing
had been done, because 'not doing is no trespass'[52] the case of the debtor who
had not paid money and the bailee who still had the goods undamaged posed
seemingly insoluble problems. Turning a defaulting debtor, however innocent,
into a tortfeasor was substantially achieved in *Slade's case*.[53] The case of the
possessor who had come to the goods otherwise than by bailment and still had
them, unharmed and unused, was inconclusively considered in *Eas(t)on v
Newman*[54] in 1596 using the trover fiction from the detinue cases—trover and
conversion—but the issue was settled in 1614 when a bailee in the same position
was firmly locked into the law of tort in *Isaack v Clark*.[55]

V

The plaintiff counted that on 9 February 1608 he was possessed of a bag of
money which on 12 February he lost, and which came to the hands of the
defendant, who on 28 February converted it to his own use.[56] The defendant
pleaded not guilty and the jury found a special verdict. Adams had recovered
judgment elsewhere against Lewis. Process was issued against Lewis who could
not be found, so Clark, a court official, proceeded against Watkins, one of
Lewis's pledges, and took three buts of sack in execution. Isaack, who was present
at this event, in order to prevent the sack from being sold, offered Clark a purse
containing money which he pawned and deposited with him[57] until the next
court day on 13 March as a pledge for the re-delivery of the sack, if Watkins had
by that time procured the sparing of the levying of the execution. Watkins had
not procured the concession from Adams, but Isaack had none the less
demanded the return of the purse and Clark had refused to hand it over,[58] which

[51] *Davies v Perpetual Trustee* [1959] AC 439.
[52] The *Six Carpenters Case* (1610) 8 Co Rep 146a, 147a.   [53] n 30.
[54] HLS MS 110, fo 218v (B&M 537); Cro Eliz 495; Moo KB 460; Goulds 152. Those who
have not yet tried to search electronically for cases in this period are warned that contemporaries
appear not to have been that bothered about the spelling of names in this context any more than in
any other. Professor Baker will sometimes give yet a further spelling when reproducing the record.
[55] 2 Bulstrode 306; 1 Rolle 59; Moore 841. An action by bill even though a writ would have
been available.
[56] Although the action is described by the reporters as an action on the case on trover or trover
and conversion, there is no reported allegation even in Bultrode's very full report that the defendant
found the bag.   [57] On 12 February?
[58] On 28 February?

Isaack said was a conversion to his own use. There was a challenge that Isaack had not made it clear whether he was seeking the return of money in a bag, or money and a bag since there was a view that money out of a bag was only recoverable in debt,[59] but this was brushed aside and the court focussed on the nature of the wrong, if any.

It had been said in 1609[60] that it was the common experience, that the detention of goods from an owner, after request, could be sufficient evidence to maintain a conversion on the grounds that the detainer claimed them as his own, and so used them. This idea was now developed using the presumption laid down in the *Chancellor of Oxford's case*[61] in the previous year, that refusal to deliver was not itself a conversion, but was evidence that the defendant was setting himself up against the plaintiff—a case where the purpose of the denial overcame the lack of action perhaps. The plaintiff ingeniously argued that for money it was not possible to draw this distinction, as it was for specific chattels, because money was not identifiable, and so presumably refusal to deliver it would always be a conversion. But this was not picked up, possibly because the court took the view that the money was indeed in the bag. What was picked up, expressly by Croke J but implicitly perhaps in the language of 'privity'[62] between the bailor and bailee, was the analogy with denial in the land law. The plaintiff argued that 'he who takes from me my possession and profit, takes from me my property, so here this denial takes from me possession and profit and is thus a conversion'. There is a vacant slot in the text for a Littleton reference followed by one to *Maund's case*[63] and then the bold assertion that if a rent seck is demanded and not paid, that is a denial in law and is also a disseisin and the assize lies for it.[64] Croke J[65] asserts that there can be no conversion so

---

[59] In detinue, orthodoxy said money at large could not be recovered: *Banks v Whetston* (1596) Cro Eliz 457. But in the action on the case there was still some confusion. In *Holiday v Hicks* (1600) Cro Eliz 638, 661, 746 it is reported at 661 and 746 that this action only lay for money which was 'found' if it was in a bag or chest, (the p 661 report 'pre-reporting' the p 746 decision) since, as in detinue, loss of possession was loss of property. A manuscript version of the Exchequer Chamber report is in B&M at 537. But in *Hall v Dean and Wood* (1601) Cro Eliz 841 [*Hall v Wood*] Owen 131 the Exchequer Chamber decision appears to have been distinguished and not followed and the action allowed for loose money. Haughton and Coke JJ in *Isaack* are recorded in Rolle as saying it is a common matter for money to be recovered in this action. The matter was put beyond doubt in this sense in *Kinaston v Moore* (1627) Cro Car 89.   [60] *Agar v Lisle*, Hobart 187.

[61] (1613), 10 Co Rep 53a, 56ba: ' . . . the Chief Justice held, that if A. brings an action on the case against B. upon trover and conversion of plate, jewels, &c. and the defendant pleads not guilty, now it is good evidence primâ facie, to prove a conversion that the plaintiff requested the defendant to deliver them, and he refused, and therefore it shall be presumed that he has converted them to his use. But yet it is but evidence; and if it be found by special verdict in such case, that the plaintiff requested them of the defendant, and he refused, it is not a matter upon which the Court can judge any conversion: for the conversion ought to alter the action of detinue to a trespass upon the case, which a denial cannot do in law; for in every action of detinue there is alleged in the declaration a request and refusal, yet it is good evidence, as has been said, and so has always been allowed to prove a conversion, that the plaintiff demanded the goods, and the defendant refused to deliver them.'

[62] Privity of estate between landlord and tenant was by now well established as a phrase as well as a concept: *Brediman's Case* (1607) 6 Co Rep 56b.   [63] n 21.

[64] Rolle 60 (translated).   [65] At 311.

long as the privity of bailment remains, but if this is destroyed, it would be possible. Denial destroyed the privity: Littleton said denyer shall make a disseisin and 'if it be so in real things, *a fortiori* it shall be so in personals'. But the judges agreed that here the denial was justified and did not have the effect sought by the plaintiff, who thus took nothing by his bill. Courts would now have to formulate a coherent theory of when refusal to deliver or other wrongful act was a conversion and when not. Detinue would lie for the refusals which were not wrongs in this sense. But the wrong had no physical manifestation: not doing was now trespass.

The new metaphysics had been assisted by drawing on the law of real property. The analogy with the denial of rent is weaker than that with the denial of the landlord's title by the lessee which would terminate the lease. It may be that this was not used because the law on denials by tenants was not as clear as it seemed to be to later generations, but in the highly politically charged context of this dispute between the courts, even in its dying stages, any analogy might have been enough, and certainly the language of termination of privity of bailment must have raised powerful echoes from the law of leases, where there seem to be other complications.[66] The contractual reasoning used in the *British Telecommunications* case,[67] in its insistence on looking at the whole picture and not on the simple outward act, looks remarkably similar to that used to distinguish refusals that were denials from those that were not, but from a different and commercially more useful angle. Wrongful acts are not to be taken at face value but are to be investigated to see their true meaning. The reasoning in *Isaack* might have been useful support for the judge in the BT dilemma.

VI

The Romans did this differently and probably better. First, as to procedure, they did not have conflicting proof regimes and so the pressures put on the common law by wager were absent. Perhaps for that reason there does not appear to have been a double remedies rule and it was only in areas where defendants might be specially adversely affected by giving a plaintiff a choice such as in the one serious oddity of the Roman system, its highly penal delict of theft, was special care taken to define that delict and its close compensatory neighbour, wrongful damage to property, in such a way as to keep the theft delict from encroachment.

---

[66] While lessors should in this period recover their rent by the action of debt, from which wager was excluded, and could not use the assize of novel disseisin, holders of a rent seck or rent charge ought at first sight to use debt also, but it was accepted, apparently without debate since Littleton's time, that the assize was their proper remedy. AWB Simpson, *A History of the Common Law of Contract* (1975) 17–18, 84–7, 171–3, 300–1; WF Finlason (ed), *Reeves' History of English Law* (1869) vol 2 566.   [67] n 5.

Elsewhere plaintiffs were able to choose the most suitable action into which they could slip their complaint.[68]

The Roman finder of a moveable lost by its owner would face a proprietary action for the recovery of its value and some good faith possessors faced with a similar loss would, under strict conditions and for a limited period, receive a quasi-proprietary remedy courtesy of praetorian innovations. The less well-qualified possessor who had recently lost possession might also receive possessory protection by interdict.[69] One who picked up and/or used property which had been lost but not abandoned, and who thought as much, would be guilty of theft, but if he were innocent would be liable only to the proprietary or possessory remedies.[70] Owners or possessors of moveable or immoveable property deprived by others would bring remedies in the law of property as above, plus any remedy for the delict under which they might have been deprived, though land could not be stolen. The finder who had innocently lost possession before demand was made of him appears to have quite rightly escaped all liability, just as had his common law innocent occupier-turned-grantor of freehold land.[71]

Turning to transaction-based liability, the medieval common law, outside the freehold estates, focussed on the twin concepts of term of years and bailment. The Roman holder of property might be such as the result of a usufruct (or its reduced version, usus), a hire, a mandate, a deposit, a loan for consumption, a loan for use, a pledge, or a precarium to name but a few.[72] Apart from usufruct, which led an uneasy existence allegedly in the law of property, these were different contracts with their own special rules, but the law allowed a custodian whose actions transgressed too far from the terms of his holding to be held liable also in delict. There were some fine lines. We are told for instance that one holding a horse under a loan for use who used a horse to go to war when he had asked for the loan to go to his country house, would be liable for the death of the horse in those circumstances but was also liable in delict for the theft of the use of the horse.[73] The holder who damaged, however, could not escape contractual liability by returning damaged goods and again might even be liable in delict if the damage was caused by use outside the scope of the transaction.[74] And torn clothes attracted delictal liability for the whole value.[75] If the opposite was indeed

---

[68] See eg D.7.1.66; D.16.3.1.21–2; D.13.6.18.1; D.19.2.25.5. Occasionally he might get two actions: D.9.2.23.9.
[69] JAC Thomas, *Textbook of Roman Law* (1976) 136–7, 91, 147, 149–50.
[70] D.47.2.43.5–8, though if he claims a reward for finding it, he sails close to the legal wind.
[71] Though he might have been liable for mesne profits.
[72] Familiar to common lawyers via the judgment of Holt CJ in *Coggs v Bernard* (1703) 3 Ld Raym 909.
[73] D.13.6.5.7–8; D.47.2.40, 83; D.47.2.1.3; D.7.8.12.4. This is the common law's ride to Carlisle: n 47.
[74] D.16.3.1.16; D.13.6.3.1. The mule driver who overloads mules D.19.2.30.2 though in a sombre prediction of later law in England on liability for highway accidents, only the driver of the mules could be liable in delict; the hirer, if different, was liable only on the contract.
[75] D.9.2.27.18.

true in detinue, this failure to distinguish the proprietary from the transactional aspects of bailment and to see the tortious possibilities looks doubly foolish, given the existence of the Roman precedent. Nor does any of this seem to depend on any notion of whether a new thing had been created by the wrongdoer. Putting soil in wine certainly created delictal liability for the whole value,[76] as indeed it must in England, and converting money to one's own use was already known.[77] But usufruct could be ended by a fundamental change in the character of the subject-matter or by its destruction, a rule which may be similar to the notion exercising the English judges in the 1470s.[78]

And transaction-based liability knew nothing of simple denial of title as a delict. The holder under a transaction who was held to account and who simply denied the title of the person by whose consent he came into control of the property, seems to have been talking off the point and faced no special penalty; if he was liable under the contract or proprietary arrangement under which he was in control of the property his denial could not affect that liability either way. Indeed in the real contracts[79] such as deposit, since possession was not transferred it did not matter whether the depositor was a thief or someone who only themselves held under a contract.[80] A depositee was obliged to return the property on demand and denial would generate liability, but this was contractual not delictal. And there may be good reasons for not returning it; for instance if the goods were in a warehouse which was closed when demand was made. But in that case you had to restore them before judgment to escape liability.[81] And he might also escape liability if he were not persuaded that the person making the demand was properly authorized to do so.[82] And in hire, a carrier of wine who was challenged by a claim to the wine from a third party and who put the wine under his own seal and that of the third party into a warehouse, presumably awaiting the outcome, would be liable on the contract of hire for failure to deliver or return, unless his actions lacked an element of negligence.[83] And there was some anxiety about depositors who were thieves: should the depositee hand back to the thief or to the true owner once he discovers the facts? On the face of it, contractual principle said it had to be given to the thief, but since justice gives to everyone his own, it was thought in this case it should be handed to the true owner.[84]

The general principle 'give it back and then litigate title' is clearly stated in the Code.[85] The nearest we get to tort-like penalties is the provision of the Emperor Zeno, who in a thought-mode similar to that which governed litigation under the lex Aquilia (and maybe similar to that of the common law judges awarding the winning litigator his costs against the loser), ruled that in hire or *precarium*, if

---

[76] D.9.2.27.15.   [77] D.16.3.25.1.   [78] D.7.4.5.2–3.
[79] Those created by consensual delivery of a thing.   [80] Thomas (n 67) 276.
[81] D.16.3.1.21–2.   [82] D.16.3.13.   [83] D.19.2.11.3.
[84] D.16.3.31.1 though if the depositee turned out to be the true owner, the thief did not get it back even on principle. And see Inst 1.1.pr.   [85] C.4.65.25.

the holder or his heir refused to hand the subject-matter back until after final judgment had been entered against him, he would be liable for double the value of the thing.[86]

So to Roman eyes, *Isaack v Clarke* itself could have played out as follows, and on these facts the result in both systems is similar. Isaack had pleaded three days possession of the purse. If he was confident that he was its owner, he could sue in a proprietary action asserting ownership but he would have failed in an interdict since he had handed the purse over. Clark would then have pleaded the conditional contract for which the condition had not yet been performed. He would have won on that point and Isaack's ownership would have stood him in no avail. If he had sued on the contract,[87] the question of his title would have been quite irrelevant. If Clark had received the goods under a contract to return them on the happening of a given event and that event had not occurred, absent the intervention of a third party, Clarke's denial of Isaack's title would not only have been irrelevant, but, in Rome, laughably so.[88]

---

[86] C.4.65.33.   [87] This would be *pignus*: Thomas (n 69) 330–2.
[88] If the reaction of Professor Tony Honoré on hearing of such a scenario, is a good guide, which it is.

31

Rumford Market and the Genesis of Fiduciary Obligations

*Joshua Getzler**

Peter Birks's writings on English legal history, which stand alongside his studies of classical Roman law, are a model for historians of the law. His rationalization of the modern law of unjust enrichment drew from a deep knowledge of the historical sources of that law. Peter's blend of ancient and modern sensibilities in his jurisprudence was irresistible. Perhaps every true *avant garde* must be imbued with tradition. This essay examines the origins and contours of fiduciary law, using Peter's theory of fiduciary obligation as a counterpoint, and drawing on Peter's legal history as an inspiration.

1. Fiduciary Export

Peter Birks's concept of fiduciary law was articulated with great clarity in a lecture delivered at the Hebrew University in May 2000.[1] There he stated: 'A fiduciary relationship is a relationship analogous to that between express trustee and beneficiary, and a fiduciary obligation is a trustee-like obligation exported by analogy . . . its function is to export the incidents of the express trust to new situations'.[2]

Having set out the derivation of fiduciary obligations, Birks then turned to the content of such obligations. He discriminated between three tiers of other-regarding conduct or altruism demanded by private law—a negative obligation to do no harm, a positive obligation to act with due care and skill where one has assumed a special responsibility, and a duty to act both positively and

---

* Fellow and Tutor in Law, St Hugh's College, Oxford.

I thank Hamilton Bryson, Andrew Burrows, Emily Coates, James Edelman, Mark McGaw, Michael Macnair, James Oldham, and Olivia Robinson for their invaluable help.

[1] P Birks, 'The Content of Fiduciary Obligation' (2000) 34 Israel L Rev 3; and see P Birks, *An Introduction to the Law of Restitution* (rev edn, 1989) 332–3, 338–43, 380–9.
[2] 'Content of Fiduciary Obligation' (n 1) 8.

disinterestedly, focussing exclusively on the interests of a beneficiary.[3] The higher duty of disinterestedness was 'parasitic', in that it existed to ensure that in certain sensitive situations self-interest would not interfere with correct performance of the duties of the fiduciary 'to preserve and promote'.[4] He cautioned against running these distinct duty categories together, and in particular against describing the duties of care and skill that might apply to a fiduciary as elements of the duty of disinterestedness, especially since the latter duty attracted especially stringent equitable remedies and procedures. At the same time Birks allowed that a fiduciary's standard of care and skill might be fine-tuned upwards to allow for the heavier demands of reasonableness in a close or trusting relationship.

No one can deny the elegance of Birks's analysis. He puts a case that must be addressed. One may argue over whether the duties of a fiduciary can so neatly be split between tiers two and three—and also whether such a division of care from loyalty sends the wrong policy message to those entrusted with the affairs of others.[5] However, my purpose here is not to revisit the care–loyalty debate, but rather to examine the 'export' and 'trust-like' metaphors used at the start of Birks's analysis. My main claim is that Birks's fertile metaphor can lend us more than one perspective. Borrowing his linguistic form, the perspective I wish to pursue may be put thus: 'A trust relationship is a fiduciary obligation exported by analogy to custodial relationships . . . its function is to export the incidents of the fiduciary obligation to new situations'.

---

[3] Birks was influenced here by P Finn, 'The Fiduciary Principle' in TG Youdan, *Equity, Fiduciaries, and Trusts* (1989) 1. In 'Content of Fiduciary Obligation' (n 1) 5 at n 4 he wrote: 'I acknowledge a great debt to this important paper, albeit arriving at different results. Finn seeks to create a hierarchy of different obligations within the sub-class of those "imposed on a person in his voluntary or consensual relationships with another" . . . he finds that hierarchy in standards expressed in "unconscionable", "good faith" and "fiduciary". By contrast the present exercise seeks to locate fiduciary obligations in the class of all obligations. It takes a different view of the core fiduciary obligation . . . and the three-tier hierarchy which it detects is quite different.'

[4] The model of fiduciary duties as protecting or fencing other duties is developed in M Conaglen, 'The Nature and Function of Fiduciary Loyalty' (2005) 121 LQR 452; and M Conaglen, 'Locating Loyalty: Fiduciary Protection of Non-Fiduciary Duties' (Cambridge PhD thesis, 2003) 137–52.

[5] For arguments locating duties of care within the fiduciary core see: J Getzler, 'Equitable Compensation and the Regulation of Fiduciary Relationships' in P Birks and F Rose (eds), *Restitution and Equity Vol 1: Resulting Trusts and Equitable Compensation* (2000) 235; J Getzler, 'Duty of Care' in P Birks and A Pretto (eds), *Breach of Trust* (2002) 41; J Getzler, 'Am I my Beneficiary's Keeper? Fusion and Loss-Based Fiduciary Remedies' in S Degeling and J Edelman (eds), *Equity in Commercial Law* (2005) 239; JD Heydon, 'Are the Duties of Company Directors to Exercise Care and Skill Fiduciary?' ibid 185. For the contrary view see G McCormack, 'The Liability of Trustees for Gross Negligence' [1998] Conv 100; L Smith, 'The Motive, Not the Deed' in J Getzler (ed), *Rationalizing Property, Equity and Trusts* (2003) 53; Conaglen, 'Fiduciary Loyalty' and *Locating Loyalty* (n 4); and see in particular Kam Fan Sin, 'Equitable Negligence: Tentative Thoughts from Landmarks' in K Sin (ed), *Legal Explorations: Essays in Honour of Professor Michael Chesterman* (2003) 99. P Birks, 'Negligence in the Eighteenth Century Common Law' in EJH Schrage (ed), *Negligence. The Comparative Legal History of the Law of Tort* (2001) 173, 193–6, acknowledges that the 'reasonableness' standard of the common law tort of negligence may have developed through the 'prudence' standard of trusteeship.

My technique in articulating and defending this model will be to delve into the historical evolution of fiduciary law. In pursuing this enquiry we must be sensitive to terminology. Birks pointed out the many ways in which the concept of faithfulness appeared in legal language.[6] The word 'fiduciary' or its synonyms were not necessarily used to identify what were in effect fiduciary relations in earlier law. Fiduciary concepts—like unjust enrichment concepts—were dispersed and scattered throughout the common law-equity system, just as they were scattered under various labels through Roman law.[7]

One historical line of enquiry may briefly be mentioned in order to be put to one side. It could be claimed that fiduciary obligations and trusts share a common origin in English Chancery jurisdiction, as *in personam* duties of conscience. The classical notion that 'equity acts *in personam*' meant that Chancery ordered the person affected by conscience to desist from claiming the full extent of his or her legal rights, or else be subjected to a contempt order binding the person, that is the body.[8] Equitable duties of good faith were thereby generated in silhouette, as it were, by annulling, suspending, or otherwise restraining amorally exercised legal rights.[9] On this classical analysis, the institution of the trust can be modelled as a multiplication of fiduciary duties reaching beyond the original obligee to bind third parties, and thus yielding to the obligor a title comprising 'multital' legal relations, to use Hohfeldian language.[10] The trust title is constructed of a series of binding personal, good faith claims against nearly all takers of trusts' assets, through the operation of the doctrine of notice that allows tracing and following of trust property and constitution of new trusts to protect the claims to the *res* or value of assets in third party hands.[11]

Birks criticized the dual equity-law model with a unique ferocity,[12] in particular rejecting the model of the trust as something less than property, as merely an

[6] 'Content of Fiduciary Obligation' (n 1) 6–14.

[7] cf D Johnston, 'Trusts and Trust-Like Devices in Roman Law' in R Helmholz and R Zimmermann (eds), *Itinera Fiduciae: Trust and Treuhand in Historical Perspective* (1998) 45; D Johnston, *The Roman Law of Trusts* (1988). The main territory of Roman 'trusts' was testamentary; see further below (n 97).

[8] The classical exposition is FW Maitland, *Equity: A Course of Lectures* (2nd rev edn, J Brunyate (ed), 1936). The *in personam* actions of Chancery must therefore be contrasted with the Roman concept of an action *in personam* as a claim that one person ought to give another something, or do something: J.4.6, P Birks and G McLeod (trs), *The Institutes of Justinian* (London 1997) 129.

[9] J Getzler, 'Patterns of Fusion' in P Birks (ed), *The Classification of Obligations* (1997) 157. An argument that good motive remains the underpinning theory of modern fiduciary law is offered by Smith, 'Motive' (n 5) 53, criticized in Conaglen, 'Fiduciary Loyalty' (n 4) 464–5, 473–5.

[10] WN Hohfeld, *Fundamental Legal Conceptions as Applied in Judicial Reasoning* (Cooke (ed), 1919) 67–114. Hohfeld was withering in his dismissal of the traditional language of trusts and property: ibid 23–31; WN Hohfeld, 'The Relations between Equity and Law' (1913) 11 Michigan L Rev 537; cf T Honoré, 'Trusts: The Inessentials' in *Rationalizing Property, Equity and Trusts* (n 5) 7, 15–20.

[11] cf L Smith, 'Unjust Enrichment, Property and the Structure of Trusts' (2000) 116 LQR 412; L Smith, 'Transfers' in *Breach of Trust* (n 5) 111.

[12] P Birks, 'Equity in the Modern Law: An Exercise in Taxonomy' (1996) 26 UWA L Rev 1; P Birks, 'Equity, Conscience, and Unjust Enrichment' (1999) 23 MelbU L Rev 1.

aggregation of defeasible equitable obligations.[13] Perhaps one of his most telling
insights was how so-called *in personam* actions, whether emanating from Chancery
or common law, and which he preferred to classify simply as wrong-based claims,
yielded the equivalent of a *vindicatio*, operating especially in the field of personal
property.[14] There are further reasons to question the classical theory that equitable
duties, whether fiduciary obligations or full-blown trusteeships, all derive from the
original source of restraint of unconscionable legal rights. Stand-alone fiduciary
obligations often enjoin positive performance of managerial duties and therefore do
not easily fit the *in personam* restraint model. Historically this is because much of
fiduciary law emerged from the action and remedies of account, and account with
its contractual and obligational overtones typically required positive performance as
well as imposing forbearances and prohibitions.[15] It was Birks who restored to
prominence the importance of the actions of account.[16]

   If we are to discard the classical language of fiduciary obligation as the most
demanding equitable requirement of good faith, then it might be helpful to set
out the abstract function of such obligations, conscious that 'every definition is
dangerous in law'.[17] Adapting Birks's own careful approach, we may state that a
fiduciary obligation is a legal requirement that a person in a fiduciary position
should promote exclusively the beneficiary's interests, and refrain from allowing
any self-interest or rival interests to touch or affect his or her conduct. Limits on
the reach of this demanding duty are necessary: the fiduciary obligation is
confined to the fiduciary parts of a relationship;[18] the obligation will take on
variable intensities in different contexts;[19] and self-interest or rival interests may

   [13] P Birks, 'Receipt' in *Breach of Trust* (n 5) 213, esp 233–9.
   [14] P Birks, 'Personal Property: Proprietary Rights and Remedies' (2000) 11 KCLJ 1.
   [15] One may put to one side the idea evoked in recent Australian law that fiduciary relationships
are merely proscriptive (eg *Breen v Williams* (1996) 186 CLR 71, 113 (HCA); *Pilmer v Duke Group
Ltd (In Liq)* (2001) 207 CLR 165, 197–9 (HCA); Finn, 'The Fiduciary Principle' (n 3) 24–31).
This model is questionable both historically and analytically; for one, the line between proscriptive
and prescriptive duties is as hazy as that between omission and commission. See further Getzler,
'Am I my Beneficiary's Keeper?' (n 5); D DeMott, 'Fiduciary Obligation in the High Court of
Australia' in P Cane (ed), *Centenary Essays for the High Court of Australia* (2004) 277.
   [16] P Birks, 'Restitution for Wrongs' in EJH Schrage (ed), *Unjust Enrichment. The Comparative
Legal History of the Law of Restitution* (2nd edn, 1999) 171, 177–9, 187–91; P Birks, 'Equity in the
Modern Law' (n 12) 45–8; and see also P Millett, 'Equity's Place in the Law of Commerce' (1998)
114 LQR 214, 225–7; R Chambers, 'Liability' in *Breach of Trust* (n 5) 1; SB Elliott and C Mitchell,
'Remedies for Dishonest Assistance' (2004) 67 MLR 16, 23–34.
   [17] Birks, 'Content of Fiduciary Obligation' (n 1) 13, citing Javolenus D.50.17.202. The call for
definition was resisted by P Finn, *Fiduciary Obligations* (1977) 1, instead relying on fine-spun analysis
of the legal purposes of fiduciary rules. Judges and jurists have sometimes attempted to reduce fiduciary
obligations to a monotonic theory; see surveys in Conaglen, 'Fiduciary Loyalty' (n 4) 452–60 and
G Moffat, G Bean, and J Dewar, *Trusts Law: Texts and Materials* (4th edn 2005) 799–851. A *via
media* can be located between theory-led reductionism and pragmatic exemplification.
   [18] *Birtchnell v Equity Trustee Executors and Agency Co Ltd* (1929) 42 CLR 384, 408 per Dixon J;
New Zealand Netherlands Society 'Oranje' Inc v Kuys [1973] 1 WLR 1126 at 1130 per Lord
Wilberforce (PC).
   [19] *Re Coomber* [1911] 1 Ch 723, 728 per Fletcher Moulton LJ; AW Scott, 'The Trustee's Duty
of Loyalty' (1936) 49 Harvard L Rev 521.

be permitted if clearly disclosed and allowed by the beneficiary, or perhaps allowed by accepted general practice or by approval of a court or legislature.[20] Typically the fiduciary will have a continuing relationship with the beneficiary that resists complete specification by agreement or contract and instead bestows discretions;[21] and the fiduciary will generally have strong powers to change the beneficiary's legal position and affect his or her interests unilaterally. Because of these great powers it is often difficult for the beneficiary to monitor the fiduciary's conduct of his or her business, hence strong remedies are accorded to the beneficiary to restore balance to the relationship. A dialectic is at work: the fiduciary can only serve the beneficiary if armed with extensive powers, and the beneficiary can only hold the fiduciary to account if the fiduciary is hemmed in by potent duties and remedies.

2. The *Rumford Market* Case

The duties to act exclusively in the beneficiary's interest and not to profit from a fiduciary office are at the core of classical fiduciary obligation. Yet it was an extraordinarily cryptic case that established the no-profit rule, and it took a long time for the rule to be clarified and adopted into the fabric of the law.

Keech v Sandford was decided by Lord Chancellor King on 31 October 1726. The judgment is reported with frustrating brevity. Nominate reports were scanty in this period; the apparent absence of any manuscript sources may also suggest that the decision did not strike a chord at the time.[22] A trustee was devised a term lease over the profits of Rumford Market, to hold on trust for an infant. When the trustee asked for a renewal of the term for the cestui que use, the lessor refused, on the ground that he would not have a proper remedy to defend his interest. Distress could not be levied for recovery of such a profit, being an incorporeal hereditament, and covenant could not be used since the lessee was to be an infant lacking the requisite contractual capacity. Thus it appears that the renewed estate being sought was not of the legal leasehold estate in the hands of the trustee to hold for the cestui, but rather of a legal estate to be vested in the infant. Since the lease could not be got in for the infant, the trustee in the end

[20] Here we can compare the approach of the Privy Council in *Kelly v Cooper* [1993] AC 205 with that of the House of Lords in *Hilton v Barker Booth & Eastwood* [2005] 1 WLR 567; see J Getzler, 'Inconsistent Fiduciary Duties and Implied Consent' (2006) 122 LQR 1.

[21] Bare trusts of limited duration for a specific purpose, eg escrow accounts, are possible exceptions, but these may be fitted into the proffered model as trusts of narrow fiduciary scope and intensity.

[22] cf J Oldham, 'Underreported and Underrated: The Court of Common Pleas in the Eighteenth Century' in H Hartog and WE Nelson (eds) *Law as Culture and Culture as Law* (2000) 119–46. Much work remains to be done on the equity judges' trial notebooks, the potential value of which is demonstrated by James Oldham's trail-blazing work on Lord Mansfield. Lord Eldon's notebooks, now at Georgetown University Law Center, await due scholarly attention.

had the lease renewed for himself. He was ordered by the court to hold the lease on a constructive trust to convey to the infant, and further to account for all profits. Lord King stated:

I must consider this as a trust for the infant; for I very well see, if a trustee, on the refusal to renew, might have a lease to himself, few trust-estates would be renewed to *cestui que* use; though I do not say there is a fraud in this case, yet he should rather have let run out, than to have had the lease to himself. This may seem hard, that the trustee is the only person of all mankind who might not have the lease: but it is very proper that rule should be strictly pursued, and not in the least relaxed; for it is very obvious what would be the consequence of letting trustees have the lease, on refusal to *cestui que* use.[23]

What, then, was the 'very obvious consequence' of allowing the trustee an opportunity derived from his office that would not have been available to his cestui? It was not obvious to earlier courts; in 1680 it was stated to be old doctrine that the trustee and guardian of an infant could buy the infant's estate through a third party.[24] Cretney[25] has surmised that the unstated premise of the *Keech* judgment was the court's concern over appropriation to the trustee of the substantive benefit of 'tenant's right'. This was the customary, non-legal, but none the less firm entitlement to roll over finite leases and thus maintain possession over long stretches of time across lives and generations. A trustee who used his legal title and fiduciary position to renew a lease was taking this benefit to himself and exploiting his office to do so.[26] Cretney acknowledges that the *Keech* doctrine was always put at a far higher level of generality than simply policing appropriation of tenant right—for example, that the larger benefit of the new lease grew from the root of the former lease, or was won by the advantages accruing from control of the former lease,[27] and hence was part of the beneficiary's estate. Equity recognized this link between the consecutive estates by automatic imposition of constructive trust, and refused to allow proof that the taking of the interest by a fiduciary caused no harm to the beneficiary.

---

[23] (1726) Select Case Temp King 61, 62–3; 25 ER 223, 223–4. The alternative report of *Keech v Sandford*, in 2 Equity Cases Abridged 741, 22 ER 629, is clearly derived from Select Case Temp King and adds nothing to our knowledge of the case.

[24] '[T]his shall not be taken to be a trust for the infant, for he is at liberty to purchase it as well as any body else': *Lesley's Case* (1680) 2 Freeman 52, 22 ER 1053. The same principle, in what might be the same case, is reported in *Combes v Throckmorton* (1680) 2 Equity Cases Abridged 742, 22 ER 630.

[25] S Cretney, 'The Rationale of Keech v. Sandford' (1969) 33 Conveyancer (NS) 161. Cretney's arguments and sources were adumbrated in WG Hart, 'The Development of the Rule in *Keech v Sandford*' (1905) 21 LQR 258.

[26] See Lord Hardwicke's speech referring to *Keech* in *Norris v Le Neve Ridgeway* (1745) Temp Hardwicke 322, 330–31; 27 ER 843, 846 (HL), stating: 'the equity of those cases is grounded on the supposed tenant's right or expectation, and the known usage of renewal: For though the tenants have properly no right, yet he is always preferred, and the ground is, that the person who settles the term in trust has a view to the courtesy in the renewal, the renewal enuring to the benefit of all the trusts'. An early instance of sensitivity to tenant's right is afforded by *Stokes v Clarke* [1701] Colles 192, 1 ER 245 (HL).   [27] *In Re Biss* [1903] 2 ch 40, 60–1 per Romer LJ pursues this analysis.

Harm was not the root of title; title was. And if a fiduciary agent without title made a profit from office, equity used constructive trust to create a title.[28]

The brevity of reasoning in Lord King's judgment in *Keech* was not perhaps atypical. King was regarded as a poor chancellor with a weak command of equitable doctrine. Lord Hervey, who bore a partisan hostility to King, commented: 'He had such a diffidence of himself that he did not dare to do right, for fear of doing wrong; decrees were always extorted from him; and had he been let alone he would never have given any suitor his due, for fear of giving him what was not so'.[29]

There were other critical stories about King, such as that he found the effort of learning equity late in life to be a strain that helped bring on the stroke that killed him; or that he dozed in court whilst senior counsel settled his decrees. These stories may exaggerate. None the less it is true that King came to the Woolsack as a political appointee from the Court of Common Pleas, without being steeped in the doctrines and practice of equity to the extent of other, greater chancellors of the seventeenth and eighteenth centuries. But his perceived weakness may have resulted not from incompetence, but rather from a conscious policy of legal rigorism, judicial restraint, and deference to the common law, so to avoid the jurisdictional attacks that dogged his disgraced predecessor Lord Macclesfield. This policy may explain why he constantly sent Chancery suits away for trial at law, or else reserved points for a conference of judges. Whatever the intention, the consequence was an intolerable backlog of cases; moreover his muddling of common-law and equitable testamentary doctrines had to be corrected by his successors. But for all that, King's judgment in *Keech* has won him a place in the history of equity.[30]

In his early twenties Peter King had shown promise as a gifted theologian and historian of patristics. His family steered him from a church career to the law, and he entered Middle Temple around age 25, and also studied civil law at Leiden. His cousin John Locke mentored him, and King imbibed Locke's philosophical theology and engaged in a long correspondence with him. Locke introduced him to Whig grandees, to judges such as Lord Chancellor Somers, and to the metropolitan intelligentsia including Isaac Newton. In return King

[28] *Bulkley v Wilford* (1834) 2 Cl & Fin 102, 177; 6 ER 1094, 1122 per Eldon LC; Maitland, *Equity* (n 8) 80–4. The modern debate over proprietary remedies for bribes, and the conflict between *Lister & Co v Stubbs* (1890) 45 Ch D 1 (CA) and *A-G Hong Kong v Reid* [1994] 1 AC 324 (PC), raise issues concerning the nature of constructive trust titles that cannot be explored here; see further P Birks, 'Property in the Profits of Wrongdoing' (1994) 24 UWA L Rev 8.
[29] J Hervey, *Memoirs of the Reign of George the Second* (JW Croker (ed), 1848) i, 286.
[30] For details of King's career and biography I have relied on: Hervey, *Memoirs* (n 29) i, 281–6; J Campbell *Lives of the Lord Chancellors* (1846) iv, 567–647; E Foss, *The Judges of England* (1864) viii, 41–4, 132–8; WS Holdsworth, *A History of English Law* (1922–66) i, 439–42, xii, 206–14; Oldham, 'Underreported and Underrated' (n 22); M Macnair, 'Lord King and Lord Talbot: An Eighteenth Century Attempt to Reduce Delay in Equity and its General Lessons' in CH van Rhee (ed), *The Law's Delay* (2004) 181–93; D Lemmings, 'Peter King' *New Dictionary of National Biography* (2005 web edn); M Macnair, 'Charles Talbot' ibid; PDG Thomas 'Philip Yorke' ibid.

managed Locke's affairs and investments in London, and was later to assist in the editing of his posthumous work. King maintained his evangelistic religious side; he helped found the Society for the Propagation of the Gospel in Foreign Parts in 1701,[31] and the next year published his highly influential *History of the Apostles Creed*.[32] King's connections and natural talent led him to success as a junior appearing before King's Bench in both private and criminal matters, with a reputation for forceful technical argumentation. Political patronage won him a seat in the Commons in 1704. As a strong Whig he criticized the Commons use of parliamentary privilege to defend corrupt elections in the *Aylesbury Voter's case*.[33] King followed Holt CJ and the Lords in pressing for justiciability of voting rights. He defended religious toleration and freedom against Tory divines in 1710. Throughout his political career he hounded Tory and Crown administrators for their corruption, place-getting, and inefficiency in serving the public. He was a particular enemy of the sale and exploitation of public offices. As a barrister he defended freedom of speech cases against the Crown. His Whig tendencies bought him Queen Anne's enmity and blocked his preferment as attorney or judge for the Crown, but after George I's accession he was appointed chief justice of the Court of Common Pleas in 1714 on Cowper LC's nomination. King helped try the Jacobite rebels, recommending clemency. He was a proficient and creative common-law judge, forming a bridge between Holt and Mansfield in his decisions on insurance, contract, and bills and notes.

King was raised to the Lord Chancellorship in 1725 following the fall of Lord Macclesfield for corruption. This was one year before he decided *Keech*. King had presided over Macclesfield's impeachment in the Lords, and his fair conduct recommended him for the task of restoring the tainted reputation of the Court of Chancery. King quickly achieved some lasting and much-needed reforms. The Chancery officials had treated their own fiduciary custodianship of litigants' money as merely a personal obligation to pay back a certain sum, and saw nothing wrong with trying to profit from custody of the cash; indeed this profit stream was seen as an emolument of office that helped pay off the costs of purchasing such office. Monies paid into court were commonly treated as personal loans, and were too often punted on stock markets and in gaming houses. King assaulted this entrenched venal culture from the start of his chancellorship. He did not exercise his customary power to sell the masterships as capital investments, but added £12,000 to his £6,000 pension in substitution. He required that litigants' monies be paid into a separate fund of the Bank of England, appointed an accountant to

---

[31] Interestingly King's Chancery deputy Jekyll, who served as Master of the Rolls from 1717 to 1738, was also a member of the Society, and was counted intellectually as a dissenter: T Keirn, 'Sir Joseph Jekyll' *New Dictionary of National Biography* (2005 web edn).

[32] P King, *The History of the Apostles Creed* (1702). King earlier published anonymously *An Enquiry into the Constitution, Discipline, Unity & Worship of the Primitive Church* (1691–2).

[33] *Ashby v White* (*the Aylesbury Voter's case*) (1703) 6 Mod 45, 87 ER 810; 2 Ld Raym 938, 92 ER 126; Holt KB 524, 90 ER 1188 (KB), discussed in J Getzler, *A History of Water Rights at Common Law* (2004) 146–8.

control all payments and securities brought into court, and took measures to indemnify any suitor whose money was lost by an official's bankruptcy or insolvency. He may have instigated moves by Parliament in the 1730s to have all legal proceedings conducted in English, and to control the exorbitant expenses and delays of litigation in equity and the common law.

Can King LC's career throw light on the *Keech* decision? The idea that profit from office should be barred can plausibly be connected to King's experience battling the abuses of the masters in Chancery. In this decade the business classes were still reeling from the disintegration of confidence in the capital markets following the South Sea Bubble of 1720.[34] It emerged that Chancery masters had scandalously lost in the Bubble some £100,871 of suitors' payments into court.[35] King's attacks on the sinecurism, speculation, and corruption of the officials of Chancery may conceivably be connected to the prophylactic policy announced in *Keech* at the start of his chancellorship. We can also find a run of stringently moralistic decisions disciplining trustees, guardians, co-owners, mortgagees and so on, in the months preceding *Keech*,[36] suggesting that King was pursuing a praetorian policy of enforcing commercial and fiduciary honesty. Yet we should be cautious in making the connection between public or personal morality on the one hand and the creation of private law doctrine on the other. The upright, devout King ended his career pilloried as a corrupt as well as ineffective judge himself, grasping for bribes and preferring his son to a government post.[37] His critics suggested that he opposed the graft of others but not his own. Yet it may still be that as he strove to establish his authority over Chancery in 1725–6, he wished to be seen as acting against corruption, and that cases such as *Keech* signalled that intention. The decay of King's judicial career, a full decade after *Keech* was decided, possibly forms a separate and severable phase.

[34] The impact of the Bubble on the law is examined in R Harris, *Industrializing English Law: Entrepreneurship and Business Organization, 1720–1844* (2000) esp 60–81. Certainly the events of 1720 reached into the minds of trusts lawyers. Hardwicke LC wryly commented, 'But it is well known, that during the golden dream, people were so infatuated as to look upon imaginary wealth as equally valuable with so much money'. He refused to compensate beneficiaries' losses in the Bubble where trustees acted as investment agents: *Jackson v Jackson* (1737) 1 Atkyns 513, 26 ER 324.

[35] Campbell, *Lives of the Lord Chancellors* (n 30) 608; Foss, *Judges* (n 30) 136; Holdsworth, *History* n (30) i, 439–42, citing (at 440) Parl Papers vol 31, 137 App No 4 (1860) (Order of Lord Chancellor 19 January 1749).

[36] See eg *Whitackre v Whitackre* (1725) Select Cases Temp King 13, 25 ER 195; *Pugh v Ryal* (1725) Select Cases Temp King 40, 25 ER 211; *Wood's Case* (1725) Select Cases Temp King 46, 25 ER 214; *Combs's Case* (1725) Select Cases Temp King 46, 25 ER 214; *Macarte v Gibson* (1725) Select Cases Temp King 50, 25 ER 217; *Western v Cartwright* (1725) Select Cases Temp King 34, 25 ER 207; *Eden v Foster* (1725) Select Cases Temp King 36, 25 ER 208.

[37] Adjustments need to be made for a different public morality at that time. Lord Hardwicke, the greatest eighteenth-century chancellor, found legal posts for his children and reached for titles and emoluments, but was not counted a corrupt chancellor; by contrast Lord Brougham in the next century was accused of preferring a nephew to a Chancery sinecure, undermining his campaign against inefficiency and patronage in the legal system. See Thomas, 'Philip Yorke' (n 30), and J Getzler, 'Edward Burtenshaw Sugden' *New Dictionary of National Biography* (2005 web edn).

3. Take-up, Expansion, and Justification

Historically the *Rumford Market* case has been received as embodying a policy of
prophylaxis, or preventative sanction through profit-stripping that takes away all
incentive for a fiduciary to consider how he might gain from his position.[38] The
policy can also be put in evidential terms: Lord Eldon later opined that fiduciary
law prohibits all profit-taking because the stronger party to a fiduciary relationship controls all evidence of the relationship and can easily conceal
wrongdoing from the vulnerable party or the court.[39] In different language we
can say that the costs of monitoring a fiduciary are high, since the fiduciary has
extensive powers and discretionary control over the running of the relationship,
including extensive powers to deal with the beneficial assets. It is therefore difficult to protect the vulnerable beneficiary, precisely because proof of wrongdoing is elusive where the wrongdoer has strong control over the evidence of
dealings. Equity therefore applies a stern rule forbidding all fiduciary profit-
taking, however innocent in intent and even where the profit does not subtract
from the beneficiary's assets, in order to redress the power imbalance within the
fiduciary relationship that derives from the difficulty of monitoring the fiduciary's actions as plenary agent. That *Keech* is the *fons et origo* of this doctrine is
especially striking since the court conceded in that case that 'there was clear proof
of the refusal to renew for the benefit of the infant' and Lord King avowed that
'I do not say there is a fraud in this case'. In other words, information monitoring the fiduciary's behaviour was readily available in this particular instance;
yet the prohibition of profit was applied none the less and erected into a general
rule. The rule does not seem to have been followed before Lord King enunciated
it in 1726.[40] The rule has become unpopular with modern commentators, who
have argued that the automatic finding of impropriety should be replaced by a
rebuttable presumption, partly because modern law and accounting is more apt
to deal with fiduciary power; partly out of unease at the penal or deterrent
application of private law remedies to pursue public policy goals.[41] But
equity has maintained the rule, allowing only informed consent to suspend its
operation.

[38] G Jones, 'Unjust Enrichment and the Fiduciary's Duty of Loyalty' (1968) 84 LQR 472; G
Jones, 'The Role of Equity in the English Law of Restitution' in *Unjust Enrichment* (n 16) 149,
158–60; J Edelman, *Gain-Based Damages* (2002) 65–111, 191–3, 207–16.

[39] *Ex parte James* (1803) 8 Vesey Junior 337, 345; 32 ER 385, 388; *Ex parte Hughes* (1802) 6
Vesey Junior 617, 31 ER 1223; *Ex parte Lacey* (1801) 6 Vesey Junior 625, 31 ER 1228. Lord Eldon
drew from Lord Hardwicke's judgment in *Whelpdale v Cookson* (1747) 1 Vesey Senior 9, 27 ER
856; see below, text accompanying (nn 57–65).

[40] Cretney collects seventeenth–century cases at odds with *Keech* in 'Rationale' (n 25) 178.

[41] eg Cretney, 'Rationale' (n 25) 161–3, 178; Finn, *Fiduciary Obligations* (n 17) 246–51, 259–
65; Smith, 'Motive' (n 5) 57–64, 73–80; cf Conaglen, 'Fiduciary Loyalty' (n 4) 460–71. The Court
of Appeal was concerned about deterrent overkill, yet maintained the full rigour of the no-profit
rule in *Re Biss* [1903] 2 Ch 40.

Despite the ubiquity of the *Keech* rule today, at the time the decision may have been regarded as marginal.[42] For example in 1728 the case of *Rakestraw v Brewer*[43] came before Chancery concerning a lease mortgagee who bought the lease reversion. He had to account for it to the mortgagor, but Jekyll MR, and on appeal King LC himself, did not cite *Keech*, instead speaking in general terms of protecting the mortgagor's title from the mortgagee who was exploiting his legal title to take undue advantage in getting in a new lease. In 1732 in *Mansel v Mansel*[44] a life tenant joined with the trustees protecting the contingent remainders to convey the estate to her husband and so destroy the remainders. The court nullified the conveyance and decreed that an estate tail be held on trust for the issue, citing *Keech*. It was acknowledged that Harcourt LK, supported by older authorities, had thought differently in a case of 1710;[45] but King LC, sitting with Raymond CJ and Reynolds CB, seemed to have thought that the Rumford Market case now pushed equity to take a stronger stance against trustees exercising legal powers in a fashion inimical to beneficiaries.[46] Lord Hardwicke in 1745 stated that 'the case of Rumford market was a very strong case', but he distinguished the appropriation of the lessee's customary expectation of a lease renewal from a case where a trustee bought the reversion of a life interest, where there was no such expectation.[47] Other cases did hold that purchase of the freehold was caught by the *Keech* rule as the opportunity to buy had come to the trustee through his office, expropriating the good will a reversioner might have toward a life tenant.[48] In 1768 it was held that a life tenant under a settlement who won a further term of a Crown lease held the renewal for the settlement, because 'the additional term was to be considered as an ingraftment upon the old term, on the principle which prevailed in the case of Rumford Market'.[49] *Keech* was approved as a 'strong case' by Lord Apsley in 1773 on a like issue of a life tenant renewing.[50] Lord Thurlow later described such a renewal as 'making an unconscientious benefit of the estate', citing the Rumford Market case as 'the first and most notorious case on this subject', even though the life tenant was not obliged to seek renewal for the settlement in the first place. The trustee's actual intentions would not be measured in order to determine whether there had been an illegitimate exploitation of position.[51]

---

[42] cf Hart, 'The Development of the Rule in *Keech v. Sandford*' (n 25).

[43] (1728) 2 Peere Williams 511, 24 ER 839. In the same year King LC avoided the renewal of a lease by a remainderman, which would have denied a widow with the life estate a chance to extend the lease, again without mentioning *Keech*. See *Addis v Clement* (1728) 2 Peere Williams 456, 24 ER 811.   [44] (1732) 2 Barnardiston KB 186, 94 ER 438.

[45] *Pye v Georges* (1710) 1 Equity Cases Abridged 385, 21 ER 1120.

[46] *Mansel v Mansel* (1732) 2 Barnardiston KB 186, 188; 94 ER 438, 339.

[47] *Norris v Le Neve Ridgeway* (1745) Temp Hardwicke 322, 27 ER 843 (HL), affirming *Norris v Le Neve* (1743) 3 Atkyns 26, 26 ER 818 (Hardwicke LC). See above, text accompanying (nn 25–8).

[48] See Cretney, 'Rationale' (n 25).

[49] *Taster v Marriott* (1768) Ambler 668, 27 ER 433 (Sewell MR, aff'd Camden LC).

[50] *Owen v Williams* (1773) Ambler 734, 737; 27 ER 474, 476 (LC). By the time we get to *Randall v Russell* (1817) 3 Merivale 190, 36 ER 73 the restraint of the life tenant in renewing was seen as orthodox.   [51] *Stone v Theed* (1787) 2 Brown CC 243, 29 ER 135 (LC).

For all this swell of affirmation in the case-law, doubts still seemed to arise as to the reach of the no-profit principle.[52] In 1782 Lord Thurlow found that an executor with a power to sell assets had to keep the sale proceeds segregated as an equitable estate, and not mix the proceeds into his own legal estate and account for the value simply as a debt.[53] He found that prior authorities formed a conflicting morass giving no guidance on this point; interestingly the *Keech* doctrine was not mentioned, perhaps because the trustee-like duties of executors were seen as distinct from those of *inter vivos* trustees and guardians. Lord Thurlow referred to the 1768 case of *Silk v Prime*,[54] where 'Lord Camden . . . sifted all the cases and settled the point that the circumstance of giving the real estate *by any means* to the executor, shall not occasion the produce of it when sold, to be applied as [legal assets], but it must nevertheless be considered as equitable assets'. Thurlow affirmed this rule, and added this order: 'To make this still clearer, [t]he rents and profits in the hands of the devisees are assets before the sale. Legal assets they cannot be, for the executors have no right to receive them. They must therefore be equitable assets'.[55] Thurlow LC later hardened his position, stating that a trustee in any wise could never buy trust property.[56]

In the important 1795 case of *York Buildings Company v Mackenzie*[57] the House of Lords reviewed a Scots case where a solicitor acting as common agent for a court sale of an insolvent estate had to account to the creditors for property of the estate he had bought for himself. The Lords built on the authority of *Keech* to make a strong general statement of the no-profit and no-conflict rules. It was held to be a natural law of all civil societies, found in all developed legal systems, to bar an agent or trustee from benefiting from the entrustment;[58] and the bar was to be conclusive in order to avoid all evidential problems.[59] The evidential

---

[52] Difficulties in framing the *Keech* doctrine were not helped by incomplete and sometimes incoherent law reporting, as in *Blewett v Millett* (1774) 7 Brown PC 367, 3 ER 238.

[53] *Newton v Bennet* (1782) 1 Brown CC 135, 28 ER 1035. The use of common-law remedies to compel executors to transfer legacies was explored that same year in *Hawkes v Saunders* (1782) 1 Cowp 289, 98 ER 1091 per Buller J.

[54] Reported briefly as *Silk v Pryme* (1768) 2 Collyer 511, 63 ER 838 and (1766) 2 Collyer 509, 63 ER 837.

[55] *Newton v Bennet* (1782) 1 Brown CC 135, 141; 28 ER 1035, 1040.

[56] *Fox v Mackreth* (1788) 2 Brown CC 400, 29 ER 224 (MR); (1789) 1 Vesey Junior 69, 30 ER 234; (1791) 4 Brown PC 258, 2 ER 175 (LC).

[57] (1795) 8 Brown PC 42, 3 ER 432. See also *Whichcote v Lawrence* (1798) 1 Vesey Junior Supplement 422, 34 ER 856 per Loughborough LC.

[58] *York Buildings Company v Mackenzie* (1795) 8 Brown PC 42, 63; 3 ER 432, 446: '[A] person cannot be both judge and party. No man can serve two masters. He that is entrusted with the interest of others, cannot be allowed to make the business an object of interest to himself; because from the frailty of nature, one who has the power, will be too readily seized with the inclination to use the opportunity for serving his own interest at the expence of those for whom he is entrusted'.

[59] (1795) 8 Brown PC 42, 64; 3 ER 432, 446: 'The danger of temptation, from the facility and advantages for doing wrong which a particular situation affords, does, out of the mere necessity of the case, work a disqualification; nothing less than incapacity being able to shut the door against temptation where the danger is imminent, and the security against discovery great, as it must be

point was derived from a decision of Lord Hardwicke,[60] nullifying a sale made at auction of an estate to pay debts, where an agent of the trustee bought the assets. Though it was proved that the highest bidder won, the sale could not stand without the consent of the creditors, 'for he [Hardwicke] knew the dangerous consequence: nor is it enough for the trustee to say, you cannot prove any fraud, as it is in his own power to conceal it'.

The *Keech* principle was further generalized to all fiduciaries in the early nineteenth century.[61] Lord Eldon's 1808 judgment of *Crawshay v Collins*[62] stated that on dissolution of a partnership the partners became tenants in common with an obligation to deal with the whole of the stock, and each to account to the group. '[T]he right is, not to an individual proportion of a specific article, but to an account: the property to be made the most of, and divided'. *Crawshay* became a leading case, and *Keech* itself was not often relied upon as authority, though it was occasionally cited by counsel.[63] It was significant that, in the important case of *Ex parte James* of 1803, Lord Eldon adverted to the *Keech* doctrine regarding trustee purchase of a lease reversion as possibly a uniquely strong version of the larger doctrine repressing self-dealing by a trustee, and he acknowledged that the authorities conflicted as to whether the trustee had to derive a real advantage for the rule to operate. Eldon reiterated Hardwicke's theory that the *Keech* doctrine was designed to leapfrog the absence of evidence of fiduciary fraud.[64] It was this version of the doctrine that was adopted into modern English law by Lord Russell in *Regal (Hastings) Ltd v Gulliver*.[65]

where the difficulty of prevention or remedy is inherent to the very situation which creates the danger. The wise policy of the law has therefore put the sting of a disability into the temptation as a defensive weapon against the strength of the danger which lies in the situation'.

[60] *Whelpdale v Cookson* (1747) 1 Vesey Senior 9, 27 ER 856.

[61] See eg *Nesbitt v Tredennick* (1808) [1803–13] All ER Rep 782; *O'Reilly v Fetherston* (1830) 4 Bligh NS 161, 5 ER 58; AW Scott and WF Fratcher *The Law of Trusts* (4th edn, 1987) 2A 170 at ¶ 311.

[62] (1808) 15 Vesey Junior 218, 229, 33 ER 736, 741, argued successfully by Sir Samuel Romilly, who also won in *Featherstonhaugh v Fenwick* (1810) 17 Vesey Junior 298, 34 ER 115 where Sir William Grant MR adopted the doctrine.

[63] eg *Webb v Lugar* (1836) 2 Younge and Collyer Exchequer 247, 160 ER 389; *Stears v South Essex Gas-Light Company* (1860) 9 Common Bench NS 180, 142 ER 70.

[64] *Ex parte James* (1803) 8 Vesey Junior 337, 345; 32 ER 385, 388: '[P]urchases by trustees, assignees, and persons having a confidential character ... [are] not permitted in any case however honest the circumstances; the general interests of justice requiring [them] to be destroyed in every instance; as no Court is equal to the examination and ascertainment of the truth in much the greater number of cases'. Lord Eldon made the evidential point a number of times with great force; see also *Ex parte Hughes* (1802) 6 Vesey Junior 617, 31 ER 1223 (forbidding a creditor to use his knowledge of the bankrupt estate to buy assets in auction), and *Ex parte Lacey* (1801) 6 Vesey Junior 625, 31 ER 1228 (same, regarding purchase by assignee in bankruptcy). Lord Eldon later developed the idea that a trustee might honestly conceal wrongdoing from himself through failing to reach an objective standard: *Bulkley v Wilford* (1834) 2 Cl & Fin 102, 177; 6 ER 1094, 1122; SC 8 Bligh NS 111, 143; 5 ER 888, 899–900 (HL).

[65] *Regal (Hastings) Ltd v Gulliver* [1967] 2 AC 46; see also *In Re Biss* [1903] 2 Ch 40, 60–1 per Romer LJ; cf *Bray v Ford* [1896] AC 44, 51 per Lord Herschell (HL), stating that the 'inflexible

4. The Sources of Fiduciary Obligation

We can now better see why Lord King decided *Keech v Sandford* as he did, and how his creation of a no-profits rule for lease renewals was developed over a century into a doctrine of general application to fiduciary circumstances. But the case-law flowing from *Keech* hardly explored the foundations of the doctrine. Apart from the evidential theory, we do not learn the reason for its triumph. For this we must look back to the period before the eighteenth century.

We can isolate perhaps four historical sources or models[66] influencing the development of fiduciary obligations, including the duty not to profit from a dominant position.[67] First, fiduciary obligations regulated the relationships of *co-owners*, or any persons who split or share between them ownership interests in a single asset. Secondly, fiduciary obligations protected minors under wardship and guardianship law, and later came to regulate relationships based generally on unequal *personal status* including many relationships of presumed undue influence.[68] Thirdly, fiduciary obligations could be based on duties to *account*, which stopped opportunistic parties from exploiting bargaining or possessory advantages.[69] Such duties could involve *custody*, especially of non-fungible assets, or *powers* without custody, with bailment and agency being two dominant examples. And finally, much fiduciary law was generated by the control of *office-holders* where there were no obvious persons with standing to enforce duties of loyalty and due performance. *Public office* and *corporate direction*, which were both seen as akin to the public or charitable trust, were examples of this, where diffuse beneficiaries might not have effective correlative rights of enforcement against the person wielding powers. *Testamentary executors* were another important sub-category, whose duty to carry out the will of the deceased had to be enforced over time in relation to numbers of heirs with disparate interests over dispersed, unconverted assets.

The medieval use over land or other assets, and its child the modern trust, could draw on any or all of these fiduciary sources. Lawyers did not need the

---

rule' of *Keech* might none the less be lifted to allow the trustee a remuneration or profit from office with the express agreement of cestuis.

[66] One hesitates to describe them as *causae*, or 'events' using Birksian terminology, as they do not form exclusive and self-sufficient categories or discrete sets of fact triggering legal consequences. cf Birks, *Introduction* (n 1) 6–7.

[67] Sealy's classic pair of articles provide a different classification that has influenced this analysis: see LS Sealy, 'Fiduciary Relationships' [1962] CLJ 69; 'Some Principles of Fiduciary Obligation' [1963] CLJ 119.

[68] Today we may feel unease at application of fiduciary language to describe relations of influence and confidence: see P Birks, 'The New Equity and the Need for Certainty' [1987] Cambridge Lectures 309. The historical connections of these doctrines requires investigation; a start is made in Finn, *Fiduciary Obligations* (n 17) 82–8; Sealy, 'Fiduciary Relationships' (n 67) 78–9.

[69] cf P Birks, 'Restitutionary Damages for Breach of Contract: *Snepp* and the Fusion of Law and Equity' [1987] LMCLQ 421.

model of the custodial trust before them in order to invent fiduciary duties; quite the reverse, the prior existence of fiduciary duties suggested the creation of the trust. The label that was applied in any particular case might be confidence, or express, implied, or constructive trust, or increasingly from 1800, 'fiduciary' duty.[70] But labels do not always reveal the contents of their vessels. The next task is to study more closely the nature of these four models.

4.1. The Co-ownership Model

Where parties share the ownership of an asset, and each has authority to deal with that asset, each has a potent continuing power to affect the other's interests. The law responds by shackling this power and forcing each to guard the interests of the other—a mutual fiduciary relationship akin to modern partnership.[71] This phenomenon stretches back in legal time and is not a product of trust institutions, but rather of the simple possibility of ownership by more than one person.[72] Maitland noted how in medieval law co-ownership so often leads to the recognition of an entity with its own internal law to protect the stakeholders, and built from this a Germanic realist theory of the corporation.[73] Roman law had a conceptual commitment to undivided *dominium*.[74] But even Roman law had to accommodate shared ownerships, with remedies to protect co-owners from each other or even to allow them to take out their shares, for example from a mixture. There was also the splitting of ownership between a *dominus* and owners of servitudes and usufructs, which lesser interests were eventually accorded their own real remedies against strangers.[75] In the law of obligations too the Roman jurists could recognize sharing of intangible assets and legal balancing

---

[70] The early textbooks provide good information as to usage of the language of fiduciaries and constructive trusts: see J Fonblanque, *A Treatise of Equity* (5th edn, 1820) ii, 167–203; G Spence, *The Equitable Jurisdiction of the Court of Chancery* (1849) 294–310; J Story, *Commentaries on Equity Jurisprudence* (1st English edn by WE Grigsby, 1884) 194–219.

[71] It is noticeable that the common law for long could not decide the basis of property-holding within partnerships; these were agreed to be composed of mutual agency relations, but the courts dithered between applying joint, several, and joint and several property regimes to the partnership assets. See J Getzler and M Macnair, 'The Firm as an Entity before the Companies Acts' in P Brand, K Costello, and WN Osborough (eds), *Adventures of the Law* (2005) 267.

[72] eg Lord Nottingham *c* 1672: 'The Common Law raises a trust between tenants in common of a personal chattel'. See DEC Yale (ed), *Lord Nottingham's 'Manual of Chancery Practice' and 'Prolegomena of Chancery and Equity'* (1965) 244.

[73] FW Maitland, *Domesday Book and Beyond* (1897, repr 1987) 341–56; J Getzler, 'Law, History and the Social Sciences: Intellectual Traditions of Late Nineteenth- and Early Twentieth-Century Europe' in M Lobban and A Lewis (eds), *Law and History: Current Legal Issues* 6 (2003) 215, 242–8.

[74] P Birks, 'The Roman Law Concept of Dominium and the Idea of Absolute Ownership' [1985] Acta Juridica 1, 7–15.

[75] On the limited scope and uncertain juridical nature of common ownership in Roman law, whether in partnerships or joint inheritances, see WW Buckland, *Textbook of Roman Law* (3rd edn, PG Stein (ed), 1963) 539–41; on the *iure in re aliena* see A Rodger, *Owners and Neighbours in Roman Law* (1972).

of power between the sharers. Birks illuminated the role of the second chapter of the lex Aquilia giving recourse to a person whose co-obligor the adstipulator had wrongly released a debt. Birks's thesis was that the adstipulator could collude with the debtor to compromise the debt obligation using silver coinage at a low discretionary conversion rate, with a kick-back to the adstipulator as a reward for the collusion. The fraud was hard to detect by the stipulator, hence the Aquilian award of double damages as a deterrent. This action can be seen as an obligational version of co-owners being required to respect each other's interests.[76]

The insights found in earlier co-ownership regimes can help us grasp the main terrain of the doctrine of *Keech v Sandford* in its first hundred years—regulation of advantage taking in an array of split ownership cases involving renewals and purchases of leases and residues where one party, whether joint owner, lessor, mortgagee, trustee for sale, or other, has acted on an estate without proper concern for the impact on a co-owner's estate or interest. The details form much of the bulk of pre-1800 English Chancery jurisdiction, demonstrating how co-ownership and fiduciary law are thoroughly imbricated.

4.2. The Status Model

Relationships of dependence and subordination in a legalistic culture will swiftly generate rules to govern how far the superior can control the inferior.[77] In Marc Bloch's striking portrayal, feudalism, or the exchange of land for services under a relationship of subordination of tenant to lord, was 'born muzzled' in Western Europe, restrained by law or legally enforced custom.[78] This legalistic feudalism has been described as contractual, but fealty and homage can also be cast as a type of fiduciary relationship. One of the duties of the lord was to protect and give justice to his tenants; and the tenants in return had to give service and fealty to the lord. Rent supporting the lord was thus a surrogate for tax, as the lordship was also a form of government. Fundamental breach of this solemn fiduciary relationship was treason. Much of the history of English feudalism concerns the Crown's use of law to buttress feudal obligations,[79] and also the attempts of lords to improve their fiscal position by exploiting or evading the feudal incidents. These incidents were the special obligations that accrued to a tenant at key moments such as entry to a fee on

---

[76] P Birks, 'Wrongful Loss by Co-Promisees' (1994) 22 Index 181.

[77] Roman slave law, defining humans as ordinary property, is an unsettling counter-example: see WW Buckland, *The Roman Law of Slavery* (1908); P Birks, 'An Unacceptable Face of Human Property' in P Birks (ed), *New Perspectives in the Roman Law of Property: Essays for Barry Nicholas* (1989) 61.

[78] M Bloch, *Feudal Society*, 2 vols (1st edn, 1939–40, LA Manyon (trs), 1961); M Bloch, 'Personal Liberty and Servitude in the Middle Ages' in *Slavery and Serfdom in the Middle Ages: Selected Essays by Marc Bloch* (WR Beer (trs), 1975) 33.

[79] SFC Milsom, *The Legal Framework of English Feudalism* (1976); RC Palmer, *English Law in the Age of the Black Death, 1348–1381: A Transformation of Governance and Law* (1993).

death of an ancestor, known as relief and primer seisin, or fines for *inter vivos* transfer. The further incidents of wardship and marriage were incurred where land was left to an under-age heir. The lord then took the seisin of the land and had a putative duty to stand as guardian of land and heir until majority. Lords could not by law commit waste undermining the value of the land capital (though they commonly did), but if the fee was in knight service the lord could pocket the profits, as well as arrange a marriage or force the heir to pay if the proposed marriage was not wanted. Leases were suspended for the currency of the wardship. However for socage or non-military tenures the lord had to account to the heir for all estate profits taken between the ages of 14 and 21, a rule that crystallized in the early thirteenth century. Legislation was passed continuously to enforce and regulate the feudal incidents and protect Crown and lordly revenues from mortmain, uses, and other evasions, and account remedies buttressed by legislation were used to control socage wardships.[80] The legally regulated subordinations of feudalism provided a vocabulary of fiduciary concepts for other forms of subordination. The use and trust were developed largely to undermine feudal incidents, and in attempting to shore up those obligations the Crown ended up fuelling the rise of enforceable split titles, enforced as obligations of good faith in Chancery.[81]

4.3. The Accountability Model

We have noted that Birks identified the action of account as the main vehicle by which trust assets were defended using the law of obligations. I remember first discussing the actions of account with Peter on a trip to the Australian bush sometime in the mid-1990s. He became particularly fascinated that day with taxonomizing the platypus he encountered. On his home territory of English private law, he teased out the delicate relationships between indebitatus assumpsit, debt proper, and account in sixteenth and seventeenth century common law, as he sought to build sure foundations for a law of obligations that

---

[80] Magna Carta 1215 cl 2–5; 9 Henry III 1225 confirmed 25 Edw I 1297; Provisions of Merton 1236 cc 5–7; and note esp Provisions of Westminster 1259 cl 12, reissued in 1263–4 cl 12 and also in the Statute of Marlborough 1267 c 17: 'It has also been provided that, if land which is held in socage is in the wardship of the kinsmen of the heir because the heir is under age, those guardians may not make waste or sale or any destruction of that inheritance but are to keep it safely for the benefit of the said heir, so that when he shall come of age, they are to answer him through a lawful accounting (*'per legitimam computacionem'*) for the issues of the said inheritance with due allowance made to those guardians of their reasonable expenses'.
See P Brand, *Kings, Barons and Justices: The Making and Enforcement of Legislation in Thirteenth-Century England* (2003) 62–9 (on account actions), 348–61 (on accountability of socage guardians), 422–3, 476–7 (texts of legislation and translations).
[81] Statute on Feoffment to Uses 1484; Statute of Uses 1536. For an acute overview see JH Baker, *The Oxford History of the Laws of England Vol VI 1483–1558* (2003) 661–86; for details see J Biancalana, 'Medieval Uses' in *Itinera Fiduciae* (n 7) 111; N Jones, 'Trusts in England after the Statute of Uses: A View from the 16th Century' ibid 173; M Macnair, 'The Conceptual Basis of Trusts in the Later 17th and Early 18th Centuries' ibid 207.

could seize profits won through civil wrongs.[82] In the end he argued that the account model of stewardship of an asset was too arcanely historical for present use, and ought to be overlaid or replaced by modern categories of loss- or gain-based damages.[83] Yet his original insight that we cannot understand our law without knowledge of account has not lost its force.

Account today seems to us a remedial response, but originally it had substantive connotations, being a feudal action to control bailiffs of farms, guardians of estates, bailees and factors of goods, and similar persons with control over another's assets. Account meant they had to state how they had managed those assets, and restore to owners assets that had been lost or their value; or to add in profits that had been diverted or that ought to have been gathered in.[84] Biancalana has shown how, in the pre-Chancery world of the thirteenth century, various forms of *custodia* appeared to allow a custodian to manage an asset and be controlled in that management—without taking seisin or title, which might bring adverse reactions from lords wary of subinfeudations, or reduce the availability of real remedies to defend titles, or disrupt the balance of power between generations in a family. Account-like actions were one way to enforce such *custodia* in addition to covenant between the parties. The *custodia* may be seen as a form of fiduciary management without passing of title, and were commonly employed until the rise of the use and the decline of feudal relationships rendered these devices otiose.[85]

A significant Year Book case of 1320 shows how very early in the history of the common law the claim of a beneficiary could be enforced using account yet without any privity between the parties. An under-age heir had his legacy placed by the executors in the hands of a bailee, with instructions for the money to be kept until the beneficiary came of age. The bailee refused to pay, defending that he had not been a receiver nor a bailee to the beneficiary and the beneficiary had never had possession or title to the money. Stonore J held that since a bailment could not be enforced, 'It is therefore necessary that the person in whose name the monies were bailed should have an action [of account], for otherwise you would be answerable to nobody, and this would be against the law'.[86] By allowing account without privity of receipt or bailment, in effect a custody with

---

[82] Birks, 'Restitution for Wrongs' (n 16).

[83] P Birks, *Unjust Enrichment* (2nd edn, 2005) 293–5 ('accountability is dying and there is no point in trying to turn the clock back').

[84] Much work remains to be done in understanding this field. Invaluable material on early use of account in commercial law is uncovered in SB Elliott *Compensation Claims Against Trustees* (Oxford DPhil thesis 2002) esp ch 2; and M McGaw, *A History of the Common Law of Agency* (Oxford DPhil thesis 2005) esp 60–75. For account and insolvency in Chancery in a later period see Getzler and Macnair 'The Firm as an Entity' (n 71).

[85] J Biancalana, 'Thirteenth-Century *Custodia*' (2001) 22 J Legal History 14; Biancalana 'Medieval Uses' (n 81).

[86] *Robert le Taillour v Alexander atte Medwe* (1320) in SJ Stoljar and LJ Downer (eds), *Year Books of Edward II* (104 Selden Soc 1988) 39–42, discussed at pp xi–xiv; cf SJ Stoljar, 'The Transformations of Account' (1964) 80 LQR 203.

fiduciary qualities was being recognized. Actions of account was thus used to give remedies against both contracting parties and parties outside privity, who exploited their control of assets in a transaction to take an unfair advantage; they could be required to disgorge as if they had stood as agents. Account in both law and equity thus yielded effective remedies against fiduciaries including trustees and partners. In the hands of Lord Nottingham much later the accounting remedies against fiduciaries flowered into full-blown proprietary remedies to enforce trusts.[87]

4.4. The Office Model

The 1742 case of *Charitable Corporation v Sutton*[88] has been identified as one of the earliest cases where fiduciary office was identified as a category running alongside trusteeship of property. In that case the directors of a corporation, through grossly negligent lack of supervision of servants of the corporation, allowed fraudulent loans to be made on fictitious or inadequate securities and so undermined the capital of the corporation, which had been set up by Crown charter to make loans to the worthy poor. Over half the capital of £600,000 was so lost. Lord Hardwicke, borrowing from civilian categories of the degrees of negligence, found that the directors had been grossly negligent and therefore culpable of a kind of fraud or breach of trust. He assimilated nonfeasance in failing to supervise with misfeasance of office. The telling portion of his judgment involves extension of jurisdiction to the directors as 'agents' or 'trustees': 'By accepting of a trust of this sort, a person is obliged to execute it with fidelity and reasonable diligence; and it is no excuse to say that they had no benefit from it, but that it was merely honorary; and therefore they are within the case of common trustees'.[89] The office of director was not governmental, but like the Bank of England or the great trading companies had sufficient impact on the public to require stern legal regulation through trust law.[90] The directors were to be liable for misfeasance and nonfeasance of duty, and were also to be jointly liable even though they each breached their duty in distinct fashion and each had

---

[87] See *Nottingham's Chancery Cases* (73 Selden Soc 1957) i, Cases 105, 120, 198, 294, 303, 340, 341, 480; DEC Yale, 'Introduction' to *Nottingham's Chancery Cases* (79 Selden Soc 1961) ii, 195–207, Cases 651, 817, 824, 880, 961, 987, 1039, 1061, 1150.

[88] (1742) 2 Atk 400, 26 ER 642 per Hardwicke LC.

[89] The *ex lege* quality of this obligation is stressed by Birks in his analysis of the case in 'Negligence' (n 5) 193–4.

[90] (1742) 2 Atk 400, 405; 26 ER 642, 644: 'I take the employment of a director to be of a mixed nature: it partakes of the nature of a publick office, as it arises from the charter of the crown. But it cannot be said to be an employment affecting the public government; and for this reason none of the directors of the great companies, the *Bank, South-sea, &c.* are required to qualify themselves by taking-the sacrament. Therefore committee-men are most properly agents to those who employ them in this trust, and who empower them to direct and superintend the affairs of the corporation. In this respect they may be guilty of acts of commission or omission, of mal-feasance or non-feasance'.

a different proportionate blame for the disaster.[91] This strong solidary liability was a key step in the use of fiduciary relations to construct entities in law.

Equity also constructed joint and several liabilities for partners and participants in deeds of trust ventures through its control of insolvency procedures, and thereby created a nascent fiduciary law to govern trading entities that was complete by 1800, if not by 1700.[92] It was the necessity of aggregating individual investors and directors into entities that could sue and be sued that was a major forcing house for the development of fiduciary theory, and these developments took place as an experiment independent of liabilities of trustees proper.[93]

The law of public office was regulated by different writs such as quo warranto and trespassory actions[94] until well into the mid-nineteenth century when fresh public-law techniques of judicial review based on King's Bench writs of prohibition, certiorari, and mandamus were developed.[95] The content of the modern rules for judicial review of administrative powers were lifted from Chancery doctrine concerning exercise of trust powers. Powers themselves were developed simultaneously as a fiduciary adjunct to trust law proper and were inserted into trusts to make them more flexible in the era of strict settlement.[96]

Testamentary executorship may lay claim to being the main forcing house of fiduciary concepts in Roman[97] and early medieval law. Helmholz has shown how the church helped develop testamentary uses using Romano-canonical procedure, as part of its concern to protect the dying wishes of testators and the solemn undertakings of those in whom they reposed their trust to carry out their will.[98]

---

[91] (1742) 2 Atk 400, 406; 26 ER 642, 645: 'Nor will I ever determine that a court of equity cannot lay hold of every breach of trust, let the person be guilty of it either in a private, or public capacity . . . I will never determine that frauds of this kind are out of the reach of courts of law or equity, for an intolerable grievance would follow from such a determination'.

[92] Getzler and Macnair, 'The Firm as Entity' (n 71).

[93] cf Harris, *Industrializing English Law* (n 34) 14–36, 137–67.

[94] See eg *Lane v Cotton* (1701) 12 Modern 472, 88 ER 1458, where action on the case was used against an officer of the Post Office, with pre-1700 authorities on accountability of office-holders analysed closely by Holt CJ.

[95] See *Darley v Regina* (1845–6) 12 Clark and Finnelly 520, 8 ER 1513 (Exch Ch Ireland); *Julius v Lord Bishop of Oxford* [1880] All ER Rep 43 (HL). In *R v Windham* (1776) 1 Cowp 377; 98 ER 1139 (KB), Lord Mansfield CJ investigated the interplay between the common-law prerogative writs and fiduciary and equitable remedies that could be levied against officers of a corporation with public functions (in this case, Wadham College, Oxford).

[96] E Sugden, *Practical Treatise on Powers* (1808) is a key work summarizing the law since Lord Nottingham.

[97] Johnston analyses the growth of fiduciary devices in Roman law in *Roman Law of Trusts* (n 7) esp 256–8, and sees parallels, probably unconscious, with English Chancery practice, with the important distinction that devices such as *fideicommissa* were testamentary devices designed to avoid restrictions on selection of heirs and scope of legacies, and were not used for *inter vivos* purposes. *Usufructus* and the other servitudes could serve *inter vivos* calls for split title; these *iura in re* are summarized in JAC Thomas, *Textbook of Roman Law* (1976) 195–210.

[98] R Helmholz, 'Trusts in the English Ecclesiastical Courts 1300–1640' in *Itinera Fiduciae* (n 7) 153; R Helmholz, *Oxford History of the Laws of England Vol 1: The Canon Law and Ecclesiastical Jurisdiction from 597 to the 1640s* (2004) 417–24.

Biancalana's recent work on thirteenth century *custodia* demonstrates how fiduciary concepts of agency could do the same work, without seisin or title being vested in the executors.[99] This body of fiduciary law therefore can be seen to precede uses and trusts in their Chancery forms. What finally emerged was the peculiar English system of vesting title in the executors as trustees and making them personal representatives of the estate, a form of trusteeship that gave stronger powers and more demanding duties in running the deceased estate than was the case anywhere else in Europe.[100] There is a mild paradox here: English respect for the individual property-holder and his or her freedom of testation required strong fiduciaries to carry out the will, and the need for fiduciaries laid the groundwork for the invention of the trust that could split titles and disperse powers over property; whilst European systems had undivided *dominium*, weakened freedom of testation, and a muted law of fiduciaries and trusts.

5. The Value of Loyalty

These four models of relationship provided the raw juristic materials for English law to develop both the law of trusts as a vast expansion of our proprietary concepts, and the fiduciary doctrines of management that govern much of our commercial world today. Both fiduciary and trust institutions are hard to imagine without strong legal norms forbidding trusted persons to profit from or exploit their dominant position. The fiduciary principle barring profit was stated starkly enough in the trust case of *Keech*, but we can now see that it stretches far back behind that leading case, and indeed that the principle precedes trusteeship itself. If Birks could seem to doubt the independence of fiduciary law from the institutions of trust, contract, and tort, his scholarly historical work on account and restitution for wrongs demonstrates how deeply went the law's commitment to repress undue advantage-taking in close relationships. The great American trusts scholar John Langbein has now argued that it is time for the anti-profit rule of *Keech* to go. The nub of his argument is that modern accounting and discovery procedures are so penetrating that monitoring of the fiduciary through private actions or normal contractual discipline suffices and the sole interest standard for protecting the beneficiary is too constricting. He claims that the *Keech* rule prohibiting profit-taking may actually inhibit a fiduciary from acting vigorously in the best interests of his beneficiaries.[101] There is a great weight of

[99] Biancalana, '*Custodia*' (n 85).
[100] R Zimmermann, '*Heres Fiduciarius?* Rise and Fall of the Testamentary Executor' in *Itinera Fiduciae* (n 7) 267.
[101] JH Langbein, 'Questioning the Trust Law Duty of Loyalty: Sole Interest or Best Interest?' (2005) 114 Yale LJ 929; JH Langbein, 'Mandatory Rules in the Law of Trusts' (2004) 98 NWU L Rev 1105.

English legal history—and some recent frauds in corporate America—to suggest that his call for abolition is premature.[102]

Peter Birks was certainly no enemy of the fiduciary principle, notwithstanding the fact that it appears in our law as a peculiarly moralistic doctrine. What worried him was the tendency of undiscriminating moralistic argument to descend into a formless anarchy of opinion, too often a prelude to power-mongering and tyranny. Hence, perhaps, his desire to speak of disinterested service rather than simply altruism or loyalty as the hallmark of the fiduciary. I had a presage of Peter's views when I asked him once what he made of Cardozo's famous encomium of the fiduciary duty as a mystical vehicle to a higher commercial morality.[103] 'So much the worse for Cardozo', was Peter's confident verdict. Rather one must describe the moral imperatives of the law in careful and constrained juristic terms, so as to allow the law a neutrality that guarantees its authority and effectiveness.

Peter was passionate in his advocacy of a reasoned law, built on secure historical foundations and refined by scholarly debate, always seeking a better understanding and open to new arguments. He gave and in turn inspired strong loyalty and affection as he shared with friends and colleagues his ideal. This is a precious legacy.

---

[102] In *Murad v Al-Saraj* [2005] EWCA Civ 959 at [81]–[83] Arden LJ maintained the *Keech* rule as applied in *Regal (Hastings) Limited v Gulliver* [1967] 2 AC 46 and *Boardman v Phipps* [1967] 2 AC 46, but suggested that its reach might be palliated in a future case. Jonathan Parker LJ agreed and held that the accounting of profits from fiduciary breach should be judged on a but-for causal model and not permit apportionment beyond possible allowance for an errant fiduciary's skill, effort, and resources (following *Warman International Ltd v Dwyer* [1994–5] 182 CLR 546 (High Court of Australia)). Clarke LJ (dissenting) would have used *Warman* as a lever to allow full apportionment of profits. Leave to appeal to the House of Lords was refused. *Murad* suggests that contest over the shape of the *Keech* doctrine in English law, ignited in *Boardman v Phipps* [1967] 2 AC 46, will continue.

[103] *Meinhard v Salmon* 164 NE 545, 546 (NY 1928) (Cardozo J).

32

Slavery and the Roman Law of Evidence in Eighteenth-Century Scotland

*John W Cairns**

In the 1760s Sir William Blackstone wrote:

There is nothing which so generally strikes the imagination, and engages the affections of mankind, as the right of property; or that sole and despotic dominion which one man claims and exercises over the external things of the world, in total exclusion of the right of any other individual in the universe.[1]

The nature of the 'sole and despotic dominion' in Roman law exercised the mind of Peter Birks, leading to a classic essay in 1985 on absolute *dominium*.[2] It is a fine example of the analytical, rational, and enquiring qualities of his intellect, which, together with boundless enthusiasm, produced the results in both Roman law and unjustified enrichment that made him in so many ways a scholar without peer in British academic life. These qualities became abundantly clear to me in the years Peter and I were colleagues in Edinburgh—not only in formal business and work, but also over the bottle of wine we would sometimes share in the evening in his room in Old College, when we had both been working late.

1. Slavery in Roman Law and its Reception

One object of 'sole and despotic dominion' in Roman law was the slave. As objects of ownership, slaves possessed the valuable attributes of volition, intellect, mobility, and dexterity. These very attributes, however, presented particular

* Professor of Legal History, University of Edinburgh. The author gratefully acknowledges the assistance of the British Academy. He is indebted to Professor Roderick Paisley of Aberdeen who first drew the printed report of *Stewart Nicolson v Stewart Nicolson* (1770) Mor 16770 to his attention; to the Keeper of the Records of Scotland for permission to cite and quote from unpublished records under his care; and to the Keeper of the Advocates Library for access to the Faculty of Advocates' collection of Session Papers. He has also benefited much from the comments of Alan Rodger.

[1] W Blackstone, *Commentaries on the Laws of England*, 4 vols (1765–9) vol 2, 2.
[2] P Birks, 'The Roman Law Concept of Dominium and the Idea of Absolute Ownership' 1985 Acta Juridica 1.

problems. Slaves could cheat, lie, commit delicts and crimes, run away, and combine and plot against their owners. All this had to be regulated in some way to minimise harm both to owners and innocent parties. Discipline was preserved in theory through severity and the slaves' lack of enforceable rights. Examples of harsh treatment are well known. There is the tradition that all the slaves in a house had to be put to death if one had killed their master, while the *Senatusconsultum Silanianum* provided for the torture of all the slaves in a household if the master or someone under his paternal authority had been murdered (other than by poison).[3]

1.1. Slaves as Witnesses

In Roman law the general rule was that slaves were rejected as witnesses. This was required by the peculiar problems posed by slaves as rational beings. They might act against the interests of their owners through spite or they might act dishonestly in favour of their owners through fear of the consequences if they did not do so. Or else they were simply regarded as unreliable and unacceptable because of their position in life.[4] This section examines some of the relevant texts and some of the problems they pose.

Any broad statement that slaves were inadmissible as witnesses is Justinianic:

If he who wishes to give evidence is indeed said to be of servile status and it is said that he has been shown to be free, if this is from birth, his evidence should be taken, but the point about his status should be reserved so that, if it comes to be seen that he is of servile status, his evidence should be treated as if it had not been given.[5]

Likewise, Justinian's Code added a sentence to a constitution of 409 CE which had said that witnesses to crimes must be free unless they were implicated in the crime: 'It is the same in law if witnesses are produced by either party in pecuniary causes'.[6]

Of course, such a general rule was not entirely practical, given the importance of slaves in Roman domestic and commercial life. Just as Peter argued that a certain measure of pragmatism—rather than high ideals—led to the Roman law's acceptance that the offspring of slaves were not counted *in fructu*, so some accommodation had to be made as regards evidence by slaves.[7] They were accordingly permitted as witnesses *de suo facto*, that is, in those matters with

---

[3] WW Buckland, *The Roman Law of Slavery* (1908) 94–5.

[4] What follows relies on ibid 86–91; A Watson, *Roman Slave Law* (1987) 84–6.

[5] Nov.90.6: Si vero dicatur servilis esse fortunae qui testari voluerit, is vero liber affirmetur constitutus, si quidem ex nativitate, impleatur quidem testimonium, disputationum vero de statu servata ratione, ut si apparuerit fortunae servilis esse, eius testimonium ac si neque datum fuerit ita sit (539 CE).

[6] C.4.20.11.1, probably reflecting C.4.20.16 (perhaps of 527 CE): Idem iuris est et si in pecuniaria causa testes ab alterutra parte producendi sunt.

[7] P Birks, 'An Unacceptable Face of Human Property' in P Birks (ed), *New Perspectives in the Roman Law of Property: Essays for Barry Nicholas* (1989) 61, 72–3.

which they were themselves concerned. Modestinus wrote: 'The answer of a slave must then be relied on when there is no other proof to establish the truth'.[8] If the inscription is to be trusted,[9] Modestinus would have made the remark in relation to some economic activity in which slaves were involved and in relation to which they were the only witnesses. A constitution of 294 CE proclaimed: 'The power to interrogate slaves about matters with which they are concerned not only in criminal but also in pecuniary causes (such as when the property is delivered to others by a slave on account of a deposit or loan or in other circumstances authorised by law) cannot be doubted'.[10] The *Sententiae Pauli* explained: 'Equitable reason demonstrates that a slave may be questioned about his actions and about himself; for no one ought to be prejudiced who has either loaned or deposited something through a slave without security'.[11] In fact, slaves could be examined as witnesses in a variety of circumstances, although no definitive list of those circumstances may be found. It is clear, however, that slaves could be questioned on: the issue of who owned them;[12] matters relating to guardianship (*tutela*) and disputes over an inheritance;[13] and matters arising out of the *Edictum Carbonianum* relating to the time of a birth.[14] In 535 CE Justinian permitted slaves to be examined on the accuracy of the inventory of the deceased's estate drawn up by the heir.[15] From these texts one can deduce that slaves were permitted as witnesses in matters likely to be especially within their knowledge, whether commercial or domestic.

Where the testimony of a slave was admitted, it had to be taken under torture: 'Should the circumstances of the thing be such that we are compelled to admit a gladiator or similar person as a witness, his evidence is not to be believed without torture'.[16] Not all the texts specifically mention torture, but enough do to indicate that it was normally required when a slave gave evidence.[17]

These texts strongly suggest that slaves were permitted as witnesses in only a determinate number of cases. The text of Modestinus might suggest the

---

[8] D.22.5.7, Modestinus 3 *regularum*: Servi responso tunc credendum est, cum alia probatio ad eruendam veritatem non est.

[9] In book 3 Modestinus deals with various aspects of obligations. See O Lenel, *Palingenesia Iuris Civilis* (1889) vol 1 734–5. But Lenel plausibly suggests that the inscription is erroneous and that the text actually comes from book 8 where Modestinus dealt with various problems of proof under the general heading *de criminibus*. See *Palingenesia* vol 1, 737, fragment 247.

[10] C.9.41.15: Interrogari servos de facto suo non solum in criminali causa, sed etiam in pecuniaria (veluti quando per eum depositi vel commodati nomine vel in aliis causis legibus cognitis res aliis praestitae sunt) posse non ambigitur (294 CE).

[11] P.S.5.16.1: Servum de facto in se interrogari posse ratio aequitatis ostendit: nec enim ei obesse debet, qui per servum aliquid sine cautione commodat vel deponit.

[12] C.3.32.10 (290 CE); C.9.41.12 (291 CE).

[13] P.S.5.15.6; P.S.5.16.2; D.34.9.5.15, Paul 1 *de iure fisci*; D.48.10.24, Scaevola 22 *digestorum*; C.9.41.13 (293 CE). [14] D.37.10.3.5, Ulpian 41 *ad edictum*.

[15] Nov.1.2.

[16] D.22.5.21.2, Arcadius *libro singulari de testibus*: Si ea rei condicio sit, ubi harenarium testem vel similem personam admittere cogimur, sine tormentis testimonio eius credendum non est.

[17] See eg C.3.32.10; C.9.41.12; P.S.5.15.6; P.S.5.16.2.

contrary, but the other texts would be pointless and the blanket prohibitions would be misleading, if this were not the position. A further text[18] is also ambiguous: the Latin could be taken as meaning either that a slave may be tortured in a *pecuniaria causa* if the truth cannot otherwise be discovered or that a slave should not be tortured in a matter concerning money if the truth can be discovered in some other way. Again, however, the emphasis in the other texts, on whether the circumstances were such that slave testimony was admissible at all, suggests that the second interpretation is probably the correct one. The texts do, however, present a measure of (at least) apparent inconsistency—but it need not be considered further here.

1.2. Slaves as Witnesses in the Ius Commune

By the later sixteenth century, the important work on proof of Mascardus provided an interpretation and synthesis of the medieval reading of the Roman texts:

Slaves are rejected as witnesses, because they are held for nothing by the civil law, and excluded from all legal responsibilities.... For slavery is comparable almost with death according to the Roman law. Decius ... says that a slave cannot be an arbiter, judge, notary, executor, guardian, soldier, ambassador, or witness; for that reason the evidence of a slave is null *ipso iure*, albeit it is not opposed by a party, as Angelus [and many others] state.

The first exception to this general rule is when a slave is commonly reputed free: in these circumstances his testimony is valid, and cannot be impugned later if his servitude is discovered....

The second exception is when the truth cannot otherwise be uncovered; in these circumstances the slave's evidence is admitted in support, but the suit should be of that kind, in which the truth cannot otherwise be got at—neither by experience nor custom....

The third exception concerns serious crimes, in which, on account of the atrocious nature of the charge, witnesses are admitted who would otherwise not be permitted, such as in heresy, lese-majesty, assassination, sacrilege; a slave can accordingly be examined in these cases, lest others be unjustly accused of the crime....

The fourth exception is when a slave gives evidence about matters concerning his own affairs, with torture and the other presumptions....[19]

---

[18] D.48.18.9 pr, Marcian 2 *de iudiciis publicis*: Divus Pius rescripsit posse de servis haberi quaestionem in pecuniaria causa, si aliter veritas inveniri non possit. quod et aliis rescriptis cavetur. sed hoc ita est, ut non facile in re pecuniaria quaestio habeatur: sed si aliter veritas inveniri non possit nisi per tormenta, licet habere quaestionem, ut et divus Severus scripsit. licet itaque et de servis alienis haberi quaestionem, si ita res suadeat. See Buckland, *Law of Slavery* (n 3) 86; Watson, *Slave Law* (n 4) 85.

[19] J Mascardus, *Conclusiones probationum omnium quibusvis in utroque foro versantibus... necessariae... iisdem additiones JA Ricii... et B Nigri... insertae sunt. Accedit repertorium universale*, 4 vols (1661), vol 3, 245–50, conclusio 1365: Octavo a testimonio repelluntur servi; quia jure civili pro nihilo habentur, & ab omnibus officiis arcentur.... Servitus enim morti fere comparatur, quoad jus Romanum.... Dec.... dicit servum, arbitrum, judicem, tabellionem, executorem, tutorem, militem, nuncium, testem esse non posse; qua propter testimonium servi ipso jure nullum est, licet a parte non opponatur, ut inquit Angel.... Limitatur primo, ut non procedat, quando servus communi opinione liber reputabatur: tunc enim ejus testimonium valebit, & detecta

A comparable synthesis, if different in detailed result, is found in the work of Johannes Voet. He wrote:

> The Civil law [*lex civilis*] does not allow slaves to be witnesses. So much is that so that if there is a doubt about the status of a witness brought forward as to whether he is a free man or a slave, he is indeed heard, and the evidence regarded as complete if thereafter he is declared free; but if he is declared a slave it is *ipso jure* void. Exceptions are when the cause is an uphill one and concerns the benefit of the commonwealth; or when other proofs are lacking. In other matters however the truth can be searched out from them by torture. Nor does anything prevent their giving evidence after they have become free on things which they have seen or heard while in slavery.[20]

In principle, the *ius commune* accepted that, in general, a slave could not be a witness.[21] A slave could, however, be a witness in serious criminal proceedings, in matters in which there is no other means of proof and in other matters if tortured. While Voet stated that the last can apply in any case, Mascardus stressed that it could only be in relation to his own affairs (*de facto suo*). This appears to make more sense in view of the general prohibition. Present purposes do not require further discussion of such differences of detail.

2. Slavery in the New World

Slavery had persisted in the Mediterranean region through the Middle Ages to the time of Mascardus and beyond. Christian Europeans, including Scots, were enslaved in large numbers, most famously, by the Barbary corsairs. Muslims too

servitute deinde impugnari non poterit, ... Limitatur secundo, ut non procedat, quando veritas aliter haberi non potest; quia tunc in subsidium servus admittitur, sed oportet, quod hujusmodi actus sit, in quo nec actu, nec habitu veritas aliter haberi non potest .... Limitatur tertio, ut non procedat in criminibus exceptis, in quibus ob atrocitatem criminis testes alias inhabiles admittuntur, ut est crimen haeresis, laesae majestatis, assassini, sacrilegii; in his ergo servus examinari poterit, si iniquitus alias sit de crimine diffamatus .... Limitatur quarto, ut non procedat, quando servus deponit de facto proprio, cum tormentis, & aliis praesumptionibus .... The ellipses are where references to Roman texts and legal literature have been omitted. In the first edition of 1588, this is conclusio 1358 in vol 3, fos 271v–274r.

[20] J Voet, *The Selective Voet: Being the Commentary on the Pandects*, translated by P Gane, 8 vols (1955–8) vol 3, 762; J Voet, *Commentarius ad pandectas: in quo, praeter romani juris principia ac controversias illustriores, jus etiam hodiernum, et praecipuae fori quaestiones excutiuntur* (1731) 22.5.2: Servos lex civilis non patitur testes esse; adeo ut, si de statu testis producti dubitetur, liberne an servus sit, audiatur quidem, & perfectum habeatur testimonium, si deinde liber pronuncietur; si vero servus, ipso jure nullum sit .... Nisi causa sit ardua ad rei publicae spectans utilitatem; aut aliae desint probationes .... In caeteris tamen veritas ex iis per tormenta inquiri potest. ... neque quicquam intercedit, quo minus liberi facti de illis deponant, quae in servitute viderint audiverintve. The ellipses mark deleted references to Roman texts.

[21] For a fascinating example, taking into account some other problems at issue here, see G Hemmy, *De Testimoniis: The Testimony of Aethiopians, Chinese and other Pagans as well as the Hottentots inhabiting the Cape of Good Hope, likewise about the Complaints of East Indian Slaves. A Thesis Presented to the University of Leiden in 1770 for the Degree of Doctor of Both Laws*, ed and trans M Hewett (1998) 18–20.

were enslaved in Spain, Portugal, and Italy, and they were often kept in order to be exchanged for European slaves. Black African and other slaves, such as Russian and Circassian, were also found in Italy, Spain, and the Muslim world.[22] In northern Europe, however, slavery as such had vanished by 1600, even though forms of serfdom remained in some areas.[23]

By the time Mascardus compiled his *Conclusiones*, the Western European nations had started to develop the triangular trade in African slaves, taking them to the New World, where they worked, particularly, on plantations producing the luxury goods of sugar and tobacco. The final quarter of the seventeenth century saw a tremendous increase in this trade.[24] During the seventeenth century England became an important slave-trading nation, with Bristol and London as major ports for the trade. One of the British triumphs in the Treaty of Utrecht of 1713, which concluded the War of the Spanish Succession, was acquisition of the *asiento*, the all-important contract to import slaves into the Spanish Indies. During the eighteenth century, with the continuing rapid expansion of the trade, Liverpool grew into a great slaving port.[25]

The origins and development of the laws on slavery in the New World varied, depending on the colonial power. This has led to a series of debates, notably that sparked by the famous thesis of Frank Tannenbaum that slavery in the Spanish and French colonies was less harsh than that in the English. He argued that this was because Roman law had been received in the Spanish and French colonies and the Roman Catholic church was influential there, while, in contrast, in the English colonies the laws were made by local assemblies dominated by slave owners.[26]

---

[22] See C Verlinden, *L'esclavage dans l'Europe médiévale*, 2 vols (1955–77); B Lewis, *Race and Slavery in the Middle East: An Historical Inquiry* (1990); RC Davis, *Christian Slaves, Muslim Masters: White Slavery in the Mediterranean, The Barabary Coast, and Italy, 1500–1800* (2003); I Origo, 'The Domestic Enemy: The Eastern Slaves in Tuscany in the Fourteenth and Fifteenth Centuries' (1955) 30 Speculum 321; DG Blumenthal, 'Implements of Labor, Instruments of Honor: Muslim, Eastern and Black African Slaves in Fifteenth-Century Valencia', unpublished PhD thesis, University of Toronto (2000); H Thomas, *The Slave Trade: The History of the Atlantic Slave Trade, 1440–1870* (1997) 33–48; D Masson (ed), *Register of the Privy Council of Scotland*, 2nd series, vol 1 (1899) 69, 70, 78, 79, 126–7, 145, 597; J Dalrymple, Viscount Stair, *The Institutions of the Law of Scotland* (2nd edn, 1693, ed DM Walker, 1981) 1.3.11.

[23] Bloch's famous thesis about the move from slavery to serfdom by about 1000 really only works for parts of north-west Europe: see M Bloch, 'How and Why Ancient Slavery Came to an End' in *Slavery and Serfdom in the Middle Ages*, translated by WR Beer (1975) 1–31. More research may alter this picture: in G Donaldson (ed), *St Andrews Formulare 1514–1546*, vol II (1944) 304–5 there is a style for a contract for sale of a Russian slave (no 518), probably to Robert Forman, Dean of Glasgow. (I am indebted to GL Gretton for bringing this to my attention.)

[24] See eg Thomas, *Slave Trade* (n 22) 49–231.

[25] ibid 243–5; D Richardson, *Bristol, Africa and the Eighteenth Century Slave Trade*, 4 vols (1986–96); D Richardson, 'Slavery and Bristol's "Golden Age"' (2005) 26 Slavery and Abolition 35; CN Parkinson, *The Rise of the Port of Liverpool* (1952). Smaller ports were also involved in the slave trade: N Tattersfield, *The Forgotten Trade: Comprising the Log of the* Daniel and Henry *of 1700 and Accounts of the Slave Trade from the Minor Ports of England* (1991).

[26] F Tannenbaum, *Slave and Citizen: The Negro in the Americas* (1947); see EV Goveia, 'The West Indian Slave Laws of the 18th Century' in EV Goveia and CJ Bartlett, *The West Indian Slave Laws of the 18th Century. A New Balance of Power: The 19th Century* (1970) 7.

Whether Tannenbaum was exactly correct about France is questionable.[27] Much can also be debated about the origins of the laws on slavery in the English colonies.[28] It is important to be aware that whatever their different legal regimes, all these slave-owning societies required detailed regulation of slavery.[29]

2.1. Scots and Slavery in the New World

While there were slaving voyages from Scotland, no Scottish port developed into a great slaving port to rival London, Bristol, or Liverpool.[30] Many Scots were, however, not only involved but prominent in the trade from an English base.[31] By the mid-eighteenth century, the London-based Scot, Richard Oswald, became a major trader as a result of his partnership with four fellow Scots and a single Englishman.[32] It was a former Scots merchant in Virginia, who regularly traded in slaves, who claimed rights over Somerset in the famous English case.[33] Scots also invested heavily in land in the Caribbean sugar islands and the Chesapeake region.[34] For example, in Grenada, which had been ceded by France in 1763, already by 1772 Scots formed 21 per cent of the total land-holding population and 57 per cent of the British land-holding population. Indeed they owned 40 per cent of the land planted with sugar and coffee.[35] But even in the established colony of Jamaica, by 1754 Scots had come to own a quarter of the

[27] See eg VV Palmer, 'The Origins and Authors of the Code Noir' (1995) 56 Louisiana Law Review 363; cf A Watson, 'Origins of the Code Noir Revisited' (1997) 71 Tulane Law Review 1041; H Baade, 'The *Gens de Couleur* of Louisiana: Comparative Slave Law in Microcosm' (1996) 18 Cardozo Law Review 535; TN Ingersoll, 'Slave Codes and Judicial Practice in New Orleans, 1718–1807' (1995) 13 Law and History Review 23.

[28] See eg TD Morris, ' "Villeinage . . . as it existed in England, reflects but little light on our subject:" The Problem of the "Sources" of Southern Slave Law' (1988) 32 American Journal of Legal History 95; JA Bush, 'Free to Enslave: The Foundations of Colonial American Slave Law' (1993) 5 Yale Journal of Law and the Humanities 417; BJ Nicholson, 'Legal Borrowing and the Origins of Slave Law in the British Colonies' (1994) 38 American Journal of Legal History 38; JA Bush, 'The First Slave (And Why He Matters)' (1996) 18 Cardozo Law Review 599; WM Wiecek, 'The Origins of the Law of Slavery in British North America' (1996) 17 Cardozo Law Review 1711.

[29] See further A Watson, *Slave Law in the Americas* (1989).

[30] M Duffill, 'The Africa Trade from the Ports of Scotland, 1706–66' (2004) 25 Slavery and Abolition 102; EJ Graham, *A Maritime History of Scotland, 1650–1790* (2002) 174–8, 193–4; D Hancock, 'Scots in the Slave Trade' in NC Landsman (ed), *Nation and Province in the First British Empire: Scotland and the Americas, 1600–1800* (2001) 60, 62–3.

[31] Thomas, *Slave Trade* (n 22) 242–3; Hancock 'Scots in the Slave Trade' (n 30) 62–5.

[32] Hancock, 'Scots in the Slave Trade' (n 30) 65–83; D Hancock, *Citizens of the World: London Merchants and the Integration of the British Atlantic Community, 1735–1785* (1995) 172–220. For another Scottish slave trader's career, see IA Akinjogbin, 'Archibald Dalzel: Slave Trader and Historian of Dahomey' (1966) 7 Journal of African History 67.

[33] MS Wiener, 'New Biographical Evidence on *Somerset's Case*' (2002) 23 Slavery and Abolition, 121, 127–8.

[34] AR Karras, *Sojourners in the Sun: Scottish Migrants in Jamaica and the Chesapeake, 1740–1800* (1992).

[35] Hancock 'Scots in the Slave Trade' (n 30) 64. For one Scot's experience in Grenada, see M Quintanilla, 'The World of Alexander Campbell: An Eighteenth-Century Grenadian Planter' (2003) 35 Albion 229.

land.[36] The plantations on the Caribbean islands badly needed physicians and surgeons to treat the slaves: this need was met by many Scots medical graduates, who used their opportunities to acquire slaves and plantations.[37] Indeed, the presence of Scots in numbers attracted other Scots through networks of patronage as merchants, lawyers, artisans, and so on.[38]

Scottish involvement in the slave trade and in the Caribbean and southern parts of British North America led to the presence of a small number of black men (and some women) in Scotland. While it is possible that some had found their own way to Scotland for their own purposes, most about whom information is available were either brought from slave-owning colonies as personal servants or were sent to Scotland to be trained in a useful skill. An example of the first would be 'Black Tom', who took the name David Spence on baptism. He was brought as a servant from Grenada by Dr David Dalrymple to assist him on the voyage home.[39] An example of the second would be Cato, sent from Jamaica in 1735 to be apprenticed as a millwright to Joseph Foggo at Jock's Lodge, near Edinburgh.[40]

2.2. The Legal Position of Black Slaves in Scotland

In 1778, in *Knight v Wedderburn* the Court of Session decided definitively that no one could be held as a slave in Scotland.[41] Before that, however, those who either sent or brought such individuals to Scotland undoubtedly considered that they continued to hold them as slaves. Thus Scottish newspapers carried advertisements about runaway slaves and announcing that slaves were for sale.[42] Those who claimed ownership of such men and women appear to have had every expectation that the rights they claimed were enforceable.

All European slave-trading nations and powers with colonial empires in which there were slaves faced the problem of deciding the status of slaves brought home from the colonies if slavery was not recognized at home. In France the issue was directly confronted, and there was specific legislation to resolve the problem, whether satisfactorily or not being a different issue.[43] In Britain, however,

---

[36] See, CA Whatley, *Scottish Society 1707–1830: Beyond Jacobitism, Towards Industrialisation* (2000) 110.   [37] Karras, *Sojourners in the Sun* (n 34) 55–60.

[38] ibid 11, 118–69.

[39] AS Cunningham, *Rambles in the Parishes of Scoonie and Wemyss* (1905) 154–6; National Archives of Scotland [hereafter NAS] CS236/D/4/3 and CS236/S/3/13.

[40] See A Mountier to E Burd, 11 January 1735, in NAS RH15/54/9. The indenture, for four years, is found in NAS RH15/54/26. I owe these references initially to the kindness of RB Baker.

[41] (1778) Mor 14545. For a brief discussion, see JW Cairns, 'Stoicism, Slavery, and Law: Grotian Jurisprudence and its Reception' in HW Blom and LC Winkel (eds), *Grotius and the Stoa* (2004) 197, 224–30.

[42] 27 October 1755, *Glasgow Courant*: for sale 'Black Negroe Boy'; 7 September 1768, *Edinburgh Advertiser*: Runaway 'Negroe Slave'.

[43] S Peabody, *'There Are No Slaves in France': The Political Culture of Race and Slavery in the Ancien Régime* (1996) 11–56. For the Netherlands, see AH Huussen, 'The Dutch Constitution of 1798 and the Problem of Slavery' (1999) 67 T v R 99, 104–7.

though there were many statutes governing the African trade, the status of black people was not regulated by legislation. In England, the attitude of the courts can be described as varying.[44] In 1729, however, the two law officers of the Crown in England gave this opinion:

We are of opinion that a slave by coming from the West Indies to Great Britain or Ireland, either with or without his master, doth not become free, and that his master's property or right in him is not therefore determined or varied, and that Baptism doth not bestow freedom on him nor make any alteration in his temporal condition in these Kingdoms; we are also of opinion that the Master may legally compel him to return again to the plantations.[45]

The exact status of this opinion was open to question.[46]

Even supposing it was correct that black slaves from the colonies remained slaves after arriving in both England and Scotland, much was still left unclear. As a minimum requirement for enforcing their owners' rights, such men and women could be bought and sold and recovered as runaways. Moreover, their behaviour could be regulated by the potent threat to return them to the colonies and to sell them there as slaves. Nevertheless, there was no law to regulate the exercise of slavery.[47] One can identify obvious problems: what were a master's or mistress's rights of chastisement? Could slaves be manumitted? If so, how? And—the point at issue here—could such slaves give evidence in court? If so, how?

2.3. The Particular Problem of Testimony

In the British Caribbean and in British North America, the testimony of slaves (and free blacks) was recognized as creating a particular problem. In the mainland colonies, this matter was usually governed by legislation. While there was some variation, in general they were prohibited from testifying against white people and might usually testify only against other blacks, slave or free. Some colonies only allowed their testimony in serious criminal offences; statutes sometimes required it to be corroborated, or left its probative value to the decision of the court.[48] In New York, for example, a slave was allowed to give evidence only in the trial of another slave: no slave could be a witness against or

---

[44] See E Fiddes, 'Lord Mansfield and the Somersett Case' (1934) 50 LQR 499; WM Wiecek, '*Somerset*: Lord Mansfield and the Legitimacy of Slavery in the Anglo-American World' (1974) 42 University of Chicago Law Review 86, 88–95; J Oldham, 'New Light on Mansfield and Slavery' (1988) 27 Journal of British Studies 45, 48–53.

[45] Found quoted in RA Fisher, 'Granville Sharp and Lord Mansfield' (1943) 28 Journal of Negro History 381, 384. A virtually identical version is quoted in *Knight v Wedderburn* (1778) Mor 14545, 14547.   [46] Fiddes, 'Lord Mansfield' (n 44) 501–2.

[47] On this see S Drescher, 'Manumission in a Society without Slave Law: Eighteenth Century England' (1989) 10 Slavery and Abolition 85.

[48] WM Wiecek, 'The Statutory Law of Slavery and Race in the Thirteen Mainland Colonies of British America' (1977) 34 William and Mary Quarterly 258, 269.

on behalf of any free person in a civil or criminal trial.[49] It took a while for such a general approach to be achieved. Thus, in Virginia in 1705 statute provided that 'popish recusants convict, negroes, mulattoes and Indian servants, and others, not being Christians, shall be deemed and taken to be persons incapable in law, to be witnesses in any cases whatsoever'. Here the focus was on absence of Christian belief barring from testifying because of inability to take an oath: Christian blacks were allowed to testify. In 1732, however, it was enacted that since black men and women 'are people of such base and corrupt natures, that the credit of their testimony cannot be certainly depended upon', they could only testify in the trial of a slave for a capital offence.[50] In the Caribbean colonies also, slaves were generally only able to give testimony against each other and then not under oath.[51] Restriction on black testimony was undoubtedly a prerequisite to maintenance of slavery, only to be relaxed in very exceptional circumstances.[52] It is notable that, when the British Government started to put pressure on the West Indian Colonies to ameliorate slavery, one measure proposed was the admission of slave evidence.[53]

3. Slaves and Testimony in Scotland

The issue of the admissibility of evidence by an alleged slave arose in the Commissary Court in Edinburgh in 1770 in *Stewart Nicolson v Stewart Nicolson*.[54] This was a bitterly fought action in which Houston Stewart Nicolson sought to divorce his wife Margaret Porterfield or Stewart Nicolson.[55] Both parties were from the Scottish landed classes, he being the second son of Sir Michael Stewart, Baronet, she the daughter of Boyd Porterfield, Esq, of Porterfield.[56] She was alleged to have committed adultery with William Graham, the young grieve (factor or overseer) of Sir William Maxwell of Springkell in Dumfriesshire during 1768. Lady Maxwell was Houston Stewart Nicolson's sister.[57]

[49] E Olson, 'The Slave Code in Colonial New York' (1944) 29 Journal of Negro History 147, 150.
[50] A Hast, 'The Legal Status of the Negro in Virginia 1705–1765' (1969) 54 Journal of Negro History 217, 225–6.
[51] See eg DB Gaspar, *Bondmen and Rebels: A Study of Master–Slave Relations in Antigua, With Implications for Colonial British America* (1985) 11–12.
[52] N Zacek, 'Voices and Silences: The Problem of Slave Testimony in the English West Indian Law Court' (2003) 24 Slavery and Abolition 24; RN Buckley, 'The Admission of Slave Testimony at British Military Courts in the West Indies, 1800–1809' in DB Gaspar and DP Geggus (eds), *A Turbulent Time: The French Revolution and the Greater Caribbean* (1997) 226.
[53] C Levy, 'Slavery and the Emancipation Movement in Barbados, 1650–1833' (1970) 55 Journal of Negro History 1, 10.   [54] (1770) Mor 16770.
[55] There is a brief account of the case from a different perspective in L Leneman, *Alienated Affections: The Scottish Experience of Divorce and Separation, 1684–1830* (1998) 174–9.
[56] GE C[okayne], *Complete Baronetage*, 6 vols (1900–9) vol 4, 261.
[57] ibid, vol 4, 320.

The action was three times advocated from the Commissaries to the Court of Session, with one interlocutor of the Lords of Session appealed to the House of Lords. Mainly at issue was the hability (admissibility) of witnesses against Mrs Stewart Nicolson, most of whom were servants in the employ of Sir William. Among the witnesses to whom she objected, along with Graham and the Maxwells, was Latchemo, allegedly the slave of Sir William. Graham raised a particular problem as the alleged paramour, but the others would normally have been habile, since servants were inadmissible only as witnesses in favour of their employers.[58] With some justification, however, Mrs Stewart Nicolson argued that it was the Maxwells who had enthusiastically promoted the action of divorce against her. The Commissaries obviously had reservations about the evidence of the Maxwells; but their evidence, that of Graham, and of their undoubtedly free servants was allowed. In the result, the Commissaries held that the adultery had been proved.[59]

3.1. Latchemo

Whatever evidence Latchemo may have been able to offer obviously strongly supported Mr Stewart Nicolson's case. Thus the issue of his hability as a witness was advocated to the Session and appealed to the House of Lords. Further, pending decision on this, Helen Laing, one of Sir William Maxwell's other servants, was asked to report what it was that Latchemo had said that had led her to believe that Mrs Stewart Nicolson was too familiar with Graham. The defender understandably objected to this attempt to introduce his evidence in this fashion.[60]

---

[58] See [A McDouall, Lord Bankton], *An Institute of the Laws of Scotland*, 3 vols (1751–3) 4.30.8.

[59] This account is drawn (1) from the Extracted Decreet of Divorce, *Houston Stewart Nicolson v Mrs Margaret Porterfield*, 22 August 1771, Commissary of Edinburgh. Consistorial Decreets, vol 12 8 March 1769–18 December 1771, NAS CC8/5/12, which sets out the process and evidence at length and (2) the following printed papers produced for proceedings before the Court of Session preserved in Edinburgh, in the Advocates Library, Session Papers, Campbell Collection, 1770, vol 19: *Bill of Advocation Houston Stewart-Nicolson, Esq; against Mrs Margaret Porterfield* (no 61); *Answers for Mrs Stewart-Nicolson, to the Bill of Advocation for Houston Stewart-Nicolson, Esq* (no 62); *Objections for Mrs Stewart-Nicolson, to Witnesses proposed to be adduced against her by Mr Stewart-Nicolson* (no 63); *Answers for Houston Stewart-Nicolson, to the Objections for Mrs Stewart-Nicolson* (no 64); *Unto the Right Honourable the Lords Commissaries of Edinburgh, The Petition of Mrs Stewart Nicolson . . .* (no 64/1); *Answers for Houston Stewart-Nicolson to the Petition of Mrs Stewart Nicolson* (no 64/2); *Replies for Mrs Stewart-Nicolson, to the Answers for Mr Stewart-Nicolson* (no 65); *Bill of Advocation, Mrs Stewart-Nicolson against Houston Stewart-Nicolson, Esq* (no 66); *Answers for Houston Stewart-Nicolson, Esq; to the Bill of Advocation for Mrs Nicolson* (no 67); *Replies for Mrs Stewart-Nicolson, to the Answers of Mr Stewart-Nicolson* (no 68); *Memorial for Houston Stewart-Nicolson, Esq; against Mrs Stewart-Nicolson* (no 69); and *Memorial for Mrs Margaret Porterfield, spouse of Houston Stewart-Nicolson of Carnock, defender; against the said Houston Stewart-Nicolson, Pursuer* (no 70). The volume of extracted decreets is unpaginated, so it is not possible to provide pin-point references. All citations will therefore be to the volume as a whole. It is possible to identify the individual Session Papers, which are paginated, from their title and from the (MS) number assigned them in the volume of the Campbell Collection.

[60] NAS CC8/5/12.

Latchemo's possession of what is probably an African name is significant.[61] It does not necessarily indicate that he was born in West Africa, as African names often continued in use among slaves born in the Caribbean.[62] But it indicates he was not a baptized Christian. Mrs Stewart Nicolson objected to him on three grounds: first, because he was not a Christian and could not be bound by an oath; secondly, because he was a slave 'and the slave of her accusers' (ie of the Maxwells); and thirdly, because he was within the King's unlaw, having no property and 'being incapable of any' (presumably as a slave).[63]

The third objection was not very important and was easily met by the pursuer.[64] It was based on the proposition that no one who was not worth £10 Scots could be a witness since he could not pay the common fine for absence from court. Bankton commented that this objection 'was much more respected formerly than at this day', so that if the witness's 'veracity is otherwise unsuspected, he will not be rejected on that head; especially, if he be in service, or have a trade, or even be a day-labourer'. Only a common beggar would be rejected.[65] The importance of the objection for the defender was, however, that it introduced consideration of Latchemo's financial status, which would underscore the claim that he was a slave without resources.

The first ground was, however, of great importance, both on its own and in support of the second. Latchemo was to be rejected as a witness, since 'Pagans...cannot possibly be bound by the solemn oath, founded upon the tenets and faith of our holy religion' which was administered to witnesses.[66] It was admitted that Latchemo was not baptized; but for Houston Stewart Nicolson it was argued:

The pursuer has reason to believe, that the witness in question will depone, that he believes in a God, and owns the Christian religion: And the pursuer has been informed, that, for several years past, this witness has been desirous of being baptized, and has applied to several clergymen for that purpose; as to which they demurred, till his master gave his consent: That consent his master never intended to with-hold; but it has been delayed from time to time...[67]

---

[61] It is just possible that it is a version of Lachimo, a character (a villainous Roman nobleman) in Shakespeare's *Cymbeline*; but this seems unlikely. It is difficult to identify African names, often erratically spelled, from European sources; but I owe to the kindness of Professor Robin Law of the University of Stirling the speculation that this may be a version of the Yoruba name (O)lajumo, though he stresses that other speculative matches may be possible. I have not yet pursued the matter further.

[62] See JS Handler and J Jacoby, 'Slave Names and Naming in Barbados, 1650–1830' (1996) 53 William and Mary Quarterly 685.

[63] *Objections for Mrs Stewart-Nicolson, to Witnesses* (no 63) (n 59) 13.

[64] *Answers for Houston Stewart-Nicolson, to the Objections for Mrs Stewart-Nicolson* (no 64) (n 59) 38–9.   [65] Bankton, *Institute* (n 58) 4.30.21.

[66] *Objections for Mrs Stewart-Nicolson, to Witnesses* (no 63) (n 59) 13; see also *Bill of Advocation, Mrs Stewart-Nicolson* (no 66) (n 59) 11–12. Bankton, *Institute* (n 58) 4.30.4 discusses the Scots law on the point.

[67] *Answers for Houston Stewart-Nicolson, to the Objections for Mrs Stewart-Nicolson* (no 64) (n 59) 38.

The Commissaries allowed Latchemo to be examined on his knowledge of the tenets of the Christian faith before a decision was to be made on whether or not his evidence could be taken. So far so good for the pursuer. This none the less raised a problem. The fact that Latchemo had wished to be baptized, but his master had never consented tended to support the defender's claim that he was indeed held as a slave. This was because there was a popular, if inaccurate, belief that baptism freed from slavery. Masters were often wary of allowing the baptism of their slaves lest it affect their behaviour and make them more difficult to control.[68]

In her Objections, the defender stated of Latchemo that '[h]is being a slave is also a good objection, independent of the other. By the Civil law, slaves were never received without being put to the torture; and even then it was only *super facto proprio*'. For this, counsel cited the first part of the *conclusio* of Mascardus and the passage of Voet quoted above, along with a purported statute of Robert I relating to serfs.[69] The pursuer's Answers countered:

For, as to the argument, that he is a slave, there is no proper slavery known in this country: A servitude for life is known, but no slavery. It is a great question, but that a Black, the moment he sets his foot upon British ground, becomes *immediately* free. This was the subject of a hearing before the Court of Session some years ago; but the determination was prevented by the death of the Negro. It is again before the court upon memorials; and, in that case, the master does not plead the right to any more than the service of the Negro for life; not that he has *jus vitae et necis* over him, or that the Negro is incapable of property.[70]

The first case to which this refers was *Sheddan v Montgomery* which, because of the death of the alleged slave, had indeed left undecided the question of the freedom in Scotland of slaves from the colonies.[71] The second, *Spence v Dalrymple* (1770), also ultimately left the issue undecided, this time because of the death of the master.[72] In this case, however, what was at issue was Dalrymple's right to send Spence to the West Indies against his will, the very issue at stake in *Somerset*'s case. The defender's replies added nothing that need be noted here.[73]

[68] See eg WR Riddell, 'The Baptism of Slaves in Prince Edward Island' (1921) 6 Journal of Negro History 307.

[69] *Objections for Mrs Stewart-Nicolson, to Witnesses* (no 63) (n 59) 14; Mascardus, *Conclusio* 1365 (n 19) § 14; Voet, *ad Pandectas* (n 20) 20.5.2; 'The Secund Statutes of King Robert the First', c 34, as found in *Regiam Majestatem. The Auld Lawes and Constitutions of Scotland, Faithfullie Collected Furth of the Register and Other Auld Authentick Bukes . . . Be Sr. John Skene of Curriehill* (1609) fol 35 (second sequence of foliation). The Latin was *servi*, translated here as 'bondmen (*or slaves*)', but referring to *nativi*: see *Regiam Majestatem Scotiae, Veteres leges et constitutiones, ex archivis publicis, et antiquis libris manuscriptis collectae, recognitae . . . opera et studio Joannis Skenaei* (1609) fol 46 (second sequence of foliation).

[70] *Answers for Houston Stewart-Nicolson, to the Objections for Mrs Stewart-Nicolson* (no 64) (n 59) 38.

[71] *Sheddan v A Negro* (1757) Mor 14545. For a preliminary discussion of this case, see Cairns, 'Stoicism, Slavery, and Law' (n 41) 222–4.

[72] See the material in the unextracted process in the Court of Session in NAS CS236/S/3/13 and CS236/D/4/3. The memorials do not appear to have survived. The production of them may have become superfluous because of Dalrymple's death.

[73] *Replies for Mrs Stewart-Nicolson* (no 65) (n 59) 15.

The defender's bill of advocation added to her earlier arguments:

Had this witness been the slave of the pursuer, there could have been no doubt of the validity of the objection; and as it has been already shown, that his master and mistress are closely connected with the pursuer, have a patrimonial interest in the cause, and that his mistress, in particular, considers this cause as her own, it is submitted, if the objection does not fall to be considered in the same light as if he was the slave of the pursuer.[74]

The pursuer's Answers to the Bill on this point merely referred to his Answers to the pursuer's Objections.[75] In her Replies, the defender developed the issue further (omitting here discussion of the issue of whether he was a Christian):

[H]ad this witness been the slave of the pursuer, there could have been no doubt of the validity of the Objection. *Julius Paulus in recpt. Sentent. ad filium*, writes, 'Suspectos gratiae testes, & eos vel maxime, quos accusator de domo produxerit, vel vitae humilitas infamaverit interrogari non placuit. In testibus enim & vitae qualitas spectari debet & dignitas.'[76] Such is the Disposition of the Civil law; and by our own law, even tenants, if they were moveable, could not be received as witnesses for their masters.

In the present case, although this person is not the slave of the pursuer, yet as it has been shown, by the letters produced, that his mistress considers this cause as her own, he must be subject to the same rule as if the process were in her name.

But the objection does not rest here alone: for this witness is not in the state of a menial servant, or of a moveable tenant; he is a slave; and without pleading the point so high as to maintain, that he is in the same condition as a slave by the Roman law, or that the master has over him the *jus vitae et necis*, or even the power of maltreating him; yet surely it will be admitted, that his master has the power of his service for life, may reclaim him if he runs away, may dispose of these services, and may send him to any place of the world he pleases. This was the opinion of a very great man lately at the head of the law in England; and if the defender is not misinformed, it was that great man's opinion, that even baptism would not alter or impair the master's right; though indeed it is unnecessary to mention that circumstance, as it is admitted that this man is not baptized.[77] So standing the case, this man is, and must look upon himself to be, in the absolute disposal of his master. He can have no property of his own, for his service is not his own; he has no character to sustain or lose. Is this a person upon whose *dictum* the defender's character, and every thing dear to her, must depend?[78]

[74] *Bill of Advocation Mrs Stewart-Nicolson* (no 66) (n 59) 11.
[75] *Answers for Houston Stewart-Nicolson . . . to the Bill* (no 67) (n 59) 19.
[76] I have checked and corrected the quotation against the edition: *Iulii Pauli Patauini Sententiarum receptarum ad filium, libri quinque* (Nuremberg, 1594) 247 (V xv 1), although it is unclear which edition would have been used: 'Those witnesses whom the accuser produces from his home are suspected above all others of partiality, as are those whose humble life makes them of poor repute. Neither should give evidence, for station in life and rank should be looked at in a witness.'
[77] This is a reference to the opinion of the English law officers quoted above at n 44, and in particular to Philip Yorke, Lord Hardwicke, who became Lord Chancellor (as indeed had the other law officer before him).   [78] *Replies for Mrs Stewart-Nicolson* (no 68) (n 59) 21–2.

3.2. Analysis of the Debate over Latchemo

The strategies of the parties' lawyers in arguing over whether or not Latchemo was a habile witness are clear. On behalf of the pursuer it was stressed that, though not baptized, he was indeed a Christian and, secondly, he was not a slave, since proper slavery—identified with the *ius vitae et necis*—was not known in Scotland. Rather, he was in servitude for life. Here Mr Stewart Nicolson's lawyer had a difficult task. As the issue of baptism indicated, Sir William Maxwell probably considered that he held Latchemo as a slave. If the lawyer admitted this, there would be a problem since the Roman texts and their civilian interpreters stressed that, as a matter of principle, slaves could not give testimony. Further, the main exceptions to this general rule—testimony *de facto suo* and when other proof was lacking—were inapplicable in this case. On the other hand, the lawyer did not wish to argue that Latchemo was simply a regular servant: this would be to deny Sir William any rights he claimed in Latchemo. This led to the assertion, indirectly rather than expressly articulated, that Latchemo was in perpetual servitude, a status different from slavery.

This was not such a remarkable argument as it might seem. The *usus modernus pandectarum* generally recognized contracts of perpetual service, although some contradictory texts could be found in the *Corpus Juris*.[79] Further, natural law was also sympathetic to such arguments: a man might be born free, but he could use his will to make a contract to subject himself to perpetual servitude.[80] Grotius, whose writings undoubtedly underpinned the pursuer's arguments on this point, stressed that in these circumstances the master, according to the *ius naturale*, would not have the *ius vitae ac necis*, although human laws might grant it to him.[81] Though not discussed by the parties, the fact that Scots law recognized that colliers and salters were potentially bound to serve for life supported such a view;[82] on the other hand, the fact this was by virtue of a statute opened up the possibility of the contrary argument. Thus the Court of Session had accepted the peculiar status of colliers and salters because of its statutory basis[83] but it had rejected a similar contractual arrangement among tacksmen of fishing boats.[84]

[79] EJ Cohn, 'Contracts of Service for Life in Comparative Jurisprudence' (1938) 20 Journal of Comparative Legislation and International Law 45, 47–9.
[80] See eg H Grotius, *De iure belli ac pacis libri tres* 2.5.27: edn used, by BJA de Kanter-van Hettinga Tromp, with new notes added by R Feenstra and CE Persenaire with the assistance of E Arps-De Wilde (1993) 256–7; Stair, *Institutions* (n 22) 1.2.5–11. See Cairns, 'Stoicism, Slavery, and Law' (n 41) 207–8, 220–2.   [81] Grotius, *De iure belli ac pacis* (n 80) 2.5.27–8.
[82] Act 1606, c 10 and Act 1661, c 333 respectively in *Acts of the Parliaments of Scotland*, 12 vols (1814–75) vol 4 286–7, vol 7 304. See BF Duckham, 'Serfdom in Eighteenth-Century Scotland' (1969) 54 *History* 177; CA Whatley, 'The Dark Side of the Enlightenment? Sorting out Serfdom' in TM Devine and JR Young (eds), *Eighteenth Century Scotland: New Perspectives* (1999) 259.
[83] *Laird of Caprington v Geddew* (1632) Mor 9454.
[84] *Allen and Mearns v Skene and Burnet* (1728) Mor 9454.

John Erskine, Professor of Scots Law in the University of Edinburgh from 1732–65, wrote in his *Institute*, posthumously published in 1773:

[I]t is hard to conceive, how an engagement of that sort, which is to last for life, is more inconsistent with liberty, than one which is to expire after twenty or thirty years. And there appears nothing repugnant either to reason, or to the peculiar doctrines of Christianity, in a contract by which one binds himself to perpetual service under a master, who, on his part, is obliged to maintain the other in all the necessaries of life. . . . [85]

For this he cited the authority of Grotius.[86] If Mr Stewart Nicolson's lawyer chose in this way not to make it clear whether Latchemo was in perpetual service, this was presumably because Latechemo had not actually voluntarily engaged for such a status. It was better simply to deny 'Roman' slavery and point out that, in the contemporary case about returning a black man to the West Indies, only perpetual service was claimed.

Mrs Stewart Nicolson's argument on the point was simple in its essentials. Latchemo was a slave. There was no special regulation in Scotland dealing with the testimony of slaves. Since this was so, what should be done? In objecting to the admissibility of the evidence of Sir William and Lady Maxwell, Mrs Stewart Nicolson's lawyer had stated, citing Voet on witnesses, that 'the Civil Law . . . with us has the greatest weight particularly in our Consistorial Courts'.[87] One may note that the accounts of Voet and Bankton on the admissibility of witnesses essentially were perfectly compatible: the Scots law on the hability of witnesses derived in the main from the rules of the *ius commune*. This being the case, it followed that it was reasonable to look to the views of Civilians, such as Mascardus and Voet, as authoritative on the issue. This led to the conclusion that Latchemo should simply be excluded as inhabile. Further, it was pointed, that, if indeed one of the exceptions to the general rule applied, the law required that the slave be tortured. It is fair to assume that no one seriously envisaged this happening, if for no other reason than that torture was simply not possible in Scottish judicial proceedings, whether civil or criminal.[88] The issue of torture was presumably raised, however, in order to emphasize just how unreliable any evidence by a man in Latchemo's position would be, and how it ought not to be used to the detriment of the defender.

On Mrs Stewart Nicolson's behalf it was also pointed out that, even if the Roman *ius vitae et necis* did not exist over Latchemo in Scots law, Sir William had the 'power of his service for life', could reclaim him if he ran away, could sell him, and could send him abroad. We know that all of these powers were indeed exercised by masters in Scotland. They went to the heart of the preservation of

---

[85] J Erskine, *An Institute of the Law of Scotland. In Four Books. In the order of Sir George Mackenzie's Institutions of that Law* (1773) 1.7.62.

[86] Grotius, *De iure belli ac pacis* (n 80) 2.5.27.   [87] NAS CC8/5/12.

[88] In Antigua the legislature passed an act to authorize the torture of slaves in 1736, though this appears to have been more for purposes of investigation rather than as a routine mode of proof: Gaspar, *Bondmen and Rebels* (n 51) 21–2.

their power over black slaves. This claim by the defender emphasized that perpetual service was indeed a form of slavery which was virtually identical to slavery in the colonies—and Latchemo could be sent back to the colonies for sale if he displeased Sir William and Lady Maxwell. The aim was to stress that even were Latchemo in principle a habile witness, his position in life rendered him far too vulnerable for his evidence to be reliable or credible: he would not dare to refuse to do what the Maxwells wanted in case he soon found himself on a ship taking him to the West Indies to be sold into labour on a sugar plantation.

This aspect of the defender's argument was indeed quite powerful, since the assertion, based on Grotius, that there was no 'true' slavery in Scotland because masters did not have the *ius vitae et necis*, was weak, if perpetual servitude was accepted. After all, whatever the social realities may have been, neither in the Caribbean nor in the North American slave states did masters in theory have a simple *ius vitae et necis*;[89] nor latterly had they had that right in Roman law—though, as Peter pointed out, the actual enforcement of any restraint was questionable.[90] Houston Stewart Nicolson's lawyer was identifying slavery with what Thomas Cobb was later (in 1858) to call 'absolute or pure slavery', which he pointed out did not exist in America or in any other of the 'civilized nations of the world'.[91] His claim was overstated.

Lord Hailes's interlocutor refusing the defender's bill of advocation stated:

> The Lord Ordinary, after advising with the Lords, refuses this bill with respect to . . . Latchimo [*sic*] the negro being examined as [a witness] in this cause; and so far remits the cause to the Commissaries *simpliciter*.[92]

As is usual, there is no indication as to the Lords' reasons for this. Ilay Campbell, one of Mrs Stewart Nicolson's counsel, recorded on his copy of his client's printed *Replies*, what may be the view of a judge in the Inner House: 'as to Black being a Slave no good objection—a Persona standi different from Bondman in Plantations. If believes in a Supreme Deity, enough tho not a Christian ought to take proof of a Clergyman as to his belief'.[93] It is difficult to make much of this; it may even be a note of the argument of one of the counsel, since below it Campbell noted (illegibly) the view of the Lord President, who normally delivered his speech first, followed by the names of a number of other judges. It none the less must indicate the type of thinking that influenced the decision to remit *simpliciter*.[94]

---

[89] See eg Goveia, 'West Indian Slave Laws' (n 26) 25, 28–33; Nicholson, 'Slave Law in the British Colonies' (n 28) 49–53; JB Wahl, 'Legal Constraints on Slave Masters: The Problem of Social Cost' (1997) 41 American Journal of Legal History 1.

[90] Buckland, *Law of Slavery* (n 3) 36–9; Birks, 'Absolute Ownership' (n 2) 18.

[91] TRR Cobb, *An Inquiry into the Law of Negro Slavery in the United States of America*, introd by P Finkelman (1999) 3–4 (§ 1), 83–4 (§ 86).

[92] *Stewart Nicolson v Stewart Nicolson* (1770) Mor 16770, 16774.

[93] *Replies for Mrs Stewart-Nicolson* (no 65) (n 59) MS notes on the verso of 15.

[94] Both parties had some of the most distinguished advocates of the day as their counsel in the Court of Session: for the pursuer: James Montgomery (Lord Advocate), Alexander Lockhart (Dean

It is important to note that no formal decision was made as to whether or not Latchemo would be admitted as a witness. Supposing it had been decided that he did have sufficient Christian religious belief to understand the nature of the oath and be bound by it, there presumably would have been an examination *in initialibus*, exploring his motivations and reliability as a witness. This might not have been entirely welcome to the pursuer since it might have opened up the question of the status of Latchemo in a very direct way. One cannot imagine that the Maxwells would have relished Latchemo being asked whether he was in perpetual servitude, and, if so, whether this was through his own will. Such a line of questioning could have led to some very awkward answers. Further, it may well be that the defender's lawyers—Henry Dundas and John Swinton, as well as Campbell—were also glad not to have to explore this issue further. A few years later, Henry Dundas was to give a brilliant speech on behalf of Joseph Knight in the case in which he asserted his freedom from slavery or perpetual service.[95] Dundas, as an advocate, may have had no particular commitment to this cause, and been simply acting in the best interests of his client. This does not appear to have been the case, however, with John Swinton. As Sheriff-Depute of Perthshire, he was to rule in favour of Knight in 1774:

That the State of Slavery is not recognised by the Laws of this Kingdom and is inconsistent with the principles thereof and Found That the Regulations in Jamaica concerning slaves do not extend to this Kingdom and repelled the Defender's Claim to perpetual Service . . . and decerned.[96]

This ruling, directly contrary to that of the Sheriff-Substitute, and far broader than was necessary to decide in favour of Knight, suggests that Swinton had a clear, perhaps ideological, commitment to freedom for someone in Latchemo's position. If so, for their own reasons, Mrs Stewart Nicholson's counsel may have preferred, so far as possible, to avoid any ruling by which the Court decided formally that Latchemo was a slave, or in which it upheld his perpetual servitude. The comment by a judge (if it indeed be that) recorded by Campbell, though apparently acknowledging that Latchemo had a different legal *persona* from a 'bondman in [the] Plantations', may be read as accepting his servile status.[97] This could have had worrying implications if the point were to come to a formal decision. It was thus probably in no one's interest to have Latchemo questioned.

of Faculty), John Maclaurin; for the defender: Henry Dundas, Solicitor General; Ilay Campbell, John Swinton. Most of the pleading before the Commissaries was by the parties' procurators, John Euston for the pursuer, and John Watson for the defender, who will have been members of the Society of Solicitors at Law, who had a privilege for pleading before the Commissaries. For difficult issues in the case, some of the advocates can be found appearing before the Commissaries.

[95] 21 Feb 1776 Caledonian Mercury. For a discussion of *Knight v Wedderburn* (1778) Mor 14545, see Cairns, 'Stoicism, Slavery, and Law' (n 41) 224–30.

[96] (MS) Extract Process Joseph Knight against Sir John Wedderburn of Ballendean, Bart 1774, 27–8, in NAS CS235/K/2/2 (contractions extended); see also Diet Book, Sheriff Court of Perthshire, 20 May 1774, NAS SC49/1/64.

[97] *Replies for Mrs Stewart-Nicolson* (no 65) (n 59) MS notes on the verso of 15.

4. Conclusion

To permit slavery is to create an institution of property that inevitably involves 'deviation from the proprietary logic'. It simply is not possible to treat slaves exactly like cattle or sheep. Given Peter Birks's commitment to analysing and plotting the law's varied and differing maps, it was inevitable that what was entailed in any such deviation should have attracted his attention. Legal systems that draw the line of property in such a way as to accept ownership of human beings have then to regulate slavery as an institution.[98] Thus, in 1807, for the sake of certainty, the territorial legislature of the future state of Louisiana enacted a relatively detailed *Code Noir*, which imposed a number of duties on owners, including duties to sick slaves and a provision preventing the sale of children under 10 years separately from their mothers. Slaves were, however, specifically classed as 'real estate' for purposes of mortgages and a whole series of other provisions in the public interest regulated the exercise of the proprietary rights of slavery in a relatively detailed way, with various civil and criminal consequences for disobedience. Section 16 thus laid down that 'no slaves shall be parties to a suit in civil matters, either as plaintiffs or defendants, nor be witness in any civil or criminal matters against any white persons'. There was even a separate detailed section relating to the prosecution of criminal offences by and against slaves, while in section 11 the very Roman provision, discussed by Peter, on the ownership of children born to a female slave subject to a usufruct was enacted to prevent the face of human property becoming too unacceptable.[99]

It was this type of detailed regulation that Scotland lacked. In so far as the Scottish legal system can be seen as accepting the status of slave, it singularly failed to provide any kind of *Code Noir* to regulate the problems arising from the fact that slaves were human. No doubt to have attempted to do so was politically

---

[98] Birks, 'Unacceptable Face of Human Property' (n 7) 61.

[99] Black Code. An Act prescribing the rules and conduct to be observed with respect to negroes and other slaves of this territory, c 33, in *Acts Passed at the First Session of the First Legislature of the Territory of Orleans* (1806) 150–212; see further An Act to regulate the conditions and forms of the emancipation of slaves, c 10, and An Act to amend the Act entitled 'An act prescribing the rules and conduct to be observed with respect to negroes and other slaves of this territory', c 30, in *Acts Passed at the Second Session of the First Legislature of the Territory of Orleans* (1807) 82–8, 186–90. On the complex question of slavery in Louisiana in the colonial and then American period, which raises many questions concerning various theses on New World slavery, see eg H Baade, 'The Law of Slavery in Spanish Luisiana, 1769–1803' in EF Haas (ed), *Louisiana's Legal Heritage* (1983) 43; Ingersoll, 'Slave Codes and Judicial Practice' (n 27); H Baade, '*Gens de Couleur of Louisiana*' (n 27); GC Din, *Spaniards, Planters, and Slaves: The Spanish Regulation of Slavery in Louisiana, 1763–1803* (1999). JK Schafer, *Slavery, the Civil Law, and the Supreme Court of Louisiana* (1994) traces development away from the Spanish and French regulations on slavery. That slaves were classed as real estate and could be mortgaged was of immense importance economically: RH Kilbourne, *Debt Investment, Slaves: Credit Relations in East Feliciana Parish, Louisiana, 1825–1885* (1995).

impossible; but the failure had consequences that were troubling both for alleged owners and alleged slaves. Scots law simply did not have the resources within itself to regulate slavery in the detailed way of a New World *Code Noir*. Scots lawyers' practice of turning to Roman law and the law of nature and nations to elaborate and develop arguments, especially when the law seemed deficient in some way, did not help. This was so even though Roman law had many provisions on slavery. The problem was that these presupposed institutions, such as torture, which were neither known nor acceptable to Scots law. Discipline and control over slaves could only be exercised through their sale, or its threat, especially after shipment to the colonies; slaves could only resort to flight, in the absence of regulations on their treatment. Matters such as the giving of evidence were left completely obscure, leading to the problems discussed above. Human property had many unacceptable faces, particularly in a system of slavery without a slave law.

33

Sir William Jones and the
Nature of Law

*David Ibbetson**

It is impossible to have been a close colleague of Peter's without having been disagreed with by him on occasion, robustly and passionately. This essay is the product of one such being-disagreed-with, on the subject of the use in Sir William Jones's *Essay on the Law of Bailments* (1781) of the duty to take care as an analytical tool within the context of the developing tort of negligence of the late-eighteenth and early-nineteenth centuries.[1] Peter's position, as I remember it, was that the duty of care was essential in a proper formulation of negligence liability, and that Jones's use of it was a reflection of the fact that he was perhaps the first English lawyer to grasp this fundamental truth. My (more muted) view, again as I remember it, was that the duty of care was not essential to the description of negligence liability, that Jones had borrowed it from Roman law, and that its centrality in the nineteenth-century structure of the rules of negligence was to some extent the consequence of the use which he had made of it in the *Essay on the Law of Bailments*. I suspect neither of us was convinced by the other—such is the nature of academic debate—but the discussion led at least one of us to a more pointed reconsideration of Jones's text.

'Taxonomy' is not a word which was known to Jones,[2] but if it had been we may be sure that he would have asserted its centrality to the organization of knowledge. In the late 1780s he became throroughly acquainted with Linnaeus' systematics, on the basis of which he contributed substantially to the classi-fication of the plants of India.[3] The same concern with accurate classification

* Regius Professor of Civil Law, University of Cambridge; Fellow of Corpus Christi College, Cambridge. I am grateful to Stelios Tofaris for commenting on an earlier draft of this essay.

[1] Giving rise to it were the remarks later published in P Birks, 'Negligence in the Eighteenth Century Common Law' in EJH Schrage (ed), *Negligence: The Comparative Legal History of the Law of Torts* (2001) 173, 194–6; D Ibbetson, 'The Tort of Negligence in the Common Law in the Nineteenth and Twentieth Centuries' ibid 229, 231.

[2] The earliest dated examples of 'taxonomy' in the *Oxford English Dictionary* come from the beginning of the nineteenth century, some twenty years after Jones's death.

[3] G Cannon (ed), *The Letters of Sir William Jones* (1970) 892; 'Catalogue of Indian Plants' in *Works* (1807) 5.55–61; 'Botanical Observations on Select Indian Plants' in *Works* 5.62–162.

based on precise observation and description is visible in his paper 'On the Pangolin of Bahar',[4] in which he reported on his analysis of a specimen of pangolin and argued that it was a different variety, perhaps a different species, from that described by Buffon in his *Natural History of Animals, Vegetables and Minerals.*[5] Jones's classification was not merely descriptive; he was as concerned with explaining similarities as he was with noting differences. The most notable example of this is his well-known suggestion that the linguistic similarities between Latin, Greek, and Sanskrit were the result of there having been a single proto-language, now disappeared, from which they had all derived.[6] In the same way he postulated a common source for Greek and Indian philosophy: '[N]or is it possible to read the Vedanta, or the many fine compositions in illustration of it, without believing, that Pythagoras and Plato derived their sublime theories from the same fountains with the sages of India'.[7]

The application of this taxonomic approach to the law was a primary concern of Peter's, and much of what he said and wrote on the subject has its parallels in Jones's multifarious writings. It is striking, though, that Jones himself never explicitly wrote about law in this way. To a degree this may have been no more than an accident of chronology in that his most important writing on law, the *Essay on the Law of Bailments*, antedated by several years the work on natural history in which his concern for taxonomy is most marked, while his legal writings in the latter part of his life took the form of editions of texts translated from Sanskrit and Arabic, a genre in which it was impossible to display any organizational originality. None the less, that can be only one part of the

---

⁴ *Works* 4.356–359.

⁵ GLL de Buffon, *Histoire Naturale Générale et Particulière* (1763) vol 10 180–6 (*Natural History of Animals, Vegetables and Minerals* (W Kenrick and J Murdoch (trs) 1775–6) vol 3 30–3). Jones refers expressly to Buffon, and to the abridged translation in Oliver Goldsmith's *History of Animated Nature* (2nd edn, 1779), vol 4 116–24. The features of Buffon's animal to which Jones draws attention are those referred to by Goldsmith, and I suspect that this may have been his immediate source; but some of the points Jones makes are found in Buffon though not in Goldsmith, so it seems clear that he had recourse to the original text too. For the pangolin, see RM Nowak, *Walker's Mammals of the World* (6th edn, 1999) vol 2 1239–42. It is likely that Jones's animal was not in fact a different variety or species from that described by Buffon.

⁶ 'Third Anniversary Discourse' in *Works* 3.24, 35: 'The *Sanscrit* language, whatever be its antiquity, is of a wonderful structure; more perfect than the *Greek*, more copious than the *Latin*, and more exquisitely refined than either, yet bearing to both of them a stronger affinity, both in the roots of verbs and in the forms of grammar, than could possibly have been produced by accident; so strong indeed, that no philologer could examine them all three, without believing them to have sprung from a common source which, perhaps, no longer exists; there is a similar reason, though not quite so forcible, for supposing that both the *Gothick* and the *Celtick*, though blended with a very different idiom, had the same origin with *Sanscrit*, and the old *Persian* might be added to the same family'. See in particular Anna Morpurgo Davies, *Nineteenth-Century Linguistics* (= Giulio Lepschy (ed), *History of Linguistics* vol 4) (1998) 46–47; R Rocher, 'Nathaniel Brassey Halhed, Sir William Jones and Comparative Indo-European Linguistics' in J Bingen, A Coupez, and F Mawet (eds), *Recherches de Linguistique: Hommages à Maurice Leroy* (1980) 173; R Rocher, *Orientalism, Poetry, and the Millennium: The Checkered Life of Nathaniel Brassey Halhed, 1751–1830* (1983) 293–309.

⁷ 'Third Anniversary Discourse' in *Works* 3.25, 37. The same point is made about their mythological systems in 'On the Gods of Greece, Italy and India' in *Works* 3.319.

explanation. In addition, Jones was substantially wedded to a model of law which downplayed differences and distinctions, one in which there was little place for any sense of historical development or evolution; and although there are clear hints that he moved away from this model in his later years, he was never to abandon it completely.

Jones's life divides neatly into two parts.[8] Born in 1746, by the time he was in his twenties he had a considerable reputation as a scholar of Arabic and Persian language and literature, remarked upon in 1774 by a reviewer of his *Poeseos Asiaticae Commentariorum Libri Sex*.[9] None the less, recognizing that the pursuit of letters would never make him rich, he followed the advice of family and friends and turned to the law. He was called to the Bar in 1774, by which time he wrote that he had left idle all his books and manuscripts which were not relevant to the law.[10] He built up a reasonable, if not spectacular, practice at the Bar, in 1782 estimating that he was earning from this a steady £400 per year.[11] It was towards the end of this period that he wrote the *Essay on the Law of Bailments*. The turning point in Jones's life occurred in 1783, when (after several years of lobbying) he was appointed to the Bench of the Supreme Court of Bengal and moved to Calcutta. Once there, alongside his judicial work, he turned to the study of all things Indian. He was one of the first Westerners to master Sanskrit, and so one of the first to be able to approach Indian materials on their own terms.[12] As founder and first president of the Asiatic Society of Bengal, it has been said that he 'invaded almost every branch of learning',[13] that he was the first 'Interpreter of India to the West'.[14] By the time of his early death, in 1794, it was once again as an oriental scholar or Indologist that he was primarily known in England.[15]

This essay will follow the two halves of Jones's life. The first part focuses on his approach to law before the move to India, concentrating on the *Essay on the Law of Bailments*. The second, briefer, part examines his conception of law after his appointment to the Bench in Calcutta.

---

[8] The standard biography of Jones is G Cannon, *The Life and Mind of Oriental Jones* (1990). Except where otherwise stated, this is the source of the biographical information in the following paragraph.   [9] (1774) 44 Gentleman's Magazine 579.

[10] *Letters* 163 (translation at 166).

[11] *Letters* 598. Such an income would have been fairly typical of the young barrister destined for a very successful career: D Duman, *The Judicial Bench in England 1727–1875* (1982) 58–9, 104–10.

[12] W Halbfass, *India and Europe: An Essay in Understanding* (1988) 62. For differing interpretations of Jones's 'Orientalism', see E Said, *Orientalism* (1995) 76–9; J Majeed, *Ungoverned Imaginings: James Mill's* The History of British India *and Orientalism* (1992) 11–46; K Teltscher, *India Inscribed* (1995) 192–228.   [13] OP Kejariwal, The *Asiatic Society of Bengal* (1988) 35.

[14] LSR Krishna Sastry, *Sir William Jones: Interpreter of India to the West* (1998).

[15] See eg the obituary notices in (1795) 65 Gentleman's Magazine 347 ('the most eminent Oriental scholar in this or perhaps any other age') and (1797) 31 European Magazine 40 ('In Sir William Jones, India has lost her greatest ornament, the Commentator of her Poetry, the Investigator of her History, and the Elucidator of her Antiquities, her Laws, her Manners, and her Opinions').

1. Jones the English Lawyer

Jones's letters of the late 1770s, together with a surviving notebook from about 1775, contain a sprinkling of hints about his thoughts as to the nature of law. We may distil out two features. First, there is what we might regard as a strong streak of anti-historicism. In his notebook of 1775, one year after his call to the Bar, he sketched out a plan to edit and publish a series of the ancient treatises of English law: Glanville, Bracton, Horne's *Mirror of Justices*, Britton, Fleta, Hengham, Littleton, and Fortescue.[16] It is possible that his surviving translation of Littleton's *Tenures*, which looks to have been intended for publication, was a spur from this plan, though it is impossible to know.[17] It may be that this was meant as a purely scholarly exercise, though such an explanation would sit ill with the professed putting aside of all of his unpractical work on Arabic and Persian. No doubt, too, these were the 'favourite Law-Classicks' which he was studying while on holiday in Margate in 1774,[18] presumably with a view to making use of them in the legal practice which he hoped would come his way after his call to the Bar earlier that year. Secondly, in a letter of 1779 he displayed a respectful antipathy towards Blackstone's model of the law. This was, according to the *Commentaries*, divided into two parts, the changeless law of nature which had been laid down by God and the municipal or civil law particular to each state.[19] Jones did not dissent from the first of these, but he disagreed with Blackstone's characterization of the municipal or civil law in terms of rules laid down by a superior power. Jones's preference was to define it as 'The Will of the whole community as far as it can be collected with convenience',[20] thereby aligning himself more with Rousseau than with Hobbes. One of the consequences of this he fleshed out in another letter three years later:

[T]he common law is the collected wisdom of many centuries, having been used and approved by successive generations; but the statutes frequently contain the whims of a few leading men, and sometimes of the mere individuals employed to draw them.[21]

Both of these features are central to the thinking of the *Essay on the Law of Bailments*.

The *Essay on the Law of Bailments* is a work which fits four-square within the Natural law tradition of English legal writing in the later eighteenth century.[22] Its topic was not, as might be supposed, the totality of the law of bailment, the collectivity of rules applicable to the situation where one person had possession

[16] B[ritish] L[ibrary] MS Add 8889 f 5; at f 4v he had listed the whereabouts of some manuscripts of these works. The manuscript probably dates from 1775.
[17] BL 708.g 22–6. Jones had crafted his own title page in manuscript, together with instructions for typesetting. [18] *Letters* 156.
[19] William Blackstone, *Commentaries* 1.39, 44. [20] *Letters* 333–4. [21] *Letters* 553.
[22] DJ Ibbetson, 'Natural Law and Common Law' (2001) 5 Edinburgh Law Review 1.

of goods belonging to another. It was in fact concerned with one particular aspect of the bailment relationship, the standard of care to be demanded of a bailee.[23] From a taxonomical point of view it is a particularly interesting subject, for in the institutional scheme of Roman law it was a question discussed within the law of contracts whereas in English law issues of the bailee's liability fell, formally at least, within the action of trespass on the case and constituted part of what we would call the law of torts. It is not impossible that Jones's choice of topic stemmed from a recognition that any attempt to arrange the legal rules of different legal systems in a rational order would necessitate the use of categories different from those used by any particular system, though this is not what he himself said. His own explanation was that he was filling a perceived gap in Blackstone,[24] and it may be that we should just accept this at face value. If anything, Jones saw the problem in Roman terms, as one lying within the law of contract, making reference in the opening sentence of the work to 'that contract, which lawyers call bailment',[25] and in general putting the analysis of Roman law at the centre of his reasoning.

In common with other writers within the Natural law tradition, Jones believed that law was a science and not simply a set of unconnected rules, and that as a science it must be reducible to a set of identifiable principles whose validity could be determined both by reason and by observation:

[I]f law be a science, and really deserve so sublime a name, it must be founded on principle, and claim an exalted rank in the empire of reason; but, if it be merely an unconnected series of decrees and ordinances, its use may remain, though its dignity be lessened, and He will become the greatest lawyer, who has the strongest habitual, or artificial, memory.[26]

Given the primacy of principle and reason in determining the proper rules, there was little independent scope for authority, though there was a grudging recognition that the law could not function on the basis of reason alone: sometimes authority was needed in order to give clear guidance in situations where reason did not give a single answer.[27] It followed from this starting point that Jones's interpretation of English cases and Roman texts was very heavily coloured by his preconceptions as to what reason demanded.

---

[23] Compare the subheadings of the title Bailment in Charles Viner's *Abridgment*:

> Bailee. Answerable in what Cases
> Bailee. Who; and his Power and Interest
> The Several Sorts of Bailments
> Revocable. Or Property altered. In what Cases.
> Actions and Pleadings.

[24] *Bailments* 3. References are to the pagination of the first edition (1781).
[25] *Bailments* 2.
[26] *Bailments* 123–4; cf 117. And note p 3, describing Blackstone's *Commentaries* as 'the most correct and beautiful outline, that ever was exhibited of any human science'.
[27] *Bailments* 60.

The belief that law was a science, in this sense, grounded the structure of Jones's whole argument. He framed his reasoning according to a tripartite model traceable back to the German jurist Johann Gotlieb Heineccius, whose work was influential in University College, Oxford, where Jones was by then a fellow.[28] First came an analytical part, in which the subject was sketched out according to the first principles of natural reason; this was followed by an historical, or empirical, part, in which it was shown how the rules of developed legal systems conformed to this natural model; finally there was a relatively brief synthetic part, formulating a set of rules based on his conclusions in the first two parts.[29] The closeness of this to the approach recommended by George Turnbull, the translator of Heineccius, is immediately visible:

And it would not certainly be an improper way of studying our laws first to get well acquainted with the laws of nature (large commentaries upon which are generally at the same time commentaries upon the Roman laws, the examples being commonly taken from thence), and then to go over the same laws of nature again in order, and to enquire into our laws under each head, and try them by the laws of nature, as the Roman laws are commonly canvassed by the maxims of natural equity, in treatises upon universal law.[30]

The analytical part began with the definition of bailment as a relationship incorporating an obligation on the part of the borrower to return the property to the lender in due time. From this Jones deduced three conclusions:

(a) the bailee must keep the property, and be responsible to the bailor should it be lost or damaged;
(b) his responsibility only arose if the loss or damage was due to his fault through not exercising a proper degree of care;
(c) the measure of care required of the bailee depended on the type of bailment.[31]

None of these conclusions was remotely obvious. The first might perhaps be admitted so far as the loss of the property was concerned, but there was nothing in the definition of bailment to entail liability for damage. The second was based on Jones's assumption, that 'the bounds of justice would in most cases be transgressed, if he were made answerable for the loss of it without his fault'. While it was a commonplace in the main strand of Natural law thinking that what we would call tortious liability depended on fault, at the beginning of the

---

[28] R Eden, *Jurisprudentia Philologica* (1744) vi. For Eden's dependence on Heineccius, see JL Barton, 'Legal Studies' in LS Sutherland and LG Mitchell (eds), *The History of the University of Oxford* Vol V: *The Eighteenth Century* (1986) 599.

[29] [4]. For this tripartite approach, see K Haakonssen, *Natural Law and Moral Philosophy* (1996) 85–90.

[30] G Turnbull, 'A Supplement concerning the Duties of Subjects and Magistrates' in G Heineccius, *A Methodical System of Universal Law: Or, the Laws of Nature and Nations deduced from Certain Principles, and applied to Proper Cases* (translated by G Turnbull, 1763), vol 2 230–1, quoted in T Hochstrasser, *Natural Law Theories in the Early Enlightenment* (2000) 16–17.

[31] *Bailments* 5.

eighteenth century Christian Thomasius had argued strongly against this supposition;[32] so it was not something that could just be taken for granted. A further difficulty was that where the bailment had arisen out of a contract, orthodox Natural law theory would say that the degree of care required of the bailee should have depended on the agreement between the parties. Jones recognized this, but attempted to slip the noose by supposing that it was a 'fair presumption' that the parties had intended to incorporate the fault principle into their contract,[33] a step which there was absolutely no warrant for taking.[34] His third conclusion was no less question-begging, but he moved on from it to identify three distinct levels of care that might be demanded: ordinary care, more than ordinary care, and less than ordinary care. Which one of these should apply in any particular case depended on whether the bailment was of benefit to one or both of the parties.[35] Throughout this purportedly axiomatic section, the boot-strapping character of the reasoning is utterly transparent. Jones was anything but a fool, and the fact that he proceeded to argue in this way reveals just how strongly he was committed to the supposition that normative rules could be deduced from first principles and just how easy it was to slide from this to the conclusion that that which was familiar (in this case the basic Roman law rules of the liability of the borrower of goods) was necessarily also true.

The second stage of Jones's reasoning, the historical or empirical, involved the demonstration that the liability rules of 'nations most eminent for legal wisdom',[36] particularly the English and the Roman, were in conformity with the analytical framework which he had deduced. His anchor-point was Roman law, though it is likely that this was because he believed—like his older Oxford colleague Thomas Bever—that the principles of Natural law (or 'jurisprudence') were most usefully exemplified through the reasoning of Roman jurists.[37] Superficially at least, his study of this is a tour de force, far more sophisticated in its engagement with the Roman texts and with the scholarly literature of continental Europe than anything else on the subject being written in England at the time.[38] A significant part of this treatment involved a minute examination of a text of Ulpian in Justinian's Digest, D.50.17.23, where there was a difference

---

[32] Grotius, *De Jure Belli ac Pacis* 2.17.1; Pufendorf, *De Jure Naturae et Gentium* 3.1.6; cf Thomasius, *Larva Legis Aquiliae* esp at s 2. [33] *Bailments* 11.

[34] The problem had been pointed out by the German scholar Nicolaus Gundling, and discussed in Jean Barbeyrac's note incorporated in the fifth edition of the English translation of Pufendorf's *De Jure Naturae et Gentium: On the Law of Nature and Nations* (1749) V.IV.3 (485 n 8, at 486).

[35] *Bailments* 5–10. More accurately, he recognized there was an infinite continuum of degrees of care, but argued that for practical convenience the law should reduce them to these three. See in particular p 9. [36] *Bailments* 11, 111.

[37] Thomas Bever, *A Discourse on the Study of Jurisprudence and the Civil Law* (1766) 2. So too George Turnbull (n 30).

[38] *Bailments* 12–34. This may, though, be no more than superficial: he appears to have relied very heavily on the *In Titulum Pandectarum De Diversis Regulis Iuris Antiqui Commentarius* of Jacques Godefroy (Gothofredus) (ed Geneva, 1612) 97–147, though disagreeing with his conclusions.

between the received text of the medieval jurists and the oldest manuscript, the Florentine.[39] Jones spent several pages discussing which version was the more accurate, eventually coming down in favour of the traditional reading rather than that of the Florentine.[40] This led him to define the three grades of responsibility: *culpa lata*, or gross neglect, the omission of that care, which even inattentive and thoughtless men never fail to take of their own property; *culpa levis*, or ordinary neglect, the want of that diligence, which the generality of mankind use in their own concerns; and *culpa levissima*, slight neglect, the omission of that care, which very attentive and vigilant persons take of their own goods.[41] Where the contract was beneficial solely to the bailor, the bailee was liable for nothing less than gross neglect; where the contract was for the benefit of both parties, the bailee was liable for ordinary neglect; and where it was for the benefit of the bailee alone he was liable for *culpa levissima*, any slight neglect.[42] Although there is no denying the depth of his scholarship throughout this section, his conclusions are ineluctably orthodox, hardly departing from the exposition found in Vinnius' Commentary on the Institutes: his division of responsibility into three grades, his definition of each of these, and his identification of the circumstances in which each applied.[43]

Given the structure of Jones's reasoning thus far, it is not surprising that his treatment of English law[44] fits into the pattern set by the analysis of natural reason and the exposition of Roman law. The ground had been prepared for this before his section on Roman law, where he had written that, although Roman law had no formal authority in Westminster Hall, where 'rational law' was in issue resort might be had to the wisdom of ancient jurists: 'What is good sense, in one age, must be good sense, all circumstances remaining, in another; and pure unsophisticated reason is the same in Italy and in England, in the mind of a Papinian and of a Blackstone'.[45] His opening strategy was to divide bailments up into different types, following the Roman model, in order to determine what standard of care was appropriate to each of them.[46] Such an approach had the authority of Holt CJ, in the great case of *Coggs v Bernard* in 1703,[47] and although Jones did not slavishly follow the categories identified by Holt he was happy to hold out his own work as a commentary on that judgment.[48] The effect

---

[39] The Vulgate text reads *Contractus quidam dolum malum dumtaxat recipiunt, quidam et dolum et culpam. Dolum tantum: depositum et precarium. Dolum et culpam mandatum, commodatum, venditum, pignori acceptum, locatum, item dotis datio, tutelae, negotia gesta: in his quidam et diligentiam. Societas et rerum communio et dolum et culpam recipit.* The Florentine is the same, except that it reads *quidem* rather than *quidam* in the penultimate sentence.   [40] *Bailments* 17–20.
[41] *Bailments* 21–2.   [42] *Bailments* 22–4.
[43] A Vinnius, *In Quatuor Libros Institutionum Imperialium Commentarius* 3.15.2, no 12.
[44] *Bailments* 34–111.
[45] *Bailments* 14. Cf *Letters* 796, where he was to claim that Justinian's law was the source of much of the law of England: below, text at n 105.   [46] *Bailments* 35–7.
[47] (1703) 2 Ld Raym 909, 3 Ld Raym 163, 1 Com 133, 1 Salk 26, 2 Salk 735, 3 Salk 11, 3 Salk 268, Holt KB 13, Holt KB 131, Holt 528. The principal report, which was the one explicitly cited by Jones, is 2 Ld Raym 909.   [48] *Bailments* 59.

of this was to facilitate the shaping of English law according to the Roman model, and since Holt himself had substantially borrowed the Roman rules, both directly from Justinian's Institutes and Vinnius' Commentary on them and indirectly through Bracton, the fit was all the easier.[49]

Jones's technique for dealing with English material is well illustrated by his treatment of the first type of bailment with which he dealt, the contract of deposit, that is, a gratuitous bailment for safe-keeping.[50] His starting-point was *Bonion's Case*, a case of 1315 reported in the Vulgate Year Book and in Fitzherbert's Abridgment.[51] This was an action of detinue for goods which had been bailed to the defendant. The defendant pleaded that the goods (including, somewhat surprisingly, a bed) had been bailed to her in a locked box, of which the plaintiff had taken the key away with him, and that thieves had broken into the box and stolen the contents along with other goods of the defendant's. To this the plaintiff replied that the box had not been locked, on which the defendant joined issue. It was not obvious why the question whether the box was locked or not made a difference, but it had been explained away in a case reported by Coke on the basis that a depositor who had locked the box and taken away the key (if this was the case) would have demonstrated thereby that he did not trust the depositee with the goods.[52] Holt CJ had taken a more robust view, saying simply that the fact that it was in a box should not have made any difference.[53] Jones's approach to the problem of the case was to refer to a dispute between the Roman jurists Trebatius and Labeo.[54] Trebatius had said that where goods were deposited in a sealed chest the depositor might only bring an *actio depositi* for the chest and its contents, whereas Labeo had argued that an *actio depositi* might be brought claiming the contents alone. As Jones realized, this dispute related purely to the formal question of how the Roman *actio depositi* ought to be framed and had absolutely nothing to do with the circumstances in which the depositee ought to be liable for the loss;[55] but, he said, it might make a difference to the standard of care demanded of the depositee if the chest was sealed and he did not know what it contained, for a person who knew that he had a box of valuable jewels might be required to exercise greater care in their custody, so that he might be found guilty of gross negligence where one who thought he had only relatively worthless items would not be. The seventeenth-century French jurist Jean Domat had, according to Jones, interpreted the

---

[49] Holt's judgment can also be seen as prefiguring Jones's argument in its willingness to use congruity with reason and with the law in other countries as justifications for recognizing something as the law of England; see in particular 2 Ld Raym 909, 915.   [50] *Bailments* 36–52.

[51] YB P 8 Edw II f 275; Fitz Abr, *Detinue* 59. There is a modern edition based on the manuscripts which confirms the Vulgate report in all material ways: *Bowdon v Pelleter*, YB P 8 Edw II (41 SS) 136.   [52] *Southcote v Bennett* (1601) 4 Co Rep 83b, 84.

[53] *Coggs v Bernard* (1703) 2 Ld Raym 909, 914.   [54] D.16.3.1.41.

[55] *Bailments* 38. The issue would have arisen where some single item had been taken from the chest. cf D.47.2.21 pr–21.8, referring at 21 pr to a similar approach of Trebatius.

Roman text in this way,[56] all of which went to show that *Bonion's Case* was wrong. The rule of reason was that where there was a gratuitous deposit the bailee should be liable only for *culpa lata*, gross neglect. Since the goods had been stolen the depositee could not have been guilty of this, and hence she should not have been liable. The inadequacy of the argument is, to the eyes of the lawyer of the twenty-first century accustomed to identifying authoritative propositions by interpreting cases on their own terms, astonishing. It can only be explained on the basis that Jones's notion of the authority of a case was either very much weaker than our notion or very different from it. Where reason dictated a conclusion different from that reached in a case, it was the rule derived from the case that had to give way.

Jones then turned his attention to the form of the rule in Coke's Commentary on Littleton, reflecting the decision of the Court of King's Bench in *Southcote v Bennett* as reported by Coke.[57] For him, the depositee was liable if the goods were stolen unless he had received them explicitly to look after as he looked after his own goods. This, said Jones, was wrong for three reasons: it was repugnant to natural reason and the laws of other nations; it was based upon chance remarks in the Year Books, 'broken cases', and 'mere conversations on the bench'; and *Southcote's Case* did not itself justify the rule which Coke had derived from it.[58] Neither the second nor the third reason has much substance to it. As a matter of history, probably, Coke's interpretation of the case was correct, and at the very least it was plausible;[59] and the dismissal of the Year Book evidence as 'mere conversations on the bench' was rather too obviously a glib means to get round inconvenient case-law. The only real justification for the rejection of Coke's version of the rule was the first one, that it was contrary to natural reason and the law elsewhere. But since the whole point of Jones's argument was to show that the Common law was like other developed legal systems and consistent with reason, the rejection of Coke's position simply on the grounds that it was contrary to reason was quite perfectly circular.[60] Transparently, the demonstration that as a matter of English law the liability of the depositee was limited to cases of gross negligence was very flimsy, grounded on little more than an assertion that this was what natural reason demanded. Case-law to the contrary, even principles associated with an authority as high as Sir Edward Coke, were

[56] J Domat, *Les Loix Civiles dans leur Ordre Naturel* I.7.1.17. I believe this to be a misinterpretation of Domat, but the point is not material to the present argument.

[57] 4 Co Rep 83b; Co Litt 89.

[58] *Bailments* 41. Holt CJ had made a similar criticism of *Southcote v Bennett*: (1703) 2 Ld Raym 909, 913. But for him the case represented a 'great authority against me', which had to be avoided; once *Coggs v Bernard* had been decided, the authority of *Southcote v Bennett* was enormously weakened, and there was no necessity for Jones to make the similar argument.

[59] DJ Ibbetson, 'Fault and Absolute Liability in Pre-Modern Contract Law' (1997) 18 (2) Journal of Legal History 1, 17.

[60] No less circular was the continuation of his argument (*Bailments* 47–50): the general rule of liability for gross negligence was qualified by a number of exceptions, all of which were substantially derived from texts of Roman law without reference to English authority.

padded away with a veneer of learning but with almost nothing at all which could pass muster as a serious argument.

Similar comments could be made about his reasoning when dealing with the other forms of bailment. Underpinning all of his arguments are two dominant characteristics: a significant lack of historical perspective in dealing with English law; and a violent syncretism which caused him to run together his interpretation of English and Roman law, commonly twisting either or both of them in the process of fitting them to each other and to his preconceived notion of what natural law demanded.

Jones's ahistoricism in the analysis of English law is well brought out in his treatment of liability arising out of a mandate or commission, where one person did an act at the request of another (in this context, an act involving having the custody of the other's property).[61] In this context he discusses *Watkin's Case* in 1425,[62] where in an action on the case against a builder who had failed to build a mill in accordance with his undertaking to do so the distinction was drawn between misfeasance and pure nonfeasance. Where the defendant promisor had misperformed his obligation, it was said by Martin J, the action on the case would lie, but it would not do so where he had simply omitted to do anything. This was a perfectly orthodox statement of fifteenth-century law,[63] at least until a chance remark of Fineux CJ in 1499 heralded a volte face on the actionability of cases of nonfeasance.[64] Jones did not advert at all to this historical shift, asserting simply that 'authority' and 'reason' convinced him that the supposition of Martin J that the action on the case would not lie for nonfeasance was wrong.[65]

Jones's syncretism was all-pervasive. His section on *commodatum*, loan for use, begins with the statement that there is little that needs to be said since English law and Roman law are identical in imposing liability for the slightest negligence.[66] There is, though, no demonstration of this. The working out of the theme involves a reassertion of the rule, dismissing the opinions of those continental writers who had argued for something different. Pufendorf, and following him Barbeyrac, had been guilty of 'much idle reasoning, which I am not idle enough to transcribe' in suggesting that the bailee might be liable without fault if the bailed goods were destroyed while the bailee's own property was left unscathed; Pothier, it was said, had shown the good sense of the orthodox analysis.[67] The bailee would not normally be liable if robbed of the goods, though in *Doctor and Student* Christopher St Germain had made the point that even in this case liability would arise if the borrower had been foolish enough to

[61] *Bailments* 54–6.   [62] YB H 3 Hen VI 36b, 37a; Stath Abr *Accions sur le cas*, pl 20.

[63] AWB Simpson, *A History of the Common Law of Contract* (1975) 248, esp at n 1.

[64] Fitz Abr, *Accion sur le Case*, 45, YB 21 Hen VII f 41, cited by Jones from Brooke's Abridgment, *Accion sur le Case* 72.

[65] *Bailments* 55. The distinction between misfeasance and nonfeasance, and the change at the end of the fifteenth century, was to be clearly noticed in John Reeves, *A History of the English Law* (1783–4) 2.394.   [66] *Bailments* 64; cf 66–7.

[67] *Bailments* 66–7.

leave the high road and pass through a dark thicket; this was plausible, but St Germain's example had been (as Jones recognized) drawn from the Canonist *Summa Rosella* so was hardly an independent testimony to the rule of English law.[68] More generally, his discussions of both pledge and hire begin with, and are largely dependent on, the assumption that the English law and that of other sophisticated legal systems embodies the general principles which Jones had derived from reason in the analytical introduction to the essay.[69] 'Natural reason and the wisdom of nations's dictated that a pledgee should be liable for the failure to take reasonable care; this is the rule found in Bracton,[70] and although this was copied straight out of Justinian's Institutes 3.14.4 it was said that it must be taken as representing English law, for it was Bracton's practice only to reproduce Roman law when English law was in conformity with it.[71] No reason is given for this supposition, in its nature incapable of proof since Jones's picture of the law of the thirteenth century was derived exclusively from Bracton itself. The approach to hire is not dissimilar, beginning with the question-begging statement that 'the harmonious consent of nations will be interrupted, and one object of this essay defeated, if the laws of England shall be found, on a fair inquiry, to demand of the hirer a more than ordinary degree of diligence'.[72] Modern writers and judges, wrote Jones, were misguided in their opinion that what was required was the exercise of all imaginable care, a test which had been derived from Bracton.[73] As with pledge, Bracton's rule here was derived directly from Justinian's Institutes, from 3.24.5; but this time Bracton was wrong, as also was Justinian. The requirement that the hirer should take the care of a *diligentissimus paterfamilias* was ultimately traceable back to Gaius, who was, it was said, prone to the use of unnecessary superlatives. Better, according to Jones, was the version of the text found in Theophilus's Paraphrase of the Institutes, where only ordinary diligence was required. So interpreted, English and Roman law were in harmony with the book of Exodus, where a clear distinction was drawn between hiring and borrowing.[74]

As Jones's attitude to Bracton might suggest, his assumptions about what the correct rules were led him to interpret evidence in the way which was most consistent with his theory. Since his analytical position was largely derived from Roman law, it followed that it was primarily English law which attracted his critical attention.[75] There are many examples of this. In discussing pledge, for instance, Jones found that a Year Book case of 1355 seemed to have adopted a different liability rule than that which was dictated by 'natural reason', treating a pledgee as not liable if his own goods were taken as well as those of the pledgor.[76]

---

[68] *Bailments* 68.   [69] Above 624–5.   [70] *Bracton* f 99b (ed Thorne, 2.284).
[71] *Bailments* 71–2.   [72] *Bailments* 86.
[73] F Buller, *Introduction to the Law of Trials at Nisi Prius* (2nd edn, 1775) 72; *Coggs v Bernard* (1703) 2 Ld Raym 909, 916; *Bracton* f 62b (ed Thorne, 2.184).   [74] *Bailments* 87–8.
[75] Though Roman law too does come in for some critical reconstruction: eg *Bailments* 77, 87.
[76] YB 29 Lib Ass 28; *Bailments* 77–9.

Had this been right, Jones said, it would have destroyed the harmony of his system. Hence he asserted that it was wrong, citing statements from Bracton, Doctor and Student, and a dictum of Holt CJ in *Coggs v Bernard*—all of them, it should be noted, sources which were heavily dependent on the rules of Roman law out of which Jones had fashioned his analytical conclusions. A later Year Book case had drawn a distinction between situations where the goods were stolen and where they were taken by robbery, holding the bailee liable in the former and not in the latter;[77] but this was not a case of pledge, so it was hardly relevant to the resolution of Jones's problem. In any event, he said, the 1355 case was not a simple case of theft at all, but a case of violent robbery, as was 'confirmed beyond any doubt' by the sidenote in Brooke's Abridgment of the case, 'Who shall bear the loss when the goods are robbed'.[78] But no reason is given why weight should be placed on Brooke, writing some two centuries after the case had been decided, rather than on the words of the Year Book report itself. The best that can be said about Jones's reasoning here is that he does give reasons for saying that the case is wrong. Even that is lacking in his treatment of a series of cases dealing with the liability of carriers, where the 'true' reasons for the decisions are repeatedly said to be different from the reason given in the cases themselves.[79]

Roman law and English law having been dealt with, and having been shown to conform to natural reason, the third sub-division of the historical or empirical section of the *Law of Bailments* focused on less developed legal systems, those normally described as 'barbarous'.[80] In it Jones cited passages from the laws of the Visigoths and Bavarians, from capitularies of Louis the Pious, from the Gothic and Welsh laws, and from the Hindu laws known to him from Halhed's *Code of Gentoo Laws*.[81] There was no real necessity for this, for it was no part of his argument that the laws of all nations approximated to natural reason; but that similar rules might be found even in what he regarded as unsophisticated systems could be seen as adding a measure of support to his conclusions about the rationality of English and Roman law. In truth, though, they were unconnected wisps of evidence pulled out because they chanced to fit with conclusions which had already been reached. The real interest, from the point of view of Jones's future endeavours, lies in the closing remarks of the section:

All these provisions are consonant to the principles established in this essay; and I cannot help thinking, that a clear and concise treatise, written in the Persian or Arabian language, on the law of Contracts, and evincing the general conformity between the Asiatick and European systems, would contribute, as much as any regulation whatever, to bring our

---

[77] YB M 10 Hen VI f 21 pl 69.   [78] Br Abr, *Bailment* 7.
[79] *Bailments* 105–8, discussing *Dale v Hall* (1750) 1 Wils 281; *Gibbon v Paynton* (1769) Burr 2298; *Rich v Kneeland* (1613) Hob 30, Cro Jac 330; *Barcroft's Case*, cited in *Kenrig v Eggleston* (1648) Alleyn 93.   [80] *Bailments* 111–16.
[81] On the last of these, it is worth noting that Jones referred to the unpublished Persian text, which he must surely have had from Halhed, as well as the English translation.

English law into good odour among those, whose fate it is to be under our dominion, and whose happiness ought to be a serious and continual object of our care.[82]

There is little need to pause over the third section of the work, the synthetic,[83] which merely summarized what had earlier been argued, adding nothing of any substance to it.

The *Essay on the Law of Bailments* was designed by Jones to be a work of English law, filling what he perceived as a lacuna in Blackstone's *Commentaries*;[84] and two years after its publication, in a memorandum 'Objects of Enquiry during my Residence in Asia' written on his voyage to India, he referred to it as the model of a series of treatises or essays described as 'Elements of the Laws of England'.[85] We may take it, therefore, that he believed that his design had been accomplished, and that it actually was a work of English law. It was, though, very different from any work of English law which had preceded it. Most obviously, it departed from the traditional Common law treatise, whose function was simply to describe rules without making any attempt to link them together as parts of a coherent whole with a rational structure, making use of Roman law and the writings of seventeenth- and eighteenth-century Natural lawyers as a source of its ideas. In no way was this unusual for a post-Blackstonian treatise, though, let alone unique.[86] What marked it out was not so much the fact that it made use of Natural law or Roman law, but the way in which it did so. Blackstone, for example, had used Natural law to give structure to his *Commentaries*, but in the main the substantive rules which he had built on the Natural law base were orthodoxly English.[87] English contract law, beginning with Henry Ballow's *Treatise on Equity* in 1737, was substantially constructed around a skeletal framework provided by Natural law, largely from the writings of Samuel Pufendorf and (later) Robert-Joseph Pothier; but the rules hung on this framework had a plausible Common-law pedigree behind them.[88] The same could be said about the crystallization of the idea of negligence as the heart of the law of torts: although the articulation of the idea was fairly clearly derived from Natural lawyers, especially from Pufendorf, its basic elements could without violence be identified in the older Common law.[89] Ideas of copyright were to a considerable degree derived from Natural law thinking, providing solutions to problems which the earlier Common law had left untouched. Jones's work was

---

[82] *Bailments* 116; cf 99–100 to the same effect. Jones did recognize, though, that in some areas of the law there were appreciable differences between the systems in fields such as inheritance.

[83] *Bailments* 116–23.   [84] *Bailments* 3.   [85] *Works* 2.3–4, at 4.

[86] D Lieberman, *The Province of Legislation Determined* (1989) esp at 36–9; M Lobban, *The Common Law and English Jurisprudence 1760–1850* (1991) 17–46.

[87] For Blackstone's Natural law, as well as the works of Lieberman and Lobban cited above, see NE Simmonds, 'Reason, History and Privilege: Blackstone's Debt to Natural Law' (1988) 105 ZSS (Germ Abt) 200.

[88] AWB Simpson, 'Innovation in Nineteenth Century Contract Law' (1975) 91 LQR 249; J Gordley, *The Philosophical Origins of Modern Contract Doctrine* (1991); DJ Ibbetson, *Historical Introduction to the Law of Obligations* (1999) 217–19, 220–36.

[89] Ibbetson, *Historical Introduction to the Law of Obligations* (n 88) 164–8.

different from all of these. For him Natural law did not simply provide a structure, or a set of model rules which might be adopted where there was no relevant English law; it provided a moral framework through which English law could be interpreted, and a set of rules which, all other things being equal, could be supposed to apply as positive law in England. Such a strong approach to the relationship between Natural law and positive law is similar to that espoused by the Scottish lawyer George Turnbull, in his notes to the English translation of Heineccius' *Methodical System of Universal Law*:

[T]he proper way of studying the laws of any particular country is by comparing them all along with the dictates of the law of nature concerning the same cases, in an orderly way, proceeding from simple to more and more complex cases gradually. Whence it is evident, that one well versed in the knowledge of natural law, can never be at a loss to find what ought to be the general positive law in certain cases, and how positive law ought to be interpreted in cases, which, tho' not expressly excepted in a law, which must be general, yet are in the nature of things excepted.[90]

Turnbull, like Jones, believed that the principles of Natural law were reflected in the practice of civilized nations,[91] though he did not accept the view taken by Grotius and traceable back to Cicero, that Natural law could be deduced from the general practice of nations: the fact that all nations agreed on something was irrelevant in showing that it conformed to the divine will, which was the source of all principles of Natural law.[92] But in one way Jones may have gone further than Turnbull. In his interpretative stance, he got very close to treating Natural law as something which could displace what appeared to be Common law rules: cases which reached results, or used reasoning, inconsistent with his principles could simply be dismissed as wrong or misguided, writers as authoritative as Bracton and Coke discarded when they said things which disagreed with his model. There is an obvious instability in Jones's position. On the one hand, he clearly allowed the possibility of English law being in conflict with Natural law, for otherwise there would have been no purpose in going beyond the bare exegesis of Natural law itself. On the other, he got very close to denying the reality of such conflict in his repeated interpretations of English cases in line with his perceptions of Natural law. At only one point in the *Essay* does he confront this tension, commenting on a remark of Powell J in *Coggs v Bernard*:[93]

[F]or nothing, said Mr. Justice Powell emphatically, is law, that is not reason; a maxim, in theory excellent, but in practice dangerous, as many rules, true in the abstract, are false

---

[90] G Heineccius, *A Methodical System of Universal Law: Or, the Laws of Nature and Nations deduced from Certain Principles, and applied to Proper Cases* (translated by G Turnbull, 1763) vol 1 322–3, quoted in part in T Hochstrasser, *Natural Law Theories in the Early Enlightenment* (2000) 17.

[91] 'Of the Nature and Origine of Moral and Civil Laws' in Heineccius, *Methodical System of Universal Law* (n 90) 2.320.

[92] Grotius, *De Jure Belli ac Pacis*, Prologomenon § 40; Cicero, *Tusculanae Disputationes* 1.13; Heineccius, *Methodical System of Universal Law* (n 90) 1.47–8.

[93] (1703) 2 Ld Raym 909, 911.

in the concrete; for, since the reason of Titius may, and frequently does, differ from the reason of Septimius, no man, who is not a lawyer, would ever know how to act, and no man, who is a lawyer, would in many instances know what to advise, unless courts were bound by authority, as firmly as the pagan deities were supposed to be bound by the decrees of fate.[94]

For all that this constitutes a justification for argument from authority, it is none the less only a pragmatic qualification to the primacy of reason. We are, therefore, left with the sense that when Jones described law as a science[95] he believed not simply that it was capable of rational analysis, which might mean no more than that its rules satisfied a test of coherence within an abstract framework, but that it was consistent with a conception of justice which was itself deducible by reason.[96]

2. Jones and India

The *Essay on the Law of Bailments* was Jones's only published work of English law. His later legal works consisted solely of translations: *The Mahomedan Law of Succession to Property of Intestates* (1782),[97] *Al Sirájiyyah; or the Mohammedan Law of Inheritance* (1792),[98] and *Institutes of Hindu Law; or the Ordinances of Menu* (1794),[99] to which should be added the *Digest of Hindu Law on Contracts and Successions* (1797–8) which was begun under Jones's direction and completed after his death by Henry Colebrooke. Of these the most important was the *Institutes of Hindu Law*, a translation of the Sanskrit text known as the *Mānava-Dharmaśāstra* or *Manusmṛti*.[100] In the absence of any discursive work like the *Essay on the Law of Bailments* it is not easy to extract Jones's conception of law with any certainty, but there are sufficient hints in his translations and in his letters to enable us to sketch its outline.

The most notable feature of the *Essay on the Law of Bailments*, it has been argued, was its syncretism, hardly distinguishing between the rules of different systems. Moreover, although Jones was there primarily concerned with the similarities between English and Roman law, he had suggested that, at least in

[94] *Bailments* 60.   [95] Above, at n 26.
[96] NE Simmonds, *The Decline of Juridical Reason* (1984) 19–22.   [97] *Works* 8. 159–96.
[98] *Works* 3. 197–321.   [99] *Works* 7. 75–8.158.
[100] This was not the first Sanskrit legal or quasi-legal text to be translated into English. In 1776 there had appeared Nathaniel Brassey Halhed's *Code of Gentoo Laws*, a direct response to the need for some sort of text dealing with Hindu laws which could be used by English lawyers and administrators when they were required to decide cases according to Hindu law. But the *Code of Gentoo Laws* was something of an artificial text, a work prepared to order by a commission of pandits, experts in *dharma*, rather than a text of genuine authority for Hindus. It was, moreover, translated from Sanskrit into Persian, perhaps via Bengali, and only thence translated into English by Halhed, suffering a good deal of re-ordering on the way. See Rocher, *Orientalism, Poetry, and the Millennium* (n 6), 48–72; R Rocher, 'The Vivādārṇavasetu, Chapters 1 and 2' (1980–1) 44–5 Brahmavidya 63, 69–71.

some fields, there was a 'general conformity between the Asiatick and European systems',[101] based on his knowledge of Arabic and Persian texts. Once in India, though, he was to emphasize differences rather than similarities. He was committed to a belief that Indians should be governed by their own laws, a theoretical position similar to that of Montesquieu, a copy of whose works was probably in his library.[102] As he outlined in a memorandum to Edmund Burke soon after his arrival in India:

A system of liberty, forced upon a people invincibly attached to opposite habits, would in truth be a system of cruel tyranny.

Any system of judicature effecting the natives in Bengal, and not having for its basis the old Mogul constitution, would be dangerous and impracticable.

All original jurisdiction against natives without the Mahratta ditch, except for that exercised by the courts of Diwāneī Adālet according to forms used and approved, will produce confusion and misery.[103]

This was not merely theory. English judges in Calcutta, Madras, and Bombay were required to apply Hindu (or, where appropriate, Muslim) law in cases involving contracts or inheritance, and Jones took this obligation seriously: once he had mastered Sanskrit he would refer to Hindu texts himself.[104] There is not the slightest reminiscence of the syncretism of the *Essay on the Law of Bailments*. Indian law was different, and Jones had a conscientious respect for that difference. There was also, perhaps, a shift in his understanding of the relationship between English and Roman law: in a letter of 1788 he stated quite explicitly that English law was largely derived from that of Justinian, despite the timidity of English lawyers in acknowledging it,[105] a marked contrast with his unhistorical approach in the *Essay*.

This is not to say that Jones left all of his preconceptions behind, as his translations of Sanskrit terms sometimes slip inappropriately into the technical terminology of Roman or English law. The first two titles of litigation in *Manu* I.4 Jones translates as 'debt, on loans for consumption' and 'deposits, and loans for use',[106] directly borrowing the Romans' *mutuum, depositum*, and *commodatum*. Contrast the more literal, and less Romanized, modern translation of Olivelle: 'non-payment of debts' and 'deposits'.[107] In the same context, when proposing to

---

[101] Above, at n 82.

[102] [R H Evans], *Catalogue of the Library of the Late Sir William Jones* (1831), Item 232. We cannot be completely certain that the work had actually belonged to Jones, since his widow continued to add to his library after his death.

[103] 'The Best Practicable System of Judicature for India' in Garland Cannon, 'Sir William Jones and Edmund Burke' (1957) 54 Modern Philology 165, 185–6 (reproduced in *Letters* 643). Similar sentiments are expressed in his Charge to the Calcutta Grand Jury in 1783 (*Works* 7.4), and in his preface to the *Institutes of Hindu Law* (*Works* 7. 75).

[104] DJ Ibbetson, 'Sir William Jones as a Comparative Lawyer' in A Murray (ed), *Sir William Jones* (1998) 23 n 23; R Rocher, 'Weaving Knowledge: Sir William Jones and Indian Pandits' in G Cannon and KR Brine (eds), *Objects of Enquiry* (1995) 57.   [105] *Letters* 796.

[106] *Works* 7. 330.   [107] P Olivelle, *Manu's Code of Law* (2005) 167.

Cornwallis the making of a Digest in 1788 he referred to the need for greater information than was hitherto available on the 'twelve different Contracts, to which Ulpian has given specifick names, and on all the others, which, though not specifically named, are reducible to four general heads'.[108] This was more or less good Roman law, but it bore not the slightest resemblance to the way in which Hindu scholars had organized their material on contracts. Though Roman law provided most of his patterns, inappropriate usage of English terminology can be seen too, as in the translation of *Manu* VIII.266,[109] where Jones renders as 'defamatory words' a phrase referring to abusive language far better translated as 'verbal assault'.[110] Despite his clear recognition that Indian law was different from Roman law or English law, in his approach to Hindu law he may have made an unspoken assumption that the basic building blocks of all three were the same.

Jones was not quite so respectful of Indian traditions when it came to procedure. One strong reason for his reading of texts for himself and his preparation of translations for others was that he had no faith in the native pandits, believing that they could not be trusted to act disinterestedly.[111] It was only if English judges could read the texts for themselves that it was possible to neutralize what he perceived to be native corruption. Indians might be entitled to be governed by their own laws; but their own people could not be trusted to administer them. Similarly, although Indians might be governed by their own substantive law, this did not displace English procedural norms. So, in his Charge to the Grand Jury at Calcutta in 1792, he lauded the English jury as the final protection of the British constitution from total shipwreck, moving from there to criticize summary jurisdiction in India: 'a difference in faith or complexion can make no difference in justice and right'.[112] If the *Essay on the Law of Bailments* was underpinned by a conception of substantive justice at the heart of legal rules, in India he seems to have been committed to a belief that justice lay in fair process.

Though recognizing the differences between Hindu law and English or Roman law so far as its content was concerned, the publication of *Manu* as the *Institutes of Hindu Law* and the preparation of a Digest points to the adoption of a Roman model of legal literature, but we should not be too hasty to assume that there was no more to it than this.[113] No doubt the initial idea for a Digest came from Roman law, but by 1786 it had taken on a decidedly Indian garb. By this time Jones had become aware of the Indians' own tradition of the compilation of Digests, referring in a letter of that year to the work of the sixteenth-century Bengali scholar Raghunandana.[114] He had obtained in addition the Sanskrit

---

[108] *Letters* 797.   [109] *Works* 7. 374.   [110] Olivelle, *Manu' Code of Law* (n 107) 181.
[111] Majeed, *Ungoverned Imaginings* (n 12) 19–20; Rocher, 'Sir William Jones and Indian Pandits' (n 104). For examples, see *Letters* 664, 683–4, 699, 720, 795.
[112] *Works* 7. 68–9 (quote at 69).
[113] I have been guilty of such a hasty assumption: 'Sir William Jones as a Comparative Lawyer' (n 104) 19, 31.
[114] *Letters* 722. On the Indian digests, see R Lingat, *The Classical Law of India* (translated by JDM Derrett, 1973) 115–22.

original on which Halhed's *Code of Gentoo Laws* had been based, the *Vivá-darnava Sétu*, a work which belonged firmly within the same Digest tradition as Raghunandana.[115] Whereas the Digest of Justinian was simply a collection of extracts from juristic texts brought together as a body of rules of law, the Indian Digests consisted of texts together with a commentary in which the compiler attempted to explain and reconcile the conflicting opinions;[116] and it was this, Indian, model which was followed by the Digest worked on by Jones and published by Colebrooke. Jones might, perhaps, have thought of an institutional work in the Roman tradition, too, but there is no good reason to think that his translation of *Manu* was planned in this way. It is true that in a letter of 1786, writing of his intention to make the translation, he expressed concern that those who did not know him might suspect that he was seeking fame or patronage by setting himself up as the Justinian of India,[117] but his point here relates to the production of a legal text at all, not a legal text on an explicitly Roman model. Although he did link the production of his Digest with his translation of *Manu* (and other legal works),[118] neither here nor elsewhere at this time does he seem to have been suggesting that *Manu* was thought of as an institutional work. Not until 1792 do we find him referring explicitly to his *Institutes of Hindu Law*,[119] and it was only in the preface to his edition that he drew the express link with the Institutes of Justinian. It is hard to believe that he had really come to think of *Manu* as an institutional text on the Justinianic model, since even the most cursory glance at the two texts shows them to be very different. It is altogether more likely that he adopted the *Institutes of Hindu Law* as a convenient title, passing it off to a Western audience in a more or less familiar guise.

The second feature of the *Essay on the Law of Bailments* was its ahistoricism, disregarding the ways in which law might have changed over time. Unlike his syncretism, this aspect did carry across into Jones's approach to the law in India. Despite being of extreme antiquity—Jones writes of its being believed to be many millions of years old, though he himself dated it to 880 BC[120]—*Manu* could still be passed off as an Institute, a basic primer, of Indian law as it existed at the end of the eighteenth century. Similarly, his projected Digest was at first planned to be constructed by cutting and pasting from a small number of classical texts, each with one well-respected commentary, very much in the manner that Justinian's Digest had been constructed from the writings of classical Roman jurists,[121] without any concern that the works selected might have been written at different epochs. That said, though, there was probably more justification for treating Hindu law in this way than there was for thinking that

[115] R Rocher, 'The Vivādārṇavasetu, Chapters 1 and 2' (1980–1) 44–5 Brahmavidya 63.
[116] See eg L Rocher (ed), *Jīmūtavāna's Dāyabhāga: The Hindu Law of Inheritance in Bengal* (2004).   [117] *Letters* 699.
[118] *Letters* 794–800.   [119] *Letters* 908.
[120] *Letters* 747; *Works* 7. 79. Modern scholarship, based on evidence unavailable to Jones, places it somewhere around AD 200: Olivelle, *Manu's Code of Law* (n 107) 20–5, with references to earlier scholars.   [121] *Letters* 721–2.

David Ibbetson

English law could be derived from the classical legal texts which he had once intended to edit and publish.[122] As the latest editor of the text has argued, *Manu* had been the 'dominant voice on *dharma* for close to two millennia', by a very clear margin the most frequently quoted work within the tradition;[123] to see it as the foundation text did not involve any serious wrench with the way in which Indian scholars themselves had used it. So too his Digest, at least in the form in which it was finally constructed and published, adhered closely to the traditional Indian form of Digest literature, in which the commentator collected together the various texts and attempted to reconcile the apparently conflicting opinions found within them.

For all of this, it has to be admitted that at the most basic level Jones did not discard his eurocentric assumptions about the nature of law.[124] Law, for him, was to be found in an authoritative text or set of texts, and the office of the judge was simply to apply this law to the facts of any dispute.[125] Within the Hindu tradition, though, a far more important role was played by interpretation, using the classical texts as reference points rather than sources of formal rules.[126] His frustration with what he perceived as the venality of native lawyers was at least partly the consequence of his failure to recognize the nature of the endeavour in which they were involved. To see *Manu* as a law-book at all, in the Western understanding, is in any event questionable. As a work of *dharma*, its focus was right living, in the broadest sense,[127] and only about one-sixth of the work, that dealing with the duties of a King and within that the grounds for litigation,[128] was concerned with law in the way in which an English Common lawyer would have conceived of it.

It would be unfair to judge Jones too harshly for this. As a judge whose upbringing had been in the Common law, he was almost bound to look for some authoritative source of rules; and when his scholarship consisted largely in the identification of the dominant texts and their translation, there was little scope for anything in the way of nuanced interpretation. His only real fault was the use of the title *Institutes of Hindu Law* for his edition of *Manu*; but this, it has been suggested, may have been an afterthought. If there was a point at which his

---

[122] Above 622.   [123] Olivelle, *Manu's Code of Law* (n 107) 70.

[124] BS Cohn, *Colonialism and its Forms of Knowledge* (1996) 68–71.

[125] Cohn contrasts Jones's rather rigid approach to Indian law with the flexibility of the English Common law; this might accurately reflect the nature of the Common law, but it was not Jones's conception of it. For him, the value of case-law was not that it allowed adaptation to changing circumstances, but that it enabled good rules to become embedded through long use, whereas legislation was too easily framed in such a way as to deal with immediate problems without thought for the integrity of the system as a whole. See above, at n 21.

[126] Lingat, *Classical Law of India* (n 114) 143–75.

[127] On *dharma*, see Lingat, *Classical Law of India* (n 114) 3–7; JDM Derrett, *Religion, Law and the State in India* (1999) 75-96. The classic study is PV Kane, *History of Dharmasastra* (1930–62), esp vol 3.

[128] VIII.4–7; VIII.47–IX.250. On the origins of this section outside the tradition of *dharma-śāstra*, see Olivelle, *Manu's Code of Law* (n 107) 46–50.

interpretation faltered, it was in his understanding of the nature of English law, where he inclined to give too great a role to Natural law and too little a role to authority. If anything, his work in India gave him a degree of relativism in his approach to the law. It is possible that, had he lived longer, he would have formulated a theory of the relationship between legal systems, analogous to his description of the relationship between the Latin, Greek, and Sanskrit languages, discarding the assumptions about the static nature of law found in the *Essay on the Law of Bailments;* but this can be no more than a speculation.

The Publications of Peter Birks
1969–2005

Compiled by Eric Descheemaeker

BOOKS

1985   *An Introduction to the Law of Restitution* (Oxford: Clarendon Press, 1985)

1986   (ed with N MacCormick) *The Legal Mind: Essays for Tony Honoré* (Oxford: Clarendon Press, 1986)

1987   (tr with G McLeod) *Justinian's Institutes* (London: Duckworth and Ithaca, NY: Cornell University Press, 1987)

1989   *An Introduction to the Law of Restitution* (revised edn, Oxford: Clarendon Press, 1989)

       (ed) *New Perspectives in the Roman Law of Property: Essays for Barry Nicholas* (Oxford: Clarendon Press, 1989)

1992   *Restitution—The Future* (Annandale, NSW: Federation Press, 1992)

       (ed) *Examining the Law Syllabus: The Core* (Oxford: Oxford University Press, 1992)

1993   (ed) *Examining the Law Syllabus: Beyond the Core* (Oxford: Oxford University Press, 1993)

       (ed) *The Life of the Law* (London *et al*: Hambledon, 1993)

1994   (with R Chambers) *Restitution Research Resource* (Oxford: Mansfield Press, 1994)

       (ed) *The Frontiers of Liability*, 1 (Oxford: Oxford University Press, 1994)

       (ed) *The Frontiers of Liability*, 2 (Oxford: Oxford University Press, 1994)

       (ed) *Reviewing Legal Education* (Oxford: Oxford University Press, 1994)

1995   (ed) *Laundering and Tracing* (Oxford: Clarendon Press, 1995)

       (ed) *Pressing Problems in the Law*, 1: *Criminal Justice and Human Rights* (Oxford: Oxford University Press, 1995)

1996   (ed) *Pressing Problems in the Law*, 2: *What are Law Schools For?* (Oxford: Oxford University Press, 1996)

       (ed) *Wrongs and Remedies in the Twenty-First Century* (Oxford: Clarendon Press, 1996)

1997   (with R Chambers) *Restitution Research Resource* (2nd edn, Oxford: Mansfield Press, 1997)

       (ed) *The Classification of Obligations* (Oxford: Clarendon Press, 1997)

       (ed) *Privacy and Loyalty* (Oxford: Clarendon Press, 1997)

2000   (ed with F Rose) *Restitution and Equity*, 1: *Resulting Trusts and Equitable Compensation* (London: Mansfield Press, 2000) (ed) *English Private Law*, 1: *Sources of Law—The Law of Persons—The Law of Property*, 2: *The Law of Obligations—Litigation* (Oxford: Oxford University Press, 2000)

(ed with F Rose) *Lessons of the Swaps Litigation* (London: Mansfield Press, 2000)

2002 *The Foundations of Unjust Enrichment: Six Centennial Lectures* (Wellington: Victoria University Press, 2002)

(ed with A Pretto) *Breach of Trust* (Oxford *et al*: Hart, 2002)

(ed) *English Private Law, First Updating Supplement* (Oxford: Oxford University Press, 2002)

(ed with A Pretto) *Themes in Comparative Law: In Honour of Bernard Rudden* (Oxford: Oxford University Press, 2002)

2003 *Unjust Enrichment* (Oxford: Oxford University Press, 2003)

2004 (ed) *English Private Law, Second Cumulative Updating Supplement* (Oxford: Oxford University Press, 2004)

2005 *Unjust Enrichment* (2nd edn, Oxford: Oxford University Press, 2005)

CONTRIBUTIONS TO BOOKS

1974 'Lucius Veratius and the *Lex Aebutia*' in A Watson (ed), *Daube Noster: Essays in Legal History for David Daube* (Edinburgh *et al*: Scottish Academic Press, 1974) 39–48

1983 'Obligations: One Tier or Two?' in PG Stein and ADE Lewis (eds), *Studies in Justinian's Institutes in Memory of JAC Thomas* (London: Sweet & Maxwell, 1983) 18–38

1984 'The Case of the Filched Pedigree: D.47.2.52.20' in *Sodalitas: Scritti in Onore di Antonio Guarino* (Naples: Jovene Editore, 1984) 731–48

1985 Translation of books 12 and 13 in A Watson (ed), *The Digest of Justinian*, 1 (Philadelphia: University of Pennsylvania Press, 1985) 357–414. Reprinted in the 1998 revised English-language edition

1986 'Fictions Ancient and Modern' in N MacCormick and P Birks (eds), *The Legal Mind: Essays for Tony Honoré* (Oxford: Clarendon Press, 1986) 83–101

1987 'Introduction' in W Fulbeck, *Fulbeck's Direction, or Preparative to the Study of the Law* (Aldershot: Wildwood House, 1987) pp iii–xviii

'Introduction' in P Birks and G McLeod (tr) *Justinian's Institutes* (London: Duckworth and Ithaca, NY: Cornell University Press, 1987) 7–28

1989 'The New Equity and the Need for Certainty' in FE McArdle (ed), *The Cambridge Lectures 1987* (Montréal: Éditions Yvon Blais, 1989) 309–22

'An Unacceptable Face of Human Property' in P Birks (ed), *New Perspectives in the Roman Law of Property: Essays for Barry Nicholas* (Oxford: Clarendon Press, 1989) 61–73

1990 'Restitution from the Executive: A Tercentenary Footnote to the Bill of Rights' in PD Finn (ed), *Essays on Restitution* (North Ryde, NSW: Law Book Co, 1990) 164–205

1991 'In Defence of Free Acceptance' in A Burrows (ed), *Essays on the Law of Restitution* (Oxford: Clarendon Press, 1991) 105–46

1992 'Civil Wrongs: A New World' in *Butterworth Lectures 1990–91* (London *et al*: Butterworths, 1992) 55–112

'Restitution and Resulting Trusts' in S Goldstein (ed), *Equity and Contemporary Legal Developments* (Jerusalem: The Harry and Michael Sacher Institute for Legislative Research and Comparative Law, 1992) 335–73. Reprinted in P Birks and F Rose (eds), *Restitution and Equity*, 1: *Resulting Trusts and Equitable Compensation* (London: Mansfield Press, 2000) 265–83

'Trusts in the Recovery of Misapplied Assets: Tracing, Trusts, and Restitution' in E McKendrick (ed), *Commercial Aspects of Trusts and Fiduciary Obligations* (Oxford: Clarendon Press, 1992) 149–66

'Introduction' in P Birks (ed), *Examining the Law Syllabus: The Core* (Oxford: Oxford University Press, 1992) 7–10

1993   'Mixtures' in N Palmer and E McKendrick (eds), *Interests in Goods* (London *et al*: Lloyd's of London Press, 1993) 449–68

'A Decade of Turmoil in Legal Education' in P Birks (ed), *Examining the Law Syllabus: Beyond the Core* (Oxford: Oxford University Press, 1993) 9–17

1994   'The Historical Context' in P Birks (ed), *Reviewing Legal Education* (Oxford: Oxford University Press, 1994) 1–8

'Short-Cuts' in P Birks (ed), *Reviewing Legal Education* (Oxford: Oxford University Press, 1994) 20–36

'Gifts of Other People's Money' in P Birks (ed), *The Frontiers of Liability*, 1 (Oxford: Oxford University Press, 1994) 31–40

'Proprietary Rights as Remedies' in P Birks (ed), *The Frontiers of Liability*, 2 (Oxford: Oxford University Press, 1994) 214–223

'The Edictal Rubric "*Ad Legem Aquiliam*"' in R Pérez-Bustamente (ed), *Estudios de historia del derecho europeo: homenaje al professor Gonzalo Martínez Díez*, 1 (Madrid: Editorial Complutense, 1994), 81–9

'Peter Stein, Regius Professor of Civil Law in the University of Cambridge, 1968–1993' in ADE Lewis and DJ Ibbetson (eds), *The Roman Law Tradition* (Cambridge: Cambridge University Press, 1994) p xi

'Doing and Causing to be Done' in ADE Lewis and DJ Ibbetson (eds), *The Roman Law Tradition* (Cambridge: Cambridge University Press, 1994) 31–53

1995   (with NY Chin) 'On the Nature of Undue Influence' in J Beatson and D Friedmann (eds), *Good Faith and Fault in Contract Law* (Oxford: Clarendon Press, 1995) 57–97

'Legal Education in England and Scotland' in SCJJ Kortmann (ed), *Legal Education in the Netherlands in a Comparative Perspective* (Nijmegen: Grotius Academy, 1995) 15–35

'Restitution for Wrongs' in EJH Schrage (ed), *Unjust Enrichment: The Comparative Legal History of the Law of Restitution* (Berlin: Duncker & Humblot, 1995) 171–96. Reprinted in the 2nd edn of the book (1999)

'Ulpian 18 *ad Edictum*: Introducing *Damnum Iniuria*' in R Feenstra, AS Hartkamp, JE Spruit, PJ Sijpesteijn, and LC Winkel (eds), *Collatio Iuris Romani*, 1 (Amsterdam: Gieben, 1995) 17–36

'The Foundation of Legal Rationality in Scotland' in R Evans-Jones (ed), *The Civil Law Tradition in Scotland* (Edinburgh: Stair Society, 1995) 81–99

'Overview: Tracing, Claiming and Defences' in P Birks (ed), *Laundering and Tracing* (Oxford: Clarendon Press, 1995) 289–348

1996   'Change of Position, the Nature of the Defence and its Relationship to other
       Defences' in M McInnes (ed), *Restitution: Developments in Unjust Enrichment*
       (Sydney: LBC Information Services, 1996) 49–74
       'Failure of Consideration' in F Rose (ed), *Consensus ad Idem: Essays in the Law of
       Contract in Honour of Guenter Treitel* (London: Sweet & Maxwell, 1996) 179–202
       'The Concept of a Civil Wrong' in D Owen (ed), *Philosophical Foundations of
       Tort Law* (Oxford: Clarendon Press, 1996) 29–52

1997   'This Heap of Good Learning: The Jurist in the Common Law Tradition' in BS
       Markesinis (ed), *The Clifford Chance Lectures*, 2: *Law Making, Law Finding and
       Law Shaping: The Diverse Influences* (Oxford: Oxford University Press, 1997)
       113–38
       'More Logic and Less Experience: The Difference between Scots Law and English
       Law' in DL Carey Miller and R Zimmermann (eds), *The Civilian Tradition and
       Scots Law: Aberdeen Quincentenary Essays* (Berlin: Duncker & Humblot, 1997)
       167–90
       'Change of Position and Surviving Enrichment' in W Swadling (ed), *The Limits
       of Restitutionary Claims: A Comparative Analysis* (United Kingdom Comparative
       Law Series, No 17, London: United Kingdom National Committee of Com-
       parative Law, 1997) 36–63
       'The Necessity of a Unitary Law of Tracing' in R Cranston (ed), *Making
       Commercial Law: Essays in Honour of Roy Goode* (Oxford: Clarendon Press, 1997)
       249–58
       'Definition and Division: A Meditation on *Institutes* 3.13' in P Birks (ed), *The
       Classification of Obligations* (Oxford: Clarendon Press, 1997) 1–36

1998   'Before we Begin: Five Keys to Land Law' in S Bright and J Dewar (eds), *Land
       Law: Themes and Perspectives* (Oxford: Oxford University Press, 1998) 457–86
       'Mixtures' in N Palmer and E McKendrick (eds), *Interests in Goods* (2nd edn,
       London *et al*: Lloyd's of London Press, 1998) 227–49 (2nd edn of the 1993
       article, above)
       'Misnomer' in WR Cornish, R Nolan, J O'Sullivan, and G Virgo (eds), *Resti-
       tution, Past, Present and Future: Essays in Honour of Gareth Jones* (Oxford: Hart,
       1998) 1–30
       'The Burden on the Bank' in F Rose (ed), *Restitution and Banking Law* (Oxford:
       Mansfield Press, 1998) 189–232
       'Can we get Nearer to the Text of the *Lex Aquilia*?' in BCM Jacobs and EC
       Coppens (eds), *Een rijk gerecht: opstellen aangeboden aan prof. mr. P. L. Nève*
       (Nijmegen: Gerard Noodt Instituut, 1998) 25–41
       'Large Scale Fraud: Sharpening the Weapons of Restitution' in JJ Norton (ed),
       Yearbook of International Financial and Economic Law 1996 (London: Kluwer
       Law, 1998) 291–315

1999   'The Role of Fault in the Law of Unjust Enrichment' in W Swadling and G Jones
       (eds), *The Search for Principle: Essays in Honour of Lord Goff of Chieveley* (Oxford:
       Oxford University Press, 1999) 235–75

2000   'Private Law' in P Birks and F Rose (eds), *Lessons of the Swaps Litigation* (London:
       Mansfield Press, 2000) 1–45
       'Introduction' in P Birks (ed), *English Private Law*, 1 (Oxford: Oxford University
       Press, 2000) pp xxxv–li

(with C Mitchell) 'Unjust Enrichment' in P Birks (ed), *English Private Law*, 2 (Oxford: Oxford University Press, 2000) 525–635

'Epilogue' in P Birks and F Rose (eds), *Restitution and Equity*, 1: *Resulting Trusts and Equitable Compensation* (London: Mansfield Press, 2000) 261–2

2001   'Negligence in the Eighteenth Century Common Law' in EJH Schrage (ed), *Negligence: The Comparative Legal History of the Law of Torts* (Berlin: Duncker & Humblot, 2001) 173–227

2002   (with C Mitchell) 'Unjust Enrichment' in P Birks (ed), *English Private Law, First Updating Supplement* (Oxford: Oxford University Press, 2002) 99–108

' "At the Expense of the Claimant": Direct and Indirect Enrichment in English Law' in D Johnston and R Zimmermann (eds), *Unjustified Enrichment: Key Issues in Comparative Perspective* (Cambridge: Cambridge University Press, 2002) 493–525. Originally published in (2000) 1 Oxford University Comparative Law Forum at http://ouclf.iuscomp.org/articles/birks.shtml

'Receipt' in P Birks and A Pretto (eds), *Breach of Trust* (Oxford *et al*: Hart, 2002) 213–40

'Comparative Unjust Enrichment' in P Birks and A Pretto (eds), *Themes in Comparative Law: In Honour of Bernard Rudden* (Oxford: Oxford University Press, 2002) 137–51

2003   'Restitution of Unjust Enrichment' in A Burrows and E Peel (eds), *Commercial Remedies: Current Issues and Problems* (Oxford: Oxford University Press, 2003) 131–69

'Events and Responses: The Case of Trusts' in C Wasserstein and I Gilead (eds), *Classification of Private Law: Bases of Liability and Remedies* (Jerusalem: The Harry and Michael Sacher Institute for Legislative Research and Comparative Law, 2003) 159–87

2004   'Series Editor's Foreword' in D Feldman (ed), *English Public Law* (Oxford: Oxford University Press, 2004) pp vii–viii

'Retrieving Tied Money' in W Swadling (ed), *The Quistclose Trust: Critical Essays* (Oxford *et al*: Hart, 2004) 121–43

(with C Mitchell) 'Unjust Enrichment' in P Birks (ed), *English Private Law, Second Cumulative Updating Supplement* (Oxford: Oxford University Press, 2004) 157–77

'Roman Law in Twentieth-Century Britain' in J Beatson and R Zimmermann (eds), *Jurists Uprooted: German-Speaking Emigré Lawyers in Twentieth-Century Britain* (Oxford: Oxford University Press, 2004) 249–68

ARTICLES AND CASE NOTES

1969   'From *Legis Actio* to *Formula*' (1969) 4 Irish Jurist (NS) 356–67

'The Early History of *Iniuria*' (1969) 37 Tijdschrift voor Rechtsgeschiedenis 163–208

'The Problem of Quasi-Delict' (1969) 22 CLP 164–80

1971   '*Negotiorum Gestio* and the Common Law' (1971) 24 CLP 110–32

'English Beginnings and Roman Parallels' (1971) 6 Irish Jurist (NS) 147–62

1972   'The Recovery of Carelessly Mistaken Payments' (1972) 25 CLP 179–99

1973   'A Note on the Development of *Furtum*' (1973) 8 Irish Jurist (NS) 349–55
1974   'Restitution for Services' (1974) 27 CLP 13–36
1975   'No Shield for a Stranger' (1975) 1 Poly LR 39–44
1976   (with J Beatson) 'Unrequested Payment of Another's Debt' (1976) 92 LQR
        188–212
        '*Infamandi Causa Facta* in Disguise' (1976) Acta Juridica 83–104
1980   'Restitution from Public Authorities' (1980) 33 CLP 191–211
1981   'Other Men's Meat: Aquilian Liability for Proper Use' (1981) 16 Irish Jurist
        (NS) 141–85
1982   'Restitution and Wrongs' (1982) 35 CLP 53–76
1983   'Restitution and the Freedom of Contract' (1983) 36 CLP 141–62
        'Honoré's Ulpian' (1983) 18 Irish Jurist (NS) 151–81
1984   'English and Roman Learning in *Moses* v *Macferlan*' (1984) 37 CLP 1–28
        'A New Argument for A Narrow View of *Litem Suam Facere*' (1984) 52 Tijds-
        chrift voor Rechtsgeschiedenis 373–87
        (with A Rodger and JS Richardson) 'Further Aspects of the *Tabula Contrebiensis*'
        (1984) 74 Journal of Roman Studies 45–73
1985   'Restitution: A View of the Scots Law' (1985) 38 CLP 57–82
        'Six Questions in Search of a Subject' [1985] Juridical Review 227–52
        'Unjust Enrichment—A Reply to Mr Hedley' (1985) 5 LS 67–76 (Reply to
        S Hedley, 'Unjust Enrichment as the Basis of Restitution—An Overworked
        Concept' (1985) 5 LS 56–66)
        'A Point of Aquilian Pleading' (1985) 36 IVRA 97–107
        'Cooking the Meat: Aquilian Liability for Hearths and Ovens' (1985) 20 Irish
        Jurist (NS) 352–77
        'The Roman Concept of *Dominium* and the Idea of Absolute Ownership' [1985]
        Acta Juridica 1–38
1986   (with G McLeod) 'The Implied Contract Theory of Quasi-Contract: Civilian
        Opinion Current in the Century before Blackstone' (1986) 6 OJLS 46–85
1987   'Restitutionary Damages for Breach of Contract: *Snepp* and the Fusion of Law
        and Equity' [1987] LMCLQ 421–42
1988   'New Light on the Roman Legal System: The Appointment of Judges' (1988) 47
        CLJ 36–60
        'Ulpius Marcellus and an Ancient Mystery—Part I: Multiple Transfer and
        Threefold Mancipation' (1988) 23 Irish Jurist (NS) 99–128
        'Personal Restitution in Equity' [1988] LMCLQ 128–35
1989   'Misdirected Funds: Restitution from the Recipient' [1989] LMCLQ 296–341
        '3 × 1 = 3: An Arithmetical Solution to the Problem of Threefold Mancipation'
        (1989) 40 IVRA 55–63 (part II of 'Ulpius Marcellus and an Ancient Mystery',
        above)
        'Misdirected Funds' (1989) 105 LQR 352–6
        'Misdirected Funds Again' (1989) 105 LQR 528–34
        'A Lifelong Obligation of Confidence' (1989) 105 LQR 501–8
1990   'Restitution after Ineffective Contracts: Issues for the 1990s' (1990) 2 Journal of
        Contract Law 227–40

'The Independence of Restitutionary Causes of Actions' (1990) 16 University of Queensland Law Journal 1–26

'Restitution without Counter–Restitution' [1990] LMCLQ 330–8

'The Travails of Duress' [1990] LMCLQ 342–51

'The Remedies for Abuse of Confidential Information' [1990] LMCLQ 460–5

1991　'The English Recognition of Unjust Enrichment' [1991] LMCLQ 473–507

1992　'Legal Education' (1992) 109 LQR 521–4

'Studying Law in Germany' (1992) 26 Law Teacher 215–18

' "When Money is Paid in Pursuance of a Void Authority..."—A Duty to Repay?' [1992] PL 580–91

'The Condition of the English Law of Unjust Enrichment' [1992] Acta Juridica 1–22 (= TW Bennett, DJ Devine, DB Hutchison, I Leeman, CM Murray, and D van Zyl Smit (eds), *Festschrift Wouter de Vos* (Cape Town *et al*: Juta & Co, 1992))

'Mixing and Tracing: Property and Restitution' (1992) 45 CLP 69–98

'The Model Pleading of the Action for Wrongful Loss' (1992) 25–7 Irish Jurist (NS) 311–28 (= *Liber Memorialis John M Kelly*)

'The One–Year Lawyer' (1992) 142 NLJ 1015

1993　'Konkurrierende Strategien und Interessen: Das Irrtumserfordernis im Bereicherungsrecht des common law' (1993) 1 Zeitschrift für Europäisches Privatrecht 554–73 (translated by R Zimmermann)

'No Consideration: Restitution after Void Contracts' (1993) 23 University of Western Australia Law Review 195–234

'Persistent Problems in Misdirected Money: A Quintet' [1993] LMCLQ 218–37

'Restitution: Dynamics of the Modern Law' (1993) 46 CLP 157–82

'Obligations and Property in Equity: *Lister* v *Stubbs* in the Limelight' [1993] LMCLQ 30–3

'Modernising the Law of Restitution' (1993) 109 LQR 164–8

'Profits of Breach of Contract' (1993) 109 LQR 518–21

(with F Rose) 'Editorial' (1993) 1 Restitution Law Review 1–6

'Mr Justice Willes' Dream' (1993) 6 SPTL Reporter 27–30

'The Rise and Rise of the Non-Law Graduate' (1993) 7 SPTL Reporter 3–4

'Qualifying Degrees: New Proposals for 1995' (1993) 7 SPTL Reporter 14–15

1994　'Adjudication and Interpretation in the Common Law: A Century of Change' (1994) 14 LS 156–79. Reprinted in BS Markesinis (ed), *The Clifford Chance Lectures*, 1: *Bridging the Channel* (Oxford: Oxford University Press, 1996) 135–64

'Major Developments in the Law of Restitution' (1994) 6 Singapore Academy of Law Journal 253–71

'Property in the Profits of Wrongdoing' (1994) 24 University of Western Australia Law Review 8–16

'Wrongful Loss by Co–Promisees' (1994) 22 Index 181–8

'*In rem* or *in personam*? *Webb* v *Webb*' (1994) 8 Trust Law International 99–101

(with F Rose) 'Editorial' (1994) 2 Restitution Law Review 1–2

'To Be Built on Sand: The Future Form of the CPE' (1994) 8 SPTL Reporter 1–4

'The Consolation of Cassandra' (1994) 9 SPTL Reporter 28–9

1995   'Establishing a Proprietary Base (*Re Goldcorp*)' (1995) 3 Restitution Law Review
       83–93
       'Tracing, Subrogation and Change of Position (*Boscawen* v *Bajwa, Abbey
       National plc* v *Boscawen*)' (1995) 9 Trust Law International 124–6
       'Tracing Misused (*Bank Tejarat* v *Hong Kong and Shanghai Banking Corp*)'
       (1995) 9 Trust Law International 91–5
       'Shallow Foundations' (1995) 111 LQR 371–5
       'Compulsory Subjects: Will the Seven Foundations ever Crumble?' (1995) 1
       Web Journal of Current Legal Issues at http://webjcli.ncl.ac.uk/articles1/
       birks1.html. Reprinted in MJ Allen (ed), *The Web Journal of Current Legal Issues:
       1995 Yearbook* (London: Blackstone, 1996) 38–47
       'Proprietary Restitution: An Intelligible Approach' (1995) 9 Trust Law Inter-
       national 43–9
       'Villainy with a Smiling Cheek' (1995) 10 SPTL Reporter 16–18
1996   'Accessory Liability' [1996] LMCLQ 1–6
       'The Proceeds of Mortgage Fraud' (1996) 10 Trust Law International 2–5
       'Trusts Raised to Reverse Unjust Enrichment: The *Westdeutsche* Case' (1996) 4
       Restitution Law Review 3–26
       'Equity in the Modern Law: An Exercise in Taxonomy' (1996) 26 University of
       Western Australia Law Review 1–99
       'Inconsistency between Compensation and Restitution' (1996) 112 LQR 375–8
       'ACLEC: The Research Dimension' (1996) 13 SPTL Reporter 16–17
       'The Imitation of King James II & VII, or, On Not Giving a **** for the Rule of
       Law' (1996) 12 SPTL Reporter 19–22
       (with W Swadling) 'Restitution' [1996] All ER Rev 366–95
1997   'Unjust Factors and Wrongs: Pecuniary Rescission for Undue Influence' (1997) 5
       Restitution Law Review 72–9
       'Obligations Arising without Agreement under the Louisiana Civil Code' (1997)
       5 Restitution Law Review 222–8
       'On Taking Seriously the Difference between Tracing and Claiming' (1997) 11
       Trust Law International 2–9
       'Property and Unjust Enrichment: Categorical Truths' [1997] New Zealand Law
       Review 623–67
       'Harassment and Hubris: The Right to an Equality of Respect' (1997) 32 Irish
       Jurist (NS) 1–45 (revised version of the 1996 pamphlet, below)
       (with W Swadling) 'Restitution' [1997] All ER Rev 385–407
1998   'Notice and Onus in *O'Brien*' (1998) 12 Trust Law International 1–15
       'The End of the Remedial Constructive Trust?' (1998) 12 Trust Law Interna-
       tional 201–15
       'The Academic and the Practitioner' (1998) 16 SPTL Reporter 21–6 (abridged
       version of the 1999 LS article, below)
       (with W Swadling) 'Restitution' [1998] All ER Rev 390–416
1999   'The Academic and the Practitioner' (1999) 8 LS 397–414
       'Equity, Conscience, and Unjust Enrichment' (1999) 23 Melbourne University
       Law Review 1–29

'The Law of Restitution at the End of an Epoch' (1999) 28 University of Western Australia Law Review 13–64

'The Law of Unjust Enrichment: A Millennial Resolution' (1999) 40 Singapore Journal of Legal Studies 318–32

(with W Swadling) 'Restitution' [1999] All ER Rev 312–26

2000   'The Content of Fiduciary Obligation' (2000) 34 Israel Law Review 3–38

'Personal Property: Proprietary Rights and Remedies' (2000) 11 King's College Law Journal 1–18

'Three Kinds of Objection to Discretionary Remedialism' (2000) 29 University of Western Australia Law Review 1–17

'Mistakes of Law' (2000) 53 CLP 205–36

'Recovering Value Transferred under an Illegal Contract' (2000) 1 Theoretical Inquiries in Law 155–204

'Rights, Wrongs, and Remedies' (2000) 20 OJLS 1–37

'A Bank's Mistaken Payments: Two Recent Cases and their Implications' (2000) 6 New Zealand Business Law Quarterly 155–65

(with W Swadling) 'Restitution' [2000] All ER Rev 315–31

2001   'Knowing Receipt: Re Montagu's Settlement Trusts Revisited' (2001) 1 Global Jurist Advances at http://www.bepress.com/gj/advances/vol1/iss2/art2

'Property, Unjust Enrichment, and Tracing' (2001) 54 CLP 231–54

'Unjust Enrichment and Wrongful Enrichment' (2001) 79 Texas Law Review 1767–94

(with W Swadling) 'Restitution' [2001] All ER Rev 322–33

2002   'Failure of Consideration and its Place on the Map' (2002) 2 Oxford University Commonwealth Law Journal 1–13

'The Content of Fiduciary Obligation' (2002) 16 Trust Law International 34–52 (abbreviated version of the 2000 Israel Law Review article, above)

(with W Swadling) 'Restitution' [2002] All ER Rev 315–27

2003   'A Letter to America: The New Restatement of Restitution' (2003) 3 Global Jurist Frontiers at http://www.bepress.com/gj/frontiers/vol3/iss2/art2

2004   'Undue Influence as Wrongful Exploitation' (2004) 120 LQR 34–7

'Change of Position: The Two Central Questions' (2004) 120 LQR 373–8

PAMPHLETS

1995   *The Structure of the English Law of Unjust Enrichment* (Nijmegen: Centrum voor postdoctoral onderwijs, 1995)

1996   *Harassment and Hubris: The Right to an Equality of Respect, Being the Second John Maurice Kelly Memorial Lecture* (Dublin: University College Dublin, Faculty of Law, 1996)

BOOK REVIEWS AND REVIEW ARTICLES

1972   A Watson, *Roman Private Law around 200 BC* (Edinburgh: Edinburgh University Press, 1971) in (1972) 88 LQR 293–4

1973   AHM Jones, *The Criminal Courts of the Roman Republic and Principate* (Oxford: Blackwell, 1972) in (1973) 89 LQR 440–1

1978   JM Kelly, *Studies in the Civil Judicature of the Roman Republic* (Oxford: Clarendon Press, 1976) in (1978) 28 Classical Review (NS) 97–8

1983   T Honoré, *Tribonian* (London: Duckworth, 1978) in (1983) 33 Classical Review (NS) 246–9

1984   F Lyall, *Slaves, Citizens, Sons: Legal Metaphors in the Epistles* (Grand Rapids, Mich.: Academie Books, 1984) in (1984) 18 Irish Jurist (NS) 140–3

1985   P Stein, *Legal Institutions: The Development of Dispute Settlement* (London: Butterworths, 1984) in (1985) 5 LS 238–41

1986   DM Walker, *The Scottish Jurists* (Edinburgh: W Green, 1985) in (1986) 7 Journal of Legal History 238–40

1987   'An Enemy of Promises' (review of PS Atiyah, *Essays on Contract* (Oxford: Clarendon Press, 1986)) in *Times Literary Supplement*, 23–9 October 1987, 1173
        'The Rise of the Roman Jurists' (review of BW Frier, *The Rise of the Roman Jurists: Studies in Cicero's pro Caecina* (Princeton: Princeton University Press, 1985)) in (1987) 7 OJLS 444–53

1990   D Johnston, *The Roman Law of Trusts* (Oxford: Clarendon Press, 1988) in (1990) 10 LS 353–6

1992   RA Bauman, *Lawyers and Politics in the Early Roman Empire: A Study of Relations between the Roman Jurists and the Emperors from Augustus to Hadrian* (Munich: CH Beck, 1989) in (1992) 82 Journal of Roman Studies 260–2
        R Zimmermann, *The Law of Obligations: Roman Foundations of the Civilian Tradition* (Cape Town: Juta & Co, 1990) in (1992) 13 Journal of Legal History 311–14

1996   'Pharisees on the Bench' (review of AWB Simpson, *Leading Cases in the Common Law* (Oxford: Clarendon Press, 1995)) in *Times Literary Supplement*, 8 March 1996, 29

1997   (with various authors) 'The First Australian Textbook on Restitution' (review of K Mason and JW Carter, *Restitution Law in Australia* (Sydney: Butterworths, 1995)) in (1997) 5 Restitution Law Review 229–48

1999   DM Wright, *The Remedial Constructive Trust* (Sydney: Butterworths, 1998) in (1999) 115 LQR 681–8

2003   C Rotherham, *Proprietary Remedies in Context: A Study in the Judicial Redistribution of Property Rights* (Oxford et al: Hart, 2002) in (2003) 119 LQR 156–61

2004   RP Meagher, JD Heydon and MJ Leeming (eds), *Meagher, Gummow and Lehane's Equity Doctrines and Remedies* (4th edn, Sydney: Butterworths LexisNexis, 2002) in (2004) 120 LQR 344–8

LETTERS

1983   'Ulpian' *Times Literary Supplement*, 4 March 1983, 215 (re: A Watson, 'Not a Week Without a Book' *Times Literary Supplement*, 18 February 1983, 164 = review of T Honoré, *Ulpian* (Oxford: Clarendon Press, 1982))

1986   'Roman Law' *Times Literary Supplement*, 17 October 1986, 1163 (re: R Seager, 'The Greece and Rome Tome' *Times Literary Supplement*, 3 October 1986, 1108 = review of J Boardman, J Griffin, and O Murray (eds), *The Oxford History of the Classical World* (Oxford: Oxford University Press, 1986))

1992　'One-Year Lawyers' (1992) 142 NLJ 1152 (postscript to the article at 1015, above)

'A Law unto Itself' *Times Higher Education Supplement*, 28 August 1992, 17

PERSONALIA

1996　(with R Buckley) 'Professor RFV Heuston' (1996) 12 SPTL Reporter 45–6

2004　'John Kieran Barry Moylan Nicholas (1919–2002)' (2004) 124 Proceedings of the British Academy 219–42

Index